Companies Act 2014: 2018 Edition

Companies Act 2014: 2018 Edition

Bloomsbury Professional

BLOOMSBURY PROFESSIONAL
An imprint of Bloomsbury Publishing Plc

The Fitzwilliam Business Centre, 26 Upper Pembroke Street, Dublin 2, Ireland
41–43 Boltro Road, Haywards Heath, RH16 1BJ, UK

BLOOMSBURY and the Diana logo are trademarks of Bloomsbury Publishing Plc

British Library Cataloguing-in-Publication Data
A catalogue record for this book is available from the British Library.

ISBN: PB: 978 152650 922 2
epub: 978 152650 923 9
epdf: 978 152650 924 6

Typeset by Marlex Editorial Services Ltd, Dublin, Ireland
Printed and bound by CPI Group (UK) Ltd, Croydon, CR0 4YY

Contents Overview

Companies Act 2014

Companies Act 2014

Number 38 of 2014

CONTENTS

Section

PART 1
PRELIMINARY AND GENERAL

PART 2
INCORPORATION AND REGISTRATION

Chapter 1
Preliminary

Chapter 2
Incorporation and consequential matters

Notes

* Sections in square brackets have been repealed.

Chapter 3
Corporate capacity and authority

Chapter 4
Contracts and other transactions

Chapter 5
Company name, registered office and service of documents

Chapter 6
Conversion of existing private company to private company limited by shares to which Parts 1 to 15 apply

PART 3
SHARE CAPITAL, SHARES AND CERTAIN OTHER INSTRUMENTS

Chapter 1
Preliminary and interpretation

Chapter 2
Offers of securities to the public

Chapter 3
Allotment of shares

Chapter 4
Variation in capital

Chapter 5
Transfer of shares

Chapter 6
Acquisition of own shares

Chapter 7
Distributions

PART 4
CORPORATE GOVERNANCE

Chapter 1
Preliminary

Chapter 2
Directors and secretaries

Chapter 3
Service contracts and remuneration

Chapter 4
Proceedings of directors

Chapter 5
Members

Chapter 6
General meetings and resolutions

Chapter 7
Summary Approval Procedure

Chapter 3
Evidential provisions with respect to loans, other transactions, etc., between company and directors

Chapter 4
Substantive prohibitions or restrictions on loans to directors and other particular transactions involving conflict of interest

Chapter 1A
Qualification of company based on size of company

Chapter 2
Accounting records

Chapter 3
Financial year

Chapter 4
Statutory financial statements

Chapter 5
Group financial statements: exemptions and exclusions

Chapter 6
Disclosure of directors' remuneration and transactions

Chapter 7
Disclosure required in notes to financial statements of other matters

Chapter 8
Approval of statutory financial statements

Chapter 9
Directors' report

Chapter 10
Obligation to have statutory financial statements audited

Chapter 11
Statutory auditors' report

Chapter 12
Publication of financial statements

Chapter 13
Annual return and documents annexed to it

Chapter 14
Exclusions, exemptions and special arrangements with regard to public disclosure of financial information

Chapter 15
Audit exemption

Chapter 16
Special audit exemption for dormant companies

Chapter 17
Revision of defective statutory financial statements

Chapter 18
Appointment of statutory auditors

Chapter 19
Rights, obligations and duties of statutory auditors

Chapter 20
Removal and resignation of statutory auditors

Chapter 21
Notification to Supervisory Authority of certain matters and auditors acting while subject to disqualification order

Chapter 22
False statements — offence

Chapter 23
Transitional

PART 7

CHARGES AND DEBENTURES

Chapter 1
Interpretation

Chapter 2
Registration of charges and priority

Chapter 3
Provisions as to debentures

PART 9
REORGANISATIONS, ACQUISITIONS, MERGERS AND DIVISIONS

Chapter 1
Schemes of Arrangement

Chapter 2
Acquisitions

Chapter 3
Mergers

Chapter 4
Divisions

PART 10
EXAMINERSHIPS

Chapter 1
Interpretation

Chapter 2
Appointment of examiner

Chapter 3
Powers of examiner

Chapter 4
Liability of third parties for debts of a company in examination

Chapter 5
Conclusion of examinership

PART 11
WINDING UP

Chapter 1
Preliminary and interpretation

Chapter 2
Winding up by court

Chapter 3
Members' voluntary winding up

Chapter 4
Creditors' voluntary winding up

Chapter 5
Conduct of winding up

Chapter 6
Realisation of assets and related matters

Chapter 7
Distribution

Chapter 8
Liquidators

Chapter 9
Contributories

Chapter 10
Committee of inspection

Chapter 11
Court's powers

Chapter 12
Provisions supplemental to conduct of winding up

Chapter 13
General rules as to meetings of members, contributories and creditors of a company in liquidation

Chapter 14
Completion of winding up

Chapter 15
Provisions related to the Insolvency Regulation

Chapter 16
Offences by officers of companies in liquidation, offences of fraudulent trading and certain other offences, referrals to D.P.P., etc.

PART 12
STRIKE OFF AND RESTORATION

Chapter 1
Strike off of company

Chapter 2
Restoration of company to register

Chapter 3
Miscellaneous

PART 13
INVESTIGATIONS

Chapter 1
Preliminary

Chapter 2
Investigations by court appointed inspectors

Chapter 3
Investigations initiated by Director

Chapter 4
Miscellaneous provisions

PART 14
COMPLIANCE AND ENFORCEMENT

Chapter 1
Compliance and protective orders

Chapter 2
Disclosure orders

Chapter 3
Restrictions on directors of insolvent companies

Chapter 4
Disqualification generally

Chapter 5
Disqualification and restriction undertakings

Chapter 6
Enforcement in relation to disqualification and restriction

Chapter 7
Provisions relating to offences generally

Chapter 8
Provision for enforcement of section 27(1) and additional general offences

Chapter 9
Evidential matters

PART 15

FUNCTIONS OF REGISTRAR AND OF REGULATORY AND ADVISORY BODIES

Chapter 1
Registrar of Companies

Chapter 3
Director of Corporate Enforcement

Chapter 4
Company Law Review Group

PART 16

DESIGNATED ACTIVITY COMPANIES

Chapter 1
Preliminary and definitions

Chapter 2
Incorporation and consequential matters

Chapter 3
Share capital

Chapter 4
Corporate governance

Chapter 4
Interests in shares: disclosure of individual and group acquisitions

Chapter 5
Acquisition of own shares and certain acquisitions by subsidiaries

Chapter 6
Distribution by a PLC

Chapter 7
Uncertificated securities

Chapter 8
Corporate governance

Chapter 9
Duties of directors and other officers

Chapter 10
Financial statements, annual return and audit

Chapter 11
Debentures

Chapter 12
Examinerships

Chapter 13
Reorganisations

Chapter 14
Strike off and restoration

Chapter 15
Investigations

Chapter 16
Mergers

Chapter 17
Divisions

Chapter 3
Share capital

Chapter 4
Corporate governance

Chapter 5
Financial statements, annual return and audit

Chapter 3
Share capital

Chapter 4
Corporate governance

Chapter 5
Financial statements, annual return and audit

Chapter 6
Winding up

Chapter 7
Examinerships

Chapter 8
Investigations

Chapter 9
Public offers of securities, market abuse, etc.

PART 20

RE-REGISTRATION

Chapter 1
Interpretation

Chapter 2
General provisions as to re-registration

Chapter 3
Special requirements for re-registration

PART 21

EXTERNAL COMPANIES

Chapter 1
Preliminary

Chapter 2
Filing obligations of external companies

Chapter 3
Disclosure in certain business documents and translation of documents

Chapter 4
Service of documents

Chapter 5
Compliance

PART 22

UNREGISTERED COMPANIES AND JOINT STOCK COMPANIES

Chapter 1
Application of Act to unregistered companies

Chapter 2
Registration of certain bodies (other than joint stock companies) as companies

Chapter 3
Winding up of unregistered company

Chapter 4
Provisions concerning companies registered, but not formed, under former Acts and certain other existing companies

Chapter 5
Registration of joint stock companies under this Act

PART 23

PUBLIC OFFERS OF SECURITIES, FINANCIAL REPORTING BY TRADED COMPANIES, PREVENTION OF MARKET ABUSE, ETC.

Chapter 1
Public offers of securities

Chapter 2
Market abuse

Chapter 3
Requirement for corporate governance statement and application of certain provisions of Parts 5 and 6 where company is a traded company

Chapter 4
Transparency requirements regarding issuers of securities admitted to trading on certain markets

Chapter 5
Application of section 393 to a company to which Part 23 applies 1092

PART 24

INVESTMENT COMPANIES

Chapter 1
Preliminary and interpretation

Chapter 2
Incorporation and registration

Chapter 3
Share capital

Chapter 4
Financial statements

Chapter 5
Winding up

Chapter 6
Restoration

Chapter 7
Public offers of securities, prevention of market abuse, etc.

Chapter 8
Umbrella funds and sub-funds

Chapter 9
Migration of funds

PART 25

MISCELLANEOUS

Chapter 1
Provisions concerning foreign insolvency proceedings (including those covered by the Insolvency Regulation)

Chapter 2
Other miscellaneous provisions

PART 26
PAYMENTS TO GOVERNMENTS

Chapter 1
Preliminary

Chapter 2
Obligation to prepare payment reports

Chapter 3
Content of payment reports

Chapter 4
Payment reports: Exemptions and exclusions

Chapter 3
Aptitude Test

Chapter 4
Withdrawal of Approval

Chapter 5
Public Register

Chapter 6
Standards for statutory auditors

Chapter 7
Quality assurance

Chapter 8
Investigations and sanctions

Chapter 9
Actions to be taken after decision by recognised accountancy body that statutory auditor or audit firm of public-interest entity has committed relevant contravention

Chapter 10
Appointment of statutory auditors or audit firms

Chapter 11
Confidentiality and professional secrecy

Chapter 17
Cooperation with other Member States

Chapter 18
Mutual recognition of regulatory arrangements between Member States

Chapter 19
Transfer of audit working papers, etc., to third-country competent authorities

Chapter 20
International aspects

Chapter 21
Registration and oversight of third-country auditors and third-country audit entities

SCHEDULE 5
LIST OF COMPANIES FOR CERTAIN PURPOSES OF ACT (INCLUDING, IN PARTICULAR, SECTIONS 142, 350, 362 AND 510)

SCHEDULE 6
FURTHER SAVINGS AND TRANSITIONAL PROVISIONS

SCHEDULE 7
FORM OF CONSTITUTION OF DESIGNATED ACTIVITY COMPANY LIMITED BY SHARES

SCHEDULE 8
FORM OF CONSTITUTION OF DESIGNATED ACTIVITY COMPANY LIMITED BY GUARANTEE

SCHEDULE 9
FORM OF CONSTITUTION OF PUBLIC LIMITED COMPANY

SCHEDULE 10
FORM OF CONSTITUTION OF COMPANY LIMITED BY GUARANTEE

SCHEDULE 11
FORM OF CONSTITUTION OF PRIVATE UNLIMITED COMPANY HAVING A SHARE CAPITAL

SCHEDULE 12
FORM OF CONSTITUTION OF PUBLIC UNLIMITED COMPANY HAVING A SHARE CAPITAL

SCHEDULE 13
FORM OF CONSTITUTION OF PUBLIC UNLIMITED COMPANY NOT HAVING A SHARE CAPITAL

SCHEDULE 14
PROVISIONS APPLIED TO UNREGISTERED COMPANIES

Schedule 15

Repeals and Revocation In relation to Unregistered Companies

Part 1

Statutes repealed

Part 2

Instruments or charters revoked

Schedule 16

Form of Constitution of Investment Company

Schedule 17

Conditions to be Satisfied for Application of Segregated Liability to Sub-funds of Investment Company Trading before 30 June 2005

Schedule 18

Table of Activities Relevant to the Definitions of "logging Undertaking" and "mining or Quarrying Undertaking" in Section 1449

Schedule 19

Standards Relating to Training and Qualifications for Approval of Individual as Statutory Auditor

Schedule 20

Information Required, by Chapter 5 of Part 27, to be Supplied And Entered in a Public Register

Acts Referred to

Arbitration Act 2010 (No. 1)

Assurance Companies Act 1909 (9 Edw. 7. c. 42)

Bank Act 1892 (56 Vic. c. 48.)

Bank Notes (Ireland) Act 1864 (28 Vic. c. 78)

Bank of Ireland Act 1781 (22 Geo. III, c. 16)

Bank of Ireland Act 1791 (Geo. III, c. 22)

Bank of Ireland Act 1797 (Geo. III, c. 50)

Bank of Ireland Act 1808 (Geo. III, c. 103)

Bank of Ireland Act 1821 (Geo. IV, c. 72)

Bank of Ireland Act 1860 (24 Vic. c. 31)

Bank of Ireland Act 1929 (No. 4 (Private))

Bank of Ireland Act 1935 (No. 1 (Private))

Bank of Ireland Charter Amendment Act 1872 (36 Vic. c. 5)

Bankers' (Ireland) Act 1845 (Vic. c. 37)

Bankruptcy Act 1988 (No. 27)

Building Societies Act 1989 (No. 17)

Capital Acquisitions Tax Consolidation Act 2003 (No. 1)

Capital Gains Tax Acts

Central Bank Act 1942 (No. 22)

Central Bank Act 1971 (No. 24)

Central Bank Act 1989 (No. 16)

Central Bank Acts 1942 to 2010

Central Bank and Financial Services Authority of Ireland Act 2003 (No. 12)

Central Bank Reform Act 2010 (No. 23)

Charities Act 1961 (No. 17)

Charities Act 2009 (No. 6)

Chartered Companies Act 1837 (1 Vic. c. 73)

Civil Liability Act 1961 (No. 41)

Civil Partnership and Certain Rights and Obligations of Cohabitants Act 2010 (No. 24)

Civil Service Regulation Acts 1956 to 2005

Commissions of Investigation Act 2004 (No. 23)

Committees of the Houses of the Oireachtas (Compellability, Privileges and Immunities of Witnesses) Act 1997 (No. 17)

Companies (Amendment) Act 1977 (No. 31)

Companies (Amendment) (No. 2) Act 1999 (No. 30)

Companies (Amendment) Act 1982 (No. 10)

Companies (Amendment) Act 1983 (No. 13)

Companies (Amendment) Act 1986 (No. 25)

Companies (Amendment) Act 1990 (No. 27)

Companies (Amendment) Act 1999 (No. 8)

Companies (Amendment) Act 2009 (No. 20)

Companies (Amendment) Act 2012 (No. 22)

Companies (Auditing and Accounting) Act 2003 (No. 44)

Companies (Consolidation) Act 1908 (8 Edw. 7 c. 69)

Companies (Miscellaneous Provisions) Act 2009 (No. 45)

Companies (Miscellaneous Provisions) Act 2013 (No. 46)

Companies Act 1862 (26 Vic. c. 89)

Companies Act 1879 (43 Vic. c. 76)

Companies Act 1963 (No. 33)

Companies Act 1990 (No. 33)

Companies Acts

Companies Acts 1963 to 2005

Company Law Enforcement Act 2001 (No. 28)

Comptroller and Auditor General (Amendment) Act 1993 (No. 8)

Consumer Credit Act 1995 (No. 24)

Courts of Justice Act 1924 (No. 10)

Courts of Justice Act 1936 (No. 48)

Criminal Procedure Act 1967 (No. 12)

Customs Acts

Data Protection Acts 1988 to 2018

Diplomatic and Consular Officers (Provision of Services) Act 1993 (No. 33)

Economic and Monetary Union Act 1998 (No. 38)

Electoral Act 1997 (No. 25)

Electronic Commerce Act 2000 (No. 27)

Ethics in Public Office Act 1995 (No. 22)

European Communities Act 1972 (No. 27)

European Parliament Elections Act 1997 (No. 2)

Exchange Control Acts 1954 to 1990

Finance Act 1961 (No. 23)

Finance Act 2003 (No. 3)

Finance Act 2011 (No. 6)

Finance (Local Property Tax) Act 2012 (No. 52)

Friendly Societies Acts 1896 to 2014

Hire Purchase Act 1946 (No. 16)

Industrial and Provident Societies Acts 1893 to 2014

Insurance Act 1936 (No. 45)

Insurance Act 1989 (No. 3)

Insurance Acts 1909 to 2000

Interpretation Act 2005 (No. 23)

Investment Funds, Companies and Miscellaneous Provisions Act 2005 (No. 12)

Investment Funds, Companies and Miscellaneous Provisions Act 2006 (No. 41)

Investment Intermediaries Act 1995 (No. 11)

Investment Limited Partnerships Act 1994 (No. 24)

Irish Takeover Panel Act 1997 (No. 5)

Joint Stock Banking Companies Act 1857 (21 Vic. c. 80)

Joint Stock Companies Act 1856 (19 Vic. c. 47)

Joint Stock Companies Acts

Land and Conveyancing Law Reform Act 2009 (No. 27)

Limited Partnerships Act 1907 (7 Edw. 7, c. 24)

Local Government Act 2001 (No. 37)

Mercantile Marine Act 1955 (No. 29)

Multi-Unit Developments Act 2011 (No. 2)

National Archives Act 1986 (No. 11)

National Asset Management Agency Act 2009 (No. 34)

Netting of Financial Contracts Act 1995 (No. 25)

Official Languages Act 2003 (No. 32)

Organisation of Working Time Act 1997 (No. 20)

Partnership Act 1890 (4 Vict., c. 39)

Petty Sessions (Ireland) Act 1851 (14 & 15 Vict., c. 93)

Post Office Savings Bank Acts 1861 to 1958

Public Service Management (Recruitment and Appointments) Act 2004 (No. 33)

Registration of Business Names Act 1963 (No. 30)

Registration of Deeds and Title Act 2006 (No. 12)

Registration of Title Act 1964 (No. 16)

Social Welfare Acts

Social Welfare Consolidation Act 2005 (No. 26)

Solicitors Act 1954 (No. 36)

Solicitors Acts 1954 to 2002

Stamp Duties Consolidation Act 1999 (No. 31)

State Property Act 1954 (No. 25)

Statute Law (Restatement) Act 2002 (No. 33)

Statutory Declarations Act 1938 (No. 37)

Stock Transfer Act 1963 (No. 34)

Succession Act 1965 (No. 27)

Supreme Court of Judicature (Ireland) Act 1877 (41 Vict., c. 57)

Tax Acts

Taxes Consolidation Act 1997 (No. 39)

Trade Union Acts 1871 to 1990

Tribunals of Inquiry (Evidence) Acts 1921 to 2004

Trustee Savings Banks Act 1989 (No. 21)

Unit Trusts Act 1990 (No. 37)

Value-Added Tax Acts

Value-Added Tax Consolidation Act 2010 (No. 31)

Companies Act 2014

Number 38 of 2014

An Act to consolidate, with amendments, certain enactments relating to companies and to provide for related matters.

23rd December 2014

Be it enacted by the Oireachtas as follows:

PART 1
PRELIMINARY AND GENERAL

1 Short title and commencement

(1) This Act may be cited as the Companies Act 2014.

(2) This Act shall come into operation on such day or days as the Minister may appoint by order or orders either generally or with reference to any particular purpose or provision and different days may be so appointed for different purposes or different provisions.

(3) Without prejudice to the generality of *subsection (2)*, an order or orders under that subsection may appoint different days for the coming into operation of *section 4* or *1325* so as to effect the repeal or revocation provided by *section 4* or *1325* of—

(a) an enactment specified in *Part 1* or *Part 2* of *Schedule 2* or in *Schedule 15*, as the case may be, on different days for different purposes; or

(b) different provisions of an enactment specified in *Part 1* or *Part 2* of *Schedule 2* or in *Schedule 15*, as the case may be, on different days.

2 Interpretation generally

(1) In this Act—

[...][a]

"Acting Director" means a person appointed under *section 948* as the Acting Director of Corporate Enforcement;

"Act of 1963" means the Companies Act 1963;

"Act of 1990" means the Companies Act 1990;

"agent" does not include a person's counsel acting as such;

"amendment", in relation to a constitution, includes an alteration and a deletion;

"annual general meeting" means the meeting provided for in *section 175*;

"annual return" has the meaning given to it by *section 342*;

"annual return date" has the meaning given to it by *section 343*;

"appropriate rate", in relation to interest, means—

(a) subject to *paragraph (b)*, 5 per cent per annum; or

(b) such other rate as may be specified by order made by the Minister under *subsection (7)*;

"articles" means articles of association;

"assignee in bankruptcy" means the Official Assignee (within the meaning of the Bankruptcy Act 1988) or a creditors' assignee (within the meaning of that Act);

"authorised market operator" means a market operator (within the meaning of Directive 2004/39/EC of the European Parliament and of the Council of 21 April 2004) who, for the time being, is authorised under—

(a) the European Communities (Markets in Financial Instruments) Regulations 2007 (S.I. No. 60 of 2007); or

(b) the measures adopted by another Member State to implement that Directive,

to operate the business of a regulated market (within the meaning of that Directive);

["Bank Recovery and Resolution Regulations" means the European Union (Bank Recovery and Resolution) Regulations 2015 (S.I. No. 289 of 2015);][b]

"Bankruptcy Acts" means the Bankruptcy Act 1988 and any enactment amending or extending that Act;

"book and paper" and "book or paper" includes deeds, writings and documents and, where not separately mentioned in the provision concerned, accounting records;

"books and documents" and "books or documents" includes deeds, writings and records made in any other manner and, where not separately mentioned in the provision concerned, accounting records;

"called-up share capital", in relation to a company, means so much of its share capital as equals the aggregate amount of the calls made on its shares, whether or not those calls have been paid, together with any share capital paid up without being called and any share capital to be paid on a specified future date under the company's constitution, the terms of allotment of the relevant shares or any other arrangements for payment of those shares, and "uncalled share capital" shall be read accordingly;

"category 1 offence" means an offence the penalties for which are specified in *section 871(1)*;

"category 2 offence" means an offence the penalties for which are specified in *section 871(2)*;

"category 3 offence" means an offence the penalties for which are specified in *section 871(3)*;

"category 4 offence" means an offence the penalties for which are specified in *section 871(4)*;

"Central Bank" means the Central Bank of Ireland;

"child" includes a step-child and an adopted child and "son", "daughter" and "parent" shall be read accordingly;

"civil partner" has the meaning given to it by the Civil Partnership and Certain Rights and Obligations of Cohabitants Act 2010;

"Community act" means an act adopted by an institution of the European Union;

"company"—

(a) in *Parts 2* to *14*, shall be read in accordance with *section 10*;

(b) subject to the foregoing, means a company formed and registered under this Act, or an existing company;

"company having a sole director" shall be read in accordance with *subsection (8)*;

"constitution" means the constitution of a company as provided for in *section 19* or, in the case of a company that is not a private company limited by shares, as provided for in *Part 16*, *17*, *18*, *19* or *24*, as appropriate;

"contravention" includes a failure to comply;

"contributory" has the meaning given to it by *section 559*;

"court"—

(a) without prejudice to *paragraphs (b)* and *(c)*, where used in any provision of this Act in relation to a company, means—

(i) the High Court; or

(ii) where another court is specified for the purposes of that provision — that court;

(b) where used in relation to proceedings for an offence, means—

(i) in the case of an offence that is being prosecuted summarily — the District Court; or

(ii) in any other case — the court with jurisdiction in the matter concerned;

(c) where used in connection with proceedings for a debt or the recovery of a sum otherwise provided by this Act to be recoverable and a particular court or a court of competent jurisdiction is not specified for the purpose, means any court of competent jurisdiction;

"CRO Gazette" means the Companies Registration Office Gazette referred to in *section 887(7)*;

"debenture" includes debenture stock, bonds and any other securities of a company whether constituting a charge on the assets of the company or not;

"*de facto* director" shall be read in accordance with *section 222*;

"deliver" includes send or forward and, in the case of a requirement to deliver a document, notice or thing to the Registrar, where the provision concerned itself does not indicate that that is the purpose of its delivery, means deliver the document, notice or thing to the Registrar for the purposes of its registration;

"director" includes any person occupying the position of director by whatever name called;

"Director" means the Director of Corporate Enforcement (but that title appears set out in full in any provision where it is desirable to avoid confusion or otherwise to provide clarity on the matter) and includes an Acting Director while so acting and, in relation to a particular power of the Director, a delegate to whom the power is delegated under *section [952]*[c];

"document" includes summons, notice, order and other legal process, and register;

"EEA Agreement" means the Agreement on the European Economic Area signed at Oporto on 2 May 1992, as adjusted by the Protocol signed at Brussels on 17 March 1993;

"EEA state" means a state, including the State, which is a contracting party to the EEA Agreement;

"electronic means" or "electronic communications" includes the use of electronic mail;

"enactment" means a statute or an instrument made under a power conferred by a statute;

"examiner" means an examiner appointed under *section 509* or *517*;

"existing company" means a company formed and registered in a register kept in the State under the Joint Stock Companies Acts, the Companies Act 1862, the Companies (Consolidation) Act 1908 or the Act of 1963;

"extended notice" has the meaning given to it by *section 396*;

"extraordinary general meeting" shall be read in accordance with *section 177*;

"financial year" shall be read in accordance with *section 288*;

"hire-purchase agreement" has the same meaning as it has in the Consumer Credit Act 1995;

"holding company" has the meaning given to it by *section 8*;

"insolvency proceedings", other than in *Chapter 15* of *Part 11*, means insolvency proceedings opened under Article 3 of the Insolvency Regulation in a Member State, other than the State and Denmark, where the proceedings relate to a body corporate;

"Insolvency Regulation" means Council Regulation (EC) No. 1346/2000 of 29 May 2000 on insolvency proceedings;

"Joint Stock Companies Acts" means the Joint Stock Companies Act 1856, the Joint Stock Companies Acts 1856, 1857, the Joint Stock Banking Companies Act 1857 and the Act to enable Joint Stock Banking Companies to be formed on the principle of limited liability, or any one or more of those Acts as the case may require, but does not include the Act 7 & 8 Victoria, Chapter 110;

"limited company" means a company the liability of whose members is limited;

"members' voluntary winding up" has the meaning given to it by *section 559(1)*;

"memorandum" means memorandum of association;

"Minister", other than in *Parts 23* and *24*, means the Minister for Jobs, Enterprise and Innovation;

"officer", in relation to a body corporate, includes a director or secretary;

"officer of the Director" means—

(a) an officer of the Minister assigned to the Director;

(b) a member of An Garda Síochána seconded to the Director; or

(c) a person employed by the Minister or the Director under a contract for service or otherwise, to assist the Director in performing functions of the Director under this Act or any other enactment;

"ordinary resolution" has the meaning given to it by *section 191*;

"prescribed"—

(a) subject to *paragraphs (b)*, *(c)* and *(d)*, means prescribed by regulations made by the Minister;

(b) in *Part 11*, unless a power of the Supervisory Authority to prescribe by regulations is provided or that Part otherwise makes express provision—

(i) means prescribed by rules of court; and

(ii) where a power of the Minister to prescribe is provided, means prescribed by the means referred to in *paragraph (a)*;

(c) in *Part 15*, where a power of the Minister to prescribe is provided or the provision in which the expression appears does not indicate otherwise, means prescribed by the means referred to in *paragraph (a)*; and

(d) in *Parts 23* and *24*, means prescribed by regulations made by the Minister for Finance;

"printed" includes reproduced in any legible and durable form approved by the Registrar;

"prior Companies Acts" means—

(a) the Companies Acts 1963 to 2005;

(b) Parts 2 and 3 of the Investment Funds, Companies and Miscellaneous Provisions Act 2006;

(c) the Companies (Amendment) Act 2009;

(d) the Companies (Miscellaneous Provisions) Act 2009;

(e) the Companies (Amendment) Act 2012;

(f) the Companies (Miscellaneous Provisions) Act 2013; and

(g) every other enactment passed or made before the commencement of this section which provides that it is to be read as one with the Companies Acts;

"private company limited by shares" means, unless otherwise indicated, a private company limited by shares registered under *Part 2* as distinct from a designated activity company of the type referred to in *section 965(2)(a)*;

"prospectus" means a document or documents in such form and containing such information as may be required by or under Irish prospectus law or EU prospectus law (within the meaning of *Chapter 1* of *Part 23*), howsoever the document or documents are constituted, but does not include any advertisements in newspapers or journals derived from the foregoing;

"public holiday" means a day which is a public holiday under the Organisation of Working Time Act 1997;

["public-interest entity" has the meaning given to it by Part 27;][d]

"public limited company" includes (in *Parts 2* to *15*) an investment company within the meaning of *Part 24*;

"receiver of the property of a company" shall be read in accordance with *subsection (9)*;

"register" shall be read in accordance with *section 887(2)*;

"registered office", in relation to a company, means the office provided for in *section 50*;

"Registrar" means—

(a) the registrar appointed under *section 887(3)*; or

(b) the person referred to in *subsection (6)* (which relates to the existing Registrar of Companies) of *section 887* for so long as the person holds office in accordance with *subsection (5)* of that section;

["Regulation (EU) 2016/679" means Regulation (EU) 2016/679 of the European Parliament and of the Council of 27 April 2016 on the protection of natural persons with regard to the processing of personal data and on the free movement of such data and repealing Directive 95/46/EC (General Data Protection Regulation);][e]

"related company" shall be read in accordance with *subsections (10)* and *(11)*;

"resolution for voluntary winding up" means a resolution referred to in—

(a) *section 202(1)(a)(i)* as it relates to *section 579*; or

(b) *section 580(1) or 586(2)*,

to wind up a company voluntarily;

"sealed", other than in provisions governing the use of a company's common seal or of any official seal of it, means executed in the manner specified in section 64 of the Land and Conveyancing Law Reform Act 2009 (but only to the extent that that section 64 obviates the need for a seal);

"shadow director" shall be read in accordance with *section 221*;

"share" means share in the share capital of a company, and includes stock except where a distinction between stock and shares is express or implied;

"single-member company" has the meaning given to it by *section 196*;

"special resolution" has the meaning given to it by *section 191*;

["statutory auditor" means an individual or a firm (within the meaning of *Part 27*) that stands approved as a statutory auditor or statutory audit firm, as the case may be, under *Part 27*, and includes a firm registered in accordance with *section 1465*;][f]

"subscribe" includes, where the means of authentication referred to in *section 888* are employed, subscribe in the prescribed non-legible form;

"subsidiary" has the meaning given to it by *section 7*;

"Summary Approval Procedure" has the meaning given to it by *section 202*;

"Supervisory Authority" has the meaning given to it by *section 900(1)*;

"system of interconnection of registers" means the system of interconnection of central commercial and companies registers established in accordance with Article 4a(2) of Directive 2009/101/EC of the European Parliament and of the Council of 16 September 2009;

"undischarged bankrupt" means a person who is declared bankrupt by a court of competent jurisdiction, within the State or elsewhere, and who has not obtained a certificate of discharge or its equivalent in the relevant jurisdiction;

"written resolution" has the meaning given to it by *section 191(8)*.

(2) A word or expression used in *Part 6* and also used in another Part of this Act has, in that other Part, the same meaning as it has in *Part 6*.

(3) A reference in this Act to Table A in the First Schedule to the Act of 1963 shall, where appropriate, be read as a reference to Tábla A in that Schedule.

(4) References in this Act to a body corporate or to a corporation shall be read as not including a corporation sole, but as including a company or body corporate incorporated outside the State.

(5) Any provision of this Act overriding or interpreting a company's constitution shall, except as provided by this Act, apply in relation to the constitution in force on the provision's commencement as well as to regulations of the constitution coming into force thereafter.

(6) References in this Act to a person being in partnership with another are references to the person's being in partnership, within the meaning of section 1(1) of the Partnership Act 1890, with that person and references to a partner of a person shall be read accordingly.

(7) The Minister may, by order, specify a rate of interest for the purposes of *paragraph (b)* of the definition of "appropriate rate" in *subsection (1)*.

(8) In this Act a reference to a company having a sole director is a reference to its having, for the time being and for whatever reason, a single director (and this applies notwithstanding a stipulation in the constitution that there be 2 directors, or a greater number).

(9) In this Act a reference to a receiver of the property of a company includes—

- (a) a reference to—
  - (i) a receiver and manager of the property of a company; or
  - (ii) a manager of the property of a company;
- (b) a reference to a receiver or to a receiver and manager or to a manager, of part only of that property; and
- (c) a reference to a receiver only of the income arising from that property or from part of it.

(10) For the purposes of this Act, a company is related to another company if—

(a) that other company is its holding company or subsidiary; or

(b) more than half in nominal value of its equity share capital (within the meaning of *section 7(11)*) is held by the other company and companies related to that other company (whether directly or indirectly, but other than in a fiduciary capacity); or

(c) more than half in nominal value of the equity share capital (within the meaning of *section 7(11)*) of each of them is held by members of the other (whether directly or indirectly, but other than in a fiduciary capacity); or

(d) that other company or a company or companies related to that other company, or that other company together with a company or companies related to it, are entitled to exercise or control the exercise of more than one half of the voting power at any general meeting of the company; or

(e) the businesses of the companies have been so carried on that the separate business of each company, or a substantial part thereof, is not readily identifiable; or

(f) there is another body corporate to which both companies are related,

and "related company" has a corresponding meaning; for the purpose of any preceding paragraph of this subsection that contains a reference to a company being related to another, the provisions of this subsection also apply to the construction of each such reference.

(11) For the purposes of *subsection (10)* "company" includes any body that is capable of being wound up under this Act.

Amendments

a Definition of "2016 Audits Regulations" deleted by C(SA)A 2018, s 4(a).

b Definition of "Bank Recovery and Resolution Regulations" inserted by the European Union (Bank Recovery and Resolution) Regulations 2015 (SI 289/2015), reg 189(1), with effect from 15 July 2015.

c Figure of "952" substituted for "954" by C(A)A 2017, s 98(a).

d Definition of "public-interest entity" inserted by C(SA)A 2018, s 4(c).

e Definition of "Regulation (EU) 2016/679" inserted by C(SA)A 2018, s 4(c).

f Definition of "statutory auditor" substituted by C(SA)A 2018, s 4(b).

3 Periods of time

(1) Where the time limited by any provision of this Act for the doing of anything expires on a Saturday, a Sunday or a public holiday, the time so limited shall extend to and the thing may be done on the first following day that is not a Saturday, a Sunday or a public holiday.

(2) Where in this Act anything is required or allowed to be done within a number of days not exceeding 6, a day that is a Saturday, a Sunday or a public holiday shall not be reckoned in computing that number.

4 Repeals and revocations

(1) The Acts of the Oireachtas specified in *Part 1* of *Schedule 2* are repealed to the extent specified in the third column of that Part.

(2) The statutory instruments specified in *Part 2* of *Schedule 2* are revoked to the extent specified in the third column of that Part.

(3) This section is in addition to *section 1325* and *Schedule 15* (repeals related to an unregistered company becoming registered under this Act).

5 Savings and transitional provisions

(1) As provided under *Part 17*, *18*, *19* or *24*, as appropriate, the repeal by this Act of any enactment shall not affect the incorporation of any company registered under any enactment so repealed.

(2) The effect of this Act in relation to a private company limited by shares incorporated under any former enactment relating to companies is provided for in *Chapter 6* of *Part 2*.

(3) Any document referring to any former enactment relating to companies shall be read as referring to the corresponding enactment of this Act.

(4) Any person, appointed to any office under or by virtue of any former enactment relating to companies, who is in office immediately before the commencement of the provision concerned of this Act, shall be deemed to have been appointed to that office under or by virtue of the provision concerned of this Act.

(5) Any register, kept under any former enactment relating to companies, shall be deemed part of the register to be kept under the corresponding provision of this Act.

(6) All funds and accounts constituted under this Act shall be deemed to be in continuation of the corresponding funds and accounts constituted under the former enactments relating to companies.

(7) *Schedule 6* contains further savings and transitional provisions and shall have effect accordingly.

(8) This section is without prejudice to—

(a) the generality of the Interpretation Act 2005 and, in particular, section 27 of it; and

(b) the special provision made in certain provisions of this Act for transitional matters as they relate to those provisions.

(9) In this section "former enactment relating to companies" means any enactment repealed or revoked by this Act and any enactment repealed or revoked by the Act of 1963 or the Companies (Consolidation) Act 1908.

6 Construction of references in other Acts to companies registered under Companies (Consolidation) Act 1908 and Act of 1963

(1) References in any Act, other than this Act, to a company formed and registered, or registered, under the Companies (Consolidation) Act 1908 or the Act of 1963

shall, unless the contrary intention appears, be read as references to a company formed and registered, or registered, under whichever of those Acts is appropriate or this Act.

(2) *Subsection (1)* applies despite section 26(2)(f) of the Interpretation Act 2005 (which provides that where an Act repeals and re-enacts, with or without modification, any provisions of a former Act, references in any other Act to the provisions so repealed shall, unless the contrary intention appears, be read as references to the provisions of the new Act relating to the same subject-matter as that of the former Act).

7 Definition of "subsidiary"

(1) In this section the expressions "superior company" and "lower company" are used solely to assist the understanding of its terms and—

(a) are not indicative of the status (in any manner not relevant to this section) of the respective companies vis a vis one another; and

(b) do not constitute definitions to which regard must be had for any other purpose of this Act.

(2) For the purposes of this Act, a company (the "lower company") is, subject to *subsection (5)*, a subsidiary of another (the "superior company") if, but only if—

(a) the superior company—

(i) is a shareholder or member of it and controls the composition of its board of directors; or

(ii) holds more than half in nominal value of its equity share capital; or

(iii) holds more than half in nominal value of its shares carrying voting rights (other than voting rights which arise only in specified circumstances); or

(iv) holds a majority of the shareholders' or members' voting rights in the lower company; or

(v) is a shareholder or member of it and controls alone, pursuant to an agreement with other shareholders or members, a majority of the shareholders' or members' voting rights;

or

(b) the superior company has the right to exercise a dominant influence over it—

(i) by virtue of provisions contained in the lower company's constitution; or

(ii) by virtue of a control contract;

or

(c) the superior company has the power to exercise, or actually exercises, dominant influence or control over it; or

(d) the superior company and the lower company are managed by the superior company on a unified basis; or

(e) the lower company is a subsidiary (by virtue of the application of any of the provisions of this section) of any company which is the superior company's subsidiary (by virtue of such application).

(3) For the purposes of *subsection (2)(a)(i)*, the composition of the lower company's board of directors shall be regarded as being controlled by the superior company if, but only if, the latter company, by the exercise of some power exercisable by it without the consent or concurrence of any other person, can appoint or remove the holders of all or a majority of the directorships.

(4) In applying *subsection (3)*, the superior company shall be deemed to have power to appoint to a directorship in relation to which any of the following conditions is satisfied—

(a) that a person cannot be appointed to the directorship without the exercise in his or her favour by the superior company of such a power as is mentioned in that subsection; or

(b) that a person's appointment to the directorship follows necessarily from his or her appointment as director of the superior company.

(5) In determining whether the lower company is a subsidiary of the superior company—

(a) any shares held or power exercisable by the superior company in a fiduciary capacity shall be treated as not held or exercisable by it;

(b) subject to *paragraphs (c)* and *(d)*, any shares held or power exercisable—

[(i) by any person as a nominee for the superior company or by any person acting in that person's own name but on behalf of the superior company (except where, in either case, the superior company is concerned only in a fiduciary capacity), or][a]

(ii) by, or by a nominee for, [or by any person acting in that person's own name but on behalf of,][b] a subsidiary of the superior company, not being a subsidiary which is concerned only in a fiduciary capacity,

shall be treated as held or exercisable by the superior company;

(c) any shares held or power exercisable by the superior company or a nominee for the superior company or a subsidiary of it shall be treated as not held or exercisable by the superior company where the shares are so held or the power is so exercisable by way of security but only if such power or the rights attaching to such shares are exercised in accordance with instructions received from the person providing the security;

(d) any shares held or power exercisable by the superior company or by a nominee for the superior company or a subsidiary of it shall be treated as not held or exercisable by the superior company if the ordinary business of the superior company or its subsidiary, as the case may be, includes the lending of money and the shares are so held or the power is so exercisable by way of security but only if such power or the rights attaching to such shares are exercised in the interests of the person providing the security.

(6) For the purposes of *subsection (2)(a)(iv)* and *(v)*, the total of the voting rights of the shareholders or members in the lower company shall be reduced by the following—

(a) the voting rights attached to shares held by the lower company in itself; and

(b) the voting rights attached to shares held in the lower company by any of its subsidiaries; and

(c) the voting rights attached to shares held by a person acting in his or her own name but on behalf of the lower company or one of the lower company's own subsidiaries.

(7) For the purposes of *subsection (2)(b)*, a company shall not be regarded as having the right to exercise a dominant influence over another company unless it has a right to give directions with respect to the operating and financial policies of that other company which its directors are obliged to comply with.

(8) In *subsection (2)(b)* "control contract" means a contract in writing conferring such a right as is there referred to which—

(a) is of a kind authorised by the constitution of the company in relation to which the right is exercisable; and

(b) is permitted by the law under which that company is established.

(9) *Subsection (7)* shall not be read as affecting the construction of the expression "actually exercises dominant influence" in *subsection (2)(c)*.

(10) If a document created before the commencement of this section defines the expression "subsidiary" by reference to section 155 of the Act of 1963, then, for the avoidance of doubt, the construction provided in respect of that expression by the document is not affected by this section in the absence of an agreement to the contrary by the parties to the document.

(11) In this section—

"company" includes any body corporate;

"equity share capital" means, in relation to a company, its issued share capital excluding any part of it which, neither as respects dividends nor as respects capital, carries any right to participate beyond a specified amount in a distribution.

Amendments

a Section 5(b)(i) substituted by C(A)A 2017, s 4(a).

b Words inserted by C(A)A 2017, s 4(b).

---

8 Definitions of "holding company", "wholly owned subsidiary" and "group of companies"

(1) For the purposes of this Act, a company is another company's holding company if, but only if, that other is its subsidiary.

(2) For the purposes of this Act, a company is another company's wholly owned subsidiary if, but only if, the company has no members except—

(a) that other company; or

(b) companies that are wholly-owned subsidiaries (by virtue of the application of this subsection to them) of that other company; or

(c) nominees of any company referred to in *paragraph (a)* or *(b)*; or

(d) a mixture of what is referred to in 2 or more of the foregoing paragraphs.

(3) For the purposes of this Act "group of companies" means a holding company and its one or more subsidiaries.

(4) If a document created before the commencement of this section defines the expression "holding company" by reference to section 155 of the Act of 1963, then, for the avoidance of doubt, the construction provided in respect of that expression by the document is not affected by this section in the absence of an agreement to the contrary by the parties to the document.

(5) In this section "company" has the same meaning as it has in *section 7.*

9 Act structured to facilitate its use in relation to most common type of company

(1) Subject to *subsections (3)* and *(4)*, all of the law in this Act in relation to private companies limited by shares is to be found in *Parts 1* to *14* (or instruments under them) and *Schedules 1* to *6.*

(2) Subject to *subsection (3)*, all of the law in this Act in relation to other types of company is to be found amongst the provisions of—

[(a) *Parts 16* to *26* (or instruments under them) and *Schedules 7* to *18*; and][a]

(b) *Parts 1* to *14* (or instruments under them) and *Schedules 1* to *6* as applied or adapted by *Parts 16* to *25.*

(3) *Part 15* (Functions of Registrar and of regulatory and advisory bodies) applies to both—

(a) private companies limited by shares; and

(b) other types of company,

as well as to certain undertakings to which the European Communities (Accounts) Regulations 1993 (S.I. No. 396 of 1993), as amended, apply.

(4) Exceptionally, provisions either—

(a) of a miscellaneous nature arising out of the relationship between a private company limited by shares and another company type (such as provisions for re-registration); or

(b) which it would not otherwise be practicable to include in *Parts 1* to *14* (such as provisions for a merger between a public limited company and a private company limited by shares),

will be found in [*Parts 16* to *26*].[b]

(5) References in *Chapter 6* of *Part 2*, however expressed, to this Part and *Parts 2* to *15* having application to a private company limited by shares shall not be read as excluding the application to such a company of provisions of the kind mentioned in *subsection (4)*.

Amendments

a Section 9(2)(a) substituted by C(A)A 2017, s 5(a).

b Words substituted by C(A)A 2017, s 5(b) (previously: "*Parts 16* to *252*").

10 Reference in *Parts 2* to *14* to company to mean private company limited by shares

(1) Unless expressly provided otherwise, a reference in *Parts 2* to *14* to a company is a reference to a private company limited by shares.

(2) For the avoidance of doubt, *subsection (1)* does not apply to the construction of—

(a) the expression "holding company", where that expression is used without qualification, in *Parts 2* to *14*; or

(b) any related expression, where used without qualification, in those Parts.

11 Construction of references to directors, board of directors and interpretation of certain other plural forms

(1) References in this Act to the directors of a company shall, where the company has a sole director, be read as references to the director of the company.

(2) References in this Act to the board of directors of a company shall, where the company has a sole director, be read as references to the director of the company.

(3) References in this Act to the members of a company, or the subscribers to a company's constitution, shall, where the company has a sole member or where there is a single subscriber to its constitution, be read as references to the member of the company or the subscriber to its constitution, as the case may be.

(4) This section is in addition to, and does not derogate from, any special provision in this Act as to the construction of the expression "director" or "member" in a particular case.

(5) This section is without prejudice to the generality of section 18(a) of the Interpretation Act 2005.

12 Regulations and orders

(1) Subject to *subsection (2)*, the Minister may make regulations prescribing anything referred to in this Act as prescribed or to be prescribed.

(2) *Subsection (1)* does not apply to anything that *Part 11* or *15* provides is to be prescribed by another authority.

(3) Every regulation made by the Minister under this Act (other than a regulation referred to in *section 946*, *1313* or *1321*) or order made by the Minister under this Act (other than an order under *section 1(2)* or *16(1)*) shall be laid before each House of the Oireachtas as soon as may be after it is made and, if a resolution annulling the regulation or order is passed by either such House within the next 21 days on which that House has sat after the regulation or order is laid before it, the regulation or order shall be annulled accordingly but without prejudice to the validity of anything previously done thereunder.

13 Authentication of certain official documents

Any approval, sanction, direction or licence or revocation of licence which, under this Act, may be given or made by the Minister may be signed by any person authorised in that behalf by the Minister.

14 Expenses

The expenses incurred by the Minister in the administration of this Act shall, to such extent as may be sanctioned by the Minister for Public Expenditure and Reform, be paid out of moneys provided by the Oireachtas.

PART 2
INCORPORATION AND REGISTRATION

Chapter 1
Preliminary

15 Definitions (*Part 2*)

In this Part—

"activity" means any activity that a company may be lawfully formed to carry on and includes the holding, acquisition or disposal of property of whatsoever kind;

"existing private company" means a private company limited by shares which—

(a) was incorporated under any former enactment relating to companies (within the meaning of *section 5*); and

(b) is in existence at the commencement of this section,

but does not include such a company where, subsequent to that commencement, it re-registers as another type of company;

"registered person" shall be read in accordance with *section 39(2)*;

"relevant classification system" means NACE Rev. 2, that is to say, the common basis for statistical classifications of economic activities within the European Community set out in the Annex to Council Regulation (EEC) No. 3037/90 of 9 October 1990 on the statistical classification of economic activities in the European Community, as amended for the time being;

"transition period" means the period expiring 18 months after the commencement of this section.

16 Extension of transition period in the event of difficulties

(1) If, in any respect, any difficulties arise in the operation of the provisions of the Act which, in the opinion of the Minister, necessitate the giving of more time for affected or interested parties to undertake any necessary actions or procedures in the period provided for in the definition of "transition period" in *section 15*, the Minister may by order substitute a longer period (but not a period of longer than 30 months) for the period mentioned in that definition.

(2) Where it is proposed to make an order under this section, a draft of the order shall be laid before each House of the Oireachtas and the order shall not be made unless a resolution approving of the draft has been passed by each such House.

Chapter 2
Incorporation and consequential matters

17 Way of forming private company limited by shares

(1) A company may be formed for any lawful purpose by any person or persons subscribing to a constitution and complying with the requirements of this Part as to registration of a company.

(2) The liability of a member of a company at any time shall be limited to the amount, if any, unpaid on the shares registered in the member's name at that time.

(3) *Subsection (2)* is without prejudice to any other liability to which a member may be subject as provided by this Act.

(4) The number of members of a company shall not exceed 149 but, in reckoning that limit, there shall be disregarded any of the following persons.

(5) Those persons are—

(a) a person in the employment of the company who is a member of it;

(b) a person who, having been formerly in the employment of the company, was, while in that employment, and has continued after the termination of the employment to be, a member of it.

(6) Where 2 or more persons hold one or more shares in a company jointly, they shall, for the purposes of this section, be treated as a single member.

(7) Any registration of a person as a member of a company in excess of the limit provided by *subsection (4)* shall be void.

18 Company to carry on activity in the State and prohibition of certain activities

(1) A company shall not be formed or registered unless it appears to the Registrar that the company, when registered, will carry on an activity in the State.

(2) A company shall not carry on the activity of a credit institution or an insurance undertaking.

19 Form of the constitution

(1) The constitution of a company shall state—

(a) the company's name;

(b) that it is a private company limited by shares registered under this Part;

(c) that the liability of its members is limited;

(d) as respects its share capital, either—

(i) the amount of share capital with which it proposes to be registered ("its authorised share capital"), and the division of that capital into shares of a fixed amount specified in the constitution, or

(ii) without stating such amount, that the share capital of the company shall, at the time of its registration, stand divided into shares of a fixed amount specified in the constitution;

(e) the number of shares (which shall not be less than one) taken by each subscriber to the constitution; and

(f) if the company adopts supplemental regulations, those regulations.

(2) The constitution shall—

(a) be in a form in accordance with the form set out in *Schedule 1* or as near to it as circumstances permit;

(b) be divided into paragraphs numbered consecutively; and

(c) either—

(i) be signed by each subscriber in the presence of at least one witness who shall attest the signature; or

(ii) be authenticated in the manner referred to in *section 888*.

(3) Where, subsequent to its registration, an amendment of the constitution is made affecting the matter of share capital, or another matter, referred to in *subsection (1)*, that subsection shall be read as requiring the constitution to state the matter as it stands in consequence of that amendment.

20 Restriction on amendment of constitution

A company may not amend the provisions contained in its constitution except in the cases, in the manner and to the extent for which express provision is made in this Act.

21 Registration of constitution

(1) The constitution of a company shall be delivered for registration to the Registrar together with—

(a) the statement and consent referred to in *section 22*; and

(b) the declaration referred to in *section 24*, and, where appropriate—

(i) the bond referred to in *section 22(6)*;

(ii) the statement referred to in *section 23*.

(2) The Registrar shall not register a constitution delivered for registration under this section unless he or she is satisfied that all the requirements of this Act in respect of registration and of matters precedent and incidental thereto have been complied with.

22 Statement to be delivered with constitution

(1) In this section—

(a) a reference to a statement is to the statement required to be delivered by *section 21(1)(a)*; and

(b) a reference to a company is to the company to which such statement relates.

(2) The statement shall be in the prescribed form and shall state:

(a) the name of each of the persons who are to be the first directors of the company;

(b) the name of the person who is, or of each of the persons who are, to be the first secretary or joint secretaries of the company;

(c) the name of the person (if any) who is, or of each of the persons (if any) who are, to be the first assistant or deputy secretary or secretaries of the company;

(d) the address of the company's registered office; and

(e) the place (whether in the State or not) where the central administration of the company will normally be carried on, and the particulars (in relation to any foregoing person) specified in *subsection (3)* and any other particulars that may be prescribed in relation to such a person or in relation to any other foregoing matter.

(3) The particulars referred to in *subsection (2)* are—

(a) in relation to a person named as director of the company concerned, all particulars which are, in relation to a director, required pursuant to *subsection (2)* of *section 149* to be contained in the register kept under that section;

(b) in relation to a person named as secretary, or as one of the joint secretaries, all particulars which are, in relation to the secretary or to each joint secretary, required pursuant to *subsection (5)* of *section 149* to be contained in the register kept under that section; and

(c) in relation to a person named as assistant or deputy secretary, all particulars which are, in relation to an assistant or deputy secretary, required pursuant to *subsection (7)* of *section 149* to be contained in the register kept under that section.

(4) Where the constitution is delivered, pursuant to *section 21*, to the Registrar by a person (the "agent") as agent for the person or persons who have subscribed to the constitution, the statement shall so specify and shall specify the name and address of the agent.

(5) *Subsections (2)* and *(3)* are without prejudice to *subsection (7)*.

(6) Where no person referred to in *subsection (2)(a)* is resident in an EEA state, there shall be delivered for registration a bond as provided by *section 137(2)*.

(7) In respect of the activity, or one of the activities, to be carried on by the company in the State, the statement shall contain the following particulars:

(a) if it appears to the person making the statement that the activity belongs to a division, group and class appearing in the relevant classification system—

(i) the general nature of the activity; and

(ii) the division, group and class in that system to which the activity belongs;

(b) if it appears to that person that the activity does not belong to any such division, group and class, a precise description of the activity;

(c) the place or places in the State where it is proposed to carry on the activity.

(8) For the purposes of *subsection (7)*, if the purpose or one of the purposes for which the company is being formed is the carrying on of 2 or more activities in the State, the particulars in respect of the matters referred to in *paragraphs (a)* to *(c)* of that subsection to be given in the statement shall be the particulars that relate to whichever of those activities the person making the statement considers to be the principal activity for which the company is being formed to carry on in the State.

(9) The statement shall—

(a) be signed by or on behalf of each subscriber to the constitution of the company or be authenticated in the manner referred to in *section 888*; and

(b) be accompanied by a consent that is either—

(i) signed by each of the persons named in the statement as a director, secretary or joint secretary or assistant or deputy secretary to act in that capacity, or

(ii) authenticated in the manner referred to in *section 888*.

(10) *Section 223(3)*, in the case of a director, and *section 226(5)*, in the case of a secretary, requires the inclusion of a particular statement in a foregoing consent by him or her.

23 Additional statement to be furnished in certain circumstances

(1) If any person named in the statement to be delivered under *section 21(1)(a)* as a director of the company concerned is a person who is disqualified under the law of another state (whether pursuant to an order of a judge or a tribunal or otherwise) from being appointed or acting as a director or secretary of a body corporate or an undertaking, that person has the following obligation.

(2) That obligation is to ensure that the foregoing statement is accompanied by (but as a separate document from that statement) a statement in the prescribed form signed by him or her, or authenticated in the manner referred to in *section 888*, specifying—

(a) the jurisdiction in which he or she is so disqualified;

(b) the date on which he or she became so disqualified; and

(c) the period for which he or she is so disqualified.

24 Declaration to be made to Registrar

(1) In this section—

(a) a reference to a declaration is to the declaration required to be delivered by *section 21(1)(b)*; and

(b) a reference to a company is to the company to which such declaration relates.

(2) The declaration shall state that—

(a) all the requirements in respect of registration of the company and of matters precedent and incidental thereto have been complied with;

(b) the purpose, or one of the purposes, for which the company is being formed is the carrying on by it of an activity in the State; and

(c) the particulars contained in the statement delivered under *section 21(1)(a)* are correct.

(3) The declaration shall be made by—

(a) one of the persons named in the statement delivered under *section 21(1)(a)* as directors of the company;

(b) the person or, as the case may be, one of the persons named in that statement as secretary or joint secretaries of the company; or

(c) the solicitor, if any, engaged in the formation of the company.

(4) The Registrar may accept the declaration as sufficient evidence that all the requirements in respect of registration of the company and of matters precedent and

incidental thereto have been complied with and, in particular, that there have been complied with—

(a) the requirements mentioned in *section 22* and, where appropriate, *section 23*; and

(b) the requirement mentioned in *section 18*.

25 Effect of registration

(1) On the registration of the constitution of a company, the Registrar shall certify in writing that the company is incorporated and shall issue to the company a certificate of incorporation in respect of it.

(2) From the date of incorporation mentioned in the certificate of incorporation, the subscriber or subscribers to the constitution, together with such other persons as may from time to time become members of the company, shall be a body corporate with the name contained in the constitution, having perpetual succession and a common seal.

(3) The certificate of incorporation issued under *subsection (1)* shall state that the company is a private company limited by shares.

(4) A certificate of incorporation issued under *subsection (1)* shall be conclusive evidence that the requirements of *section 21* have been complied with, and that the company is duly registered under this Act.

(5) The persons who are specified in the statement required to be delivered to the Registrar by *section 21(1)(a)* as the director or directors, secretary or joint secretaries or assistant or deputy secretary or secretaries of the company to which the statement refers shall, on the incorporation of the company, be deemed to have been appointed as the first director or directors, secretary or joint secretaries or assistant or deputy secretary or secretaries, as the case may be, of the company.

(6) Any indication in the constitution, as delivered under *section 21* for registration, specifying a person as a director or secretary (including any assistant or deputy secretary) of a company shall be void unless such person is specified as a director or as secretary (or, as the case may be, assistant or deputy secretary) in the foregoing statement.

(7) *Subsection (5)* does not operate to deem a person appointed as a director or secretary (including any assistant or deputy secretary) of a company where—

(a) he or she is disqualified under this Act from being appointed a director, secretary, assistant or deputy secretary, as the case may be, of a company; or

(b) in the case of a director or secretary, a provision of this Act provides that the person's appointment as such in the circumstances is void.

26 Provisions as to names of companies

(1) The name of a company shall end with one of the following:

— limited;

— teoranta.

(2) The word "limited" may be abbreviated to "ltd." (including that abbreviation in capitalised form) in any usage after the company's registration by any person including the company.

(3) The word "teoranta" may be abbreviated to "teo." (including that abbreviation in capitalised form) in any usage after the company's registration by any person including the company.

(4) A company carrying on business under a name other than its corporate name shall register in the manner directed by law for the registration of business names but the use of the abbreviation set out in *subsection (2)* or *(3)* shall not of itself render such registration necessary.

(5) No company shall be registered on—

(a) its incorporation; or

(b) should such occur, its re-registration, merger or division,

by a name which, in the opinion of the Registrar, is undesirable.

(6) An appeal shall lie to the court against a refusal by the Registrar to register a company (in any of the circumstances referred to in *paragraph (a)* or *(b)* of *subsection (5)*) on the ground there referred to.

27 Trading under a misleading name

(1) Neither a body that is not a company nor an individual shall carry on any trade, profession or business under a name which includes, as its last part, the word "limited" or the words "company limited by shares" or any abbreviations of any of the foregoing words.

(2) If a body or individual contravenes *subsection (1)*, the body or individual and, in the case of a body, any officer of it who is in default, shall be guilty of a category 3 offence.

(3) *Subsection (1)* as it relates to the use of the word "limited", or any abbreviation of that word, shall not apply to a society registered under the Industrial and Provident Societies Acts 1893 to 2014.

[(3A) Subsection (1) as it relates to the use of the word 'limited', or any abbreviation of that word, shall not apply to a limited liability partnership (within the meaning of the Legal Services Regulation Act 2015).][a]

(4) A company shall not, in the following circumstances, use a name which may reasonably be expected to give the impression that it is any type of company other than a private company limited by shares or that it is any other form of body corporate.

(5) Those circumstances are circumstances in which the fact that it is a private company limited by shares is likely to be material to any person.

(6) If a company contravenes *subsection (4)*, the company and any officer of it who is in default shall be guilty of a category 3 offence.

(7) *Subsection (1)* shall not apply to any company—

(a) to which *Part 21* applies, and

(b) which has provisions in its constitution that would entitle it to rank as a private company limited by shares (whether under this Part or *Part 16*) if it had been registered in the State.

Amendments

a Subsection (3A) inserted by Legal Services Regulation Act 2015, s 132, not yet commenced as of date of publication of this book.

28 Reservation of a company name

(1) In this section—

"reserved" means reserved under *subsection (4)* for the particular purpose mentioned in *subsection (2)*;

"specified period" means the period specified in the relevant notification made by the Registrar under *subsection (5)*.

(2) A person may apply to the Registrar to reserve a specified name for either of the following purposes, namely—

(a) the purpose of a company that is proposed to be formed by that person being incorporated with that name;

(b) the purpose of a company changing its name to that name,

and, in either such case, such an application shall be accompanied by the prescribed fee.

(3) In *subsection (2)*, "person" means, for the purposes of *paragraph (b)* of it, the company referred to in that paragraph.

(4) On the making of such an application, the Registrar may, subject to *subsection (7)*, determine that the name specified in the application shall be reserved for the particular purpose mentioned in *subsection (2)*.

(5) That determination shall be notified to the applicant by the Registrar and that notification shall specify the period for which the name is reserved.

(6) The specified period shall not be greater than 28 days and shall be expressed to begin on the making of the notification.

(7) A name shall not be reserved that, in the opinion of the Registrar, is undesirable.

(8) A person in whose favour a name has been reserved may, before the expiry of the specified period, apply to the Registrar for an extension of the specified period; such an application shall be accompanied by the prescribed fee.

(9) On the making of such an application, the Registrar may, if he or she considers it appropriate to do so, extend the specified period for such number of days (not exceeding 28 days) as the Registrar determines and specifies in a notification of the determination to the applicant.

29 Effect of reservation of name

(1) During the specified period and any extension under *section 28(9)* of that period, a company shall neither—

(a) be incorporated with a particular reserved name save on application of the person in whose favour that name has been reserved; nor

(b) be incorporated with a name that, in the opinion of the Registrar, is too like a particular reserved name.

(2) During the specified period and any extension under *section 28(9)* of that period, a company shall neither—

(a) change its name to a particular reserved name (unless it is the company in whose favour the name has been reserved); nor

(b) change its name to a name that, in the opinion of the Registrar, is too like a particular reserved name.

(3) If an application for the incorporation of a company with a name that has been reserved under *section 28* is received by the Registrar during the specified period (or any extension of it granted under *section 28(9)*) from the person in whose favour the name has been so reserved, the fee payable to the Registrar in respect of that incorporation shall be reduced by an amount equal to the amount of the fee paid under *section 28(2)* in respect of the reservation of that name.

(4) In this section "reserved" and "specified period" have the same meaning as they have in *section 28*.

30 Change of name

(1) A company may, by special resolution and with the approval of the Registrar, signified in writing, change its name.

(2) *Subsection (3)* applies if, through inadvertence or otherwise, a company is registered by a name (whether on its first registration, or on its registration by a new name) which, in the opinion of the Registrar, is too like the name by which a company in existence is already registered.

(3) Where this subsection applies the first-mentioned company in *subsection (2)*—

(a) with the approval of the Registrar — may change its name; or

(b) if, within 6 months after the date of its being registered by the first-mentioned name in *subsection (2)*, the Registrar directs it to do so — shall change its name.

(4) A direction under *subsection (3)(b)* shall be complied with within a period of 6 weeks after the date of its being given or such longer period as the Registrar may think fit to allow.

(5) Where a company changes its name under this section, the Registrar shall enter the new name in the register in place of the former name, and shall issue a certificate of incorporation altered to meet the circumstances of the case.

(6) A change of name by a company under this section shall not affect any rights or obligations of the company, or render defective any legal proceedings by or against the company, and any legal proceedings which might have been continued or commenced against it by its former name may be continued or commenced against it by its new name.

(7) A company which was registered by a name specified by statute, may, notwithstanding anything contained in that statute, change its name in accordance with *subsection (1)*, but, if the Registrar is of the opinion that any Minister of the Government is concerned in the administration of the statute which specified the name of the company, the Registrar shall not approve of the change of name save after consultation with that Minister of the Government.

(8) If a company fails to comply with a direction under *subsection (3)(b)* within the period provided under *subsection (4)*, the company and any officer of it who is in default shall be guilty of a category 4 offence.

31 Effect of constitution

(1) Subject to the provisions of this Act, the constitution shall, when registered, bind the company and the members of it to the same extent as if it had been signed and sealed by each member, and contained covenants by the company and each member to observe all the provisions of the constitution and any provision of this Act as to the governance of the company.

(2) For the avoidance of doubt, in *subsection (1)* the reference to any provision of this Act as to the governance of the company includes a reference to any provision of this Act that commences with words to the effect that the provision applies save where the company's constitution provides otherwise or otherwise contains a qualification on the provision's application by reference to the company's constitution.

(3) All money payable by any member to the company under the constitution shall be a debt due from him or her to the company.

(4) An action to recover a debt created by this section shall not be brought after the expiration of 12 years after the date on which the cause of action accrued.

32 Amendment of constitution by special resolution

(1) Subject to the provisions of this Act, a company may by special resolution amend its constitution.

(2) Any amendment so made of the constitution shall, subject to the provisions of this Act, be as valid as if originally contained therein, and be subject in like manner to amendment by special resolution.

(3) Where any amendment is made to a company's constitution notice of which *section 33* requires to be published as therein mentioned, the company shall deliver to the Registrar, in addition to the amendment, a copy of the text of the constitution as so amended.

(4) Subject to *subsection (5)*, and notwithstanding anything in the constitution of a company, no member of the company shall be bound by an amendment made to the

constitution after the date on which he or she became a member, if and so far as the amendment—

(a) requires him or her to take or subscribe for more shares than the number held by him or her at the date on which the amendment is made, or

(b) in any way increases his or her liability as at the date referred to in *paragraph (a)* to—

(i) contribute to the share capital of the company, or

(ii) otherwise pay money to the company.

(5) *Subsection (4)* shall not apply in any case where the member agrees in writing, either before or after the amendment is made, to be bound by the amendment.

33 Publication of notices

(1) The Registrar shall publish in the CRO Gazette notice of the delivery to or the issue by the Registrar of the following documents and particulars—

(a) any certificate of incorporation of the company;

(b) the constitution of the company;

(c) any document making or evidencing an amendment of its constitution;

(d) every amended text of its constitution;

(e) any return relating to its register of directors or notification of a change among its directors;

(f) any return relating to the persons, other than the board of directors, authorised to enter into transactions binding the company, or notification of a change among such persons;

(g) its annual return and the financial statements that are required to be published in accordance with *Part 6*;

(h) any notice of the situation of its registered office, or of any change therein;

(i) any copy of a winding up order in respect of the company;

(j) any copy of an order for the dissolution of the company on a winding up;

(k) any return by the liquidator of the final meeting of the company on a winding up;

(l) any notice of the appointment of a liquidator in a voluntary winding up of the company.

(2) The publication referred to in *subsection (1)* shall occur within 10 days after the date of the relevant delivery or issue.

34 Language of documents filed with Registrar

(1) Without prejudice to any other provisions on the language of documents, any document delivered to the Registrar shall be in the Irish or English language.

(2) A translation of any such document may be delivered to the Registrar in any official language of the European Union.

(3) Every translation referred to in *subsection (2)* shall be certified, in a manner approved by the Registrar, to be a correct translation.

(4) In any case of a discrepancy between a document delivered as mentioned in *subsection (1)* and a translation of it delivered pursuant to *subsection (2)*, the latter may not be relied upon by the company against a third party. A third party may, nevertheless, rely on that translation against the company, unless the company proves that the third party had knowledge of the document delivered as mentioned in *subsection (1)*.

(5) In *subsection (4)*, "third party" means a person other than the company or a member, officer or employee of it.

35 Authorisation of an electronic filing agent

(1) A company may authorise a person (who shall be known and is in this Act referred to as an "electronic filing agent") to do the following acts on its behalf.

(2) Those acts are—

(a) the electronic signing of documents that are required or authorised, by or under this Act or any other enactment, to be delivered by the company to the Registrar; and

(b) the delivery to the Registrar, by electronic means, of those documents so signed.

(3) The authorisation of a firm (not being a body corporate) by its firm name to do the foregoing acts on behalf of a company shall operate to authorise the following persons to do those acts on the company's behalf, namely those persons who are from time to time during the currency of the authorisation the partners in that firm as from time to time constituted.

(4) Subject to the following conditions being satisfied, an act of the foregoing kind done by such an agent on behalf of a company pursuant to an authorisation by the company under this section that is in force shall be as valid in law as if it had been done by the company (and the requirements of this Act or the other enactment concerned with respect to the doing of the act have otherwise been complied with (such as with regard to the period within which the act is to be done)).

(5) The conditions mentioned in *subsection (4)* are—

(a) that prior to the first instance of the electronic filing agent's doing of an act of the kind referred to in *subsection (2)*, pursuant to an authorisation by the company concerned under this section, the authorisation of the agent has been notified by the company to the Registrar in the prescribed form; and

(b) the doing of the act complies with any requirements of the Registrar of the kind referred to in sections 12(2)(b) and 13(2)(a) of the Electronic Commerce Act 2000.

(6) It shall be the joint responsibility of a company and the electronic filing agent authorised by it under this section to manage the control of the documents referred to in *subsection (2)*.

[(7) An electronic filing agent shall not, by virtue of his or her authorisation under this section to act as such, be regarded as an officer or servant of the company concerned for the purposes of [section 1535(2) or (3)].[b]][a]

Amendments

a Subsection (7) substituted by the European Union (Statutory Audits) (Directive 2006/43/EC, as amended by Directive 2014/56/EU, and Regulation (EU) No 537/2014) Regulations 2016 (SI 312/2016), reg 7, with effect from 17 June 2016.

b Words substituted by C(SA)A 2018, s 5.

---

36 Revocation of the authorisation of an electronic filing agent

(1) A company may revoke an authorisation by it under *section 35* of an electronic filing agent.

(2) Such a revocation by a company shall be notified by it, in the prescribed form, to the Registrar.

(3) Unless and until the revocation is so notified to the Registrar, the authorisation concerned shall be deemed to subsist and, accordingly, to be still in force for the purposes of *section 35(4)*.

(4) If a revocation, in accordance with this section, of an authorisation under *section 35* constitutes a breach of contract or otherwise gives rise to a liability being incurred—

(a) the fact that it constitutes such a breach or otherwise gives rise to a liability being incurred does not affect the validity of the revocation for the purposes of *section 35*; and

(b) the fact of the revocation being so valid does not remove or otherwise affect any cause of action in respect of that breach or the incurring of that liability.

37 Copies of constitution to be given to members

(1) A company shall, on being so requested by any member, send to him or her a copy of its constitution—

(a) free of charge, and

(b) in the event of a second or subsequent such request by the member (the first request by him or her having been complied with) on payment to it of €5.00.

(2) Where an amendment is made of the constitution of a company, every copy of the constitution issued after the date of the amendment shall be in accordance with the amendment.

(3) If a company contravenes this section, the company and any officer of it who is in default shall be guilty of a category 4 offence.

Chapter 3
Corporate capacity and authority

38 Capacity of private company limited by shares

(1) Subject to *subsection (2)*, notwithstanding anything contained in its constitution a company shall have, whether acting inside or outside of the State—

(a) full and unlimited capacity to carry on and undertake any business or activity, do any act or enter into any transaction; and

(b) for the purposes of *paragraph (a)*, full rights, powers and privileges.

(2) Nothing in *subsection (1)* shall relieve a company from any duty or obligation under any enactment or the general law.

39 Registered person

(1) Where the board of directors of a company authorises any person as being a person entitled to bind the company (not being an entitlement to bind that is, expressly or impliedly, restricted to a particular transaction or class of transactions), the company may notify the Registrar in the prescribed form of the authorisation and the Registrar shall register the authorisation.

(2) A person so authorised, where his or her authorisation is registered in the foregoing manner, is referred to in this Act as a "registered person"; where, in a provision of this Act, that expression appears without qualification, it shall be taken as a reference to a registered person authorised by the board of the directors of the company to which the provision falls to be applied.

(3) Where the board of directors of a company revokes an authorisation of a person as a person entitled to bind the company (being an authorisation notified to the Registrar in the prescribed form), the person shall, notwithstanding that revocation, continue to be regarded for the purposes of this Act as a registered person unless and until the company notifies the Registrar in the prescribed form of that revocation.

(4) References in this section to a person's entitlement to bind the company are references to his or her authority to exercise any power of the company and to authorise others to do so.

(5) In *subsection (4)* "power of the company" does not include—

(a) any power of management of the company exercisable by its board of directors (as distinct from any power of the board to enter into transactions with third parties), or

(b) a power of the company which this Act requires to be exercised otherwise than by its board of directors.

(6) For the avoidance of doubt, for the purposes of this section the provisions of a company's constitution with regard to a person's office or powers shall not, in themselves, be taken as an authorisation by the board of the directors of the company of the person as a person entitled to bind the company.

40 Persons authorised to bind company

(1) For the purposes of any question whether a transaction fails to bind a company because of an alleged lack of authority on the part of the person who exercised (or purported to exercise) the company's powers, the following, namely—

(a) the board of directors of the company; and

(b) any registered person,

shall each be deemed to have authority to exercise any power of the company and to authorise others to do so.

(2) *Subsection (1)* applies regardless of any limitations in the company's constitution on the board's authority or a registered person's authority, but subject to *subsections (5)* and *(8)*.

(3) *Subsection (1)* is not to be read as preventing the exercise of a company's powers otherwise than by the board, a registered person or a person authorised by the board or by a registered person, where authority for that exercise exists.

(4) *Subsection (1)* does not affect—

(a) a director's duties (including a director's duty to observe any limitations in the company's constitution on the board's authority), or his or her liability in respect of any breach of those duties; or

(b) any duty arising on the part of any other person concerned in the transaction (including the registered person) or his or her liability in respect of any breach of that duty.

(5) Where a company is purportedly a party to a transaction—

(a) in connection with which the board of directors exceeded limitations in the company's constitution on their authority; and

(b) to which a person referred to in *subsection (6)* is also a party,

subsection (1) does not apply in favour of the person so referred to.

(6) Each of the following is a person mentioned in *subsection (5)(b)*:

(a) a director or shadow director of the company or of its holding company;

(b) a person connected with such a director;

(c) a registered person;

(d) a person connected with a registered person,

and in this subsection references to a person's being connected with—

(i) a director or shadow director are to be read in accordance with *section 220*; or

(ii) a registered person are to be read in accordance with *section 220* as that section is applied by *subsection (7)*.

(7) For the purpose of *subsection (6)(ii), section 220* applies as if—

(a) for each reference in *subsections (1)*, *(2)*, *(3)* and *(8)* to a director of a company there were substituted a reference to the registered person;

(b) for the first reference and the third reference in *subsection (5)* to a director of a company there were substituted a reference to the registered person;

(c) the references in *subsection (5)* to another director or directors included references to one or more other registered persons; and

(d) the reference in *subsection (6)(b)* to a director included a reference to a registered person.

(8) In *subsection (1)* "power of the company" does not include—

(a) with reference to any registered person, the power of management referred to in *section 39(5)(a)*, and

(b) with reference to the board of directors or any registered person, the power referred to in *section 39(5)(b)*.

(9) Without prejudice to *subsection (1)*, in determining any question whether a person had ostensible authority to exercise any of a company's powers in a given case, no reference may be made to the company's constitution.

(10) In this section a reference—

(a) to limitations in a company's constitution includes a reference to limitations deriving from—

(i) a resolution of the company or of any class of its members; or

(ii) any agreement between the members of the company or of any class of its members;

(b) to a transaction includes a reference to any act or omission.

(11) This section is in addition to, and not in substitution for, the Rule in *Royal British Bank v. Turquand.*

41 Powers of attorney

(1) Notwithstanding anything in its constitution, a company may empower any person, either generally or in respect of any specified matters, as its attorney, to execute deeds or do any other matter on its behalf in any place whether inside or outside the State.

(2) A deed signed by such attorney on behalf of the company shall bind the company and have the same effect as if it were under its common seal.

Chapter 4
Contracts and other transactions

42 Form of contracts

(1) Contracts on behalf of a company may be made as follows—

(a) a contract which, if made between natural persons, would be by law required to be in writing and to be under seal, may be made on behalf of the company in writing under the common seal of the company;

(b) a contract which, if made between natural persons, would be by law required to be in writing, signed by the parties to be charged therewith, may be made on behalf of the company in writing, signed by any person acting under its authority, express or implied;

(c) a contract which, if made between natural persons, would by law be valid although made by parol only, and not reduced into writing may be made by parol on behalf of the company by any person acting under its authority, express or implied.

(2) A contract made according to this section shall bind the company and its successors and all other parties to it.

(3) A contract made according to this section may be varied or discharged in the same manner in which it is authorised by this section to be made.

43 The common seal

(1) A company shall have a common seal or seals that shall state the company's name, engraved in legible characters.

(2) Save as otherwise provided by this Act or by the constitution of the company—

(a) a company's seal shall be used only by the authority of its directors, or of a committee of its directors authorised by its directors in that behalf; and

(b) any instrument to which a company's seal shall be affixed shall be—

(i) signed by a director of it or by some other person appointed for the purpose by its directors or by a foregoing committee of them; and

(ii) be countersigned by the secretary or by a second (if any) director of it or by some other person appointed for the purpose by its directors or by a foregoing committee of them.

(3) Save as otherwise provided by the constitution of the company, if there be a registered person in relation to a company, the company's seal may be used by such person and any instrument to which the company's seal shall be affixed when it is used by the registered person shall be signed by that person and countersigned—

(a) by the secretary or a director of the company; or

(b) by some other person appointed for the purpose by its directors or a committee of its directors authorised by its directors in that behalf.

44 Power for company to have official seal for use abroad

(1) In this section—

"official seal", in relation to a company, means the official seal referred to in *subsection (2)*;

"place abroad" means any territory, district or place not situate in the State.

(2) A company may, if authorised by its constitution, have for use in any place abroad an official seal which shall resemble the common seal of the company with the addition on its face of the name of every place abroad where it is to be used.

(3) A deed or other document to which an official seal is duly affixed shall bind the company as if it had been sealed with the common seal of the company.

(4) A company having an official seal for use in any place abroad may, by writing under its common seal, authorise any person appointed for the purpose in that place (the "agent") to affix the official seal to any deed or other document to which the company is party in that place.

(5) The authority of the agent shall, as between the company and any person dealing with the agent, continue during the period, if any, mentioned in the instrument conferring the authority, or, if no period is there mentioned, then until the notice of revocation or determination of the agent's authority has been given to the person dealing with him or her.

(6) The person affixing an official seal shall, by writing under his or her hand, certify on the deed or other instrument to which the seal is affixed, the date on which and the place at which it is affixed.

45 Pre-incorporation contracts

(1) Any contract or other transaction (including any application to any lawful authority) purporting to be entered into by a company prior to its formation, or by any person on behalf of the company prior to its formation, may be ratified by the company after its formation.

(2) Upon such contract or other transaction being so ratified, the company shall become bound by it and entitled to the benefit of it as if the company had been in existence at the date of such contract or other transaction and had been a party to it.

(3) Prior to such ratification (if any) by the company, the person or persons who purported to act in the name or on behalf of the company shall, in the absence of express agreement to the contrary, be personally bound by the contract or other transaction and entitled to the benefit of it.

46 Bills of exchange and promissory notes

A bill of exchange or promissory note shall be deemed to have been made, accepted or endorsed on behalf of a company, if made, accepted or endorsed in the name of or by or on behalf or on account of, the company by a person acting under its authority.

47 Liability for use of incorrect company name

(1) If an officer of a company or any person on its behalf does any of the following things, the officer or person shall be guilty of a category 4 offence.

(2) Those things are:

(a) uses or authorises the use of any seal purporting to be a seal of the company on which its name is not engraved in legible characters;

(b) issues or authorises the issue of any business letter of the company or any notice or other official publication of the company, or signs or authorises to be signed on behalf of the company any bill of exchange, promissory note, endorsement, cheque or order for money or goods, in which its name is not mentioned in the manner described in *section 49*;

(c) issues or authorises the issue of any invoice, receipt or letter of credit of the company in which its name is not mentioned in the manner described in *section 49*.

(3) In the circumstances of his or her doing a relevant thing mentioned in *subsection (2)(b)*, the officer or other person shall be personally liable to the holder of the bill of exchange, promissory note, cheque or order for money or goods for the amount thereof unless—

(a) it is duly paid by the company; or

(b) it appears to the court that no injustice will be done by imposing liability for the amount on the company.

48 Authentication by company of documents

A document or proceeding requiring authentication by a company may be signed by a director, secretary, registered person or other authorised officer of the company, and need not be under its common seal.

Chapter 5
Company name, registered office and service of documents

49 Publication of name by company

(1) A company—

(a) shall display its name in a conspicuous position, in letters easily legible, outside every office or place in which its business is carried on and at its registered office; and

(b) shall have its name mentioned in legible characters in each of the following:

(i) all notices and other official publications of the company;

(ii) all bills of exchange, promissory notes, endorsements, cheques and orders for money or goods purporting to be signed by or on behalf of the company;

(iii) all invoices, receipts and letters of credit of the company.

(2) If a company contravenes *subsection (1)(a)* or *(b)*, the company and any officer of it who is in default shall be guilty of a category 4 offence.

(3) The use of the abbreviation "ltd" instead of "limited" or "teo" instead of "teoranta" shall not be regarded as constituting a contravention of this section.

(4) This section is without prejudice to *section 151*.

50 Registered office of company

(1) A company shall, at all times, have a registered office in the State to which all communications and notices may be addressed.

(2) Particulars of the situation of the company's registered office shall be specified in the statement delivered pursuant to *section 21(1)(a)* prior to the incorporation of the company.

(3) Notice of any change in the situation of the registered office of a company shall be given in the prescribed form, within 14 days after the date of the change, to the Registrar who shall record that change.

(4) A company's registered office may be constituted by a statement (contained in the statement or notice referred to in *subsection (2)* or *(3)*) to the effect that the office is care of a specified agent, being a company formed and registered under this Act, or an existing company, and which is approved for this purpose by the Registrar; where a registered office is constituted by those means, references in this Act to the situation of the company's registered office shall be read accordingly.

(5) The notification to the Registrar by the agent approved for that purpose of any change in the situation of the agent's registered office shall, if made in the form prescribed for the purpose of *subsection (3)* and within the period there mentioned, be regarded as constituting compliance by the company concerned with *subsection (3)*.

(6) If default is made in complying with this section, the company concerned and any officer of it who is in default shall be guilty of a category 4 offence.

51 Service of documents

(1) A document may be served on a company—

(a) by leaving it at or sending it by post to the registered office of the company; or

(b) if the company has not given notice to the Registrar of the situation of its registered office, by delivering it to the Registrar.

(2) For the purposes of this section, any document left at or sent by post to the place for the time being recorded by the Registrar as the situation of the registered office of a company shall be deemed to have been left at or sent by post to the registered office of the company notwithstanding that the situation of its registered office may have changed.

(3) It shall be the duty of the Registrar to enter on the register a document that has, by the means referred to in *subsection (1)(b)*, been served on a company.

52 Security for costs

Where a company is plaintiff in any action or other legal proceeding, any judge having jurisdiction in the matter, may, if it appears by credible testimony that there is reason to believe that the company will be unable to pay the costs of the defendant if successful in his or her defence, require security to be given for those costs and may stay all proceedings until the security is given.

53 Enforcement of orders and judgments against companies and their officers

(1) Any judgment or order against a company wilfully disobeyed may, by leave of the court, be enforced by—

(a) sequestration against the property of the company,

(b) attachment against the directors or other officers of the company, or

(c) sequestration against the property of such directors or other officers.

(2) An application may not be made, in the foregoing circumstances, for attachment against directors or other officers or for sequestration against their property unless the judgment or order of the court to which the application relates has contained a statement indicating the liability of such persons or of their property to attachment or sequestration, as the case may be, should the judgment or order be disobeyed by the company.

(3) In this section "attachment" and "sequestration" have the same meaning as they have in rules of court concerning the jurisdiction of the High Court and the Supreme Court.

Chapter 6
Conversion of existing private company to private company limited by shares to which Parts 1 to 15 apply

54 Interpretation (*Chapter 6*)

(1) In this Chapter—

"mandatory provision" means a provision of any of *Part 1*, this Part or *Parts 3* to *14* that is not an optional provision;

"optional provision" means a provision of any of *Part 1*, this Part or *Parts 3* to *14* that—

(a) contains a statement to the effect, or is governed by provision elsewhere to the effect, that the provision applies save to the extent that the constitution provides otherwise or unless the constitution states otherwise; or

(b) is otherwise of such import;

"Table A" means Table A in the First Schedule to the Act of 1963.

(2) A reference in this Chapter to a designated activity company is a reference to a designated activity company limited by shares.

(3) A reference in this Chapter to Table A includes, where appropriate, a reference to any Table referred to in section 3(9)(b), (c) or (d) of the Act of 1963.

55 Status of existing private companies at end of transition period: general principle

As provided for in *section 61*, on the expiry of the transition period, unless it has re-registered as a designated activity company or one of the other circumstances specified in that section prevent the following happening—

(a) an existing private company shall be deemed to have a constitution that comprises the provisions of its existing memorandum (other than the provisions excepted by *subsection (1)(a)* of that section) and of its existing articles and subject to *subsection (3)* of that section;

(b) the company's constitution, as so constituted of those provisions, shall be deemed to satisfy the requirements of *section 19* as to the form of a company's constitution, and the company shall be deemed to have become a private company limited by shares to which this Part and *Parts 1* and *3* to *15* apply.

56 Conversion of existing private companies to designated activity companies: duties and powers in that regard

(1) An existing private company may re-register as a designated activity company by passing an ordinary resolution, not later than 3 months before the expiry of the transition period, resolving that the company be so registered; if it so re-registers, pursuant to such a resolution, before the expiry of the transition period, *Part 16* shall, as provided in *section 63(9)*, apply to it.

(2) An existing private company shall re-register as a designated activity company before the expiry of the transition period if, not later than 3 months before the expiry of that period, a notice in writing requiring it to do so is served on it by a member or members holding shares in the company that confer, in aggregate, more than 25 per cent of the total voting rights in the company; on its so re-registering, in compliance with that notice, *Part 16* shall, as provided in *section 63(9)*, apply to it.

(3) Without prejudice to *subsections (1)* and *(2)* but subject to *subsection (4)*, where anything is done by an existing private company, being a thing which (if the company were a private company limited by shares to which this Part and *Parts 1* and *3* to *15* apply) would not be in compliance with *section 68*, then the company shall re-register as a designated activity company before the expiry of the transition period and upon its so doing *Part 16* shall, as provided in *section 63(9)*, apply to it.

(4) Instead of re-registering as a designated activity company as mentioned in *subsection (3)*, an existing private company referred to in that subsection may, by passing a special resolution and otherwise complying with the requirements of *Part 20*, re-register as a type of company that is not a designated activity company before the expiry of the transition period.

(5) The reference in *subsection (2)* to a voting right in a company shall be read as a reference to a right exercisable for the time being to cast a vote at general meetings of members of the company, not being such a right that is exercisable only in special circumstances.

57 Relief where company does not re-register as a designated activity company

(1) Where an existing private company does not, before the expiry of the transition period, re-register as a designated activity company under *section 56* (whether it is obliged under that section to do so or not), the person or persons referred to in *subsection (2)* may apply to the court for an order directing that it shall re-register as such a company and the court shall, unless cause is shown to the contrary, make the order sought or make such other order as seems just.

(2) The persons mentioned in *subsection (1)* are—

(a) one or more members of the company who hold, or together hold, not less than 15 per cent in nominal value of the company's issued share capital or any class thereof; or

(b) one or more creditors of the company who hold, or together hold, not less than 15 per cent of the company's debentures entitling the holders to object to alterations of its objects.

58 Applicable laws during transition period

(1) During the period beginning on the commencement of this Part and ending on the expiry of the transition period, *Part 16* shall, subject to *subsection (3)* and without prejudice to *subsection (7)*, apply to an existing private company as if it were a designated activity company, unless and until there is delivered to the Registrar, in accordance with this Chapter, a constitution in respect of it in the form provided under *section 19*.

(2) If there is so delivered to the Registrar such a constitution in respect of that company then, on and from such delivery, this Part and *Parts 1* and *3* to *15* shall apply to that company.

(3) The provisions of the prior Companies Acts relating to the use of limited or teoranta (or their abbreviations) shall apply as respects the name of an existing private company referred to in *subsection (1)* during the period referred to in that subsection and not the provisions of *section 969* and the other relevant provisions of *Part 16*.

(4) The reference in *subsection (3)* to provisions relating to the use of any words includes a reference to provisions conferring an exemption from the use of those words.

(5) An existing private company that has adopted, or is deemed to have adopted, in whole or in part, the regulations of Table A as its articles, shall, despite the repeal of the Act of 1963, continue to be governed by those regulations (or the parts of them concerned) after the repeal of that Act and, without prejudice to *subsection (8)*, before the expiry of the transition period unless and until—

(a) there is delivered to the Registrar, in accordance with this Chapter, a constitution in respect of it in the form provided under *section 19*; or

(b) it re-registers as another type of company,

but, as regards the company continuing to be governed by the foregoing regulations—

(i) this is save to the extent that those regulations are inconsistent with a mandatory provision;

(ii) those regulations may be altered or added to under and in accordance with the conditions under which articles, whenever registered, are permitted by *Part 16* to be altered or added to; and

(iii) references in those regulations to any provision of the prior Companies Acts shall be read as references to the corresponding provision of this Act.

(6) Subject to *paragraphs (ii)* and *(iii)* of that subsection, the regulations referred to in *subsection (5)* shall be interpreted according to the form in which they existed on the date of repeal of the Act of 1963.

(7) To take account of any interregnum between—

(a) the delivery (in accordance with this Chapter and in the form provided under *section 19*) of a constitution in respect of an existing private company to the Registrar for registration; and

(b) its registration by the Registrar,

it is declared that *subsections (1)* and *(2)* operate, and are to be read as operating, so as also to provide that *Part 16* applies, subject to *subsection (3)*, to that company as if it were a designated activity company during any such interregnum (and accordingly that the application of this Part, and *Parts 1* and *3* to *15*, to it is postponed until that registration is effected).

(8) Likewise, to take account of any similar interregnum in the case of *subsection (5)*, it is declared that that subsection operates, and is to be read as operating, so as also to provide that the whole or part (as the case may be) of the regulations of Table A continue to govern the company concerned during any such interregnum.

(9) For the avoidance of doubt, the application of *Part 16*, in the circumstances under this section where that Part is stated to apply and notwithstanding that the course of action of delivering a constitution of the kind referred to in *subsection (1)* will not be adopted by such a company, extends to an existing private company falling within *subsection (10)* but—

(a) the application of *Part 16* to such a company does not affect the application of the provisions of the statute referred to in *subsection (10)* (or any other relevant statute) to the company; and

(b) if, by virtue of the foregoing statute, the company was not required to include the word "limited" or "teoranta" in its name, that exemption is not affected by anything in this section or *Part 16*.

(10) The existing private company referred to in *subsection (9)* is one that has been incorporated under a former enactment relating to companies (within the meaning of *section 5*) pursuant to, or in compliance with a requirement of, any statute.

59 Adoption of new constitution by members

(1) An existing private company—

(a) by special resolution passed in accordance with its existing memorandum and articles; and

(b) subject to compliance with the provisions of *Part 16* as to the variation of rights and obligations of members,

may, after the commencement of this Part, adopt a new constitution in the form provided under *section 19*; where it does so and delivers, in the prescribed form, before the expiry of the transition period, the constitution to the Registrar for registration, it shall, on the constitution's registration, become a private company limited by shares to which this Part and *Parts 1* and *3* to *15* apply.

(2) The constitution need not contain any supplemental regulations, to the extent that the provisions of this Part and *Parts 1* and *3* to *15* regulate the matters which would be governed by those regulations; for the avoidance of doubt, the requirements of *sections*

19 and *26(1)* relating to a company's name shall apply despite any exemption of the kind referred to in *section 61(3)* that had been enjoyed by the company under the prior Companies Acts.

(3) On registration of its constitution under this section, the Registrar shall issue to the company a certificate of incorporation in respect of it stating that the company is a private company limited by shares registered under this Part.

60 Preparation, registration, etc. of new constitution by directors

(1) The directors of an existing private company shall do each of the things specified in *subsection (2)* before the expiry of the transition period, unless the company—

(a) has already adopted a constitution in accordance with *section 59(1)*; or

(b) is required, under *section 56(2)* or *(3)*, to re-register as a designated activity company; or

(c) is proceeding, in accordance with a resolution passed pursuant to *section 56(1)*, to re-register as such a company or is proceeding, in accordance with *section 56(4)* and *Part 20*, to re-register as another type of company; or

(d) is required by an order made under *section 57* to re-register as a designated activity company or proceedings under that section are pending in relation to it.

(2) The things referred to in *subsection (1)* are—

(a) prepare a constitution for the company in the form provided under *section 19*;

(b) deliver a copy of such constitution to each member; and

(c) deliver, in the prescribed form, the constitution to the Registrar for registration,

and, where the things in the foregoing paragraphs are done (including the delivery of the constitution to the Registrar for registration), the company shall, on the constitution's registration, become a private company limited by shares to which this Part and *Parts 1* and *3* to *15* apply, and the Registrar shall issue to it a certificate of incorporation in respect of it stating that it is a private company limited by shares registered under this Part.

(3) The provisions of that constitution of the company, to be prepared by the directors as mentioned in *subsection (2)(a)*, shall consist solely of—

(a) the provisions of its existing memorandum, other than provisions that—

(i) contain its objects; or

(ii) provide for, or prohibit, the alteration of all or any of the provisions of its memorandum or articles;

and

(b) the provisions of its existing articles,

but, despite any exemption of the kind referred to in *section 61(3)* that had been enjoyed by the company under the prior Companies Acts, nothing in this subsection shall be read as overriding the requirements of *sections 19* and *26(1)* relating to a company's name.

(4) If, by reason of the company not having registered articles, the regulations in Table A are deemed to be the articles of the company, the constitution prepared under *subsection (2)(a)* shall state that the articles of the company comprise those regulations.

(5) If the existing articles do not exclude or modify the regulations contained in the Table A, those regulations shall, so far as applicable, be the regulations of the existing private company in the same manner and to the same extent as if they were contained in the constitution prepared under *subsection (2)(a)*.

(6) For the purposes of *subsections (4)* and *(5)* and without prejudice to their application otherwise by a provision of this Chapter, the regulations contained in Table A shall, despite the repeal of the Act of 1963, continue in force but, as regards the company continuing, by virtue of *subsection (4)* or *(5)*, to be governed (in whole or in part) by the foregoing regulations—

(a) this is save to the extent that those regulations are inconsistent with a mandatory provision;

(b) those regulations may be altered or added to under and in accordance with the conditions under which the company's constitution is permitted by *section 32* to be altered or added to; and

(c) references in those regulations to any provision of the prior Companies Acts shall be read as references to the corresponding provision of this Act.

(7) Subject to *paragraphs (b)* and *(c)* of that subsection, the regulations referred to in *subsection (6)* shall be interpreted according to the form in which they existed on the date of repeal of the Act of 1963.

61 Deemed constitution

(1) Where there has not been delivered to the Registrar a constitution (in the form provided under *section 19*) in respect of an existing private company for registration within the transition period then, subject to *subsection (4)*, from the expiry of that period—

(a) the existing private company shall be deemed to have, in place of its existing memorandum and articles, a constitution that comprises—

(i) the provisions of its existing memorandum, other than provisions that—

(I) contain its objects; or

(II) provide for, or prohibit, the alteration of all or any of the provisions of its memorandum or articles;

and

(ii) the provisions of its existing articles;

and

(b) its constitution, as so constituted of those provisions, shall be deemed to satisfy the requirements of *section 19* as to the form of a company's constitution, and the company shall be deemed to have become a private company limited by shares to which this Part and *Parts 1* and *3* to *15* apply.

(2) In those circumstances the Registrar shall issue to the company a certificate of incorporation in respect of it stating that the company is a private company limited by shares registered under this Part.

(3) Notwithstanding—

(a) section 24, as originally enacted, of the Act of 1963; or

(b) section 24, inserted in the Act of 1963 by section 88(1) of the Company Law Enforcement Act 2001, in place of the first-mentioned section,

and the continuing effect, for certain other types of company, provided elsewhere by this Act of an exemption conferred by or under either such section, any such exemption (whatever its basis) enjoyed, immediately before the expiry of the transition period, by an existing private company to which *subsection (1)* applies shall cease on that expiry; accordingly *subsection (1)(a)* shall be read as requiring such a company's name to end with "limited" or "teoranta", as appropriate, and *subsection (2)* shall have effect subject to this subsection.

(4) *Subsection (1)* shall not apply if—

(a) the existing company has re-registered before the expiry of the transition period as a designated activity company in accordance with *section 56(1)* or as another type of company in accordance with *section 56(4)* and *Part 20*;

(b) the existing company is required under *section 56(2)* or *(3)* to re-register as such a company and has so re-registered; or

(c) its operation would be inconsistent with an order of the court made under *section 57* or otherwise.

(5) If, by reason of *section 58*, an existing private company was, immediately before the expiry of the transition period or, if later, the end of the interregnum referred to in *section 58(8)*, governed (in whole or in part) by the regulations contained in Table A, then for the purposes of this section and without prejudice to their application otherwise by a provision of this Chapter, those regulations shall, despite the repeal of the Act of 1963, continue in force and the existing articles of the company shall be deemed to comprise the whole of those regulations or, as the case may be, to include the parts concerned of those regulations, but—

(a) this is save to the extent that those regulations are inconsistent with a mandatory provision;

(b) those regulations may be altered or added to under and in accordance with the conditions under which the company's constitution is permitted by *section 32* to be altered or added to; and

(c) references in those regulations to any provision of the prior Companies Acts shall be read as references to the corresponding provision of this Act.

(6) Subject to *paragraphs (b)* and *(c)* of that subsection, the regulations referred to in *subsection (5)* shall be interpreted according to the form in which they existed on the date of repeal of the Act of 1963.

62 Relief for members and creditors

(1) Without limiting the generality of *section 212*, if any member of a company considers that his or her rights or obligations have been prejudiced by—

(a) the exercise of any power under this Chapter;

(b) the non-exercise of any such power; or

(c) the exercise of any such power in a particular manner,

by the company or the directors of it, the member may apply to the court for an order under *section 212*.

(2) In any such application where it is proved that the directors of the company have failed to comply with *section 60* then, unless the members of the company have adopted a new constitution in accordance with *section 59(1)*, it shall be presumed, until the contrary is proved, that the directors have exercised their powers in a manner oppressive to the applicant or in disregard of his or her interests as a member.

(3) Where in relation to an existing private company a constitution in the form provided under *section 19* comes into being, the person or persons referred to in *subsection (5)* may apply under this subsection to the court for relief if the constitution prejudices any interest of the person or persons (but only if the person or persons has or have a legal or equitable right to that interest).

(4) On the hearing of an application under *subsection (3)*, the court may grant such relief to the applicant or applicants as the court thinks just.

(5) The persons mentioned in *subsection (3)* are one or more creditors of the company who hold, or together hold, not less than 15 per cent of the company's debentures entitling the holders to object to alterations of its objects.

(6) The jurisdiction of the court under *section 212* as provided for under *subsection (1)* and the jurisdiction of the court under *subsection (3)* shall each be exercised having regard to, and, where appropriate subject to, any exercise by the court of its jurisdiction under *section 57* in relation to the company concerned.

(7) In this section a reference to a constitution in the form provided under *section 19* coming into being is a reference to such a constitution coming into being by reason of—

(a) its being adopted and registered under *section 59*; or

(b) its being prepared by the directors and registered under *section 60*; or

(c) the operation of *section 61*.

63 Procedure for re-registration as designated activity company under this Chapter

(1) This section contains the procedure for re-registration by an existing private company as a designated activity company under *section 56(1)*, *(2)* or *(3)* or pursuant to an order of the court under *section 57(1)*.

(2) Either—

(a) in the case of re-registration under *section 56(1)*, the ordinary resolution referred to in that provision; or

(b) in the case of re-registration under *subsection (2)* or *(3)* of *section 56* or pursuant to an order of the court under *section 57(1)*, a resolution of the directors of the company passed for the purpose in consequence of that subsection's operation or that order,

shall alter the company's memorandum so that it states that the company is to be a designated activity company and shall, unless this Act provides that on re-registration the company shall continue to enjoy an exemption conferred by or under either of the sections referred to in *section 61(3)*, alter that document and the articles so that there is substituted "designated activity company" or "cuideachta ghníomhaíochta ainmnithe" for "limited" or "teoranta", as the case may be, in the company's name.

(3) An application for the purpose of re-registration, in the prescribed form and signed by a director or secretary of the company, shall be delivered by the company to the Registrar together with the documents specified in *subsection (4)*.

(4) Those documents are—

(a) a copy of the ordinary resolution or the resolution of the directors referred to in *subsection (2)(a)* or *(b)*;

(b) a copy of the memorandum and articles of the company as altered by the resolution; and

(c) a statement in the prescribed form (in this section referred to as a "statement of compliance") by a director or secretary of the company that the requirements of this Chapter as to re-registration as a designated activity company have been complied with by the company, including the passing of the resolution referred to in *paragraph (a)*.

(5) The Registrar may accept the statement of compliance as sufficient evidence that the resolution referred to in *subsection (4)(a)* has been duly passed and the other conditions of this Chapter for re-registration as a designated activity company have been satisfied and that the company is entitled to be re-registered as that type of company.

(6) If, on an application under *subsection (3)* for re-registration of an existing private company as a designated activity company, the Registrar is satisfied that a company is entitled to be so re-registered, the Registrar shall—

(a) retain the application and the other documents delivered to him or her under this section; and

(b) issue to the company a certificate of incorporation in respect of it, being a certificate of incorporation that—

(i) is altered to meet the circumstances of the case; and

(ii) states that it is issued on re-registration of the company and the date on which it is issued.

(7) If the existing private company had not registered articles and, by reason of *section 58*, the regulations in Table A are, immediately before the making by the company of an application under *subsection (3)*, deemed to be its articles, then each of the references in the preceding subsections of this section to articles shall be disregarded, but in such a case the application under *subsection (3)* shall be accompanied by a statement in the prescribed form that the articles of the company comprise those regulations.

(8) Upon the issue to a company of a certificate of incorporation on re-registration under *subsection (6)*—

(a) the company shall, by virtue of the issue of that certificate, become a designated activity company; and

(b) any alterations in the memorandum and articles set out in the resolution concerned shall take effect accordingly.

(9) A certificate of incorporation issued on re-registration to a company under *subsection (6)* shall be conclusive evidence—

(a) that the requirements of this Chapter as to re-registration and of matters precedent and incidental thereto have been complied with; and

(b) that the company is the type of company which is set out in the certificate,

and, accordingly, without prejudice to *section 58*, *Part 16*, on and from the issue of the certificate, shall apply to the company as a designated activity company.

(10) If, by reason of *section 58*, an existing private company was, immediately before the making by the company of an application under *subsection (3)*, governed (in whole or in part) by the regulations contained in Table A, then for the purposes of this section and in addition to the other cases where their continuance in force for a particular purpose is provided for by this Chapter, those regulations shall, despite the repeal of the Act of 1963, continue in force and upon the issue of the aforementioned certificate of incorporation the articles of the designated activity company shall be deemed to comprise the whole of those regulations or, as the case may be, to include the parts concerned of those regulations, but—

(a) this is save to the extent that those regulations are inconsistent with a mandatory provision;

(b) those regulations may be altered or added to under and in accordance with the conditions under which the designated activity company's articles are permitted by *Part 16* to be altered or added to; and

(c) references in those regulations to any provision of the prior Companies Acts shall be read as references to the corresponding provision of this Act.

(11) Subject to *paragraphs (b)* and *(c)* of that subsection, the regulations referred to in *subsection (10)* shall be interpreted according to the form in which they existed on the date of repeal of the Act of 1963.

(12) The re-registration of an existing private company as a designated activity company pursuant to this Chapter shall not affect any rights or obligations of the company or render defective any legal proceedings by or against the company, and

any legal proceedings which might have been continued or commenced against it in its former status may be continued or commenced against it in its new status.

(13) The procedures under this section may be followed, after consultation by the company with the relevant Minister, by an existing private company that has been incorporated under a former enactment relating to companies (within the meaning of *section 5*) pursuant to, or in compliance with a requirement of, any statute (in *subsection (11)* referred to as the "relevant statute") and may be so followed notwithstanding that statute but—

(a) the provisions otherwise of that statute (and any other relevant statute) shall apply to the designated activity company that the foregoing company re-registers as under this section as they apply to the foregoing company before such re-registration; and

(b) if the foregoing company is a company to which *section 1446* applies, the provision made by *subsection (1)* requiring the substitution of certain words in its name shall be taken to be omitted from that subsection.

(14) In *subsection (13)* "relevant Minister" means the Minister of the Government concerned in the administration of the relevant statute.

(15) For the avoidance of doubt, references in *Part 6*, and in particular *section 349* (which exempts a company from having to annex financial statements to its first annual return), to the incorporation of a company are references to its original incorporation.

PART 3
SHARE CAPITAL, SHARES AND CERTAIN OTHER INSTRUMENTS

Chapter 1
Preliminary and interpretation

64 Interpretation (*Part 3*)

(1) In this Part—

"capital conversion reserve fund", in relation to a company, means the amount equivalent to the aggregate diminution in share capital consequential upon renominalisation of share capital under section 26 of the Economic and Monetary Union Act 1998;

"cash" includes funds in any currency or currencies;

"company capital", in relation to a company, means—

(a) the aggregate value, expressed as a currency amount, of the consideration received by the company in respect of the allotment of shares of the company; and

(b) that part of the company's undenominated capital constituted by the transfer of sums referred to in *sections 106(4)* and *108(3)*,

and *subsection (2)* supplements this definition;

"employees' share scheme" means any scheme, for the time being in force, in accordance with which a company encourages or facilitates the holding of shares in, or debentures of, the company or its holding company by or for the benefit of employees or former employees of the company or of any subsidiary of the company including any person who is or was a director holding a salaried employment or office in the company or any subsidiary of the company;

"nominal value", in relation to a share, means a monetary amount, expressed as an amount, multiple, fraction or percentage of any currency or currencies or combination thereof;

"parent public company" means a public limited company which has one or more private limited subsidiaries;

"private limited subsidiary" means a subsidiary that is a private company limited by shares but, for the purposes of this definition, a company shall not be regarded as a subsidiary if it is such only by virtue of *section 7(2)(a)(ii)* or *(e)*;

"redeemable shares" includes shares which are liable at the option of the company or the shareholder to be redeemed;

"securities" means—

(a) shares in a company;

(b) debentures of a company, including debenture stock, bonds and any other debt instruments of a company whether constituting a charge on the assets of the company or not;

(c) those classes of securities which are negotiable on the capital market, such as:

(i) shares in bodies corporate and other securities equivalent to shares in bodies corporate, partnerships or other entities, and depositary receipts in respect of shares;

(ii) bonds or other forms of securitised debt, including depositary receipts in respect of such securities;

(iii) any other securities giving the right to acquire or sell any such transferable securities or giving rise to a cash settlement determined by reference to transferable securities, currencies, interest rates or yields, commodities or other indices or measures with the exception of instruments of payment;

"share capital", in relation to a company, means the aggregate amount or value of the nominal value of shares of the company;

"undenominated capital", in relation to a company, means the amount of the company capital from time to time which is in excess of the nominal value of its issued shares and shall be deemed to include any sum transferred as referred to in *sections 106(4)* and *108(3)*.

(2) There is included in the definition of "company capital" in *subsection (1)* any amounts standing, immediately before the commencement of this section, to the credit of—

(a) the company's share premium account (within the meaning of the prior Companies Acts);

(b) its capital redemption reserve fund (within the meaning of those Acts); and

(c) its capital conversion reserve fund.

(3) For the purposes of this Part a share in a company shall be taken to have been paid up (as to its nominal value or any premium on it) in cash or allotted for cash if the consideration for the allotment or the payment up is—

(a) cash received by the company; or

(b) a cheque received by the company in good faith which the directors have no reason for suspecting will not be paid; or

(c) the release of a liability of the company for a liquidated sum; or

(d) an undertaking to pay cash to the company on demand or at an identified or identifiable future date which the directors have no reason for suspecting will not be complied with.

(4) In relation to the allotment or payment up of any shares in a company, references in this Act, other than in *section 69(12)(c)*, to consideration other than cash and to the payment up of shares and premiums on shares otherwise than in cash include references to the payment of, or an undertaking to pay, cash to any person other than the company.

65 Powers to convert shares into stock, etc.

(1) Each provision of this section applies save to the extent that the company's constitution provides otherwise.

(2) A company may, by ordinary resolution—

(a) convert any of its paid up shares into stock; and

(b) reconvert any stock into paid up shares of any denomination.

(3) Subject to *subsection (4)*, the holders of stock may transfer the stock, or any part of it, in the same manner and subject to the same regulations as, and subject to which the shares from which the stock arose might, previously to conversion, have been transferred, or as near thereto as circumstances admit.

(4) The directors of a company may from time to time fix the minimum amount of stock that is capable of being transferred but any such minimum so fixed shall not exceed the nominal amount of each share from which the stock arose.

(5) Subject to *subsection (6)*, the holders of stock shall, according to the amount of stock held by them, have the same rights, privileges and advantages in relation to dividends, voting at meetings of the company and other matters as if they held the shares from which the stock arose.

(6) No such right, privilege or advantage (except participation in the dividends and profits of the company and in the assets on winding up) shall be conferred by an amount of stock which would not, if existing in shares, have conferred that right, privilege or advantage.

(7) Such of the regulations of a company as are applicable to paid up shares shall apply to stock of the company, and the words "share" and "shareholder" in those regulations shall be read as including "stock" and "stockholder", respectively.

66 Shares

(1) Shares in the capital of a company shall have a nominal value.

(2) A company may allot shares—

(a) of different nominal values;

(b) of different currencies;

(c) with different amounts payable on them; or

(d) with a combination of 2 or more of the foregoing characteristics.

(3) Without prejudice to any special rights previously conferred on the holders of any existing shares or class of shares, any share in a company may be issued with such preferred, deferred or other special rights or such restrictions, whether in regard to dividend, voting, return of capital or otherwise, as the company may from time to time by ordinary resolution determine.

(4) Save to the extent that its constitution provides otherwise, a company may allot shares that are redeemable (which shall be known, and are referred to in this Act, as "redeemable shares").

(5) The shares or other interest of any member in a company shall be personal estate and shall not be of the nature of real estate.

(6) Except as required by law, no person shall be recognised by a company as holding any share upon any trust and the company shall not be bound by or be compelled in any way to recognise (even when having notice of it)—

(a) any equitable, contingent, future or partial interest in any share or any interest in any fractional part of a share; or

(b) save only as this Act or other law otherwise provides, any other rights in respect of any share, except an absolute right to the entirety of it in the registered holder.

(7) *Subsection (6)* shall not preclude the company from requiring a member or a transferee of shares to furnish the company with information as to the beneficial ownership of any share when such information is reasonably required by the company.

(8) In *subsections (9)* and *(10)* "bearer instrument" means an instrument, in relation to shares of a company, which entitles or purports to entitle the bearer thereof to transfer the shares that are specified in the instrument by delivery of the instrument.

(9) A company shall not have power to issue any bearer instrument.

(10) If a company purports to issue a bearer instrument, the shares that are specified in the instrument shall be deemed not to have been allotted or issued, and the amount subscribed therefor (and in the case of a non-cash asset subscribed therefor, the cash value of that asset) shall be due as a debt of the company to the purported subscriber thereof.

67 Numbering of shares

(1) Subject to *subsections (2)* and *(3)*, each share in a company shall be distinguished by its appropriate number.

(2) If at any time, all the issued shares in a company or all the issued shares in it of a particular class are fully paid up and rank *pari passu* for all purposes, none of those shares need thereafter have a distinguishing number, so long as it—

(a) remains fully paid up; and

(b) ranks *pari passu* for all purposes with all shares of the same class for the time being issued and fully paid up.

(3) Where new shares are issued by a company on the terms that, within a period not exceeding 12 months, they will rank *pari passu* for all purposes with all the existing shares, or with all the existing shares of a particular class in the company, neither the new shares nor the corresponding existing shares need have distinguishing numbers so long as all of them are fully paid up and rank *pari passu*.

(4) However, in the circumstances mentioned in *subsection (3)*, the share certificates of the new shares shall, if not numbered, be appropriately worded or enfaced.

Chapter 2
Offers of securities to the public

68 Limitation on offers of securities to the public

(1) Subject to the provisions of this section, a company shall not—

(a) make—

(i) any invitation to the public to subscribe for; or

(ii) any offer to the public of,

any shares, debentures or other securities of the company; or

(b) allot, or agree to allot, (whether for cash or otherwise) any shares in or debentures of the company with a view to all or any of those shares or debentures being offered for sale to the public or being the subject of an invitation to the public to subscribe for them.

(2) [Subject to *subsection (8A)*, a company shall][a]—

(a) neither apply to have securities (or interests in them) admitted to trading or to be listed on; nor

(b) have securities (or interests in them) admitted to trading or listed on,

any market, whether a regulated market or not, in the State or elsewhere.

(3) *Subsection (1)* shall not apply to any of the following offers or allotments of debentures by a company (wherever they may be made)—

(a) an offer of debentures addressed solely to qualified investors;

(b) an offer of debentures addressed to fewer than 150 persons, other than qualified investors;

(c) an offer of debentures addressed to investors who acquire securities for a total consideration of at least €100,000 per investor, for each separate offer;

(d) an offer of debentures whose denomination per unit amounts to at least €100,000;

(e) an offer of debentures with a total consideration in the European Union less than €100,000, which shall be calculated over a period of 12 months;

(f) an allotment of debentures, or an agreement to make such an allotment, with a view to those debentures being the subject of any one or more of the offers referred to in *paragraphs (a)* to *(e)*,

and the reference in this subsection to an offer of debentures includes an invitation to subscribe for them.

(4) *Subsection (1)* shall not apply to—

(a) an offer of shares by a company (of any amount or wherever it may be made), being an offer addressed to—

(i) qualified investors; or

(ii) 149 or fewer persons; or

(iii) both qualified investors and 149 or fewer other persons;

or

(b) an allotment of shares, or an agreement to make such an allotment, with a view to those shares being the subject of an offer referred to in *paragraph (a)*,

and the reference in this subsection to an offer of shares includes an invitation to subscribe for them.

(5) *Subsection (1)* shall not apply to an offer by a company of those classes of instruments which are normally dealt in on the money market (such as treasury bills, certificates of deposit and commercial papers) having a maturity of less than 12 months, and the reference in this subsection to an offer of instruments includes an invitation to subscribe for them.

(6) A word or expression that is used in this section and is also used in the Prospectus (Directive 2003/71/EC) Regulations 2005 (S.I. No. 324 of 2005) shall have in this section the same meaning as it has in those Regulations.

(7) For the purposes of *subsection (6)*, the Regulations referred to in that subsection shall have effect as if Regulation 8 were omitted therefrom.

(8) Nothing in this section shall affect the validity of any allotment or sale of securities or of any agreement to allot or sell securities.

[(8A) *Subsection (2)* shall not apply to securities (or interests in them) which were, prior to 1 June 2015, admitted to trading or listed on any market, whether a regulated market or not, in the State or elsewhere.][b]

(9) If a company contravenes *subsection (1)* or *(2)*, the company and any officer of it who is in default shall be guilty of a category 2 offence.

Amendments

a Words substituted by C(A)A 2017, s 6(a) (previously: "A company shall—").
b Subsection (8A) added by C(A)A 2017, s 6(b).

Chapter 3
Allotment of shares

69 Allotment of shares

(1) No shares may be allotted by a company unless the allotment is authorised, either specifically or pursuant to a general authority, by ordinary resolution or by the constitution of the company.

(2) Without prejudice to *subsection (1)*, in the case of a company whose constitution states an authorised share capital, no shares may be allotted by the company unless those shares are comprised in the authorised but unissued share capital of the company.

(3) An authorisation for the purposes of *subsection (1)* (whether conferred by an ordinary resolution or the constitution) may stipulate a period during which the allotment may occur; if it so stipulates, then allotments occurring outside that period are not authorised by it.

(4) Save to the extent that the constitution of the company provides otherwise—

(a) shares of a company may only be allotted by the directors of the company;

(b) the directors of a company may allot, grant options over or otherwise dispose of shares to such persons, on such terms and conditions and at such times as they may consider to be in the best interests of the company and its shareholders.

(5) Any director of a company who knowingly contravenes, or knowingly permits or authorises a contravention of, a preceding provision of this section shall be guilty of a category 3 offence.

(6) Subject to *subsections (8)* and *(12)* and *section 70*, a company proposing to allot any shares—

(a) shall not allot any of those shares, on any terms—

(i) to any non-member, unless it has made an offer to each person who holds relevant shares, of the class concerned, in the company to allot to him or her, on the same or more favourable terms, a proportion of those relevant shares which is, as nearly as practicable, equal to the proportion in nominal value held by him or her of the aggregate of the shares of that class; or

(ii) to any person who holds shares in the company, unless it has made an offer to each person who holds relevant shares, of the class concerned, in the company to allot to him or her, on the same terms, a proportion of those shares which is, as nearly as practicable, equal to the proportion in nominal value held by him or her of the aggregate of the relevant shares of that class;

and

(b) shall not allot any of those shares to any person unless the period during which any such offer may be accepted (not being less than 14 days) has expired or the company has received notice of the acceptance or refusal of every offer so made.

(7) In—

(a) *subsection (6)* "relevant shares", in relation to a company, means shares in the company other than shares which as respects dividends and capital carry a right to participate only to a specified amount in a distribution;

(b) *subsection (6)(a)(ii)* "non-member" means a person who is not a holder of shares (as that expression is to be read by virtue of *section 70(4)*) in the company.

(8) Where a company's constitution contains provisions which—

(a) require that the company, when proposing to allot shares of a particular class, shall not allot those shares unless it makes an offer of those shares to existing holders of shares of that class; and

(b) specify that the minimum period during which that offer may be accepted is not less than 14 days,

then *subsection (6)* shall not apply to any allotments made in compliance with such provisions.

(9) An offer which is required by—

(a) *subsection (6)*; or

(b) the provisions of the company's constitution referred to in *subsection (8)*,

to be made to any person shall be made by serving it on him or her in the same manner in which notices are authorised to be given by *sections 180, 181* and *218*.

(10) Any such offer as is mentioned in *subsection (6)* or *(8)* shall not be withdrawn before the end of the period that the offer referred to in *subsection (6)* or, as the case may be, the provisions of the company's constitution referred to in *subsection (8)* specify as the period within which it may be accepted.

(11) Nothing in *subsection (6)(b), (9)* or *(10)* shall invalidate provisions of the company's constitution referred to in *subsection (8)* by reason that those provisions require or authorise an offer thereunder to be made in contravention of one or more of those subsections, but, to the extent that those provisions require or authorise such an offer to be so made, they shall be of no effect.

(12) *Subsection (6)* shall not apply—

(a) to the extent that—

(i) the constitution of the company,

(ii) a special resolution, or

(iii) the terms of issue of already allotted shares,

provides or provide (either generally or in respect of a particular allotment or class of allotments), to the extent so provided;

(b) to allotments of shares for a consideration wholly or partly paid for, otherwise than in cash;

(c) to allotments of shares to the subscriber or subscribers to the company's constitution upon the company's incorporation, being the shares taken by that subscriber or those subscribers before such incorporation;

(d) to allotments of shares to persons in pursuance of the terms of an employees' share scheme established by the company;

(e) to allotments of bonus shares.

70 Supplemental and additional provisions as regards allotments

(1) Shares which a company has offered to allot to a holder of shares in the company may be allotted to that holder or anyone in whose favour that holder has renounced his or her right to their allotment without contravening *section 69(6)(b)*.

(2) Notwithstanding that any authorisation conferred by a resolution or the constitution such as is mentioned in *section 69(1)* has expired, the directors of a company may allot shares in pursuance of an offer or agreement previously made by the company, if that authorisation enabled the company to make an offer or agreement which would or might require shares to be allotted after the authorisation's expiry.

(3) For the purposes of *section 69* and this section—

(a) "allot" includes "agreement to allot" (other than an agreement made subject to the passing of an ordinary or special resolution);

(b) "shares" includes a right to subscribe for shares or to convert securities into shares,

and with the effect that—

(i) in the case of *paragraph (a)*, if an agreement to allot shares is entered into in compliance with *section 69*, *subsections (3)*, *(4)* and *(6)* of that section shall not apply to an allotment of shares pursuant to that agreement; and

(ii) in the case of *paragraph (b)*, if a right to subscribe for shares, or to convert securities into shares, is granted in compliance with *section 69*, *subsections (3)*, *(4)* and *(6)* of that section shall not apply to an allotment of shares pursuant to the exercise of that right.

(4) References in *section 69* and this section (however expressed) to the holder of shares or the holder of shares of any class shall be read as including references to any person who held shares or, as the case may be, shares of that class on any day within the period of 28 days ending with the day immediately preceding the date of the offer which is specified by the directors of the company concerned as being the record date for the purposes of the offer.

(5) A resolution of a company to give, vary, revoke or renew an authority for the purposes of *section 69(1)* may, notwithstanding that it alters the company's constitution, be an ordinary resolution.

(6) Where a company allots shares, the shares shall be taken, for the purposes of this Act, to be allotted when a person acquires the unconditional right to be included in the company's register of members in respect of those shares.

(7) Where a company allots shares, it shall, within 30 days after the date of allotment, deliver particulars of the allotment in the prescribed form to the Registrar.

(8) If a company fails to comply with *subsection (7)*, the company and any officer of it who is in default shall be guilty of a category 4 offence.

(9) Nothing in *section 69* or this section shall affect the validity of any allotment of shares.

(10) Where there is a contravention of *section 69(6)*, the company and every officer of the company who knowingly authorised or permitted the contravention, shall be jointly and severally liable to compensate any person to whom an offer should have been made under *section 69(6)* for any loss, damage, costs or expenses which that person has sustained or incurred by reason of the contravention.

(11) No proceedings to recover any such loss, damage, costs or expenses shall be commenced after the expiration of 2 years after the date of the delivery to the Registrar of the return of allotments in question or, where shares are agreed to be allotted, the agreement.

(12) If, before the commencement of *section 69*, the directors of a company have been granted authority, pursuant to section 20 of the Act of 1983, to allot relevant securities (within the meaning of that section 20) and that authority is in force immediately before that commencement—

(a) neither *section 69* nor this section shall apply to the allotment, after that commencement, of relevant securities by the directors pursuant to that authority (which authority shall, in accordance with its terms, be taken to remain in force); and

(b) section 20 (other than subsections (4) and (9) thereof), and sections 23 and 24, of the Act of 1983 shall apply to that authority and any allotment of relevant securities on foot thereof,

but, on the expiry of that authority, *section 69* and this section shall apply to any allotment thereafter of shares in the company (or the grant of any right to subscribe for shares in the company or to convert securities into such shares).

(13) For the purposes of *subsection (12)*—

(a) "Act of 1983" means the Companies (Amendment) Act 1983;

(b) the reference to the grant of an authority includes a reference to the conferral, by the articles of the company, of an authority; and

(c) the exclusion of the application of section 20(4) of the Act of 1983 by *paragraph (b)* of *subsection (12)* shall not be taken as preventing the renewal of the authority concerned under *section 69* and this section, but if that authority is so renewed, *section 69* and this section shall apply to any allotment, or the grant of any right, as mentioned in *subsection (12)*, that occurs after that renewal of authority on foot thereof.

71 Payment of shares

(1) Shares may be paid up in money or money's worth (including goodwill and expertise).

(2) Shares of a company shall not be allotted at a discount to their nominal value.

(3) Where shares are allotted in contravention of *subsection (2)*, the allottee shall be liable to pay the company concerned an amount equal to the amount of the discount and interest thereon at the appropriate rate.

(4) *Subsections (1)* and *(2)* shall not prevent a company from allotting bonus shares as provided by this Part.

(5) Subject to *sections 72*, *73* and *75*, any value received in respect of the allotment of a share in excess of its nominal value shall be credited to and form part of undenominated capital of the company and, for that purpose, shall be transferred to an account which shall be known, and in this Act is referred to, as the "share premium account".

(6) Where any person becomes a holder of any shares in respect of which—

- (a) there has been a contravention of this section; and
- (b) by virtue of that contravention, another is liable to pay any amount under this section,

the first-mentioned person in this subsection also shall be liable to pay that amount (jointly and severally with any other person so liable) unless either that first-mentioned person is a purchaser for value and, at the time of the purchase, he or she did not have actual notice of the contravention or he or she derived title to the shares (directly or indirectly) from a person who became a holder of them after the contravention and was not so liable.

(7) Where a company contravenes any of the provisions of this section, the company and any officer of it who is in default shall be guilty of a category 3 offence.

72 Restriction of *section 71(5)* in the case of mergers

(1) This section applies where the issuing company has secured at least a 90 per cent equity share capital holding in another company in pursuance of an arrangement providing for the allotment of equity share capital in the issuing company, on terms that the consideration for the shares allotted is to be provided—

- (a) by the issue or transfer to the issuing company of equity shares in the other company; or
- (b) by the cancellation of any such shares not held by the issuing company.

(2) If the equity shares in the issuing company, allotted in pursuance of the arrangement in consideration for the acquisition or cancellation of equity shares in the other company, are issued at a premium *section 71(5)* does not apply to the premiums on those shares.

(3) Where the arrangement also provides for the allotment of any shares in the issuing company on terms that the consideration for those shares is to be provided by the issue or transfer to the issuing company of non-equity shares in the other company or by the cancellation of any such shares in that company not held by the issuing company, the restriction on the application of *section 71(5)* provided by *subsection (2)* extends to any shares in the issuing company allotted on those terms in pursuance of the arrangement.

(4) Subject to *subsection (5)*, the issuing company ("company X") is to be regarded for purposes of this section as having secured at least a 90 per cent equity share capital holding in another company ("company Y") in pursuance of such an arrangement

as is mentioned in *subsection (1)* if in consequence of an acquisition or cancellation of equity shares in company Y (in pursuance of that arrangement)—

(a) company X holds equity shares in company Y (whether all or any of those shares were acquired in pursuance of that arrangement, or not); and

(b) the aggregate nominal value of the equity shares so held by company X equals 90 per cent or more of the nominal value of company Y's equity share capital (excluding any shares in company Y held as treasury shares).

(5) Where the equity share capital of the other company is divided into different classes of shares, this section does not apply unless the requirements of *subsection (1)* are satisfied in relation to each of those classes of shares taken separately.

(6) Shares held by a company which is the issuing company's holding company or subsidiary, or a subsidiary of the issuing company's holding company, or by its or their nominees, are to be regarded for purposes of this section as held by the issuing company.

[(7) In relation to a company and its shares and capital, the following definitions apply for the purposes of this section:

"arrangement" means any agreement, scheme or arrangement (including an arrangement sanctioned under *section 453* or *601*);

"company", other than in relation to the issuing company, includes any body corporate;

"equity share capital" means the company's issued share capital excluding any part of it which, neither as respects dividends nor as respects capital, carries any right to participate beyond a specified amount in a distribution;

"equity shares" means shares comprised in the company's equity share capital;

"non-equity shares" means shares (of any class) not comprised in the company's equity share capital.][a]

(8) This section does not apply if the issue of shares took place before the commencement of this section.

Amendments

a Subsection (7) substituted by C(A)A 2017, s 7.

---

73 Restriction of *section 71(5)* in the case of group reconstructions

(1) This section applies where the issuing company—

(a) is a wholly-owned subsidiary of a body corporate (the "holding company"); and

(b) allots shares to the holding company or to another wholly-owned subsidiary of the holding company in consideration for the transfer to the issuing company of assets other than cash, being assets of any body corporate (the "transferor") which is a member of the group which comprises the holding company and all its wholly-owned subsidiaries.

(2) Where the shares in the issuing company, allotted in consideration for the transfer, are issued at a premium, the issuing company is not required by *section 71(5)* to credit to undenominated capital any amount in excess of the minimum premium value.

(3) In *subsection (2)* the "minimum premium value" means the amount (if any) by which the base value of the consideration for the shares allotted exceeds the aggregate nominal value of those shares.

(4) For the purposes of *subsection (3)*, the base value of the consideration for the shares allotted is the amount by which the base value of the assets transferred exceeds the base value of any liabilities of the transferor assumed by the issuing company as part of the consideration for the assets transferred.

(5) For the purposes of *subsection (4)*—

(a) the base value of assets transferred is to be taken as—

(i) the cost of those assets to the transferor; or

(ii) the amount at which those assets are stated in the transferor's accounting records immediately before the transfer, whichever is the less,

and

(b) the base value of the liabilities assumed is to be taken as the amount at which they are stated in the transferor's accounting records immediately before the transfer.

(6) *Section 72* shall not apply to a case falling within this section.

74 Supplementary provisions in relation to *sections 72* and *73*

(1) An amount corresponding to one representing the premiums or part of the premiums on shares issued by an issuing company which, by virtue of *section 72* or *73*, is not included in the issuing company's undenominated capital may also be disregarded in determining the amount at which any shares or other consideration provided for the shares issued is to be included in the company's balance sheet.

(2) References in *sections 72* and *73* (however expressed) to—

(a) the acquisition by a company of shares in a body corporate; and

(b) the issue or allotment of shares to, or the transfer of shares to or by, a company or other body corporate,

include (respectively) the acquisition of any of those shares by, and the issue or allotment or (as the case may be) the transfer of any of those shares to or by, nominees of that company or body corporate; and the reference in *section 72* to the company transferring the shares is to be read accordingly.

(3) References in *sections 72* and *73* to the transfer of shares in a body corporate include the transfer of a right to be included in the body corporate's register of members in respect of those shares.

75 Restriction of *section 71(5)* in the case of shares allotted in return for acquisition of issued shares of body corporate

(1) This section applies where—

(a) a company (the "issuer") allots and issues shares to the shareholders of a body corporate in consideration for the acquisition by the issuer of all of the issued shares in the body corporate (the "acquired shares") such that the body corporate becomes the wholly-owned subsidiary of the issuer;

(b) the consolidated assets and liabilities of the issuer immediately after those shares are issued are exactly, except for any permitted cash payments, the same as—

(i) if the body corporate was itself a holding company, the consolidated assets and liabilities of the body corporate immediately before those shares were issued, or

(ii) if the body corporate was not a holding company, the assets and liabilities of the body corporate immediately before those shares were issued;

(c) the absolute and relative interests that the shareholders in the body corporate have in the consolidated assets and liabilities of the issuer are in proportion to (or as nearly as may be in proportion to) the interest they had in—

(i) if the body corporate was itself a holding company, the consolidated assets and liabilities of the body corporate immediately before the shares were issued;

(ii) if the body corporate was not a holding company, the assets and liabilities of the body corporate immediately before the shares were issued;

and

(d) the issuer does not account for its investment in the body corporate at fair value in the issuer's entity financial statements.

(2) Where the shares in the issuer allotted in consideration for the acquisition of the acquired shares are issued at a premium, the issuer—

(a) is not required by *section 71(5)* to credit to undenominated capital any amount in excess of the minimum premium value; and

(b) may disregard any such amount in determining the amount at which the shares or other consideration provided for the acquired shares is to be included in the issuer's entity financial statements and, if such are prepared, group financial statements.

(3) Nothing in this section shall permit any share in the issuer to be issued at a discount to the share's nominal value.

(4) In this section—

"base value of the consideration", in relation to shares allotted by an issuer, means the carrying value of the assets and liabilities that would be shown in the balance sheet of the body corporate if that body corporate were to prepare entity financial statements in accordance with *Part 6* immediately before the issue of the shares;

"consolidated assets and liabilities", in relation to a holding company, means the assets and liabilities included in the group financial statements of the holding company prepared under *section 293*;

"minimum premium value", in relation to shares allotted, means the amount (if any) by which the base value of the consideration for the acquisition of the acquired shares exceeds the aggregate nominal value of the shares issued;

"permitted cash payments" means—

(a) cash payments to shareholders of the body corporate in relation to fractional share entitlements in the body corporate that are not being replicated in the issuer, whether on account of different nominal values of shares or otherwise;

(b) such cash payments as may be ordered or permitted by the court, including by reason of the imposition on the issuer of disproportionate expense arising from compliance with requirements with respect to a prospectus or similar requirements.

76 Treatment of premiums paid on shares issued before a certain date

(1) Where before 1 April 1964 a company had issued any shares at a premium, *section 71(5)* (and the exceptions to that provision in *sections 72* to *75*) shall apply as if the shares had been issued after that date, but this is subject to *subsection (2)*.

(2) Where any part of a premium referred to in *subsection (1)* had been applied as mentioned in section 62(2) of the Act of 1963 such that it did not, on 1 April 1964, form an identifiable part of the company's reserves (within the meaning of the Sixth Schedule to the Act of 1963) then that part shall continue to be disregarded in determining the sum to be included in the share premium account.

77 Calls on shares

(1) Each provision of this section and of *section 78* applies save to the extent that the company's constitution provides otherwise.

(2) Subject to *subsection (3)*, the directors of a company may from time to time make calls upon the members in respect of any moneys unpaid on their shares (whether on account of the nominal value of the shares or by way of premium).

(3) *Subsection (2)* does not apply to shares where the conditions of allotment of them provide for the payment of moneys in respect of them at fixed times.

(4) Each member shall (subject to receiving at least 30 days' notice specifying the time or times and place of payment) pay to the company, at the time or times and place so specified, the amount called on the shares.

(5) A call may be revoked or postponed, as the directors of the company may determine.

(6) A call shall be deemed to have been made at the time when the resolution of the directors authorising the call was passed and may be required to be paid by instalments.

(7) The joint holders of a share shall be jointly and severally liable to pay all calls in respect of it.

(8) If a sum called in respect of a share is not paid before or on the day appointed for payment of it, the person from whom the sum is due shall pay interest on the sum from the day appointed for payment of it to the time of actual payment of such rate, not exceeding the appropriate rate, as the directors of the company may determine, but the directors may waive payment of such interest wholly or in part.

78 Supplemental provisions in relation to calls

(1) Any sum which, by the terms of issue of a share, becomes payable on allotment or at any fixed date (whether on account of the nominal value of the share or by way of premium) shall, for the purposes of this Act, be deemed to be a call duly made and payable on the date on which, by the terms of issue, that sum becomes payable.

(2) In case of non payment of such a sum, all the relevant provisions of this Act as to payment of interest and expenses, forfeiture or otherwise, shall apply as if such sum had become payable by virtue of a call duly made and notified.

(3) The directors of a company may, on the issue of shares, differentiate between the holders of different classes as to the amount of calls to be paid and the times of payment.

(4) The directors of a company may, if they think fit—

(a) receive from any member willing to advance such moneys, all or any part of the moneys uncalled and unpaid upon any shares held by him or her; and

(b) pay, upon all or any of the money so advanced (until the amount concerned would, but for such advance, become payable) interest at such rate (not exceeding, unless the company in a general meeting otherwise directs, the appropriate rate) as may be agreed upon between the directors and the member paying such moneys in advance.

79 Further provisions about calls (different times and amounts of calls)

Save to the extent that the company's constitution provides otherwise, a company may—

(a) make arrangements on the issue of shares for a difference between the shareholders in the amounts and times of payment of calls on their shares;

(b) accept from any member the whole or a part of the amount remaining unpaid on any shares held by him or her, although no part of that amount has been called up;

(c) pay a dividend in proportion to the amount paid up on each share where a larger amount is paid up on some shares than on others; and

(d) by special resolution determine that any portion of its share capital which has not been already called up shall not be capable of being called up except in the event and for the purposes of the company being wound up; upon the company doing so, that portion of its share capital shall not be capable of being called up except in that event and for those purposes.

80 Lien

(1) Each provision of this section applies save to the extent that the company's constitution provides otherwise.

(2) A company shall have a first and paramount lien on every share (not being a fully paid share) for all moneys (whether immediately payable or not) called, or payable at a fixed time, in respect of that share.

(3) The directors of a company may at any time declare any share in the company to be wholly or in part exempt from *subsection (2)*.

(4) A company's lien on a share shall extend to all dividends payable on it.

(5) A company may sell, in such manner as the directors of the company think fit, any shares on which the company has a lien, but no sale shall be made unless—

- (a) a sum in respect of which the lien exists is immediately payable; and
- (b) the following conditions are satisfied.

(6) Those conditions are—

- (a) a notice in writing, stating and demanding payment of such part of the amount in respect of which the lien exists as is immediately payable, has been given to the registered holder for the time being of the share, or the person entitled thereto by reason of his or her death or bankruptcy; and
- (b) a period of 14 days after the date of giving of that notice has expired.

(7) The following provisions apply in relation to a sale referred to in *subsection (5)*—

- (a) to give effect to any such sale, the directors may authorise some person to transfer the shares sold to the purchaser of them;
- (b) the purchaser shall be registered as the holder of the shares comprised in any such transfer;
- (c) the purchaser shall not be bound to see to the application of the purchase money, nor shall his or her title to the shares be affected by any irregularity or invalidity in the proceedings in reference to the sale; and
- (d) the proceeds of the sale shall be received by the company and applied in payment of such part of the amount in respect of which the lien exists as is immediately payable, and the residue, if any, shall (subject to a like lien for sums not immediately payable as existed upon the shares before the sale) be paid to the person entitled to the shares at the date of the sale.

81 Forfeiture of shares

(1) Each provision of this section applies save to the extent that the company's constitution provides otherwise.

(2) If a member of a company fails to pay any call or instalment of a call on the day appointed for payment of it, the directors of the company may, at any time thereafter during such time as any part of the call or instalment remains unpaid, serve a notice on the member requiring payment of so much of the call or instalment as is unpaid, together with any interest which may have accrued.

(3) That notice shall—

(a) specify a further day (not earlier than the expiration of 14 days after the date of service of the notice) on or before which the payment required by the notice is to be made; and

(b) state that, if the amount concerned is not paid by the day so specified, the shares in respect of which the call was made will be liable to be forfeited.

(4) If the requirements of that notice are not complied with, any share in respect of which the notice has been served may at any time after the day so specified (but before, should it occur, the payment required by the notice has been made) be forfeited by a resolution of the directors of the company to that effect.

(5) A forfeited share may be sold or otherwise disposed of on such terms and in such manner as the directors of the company think fit, and at any time before a sale or disposition the forfeiture may be cancelled on such terms as the directors think fit.

(6) A person whose shares have been forfeited shall cease to be a member of the company in respect of the forfeited shares, but shall, notwithstanding, remain liable to pay to the company all moneys which, at the date of forfeiture, were payable by him or her to the company in respect of the shares, but his or her liability shall cease if and when the company shall have received payment in full of all such moneys in respect of the shares.

(7) A statement in writing that the maker of the statement is a director or the secretary of the company, and that a share in the company has been duly forfeited on a date stated in the statement, shall be conclusive evidence of the facts stated in it as against all persons claiming to be entitled to the share.

(8) The following provisions apply in relation to a sale or other disposition of a share referred to in *subsection (5)*:

(a) the company may receive the consideration, if any, given for the share on the sale or other disposition of it and may execute a transfer of the share in favour of the person to whom the share is sold or otherwise disposed of (the "disponee");

(b) upon such execution, the disponee shall be registered as the holder of the share;

(c) the disponee shall not be bound to see to the application of the purchase money, if any, nor shall his or her title to the share be affected by any irregularity or invalidity in the proceedings in reference to the forfeiture, sale or disposal of the share.

82 Financial assistance for acquisition of shares

(1) In *subsection (2)* "acquisition", in relation to shares, means acquisition by subscription, purchase, exchange or otherwise.

(2) It shall not be lawful for a company to give any financial assistance for the purpose of an acquisition made or to be made by any person of any shares in the company, or, where the company is a subsidiary, in its holding company.

(3) *Subsection (2)* is subject to *subsections (5)* and *(6)*.

(4) The prohibition in *subsection (2)* applies whether the financial assistance is given—

(a) directly or indirectly; or

(b) by means of a loan or guarantee, the provision of security or otherwise.

(5) *Subsection (2)* does not prohibit the giving of financial assistance in relation to the acquisition of shares in a company or its holding company if—

(a) the company's principal purpose in giving the assistance is not to give it for the purpose of any such acquisition; or

(b) the giving of the assistance for that purpose is only an incidental part of some larger purpose of the company,

and the assistance is given in good faith in the interests of the company.

(6) Without prejudice to the generality of *subsection (5)*, *subsection (2)* does not prohibit—

(a) the giving of financial assistance in accordance with the Summary Approval Procedure;

(b) the payment by a company of a dividend or making by it of any distribution out of profits of the company available for distribution;

(c) the discharge by a company of a liability lawfully incurred by it;

(d) the—

(i) purchase under *section 105*; or

(ii) redemption under *section 105* or *108*,

of own shares or the giving of financial assistance, by means of a loan or guarantee, the provision of security or otherwise, for the purpose of such purchase or redemption;

(e) where the lending of money is part of the ordinary business of the company, the lending of money by a company in the ordinary course of its business;

(f) the provision by a company, in accordance with any scheme for the time being in force, of money for the purchase of, or subscription for, fully paid shares in the company or its holding company, being a purchase or subscription of or for shares to be held by or for the benefit of employees or former employees of the company or of any subsidiary of the company including any person who is or was a director holding a salaried employment or office in the company or any subsidiary of the company;

(g) the making by a company of loans to persons, other than directors, *bona fide* in the employment of the company or any subsidiary of the company with a view to enabling those persons to purchase or subscribe for fully paid shares in the company or its holding company to be held by themselves as beneficial owners thereof;

(h) the giving of financial assistance—

(i) by means of a loan or guarantee, the provision of security or otherwise to discharge the liability under, or effect that which is commonly known as a refinancing of, any arrangement or transaction that gave rise to the provision of financial assistance, being financial assistance referred to in *subsection (2)* that has already been given by the company in accordance with the Summary Approval Procedure or section 60(2) of the Act of 1963; or

(ii) by means of any subsequent loan or guarantee, provision of security or otherwise to effect a refinancing of—

(I) refinancing referred to *subparagraph (i)*; or

(II) refinancing referred to in this subparagraph that has been previously effected (and this subparagraph shall be read as permitting the giving of financial assistance to effect such subsequent refinancing any number of times);

(i) the making or giving by a company of one or more representations, warranties or indemnities to a person (or any affiliate of, or person otherwise connected with, the first-mentioned person or a director of such an affiliate or connected person that is a body corporate) who has purchased or subscribed for, or proposes to purchase or subscribe for, shares in the company or its holding company for the purpose of or in connection with that purchase or subscription;

(j) the payment by a company of fees and expenses of—

(i) the advisers to any subscriber for, or purchaser of, shares in the company that are incurred in connection with his or her subscription for, or purchase of, such shares; or

(ii) the advisers to the company or its holding company that are incurred in connection with that subscription or purchase;

(k) the incurring of any expense by a company in order to facilitate the admission to, or the continuance of, a trading facility of securities of its holding company on a stock exchange or securities market, including the expenses associated with the preparation and filing of documents required under the laws of any jurisdiction in which the securities in question are admitted to trading or are afforded a trading facility;

(l) the incurring of any expenses by a company in order to ensure compliance by the company or its holding company with the Irish Takeover Panel Act 1997 or an instrument thereunder or any measures for the time being adopted by the State to implement Directive 2004/25/EC of the European Parliament and of the Council of 21 April 2004 on takeover bids;

(m) the reimbursement by a private limited subsidiary of an offeree (within the meaning of the Irish Takeover Panel Act 1997) of expenses of an offeror (within the meaning of that Act) pursuant to an agreement approved by, or on terms approved by, the Irish Takeover Panel;

(n) in connection with an allotment of shares by a parent public company, the payment by a private limited subsidiary of that company of commissions, not exceeding 10 per cent of the money received in respect of such allotment, to intermediaries, and the payment by that subsidiary of professional fees;

(o) to the extent that provision of this kind is not authorised by *paragraph (f)* or *(g)*, the provision of financial assistance by a holding company or a subsidiary of it in connection with the holding company or subsidiary purchasing or subscribing for shares in the holding company on behalf of—

(i) the present or former employees of the holding company or any subsidiary of it;

(ii) an employees' share scheme; or

(iii) an employee share ownership trust referred to in section 519 of the Taxes Consolidation Act 1997.

(7) Subject to *subsection (8)*, a private limited subsidiary shall not provide financial assistance in accordance with the Summary Approval Procedure for the purpose of the acquisition of shares in its parent public company.

(8) The Minister may, by regulations, specify circumstances in which a private limited subsidiary, in cases falling within *subsection (7)*, may avail itself of the Summary Approval Procedure.

(9) Any transaction in contravention of this section shall be voidable at the instance of the company against any person (whether a party to the transaction or not) who had notice of the facts which constitute such contravention.

(10) Nothing in this section shall affect the operation of *sections 84* to *87*.

(11) If a company contravenes this section, the company and any officer of it who is in default shall be guilty of a category 2 offence.

Chapter 4
Variation in capital

83 Variation of company capital

(1) Save to the extent that its constitution otherwise provides, a company may, by ordinary resolution, do any one or more of the following, from time to time—

(a) consolidate and divide all or any of its shares into shares of a larger nominal value than its existing shares;

(b) subdivide its shares, or any of them, into shares of a smaller nominal value, so however, that in the subdivision the proportion between the amount paid and the amount, if any, unpaid on each reduced share shall be the same as it was in the case of the share from which the reduced share is derived;

(c) increase the nominal value of any of its shares by the addition to them of any undenominated capital;

(d) reduce the nominal value of any of its shares by the deduction from them of any part of that value, subject to the crediting of the amount of the deduction to undenominated capital, other than the share premium account;

(e) convert any undenominated capital into shares for allotment as bonus shares to holders of existing shares;

(f) in the case of a company whose constitution states an authorised share capital (in addition to its power to do any of the foregoing things)—

(i) increase its share capital by new shares of such amount as it thinks expedient; or

(ii) cancel shares of its share capital which, at the date of the passing of the resolution, have not been taken or agreed to be taken by any person, and diminish the amount of its share capital by the amount of the shares so cancelled.

(2) A cancellation of share capital under *subsection (1)(f)(ii)* shall be deemed not to be a reduction of company capital within the meaning of this Act.

(3) Save to the extent that its constitution otherwise provides, a company may, by special resolution, and subject to the provisions of this Act governing the variation of rights attached to classes of shares and the amendment of a company's constitution, convert any of its shares into redeemable shares.

(4) Such a conversion shall not have effect with respect to any shares, the holder of which notifies the company, before the date of conversion, of his or her unwillingness to have his or her shares converted but, subject to that and the other provisions of this section, the conversion shall have effect according to its terms.

(5) *Subsection (4)* shall not, where a shareholder objects to a conversion, prejudice any right he or she may have under this Act or otherwise to invoke the jurisdiction of the court to set aside the conversion or otherwise provide relief in respect of it.

(6) A company shall deliver particulars, in the prescribed form, of any resolution referred to in *subsection (1)* to the Registrar within 30 days after the date of its being passed by the company.

(7) If a company contravenes *subsection (6)*, the company and any officer of it who is in default shall be guilty of a category 3 offence.

84 Reduction in company capital

(1) Save to the extent that its constitution otherwise provides, a company may, subject to the provisions of this section and *sections 85* to *87*, reduce its company capital in any way it thinks expedient and, without prejudice to the generality of the foregoing, may thereby—

(a) extinguish or reduce the liability on any of its shares in respect of share capital not paid up;

(b) either with or without extinguishing or reducing liability on any of its shares, cancel any paid up company capital which is lost or unrepresented by available assets; or

(c) either with or without extinguishing or reducing liability on any of its shares, pay off any paid up company capital which is in excess of the wants of the company.

(2) A reduction of company capital under this section shall be effected either by the company—

(a) employing the Summary Approval Procedure; or

(b) passing a special resolution that is confirmed by the court.

(3) Where the reduction has been approved by the Summary Approval Procedure, the reduction shall take effect—

(a) if no date is specified in that behalf in the special resolution referred to in *section 202(1)(a)(i)*, on the expiry of 12 months after the date of the passing of the special resolution; or

(b) if such a date is so specified, on that date.

(4) A company shall not purport to reduce its company capital otherwise than as provided for by this section.

(5) Any transaction in contravention of this section shall be voidable at the instance of the company against any person (whether a party to the transaction or not) who had actual notice of the facts which constitute such contravention.

(6) If a company contravenes this section, the company and any officer of it who is in default shall be guilty of a category 3 offence.

85 Application to court for confirming order, objections by creditors and settlement of list of such creditors

(1) Where a company has passed a special resolution under *section 84(2)(b)* for reducing its company capital it may apply to the court for an order confirming the resolution.

[(2) If a company proposes to apply to the court for an order confirming the resolution, it shall cause notice of its intention to make such an application—

(a) to be advertised once at least in one daily newspaper circulating in the district where the registered office or principal place of business of the company is situated, and

(b) to be notified by electronic means to all creditors of the company who are resident, or have their principal place of business, outside the State,

and that advertisement and that notification shall indicate a means by which there will be notified by the company to any inquirer the date on which that hearing will take place (or any change in the date of such) and the company shall, accordingly, notify to any inquirer, by those means, the first-mentioned date on request being made by the inquirer therefor (and shall make satisfactory arrangements with the inquirer for the notification, by these means or such other means as may be agreed between them, to the inquirer of a change in that date).][a]

(3) In determining any preliminary application for directions as to the hearing of an application under this section, the court shall have regard to compliance by the company with the requirements of *subsection (2)*.

(4) Where the proposed reduction of the company's company capital involves either diminution of liability in respect of unpaid company capital, or the payment to any

shareholder of any paid up company capital, and in any other case if the court so directs, the following provisions shall have effect (but subject to *subsection (5)*)—

(a) every creditor of the company who—

(i) at the date fixed by the court, is entitled to a debt or claim that, if that date were the commencement of the winding up of the company, would be admissible in proof against the company; and

(ii) can credibly demonstrate that the proposed reduction in company capital would be likely to put the satisfaction of that debt or claim at risk, and that no adequate safeguards have been obtained from the company,

is entitled to object to the reduction,

(b) the court shall settle a list of creditors entitled to object, and for that purpose may publish notices fixing a day or days within which creditors are to claim to be entered on the list or are to be excluded from the right of objecting to the reduction of company capital, and

(c) where a creditor entered on the list whose debt or claim is not discharged or has not terminated does not consent to the confirmation, the court may, if it thinks fit, dispense with the consent of that creditor, on the company securing payment of his or her debt or claim by appropriating, as the court may direct, the following amount—

(i) if the company admits the full amount of the debt or claim, or, though not admitting it, is willing to provide for it, then the full amount of the debt or claim;

(ii) if the company does not admit and is not willing to provide for the full amount of the debt or claim, or, if the amount is contingent or not ascertained, then an amount fixed by the court after the like inquiry and adjudication as if the company were being wound up by the court.

(5) Where a proposed reduction of company capital involves either the diminution of any liability in respect of unpaid company capital or the payment to any shareholder of any paid up company capital, the court may, if, having regard to any special circumstances of the case, it thinks proper so to do, direct that *subsection (4)* shall not apply as regards any class or any classes of creditors.

(6) If satisfied that the following requirement is satisfied, the court may make an order confirming the resolution on such terms and conditions as it thinks fit.

(7) That requirement is that, in relation to every creditor of the company who, under this section is entitled to object to the confirmation, either—

(a) the creditor's consent to the confirmation has been obtained, or

(b) the creditor's debt or claim has been discharged or has terminated, or has been secured.

(8) Where the court makes an order confirming the resolution, it may make an order requiring the company to publish, as the court directs, the reasons for reduction of its company capital or such other information in regard thereto as the court may

think expedient, with a view to giving proper information to the public, and if the court thinks fit, the causes which led to that reduction.

(9) References in this section to a debt or claim having terminated are references to the debt or claim ceasing to be enforceable or to its otherwise determining.

Amendments

a Subsection (2) substituted by C(A)A 2017, s 8.

---

86 Registration of order and minute of reduction

(1) On the doing of both of the following—

(a) the production to the Registrar of an order of the court under *section 85* confirming the resolution of the company with respect to reduction of its company capital; and

(b) the delivery to the Registrar of a copy of the order and of a minute approved by the court showing, with respect to the company capital of the company as altered by the order—

(i) the amount of the share capital;

(ii) the number of shares into which it is to be divided and the amount of each share; and

(iii) the amount, if any, at the date of the registration deemed to be paid up on each share,

the Registrar shall register the order and minute.

(2) On the registration of the order and minute and not before, the resolution for reducing company capital as confirmed by the order so registered shall take effect.

(3) Notice of the registration of the order and minute shall be published in such manner as the court may direct.

(4) The Registrar shall issue a certificate with respect to the registration of the order and minute, and that certificate shall be conclusive evidence that all the requirements of this Act relating to reduction of company capital have been complied with, and that the share capital of the company is such as is stated in the minute.

(5) The minute, when registered, shall be deemed to be substituted for the corresponding part of the constitution of the company and shall be valid and capable of amendment as if it had been originally contained in it.

(6) The substitution of any such minute for part of the constitution of the company shall be deemed to be an amendment of the constitution within the meaning of *section 37(2)*.

87 Liability of members in respect of reduced calls

(1) In this section—

"confirmation" means confirmation by the court under *section 85* of a resolution for reduction of company capital;

"minute" means the minute referred to in *section 86(1)(b)*.

(2) Subject to *subsection (3)*, in the case of a reduction of company capital where future calls have been reduced, a member of the company, past or present, shall not be liable in respect of any share to any call or contribution exceeding in amount the difference, if any, between the amount of the share, as fixed by the minute and the amount paid, or the reduced amount, if any, which is to be deemed to have been paid, on the share, as the case may be.

(3) If any creditor entitled, in respect of any debt or claim, to object to the confirmation, is, by reason of his or her not being aware of the proceedings for the confirmation or of their nature and effect with respect to his or her debt or claim, not entered on the list of creditors, and, after the reduction, the company is unable, within the meaning of the provisions of this Act relating to winding up by the court, to pay the amount of his or her debt or claim, then—

(a) every person who was a member of the company at the date of the delivery for registration of the order in respect of the confirmation and the minute, shall be liable to contribute for the payment of that debt or claim an amount not exceeding the amount which he or she would have been liable to contribute if the company had commenced to be wound up on the day before that date; and

(b) if the company is wound up, the court, on the application of any such creditor and proof of his or her not being aware as mentioned in this subsection may, if it thinks fit, settle accordingly a list of persons so liable to contribute, and make and enforce calls and orders on the contributories settled on the list, as if they were ordinary contributories in a winding up.

(4) Nothing in this section shall affect the rights of the contributories among themselves.

(5) If any officer of the company—

(a) intentionally conceals the name of any creditor entitled to object to the confirmation; or

(b) intentionally misrepresents the nature or amount of the debt or claim of any creditor,

he or she shall be guilty of a category 2 offence.

88 Variation of rights attached to special classes of shares

(1) This section shall have effect with respect to the variation of the rights attached to any class of shares in a company whose share capital is divided into shares of different classes, whether or not the company is being wound up.

(2) Where the rights are attached to a class of shares in the company otherwise than by the constitution, and the constitution does not contain provisions with respect to the variation of the rights, those rights may be varied if, but only if—

(a) the holders of 75 per cent, in nominal value, of the issued shares of that class, consent in writing to the variation; or

(b) a special resolution, passed at a separate general meeting of the holders of that class, sanctions the variation,

and any requirement (however it is imposed) in relation to the variation of those rights is complied with, to the extent that it is not comprised in the requirements in *paragraphs (a)* and *(b)*.

(3) Where—

(a) the rights are attached to a class of shares in the company by the constitution or otherwise;

(b) the constitution contains provision for the variation of those rights; and

(c) the variation of those rights is connected with the giving, variation, revocation or renewal of an authority for the purposes of *section 69(1)* or with a reduction of the company's company capital by either of the means referred to in *section 84*,

those rights shall not be varied unless—

(i) the requirement in *subsection (2)(a)* or *(b)* is satisfied; and

(ii) any requirement of the constitution in relation to the variation of rights of that class is complied with to the extent that it is not comprised in the requirement in *subsection (2)(a)* or *(b)*.

(4) Where the rights are attached to a class of shares in the company by the constitution or otherwise and—

(a) where they are so attached by the constitution, it contains provision with respect to their variation which had been included in the constitution at the time of the company's original incorporation; or

(b) where they are so attached otherwise, the constitution contains such provision (whenever first so included),

and in either case the variation is not connected as mentioned in *subsection (3)(c)*, those rights may only be varied in accordance with that provision of the constitution.

(5) Where the rights are attached to a class of shares in the company by the constitution and it does not contain provisions with respect to the variation of the rights, those rights may be varied if all the members of the company agree to the variation.

(6) Where a resolution referred to in any of the preceding subsections is to be proposed at a meeting of members holding a particular class of shares—

(a) the necessary quorum at any such meeting, other than an adjourned meeting, shall be 2 persons holding or representing by proxy at least one-third in nominal value of the issued shares of the class in question and at an adjourned meeting one person holding shares of the class in question or his or her proxy;

(b) any holder of shares of the class in question present in person or by proxy may demand a poll.

(7) Any amendment of a provision contained in the constitution of a company for the variation of the rights attached to a class of shares or the insertion of any such provision into the company's constitution shall itself be treated as a variation of those rights.

(8) References to the variation of the rights attached to a class of shares in—

(a) this section; and

(b) except where the context otherwise requires, in any provision for the variation of the rights attached to a class of shares contained in the company's constitution,

shall include references to their abrogation.

(9) Nothing in *subsections (2)* to *(5)* shall be read as derogating from the powers of the court under *sections 212*, *451* and *455*.

(10) Save where the company's constitution provides otherwise, the rights conferred upon the holders of the shares of any class issued by a company with preferred or other rights shall not, unless otherwise expressly provided by the terms of issue of the shares of that class, be deemed to be varied by the creation or issue of further shares ranking *pari passu* therewith.

89 Rights of holders of special classes of shares

(1) If in the case of a company, the share capital of which is divided into different classes of shares, the rights attached to any such class of shares are at any time varied pursuant to *section 88*, one or more members who hold, or together hold, not less than 10 per cent of the issued shares of that class, being members who did not consent to or vote in favour of the resolution for the variation, may apply to the court to have the variation cancelled.

(2) Where any such application is made, the variation shall not have effect unless and until it is confirmed by the court.

(3) An application under this section shall be made within 28 days (or such longer period as the court, on application made to it by any member before the expiry of the first mentioned 28 days, may allow) after the date on which the consent was given or the resolution was passed, as the case may be, and may be made on behalf of the members entitled to make the application by such one or more of their number as they may appoint in writing for the purpose.

(4) On any such application the court, after hearing the applicant and any other persons who apply to the court to be heard and appear to the court to be interested in the application, may, if it is satisfied having regard to all the circumstances of the case that the variation would unfairly prejudice the shareholders of the class represented by the applicant, disallow the variation and shall, if not so satisfied, confirm the variation.

(5) The decision of the court on any such application shall be final but an appeal shall lie to the Supreme Court from the determination of the court on a question of law.

(6) The company shall, within 21 days after the date on which an order is made by the court on any such application, deliver a certified copy of the order to the Registrar.

(7) If a company contravenes *subsection (6)*, the company and any officer of it who is in default shall be guilty of a category 4 offence.

(8) In this section "variation" includes abrogation, and "varied" shall be read accordingly.

90 Registration of particulars of special rights

(1) Where a company allots shares with rights which are not stated in its constitution or in any resolution or agreement to which *section 198* applies, the company shall, unless the shares are in all respects uniform with shares previously allotted, deliver to the Registrar, within 30 days after the date of allotting the shares, a statement in the prescribed form containing particulars of those rights.

(2) Shares allotted with such rights shall not be treated for the purposes of *subsection (1)* as different from shares previously allotted by reason only of the fact that the former do not carry the same rights to dividends as the latter during the 12 months after the date of the former's allotment.

(3) Where the rights attached to any shares of a company are varied otherwise than by an amendment of the company's constitution or by resolution or agreement to which *section 198* applies, the company shall within 30 days after the date on which the variation is made, deliver to the Registrar a statement in the prescribed form containing particulars of the variation.

(4) Where a company (otherwise than by any such amendment, resolution or agreement as is mentioned in *subsection (3)*) assigns a name or other designation, or a new name or other designation, to any class of its shares it shall, within 30 days after the date of doing so, deliver to the Registrar a notice in the prescribed form giving particulars thereof.

(5) If a company contravenes this section, the company and any officer of it who is in default shall be guilty of a category 4 offence.

91 Variation of company capital on reorganisation

(1) Subject to *subsection (3)*, a company (the "relevant company") may for any purpose (with the result that its company capital is thereby re-organised) transfer or dispose of—

(a) one or more assets;

(b) an undertaking or part of an undertaking; or

(c) a combination of assets and liabilities,

to a body corporate, on the terms that the consideration (or part of the consideration) therefor is as follows.

(2) That consideration (or part of consideration) is one comprising shares or other securities of that body corporate paid (by the allotment of them) to the members of the relevant company or of its holding company rather than to the relevant company.

(3) *Subsection (2)* applies whether or not the terms of the transfer or disposal referred to in *subsection (1)* also involve the payment of cash to the members of the relevant company or of its holding company or the relevant company.

(4) A transaction to which *subsection (1)* applies shall not be undertaken unless it is—

(a) approved by the relevant company by employing the Summary Approval Procedure; or

(b) approved by special resolution passed by the relevant company that is confirmed by the court under *section 85* as if that resolution were providing for a reduction of the company's company capital (and the provisions of *sections 84* to *87* shall apply accordingly with the necessary modifications).

(5) Where such a transaction is so approved or confirmed by order of the court under *section 85*, there shall be deducted from such of the relevant company's reserves and company capital as the relevant company shall, by ordinary resolution, resolve an amount equivalent to the value (as stated in, or ascertainable from, the accounting records of the company immediately before the transfer or disposal) of the transferred or disposed asset or assets, undertaking or part of an undertaking mentioned in *subsection (1)*.

(6) Any transaction in contravention of this section shall be voidable at the instance of the relevant company against any person (whether a party to the transaction or not) who had notice of the facts which constitute such contravention.

92 Notice to Registrar of certain alterations of share capital

(1) If a company has—

(a) consolidated and divided its share capital into shares of larger amount than its existing shares; or

(b) converted any shares into stock; or

(c) reconverted stock into shares; or

(d) subdivided its shares or any of them; or

(e) redeemed any redeemable shares; or

(f) redeemed any preference shares; or

(g) cancelled any shares, otherwise than in connection with a reduction of company capital referred to in *section 84*,

it shall, within 30 days after the date of so doing, give notice thereof to the Registrar specifying, as the case may be, the shares consolidated, divided, converted, subdivided, redeemed or cancelled, or the stock reconverted.

(2) If a company contravenes this section, the company and any officer of it who is in default shall be guilty of a category 3 offence.

93 Notice of increase of share capital

(1) This section applies to a company whose constitution states an authorised share capital.

(2) If a company, whether its shares have or have not been converted into stock, has increased its share capital above the registered capital, it shall, within 30 days after the date on which it passes the resolution increasing its share capital, give to the Registrar notice of the increase and the Registrar shall record the increase.

(3) That notice shall include such particulars as may be prescribed with respect to the classes of shares affected, and the conditions subject to which the new shares have been or are to be issued.

(4) If a company contravenes this section, the company and any officer of it who is in default shall be guilty of a category 3 offence.

[(5) This section shall not have effect in respect of a company to which the resolution tools, powers or mechanisms provided for in Part 4 of the Bank Recovery and Resolution Regulations are applied or exercised.][a]

Amendments

a Subsection (5) inserted by European Union (Bank Recovery and Resolution) Regulations 2015 (SI 289/2015), reg 189(2), with effect from 15 July 2015.

Chapter 5
Transfer of shares

94 Transfer of shares and debentures

(1) Subject to any restrictions in the company's constitution and this section, a member may transfer all or any of his or her shares in the company by instrument in writing in any usual or common form or any other form which the directors of the company may approve.

(2) The instrument of transfer of any share shall be executed by or on behalf of the transferor, save that if the share concerned (or one or more of the shares concerned) is not fully paid, the instrument shall be executed by or on behalf of the transferor and the transferee.

(3) The transferor shall be deemed to remain the holder of the share until the name of the transferee is entered in the register in respect thereof.

(4) A company shall not register a transfer of shares in or debentures of the company unless a proper instrument of transfer has been delivered to the company.

(5) Nothing in *subsection (4)* shall prejudice any power of the company to register as shareholder or debenture holder, any person to whom the right to any shares in, or debentures of the company, has been transmitted by operation of law.

(6) A transfer of the share or other interest of a deceased member of a company made by his or her personal representative shall, although the personal representative is not himself or herself a member of the company, be as valid as if the personal representative had been such a member at the time of the execution of the instrument of transfer.

(7) On application of the transferor of any share or interest in a company, the company shall enter in its register of members, the name of the transferee in the same manner and subject to the same conditions as if the application for the entry were made by the transferee.

(8) Save to the extent that a company's constitution regulates the execution of instruments by any particular company or other body corporate, this section is without prejudice to the Stock Transfer Act 1963.

95 Restrictions on transfer

(1) Save where the constitution of the company provides otherwise—

(a) the directors of a company may in their absolute discretion and without assigning any reason for doing so, decline to register the transfer of any share;

(b) the directors' power to decline to register a transfer of shares (other than on account of a matter specified in *subsection (2)*) shall cease to be exercisable on the expiry of 2 months after the date of delivery to the company of the instrument of transfer of the share.

(2) The directors of a company may decline to register any instrument of transfer unless—

(a) a fee of €10.00 or such lesser sum as the directors may from time to time require, is paid to the company in respect of it;

(b) the instrument of transfer is accompanied by the certificate of the shares to which it relates and such other evidence as the directors may reasonably require to show the right of the transferor to make the transfer; and

(c) the instrument of transfer is in respect of one class of share only.

(3) If the directors refuse to register a transfer they shall, within 2 months after the date on which the transfer was lodged with the company, send to the transferee notice of the refusal.

(4) The registration of transfers of shares in a company may be suspended at such times and for such periods, not exceeding in the whole 30 days in each year, as the directors of the company may from time to time determine.

96 Transmission of shares

(1) *Subsections (2)* to *(11)* apply save to the extent that the company's constitution provides otherwise.

(2) In the case of the death of a member, the survivor or survivors where the deceased was a joint holder, and the personal representatives of the deceased where he or she

was a sole holder, shall be the only persons recognised by the company as having any title to his or her interest in the shares.

(3) Nothing in *subsection (2)* shall release the estate of a deceased joint holder from any liability in respect of any share which had been jointly held by him or her with other persons.

(4) Any person becoming entitled to a share in consequence of the death or bankruptcy of a member may, upon such evidence being produced as may from time to time properly be required by the directors of the company and subject to *subsection (5)*, elect either—

(a) to be registered himself or herself as holder of the share; or

(b) to have some person nominated by him or her (being a person who consents to being so registered) registered as the transferee thereof.

(5) The directors of the company shall, in either of those cases, have the same right to decline or suspend registration as they would have had in the case of a transfer of the share by that member before his or her death or bankruptcy, as the case may be.

(6) If the person becoming entitled as mentioned in *subsection (4)*—

(a) elects to be registered himself or herself, the person shall furnish to the company a notice in writing signed by him or her stating that he or she so elects; or

(b) elects to have another person registered, the person shall testify his or her election by executing to that other person a transfer of the share.

(7) All the limitations, restrictions and provisions of this Chapter relating to the right to transfer and the registration of a transfer of a share shall be applicable to a notice or transfer referred to in *subsection (6)* as if the death or bankruptcy of the member concerned had not occurred and the notice or transfer were a transfer signed by that member.

(8) Subject to *subsections (9)* and *(10)*, a person becoming entitled to a share by reason of the death or bankruptcy of the holder shall be entitled to the same dividends and other advantages to which he or she would be entitled if he or she were the registered holder of the share.

(9) Such a person shall not, before being registered as a member in respect of the share, be entitled in respect of it to exercise any right conferred by membership in relation to meetings of the company.

(10) The directors of the company may at any time serve a notice on any such person requiring the person to make the election provided for by *subsection (4)* and, if the person does not make that election (and proceed to do, consequent on that election, whichever of the things mentioned in *subsection (6)* is appropriate) within 90 days after the date of service of the notice, the directors may thereupon withhold payment of all dividends, bonuses or other moneys payable in respect of the share until the requirements of the notice have been complied with.

(11) The company may charge a fee not exceeding €10.00 on the registration of every probate, letters of administration, certificate of death, power of attorney, notice as to stock or other instrument or order.

(12) The production to a company of any document which is by law sufficient evidence of probate of the will or letters of administration of the estate of a deceased person having been granted to some person shall be accepted by the company, notwithstanding anything in its constitution, as sufficient evidence of the grant.

97 Transmission of shares in special circumstances (including cases of mergers)

(1) The Minister may prescribe procedures whereby the registration of shares in a company may be validly effected in the following cases:

(a) cases of a death of the sole member of a single-member company where that member had been the only director of the company;

(b) other cases of difficulty in effecting such registration.

(2) Without prejudice to this matter being provided for by the exercise of the Minister's powers under *subsection (1)* (and subject, in that eventuality, to any regulations made in pursuance thereof), nothing in *section 96* prejudices the adoption of alternative procedures to those specified in that section with respect to the registering of a transfer of shares in a company held by another company that are transmitted by operation of law in consequence of a merger between those companies.

(3) Save to the extent that the constitution of the second-mentioned company in *subsection (2)* provides otherwise and subject—

(a) as mentioned in *subsection (2)*; and

(b) in every case (that is to say, irrespective of what that constitution or those regulations provide), to any order made by the court in respect of the matter concerned under *Part 9*,

those alternative procedures shall be such as the directors of that second-mentioned company determine.

98 Certification of shares

(1) The certification by a company of any instrument of transfer of shares in, or debentures of, the company shall be taken as a representation by the company to any person acting on the faith of the certification that there have been produced to the company such documents as on the face of them show a *prima facie* title to the shares or debentures in the transferor named in the instrument of transfer, but not as a representation that the transferor has any title to the shares or debentures.

(2) Where any person acts on the faith of a false certification by a company made negligently, the company shall be under the same liability to him or her as if the certification had been made fraudulently.

(3) For the purposes of this section—

(a) an instrument of transfer shall be deemed to be certificated if it bears the words "certificate lodged" or words to the like effect;

(b) the certification of an instrument of transfer shall be deemed to be made by a company if—

(i) the person issuing the instrument is a person authorised to issue certificated instruments of transfer on the company's behalf; and

(ii) the certification is signed by a person authorised to certificate transfers on the company's behalf or by any officer or employee either of the company or of a body corporate so authorised;

(c) a certification shall be deemed to be signed by any person if—

(i) it purports to be authenticated by his or her signature or initials (whether handwritten or not); and

(ii) it is not shown that the signature or initials was or were placed there neither by himself or herself nor by any person authorised to use the signature or initials for the purpose of certificating transfers on the company's behalf.

99 Share certificates

(1) A certificate under the common seal of the company specifying any shares held by any member shall be *prima facie* evidence of the title of the member to the shares.

(2) A company shall, within 2 months after the date—

(a) of allotment of any of its shares or debentures; or

(b) on which a transfer of any such shares or debentures is lodged with the company,

complete and have ready for delivery the certificates of all shares and debentures allotted or, as the case may be, transferred, unless the conditions of issue of the shares or debentures otherwise provide.

(3) In *subsection (2)* "transfer" means a transfer that is (where appropriate) duly stamped and is otherwise valid and does not include such a transfer as the company is, for any reason, entitled to refuse to register and does not register.

(4) If any company on which a notice has been served requiring the company to make good any default in complying with the provisions of *subsection (2)*, fails to make good the default within 10 days after the date of service of the notice, the person entitled to have the certificates or the debentures delivered to him or her may apply to the court for, and the court on such an application may grant, the following order.

(5) That order is one directing the company and any officer of the company specified in the order to make good the default within such time as may be specified in the order, and any such order may provide that all costs of and incidental to the application shall be borne by the company or by any officer of it responsible for the default.

(6) If a share certificate is defaced, lost or destroyed, it may be renewed on payment of €10.00 or such lesser sum and on such terms (if any) as to evidence and indemnity and the payment of out-of-pocket expenses of the company of investigating evidence as the directors of the company think fit.

(7) If a member of a company so requests, the member shall be entitled to receive from the company one or more certificates for one or more shares held by the member upon payment, in respect of each certificate, of €10.00 or such lesser sum as the directors of the company think fit.

(8) In respect of a share or shares in a company held jointly by several persons—

(a) the company shall not be bound to issue more than one certificate; and

(b) delivery by the company of a certificate for a share to one of several joint holders shall be sufficient delivery to all such holders.

(9) If a company contravenes *subsection (2)*, the company and any officer of it who is in default shall be guilty of a category 4 offence.

100 Rectification of dealings in shares

(1) If—

(a) a company has created, allotted, acquired or cancelled any of its shares; and

(b) there is reason to apprehend that such shares were invalidly created, allotted, acquired or cancelled,

the court may, on the application of any of the following persons, declare that such creation, allotment, acquisition or cancellation shall be valid for all purposes if the court is satisfied that it would be just and equitable to do so.

(2) The persons who may make such an application are—

(a) the company;

(b) any holder or former holder of such shares;

(c) any member or former member or creditor of the company;

(d) the liquidator of the company.

(3) Where such a declaration is made, the shares shall from the creation, allotment, acquisition or cancellation thereof, as the case may be, be deemed to have been validly created, allotted, acquired or cancelled.

(4) The grant of relief by the court under this section shall, if the court so directs, not have the effect of relieving the company or its officers of any liability incurred under this Act.

(5) In this section "acquired", in relation to shares, means acquired by redemption, purchase, surrender, forfeiture or other means.

101 Personation of shareholder: offence

If any person falsely and deceitfully personates any owner of any share or interest in a company and thereby—

(a) obtains or endeavours to obtain any such share or interest;

(b) receives or endeavours to receive any money due to any such owner; or

(c) votes at any meeting as if the person were the true and lawful owner,

he or she shall be guilty of a category 2 offence.

Chapter 6
Acquisition of own shares

102 Company acquiring its own shares, etc. — permissible circumstances and prohibitions

(1) Subject to the provisions of this Chapter, a company may acquire its own fully paid shares—

(a) by transfer or surrender to the company otherwise than for valuable consideration;

(b) by cancellation pursuant to a reduction of company capital by either of the means referred to in *section 84*;

(c) pursuant to an order of the court under *section 212*;

(d) where those shares are redeemable shares, by redemption or purchase under *section 105*;

(e) by purchase under *section 105*;

(f) where those shares are preference shares referred to in *section 108*, by redemption under that section; or

(g) pursuant to a merger or division under *Chapter 3* or *4* of *Part 9*.

(2) Without prejudice to the powers of a company with respect to forfeiture of its own shares as provided by this Part or to accept any of its own shares surrendered in lieu for failure to pay any sum payable in respect of those shares, a company may not acquire any of its own shares otherwise than as described in the preceding subsection, but nothing in that subsection or any other provision of this section affects the lawfulness of a merger effected in accordance with *Chapter 3* of *Part 9* or a scheme of arrangement sanctioned under that Part.

(3) If a company purports to act in contravention of *subsection (2)*, the company and any officer of it who is in default shall be guilty of a category 2 offence and the purported acquisition is void.

(4) Subject to *section 103*, a private limited subsidiary shall not—

(a) subscribe for the shares of its parent public company; or

(b) purchase shares in its parent public company which are not fully paid.

(5) If a private limited subsidiary purports to act in contravention of *subsection (4)(a)*, that subsidiary and any officer of it who is in default shall be guilty of a category 2 offence and the purported subscription is void.

(6) Where shares in a parent public company are subscribed for by a nominee of a private limited subsidiary, then for all purposes the shares shall be treated as held by the nominee on his or her own account and the private limited subsidiary shall be regarded as having no beneficial interest in them, and the provisions of *section 104* shall, with any necessary modifications, apply.

(7) Without prejudice to any other requirements contained in or penalties imposed by this Act, where a private limited subsidiary purchases, subscribes for or holds shares in its parent public company, and—

(a) in the case of a purchase, the shares were not fully paid when they were purchased; or

(b) the authorisation required by *section 114(3)* has not been obtained; or

(c) by virtue of their being treated (under *subsection (2)* of *section 109*) as shares held as treasury shares by the parent public company for the purposes of the limit provided by *subsection (1)* of that section, that limit is exceeded by the parent public company; or

(d) the purchase or subscription was in contravention of *section 82(7)*,

then, unless the shares or any interest of the private limited subsidiary in them are previously disposed of, the provisions of *sections 1040* and *1041* shall apply to the private limited subsidiary in respect of such shares, with the modification that the "relevant period" (as that expression is used in those sections) in relation to any shares shall be 12 months and with any other necessary modifications.

103 Supplemental provisions in relation to *section 102*

(1) *Section 102* shall not affect or prohibit—

(a) subject to *subsection (2)*, the subscription for, acquisition or holding of shares in its parent public company by a private limited subsidiary where the private limited subsidiary is concerned as personal representative or where it is concerned as trustee;

(b) without prejudice to *subsection (3)*, the allotment to, or holding by, a private limited subsidiary of shares in its parent public company in the circumstances set out in *section 113(6)*;

(c) the subscription, acquisition or holding of shares in its parent public company by a private limited subsidiary where the subscription, acquisition or holding is effected on behalf of a person other than the person subscribing, acquiring or holding the shares, who is neither the parent public company itself nor a subsidiary of that parent public company; or

(d) the subscription, acquisition or holding of shares in its parent public company by a private limited subsidiary which is a member of an authorised market operator acting in its capacity as a professional dealer in securities in the normal course of its business.

(2) The restriction on the application of *section 102* by *subsection (1)(a)* does not have effect (in the case of a trust) if the parent public company or a subsidiary of it is beneficially interested under the trust and is not so interested only by way of security for the purposes of a transaction entered into by it in the ordinary course of a business which includes the lending of money.

(3) Where shares in a parent public company—

(a) are allotted to, or held by, a private limited subsidiary as mentioned in *subsection (1)(b)*; and

(b) by virtue of their being treated (under *subsection (2)* of *section 109*) as shares held as treasury shares by the parent public company for the purposes of the limit provided by *subsection (1)* of that section, that limit is exceeded by the parent public company,

then, unless the shares or any interest of the private limited subsidiary in them are previously disposed of, the provisions of *sections 1040* and *1041* shall apply to the private limited subsidiary in respect of such shares, with the modification that the "relevant period" (as that expression is used in those sections) in relation to any shares shall be 3 years and with any other necessary modifications.

104 Shares of a company held by a nominee of a company

(1) Subject to *subsection (5)*, where shares in a company are issued to a nominee of the company or are acquired by a nominee of the company from a third party as partly paid up, then for all purposes the shares shall be treated as held by the nominee on his or her own account and the company shall be regarded as having no beneficial interest in them.

(2) If a person is called on to pay any amount for the purpose of paying up, or paying any premium on, any shares in a company which were issued to him or her, or which he or she otherwise acquired, as the nominee of the company and he or she fails to pay that amount within 21 days after the date on which he or she is called on to do so, then—

(a) if the shares were issued to him or her as a subscriber to the constitution by virtue of an undertaking of his or hers in the constitution, the other subscribers, if any, to the constitution; or

(b) if the shares were otherwise issued to or acquired by him or her, the directors of the company at the time of the issue or acquisition,

shall be jointly and severally liable with him or her to pay that amount.

(3) If in proceedings for the recovery of any such amount from any such subscriber or director under this section, it appears to the court that he or she is or may be liable to pay that amount, but that he or she has acted honestly and reasonably and that, having regard to all the circumstances of the case, he or she ought fairly to be excused from liability, the court may relieve him or her, either wholly or partly, from his or her liability on such terms as the court thinks fit.

(4) Where any such subscriber or director has reason to apprehend that a claim will or might be made for the recovery of any such amount from him or her, he or she may apply to the court for relief and on the application the court shall have the same power to relieve him or her as it would have had in proceedings for the recovery of that amount.

(5) *Subsections (1)* and *(2)* shall not apply—

(a) to shares acquired by a nominee of a company where the company has no beneficial interest in those shares (disregarding any right which the company itself may have as trustee, whether as personal representative or otherwise, to recover its expenses or be remunerated out of the trust property); or

(b) to shares issued in consequence of an application made for them before 13 October 1983 or transferred in pursuance of an agreement to acquire them made before that date.

105 Acquisition of own shares

(1) A company may acquire its own shares by purchase, or in the case of redeemable shares, by redemption or purchase.

(2) Any such acquisition is subject to payment in respect of the shares' acquisition being made out of—

(a) profits available for distribution; or

(b) where the company proposes to cancel, pursuant to *section 106*, shares on their acquisition, the proceeds of a fresh issue of shares made for the purposes of the acquisition, but subject to the restriction contained in *subsection (3)* as respects such proceeds being used to pay a premium there referred to.

(3) Where the shares being acquired were issued at a premium, some or all of the premium payable on their acquisition (being an acquisition to which *subsection (2)(b)* applies) may be paid out of the proceeds of a fresh issue of shares made for the purposes of the acquisition, up to an amount equal to—

(a) the aggregate of the premiums received by the company on the issue of the shares acquired; or

(b) the current amount of the company's undenominated capital (including any sum transferred to its share premium account in respect of premiums on the new shares),

whichever is less, and in any such case the amount of the company's share premium account or other undenominated capital shall be reduced by a sum corresponding (or by sums in the aggregate corresponding) to the amount of any payment made by virtue of this subsection out of the proceeds of the issue of the new shares.

(4) Subject to this Part, the acquisition by a company of its own shares shall be authorised by—

(a) the constitution of the company;

(b) the rights attaching to the shares in question; or

(c) a special resolution.

(5) A special resolution under *subsection (4)* shall not be effective for the purposes of this section if any member of the company holding shares to which the resolution

relates exercises the voting rights carried by any of those shares in voting on the resolution and the resolution would not have been passed if he or she had not done so.

(6) With respect to *subsection (4)* and the matter of passing a special resolution for the purpose thereof by the written means provided for under this Act—

(a) the procedure under *section 193* (unanimous written resolutions) is not available for that purpose;

(b) if a resolution referred to in *section 194* (majority written resolutions) for the purpose of *subsection (4)* is signed by a member of the company who holds shares to which the resolution relates, then, in determining whether the requirement under *section 194(4)(a)(ii)* — that the resolution be signed by the requisite majority — has been fulfilled, no account shall be taken of the percentage of voting rights conferred by the foregoing shares of that member.

(7) Notwithstanding anything contained in *section 189* or in the company's constitution, any member holding one or more shares in the company conferring the right to vote at the meeting concerned may demand a poll on a special resolution under *subsection(4).*

(8) Where a purchase of shares is proposed to be authorised by special resolution—

(a) the proposed contract of purchase or, if the contract is not in writing, a written memorandum of its terms shall be furnished to the members of the company on request or made available for inspection by the members at the registered office of the company from the date of the notice of the meeting at which the resolution is to be proposed and at the meeting itself;

(b) any memorandum of the terms of the contract of purchase made available for the purposes of *paragraph (a)* shall include the names of any members holding shares to which the contract relates, and any copy of the contract made available for those purposes shall have annexed to it a written memorandum specifying any such names which do not appear in the contract itself.

(9) With respect to the proposed authorisation of a purchase of shares by a resolution referred to in *section 194*, the requirements of *subsection (8)* shall also apply but with the modification that in *paragraph (a)* of that subsection "during the period of 21 days before the date of the signing of the resolution by the last member to sign" shall be substituted for "from the date of the notice of the meeting at which the resolution is to be proposed and at the meeting itself".

(10) A company may agree to a variation of an existing contract of purchase authorised pursuant to a special resolution under this section only if the variation is authorised by special resolution of the company before it is agreed to, and *subsections (5)* to *(9)* shall apply in relation to that authority, save that a copy or memorandum (as the case may require) of the existing contract shall also be available for inspection in accordance with *subsection (8).*

(11) A company shall only make a purchase of its own shares in pursuance of an option if the terms of the option have been authorised by a special resolution of the company in accordance with *subsections (5)* to *(9)* and, for the purposes of this subsection,

subsection (8) shall have effect as if the references in it to the contract of purchase were references to the contract under which the option arises.

(12) In *subsection (11)* "option" means an entitlement of the company, or an obligation on the part of the company, to purchase any of its shares that may arise under a contract entered into, being a contract that does not amount to a contract to purchase those shares.

106 Supplemental provisions in relation to *section 105*

(1) Shares acquired by a company under *section 105*, or otherwise acquired by it under *section 102(1)(a)*, shall be cancelled or held by it (as "treasury shares").

(2) Where a company—

(a) has acquired, under *section 105*, shares and cancelled them; or

(b) is about to so acquire shares and cancel them upon their acquisition,

it shall have power to issue shares up to the nominal amount of the shares so acquired, or to be so acquired, as if those shares had never been issued.

(3) No cancellation of shares under *subsection (1)* shall be taken as reducing the amount of the company's authorised share capital (if any).

(4) Where the shares are—

(a) under *section 105*, acquired wholly out of the profits available for distribution; or

(b) under *section 105*, acquired wholly or partly out of the proceeds of a fresh issue and the aggregate amount of those proceeds (disregarding any part of those proceeds used to pay any premium on the acquisition) is less than the aggregate nominal value of the shares acquired (the "aggregable difference"),

then a sum equal to, in the case of *paragraph (a)*, the nominal value of the shares acquired and, in the case of *paragraph (b)*, the aggregable difference shall be transferred to undenominated capital of the company, other than its share premium account.

(5) The amount by which the consideration paid for the acquisition of redeemable preference shares allotted before 1 February 1990 exceeds the consideration received by the company on the issue of those shares may be paid from undenominated capital.

(6) *Section 105* shall not apply to the redemption of preference shares referred to in *section 108* and no such shares may be the subject of purchase under *section 105*.

107 Assignment or release of company's right to purchase own shares

(1) Any purported assignment of the rights of a company under any contract authorised under *section 105* shall be void.

(2) Nothing in *subsection (1)* shall prevent a company from releasing its right under any contract authorised under *section 105* provided that the release has been authorised by special resolution of the company before the release is entered into, and any such

purported release by a company which has not been authorised in that manner shall be void.

(3) *Subsections (5)* to *(9)* of *section 105* shall apply to a resolution under *subsection (2)* and, for the purposes of this subsection, *subsection (8)* of *section 105* shall have effect as if the references in it to the contract of purchase were references to the release concerned.

108 Power to redeem preference shares issued before 5 May 1959

(1) Subject to the provisions of this section, a company may, if so authorised by its constitution, redeem any preference shares issued by it before 5 May 1959 provided that—

(a) no such shares shall be redeemed except out of profits of the company which would otherwise be available for distribution or out of the proceeds of a fresh issue of shares made for the purposes of the redemption;

(b) no such shares shall be redeemed at a sum greater than the issue price of such shares;

(c) the redemption of such shares and the terms and the manner of the redemption shall have been authorised by a special resolution of the company;

(d) notice of the meeting at which the special resolution referred to in *paragraph (c)* is to be proposed and a copy of that resolution shall be published in *Iris Oifigiúil* and in at least one daily newspaper circulating in the district in which the registered office of the company is situated not less than 14 days and not more than 30 days before the date of the meeting;

(e) no holder of such shares shall be obliged to accept redemption of them;

(f) the redemption shall have been sanctioned by the court.

(2) The powers conferred by this section may be availed of only by means of an offer made to all the holders of the preference shares concerned.

(3) Where any such shares are redeemed otherwise than out of the proceeds of a fresh issue, there shall, out of profits which would otherwise have been available for distribution be transferred to undenominated capital, other than the share premium account a sum equal to the nominal amount of the shares redeemed.

(4) Subject to the provisions of this section, the redemption of preference shares under this section may be effected on such terms and in such manner as may be provided by the special resolution referred to in *subsection (1)(c)*.

(5) The redemption of preference shares under this section by a company shall not be taken as reducing the amount of the company's authorised share capital (if any).

(6) Where in pursuance of this section a company has redeemed or is about to redeem any preference shares, it shall have power to issue shares up to the nominal amount of the shares redeemed or to be redeemed as if those shares had never been issued.

109 Treasury shares

(1) The nominal value of treasury shares held by a company may not, at any one time, exceed 10 per cent of its company capital.

(2) For the purposes of *subsection (1)*, the following shall also be deemed to be treasury shares held by the company—

(a) shares held in the company by any subsidiary in pursuance of *section 114*;

(b) shares held in the company by any person acting in his or her own name but on the company's behalf.

(3) For the purposes of *subsection (1)*, shares of the company acquired by it otherwise than for valuable consideration shall not be deemed to be treasury shares.

(4) For so long as the company holds shares as treasury shares—

(a) the company shall not exercise any voting rights in respect of those shares and any purported exercise of those rights shall be void; and

(b) no dividend or other payment (including any payment in a winding up of the company) shall be payable to the company in respect of those shares.

(5) The manner in which shares held by a company as treasury shares are to be treated in the company's entity financial statements is provided for in *section 320(1)* (which also contains provision restricting the profits available for distribution by reference to the accounting treatment of such shares there provided).

(6) Treasury shares may either be—

(a) cancelled by the company in which case *section 106* shall apply as if the shares had been cancelled on their acquisition; or

(b) subject to *subsections (7)* to *(9)*, re-issued as shares of any class or classes.

(7) A re-issue of shares under this section shall be deemed for all the purposes of this Act to be an issue of shares but the issued share capital of the company shall not be regarded for any purpose as having been increased by the re-issue of the shares.

(8) Unless the case falls within *subsection (9)*, the maximum and minimum prices at which treasury shares may be re-allotted (the "re-allotment price range") shall be determined by special resolution of the company passed before any contract for the re-allotment of the shares is entered into.

(9) In a case where the whole or a part of the treasury shares to be re-allotted are derived from shares acquired by the company under this Part on foot of the authority of a special resolution of the company, the re-allotment price range of the whole or such part (as the case may be) of those shares shall be determined by special resolution of the company passed at the meeting at which the first-mentioned resolution in this subsection has been passed.

(10) Any determination referred to in *subsection (8)* or *(9)*—

(a) may fix different maximum and minimum prices for different shares; and

(b) shall, for the purposes of *subsection (8)* or *(9)*, as the case may be, remain effective with respect to those shares for the requisite period.

(11) The company may from time to time, by special resolution, vary or renew a determination of re-allotment price range under *subsection (8)* or *(9)* with respect to particular treasury shares before any contract for re-allotment of those shares is entered into and any such variation or renewal shall, for the purposes of this subsection, remain effective as a determination of the re-allotment price range of those shares for the requisite period.

(12) A re-allotment by a company of treasury shares in contravention of *subsection (8)*, *(9)*, *(10)* or *(11)* shall be unlawful.

(13) In this section "requisite period" means the period of 18 months after the date of the passing of the resolution determining the re-allotment price range or varying or renewing (as the case may be) such determination or such lesser period as the resolution may specify.

110 Incidental payments with respect to acquisition of own shares

(1) Any payment made by a company in consideration of—

(a) acquiring any right with respect to the purchase of its own shares in pursuance of a contract authorised under *section 105*;

(b) the variation of a contract authorised under *section 105*; or

(c) the release of any of the company's obligations with respect to the purchase of any of its own shares under a contract authorised under *section 105*,

shall be unlawful if any such payment is made otherwise than out of distributable profits of the company or, in the circumstances in which the proceeds of such an issue are permitted to be used by this Part for the purpose of the purchase of the shares, the proceeds of a new issue of shares.

(2) If the requirements of *subsection (1)* are not satisfied in relation to a contract—

(a) in a case to which *paragraph (a)* of that subsection applies, no purchase by the company of its own shares in pursuance of that contract shall be lawful under this Part;

(b) in a case to which *paragraph (b)* of that subsection applies, no such purchase following the variation shall be lawful under this Part; and

(c) in a case to which *paragraph (c)* of that subsection applies, the purported release shall be void.

111 Effect of company's failure to redeem or purchase

(1) This section applies to—

(a) redeemable shares issued after 1 February 1991;

(b) shares which have been converted into redeemable shares; and

(c) shares which a company has agreed to purchase pursuant to *section 105*.

(2) Without prejudice to any other right of the holder of any shares to which this section applies, a company shall not be liable in damages in respect of any failure on its part to redeem or purchase any such shares.

(3) Neither the High Court nor the Circuit Court shall grant an order for specific performance of the terms of redemption or purchase of the shares to which this section applies if the company shows that it is unable to meet the cost of redeeming or purchasing the shares out of profits available for distribution.

(4) Where, at the commencement of the winding up of a company, any shares to which this section applies have not been redeemed or purchased then, subject to *subsections (5)*, *(6)* and *(7)*, the terms of redemption or purchase may be enforced against the company and the shares when so redeemed or purchased under this subsection shall be treated as cancelled.

(5) *Subsection (4)* shall not apply if—

(a) the terms of redemption or purchase provided for the redemption or purchase to take place at a date later than that of the commencement of the winding up; or

(b) during the period beginning with the date on which the redemption or purchase was to have taken place and ending with the commencement of the winding up, the company could not at any time have lawfully made a distribution equal in value to the price at which the shares were to have been redeemed or purchased.

(6) There shall be paid in priority to any amount for which the company is liable by virtue of *subsection (4)* to pay in respect of any shares—

(a) all other debts and liabilities of the company other than any due to members in their capacity as such; and

(b) if other shares carry rights, whether as to capital or to income, which are preferred to the rights as to capital attaching to the first-mentioned shares, any amount due in satisfaction of those preferred rights, but subject to that, any such amount shall be paid in priority to any amounts due to members in satisfaction of their rights (whether as to capital or income) as members.

(7) Where, by virtue of the application by *section 619* of the rules of bankruptcy in the winding up of insolvent companies, a creditor of a company is entitled to payment of any interest only after payment of all other debts of the company, the company's debts and liabilities shall for the purposes of *subsection (6)* include the liability to pay that interest.

112 Retention and inspection of documents

(1) A company which enters into a contract under *section 105* shall, until the expiration of 10 years after the date on which the contract has been fully performed, keep at its registered office a copy of that contract or, if it is not in writing, a memorandum of its terms.

(2) Every document required to be kept under *subsection (1)* shall during business hours be open to the inspection of any member.

(3) In the case of a refusal of an inspection of a document required under *subsection (2)*, the court may, on the application of a person who has requested an inspection and has been refused, by order require the company to allow the inspection of that document.

(4) *Section 127(1)* (access to documents during business hours) shall apply in relation to *subsection (2)* as it applies in relation to the relevant provisions of *Part 4*.

(5) If a company contravenes this section, the company and any officer of it who is in default shall be guilty of a category 3 offence.

113 Membership of holding company

(1) Subject to *section 114* and the other provisions of this Act, a company cannot be a member of a company which is its holding company, and any allotment or transfer of shares in a company to its subsidiary shall be void.

(2) Nothing in this section shall apply where the subsidiary is concerned as personal representative, or where it is concerned as trustee, unless the holding company or a subsidiary of it is beneficially interested under the trust and is not so interested only by way of security for the purposes of a transaction entered into by it in the ordinary course of a business which includes the lending of money.

(3) This section shall not prevent a subsidiary which on 5 May 1959 was a member of its holding company from continuing to be a member.

(4) This section shall not prevent a company which, at the date on which it becomes a subsidiary of another company is a member of that other company, from continuing to be a member.

(5) This section shall not prevent the subscription, acquisition or holding of shares in its parent public company by a company which is a member of an authorised market operator acting in its capacity as a professional dealer in securities in the normal course of its business.

(6) This section shall not prevent a subsidiary which is a member of its holding company from accepting and holding further shares in the capital of its holding company if—

(a) such further shares are allotted to it in consequence of a capitalisation by such holding company; and

(b) the terms of such capitalisation are such that the subsidiary is not thereby involved in any obligation to make any payment or to give other consideration for such further shares.

(7) Subject to *subsection (2)*, a subsidiary which is a member of its holding company shall have no right to vote at meetings of the holding company or any class of members of it.

(8) The manner in which shares held (in the circumstances permitted by this section) in a holding company by the subsidiary are to be treated in—

(a) the subsidiary's entity financial statements is provided for in *section 320(2)* (which also contains provision restricting the profits available for distribution by reference to the accounting treatment of such shares there provided); and

(b) the group financial statements, if any, of the holding company is provided for in *section 320(3)*.

(9) Subject to *subsection (2)*, this section shall apply in relation to a nominee for the company firstly referred to in *subsection (1)*, as if references in this section to such a company included references to a nominee for it.

(10) Where a holding company makes an offer of shares to its members, it may sell, on behalf of a subsidiary, any such shares which the subsidiary could, but for this section, have taken by virtue of shares already held by it in the holding company and pay the proceeds of sale to the subsidiary.

114 Holding by subsidiary of shares in its holding company

(1) Notwithstanding *section 82* or *113*, a company may, subject to the provisions of this section, acquire and hold shares in a company which is its holding company.

(2) The acquisition and holding by a subsidiary under *subsection (1)* of shares in its holding company shall be subject to the following conditions—

(a) the consideration for the acquisition of such shares shall be provided for out of the profits of the subsidiary available for distribution;

(b) upon the acquisition of such shares and for so long as the shares are held by the subsidiary—

(i) the subsidiary shall not exercise any voting rights in respect of the shares and any purported exercise of those rights shall be void;

(ii) the manner in which shares so held by the subsidiary are to be treated in—

(I) the subsidiary's entity financial statements is provided for in *section 320(2)* (which also contains provision restricting the profits available for distribution by reference to the accounting treatment of such shares there provided); and

(II) the group financial statements, if any, of the holding company is provided for in *section 320(3)*.

(3) A contract for the acquisition (whether by allotment or transfer) by a subsidiary of shares in its holding company shall not be entered into without being authorised in advance both by the subsidiary and its holding company and the provisions of *sections 105* and *107* shall apply, with the necessary modifications, to the granting, variation, revocation and release of such authority.

(4) For the purposes of this section and *section 320*, a subsidiary's profits available for distribution shall not include the profits attributable to any shares in the subsidiary for the time being held by the subsidiary's holding company, so far as they are profits for the period before the date on or from which the shares were acquired by the holding company.

(5) This section shall not apply to shares held by a subsidiary in its holding company in the circumstances permitted by *section 113*.

(6) No authorisation is required to be given under *subsection (3)* by any body corporate unless it is a company formed and registered under this Act or an existing company.

(7) Nothing in this section limits the operation of *section 102(4)*.

115 Civil liability for improper purchase in holding company

(1) This section applies where—

(a) the winding up of a company which has acquired shares in its holding company in accordance with *section 114* commences within 6 months after the date of such acquisition; and

(b) the company is, at the time of the commencement of the winding up, unable to pay its debts (taking into account the contingent and prospective liabilities).

(2) Where this section applies the court, on the application of a liquidator, creditor, employee or contributory of the company, may, subject to *subsection (3)*, declare that the directors of the company shall be jointly and severally liable to repay to the company the total amount paid by the company for the shares.

(3) Where it appears to the court that any person in respect of whom a declaration has been sought under *subsection (2)* believed on reasonable grounds that the acquisition referred to in *subsection (1)* was in the best interests of the company, the court may relieve him or her, either wholly or in part, from personal liability on such terms as it may think fit.

116 Return to be made to Registrar

(1) A company which has acquired shares pursuant to this Part shall, within 30 days after the date of delivery to the company of those shares, deliver to the Registrar a return in the prescribed form stating, with respect to shares of each class acquired, the number and nominal value of those shares and the date on which they were delivered to the company.

(2) Particulars of shares delivered to the company on different dates and under different contracts may be included in a single return to the Registrar.

(3) If a company contravenes this section, the company and any officer of it who is in default shall be guilty of a category 3 offence.

Chapter 7
Distributions

117 Profits available for distribution

(1) A company shall not make a distribution except out of profits available for the purpose.

(2) For the purposes of this Part, a company's profits available for distribution are its accumulated, realised profits, so far as not previously utilised by distribution or capitalisation, less its accumulated, realised losses, so far as not previously written off in a reduction or reorganisation of capital duly made.

(3) A company shall not apply an unrealised profit in paying up debentures or any amounts unpaid on any of its issued shares.

[(4) For the purposes of *subsections (2)* and *(3)*—

(a) where the company prepares Companies Act entity financial statements, any provision or value adjustment (within the meaning of *Schedule 3, 3A or 3B*, as the case may be) shall be treated as a realised loss other than a value adjustment in respect of any diminution in value of a fixed asset appearing on a revaluation of all the fixed assets or of all the fixed assets other than goodwill (and this qualification is referred to in *subsections (5)* and *(6)* as "the exception to *subsection (4)(a)*"), and

(b) where the company prepares IFRS financial statements, a provision or value adjustment of any kind shall be treated as a realised loss.][a]

(5) Subject to *section 121(6)* and the next subsection, any consideration by the directors of a company of the value at any particular time of any fixed asset of the company shall be treated as a revaluation of that asset for the purposes of determining whether any such revaluation of the company's fixed assets, as is required for the purposes of the exception to *subsection (4)(a)*, has taken place at that time.

(6) However where any such assets which have not actually been revalued are treated as revalued for those purposes by virtue of the preceding subsection, the exception to *subsection (4)(a)* shall only apply if the directors are satisfied that the aggregate value of those assets at the time in question is not less than the aggregate amount at which they are for the time being stated in the company's Companies Act entity financial statements.

(7) If, on the revaluation of a fixed asset, an unrealised profit is shown to have been made and, on or after the revaluation, a sum is written off or retained for depreciation of that asset over a period, then an amount equal to the amount by which that sum exceeds the sum which would have been so written off or retained for depreciation of that asset over that period if that profit had not been made, shall be treated for the purposes of *subsections (2)* and *(3)* as a realised profit made over that period.

(8) Where there is no record of the original cost of an asset of a company or any such record cannot be obtained without unreasonable expense or delay, then, for the purposes of determining whether the company has made a profit or loss in respect of that asset, the cost of the asset shall be taken to be the value ascribed to it in the earliest available record of its value made on or after its acquisition by the company.

(9) Notwithstanding anything in the preceding subsections of this section, but without prejudice to any contrary provision of—

(a) an order of, or undertaking given to, the court;

(b) the resolution for, or any other resolution relevant to, the reduction of company capital; or

(c) the company's constitution,

a reserve arising from the reduction of a company's company capital is to be treated, both for the purposes of this section and for purposes otherwise, as a realised profit.

(10) In this section "fixed asset" includes any other asset which is not a current asset.

Amendments

a Subsection (4) substituted by C(A)A 2017, s 91.

118 Prohibition on pre-acquisition profits or losses being treated in holding company's financial statements as profits available for distribution

(1) Subject to *subsections (3)* and *(4)*, any amount of the accumulated profits or losses attributable to any shares in a subsidiary for the time being held by a holding company or any other of its subsidiaries shall not, for any purpose, be treated in the holding company's financial statements as profits available for distribution so far as that amount relates to accumulated profits or losses for the period before the date on or as from which the shares were acquired by the company or any of its subsidiaries (which period is referred to in *subsection (2)* as the "pre-acquisition period").

(2) For the purpose of determining whether any profits or losses are to be treated as profits or losses for the pre-acquisition period, the profit or loss for any financial year of the subsidiary may, if it is not practicable to apportion it with reasonable accuracy by reference to the facts, be treated as accruing from day to day during that year and be apportioned accordingly.

(3) If the Summary Approval Procedure is followed in respect of such treatment, *subsection (1)* does not prohibit—

(a) the whole of the amount referred to in that subsection; or

(b) such proportion of that amount as is specified in the declaration referred to in *section 205*,

being treated as profits available for distribution by the holding company for the period, and the period only, referred to in *section 202(1)(a)* (as that provision applies by virtue of *section 202(2)* and *(3)*).

(4) *Subsection (1)* does not apply to the profits or losses attributable to shares in a subsidiary held by a holding company where those shares were acquired in a transaction to which *section 72, 73* or *75* applies.

119 Distributions in kind: determination of amount

(1) This section applies for determining the amount of a distribution consisting of or including, or treated as arising in consequence of, the sale, transfer or other disposition by a company of a non-cash asset where—

(a) at the time of the distribution the company has profits available for distribution; and

(b) if the amount of the distribution were to be determined in accordance with this section, the company could make the distribution without contravening this Part.

(2) The amount of the distribution (or the relevant part of it) is taken to be—

(a) in a case where the amount or value of the consideration for the disposition is not less than the book value of the asset, zero;

(b) in any other case, the amount by which the book value of the asset exceeds the amount or value of any consideration for the disposition.

(3) For the purposes of *subsection (1)(a)*, the company's profits available for distribution are treated as increased by the amount (if any) by which the amount or value of any consideration for the disposition exceeds the book value of the asset.

(4) In this section "book value", in relation to an asset, means—

(a) the amount at which the asset is stated in the relevant financial statements referred to in *section 121*; or

(b) where the asset is not stated in those financial statements at any amount, zero.

(5) The provisions of *section 121* shall have effect subject to this section.

120 Development costs shown as asset of company to be set off against company's distribution profits

(1) Subject to the following provisions of this section, where development costs are shown as an asset in a company's financial statements, any amount shown in respect of those costs shall be treated for the purposes of *section 117* as a realised loss.

(2) *Subsection (1)* shall not apply to any part of the amount referred to in that subsection representing an unrealised profit made on revaluation of the costs so referred to.

(3) *Subsection (1)* shall not apply if—

(a) there are special circumstances justifying the directors of the company concerned in deciding that the amount mentioned in respect of development costs in the company's financial statements shall not be treated as required by that subsection; and

(b) it is stated—

[(i) where the company does not qualify for the micro companies regime and prepares Companies Act entity financial statements, in the note to the statements required by *paragraph 24(2)* of *Schedule 3*, or *paragraph 24(2)* of *Schedule 3A*, as the case may be; or][a]

(ii) where the company prepares IFRS entity financial statements, in any note to those statements,

that that amount is not to be so treated, and the note explains the circumstances relied upon to justify the decision of the directors to that effect.

Amendments

a Subparagraph (3)(b)(i) substituted by C(A)A 2017, s 90(a).

121 The relevant financial statements

(1) Subject to the following provisions of this section, the question whether a distribution may be made by a company without contravening *section 117* and the amount of any distribution which may be so made shall be determined by reference to the relevant items as stated in the relevant entity financial statements, and *section 117* shall be treated as contravened in the case of a distribution unless the requirements of this section in relation to those statements are complied with in the case of that distribution.

(2) The relevant entity financial statements for any company in the case of any particular distribution are—

(a) except in a case falling within *paragraph (b)* or *(c)*, the last entity financial statements, that is to say, the statutory financial statements, respecting the company alone, prepared in accordance with the requirements of *Part 6* (and, where applicable, in accordance with the requirements of Article 4 of the IAS Regulation (within the meaning of that Part)) which were laid in respect of the last preceding financial year in respect of which statutory financial statements so prepared were laid;

(b) if that distribution would be found to contravene *section 117* if reference were made only to the last statutory financial statements, such financial statements ("interim financial statements"), respecting the company alone, as are necessary to enable a reasonable judgement to be made as to the amounts of any of the relevant items;

(c) if that distribution is proposed to be declared during the company's first financial year or before any statutory financial statements are laid in respect of that financial year, such financial statements ("initial financial statements"), respecting the company alone, as are necessary as mentioned in *paragraph (b)*.

(3) The following requirements apply where the last financial statements of a company constitute the only relevant entity financial statements in the case of any distribution, that is to say—

(a) those financial statements shall have been properly prepared or have been so prepared subject only to matters which are not material for the purpose of determining, by reference to the relevant items as stated in those statements, whether that distribution would be in contravention of *section 117*;

(b) unless the company is entitled to and has availed itself of the audit exemption under *section 360* or *365*, the statutory auditors of the company shall have made a report under *section 391* in respect of those financial statements;

(c) if, by virtue of anything referred to in that report, the report is not an unqualified report, the statutory auditors shall also have stated in writing (either at the time the report was made or subsequently) whether, in their opinion, that thing is material for the purpose of determining, by reference to the relevant items as stated in those financial statements, whether that distribution would be in contravention of *section 117*; and

(d) a copy of any such statement shall have been laid before the company in general meeting.

(4) A statement under *subsection (3)(c)* suffices for the purposes of a particular distribution, not only if it relates to a distribution which has been proposed, but also if it relates to distributions of any description which include that particular distribution, notwithstanding that at the time of the statement it has not been proposed.

(5) For the purpose of determining by reference to particular financial statements whether a proposed distribution may be made by a company, this section shall have effect, in any case where one or more distributions have already been made in pursuance of determinations made by reference to those same financial statements, as if the amount of the proposed distribution was increased by the amount of the distributions so made.

(6) Where *subsection (3)(a)* applies to the relevant entity financial statements, *section 117(5)* shall not apply for the purposes of determining whether any revaluation of the company's fixed assets affecting the amount of the relevant items as stated in those statements has taken place, unless it is stated in a note to those statements—

(a) that the directors have considered the value at any time of any fixed assets of the company without actually revaluing those assets;

(b) that they are satisfied that the aggregate value of those assets at the time in question is or was not less than the aggregate amount at which they are or were for the time being stated in the company's statutory financial statements; and

(c) that the relevant items affected are accordingly stated in the relevant financial statements on the basis that a revaluation of the company's fixed assets that, by virtue of *section 117(5)*, is deemed to have included a revaluation of the assets in question, took place at that time.

(7) In this section—

"properly prepared" means, in relation to any financial statements of a company, that they have been properly prepared in accordance with the provisions of *Part 6*;

"relevant item" means any of the following, that is to say profits, losses, assets, liabilities, provisions (within the meaning of [*Schedule 3, 3A* or *3B*, as the case may be][a]), share capital and reserves;

"reserves" includes undistributable reserves, that is to say—

(a) the company's undenominated capital;

(b) the amount by which the company's accumulated, unrealised profits, so far as not previously utilised by any capitalisation, exceed its accumulated, unrealised losses, so far as not previously written off in a reduction or reorganisation of capital duly made; and

(c) any other reserve which the company is prohibited from distributing by any enactment, other than one contained in this Part, or by its constitution.

"unqualified report", in relation to any financial statements of a company, means a report without qualification, to the effect that, in the opinion of the person making the report, the financial statements have been properly prepared, and for the purposes of this section, financial statements are laid if *section 290* has been complied with in relation to those statements.

Amendments

a Words substituted by C(A)A 2017, s 90(b) (previously: "*Schedule 3*").

---

122 Consequences of making unlawful distribution

(1) Where a distribution or part of one, made by a company to one of its members, is made in contravention of any provision of this Part and, at the time of the distribution, he or she knows or has reasonable grounds for believing that it is so made, he or she shall be liable to repay it or that part, as the case may be, to the company or (in the case of a distribution made otherwise than in cash) to pay the company a sum equal to the value of the distribution or part at that time.

(2) This section is without prejudice to any obligation imposed apart from this section on a member of a company to repay a distribution unlawfully made to him or her.

123 Meaning of "distribution", "capitalisation", etc., and supplemental provisions

(1) In this Part "distribution" means every description of distribution of a company's assets to members of the company, whether in cash or otherwise, except distributions made by way of—

(a) an issue of shares as fully or partly paid bonus shares;

(b) the redemption of preference shares pursuant to *section 108* out of the proceeds of a fresh issue of shares made for the purposes of redemption;

(c) the redemption or purchase of shares pursuant to *section 105* and the other relevant provisions of this Part out of the proceeds of a fresh issue of shares made for the purposes of the redemption or purchase;

(d) the payment pursuant to *section 106(5)* of any premium out of the company's undenominated capital on a redemption referred to in that provision; and

(e) a distribution of assets to members of the company on its winding up.

(2) In this Part "capitalisation", in relation to any profits of a company, means any of the following operations, that is to say, applying the profits in wholly or partly paying up unissued shares in the company to be allotted to members of the company as fully or partly paid bonus shares or transferring the profits to undenominated capital.

(3) In this Part references to profits and losses of any description are references respectively to profits and losses of that description made at any time and, except

where the context otherwise requires, are references respectively to revenue and capital profits and revenue and capital losses.

(4) The provisions of this Part are without prejudice to any enactment or rule of law or any provision of a company's constitution restricting the sums out of which, or the cases in which, a distribution may be made.

(5) Where a company makes a distribution of or including a non-cash asset and any part of the amount at which that asset is stated in the financial statements relevant for the purposes of the distribution in accordance with this Chapter represents an unrealised profit, that profit is to be treated as a realised profit—

(a) for the purpose of determining the lawfulness of the distribution in accordance with this Chapter (whether before or after the distribution takes place); and

(b) for the purpose of the application of [*paragraph 14(a)* of *Schedule 3, 3A* or *3B* and *paragraph 37(3)* of *Schedule 3* or *3A*, as the case may be][a] (only realised profits to be included in or transferred to the profit and loss account) in relation to anything done with a view to or in connection with the making of that distribution.

Amendments

a Words substituted by C(A)A 2017, s 90(c) (previously: "*paragraphs 14(a)* and *37(3)* of *Schedule 3*").

124 Procedures for declarations, payments, etc., of dividends and other things

(1) Each provision of this section and *section 125* applies save to the extent that the company's constitution provides otherwise.

(2) A company may, by ordinary resolution, declare dividends but no dividend shall exceed the amount recommended by the directors of the company.

(3) The directors of a company may from time to time—

(a) pay to the members such interim dividends as appear to the directors to be justified by the profits of the company, subject to *section 117*;

(b) before recommending any dividend, set aside out of the profits of the company such sums as they think proper as a reserve or reserves which shall, at the discretion of the directors, be applicable for any purpose to which the profits of the company may be properly applied, and pending such application may, at the like discretion either be employed in the business of the company or be invested in such investments as the directors may lawfully determine;

(c) without placing the profits of the company to reserve, carry forward any profits which they may think prudent not to distribute.

(4) Subject to the rights of persons, if any, entitled to shares with special rights as to dividend, all dividends shall be declared and paid according to the amounts paid or credited as paid on the shares in respect of which the dividend is paid.

(5) However no amount paid or credited as paid on a share in advance of calls shall be treated for the purposes of this section as paid on the share.

(6) All dividends shall be apportioned and paid proportionally to the amounts paid or credited as paid on the shares during any portion or portions of the period in respect of which the dividend is paid, but if any share is issued on terms providing that it shall rank for a dividend as from a particular date, such share shall rank for dividend accordingly.

(7) The directors may deduct from any dividend payable to any member, all sums of money (if any) immediately payable by him or her to the company on account of calls or otherwise in relation to the shares of the company.

125 Supplemental provisions in relation to *section 124*

(1) A general meeting of a company declaring a dividend or bonus may direct payment of such dividend or bonus wholly or partly by the distribution of specific assets and, in particular, paid up shares, debentures or debenture stock of any other company or in any one or more of such ways.

(2) The directors of the company shall give effect to such resolution, and where any difficulty arises in regard to such distribution, the directors may settle the matter as they think expedient and, in particular, may—

(a) issue fractional certificates and fix the value for distribution of such specific assets or any part of them;

(b) determine that cash payments shall be made to any members upon the footing of the value so fixed, in order to adjust the rights of all the parties; and

(c) vest any such specific assets in trustees as may seem expedient to the directors.

(3) Any dividend, interest or other moneys payable in cash in respect of any shares may be paid—

(a) by cheque or negotiable instrument sent by post directed to or otherwise delivered to the registered address of the holder, or where there are joint holders, to the registered address of that one of the joint holders who is first named on the register or to such person and to such address as the holder or the joint holders may in writing direct; or

(b) by agreement with the payee (which may either be a general agreement or one confined to specific payments), by direct transfer to a bank account nominated by the payee.

(4) Any such cheque or negotiable instrument shall be made payable to the order of the person to whom it is sent.

(5) Any one of two or more joint holders may give valid receipts for any dividends, bonuses or other moneys payable in respect of the shares held by them as joint holders, whether paid by cheque or negotiable instrument or direct transfer.

(6) No dividend shall bear interest against the company.

126 Bonus issues

(1) Each provision of this section applies save where the company's constitution provides otherwise.

(2) In *subsections (3)* and *(4)* "relevant sum" means—

(a) any sum for the time being standing to the credit of the company's undenominated capital;

(b) any of the company's profits available for distribution; or

(c) any sum representing unrealised revaluation reserves.

(3) The company in general meeting may, on the recommendation of the directors, resolve that any relevant sum be capitalised and applied on behalf of the members who would have been entitled to receive that sum if it had been distributed by way of dividend and in the same proportions in or towards paying up in full unissued shares of the company of a nominal value equal to the relevant sum capitalised (such shares to be allotted and distributed credited as fully paid up to and amongst such holders and in the proportions as aforementioned).

(4) The company in general meeting may, on the recommendation of the directors, resolve that it is desirable to capitalise any part of a relevant sum which is not available for distribution, by applying such sum in paying up in full unissued shares to be allotted as fully paid bonus shares, to those members of the company who would have been entitled to that sum if it were distributed by way of dividend (and in the same proportions).

(5) The directors of the company shall give effect to any resolution under *subsection (3)* or *(4)*.

(6) For that purpose the directors shall make—

(a) all appropriations and applications of the undivided profits resolved to be capitalised by the resolution; and

(b) all allotments and issues of fully paid shares, if any, and generally shall do all acts and things required to give effect to the resolution.

(7) Without limiting the foregoing, the directors may—

(a) make such provision as they think fit for the case of shares becoming distributable in fractions (and, again, without limiting the foregoing, may sell the shares represented by such fractions and distribute the net proceeds of such sale amongst the members otherwise entitled to such fractions in due proportions); and

(b) authorise any person to enter, on behalf of all the members concerned, into an agreement with the company providing for the allotment to them, respectively credited as fully paid up, of any further shares to which they may become entitled on the capitalisation concerned or, as the case may require, for the payment by the application thereto of their respective proportions of the profits resolved to be capitalised of the amounts remaining unpaid on their existing shares.

(8) Any agreement made under such authority shall be effective and binding on all the members concerned.

(9) Where the directors of a company have resolved to approve a *bona fide* revaluation of all the fixed assets of the company, the net capital surplus in excess of the previous book value of the assets arising from such revaluation may be—

(a) credited by the directors to undenominated capital, other than the share premium account; or

(b) used in paying up unissued shares of the company to be issued to members as fully paid bonus shares.

PART 4
CORPORATE GOVERNANCE

Chapter 1
Preliminary

127 Access to documents during business hours

(1) A reference in this Part to a document kept by a company being open to the inspection of a person, or a specified class of person, during business hours shall be read as a requirement that the document be open to such inspection subject to such reasonable restrictions as the company may in general meeting impose, but so that not less than 2 hours in each day be allowed for such inspection.

(2) *Subsection (1)* applies to the provisions of other Parts of this Act that are referred to in *Chapter 10* (which deals with, amongst other things, inspection of registers) as it applies to the provisions of this Part so referred to.

Chapter 2

Directors and secretaries

128 Directors

(1) A company shall have at least one director.

(2) If default is made by a company in complying with *subsection (1)* for 28 consecutive days, the company and any officer of it who is in default shall be guilty of a category 3 offence.

129 Secretaries

(1) A company shall have a secretary, who may be one of the directors.

(2) Anything required or authorised to be done by or to the secretary may, if the office is vacant or there is for any other reason no secretary capable of acting, be done by or to any assistant or deputy secretary or, if there is no assistant or deputy secretary capable of acting, by or to any officer of the company authorised generally or specially in that behalf by the directors.

(3) Subject to *section 25(5)*, the secretary shall be appointed by the directors of the company for such term, at such remuneration and upon such conditions as they may think fit; and any secretary so appointed may be removed by them.

(4) The directors of a company shall have a duty to ensure that the person appointed as secretary has the skills or resources necessary to discharge his or her statutory and other duties.

(5) The cases to which *subsection (4)* applies includes the case of an appointment of one of the directors of the company as secretary.

(6) Where a company has only one director, that person may not also hold the office of secretary of the company.

(7) In *subsections (2)* to *(6)* references to a secretary include references to joint secretaries.

130 Prohibition of body corporate or unincorporated body of persons being director

(1) A company shall not have as director of the company a body corporate or an unincorporated body of persons.

(2) Any purported appointment of a body corporate or an unincorporated body of persons as a director of a company shall be void.

131 Prohibition of minor being director or secretary

(1) No person shall be appointed a director or, in the case of an individual, secretary of a company unless he or she has attained the age of 18 years.

(2) Any purported appointment of a minor as a director of a company shall be void.

(3) Where—

(a) a person appointed a director of a company before the commencement of *subsection (1)* has not attained the age of 18 years when that subsection is commenced; or

(b) the office of director of a company is held otherwise by virtue of another office, and the person appointed to that other office has not attained the age of 18 years when *subsection (1)* is commenced,

that person ceases to be a director of the company on the commencement of *subsection (1)* and the company shall make the necessary consequential alteration in its register of directors and shall notify the Registrar of the change.

132 Prohibition of undischarged bankrupt being director or secretary or otherwise involved in company

(1) If any person being an undischarged bankrupt—

(a) acts as a director or secretary of a company; or

(b) directly or indirectly takes part or is concerned in the promotion, formation or management of a company,

the person shall (unless he or she does so with the leave of the court) be guilty of a category 2 offence.

(2) Where a person is convicted of an offence under *subsection (1)* the person shall be deemed to be subject to a disqualification order from the date of such conviction for such period as the court specifies if he or she was not, or was not deemed to be, subject to such an order on that date.

(3) In this section "disqualification order" has the same meaning as it has in *Chapter 4* of *Part 14*.

133 Examination as to solvency status

(1) Where the Director of Corporate Enforcement has reason to believe that a director or secretary of a company is an undischarged bankrupt, the Director of Corporate Enforcement may exercise the following power.

(2) That power is to require the director or secretary of the company to produce to the Director, by a specified date, a sworn statement by him or her of all relevant facts pertaining to the director's or secretary's financial position, both within the State and elsewhere, and, in particular, to any matter relating to bankruptcy as at a particular date.

(3) The court may, on the application of the Director of Corporate Enforcement, require a director or secretary of a company who has made a statement under *subsection (2)* to appear before it and answer on oath any question pertaining to the content of the statement.

(4) The court may, on the application of the Director of Corporate Enforcement, make a disqualification order against a director or secretary of a company, to be for such period as the court specifies, on the grounds that he or she is an undischarged bankrupt.

(5) A director or secretary of a company who fails to comply with a requirement under *subsection (2)* shall be guilty of a category 3 offence.

(6) In this section "disqualification order" has the same meaning as it has in *Chapter 4* of *Part 14*.

134 Performance of acts by person in dual capacity as director and secretary not permitted

A provision of—

(a) this Act;

(b) an instrument under it; or

(c) a company's constitution,

requiring or authorising a thing to be done by or to a director and the secretary shall not be satisfied by its being done by or to the same person acting both as director and as, or in place of, the secretary.

135 Validity of acts of director or secretary

The acts of a director or of a secretary shall be valid notwithstanding any defect which may afterwards be discovered in his or her appointment or qualification.

136 Share qualifications of directors

(1) This section applies where the constitution of a company requires a director of the company to hold a specified share qualification (the "specified qualification").

(2) Where this section applies—

(a) the office of director of a company shall be vacated if the director—

(i) does not within 2 months after the date of his or her appointment or within such shorter time as may be fixed by the constitution, obtain the specified qualification; or

(ii) ceases at any time, after the expiration of that period or shorter time so fixed, as the case may be, to hold the specified qualification;

and

(b) a person vacating office under this section shall be incapable of being re-appointed director of the company until he or she has obtained the specified qualification.

137 Company to have director resident in an EEA state

(1) Subject to *subsection (2)* and *section 140*, one, at least, of the directors for the time being of a company shall be a person who is resident in an EEA state.

(2) *Subsection (1)* shall not apply in relation to a company if the company for the time being holds a bond, in the prescribed form, in force to the value of €25,000 and which provides that, in the event of a failure by the company to pay the whole or part of each (if any) fine and penalty specified in the Table to this section, there shall become payable under the bond to a person who is, under *subsection (4)*, nominated for the purpose (the "nominated person") a sum of money for the following purpose.

(3) That purpose is the purpose of the sum being applied by the nominated person in discharging the whole or part, as the case may be, of the company's liability in respect of any such fine or penalty (and any sum that becomes so payable shall be applied by the nominated person accordingly).

(4) The nomination referred to in *subsection (2)* shall be made—

(a) by the Registrar or the Revenue Commissioners, as appropriate; or

(b) in the case of failure to pay both a fine referred to in *paragraph 1* of the Table to this section and a fine or penalty, or a fine and penalty, referred to in *paragraph 2* of that Table, jointly by the Registrar and the Revenue Commissioners.

(5) The bond referred to in *subsection (2)* may be entered into and shall have effect according to its terms notwithstanding any rule of law whereby any agreement to insure or indemnify a person in respect of any punishment or liability imposed on him or her in relation to any offence or unlawful act committed by him or her is void or unenforceable.

(6) If *subsection (1)* is not complied with, the company concerned and any officer of it who is in default shall be guilty of a category 4 offence.

(7) In this section "director" does not include an alternate director.

Table

1. A fine imposed on the company in respect of an offence under this Act committed by it.
2. (1) A fine imposed on the company in respect of an offence under section 1078 of the Taxes Consolidation Act 1997 committed by it, being an offence that consists of a failure by the company to deliver a statement which it is required to deliver under section 882 of that Act or to comply with a notice served on it under section 884 of that Act. (2) A penalty which the company has been held liable to pay under section 1071 or 1073 of the Taxes Consolidation Act 1997

138 Supplemental provisions concerning bond referred to in *section 137(2)*

(1) In this section—

"bond" means the bond referred to in *section 137(2)*;

"nominated person" means the person nominated under *section 137(4)* in relation to the bond concerned.

(2) The bond shall also provide that, in addition to the sum referred to in *section 137(2)*, there shall become payable under the bond to the nominated person, on demand being made, with the consent of the Revenue Commissioners, by him or her in that behalf, a sum of money (not exceeding such sum as the Revenue Commissioners and the Minister may sanction) for the purpose of defraying such expenses as may have been reasonably incurred by that person in carrying out his or her duties under *section 137(3)*.

(3) The nominated person shall keep all proper and usual accounts, including an income and expenditure account and a balance sheet, of all moneys received by him or her on foot of the bond and of all disbursements made by him or her from any such moneys.

(4) The Minister, after consultation with the Minister for Public Expenditure and Reform, the Revenue Commissioners and any other person who, in the opinion of the Minister, might be concerned with or interested in the matter, may prescribe—

(a) that arrangements in relation to the bond shall only be entered into with persons of a prescribed class or classes;

(b) the form of that bond and the minimum period to be specified in the bond as being the period for which it shall be valid.

(5) A copy of the bond held by a company shall be appended—

(a) in case none of the directors (within the meaning of *section 137*) of the company is resident in an EEA state on its incorporation, to the statement required by *section 21(1)(a)* to be delivered to the Registrar in relation to the company;

(b) in case a notification is made under *section 139* to the Registrar in relation to the company, to that notification;

(c) in case during the period to which an annual return concerning the company relates none of the directors (within the meaning of *section 137*) of the company is resident in an EEA state, to that annual return (unless such a copy has been appended to a notification under *section 139* made to the Registrar in that period).

139 Notification requirement as regards non-residency of director

(1) Without prejudice to anything in *section 149*, if a person ceases to be a director of a company and, at the time of that cessation—

(a) he or she is resident in an EEA state; and

(b) either—

(i) he or she was the sole director, or

(ii) to his or her knowledge, no other director of the company is resident in an EEA state,

that person shall, within 14 days after the date of that cessation, notify, in writing, the Registrar of that cessation and the matter referred to in *paragraph (b)(i)* or *(ii)*, as the case may be.

(2) A notification in writing to the Registrar of the matter referred to in *subsection (1)(b)(i)* or *(ii)* shall not, of itself, be regarded as constituting defamatory matter.

(3) If a person fails to comply with *subsection (1)*, he or she shall be jointly and severally liable with the company of which he or she has ceased to be director for any fine or penalty referred to in *section 137(2)* imposed on the company, or which it is held liable to pay, after that cessation.

(4) Any such fine or penalty for which that person is so liable may be recovered by the Registrar or the Revenue Commissioners, as appropriate, from him or her as a simple contract debt in any court of competent jurisdiction.

(5) In this section "director" does not include an alternate director.

140 Exception to *section 137* — companies having real and continuous link with economic activity in State

(1) *Section 137(1)* shall not apply in relation to a company in respect of which there is in force a certificate under this section.

(2) The Registrar may grant to a company, on application in the prescribed form being made by it in that behalf, a certificate stating that the company has a real and continuous link with one or more economic activities that are being carried on in the State.

(3) The Registrar shall not grant such a certificate unless the company concerned tenders proof to him or her that it has such a link.

(4) A statement referred to in *subsection (5)* that is tendered by the applicant shall be deemed to be proof, for the purposes of *subsection (3)*, that the applicant has such a link.

(5) That statement is a statement in writing that has been given to the company concerned by the Revenue Commissioners within the period of 2 months ending before the date on which an application is made under *subsection (2)* by the company and which states that the Revenue Commissioners have reasonable grounds to believe that the company has a real and continuous link with one or more economic activities being carried on in the State.

(6) If, in consequence of information that has come into the possession of the Registrar, the Registrar is of opinion that a company in respect of which a certificate under *subsection (2)* has been granted has ceased to have a real and continuous link with any economic activity being carried on in the State, he or she shall revoke that certificate.

(7) If, in consequence of information that has come into their possession, the Revenue Commissioners are of opinion that a company in respect of which a certificate under *subsection (2)* has been granted has ceased to have a real and continuous link with any economic activity being carried on in the State, the following applies—

(a) the Commissioners may give a notice in writing to the Registrar stating that they are of that opinion; and

(b) such a notice that is received by the Registrar shall constitute information in his or her possession for the purposes of *subsection (6)*.

(8) *Subsection (7)(a)* has effect notwithstanding any obligations as to secrecy or other restrictions upon disclosure of information imposed by or under statute or otherwise.

(9) For the purposes of this section a company has a real and continuous link with an economic activity that is being carried on in the State if one or more of the following conditions are satisfied by it—

(a) the affairs of the company are managed by one or more persons from a place of business established in the State and that person or those persons is or are authorised by the company to act on its behalf;

(b) the company carries on a trade in the State;

(c) the company is a subsidiary or a holding company of a company or other body corporate that satisfies either or both of the conditions specified in *paragraphs (a)* and *(b)*;

(d) the company is a subsidiary of a company, another subsidiary of which satisfies either or both of the conditions specified in *paragraphs (a)* and *(b)*.

141 Provisions for determining whether director resident in State

(1) So far as it is the person's residence in the State that falls to be determined for the purposes of those sections, for the purposes of *sections 137* and *139* a person is resident in the State at a particular time (the "relevant time") if—

(a) he or she is present in the State at—

(i) any one time or several times in the period of 12 months preceding the relevant time (the "immediate 12 month period") for a period in the aggregate amounting to 183 days or more; or

(ii) any one time or several times—

(I) in the immediate 12 month period; and

(II) in the period of 12 months preceding the immediate 12 month period (the "previous 12 month period"),

for a period (being a period comprising in the aggregate the number of days on which the person is present in the State in the immediate 12 month period and the number of days on which the person was present in the State in the previous 12 month period) in the aggregate amounting to 280 days or more; or

(b) that time is in a year of assessment (within the meaning of the Taxes Consolidation Act 1997) in respect of which the person has made an election under section 819(3) of that Act.

(2) Notwithstanding *subsection (1)(a)(ii)*, where in the immediate 12 month period concerned a person is present in the State at any one time or several times for a period in the aggregate amounting to not more than 30 days—

(a) the person shall not be resident in the State, for the purposes of *section 137* or *139*, at the relevant time concerned; and

(b) no account shall be taken of the period for the purposes of the aggregate mentioned in *subsection (1)(a)(ii)*.

(3) For the purposes of *subsections (1)* and *(2)*—

(a) references in this section to a person's being present in the State are references to the person's being personally present in the State; and

(b) a person shall be deemed to be present in the State for a day if the person is present in the State at any time during that day.

142 Limitation on number of directorships

(1) A person shall not, at a particular time, be a director of more than—

(a) 25 private companies limited by shares; or

(b) 25 companies, one, or more than one, of which is a private company limited by shares and one, or more than one, of which is any other type of company capable of being wound up under this Act.

(2) *Subsections (3)* to *(7)* apply in reckoning, for the purposes of *subsection (1)* (the "relevant purposes"), the number of companies of which the person concerned is a director at a particular time (the "relevant time") and a reference in them to a company, without qualification, includes a reference to any type of company capable of being wound up under this Act.

(3) Without prejudice to the following subsections, there shall not be included for the relevant purposes any of the following companies of which the person is a director at the relevant time, namely—

(a) a public limited company;

(b) a company in respect of which a certificate under *section 140* is in force.

(4) There shall not be included, for the relevant purposes, any company of which the person is a director at the relevant time (not being a time that is before the date of the giving of the certificate or direction referred to subsequently in this subsection) if—

(a) the person, or the company, delivers to the Registrar a notice, in the prescribed form, stating that the company is a company falling within one or more of the categories of company specified in the Table to this section; and

(b) either—

(i) the Registrar, having considered that notice and having made such enquiries as he or she thinks fit, certifies in writing, or as the case may be the Minister under *subsection (7)* so certifies, that the company is a company falling within one or more of the foregoing categories; or

(ii) the Minister directs, under *subsection (7)*, that the company is not to be included amongst the companies for the relevant purposes.

(5) There shall, for the relevant purposes, be counted as the one company of which the person is a director at the relevant time, 2 or more companies of which he or she is a director at that time if one of those companies is the holding company of the other or others.

(6) For the purposes of *subsection (4)(b)(i)*, the Registrar may accept as sufficient evidence that the company concerned falls within a category of company specified in the Table to this section a declaration, in the prescribed form, to that effect made by an officer of the company or the other person referred to in *subsection (4)(a)*.

(7) If the Registrar refuses to certify that the company to which a notice under *subsection (4)(a)* relates is a company falling within a category of company specified in the Table to this section, the company or the person referred to in *subsection (4)(a)* may appeal to the Minister against such a refusal and the Minister may, having considered the matter and made such enquiries as he or she thinks fit, do one of the following:

(a) confirm the decision of the Registrar;

(b) certify in writing that the company is a company falling within a foregoing category; or

(c) notwithstanding that he or she confirms the decision of the Registrar, direct that the company is not to be included amongst the companies that shall be reckoned for the purposes of *subsection (1)* in so far as that subsection applies to the person concerned but shall only give such a direction if—

(i) the person concerned was a director of the company before 18 April 2000; and

(ii) in the opinion of the Minister the inclusion of the company amongst the companies that shall be reckoned for the purposes of *subsection (1)*, in so far as that subsection applies to the person concerned, would result in serious injustice or hardship to that person; and

(iii) the giving of the direction would not operate against the common good.

(8) A notice referred to in *subsection (4)(a)* may, for the purposes of that provision, be delivered to the Registrar before the person concerned becomes a director of the company to which the notice relates.

Table

A company that is the holder of a licence under section 9 of the Central Bank Act 1971 or is exempt from the requirement under that Act to hold such a licence.
A company falling within any provision (in so far as applicable to a private company limited by shares) of *Schedule 5*.

143 Sanctions for contravention of *section 142* and supplemental provisions

(1) If a person, in contravention of *section 142(1)*, purports to become, or purports to remain, a director of one or more companies he or she shall be guilty of a category 4 offence.

(2) An appointment of a person as a director of a company shall, if it contravenes *section 142(1)*, be void.

(3) For the avoidance of doubt—

(a) each purported appointment, in excess of the limit (reckoned in accordance with *section 142(3)* to *(7)*) that is provided for by *section 142(1)*, of a person as a director of a company shall constitute a separate contravention of *section 142(1)*;

(b) an appointment, not in excess of the foregoing limit, of a person as a director of a company shall not, by virtue of this section, become unlawful, be rendered void or cease to have effect by reason of a subsequent appointment, in excess of that limit, of the person as a director of a company.

(4) If—

(a) the appointments of a person as a director of 2 or more companies are made at the same time; or

(b) the times at which the appointments of a person as a director of 2 or more companies were made are not capable of being distinguished from one another,

then those appointments shall, for the purposes of *section 142*, be deemed to have been made at different times on the day concerned and in the same order as the order in which the companies to which the appointments relate were registered under this Act, the prior Companies Acts or any other former enactment relating to companies (within the meaning of *section 5*), as the case may be.

(5) A reference in this section to a company includes a reference to any type of company capable of being wound up under this Act.

144 Appointment of director

(1) Any purported appointment of a director without that director's consent shall be void.

(2) Subject to *subsection (1)*, the first directors of a company shall be those persons determined in writing by the subscribers of the constitution or a majority of them.

(3) Save to the extent that the company's constitution provides otherwise and subject to *subsection (5)* in the case of a single-member company—

(a) subsequent directors of a company may be appointed by the members in general meeting, provided that no person other than a director retiring at the meeting shall, save where recommended by the directors, be eligible for election to the office of director at any general meeting unless the requirements of *subsection (4)* as to his or her eligibility for that purpose have been complied with;

(b) the directors of the company may from time to time appoint any person to be a director of the company, either to fill a casual vacancy or as an addition to the existing directors, but so that the total number of directors of the company shall not at any time exceed the number, if any, provided for in its constitution;

(c) any director appointed as mentioned in *paragraph (b)* shall hold office only until the next following annual general meeting, and shall then be eligible for re-election;

(d) the company may from time to time, by ordinary resolution, increase or reduce the number of directors;

(e) the company may, by ordinary resolution, appoint another person in place of a director removed from office under *section 146* and, without prejudice to the powers of the directors under *subsection (3)(b)*, the company in general meeting may appoint any person to be a director either to fill a casual vacancy or as an additional director.

(4) The following are the requirements mentioned in *subsection (3)(a)* for the eligibility of a person (the "person concerned") for election as a director at a general meeting, namely, not less than 3 nor more than 21 days before the day appointed for the meeting there shall have been left at the company's registered office—

(a) notice in writing signed by a member of the company duly qualified to attend and vote at the meeting for which such notice is given, of his or her intention to propose the person concerned for such election; and

(b) notice in writing signed by the person concerned of his or her willingness to be so elected.

(5) Subject to *subsection (1)*, in the case of a single-member company, the sole member may appoint a person to be a director of the company by serving a notice in writing on the company which states that the named person is appointed director and this applies notwithstanding anything in *subsection (3)* (save for the requirement of it that any limit for the time being on the number of the directors is to be observed) or *subsection (4)*.

145 Appointment of directors to be voted on individually

(1) At a general meeting of a company, a motion for the appointment of 2 or more persons as directors of the company by a single resolution shall not be made, unless a resolution that it shall be so made has first been agreed to by the meeting without any vote being given against it.

(2) Subject to *subsections (3)* and *(4)*, a resolution moved in contravention of this section shall be void, whether or not its being so moved was objected to at the time.

(3) *Subsection (2)* shall not be taken as excluding the operation of *section 135*.

(4) Where a resolution moved in contravention of this section is passed, no provision for the automatic re-appointment of retiring directors in default of another appointment shall apply.

(5) For the purposes of this section, a motion for approving a person's appointment or for nominating a person for appointment shall be treated as a motion for his or her appointment.

(6) Nothing in this section shall apply to a resolution amending the company's constitution.

146 Removal of directors

(1) A company may by ordinary resolution remove a director before the expiration of his or her period of office notwithstanding anything in its constitution or in any agreement between it and him or her.

(2) *Subsection (1)* shall not authorise the removal of a director holding office for life.

(3) In the case of a resolution to remove a director under this section or to appoint somebody instead of the director so removed at the meeting at which he or she is removed the following provisions shall apply—

(a) the company shall be given not less than 28 days' notice of the intention to move any such resolution except when the directors of the company have resolved to submit it;

(b) on receipt of notice of such an intended resolution, the company shall forthwith send a copy of it to the director concerned, and the director (whether or not he or she is a member of the company) shall be entitled to be heard on the resolution at the meeting; and

(c) the company shall give its members notice of any such resolution at the same time and in the same manner as it gives notice of the meeting or, if that is not practicable, shall give them notice of it, either by advertisement in a daily newspaper circulating in the district in which the registered office of the company is situated or in any other manner allowed by this Act or by the constitution, not less than 21 days before the date of the meeting.

(4) Any such resolution that is passed that does not comply with the foregoing provisions shall, subject to *subsection (5)*, not be effective.

(5) If, after notice of the intention to move such a resolution has been given to the company, a meeting is called for a date 28 days or less after the notice has been given, the notice, though not given within the time required by *subsection (3)(a)*, shall be deemed to have been properly given for the purposes of that provision.

(6) Subject to *subsection (8)*, where notice is given of an intended resolution to remove a director under this section and the director concerned makes in relation to that resolution representations in writing to the company (not exceeding a reasonable length) and requests their notification to the members of the company, the company shall, unless the representations are received by it too late for it to do so—

(a) in any notice of the resolution given to members of the company, state the fact of the representations having been made; and

(b) send a copy of the representations to every member of the company to whom notice of the meeting is sent (whether before or after receipt of the representations by the company).

(7) If a copy of the representations is not sent as mentioned in *subsection (6)* (either because they were received too late or because of the company's default) the director concerned may, without prejudice to his or her right to be heard orally, require that the representations shall be read out at the meeting concerned.

(8) Copies of the representations need not be sent out, and the representations need not be read out at the meeting concerned, as mentioned in *subsection (6)* or *(7)*, if, on the application either of the company or of any other person who claims to be aggrieved, the court is satisfied that the rights conferred by this section are being abused to secure needless publicity for defamatory matter and orders that those things need not be done.

(9) The court may order the company's costs on such an application to be paid in whole or in part by the director concerned, notwithstanding that he or she is not a party to the application.

(10) A vacancy created by the removal of a director under this section may be filled at the meeting at which he or she is removed and, if not so filled, may be filled as a casual vacancy.

(11) A person appointed director in place of a person removed under this section shall be treated, for the purpose of determining the time at which he or she or any other director is to retire, as if he or she had become director on the day on which the person in whose place he or she is appointed was last appointed director.

147 Compensation for wrongful termination, other powers of removal not affected by *section 146*

Nothing in *section 146* shall be taken—

(a) as depriving a person removed under it of compensation or damages payable to him or her, or any other remedy available to the person, in respect of the termination of his or her appointment as director or of any appointment terminating with that as director; or

(b) as derogating from any power to remove a director that may exist apart from that section.

148 Vacation of office

(1) In addition to the case provided by *section 136* (share qualification of directors), the office of director shall be vacated if the director—

(a) is adjudicated bankrupt or being a bankrupt has not obtained a certificate of discharge in the relevant jurisdiction; or

(b) becomes or is deemed to be subject to a disqualification order within the meaning of *Chapter 4* of *Part 14*.

(2) Save to the extent that the company's constitution provides otherwise, the office of director shall be vacated if—

(a) the director resigns his or her office by notice in writing to the company; or

(b) the health of the director is such that he or she can no longer be reasonably regarded as possessing an adequate decision making capacity; or

(c) a declaration of restriction is made in relation to the director and the directors, at any time during the currency of the declaration, resolve that his or her office be vacated; or

(d) the director is sentenced to a term of imprisonment following conviction of an indictable offence; or

(e) the director is for more than 6 months absent, without the permission of the directors, from meetings of the directors held during that period.

(3) In *subsection (2)(d)* the reference to a term of imprisonment includes a reference to such a term that is suspended.

149 Register of directors and secretaries

(1) A company shall keep a register (the "register") of its directors and secretaries and, if any, its assistant and deputy secretaries.

(2) Subject to *subsection (4)* and *section 150(11)*, the register shall contain the following particulars relating to each director:

(a) his or her present forename and surname and any former forename and surname;

(b) his or her date of birth;

(c) his or her usual residential address;

(d) his or her nationality;

(e) his or her business occupation, if any; and

(f) particulars of any other directorships of bodies corporate, whether incorporated in the State or elsewhere, held by him or her or which have been held by him or her.

(3) *Sections 215* to *217* (rights of inspection, requests for copies, etc.) apply to the register.

(4) It shall not be necessary for the register to contain on any day particulars of any directorship—

(a) which has not been held by a director at any time during the 5 years preceding that day;

(b) which is held or was held by a director in bodies corporate of which the company is or was the wholly owned subsidiary or which are or were the wholly owned subsidiaries either of the company or of another body corporate of which the company is or was the wholly owned subsidiary.

(5) Subject to *subsection (6)* and *section 150(11)*, the register shall contain the following particulars relating to the secretary or, where there are joint secretaries, in relation to each of them—

(a) in the case of an individual—

(i) his or her present forename and surname and any former forename and surname;

(ii) his or her usual residential address; and

(iii) his or her date of birth,

and

(b) in the case of a body corporate, the corporate name and, if the body corporate is registered—

(i) its registered office;

(ii) the register in which it is registered; and

(iii) the number under which it is registered in that register.

(6) Where all the partners in a firm are joint secretaries of a company, the name and principal office of the firm may be stated instead of the particulars referred to in *subsection (5)*.

(7) In relation to any assistant or deputy secretary the same particulars shall be contained in the register as respects the assistant or deputy secretary as are required by *subsection (5)* to be contained in the register as respects a secretary or joint secretary.

(8) The company shall, within the period of 14 days after the date of the happening of—

(a) any change among its directors or in its secretary or assistant or deputy secretary; or

(b) any change in any of the particulars contained in the register,

send to the Registrar a notification in the prescribed form of the change and of the date on which it occurred.

(9) In the case of a person who is a director of more than one company (the "relevant companies") the following provisions apply—

(a) the person may send a notification in the prescribed form to the Registrar of a change in his or her usual residential address or of a change in his or her name and (in each case) of the date on which the change occurred;

(b) if such a notification is sent to the Registrar and the relevant companies are listed in the notification as being companies of which the person is a director—

(i) each of the relevant companies shall be relieved, as respects, and only as respects, that particular change or, as the case may be, those particular changes, of the obligation under *subsection (8)* to send a notification of it or them to the Registrar; and

(ii) the Registrar may proceed to record the relevant change or changes concerning the person in relation to each of the relevant companies.

(10) A notification sent to the Registrar pursuant to *subsection (8)* of the appointment of a person as a director, secretary, joint secretary or assistant or deputy secretary of a company shall be accompanied by a consent signed by that person to act as director or secretary or assistant or deputy secretary or, where all the partners in a firm have been

appointed joint secretaries of a company, by one partner on behalf of the firm, as the case may be.

(11) *Section 223(3)*, in the case of a director, and *section 226(5)*, in the case of a secretary, requires the inclusion of a particular statement in a foregoing consent by him or her.

(12) For the purposes of this section—

(a) in the case of a person usually known by a title different from his or her surname, the expression "surname" means that title;

(b) references to a "former forename" or "surname" do not include—

(i) in the case of a person usually known by a title different from his or her surname, the name by which he or she was known previous to the adoption of or succession to the title; or

(ii) in the case of any person, a former forename or surname where that name or surname was changed or disused before the person bearing the name attained the age of 18 years or has been changed or disused for a period of not less than 20 years, or

(iii) in the case of a married person or civil partner, the name or surname by which he or she was known previously to his or her marriage or civil partnership.

150 Supplemental provisions (including offences) in relation to *section 149*

(1) Without prejudice to the generality of *section 149(8)*, a change among the directors for the purposes of that provision shall be deemed to include the case of a director's becoming disqualified under the law of another state (whether pursuant to an order of a judge or a tribunal or otherwise) from being appointed or acting as a director or secretary of a body corporate or an undertaking; accordingly, in such a case, the notice under *section 149(8)* shall state, in relation to the director concerned—

(a) the jurisdiction in which he or she has become so disqualified;

(b) the date on which he or she has become so disqualified; and

(c) the period for which he or she has become so disqualified.

(2) Without prejudice to *subsection (1)* and to the requirement under *section 149(10)* that the notification be accompanied by the consent there referred to, if—

(a) the notification to be sent to the Registrar pursuant to *section 149(8)* is a notification of the appointment of a person as a director of a company; and

(b) that person is a person who is disqualified under the law of another state (whether pursuant to an order of a judge or a tribunal or otherwise) from being appointed or acting as a director or secretary of a body corporate or an undertaking,

that person shall ensure that the notification is accompanied by (but as a separate document from that notification) a statement in the prescribed form signed by the person specifying—

(i) the jurisdiction in which he or she is so disqualified;

(ii) the date on which he or she became so disqualified; and

(iii) the period for which he or she is so disqualified.

(3) It shall be the duty of each director and secretary and assistant or deputy secretary, if any, of a company to give information in writing to the company as soon as may be of such matters as may be necessary to enable the company to comply with *section 149* and the preceding subsections of this section.

(4) If default is made in complying with *section 149(1)*, *(2)*, *(5)*, *(7)*, *(8)* or *(10)*, the company concerned and any officer of it who is in default shall be guilty of a category 3 offence.

(5) A person who fails to comply with *subsection (1)* shall be guilty of a category 3 offence.

(6) If the second mentioned person in *subsection (2)* fails to comply with that subsection, he or she shall be guilty of a category 3 offence.

(7) A person who fails to comply with *subsection (3)* shall be guilty of a category 3 offence.

(8) Without prejudice to *subsection (3)* or *(6)* and notwithstanding anything in *subsection (2)*, it shall be the duty of a company to make reasonable enquiries of a person, on his or her appointment as director of the company, so as to ascertain whether the requirements of *subsection (2)* fall to be complied with by that person in relation to that appointment (but a failure of the company to do so does not relieve the person of his or her obligations under that subsection).

(9) If a person appointed a director of a company before the commencement of this section has, subsequent to his or her appointment but before that commencement, become disqualified under the law of another state (whether pursuant to an order of a judge or a tribunal or otherwise) from being appointed or acting as director or secretary of a body corporate or an undertaking, then *subsection (1)* shall apply to such a case as it applies to a case of a director becoming so disqualified after that commencement.

(10) For the purpose of the application of *subsection (1)* to the case first-mentioned in the preceding subsection, *section 149* shall apply as if the following subsection were substituted for *subsection (8)*:

> "(8) The company shall, within the period of 3 months after the commencement of this section, send to the Registrar a notification in the prescribed form of the change and of the date on which it occurred.".

(11) The Minister may make regulations providing that any requirement of this Act that the usual residential address of an officer of a company appear on the register referred to in *section 149(1)* or the register kept by the Registrar shall not apply in relation to a particular person who is such an officer if—

(a) in accordance with a procedure provided in the regulations for this purpose, it is determined that the circumstances concerning the personal safety or security of the person warrant the application of the foregoing exemption in respect of him or her; and

(b) such other conditions (if any) as are specified in the regulations for the application of the foregoing exemption are satisfied.

(12) Regulations under *subsection (11)* may contain such incidental, consequential and supplemental provisions as appear to the Minister to be necessary or expedient, including provision—

(a) so as to secure that there is not otherwise disclosed, by virtue of this Act's operation, the usual residential address of a person in respect of whom the exemption referred to in that subsection applies; and

(b) limiting the regulations' application to a usual residential address that, but for the regulations' operation, would fall to be entered, on a register referred to in that subsection, on or after a date specified in the regulations.

151 Particulars to be shown on all business letters of company

(1) Subject to *subsection (5)*, a company shall, in all business letters on or in which the company's name appears and which are sent by the company to any person, state in legible characters in relation to every director of the company the following particulars:

(a) his or her present forename, or the initials thereof, and present surname;

(b) any former forename and surnames of him or her; and

(c) his or her nationality, if not Irish.

(2) A company shall further have the following particulars on all its business letters and order forms:

(a) the name and legal form of the company;

(b) the place of registration of the company and the number under which it is registered; and

(c) the address of its registered office.

(3) If on any business letters or order forms of a company there is reference to the share capital of the company, the company shall ensure that the reference is not stated otherwise than as a reference to the issued share capital of the company that is paid up.

(4) Where a company has a website, it shall display in a prominent and easily accessible place on that website the particulars referred to in *subsection (2)(a)* to *(c)* and if there is reference in such a website to the share capital of the company—

(a) the same requirement under *subsection (3)* applies to such a reference as it applies to such a reference on business letters and order forms; and

(b) the reference shall be displayed in a prominent and easily accessible place on the website.

(5) If special circumstances exist which render it, in the opinion of the Minister, expedient that such an exemption should be granted, the Minister may, subject to such

conditions as he or she may think fit to impose and specifies in the exemption, grant, in writing, an exemption from the obligations imposed by *subsection (1)*.

(6) If a company makes default in complying with this section, the company and any officer of it who is in default shall be guilty of a category 4 offence.

(7) For the purposes of this section—

(a) "director" includes any person in accordance with whose directions or instructions the directors of the company are accustomed to act, and "officer" shall be read accordingly;

(b) "initials" includes a recognised abbreviation of a forename; and

(c) *section 149(12)* shall apply as it applies for the purposes of *section 149*.

152 Entitlement to notify Registrar of changes in directors and secretaries if section 149(8) contravened

(1) In this section "former director or secretary" means the person referred to in *subsection (2)*.

(2) This section applies where a company fails to send, in accordance with *section 149(8)*, a notification, in the prescribed form, to the Registrar of the fact of a person's having ceased, for whatever reason, to be a director or secretary of the company and of the date on which that event occurred.

(3) Where this section applies, the former director or secretary may serve on the company a notice—

(a) requesting it to send forthwith the notification of the matters mentioned in *subsection (2)*, in the prescribed form, to the Registrar; and

(b) stating that if the company fails to comply with that request within 21 days after the date of service of the notice on it, he or she will forward to the Registrar and to every person who, to his or her knowledge, is an officer of the company a copy of any notice of resignation by him or her as a director or secretary of the company or any other documentary proof of his or her having ceased to be such a director or secretary, together with—

(i) in the case of the Registrar, such additional information as may be prescribed (which may include a declaration made by the person stating the names of the persons who, to the knowledge of the person, are officers of the company); and

(ii) in the case of every other person forwarded as mentioned above, a written request of the person that he or she take such steps as will ensure that the failure of the company to comply with the notice continues no further.

(4) If a company fails to comply with a request made of it under a notice referred to in *subsection (3)*, the former director or secretary may forward to the Registrar and to every person who, to his or her knowledge, is an officer of the company a copy of the notice of resignation or other documentary proof referred to in *subsection (3)(b)* if, but only if, there is forwarded together with that notice or proof—

(a) in the case of the Registrar, the additional information referred to in *subsection (3)(b)(i)*; and

(b) in the case of every other such person, the written request referred to in *subsection(3)(b)(ii)*.

(5) No notice of resignation or other documentary proof of a person's having ceased to be a director or secretary of a company which is forwarded to the Registrar by that person (other than such a notice or other proof which is forwarded by him or her under and in accordance with the preceding subsections or *section 139*) shall be considered by the Registrar.

(6) No additional information referred to in *subsection (3)(b)(i)* that is—

(a) included in a notice of resignation or other documentary proof referred to in this section; and

(b) forwarded, under and in accordance with the foregoing provisions of this section, to the Registrar,

shall, of itself, be regarded as constituting defamatory matter.

153 Provisions as to assignment of office by directors

(1) This section applies to any provision of—

(a) the constitution of a company, or

(b) any agreement entered into between a company and any person,

under which a director of the company is enabled to assign his or her office as such to another person.

(2) Any assignment of office made in pursuance of a provision to which this section applies shall, notwithstanding anything to the contrary contained in the provision, be of no effect unless and until it is approved by a special resolution of the company.

Chapter 3
Service contracts and remuneration

154 Copies of directors' service contracts

(1) Subject to the provisions of this section, a company shall keep—

(a) in the case of each director whose contract of service with the company is in writing, a copy of that contract;

(b) in the case of each director whose contract of service with the company is not in writing, a written memorandum setting out the terms of that contract;

(c) in the case of each director who is employed under a contract of service with a subsidiary of the company, a copy of that contract or, if it is not in writing, a written memorandum setting out the terms of that contract;

(d) a copy or written memorandum, as the case may be, of any variation of any contract of service referred to in *paragraph (a)*, *(b)* or *(c)*, and all copies and memoranda kept by a company in pursuance of this subsection shall be kept at the same place.

(2) *Sections 215* to *217* (rights of inspection, etc.) apply to those copies and memoranda.

(3) Where a contract of service is only partially in writing, *paragraphs (a)*, *(b)*, *(c)* and *(d)*, as appropriate, of *subsection (1)*, and *subsection (4)* shall also apply to such a contract.

(4) *Subsection (1)* shall not apply in relation to a director's contract of service with the company or with a subsidiary of the company if that contract required him or her to work wholly or mainly outside the State, but the company shall keep a memorandum—

(a) in the case of a contract of service with the company, setting out the name of the director and the provisions of the contract relating to its duration;

(b) in the case of a contract of service with a subsidiary of the company, setting out the name of the director, the name and place of incorporation of the subsidiary and the provisions of the contract relating to its duration,

at the same place as copies and the memoranda are kept by the company in pursuance of *subsection (1)*.

(5) If default is made in complying with *subsection (1)* or *(4)*, the company concerned and any officer of it who is in default shall be guilty of a category 3 offence.

(6) This section shall not require to be kept—

(a) a copy of, or memorandum setting out the terms of, a contract; or

(b) a copy of, or memorandum setting out the terms of a variation of, a contract,

at a time at which the unexpired portion of the term for which the contract is to be in force is less than 3 years or at a time at which the contract can, within the next ensuing 3 years, be terminated by the company without payment of compensation.

155 Remuneration of directors

(1) Each provision of this section applies save to the extent that the company's constitution provides otherwise.

(2) The remuneration of the directors of a company shall be such as is determined, from time to time, by the board of directors and such remuneration shall be deemed to accrue from day to day.

(3) The directors of a company may also be paid all travelling, hotel and other expenses properly incurred by them—

(a) in attending and returning from—

(i) meetings of the directors or any committee referred to in *section 160(9)*; or

(ii) general meetings of the company,

or

(b) otherwise in connection with the business of the company.

156 Prohibition of tax-free payments to directors

(1) It shall not be lawful for a company to pay a director of the company remuneration (whether as director or otherwise)—

(a) free of income tax or the universal social charge, or

(b) otherwise calculated by reference to or varying with the amount of his or her income tax or to or with the rate of income tax,

except under a contract which was in force on 31 March 1962 and provides expressly and not by reference to the constitution for payment of remuneration in that manner.

(2) Any provision contained in—

(a) a company's constitution;

(b) any contract other than such a contract as is mentioned in *subsection (1)*; or

(c) any resolution of a company or a company's directors,

for payment to a director of remuneration in the manner referred to in *subsection (1)* shall have effect as if it provided for payment, as a gross sum subject to income tax and the universal social charge, of the net sum for which it actually provides.

Chapter 4
Proceedings of directors

157 *Sections 158* to *165* to apply save where constitution provides otherwise

Each subsequent provision of this Chapter (other than *sections 166* and *167*) applies save to the extent that the company's constitution provides otherwise.

158 General power of management and delegation

(1) The business of a company shall be managed by its directors, who may pay all expenses incurred in promoting and registering the company and may exercise all such powers of the company as are not, by this Act or by the constitution, required to be exercised by the company in general meeting, but subject to—

(a) any regulations contained in the constitution;

(b) the provisions of this Act; and

(c) such directions, not being inconsistent with the foregoing regulations or provisions, as the company in general meeting may (by special resolution) give.

(2) However, no direction given by the company in general meeting under *subsection (1)(c)* shall invalidate any prior act of the directors which would have been valid if that direction had not been given.

(3) Without prejudice to the generality of that subsection, *subsection (1)* operates to enable, subject to a limitation (if any) arising under any of *paragraphs (a)* to *(c)* of it, the directors of the company to exercise all powers of the company to borrow money and to mortgage or charge its undertaking, property and uncalled capital, or any part thereof.

(4) Without prejudice to *section 40*, the directors may delegate any of their powers to such person or persons as they think fit, including committees; any such committee

shall, in the exercise of the powers so delegated, conform to any regulations that may be imposed on it by the directors.

(5) The reference in *subsection (1)* to a power of the company required to be exercised by the company in general meeting includes a reference to a power of the company that, but for the power of the members to pass a written resolution to effect the first-mentioned power's exercise, would be required to be exercised by the company in general meeting.

159 Managing director

(1) The directors of a company may from time to time appoint one or more of themselves to the office of managing director (by whatever name called) for such period and on such terms as to remuneration and otherwise as they see fit, and, subject to the terms of any agreement entered into in any particular case, may revoke such appointment.

(2) Without prejudice to any claim the person so appointed may have for damages for breach of any contract of service between the person and the company, the person's appointment shall cease upon his or her ceasing, from any cause, to be a director of the company.

(3) A managing director of a company shall receive such remuneration whether by way of salary, commission or participation in the profits, or partly in one way and partly in another, as the directors may determine.

(4) Without prejudice to *section 40*, the directors may confer upon a managing director any of the powers exercisable by them upon such terms and conditions and with such restrictions as they may think fit.

(5) In conferring any such powers, the directors may specify that the conferral is to operate either—

(a) so that the powers concerned may be exercised concurrently by them and the managing director; or

(b) to the exclusion of their own such powers.

(6) The directors may—

(a) revoke any conferral of powers under *subsection (4)*; or

(b) amend any such conferral (whether as to the powers conferred or the terms, conditions or restrictions subject to which the conferral is made).

160 Meetings of directors and committees

(1) The directors of a company may meet together for the dispatch of business, adjourn and otherwise regulate their meetings as they think fit.

(2) Questions arising at any such meeting shall be decided by a majority of votes and where there is an equality of votes, the chairperson shall have a second or casting vote.

(3) A director may, and the secretary on the requisition of a director shall, at any time summon a meeting of the directors.

(4) All directors shall be entitled to reasonable notice of any meeting of the directors but, if the directors so resolve, it shall not be necessary to give notice of a meeting of directors to any director who, being resident in the State, is for the time being absent from the State.

(5) Nothing in *subsection (4)* or any other provision of this Act enables a person, other than a director of the company concerned, to object to the notice given for any meeting of the directors.

(6) The quorum necessary for the transaction of the business of the directors may be fixed by the directors, and unless so fixed shall be 2 but, where the company has a sole director, the quorum shall be one.

(7) The continuing directors may act notwithstanding any vacancy in their number but, if and so long as their number is reduced below the number fixed by or pursuant to this Act as the necessary quorum of directors, the continuing directors or director may act for the purpose of increasing the number of directors to that number or of summoning a general meeting of the company but for no other purpose.

(8) The directors may elect a chairperson of their meetings and determine the period for which he or she is to hold office, but if no such chairperson is elected, or, if at any meeting the chairperson is not present within 15 minutes after the time appointed for holding it, the directors present may choose one of their number to be chairperson of the meeting.

(9) The directors may establish one or more committees consisting in whole or in part of members of the board of directors.

(10) A committee established under *subsection (9)* (a "committee") may elect a chairperson of its meetings; if no such chairperson is elected, or if at any meeting the chairperson is not present within 15 minutes after the time appointed for holding it, the members of the committee present may choose one of their number to be chairperson of the meeting.

(11) A committee may meet and adjourn as it thinks proper.

(12) Questions arising at any meeting of a committee shall be determined by a majority of votes of the members of the committee present, and where there is an equality of votes, the chairperson shall have a second or casting vote.

161 Supplemental provisions about meetings (including provision for acting by means of written resolutions)

(1) A resolution in writing signed by all the directors of a company, or by all the members of a committee of them, and who are for the time being entitled to receive notice of a meeting of the directors or, as the case may be, of such a committee, shall be as valid as if it had been passed at a meeting of the directors or such a committee duly convened and held.

(2) Subject to *subsection (3)*, where one or more of the directors (other than a majority of them) would not, by reason of—

(a) this Act or any other enactment;
(b) the company's constitution; or
(c) a rule of law,

be permitted to vote on a resolution such as is referred to in *subsection (1)*, if it were sought to pass the resolution at a meeting of the directors duly convened and held, then such a resolution, notwithstanding anything in *subsection (1)*, shall be valid for the purposes of that subsection if the resolution is signed by those of the directors who would have been permitted to vote on it had it been sought to pass it at such a meeting.

(3) In a case falling within *subsection (2)*, the resolution shall state the name of each director who did not sign it and the basis on which he or she did not sign it.

(4) For the avoidance of doubt, nothing in the preceding subsections dealing with a resolution that is signed by other than all of the directors shall be read as making available, in the case of an equality of votes, a second or casting vote to the one of their number who would, or might have been, if a meeting had been held to transact the business concerned, chairperson of that meeting.

(5) The resolution referred to in *subsection (1)* may consist of several documents in like form each signed by one or more directors and for all purposes shall take effect from the time that it is signed by the last director.

(6) A meeting of the directors or of a committee referred to in *section 160(9)* may consist of a conference between some or all of the directors or, as the case may be, members of the committee who are not all in one place, but each of whom is able (directly or by means of telephonic, video or other electronic communication) to speak to each of the others and to be heard by each of the others and—

(a) a director or member of the committee taking part in such a conference shall be deemed to be present in person at the meeting and shall be entitled to vote and be counted in a quorum accordingly; and
(b) such a meeting shall be deemed to take place—
   (i) where the largest group of those participating in the conference is assembled;
   (ii) if there is no such group, where the chairperson of the meeting then is;
   (iii) if neither *subparagraph (i)* or *(ii)* applies, in such location as the meeting itself decides.

(7) Subject to the other provisions of this Act, a director may vote in respect of any contract, appointment or arrangement in which he or she is interested and he or she shall be counted in the quorum present at the meeting.

(8) The directors of a company may exercise the voting powers conferred by the shares of any other company held or owned by the company in such manner in all respects as they think fit and, in particular, they may exercise the voting powers in favour of any resolution—

(a) appointing the directors or any of them as directors or officers of such other company; or

(b) providing for the payment of remuneration or pensions to the directors or officers of such other company.

(9) Any director of the company may vote in favour of the exercise of such voting rights notwithstanding that he or she may be or may be about to become a director or officer of the other company referred to in *subsection (8)* and as such or in any other way is or may be interested in the exercise of such voting rights in the foregoing manner.

162 Holding of any other office or place of profit under the company by director

(1) A director of a company may hold any other office or place of profit under the company (other than the office of statutory auditor) in conjunction with his or her office of director for such period and on such terms as to remuneration and otherwise as the directors of the company may determine.

(2) No director of a company or intending such director shall be disqualified by his or her office from contracting with the company either with regard to his or her tenure of any such other office or place of profit or as vendor, purchaser or otherwise.

(3) In particular, neither shall—

(a) any contract with respect to any of the matters referred to in *subsection (2)*, nor any contract or arrangement entered into by or on behalf of the company in which a director is in any way interested, be liable to be avoided, nor

(b) a director so contracting or being so interested be liable to account to the company for any profit realised by any such contract or arrangement,

by reason of such director holding that office or of the fiduciary relation thereby established.

163 Counting of director in quorum and voting at meeting at which director is appointed

A director of a company, notwithstanding his or her interest, may be counted in the quorum present at any meeting at which—

(a) that director or any other director is appointed to hold any such office or place of profit under the company as is mentioned in *section 162(1)*, or

(b) the terms of any such appointment are arranged,

and he or she may vote on any such appointment or arrangement other than his or her own appointment or the arrangement of the terms of it.

164 Signing, drawing, etc., of negotiable instruments and receipts

Each—

(a) cheque, promissory note, draft, bill of exchange or other negotiable instrument, and

(b) receipt for moneys paid to the company,

shall be signed, drawn, accepted, endorsed or otherwise executed, as the case may be, by such person or persons and in such manner as the directors of the company shall from time to time by resolution determine.

165 Alternate directors

(1) Any director (the "appointer") of a company may from time to time appoint any other director of it or, with the approval of a majority of its directors, any other person to be an alternate director (the "appointee") as respects him or her.

(2) Only one person may stand appointed at a particular time to be an alternate director as respects a particular director.

(3) The appointee, while he or she holds office as an alternate director, shall be entitled—

(a) to notice of meetings of the directors of the company,

(b) to attend at such meetings as a director, and

(c) in place of the appointer, to vote at such meetings as a director,

but shall not be entitled to be remunerated otherwise than out of the remuneration of the appointer.

(4) Any appointment under this section shall be effected by notice in writing given by the appointer to the company.

(5) Any appointment so made may be revoked at any time by the appointer or by a majority of the other directors or by the company in general meeting.

(6) Revocation of such an appointment by the appointer shall be effected by notice in writing given by the appointer to the company.

166 Minutes of proceedings of directors

(1) A company shall cause minutes to be entered in books kept for that purpose of—

(a) all appointments of officers made by its directors;

(b) the names of the directors present at each meeting of its directors and of any committee of the directors;

(c) all resolutions and proceedings at all meetings of its directors and of committees of directors.

(2) Such minutes shall be entered in the foregoing books as soon as may be after the appointment concerned is made, the meeting concerned has been held or the resolution concerned has been passed.

(3) Any such minute, if purporting to be signed by the chairperson of the meeting at which the proceedings were had, or by the chairperson of the next succeeding meeting, shall be evidence of the proceedings.

(4) Where minutes have been made in accordance with this section of the proceedings at any meeting of directors or committee of directors, then, until the contrary is proved—

(a) the meeting shall be deemed to have been duly held and convened;

(b) all proceedings had at the meeting shall be deemed to have been duly had; and

(c) all appointments of officers made by its directors at the meeting shall be deemed to be valid.

(5) A company shall, if required by the Director of Corporate Enforcement, produce to the Director for inspection the book or books kept in accordance with *subsection (1)* by it and shall give to the Director of Corporate Enforcement such facilities for inspecting and taking copies of the contents of the book or books as the Director may require.

(6) If a company fails to comply with *subsection (1)* or with a requirement made of it under *subsection (5)*, the company and any officer of it who is in default shall be guilty of a category 4 offence.

167 Audit committees

(1) In this section—

"amount of turnover" and "balance sheet total" have the same meanings as they have in [*section 275*][a];

"[relevant company][c]" means either of the following—

(a) a company that, in both the most recent financial year of the company and the immediately preceding financial year, meets the following criteria—

(i) the balance sheet total of that company exceeds for the year—

(I) subject to *clause (II)*, €25,000,000; or

(II) if an amount is prescribed under [*section 943(1)(i)*][b], the prescribed amount;

and

(ii) the amount of turnover of that company exceeds for the year—

(I) subject to *clause (II)*, €50,000,000; or

(II) if an amount is prescribed under [*section 943(1)(i)*][b], the prescribed amount;

or

(b) a company which has one or more subsidiary undertakings, if the company and all those subsidiary undertakings together, in both the most recent financial year of that company and the immediately preceding financial year, meet the criteria set out in *paragraph (a)*.

(2) The board of directors of a [relevant company][c] shall either—

(a) establish a committee (an "audit committee") that—

(i) has at least the responsibilities specified in *subsection (7)*; and

(ii) otherwise meets the requirements of this section;

or

(b) decide not to establish such a committee.

(3) The board of directors of a [relevant company][c] shall state in their report under *section 325*—

(a) whether the company has established an audit committee or decided not to do so;

(b) if the company has decided not to establish an audit committee, the reasons for that decision.

(4) The members of the audit committee shall include at least one independent director of the [relevant company][c], that is to say, a person who—

(a) is a non-executive director of it; and

(b) otherwise possesses the requisite degree of independence (particularly with regard to his or her satisfying the condition in *subsection (5)*) so as to be able to contribute effectively to the committee's functions.

(5) The condition referred to in *subsection (4)(b)* is that the director there referred to does not have, and at no time during the period of 3 years preceding his or her appointment to the committee did have—

(a) a material business relationship with the [relevant company][c], either directly, or as a partner, shareholder, director (other than as a non-executive director) or senior employee of a body that has such a relationship with the company; or

(b) a position of employment in the [relevant company][c].

(6) The director referred to in *subsection (4)* (or, where there is more than one director of the kind referred to in that subsection, one of them) shall be a person who has competence in accounting or auditing.

(7) Without prejudice to the responsibility of the board of directors, the responsibilities of the audit committee shall include:

(a) the monitoring of the financial reporting process;

(b) the monitoring of the effectiveness of the [relevant company][c]'s systems of internal control, internal audit and risk management;

(c) the monitoring of the statutory audit of the [relevant company][c]'s statutory financial statements; and

(d) the review and monitoring of the independence of the statutory auditors and in particular the provision of additional services to the [relevant company][c].

(8) If an audit committee is established, any proposal of the board of directors of the [relevant company][c] with respect to the appointment of statutory auditors to the company shall be based on a recommendation made to the board by the audit committee.

(9) The statutory auditors shall report to the audit committee of the [relevant company][c] on key matters arising from the statutory audit of the company, and, in particular, on material weaknesses in internal control in relation to the financial reporting process.

(10) For the purposes of *subsections (4)* and *(5)(a)*, a non-executive director is a director who is not engaged in the daily management of the [relevant company][c] or body concerned, as the case may be.

(11) Where a director of a [relevant company][c] fails to take all reasonable steps to comply with the requirements of *subsection (3)*, the director shall be guilty of a category 3 offence.

Amendments

a Words substituted by C(A)A 2017, s 9(a)(i) (previously: "*section 350*").
b Words substituted by C(A)A 2017, s 9(a)(ii) (previously: "*section 945(1)(k)*").
c Words substituted by C(A)A 2017, s 9(b) (previously: "large company").

Chapter 5
Members

168 Definition of member

(1) The subscribers to the constitution of a company shall be deemed to have agreed to become members of the company, and, on its registration, shall be entered as members in its register of members.

(2) Every other person who agrees to become a member of a company, and whose name is entered in its register of members, shall be a member of the company.

169 Register of members

(1) Subject to *subsection (5)*, a company shall keep a register of its members and enter in it the following particulars:

(a) the names, addresses of the members and a statement of the shares held by each member, distinguishing each share by its number so long as the share has a number, and of the amount paid or agreed to be considered as paid on the shares of each member;

(b) the date at which each person was entered in the register as a member; and

(c) the date at which any person ceased to be a member.

(2) *Sections 215* to *217* (rights of inspection, requests for copies, etc.) apply to the register of members.

(3) The entries required under *paragraphs (a)* and *(b)* of *subsection (1)* shall be made within 28 days after the date of conclusion of the agreement with the company to become a member or, in the case of a subscriber of the constitution, within 28 days after the date of registration of the company.

(4) The entry required under *subsection (1)(c)* shall be made—

(a) within 28 days after the date when the person concerned ceased to be a member; or

(b) if the person ceased to be a member otherwise than as a result of action by the company, within 28 days after the date of production to the company of evidence satisfactory to the company of the occurrence of the event whereby the person ceased to be a member.

(5) Where the company has converted any of its shares into stock and given notice of the conversion to the Registrar, the register shall show the amount of stock held by

each member instead of the amount of shares and the particulars relating to shares specified in *subsection (1)(a)*.

(6) Where a company makes default in complying with any of the requirements of *subsection (1)* or *subsections (3)* to *(5)*, the company and any officer of it who is in default shall be guilty of a category 3 offence.

170 Trusts not to be entered on register of members

No notice of any trust, express, implied or constructive, shall be entered—

(a) on the register of members or be receivable by the keeper of the register; or

(b) on any register kept by the Registrar.

171 Register to be evidence

The register of members shall be *prima facie* evidence of any matters by this Act directed or authorised to be inserted in it.

172 Consequences of failure to comply with requirements as to register owing to agent's default

(1) Where—

(a) by virtue of *section 216(2)* the register of members is kept by some person other than the company concerned; and

(b) by reason of any default of that other person a failure on the part of the company to comply with *section 169* or *216*, or with any requirements of this Act as to the production of the register, occurs amounting to the commission of an offence under this Act by the company,

that other person shall also be guilty of an offence and may be charged with and convicted of it whether or not proceedings for an offence are brought against the company.

(2) A person guilty of an offence under *subsection (1)* shall be liable on conviction to the same range of fines and other penalties provided in this Act that the company referred to in *subsection (1)* is or would be liable in respect of that offence.

(3) The power of the court under this Act to require compliance with the provision concerned shall extend to the making of orders against the person referred to in *subsection (1)* and his or her officers and servants.

173 Rectification of register

(1) If—

(a) the name of any person is, without sufficient cause, entered in the register of members or omitted from it, in contravention of *subsections (1)* and *(3)* of *section 169*, or

(b) default is made in entering on the register, within the period fixed by *subsection (4)* of *section 169*, the fact of any person's having ceased to be a member, the person aggrieved, or any member of the company, or the company, may apply to the court for rectification of the register.

(2) Where an application is made under this section, the court may either refuse the application or may order rectification of the register and payment by the company of compensation for any loss sustained by any party aggrieved.

(3) On an application under this section the court may decide any question relating to the title of any person who is a party to the application to have his or her name entered in or omitted from the register (whether the question arises between members or alleged members, or between members or alleged members on the one hand and the company on the other hand) and generally may decide any question necessary or expedient to be decided for rectification of the register.

(4) The court when making an order for rectification of the register shall by its order direct, if appropriate, notice of the rectification to be given to the Registrar.

(5) A company may, without application to the court, at any time rectify any error or omission in the register but such a rectification shall not adversely affect any person unless he or she agrees to the rectification made.

(6) The company shall, within 21 days after the date on which the rectification under *subsection (5)* has been made, give notice, in the prescribed form, of the rectification to the Registrar if the error or omission referred to in *subsection (5)* also occurs in any document forwarded by the company to the Registrar.

(7) Without prejudice to the generality of *subsection (5)*, a rectification may be effected by the company under that subsection of an error or omission that relates to the amount of the company's issued share capital (whether it consists of an overstatement or understatement of it) and *subsection (6)* shall apply, in the circumstances there set out, in the event of such a rectification.

174 Power to close register

A company may, on giving notice by advertisement in some newspaper circulating in the district in which the registered office of the company is situate, close the register of members for any time or times not exceeding in the whole 30 days in each year.

Chapter 6
General meetings and resolutions

175 Annual general meeting

(1) Subject to *subsections (2)* and *(3)*, a company shall in each year hold a general meeting as its annual general meeting in addition to any other meetings in that year and shall specify the meeting as such in the notices calling it and not more than 15 months shall elapse between the date of one annual general meeting of a company and that of the next.

(2) So long as a company holds its first annual general meeting within 18 months after the date of its incorporation, it need not hold it in the year of its incorporation or in the following year.

(3) A company need not hold an annual general meeting in any year where all the members entitled (at the date of the written resolution referred to in this subsection) to attend and vote at such general meeting sign, before the latest date for the holding of that meeting, a written resolution under *section 193*—

(a) acknowledging receipt of the financial statements that would have been laid before that meeting;

(b) resolving all such matters as would have been resolved at that meeting; and

(c) confirming no change is proposed in the appointment of the person (if any) who, at the date of the resolution, stands appointed as statutory auditor of the company.

(4) Without prejudice to any specific provision of this Act providing for the contingency of an annual general meeting being so dispensed with, where a provision of this Act requires that a thing is to be done at an annual general meeting, then, if the thing is dealt with in the foregoing resolution (whether by virtue of the matter being resolved in the resolution, the members' acknowledging receipt of a notice, report or other documentation or, as the case may require, howsoever otherwise), that requirement shall be regarded as having been complied with.

(5) If default is made in holding a meeting of the company in accordance with *subsection (1)*, the Director of Corporate Enforcement may, on the application of any member of the company, call or direct the calling of a general meeting of the company and give such ancillary or consequential directions as the Director of Corporate Enforcement thinks expedient, including directions modifying or supplementing the operation of the company's constitution in relation to the calling, holding and conducting of the meeting.

(6) The directions which may be given under *subsection (5)* may include a direction that one member of the company present in person or by proxy shall be deemed to constitute a meeting.

(7) A general meeting held in pursuance of *subsection (5)* shall, subject to any directions of the Director of Corporate Enforcement and *subsection (8)*, be deemed to be an annual general meeting of the company.

(8) Where a meeting so held is not held in the year in which the default in holding the company's annual general meeting occurred, the meeting so held shall not be treated as the annual general meeting for the year in which it is held unless, at that meeting, the company resolves that it shall be so treated.

(9) Where a company resolves that a meeting shall be so treated, a copy of the resolution shall, within 21 days after the date of passing of it, be delivered by it to the Registrar.

(10) If default is made in holding a meeting of the company in accordance with *subsection (1)*, or in complying with any direction of the Director of Corporate Enforcement under *subsection (5)*, the company and any officer of it who is in default shall be guilty of a category 3 offence.

(11) If default is made by a company in complying with *subsection (9)*, the company and any officer of it who is in default shall be guilty of a category 4 offence.

176 The location and means for holding general meetings

(1) Subject to the provisions of this section, an annual general meeting of a company or an extraordinary general meeting of it may be held inside or outside of the State.

(2) If a company holds its annual general meeting or any extraordinary general meeting outside of the State then, unless all of the members entitled to attend and vote at such meeting consent in writing to its being held outside of the State, the company has the following duty.

(3) That duty is to make, at the company's expense, all necessary arrangements to ensure that members can by technological means participate in any such meeting without leaving the State.

(4) A meeting referred to in *subsection (1)* may be held in 2 or more venues (whether inside or outside of the State) at the same time using any technology that provides members, as a whole, with a reasonable opportunity to participate.

177 Extraordinary general meetings

(1) All general meetings of a company, other than annual general meetings, shall be known, and in this Act are referred to, as "extraordinary general meetings".

(2) The directors of a company may, whenever they think fit, convene an extraordinary general meeting.

(3) If, at any time, there are not sufficient directors capable of acting to form a quorum, any director of the company or any member of it may convene an extraordinary general meeting in the same manner as nearly as possible as that in which meetings may be convened by the directors.

178 Convening of extraordinary general meetings by members

(1) The rights conferred—

(a) by *subsection (2)* on a member or members have effect save where the constitution of the company provides otherwise; and

(b) by *subsections (3)* to *(7)* on a member or members (and the corresponding duties on the part of the directors) have effect notwithstanding anything in the constitution of the company.

(2) One or more members of a company holding, or together holding, at any time not less than 50 per cent (or such other percentage as may be specified in the constitution) of the paid up share capital of the company as, at that time, carries the right of voting at general meetings of the company may convene an extraordinary general meeting of the company.

(3) The directors of a company shall, on the requisition of one or more members holding, or together holding, at the date of the deposit of the requisition, not less than 10 per cent of the paid up share capital of the company, as at the date of the deposit

carries the right of voting at general meetings of the company, forthwith proceed duly to convene an extraordinary general meeting of the company.

(4) The requisition shall state the objects of the meeting and shall be signed by the requisitionists and deposited at the registered office of the company and may consist of several documents in like form each signed by one or more requisitionists.

(5) If the directors do not within 21 days after the date of the deposit of the requisition proceed duly to convene a meeting to be held within 2 months after that date (the "requisition date"), the requisitionists, or any of them representing more than 50 per cent of the total voting rights of all of them, may themselves convene a meeting, but any meeting so convened shall not be held after the expiration of 3 months after the requisition date.

(6) Any reasonable expenses incurred by the requisitionists by reason of the failure of the directors duly to convene a meeting shall be repaid to the requisitionists by the company and any sum so repaid shall be retained by the company out of any sums due or to become due from the company by way of fees or other remuneration in respect of their services to such of the directors as were in default.

(7) For the purposes of *subsections (3)* to *(6)*, the directors shall, in the case of a meeting at which a resolution is to be proposed as a special resolution, be deemed not to have duly convened the meeting if they do not give such notice of it as is required by *section 181*.

(8) A meeting convened under *subsection (2)* or *(5)* shall be convened in the same manner as nearly as possible as that in which meetings are to be convened by directors.

179 Power of court to convene meeting

(1) Subject to *subsection (2)*, the court may on application being made to it by any of the persons specified in *subsection (3)*, or of its own motion, make an order requiring a general meeting of a company to be called, held and conducted in any manner that the court thinks fit.

(2) An order shall not be made under *subsection (1)* unless the court is satisfied that for any reason it is impracticable or otherwise undesirable—

(a) for any person to call a general meeting of the company in any manner in which meetings of that company may be called; or

(b) to conduct a general meeting of the company in any manner provided by this Act or the company's constitution.

(3) The persons referred to in *subsection (1)* are—

(a) a director of the company referred to in that subsection (the "company");

(b) a member of the company who would be entitled to vote at a general meeting of it;

(c) the personal representative of a deceased member of the company, which member would, but for his or her death, be entitled to vote at such a meeting; and

(d) the assignee in bankruptcy of a bankrupt member of the company, which member would be entitled to vote at such a meeting.

(4) Where an order under *subsection (1)* is made, the court may give such ancillary or consequential directions as it thinks expedient.

(5) Such directions may include a direction that one member of the company, or the personal representative of a deceased member of the company or the assignee in bankruptcy of a bankrupt member of it, present in person or by proxy, is a quorum.

(6) A meeting called, held and conducted in accordance with an order under *subsection (1)* is for all purposes to be taken as a meeting of the company duly called, held and conducted.

180 Persons entitled to notice of general meetings

(1) Notice of every general meeting of a company ("relevant notice") shall be given to—

(a) every member;

(b) the personal representative of a deceased member of the company, which member would, but for his or her death, be entitled to vote at the meeting;

(c) the assignee in bankruptcy of a bankrupt member of the company (being a bankrupt member who is entitled to vote at the meeting); and

(d) the directors and secretary of the company.

(2) Relevant notice may, in the case of joint holders of a share, be given by giving the notice to the joint holder first named in the register in respect of the share.

(3) Relevant notice may be given by the company to the persons entitled to a share in consequence of the death or bankruptcy of a member by sending it through the post in a prepaid letter addressed to them by name or by the title of representatives of the deceased or assignee in bankruptcy or by any like description at the address supplied for the purpose by the persons claiming to be so entitled.

(4) Until such an address has been so supplied, relevant notice may be given to those persons by giving the notice in any manner in which it might have been given if the death or bankruptcy concerned had not occurred.

(5) Unless its constitution provides otherwise, no person, other than any person specified in the preceding subsections, shall be entitled to receive notices of general meetings of a company but this is without prejudice to *subsection (6)*.

(6) Unless the company is entitled to and has availed itself of the audit exemption under *section 360* or *365* (and, where relevant, *section 399* has been complied with in that regard), the statutory auditors of a company shall be entitled to—

(a) attend any general meeting of a company;

(b) receive all notices of, and other communications relating to, any general meeting which any member of the company is entitled to receive; and

(c) be heard at any general meeting which they attend on any part of the business of the meeting which concerns them as statutory auditors.

181 Notice of general meetings

(1) Save where the constitution of the company makes provision for the giving of greater notice, a meeting of a company, other than an adjourned meeting, shall be called—

(a) in the case of the annual general meeting or an extraordinary general meeting for the passing of a special resolution, by not less than 21 days' notice;

(b) in the case of any other extraordinary general meeting, by not less than 7 days' notice.

(2) A meeting of a company shall, notwithstanding that it is called by shorter notice than that specified in *subsection (1)*, be deemed to have been duly called if it is so agreed by—

(a) all the members entitled to attend and vote at the meeting; and

(b) unless no statutory auditors of the company stand appointed in consequence of the company availing itself of the audit exemption under *section 360* or *365* (and, where relevant, *section 399* has been complied with in that regard), the statutory auditors of the company.

(3) Where notice of a meeting is given by posting it by ordinary prepaid post to the registered address of a member, then, for the purposes of any issue as to whether the correct period of notice for that meeting has been given, the giving of the notice shall be deemed to have been effected on the expiration of 24 hours following posting.

(4) In determining whether the correct period of notice has been given by a notice of a meeting, neither the day on which the notice is served nor the day of the meeting for which it is given shall be counted.

(5) The notice of a meeting shall specify—

(a) the place, the date and the time of the meeting;

(b) the general nature of the business to be transacted at the meeting;

(c) in the case of a proposed special resolution, the text or substance of that proposed special resolution; and

(d) with reasonable prominence a statement that—

(i) a member entitled to attend and vote is entitled to appoint a proxy using the form set out in *section 184* or, where that is allowed, one or more proxies, to attend, speak and vote instead of him or her;

(ii) a proxy need not be a member; and

(iii) the time by which the proxy must be received at the company's registered office or some other place within the State as is specified in the statement for that purpose.

(6) Save to the extent that the company's constitution provides otherwise, the accidental omission to give notice of a meeting to, or the non-receipt of notice of a meeting by, any person entitled to receive notice shall not invalidate the proceedings at the meeting.

182 Quorum

(1) No business shall be transacted at any general meeting of a company unless a quorum of members is present at the time when the meeting proceeds to business.

(2) Save to the extent that its constitution provides otherwise or in a case falling within *subsection (3)*, 2 members of a company present in person or by proxy at a general meeting of it shall be a quorum.

(3) In the case of a single-member company, one member of the company present in person or by proxy at a general meeting of it shall be a quorum.

(4) *Subsection (5)* shall apply unless the company's constitution provides otherwise.

(5) Save to the extent that the company's constitution provides otherwise, if within 15 minutes after the time appointed for a general meeting a quorum is not present, then—

- (a) where the meeting has been convened upon the requisition of members, the meeting shall be dissolved;
- (b) in any other case—
  - (i) the meeting shall stand adjourned to the same day in the next week, at the same time and place or to such other day and at such other time and place as the directors may determine; and
  - (ii) if at the adjourned meeting a quorum is not present within half an hour after the time appointed for the meeting, the members present shall be a quorum.

183 Proxies

(1) Subject to *subsection (3)*, any member of a company entitled to attend and vote at a meeting of the company shall be entitled to appoint another person (whether a member or not) as his or her proxy to attend and vote instead of him or her.

(2) A proxy so appointed shall have the same right as the member to speak at the meeting and to vote on a show of hands and on a poll.

(3) Unless the company's constitution otherwise provides, a member of a company shall not be entitled to appoint more than one proxy to attend on the same occasion.

(4) The instrument appointing a proxy (the "instrument of proxy") shall be in writing—

- (a) under the hand of the appointer or of his or her attorney duly authorised in writing; or
- (b) if the appointer is a body corporate, either under seal of the body corporate or under the hand of an officer or attorney of it duly authorised in writing.

(5) The instrument of proxy and the power of attorney or other authority, if any, under which it is signed, or a notarially certified copy of that power or authority, shall be deposited at the registered office of the company concerned or at such other place within the State as is specified for that purpose in the notice convening the meeting, and shall be so deposited not later than the following time.

(6) That time is—

(a) 48 hours (or such lesser period as the company's constitution may provide) before the time for holding the meeting or adjourned meeting at which the person named in the instrument proposes to vote; or

(b) in the case of a poll, 48 hours (or such lesser period as the company's constitution may provide) before the time appointed for the taking of the poll.

(7) The depositing of the instrument of proxy referred to in *subsection (5)* may, rather than its being effected by sending or delivering the instrument, be effected by communicating the instrument to the company by electronic means, and this subsection likewise applies to the depositing of anything else referred to in *subsection (5)*.

(8) If *subsection (5)* or *(6)* is not complied with, the instrument of proxy shall not be treated as valid.

(9) Subject to *subsection (10)*, a vote given in accordance with the terms of an instrument of proxy shall be valid notwithstanding the [previous death of the appointer][a] or revocation of the proxy or of the authority under which the proxy was executed or the transfer of the share in respect of which the proxy is given.

(10) *Subsection (9)* does not apply if notice in writing of [such death, revocation or transfer][b] as is mentioned in that subsection is received by the company concerned at its registered office before the commencement of the meeting or adjourned meeting at which the proxy is used.

(11) Subject to *subsection (12)*, if, for the purpose of any meeting of a company, invitations to appoint as proxy a person or one of a number of persons specified in the invitations are issued at the company's expense to some only of the members entitled to be sent a notice of the meeting and to vote at it by proxy, any officer of the company who knowingly and intentionally authorises or permits their issue in that manner shall be guilty of a category 3 offence.

(12) An officer shall not be guilty of an offence under *subsection (11)* by reason only of the issue to a member, at his or her request in writing, of a form of appointment naming the proxy or of a list of persons willing to act as proxy if the form or list is available on request in writing to every member entitled to vote at the meeting by proxy.

Amendments

a Words substituted by C(A)A 2017, s 98(b)(i) (previously: "previous death or insanity of the appointer").

b Words substituted by C(A)A 2017, s 98(b)(ii) (previously: "such death, insanity, revocation or transfer").

---

184 Form of proxy

An instrument appointing a proxy shall be in the following form or a form as near to it as circumstances permit—

[name of company] ("the Company")

[name of member] ("the Member") of [address of member] being a member of the Company hereby appoint/s [name and address of proxy] or failing him or her

[name and address of alternative proxy] as the proxy of the Member to attend, speak and vote for the Member on behalf of the Member at the (annual or extraordinary, as the case may be) general meeting of the Company to be held on the [date of meeting] and at any adjournment of the meeting.

The proxy is to vote as follows:

Voting Instructions to Proxy (choice to be marked with an 'x')			
Number or description of resolution:	In Favour	Abstain	Against
1			
2			
3			
Unless otherwise instructed the proxy will vote as he or she thinks fit.			
Signature of member			
Dated: [date]			

185 Representation of bodies corporate at meetings of companies

(1) A body corporate may, if it is a member of a company, by resolution of its directors or other governing body authorise such person (in this section referred to as an "authorised person") as it thinks fit to act as its representative at any meeting of the company or at any meeting of any class of members of the company.

(2) A body corporate may, if it is a creditor (including a holder of debentures) of a company, by resolution of its directors or other governing body authorise such person (in this section also referred to as an "authorised person") as it thinks fit to act as its representative at any meeting of any creditors of the company held in pursuance of this Act or the provisions contained in any debenture or trust deed, as the case may be.

(3) An authorised person shall be entitled to exercise the same powers on behalf of the body corporate which he or she represents as that body corporate could exercise if it were an individual member of the company, creditor or holder of debentures of the company.

(4) The chairperson of a meeting may require a person claiming to be an authorised person within the meaning of this section to produce such evidence of the

person's authority as such as the chairperson may reasonably specify and, if such evidence is not produced, the chairperson may exclude such person from the meeting.

186 The business of the annual general meeting

The business of the annual general meeting shall include—

(a) the consideration of the company's statutory financial statements and the report of the directors and, unless the company is entitled to and has availed itself of the audit exemption under *section 360* or *365*, the report of the statutory auditors on those statements and that report;

(b) the review by the members of the company's affairs;

(c) save where the company's constitution provides otherwise—

(i) the declaration of a dividend (if any) of an amount not exceeding the amount recommended by the directors; and

(ii) the authorisation of the directors to approve the remuneration of the statutory auditors (if any);

(d) where the company's constitution so provides, the election and re-election of directors;

(e) save where the company is entitled to and has availed itself of the exemption referred to in *paragraph (a)*, the appointment or re-appointment of statutory auditors; and

(f) where the company's constitution so provides, the remuneration of the directors.

187 Proceedings at meetings

(1) Each provision of this section applies save to the extent that the company's constitution provides otherwise.

(2) The chairperson, if any, of the board of directors shall preside as chairperson at every general meeting of the company, or if there is no such chairperson, or if he or she is not present within 15 minutes after the time appointed for the holding of the meeting or is unwilling to act, the directors present shall elect one of their number to be chairperson of the meeting.

(3) If at any meeting no director is willing to act as chairperson or if no director is present within 15 minutes after the time appointed for holding the meeting, the members present shall choose one of their number to be chairperson of the meeting.

(4) The chairperson may, with the consent of any meeting at which a quorum is present, and shall if so directed by the meeting, adjourn the meeting from time to time and from place to place.

(5) However no business shall be transacted at any adjourned meeting other than the business left unfinished at the meeting from which the adjournment took place.

(6) When a meeting is adjourned for 30 days or more, notice of the adjourned meeting shall be given as in the case of an original meeting but, subject to that, it shall not be necessary to give any notice of an adjournment or of the business to be transacted at an adjourned meeting.

(7) Unless a poll is demanded in accordance with *section 189*, at any general meeting—

(a) a resolution put to the vote of the meeting shall be decided on a show of hands;

and

(b) a declaration by the chairperson that a resolution has, on a show of hands, been carried or carried unanimously, or by a particular majority, or lost, and an entry to that effect in the book containing the minutes of the proceedings of the company shall be conclusive evidence of the fact without proof of the number or proportion of the votes recorded in favour of or against such resolution.

(8) Where there is an equality of votes, whether on a show of hands or on a poll, the chairperson of the meeting at which the show of hands takes place or at which the poll is demanded, shall be entitled to a second or casting vote.

188 Votes of members

(1) Each provision of this section applies save to the extent that the company's constitution provides otherwise.

(2) Subject to any rights or restrictions for the time being attached to any class or classes of shares, where a matter is being decided—

(a) on a show of hands, every member present in person and every proxy shall have one vote, but so that no individual member shall have more than one vote; and

(b) on a poll, every member shall, whether present in person or by proxy, have one vote for each share of which he or she is the holder or for each €15 of stock held by him or her, as the case may be.

(3) Where there are joint holders of a share, the vote of the senior who tenders a vote, whether in person or by proxy, shall be accepted to the exclusion of the votes of the other joint holders; and for this purpose, seniority shall be determined by the order in which the names of the joint holders stand in the register of members.

(4) Each of the following:

(a) a member of unsound mind;

(b) a member who has made an enduring power of attorney;

(c) a member in respect of whom an order has been made by any court having jurisdiction in cases of unsound mind;

may vote, whether on a show of hands or on a poll, by his or her committee, donee of an enduring power of attorney, receiver, guardian or other person appointed by the foregoing court.

(5) Any such committee, donee of an enduring power of attorney, receiver, guardian, or other person may speak and vote by proxy, whether on a show of hands or on a poll.

(6) No member shall be entitled to vote at any general meeting of a company unless all calls or other sums immediately payable by him or her in respect of shares in the company have been paid.

(7) No objection shall be raised to the qualification of any voter except at the meeting or adjourned meeting at which the vote objected to is given or tendered, and every vote not disallowed at such meeting shall be valid for all purposes.

(8) Any such objection made in due time shall be referred to the chairperson of the meeting, whose decision shall be final and conclusive.

189 Right to demand a poll

(1) At a meeting, a poll may be demanded in relation to a matter (whether before or on the declaration of the result of the show of hands in relation to it).

(2) A demand for such a poll may be made by—

(a) the chairperson of the meeting;

(b) at least 3 members present in person or by proxy;

(c) any member or members present in person or by proxy and representing not less than 10 per cent of the total voting rights of all the members of the company concerned having the right to vote at the meeting; or

(d) a member or members holding shares in the company concerned conferring the right to vote at the meeting, being shares on which an aggregate sum has been paid up equal to not less than 10 per cent of the total sum paid up on all the shares conferring that right.

(3) A demand for such a poll may be withdrawn by the person or persons who have made the demand.

(4) Subject to *subsection (5)*, if a poll is duly demanded it shall be taken in such manner as the chairperson of the meeting directs, and the result of the poll shall be deemed to be the resolution, in relation to the matter concerned, of the meeting at which the poll was demanded.

(5) A poll demanded with regard to the election of a chairperson or on a question of adjournment shall be taken forthwith.

(6) A poll demanded on any other question shall be taken at such time as the chairperson of the meeting directs, and any business other than that on which a poll is demanded may be proceeded with pending the taking of the poll.

(7) The instrument appointing a proxy to vote at a meeting of a company shall be deemed also to confer authority to demand or join in demanding a poll, and for the purposes of *subsections (2)* and *(3)*, a demand by a person as proxy for a member shall be the same as a demand by the member.

190 Voting on a poll

On a poll taken at a meeting of a company or a meeting of any class of members of a company, a member, whether present in person or by proxy, entitled to more than one vote need not, if he or she votes—

(a) use all his or her votes; or
(b) cast all the votes he or she uses in the same way.

191 Resolutions — ordinary resolutions, special resolutions, etc., — meaning

(1) In this Act "ordinary resolution" means a resolution passed by a simple majority of the votes cast by members of a company as, being entitled to do so, vote in person or by proxy at a general meeting of the company.

(2) In this Act "special resolution" means a resolution—

(a) that is referred to as such in this Act, or is required (whether by this Act or by a company's constitution or otherwise) to be passed as a special resolution; and
(b) that satisfies the condition specified in [*subsection (3) or (3A)*;][a] and
(c) without prejudice to *subsections (4)* and *(5)*, as respects which notice of the meeting at which the resolution is proposed to be passed has been given in accordance with *section 181(1)(a)* and *(5)*.

(3) The condition referred to in *subsection (2)(b)* is that the resolution is passed by not less than 75 per cent of the votes cast by such members of the company concerned as, being entitled to do so, vote in person or by proxy at a general meeting of it.

[(3A) Where section 1102(3) applies, the condition referred to in subsection (2)(b) is that the resolution is passed by not less than two-thirds of the votes cast by such members of the company concerned as, being entitled to do so, vote in person or by proxy at a general meeting of it.][b]

(4) Notwithstanding *section 181(1)(a)*, for the purposes of *subsection (2)(c)* a resolution may be proposed and passed as a special resolution at a meeting of which less than 21 days' notice has been given if it is so agreed by a majority in number of the members having the right to attend and vote at any such meeting, being a majority either—

(a) together holding not less than 90 per cent in nominal value of the shares giving that right; or
(b) together representing not less than 90 per cent of the total voting rights at that meeting of all the members.

(5) Nothing in either *subsection (2)(c)* (as it relates to *section 181(1)(a)*) or *(4)* prevents a special resolution from being regarded as having been passed (in a case where less than 21 days' notice of the meeting has been given) in the following circumstances:

(a) the agreement referred to in *section 181(2)* exists as regards the meeting; and
(b) the condition specified in *subsection (3)* is satisfied in relation to the resolution.

(6) The terms of any resolution (whether special or otherwise) before a general meeting may be amended by ordinary resolution moved at the meeting provided that the terms of the resolution as amended will still be such that adequate notice of the intention to pass the same can be deemed to have been given.

(7) Any reference to an extraordinary resolution contained in any statute which was passed or document which existed before 1 April 1964 shall, in relation to a resolution passed on or after that date, be deemed to be a reference to a special resolution.

(8) In this Act "written resolution" means either an ordinary resolution or a special resolution passed in accordance with *section 193* or *194*.

Amendments

a Words "subsection (3) or (3A)" substituted for "subsection (3)" by European Union (Bank Recovery and Resolution) Regulations 2015, reg 189(3)(a), with effect from 15 July 2015.

b Subsection (3A) inserted by European Union (Bank Recovery and Resolution) Regulations 2015, reg 189(3)(b), with effect from 15 July 2015.

---

192 Resolutions passed at adjourned meetings

Where a resolution is passed at an adjourned general meeting, the resolution shall for all purposes be treated as having been passed on the date on which it was in fact passed and shall not be deemed to have been passed on any earlier date.

193 Unanimous written resolutions

(1) Notwithstanding any provision to the contrary in this Act—

(a) a resolution in writing signed by all the members of a company for the time being entitled to attend and vote on such resolution at a general meeting (or being bodies corporate by their duly appointed representatives) shall be as valid and effective for all purposes as if the resolution had been passed at a general meeting of the company duly convened and held; and

(b) if described as a special resolution shall be deemed to be a special resolution within the meaning of this Act.

(2) For the avoidance of doubt, the reference in *subsection (1)* to a provision to the contrary includes a reference to a provision that stipulates that the company in general meeting, or the members of the company in general meeting, must have passed the resolution concerned.

(3) A resolution passed in accordance with *subsection (1)* may consist of several documents in like form each signed by one or more members.

(4) A resolution passed in accordance with *subsection (1)* shall be deemed to have been passed at a meeting held on the date on which it was signed by the last member to sign, and, where the resolution states a date as being the date of his or her signature thereof by any member, the statement shall be *prima facie* evidence that it was signed by him or her on that date.

(5) If a resolution passed in accordance with *subsection (1)* is not contemporaneously signed, the company shall notify the members, within 21 days after the date of

delivery to it of the documents referred to in *subsection (6)*, of the fact that the resolution has been passed.

(6) The signatories of a resolution passed in accordance with *subsection (1)* shall, within 14 days after the date of its passing, procure delivery to the company of the documents constituting the written resolution; without prejudice to the use of the other means of delivery generally permitted by this Act, such delivery may be effected by electronic mail or the use of a facsimile machine.

(7) The company shall retain those documents as if they constituted the minutes of the proceedings of a general meeting of the company; without prejudice to the requirement (by virtue of *section 199(1)*) that the terms of the resolution concerned be entered in books kept for the purpose, the requirement under this subsection that the foregoing documents be retained shall be read as requiring those documents to be kept with the foregoing books.

(8) It is immaterial, as regards the resolution's validity, whether *subsection (5)*, *(6)* or *(7)* is complied with.

(9) If a company fails to comply with *subsection (5)*, the company and any officer of it who is in default shall be guilty of a category 4 offence.

(10) If a signatory fails to take all reasonable steps to procure the delivery to the company, in accordance with *subsection (6)*, of the documents referred to in that subsection, the signatory shall be guilty of a category 4 offence.

(11) This section does not apply to—

(a) a resolution to remove a director;

(b) a resolution to effect the removal of a statutory auditor from office, or so as not to continue him or her in office, as mentioned in *section 382(2)*, *383(2)(b)* or *394*.

(12) Nothing in this section affects any rule of law as to—

(a) things done otherwise than by passing a resolution;

(b) circumstances in which a resolution is or is not treated as having been passed; or

(c) cases in which a person is precluded from alleging that a resolution has not been duly passed.

194 Majority written resolutions

(1) Notwithstanding any provision to the contrary in this Act, a resolution in writing—

(a) that is—

(i) described as being an ordinary resolution, and

(ii) signed by the requisite majority of members of the company concerned, and

(b) in respect of which the condition specified in *subsection (7)* is satisfied,

shall be as valid and effective for all purposes as if the resolution had been passed at a general meeting of the company duly convened and held.

(2) For the avoidance of doubt, the reference in *subsection (1)* to a provision to the contrary includes a reference to a provision that stipulates that the company in general meeting, or the members of the company in general meeting, must have passed the resolution concerned.

(3) In *subsection (1)* "requisite majority of members" means a member or members who alone or together, at the time of the signing of the resolution concerned, represent more than 50 per cent of the total voting rights of all the members who, at that time, would have the right to attend and vote at a general meeting of the company (or being bodies corporate by their duly appointed representatives).

(4) Notwithstanding any provision to the contrary in this Act, a resolution in writing—

(a) that is—

(i) described as being a special resolution, and

(ii) signed by the requisite majority of members,

and

(b) in respect of which the condition specified in *subsection (7)* is satisfied,

shall be as valid and effective for all purposes as if the resolution had been passed at a general meeting of the company duly convened and held.

(5) For the avoidance of doubt, the reference in *subsection (4)* to a provision to the contrary includes a reference to a provision that stipulates that the company in general meeting, or the members of the company in general meeting, must have passed the resolution concerned.

(6) In *subsection (4)* "requisite majority of members" means a member or members who alone or together, at the time of the signing of the resolution concerned, represent at least 75 per cent of the total voting rights of all the members who, at that time, would have the right to attend and vote at a general meeting of the company (or being bodies corporate by their duly appointed representatives).

(7) The condition referred to in *subsections (1)(b)* and *(4)(b)* is that all members of the company concerned entitled to attend and vote on the resolution referred to in *subsection (1)* or *(4)*, as the case may be, have been circulated, by the directors or the other person proposing it, with the proposed text of the resolution and an explanation of its main purpose.

(8) A resolution passed in accordance with *subsection (1)* or *(4)* may consist of several documents in like form each signed by one or more members.

(9) Without prejudice to *section 195(5)*, a resolution passed—

(a) in accordance with *subsection (1)*, shall be deemed to have been passed, subject to *subsection (10)*, at a meeting held 7 days after the date on which it was signed by the last member to sign, or

(b) in accordance with *subsection (4)*, shall be deemed to have been passed, subject to *subsection (10)*, at a meeting held 21 days after the date on which it was signed by the last member to sign, and where the resolution states a date as being the date of his or her signature thereof by any member the statement shall be *prima facie* evidence that it was signed by him or her on that date.

(10) Without prejudice to *section 195(5)*, if—

(a) a date earlier than that referred to in *subsection (9)(a)* or *(b)* (not being earlier than the date on which the resolution was signed by the last member to sign) is specified in the resolution referred to in *subsection (1)* or *(4)* as the date on which it shall have been deemed to have been passed,

(b) all members of the company concerned entitled to attend and vote on that resolution state, in a written waiver signed by each of them, that the application of *subsection (9)* is waived, and

(c) there accompanies the delivery to the company under *subsection (3)* of *section 195* of the documents referred to in that subsection that written waiver (which may be so delivered to the company by any of the means referred to in that subsection),

then the resolution shall be deemed to have been passed on the date specified in it.

(11) A written waiver under *subsection (10)* may consist of several documents in like form each signed by one or more members.

195 Supplemental provisions in relation to *section 194*

(1) *Section 194* does not apply to—

(a) a resolution to remove a director;

(b) a resolution to effect the removal of a statutory auditor from office, or so as not to continue him or her in office, as mentioned in *section 382(2)*, *383(2)(b)* or *394*.

(2) Within 3 days after the date of the delivery to it of the documents referred to in *subsection (3)*, the company shall notify every member of—

(a) the fact of the resolution concerned having been signed by the requisite majority of members (within the meaning of *section 194(3)* or *(6)*, as the case may be); and

(b) the date that the resolution will, by virtue of *section 194*, be deemed to have been passed.

(3) The signatories of a resolution passed in accordance with *section 194(1)* or *(4)* shall procure delivery to the company of the documents constituting the written resolution; without prejudice to the use of the other means of delivery generally permitted by this Act, such delivery may be effected by electronic mail or the use of a facsimile machine.

(4) The company shall retain those documents as if they constituted the minutes of the proceedings of a general meeting of the company; without prejudice to the requirement (by virtue of *section 199(1)*) that the terms of the resolution concerned be entered in books kept for the purpose, the requirement under this subsection that the

foregoing documents be retained shall be read as requiring those documents to be kept with the foregoing books.

(5) Unless and until *subsection (3)* is complied with, a resolution passed in accordance with *section 194(1)* or *(4)* shall not have effect; however it is immaterial, as regards the resolution's validity, whether *subsection (2)* or *(4)* is complied with.

(6) Where *subsection (10)* of *section 194* applies, the reference in *subsection (5)* to *subsection (3)* shall be read as including a reference to *paragraph (c)* of that *subsection (10)*.

(7) If a company fails to comply with *subsection (2)*, the company and any officer of it who is in default shall be guilty of a category 4 offence.

196 Single-member companies — absence of need to hold general meetings, etc.

(1) In this Act "single-member company" means a company which, for whatever reason, has, for the time being, a sole member (and this applies notwithstanding a stipulation in the constitution that there be 2 members, or a greater number).

(2) Subject to *subsection (3)*, all the powers exercisable by a company in general meeting under this Act or otherwise shall be exercisable, in the case of a single-member company, by the sole member without the need to hold a general meeting for that purpose; for the avoidance of doubt this subsection extends to the exercise of the power under *section 146* to remove a director and, accordingly, any of the procedures under that section concerning notice to the director or the making of representations by the director shall not apply in the case of a single-member company but this is without prejudice to the application of the requirements of procedural fairness to the exercise of that power of removal by the sole member and *section 147*.

(3) *Subsection (2)* shall not empower the sole member of a single-member company to exercise the powers under *section 382(2)*, *383(2)(b)* or *394* to remove a statutory auditor from, or not continue a statutory auditor in, office without holding the requisite meeting provided for in the section concerned.

(4) Subject to *subsection (3)*, any provision of this Act which—

(a) enables or requires any matter to be done or to be decided by a company in general meeting, or

(b) requires any matter to be decided by a resolution of the company,

shall be deemed to be satisfied, in the case of a single-member company, by a decision of the member which is drawn up in writing and notified to the company in accordance with this section.

(5) Where the sole member of a single-member company takes any decision which has effect, pursuant to *subsections (2)* and *(4)*, as if agreed by the company in general meeting, the member shall provide the company with a written record of that decision, unless the decision is taken by way of written resolution which the member has already forwarded to the company.

(6) Where the sole member notifies to the company of which he or she is such member a decision taken by way of written resolution, or, pursuant to *subsection (5)*, a written record of a decision taken by him or her, the notification shall be recorded and retained by the company in a book or by some other suitable means maintained for the purpose, and the one or more records so retained shall—

(a) be deemed to be the books kept by the company pursuant to *section 199*, or

(b) where (at any subsequent or prior time when the company is, or was, not a single-member company) that section has or had application to proceedings of its members, be kept with the books kept by the company pursuant to *section 199*,

and, either case, *subsection (5)* of that section applies to those records as it applies to books generally of a company under that section.

(7) Where—

(a) the sole member of a single-member company exercises or discharges, by virtue of this section, any power, right or obligation, and

(b) such exercise or discharge involves or consists of the passing of a resolution, or the sole member's agreeing to a thing, to which *section 198* applies,

such exercise or discharge shall, within 15 days after the date of the exercise or discharge, be notified by the company in writing to the Registrar and be recorded by the Registrar.

(8) If—

(a) the sole member fails to comply with *subsection (5)*, or

(b) a company fails to comply with *subsection (6)* or *(7)*,

then (irrespective of whether the case falls within *paragraph (a)* or *(b)*) the sole member, the company and any officer of it who is in default shall be guilty of a category 4 offence.

(9) Failure by the sole member to comply with *subsection (5)* shall not affect the validity of any decision referred to in that subsection.

197 Application of this Part to class meetings

(1) The provisions of this Part, and the provisions of the constitution of a company relating to general meetings, shall, as far as applicable, apply in relation to any meeting of any class of member of the company.

(2) *Subsection (1)* operates so that all of *section 198*, in so far as it relates to *subsection (4)(c)* of that section, applies in relation to any meeting of any class of member of the company but does not operate to apply (if those provisions would otherwise be so applicable) the provisions of that section apart from the foregoing to any such meeting.

198 Registration of, and obligation of company to supply copies of, certain resolutions and agreements

(1) A copy of every resolution or agreement to which this section applies shall, within 15 days after the date of passing or making of it, be forwarded by the company concerned to the Registrar and recorded by the Registrar.

(2) A copy of every such resolution or agreement for the time being in force shall be embodied in, or annexed to, every copy of the constitution of the company concerned issued by it after the passing of the resolution or the making of the agreement.

(3) A copy of every such resolution or agreement shall be forwarded by the company concerned to any member of it, at his or her request, on payment of €10.00 or such lesser sum as the company may direct.

(4) This section applies to—

(a) resolutions that are required by this Act or a company's constitution to be special resolutions;

(b) resolutions which have been agreed to by all the members of a company, but which, if not so agreed to, would not have been effective for their purpose unless they had been passed as special resolutions;

(c) resolutions or agreements which have been agreed to by all the members of some class of shareholders but which if not so agreed to, would not have been effective for their purpose unless they had been passed by some particular majority or otherwise in some particular manner, and all resolutions or agreements which effectively bind all the members of any class of shareholders though not agreed to by all those members;

(d) resolutions increasing or decreasing the authorised share capital (if any) of a company;

(e) resolutions conferring authority for the allotment of shares;

(f) resolutions that a company be wound up voluntarily passed under *section 580*;

(g) resolutions attaching rights or restrictions to any share;

(h) resolutions varying any such right or restriction;

(i) resolutions classifying any unclassified share;

(j) resolutions converting shares of one class into shares of another class;

(k) resolutions converting share capital into stock and resolutions converting stock into share capital.

(5) If a company fails to comply with *subsection (1)*, *(2)* or *(3)*, the company and any officer of it who is in default shall be guilty of a category 4 offence.

(6) For the purposes of *subsection (5)*, a liquidator of a company shall be deemed to be an officer of the company.

199 Minutes of proceedings of meetings of a company

(1) A company shall, as soon as may be after their holding or passing, cause—

(a) minutes of all proceedings of general meetings of it, and
(b) the terms of all resolutions of it,

to be entered in books kept for that purpose; all such books kept by a company in pursuance of this subsection shall be kept at the same place.

(2) *Sections 215* to *217* (rights of inspection, requests for copies, etc.) apply to those books.

(3) Any such minute, if purporting to be signed by the chairperson of the meeting at which the proceedings were had, or by the chairperson of the next succeeding meeting, shall be evidence of the proceedings.

(4) Where minutes have been made in accordance with this section of the proceedings at any general meeting of a company then, until the contrary is proved—

(a) the meeting shall be deemed to have been duly held and convened;
(b) all proceedings had at the meeting shall be deemed to have been duly had; and
(c) all appointments of directors or liquidators shall be deemed to be valid.

(5) A company shall, if required by the Director of Corporate Enforcement, produce to the Director for inspection the book or books kept in accordance with *subsection (1)* by it and shall give the Director of Corporate Enforcement such facilities for inspecting and taking copies of the contents of the book or books as the Director may require.

(6) If a company fails to comply with *subsection (1)* or with a requirement made of it under *subsection (5)*, the company and any officer of it who is in default shall be guilty of a category 4 offence.

Chapter 7
Summary Approval Procedure

200 Interpretation (*Chapter 7*)

(1) In this Chapter—

"common draft terms of merger" means the common draft terms of merger referred to in *section 466(1)*;

"declaration" means a declaration referred to in *section 202(1)(b)*;

"merger" means a merger under *Chapter 3* of *Part 9*;

"merging companies" has the same meaning as it has in *Chapter 3* of *Part 9*;

"restricted activity" means an activity that is specified in—

(a) *section 82* (financial assistance for acquisition of shares);
(b) *section 84* (reduction in company capital);
(c) *section 91* (variation of company capital on reorganisations);

(d) *section 118* (prohibition on pre-acquisition profits or losses being treated in holding company's financial statements as profits available for distribution);

(e) *section 239* (prohibition of loans, etc., to directors and connected persons);

(f) *section 464* (merger may not be put into effect save in accordance with the relevant provisions of this Act); or

(g) *section 579* (procedure for and commencement of members' voluntary winding up);

the carrying on of which is expressed by a provision of this Act to be either—

(i) prohibited unless carried on in accordance with the Summary Approval Procedure; or

(ii) authorised subject to a specified requirement that the Summary Approval Procedure be employed or, in the case of *section 84*, *91* or *464*, that the Summary Approval Procedure be employed if the alternative procedure specified in *section 84(2)(b)*, *91(4)(b)* or, as the case may be, *464(1)(b)* is not employed;

"Summary Approval Procedure" shall be read in accordance with *section 202*;

"written means for passing the resolution" means—

(a) other than in the case of a merger, the means under *section 193* or *194(4)* for passing a special resolution;

(b) in the case of a merger, the means under *section 193* for passing a unanimous resolution.

(2) A reference in the definition of "restricted activity" in *subsection (1)* to an activity—

(a) subject to *paragraph (b)*, includes a reference to a procedure, transaction or arrangement;

(b) in the case of the activity falling within *paragraph (g)* of that definition, is a reference to the commencement of a members' voluntary winding up.

201 *Chapter 7* — what it does

(1) This Chapter sets out the way in which a company can, by—

(a) its members passing a special resolution, and

(b) its directors making a certain declaration,

either—

(i) permit the carrying on of a restricted activity (not being a merger) that is otherwise prohibited, or

(ii) fulfil the requirement specified in the provision concerned for the restricted activity (not being a merger) to be authorised,

as the case may be.

(2) In a case where the restricted activity is a merger, this Chapter sets out the way in which each of the merging companies can, by—

(a) every member of it entitled to vote at a general meeting of the company voting in favour of a resolution at such a meeting, and

(b) its directors making a certain declaration,

authorise, as provided in *section 464(1)*, the merger to be put in effect without certain procedures under *Chapter 3* of *Part 9* having to be employed.

(3) The provisions of this Chapter shall be read and shall operate so that a restricted activity may be carried on at a time falling before compliance with the requirement (arising under *section 203*, *204*, *205*, *206* or *207* as the case may be) that a copy of the appropriate declaration be delivered to the Registrar; however — should a failure to comply with that requirement occur — that failure then invalidates the carrying on of the activity, but this is without prejudice to the power of validation conferred subsequently by this Chapter on the court.

202 Summary Approval Procedure

(1) In this Act "Summary Approval Procedure" means the procedure whereby the following conditions are satisfied:

(a) authority for the carrying on of the restricted activity has been conferred by—

(i) other than in the case of a merger, a special resolution of the company; or

(ii) in the case of a merger, a resolution of each of the merging companies which every member of the company entitled to vote at a general meeting of it has voted in favour of (a "unanimous resolution");

being a special resolution or unanimous resolution passed not more than, subject to *subsections (2)* and *(3)*, 12 months prior to the commencement of the carrying on by the company, or as the case may be, by each of the merging companies of the activity; and

(b) either—

(i) the company or, as the case may be, each of the merging companies has forwarded with each notice of the meeting at which the special resolution or other foregoing resolution is to be considered, or

(ii) if the written means for passing the resolution is used, the company or, as the case may be, each of the merging companies has appended to the proposed text of the resolution,

a copy of a declaration which complies with *subsection (6)* and the other relevant provisions of this Chapter as regards its contents or the documents to be attached to it.

(2) In computing the period of 12 months referred to in *subsection (1)(a)* there shall be disregarded, where an application is made in accordance with *section 211* to cancel the special resolution, the period beginning on the date of the making of that application and ending on—

(a) the date of confirmation of the special resolution by the court on that application;

or

(b) if such an application so made is withdrawn, the date of that withdrawal.

(3) If the restricted activity is that referred to in *paragraph (d)* of the definition of that expression in *section 200(1)*, the reference in *subsection (1)(a)* to 12 months shall be read as a reference to—

(a) subject to *paragraph (b)*, 60 days; or

(b) if—

(i) one or more members who hold, or together hold, more than 90 per cent in nominal value of each class of issued shares of the company and entitled to vote at general meetings of the company have voted in favour of the special resolution referred to in *subsection (1)(a)*, or

(ii) that resolution has been passed by the means provided under *section 193*,

30 days,

but *subsection (2)* applies as regards computing that period of 60 or 30 days as it applies as regards computing the period of 12 months referred to in *subsection (2)*.

(4) *Subsection (1)* is, in the case of a merger, without prejudice to the procedures set out in *Chapter 3* of *Part 9* that must be followed before the resolution referred to in *paragraph (a)(ii)* of that subsection may be passed.

(5) In the case of a merger, on the delivery, in accordance with *section 206*, to the Registrar of each declaration referred to in that section, the Registrar shall register the dissolution of the transferor company or companies concerned.

(6) The declaration referred to in *subsection (1)(b)* is a declaration in writing that is made at a meeting of the directors held—

(a) not earlier than 30 days before the date of the meeting referred to in *subsection (1)(b)*, or

(b) if the written means for passing the resolution is used, not earlier than 30 days before the date of the signing of the resolution by the last member to sign,

and that is made by the directors or, in the case of a company having more than 2 directors, by a majority of the directors.

(7) The terms of the resolution referred to in *subsection (1)(a)(ii)* (which deals with a case of a merger) shall be that the common draft terms of merger are approved.

203 Declaration to be made in the case of financial assistance for acquisition of shares or transaction with directors

(1) Where the restricted activity is a transaction or arrangement that would otherwise be prohibited by *section 82(2)* or *239*, the declaration shall state—

(a) the circumstances in which the transaction or arrangement is to be entered into;

(b) the nature of the transaction or arrangement;

(c) the person or persons to or for whom the transaction or arrangement is to be made;

(d) the purpose for which the company is entering into the transaction or arrangement;

(e) the nature of the benefit which will accrue to the company directly or indirectly from entering into the transaction or arrangement; and

(f) that the declarants have made a full inquiry into the affairs of the company and that, having done so, they have formed the opinion that the company, having entered into the transaction or arrangement (the "relevant act"), will be able to pay or discharge its debts and other liabilities in full as they fall due during the period of 12 months after the date of the relevant act.

(2) For the purposes of a declaration under this section, in determining whether or not a company will be able to pay or discharge its debts and other liabilities in full, the declarants shall not be required to assume (in circumstances where the following are relevant) either that the company will be called upon to pay moneys on foot of a guarantee given or, as the case may be, that security given will be realised.

(3) A copy of the declaration under this section shall be delivered to the Registrar not later than 21 days after the date on which the carrying on of the restricted activity concerned is commenced.

(4) On application to it by any interested party, the court may, in any case where there has been a failure to comply with *subsection (3)*, declare that the carrying on of the restricted activity concerned shall be valid for all purposes if the court is satisfied that it would be just and equitable to do so.

204 Declaration to be made in the case of a reduction in company capital or variation of company capital on reorganisation

(1) Where the restricted activity is a reduction in company capital referred to in *section 84(1)* or a transfer or disposal referred to in *section 91(1)*, the declaration shall state—

(a) the circumstances in which the transaction or arrangement is to be entered into;

(b) the nature of the transaction or arrangement;

(c) the person or persons to or for whom the transaction or arrangement is to be made;

(d) the total amount of the company's assets and liabilities as at the latest practicable date before the date of making of the declaration and in any event at a date not more than 3 months before the date of that making;

(e) the anticipated total amount of the company's assets and liabilities immediately after the restricted activity having taken place;

(f) that the declarants have made a full inquiry into the affairs of the company and that, having done so, they have formed the opinion that the company, after the restricted activity has taken place, will be able to pay or discharge its debts and other liabilities (being the debts and liabilities identified for the purposes of *paragraph (d)* and so far as not already paid or discharged) in full as they fall due during the period of 12 months after the date of that event; and

(g) that the declarants do not have actual or constructive notice that the company will incur any material, extraordinary, future liability within the period of 12 months after the date of the making of the declaration.

(2) A copy of the declaration under this section shall be delivered to the Registrar not later than 21 days after the date on which the carrying on of the restricted activity concerned is commenced; if a failure to comply with this subsection occurs, a like power to that under *section 203(4)* is available to the court to declare valid for all purposes the carrying on of the activity.

205 Declaration to be made in the case of treatment of pre-acquisition profits or losses in a manner otherwise prohibited by *section 118(1)*

(1) Where the restricted activity is to provide in a company's financial statements a treatment that is otherwise prohibited by *section 118(1)* of the profits or losses attributable to shares of a subsidiary of the company for the period referred to in *section 118(2)* as the "pre-acquisition period", the declaration shall state—

(a) the amount of the profits or losses that will be subject to the alternative treatment and the amount so stated is referred to in this section as the "proposed distribution";

(b) the total amount of the company's assets and liabilities as stated in its last statutory financial statements or interim financial statements properly prepared as of a date specified in the declaration, and the date so specified shall be the date which is the latest practicable date before the date of making of the declaration and in any event shall not be a date more than 3 months before the date of such making;

(c) that the declarants have made a full inquiry into the affairs of the company and that, having done so, they have formed the opinion that, if the company were to make the proposed distribution within 2 months after the date of the making of the declaration, the company would be able to pay or discharge its debts and other liabilities included in the financial statements referred to in *paragraph (b)* as they fall due during the period of 12 months after the date of that distribution.

(2) In determining whether or not a company will be able to pay or discharge its debts and other liabilities as they fall due, the declarants shall be required to consider the likelihood (in circumstances where the following are relevant) either that the company will be called upon to pay moneys on foot of a guarantee given or, as the case may be, that security given will be realised.

(3) The reference in *subsection (1)(b)* to a company's last statutory financial statements or interim financial statements or to their being properly prepared shall be read in accordance with *section 121*.

(4) A copy of the declaration under this section shall be delivered to the Registrar not later than 21 days after the date on which the carrying on of the restricted activity concerned is commenced; if a failure to comply with this subsection occurs, a like power to that under *section 203(4)* is available to the court to declare valid for all purposes the carrying on of the activity.

206 Declaration to be made in the case of merger of company

(1) Where the restricted activity is to effect a merger, each declaration (that is to say, each declaration by the directors (or a majority of them) of each merging company) shall state—

(a) the total amount of the assets and liabilities of the merging company in question as at the latest practicable date before the date of making of the declaration and in any event at a date not more than 3 months before the date of that making; and

(b) that the declarants have made a full inquiry into the affairs of the company and the other merging companies and that, having done so, they have formed the opinion that the successor company (within the meaning of *Chapter 3* of *Part 9*) will be able to pay or discharge the debts and other liabilities of it and the transferor company or companies in full as they fall due during the period of 12 months after the date on which the merger takes effect.

(2) A copy of each declaration under this section shall be delivered to the Registrar not later than 21 days after the date on which the carrying on of the restricted activity concerned is commenced; if a failure to comply with this subsection occurs, a like power to that under *section 203(4)* is available to the court to declare valid for all purposes the carrying on of the activity.

207 Declaration to be made in the case of members' winding up of solvent company

(1) Where the restricted activity is to wind up a company in a members' voluntary winding up under *section 579*, the declaration shall state—

(a) the total amount of the company's assets and liabilities as at the latest practicable date before the date of making of the declaration and in any event at a date not more than 3 months before the date of that making; and

(b) that the declarants have made a full inquiry into the affairs of the company and that, having done so, they have formed the opinion that the company will be able to pay or discharge its debts and other liabilities in full within such period not exceeding 12 months after the commencement of the winding up as may be specified in the declaration.

(2) A copy of the declaration under this section shall be delivered to the Registrar not later than 21 days after the date on which the carrying on of the restricted activity concerned is commenced; if a failure to comply with this subsection occurs, a like power to that under *section 203(4)* is available to the court to declare valid for all purposes the carrying on of the activity.

208 Condition to be satisfied common to declarations referred to in *section 204, 205* or *207*

A declaration referred to in *section 204, 205* or *207* shall have no effect for the purposes of this Act unless it is accompanied by a report—

(a) drawn up in the prescribed form, by a person who is qualified at the time of the report to be appointed, or to continue to be, the statutory auditor of the company; and

(b) which shall state whether, in the opinion of that person, the declaration is not unreasonable.

209 Condition to be satisfied in relation to declaration referred to in *section 206*

(1) A declaration referred to in *section 206* shall have no effect for the purposes of this Act unless it is accompanied by a document prepared by the declarants either—

(a) confirming that the common draft terms of merger provide for such particulars of each relevant matter as will enable each of the prescribed effects provisions to operate without difficulty in relation to the merger; or

(b) specifying such particulars of each relevant matter as will enable each of those effects provisions to operate without difficulty in relation to the merger.

(2) In *subsection (1)* "prescribed effects provisions" means *subsection (3)(a)* to *(i)* of *section 480* as that subsection has effect by virtue of *section 472(2)*.

210 Civil sanctions where opinion as to solvency stated in declaration without reasonable grounds

(1) Where a director of a company makes a declaration without having reasonable grounds for the opinion referred to in *section 203(1)(f), 204(1)(f), 205(1)(c), 206(1)(b)* or *207(1)(b)*, as the case may be, the court, on the application of—

(a) a liquidator, creditor, member or contributory of the company or, in the case of the opinion referred to in *section 206(1)(b)*, of the successor company (within the meaning of *Chapter 3* of *Part 9*), or

(b) the Director of Corporate Enforcement,

may declare that the director shall be personally responsible, without any limitation of liability, for all or any of the debts or other liabilities of the company or successor company, as the case may be.

(2) If a company or, as the case may be, a successor company (within the foregoing meaning) is wound up within 12 months after the date of the making of a declaration and its debts are not paid or provided for in full within 12 months after the commencement of the winding up, it shall be presumed, until the contrary is shown, that each director of, as appropriate—

(a) the company, or

(b) the merging companies,

who made the declaration did not have reasonable grounds for the opinion referred to in *section 203(1)(f), 204(1)(f), 205(1)(c), 206(1)(b)* or *207(1)(b)*, as the case may be.

(3) If the court makes a declaration under *subsection (1)*, it may give such further directions as it thinks proper for the purpose of giving effect to the declaration.

211 Moratorium on certain restricted activities being carried on and applications to court to cancel special resolution

(1) This section shall apply unless the restricted activity—

(a) is to effect a merger; or

(b) has the authority of a special resolution referred to in *section 202(1)(a)(i)* passed by the means provided under *section 193*.

(2) Unless one or more members who hold, or together hold, more than 90 per cent in nominal value of each class of issued shares of the company and entitled to vote at general meetings of the company have voted in favour of the special resolution referred to in *section 202(1)(a)*, the company shall not proceed to carry on the restricted activity—

(a) subject to *paragraph (b)*, until the expiry of 30 days after the date on which the special resolution has been passed; or

(b) if an application under *subsection (3)* is made, until the application has been disposed of by the court (and then only (unless the application is withdrawn) to the extent, if any, that authority for its being proceeded with is provided by a confirmation of the special resolution by the court on that application).

(3) An application may be made to the court in accordance with this section for the cancellation of the special resolution.

(4) Subject to *subsection (5)*, an application under *subsection (3)* may be made by one or more members who held, or together held, not less than 10 per cent in nominal value of the company's issued share capital, or any class thereof, at the date of the passing of the special resolution and hold, or together hold, not less than that percentage in nominal value of the foregoing on the date of the making of the application.

(5) An application shall not be made under *subsection (3)* by a person who has consented to, or voted in favour of, the special resolution.

(6) An application under *subsection (3)* shall be made within 30 days after the date on which the special resolution was passed and may be made on behalf of the persons entitled to make the application by such one or more of their number as they may appoint in writing for the purpose.

(7) On the hearing of an application under *subsection (3)*, the court may, as it thinks fit—

(a) confirm the special resolution;

(b) confirm the special resolution as respects only specified parts or aspects of the restricted activity to which it relates; or

(c) cancel the special resolution.

Chapter 8
Protection for minorities

212 Remedy in case of oppression

(1) Any member of a company who complains that the affairs of the company are being conducted or that the powers of the directors of the company are being exercised—

(a) in a manner oppressive to him or her or any of the members (including himself or herself), or

(b) in disregard of his or her or their interests as members,

may apply to the court for an order under this section.

(2) If, on an application under *subsection (1)*, the court is of opinion that the company's affairs are being conducted or the directors' powers are being exercised in a manner that is mentioned in *subsection (1)(a)* or *(b)*, the court may, with a view to bringing to an end the matters complained of, make such order or orders as it thinks fit.

(3) The orders which a court may so make include an order—

(a) directing or prohibiting any act or cancelling or varying any transaction;

(b) for regulating the conduct of the company's affairs in future;

(c) for the purchase of the shares of any members of the company by other members of the company or by the company and, in the case of a purchase by the company, for the reduction accordingly of the company's capital; and

(d) for the payment of compensation.

(4) Where an order under this section makes any amendment of any company's constitution, then, notwithstanding anything in any other provision of this Act, but subject to the provisions of the order, the company concerned shall not have power, without the leave of the court, to make any further amendment of the constitution, inconsistent with the provisions of the order.

(5) However, subject to the foregoing subsection, the amendment made by the order shall be of the same effect as if duly made by resolution of the company, and the provisions of this Act shall apply to the constitution as so amended accordingly.

(6) A certified copy of any order under this section amending or giving leave to amend a company's constitution shall, within 21 days after the date of the making of the order, be delivered by the company to the Registrar.

(7) If a company fails to comply with *subsection (6)*, the company and any officer of it who is in default shall be guilty of a category 4 offence.

(8) Each of the following—

(a) the personal representative of a person who, at the date of his or her death, was a member of a company, or

(b) any trustee of, or person beneficially interested in, the shares of a company by virtue of the will or intestacy of any such person, may apply to the court under *subsection (1)* for an order under this section and, accordingly, any reference in that subsection to a member of a company shall be read as including a reference to any such personal representative, trustee or person beneficially interested as mentioned in *paragraph (a)* or *(b)* or to all of them.

(9) If, in the opinion of the court, the hearing of proceedings under this section would involve the disclosure of information the publication of which would be seriously prejudicial to the legitimate interests of the company, the court may order that the hearing of the proceedings or any part of them shall be *in camera*.

Chapter 9
Form of registers, indices and minute books

213 Form of registers, minutes, etc.

(1) Any register, index or minute book required by this Act to be kept by a company or by the Registrar may be kept either by making entries in bound books or by recording the matters in question in any other manner.

(2) Where any register, index or minute book to be kept by a company is not kept by making entries in a bound book but by some other means, adequate precautions shall be taken for guarding against falsification and facilitating discovery of such falsification, should it occur.

(3) If default is made in complying with *subsection (2)*, the company concerned and any officer of it who is in default shall be guilty of a category 3 offence.

214 Use of computers, etc., for certain company records

(1) Subject to *subsections (2)* and *(6)*, the power conferred on a company by *section 213(1)* to keep a register or other record by recording the matters in question otherwise than by making entries in bound books includes power to keep the register or other record by recording the matters in question otherwise than in a legible form so long as the recording is capable of being reproduced in a legible form.

(2) *Subsection (1)* does not apply to the books required to be kept by *section 199* for the purpose mentioned in *subsection (1)* of that section.

(3) Any provision of an instrument made by a company before 3 April 1978 which requires a register of holders of debentures of the company to be kept in a legible form shall be read as requiring the register to be kept in a legible or non-legible form (but so that, if it is kept in non-legible form, it shall be capable of being reproduced in legible form).

(4) If the power under *subsection (1)* is availed of by a company, any duty imposed on the company by or under this Act to allow inspection of, or to furnish a copy of, the register or other record concerned kept by the company otherwise than in legible form, or any part of it, shall be treated as a duty to allow inspection of, or to furnish, a reproduction of the recording or of the relevant part of it in a legible form.

(5) *Subsection (6)* does not apply—

(a) if the services to the other computer there mentioned are provided by means of the technology commonly known as cloud computing or by any other distance hosting solution; or

(b) to the extent that regulations under *subsection (7)* provide that it shall not apply.

(6) Any computer (the "server computer") that provides services to another computer, being services the provision of which to the latter is necessary so that the information of the kind referred in *subsection (1)* stored in the latter can be accessed at all times, shall be kept in a place in the State.

(7) The Minister may, by regulations, make such provision, being provision in addition to *subsection (4)*, as he or she considers appropriate in connection with such registers or other records as are mentioned in that subsection and are kept as there mentioned and may also, by regulations, provide for such exceptions to *subsection (6)* as he or she considers appropriate.

Chapter 10
Inspection of registers, provision of copies of information in them and service of notices

215 Definitions for purposes of *section 216* concerning registers, etc. and construction of reference to company keeping registers, etc.

In—

(a) *section 216*—

"copies of directors' service contracts and memoranda" means the copies of directors' service contracts and memoranda kept by the company pursuant to *section 154*;

"copies of instruments creating charges" means the copies of instruments creating charges kept by the company pursuant to *section 418* (including copies of any relevant judgment mortgage documentation referred to in that section);

"directors' and secretaries' register" means the register of directors and secretaries kept by the company pursuant to *section 149*;

"disclosable interests register" means the register of interests kept by the company pursuant to *section 267*;

"members' register" means the register of members kept by the company pursuant to *section 169*;

"minutes of meetings" means the books kept by the company pursuant to *section 199* (including any records referred to in *section 196(6)*) and—

(i) the documents, if any, required by *section 193(7)* (documents relating to unanimous written resolutions), and

(ii) the documents, if any, required by *section 195(4)* (documents relating to majority written resolutions),

to be kept with those books;

(b) this section a reference to any foregoing register or document being kept by the company includes a reference to the register or document being kept by another on the company's behalf pursuant to *section 216(2)*;

(c) this section and *section 216* a reference to keeping includes a reference to maintaining; and

(d) *section 216(3)* the requirement thereunder to keep a register or other document at a place shall be deemed to be complied with if, by means of any computer, the register or document is (at that place) capable of being reproduced in legible form and inspected in that form, and references elsewhere in *section 216* and this Chapter to the keeping of a register or other document, and the inspection of it, shall be read accordingly.

216 Where registers and other documents to be kept, right to inspect them, etc.

(1) This section applies to—

(a) the copies of directors' service contracts and memoranda;

(b) the copies of instruments creating charges;

(c) the directors' and secretaries' register;

(d) the disclosable interests register;

(e) the members' register; and

(f) the minutes of meetings.

(2) An obligation imposed on a company under this Act to keep a register or document to which this section applies may be discharged by another person keeping, on its behalf, the register or document.

(3) Subject to *subsections (4)* and *(5)*, a register or document to which this section applies shall be kept at—

(a) the registered office of the company;

(b) its principal place of business within the State; or

(c) another place within the State.

(4) Where the register or document is kept by another person on behalf of the company pursuant to *subsection (2)*, the place at which that register or document is kept by that person shall be a place within the State.

(5) In a case where a company keeps several of the registers or documents (or both) to which this section applies at a place other than that referred to in *subsection (3)(a)* or *(b)*, those registers or documents (or both) shall be kept by it at a single place.

(6) Where a register or document to which this section applies is kept at a place referred to in *subsection (3)(b)* or *(c)* or *subsection (4)*, the company shall send a notice to the Registrar in the prescribed form of that place and of any change in that place.

(7) A register or document to which this section applies shall, during business hours (except, in the case of the members' register, when it is closed under *section 174*), be open to inspection in accordance with *subsections (8)* to *(10)*.

(8) Every such register or document shall be open to the inspection of any member of the company without charge.

(9) The following shall be open to the inspection of any other person, on payment of the relevant fee:

(a) the directors' and secretaries' register;
(b) the disclosable interests register;
(c) the members' register.

(10) The copies of instruments creating charges shall be open to the inspection of any creditor of the company without charge.

(11) A member of the company may request a copy, or a copy of any part, of—

(a) the directors' and secretaries' register;
(b) the disclosable interests register;
(c) the members' register; or
(d) the minutes of meetings.

(12) Any other person may request a copy, or a copy of any part, of—

(a) the directors' and secretaries' register;
(b) the disclosable interests register; or
(c) the members' register.

(13) A company shall, within 10 days after the date of receipt of a request under *subsection (11)* or *(12)* and on payment to it of the relevant fee by the requester, cause to be sent to the requester the copy, or part of it, concerned.

217 Supplemental provisions in relation to *section 216* — "relevant fee", power to alter the amount of it, offences, etc.

(1) In *section 216* "relevant fee" means—

(a) in a case falling within *subsection (9)* of that section—
   (i) where one register is inspected, €10.00 or such less sum as the company may determine; or
   (ii) subject to *subsection (2)*, where more than one register is inspected on the same day or in any period of 24 consecutive hours, €15.00 or such less sum as the company may determine;

(b) in a case falling within *subsection (13)* of that section, €10.00 per copy or such less sum as the company may determine.

(2) *Subsection (1)(a)(ii)* only applies if—

(a) the inspections concerned are made by, or on behalf of, the same person; and
(b) at the time the first request for inspection is made (by, or on behalf of, the same person) during the period concerned it is indicated to the company that more than one register will be inspected (by, or on behalf of, that person) during that period.

(3) If a company fails to comply with any of *subsections (3)* to *(10)*, or *subsection (13)*, of *section 216*, the company and any officer of it who is in default shall be guilty of a category 3 offence.

(4) The court may, on application being made to it, make the following orders:

(a) in the case of a failure to comply with any of *subsections (7)* to *(10)* of *section 216*, an order compelling an immediate inspection of the register or document concerned;

(b) in the case of a failure to comply with *section 216(13)*, an order directing that the copy requested be sent to the person requesting it.

(5) Subject to *subsections (6)* to *(8)*, the Minister may, by order, alter a sum specified in *paragraph (a)* or *(b)* of the definition of "relevant fee" in this section.

(6) An order under *subsection (5)* may only be made, at a particular time (the "relevant time"), if it appears to the Minister the changes in the value of money generally in the State that have occurred during the period beginning—

(a) on this Act's passing, or

(b) if the powers under that subsection have previously been exercised, immediately after their last previous exercise,

and ending at the relevant time warrant the exercise of powers under that subsection for the following purpose.

(7) That purpose is to relieve companies of an additional financial expense that they would otherwise incur (by reason of the foregoing changes) in complying with the provisions specified in the definition of "relevant fee" in this section if the powers under *subsection (5)* were not exercised at the relevant time.

(8) Without prejudice to *subsections (6)* and *(7)*, in making any order under *subsection (5)*, the Minister shall take into account the general costs incurred by a company in facilitating the inspection, or providing copies, of the registers or other documents referred to in the provisions specified in the definition of "relevant fee" in this section.

218 Service of notices on members

(1) *Subsections (3)* and *(4)* shall apply to any case in which a provision of this Act, or of the company's constitution, requires or authorises a notice to be served on or given to a member of the company by the company, or an officer of it, but save to the extent that the constitution provides otherwise.

(2) *Subsection (5)* shall only apply if there is contained in the company's constitution a provision to the effect that it shall apply (but nothing in this subsection shall prevent alternative and reasonable provision being made in the constitution with regard to one or more of the matters set out in that subsection and, to the extent that such alternative and reasonable provision is made, that provision shall apply instead of that subsection).

(3) A notice referred to in *subsection (1)* shall, save where the means of serving or giving it specified in *paragraph (d)* is used, be in writing and may be served on or given to the member in one of the following ways:

(a) by delivering it to the member;

(b) by leaving it at the registered address of the member;

(c) by sending it by post in a prepaid letter to the registered address of the member; or

(d) if the company's constitution permits the use of electronic means to serve or give the notice or the conditions specified in *subsection (4)* are satisfied, by electronic means.

(4) The conditions referred to in *subsection (3)(d)* are—

(a) the member has consented in writing to the company, or the officer of it, using electronic means to serve or give notices in relation to him or her;

(b) at the time the electronic means are used to serve or give the notice in relation to the member, no notice in writing has been received by the company or the officer concerned from the member stating he or she has withdrawn the consent referred to in *paragraph (a)*; and

(c) the particular means used to serve or give the notice electronically are those that the member has consented to.

(5) Any notice served or given in accordance with *subsection (3)* shall be deemed, in the absence of any agreement to the contrary between the company (or, as the case may be, the officer of it) and the member, to have been served or given—

(a) in the case of its being delivered, at the time of delivery (or, if delivery is refused, when tendered);

(b) in the case of its being left, at the time that it is left;

(c) in the case of its being posted (to an address in the State) on any day other than a Friday, Saturday or Sunday, 24 hours after despatch and in the case of its being posted (to such an address)—

(i) on a Friday – 72 hours after despatch; or

(ii) on a Saturday or Sunday – 48 hours after despatch;

(d) in the case of electronic means being used in relation to it, 12 hours after despatch,

but this subsection is without prejudice to *section 181(3)*.

(6) In this section "registered address", in relation to a member, means the address of the member as entered in the register of members.

PART 5
DUTIES OF DIRECTORS AND OTHER OFFICERS

Chapter 1
Preliminary and definitions

219 Interpretation and application (*Part 5*)

(1) In this Part—

"credit transaction" has the meaning given to it by *subsection (3)*;

"guarantee" includes an indemnity;

"quasi-loan" has the meaning given to it by *subsection (2)*.

(2) For the purposes of this Part—

(a) a quasi-loan is a transaction under which one party (the "creditor") agrees to pay, or pays otherwise than in pursuance of an agreement, a sum for another (the "borrower") or agrees to reimburse or reimburses otherwise than in pursuance of an agreement, expenditure incurred by another party for another (the "borrower")—

(i) on terms that the borrower (or a person on his behalf) will reimburse the creditor; or

(ii) in circumstances giving rise to a liability on the borrower to reimburse the creditor;

(b) any reference to the person to whom a quasi-loan is made is a reference to the borrower; and

(c) the liabilities of a borrower under a quasi-loan include the liabilities of any person who has agreed to reimburse the creditor on behalf of the borrower.

(3) For the purposes of this Part a credit transaction is, subject to *subsection (4)*, a transaction under which one party (the "creditor")—

(a) supplies any goods or sells any land under, as the case may be, a hire-purchase agreement or conditional sale agreement;

(b) leases or licenses the use of land or hires goods in return for periodical payments;

(c) otherwise disposes of land or supplies goods or services, on the understanding that payment (whether in a lump sum or instalments or by way of periodical payments or otherwise) is to be deferred.

(4) For the purposes of this Part a lease of land which reserves a nominal annual rent of not more than €100 is not a credit transaction where a company grants the lease in return for a premium or capital payment which represents the open market value of the land thereby disposed of by the company.

(5) For the purposes of this Part the value of a transaction or arrangement is—

(a) in the case of a loan, the principal of the loan;

(b) in the case of a quasi-loan, the amount or maximum amount which the person to whom the quasi-loan is made is liable to reimburse the creditor;

(c) in the case of a transaction or arrangement other than a loan or quasi-loan or a transaction or arrangement falling within *paragraph (d)* or *(e)*, the price which it is reasonable to expect could be obtained for the goods, land or services to which the transaction or arrangement relates if they had been supplied at the time the transaction or arrangement is entered into in the ordinary course of business and on the same terms (apart from price) as they have been supplied or are to be supplied under the transaction or arrangement in question;

(d) in the case of a guarantee or security, the amount guaranteed or secured;

(e) in the case of an arrangement to which *section 239(2)* or *(3)* applies, the value of the transaction to which the arrangement relates less any amount by which the liabilities under the arrangement or transaction of the person for whom the transaction was made have been reduced.

(6) For the purposes of *subsection (5)*, the value of a transaction or arrangement (or, as the case may be, of a transaction to which an arrangement relates) which is not capable of being expressed as a specific sum of money, whether because the amount of any liability arising under the transaction or arrangement is unascertainable or for any other reason, shall be deemed to exceed €65,000, and this subsection applies irrespective of whether any liability under the transaction or arrangement has been reduced.

(7) For the purposes of this Part, a transaction or arrangement is made for a person if—

(a) in the case of a loan or quasi-loan, it is made to him or her;

(b) in the case of a credit transaction, he or she is the person to whom goods or services are supplied, or land is sold or otherwise disposed of, under the transaction;

(c) in the case of a guarantee or security, it is entered into or provided in connection with a loan or quasi-loan made to him or her or a credit transaction made for him or her;

(d) in the case of an arrangement to which *section 239(2)* or *(3)* applies, the transaction to which the arrangement relates was made for him or her; and

(e) in the case of any other transaction or arrangement for the supply or transfer of goods, land or services (or any interest therein), he or she is the person to whom the goods, land or services (or the interest) are supplied or transferred.

(8) This Part does not apply to arrangements or transactions entered into before 1 February 1991 but, for the purposes of determining whether an arrangement is one to which *section 239(2)* or *(3)* applies, the transaction to which the arrangement relates shall, if it was entered into before 1 February 1991, be deemed to have been entered into after that date.

(9) This Part shall have effect in relation to an arrangement or transaction whether governed by the law of the State or of another country.

220 Connected persons

(1) For the purposes of this Part (and without prejudice to *subsection (3)*), a person is connected with a director of a company if, but only if, the person (not being himself or herself a director of the company) is—

(a) that director's spouse, civil partner, parent, brother, sister or child;

(b) a person acting in his or her capacity as the trustee of any trust, the principal beneficiaries of which are that director, the spouse (or civil partner) or any children of that director or any body corporate which that director controls; or

(c) in partnership with that director.

(2) In *subsection (1)(a)* and *(b)* "child", in relation to a director, shall be deemed to include a child of the director's civil partner who is ordinarily resident with the director and the civil partner.

(3) A body corporate shall also be, for the purposes of this Part, connected with a director of a company if it is controlled by that director or by another body corporate that is controlled by that director.

(4) For the avoidance of doubt, *subsection (3)* is without prejudice to the application of section 18(c) of the Interpretation Act 2005 ("person" to include body corporate, etc.) to *subsection (1)(b)*.

(5) For the purposes of this section, a director of a company controls a body corporate if, but only if, he or she is, alone or together with any other director or directors of the company or any person connected with the director or such other director or directors—

(a) interested in one-half or more of the equity share capital of that body; or

(b) entitled to exercise or control the exercise of one-half or more of the voting power at any general meeting of that body.

(6) In *subsection (5)*—

(a) "equity share capital" has the same meaning as it has in *section 7*; and

(b) references to voting power exercised by a director shall be read as including references to voting power exercised by another body corporate which that director controls.

(7) For the purpose of *subsections (5)(b)* and *(6)(b)* "voting power" does not include any power to vote which arises only in specified circumstances.

(8) It shall be presumed, for the purposes of this Part, until the contrary is shown, that the sole member of a single-member company is a person connected with a director of that company.

221 Shadow directors

(1) Subject to *subsection (2)*, a person in accordance with whose directions or instructions the directors of a company are accustomed to act (in this Act referred to as a "shadow director") shall be treated for the purposes of this Part as a director of

the company unless the directors are accustomed so to act by reason only that they do so on advice given by him or her in a professional capacity.

(2) A body corporate is not to be regarded as a shadow director of any of its subsidiaries.

(3) *Section 231* shall apply in relation to a shadow director of a company as it applies in relation to a director of a company, except that the shadow director shall declare his or her interest, not at a meeting of the directors, but by a notice in writing to the directors which is either—

(a) a specific notice given before the date of the meeting at which, if he or she had been a director, the declaration would be required by *subsection (3)* of that section to be made; or

(b) a notice which under *subsection (4)* of that section falls to be treated as a sufficient declaration of that interest or would fall to be so treated apart from the qualification of that *subsection (4)* contained in *subsection (5)* of that section.

(4) As respects a declaration made by either of the means referred to in *subsection (3)*, *section 166* shall have effect as if the declaration had been made at the meeting in question and had accordingly formed part of the proceedings at that meeting.

222 *De facto* director

(1) Without limiting the manner in which the expression "director" is to be read by virtue of *section 2(1)*, a person who occupies the position of director of a company but who has not been formally appointed as such director shall, subject to *subsection (4)*, be treated, for the purposes of this Part, as a director of the company.

(2) In particular, *section 231* shall apply in relation to such a director as it applies in relation to directors generally.

(3) A person who is, by virtue of *subsection (1)*, treated, for the purposes of this Part, as a director of a company is in this Act referred to as a *de facto* director.

(4) A person shall not be a *de facto* director of a company by reason only of the fact that he or she gives advice in a professional capacity to the company or any of the directors of it.

Chapter 2
General duties of directors and secretaries and liabilities of them and other officers

223 Duty of each director

(1) It is the duty of each director of a company to ensure that this Act is complied with by the company.

(2) The breach by a director of the duty under *subsection (1)* shall not of itself affect—

(a) the validity of any contract or other transaction, or

(b) the enforceability, other than by the director in breach of that duty, of any contract or other transaction by any person, but nothing in this subsection affects the principles of liability of a third party where he or she has been an accessory to a breach of duty or has knowingly received a benefit therefrom.

(3) The consent in respect of a director to accompany—

(a) a statement under *section 21(1)(a)*, and

(b) a notification under *section 149(8)*,

shall include a statement by the director (immediately above his or her signature on the consent) in the following terms:

"I acknowledge that, as a director, I have legal duties and obligations imposed by the Companies Act, other statutes and at common law.".

224 Directors to have regard to interests of employees

(1) The matters to which the directors of a company are to have regard in the performance of their functions shall include the interests of the company's employees in general, as well as the interests of its members.

(2) Accordingly, the duty imposed by this section on the directors shall be owed by them to the company (and the company alone) and shall be enforceable in the same way as any other fiduciary duty owed to a company by its directors.

225 Directors' compliance statement and related statement

(1) In this section—

"amount of turnover" and "balance sheet total" have the same meanings as they have in [*section 275*][a];

"relevant obligations", in relation to a company, means the company's obligations under—

(a) this Act, where a failure to comply with any such obligation would (were it to occur) be—

(i) a category 1 offence or a category 2 offence; or

(ii) a serious Market Abuse offence or a serious Prospectus offence;

and

(b) tax law;

"serious Market Abuse offence" means an offence referred to in *section 1368*;

"serious Prospectus offence" means an offence referred to in *section 1356*;

"tax law" means—

(a) the Customs Acts;

(b) the statutes relating to the duties of excise and to the management of those duties;

(c) the Tax Acts;

(d) the Capital Gains Tax Acts;

(e) the Value-Added Tax Acts;

(f) the Capital Acquisitions Tax Consolidation Act 2003 and the enactments amending or extending that Act;

(g) the Stamp Duties Consolidation Act 1999 and the enactments amending or extending that Act; and

(h) any instruments made under an enactment referred to in any of *paragraphs (a)* to *(g)* or made under any other enactment and relating to tax.

(2) The directors of a company to which this section applies shall also include in their report under *section 325* a statement—

(a) acknowledging that they are responsible for securing the company's compliance with its relevant obligations; and

(b) with respect to each of the things specified in *subsection (3)*, confirming that the thing has been done or, if it has not been done, specifying the reasons why it has not been done.

(3) The things mentioned in *subsection (2)(b)* are—

(a) the drawing up of a statement (to be known, and in this Act referred to as, a "compliance policy statement") setting out the company's policies (that, in the directors' opinion, are appropriate to the company) respecting compliance by the company with its relevant obligations;

(b) the putting in place of appropriate arrangements or structures that are, in the directors' opinion, designed to secure material compliance with the company's relevant obligations; and

(c) the conducting of a review, during the financial year to which the report referred to in *subsection (2)* relates, of any arrangements or structures referred to in *paragraph (b)* that have been put in place.

(4) The arrangements or structures referred to in *subsection (3)(b)* may, if the directors of the company in their discretion so decide, include reliance on the advice of one or more than one person employed by the company or retained by it under a contract for services, being a person who appears to the directors to have the requisite knowledge and experience to advise the company on compliance with its relevant obligations.

(5) For the purposes of this section, the arrangements or structures referred to in *subsection (3)(b)* shall be regarded as being designed to secure material compliance by the company concerned with its relevant obligations if they provide a reasonable assurance of compliance in all material respects with those obligations.

(6) If default is made in complying with *subsection (2)*, each director to whom the default is attributable shall be guilty of a category 3 offence.

(7) Subject to *subsection (8)*, this section shall apply to a company if, in respect of the financial year of the company to which the report referred to in *subsection (2)* relates—

(a) its balance sheet total for the year exceeds—

(i) subject to *subparagraph (ii)*, €12,500,000; or

(ii) if an amount is prescribed under *section 943(1)(i)*, the prescribed amount;

and

(b) the amount of its turnover for the year exceeds—

(i) subject to *subparagraph (ii)*, €25,000,000; or

(ii) if an amount is prescribed under *section 943(1)(i)*, the prescribed amount.

(8) This section does not apply to any company that is of a class exempted under *section 943(1)(g)* from this section.

Amendments

a Words substituted by C(A)A 2017, s 88(a)(i) (previously: "*section 350*").

226 Duties of secretary

(1) The duties of the secretary of a company shall, without derogating from the secretary's statutory and other legal duties, be such duties as are delegated to the secretary, from time to time, by the board of directors of the company.

(2) Without prejudice to the generality of *section 129(4)*, the directors of a company shall, in their appointment of a secretary, have a duty to ensure that the person appointed has the skills necessary so as to enable him or her maintain (or procure the maintenance of) the records (other than accounting records) required to be kept under this Act in relation to the company.

(3) The cases to which *subsection (2)* applies includes the case of an appointment of one of the directors of the company as secretary.

(4) In *subsections (1)* to *(3)* references to a secretary include references to joint secretaries.

(5) The consent in respect of a secretary or joint secretaries to accompany—

(a) a statement under *section 21(1)(a)*, and

(b) a notification under *section 149(8)*,

shall include a statement by the secretary or secretaries (immediately above the signature or signatures of the secretary or secretaries on the consent) in the following terms:

> "I/We acknowledge that, as a secretary, I/we have legal duties and obligations imposed by the Companies Act, other statutes and at common law.".

227 Fiduciary duties of directors — provisions introductory to *section 228*

(1) Without prejudice to the provisions of any enactment (including this Act), a director of a company shall owe the duties set out in *section 228* (the "relevant duties") to the company (and the company alone).

(2) The breach by a director of the relevant duties shall not of itself affect—

(a) the validity of any contract or other transaction, or

(b) the enforceability, other than by the director in breach of that duty, of any contract or other transaction by any person,

but nothing in this subsection affects the principles of liability of a third party where he or she has been an accessory to a breach of duty or has knowingly received a benefit therefrom.

(3) The relevant duties shall be enforced in the same way as any other fiduciary duty owed to a company by its directors.

(4) The relevant duties (other than those set out in *section 228(1)(b) and (h)*) are based on certain common law rules and equitable principles as they apply in relation to the directors of companies and shall have effect in place of those rules and principles as regards the duties owed to a company by a director.

(5) The relevant duties (other than those set out in *section 228(1)(b) and (h)*) shall be interpreted, and the provisions concerned of *section 228* shall be applied, in the same way as common law rules or equitable principles; regard shall be had to the corresponding common law rules and equitable principles in interpreting those duties and applying those provisions.

228 Statement of principal fiduciary duties of directors

(1) A director of a company shall—

(a) act in good faith in what the director considers to be the interests of the company;

(b) act honestly and responsibly in relation to the conduct of the affairs of the company;

(c) act in accordance with the company's constitution and exercise his or her powers only for the purposes allowed by law;

(d) not use the company's property, information or opportunities for his or her own or anyone else's benefit unless—

(i) this is expressly permitted by the company's constitution; or

(ii) the use has been approved by a resolution of the company in general meeting;

(e) not agree to restrict the director's power to exercise an independent judgment unless—

(i) this is expressly permitted by the company's constitution;

(ii) the case concerned falls within *subsection (2)*; or

(iii) the director's agreeing to such has been approved by a resolution of the company in general meeting;

(f) avoid any conflict between the director's duties to the company and the director's other (including personal) interests unless the director is released from his or her duty to the company in relation to the matter concerned, whether in accordance with provisions of the company's constitution in that behalf or by a resolution of it in general meeting;

(g) exercise the care, skill and diligence which would be exercised in the same circumstances by a reasonable person having both—

(i) the knowledge and experience that may reasonably be expected of a person in the same position as the director; and

(ii) the knowledge and experience which the director has;

and

(h) in addition to the duty under *section 224* (duty to have regard to the interests of its employees in general), have regard to the interests of its members.

(2) If a director of a company considers in good faith that it is in the interests of the company for a transaction or engagement to be entered into and carried into effect, a director may restrict the director's power to exercise an independent judgment in the future by agreeing to act in a particular way to achieve this.

(3) Without prejudice to the director's duty under *subsection (1)(a)* to act in good faith in what the director considers to be the interests of the company, a director of a company may have regard to the interests of a particular member of the company in the following circumstances.

(4) Those circumstances are where the director has been appointed or nominated for appointment by that member, being a member who has an entitlement to so appoint or nominate under the company's constitution or a shareholders' agreement.

229 Other interests of directors

(1) Save to the extent that the company's constitution provides otherwise, a director of a company may be or become a director or other officer of, or otherwise interested in, any company promoted by the company or in which the company may be interested as shareholder or otherwise; but neither this subsection nor anything in the company's constitution governing the foregoing matter overrides *section 228*.

(2) No such director shall be accountable to the company for any remuneration or other benefits received by him or her as a director or officer of, or from his or her interest in, such other company unless the company otherwise directs.

230 Power of director to act in a professional capacity for company

Save to the extent that the company's constitution provides otherwise—

(a) any director may act by himself or herself, or his or her firm, in a professional capacity for the company of which he or she is a director, and

(b) any director, in such a case, or his or her firm, shall be entitled to remuneration for professional services as if he or she were not a director,

but nothing in this section authorises a director, or his or her firm, to act as statutory auditor of a company of which he or she is director.

231 Duty of director to disclose his or her interest in contracts made by company

(1) It shall be the duty of a director of a company who is in any way, whether directly or indirectly, interested in a contract or proposed contract with the company, to declare the nature of his or her interest at a meeting of the directors of the company.

(2) *Subsection (1)* does not apply in relation to an interest that cannot reasonably be regarded as likely to give rise to a conflict of interest.

(3) The declaration required by this section to be made by a director shall—

(a) in the case of a proposed contract, be made at the meeting of the directors at which the question of entering into the contract is first taken into consideration or, if the director was not at the date of that meeting interested in the proposed contract, at the next meeting of the directors held after he or she became so interested; and

(b) in the case of his or her becoming interested in a contract after it is made, be made at the first meeting of the directors held after the director becomes so interested.

(4) Subject to *subsection (5)*, for the purposes of this section a general notice given to the directors of a company by a director to the effect that—

(a) he or she is a member of a specified company or firm and is to be regarded as interested in any contract which may, after the date of the notice, be made with that company or firm, or

(b) he or she is to be regarded as interested in any contract which may, after the date of the notice, be made with a specified person who is connected with him or her,

shall be deemed to be a sufficient declaration of interest in relation to any such contract.

(5) No such notice as is mentioned in *subsection (4)* shall be of effect unless it is given at the meeting of directors or the director takes reasonable steps to secure that it is brought up and read at the next meeting of the directors after it is given.

(6) A copy of every declaration made and notice given in pursuance of this section shall, within 3 days after the date of making or giving of it, be entered into a book kept by the company for this purpose.

(7) That book shall be open for inspection, without any charge, by any director, secretary, statutory auditor or member of the company at the registered office of the company and shall be produced at—

(a) every general meeting of the company; and

(b) any meeting of its directors if any of its directors so requests in sufficient time to enable the book to be available at the meeting.

(8) A company shall, if required by the Director of Corporate Enforcement, produce to the Director for inspection the book kept by it in accordance with *subsection (6)* and shall give the Director such facilities for inspecting and taking copies of the contents of the book as the Director may require.

(9) Nothing in this section shall be taken to prejudice the operation of any enactment or rule of law restricting directors of a company from having interests in contracts with the company.

(10) Any reference in this section to a contract—

(a) shall be read as excluding a reference to a contract the decision as to whether to enter into it is taken, or falls to be taken, other than by the board of directors or a committee of which the first-mentioned director in *subsection (1)* is a member;

(b) shall be read as including a reference to any transaction or arrangement, whether or not constituting a contract, but, in a case where the transaction or arrangement does not constitute a contract, a like limitation to that which applies under *paragraph (a)* applies to the construction of reference provided by this paragraph.

(11) For the purposes of this section, a transaction or arrangement of a kind described in *section 239* made by a company for a director of the company or a person connected with such a director shall, if it would not otherwise be so treated (and whether or not prohibited by that section), be treated as a transaction or arrangement in which that director is interested.

232 Breaches of certain duties: liability to account and indemnify

(1) Subject to *section 233*, where a director of a company acts in breach of his or her duty under *section 228(1)(a), (c), (d), (e), (f)* or *(g)*, he or she shall be liable to do either or both (as the corresponding common law rule or equitable principle with respect to the matter would have required) of the following things, namely—

(a) account to the company for any gain which he or she makes directly or indirectly from the breach of duty;

(b) indemnify the company for any loss or damage resulting from that breach.

(2) Subject to *subsection (6)*, where a company enters into a transaction or arrangement contrary to *section 238* or *239* with—

(a) a director of the company,

(b) a director of its holding company, or

(c) a person connected with a director of the company or its holding company,

that director and the person so connected and any other director of the company who authorised the transaction or arrangement (or, as the case may be, any transaction entered into in pursuance of the arrangement) shall be liable—

(i) to account to the company for any gain which he or she makes directly or indirectly from the transaction or arrangement;

(ii) (jointly and severally with any other person liable under this subsection) to indemnify the company for any loss or damage resulting from the transaction or arrangement; or

(iii) to do both of those things as the circumstances may require.

(3) Subject to *section 233*, where a company makes a payment to a director contrary to *section 251* or *252* that director shall be liable—

(a) to account to the company for any gain which he or she makes directly or indirectly from the payment,

(b) to indemnify the company for any loss or damage resulting from the payment, or

(c) to do both of those things as the circumstances may require,

and, in the case of section 252, this is without prejudice to subsection (3) of that section.

(4) *Subsection (2)* applies irrespective of whether the transaction or arrangement concerned has been avoided.

(5) *Subsections (1)* to *(3)* are without prejudice to—

(a) the company's right at common law to claim damages for breach of duty, or

(b) the company's right to make an application seeking the grant of equitable relief,

but the provisions of this section shall not be read as having the combined effect of enabling the company to be afforded more compensation for any damage or injury, or more protection of any proprietary right, than is just and equitable in the circumstances.

(6) Where a transaction or arrangement is entered into by a company and a person connected with a director of the company or of its holding company in contravention of *section 238* or *239*—

(a) that director shall not be liable under *subsection (2)* (or under any law referred to in *subsection (5)*) if he or she shows that he or she took all reasonable steps to secure the company's compliance with *section 238* or *239*, as the case may be, and

(b) in any case, a person so connected and any such other director as is mentioned in *subsection (2)* shall not be so liable if he or she shows that, at the time the transaction or arrangement was entered into (or, as the case may be, at the time the particular transaction was entered into in pursuance of the arrangement), he or she did not know the relevant circumstances constituting the contravention.

233 Power of court to grant relief to officers of company

(1) This section applies to any proceedings for negligence, default, breach of duty or breach of trust against an officer of a company.

(2) In proceedings to which this section applies the court hearing the proceedings has the power of granting relief provided under *subsection (3)* if it appears to the court that the officer concerned is or may be liable in respect of the negligence, default, breach of duty or breach of trust (the "wrong concerned") but that he or she has acted honestly and reasonably and that, having regard to all the circumstances of the case (including those connected with his or her appointment), he or she ought fairly to be excused for the wrong concerned.

(3) The power referred to in *subsection (2)* is to relieve the officer concerned, either wholly or partly, from his or her liability in respect of the wrong concerned on such terms as the court may think fit.

234 Anticipated claim: similar power of relief as under *section 233*

(1) If an officer of a company has reason to apprehend that any claim will or might be made against him or her in respect of any negligence, default, breach of duty or breach of trust (the "wrong concerned") he or she may make the following application to the court.

(2) That application is an application to be relieved of liability in respect of the wrong concerned; on the making of such an application the court shall have the same power to relieve the applicant as it would have had (by virtue of *section 233*) if it had been a court before which proceedings against that person for the wrong concerned had been brought.

235 Any provision exempting officers of company from liability void (subject to exceptions)

(1) Subject to the provisions of this section, the following provision shall be void, namely, any provision:

(a) purporting to exempt any officer of a company from; or

(b) purporting to indemnify such an officer against;

any liability which by virtue of any enactment or rule of law would otherwise attach to him or her in respect of any negligence, default, breach of duty or breach of trust of which he or she may be guilty in relation to the company.

(2) *Subsection (1)* applies whether the provision concerned is contained in the constitution of a company or a contract with a company or otherwise.

(3) Notwithstanding *subsection (1)*, a company may, in pursuance of any such provision as is mentioned in that subsection, indemnify any officer of the company against any liability incurred by him or her—

(a) in defending proceedings, whether civil or criminal, in which judgment is given in his or her favour or in which he or she is acquitted; or

(b) in connection with any proceedings or application referred to in, or under, *section 233* or *234* in which relief is granted to him or her by the court.

(4) Notwithstanding *subsection (1)*, a company may purchase and maintain for any of its officers insurance in respect of any liability referred to in that subsection.

(5) Notwithstanding any provision contained in any enactment, the constitution of a company or otherwise, a director may be counted in the quorum and may vote on any resolution to purchase or maintain any insurance under which the director might benefit.

(6) For the avoidance of doubt, if—

(a) any business, trade or activity has been carried on by means of a company, or other body corporate, registered or formed under the laws of another country,

(b) the period for which that business, trade or activity was so carried on was not less than 12 months preceding the date on which this subsection falls to be applied,

(c) a provision of the kind referred to in *subsection (1)(a)* or *(b)* in relation to officers of the company or other body corporate was in being and valid under the laws of that country, and

(d) a private company limited by shares is formed and registered to carry on that business, trade or activity,

then nothing in this section invalidates the operation of the provision referred to in *paragraph (c)* in respect of any negligence, default, breach of duty or breach of trust occurring before that private company limited by shares is formed and registered.

(7) Any directors' and officers' insurance purchased or maintained by a company before 6 April 2004 is as valid and effective as it would have been if this section had been in operation when that insurance was purchased or maintained.

(8) In this section—

(a) "officer" includes a statutory auditor,

(b) a reference to an officer includes a reference to any former or current officer of the company.

Chapter 3
Evidential provisions with respect to loans, other transactions, etc., between company and directors

236 Loans, etc., by company to directors: evidential provisions

(1) In this section "relevant proceedings" means civil proceedings in which it is claimed that a company has made a loan or quasi-loan to—

(a) a director of the company, or

(b) a director of its holding company, or

(c) a person connected with a director of any such company.

(2) In relevant proceedings if the terms of the loan or quasi-loan are not in writing then it shall be presumed, until the contrary is proved, that—

(a) the loan or quasi-loan is repayable on demand, and

(b) for any period before repayment of the amount of the loan or quasi-loan (or for any period before repayment of part of that amount) the amount or part has borne interest at the appropriate rate.

(3) In relevant proceedings if the terms of the loan or quasi-loan are in writing or partially in writing but—

(a) the case is one in which those terms are ambiguous with respect to the time at which, or the circumstances under which, the loan or quasi-loan is to be repaid, then it shall be presumed, until the contrary is proved, that the loan or quasi-loan is repayable on demand, or

(b) the case is one in which those terms are ambiguous with respect to whether, or the extent to which, the loan or quasi-loan bears interest, then it shall be presumed, until the contrary is proved, that for any period before repayment of the amount of the loan or quasi-loan (or for any period before repayment of part of that amount) the amount or part has borne interest at the appropriate rate.

(4) If the case referred to in *paragraph (a)* of *subsection (3)* and the case referred to in *paragraph (b)* of that subsection both apply then both of the presumptions provided by that subsection shall apply.

(5) References in *subsection (3)* to the terms of a loan or quasi-loan being ambiguous with respect to a matter shall, if the terms of the loan or quasi-loan are partially in writing, be deemed to include references to the following case.

(6) That case is one in which—

(a) the written terms of the loan or quasi-loan do not make provision in respect of the matter concerned, and

(b) provision in respect of that matter is alleged to be made by those of the terms of the loan or quasi-loan that are not in writing.

237 Loans, etc., by directors or connected persons to company or holding company: evidential provisions

(1) In this section "relevant proceedings" means civil proceedings in which it is claimed that a transaction or arrangement entered into, or alleged to have been entered into—

(a) by a director of a company with the company or its holding company, or

(b) by a person connected with such director with that company or its holding company (the "related person"),

constitutes a loan or quasi-loan by the director or (as appropriate) the related person to that company or its holding company, as the case may be.

(2) In relevant proceedings, if the terms of the transaction or arrangement concerned either—

(a) are not in writing, or

(b) are in writing, or partially in writing, but are ambiguous as to whether the transaction or arrangement constitutes a loan or quasi-loan or not (or as to whether it constitutes a quasi-loan as distinct from a loan),

then it shall be presumed, until the contrary is proved, that the transaction or arrangement constitutes neither a loan nor a quasi-loan to the company or its holding company, as the case may be.

(3) In relevant proceedings, where it is proved that a loan or a quasi-loan was made to the company or its holding company by the director of the first-mentioned company or the related person (whether the terms of the loan or quasi-loan are in writing, partially in writing or wholly oral) then, if—

(a) the case is one in which those terms are ambiguous with respect to whether, or the extent to which, the loan or quasi-loan bears interest, it shall be presumed, until the contrary is proved, that the loan or quasi-loan bears no interest,

(b) the case is one in which those terms are ambiguous with respect to whether, or the extent to which, the loan or quasi-loan is secured, it shall be presumed, until the contrary is proved, that the loan or quasi-loan is not secured, or

(c) in the event that the loan or quasi-loan is proved to be secured and the case is one in which those terms are ambiguous with respect to the priority that the security concerned is to have as against other indebtedness of the company, it shall be presumed, until the contrary is proved, that the loan or quasi-loan is subordinate to all other indebtedness of the company.

(4) If more than one of the cases referred to in *paragraphs (a)* to *(c)* of *subsection (3)* apply then each of the presumptions provided by the applicable paragraphs shall apply.

(5) The reference in *subsection (2)(b)* to the terms of a transaction or arrangement being ambiguous as to whether the transaction or arrangement constitutes a loan or quasi-loan or not (or as to whether it constitutes a quasi-loan as distinct from a loan) shall, if the terms of the transaction or arrangement are partially in writing, be deemed to include a reference to the following case.

(6) That case is one in which—

(a) the written terms of the transaction or arrangement do not specify what the nature of the transaction or arrangement is, and

(b) the nature of the transaction or arrangement is alleged to be specified by those of its terms that are not in writing.

(7) References in *subsection (3)* to the terms of a loan or quasi-loan being ambiguous with respect to a matter shall, if the terms of the loan or quasi-loan are partially in writing, be deemed to include references to the following case.

(8) That case is one in which—

(a) the written terms of the loan or quasi-loan do not make provision in respect of the matter concerned, and

(b) provision in respect of that matter is alleged to be made by those of the terms of the loan or quasi-loan that are not in writing.

Chapter 4

Substantive prohibitions or restrictions on loans to directors and other particular transactions involving conflict of interest

238 Substantial transactions in respect of non-cash assets and involving directors, etc.

(1) Subject to *subsections (4)* and *(5)*, a company (the "relevant company") shall not enter into an arrangement under which—

(a) a director of the relevant company or of its holding company, or a person connected with such a director, acquires or is to acquire, one or more non-cash assets of the requisite value from the relevant company, or

(b) the relevant company acquires or is to acquire, one or more non-cash assets of the requisite value from such a director or a person so connected,

unless the arrangement is first approved—

(i) by a resolution of the relevant company in general meeting, and

(ii) if the director or connected person is a director of its holding company or a person connected with such a director, by a resolution of the holding company in general meeting.

(2) For the purposes of this section a non-cash asset is of the requisite value if at the time the arrangement in question is entered into its value is not less than €5,000 but, subject to that, exceeds €65,000 or 10 per cent of the amount of the relevant company's relevant assets, and for those purposes the amount of a company's relevant assets is—

(a) except in a case falling within *paragraph (b)*, the value of its net assets determined by reference to the entity financial statements prepared under *section 290* and laid in accordance with *section 341* in respect of the last preceding financial year in respect of which such entity financial statements were so laid,

(b) where no entity financial statements have been prepared and laid under the foregoing sections before that time, the amount of its called-up share capital.

(3) An arrangement entered into by a company in contravention of this section and any transaction entered into in pursuance of the arrangement (whether by the company or any other person) shall be voidable at the instance of the company unless—

(a) restitution of any money or any other asset which is the subject-matter of the arrangement or transaction is no longer possible or the company has been indemnified in pursuance of *section 232* by any other person for the loss or damage suffered by it, or

(b) any rights acquired *bona fide* for value and without actual notice of the contravention by any person who is not a party to the arrangement or transaction would be affected by its avoidance, or

(c) the arrangement is affirmed by a resolution of the company in general meeting passed within a reasonable period of time after the date on which the arrangement is entered into and, if it is an arrangement for the transfer of an asset to or by a director of its holding company or a person who is connected with such a director, is affirmed by a resolution of the holding company in general meeting passed within a reasonable period of time after that date.

(4) *Subsection (1)* shall not apply in relation to any arrangement for the acquisition of a non-cash asset—

(a) if the non-cash asset in question is or is to be acquired—

(i) by a holding company from any of its wholly owned subsidiaries, or

(ii) from a holding company by any of its wholly owned subsidiaries, or

(iii) by one wholly owned subsidiary of a holding company from another wholly owned subsidiary of that holding company,

or

(b) if the arrangement is entered into by a company which is being wound up unless the winding up is a members' voluntary winding up, or

(c) if the arrangement involves the disposal of a company's assets by a receiver.

(5) *Subsection (1)(a)* shall not apply in relation to any arrangement under which a person acquires or is to acquire an asset from a company of which he or she is a member if the arrangement is made with that person in his or her character as such member.

(6) Without prejudice to *subsection (7)*, no approval is required to be given under this section by any body corporate unless it is a company formed and registered under this Act or an existing company.

(7) No approval is required to be given under this section by a wholly owned subsidiary of any body corporate.

(8) In this section—

(a) "non-cash asset" means any property or interest in property other than cash, and for this purpose "cash" includes foreign currency,

(b) any reference to the acquisition of a non-cash asset includes a reference to the creation or extinction of an estate or interest in, or a right over, any property and also a reference to the discharge of any person's liability other than a liability for a liquidated sum, and

(c) "net assets", in relation to a company, means the aggregate of the company's assets less the aggregate of its liabilities, and for this purpose "liabilities" includes—

(i) where the company prepares Companies Act entity financial statements, any provision for liabilities (within the meaning of [*paragraph 80* of *Schedule 3*, *paragraph 65* of *Schedule 3A* or *paragraph 39* of *Schedule 3B*, as the case may be][a]) that is made in those financial statements,

(ii) where the company prepares IFRS entity financial statements, any provision that is made in those financial statements.

Amendments

a Words substituted by C(A)A 2017, s 90(d) (previously: "*paragraph 82* of *Schedule 3*").

239 Prohibition of loans, etc., to directors and connected persons

(1) Except as provided by *section 240* and *sections 242* to *245*, a company shall not—

(a) make a loan or a quasi-loan to a director of the company or of its holding company or to a person connected with such a director,

(b) enter into a credit transaction as creditor for such a director or a person so connected,

(c) enter into a guarantee or provide any security in connection with a loan, quasi-loan or credit transaction made by any other person for such a director or a person so connected.

(2) A company shall not arrange for the assignment to it or the assumption by it of any rights, obligations or liabilities under a transaction which, if it had been entered into by the company, would have contravened *subsection (1)*, but, for the purposes of this Part, the transaction shall be treated as having been entered into on the date of the arrangement.

(3) A company shall not take part in any arrangement under which—

(a) another person enters into a transaction which, if it had been entered into by the company, would have contravened *subsection (1)* or *(2)*, and

(b) that other person, in pursuance of the arrangement, has obtained or is to obtain any benefit from the company or its holding company or a subsidiary of the company or its holding company.

240 Arrangements of certain value

(1) *Section 239* does not prohibit a company from entering into an arrangement with a director or a person connected with a director (whether, in either case, a director of the company or of its holding company) if—

(a) the value of the arrangement, or

(b) in a case where there are other arrangements entered into by the company with any director of the company, or any person connected with a director, the value of the arrangement and the total amount outstanding under those other arrangements,

is, or, as the case may be, is together, less than 10 per cent of the company's relevant assets.

(2) For the purposes of this section—

(a) a company enters an arrangement with a person if it—

(i) makes a loan or quasi-loan to or enters into a credit transaction as creditor for that person, or

(ii) enters into a guarantee or provides any security in connection with a loan, quasi-loan or credit transaction made for that person by any other person,

(b) the amount of a company's relevant assets shall be determined in accordance with *section 238(2)*; and

(c) there shall not be reckoned any arrangement entered into in accordance with the Summary Approval Procedure.

241 Reduction in amount of company's relevant assets

(1) This section applies to a company in respect of which the total amount outstanding under any arrangements referred to in *section 240* comes to exceed 10 per cent of the company's relevant assets for any reason but in particular because the value of those assets has fallen.

(2) The reference in *subsection (1)* to arrangements referred to in *section 240* does not include a reference to any arrangement or arrangements entered into in accordance with the Summary Approval Procedure.

(3) Where the directors of a company to which this section applies become aware, or ought reasonably to become aware, that there exists the situation referred to in *subsection (1)*, it shall be the duty of the company, its directors and any persons for whom the arrangements referred to in that subsection were made, to do the thing referred to in *subsection (4)* within the period specified in *subsection (5)*.

(4) The thing mentioned in *subsection (3)* is to amend the terms of the arrangements concerned so that the total amount outstanding under the arrangements again falls within the percentage limit referred to in *subsection (1)*.

(5) The period mentioned in *subsection (3)* is 2 months after the date that the directors become aware or ought reasonably to have become aware that the situation concerned referred to in *subsection (1)* exists.

(6) Where the terms of the arrangements referred to in *subsection (4)* are not amended within the period specified in *subsection (5)*, the arrangements shall be voidable at the instance of the company; but the same restrictions apply to this right of the company to avoid as are contained in *paragraphs (a)* and *(b)* of *section 246* on the right to avoid under that section.

242 Availability of Summary Approval Procedure to permit loans, etc.

Section 239 does not prohibit a company from—

(a) making a loan or quasi-loan,

(b) entering into a credit transaction, or

(c) entering into a guarantee or providing any security,

of the kind described in *subsection (1)* of that section if the Summary Approval Procedure is followed in respect of the doing of the thing referred to in *paragraph (a)*, *(b)* or *(c)*, as the case may be.

243 Intra-group transactions

(1) *Section 239* does not prohibit a company from—

(a) making a loan or quasi-loan to any body corporate which is its holding company, subsidiary or a subsidiary of its holding company, or

(b) entering into a guarantee or providing any security in connection with a loan or quasi-loan made by any person to any body corporate which is its holding company, subsidiary or a subsidiary of its holding company.

(2) *Section 239* does not prohibit a company from—

(a) entering into a credit transaction as creditor for any body corporate which is its holding company, subsidiary or a subsidiary of its holding company, or

(b) entering into a guarantee or providing any security in connection with any credit transaction made by any other person for any body corporate which is its holding company, subsidiary or a subsidiary of its holding company.

244 Directors' expenses

(1) *Section 239* does not prohibit a company from doing anything—

(a) to provide any of its directors with funds to meet vouched expenditure properly incurred or to be incurred by him or her—

(i) for the purposes of the company, or

(ii) for the purpose of enabling him or her properly to perform his or her duties as an officer of the company,

or

(b) to enable any of its directors to avoid incurring such expenditure.

(2) Where a company enters into any transaction that is permitted by *subsection (1)*, any liability falling on any person arising from any such transaction shall be discharged by him or her within 6 months after the date on which it was incurred.

(3) A person who contravenes *subsection (2)* shall be guilty of a category 4 offence.

245 Business transactions

(1) *Section 239* does not prohibit a company from—

(a) making a loan or quasi-loan,

(b) entering into a credit transaction, or

(c) entering into a guarantee or providing any security,

of the kind described in that section if the following 2 conditions are satisfied.

(2) Those conditions are—

(a) the company enters into the transaction concerned in the ordinary course of its business, and

(b) the value of the transaction is not greater, and the terms on which it is entered into are no more favourable, in respect of the person for whom the transaction is made, than that or those which—

(i) the company ordinarily offers, or

(ii) it is not unreasonable to expect the company to have offered,

to or in respect of a person of the same financial standing as that person but unconnected with the company.

246 Transaction or arrangement in breach of *section 239* voidable at instance of company

If a company enters into a transaction or arrangement in contravention of *section 239* the transaction or arrangement shall be voidable at the instance of the company unless—

(a) restitution of any money or any other asset which is the subject matter of the arrangement or transaction is no longer possible, or the company has been indemnified in pursuance of *section 232* for the loss or damage suffered by it, or

(b) any rights acquired *bona fide* for value and without actual notice of the contravention by any person other than the person for whom the transaction or arrangement was made would be affected by its avoidance.

247 Personal liability for company debts in certain cases

(1) If—

(a) a company is being wound up and is unable to pay its debts, and

(b) the court considers that any arrangement of a kind described in *section 240(2)(a)* has contributed materially to the company's inability to pay its debts or has substantially impeded the orderly winding up of it,

the court, on the application of the liquidator or any creditor or contributory of the company, may, if it thinks it proper to do so, make the following declaration.

(2) That declaration is a declaration that any person for whose benefit the arrangement was made shall be personally liable, without any limitation of liability, for all or such part as may be specified by the court, of the debts and other liabilities of the company.

(3) In deciding whether to make a declaration under this section, the court shall have particular regard to whether and to what extent, any outstanding liabilities arising under any arrangement referred to in *subsection (1)* were discharged before the commencement of the winding up.

(4) In deciding the extent of any personal liability under this section, the court shall have particular regard to the extent to which the arrangement in question contributed materially to the company's inability to pay its debts or substantially impeded the orderly winding up of the company.

248 Offence for contravention of *section 239*

If a company enters into a transaction or arrangement that contravenes *section 239*, any officer of it who is in default shall be guilty of a category 2 offence.

249 Contracts of employment of directors — control by members over guaranteed periods of employment

(1) In this section "relevant term" means a term by which a director's employment with the company of which he or she is a director or, where he or she is the director of a holding company, his or her employment by any company comprised in the group, is to

continue or may be continued, otherwise than at the instance of the company, for a period exceeding 5 years during which the employment—

(a) cannot be terminated by the company by the giving of notice, or

(b) can be so terminated only in specified circumstances.

(2) References in *subsection (1)* to employment being continued (or its potential to be continued) are references to its being continued (or its potential to be continued) whether under the original agreement concerned or under a new agreement entered into in pursuance of the original agreement concerned.

(3) A company shall not incorporate in any agreement a relevant term unless the term is first approved by a resolution of the company in general meeting and, in the case of a director of a holding company, by a resolution of that company in general meeting.

(4) A resolution of a company approving a relevant term shall not be passed at a general meeting of the company unless a written memorandum, setting out the proposed agreement incorporating the term, is available for inspection by members of the company both—

(a) at the registered office of the company for not less than the period of 15 days ending before the date of the meeting, and

(b) at the meeting itself.

(5) If it is proposed to use the means under *section 193* or *194*, in lieu of passing a resolution at a general meeting of the company, to approve a relevant term those means shall not be used unless a written memorandum setting out the proposed agreement incorporating the relevant term has been circulated to the members of the company (being those entitled to attend and vote at a general meeting of the company) with the proposal for the written resolution.

(6) A term incorporated in an agreement in contravention of this section shall, to the extent that it contravenes this section, be void and the agreement shall be deemed to contain a term entitling the company to terminate it at any time by the giving of reasonable notice.

(7) No approval is required to be given under this section by any body corporate unless it is a company formed and registered under this Act, an existing company or a wholly owned subsidiary of a body corporate.

(8) For the purposes of this section—

"employment" includes employment under a contract for services;

"group", in relation to a director of a holding company, means the group which consists of that company and its subsidiaries.

250 Anti-avoidance provision — section 249

(1) In any case where—

(a) a person is or is to be employed with a company under an agreement which cannot be terminated by the company by the giving of notice or can be so terminated only in specified circumstances, and

(b) more than 6 months before the expiration of the period for which he or she is or is to be so employed, the company enters into a further agreement (otherwise than in pursuance of a right conferred by or by virtue of the original agreement on the other party to it) under which he or she is to be employed with the company, or where he or she is a director of a holding company, within the group,

the definition of "relevant term" in *section 249* shall apply as if to the period for which the person is to be employed under that further agreement there were added a further period equal to the unexpired period of the original agreement.

(2) Where *subsection (1)* has effect in relation to the definition of "relevant term" in *section 249*, *subsection (6)* of that section has effect as if there were substituted "the agreement and the original agreement referred to in *section 250(1)* shall each be deemed to contain a term entitling the company to terminate it at any time by the giving of reasonable notice" for "the agreement shall be deemed to contain a term entitling the company to terminate it at any time by the giving of reasonable notice".

(3) For the purposes of this section "employment" and "group" have the same meaning as they have for the purposes of *section 249*.

251 Approval of company necessary for payment by it to director or directors' dependants for loss of office

(1) It shall not be lawful for a company to make to any director of the company any payment by way of compensation for loss of office or as consideration for or in connection with his or her retirement from office, unless the following conditions are first satisfied.

(2) Those conditions are—

(a) particulars relating to the proposed payment (including the amount of it) are disclosed to the members of the company, and

(b) the proposal is approved by resolution of the company in general meeting.

(3) Without prejudice to the exceptions provided for by *section 254(5)*, a payment made *bona fide* in discharge of an existing legal obligation does not fall within this section.

252 Approval of company necessary for payment to director of compensation in connection with transfer of property

(1) It shall not be lawful in connection with the transfer of the whole or any part of the undertaking or property of a company for any payment to be made to any director of the company by way of compensation for loss of office or as consideration for or in connection with his or her retirement from office, unless the following conditions are first satisfied.

(2) Those conditions are—

(a) particulars relating to the proposed payment (including the amount of it) are disclosed to the members of the company, and

(b) the proposal is approved by resolution of the company in general meeting.

(3) Where a payment which is not lawful under *subsection (1)* is made to a director of a company the amount received shall be deemed to have been received by him or her in trust for the company.

(4) Without prejudice to the exceptions provided for by *section 254(5)*, a payment made *bona fide* in discharge of an existing legal obligation does not fall within this section.

253 Duty of director to disclose to company payments to be made to him or her in connection with transfer of shares in company

(1) The following duty arises on the part of a director where, in connection with the transfer to any persons of all or any of the shares in a company being a transfer resulting from:

(a) an offer made to the general body of shareholders, or

(b) an offer made by or on behalf of some other body corporate with a view to the company becoming its subsidiary or a subsidiary of its holding company, or

(c) an offer made by or on behalf of an individual with a view to his or her obtaining the right to exercise or control the exercise of not less than one-third of the voting power at any general meeting of the company, or

(d) any other offer which is conditional on acceptance to a given extent,

a payment is to be made to that director of the company by way of compensation for loss of office or as a consideration for or in connection with his or her retirement from office.

(2) That duty on the part of that director is to take all reasonable steps to secure that particulars of the proposed payment (including the amount of it) are included in or sent with any notice of the offer made for their shares which is given to any shareholders.

(3) Without prejudice to the exceptions provided for by *section 254(5)*, a payment to be made, or that is made, *bona fide* in discharge of an existing legal obligation does not fall within this section.

(4) If—

(a) any such director fails to take reasonable steps as mentioned in *subsection (2)*, or

(b) any person who has been properly required by any such director to include the particulars specified in that subsection in, or send them with, any such notice so mentioned fails to do so,

he or she shall be guilty of a category 3 offence.

(5) Unless—

(a) the requirements of *subsections (1)* and *(2)* are complied with in relation to any such payment as is mentioned in *subsection (1)*, and

(b) the making of the proposed payment is, before the transfer of any shares in pursuance of the offer, approved by a meeting summoned for the purpose of the holders of the shares to which the offer relates and of other holders of shares of the same class as any of those shares,

any sum received by the director on account of the payment shall be deemed to have been received by him or her in trust for any persons who have sold their shares as a result of the offer made and the expenses incurred by him or her in distributing that sum amongst those persons shall be borne by him or her and not retained out of that sum.

(6) Where the shareholders referred to in *paragraph (b)* of *subsection (5)* are not all the members of the company and no provision is made by the constitution for summoning or regulating such a meeting as is mentioned in that paragraph, the provisions of—

(a) this Part and the rest of *Parts 1* to *14*, and

(b) the company's constitution,

relating to general meetings of the company shall, for that purpose, apply to the meeting either without modification or with such modifications as the Director of Corporate Enforcement, on the application of any person concerned, may direct for the purpose of adapting them to the circumstances of the meeting.

(7) If at a meeting summoned for the purpose of approving any payment as required by *paragraph (b)* of *subsection (5)*, a quorum is not present and after the meeting has been adjourned to a later date a quorum is again not present, the payment shall be deemed for the purposes of that subsection to have been approved.

254 "Existing legal obligation"— definition and other provisions in relation to *sections 251* to *253*

(1) "Existing legal obligation" for the purposes of—

(a) *section 251(3)*, means an obligation of the company concerned, or any body corporate associated with it, that was not entered into in connection with, or in consequence of, the event giving rise to the payment for loss of office in question,

(b) *sections 252(4)* and *253(3)*, means an obligation of the person making, or proposing to make, the payment that was not entered into for the purposes of, in connection with or in consequence of, the transfer in question.

(2) In the case of a payment to which both *sections 251* and *252* apply, or to which both *sections 251* and *253* apply, *paragraph (a)* of *subsection (1)* and not *paragraph (b)* of it shall have effect.

(3) Where in proceedings for the recovery of any payment which it is alleged is recoverable as having, by virtue of—

(a) *subsections (1)* and *(3)* of *section 252*, or

(b) *subsections (1)*, *(2)* and *(5)* of *section 253*,

been received by any person in trust, it is shown that—

(i) the payment was made in pursuance of any arrangement entered into as part of the agreement for the transfer in question or within one year before or 2 years after the date of that agreement or the offer leading to it, and

(ii) the company or any person to whom the transfer was made was privy to that arrangement,

the payment shall be deemed, except in so far as the contrary is shown, to be one to which the subsections concerned apply.

(4) If, in connection with any such transfer as is mentioned in *section 252* or *253*—

(a) the price to be paid to a director of the company for any shares in the company held by him or her is in excess of the price which could at the time have been obtained by other holders of the like shares, or

(b) any valuable consideration is given to any such director,

the excess or the money value of the consideration, as the case may be, shall, for the purposes of that section, be deemed to have been a payment made to him or her by way of compensation for loss of office or as consideration for or in connection with his or her retirement from office.

(5) References in *sections 251* to *253* to payments to any director of a company by way of compensation for loss of office or as consideration for or in connection with his or her retirement from office include references to payments to him or her by way of compensation for—

(a) loss of office as director of the company,

(b) the loss, while director of the company, or on or in connection with his or her ceasing to be a director of the company, of any other office in connection with the management of the company's affairs or of any office as director or otherwise in connection with the management of the affairs of any subsidiary,

but do not include references to any *bona fide* payment by way of—

(i) damages for breach of contract, or

(ii) pension in respect of past services,

and, for the purposes of this subsection, "pension" includes any superannuation allowance, superannuation gratuity or similar payment.

(6) Nothing in *section 251* or *252* shall be taken to prejudice—

(a) the operation of any rule of law requiring disclosure to be made with respect to any such payments as are mentioned in that section or with respect to any other like payments made or to be made to the directors of a company, or

(b) the operation of any rule of law or enactment in relation to the accountability (if any) of any director for any such payment received by him or her.

(7) References in *sections 251* to *253* and this section to a director include references to a past director.

(8) For the purposes of *subsection (1)(a)* a body corporate is associated with a company if one is the subsidiary of the other or both are subsidiaries of the same body corporate.

255 Contracts with sole members

(1) Subject to *subsection (2)*, where a single-member company enters into a contract with the sole member of the company and the sole member also represents the company

in the transaction, whether as a director or otherwise, the single-member company shall, unless the contract is in writing, ensure that the terms of the contract are forthwith set out in a written memorandum or are recorded in the minutes of the first meeting of the directors of the company following the making of the contract.

(2) *Subsection (1)* shall not apply to contracts entered into in the ordinary course of the company's business.

(3) If a company fails to comply with *subsection (1)*, the company and any officer of it who is in default shall be guilty of a category 3 offence.

(4) Subject to *subsection (5)*, nothing in this section shall be taken to prejudice the operation of any other enactment (including a provision of this Act) or rule of law applying to contracts between a company and a director of that company.

(5) Failure to comply with *subsection (1)* with respect to a contract shall not affect the validity of that contract.

Chapter 5
Disclosure of interests in shares and debentures

256 Interpretation generally (*Chapter 5*)

(1) In this Chapter—

(a) "body corporate of the same group" means, in relation to a company, a body corporate which belongs to the same group of companies as that company belongs to;

(b) "child" does not include a person who has attained the age of majority; and

(c) a reference to a child of a director or secretary shall be deemed to include a reference to a child of the director's civil partner or (as the case may be) the secretary's civil partner who is ordinarily resident with (as the case may be)—

(i) the director and the civil partner, or

(ii) the secretary and the civil partner.

(2) For the avoidance of doubt, the use of the words "aggregate interest" in any provision of this Chapter, with reference to the interest of a director or secretary and the spouse (or civil partner) and children of the director or secretary in shares or debentures, does not operate to limit the provision's effect (and, accordingly, does not prevent the director or secretary having the benefit of the provision) in either the situation where—

(a) the director or secretary alone has an interest in shares or debentures reckonable for the purposes of the provision, or

(b) one or more, but not all, of any foregoing class of persons has or have alone such a reckonable interest.

257 "Disclosable interest" — meaning of that term

(1) Subject to *section 260*, in this Chapter "disclosable interest" means, in relation to shares or debentures, any interest of any kind whatsoever in shares in, or debentures of, a body corporate.

(2) For that purpose there shall be disregarded any restraints or restrictions to which the exercise of any right attached to the interest is or may be subject.

(3) It is also immaterial—

(a) whether or not the interest is held alone, jointly or in common with any other person, or

(b) whether the shares or debentures are identifiable or not.

258 Circumstances in which person is to be regarded as having disclosable interest in shares or debentures

(1) Without prejudice to the other circumstances in which a person may have such an interest, a person shall, for the purposes of this Chapter, be regarded as having a disclosable interest in shares or debentures if—

(a) the person enters into a contract for the purchase by him or her of them (whether for cash or other consideration),

(b) the person is the registered holder or joint holder of them,

(c) not being the registered holder, the person is entitled to exercise any right conferred by the holding of those shares or debentures or is entitled to control the exercise of any such right,

(d) a body corporate is interested in them and—

(i) that body corporate or its directors are accustomed to act in accordance with the person's directions or instructions, or

(ii) the person is entitled to exercise or control the exercise of one third or more of the voting power at general meetings of that body corporate,

(e) otherwise than by virtue of having an interest under a trust—

(i) the person has a right to call for delivery of the shares or debentures to himself or herself or to his or her order, or

(ii) the person has a right to acquire an interest in shares or debentures, or is under an obligation to take an interest in shares or debentures,

whether in any case the right or obligation is conditional or absolute,

(f) the person is a beneficiary of a trust and—

(i) the property held on trust for that beneficiary includes any interest in shares or debentures, and

(ii) that person, apart from this paragraph, does not have an interest in the shares or debentures.

(2) For the purpose of *subsection (1)(c)*, a person shall be taken to be entitled to exercise or control the exercise of any right conferred by the holding of shares or debentures if he or she—

(a) has a right (whether subject to conditions or not), the exercise of which would make him or her so entitled, or

(b) is under an obligation (whether so subject or not), the fulfilment of which would make him or her so entitled.

(3) For the purpose of *subsection (1)(d)*—

(a) "voting power" does not include any power to vote which arises only in specified circumstances,

(b) where a person is entitled to exercise or control the exercise of one third or more of the voting power at general meetings of a body corporate and that body corporate is entitled to exercise or control the exercise of any of the voting power at general meetings of another body corporate (the "relevant voting power"), then, for the purposes of that provision, the relevant voting power shall be taken to be exercisable by that person.

259 Circumstances in which person shall be regarded as having ceased to have disclosable interest

A person shall, amongst other circumstances, be taken to have ceased to have a disclosable interest in shares or debentures for the purposes of this Chapter upon—

(a) delivery to another person's order of the shares or debentures in fulfilment of a contract for the purchase of them by that other person or in satisfaction of a right of his or her to call for delivery of them, or

(b) failure by another person to deliver the shares or debentures in accordance with the terms of a contract or pursuant to a right to call for delivery of them, or

(c) the lapse of that person's right to call for delivery of the shares or debentures.

260 Interests that are not disclosable interests for the purposes of this Chapter

The following interests shall not constitute disclosable interests for the purposes of this Chapter—

(a) where property is held on trust and an interest in shares or debentures is comprised in that property—

(i) an interest in reversion or remainder,

(ii) an interest of a bare trustee, or

(iii) any discretionary interest,

(b) an interest of a person subsisting by virtue of—

(i) his or her holding—

(I) units in an authorised unit trust scheme within the meaning of the Unit Trusts Act 1990,

(II) units in an undertaking for collective investment in transferable securities within the meaning of the European Communities (Undertakings for Collective Investment in Transferable Securities) Regulations 2011 (S.I. No. 352 of 2011), or

(III) shares in an investment company within the meaning of *Part 24*,

or

(ii) a scheme made under section 46 of the Charities Act 1961,

(c) an interest for the life of himself or herself or of another person under a settlement in the case of which the property comprised in the settlement consists of or includes shares or debentures, and—

(i) the settlement is irrevocable, and

(ii) the settlor (within the meaning of section 10 of the Taxes Consolidation Act 1997) has no interest in any income arising under, or property comprised in, the settlement,

(d) an interest in shares or debentures held by a member of an authorised market operator carrying on business as a stock broker which is held by way of security only for the purposes of a transaction entered into by the person or other body concerned in the ordinary course of business of such person or other body,

(e) any power or discretion vested in a person by virtue only of such person having been duly appointed as or acting as—

(i) an attorney of a person with an interest in shares or debentures,

(ii) a proxy of a member of, or holder of debentures in, a company or a representative of a body corporate which is a member of the holder of debentures of a company,

(f) any interest in shares in, or debentures of, a body corporate where the aggregate interest of the director or secretary and spouse (or civil partner) and children of such director or secretary is in—

(i) shares representing 1 per cent or less, in nominal value, of the body corporate's issued share capital of a class carrying rights to vote in all circumstances at general meetings of the body corporate (provided that the temporary suspension of voting rights in respect of shares comprised in issued share capital of a body corporate of any such class shall be disregarded), or

(ii) shares or debentures not carrying the right to vote at general meetings of the body corporate, save a right to vote which arises only in specified circumstances,

(g) as regards circumstances in which an offer is made in relation to shares in a body corporate, being an offer—

(i) to which the Irish Takeover Panel Act 1997 or the European Communities (Takeover Bids (Directive 2004/25/EC)) Regulations 2006 (S.I. No. 255 of 2006) applies or apply, and

(ii) which is conditional on acceptance to a given extent,

an interest in those shares that would have arisen but for the offer not being accepted to the required extent,

(h) such interests, or interests of such a class, as may be prescribed for the purposes of this subsection.

261 Duty to notify disclosable interests — first of the 5 cases in which duty arises — interests held at commencement of Chapter

(1) Subject to *subsection (3)* and *section 264*, a person who, at the commencement of this Chapter—

(a) is a director or secretary of a company, and

(b) is aware of—

(i) the person's having, or

(ii) the person's spouse or civil partner or a child of the person's having,

a disclosable interest in shares in, or debentures of, that company (the "relevant company") or a body corporate of the same group,

has the following duty.

(2) That duty is to notify the relevant company in writing of the particulars specified in *section 265* of the disclosable interest and the fact of its being so held.

(3) That duty does not arise if—

(a) the nature of the disclosable interest concerned is such as to constitute an interest of the kind specified in section 54 of the Act of 1990, and

(b) the relevant company has—

(i) before the commencement of this section, been notified, in accordance with Part IV of the Act of 1990, of the particulars required by that Part in relation to that interest, or

(ii) received, not later than 5 days after the commencement of this section, such particulars in relation to that interest by way of such a notification (being a notification sent not later than that commencement).

262 Second and third cases in which duty to notify arises — interests acquired or ceasing to be held

(1) Subject to *section 264*, a person who—

(a) is a director or secretary of a company, and

(b) becomes aware of—

(i) the person's having acquired or having ceased to have, or

(ii) the person's spouse or civil partner, or a child of the person's, having acquired or having ceased to have, a disclosable interest in shares in, or debentures of, that company (the "relevant company") or any body corporate of the same group,

has the following duty.

(2) That duty is to notify the relevant company in writing of the particulars specified in *section 265* of the disclosable interest and the fact of its being so acquired or, as the case may be, of its so ceasing to be held.

(3) Subject to *section 264*, a person who—

(a) becomes aware of—

(i) the person's having, or

(ii) the person's spouse or civil partner or a child of the person's having,

a disclosable interest in shares in, or debentures of, a company (the "relevant company") or a body corporate of the same group, and

(b) becomes a director or secretary of the relevant company (not being the secretary of the relevant company at the time of so becoming a director or not being a director at the time of so becoming the secretary of the relevant company),

has the following duty.

(4) That duty is to notify the relevant company in writing of the particulars specified in *section 265* of the disclosable interest and the fact of its being so held.

263 Fourth and fifth cases in which duty to notify arises — grant or assignment of subscription rights, etc.

(1) Subject to *section 264*, a director or secretary of a company (the "relevant company") who—

(a) (i) is granted by another body corporate of the same group a right to subscribe for shares in, or debentures of, that other body corporate, or

(ii) exercises such a right so granted,

or

(b) becomes aware of a spouse or civil partner of the director's or secretary's or a child of the director's or secretary's—

(i) having been granted by such a body corporate such a right of subscription, or

(ii) having exercised such a right so granted,

has, subject to *subsection (3)* and *(5)*, the following duty.

(2) That duty is to notify the relevant company in writing of—

(a) the grant of the right of subscription, or the exercise of it, referred to in *paragraph (a)* or *(b)* of the preceding subsection (or, as the case may be, both the things referred to in those paragraphs),

(b) the number or amount, and class, of shares or debentures involved and the consideration payable, and

(c) if *section 265(6)* applies, the address there mentioned.

(3) If a director or secretary, at the time of the thing referred to in *subsection (1)(a)* being done, is not aware of the fact of the thing being done (the "relevant fact") by reason of—

(a) in the case of the thing referred to in *subsection (1)(a)(i)*, the grantor of the right not informing the director or secretary immediately of the grant,

(b) in the case of the thing referred to in *subsection (1)(a)(ii)*, the thing being done on behalf of the director or secretary by another person pursuant to an authority conferred on the person by the director or secretary, or

(c) in either such case, other exceptional circumstances,

then the duty under *subsection (2)*, with respect to that thing, only arises on the director or secretary becoming aware of the relevant fact.

(4) However, in any proceedings (civil or criminal) it shall be presumed, unless the contrary is shown, that none of the circumstances referred to in *subsection (3)* applies.

(5) If the aggregate interest of the director or secretary and spouse (or civil partner) and children of such director or secretary in shares in the body corporate concerned (both before and after the occurrence of the event or events referred to in *subsection (2)(a)*) is such as to fall within *section 260(f)(i)*, then the duty of notification under *subsection (2)* does not arise.

(6) Subject to *section 264*, a director or secretary of a company (the "relevant company") who—

(a) enters into a contract to sell shares in, or debentures of, the relevant company or any body corporate of the same group,

(b) assigns a right granted to him or her by the relevant company or a body corporate of the same group to subscribe for shares in, or debentures of, the relevant company or such body corporate, or

(c) becomes aware of a spouse or civil partner of the director's or secretary's or a child of the director's or secretary's—

(i) having entered into a contract to sell such shares or debentures, or

(ii) having assigned a right that has been granted to the spouse, civil partner or child by the relevant company or such body corporate to subscribe for shares in, or debentures of, the relevant company or such body corporate,

has, subject to *subsection (8)* and *(10)*, the following duty.

(7) That duty is to notify the relevant company in writing of—

(a) the entering into of the contract or the assigning of the right referred to in *paragraph (a)*, *(b)* or *(c)* of the preceding subsection (or, as the case may be, the doing of 2 or more of the things referred to in those paragraphs),

(b) the number or amount, and class, of shares or debentures involved and the consideration payable, and

(c) if *section 265(6)* applies, the address there mentioned.

(8) If a director or secretary, at the time of the thing referred to in *subsection (6)(a)* or *(b)* being done, is not aware of the fact of the thing being done (the "relevant fact") by reason of—

(a) the thing being done on behalf of the director or secretary by another person pursuant to an authority conferred on the person by the director or secretary, or

(b) other exceptional circumstances,

then the duty under *subsection (7)*, with respect to that thing, only arises on the director or secretary becoming aware of the relevant fact.

(9) However, in any proceedings (civil or criminal) it shall be presumed, unless the contrary is shown, that none of the circumstances referred to in *subsection (8)* applies.

(10) If the aggregate interest of the director or secretary and spouse (or civil partner) and children of such director or secretary in shares in the body corporate concerned (before the occurrence of the event or events referred to in *subsection (7)(a)*) is such as to fall within *section 260(f)(i)*, then the duty of notification under *subsection (7)* does not arise.

264 Application of *sections 261* to *263* and exceptions to them

(1) With respect to the application of *sections 261* to *263* (by virtue of *sections 221* and *222*) to shadow directors and *de facto* directors, the making of a notification by a person under *section 261*, *262* or *263* shall not, in itself, be proof that the person making the notification is a shadow director or *de facto* director.

(2) Nothing in *sections 261* to *263* shall operate so as to impose an obligation with respect to shares in a body corporate which is the wholly owned subsidiary of another body corporate.

(3) Nothing in *sections 261* to *263* shall operate to impose an obligation on a director or secretary of a company who is granted an option to subscribe for shares in, or debentures of, that company to make any notification to that company in respect of such grant.

265 Mode of notification by directors and secretaries under this Chapter

(1) In relation to the acquisition or disposal by a director or secretary of a company of shares or debentures the means specified in *subsection (2)* shall, if the director or secretary opts to use them, constitute a sufficient notification in writing to the company, for the purposes of this Chapter, of the fact of their acquisition or disposal and the particulars of the disclosable interest.

(2) Those means are the delivery, within 30 days after the date of the instrument, to the company of an instrument of transfer in respect of the shares or debentures, being an instrument that identifies—

(a) the director or secretary by name,

(b) the shares or debentures in question,

(c) the purchase or sale price therefor, and

(d) if *subsection (6)* applies, the address there mentioned.

(3) In any case not falling within *subsection (1)* or where the director or secretary opts not to use the foregoing means in a case falling within *subsection (1)*, the following means shall be used to notify in writing, for the purpose of *section 261* or *262*, the fact of a disclosable interest being held or of its being acquired or being ceased to be held (as the case may be) and the particulars thereof.

(4) Those means are the delivery to the company concerned (within 8 days after the date of the event giving rise to the duty to make the notification) of a statement in writing by or on behalf of the director or secretary containing the following particulars:

(a) a statement that the director or secretary, or his or her spouse or civil partner or a child of the director or secretary (as the case may be) has, has acquired or has ceased to have (as the case may be) a disclosable interest in shares in, or debentures of, the company or a body corporate of the same group,

(b) the number of shares or debentures and their class, and a statement of the names of the registered holders of the shares or debentures,

(c) in the case of an acquisition or disposal of shares or debentures, the consideration payable therefor, and

(d) if *subsection (6)* applies, the address there mentioned.

(5) The notification referred to in *section 263(2)* or *(7)* shall be made to the company within 5 days after the date of the event giving rise to the duty to make the notification; in a case where the circumstances referred to in *subsection (3)* or *(8)* of *section 263* apply, the date of the event giving rise to the duty to make the notification is the date on which the director or secretary becomes aware of the relevant fact referred to in that *subsection (3)* or *(8)*.

(6) A shadow director or *de facto* director shall, in any notification made by him or her under this Chapter, specify his or her address and this applies whether the notification is in respect of himself or herself or a spouse or civil partner of such director or a child of such director.

266 Enforcement of notification obligation

(1) Where a person authorises any other person (the "agent") to acquire or dispose of, on his or her behalf, interests in shares in, or debentures of, a company, the person shall secure that the agent notifies him or her immediately of acquisitions or disposals of interests in such shares or debentures effected by the agent which will or may give rise to any duty on the person's part to make a notification under this Chapter with respect to his or her interest in those shares or debentures.

(2) Subject to the subsequent provisions of this section, where a person fails to fulfil, within the period specified by this Chapter in that behalf, a duty to which he or she is, by virtue of *section 261*, *262* or *263*, subject, no right or interest of any kind

whatsoever in respect of the shares or debentures concerned shall be enforceable by him or her, whether directly or indirectly, by action or legal proceeding.

(3) Where any right or interest is restricted under *subsection* (2)—

(a) any person in default as is mentioned in that subsection or any other person affected by such restriction may apply to the court for relief against a disability imposed by or arising out of that subsection,

(b) the court, on being satisfied that the default was accidental or due to inadvertence or some other sufficient cause or that on other grounds it is just and equitable to grant relief, may grant such relief either generally or as respects any particular right or interest, on such terms and conditions as it sees fit,

(c) where an applicant for relief under this subsection is a person referred to in *subsection (2)*, the court may not grant such relief if it appears that the default has arisen as a result of any deliberate act or omission on the part of the applicant.

(4) Where a director or secretary is in default as mentioned in *subsection (2)*, then, notwithstanding that default, that subsection shall not apply in respect of the shares or debentures concerned if the following condition is satisfied.

(5) That condition is that the identity of the director or secretary and his or her holding, acquisition and disposal (as the case may be) of the shares or debentures in question and the consideration paid or payable therefor has, from not later than 30 days after the date the duty arose, been apparent on the face of all or any of the following registers or documents of the company concerned (including some or all of them when consulted together), namely—

(a) the register of members,

(b) the register of directors and secretaries,

(c) the register of interests under *section 267*,

(d) documents made available by that company with those registers.

(6) If a company in general meeting passes a special resolution providing that the following protection shall apply in favour of a third party having the following dealing in relation to shares in, or debentures of, the company specified in the resolution then, upon production of a copy of such resolution by the secretary of the company to the third party, a third party having any dealing with the company or the registered holder of the shares or debentures in question shall be entitled to presume, without further enquiry, that—

(a) the provisions of this Chapter have been complied with in relation to the shares or debentures, and

(b) the registered holder is entitled to deal with the shares or debentures registered in his or her name.

(7) *Subsection (2)* shall not apply to a duty relating to a person ceasing to be interested in shares in, or debentures of, a company.

(8) A person who fails without reasonable excuse to comply with *subsection (1)* shall be guilty of a category 3 offence.

(9) A person who fails to fulfil, within the period specified in this Chapter in that behalf, a duty to which he or she is, by virtue of *section 261*, *262* or *263*, subject shall be guilty of a category 3 offence.

(10) Where before the commencement of this section, default has been made in complying with section 53 of the Act of 1990 in relation to shares in, or debentures of, a company, the board of directors of the company, at any time before the expiry of 18 months after that commencement, may, if authorised by an ordinary resolution of the company in that behalf, resolve that any restrictions that continue to operate (by virtue of section 58(3) of the Act of 1990) in relation to the shares or debentures shall, on and from the time of their so resolving, cease to operate if—

(a) the person upon whom the duty to make the notification concerned under that section 53 fell presents evidence (by way of affidavit or such other satisfactory means as the board may specify) to the board that the default concerned was inadvertent, and

(b) the board is satisfied from that evidence that the default was inadvertent,

and, where the board so resolves, such restrictions shall cease to operate accordingly.

267 Register of interests: contents and entries

(1) A company shall keep a register of interests (the "register of interests") for the purposes of this Chapter.

(2) *Sections 215* to *217* (rights of inspection, requests for copies, etc.) apply to the register of interests.

(3) Whenever the company receives information from a director or secretary of the company in consequence of the fulfilment of a duty to which he or she is, by virtue of *section 261*, *262* or *263*, subject, the company shall within 3 days after the date of such receipt enter in the register of interests that information and the date of the entry.

(4) A company shall, whenever it grants to a director or secretary of the company a right to subscribe for shares in, or debentures of, the company, enter in the register of interests against his or her name—

(a) the date on which the right is granted,

(b) the period during which or time at which it is exercisable,

(c) the consideration for the grant (or, if it be the case that there is no consideration, that fact), and

(d) the description of shares or debentures involved and the number or amount thereof, and the price to be paid therefor.

(5) Whenever such a right as is mentioned in *subsection (4)* is exercised by a director or secretary, the company shall enter in the register of interests against his or her name—

(a) that fact (identifying the right),

(b) the number or amount of shares or debentures in respect of which it is exercised, and

(c) if it be the case that they were registered in his or her name, that fact, and if not, the name or names of the person or persons in whose name or names they were registered, together (if they were registered in the names of 2 persons or more) with the number or amount thereof registered in the name of each of them.

(6) The register of interests shall be so made up that the entries in it against the several names inscribed in it appear in chronological order.

(7) The nature and extent of an interest recorded in the register of interests of a director or secretary in any shares or debentures shall, if he or she so requires, be recorded in that register.

(8) A company shall not, by virtue of anything done for the purposes of this section, be affected with notice of, or put upon inquiry as to, the rights of any person in relation to any shares or debentures.

(9) If default is made by a company in complying with *subsection (1)* or any of *subsections (3)* to *(7)*, the company and any officer of it who is in default shall be guilty of a category 3 offence.

268 Supplemental provisions in relation to *section 267*

(1) Unless the register under *section 267* is in such a form as to constitute in itself an index, the company shall keep an index of the names entered in it which shall—

(a) in respect of each name, contain a sufficient indication to enable the information inscribed against it to be readily found, and

(b) be kept at the same place as the register,

and the company shall, within 14 days after the date on which a name is entered in the register, make any necessary alteration in the index.

(2) In addition to the requirements of *section 216*, the register shall be, and remain, open and accessible to any person attending an annual general meeting of the company concerned at least one quarter hour before the appointed time for the commencement of the meeting and during the continuance of the meeting.

(3) If default is made by a company in complying with *subsection (1)* or *(2)*, the company and any officer of it who is in default shall be guilty of a category 3 offence.

269 Register of interests: removal of entries from it

(1) A company may remove an entry against a person's name from the register required to be kept by it under *section 267* (the "register") if more than 6 years have elapsed after the date of the entry being made, and either—

(a) that entry recorded the fact that the person in question has ceased to have an interest notifiable under this Chapter in shares in, or debentures of, the company, or

(b) it has been superseded by a later entry made under *section 267* against the same person's name, and, in a case falling within *paragraph (a)*, the company may also remove that person's name from the register.

(2) Where a company removes a name from the register pursuant to *subsection (1)*, the company shall, within 14 days after the date of that removal, make any necessary alterations in any associated index.

(3) Entries in the register shall not be deleted except in accordance with *subsections (1)* and *(2)*.

(4) If an entry is deleted from the register in contravention of *subsection (1)*, the company concerned shall restore that entry to the register as soon as is reasonable and practicable.

(5) If default is made by a company in complying with *subsection (2)*, *(3)* or *(4)*, the company and any officer of it who is in default shall be guilty of a category 3 offence.

Chapter 6

Responsibilities of officers of company — provisions explaining what being "in default" means and presumption regarding that matter

270 Meaning of "in default" in context of sanctions specified in respect of officers (whether directors or secretaries or not)

(1) For the purposes of any provision of this Act which provides that an officer of a company who is in default shall be guilty of an offence, an officer who is in default is any officer who authorises or who, in breach of his or her duty as such officer, permits the default mentioned in the provision.

(2) In this section "default" includes a refusal to do a thing or a contravention of a provision.

271 Presumption that default permitted and certain defence

(1) In this section—

(a) "basic facts concerning the default" means such of the facts, relating to the one or more acts or omissions that constituted the default, as can reasonably be regarded as indicating, at the relevant time, the general character of those acts or omissions,

(b) "permitted", in relation to the default, means permitted in breach of the defendant's duty as an officer of the company concerned,

(c) "relevant proceedings" means proceedings for an offence under a provision of this Act, being a provision which provides that an officer of a company who is in default shall be guilty of an offence,

(d) a reference to a defendant in those proceedings is a reference to—

(i) the defendant, or

(ii) if there is more than one defendant, each of the one or more persons, other than the company, alleged to be in default,

being, in every case, a person who was an officer of the company at the relevant time.

(2) In relevant proceedings, where it is proved that the defendant was aware of the basic facts concerning the default concerned, it shall be presumed that the defendant permitted the default unless the defendant shows that he or she took all reasonable steps to prevent it or that, by reason of circumstances beyond the defendant's control, was unable to do so.

PART 6
FINANCIAL STATEMENTS, ANNUAL RETURN AND AUDIT

Chapter 1
Preliminary

272 What this Part contains and use of prefixes — "Companies Act" and "IFRS"

(1) This Part contains the provisions regarding—

(a) the accounting records to be kept, and the financial statements to be prepared, by companies,

(b) the periodic returns to be made by companies to the Registrar, and

(c) the auditing of financial statements of companies and matters related to the auditing of them and, in particular, the rules governing the appointment of statutory auditors to, and their removal from, office.

(2) Those financial statements shall be prepared in accordance with (as this Part authorises)—

(a) the requirements of [*Schedule 3. 3A, 3B, 4* or *4A*, as the case may be][a] and the relevant requirements of this Part, or

(b) international financial reporting standards and the relevant requirements of this Part,

and the prefix—

(i) "Companies Act" is used in references in this Part to financial statements that must comply with the requirements referred to in *paragraph (a)*, and

(ii) "IFRS" is used in references in this Part to financial statements that must comply with the requirements referred to in *paragraph (b)*.

Amendments

a Words substituted by C(A)A 2017, s 10.

---

273 Overall limitation on discretions with respect to length of financial year and annual return date

(1) The discretions of a company under this Part with respect to the length of its financial year or to its annual return date are subject to the overall limitation that those discretions must be exercised in a manner that results in compliance by the company with the following requirement.

(2) That requirement is that which arises under *section 347(4)* relating to the earliest date to which the documents annexed to an annual return must be made up.

274 Interpretation (*Part 6*): provisions relating to financial statements

(1) In this Part—

"abridged financial statements", in relation to a company, means the financial statements of the company [prepared in accordance with *section 353*][a], as appropriate;

"balance sheet", in relation to a company, means a statement of assets, liabilities and financial position drawn up at a particular date showing the assets, liabilities and equity of the company at that date in a manner required by the financial reporting framework adopted by the company, and—

(a) for the avoidance of doubt, where the financial statements are prepared in accordance with IFRS, the expression means the statement of financial position referred to in those standards, and

(b) *subsection (3)* supplements this definition;

"Companies Act entity financial statements" shall be read in accordance with *section 290*;

"Companies Act financial statements" means Companies Act entity financial statements or Companies Act group financial statements;

"Companies Act group financial statements" shall be read in accordance with *section 293*;

"entity financial statements" means, in relation to a company, a summary (as at a particular date) respecting the company alone (as distinct from the company and any subsidiary undertakings) of its assets, liabilities and financial position, together with its profit or loss, since the date of its previous financial statements and generally comprises—

(a) a balance sheet,

(b) a profit and loss account, and

(c) other statements and notes attached to the foregoing and forming part of them,

and the expression "entity", where used in relation to such a balance sheet or profit and loss account, shall be read accordingly;

"financial reporting framework" means the collective provisions and requirements (and, in particular, the applicable accounting standards) applied in the preparation of financial statements;

"financial statements", in relation to a company, means entity financial statements and any group financial statements;

"group" means a holding undertaking and all its subsidiary undertakings;

"group financial statements" means, in relation to a holding company, a summary (as at a particular date) respecting the assets, liabilities and financial position of the company and its subsidiary undertakings as a whole, together with the profit or loss of the company and its subsidiary undertakings as a whole, since the date of the previous financial statements and generally comprises—

(a) a consolidated balance sheet,

(b) a consolidated profit and loss account, and

(c) other consolidated statements and notes attached to the foregoing and forming part of them,

and the expression "group", where used in relation to such a balance sheet or profit and loss account, shall be read accordingly;

"IAS Regulation" means Regulation (EC) No. 1606/2002 of the European Parliament and of the Council of 19 July 2002 and a reference to Article 4 of that Regulation is, in the case of a private company limited by shares, a reference to Article 5 of that Regulation;

"IFRS" means international financial reporting standards;

"IFRS entity financial statements" shall be read in accordance with *section 290*;

"IFRS financial statements" means IFRS entity financial statements or IFRS group financial statements;

"IFRS group financial statements" shall be read in accordance with *section 293*;

"international financial reporting standards" means the international financial reporting standards, within the meaning of the IAS Regulation, adopted from time to time by the Commission of the European Union in accordance with the IAS Regulation;

"non-statutory financial statements"—

(a) in relation to a company, means any balance sheet or profit and loss account, or summary or abstract of a balance sheet or profit and loss account, relating to a financial year of the company that is published by the company otherwise than as part of the statutory financial statements of the company for that financial year, and

(b) in relation to a holding company, includes any information purporting to be a consolidated balance sheet or consolidated profit and loss account, or a summary or abstract of a consolidated balance sheet or consolidated profit and loss account, of the group consisting of the holding company and its subsidiary undertakings that is published otherwise than as part of the statutory financial statements of that group for that financial year,

and "non-statutory entity financial statements" shall be read accordingly;

"profit and loss account", in relation to a company, means a statement of performance of the company showing revenues, expenses, gains and losses earned and incurred by the company during a period in a manner required by the financial reporting framework adopted by the company, and—

[(a) for the avoidance of doubt—

(i) in the case where the financial statements are prepared in accordance with IFRS, the expression means an income statement referred to in those standards, and

(ii) in the case of a company not trading for the acquisition of gain by its members, the expression means an income and expenditure account, and references to—

(I) a profit and loss account, and

(II) in the case of group financial statements, a consolidated profit and loss account,

shall be read accordingly, and][b]

(b) *subsection (4)* supplements this definition;

"statutory financial statements", in relation to a company, means—

(a) in the case of a company that is not a holding company or is a holding company that has availed itself of an exemption under this Part from the requirement to prepare group financial statements, the entity financial statements required by *section 290*, and

(b) in the case of a holding company that prepares group financial statements, the group financial statements required by *section 293* together with the entity financial statements required by *section 290*.

(2) References in this Act to financial statements giving a true and fair view are references—

(a) in the case of Companies Act entity financial statements, to the requirement under *section 291* that the entity financial statements prepared in accordance with that section give a true and fair view of the assets, liabilities, financial position and profit or loss of the company alone (as distinct from the company and any subsidiary undertakings),

(b) in the case of Companies Act group financial statements, to the requirement under *section 294* that the group financial statements prepared in accordance with that section give a true and fair view of the assets, liabilities, financial position and profit or loss of the company and the subsidiary undertakings included in the consolidation taken as a whole, so far as concerns the members of the company, and

(c) in the case of IFRS entity financial statements and IFRS group financial statements, to the equivalent requirement under international financial reporting standards to present fairly the assets, liabilities, financial position, financial performance and cash flows of the company or group concerned.

(3) References in this Part to a company's balance sheet include references to notes to the company's financial statements giving information relating to the balance sheet, being information that is both—

(a) required by any provision of this Act (including IFRS or other applicable accounting standards), and

(b) required or permitted by any such provision to be given in a note to those financial statements.

(4) References in this Part to a company's profit and loss account include references to notes to the company's financial statements giving information relating to the profit and loss account, being information that is both—

(a) required by any provision of this Act (including IFRS or other applicable accounting standards), and

(b) required or permitted by any such provision to be given in a note to those financial statements.

(5) References in this Act to an undertaking being included in—

(a) the consolidation in relation to group financial statements, or

(b) consolidated group financial statements,

shall be read as references to the undertaking being included in the financial statements by the method of full (and not proportional) consolidation, and references to an undertaking being excluded from consolidation shall be read accordingly.

(6) A requirement imposed on the directors of a company to prepare financial statements is satisfied by the financial statements being caused to be prepared by the directors.

---

a Words substituted by C(A)A 2017, s 88(e) (previously: "prepared in accordance with *section 353* or *354*").

b Words substituted by C(A)A 2017, s 11.

---

275 Interpretation (*Part 6*): other definitions and construction provisions

(1) In this Part [*and Part 26*][a]—

["Accounting Directive" means Directive 2013/34/EU of the European Parliament and of the Council of 26 June 2013[1] on the annual financial statements, consolidated financial statements and related reports of certain types of undertakings, amending Directive 2006/43/EC of the European Parliament and of the Council and repealing Council Directives 78/660/EEC and 83/349/EEC;][b]

"accounting standards" means—

(a) statements of accounting standards, and

(b) any written interpretation of those standards,

issued by a body or bodies prescribed for the purposes of this definition under *section 943(1)(h)*;

["amount of turnover", in relation to a company, means the amount of the turnover shown in the company's profit and loss account;][b]

"associated undertaking" has the meaning given to it by [*paragraph 21* of *Schedule 4* or *4A*, as the case may be][c];

"audit committee" means the committee established under *section 167*;

"audit exemption", unless expressly provided otherwise, means—

(a) other than in *Chapter 15*, the audit exemption under that Chapter or *Chapter 16*, or

(b) in *Chapter 15*, the audit exemption under that Chapter;

"audit of the statutory financial statements" means work required to fulfil the duties imposed under *section 336* on a statutory auditor of a company;

["balance sheet total", in relation to a company, means the aggregate of the amounts shown as assets in the company's balance sheet;][b]

"credit institution" means—

(a) a company or undertaking that is the holder of a licence under section 9 of the Central Bank Act 1971,

(b) a company or undertaking engaged solely in the making of hire purchase agreements ([within the meaning of the Consumer Credit Act 1995][d]) and credit sale agreements (within the meaning of that Act), in respect of goods owned by the company or undertaking,

(c) a company or undertaking engaged in the business of accepting deposits [or other repayable funds from the public and][e] granting credit for its own account, or

(d) a company or undertaking that is a trustee savings bank licensed under the Trustee Savings Banks Act 1989;

"equity share capital" or "equity shares" means, in relation to a company, its allotted share capital excluding any part of it which, neither as respects dividends nor as respects capital, carries any right to participate beyond a specified amount in a distribution;

"fellow subsidiary undertakings" means 2 or more undertakings that are subsidiary undertakings of the same holding undertaking but which are not the holding undertaking or subsidiary undertaking of each other;

"group undertaking", in relation to an undertaking, means an undertaking which is—

(a) a holding undertaking or subsidiary undertaking of that undertaking, or

(b) a subsidiary undertaking of any holding undertaking of that undertaking;

"higher holding undertaking" means an undertaking that is the holding undertaking of an undertaking that is itself a holding undertaking;

"holding undertaking" has the same meaning as "holding company" in *section 8* has save that "company" in *section 8* shall, for the purposes of this definition, include, as well as a body corporate—

(a) a partnership, and

(b) an unincorporated body of persons,

falling within the definition of "undertaking" in this subsection;

["ineligible entities" means undertakings that—

(a) have transferable securities admitted to trading on a regulated market of any Member State,

(b) are credit institutions,

(c) are insurance undertakings, or (d) are—

(i) undertakings that—

(I) fall within any of the provisions of Schedule 5, or

(II) are otherwise designated, by or under any other enactment, to be entities referred to in point (1)(d) of Article 2 of the Accounting Directive, or

(ii) undertakings that are designated, by or under the law of any other Member State, to be entities referred to in point (1)(d) of Article 2 of the Accounting Directive and 'ineligible company' shall be read accordingly;][b]

"insurance undertaking" means an undertaking that is the holder of an authorisation within the meaning of—

(a) Regulation 2 of the European Communities (Non-Life Insurance) Regulations 1976 (S.I. No. 115 of 1976),

(b) Regulation 2 of the European Communities (Non-Life Insurance) Framework Regulations 1994 (S.I. No. 359 of 1994),

(c) Regulation 2 of the European Communities (Life Assurance) Regulations 1984 (S.I. No. 57 of 1984),

[(d) Regulation 2 of the European Communities (Life Assurance) Framework Regulations 1994 (S.I. No. 360 of 1994),

(e) European Communities (Reinsurance) Regulations 2006 (S.I. No. 380 of 2006), or

(f) Regulation 3 of the European Union (Insurance and Reinsurance) Regulations 2015 (S.I. No. 485 of 2015);][f]

["large company" shall be read in accordance with *section 280H*;

"medium company" shall be read in accordance with *section 280F* or *280G*, as may be appropriate; and 'medium group' shall be read accordingly;

"micro company" shall be construed in accordance with *section 280D*;

"micro companies regime" has the meaning assigned to it by *section 280E*;][b]

"net assets", in relation to a company or group, means the total assets of the company or group less the total liabilities of it or them as shown in the financial statements of the company or group;

"participating interest" has the meaning given to it by [*paragraph 23* of *Schedule 4* or *4A* as the case may be,][g];

"publish", in relation to a document, includes issue, circulate or otherwise make it available for public inspection in a manner calculated to invite the public generally, or any class of members of the public, to read the document, and cognate words shall be read accordingly;

"regulated market" has the same meaning as it has in the European Communities (Markets in Financial Instruments) Regulations 2007 (S.I. No. 60 of 2007);

["small company" shall be read in accordance with *section 280A* or *280B*, as may be appropriate; and 'small group' shall be read accordingly;

"small companies regime" has the meaning assigned to it by section 280C;][b]

"subsidiary undertaking" has the same meaning as "subsidiary" in *section 7* has save that "company" in *section 7* shall, for the purposes of this definition, include, as well as a body corporate—

(a) a partnership, and

(b) an unincorporated body of persons,

falling within the definition of "undertaking" in this subsection;

"turnover", in relation to a company, means the amounts of revenue derived from the provision of goods and services falling within the company's ordinary activities, after deduction of—

(a) trade discounts,

(b) value-added tax, and

(c) any other taxes based on the amounts so derived,

and, in the case of a company whose ordinary activities include the making or holding of investments, includes the gross revenue derived from such activities;

"undertaking" means—

(a) any body corporate,

(b) a partnership, or

(c) an unincorporated body of persons,

engaged for gain in the production, supply or distribution of goods, the provision of services or the making or holding of investments.

(2) For the purposes of this Part, the definition of "wholly owned subsidiary" in *section 8(2)* shall apply as if each reference in that definition to a company included a reference to an undertaking.

(3) In this Part references to shares—

(a) in relation to an undertaking with share capital, are references to allotted shares,

(b) in relation to an undertaking with capital but no share capital, are references to rights to share in the capital of the undertaking, and

(c) in relation to an undertaking without capital, are references to interests—

(i) conferring any rights to share in the profits or imposing liability to contribute to the losses of the undertaking, or

(ii) giving rise to an obligation to contribute to the debts or expenses of the undertaking in the event of a winding up.

(4) In this Part references to derivative financial instruments shall be deemed to include references to commodity-based contracts that give either contracting party the right to settle in cash or some other financial instrument except when such contracts—

(a) were entered into and continue to meet the company's expected purchase, sale or usage requirements,

(b) were designed for such purpose at their inception, and

(c) are expected to be settled by delivery of the commodity.

[(5) A word or expression that is used in this Part, *Part 26* or in the *Schedules* and that is also used in the Accounting Directive shall have the same meaning in this Part, *Part 26* or in those *Schedules*, as the case may be, as it has in the Accounting Directive.][h]

(6) [...][i]

Amendments

a Words inserted by C(A)A 2017, s 12(a)(i).
b Definitions inserted by C(A)A 2017, s 12(a)(ii).
c Words substituted by C(A)A 2017, s 90(e)(i) (previously: "*paragraph 20* of *Schedule 4*").
d Words substituted by C(A)A 2017, s 12(a)(iii)(I) (previously: "(within the meaning of the Hire Purchase Act 1946)").
e Words substituted by C(A)A 2017, s 12(a)(iii)(II) (previously: "or other repayable funds or").
f Paragraphs (d) and (e) in the definition of 'insurance undertaking' substituted and paragraph (f) inserted by the European Union (Insurance and Reinsurance) Regulations 2015 (SI 485/2015), reg 316, with effect from 1 January 2016 and, so far as is necessary to secure compliance by the State with the obligations imposed by Article 308a of the Directive (as defined in the Regulations) and for the purposes of Regulation 4(7) of the Regulations, from 5 November 2015.
g Words substituted by C(A)A 2017, s 90(e)(ii) (previously: "*paragraph 22* of *Schedule 4*").
h Subsection replaced by C(A)A 2017, s 12(b).
i Subsection (6) repealed by C(A)A 2017, s 12(c).

References

1 OJ No. L 182, 29.06.2013, p.19.

276 Construction of references to realised profits

(1) It is declared, for the avoidance of doubt, that references in this Part to realised profits, in relation to a company's entity financial statements, are references to such profits of the company as fall to be treated as realised profits for the purposes of those financial statements in accordance with principles generally accepted with respect to the determination for accounting purposes of realised profits at the time when those financial statements are prepared.

(2) *Subsection (1)* is without prejudice to—

(a) the construction of any other expression by reference (where appropriate) to generally accepted accounting principles or practice, or

(b) any specific provision for the treatment of profits of any description as realised.

277 Construction of references to exemption

[(1) *Subsection (2)* is in addition to the provision made by this Part enabling certain elections to be made by a company that qualifies for the small companies regime or the micro companies regime.

(2) Any provision of this Part providing for an exemption from a requirement of this Part does not prevent the company concerned, if it so chooses, from doing the thing that the provision provides it is exempted from doing (the 'specified thing').

(3) If the company concerned chooses to do the specified thing—

(a) the provisions required by this Part to be complied with, in relation to the doing of such a thing, and

(b) the provisions specified by this Part to apply, in a case where such a thing is done, as the case may be, shall be complied with or shall apply accordingly, but this does not prejudice any provision of this Part concerning the making of an election referred to in *subsection (1)* by a company there referred to (or concerning the effect of the company's having so done).

(4) *Subsection (2)* applies whether the expression 'shall be exempt' or 'need not' or any other form of words is used in the provision concerned.][a]

Amendments

a Section 277 substituted by C(A)A 2017, s 13.

[277A Certain companies may apply provisions of Act to certain earlier financial years

(1) Subject to this section, the directors of a company may, before the operative date of the provisions of the *Act of 2017* specified in subsection (4) (the "specified provisions of the *Act of 2017*"), opt to prepare and approve statutory financial statements for the company in accordance with those specified provisions for any financial year which commenced on or after 1 January 2015.

(2) All obligations and rights that arise under this Act consequent on or in respect of financial statements having been approved by directors of a company shall likewise arise in relation to financial statements approved by directors in a case falling within subsection (1).

(3) In determining whether a company or group qualifies as—

(a) a medium company under section 280F or 280G, as the case may be,

(b) a small company under section 280A or 280B, as the case may be, or

(c) a micro company under section 280D,

in relation to a financial year to which the specified provisions of the *Act of 2017* have effect, the company or group, as may be appropriate shall be treated as having qualified as a medium company, small company or micro company, as the case may be, in any previous year in which it would have so qualified if the qualifying conditions applicable to that company or group, as the case may be, had had effect in relation to that previous year.

(4) Each of the following is a specified provision of the *Act of 2017*:

(a) *section 3*;

(b) *section 4*;

(c) *sections 10 to 12*;

(d) *sections 15 to 25*;

(e) *paragraphs (a)*, *(b)* and *(d)* of *section 26*;

(f) *sections 29* to *57*;

(g) *section 59*;

(h) *sections 62* to *64*;

(i) *sections 81* and *82*;

(j) *section 84*;

(k) *section 88*;

(l) *section 89*.

(5) In this section—

"*Act of 2017*" means the *Companies (Accounting) Act 2017*;

"operative date" means the date on which the specified provision comes into operation pursuant to an order under *section 1(2) of the Act of 2017*;

"qualifying conditions" has the same meaning as it has—

(a) in relation to a medium company, in *section 280F(7)* or *280G(10)*, as the case may be,

(b) in relation to a small company, in *section 280A(7)* or *280B(10)*, as the case may be, and

(c) in relation to a micro company, in *section 280D(7)*.][a]

Amendments

a Section 277A inserted by C(A)A 2017, s 14.

278 Accounting standards generally — power of Minister to specify

(1) The Minister may specify by regulations the accounting standards in accordance with which statutory financial statements are to be prepared but any such regulations shall not apply in any excepted case.

(2) In *subsection (1)* "excepted case" means—

(a) a case in which this Part permits (and the company concerned avails itself of that permission), or requires, statutory financial statements to be prepared in accordance with IFRS, or

(b) a case falling within *section 279* or regulations made under *section 280* and the holding company concerned avails itself of what is permitted by that section or those regulations.

279 US accounting standards may, in limited cases, be availed of for particular transitional period

(1) In this section—

"relevant holding company" means a holding company—

(a) whose securities (or whose receipts in respect of those securities) are registered with the Securities and Exchange Commission of the United States of America, or which is otherwise subject to reporting to that Commission, under the laws of the United States of [America,][a]

[(aa) which was incorporated in the State prior to the commencement of section 1 of the Companies (Amendment) Act 2017, and][b]

(b) which—

(i) prior to 4 July 2012, has not made and was not required to make an annual return to the Registrar to which accounts were required to have been annexed, or

(ii) on or after 23 December 2009 but prior to 4 July 2012, used, in accordance with the provisions of the Companies (Miscellaneous Provisions) Act 2009, US accounting standards in the preparation of its Companies Act individual accounts or its Companies Act group accounts;

"relevant financial statements" means Companies Act entity financial statements and Companies Act group financial statements;

"US accounting standards" means US generally accepted accounting principles, that is to say, the standards and interpretations, in relation to accounting and financial statements, issued by any of the following bodies constituted under the laws of the United States of America or of a territorial unit of the United States of America—

(a) the Financial Accounting Standards Board,

(b) the American Institute of Certified Public Accountants,

(c) the Securities and Exchange Commission.

(2) This section applies to the relevant financial statements of a relevant holding company that are prepared for such of its financial years after it is incorporated in the State as end or ends not later than [31 December 2030][c].

(3) To the extent that the use of US accounting standards does not contravene any provision of this Part—

(a) a true and fair view of the assets and liabilities, financial position and profit or loss of a relevant holding company may be given by the use by that company of those standards in the preparation of its Companies Act entity financial statements, and

(b) a true and fair view of the assets and liabilities, financial position and profit or loss of a relevant holding company and its subsidiary undertakings as a whole may be given by the use by that relevant holding company of those standards in the preparation of its Companies Act group financial statements.

Amendments

a Words substituted by C(A)A 2017, s 1(a) (previously: "America, and").

b Paragraph inserted by C(A)A 2017, s 1(b).

c Words inserted by C(A)A 2017, s 1(c) (previously: "31 December 2020").

---

280 Regulations may permit use of other internationally recognised accounting standards for a particular transitional period

(1) In this section "relevant financial statements" means Companies Act entity financial statements and Companies Act group financial statements.

(2) The Minister may make regulations providing for specified categories of holding companies and providing that—

(a) a true and fair view of the assets and liabilities, financial position and profit or loss of a holding company in such a category may be given by the preparation by it of its Companies Act entity financial statements for a specified number of its financial years in accordance with specified accounting standards, and

(b) a true and fair view of the assets and liabilities, financial position and profit or loss of a holding company in such a category and its subsidiary undertakings as a whole may be given by the preparation by that holding company of its Companies Act group financial statements for a specified number of its financial years in accordance with specified accounting standards.

(3) Regulations made under *subsection (2)* shall—

(a) specify the accounting standards, which shall be—

(i) internationally recognised, and

(ii) generally accepted accounting principles or practice of a jurisdiction to which a majority of the subsidiary undertakings of the holding company have a substantial connection,

(b) specify the number of financial years in respect of which the regulations apply, and the date on which the latest of such financial years shall end, which shall be not later than 31 December 2020, and

(c) provide that the preparation of such financial statements shall not contravene any provision of this Part.

[*Chapter 1A*

Qualification of company based on size of company

280A Qualification of company as small company: general

(1) A company that is not excluded by *subsection (4)* qualifies as a small company in relation to its first financial year if the qualifying conditions are satisfied in respect of that year.

(2) A company that is not excluded by *subsection (4)* qualifies as a small company in relation to a subsequent financial year (in this subsection referred to as 'relevant year') if the qualifying conditions—

(a) are satisfied in respect of the relevant year and the financial year immediately preceding the relevant year,

(b) are satisfied in respect of the relevant year and the company qualified as a small company in relation to the financial year immediately preceding the relevant year, or

(c) were satisfied in the financial year immediately preceding the relevant year and the company qualified as a small company in relation to that preceding financial year

(3) The qualifying conditions for a small company are satisfied by a company if, in relation to a financial year, it fulfils 2 or more of the following requirements:

(a) the amount of turnover of the company does not exceed €12 million;

(b) the balance sheet total of the company does not exceed €6 million;

(c) the average number of employees does not exceed 50.

(4) This section shall not apply to a company if it is—

(a) a holding company, or

(b) an ineligible company.

(5) In the application of this section to any period which is a financial year but is not in fact a year, the amount specified in *subsection (3)(a)* shall be proportionately adjusted.

(6) For the purposes of *subsection (3)(c)*, the average number of employees of a company shall be determined by applying the methods specified in *section 317* for determining the number required by *subsection (1)(a)* of that section to be stated in a note to the financial statements of a company.

(7) In this section, "qualifying conditions" mean the requirements specified in *subsection (3)*.

280B Qualification of company as small company: holding company

(1) A holding company qualifies as a small company in relation to a financial year only if the group, in respect of which it is the holding company, qualifies as a small group in relation to that same financial year.

(2) A group that is not excluded by *subsection (5)* qualifies as a small group in relation to the first financial year of the holding company if the qualifying conditions are satisfied in respect of that year.

(3) A group that is not excluded by *subsection (5)* qualifies as a small group in relation to a subsequent financial year (in this subsection referred to as "relevant year") of the holding company if the qualifying conditions—

(a) are satisfied in respect of the relevant year and the financial year immediately preceding the relevant year,

(b) are satisfied in respect of the relevant year and the group qualified as a small group in relation to the financial year immediately preceding the relevant year, or

(c) were satisfied in the financial year immediately preceding the relevant year and the group qualified as a small group in relation to that preceding financial year.

(4) The qualifying conditions for a small group are satisfied by a group if, in relation to a financial year, it fulfils 2 or more of the following requirements:

(a) the aggregate amount of turnover of the group does not exceed €12 million net (or €14.4 million gross);

(b) the aggregate balance sheet total of the group does not exceed €6 million net (or €7.2 million gross);

(c) the aggregate average number of employees of the group does not exceed 50.

(5) This section shall not apply to a holding company of a group if any member of the group is an ineligible entity.

(6) In the application of this section to any period which is a financial year but is not in fact a year, the amounts specified in *subsection (4)(a)* shall be proportionally adjusted.

(7) The aggregate figures referred to in *subsection (4)* shall be ascertained by aggregating the equivalent figures determined in accordance with *section 280A* for each member of the group.

(8) Where a group proposes to satisfy the qualifying conditions referred to in subsection (4) on the basis of the requirements of paragraphs (a) and (b) of that subsection, it may do so on the basis of either the net figures or the gross figures respectively for both of the said paragraphs.

(9) The figures for each subsidiary undertaking shall be those included in its entity financial statements for the relevant financial year—

(a) if its financial year ends with that of the holding company, that financial year, and

(b) if not, its financial year ending last before the end of the financial year of the holding company.

(10) In this section—

"first financial year of a holding company" means the first financial year at the end of which the company qualifies as a holding company by virtue of having one or more subsidiaries;

"qualifying conditions" mean the requirements referred to in *subsection (4)*.

(11) For the purposes of this section, in relation to the aggregate figures for turnover and balance sheet total—

"net" means after set-offs and other adjustments made to eliminate group transactions—

(i) in the case of Companies Act financial statements, in accordance with *Schedule 4*, and

(ii) in the case of IFRS financial statements, in accordance with international financial reporting standards; 'gross' means without those set-offs and other adjustments.

280C Small companies regime

Where a company qualifies as a small company in accordance with *section 280A* or *280B*, as may be appropriate, then, as provided in this Part, different rules may be applied (in this Act referred to as the 'small companies regime') to the company in respect of financial statements and reports for a financial year in relation to which that company so qualifies as a small company.

280D Qualification of company as micro company

(1) A company that is not excluded by *subsection (4)* qualifies as a micro company in relation to its first financial year if the qualifying conditions are satisfied in respect of that year.

(2) A company that is not excluded by *subsection (4)* qualifies as a micro company in relation to a subsequent financial year (in this subsection referred to as the 'relevant year') if the qualifying conditions—

(a) are satisfied in respect of the relevant year and the financial year immediately preceding the relevant year,

(b) are satisfied in respect of the relevant year and the company qualified as a micro company in relation to the financial year immediately preceding the relevant year, or

(c) were satisfied in the financial year immediately preceding the relevant year and the company qualified as a micro company in relation to that preceding financial year.

(3) The qualifying conditions for a micro company are satisfied by a company if, in relation to a financial year, it—

(a) qualifies for the small companies regime, and

(b) fulfils 2 or more of the following requirements:

(i) the amount of turnover of the company does not exceed €700,000;

(ii) the balance sheet total of the company does not exceed €350,000;

(iii) the average number of employees does not exceed 10.

(4) This section shall not apply to a company if it is—

(a) an investment undertaking,

(b) a financial holding undertaking,

(c) a holding company that prepares group financial statements, or

(d) a subsidiary that is included in the consolidated financial statements of a higher holding undertaking.

(5) In the application of this section to any period which is a financial year but is not in fact a year, the amount specified in *subsection (3)(b)(i)* shall be proportionately adjusted.

(6) For the purposes of *subsection (3)(b)(iii)*, the average number of employees of a company shall be determined by applying the methods specified in section 317 for determining the number required by *subsection (1)(a)* of that section to be stated in a note to the financial statements of a company.

(7) In this section, 'qualifying conditions' mean the conditions specified in subsection (3).

280E Micro companies regime

Where a company qualifies as a micro company in accordance with *section 280D*, then, as provided in this Part, different rules may be applied (in this Act referred to as the "micro companies regime") to the company in respect of financial statements and reports for a financial year in relation to which that company so qualifies as a micro company.

280F Qualification of company as medium company: general

(1) A company that is not excluded by *subsection (4)* qualifies as a medium company in relation to its first financial year if the qualifying conditions are satisfied in respect of that year.

(2) A company that is not excluded by *subsection (4)* qualifies as a medium company in relation to a subsequent financial year (in this subsection referred to as 'relevant year') if the qualifying conditions—

(a) are satisfied in respect of the relevant year and the financial year immediately preceding the relevant year,

(b) are satisfied in respect of the relevant year and the company qualified as a medium company in relation to the financial year immediately preceding the relevant year, or

(c) were satisfied in the financial year immediately preceding the relevant year and the company qualified as a medium company in relation to that preceding financial year.

(3) The qualifying conditions for a medium company are satisfied by a company if, in relation to a financial year, it fulfils 2 or more of the following requirements:

(a) the amount of turnover of the company does not exceed €40 million;

(b) the balance sheet total of the company does not exceed €20 million;

(c) the average number of employees does not exceed 250.

(4) This section shall not apply to a company if it is—

(a) a holding company,

(b) an ineligible company,

(c) a company that qualifies for the small companies regime, or

(d) a company that qualifies for the micro companies regime.

(5) In the application of this section to any period which is a financial year but is not in fact a year, the amount specified in *subsection (3)(a)* shall be proportionately adjusted.

(6) For the purposes of *subsection (3)(c)*, the average number of employees of a company shall be determined by applying the methods specified in section 317 for determining the number required by *subsection (1)(a)* of that section to be stated in a note to the financial statements of a company.

(7) In this section, "qualifying conditions" mean the conditions referred to in *subsection (3)*.

280G Qualification of company as medium company: holding company

(1) A holding company qualifies as a medium company in relation to a financial year only if the group, in respect of which it is the holding company, qualifies as a medium group.

(2) A group that is not excluded by *subsection (5)* qualifies as a medium group in relation to the first financial year of the holding company if the qualifying conditions are satisfied in respect of that year.

(3) A group that is not excluded by *subsection (5)* qualifies as a medium group in relation to a subsequent financial year (in this subsection referred to as "relevant year") of the holding company if the qualifying conditions—

(a) are satisfied in respect of the relevant year and the financial year immediately preceding the relevant year,

(b) are satisfied in respect of the relevant year and the group qualified as a medium group in relation to the financial year immediately preceding the relevant year, or

(c) were satisfied in the financial year immediately preceding the relevant year and the group qualified as a medium group in relation to that preceding financial year.

(4) The qualifying conditions for a medium group are satisfied by a group if, in relation to a financial year, it fulfils 2 or more of the following requirements:

(a) the aggregate amount of turnover of the group does not exceed €40 million net (or €48 million gross);

(b) the aggregate balance sheet total of the group does not exceed €20 million net (or €24 million gross);

(c) the aggregate average number of employees of the group does not exceed 250.

(5) This section shall not apply to the holding company of a group if any member of the group is an ineligible entity.

(6) In the application of this section to any period which is a financial year but is not in fact a year, the amounts specified in *subsection (4)(a)* shall be proportionally adjusted.

(7) The aggregate figures referred to in *subsection (4)* shall be ascertained by aggregating the equivalent figures determined in accordance with *section 280F* for each member of the group.

(8) Where a group proposes to satisfy the qualifying conditions referred to in *subsection (4)* on the basis of the requirements of paragraphs (a) and (b) of that subsection, it may do so on the basis of either the net figures or the gross figures respectively for both of the said paragraphs.

(9) The figures for each subsidiary undertaking shall be those included in its entity financial statements for the relevant financial year—

(a) if its financial year ends with that of the holding company, that financial year, and

(b) if not, its financial year ending last before the end of the financial year of the holding company.

(10) In this section—

"first financial year of a holding company" means the first financial year at the end of which the company qualifies as a holding company by virtue of having one or more subsidiaries;

"qualifying conditions" mean the conditions referred to in *subsection (4)*.

(11) For the purposes of this section, in relation to the aggregate figures for turnover and balance sheet total—

'net' means after set-offs and other adjustments made to eliminate group transactions—

(i) in the case of Companies Act financial statements, in accordance with *Schedule 4*, and

(ii) in the case of IFRS financial statements, in accordance with international financial reporting standards;

"gross" means without those set-offs and other adjustments.

280H Qualification of company as large company

A company that does not qualify as—

(a) a small company in accordance with *section 280A* or *280B*,

(b) a micro company in accordance with *section 280D*, or

(c) a medium company in accordance with *section 280F* or *280G*,

shall be deemed to be a large company.][a]

Amendments

a Chapter 1A (ss 280A–280H) inserted by C(A)A 2017, s 15.

Chapter 2
Accounting records

281 Obligation to keep adequate accounting records

A company shall keep or cause to be kept adequate accounting records.

282 Basic requirements for accounting records

(1) For the purposes of this Part, adequate accounting records are those that are sufficient to—

(a) correctly record and explain the transactions of the company,

(b) enable, at any time, the assets, liabilities, financial position and profit or loss of the company to be determined with reasonable accuracy,

(c) enable the directors to ensure that any financial statements of the company, required to be prepared under *section 290* or *293*, and any directors' report required to be prepared under *section 325*, comply with the requirements of this Act and, where applicable, Article 4 of the IAS Regulation, and

(d) enable those financial statements of the company so prepared to be audited.

(2) The accounting records shall be kept on a continuous and consistent basis, which is to say, the entries in them shall be made in a timely manner and be consistent from one period to the next; if those records are not kept by making entries in a bound book but by some other means, adequate precautions shall be taken for guarding against falsification and facilitating discovery of such falsification, should it occur.

(3) Without prejudice to the generality of *subsections (1)* and *(2)*, accounting records kept pursuant to *section 281* shall contain—

(a) entries from day to day of all sums of money received and expended by the company and the matters in respect of which the receipt and expenditure takes place,

(b) a record of the assets and liabilities of the company,

(c) if the company's business involves dealing in goods—

(i) a record of all transactions whereby goods are purchased and whereby goods are sold, showing the goods and the sellers and buyers (except buyers of goods in ordinary retail trade) in sufficient detail to enable the goods and the sellers and buyers to be identified and a record of all the invoices relating to such purchases and sales,

(ii) statements of stock held by the company at the end of each financial year and all records of stocktakings from which any such statement of stock has been, or is to be, prepared,

and

(d) if the company's business involves the provision or purchase of services, a record of all transactions whereby services are provided and whereby services are purchased, to whom they were provided or from whom they were purchased (unless provided or purchased by way of ordinary retail trade) and of all the invoices relating thereto.

(4) For the purposes of *subsections (1)* to *(3)*, adequate accounting records shall be deemed to have been maintained if they comply with those subsections and explain the company's transactions and facilitate the preparation of financial statements that give a true and fair view of the assets, liabilities, financial position and profit or loss of the company and, if relevant, the group and include any information and returns referred to in *section 283(2)*.

(5) The adequate accounting records required by *section 281* to be kept, including the information and returns referred to in this Chapter, shall be kept either—

(a) in written form in an official language of the State, or

(b) so as to enable the accounting records, including the information and returns, to be readily accessible and readily convertible into written form in an official language of the State.

(6) Subject to *subsection (7)*, any computer (the "server computer") that provides services to another computer, being services the provision of which to the latter is necessary so that the accounting records, and the other foregoing information and returns, stored in the latter can be accessed at all times, shall be kept in a place in the State.

(7) In any case where the accounting records are kept outside the State as mentioned in *section 283(2)*—

(a) save to the extent that the Minister by regulations provides otherwise, *subsection (6)* shall not apply,

(b) the Minister may by regulations impose requirements on the companies so keeping their accounting records (and which companies are not subject to *subsection (6)* by virtue of regulations under *paragraph (a)*) for the purpose of securing the effective access, in accordance with this Act, at all times to the accounting records stored in the computers concerned.

(8) A holding company which has a subsidiary undertaking in relation to which the preceding requirements of this section or similar such requirements do not apply shall take the following steps.

(9) Those steps are all reasonable steps to secure that the subsidiary undertaking keeps such adequate accounting records as will enable the directors of the holding company to ensure that any group financial statements required to be prepared under this Part comply with the requirements of this Part and, where applicable, Article 4 of the IAS Regulation.

283 Where accounting records are to be kept

(1) Subject to *subsection (2)*, a company's accounting records shall be kept at its registered office or at such other place as the directors think fit.

(2) If accounting records are kept at a place outside the State, there shall be sent to and kept at a place in the State such information and returns relating to the business dealt with in the accounting records so kept as will—

(a) disclose with reasonable accuracy the assets, liabilities, financial position and profit or loss of that business at intervals not exceeding 6 months, and

(b) enable to be prepared in accordance with this Part (and, where applicable, Article 4 of the IAS Regulation) the company's statutory financial statements required by *section 290* or *293* and the directors' report required by *section 325*.

284 Access to accounting records

(1) A company shall make its accounting records, and any information and returns referred to in *section 283(2)*, available in an official language of the State at all reasonable times for inspection without charge by the officers of the company and by other persons entitled pursuant to this Act to inspect the accounting records of the company.

(2) Where accounting records or any information and returns referred to in section *283(2)* are kept in the manner referred to in *section 282(5)(b)* the obligation under *subsection (1)* shall be read as including a requirement the company secure that the records or information are converted, without charge, into written form in an official language of the State if the person making the request so requests.

(3) No member (not being a director) shall have any right of inspecting any financial statement or accounting record of the company except—

(a) as conferred by statute or by the company's constitution, or

(b) authorised by the directors under *subsection (4)* or by the company in general meeting.

(4) The directors of a company shall from time to time determine whether and to what extent and at what times and places and under what conditions or regulations the financial statements and accounting records of the company or any of them shall be open to the inspection of its members, not being directors of the company.

285 Retention of accounting records

An accounting record required to be kept by *section 281* or information or a return referred to in *section 283(2)* shall be preserved by the company concerned for a period of at least 6 years after the end of the financial year containing the latest date to which the record, information or return relates.

286 Accounting records: offences

(1) A company that contravenes *section 281*, *282*, *283*, *284* or *285* shall be guilty of—

(a) subject to *paragraph (b)*, a category 2 offence, or

(b) if the contravention falls within a case to which *subsection (3)*, *(4)* or *(5)* relates, a category 1 offence.

(2) A director of a company who fails to take all reasonable steps to secure compliance by the company with the requirements of any of *sections 281* to *285*, or has by his or her own intentional act been the cause of any default by the company under any of them, shall be guilty of—

(a) subject to *paragraph (b)*, a category 2 offence, or

(b) if the contravention falls within a case to which *subsection (3)*, *(4)* or *(5)* relates, a category 1 offence.

(3) This subsection relates to a case in which both of the following circumstances apply—

(a) the contravention arose in relation to a company that is subsequently wound up and that company is unable to pay its debts, and

(b) the contravention has—

(i) contributed to the company's inability to pay all of its debts, or

(ii) resulted in substantial uncertainty as to the assets and liabilities of the company, or

(iii) substantially impeded the orderly winding up of the company.

(4) This subsection relates to a case in which the contravention persisted during a continuous period of 3 years or more.

(5) This subsection relates to a case in which the contravention involved the failure to correctly record and explain one or more transactions of a company the value or aggregate value of which transaction or transactions exceeded €1 million or 10 per cent of the net assets of the company, whichever is the greater.

(6) Subject to *subsection (7)*, the reference in *subsection (5)* to the net assets of the company is a reference to net assets, as defined in *section 275(1)*, of the company and for this purpose the amount of its net assets shall be ascertained by reference to the entity financial statements prepared under *section 290* and laid in accordance with *section 341* in respect of the last preceding financial year in respect of which such entity financial statements were so laid.

(7) Where no entity financial statements of the company have been prepared and laid under the foregoing sections before that time, the reference in *subsection (5)* to the net assets of the company shall be taken to be a reference to the amount of its called-up share capital at the time of the contravention.

(8) In any proceedings against a person in respect of an offence under *subsection (2)* consisting of a failure to take reasonable steps to secure compliance by a company with the requirements of any of *sections 281* to *285*, it shall be a defence to prove both of the following:

(a) that the defendant had reasonable grounds for believing and did believe that a competent and reliable person was—

(i) charged with the duty of undertaking that those requirements were complied with, and

(ii) in a position to discharge that duty,

and

(b) that the discharge of that duty by such competent and reliable person was monitored by the defendant, by means of reasonable methods properly used.

Chapter 3
Financial year

287 Financial year end date

In this and each subsequent Chapter of this Part a reference to a company's financial year end date is a reference to the last day of the financial year concerned of the company and a reference to its next financial year end date shall be read accordingly.

288 Financial year

(1) A company's first financial year is the period beginning with the date of its incorporation and ending on a date no more than 18 months after that date.

(2) Each subsequent financial year of a company begins with the day immediately after its previous financial year end date and, subject to *subsection (4)*, continues for—

(a) 12 months, or

(b) such other period, not being more than 7 days shorter or longer than 12 months, as the directors may determine to its next financial year end date,

and the power of the directors to make such a determination is referred to in *subsection (5)* as the "*subsection (2)(b)* power".

(3) Except where there are substantial reasons not to do so, which reasons shall be disclosed in the notes to the statutory financial statements of the company, the directors of a holding company shall ensure the financial year end dates of each of the subsidiary undertakings included in the consolidation concerned coincide with that of the holding company.

(4) Subject to the subsequent subsections of this section, a company may, by notice in the prescribed form, given to the Registrar, alter what for the time being is its current financial year end date or its previous financial year end date.

(5) Where a notice under *subsection (4)* is given to the Registrar then—

(a) each subsequent financial year end date shall, subject to any exercise of the *subsection (2)(b)* power or (where permitted by *subsection (10)*) further exercise of the power under *subsection (4)*, be the anniversary of the new financial year end date specified in that notice, and

(b) in consequence, the commencement of each of the financial years that follow the new financial year end date so specified is postponed or, as the case may be, brought forward by the appropriate period of time.

(6) For the purposes of *subsection (4)* a company's "previous financial year end date" means the date immediately preceding its current financial year.

(7) A notice under *subsection (4)* may not alter a financial year end date if the particular alteration specified in it would result in a financial year in excess of 18 months.

(8) A notice may not be given under *subsection (4)* in respect of a previous financial year end date if, at the date of the giving of the notice, the period for delivering to the Registrar financial statements and reports for that previous financial year has expired.

(9) Subject to *subsection (10)*, a notice under *subsection (4)* purporting to alter a company's current or previous financial year end date is not valid if given less than 5 years after the day on which there has fallen the new financial year end date specified in a previous notice given under that subsection.

(10) *Subsection (9)* does not apply to a notice given by a company—

- (a) that is a subsidiary undertaking or holding undertaking of another EEA undertaking if the new financial year end date specified coincides with that of the other EEA undertaking, or
- (b) that is being wound up, or
- (c) where the Director, on application to him or her by the company, directs that it shall not apply.

(11) In this section "EEA undertaking" means an undertaking established under the law of the State or the law of any other EEA state.

Chapter 4
Statutory financial statements

289 Statutory financial statements to give true and fair view

(1) The directors of a company shall not approve financial statements for the purposes of this Part unless they are satisfied that they give a true and fair view of the assets, liabilities and financial position, as at the end of the financial year, and profit or loss, for the financial year—

- (a) in the case of the company's entity financial statements, of the company alone (as distinct from the company and its subsidiary undertakings, if any, taken as a whole),
- (b) in the case of the company's group financial statements, of the company and all the subsidiary undertakings included in the consolidation taken as a whole, so far as concerns the members of the company.

(2) The statutory auditors of a company, in performing their functions under this Act in relation to the company's statutory financial statements, shall have regard to the directors' duty under *subsection (1)*.

290 Obligation to prepare entity financial statements under relevant financial reporting framework

(1) The directors of a company shall prepare entity financial statements for the company in respect of each financial year of it.

(2) The entity financial statements prepared under this section shall be the statutory financial statements of a company that does not prepare group financial statements under *section 293*.

(3) Subject to *subsections (5)* to *(8)* and *section 296*, a company's entity financial statements shall be prepared either (as the company elects) in accordance with—

(a) *section 291*, or

(b) international financial reporting standards and *section 292*.

(4) Entity financial statements prepared in accordance with—

(a) *section 291* shall be known, and are in this Act referred to, as "Companies Act entity financial statements" — and this also applies in any ensuing case where preparation of such statements in accordance with that section is obligatory, or

(b) international financial reporting standards and *section 292* shall be known, and are in this Act referred to, as "IFRS entity financial statements" — and this also applies in any ensuing case where preparation of such statements in accordance with those standards and that section is obligatory.

(5) In respect of a company not trading for the acquisition of gain by its members, entity financial statements shall be prepared in accordance with *section 291*.

(6) [Subject to *subsection (6A)*, after the first financial year][a] in which the directors of a company prepare IFRS entity financial statements (in this section referred to as the "first IFRS year"), all subsequent entity financial statements of the company shall be prepared in accordance with international financial reporting standards and *section 292* unless there is a relevant change of circumstances as referred to in *subsection (7)*.

[(6A) After a financial year in which the directors of a company prepare IFRS entity financial statements, the directors of the company may, notwithstanding that there is not a relevant change of circumstances as referred to in *subsection (7)*, subsequently prepare Companies Act entity financial statements for the company provided they have not changed to preparing Companies Act entity financial statements in the period of 5 years preceding the first day of that financial year.

(6B) For the purposes of calculating the 5 year period referred to in *subsection (6A)*, the reference to 'changed to Companies Act entity financial statements' shall not be read as including a reference to a change to using those financial statements which was due to a relevant change in circumstances.][b]

(7) There is a relevant change of circumstances where at any time during or after the first IFRS year—

(a) the company becomes a subsidiary undertaking of another undertaking that does not prepare IFRS financial statements,

(b) the company, having re-registered as a private company limited by shares, ceases to be a company with securities admitted to trading on a regulated market in an EEA state, or

(c) a holding undertaking of the company ceases to be an undertaking with securities admitted to trading on a regulated market in an EEA state.

(8) Where, [in accordance with *subsection (6A)* or *7*][c], Companies Act entity financial statements are prepared in relation to a company, the directors of the company may subsequently prepare IFRS entity financial statements for the company and [*subsections (6)*, *(6A)* and *(7)*][d] shall apply as if the financial year for which such IFRS entity financial statements are subsequently prepared was the first IFRS year.

Amendments

a Words substituted by C(A)A 2017, s 16(a) (previously: "After the first financial year").

b Subsections (6A) and (6B) inserted by C(A)A 2017, s 16(b).

c Words substituted by C(A)A 2017, s 16(c)(i) (previously: "following a relevant change of circumstances").

d Words substituted by C(A)A 2017, s 16(c)(ii) (previously: "*subsections (6)* and *(7)*").

291 Companies Act entity financial statements

(1) Companies Act entity financial statements in relation to a company for any financial year of it shall comprise—

(a) a balance sheet as at the financial year end date,

(b) a profit and loss account for the financial year, and

(c) any other additional statements and information required by the financial reporting framework adopted in relation to the company.

(2) Companies Act entity financial statements shall give a true and fair view of the assets, liabilities and financial position of the company as at the financial year end date and of the profit or loss of the company for the financial year.

[(3) Companies Act entity financial statements shall—

(a) as to the accounting principles to be applied, the form and content of the balance sheet and profit and loss account and the additional information to be provided by way of notes to the financial statements, comply with—

(i) in the case of a company that does not qualify for the small companies regime, the provisions of *Schedule 3*,

(ii) in the case of a company that qualifies for the small companies regime, the provisions of *Schedule 3A* or, if the company so elects, the provisions of *Schedule 3*, or

(iii) in the case of a small company that qualifies for the micro companies regime, the provisions of *Schedule 3B* or, if the company so elects, the provisions of either *Schedule 3A* or *Schedule 3*,

(b) comply with applicable accounting standards, and

(c) comply with the other provisions of this Act.][a]

[(3A) Companies Act entity financial statements shall state the following:

(a) the name and legal form of the company;

(b) the place of registration of the company and the number under which it is registered;

(c) the address of its registered office;

(d) where the company is being wound up, the information required by *section 595.*][b]

(4) Where compliance with [*Schedule 3* or *3A*, as the case may be,][c] applicable accounting standards and the other provisions of this Act as to the matters to be included in entity financial statements (or in notes to those financial statements) would not be sufficient to give a true and fair view of the matters referred to in *subsection (2)*, the necessary additional information shall be given in the entity financial statements or a note to them.

(5) If in special circumstances compliance with any of the provisions of this Act (even if additional information were provided under *subsection (4)*) is inconsistent with the requirement to give a true and fair view of the matters referred to in *subsection (2)*, the directors of the company shall depart from that provision to the extent necessary to give a true and fair view.

(6) Particulars of any departure under *subsection (5)*, the reasons for it and its effect shall be given in a note to the financial statements of the company.

[(6A) In the case of a micro company that elects to adopt the micro company regime, it shall be presumed that compliance with—

(a) *Schedule 3B*,

(b) applicable accounting standards, and

(c) the other provisions of this Act,

shall be sufficient to give a true and fair view of the matters referred to in subsection (2), and accordingly, *subsections (4)*, *(5)* and *(6)* shall not apply to a company that qualifies for the micro companies regime.][d]

(7) A company shall ensure—

(a) that its Companies Act entity financial statements include a statement as to whether they have been prepared in accordance with applicable accounting standards and identify the standards in question, and

(b) that any material departure from those standards, the effect of the departure and the reasons for it are noted in the Companies Act entity financial statements.

(8) Accounting standards are applicable to a company's entity financial statements if those standards are, in accordance with their terms, relevant to the company's circumstances and those entity financial statements.

(9) If a company fails to comply with any of *subsections (2)* to *(7)*, the company and any officer of it who is in default shall be guilty of a category 2 offence.

(10) In any proceedings against a person in respect of an offence under *subsection (9)*, it shall be a defence to prove that the defendant had reasonable grounds for believing and did believe that—

(a) a competent and reliable person was charged with the duty of ensuring that the provisions of the subsection concerned were complied with, and

(b) the latter person was in a position to discharge that duty.

(11) In *subsection (9)* "officer" includes any shadow director and *de facto* director.

Amendments

a Subsection (3) substituted by C(A)A 2017, s 17(a).
b Subsection (3A) inserted by C(A)A 2017, s 17(b).
c Words substituted by C(A)A 2017, s 17(c) (previously: "*Schedule 3*").
d Subsection (6A) inserted by C(A)A 2017, s 17(d).

---

292 IFRS entity financial statements

(1) Where the directors of a company prepare IFRS entity financial statements they shall comply with all IFRS in that regard and—

(a) shall make an unreserved statement in the notes to those entity financial statements that those financial statements have been prepared in accordance with international financial reporting standards, and

(b) shall ensure that those financial statements contain the additional information required by this Act other than that [required by *Schedules 3, 3A, 3B, 4* and *4A*][a].

(2) For the avoidance of doubt, the requirement for entity financial statements prepared in accordance with IFRS to present fairly the assets, liabilities, financial position, financial performance and cash flows is deemed to be equivalent to the true and fair view required by *section 291(2)*.

[(2A) IFRS entity financial statements shall state the following:

(a) the name and legal form of the company;

(b) the place of registration of the company and the number under which it is registered;

(c) the address of its registered office;

(d) where the company is being wound up, the information required by *section 595*.][b]

(3) If a company fails to comply with [*subsection (1)* or *(2A)*][c], the company and any officer of it who is in default shall be guilty of a category 2 offence.

(4) In any proceedings against a person in respect of an offence under *subsection (3)*, it shall be a defence to prove that the defendant had reasonable grounds for believing and did believe that—

(a) a competent and reliable person was charged with the duty of ensuring that the provisions of the subsection concerned were complied with, and

(b) the latter person was in a position to discharge that duty.

(5) In *subsection (3)* "officer" includes any shadow director and *de facto* director.

Amendments

a Words substituted by C(A)A 2017, s 18(a) (previously: "required by *Schedules 3* and *4*").

b Subsection (2A) inserted by C(A)A 2017, s 18(b).

c Words substituted by C(A)A 2017, s 18(c) (previously: "*subsection (1)*").

293 Obligation to prepare group financial statements under relevant financial reporting framework

(1) [Subject to *subsections (1A)* and *(9)*, where at the end of its financial year][a] a company is a holding company, the directors of the company, as well as preparing entity financial statements for the financial year, shall prepare group financial statements for the holding company and all its subsidiary undertakings for that financial year.

[(1A) A holding company that qualifies for the small companies regime or the micro companies regime shall be exempt from the requirements of *subsection (1)* but may, however elect to prepare group financial statements.][b]

(2) Where a holding company prepares group financial statements under this section, there shall be associated with those group financial statements the entity financial statements prepared under *section 290* and together they shall constitute the statutory financial statements of the company.

(3) Subject to *subsections (5)* to *(9)*, [a company that is required to prepare group financial statements or has elected to prepare group financial statements][c] shall prepare the statements either (as the company elects) in accordance with—

(a) *section 294*, or

(b) international financial reporting standards and *section 295*.

(4) Group financial statements prepared in accordance with—

(a) *section 294* shall be known, and are in this Act referred to, as "Companies Act group financial statements" — and this also applies in any ensuing case where preparation of such statements in accordance with that section is obligatory, or

(b) international financial reporting standards and *section 295* shall be known, and are in this Act referred to, as "IFRS group financial statements" — and this also applies in any ensuing case where preparation of such statements in accordance with those standards and that section is obligatory.

(5) In respect of a group not trading for the acquisition of gain by its members, group financial statements shall be prepared in accordance with *section 294*.

(6) [Subject to *subsection (6A)*, after the first financial year][d] in which the directors of a holding company prepare IFRS group financial statements (in this section referred to as the "first IFRS year"), all subsequent group financial statements shall be prepared in accordance with international financial reporting standards unless there is a relevant change of circumstances as referred to in *subsection (7)*.

[(6A) After a financial year in which the directors of a company prepare IFRS entity financial statements, the directors of the company may, notwithstanding that there is not a relevant change of circumstances as referred to in *subsection (7)*, subsequently prepare Companies Act entity financial statements for the company provided they have not changed to preparing Companies Act entity financial statements in the period of 5 years preceding the first day of that financial year.

(6B) For the purposes of calculating the 5 year period referred to in *subsection (6A)*, the reference to 'changed to Companies Act group financial statements' shall not be read as including a reference to a change to using those financial statements which was due to a relevant change in circumstances.][e]

(7) There is a relevant change of circumstances where at any time during or after the first IFRS year—

(a) the company becomes a subsidiary undertaking of another undertaking that does not prepare IFRS group financial statements,

(b) the company, having re-registered as a private company limited by shares, ceases to be a company with securities admitted to trading on a regulated market in an EEA state, or

(c) a holding undertaking of the company ceases to be an undertaking with securities admitted to trading on a regulated market in an EEA state.

(8) [Where Companies Act group financial statements are prepared in relation to a company in accordance with *subsection (6A)* or *(7)* as the case may be][f], the directors of the company may subsequently prepare IFRS group financial statements for the company and [*subsections (6)*, *(6A)* and *(7)*][g] shall apply as if the financial year for which such IFRS group financial statements are subsequently prepared was the first IFRS year.

(9) This section is subject to—

(a) [...][h],

(b) *section 299* (holding company that is subsidiary undertaking of undertaking registered in EEA),

(c) *section 300* (holding company that is subsidiary undertaking of undertaking registered outside EEA),

(d) *section 301* (all subsidiaries excluded from consolidation), and

(e) *section 302* (IFRS exemption).

Amendments

a Words substituted by C(A)A 2017, s 19(a) (previously: "Where at the end of its financial year").
b Subsection (1A) inserted by C(A)A 2017, s 19(b).
c Words substituted by C(A)A 2017, s 19(c) (previously: "a company that is required to prepare group financial statements").
d Words substituted by C(A)A 2017, s 19(d) (previously: "After the first financial year").
e Subsections (6A) and (6B) inserted by C(A)A 2017, s 19(e).
f Words substituted by C(A)A 2017, s 19(f)(i) (previously: "Where, following a relevant change of circumstances, Companies Act group financial statements are prepared in relation to a company").
g Words substituted by C(A)A 2017, s 19(f)(ii) (previously: "*subsections (6)* and *(7)*").
h Paragraph (9)(a) repealed by C(A)A 2017, s 19(g).

294 Companies Act group financial statements

(1) Companies Act group financial statements in relation to a holding company and its subsidiary undertakings included in the consolidation for any financial year of it shall comprise—

(a) a consolidated balance sheet dealing with the assets, liabilities and financial position of the holding company and its subsidiary undertakings (including those being wound up) as at the financial year end date,

(b) a consolidated profit and loss account dealing with the profit or loss of the holding company and its subsidiary undertakings (including those being wound up) for the financial year, and

(c) any other additional information required by the financial reporting framework adopted in relation to them.

(2) Companies Act group financial statements shall give a true and fair view of the assets, liabilities and financial position of the company and the undertakings included in the consolidation taken as a whole, as at the financial year end date and of the profit or loss of the company and those undertakings for the financial year so far as concerns the members of the company.

(3) Companies Act group financial statements shall comply with—

(a) [in the case of a holding company not qualifying for the small companies regime, the provisions of *Schedule 4*][a] as to the accounting principles to be applied, the form and content of the consolidated balance sheet and consolidated profit and loss account and the additional information to be provided by way of notes to the group financial statements,

[(aa) in the case of a holding company that qualifies for the small companies regime, the provisions of *Schedule 4A* or, if the company so elects, the provisions of *Schedule 4*,][b]

(b) applicable accounting standards, and

(c) the other provisions of this Act.

[(3A) Companies Act group financial statements shall state the following:

(a) the name and legal form of the holding company;

(b) the place of registration of the holding company and the number under which it is registered;

(c) the address of its registered office;

(d) where the holding company is being wound up, the information required by section 595.][c]

(4) Where compliance with [*Schedule 4* or *4A* as the case may be,][d] applicable accounting standards and the other provisions of this Act as to the matters to be included in group financial statements (or in notes to those financial statements) would not be sufficient to give a true and fair view of the matters referred to in *subsection (2)*, the necessary additional information shall be given in the group financial statements or a note to them.

(5) If in special circumstances compliance with any of the provisions of this Act (even if additional information were provided under *subsection (4)*) is inconsistent with the requirement to give a true and fair view of the matters referred to in *subsection (2)*, the directors of the company shall depart from that provision to the extent necessary to give a true and fair view.

(6) Particulars of any departure under *subsection (5)*, the reasons for it and its effect shall be given in a note to the financial statements.

(7) A company shall ensure—

(a) that its Companies Act group financial statements include a statement as to whether they have been prepared in accordance with applicable accounting standards and identify the standards in question, and

(b) that any material departure from those standards, the effect of the departure and the reasons for it are noted in the Companies Act group financial statements.

(8) Accounting standards are applicable to a holding company's group financial statements if those standards are, in accordance with their terms, relevant to that company's and its subsidiary undertakings' circumstances and those group financial statements.

(9) If a company fails to comply with any of *subsections (2)* to *(7)*, the company and any officer of it who is in default shall be guilty of a category 2 offence.

(10) In any proceedings against a person in respect of an offence under *subsection (9)*, it shall be a defence to prove that the defendant had reasonable grounds for believing and did believe that—

(a) a competent and reliable person was charged with the duty of ensuring that the provisions of the subsection concerned were complied with, and

(b) the latter person was in a position to discharge that duty.

(11) In *subsection (9)* "officer" includes any shadow director and *de facto* director.

Amendments

a Words substituted by C(A)A 2017, s 20(a)(i) (previously: "the provisions of *Schedule 4*").
b Paragraph (aa) inserted by C(A)A 2017, s 20(a)(ii).
c Subsection (3A) inserted by C(A)A 2017, s 20(c) (previously: "the provisions of *Schedule 4*").
d Words substituted by C(A)A 2017, s 20(b) (previously: "*Schedule 4*").

295 IFRS group financial statements

(1) Where the directors of a holding company prepare IFRS group financial statements, they shall comply with all IFRS in that regard and—

(a) shall make an unreserved statement in the notes to those group financial statements that those financial statements have been prepared in accordance with international financial reporting standards, and

(b) shall ensure that those financial statements contain the additional information required by this Act, other than that [required by *Schedules 3*, *3A*, *4* and *4A*][a].

(2) For the avoidance of doubt, the requirement for group financial statements prepared in accordance with IFRS to present fairly the assets, liabilities, financial position, financial performance and cash flows is deemed to be equivalent to the true and fair view required by *section 294(2)*.

[(2A) IFRS group financial statements shall state the following:

(a) the name and legal form of the holding company;

(b) the place of registration of the holding company and the number under which it is registered;

(c) the address of its registered office;

(d) where the holding company is being wound up, the information required by *section 595*.][b]

(3) If a company fails to comply with [*subsection (1)* or *(2A)*][c], the company and any officer of it who is in default shall be guilty of a category 2 offence.

(4) In any proceedings against a person in respect of an offence under *subsection (3)*, it shall be a defence to prove that the defendant had reasonable grounds for believing and did believe that—

(a) a competent and reliable person was charged with the duty of ensuring that the provisions of the subsection concerned were complied with, and

(b) the latter person was in a position to discharge that duty.

(5) In *subsection (3)* "officer" includes any shadow director and *de facto* director.

Amendments

a Words substituted by C(A)A 2017, s 21(a) (previously: "required by *Schedules 3* and *4*").

b Subsection (2A) inserted by C(A)A 2017, s 21(b).

c Words substituted by C(A)A 2017, s 21(c) (previously: "*subsection (1)*").

296 Consistency of financial statements

(1) Subject to the provisions of this section, the directors of a holding company shall ensure that the entity financial statements of—

(a) the holding company, and

(b) each of the subsidiary undertakings of the holding company,

are prepared using the same financial reporting framework, except to the extent that, in their opinion, there are good reasons for not doing so, and those reasons are disclosed in the entity financial statements of the holding company.

(2) As respects financial statements of subsidiary undertakings, *subsection (1)* only applies to entity financial statements of subsidiary undertakings that are required to be prepared under this Act.

(3) *Subsection (1)* does not apply—

(a) where the directors do not prepare group financial statements for the holding company, or

(b) to the financial statements of undertakings which do not trade for the acquisition of gain by the members.

(4) Where the directors of the holding company prepare IFRS group financial statements and IFRS entity financial statements for the holding company, *subsection (1)* shall have effect as if *paragraph (a)* of it were omitted.

Chapter 5
Group financial statements: exemptions and exclusions

297 Exemption from consolidation: size of group

[...][a]

Amendments

a Section 297 repealed by C(A)A 2017, s 3(1)(a).

298 Application of *section 297* in certain circumstances and cessation of exemption

[...][a]

Amendments

a Section 298 repealed by C(A)A 2017, s 3(1)(b).

299 Exemption from consolidation: holding company that is subsidiary undertaking of undertaking registered in EEA

(1) Subject to *subsection (4)*, a holding company is exempt from the requirement to prepare group financial statements if that holding company (the "lower holding company") is itself a subsidiary undertaking and its holding undertaking is established under the laws of an EEA state and one or other of the following cases applies.

(2) Those cases are—

(a) the lower holding company is a wholly owned subsidiary of that other holding undertaking,

[(aa) that other holding undertaking holds more than 90 per cent of the shares in the lower holding company and the remaining shareholders in, or members of, the lower holding company have approved the exemption,][a]

(b) that other holding undertaking holds [more than 50 per cent but not more than 90 per cent][b] of the shares in the lower holding company and notice requesting the preparation of group financial statements has not been served on the lower holding company by shareholders holding in aggregate—

(i) more than half of the remaining shares in the lower holding company, or

(ii) 5 per cent or more of the total shares in the lower holding company.

(3) The notice referred to in *subsection (2)(b)* shall be served on the lower holding company not later than 6 months after the end of the financial year before that to which it relates.

(4) *Subsection (1)* shall not apply unless the following conditions are satisfied—

(a) the lower holding company is included in consolidated accounts for a larger group drawn up to the same date, or to an earlier date in the same financial year, by a holding undertaking established under the laws of an EEA state,

(b) those accounts are drawn up and audited and the group's consolidated annual report is drawn up in accordance with—

[(i) the provisions of the Accounting Directive, or][c]

(ii) international financial reporting standards,

(c) the lower holding company [discloses in the notes to its entity financial statements][d] that it is exempt from the obligation to prepare and deliver group financial statements,

(d) the lower holding company states in its entity financial statements the name of the holding undertaking which draws up the consolidated accounts referred to in *paragraph (a)* and—

[(i) the address of the holding undertaking's registered office or, where the holding undertaking is incorporated outside the State, the registered office (howsoever described) of the undertaking in the country in which it is incorporated, or][e]

(ii) if the holding undertaking is unincorporated, the address of its principal place of business,

and

(e) the lower holding company delivers to the Registrar, within the period allowed for delivering its entity financial statements, copies of—

(i) the holding undertaking's consolidated accounts, and

(ii) the consolidated annual report,

together with the auditors' report on them.

(5) Shares held by directors of the lower holding company for the purpose of complying with any share qualification requirement shall be disregarded in determining for the purposes of *subsection (2)(a)* whether the company is a wholly owned subsidiary of another.

(6) [For the purposes of *paragraphs (aa)* and *(b)* of *subsection (2)*][f], shares held by a wholly owned subsidiary of the first-mentioned undertaking in that paragraph, or held on behalf of that undertaking or its wholly owned subsidiary, shall be attributed to that undertaking.

(7) Without prejudice to the construction provided in *subsection (8)* for the expression "consolidated annual report", references in this section to—

(a) an undertaking established under the laws of an EEA State,

(b) consolidated accounts prepared by such an undertaking, and

(c) other relevant matters in that regard,

shall, in a case where the undertaking is a company registered under this Act or an existing company, be read, respectively, as references to—

(i) the company so registered or the existing company, as the case may be,

(ii) group financial statements prepared by the company, and

(iii) the matters provided by, or referred to in, this Part or any other enactment that correspond to those relevant matters.

[(8) In this section, 'consolidated annual report' means the report prepared by management of the group in accordance with the Accounting Directive and is equivalent to the expression 'directors' report' as used in this Part.][g]

Amendments

a Paragraph (2)(aa) inserted by C(A)A 2017, s 22(a)(i).
b Words substituted by C(A)A 2017, s 22(a)(ii) (previously: "more than 50 per cent").
c Subparagraph substituted by C(A)A 2017, s 22(b)(i).
d Words substituted by C(A)A 2017, s 22(b)(ii) (previously: "discloses in its entity financial statements").
e Subparagraph substituted by C(A)A 2017, s 22(b)(iii).
f Words substituted by C(A)A 2017, s 22(c) (previously: "For the purposes of *paragraph (b)* of *subsection (2)*").
g Subsection (8) substituted by C(A)A 2017, s 22(d).

300 Exemption from consolidation: holding company that is subsidiary undertaking of undertaking registered outside EEA

(1) Subject to *subsection (4)*, a holding company is exempt from the requirement to prepare group financial statements if the holding company (the "lower holding company") is itself a subsidiary undertaking and its holding undertaking is not established under the laws of an EEA state and one or other of the following cases applies.

(2) Those cases are—

(a) the lower holding company is a wholly owned subsidiary of that other holding undertaking,

[(aa) that other holding undertaking holds more than 90 per cent of the shares in the lower holding company and the remaining shareholders in, or members of, the lower holding company have approved the exemption,][a]

(b) that other holding undertaking holds [more than 50 per cent but not more than 90 per cent][b] of the shares in the lower holding company and notice requesting the preparation of group financial statements has not been served on the lower holding company by shareholders holding in aggregate—

(i) more than half of the remaining shares in the lower holding company, or

(ii) 5 per cent or more of the total shares in the lower holding company.

(3) The notice referred to in *subsection (2)(b)* shall be served not later than 6 months after the end of the financial year before that to which it relates.

(4) *Subsection (1)* shall not apply unless the following conditions are satisfied:

(a) the lower holding company and all of its subsidiary undertakings are included in consolidated accounts for a larger group drawn up to the same date, or to an earlier date in the same financial year, by a holding undertaking;

[(b) those accounts and, where appropriate, the group's consolidated annual report are drawn up—

(i) in accordance with the Accounting Directive,

(ii) in a manner equivalent to consolidated accounts and consolidated reports so drawn up,

(iii) in accordance with international financial reporting standards, or

(iv) in accordance with accounting standards of third countries determined as equivalent to international financial reporting standards pursuant to Commission Regulation (EC) No. 1569/2007 of 21 December 2007[1] establishing a mechanism for the determination of equivalence of accounting standards applied by third country issuers of securities pursuant to Directives 2003/71/EC and 2004/109/EC of the European Parliament and of the Council;][c]

(c) the consolidated accounts are audited by one or more persons authorised to audit accounts under the laws under which the holding undertaking which draws them up is established;

(d) the lower holding company [discloses in the notes to its entity financial statements][d] that it is exempt from the obligation to prepare and deliver group financial statements;

(e) the lower holding company states in its entity financial statements the name of the holding undertaking which draws up the consolidated accounts referred to in *paragraph (a)* and—

[(i) the address of the holding undertaking's registered office and, where the holding undertaking is incorporated outside the State, the registered office (howsoever described) of the undertaking in the country in which it is incorporated, or][e]

(ii) if the holding undertaking is unincorporated, the address of its principal place of business;

and

(f) the lower holding company delivers to the Registrar, within the period allowed for delivering its entity financial statements, copies of—

(i) the other holding undertaking's consolidated accounts, and

(ii) where appropriate, the consolidated annual report,

together with the auditors' report on them.

(5) Shares held by directors of the lower holding company for the purpose of complying with any share qualification requirement shall be disregarded in determining for the purposes of *subsection (2)(a)* whether the company is a wholly owned subsidiary of another.

(6) [For the purposes of *paragraphs (aa)* and *(b)* of *subsection (2)*][f], shares held by a wholly owned subsidiary of the first-mentioned undertaking in that paragraph, or held on behalf of that undertaking or its wholly owned subsidiary, shall be attributed to that undertaking.

[(7) In this section, 'consolidated annual report' means—

(a) the report prepared by management of the group in accordance with the Accounting Directive, or

(b) the report prepared by management of the group in a manner equivalent to consolidated reports referred to in *subsection (4)(b)(ii)*,

and, in either case, is equivalent to the expression 'directors' report' as used in this Part.][g]

Amendments

a Subsection (2)(aa) inserted by C(A)A 2017, s 23(a)(i).
b Words substituted by C(A)A 2017, s 23(a)(ii) (previously: "more than 50 per cent").
c Subsection (4)(b) substituted by C(A)A 2017, s 23(b)(i).
d Words substituted by C(A)A 2017, s 23(b)(ii) (previously: "discloses in its entity financial statements").
e Subparagraph (e)(i) substituted by C(A)A 2017, s 23(b)(iii).
f Words substituted by C(A)A 2017, s 23(c) (previously: "For the purposes of *paragraph (b)* of *subsection (2)*").
g Subsection (7) substituted by C(A)A 2017, s 23(d).

References

1 OJ No. L340, 22.12.2007, p.66.

301 Exemption from consolidation: holding company with all of its subsidiary undertakings excluded from consolidation

A holding company is exempt from the requirement to prepare group financial statements if, by virtue of *section 303(2)* or *(3)*, all of its subsidiary undertakings could be excluded from the consolidation in Companies Act group financial statements.

302 Exemption from consolidation where IFRS so permits

A holding company that prepares IFRS financial statements is exempt from the requirement to prepare group financial statements in the circumstances provided, and subject to compliance with the conditions in that behalf specified, in IFRS.

303 Subsidiary undertakings included in the group financial statements

(1) In the case of Companies Act group financial statements, all of the subsidiary undertakings of the holding company shall be consolidated in the group financial statements, but this is subject to the exceptions authorised by the subsequent provisions of this section.

(2) A subsidiary undertaking may be excluded from consolidation in Companies Act group financial statements if its inclusion is not material for the purposes of giving a true and fair view; but 2 or more undertakings may be excluded only if they are not material, for those purposes, taken together.

(3) In addition, a subsidiary undertaking may be excluded from consolidation in Companies Act group financial statements where—

(a) severe long-term restrictions substantially hinder the exercise of the rights of the holding company over the assets or management of that subsidiary undertaking, or

(b) [in extremely rare cases, the information necessary][a] for the preparation of group financial statements in accordance with this Part cannot be obtained without disproportionate expense or undue delay, or

(c) the interest of the holding company is held exclusively with a view to subsequent resale.

(4) The reference in *subsection (3)(a)* to the rights of the holding company and the reference in *subsection (3)(c)* to the interest of the holding company are, respectively, to rights and interest held by or attributed to the holding company for the purposes of *section 7* (definition of subsidiary) in the absence of which it would not be the holding company.

Amendments

a Words substituted by C(A)A 2017, s 24 (previously: "the information necessary").

---

304 Treatment of entity profit and loss account where group financial statements prepared

(1) Subject to *subsection (3)*, *subsection (2)* applies with respect to the entity profit and loss account of a holding company where—

(a) [the company is required to prepare or elects to prepare (and, accordingly, does prepare)][a] group financial statements in accordance with this Act, and

(b) the notes to [the company's entity balance sheet shows][b] the company's profit or loss for the financial year determined in accordance with this Act.

(2) [The entity profit and loss account together with, in the case of a company which elects to apply the small companies regime, the information specified in *paragraphs 52* and *53* of *Schedule 3A*, and in the case of all other companies the information specified in *paragraphs 59* to *63* of *Schedule 3*][c] (information supplementing the profit and loss account) or equivalent information required by IFRS shall be approved in accordance with *section 324* (approval by board of directors) but may be omitted from the company's entity financial statements for the purposes of *section 338* (circulation of financial statements), and shall also be exempt from the requirements of—

(a) *section 339* (right of members to demand copies of financial statements),

(b) *section 341* (financial statements to be laid before members), and

(c) *section 347* (documents to be annexed to annual return).

(3) *Subsection (2)* does not apply unless the fact that it has been availed of is disclosed in the entity financial statements published with the group financial statements.

Amendments

a Words substituted by C(A)A 2017, s 25(a)(i) (previously: "the company is required to prepare and does prepare").

b Words substituted by C(A)A 2017, s 25(a)(ii) (previously: "the notes to the company's entity balance sheet show").

c Words substituted by C(A)A 2017, s 25(b) (previously: "The entity profit and loss account together with the information specified in *paragraphs 62* to *66* of *Schedule 3*").

Chapter 6
Disclosure of directors' remuneration and transactions

305 Disclosure of directors' remuneration

(1) [Subject to *subsection (14)*, the notes to the statutory financial statements][a] of a company shall disclose both for the current and the preceding financial year the following amounts in relation to directors of the company (and that expression includes the one or more persons who, at any time during the financial year concerned, were directors of it)—

(a) the aggregate amount of emoluments paid to or receivable by directors in respect of qualifying services,

(b) the aggregate amount of the gains by the directors on the exercise of share options during the financial year,

(c) the aggregate amount of the money or value of other assets, including shares but excluding share options, paid to or receivable by the directors under long term incentive schemes in respect of qualifying services,

(d) the aggregate amount of any contributions paid, treated as paid, or payable during the financial year to a retirement benefit scheme in respect of qualifying services of directors, identifying separately the amounts relating to—

(i) defined contribution schemes, and

(ii) defined benefit schemes,

and in each case showing the number of directors, if any, to whom retirement benefits are accruing under such schemes in respect of qualifying services,

(e) the aggregate amount of any compensation paid or payable to directors in respect of loss of office or other termination payments in the financial year.

(2) [Subject to *subsection (14)*, the notes to the statutory financial statements][b] of a company shall disclose both for the current and the preceding financial year the

following amounts in relation to the one or more persons who are past directors of it or past directors of its holding undertaking—

(a) the aggregate amount paid or payable for such directors' retirement benefits,

(b) the aggregate amount of any compensation paid or payable to such directors in respect of loss of office or other termination benefits.

(3) In this section "qualifying services", in relation to any person, means his or her services as a director of the company and his or her services, while director of the company, as director of any of its subsidiary undertakings or otherwise in connection with the management of the affairs of the company or any of its subsidiary undertakings.

(4) For the purpose of *subsection (1)(a)*, "emoluments", in relation to a director, includes salaries, fees and percentages, bonuses, any sums paid by way of expenses allowance in so far as those sums are chargeable to income tax, and, subject to *subsection (5)*, the estimated money value of any other benefits received by him or her otherwise than in cash.

(5) However, for the purpose of *subsection (1)(a)*, "emoluments", in relation to a director, does not include—

(a) the value of any share options granted to him or her or gains made by him or her on the exercise of share options,

(b) any contributions paid, treated as paid or payable in respect of him or her to a retirement benefit scheme or any benefits to which he or she is entitled from such a scheme,

(c) any money or other assets paid to or receivable by him or her under any long term incentive scheme.

(6) In *subsections (1)(b)* and *(c)* and *(5)(a)*—

"shares" means quoted shares (that is to say shares quoted on any securities or other market referred to in *section 1072*) or shares that are redeemable in cash or puttable in cash;

["share options" means options over quoted shares or shares that are redeemable in cash or puttable in cash.][c]

(7) In *subsection (1)(c)*, "long term incentive scheme" means any agreement or arrangement under which money or other assets may become receivable by a director and which includes one or more qualifying conditions with respect to services or performance which cannot be fulfilled within a single financial year; and for this purpose the following shall be disregarded:

(a) bonuses the amount of which falls to be determined by reference to service or performance within a single year;

(b) compensation for loss of office and other termination payments; and

(c) retirement benefits.

(8) The amount to be shown for the purpose of *subsection (2)(a)* shall not include any retirement benefits paid or receivable under a retirement benefit scheme if the scheme is

such that the contributions under it are substantially adequate for the maintenance of the scheme.

(9) However the amount to be so shown shall include any retirement benefits paid or receivable in respect of any qualifying services of a past-director of the company, whether to or by him or her, on his or her nomination or by virtue of dependence on or other connection with him or her, to or by any other person.

(10) The amount to be shown for the purpose of *subsection (2)(a)* shall distinguish between retirement benefits in respect of services as director, whether of the company or its subsidiary undertakings, and other retirement benefits.

(11) For the purposes of this section—

"contribution", in relation to a retirement benefit scheme, means any payment (including an insurance premium) made for the purposes of the scheme by or in respect of persons rendering services in respect of which retirement benefits will or may become payable under the scheme, except that it does not include any payment in respect of 2 or more persons if the amount paid in respect of each of them is not ascertainable;

"retirement benefits" includes any pension, superannuation allowance, superannuation gratuity or similar payment;

"retirement benefit scheme" means a scheme for the provision of retirement benefits in respect of services as director or otherwise which is maintained in whole or in part by means of contributions.

(12) The amounts to be shown for the purpose of *subsections (1)(e)* and *(2)(b)*—

(a) shall include any sums paid to or receivable by a director or past director—

(i) by way of compensation for loss of office or other termination payment as director of the company,

(ii) while director of the company, or on or in connection with his or her ceasing to be a director of the company, by way of—

(I) compensation for loss of any other office in connection with the management of the company's affairs or other termination payment in respect of such office, or

(II) compensation for loss of office or other termination payment as director or otherwise in connection with the management of the affairs of any of its subsidiary undertakings,

and

(b) shall distinguish between compensation or termination payments in respect of the office of director, whether of the company or of its subsidiary undertakings, and compensation or termination payments in respect of other offices,

and, for the purposes of this section, references to termination payments include references to sums paid or payable as consideration for or in connection with a person's retirement from office.

(13) The amounts to be shown for the purpose of *subsections (1)* and *(2)*—

(a) shall include all relevant sums paid by or receivable from—

(i) the company,

(ii) the company's subsidiary undertakings,

(iii) any holding undertaking of the company, and

(iv) any other person,

except sums to be accounted for to the company or any of its subsidiary undertakings or, by virtue of *section 253*, to past or present members of the company or any of its subsidiary undertakings or any class of those members, and

(b) shall distinguish, in the case of the amount to be shown for the purpose of *subsection (1)(e)* or *(2)(b)*, between the sums respectively paid by or receivable from the company, the company's subsidiary undertakings, any holding undertaking of the company and any other persons.

[(14) A company that qualifies for the micro companies regime shall be exempt from the requirements of this section.][d]

Amendments

a Words substituted by C(A)A 2017, s 26(a) (previously: "The notes to the statutory financial statements").

b Words substituted by C(A)A 2017, s 26(b) (previously: "The notes to the statutory financial statements").

c Definition 'share options' substituted by C(A)A 2017, s 26(c).

d Subsection (14) inserted by C(A)A 2017, s 26(d).

[305A Payments to third parties for services of directors

(1) Subject to *subsection (3)*, the notes to the statutory financial statements of a company shall disclose, both for the current and the preceding financial year, the aggregate amount of any consideration paid to, or receivable by, third parties for making available the services of any person—

(a) as a director of the company,

(b) as director of any of its subsidiary undertakings, or

(c) otherwise in connection with the management of the company's affairs or any of its subsidiary undertakings.

(2) The amount to be shown for the purposes of *subsection (1)* shall—

(a) include all relevant sums paid by or receivable from—

(i) the company,

(ii) the company's subsidiary undertakings,

(iii) any holding undertaking of the company, and

(iv) any other person, and

(b) distinguish between the sums respectively paid by, or receivable from, the company, the company's subsidiary undertakings, any holding undertaking of the company and any other persons.

(3) A company that qualifies for the micro companies regime shall be exempt from the requirements of this section.

(4) For the purposes of *subsection (1)*—

(a) (i) the reference to 'consideration' includes benefits otherwise than in cash and the reference to 'the aggregate amount' is to the estimated monetary value of the benefits, and

(ii) the nature of any such consideration referred to in subparagraph (i) shall be disclosed, and

(b) the reference to 'third parties' means a person other than—

(i) the director or a person connected with that director,

(ii) a body corporate controlled by that director, or

(iii) the company or any of its subsidiary undertakings.][a]

Amendments

a Section 305A inserted by C(A)A 2017, s 27.

[306 Supplemental provisions in relation to *section 305 and 305A*

(1) The amounts to be shown for the purpose of *section 305* in relation to a director shall include all amounts paid or payable to a person connected with a director within the meaning of *section 220*.

(2) The amounts to be shown for the purpose of *section 305* for any financial year shall be the sums receivable in respect of that year, whenever paid, or, in the case of sums not receivable in respect of a period, the sums paid during that year, so, however, that where—

(a) any sums are not shown in the statutory financial statements for the relevant financial year on the ground that the person receiving them is liable to account for them as mentioned in *subsection (13)(a)* of *section 305*, but the liability is thereafter wholly or partly released or is not enforced within a period of 2 years, or

(b) any sums paid by the way of expenses allowance are chargeable to income tax after the end of the relevant financial year, those sums shall, to the extent to which the liability is released or not enforced or they are chargeable as so mentioned, as the case may be, be shown in the first statutory financial statements in which it is practicable to show them and shall be distinguished from the amounts to be shown in those statements apart from this provision.

(3) Where it is necessary to do so for the purpose of making any distinction required by *sections 305*, *305A* or this section in any amount to be shown for the purpose of any one of those sections, the directors may apportion any payments between the matters in respect of which they have been paid or which are receivable or have been paid or are payable to third parties in such manner as they think appropriate.

(4) If, in the case of any statutory financial statements, the requirements of *section 305*, *305A* or this section are not complied with, it shall be the duty of the statutory auditors of the company by whom the statutory financial statements are examined to include in the report on those statements, so far as they are reasonably able to do so, a statement giving the required particulars.

(5) In *sections 305* and *305A*, any reference to a company's subsidiary undertaking—

(a) in relation to a person who is or was, while a director of the company, a director also, by virtue of the company's nomination, direct or indirect, of any other body corporate, shall, subject to paragraph (b), include that body corporate, whether or not it is or was in fact the company's subsidiary undertaking, and

(b) shall—

(i) for the purpose of *subsections (3)* to *(6)* and *(8)* to *(10)* of *section 305*, be taken as referring to a subsidiary undertaking at the time the services were rendered, and, for the purpose of *subsection (12)* of that section, be taken as referring to a subsidiary undertaking immediately before the loss of office as director of the company, and

(ii) for the purpose of *subsection (1)* of *section 305A*, be taken as referring to a subsidiary undertaking at the time the services were rendered.

(6) In *sections 305* and *305A* and this section, "director" includes any shadow director and *de facto* director.][a]

Amendments

a Section 306 substituted by C(A)A 2017, s 28.

---

307 Obligation to disclose information about directors' benefits: loans, quasi-loans, credit transactions and guarantees

(1) Subject to *sections 308* and *309*, the entity financial statements of a company shall disclose, both for the current and the preceding financial year, in the notes to the statements the particulars specified in *subsection (3)*, *(4)*, *(5)*, *(6)* or *(7)*, as appropriate, of—

(a) loans, quasi-loans and credit transactions entered into by the company with or for its directors, directors of its holding undertaking or persons connected with such directors,

(b) any agreement by the company to enter into any loans, quasi-loans and credit transactions with or for its directors, directors of its holding undertaking or persons connected with such directors,

(c) guarantees entered into and security provided by the company on behalf of its directors, directors of its holding undertaking or persons connected with such directors in connection with a loan, quasi-loan or credit transaction entered into with or for those directors or other persons,

(d) any agreement by the company to enter into guarantees or provide any security on behalf of its directors, directors of its holding undertaking or persons connected with such directors in connection with a loan, quasi-loan or credit transaction entered into with or for those directors or other persons, and

(e) any of the following arrangements made by the company or which it takes part in, namely—

(i) an assignment to it, or an assumption by it, of any rights, obligations or liabilities under a transaction which, if it had been entered into by the company, would have fallen into any of the preceding paragraphs,

(ii) an arrangement under which—

(I) another person enters into a transaction which, if it had been entered into by the company, would have fallen into any of the preceding paragraphs or *subparagraph (i)*, and

(II) that other person, in pursuance of the arrangement, has obtained or is to obtain any benefit from the company or its holding undertaking or a subsidiary undertaking of the company or its holding undertaking.

(2) Subject to *sections 308* and *309*, the group financial statements of a holding company shall disclose, both for the current and the preceding financial year, in the notes to the statements the particulars specified in *subsection (3)*, *(4)*, *(5)*, *(6)* or *(7)*, as appropriate, of—

(a) loans, quasi-loans and credit transactions entered into by the company or any of its subsidiary undertakings with or for its directors, directors of its holding undertaking or persons connected with such directors,

(b) any agreement by the company or any of its subsidiary undertakings to enter into any loans, quasi-loans and credit transactions with or for its directors, directors of its holding undertaking or persons connected with such directors,

(c) guarantees entered into and security provided by the company or any of its subsidiary undertakings on behalf of its directors, directors of its holding undertaking or persons connected with such directors in connection with a loan, quasi-loan or credit transaction entered into with or for those directors or other persons,

(d) any agreement by the company or any of its subsidiary undertakings to enter into guarantees or provide any security on behalf of its directors, directors of its holding undertaking or persons connected with such directors in connection with a loan, quasi-loan or credit transaction entered into with or for those directors or other persons, and

(e) any of the following arrangements made by the company or any of its subsidiary undertakings or which it or any of them takes part in, namely:

(i) an assignment to the company or the subsidiary undertaking, or an assumption by the company or the subsidiary undertaking, of any rights, obligations or liabilities under a transaction which, if it had been entered into by the company or undertaking, would have fallen into any of the preceding paragraphs;

(ii) an arrangement under which—

(I) another person enters into a transaction which, if it had been entered into by the company or the subsidiary undertaking (each of which is referred to in *clause (II)* as a "relevant entity"), would have fallen into any of the preceding paragraphs or *subparagraph (i)*, and

(II) that other person, in pursuance of the arrangement, has obtained or is to obtain any benefit from—

(A) if the relevant entity is the company — the company or its holding undertaking or a subsidiary undertaking of the company or its holding undertaking,

(B) if the relevant entity is the subsidiary undertaking — the subsidiary undertaking or its holding undertaking or a subsidiary undertaking of the first-mentioned subsidiary undertaking or its holding undertaking.

(3) The particulars mentioned in *subsections (1)* and *(2)* in respect of arrangements comprising loans, quasi-loans or credit transactions referred to in *paragraph (a)* of either subsection are, separately for each director or other person—

(a) the name of the person for whom the arrangements were made and where that person is or was connected with a director of the company or undertaking, the name of the director,

(b) the value of the arrangements at the beginning and end of the financial year,

(c) advances made under the arrangements during the financial year,

(d) amounts repaid under the arrangements during the financial year,

(e) the amounts of any allowance made during the financial year in respect of any failure or anticipated failure by the borrower to repay the whole or part of the outstanding amount,

(f) [amounts outstanding under the arrangements waived][a] during the financial year,

(g) an indication of the interest rate, and

(h) the arrangements' other main conditions.

(4) The particulars mentioned in *subsections (1)* and *(2)* in respect of an agreement to enter into loans, quasi-loans or credit transactions referred to in *paragraph (b)* of either subsection are, separately for each director or other person—

(a) the name of the person for whom the agreement was made and where that person is or was connected with a director of the company or undertaking, the name of the director,

(b) the value of the arrangements agreed to,

(c) an indication of the interest rate, and

(d) the agreement's other main conditions.

(5) The particulars mentioned in *subsections (1)* and *(2)* in respect of arrangements comprising guarantees entered into or security provided in connection with a loan, quasi-loan or credit transaction referred to in *paragraph (c)* of either subsection are, separately for each director or other person—

(a) the name of the person for whom the arrangements were made and where that person is or was connected with a director of the company or the undertaking, the name of the director,

(b) the amount of the maximum liability that may be incurred by the company (or any of its subsidiary undertakings),

(c) any amount paid and any liability incurred by the company (or any of its subsidiary undertakings) for the purpose of fulfilling the guarantee or on foot of the provision of security (including any loss incurred by reason of enforcement of the guarantee or loss of the security), and

(d) the arrangements' main terms.

(6) The particulars mentioned in *subsections (1)* and *(2)* in respect of agreements to enter into guarantees or provide security in connection with a loan, quasi-loan or credit transaction referred to in *paragraph (d)* of either subsection are, separately for each director or other person—

(a) the name of the person for whom the agreement was made and where that person is or was connected with a director of the company or the undertaking, the name of the director,

(b) the amount of the maximum liability that may be incurred by the company (or any of its subsidiary undertakings), and

(c) the agreement's main terms.

(7) The particulars mentioned in *subsections (1)* and *(2)* in respect of an arrangement referred to in *paragraph (e)* of either subsection are—

(a) in the case of an arrangement referred to in *subparagraph (i)* or *(ii)* of that *paragraph (e)*, whichever of the particulars specified in any of *subsections (3)* to *(6)* would have to be disclosed if the arrangement had fallen into a preceding paragraph of *subsection (1)* or, as the case may be, *subsection (2)* or (in the case of an arrangement referred to in *subparagraph (ii)* of that *paragraph (e)*) *subparagraph (i)* of that *paragraph (e)*, and

(b) in addition – in the case of an arrangement referred to in *subparagraph (ii)* of that *paragraph (e)* – the amount of the benefit referred to in that subparagraph obtained or to be obtained by the other person referred to therein.

(8) There shall also be stated, both for the current and the preceding financial year in the notes to the financial statements (whether entity or group financial statements)—

(a) the total of the amounts stated for the purposes of *paragraphs (b)* to *(f)* of *subsection (3)* (that is to say a separate total for the amounts stated for each of those paragraphs),

(b) the total of the amounts stated for the purposes of *paragraphs (b)* and *(c)* of *subsection (5)* (that is to say a separate total for the amounts stated for each of those paragraphs), and

(c) the amounts stated for the purposes of *subsection (3)(b)* expressed as a percentage of the net assets of the company at the beginning and end of the financial year.

(9) The disclosure required by *subsection (8)* is extended by *section 308(5)* to *(8)*, in the manner specified in those provisions, to persons who are officers (but not directors) of the company, holding undertaking or subsidiary undertaking concerned.

(10) Where at any time during the financial year the aggregate of the amounts outstanding under all arrangements of the type referred to in *subsections (3)(f)* and *(5)(b)* amount to more than 10 per cent of the net assets of the company, the aggregate amount shall be stated and the percentage of net assets that the total represents.

Amendments

a Words substituted by C(A)A 2017, s 29 (previously: "the maximum amount outstanding under the arrangements").

---

308 Supplemental provisions in relation to *section 307* (including certain exemptions from its terms)

(1) References in *section 307* and this section to a director of the company or the undertaking are references to the person who was a director of the company or the undertaking at any time in the financial year to which the financial statements relate (or, as the case may be, the preceding financial year) and "director" in those sections includes any shadow director and *de facto* director.

(2) The requirements of *section 307* apply in relation to every loan, quasi-loan, credit transaction or guarantee or agreement referred to in that section subsisting at any time in the financial year to which the financial statements relate (or, as the case may be, the preceding financial year)—

(a) whenever it was entered into,

(b) whether or not the person concerned was a director of the company or the undertaking in question at the time it was entered into,

(c) in the case of an arrangement entered into involving a subsidiary undertaking of that company, whether or not that undertaking was a subsidiary undertaking at the time it was entered into, and

(d) whether or not the transaction or agreement was prohibited by *section 239*.

(3) The requirements of *section 307(1)* to *(8)* do not apply in relation to an individual director and persons connected with him or her if the aggregate value of all agreements, transactions and arrangements referred to in *section 307(1)* and *(2)* did not, at any time during the financial year, exceed €7,500 for that director and those persons.

(4) Where a holding company avails itself of an exemption under this Part from the requirement to prepare group financial statements in relation to any financial year, *section 307(2)* shall have effect in relation to the company and that financial year as if "entity financial statements" were substituted for "group financial statements".

(5) In addition to, and not in derogation from any of its requirements in relation to directors, *subsection (8)* of *section 307* applies, subject to *subsection (3)* and *section 310*, to persons who are officers (but not directors) of the company, holding company or subsidiary undertaking concerned and, accordingly operates, with respect to such officers, to require to be disclosed, both for the current and the preceding financial year, in the notes to the financial statements (whether entity or group financial statements) the matters mentioned in that subsection, but separately from the disclosures under it in respect of directors.

(6) For the purposes of that application, the following provisions of *section 307* and this section have effect subject to the following modifications:

(a) the references in *section 307(1)* and *(2)* to directors are to be read as references to officers (not being directors) of the company, holding undertaking or subsidiary undertaking concerned;

(b) *subsection (3)(b)* to *(f)* and *subsection (5)(b)* and *(c)* of *section 307* are to be read as if they applied to officers (not being directors) of the company, holding undertaking or subsidiary undertaking concerned;

(c) the following references to director in this section, namely, the first and second references to director in *subsection (1)* and each such reference in *subsections (2)* and *(3)*, are to be read as references to an officer who is not a director.

(7) The operation of *subsection (8)* of *section 307*, as applied by virtue of *subsections (5)* and *(6)*, also requires the number of officers mentioned in *subsection (5)*, arrangements in respect of whom are the subject of the matters disclosed pursuant to that *subsection (8)*, as so applied, to be stated in the notes to the financial statements concerned.

(8) For the purposes of *section 307* and this section—

(a) "quasi-loan", "credit transaction", "guarantee" and "value of the arrangement" have the meanings given to them by *section 219*,

(b) *section 220* shall apply in determining whether a person is connected with a director or not,

(c) *section 219(7)* shall apply in determining whether or not a transaction or arrangement is made for a person.

309 Other arrangements and transactions in which the directors, etc., have material interest

(1) [Subject to *subsection (1A)* and *section 310*][a], the entity financial statements of a company shall disclose, both for the current and the preceding financial year, in the notes to the statements the particulars specified in *subsection (3)* of any other arrangement or transaction not dealt with by *section 305*, *307* or *308* entered into by the company in which a person, who at any time during the financial year was a director, a director of its holding undertaking or a person connected with such a director, had, directly or indirectly, a material interest.

[(1A) A company that qualifies for the micro companies regime shall be exempt from the requirements of *subsection (1)*.][b]

(2) Subject to *section 310*, the group financial statements of a holding company shall disclose, both for the current and the preceding financial year, in the notes to the statements the particulars specified in *subsection (3)* of any other arrangement or transaction not dealt with by *section 305*, *307* or *308* entered into by the company or any of its subsidiary undertakings in which a person, who at any time during the financial year was a director, a director of its holding undertaking or a person connected with such a director, had, directly or indirectly, a material interest.

(3) The particulars mentioned in *subsections (1)* and *(2)* are—

(a) particulars of the principal terms of the arrangement or transaction,

(b) the name of the director or other person with the material interest, and

(c) the nature of the interest.

(4) For the purposes of *subsections (1)* and *(2)*—

(a) an arrangement or transaction between a company and a director of the company or of its holding undertaking or a person connected with such a director shall (if it would not otherwise be so treated) be treated as an arrangement or transaction in which that director is interested, and

(b) an interest in such an arrangement or transaction is not material if in the opinion of the majority of the directors (other than that director) of the company which is preparing the financial statements in question it is not material (but without prejudice to the question whether or not such an interest is material in any case where those directors have not considered the matter).

(5) *Subsections (1)* and *(2)* do not apply in relation to the following arrangements or transactions—

(a) an arrangement or transaction between one company and another in which a director of the first company or of its subsidiary undertaking or holding undertaking is interested only by virtue of his or her being a director of the other,

(b) a contract of service between a company and one of its directors or a director of its holding undertaking or between a director of a company and any of that company's subsidiary undertakings, and

(c) an arrangement or transaction which was not entered into during the financial year concerned and which did not subsist at any time during that year.

(6) *Subsections (1)* and *(2)* do not apply to any arrangement or transaction with a company or any of its subsidiary undertakings in which a director of the company or of its holding undertaking, or a person connected with such a director, had, directly or indirectly, a material interest if—

(a) the value of each arrangement or transaction in which that director or other person had, directly or indirectly, a material interest and which was made after the commencement of the financial year with the company or any of its subsidiary undertakings, and

(b) the value of each such arrangement or transaction which was made before the commencement of the financial year less the amount (if any) by which the liabilities of the person for whom the arrangement or transaction was made have been reduced,

did not at any time during the financial year exceed in the aggregate €5,000 or, if more, did not exceed €15,000 or one per cent of the value of the net assets of the company preparing the entity or group financial statements, whichever is the less.

(7) Where a holding company avails itself of an exemption under this Part from the requirement to prepare group financial statements in relation to any financial year, *subsection (2)* shall have effect in relation to the company and that financial year as if "entity financial statements" were substituted for "group financial statements".

(8) For the purposes of this section—

(a) *section 220* shall apply in determining whether a person is connected with a director or not,

(b) "arrangement" includes an agreement, and

(c) "director" includes any shadow director and *de facto* director.

Amendments

a Words substituted by C(A)A 2017, s 30(a) (previously: "Subject to *section 310*").

b Subsection (1A) inserted by C(A)A 2017, s 30(b).

310 Credit Institutions: exceptions to disclosure by holding company under *sections 307 to 309* in the case of connected persons and certain officers

(1) As respects any financial statements prepared by any company which is the holding company of a credit institution the requirements of *section 307* do not apply in relation to any of the following to which the credit institution is a party, namely:

(a) a loan, quasi-loan or other transaction referred to in *section 307(1)(a)* or *(2)(a)* entered into with or for a person connected with a director of that holding company or institution;

(b) an agreement referred to in *section 307(1)(b)* or *(2)(b)* to enter into a loan, quasi-loan or other transaction referred to in that provision with or for a person connected with a director of that holding company or institution;

(c) a guarantee entered into or security provided as mentioned in *section 307(1)(c)* or *(2)(c)* on behalf of a person connected with any of the directors referred to in that provision (being any of the directors of the holding company or institution) in connection with a loan, quasi-loan or credit transaction entered into with or for such a person so connected;

(d) an agreement as mentioned in *section 307(1)(d)* or *(2)(d)* to enter into a guarantee or provide security on behalf of a person connected with any of the directors mentioned in that provision (being any of the directors of the holding company or institution) in connection with a loan, quasi-loan or credit transaction entered into with or for such a person so connected; or

(e) an arrangement referred to in *subparagraph (i)* or *(ii)* of *section 307(1)(e)* or *(2)(e)* where the transaction referred to in that subparagraph (that is to say, a transaction that, if it had been made by the institution, would have fallen into a preceding paragraph of *section 307(1)* or *(2)*, as the case may be, or (in the case of that *subparagraph (ii)*) that *subparagraph (i)*) was entered into with or for a person connected with a director of that holding company or institution.

(2) As respects any financial statements prepared by any company that is the holding company of a credit institution, the extension of *section 307(8)* by *section 308(5)* does not apply in relation to any transaction, arrangement or agreement made by that credit institution for or with—

(a) any of its officers, or

(b) any of the officers of the holding company.

(3) As respects any financial statements prepared by any company that is the holding company of a credit institution, the requirements of *subsection (1)* or *(2)* of *section 309* do not apply in relation to any arrangement or transaction referred to in that *subsection (1)* or *(2)* to which the credit institution is a party if the only person referred to in that *subsection (1)* or *(2)*, as the case may be, who has, directly or indirectly, a material interest in the arrangement or transaction is a person connected with any of the directors referred to in that *subsection (1)* or *(2)*, as the case may be.

(4) In a case that would fall within *subsection (3)* but for the fact that both—

(a) a person (the "connected person") connected with any of the directors referred to in *subsection (1)* or *(2)*, as the case may be, of *section 309*, and

(b) a director or directors referred to in that *subsection (1)* or *(2)*, as the case may be,

have, directly or indirectly, a material interest in the arrangement or transaction concerned to which the credit institution referred to in *subsection (3)* is a party, then the particulars of the material interest to be disclosed under *section 309* need not include the name of the connected person nor (if his or her interest is different from that of the foregoing director or directors) the nature of the connected person's interest.

(5) A word or expression used in this section and also used in *sections 307* to *309* has the same meaning in this section as it has in those sections.

311 Credit Institutions: disclosures by holding company of aggregate amounts in respect of connected persons

(1) In this section—

"relevant period" means the financial year to which the financial statements concerned relate;

"relevant persons" means persons who, at any time during the financial year to which the financial statements concerned relate, were connected with a director of the company or the institution referred to in *subsection (2)*;

"relevant transaction, arrangement or agreement" shall be read in accordance with *subsection (3)*;

"transactions, arrangements or agreements" means any of the following classes of transactions, arrangements or agreements:

(a) loans, quasi-loans or credit transactions entered into with or for relevant persons;

(b) agreements to enter into any loans, quasi-loans or credit transactions with or for relevant persons;

(c) guarantees entered into or security provided on behalf of relevant persons in connection with a loan, quasi-loan or credit transaction entered into with or for such persons;

(d) agreements to enter into guarantees or provide any security on behalf of relevant persons in connection with a loan, quasi-loan or credit transaction entered into with or for such persons;

(e) arrangements referred to in *subparagraph (i)* or *(ii)* of either *section 307(1)(e)* or *(2)(e)* where the transactions referred to in that subparagraph (that is to say, transactions that, if they had been made by the institution, would have fallen into a preceding paragraph of *section 307(1)* or *(2)*, as the case may be, or (in the case of that *subparagraph (ii)*) that *subparagraph (i)*) were entered into with or for relevant persons.

(2) The group financial statements of a company which is the holding company of a credit institution shall contain a statement, by way of notes to those statements, of the matters specified in *subsection (3)* in relation to transactions, arrangements or agreements made by the credit institution.

(3) The matters mentioned in *subsection (2)* are:

(a) the aggregate amounts outstanding at the end of the relevant period under transactions, arrangements or agreements made by the institution and coming within any particular paragraph of *subsection (1)* (which transactions, arrangements or agreements, coming within any particular such paragraph, are referred to subsequently in this section as "relevant transactions, arrangements or agreements");

(b) the aggregate maximum amounts outstanding during the relevant period under relevant transactions, arrangements or agreements made by the institution;

(c) the number of relevant persons for or with whom relevant transactions, arrangements and agreements that subsisted at the end of the relevant period were made by the institution; and

(d) the maximum number of relevant persons for or with whom relevant transactions, arrangements and agreements that subsisted at any time during the relevant period were made by the institution.

(4) A transaction, arrangement or agreement to which *subsection (2)* applies need not be included in the statement referred to in that subsection if—

(a) it is entered into by the institution concerned in the ordinary course of its business, and

(b) its value is not greater, and its terms no more favourable,

in respect of the person for or with whom it is made, than that or those which—

(i) the institution ordinarily offers, or

(ii) it is reasonable to expect the institution to have offered,

to or in respect of a person of the same financial standing but unconnected with the institution.

(5) In reckoning the aggregate maximum amounts or the maximum number of persons referred to in *subsection (3)(b)* or *(d)*, as appropriate, there shall not be counted, as the case may be—

(a) relevant transactions, arrangements and agreements made by the institution concerned for or with a person if the aggregate maximum amount outstanding during the relevant period under relevant transactions, arrangements and agreements made for or with him or her by it does not exceed €7,500, or

(b) a person for or with whom such transactions, arrangements and agreements have been so made and for whom the aggregate maximum amount outstanding as mentioned in *paragraph (a)* does not exceed the amount there mentioned.

(6) For the purposes of this section, "amount outstanding" means the amount of the outstanding liabilities of the person for or with whom the transaction, arrangement or agreement in question was made, or, in the case of a guarantee of security, the amount guaranteed or secured.

(7) Where a holding company avails itself of an exemption under this Part from the requirement to prepare group financial statements in relation to any financial year, *subsection (2)* shall have effect in relation to the company and that financial year as if "entity financial statements" were substituted for "group financial statements".

(8) A word or expression used in this section and also used in *sections 307* to *309* has the same meaning in this section as it has in those sections.

312 Credit Institutions: requirement for register, etc., in the case of holding company as respects certain information

(1) Subject to *section 313*, a company which is the holding company of a credit institution shall maintain a register containing a copy of every transaction, arrangement or agreement made by that institution of which particulars—

(a) are required by *section 307(1)* or *(2)* or *section 309(1)* or *(2)* to be disclosed, or

(b) would, but for *section 310*, be required by any such provision to be disclosed,

in the company's entity or group financial statements for the current financial year and for each of the preceding 10 financial years or, if such a transaction, arrangement or agreement is not in writing, a written memorandum setting out its terms.

(2) *Subsection (1)* shall not require a company to keep in its register a copy of any transaction, arrangement or agreement made by the credit institution for or with a connected person if—

(a) it is entered into in the ordinary course of the institution's business, and

(b) its value is not greater, and its terms no more favourable, in respect of the person for or with whom it is made, than that or those which—

(i) the institution ordinarily offers, or

(ii) it is reasonable to expect the institution to have offered,

to or in respect of a person of the same financial standing but unconnected with the institution.

(3) Subject to *section 313*, a company which is the holding company of a credit institution shall, before the annual general meeting of the holding company, make available, at its registered office for inspection by its members, the statement specified in *subsection (5)*.

(4) That statement shall be made so available for a period of not less than 15 days ending with the date of the meeting.

(5) The statement mentioned in *subsection (3)* (referred to in *subsections (6)* to *(8)* as the "statement") is one containing the particulars of transactions, arrangements and

agreements made by the credit institution which the holding company would, but for *section 310*, be required by *section 307(1)* or *(2)* or *section 309(1)* or *(2)* to disclose in its entity or group financial statements for the last complete financial year preceding the meeting referred to in that subsection.

(6) The statement shall also be made available for inspection by the members at that annual general meeting.

(7) This section shall not require the inclusion in the statement of particulars of any transaction, arrangement or agreement made by the credit institution if—

(a) it is entered into in the ordinary course of the institution's business, and

(b) its value is not greater, and its terms no more favourable, in respect of the person for or with whom it is made, than that or those which—

(i) the institution ordinarily offers, or

(ii) it is reasonable to expect the institution to have offered,

to or in respect of a person of the same financial standing but unconnected with the institution.

(8) This section shall not require the inclusion in the statement of particulars of any transaction, arrangement or agreement if, by reason of—

(a) the company's not taking advantage of *section 310*, or

(b) the company's being required by a rule, instrument, direction or requirement referred to in *section 313* to disclose such information in the following manner,

the company has included in its entity or group financial statements for the last complete financial year mentioned in *subsection (5)* the particulars referred to in *section 307(1)* or *(2)* or *section 309(1)* or *(2)*, as the case may be, of the transaction, arrangement or agreement which, but for either of those reasons, it would not have disclosed in those financial statements by virtue of *section 310*.

(9) A company shall, if required by the Director, produce to the Director for inspection the register kept by it in accordance with *subsection (1)* and shall give the Director such facilities for inspecting and taking copies of the contents of the register as the Director may require.

(10) It shall be the duty of the statutory auditors of the company to examine any such statement specified in *subsection (5)* before it is made available to the members of the company in accordance with *subsections (3)* and *(4)* and to make a report to the members on that statement; and the report shall be annexed to the statement before it is made so available.

(11) A report under *subsection (10)* shall state whether in the opinion of the statutory auditors the statement contains the particulars required by *subsection (5)* and, where their opinion is that it does not, they shall include in the report, so far as they are reasonably able to do so, a statement giving the required particulars.

(12) Where a company fails to comply with *subsection (1)*, *(3)* or *(9)*, the company and every person who at the time of that failure is a director of the company shall be guilty of a category 3 offence.

(13) In any proceedings against a person in respect of an offence under *subsection (12)* (being an offence consisting of a failure to comply with *subsection (1)* or *(3)*), it shall be a defence to prove that the defendant took all reasonable steps for securing compliance with *subsection (1)* or *(3)*, as the case may be.

(14) A word or expression used in this section and also used in *sections 307* to *309* has the same meaning in this section as it has in those sections.

313 Requirements of banking law not prejudiced by *sections 307* to *312* and minimum monetary threshold for *section 312*

(1) Nothing in *sections 307* to *312* prejudices the operation of any—

(a) rule or other instrument, or

(b) direction or requirement,

made, issued, granted or otherwise created under the Central Bank Acts 1942 to 2010 or any other enactment requiring the holding company of a credit institution to disclose particulars, whether in financial statements prepared by it or otherwise, of transactions, arrangements or agreements (whether of the kind described in *section 239* or not) entered into by the credit institution.

(2) So far as those requirements relate to *section 307(1)* or *(2)*, the requirements of *section 312(1)* or *(3)* do not apply in relation to an individual director and persons connected with him or her if the aggregate value of all arrangements, transactions and agreements referred to in *section 307(1)* and *(2)* did not at any time during the financial year exceed €7,500 for that individual director and those persons.

(3) So far as those requirements relate to any arrangement or transaction with a credit institution or any of its subsidiary undertakings in which a director of the institution or of its holding undertaking, or a person connected with such a director, had, directly or indirectly, a material interest, the requirements of *section 312(1)* or *(3)* do not apply if—

(a) the value of each such arrangement or transaction which was made after the commencement of the financial year with the institution or any of its subsidiary undertakings, and

(b) the value of each such arrangement or transaction which was made before the commencement of the financial year less the amount (if any) by which the liabilities of the person for whom the arrangement or transaction was made have been reduced,

did not at any time during the financial year exceed in the aggregate €5,000 or, if more, did not exceed €15,000 or one per cent of the value of the net assets of the company preparing the entity or group financial statements, whichever is the less.

Chapter 7
Disclosure required in notes to financial statements of other matters

314 Information on related undertakings

(1) [Subject to subsection (2A) and the other provisions of this section, where at the end of a financial year][a] of the company, a company—

(a) has a subsidiary undertaking, or

(b) holds an interest in any class of equity shares equal to 20 per cent or more of all such interests (in that class) in an undertaking that is not its subsidiary undertaking (in this section referred to as an "undertaking of substantial interest"),

a note shall be included in the statutory financial statements of the company for that year distinguishing between the subsidiary undertakings and the undertakings of substantial interest and giving the following information in relation to them:

(i) the name and registered office or, if there is no registered office, the principal place of business of each subsidiary undertaking or undertaking of substantial interest and the nature of the business carried on by it;

(ii) the identity of each class of shares held by the company in each subsidiary undertaking or undertaking of substantial interest and the proportion of the nominal value of the allotted shares in the subsidiary undertaking or undertaking of substantial interest of each such class represented by the shares of that class held by the company;

(iii) the aggregate amount of the net assets of each subsidiary undertaking or undertaking of substantial interest as at the end of the financial year of the subsidiary undertaking or undertaking of substantial interest ending with or last before the end of the financial year of the company to which the statutory financial statements relate; and

(iv) the profit or loss of the subsidiary undertaking or undertaking of substantial interest for its financial year identified in *paragraph (iii)*.

(2) [Subject to *subsection (2A)* and the other provisions of this section, the notes to the][b] statutory financial statements of a company shall contain the following particulars regarding each undertaking of which the company is a member having unlimited liability unless the information is not material to the true and fair view given by the statutory financial statements of the company:

(a) the name and registered office of each such undertaking;

(b) if the undertaking does not have a registered office, its principal place of business; and

(c) the legal form of the undertaking.

[(2A) A company that qualifies for the small companies regime or for the micro companies regime shall be exempt from the requirements of this section.][c]

(3) *Subsection (1)* is subject to *section 315* which provides for exemptions in respect of the information specified in *subsection (1)(iii)* and *(iv)*.

(4) *Subsections (1)* and *(2)* are subject to *section 316* which provides for exemptions generally in respect of the information specified in them.

(5) For the avoidance of doubt, the information required by *subsections (1)* and *(2)* is required for the financial year to which the statutory financial statements relate and comparable information for the preceding financial year need not be given.

(6) For the purposes of *paragraph (b)* of *subsection (1)*, interests held by persons acting in their own name but on behalf of the first-mentioned company in that subsection shall be deemed to be held by that company and "an interest in any class of equity shares" in *subsection (1)* includes an interest in an instrument that is convertible into equity shares as well as an option to acquire equity shares.

Amendments

a Words substituted by C(A)A 2017, s 31(a) (previously: "Where at the end of a financial year").

b Words substituted by C(A)A 2017, s 31(b) (previously: "The notes to the").

c Subsection (2A) inserted by C(A)A 2017, s 31(c).

315 Information on related undertakings: exemption from disclosures

The information on related undertakings required by paragraphs (iii) (net assets) and (iv) (profit or loss) of section 314(1) need not be given in statutory financial statements—

(a) in respect of a subsidiary undertaking of a company, if the company prepares group financial statements and either—

   (i) the subsidiary undertaking is consolidated in the statutory financial statements prepared by the company, or

   (ii) the interest of the company in the equity shares of the subsidiary undertaking is included in or in a note to the company's statutory financial statements by way of the equity method of accounting,

or

(b) in respect of a subsidiary undertaking of a company, if the company is exempt from the requirement to prepare group financial statements because it is relying on the consolidated accounts of a higher holding undertaking in accordance with *section 299* or *300* or in accordance with IFRS, and either—

   (i) the subsidiary undertaking is consolidated in the consolidated accounts of the higher holding undertaking, or

   (ii) the interest of the company in the equity shares of the subsidiary undertaking is included in or in a note to the higher holding undertaking's consolidated accounts by way of the equity method of accounting,

or

(c) in respect of an undertaking of substantial interest of a company, if the interest in the equity shares of the undertaking of substantial interest is included in or in a note to the company's statutory financial statements by way of the equity method of accounting, or

(d) [in respect of an undertaking of substantial interest of a company, if the undertaking is not required to publish its balance sheet, or][a]

(e) in relation to any undertaking, if the information required by *paragraphs (iii)* and *(iv)* of *section 314(1)* is not material to the true and fair view given by the statutory financial statements.

Amendments

a Paragraph substituted by C(A)A 2017, s 32.

---

316 Information on related undertakings: provision for certain information to be annexed to annual return

(1) If the directors of a company form the opinion that the number of undertakings in respect of which the company is required to disclose information under *section 314* is such that compliance with the provisions of that section would result in a note to the statutory financial statements of excessive length, the information mentioned in that section need only be given in such a note in respect of—

(a) the undertakings whose assets, liabilities, financial position or profit or loss, in the opinion of the directors, principally affected the amounts shown in the company's statutory financial statements, and

(b) undertakings excluded from the consolidation under *section 303(3)*.

(2) If advantage is taken of *subsection (1)*—

(a) there shall be included in the notes to the company's statutory financial statements a statement that the information given deals only with the undertakings mentioned in that subsection, and

(b) the information specified in *section 348(4)* shall be annexed to the annual return of the company to which the statutory financial statements are annexed.

(3) If a company fails to comply with *subsection (2)*, the company and any officer of it who is in default shall be guilty of a category 3 offence.

(4) In *subsection (3)* "officer" includes any shadow director and *de facto* director.

317 Disclosures of particulars of staff

(1) [Subject to *subsections (7)* and *(7A)*, the following information shall][a] be given in the notes to the entity financial statements of a company with respect to the employees of the company—

(a) the average number of persons employed by the company in the financial year concerned, and

(b) the average number of persons employed within each category of persons employed by the company in that year.

(2) In respect of all persons employed by the company during the financial year who are taken into account in determining the relevant annual number for the purposes of *subsection (1)(a)* there shall also be stated the aggregate amounts respectively of—

(a) wages and salaries paid or payable in respect of that year to those persons,

(b) social insurance costs incurred by the company on their behalf,

(c) other retirement benefit costs so incurred, and

(d) other compensation costs of those persons (such costs to be specified by type) incurred by the company in the financial year.

(3) In relation to the aggregate of all amounts stated for the purposes of *subsection (2)* there shall be shown the amount capitalised into assets and the amount treated as an expense or loss of the financial year.

(4) The categories of persons employed by the company by reference to which the number required to be disclosed by *subsection (1)(b)* is to be determined shall be such as the directors may select, having regard to the manner in which the company's activities are organised.

(5) For the purposes of *subsection (1)(a)* and *(b)*, the average number of persons employed by the company shall be determined by dividing the relevant annual number by the number of months in the financial year of the company.

(6) For the purposes of *subsection (5)*, the relevant annual number shall be determined by ascertaining for each month in the financial year of the company concerned—

(a) in the case of *subsection (1)(a)*, the number of persons employed under contracts of service by the company in that month (whether throughout the month or not), and

(b) in the case of *subsection (1)(b)*, the number of persons in the category in question of persons so employed,

and, in either case, adding together all the monthly numbers.

(7) Where the company prepares group financial statements, those group financial statements shall contain the information required by *subsections (1)* to *(3)* for the company and its subsidiary undertakings included in the consolidation taken as a whole and *subsections (4)* to *(6)* have effect as if references in them to the company were references to the company and its subsidiary undertakings included in the consolidation.

[(7A)(a) A company that qualifies for the small companies regime shall only be required to provide the information referred to in *subsection (1)(a)*.

(b) Where a company qualifies for the small companies regime but elects to prepare group financial statements—

(i) those group financial statements shall contain the information required by *subsection (1)(a)* for the company and its subsidiary undertakings included in the consolidation taken as a whole, and

(ii) *subsections (5)* and *(6)* have effect as if references in those subsections to the company were references to the company and its subsidiary undertakings included in the consolidation.

(7B) A company that qualifies for the micro companies regime shall be exempt from the requirements of this section.][b]

(8) In this section—

"retirement benefit costs" includes any expenses incurred by the company in respect of—

(a) any retirement benefit scheme established for the purpose of providing retirement benefits for persons currently or formerly employed by the company,

(b) any amounts set aside for the future payment of retirement benefits directly by the company to current or former employees, and

(c) any retirement benefits paid directly by the company to such persons without first being so set aside;

"social insurance costs" means any contribution by a company to any state social insurance, social welfare, social security or retirement benefit scheme (including provision amounting to such under the Social Welfare Acts) or to any fund or arrangement, being a fund or arrangement connected with such a scheme, and "social insurance" means any such scheme, fund or arrangement;

"wages and salaries" in a company's profit and loss account shall be determined by reference to payments made or expenses incurred in respect of all persons employed by the company during the financial year concerned who are taken into account in determining the relevant annual number for the purposes of *subsection (1)(a)*.

Amendments

a Words substituted by C(A)A 2017, s 33(a) (previously: "The following information shall").
b Subsections (7A) and (7B) inserted by C(A)A 2017, s 33(b).

---

318 Details of authorised share capital, allotted share capital and movements

(1) [Subject to subsection (9), the following information shall be given][a] in the notes to the entity financial statements of a company with respect to the company's share capital:

(a) the number and aggregate nominal value of the shares comprised in the authorised (if any) share capital;

(b) where shares of more than one class have been allotted, the number and aggregate nominal value of shares of each class allotted;

(c) in relation to each class of allotted share capital, the amount that has been called up on those shares and of this the amount that has been fully paid up at the financial year end date;

(d) an analysis of allotted and called up share capital by class between—

(i) shares presented as share capital, and

(ii) shares presented as a liability;

and

(e) where shares are held as treasury shares, the number and aggregate nominal value of the treasury shares and, where shares of more than one class have been allotted, the number and aggregate nominal value of each class held as treasury shares.

(2) In the case of any part of the allotted share capital that consists of redeemable shares, the following information shall be given:

(a) the earliest and latest dates on which the company has power to redeem those shares;

(b) whether those shares must be redeemed in any event or are liable to be redeemed at the option of the company or the shareholder and at who's option; and

(c) whether any (and, if so, what) premium is payable on redemption.

(3) If the company has allotted any shares during the financial year to which the entity financial statements relate, the following information shall be given:

(a) the reason for making the allotment;

(b) the classes of shares allotted;

(c) in respect of each class of shares, the number allotted, their aggregate nominal value and the consideration received by the company for the allotment; and

(d) whether the shares are presented as share capital or as a liability.

(4) With respect to any contingent right to the allotment of shares in the company, the following particulars shall be given:

(a) the number, description and amount of the shares in relation to which the right is exercisable;

(b) the period during which it is exercisable; and

(c) the price to be paid for the shares allotted.

(5) In *subsection (4)*, "contingent right to the allotment of shares" means any option to subscribe for shares and any other right to require the allotment of shares to any person whether arising on the conversion into shares of securities of any other description or otherwise.

(6) Subject to *subsection (7)*, where the company is a holding company, the number, description and nominal value of the shares in the company held by its subsidiary undertakings or their nominees and the consideration paid for those shares shall be disclosed in the notes to the entity financial statements of the company.

(7) *Subsection (6)* does not apply in relation to any shares—

(a) in the case of which the subsidiary undertaking is concerned as personal representative, or

(b) subject to *subsection (8)*, in the case of which the subsidiary undertaking is concerned as trustee.

(8) The restriction on the application of *subsection (6)* by *subsection (7)(b)* does not have effect if the company or a subsidiary undertaking of the company is beneficially interested under the trust and is not so interested only by way of security for the purposes of a transaction entered into by it in the ordinary course of a business which includes the lending of money.

[(9) A company that qualifies for the small companies regime or the micro companies regime shall be exempt from the requirements of this section.][b]

Amendments

a Words substituted by C(A)A 2017, s 34(a) (previously: "The following information shall be given").

b Subsection (9) inserted by C(A)A 2017, s 34(b).

---

319 Financial assistance for purchase of own shares

(1) [Subject to *subsection (4)*, the entity financial statements of a company][a] shall show the aggregate amount of financial assistance provided by the company, in the financial year to which the financial statements relate, that is permitted by *section 82* (including the aggregate amount of any outstanding loans, guarantees and securities at the financial year end date) and shall separately disclose the aggregate of—

(a) the amount of any money provided, in that financial year, by the company in accordance with a scheme referred to in *section 82(6)(f)*, and

(b) the amount of any loans referred to in *section 82(6)(g)* that have been made in that financial year by the company.

(2) [Subject to subsection (4), where a company][b] prepares group financial statements, those group financial statements shall contain the information required by *subsection (1)* for the company and its subsidiary undertakings included in the consolidation taken as a whole.

(3) The entity and group financial statements shall show for the financial year immediately preceding the financial year to which those statements relate amounts corresponding to the amounts required to be shown by *subsection (1)* in those statements for the latter year.

[(4) A company that qualifies for the small companies regime or the micro companies regime shall be exempt from the requirements of this section.][c]

Amendments

a Words substituted by C(A)A 2017, s 35(a) (previously: "The entity financial statements of a company").

b Words substituted by C(A)A 2017, s 35(b) (previously: "Where a company").
c Subsection (4) inserted by C(A)A 2017, s 35(c).

---

320 Holding of own shares or shares in holding undertaking

(1) Where a company, [a nominee of the company or a person acting in that person's own name but on behalf of the company][a], holds shares in the company or an interest in such shares, such shares or interest shall not be shown as an asset but the consideration paid for such shares or interest—

(a) shall be shown in the company's entity financial statements as a deduction from the company's capital and reserves (and the profits available for distribution shall accordingly be restricted by the amount of such deduction); and

(b) shall be shown in the company's group financial statements, if any, as a deduction from group capital and reserves.

(2) Where a company, [a nominee of the company or a person acting in that person's own name but on behalf of the company][b] holds shares in its holding undertaking or an interest in such shares, the profits of the company available for distribution shall be restricted by the amount of the consideration paid for such shares or interest.

(3) In addition to the requirements of *subsection (2)*, in the case of the holding of shares by a company, [a nominee of the company or a person acting in that person's own name but on behalf of the company, in its holding company (or the holding by a company, its nominee or a person acting in that person's own name but on behalf of the company of an interest in such shares)][c], the consideration paid for such shares or interest shall be shown in the holding company's group financial statements, if any, as a deduction from group capital and reserves.

(4) The notes to the company's entity financial statements (and, as the case may be, the group financial statements of the company or its holding company) shall give separately for the shares referred to in each of the preceding subsections—

(a) the number and aggregate nominal value of those shares and, where shares of more than one class have been acquired, the number and aggregate nominal value [each class of such shares, at the beginning and end of the financial year together with the consideration paid for such shares,][d]

[(aa) a reconciliation of the number and nominal value of each class of such shares from the beginning of the financial year to the end of the financial year showing all changes during the financial year, including further acquisitions, disposals and cancellations, in each case showing the value of the consideration paid or received, if any,

(ab) the reasons for any acquisitions made during the financial year,

(ac) the proportion of called up share capital held at the beginning and end of the financial year, and][e]

(b) particulars of any restriction on profits available for distribution by virtue of the application of subsection (1) or (2).

Amendments

a Words substituted by C(A)A 2017, s 36(a) (previously: "or a nominee of a company").
b Words substituted by C(A)A 2017, s 36(b) (previously: "or a nominee of the company").
c Words substituted by C(A)A 2017, s 36(c) (previously: "or a nominee of the company, in its holding company (or the holding by a company or its nominee of an interest in such shares)").
d Words substituted by C(A)A 2017, s 36(d)(i) (previously: "each class of such shares, and").
e Paragraphs (aa), (ab) and (ac) inserted by C(A)A 2017, s 36(d)(ii).

---

321 Disclosure of accounting policies

(1) A company shall disclose in the notes to its entity financial statements the accounting policies adopted by the company in determining—

(a) the items and amounts to be included in its balance sheet, and
(b) the items and amounts to be included in its profit and loss account.

(2) Where a company prepares group financial statements, the notes to those financial statements shall disclose the accounting policies adopted by the company in determining—

(a) the items and amounts to be included in its consolidated balance sheet, and
(b) the items and amounts to be included in its consolidated profit and loss account.

[(3) Where a company changes an accounting policy adopted by the company and has disclosed such change in the notes to the entity financial statements or group financial statements, the notes to those financial statements shall also disclose—

(a) the reason for the change in accounting policy, and
(b) to the extent practicable, the impact of the change in accounting policy on the financial statements for the current financial year and on the financial statements of preceding years.][a]

Amendments

a Subsection (3) inserted by C(A)A 2017, s 37.

---

322 Disclosure of remuneration for audit, audit-related and non-audit work

(1) In this section—

"group auditor" means the statutory auditor carrying out the audit of group financial statements;

"remuneration" includes benefits in kind, reimbursement of expenses and other payments in cash.

(2) Subject to *subsection (5)*, a company shall disclose in the notes to its entity financial statements relating to each financial year the following information:

(a) the remuneration for all work in each category specified in *subsection (3)* that was carried out—

(i) for the company,

(ii) in respect of that financial year,

by the statutory auditors of the company;

(b) the remuneration for all work in each category specified in *subsection (3)* that was carried out—

(i) for the company,

(ii) in respect of the preceding financial year,

by the statutory auditors of the company;

(c) where all or part of the remuneration referred to in *paragraph (a)* or *(b)* is in the form of a benefit in kind, the nature and estimated monetary value of the benefit.

(3) Remuneration shall be disclosed under *subsection (2)* for each of the following categories of work:

(a) the audit of entity financial statements;

(b) other assurance services;

(c) tax advisory services;

(d) other non-audit services.

(4) Where the statutory auditors of a company are a statutory audit firm (within the meaning of [Part 27][a]), any work carried out by a partner in the firm or a statutory auditor on its behalf is considered for the purposes of this section to have been carried out by the audit firm.

(5) A company need not make the disclosure required by *subsection (2)* where—

[(a) the company qualifies for the small companies regime or the micro companies regime, or][b]

[(b) the company qualifies as a medium company in accordance with section 280F or 280G, or][c]

(c) the company is a subsidiary undertaking, the holding company of which is required to prepare and does prepare group financial statements, provided that—

(i) the subsidiary undertaking is included in the group financial statements, and

(ii) the information specified in *subsection (8)* is disclosed in the notes to the group financial statements.

(6) Where a company that [qualifies as a medium company in accordance with *section 280F* or *280G*][d] does not make the disclosure of information required by *subsection (2)* it shall provide such information to the Supervisory Authority when requested so to do.

(7) A holding company that prepares group financial statements shall disclose in the notes to those statements relating to each financial year the following information:

(a) the remuneration for all work in each category specified in *subsection (8)* that was carried out in respect of that financial year by the group auditor for the holding company and the subsidiary undertakings included in the consolidation;

(b) the remuneration for all work in each category specified in *subsection (8)* that was carried out in respect of the preceding financial year by the group auditor for the holding company and those undertakings;

(c) where all or part of the remuneration referred to in *paragraph (a)* or *(b)* is in the form of a benefit in kind, the nature and estimated monetary value of the benefit.

(8) Remuneration shall be disclosed under *subsection (7)* for each of the following categories of work:

(a) the audit of the group financial statements;

(b) other assurance services;

(c) tax advisory services;

(d) other non-audit services.

(9) Where more than one statutory auditor (whether a statutory auditor or a statutory audit firm) has been appointed as the statutory auditors of a company in a single financial year, separate disclosure in respect of the remuneration of each of them shall be provided in the notes to the company's entity financial statements.

Amendments

a Words substituted by C(SA)A 2018, s 6. (previously: "the 2016 Audit Regulations").
b Paragraph (5)(a) substituted by C(A)A 2017, s 38(a)(i).
c Paragraph (5)(b) substituted by C(A)A 2017, s 38(a)(ii).
d Words substituted by C(A)A 2017, s 38(b) (previously: "is to be treated as a medium company in accordance with *section 350*").

---

323 Information on arrangements not included in balance sheet

(1) [Subject to the provisions of this section][a], the nature and business purpose of any arrangements of a company that are not included in its balance sheet and the financial impact on the company of those arrangements shall be provided in the notes to the statutory financial statements of the company if the risks or benefits arising from such arrangements are material and in so far as the disclosure of such risks or benefits is necessary for assessing the financial position of the company.

[(1A) A company that—

(a) qualifies for the small companies regime shall be exempt from the requirement to disclose the financial impact on the company of arrangements referred to in *subsection (1)*, and

(b) qualifies for the micro companies regime shall be exempt from the requirements of *subsection (1)*.][b]

(2) In the case of a holding company that prepares group financial statements—

(a) *subsection (1)* shall be read as requiring the information there referred to in respect of arrangements there referred to, whether of the company or of any subsidiary undertaking included in the consolidation, to be provided in the notes to the group financial statements in so far as the disclosure of the risks or benefits concerned is necessary for assessing the financial position, taken as a whole, of the holding company and the subsidiary undertakings included in the consolidation, and

(b) the notes to the entity financial statements of the holding company shall not be required to provide information that is provided in the notes to its group financial statements in compliance with *subsection (1)*, as it is to be read in accordance with this subsection.

Amendments

a Words substituted by C(A)A 2017, s 39(a) (previously: "Subject to *subsection (2)*,").
b Subsection (1A) inserted by C(A)A 2017, s 39(b).

Chapter 8
Approval of statutory financial statements

324 Approval and signing of statutory financial statements by board of directors

(1) [Subject to *subsection (1A)*, where the directors of a company][a] are satisfied that the statutory financial statements of the company give a true and fair view and otherwise comply with this Act or, where applicable, with Article 4 of the IAS Regulation, those statements shall be approved by the board of directors and signed on their behalf by 2 directors, where there are 2 or more directors.

[(1A) In the case of the statutory financial statements of a company that qualifies for the micro companies regime, compliance with the minimum requirements of this Act in relation to its financial statements shall be presumed to give a true and fair view for the purposes of *subsection (1)*.][b]

(2) Without prejudice to the generality of *section 11* and its application to the other provisions of this section, where the company has a sole director *subsection (1)* operates to require that director, if he or she is satisfied as to the matters referred to in that subsection in respect of the statements, to approve and sign the statutory financial statements.

(3) Where group financial statements are prepared, the group financial statements and the entity financial statements of the holding company shall be approved by the board of directors of that company at the same time.

(4) The signature or signatures evidencing approval of the financial statements by the board shall be inserted on the face of the entity balance sheet and any group balance sheet.

[(4A) If the statutory financial statements of a company that qualifies for the small companies regime or the micro companies regime, as the case may be, are prepared in accordance with the small companies regime or the micro companies regime as appropriate, the balance sheet shall contain, in a prominent position above the signature or signatures referred to in *subsection (4)*, a statement that the statutory financial statements concerned have been so prepared in accordance with the small companies regime or the micro companies regime, as may be appropriate.][c]

(5) Every copy of every balance sheet which is laid before the members in general meeting or which is otherwise circulated, published or issued shall state the names of the persons who signed the balance sheet on behalf of the board of directors.

(6) If statutory financial statements are approved which do not give a true and fair view or otherwise comply with the requirements of this Act or, where applicable, of Article 4 of the IAS Regulation, every director of the company who is party to their approval, and who knows that they do not give such view or otherwise so comply or is reckless as to whether that is so, shall be guilty of a category 2 offence.

(7) For that purpose, every director of the company at the time the statutory financial statements are approved shall be taken to be a party to their approval unless he or she shows that he or she took all reasonable steps to prevent their being approved.

(8) If any copy of a balance sheet is—

(a) laid before the members or otherwise issued, circulated or published without the balance sheet (the original of it as distinct from the copy) having been signed as required by this section or without the required statement of the signatory's name on the copy being included, or

(b) delivered to the Registrar without the balance sheet (the original of it as distinct from the copy) having been signed as required by this section or without the required statement of the signatory's name on the copy being included,

the company and any officer of it who is in default shall be guilty of a category 2 offence.

(9) *Subsection (8)* shall not prohibit the issue, circulation or publication of—

(a) a fair and accurate summary of any statutory financial statement after such statutory financial statement shall have been signed on behalf of the directors,

(b) a fair and accurate summary of the profit or loss figures for part of the company's financial year.

(10) In *subsection (8)* "officer" includes any shadow director and *de facto* director.

[(11) In this section, 'minimum requirements of this Act', in relation to a company that qualifies for the micro companies regime, means the provisions of this Act with which the company is obliged to comply, having availed of the exemptions to which it is entitled by virtue of qualifying for the micro companies regime.][d]

Amendments

a Words substituted by C(A)A 2017, s 40(a) (previously: "Where the directors of a company").
b Subsection (1A) inserted by C(A)A 2017, s 40(b).
c Subsection (4A) inserted by C(A)A 2017, s 40(c).
d Subsection (11) inserted by C(A)A 2017, s 40(d).

Chapter 9
Directors' report

325 Obligation to prepare directors' report for every financial year

(1) [Subject to subsection (1A), the directors][a] of a company shall for each financial year prepare a report (a "directors' report") dealing with the following matters:

(a) general matters in relation to the company and the directors as specified in *section 326*;

(b) a business review in accordance with *section 327*;

(c) information on the acquisition or disposal of own shares as specified in *section 328*;

(d) information on interests in shares or debentures as specified in *section 329*;

(e) statement on relevant audit information as specified in *section 330;*

and containing the notice referred to in *section 331* that (if such be the case) has been issued in that financial year in respect of the company under section 33AK of the Central Bank Act 1942.

[(1A) The directors of a company that—

(a) qualifies for the small companies regime shall not be required to include in the directors' report, a business review referred to in *subsection (1)(b)*, and

(b) qualifies for the micro companies regime shall be exempt from the requirement to prepare a directors' report under *subsection (1)* provided that the information required under *section 328* is included as a note or a footnote to the balance sheet.][b]

(2) *Subsection (1)* is in addition to the other requirements of this Act that apply in certain cases with regard to the inclusion of matters in a directors' report, namely the requirements of—

(a) *section 167(3)* (statement as to establishment or otherwise of an audit committee in the case of [a relevant private company][c]), and

(b) *section 225(2)* (directors' compliance statement in case of a company to which that section applies).

(3) For a financial year in which—

(a) the company is a holding company, and

(b) the directors of the company prepare group financial statements,

the directors shall also prepare a directors' report that is a consolidated report (a "group directors' report") dealing, to the extent provided in the following provisions of this Part, with the company and its subsidiary undertakings included in the consolidation taken as a whole.

(4) Where group financial statements are published with entity financial statements, it is sufficient to prepare the group directors' report referred to in *subsection (3)* (as distinct from that report and a directors' report in respect of the holding company as well) provided that any information relating to the holding company only, being information which would otherwise be required to be provided by *subsection (1)* or *section 167(3)* or *225(2)*, is provided in the group directors' report.

(5) A group directors' report may, where appropriate, give greater emphasis to the matters that are significant to the company and its subsidiary undertakings included in the consolidation taken as a whole.

(6) If a director fails to fulfil his or her obligation under [*subsections (1)*, *(1A)*, *(3)* or *(4)*][d], he or she shall be guilty of a category 3 offence.

(7) Without limiting the obligations of the directors of a company under this section or *subsection (6)*, it shall be the duty of a person who is a shadow director or *de facto* director of a company to ensure that the requirements of [*subsections (1)*, *(1A)*, *(3)* or *(4)*][e] are complied with in relation to the company.

(8) If a person fails to comply with his or her duty under *subsection (7)*, the person shall be guilty of a category 3 offence.

Amendments

a Words substituted by C(A)A 2017, s 41(a) (previously: "The directors").
b Subsection (1A) inserted by C(A)A 2017, s 41(b).
c Words substituted by C(A)A 2017, s 41(c) (previously: "a large private company").
d Words substituted by C(A)A 2017, s 41(d) (previously: "*subsection (1), (3)* or *(4)*").
e Words substituted by C(A)A 2017, s 41(e) (previously: "*subsection (1), (3)* or *(4)*").

---

326 Directors' report: general matters

(1) The directors' report for a financial year shall state—

(a) the names of the persons who, at any time during the financial year, were directors of the company,

(b) the principal activities of the company during the course of the year,

(c) a statement of the measures taken by the directors to secure compliance with the requirements of *sections 281* to *285*, with regard to the keeping of accounting records and the exact location of those records,

(d) the amount of any interim dividends paid by the directors during the year and the amount, if any, that the directors recommend should be paid by way of final dividend.

(2) Where relevant in a particular financial year, the directors' report shall state—

(a) particulars of any important events affecting the company which have occurred since the end of that year,

(b) an indication of the activities, if any, of the company in the field of research and development,

(c) an indication of the existence of branches (within the meaning of Council Directive 89/666/EEC) of the company outside the State and the country in which each such branch is located,

(d) political donations made during the year that are required to be disclosed by the Electoral Act 1997.

(3) [Subject to *subsection (3A)*, where material for an assessment][a] of the company's financial position and profit or loss, the directors' report shall describe the use of financial instruments by the company and discuss, in particular—

(a) the financial risk management objectives and policies of the company, including the policy for hedging each major type of forecasted transaction for which hedge accounting is used, and

(b) the exposure of the company to price risk, credit risk, liquidity risk and cash flow risk.

[(3A) A company that qualifies for the small companies regime or the micro companies regime shall be exempt from the requirements of *subsection (3)*.][b]

(4) In relation to a group directors' report, *subsections (1)(b)* and *(c)*, *(2)* and *(3)* shall have effect as if the reference to the company were a reference to the company and its subsidiary undertakings included in the consolidation.

Amendments

a Words substituted by C(A)A 2017, s 42(a) (previously: "Where material for an assessment").

b Subsection (3A) inserted by C(A)A 2017, s 42(b).

---

327 Directors' report: business review

(1) [Subject to *subsection (1A)*, the directors' report for a financial year][a] shall contain—

(a) a fair review of the business of the company, and

(b) a description of the principal risks and uncertainties facing the company.

[(1A) A company that qualifies for the small companies regime or the micro companies regime shall be exempt from the requirements of *subsection (1)*.][b]

(2) The review required by *subsection (1)* shall be a balanced and comprehensive analysis of—

(a) the development and performance of the business of the company during the financial year, and

(b) the assets and liabilities and financial position of the company at the end of the financial year,

consistent with the size and complexity of the business.

(3) The review required by *subsection (1)* shall, to the extent necessary for an understanding of such development, performance or financial position or assets and liabilities, include—

(a) an analysis of financial key performance indicators, and

(b) where appropriate, an analysis using non-financial key performance indicators, including information relating to environmental and employee matters.

[(3A) Notwithstanding the generality of *subsection (1A)*, where a company that qualifies for the small companies regime or the micro companies regime, as the case may be, elects to provide the information required by *subsection (1)*, it shall be exempt from the requirements of *subsection (3)(b)*.][c]

(4) The directors' report shall, where appropriate, include additional explanations of amounts included in the statutory financial statements of the company.

(5) The review required by *subsection (1)* shall include an indication of likely future developments in the business of the company.

(6) In relation to a group directors' report, this section has effect as if the references to the company were references to the company and its subsidiary undertakings included in the consolidation.

(7) In this section, "key performance indicators" means factors by reference to which the development, performance and financial position of the business of the company can be measured effectively.

Amendments

a Words substituted by C(A)A 2017, s 43(a) (previously: "The directors' report for a financial year").

b Subsection (1A) inserted by C(A)A 2017, s 43(b).

c Subsection (3A) inserted by C(A)A 2017, s 43(c).

---

328 Directors' report: acquisition or disposal of own shares

Where, at any time during a financial year of a company, shares in the company—

(a) are held or acquired by the company, including by forfeiture or surrender in lieu of forfeiture, or

(b) are held or acquired by any subsidiary undertaking of the company,

the directors' report with respect to that financial year of the company shall state—

(i) the number and nominal value of any shares of the company held by the company or any subsidiary undertaking at the beginning and end of the financial year together with the consideration paid for [such shares][a]

(ii) a reconciliation of the number and nominal value of such shares from the beginning of the financial year to the end of the financial year showing all changes during the year including further acquisitions, disposals and cancellations, in each case showing the value of the consideration paid or received, [if any,][b]

[(iii) the reasons for any acquisitions made during the financial year, and

(iv) the proportion of called-up share capital held at the beginning and end of the financial year.][c]

Amendments

a Words substituted by C(A)A 2017, s 44(a) (previously: "such shares, and").

b Words substituted by C(A)A 2017, s 44(b) (previously: "if any.").

c Paragraphs (iii) and (iv) inserted by C(A)A 2017, s 44(c).

---

329 Directors' report: interests in shares and debentures

(1) The directors' report in respect of a financial year shall, as respects each person who, at the end of that year, was a director of the company—

(a) state whether or not he or she was, at the end of that financial year, interested in shares in, or debentures of, the company or any group undertaking of that company,

(b) state, if he or she was so interested at the end of that year, the number and amount of shares in, and debentures of, the company and each other undertaking (specifying it) in which he or she was then interested,

(c) state whether or not he or she was, at the beginning of the financial year (or, if he or she was not then a director, when he or she became a director), interested in shares in, or debentures of, the company or any other group undertaking, and

(d) state, if he or she was so interested at either of the immediately preceding dates, the number and amount of shares in, and debentures of, the company and each other undertaking (specifying it) in which he or she was so interested at the beginning of the financial year or, as the case may be, when he or she became a director.

(2) The reference in *subsection (1)* to the time when a person became a director shall, in case of a person who became a director on more than one occasion, be read as a reference to the time when he or she first became a director.

(3) The information required by *subsection (1)* to be given in respect of the directors of the company shall also be given in respect of the person who was the secretary of the company at the end of the financial year concerned.

(4) For the purposes of this section, references to interests of a director and secretary in shares or debentures are references to all interests required to be recorded in the register of interests under *section 267* and includes interests of shadow directors and *de facto* directors required to be so registered.

330 Directors' report: statement on relevant audit information

(1) The directors' report in relation to a company shall contain a statement to the effect that, in the case of each of the persons who are directors at the time the report is approved in accordance with *section 332*—

(a) so far as the director is aware, there is no relevant audit information of which the company's statutory auditors are unaware, and

(b) the director has taken all the steps that he or she ought to have taken as a director in order to make himself or herself aware of any relevant audit information and to establish that the company's statutory auditors are aware of that information.

(2) In this section "relevant audit information" means information needed by the company's statutory auditors in connection with preparing their report.

(3) A director is regarded as having taken all the steps that he or she ought to have taken as a director in order to do the things mentioned in *subsection (1)(b)* if he or she has—

(a) made such enquiries of his or her fellow directors (if any) and of the company's statutory auditors for that purpose, and

(b) taken such other steps (if any) for that purpose,

as are required by his or her duty as a director of the company to exercise reasonable care, skill and diligence.

(4) Nothing in this section shall be read as reducing in any way the statutory and professional obligations of the statutory auditors in relation to forming their opinion on the matters specified in *section 336*.

(5) Where a directors' report containing the statement required by this section is approved in accordance with *section 332* but the statement is false, every director of the company who—

(a) knew that the statement was false, or was reckless as to whether it was false, and

(b) failed to take reasonable steps to prevent the report from being so approved,

shall be guilty of a category 2 offence.

331 Directors' report: copy to be included of any notice issued under certain banking legislation

The directors' report shall contain a copy of any Disclosure Notice issued in respect of the company under section 33AK (inserted by the Central Bank and Financial Services Authority of Ireland Act 2003 and amended by the Central Bank Reform Act 2010) of the Central Bank Act 1942 during the financial year to which the report relates.

332 Approval and signing of directors' report

(1) The directors' report and, where applicable, the group directors' report shall be approved by the board of directors making the report and signed on their behalf by 2 directors, where there are 2 or more directors.

(2) Without prejudice to the generality of *section 11* and its application to the other provisions of this section, where the company has a sole director *subsection (1)* operates to require that director to approve and sign the report or reports concerned.

(3) Every copy of every directors' report which is laid before the members in general meeting or which is otherwise circulated, published or issued shall state the names of the persons who signed it on behalf of the board of directors.

(4) If any copy of a directors' report is—

(a) laid before the members, or otherwise issued, circulated or published without the report (the original of it as distinct from the copy) having been signed as required by this section or without the required statement of the signatory's name on the copy being included, or

(b) delivered to the Registrar without the report (the original of it as distinct from the copy) having been signed as required by this section or without the required statement of the signatory's name on the copy being included,

the company and any officer of it who is in default shall be guilty of a category 3 offence.

(5) In *subsection (4)* "officer" includes any shadow director and *de facto* director.

Chapter 10
Obligation to have statutory financial statements audited

333 Statutory financial statements must be audited (unless audit exemption availed of)

The directors of a company shall arrange for the statutory financial statements of the company for a financial year to be audited by statutory auditors unless the company is entitled to, and chooses to avail itself of, the audit exemption.

334 Right of members to require audit despite audit exemption otherwise being available

(1) Any member or members of a company holding shares in the company that confer, in aggregate, not less than one-tenth of the total voting rights in the company may serve a notice in writing on the company stating that that member or those members do not

wish the audit exemption to be available to the company in a financial year specified in the notice.

(2) A notice under *subsection (1)* may be served on the company either—

(a) during the financial year immediately preceding the financial year to which the notice relates, or

(b) during the financial year to which the notice relates (but not later than 1 month before the end of that year).

(3) The reference in *subsection (1)* to a voting right in a company shall be read as a reference to a right exercisable for the time being to cast, or to control the casting of, a vote at general meetings of members of the company, not being such a right that is exercisable only in special circumstances.

(4) For the avoidance of doubt, the reference in *subsection (1)* to the one or more members not wishing the audit exemption to be available to the company in a specified financial year is, if the company is a subsidiary undertaking, a reference to their not wishing the audit exemption to be available to the subsidiary undertaking irrespective of whether its holding company and any other undertakings in the group avail themselves of the audit exemption in that year.

(5) In this section "audit exemption" does not include the dormant company audit exemption referred to in *section 365*.

335 Statement to be included in balance sheet if audit exemption availed of

(1) If a company avails itself of the audit exemption in a financial year, the balance sheet prepared by the company in respect of that year shall contain a statement by the directors of the company that, in respect of that year—

(a) the company is availing itself of the audit exemption (and the exemption shall be expressed to be "the exemption provided for by *Chapter 15* of *Part 6* of the *Companies Act 2014*"),

(b) the company is availing itself of the exemption on the grounds that *section 358* or *359*, as appropriate, is complied with,

(c) no notice under *subsection (1)* of *section 334* has, in accordance with *subsection (2)* of that section, been served on the company, and

(d) the directors acknowledge the obligations of the company, under this Act, to—

(i) keep adequate accounting records and prepare financial statements which give a true and fair view of the assets, liabilities and financial position of the company at the end of its financial year and of its profit or loss for such a year, and

(ii) otherwise comply with the provisions of this Act relating to financial statements so far as they are applicable to the company.

(2) The statement required by *subsection (1)* shall appear in the balance sheet in a position immediately above the signatures of the directors required by *section 324* or, as the case may be, the statement required by *section 355*.

(3) If *subsection (1)* or *(2)* is not complied with, the company concerned and any officer of it who is in default shall be guilty of a category 3 offence.

(4) If the company referred to in *subsection (1)* is a holding company that prepares group financial statements for the financial year concerned, that subsection shall be read as applying both to its entity balance sheet and its group balance sheet.

(5) Whenever a company has availed itself of the audit exemption in respect of a financial year, the company shall, if required by the Director of Corporate Enforcement to do so—

(a) give to the Director such access to and facilities for inspecting and taking copies of the books and documents of the company, and

(b) furnish to the Director such information,

as the Director may reasonably require for the purpose of satisfying himself or herself that the company did, in respect of that financial year, comply with *section 358* or *359*, as appropriate.

(6) If a company fails to comply with a requirement under *subsection (5),* the company and any officer of it who is in default shall be guilty of a category 4 offence.

(7) Where—

(a) the audit exemption, as referred to in *section 359(1)*, applies to a group, and

(b) any subsidiary undertaking in that group relies on that exemption (and does not have its statutory financial statements for the year concerned audited in consequence),

references in this section to a company availing itself of the audit exemption shall be read, as respects that subsidiary undertaking, as including references to such an undertaking and *subsection (3)* shall be read accordingly.

(8) In this section "audit exemption" does not include the dormant company audit exemption referred to in *section 365* but that section makes similar provision, by applying and adapting its terms, to that made by this section.

Chapter 11
Statutory auditors' report

336 Statutory auditors' report on statutory financial statements

(1) The report required by *section 391* to be made by the statutory auditors of a company on statutory financial statements to be laid before the company in general meeting shall comply with the requirements of this section.

[(2) The statutory auditors' report shall be in writing and shall—[a]

(a) [identify][b] the entity financial statements, and where appropriate, the group financial statements, that are the subject of the audit and the financial reporting framework that has been applied in their preparation,

(b) include a description of the scope of the audit identifying the auditing standards in accordance with which the audit was conducted, and

(c) identify the place of establishment of the statutory auditors who made the report.]

(3) The statutory auditors' report shall state clearly the statutory auditors' opinion as to—

(a) [subject to *subsection (3A)*, whether the statutory financial statements][c] give a true and fair view—

(i) in the case of an entity balance sheet, of the assets, liabilities and financial position of the company as at the end of the financial year,

(ii) in the case of an entity profit and loss account, of the profit or loss of the company for the financial year,

(iii) in the case of group financial statements, of the assets, liabilities and financial position as at the end of the financial year and of the profit or loss for the financial year of the undertakings included in the consolidation as a whole, so far as concerns the members of the company,

(b) whether the statutory financial statements have been properly prepared in accordance with the relevant financial reporting framework and, in particular, with the requirements of this Act (and, where applicable, Article 4 of the IAS Regulation).

[(3A) In the case of the statutory financial statements of a company that qualifies for the micro companies regime, compliance with the minimum requirements of this Act (within the meaning of *section 324(11)*) in relation to its financial statements is presumed to give a true and fair view as required by *subsection (3)*.][d]

(4) The statutory auditors' report shall also state—

(a) whether they have obtained all the information and explanations which, to the best of their knowledge and belief, are necessary for the purposes of their audit,

(b) whether, in their opinion, the accounting records of the company were sufficient to permit the financial statements to be readily and properly audited,

(c) whether, in their opinion, information and returns adequate for their audit have been received from branches of the company not visited by them, and

(d) in the case of entity financial statements, whether the company's balance sheet and, except where the exemption in *section 304* is availed of, the profit and loss account are in agreement with the accounting records and returns.

[(5) [Subject to *subsection (5B)*, the statutory auditors'][e] report shall—

(a) state whether, in their opinion, based on the work undertaken in the course of the audit—

(i) the information given in the directors' report for the financial year for which statutory financial statements are prepared is consistent with the company's statutory financial statements in respect of the financial year concerned, and

(ii) the directors' report has been prepared in accordance with applicable legal requirements,

and

(b) state whether, based on their knowledge and understanding of the company and its environment obtained in the course of the audit, they have identified material misstatements in the directors' report and, where they have so identified such misstatements, give an indication of the nature of each of such misstatements.][f]

[(5A) The statutory auditors' report shall provide a statement on any material uncertainty relating to events or conditions that may cast significant doubt about the entity's ability to continue as a going concern.][g]

[(5B) *Subsection (5)* shall not apply in the case of a company that qualifies for the micro companies regime and has availed itself of the exemption, referred to in *section 325(1A)*, from preparing a directors' report.][h]

(6) The statutory auditors' report shall—

(a) in relation to each matter referred to in *subsections (3)* to *(5)* contain a statement or opinion, as the case may be, which shall be either—

(i) unqualified, or

(ii) qualified,

and

(b) include a reference to any matters to which the statutory auditors wish to draw attention by way of emphasis without qualifying the report.

(7) For the purposes of *subsection (6)(a)(ii)*, a statement or opinion may be qualified, including to the extent of an adverse opinion or a disclaimer of opinion, where there is a disagreement or limitation in scope of work.

[(8) If in the case of any statutory financial statements—

(a) the requirements of any of *sections 305* to *312* are not complied with by a company, and

(b) the company is not a company that is entitled to, and has availed itself of, an exemption from providing the information,

the statutory auditors of the company by whom the financial statements are examined shall include in their report, so far as they are reasonably able to do so, a statement giving the required particulars.][i]

(9) Where the entity financial statements of a holding company are combined with (that is to say, associated with) the group financial statements, the statutory auditors' report on the group financial statements shall be so combined with the report on the entity financial statements.

[(9A)(a) Subject to paragraph (*b*), where the statutory audit was carried out by more than one statutory auditor, the statutory auditors shall agree on the results of the statutory audit and submit a joint report and opinion.

(b) In the case of disagreement, each statutory auditor shall submit [his or her][k] opinion in a separate paragraph of the audit report and shall state [his or her][k] reason for such disagreement.][j]

[(10) The Supervisory Authority may prescribe additional requirements, by reference to auditing standards within the meaning of *section 1461*, in relation to the content of the statutory auditors' report for all undertakings, or a class of undertakings, only—

(a) if those requirements are necessary in order to give effect to legal requirements in the State relating to the scope of statutory audits, or

(b) to the extent necessary to add to the credibility and quality of the report.][l]

Amendments

a Subsection (2) substituted by the European Union (Statutory Audits) (Directive 2006/43/EC, as amended by Directive 2014/56/EU, and Regulation (EU) No 537/2014) Regulations 2016 (SI 312/2016), reg 9(a), with effect from 17 June 2016.

b Word substituted by C(SA)A 2018, s 7(a) (previously: "include an introduction identifying").

c Words substituted by C(A)A 2017, s 45(a) (previously: "whether the statutory financial statements").

d Subsection (3A) inserted by C(A)A 2017, s 45(b).

e Words substituted by C(A)A 2017, s 45(c) (previously: "The statutory auditors'").

f Subsection (5) substituted by the European Union (Statutory Audits) (Directive 2006/43/EC, as amended by Directive 2014/56/EU, and Regulation (EU) No 537/2014) Regulations 2016 (SI 312/2016), reg 9(b), with effect from 17 June 2016.

g Subsection (5A) inserted by the European Union (Statutory Audits) (Directive 2006/43/EC, as amended by Directive 2014/56/EU, and Regulation (EU) No 537/2014) Regulations 2016 (SI 312/2016), reg 9(c), with effect from 17 June 2016.

h Subsection (5B) inserted by C(A)A 2017, s 45(d).

i Subsection (8) substituted by C(A)A 2017, s 45(e).

j Subsection (9A) inserted by the European Union (Statutory Audits) (Directive 2006/43/EC, as amended by Directive 2014/56/EU, and Regulation (EU) No 537/2014) Regulations 2016 (SI 312/2016), reg 9(d), with effect from 17 June 2016.

k Words substituted by C(SA)A 2018, s 7(b) (previously: "his, her or its").

l Subsection (10) inserted by C(SA)A 2018, s 7(c).

---

337 Signature of statutory auditor's report

(1) The report of the statutory auditor shall state the name of the statutory auditor and be signed, as provided for in *subsection (2)*, and bear the date of the signature or signatures.

[(2) Where the auditor is—[a]

(a) a statutory auditor (within the meaning of [Part 27][b]), the report shall be signed by the statutory auditor (or, where more than one, each statutory auditor), or

(b) a statutory audit firm (within the meaning of [Part 27][b]), the report shall be signed by—

(i) the statutory auditor (or, where more than one, each statutory auditor) designated by the statutory audit firm for the particular audit engagement as being primarily responsible for carrying out the statutory audit on behalf of the audit firm, or

(ii) in the case of a group audit, at least the statutory auditor (or, where more than one, each statutory auditor) designated by the statutory audit firm as being primarily responsible for carrying out the statutory audit at the level of the group,

(iii) where more than one statutory audit firm has been simultaneously engaged, by the statutory auditors designated by the statutory audit firms for the particular audit engagement as being primarily responsible for carrying out the statutory audit on behalf of the audit firm, or

(iv) in the case of a group audit, where more than one statutory audit firm has been simultaneously engaged, by the statutory auditors designated by the statutory audit firms for the particular audit engagement as being primarily responsible for carrying out the statutory audit at the level of the group,

in his or her own name, for and on behalf of the audit firm.]

(3) Every copy of the report of the statutory auditor which is laid before the members in general meeting or which is otherwise circulated, published or issued shall state the name of the statutory auditor or auditors and bear their signature and the date of the latter.

(4) The copy of the statutory auditor's report which is delivered to the Registrar shall state the name of the statutory auditor or auditors and bear their signature (in the typeset form specified in *section 347(2)*) and the date of the signature.

(5) If a copy of a statutory auditor's report—

(a) is laid before the members, or otherwise issued, circulated or published without the report (the original of it as distinct from the copy) being signed and dated as required by this section, or without the copy including the required statement of the statutory auditor's or auditors' name and the other particulars specified in *subsection (2)*, or

(b) is delivered to the Registrar without the report (the original of it as distinct from the copy) being signed and dated as required by this section, or without the copy including the required statement of the statutory auditor's or auditors' name and the other particulars specified in *subsection (3)*,

the company and any officer of it who is in default shall be guilty of a category 3 offence.

(6) In *subsection (5)* "officer" includes any shadow director and *de facto* director.

Amendments

a Subsection (2) substituted by the European Union (Statutory Audits) (Directive 2006/43/EC, as amended by Directive 2014/56/EU, and Regulation (EU) No 537/2014) Regulations 2016 (SI 312/2016), reg 10, with effect from 17 June 2016.

b Words substituted by C(SA)A 2018, s 8 (previously: "the 2016 Audit Regulations").

Chapter 12
Publication of financial statements

338 Circulation of statutory financial statements

(1) A copy of each of the documents specified in *subsection (2)* concerning the company there referred to shall be sent to—

(a) every member of the company (whether that person is or is not entitled to receive notices of general meetings of the company),

(b) every holder of debentures of the company (whether that person is or is not so entitled), and

(c) all persons, other than members or holders of debentures of the company, who are so entitled,

not less than 21 days before the date of the meeting of the company at which copies of those documents are to be laid in accordance with *section 341*.

(2) [Subject to subsection (2A), the documents][a] referred to in *subsection (1)* are—

(a) the statutory financial statements of a company for the financial year concerned,

(b) the directors' report in relation to it, including any group directors' report, for that financial year,

(c) the statutory auditors' report on those financial statements and that directors' report.

[(2A) *Subsection (2)(b)* shall not apply to a company that qualifies for the micro companies regime and has availed itself of the exemption, under *section 325(1A)*, from preparing a directors' report.][b]

(3) If the copies of the documents referred to in *subsection (1)* are sent less than 21 days before the date of the meeting referred to in that subsection they shall, notwithstanding that fact, be deemed to have been duly sent if it is so agreed by all the members entitled to attend and vote at the meeting.

(4) References in this section to sending to any person copies of the documents specified in *subsection (2)* include references to using electronic communications for sending copies of those documents to such address as may for the time being be notified to the company by that person for that purpose.

(5) Unless the company's constitution provides otherwise, copies of the foregoing documents are also to be treated, for the purposes of this section, as sent to a person where—

(a) the company and that person have agreed to his or her having access to the documents on a website (instead of their being sent to him or her),

(b) the documents are documents to which that agreement applies, and

(c) that person is notified, in a manner for the time being agreed for the purpose between him or her and the company, of—

(i) the publication of the documents on a website,

(ii) the address of that website, and

(iii) the place on that website where the documents may be accessed, and how they may be accessed.

(6) For the purposes of this section documents treated in accordance with *subsection (5)* as sent to any person are to be treated as sent to him or her not less than 21 days before the date of a meeting if, and only if—

(a) the documents are published on the website throughout a period beginning at least 21 days before the date of the meeting and ending with the conclusion of the meeting, and

(b) the notification given for the purposes of *paragraph (c)* of that subsection is given not less than 21 days before the date of the meeting.

(7) Nothing in *subsection (6)* shall invalidate the proceedings of a meeting where—

(a) any documents that are required to be published as mentioned in *paragraph (a)* of that subsection are published for a part, but not all, of the period mentioned in that paragraph, and

(b) the failure to publish those documents throughout that period is wholly attributable to circumstances which it would not be reasonable to have expected the company to prevent or avoid.

(8) Where copies of documents are sent out under this section over a period of days, references elsewhere in this Act to the day on which those copies are sent out shall be read as references to the last day of that period.

(9) If default is made in complying with this section, the company concerned and any officer of it who is in default shall be guilty of a category 3 offence.

(10) In *subsection (9)* "officer" includes any shadow director and *de facto* director.

Amendments

a Words substituted by C(A)A 2017, s 46(a) (previously: "The documents").

b Subsection (2A) inserted by C(A)A 2017, s 46(b).

---

339 Right to demand copies of financial statements and reports

(1) Any member of a company and any holder of debentures of the company shall be entitled to be furnished by the company, on demand and without charge, with a copy of—

(a) the company's statutory financial statements for the most recent financial year,

(b) [subject to *subsection (1A)*,][a] the directors' report for that year, and

(c) the statutory auditors' report for that year on those financial statements and that directors' report.

[(1A) *Subsection (1)(b)* shall not apply to a company that qualifies for the micro companies regime and has availed itself of the exemption, under *section 325(1A)*, from preparing a directors' report.][b]

(2) If the group financial statements do not deal with a subsidiary undertaking of the company, any member of the company shall be entitled to demand to be furnished by the company, without charge, with a copy of the statutory financial statements of such subsidiary undertaking for the most recent financial year which have been sent to the members of that subsidiary undertaking, together with a copy of the directors' and statutory auditors' reports.

(3) Without prejudice to *subsection (2)* but subject to *subsection (4)*, any member of the company shall be entitled to be furnished, within 14 days after the date on which he or she has made a demand in that behalf to the company, with a copy of any statutory financial statement (including every document required by law to be annexed thereto and a copy of the directors' and auditors' reports) of any subsidiary undertaking of the company laid before any annual general meeting of such subsidiary undertaking, at a charge not exceeding €3.00 for each financial year's financial statements so furnished.

(4) A member shall not be entitled to be furnished with a copy of any statements referred to in *subsection (3)* laid before an annual general meeting held more than 10 years before the date on which the demand under that subsection is made.

(5) Copies of financial statements need not be sent to any member of a company if, on the application either of the company or of any person who claims to be aggrieved, the court is satisfied that the rights conferred by this section are being abused and orders that such copies need not be sent.

(6) The court may order the company's costs on such an application to be paid in whole or in part by the member whose demands for copies of statements are the subject of the application to the court.

(7) Any obligation by virtue of *subsection (1)* or *(2)* to furnish a person with a document may, unless the company's constitution provides otherwise, be complied with by using electronic communications for sending that document to such address as may for the time being be notified to the company by that person for that purpose.

(8) If a demand made under this section by a member of a company is not complied with within 14 days after the date on which the demand is made then (unless it is proved that the member has already made a demand for and been furnished with a copy

of the financial statements for the financial year concerned) the company and any officer of it who is in default shall be guilty of a category 3 offence.

(9) In the case of any default under this section, the court may direct that the copies demanded shall be sent to the member demanding them.

(10) In *subsection (8)*, "officer" includes any shadow director and *de facto* director.

Amendments

a Words inserted by C(A)A 2017, s 47(a).

b Subsection (1A) inserted by C(A)A 2017, s 47(b).

340 Requirements in relation to publication of financial statements

(1) If a company publishes its statutory financial statements, it shall also publish with those statutory financial statements any directors' report prepared in accordance with *section 325* and any statutory auditors' report made under *section 391* in the form required by *section 336*.

(2) Where a company is required to prepare group financial statements for a financial year, it shall not publish entity financial statements for that year unless they are combined with the group financial statements and published together as the statutory financial statements of the company.

(3) Where a company publishes its abridged financial statements prepared in accordance with *section 353* [...][a], it shall also publish with those abridged financial statements any report in relation to those abridged financial statements specified in *section 356* and, if the statutory auditors of the company have refused to provide the directors of the company with a report under that section, an indication of the refusal.

(4) If a company publishes non-statutory financial statements (and that expression shall be read as including any abbreviated accounts relating to any period), it shall also publish a statement indicating—

(a) the reason for the preparation of the non-statutory financial statements,

(b) that the non-statutory financial statements are not the statutory financial statements of the company,

(c) whether statutory financial statements dealing with any financial year with which the non-statutory financial statements purport to deal have been annexed to the annual return and delivered to the Registrar and, if not, an indication of when they are likely to be so delivered,

(d) whether the statutory auditors of the company have made a report under *section 391* in the form required by *section 336* in respect of the statutory financial statements of the company which relate to any financial year with which the non-statutory financial statements purport to deal,

(e) whether any matters referred to in the statutory auditors' report were qualified or unqualified, or whether the statutory auditors' report included a reference to any matters to which the statutory auditors drew attention by way of emphasis without qualifying the report.

(5) Where a company publishes non-statutory financial statements, it shall not publish with those financial statements any such statutory auditors' report as is mentioned in *subsection (4)(d)*.

(6) Where a holding company publishes non-statutory entity financial statements dealing with the company alone (as distinct from the company and its subsidiary undertakings), it shall indicate in a note to those financial statements whether or not group financial statements have been prepared for that period and, if so, where they can be obtained.

(7) If a company fails to comply with any of *subsections (1)* to *(6)*, the company and any officer of it who is in default shall be guilty of a category 3 offence.

(8) In *subsection (7)* "officer" includes any shadow director and *de facto* director.

Amendments

a Words repealed by C(A)A 2017, s 48.

---

341 Financial statements and reports to be laid before company in general meeting

(1) The directors of a company shall, in respect of each financial year, lay before the company in general meeting copies of—

- (a) the statutory financial statements of the company for the financial year,
- (b) [subject to *subsection (1A)*, the directors' report][a], including any group directors' report, for the financial year,
- (c) the statutory auditors' report on those financial statements and that directors' report.

[(1A) *Subsection (1)(b)* shall not apply to a company that qualifies for the micro companies regime and has availed itself of the exemption, under *section 325(1A)*, from preparing a directors' report.][b]

(2) Those financial statements and those reports of the directors and the statutory auditors for a financial year shall be so laid not later than 9 months after the financial year end date.

(3) The statutory auditors' report shall be open to inspection by any member at the general meeting.

(4) Where *section 175(3)* (dispensing with the holding of an annual general meeting) is availed of, then *subsections (1)* and *(3)* shall be disregarded and *subsection (2)* shall apply as if the reference in it to the laying of financial statements by the time referred to in that subsection were a reference to those statements being provided, by that time, to all the members (entitled to attend and vote at an annual general meeting) for the purpose of their signing the written resolution referred to in *section 175(3)*.

Amendments

a Words substituted by C(A)A 2017, s 49(a) (previously: "the directors' report").
b Subsection (1A) inserted by C(A)A 2017, s 49(b).

Chapter 13
Annual return and documents annexed to it

342 Annual return

In this Act "annual return" means a return that, in accordance with the provisions of this Part, has to be made by a company to the Registrar in respect of successive periods as determined in accordance with those provisions.

343 Obligation to make annual return

(1) In this section "annual return date", in relation to a company, means the date in relation to that company as provided under *section 345* and "first annual return date", in relation to a company, shall be read accordingly.

(2) Subject to the provisions of this section, a company shall deliver to the Registrar an annual return in accordance with *subsection (4)* not later than 28 days after the annual return date of the company.

(3) However, if the annual return is made up to an earlier date than the company's annual return date, it shall be so delivered not later than 28 days after that earlier date.

(4) An annual return of a company shall—

(a) be in the prescribed form and contain the prescribed information, and

(b) be made up to a date that is not later than its annual return date,

except that the first annual return falling to be made by a company after it is incorporated shall be made up to the date that is its first annual return date.

(5) The court, on an application made (on notice to the Registrar) by a company, may, if it is satisfied that it would be just to do so, make an order extending the time for the purposes of *subsection (2)* or *(3)* in which the annual return of the company in relation to a particular period may be delivered to the Registrar; only one such order may be made as respects the particular period to which the return concerned of the company relates.

(6) Within 28 days after the date on which an order under *subsection (5)* is made, or such longer period as the court may allow on the making of the order, the company to which the order relates shall deliver a certified copy of the order to the Registrar; if the order is not received by the Registrar within whichever foregoing period is applicable it shall not be valid for the purposes of *subsection (5)*.

(7) In respect of an annual return that is to be delivered on or after the commencement of this section, the court for the purposes of *subsection (5)* shall be the District Court

for the District Court district where the registered office of the company is located or the High Court.

(8) *Subsection (2)* shall not apply in respect of any annual return date that falls during a period when the company is in the course of being wound up and a liquidator stands appointed to it.

(9) *Subsection (2)* shall not apply in respect of any annual return date that falls during a period when the company is in the course of being voluntarily struck off the register by the Registrar pursuant to *sections 731* to *733* but—

(a) *subsection (10)* has effect as regards the interpretation of this subsection, and

(b) in addition to the foregoing, the exemption conferred by this subsection shall cease to apply where the company is not ultimately dissolved on foot of that procedure or, if it is dissolved on foot thereof, where it is subsequently restored to the register.

(10) For the purposes of *subsection (9)*, the period when the company is in the course of being voluntarily struck off the register by the Registrar pursuant to *sections 731* to *733* shall only be regarded as having commenced on the publication by the Registrar of a notice under *section 732* in relation to that application.

(11) If a company fails to comply with the requirements of this section, the company and any officer of it who is in default shall be guilty of a category 3 offence.

(12) In *subsection (11)* "officer" includes any shadow director and *de facto* director.

344 Special provision for annual return delivered in a particular form

[...][a]

Amendments

a Section 344 repealed by C(SA)A 2018, s 3(a). Not yet commenced as at date of publication.

---

345 Annual return date

(1) Unless it is altered by the company or the Registrar in accordance with *section 346*, the annual return date of a company in any year shall be the date determined by this section.

(2) In the case of a company incorporated before the commencement of this section—

(a) the company's existing annual return date (as determined in accordance with the prior Companies Acts) shall be taken to be its annual return date falling next after that commencement, and

(b) the annual return date of the company, in each subsequent year, shall be the anniversary of the date referred to in *paragraph (a)*.

(3) In the case of a company incorporated on or after the commencement of this section—

(a) the first annual return date of the company shall be the date 6 months after the date of its incorporation, and

(b) the annual return date of the company, in each subsequent year, shall be the anniversary of its first annual return date.

346 Alteration of annual return date

(1) Where the annual return of a company is made up in any year to a date earlier than its annual return date, the company's annual return date shall thereafter be each anniversary of the date to which that annual return is made up unless the company—

(a) elects in the annual return to retain its existing annual return date, or

(b) establishes a new annual return date in accordance with *subsection (2)*,

but, for the avoidance of doubt, an election under *paragraph (a)* does not operate to make the next annual return date of the company fall in any year other than in the year in which it would have fallen had the election not been made.

(2) Save in the case of a company delivering its first annual return and subject to *subsections (3)* and *(4)*, a company may establish a new annual return date by delivering an annual return to the Registrar made up to its existing annual return date in accordance with *section 343(2)*, being an annual return—

(a) that is so delivered not later than [56][a] days after its existing annual return date, and

(b) to which there is annexed a notification in the prescribed form nominating the new annual return date,

but, notwithstanding anything to the contrary in this Act, the company shall not be required to annex statutory financial statements, or the other documents referred to in *section 347(1)*, to such a return.

(3) The new annual return date established pursuant to *subsection (2)* shall be a date falling within the period of 6 months following the existing annual return date.

(4) Where a company has established a new annual return date pursuant to *subsection (2)*, it shall not establish a further new annual return date pursuant to that subsection until at least 5 years have elapsed since the establishment of the first-mentioned new annual return date.

(5) Where it appears to the Registrar desirable for a holding company or a holding company's subsidiary undertaking to extend its annual return date so that the subsidiary undertaking's annual return date may correspond with that of the holding company, the Registrar may, on the application or with the consent of the directors of the company or undertaking whose annual return date is to be extended, direct that an extension is to be permitted in the case of that company or undertaking.

(6) Where the annual return date of a company or subsidiary undertaking in a year is altered pursuant to *subsection (2)* or *(5)*, its annual return date thereafter shall be each anniversary of the date so altered, but subject to any subsequent invocation, in accordance with their terms, of the preceding provisions of this section.

Amendments

a 56 days substituted for 28 days by C(SA)A 2018, s 9. Not yet commenced as at date of publication.

347 Documents to be annexed to annual return: all cases

(1) Subject to the provisions of this Part, there shall be annexed to the annual return a copy of the following documents that have been, or are to be, laid before the relevant general meeting:

(a) the statutory financial statements of the company;

(b) [subject to *subsection (1A)*, the directors' report][a], including any group directors' report; and

(c) the statutory auditors' report on those financial statements and that directors' report;

and "relevant general meeting" in this subsection means the general meeting of the company held during the period to which the annual return relates or, if the most recent statutory financial statements of the company and the other foregoing documents have not been required to be laid before such a meeting, the next general meeting held after the return's delivery to the Registrar before which those statements and other documents are required to be laid.

[(1A) *Subsection (1)(b)* shall not apply to a company that qualifies for the micro companies regime and has availed itself of the exemption, under *section 325(1A)*, from preparing a directors' report.][b]

(2) The reference in *subsection (1)* to a copy of a document is a reference to a copy that satisfies the following conditions:

(a) it is a true copy of the original save for the difference that the signature or signatures on the original, and any date or dates thereon, shall appear in typeset form on the copy; and

(b) it is accompanied by a certificate of a director and the secretary of the company, that bears the signature of the director and the secretary in electronic or written form, stating that the copy is a true copy of the original (and one such certificate relating to all of the documents mentioned in *subsection (1)* suffices and the foregoing statement need not be qualified on account of the difference permitted by *paragraph (a)* as to the form of a signature or of a date).

(3) Where any document referred to in *subsection (1)* that has been annexed to the annual return is in a language other than the English language or the Irish language, there shall be annexed to each such document a translation of it in the English language or the Irish language certified in the prescribed manner to be a correct translation.

(4) Every document annexed to the annual return in accordance with *subsection (1)* shall cover the period—

(a) in the case of the first annual return to which such documents are annexed — since the incorporation of the company, and

(b) in any other case — since the end of the period covered by the statutory financial statements annexed to the preceding annual return,

and shall be made up to a date falling not more than 9 months before the date to which the annual return is made up.

(5) If a company fails to comply with *subsection (1)*, *(3)* or *(4)*, the company and any officer of it who is in default shall be guilty of a category 3 offence.

(6) In *subsection (5)* "officer" includes any shadow director and *de facto* director.

Amendments

a Words substituted by C(A)A 2017, s 50(a) (previously: "the directors' report").

b Subsection (1A) inserted by C(A)A 2017, s 50(b).

---

348 Documents to be annexed to annual returns: certain cases

(1) Where a holding company that prepares Companies Act financial statements has availed itself of the exemption in *section 299* (subsidiary undertaking of higher EEA holding undertaking) and does not prepare group financial statements because it has relied on the following consolidated accounts and annual report prepared by a higher holding undertaking in which it and all of its subsidiary undertakings are consolidated, the holding company shall annex to its annual return a copy of the following documents:

(a) the consolidated accounts referred to in *section 299(4)(a)*;

(b) the consolidated annual report referred to in *section 299(4)(b)*; and

(c) the report of the person responsible for auditing the consolidated accounts referred to in *section 299(4)(a)*.

(2) Where a holding company that prepares Companies Act financial statements has availed itself of the exemption in *section 300* (subsidiary undertaking of higher non-EEA holding undertaking) and does not prepare group financial statements because it has relied on the following consolidated accounts and any annual report prepared by a higher holding undertaking in which it and all of its subsidiary undertakings are consolidated, the holding company shall annex to its annual return a copy of the following documents:

(a) the consolidated accounts referred to in *section 300(4)(a)*;

(b) any consolidated annual report referred to in *section 300(4)(b)*; and

(c) the report of the person or persons responsible for auditing the accounts referred to in *paragraph (a)*, being the person or persons mentioned in *section 300(4)(c)*.

(3) Where a holding company that prepares IFRS financial statements has availed itself of the exemptions in IFRS and does not prepare group financial statements because it has relied on consolidated accounts and an annual report prepared by its higher holding undertaking in which it and all of its subsidiary undertakings are consolidated, the holding company shall annex to its annual return a copy of the following documents:

(a) the consolidated accounts on which it has so relied;

(b) the consolidated annual report of the higher holding undertaking; and

(c) the report of the person or persons auditing those accounts on those accounts and that annual report.

(4) Where a company has relied on the exemption in *section 316(1)* regarding information on related undertakings, the company shall annex to the annual return to which the statutory financial statements referred to in that provision are annexed the full information concerned, that is say—

(a) the information referred to in *section 316(1)*, and

(b) the information referred to in *section 314(1)* and *(2)*, not falling within *paragraph (a)*, that it would have disclosed in the notes to those statements but for its reliance on that exemption.

(5) Where any document required to be annexed to the annual return by this section is in a language other than the English language or the Irish language, there shall be annexed to the copy of that document delivered a translation of it into the English language or the Irish language, certified in the prescribed manner to be a correct translation.

(6) If a company fails to comply with any of *subsections (1)* to *(5)*, the company and any officer of it who is in default shall be guilty of a category 3 offence.

(7) The reference in *subsection (1)*, *(2)* or *(3)* to a copy of a document is a reference to a copy that satisfies the following conditions:

(a) it is a true copy of the original save for the difference that the signature or signatures on the original, and any date or dates thereon, shall appear in typeset form on the copy; and

(b) it is accompanied by a certificate of a director and the secretary of the company, that bears the signature of the director and the secretary in electronic or written form, stating that the copy is a true copy of the original (and one such certificate relating to all of the documents mentioned in *subsection (1)*, *(2)* or *(3)*, as the case may be, suffices and the foregoing statement need not be qualified on account of the difference permitted by *paragraph (a)* as to the form of a signature or of a date).

(8) In *subsection (6)* "officer" includes any shadow director and *de facto* director.

349 First annual return: exception from requirement to annex statutory financial statements

Notwithstanding anything to the contrary in this Act, a company shall not be required to annex statutory financial statements, or the other documents referred to in *section 347(1),* to the first annual return falling to be made by the company after it is incorporated.

Chapter 14
Exclusions, exemptions and special arrangements with regard to public disclosure of financial information

350 Qualification of company as small or medium company

[...][a]

Amendments

a Section 350 repealed by C(A)A 2017, s 3(1)(c).

---

351 Exemptions in respect of directors' report in the case of small and medium companies

[...][a]

Amendments

a Section 351 repealed by C(A)A 2017, s 3(1)(d).

---

352 Exemption from filing certain information for small and medium companies

[(1) The exemption in subsection (2) is available for a company that—

(a) qualifies for the small companies regime (or the micro companies regime), and

(b) has not elected to prepare group financial statements in accordance with section 293.

(2) That exemption is an exemption from the requirement in section 347 to annex to the company's annual return the following documents:

(a) the statutory financial statements of the company;

(b) the directors' report (except where that company qualifies for the micro companies regime and has not elected to prepare the directors' report);

(c) the statutory auditors' report on those financial statements and that directors' report.

(3) If a company that qualifies for the small companies regime or the micro companies regime avails itself of the exemption provided by this section, it shall instead annex to its annual return a copy of each of the following documents:

(a) abridged financial statements prepared in accordance with section 353 and which have been approved and signed in accordance with section 355;

(b) a special statutory auditors' report prepared in accordance with section 356.

(4) A reference in subsection (3) to a copy of a document is a reference to a copy that satisfies the following conditions:

(a) it is a true copy of the original save for the difference that the signature or signatures on the original, and any date or dates thereon, shall appear in typeset form on the copy;

(b) it is accompanied by a certificate of a director and the secretary of the company, that bears the signature of the director and the secretary in electronic or written form, stating that the copy is a true copy of the original (and one such certificate relating to all of the documents mentioned in subsection (3) suffices and the foregoing statement need not be qualified on account of the difference permitted by paragraph (a) as to the form of a signature or of a date).][a]

Amendments

a Section 352 substituted by C(A)A 2017, s 51.

---

353 Abridged financial statements for a small company

(1) For the purposes of *section 352*, the abridged financial statements of a company that qualifies as a small company shall, in the manner set out in this section, be extracted from the statutory financial statements of the company prepared under *section 290*.

(2) Where the statutory financial statements of the company are IFRS financial statements, the abridged financial statements shall comprise—

(a) the balance sheet of the company,

(b) those notes to the financial statements that provide the information required by *sections 305* to *321*, [...][a]

[(c) any other notes to the financial statements including the notes relating to income statement items applicable to the small or micro company concerned, and][b]

[(d) the statement of changes in equity of the company.][c]

(3) Where the statutory financial statements of the company are Companies Act financial statements, the abridged financial statements shall comprise—

(a) the balance sheet of the company,

(b) those notes to the financial statements that provide the information required by *sections 305* to *321*,

[(c) any other notes to the financial statements, including the notes relating to profit and loss account items applicable to the small or micro company concerned and, in particular, the information required by *paragraph 53* of *Schedule 3A* in the case of a small company,][d]

[(d) the information required by *paragraph 48* of *Schedule 3A* in the case of a small company or *paragraph 33* of *Schedule 3B* in the case of a micro company, even where the company has elected to include it in the profit and loss account, and][e]

[(e) any information provided in accordance with *subsections (4)*, *(5)* and *(6)* of *section 291*.][f]

(4) *Section 274(3)* (references to balance sheet to include certain notes) does not apply to this section.

Amendments

a Word repealed by C(A)A 2017, s 52(a)(i).
b Subsection (2)(c) substituted by C(A)A 2017, s 52(a)(ii).
c Subsection (2)(d) inserted by C(A)A 2017, s 52(a)(iii).
d Subsection (3)(c) substituted by C(A)A 2017, s 52(b)(i).
e Subsection (3)(d) substituted by C(A)A 2017, s 52(b)(ii).
f Subsection (3)(e) inserted by C(A)A 2017, s 52(b)(iii).

354 Abridged financial statements for a medium company

[...][a]

Amendments

a Section 354 repealed by C(A)A 2017, s 3(1)(e).

355 Approval and signing of abridged financial statements

(1) Where the directors of a company are satisfied that the requirements of *section 353* [...][a], as appropriate, have been complied with as regards the preparation of the abridged financial statements, those financial statements shall be approved by the board of directors and signed on their behalf by 2 directors, where there are 2 or more directors.

(2) Without prejudice to the generality of *section 11* and its application to the other provisions of this section, where the company has a sole director *subsection (1)* operates to require that director, if he or she is satisfied as to the matters referred to in

that subsection in respect of the statements, to approve and sign the abridged financial statements.

(3) In addition to the preceding requirements, there shall be included the following statement on the face of the [balance sheet forming part of the abridged financial statements][b], namely a statement by the directors of the company that:

(a) they have relied on the specified exemption contained in *section 352*;

(b) they have done so on the ground that the company is entitled to the benefit of that exemption as a small company [...][c]; and

(c) the abridged financial statements have been properly prepared in accordance with *section 353* [...][d].

(4) The signatures or signature required by *subsection (1)* or *(2)*, as the case may be, shall be inserted on the face of the [balance sheet forming part of the abridged financial statements][e] immediately after the statement referred to in *subsection (3).*

(5) Every copy of every [balance sheet forming part of the abridged financial statements][f] which is approved by the board of directors or which is circulated, published or issued shall state the names of the persons who signed the balance sheet on behalf of the board of directors.

[(6) The following requirements apply to the documents annexed to the annual return under *section 352(3)* and delivered to the Registrar:

(a) the copy of the abridged financial statements required by *section 352(3)(a)* shall state the names of the directors who signed the balance sheet on behalf of the board of directors;

(b) the copy of the special statutory auditors' report required by *section 352(3)(b)* shall state the name of the statutory auditors who signed the report and, if different, the name of the statutory auditors who signed the report under *section 391*.][g]

(7) If abridged financial statements are approved which have not been prepared in accordance with the requirements of *section 353* [...][h], every director of the company who is party to their approval, and who knows that they have not been so prepared or is reckless as to whether they have been so prepared, shall be guilty of a category 2 offence.

(8) For that purpose, every director of the company at the time the abridged financial statements are approved shall be taken to be a party to their approval unless he or she shows that he or she took all reasonable steps to prevent their being approved.

(9) If the requirements of *subsection (6)* as regards documents annexed to an annual return under *section 352(3)* [...][i] are not complied with, the company concerned and any officer of it who is in default shall be guilty of a category 2 offence.

(10) In *subsection (9)* "officer" includes any shadow director and *de facto* director.

Amendments

a Words repealed by C(A)A 2017, s 53(a).
b Words substituted by C(A)A 2017, s 53(b)(i) (previously: "abridged balance sheet").
c Words repealed by C(A)A 2017, s 53(b)(ii).
d Words repealed by C(A)A 2017, s 53 (b)(iii).
e Words substituted by C(A)A 2017, s 53(c) (previously: "abridged balance sheet").
f Words substituted by C(A)A 2017, s 53(d) (previously: "abridged balance sheet").
g Subsection substituted by C(A)A 2017, s 53(e).
h Words repealed by C(A)A 2017, s 53(f).
i Words repealed by C(A)A 2017, s 53(g).

356 Special report of the statutory auditors on abridged financial statements

(1) There shall accompany abridged financial statements annexed to the annual return and delivered to the Registrar a copy of a special report of the statutory auditors of the company to the directors of it containing—

(a) a statement of the statutory auditors with respect to the matters set out in *subsection (2)* on those abridged financial statements, and

(b) a copy of the statutory auditors' report under *section 391* in the form required by *section 336*.

(2) Where—

(a) the directors of a company propose to annex to the annual return abridged financial statements for any financial year prepared pursuant to *section 353* [...][a], and

(b) the statutory auditors of the company are of opinion that the directors of the company are entitled, for that purpose, to rely on the exemption contained in *section 352* and the abridged financial statements have been properly prepared pursuant to *section 353* [...][b],

it shall be the duty of the statutory auditors of the company to state in the special report referred to in *subsection (1)* that, in the opinion of those auditors—

(i) the directors of the company are entitled to annex those abridged financial statements to the annual return, and

(ii) the abridged financial statements so annexed are properly so prepared.

(3) With respect to the statutory auditors' special report referred to in *subsection (1)* (a copy (as that expression is to be read in accordance with [*section 352(4)*][c]) of which is to be delivered to the Registrar), the original of that report shall be signed by the statutory auditors and bear the date of such signing; the requirements of *section 337(2)* with respect to the signing of the report there referred to shall also apply with respect to the signing of the special report.

(4) Every copy of the special report of the statutory auditors prepared in accordance with *subsection (1)* that is circulated, published or issued shall state the name of

the statutory auditors providing the report and, if different, the names of the statutory auditors who provided the report under *section 391*.

(5) If a company fails to comply with *subsection (1)* or *(4)*, the company and any officer of it who is in default shall be guilty of a category 2 offence.

(6) In *subsection (5)* "officer" includes any shadow director and *de facto* director.

Amendments

a Words repealed by C(A)A 2017, s 54(a).

b Words repealed by C(A)A 2017, s 54(b).

c Words substituted by C(A)A 2017, s 54(c) (previously: "*352(5)*").

---

357 Subsidiary undertakings exempted from annexing their statutory financial statements to annual return

(1) Where a company is a subsidiary undertaking of a holding undertaking that is established under the laws of an EEA state, the company shall, as respects any particular financial year of the company, stand exempted from the provisions of *sections 347* and *348* if, but only if, the following conditions are satisfied:

(a) every person who is a shareholder of the company on the date of the holding of the next annual general meeting of the company after the end of that financial year or on the next annual return date of the company after the end of that financial year, whichever is the earlier, shall declare his or her consent to the exemption;

(b) there is in force in respect of the whole of that financial year an irrevocable guarantee by the holding undertaking of all [commitments entered into by the company, including amounts shown as liabilities in the statutory financial statements][a] of the company in respect of that financial year;

(c) the company has notified in writing every person referred to in *paragraph (a)* of the guarantee;

(d) the statutory financial statements of the company for that financial year are consolidated in the consolidated accounts prepared by the holding undertaking;

(e) the exemption of the company under this section is disclosed in a note to those consolidated accounts;

(f) a notice stating that the company has availed itself of the exemption under this section in respect of that financial year together with—

  (i) a copy of the guarantee and notification referred to in *paragraphs (b)* and *(c)*, and

  (ii) a declaration by the company in writing that *paragraph (a)* has been complied with in relation to the exemption, is annexed to the annual return for the financial year made by the company to the Registrar;

(g) [the consolidated accounts of the holding undertaking are drawn up in accordance with the requirements of the Accounting Directive or in accordance with international financial reporting standards and are audited in accordance with Article 34 of that Directive; and][b]

(h) a copy of the consolidated accounts of the holding undertaking together with the report of the auditors on them are annexed to the annual return of the company referred to in *paragraph (f)*.

(2) Where any document referred to in *subsection (1)* that has been annexed to the annual return is in a language other than the English language or the Irish language, there shall be annexed to each such document a translation of it in the English language or the Irish language certified in the prescribed manner to be a correct translation.

(3) *Section 299(7)* (construction of certain references) shall apply to *subsection (1)* in a case where the holding undertaking referred to in *subsection (1)* is a company registered under this Act or an existing company.

(4) *Section 347(2)* applies for the purpose of the construction of the reference to a copy of a document in *subsection (1)(h)* of this section as it applies for the purpose of the construction of the reference to a copy of a document in *section 347(1)*.

Amendments

a Words substituted by C(A)A 2017, s 55(a) (previously: "amounts shown as liabilities in the statutory financial statements").

b Paragraph substituted by C(A)A 2017, s 55(b).

Chapter 15
Audit exemption

358 Main conditions for audit exemption — non-group situation

(1) Subject to *subsection (3)* and the other provisions of this Chapter, *section 360* (audit exemption) applies to a company in respect of its statutory financial statements for a particular financial year if the company qualifies as a small company in relation to that financial year.

(2) For the purposes of this section, whether a company qualifies as a small company shall be determined in accordance with *section [280A* and *280B*][a].

(3) *Section 360* does not apply to a company in respect of its statutory financial statements for a particular financial year during any part of which the company was a group company (within the meaning of *section 359*) unless the group qualifies, under *section 359*, as a small group in relation to that financial year (and the other relevant provisions of this Chapter are complied with).

(4) In *subsection (3)* "group", in relation to a group company, shall be read in accordance with *section 359(1)(b)*.

(5) Nothing in this section prejudices the operation of *Chapter 16* (special audit exemption for dormant companies).

Amendments

a Words substituted by C(A)A 2017, s 56 (previously: "*section 350(2), (3), (5), (7), (8), (9)* and *(10)*").

---

359 Main conditions for audit exemption — group situation

(1) In this section—

(a) "group company" means a company that is a holding company or a subsidiary undertaking; and

(b) references to the group, in relation to a group company, are references to that company, together with all its associated undertakings, and for the purposes of this paragraph undertakings are associated if one is the subsidiary undertaking of the other or both are subsidiary undertakings of a third undertaking.

(2) Subject to this Chapter, *section 360* (audit exemption) applies to any group company in respect of its statutory financial statements for a particular financial year if the [group, would qualify under *section 280B* as a small group][a] in relation to that financial year.

[...][b]

(13) Nothing in this section nor in any subsequent provision of this Chapter prejudices the operation of *Chapter 16* (special audit exemption for dormant companies).

Amendments

a Words substituted by C(A)A 2017, s 57 (previously: "group qualifies as a small group").

b Subsections (3) to (12) repealed by C(A)A 2017, s 57(b).

---

360 Audit exemption

(1) The following provisions (the "audit exemption") have effect where, by virtue of *section 358 or 359*, as appropriate, this section applies in respect of the statutory financial statements of [a company or a group company][a] for a particular financial year—

(a) without prejudice to *section 384(2)*, *section 333* (obligation to have statutory financial statements audited) shall not apply [to the entity financial statements of the company or the group company or the group financial statements of the holding company][b] in respect of that financial year, and

(b) unless and until circumstances (if any) arise by reason of which [the company or group company][c] is not entitled to the audit exemption in respect of that financial year, the provisions specified in *subsection (2)* shall not apply to [the company or group company][c] in respect of that year.

(2) The provisions mentioned in *subsection (1)* are those provisions of this Act, being provisions that—

(a) confer any powers on statutory auditors or require anything to be done by or to or as respects statutory auditors, or

(b) make provision on the basis of a report of statutory auditors having been prepared in relation to the statutory financial statements of a company in a financial year,

and, without prejudice to the generality of the foregoing, include the provisions specified in the Table to this section in so far, and only in so far, as they make provision of the foregoing kind.

Table

Section 121(3) and *(4)* (report of statutory auditors on statutory financial statements for purposes of distribution);
Section 306(4) (statement of particulars of non-compliance with *section 305* or *306*);
Section 322 (disclosure of remuneration for audit, audit-related work and non-audit work);
Section 330 (statement on relevant audit information);
Section 336 (form of statutory auditors' report);
Section 337 (signature of statutory auditor's report);
Section 338 (circulation of statutory financial statements);
Section 339 (right of members to demand copies of financial statements and reports);
Section 340 (requirements in relation to publication of financial statements);
Section 341 (financial statements and reports to be laid before company in general meeting);
Section 347 (documents to be annexed to annual return);
Section 356 (special report on abridged financial statements);
Section 380 and *sections 382* to *385* (dealing with appointment of statutory auditors);
Sections 390 to *393* (obligations of statutory auditors).

Amendments

a Words substituted by C(A)A 2017, s 58(a) (previously: "a company or a group").
b Words substituted by C(A)A 2017, s 58(b)(i) (previously: "to the company or group").
c Words substituted by C(A)A 2017, s 58(b)(ii) (previously: "the company or group").

361 Audit exemption not available where notice under *section 334* served

(1) Notwithstanding that *section 358* is complied with, a company is not entitled to the audit exemption referred to in that section in a financial year if a notice, with respect to that year, is served, under and in accordance with *section 334(1)* and *(2)*, on the company.

(2) Notwithstanding that *section 359* is complied with—

(a) a holding company and the other members of the group are not entitled to the audit exemption referred to in that section in a financial year if a notice, with respect to that year, is served, under and in accordance with *section 334(1)* and *(2)*, on the holding company (irrespective of whether such a notice is served under and in accordance with those provisions on one or more of the other members of the group),

(b) where no such notice has been served, under and in accordance with those provisions, on the holding company but one has been so served on another member of the group, then that member is not entitled to the audit exemption in the year concerned irrespective of whether its holding company and any other members of the group avail themselves of the audit exemption in that year (but this paragraph is not to be read as diminishing the extent of the audit exemption, so far as it relates to the holding company's group financial statements, that is availed of by the holding company).

362 Audit exemption not available where company or subsidiary undertaking falls within a certain category

[(1) Notwithstanding that *section 358* is complied with, a company is not entitled to the audit exemption referred to in that section if the company is a relevant securitisation company.][a]

[(2) Notwithstanding that *section 359* is complied with, a holding company and the other members of the group are not entitled to the audit exemption referred to in that section if—

(a) the holding company is a relevant securitisation company, or

(b) any of those other members is a relevant securitisation company.][b]

(3) In this section "relevant securitisation company" means—

(a) a qualifying company within the meaning of section 110 of the Taxes Consolidation Act 1997; or

(b) a financial vehicle corporation ("FVC") within the meaning of—

(i) in the period before 1 January 2015, Article 1(1) of Regulation (EC) No. 24/2009 of the European Central Bank of 19 December 2008 concerning statistics on the assets and liabilities of financial vehicle corporations engaged in securitisation transactions; or

(ii) subject to *subsection (4)*, in the period on or after 1 January 2015, Article 1(1) of Regulation (EU) No. 1075/2013 of the European Central Bank of 18 October 2013 concerning statistics on the assets and liabilities of financial vehicle corporations engaged in securitisation transactions (recast).

(4) If a Regulation is made by the European Central Bank concerning statistics on the assets and liabilities of financial vehicle corporations engaged in securitisation transactions that—

(a) contains a different definition of financial vehicle corporation ("FVC") from that referred to in *subparagraph (ii)* of *subsection (3)(b)*, the reference in that provision to that definition shall be read as a reference to the definition contained in the Regulation so made, or

(b) amends the definition so referred to, the reference in that provision to that definition shall be read as a reference to that definition as it stands so amended.

Amendments

a Subsection (1) substituted by C(A)A 2017, s 59(a).

b Subsection (2) substituted by C(A)A 2017, s 59(b).

---

363 [Audit exemption (non-group situation) not available in certain cases

(1) Subject to *subsection (2)* and notwithstanding that *section 358* is complied with, a company is not entitled to the audit exemption referred to in that section in respect of its statutory financial statements for the 2 financial years immediately succeeding a financial year (in this section referred to as the 'relevant financial year') where the company failed to deliver to the Registrar, in compliance with *section 343*, the company's annual return to which the statutory financial statements or (as appropriate) abridged financial statements for the relevant financial year are annexed.

(2) *Subsection (1)* shall not apply in the case of an annual return of a company which is the company's first annual return referred to in *section 349*.][a]

Amendments

a Section 363 substituted by C(SA)A 2018, s 10.

---

364 [Audit exemption (group situation) not available in certain cases

(1) Subject to *subsection (3)*, in this section a reference to a relevant body is a reference to the holding company or any other member of the group.

(2) Subject to *subsection (4)* and notwithstanding that *section 359* is complied with, a holding company and the other members of the group are not entitled to the audit exemption referred to in that section in respect of their statutory financial statements for the 2 financial years immediately succeeding a financial year (in this section referred to as the "relevant financial year") where any relevant body failed to deliver to the Registrar, in compliance with *section 343*, the annual return of that relevant body to which such body's statutory financial statements or (as appropriate) abridged financial statements for the relevant financial year are annexed.

(3) There shall not be reckoned as another member of the group for the purposes of this section (other than for the purposes of the expression 'other members of the group' in *subsection (2)*) a subsidiary undertaking that is not a company registered under this Act or an existing company and the construction provided for by *subsection (1)* (of references to each of the relevant bodies) shall be read accordingly.

(4) *Subsection (2)* shall not apply in the case of an annual return which is a relevant body's first annual return referred to in *section 349*.][a]

Amendments

a Section 364 substituted by C(SA)A 2018, s 10.

Chapter 16
Special audit exemption for dormant companies

365 Dormant company audit exemption

(1) Subject to *subsection (5)*, *subsection (3)* applies to a company in respect of its statutory financial statements for a financial year if the directors of the company are of the opinion that the company will satisfy the condition specified in *subsection (2)* in respect of that year and decide that the company should avail itself of *subsection (3)* in that year (and that decision is recorded by the directors in the minutes of the meeting concerned).

(2) The condition mentioned in *subsection (1)* is that in respect of the year concerned the company is dormant that is to say, during that year—

(a) it has no significant accounting transaction, and

(b) its assets and liabilities comprise only permitted assets and liabilities.

(3) The following provisions (the "dormant company audit exemption") have effect where, by virtue of the preceding subsections, this subsection applies in respect of the statutory financial statements of a company for a particular financial year—

(a) without prejudice to *section 384(2)*, *section 333* (obligation to have statutory financial statements audited) shall not apply to the company in respect of that financial year, and

(b) unless and until circumstances, if any, arise in that financial year by reason of which the company is not entitled to that audit exemption in respect of that financial year, the provisions specified in *subsection (4)* shall not apply to the company in respect of that year.

(4) The provisions mentioned in *subsection (3)* are those provisions of this Act, being provisions that—

(a) confer any powers on statutory auditors or require anything to be done by or to or as respects statutory auditors, or

(b) make provision on the basis of a report of statutory auditors having been prepared in relation to the statutory financial statements of a company in a financial year,

and, without prejudice to the generality of the foregoing, include the provisions specified in the Table to *section 360* in so far, and only in so far, as they make provision of the foregoing kind.

(5) *Section 363* shall apply for the purposes of this section as it applies for the purpose of *section 358* with the substitution in *subsection (1)*—

(a) for the reference to *section 358* being complied with of a reference to the condition specified in *subsection (2)* of this section being satisfied, and

(b) for the reference to the audit exemption referred to in *section 358* of a reference to the dormant company audit exemption.

(6) *Section 335* shall apply for the purposes of this section as it applies for the purpose of *section 358* with—

(a) the substitution, in *subsection (1)*, of the following paragraphs for *paragraphs (a)* and *(b)*:

"(a) the company is availing itself of the audit exemption (and the exemption shall be expressed to be 'the exemption provided for by *Chapter 16* of *Part 6* of the *Companies Act 2014*');

(b) the company is availing itself of the exemption on the grounds that the condition specified in *section 365(2)* is satisfied;",

and

(b) the omission of subsections (1)(c) and (7).

(7) In this section—

"permitted assets and liabilities" are investments in shares of, and amounts due to or from, other group undertakings;

"significant accounting transaction" means a transaction that is required by *sections 281* and *282* to be entered in the company's accounting records.

(8) In determining whether or when a company is dormant for the purposes of this section, there shall be disregarded—

(a) any transaction arising from the taking of shares in the company by a subscriber to the constitution as a result of an undertaking of his or her in connection with the formation of the company,

(b) any transaction consisting of the payment of—

(i) a fee to the Registrar on a change of the company's name,

(ii) a fee to the Registrar on the re-registration of the company, or

(iii) a fee to the Registrar for the registration of an annual return (including any fee of an increased amount by virtue of regulations under *section 889(6)*).

Chapter 17
Revision of defective statutory financial statements

366 Voluntary revision of defective statutory financial statements

(1) If it appears to the directors of a company that—

(a) any statutory financial statements of the company (referred to subsequently in this Chapter as the "original statutory financial statements"), or

(b) any directors' report (referred to subsequently in this Chapter as the "original directors' report"),

in respect of a particular financial year, did not comply with the requirements of this Act or, where applicable, of Article 4 of the IAS Regulation, they may prepare revised financial statements or a revised directors' report in respect of that year.

(2) Where copies of the original statutory financial statements or original directors' report have been laid before the company in general meeting or delivered to the Registrar, the revisions shall be confined to—

(a) the correction of those respects in which the original statutory financial statements or original directors' report did not comply with the requirements of this Act or, where applicable, of Article 4 of the IAS Regulation, and

(b) the making of any necessary consequential alterations.

(3) Where the reason for the revision of the statutory financial statements is—

(a) that information that should have been included by way of note to the financial statements was not so included, or

(b) information provided in a note to the financial statements was incorrect or incomplete,

then—

(i) in a case where the amounts and presentation of the profit and loss account, balance sheet or other statements required by the financial reporting framework are not affected by reason thereof — the revision may be effected by supplementary note, and

(ii) in all other cases — revised financial statements shall be prepared.

(4) Where the reason for the revision of the directors' report is—

(a) that information that should have been included in the report was not so included, or

(b) information provided in the report was incorrect or incomplete,

then—

(i) in a case where the additional information to be provided by way of revision does not affect other information included in the report — the revision may be effected by supplementary note, and

(ii) in all other cases — a revised directors' report shall be prepared.

(5) Where the statutory financial statements for any financial year are revised, the next statutory financial statements prepared after the date of revision shall refer to the fact that a previous set of financial statements was revised and provide particulars of the revision, its effect and the reasons for the revision in a note to the financial statements.

367 Content of revised financial statements or revised report

(1) Subject to *section 379*, the provisions of this Act as to the matters to be included in the statutory financial statements of a company shall apply to revised financial statements as if the revised financial statements were prepared and approved by the directors as at the date of the original statutory financial statements.

(2) In particular, *section 289* shall apply so as to require a true and fair view to be shown in the revised financial statements of the matters referred to in that section viewed as at the date of the original statutory financial statements.

(3) In the case of Companies Act financial statements, [*paragraph 14(b)* of *Schedule 3*, *3A* or *3B*, as may be appropriate,][a] shall apply to revised financial statements as if the reference in that provision to the date on which the financial statements were signed was to the date on which the original statutory financial statements were signed.

(4) The provisions of this Act as to the matters to be included in a directors' report apply to a revised directors' report as if the revised report were prepared and approved by the directors of the company as at the date of the original directors' report.

Amendments

a Words substituted by C(A)A 2017, s 62 (previously: "*paragraph 14(b)* of *Schedule 3*").

368 Approval and signature of revised financial statements

(1) *Section 324* (approval and signing of statutory financial statements) shall apply to revised financial statements save that, in the case of a revision effected by supplementary note, it shall apply as if it required a signature or signatures on the supplementary note instead of on the balance sheet.

(2) Where copies of the original statutory financial statements have been sent to members under *section 338*, laid before the members in general meeting under *section*

341 or delivered to the Registrar under *section 347*, the directors shall, before approving the revised financial statements under *section 324*, cause the following statements to be made in a prominent position in the revised financial statements or, in the case of a revision effected by supplementary note, in that note—

(a) in the case of a revision effected by replacement—

(i) a statement clearly identifying the replacement financial statements as being revised financial statements, and

(ii) statements as to the following matters:

(I) that the revised financial statements replace the original statutory financial statements for the financial year, specifying it;

(II) that they are now the statutory financial statements of the company for that financial year;

(III) that they have been prepared as at the date of the original financial statements and not as at the date of the revision and, accordingly, do not deal with events and transactions between those dates;

(IV) the respects in which the original statutory financial statements did not comply with the requirements of this Act or, where applicable, of Article 4 of the IAS Regulation; and

(V) any significant amendments made consequential upon the remedying of those defects;

(b) in the case of a revision effected by supplementary note, statements as to the following matters:

(i) that the note revises in certain respects the original statutory financial statements of the company and is to be treated as forming part of those original statutory financial statements; and

(ii) that the statutory financial statements have been revised as at the date of the original statutory financial statements and not as at the date of the revision and, accordingly, do not deal with events and transactions between those dates;

and shall, when approving the revised financial statements, cause the date on which the approval is given to be stated in them (or, in the case of revision effected by supplementary note, in that note).

(3) Without prejudice to the generality of *subsection (1)*, *subsections (8)* to *(10)* of *section 324* shall have effect as if, in addition to the references in that *subsection (8)* to the requirements as to the signing of the balance sheet and the inclusion of a statement of the signatory's name, there were included references in that subsection to each of the requirements of *paragraph (a)* or *(b)*, as the case may be, of *subsection (2)*.

369 Approval and signature of revised directors' report

(1) *Section 332* (approval and signing of directors' report) shall apply to a revised directors' report save that, in the case of a revision effected by supplementary note, it

shall apply as if it required a signature or signatures on the supplementary note instead of on the report.

(2) Where copies of the original directors' report have been sent to members under *section 338*, laid before the members in general meeting under *section 341* or delivered to the Registrar under *section 347*, the directors shall, before approving the revised directors' report under *section 332*, cause statements as to the following matters to be made in a prominent position in the revised directors' report or, in the case of a revision effected by supplementary note, in that note—

(a) in the case of a revision effected by replacement—

(i) that the revised directors' report replaces the original directors' report for the financial year, specifying it,

(ii) that it has been prepared as at the date of the original directors' report and not as at the date of the revision and, accordingly, does not deal with events and transactions between those dates,

(iii) the respects in which the original directors' report did not comply with the requirements of this Act or, where applicable, of Article 4 of the IAS Regulation, and

(iv) any significant amendments made consequential upon the remedying of those defects,

(b) in the case of a revision effected by supplementary note—

(i) that the note revises in certain respects the original directors' report of the company and is to be treated as forming part of that original directors' report, and

(ii) that the directors' report has been revised as at the date of the original directors' report and not as at the date of the revision and accordingly does not deal with events and transactions between those dates,

and shall, when approving the revised directors' report, cause the date on which the approval is given to be stated in them (or, in the case of revision effected by supplementary note, in that note).

(3) Without prejudice to the generality of *subsection (1)*, *subsections (4)* and *(5)* of *section 332* shall have effect as if, in addition to the references in that *subsection (4)* to the requirements as to the signing of the directors' report and the inclusion of the signatory's name, there were included references in that subsection to each of the requirements of *paragraph (a)* or *(b)*, as the case may be, of *subsection (2)*.

370 Statutory auditors' report on revised financial statements and revised report

(1) Subject to *section 371* and *subsection (3)*, a company's current statutory auditors shall make a report or, as the case may be, a further report of the kind referred to in *section 391*, in the form required by *section 336*, to the company's members under this section on revised financial statements prepared under *section 366*.

(2) In that case, *section 392* (assessment of accounting records) and *section 393* (reporting of offences) shall apply with the necessary modifications.

(3) Where the statutory auditors' report on the original statutory financial statements was not made by the company's current statutory auditors, the directors of the company may resolve that the report required by *subsection (1)* is to be made by the person or persons who made the first-mentioned report, provided that that person or those persons agree to do so and the person or persons would be qualified for appointment as statutory auditors of the company.

(4) Where the person or persons so qualified agree to make that report (and proceed to do so)—

(a) *subsection (2)* (application of *sections 392* and *393*) equally applies in such a case, and

(b) subsequent references in this Chapter, in relation to a report under this section, to statutory auditors shall be read as references to that person or those persons.

(5) Subject to *section 379*, a statutory auditors' report under this section shall state whether, in the statutory auditors' opinion, the revised financial statements have been properly prepared in accordance with the relevant financial reporting framework and, in particular, the provisions of this Act or, where applicable, of Article 4 of the IAS Regulation and, in relation to the latter, whether a true and fair view as at the date the original statutory financial statements were approved by the directors is given by the revised financial statements with respect to the matters set out in *section 336*.

(6) The report shall also state whether, in the statutory auditors' opinion, the original statutory financial statements failed to comply with the requirements of this Act or, where applicable, of Article 4 of the IAS Regulation in the respects identified by the directors in the statement required by *section 368(2)* to be made in the revised financial statements or supplementary note, as the case may be.

(7) The statutory auditors shall also consider whether the information contained in the directors' report for the financial year for which the revised financial statements are prepared (or where that report has been revised under this Chapter, the revised directors' report) is consistent with those financial statements, and—

(a) if they are of the opinion that it is, or

(b) if they are of the opinion that it is not,

they shall state that fact in their report under this section.

(8) *Section 337* (signature of statutory auditor's report) shall apply to a statutory auditors' report under this section as it applies to a statutory auditors' report referred to in *section 336* with the necessary modifications.

(9) A statutory auditors' report under this section shall, upon being signed under *section 337* as so applied, be, as from the date of signature, the statutory auditors' report on the statutory financial statements of the company in place of the report on the original statutory financial statements.

371 Cases where company has availed itself of audit exemption

(1) *Section 370* does not apply to a company that is entitled to, and avails itself of, the audit exemption unless *subsection (2)* applies.

(2) Where as a result of the revisions to the statutory financial statements a company which, in respect of the original statutory financial statements, was entitled to, and availed itself of, the audit exemption becomes a company which is no longer entitled to that exemption, the company shall cause a report by the statutory auditors of the company on the revised financial statements to be prepared.

(3) The report made in accordance with *subsection (2)* shall be delivered to the Registrar within 2 months after the date of the revision of the financial statements.

372 Statutory auditors' report on revised directors' report alone

(1) Subject to *subsection (2)*, a company's current statutory auditors shall make a report or, as the case may be, a further report, in the form required by *section 336*, to the company's members on any revised directors' report prepared under *section 366* if the relevant statutory financial statements have not been revised at the same time.

(2) Where the statutory auditors' report on the original statutory financial statements was not made by the company's current statutory auditors, the directors of the company may resolve that the report required by *subsection (1)* is to be made by the person or persons who made the first-mentioned report, provided that that person or those persons agree to do so and the person or persons would be qualified for appointment as statutory auditors of the company.

(3) Where the person or persons so qualified agree to make that report (and proceed to do so), subsequent references in this Chapter, in relation to a report under this section, to statutory auditors shall be read as references to that person or those persons.

(4) The report shall state that the statutory auditors have considered whether the information given in the revised report is consistent with the original statutory financial statements for the relevant year (specifying it) and—

(a) if they are of the opinion that it is, or

(b) if they are of the opinion that it is not,

they shall state that fact in their report.

(5) *Section 337* (signature of statutory auditor's report) shall apply to a statutory auditors' report under this section as it applies to a statutory auditors' report under *section 336* with the necessary modifications.

373 Effect of revision

(1) Upon the directors approving revised financial statements under *section 324* as applied by *section 368*, the provisions of this Act shall have effect as if the revised financial statements were, as from the date of their approval, the statutory financial statements of the company in place of the original statutory financial statements.

(2) In particular, the revised financial statements shall thereupon be the company's statutory financial statements for the relevant financial year for the purposes of—

(a) *section 339* (right to demand copies of financial statements and reports) and *section 340* (requirements in relation to publication of financial statements), and

(b) each of the following (but only, in each case, if the requirements of the section concerned have not been complied with prior to the date of revision)—

(i) *section 338* (circulation of statutory financial statements),

(ii) *section 341* (financial statements and reports to be laid before the members in general meeting), and

(iii) *section 347* (documents to be annexed to annual return: all cases).

(3) Upon the directors approving a revised directors' report under *section 332* as applied by *section 369*, the provisions of this Act shall have effect as if the revised report were, as from the date of its approval, the directors' report in place of the original directors' report.

(4) In particular, the revised report shall thereupon be the directors' report for the relevant financial year for the purposes of—

(a) *section 339* (right of members to demand copies of financial statements and reports), and

(b) each of the following (but only, in each case, if the requirements of the section concerned have not been complied with prior to the date of revision):

(i) *section 338* (circulation of statutory financial statements);

(ii) *section 341* (financial statements and reports to be laid before the members in general meeting); and

(iii) *section 347* (documents to be annexed to annual return: all cases).

374 Publication of revised financial statements and reports

(1) This section has effect where the directors have prepared revised financial statements or a revised directors' report under *section 366* and copies of the original statutory financial statements or original directors' report have been sent to any person under *section 338*.

(2) The directors shall send to any such person—

(a) in the case of a revision effected by replacement, a copy of the revised financial statements, or (as the case may be) the revised directors' report, together with a copy of the statutory auditors' report on those financial statements, or (as the case may be) on that report, or

(b) in the case of a revision effected by supplementary note, a copy of that note together with a copy of the statutory auditors' report on the revised financial statements, or (as the case may be) on the revised directors' report,

not more than 28 days after the date of revision.

(3) The directors shall also, not more than 28 days after the date of revision, send a copy of the revised financial statements or (as the case may be) the revised directors' report, together with a copy of the statutory auditors' report on those financial statements or (as the case may be) on that report, to any person who is not a

person entitled to receive a copy under *section 338* but who is, as at the date of revision—

(a) a member of the company,

(b) a holder of any debentures of the company, or

(c) a person who is entitled to receive notice of general meetings.

(4) If default is made in complying with this section, each of the directors who approved the revised financial statements under *section 324* as applied by *section 368* or the revised directors' report under *section 332* as applied by *section 369* shall be guilty of a category 3 offence.

(5) Where, prior to the date of revision of the original statutory financial statements, the company—

(a) had completed sending copies of those financial statements under *section 338*, references in this Act to the day on which financial statements are sent under *section 338* shall be read as references to the day on which the original statutory statements were sent under that section (applying *subsection (8)* of it as necessary) despite the fact that those financial statements have been revised, or

(b) had not completed sending copies of those financial statements under *section 338*, the foregoing references in this Act shall be read as references to the day, or the last day, on which the revised financial statements are sent under this section.

375 Laying of revised financial statements or a revised report

(1) This section has effect where the directors of a company have prepared revised financial statements or a revised directors' report under *section 366* and copies of the original statutory financial statements or directors' report have been laid before a general meeting of the company under *section 341*.

(2) A copy of the revised financial statements or (as the case may be) the revised directors' report, together with a copy of the statutory auditors' report on those financial statements, or (as the case may be) on that report, shall be laid before the next general meeting of the company held after the date of revision at which any statutory financial statements for a financial year are laid, unless the revised financial statements, or (as the case may be) the revised directors' report, have already been laid before an earlier general meeting.

376 Delivery of revised financial statements or a revised report

(1) This section has effect where the directors of a company have prepared revised financial statements or a revised directors' report under *section 366* and a copy of the original statutory financial statements or directors' report, as annexed to the company's annual return, has been delivered to the Registrar under *section 343*.

(2) The directors of the company shall, within 28 days after the date of revision, deliver to the Registrar—

(a) in the case of a revision effected by replacement, a copy of the revised financial statements or (as the case may be) the revised directors' report, together with a copy of the statutory auditors' report on those financial statements or (as the case may be) on that report, or

(b) in the case of a revision effected by supplementary note, a copy of that note, together with a copy of the statutory auditors' report on the revised financial statements or (as the case may be) on the revised report.

(3) If a director fails to comply with *subsection (2)*, he or she shall be guilty of a category 3 offence.

(4) Without limiting the obligations of the directors of a company under this section or *subsection (3)*, it shall be the duty of a person who is a shadow director or *de facto* director of a company to ensure that the requirements of *subsection (2)* are complied with in relation to the company.

(5) If a person fails to comply with his or her duty under *subsection (4)*, the person shall be guilty of a category 3 offence.

(6) If the original statutory financial statements or directors' report in respect of the company have been registered by the Registrar prior to the date of receipt by the Registrar of the revised financial statements or (as the case may be) the revised directors' report, then, despite anything in *section 373(2)*, this section shall operate so as to require—

(a) that the revised financial statements or (as the case may be) the revised directors' report be placed on the register, and

(b) notwithstanding the taking of such action, that the original statutory financial statements or directors' report continue to remain on the register.

(7) *Section 347(2)* applies for the purposes of the construction of references to a copy of a document in *subsection (2)* of this section as it applies for the purpose of the construction of the reference to a copy of a document in *section 347(1)*.

(8) In this section "date of revision" means the date of revision of the original statutory financial statements.

377 Small and medium companies

(1) This section has effect (subject to *section 379(2)*) where the directors have prepared revised financial statements under *section 366* and the company, prior to the date of revision, has, taking advantage of the exemption for a small [...][a] company conferred by *section 352*, delivered to the Registrar abridged financial statements.

(2) Where the abridged financial statements so delivered to the Registrar would, if they had been prepared by reference to the matters taken account of in the revised financial statements, not comply with the provisions of this Act or, where applicable, of Article 4 of the IAS Regulation whether because—

(a) the company would not have qualified as a small [...][b] company in the light of the revised financial statements, or

(b) the financial statements have been revised in a manner which affects the content of the abridged financial statements,

the directors of the company shall have the following duty.

(3) That duty is to cause the company either—

(a) to deliver to the Registrar, within 28 days after the date of revision, a copy of the revised financial statements, together with a copy of the directors' report and the statutory auditors' report on the revised financial statements, or

(b) if, on the basis of the revised financial statements, the company would be entitled under *section 352* to do so, to prepare revised abridged financial statements under *section 353* [...][c] and deliver them to the Registrar, together with a statement as to the effect of the revisions made,

and [*sections 352* and *353*][d] shall be read as being applicable in the circumstances referred to in *paragraph (b)* as they are applicable in circumstances not falling within this Chapter.

(4) Where the abridged financial statements would, if they had been prepared by reference to the matters taken account of in the revised financial statements, comply with the requirements of this Act, or, where that Article is applicable, the relevant requirements of this Act and the requirements of Article 4 of the IAS Regulation, the directors of the company shall have the following duty.

(5) That duty is to cause the company to deliver to the Registrar—

(a) a note stating that the statutory financial statements of the company for the relevant financial year (specifying it) have been revised in a respect which has no bearing on the abridged financial statements delivered for that year, and

(b) a copy of the statutory auditors' report on the revised financial statements.

(6) Revised abridged financial statements referred to in *subsection (3)(b)* or a note under *subsection (5)* shall be delivered to the Registrar within 28 days after the date of revision.

(7) If a director fails to comply with his or her duty under *subsection (2)* or *(4)*, he or she shall be guilty of a category 3 offence.

(8) Without limiting the obligations of the directors of a company under this section or *subsection (7)*, it shall be the duty of a person who is a shadow director or *de facto* director of a company to ensure that the requirements of *subsections (3)* and *(5)* are complied with in relation to the company.

(9) If a person fails to comply with his or her duty under *subsection (8)*, the person shall be guilty of a category 3 offence.

(10) *Section 347(2)* applies for the purposes of the construction of references to a copy of a document in *subsection (3)* or *(5)* of this section as it applies for the purpose of the construction of the reference to a copy of a document in *section 347(1)*.

(11) In this section "date of revision" means the date of revision of the original statutory financial statements.

Amendments

a Words repealed by C(A)A 2017, s 63(a) (previously: "or medium").

b Words repealed by C(A)A 2017, s 63(b) (previously: "or (as the case may be) medium").

c Words repealed by C(A)A 2017, s 63(c)(i) (previously: "or *354* as appropriate").

d Words substituted by C(A)A 2017, s 63(c)(ii) (previously: "*sections 352* to *354*").

378 Application of this Chapter in cases where audit exemption available, etc.

Where, based on the revised financial statements prepared under *section 366*, a company—

(a) is entitled to, and avails itself of, the audit exemption in respect of the financial year concerned, or

(b) would have been entitled, but for the time that it takes to complete the preparation of those revised statements resulting in the directors not being able to make a decision in accordance with *section 358(1)* or *(2)* or *section 365(1)* (as the case may be) in that regard, to avail itself of the audit exemption in respect of that year,

this Chapter shall have effect as if any reference in it to a statutory auditors' report, or to the making of such a report, were omitted.

379 Modifications of Act

(1) Where the provisions of the Act as to the matters to be included in the statutory financial statements of a company or (as the case may be) in a directors' report have been amended after the date of the original statutory financial statements or (as the case may be) directors' report but prior to the date of revision, references in *sections 366* and *370(3)* to the provisions of this Act shall be read as references to the provisions of this Act as in force at the date of approval of the original statutory financial statements or (as the case may be) directors' report.

(2) Where the provisions of *section 353* [...][a] as to the matters to be included in abridged financial statements have been amended after the date of delivery of the original abridged financial statements but prior to the date of revision of the revised financial statements or report, references in *section 370* to the provisions of this Act or to any particular provision of it shall be read as references to the provisions of this Act, or to the particular provision, as in force at the date of approval of the original abridged financial statements.

[(3) Where before the repeal of *section 354* by *section 3(1) of the Companies (Accounting) Act 2017*, a medium company referred to in *section 354* has prepared and filed abridged financial statements for a financial year in accordance with that section, the company may prepare and file revised abridged financial statements in respect of that financial year as if the said *section 354* had not been repealed.][b]

Amendments

a Words repealed by C(A)A 2017, s 64(a).

b Subsection (3) inserted by C(A)A 2017, s 64(b).

Chapter 18
Appointment of statutory auditors

380 Statutory auditors — general provisions (including as to the interpretation of provisions providing for auditors' term of office)

(1) One or more statutory auditors shall be appointed in accordance with this Chapter for each financial year of the company.

(2) For convenience of expression (but save in certain instances where use of the singular form is more appropriate) the plural form — "statutory auditors" — is used throughout this Part irrespective of the fact that a single statutory auditor has been or is to be so appointed.

(3) A reference elsewhere in this Act to statutory auditors shall be read accordingly.

(4) The appointment of a firm (not being a body corporate) by its firm name to be the statutory auditors of a company shall be deemed to be an appointment of those persons who are—

(a) from time to time during the currency of the appointment the partners in that firm as from time to time constituted, and

(b) qualified to be statutory auditors of that company.

(5) Any—

(a) reference in this Chapter to a person being appointed statutory auditor of a company to hold office until the conclusion of the next annual general meeting of the company, or

(b) provision otherwise of this Chapter stating that a person appointed statutory auditor shall hold such office until the conclusion of such a general meeting,

shall be read as meaning that the person shall hold such office until the conclusion of such a general meeting save where one of the following sooner happens—

(i) the person's resignation (in accordance with this Part) or death,

(ii) the termination of the person's office (or his or her removal otherwise from office) pursuant to this Part, or

[(iii) the person's becoming disqualified from holding office by virtue of [the relevant provisions (within the meaning of section 900)][b]][a]

[(6) A contractual clause which has the effect of restricting the choice by the general meeting of shareholders or members of a company pursuant to this Part to certain categories or lists of statutory auditors as regards the appointment of a particular statutory auditor to carry out the statutory audit of that company shall be prohibited and shall be void.][c]

Amendments

a Paragraph (5)(iii) substituted by the European Union (Statutory Audits) (Directive 2006/43/ EC, as amended by Directive 2014/56/EU, and Regulation (EU) No 537/2014) Regulations 2016 (SI 312/2016), reg 11, with effect from 17 June 2016.

b Words substituted by C(SA)A 2018, s 11(a) (previously: "the 2016 Audits Regulations").

c Subsection (6) inserted by C(SA)A 2018, s 11(b).

---

381 Remuneration of statutory auditors

(1) The remuneration of the statutory auditors—

(a) where they are appointed by the directors pursuant to this Chapter, shall be agreed with the directors,

(b) where they are—

(i) appointed by the members pursuant to this Chapter, or

(ii) deemed under *section 383(2)* to be re-appointed,

may be fixed by the members—

(I) at the annual general meeting or extraordinary general meeting concerned and thereafter at each annual general meeting subsequent to that meeting falling during the auditors' term of office, or

(II) in such other manner as the members may from time to time resolve,

or

(c) where they are appointed by the Director of Corporate Enforcement pursuant to *section 385*, may be fixed by the Director of Corporate Enforcement or, to the extent, and in the circumstances, that the Director of Corporate Enforcement authorises such to be done, by the directors or members.

(2) For the purposes of this section, any sums paid by the company in respect of the statutory auditors' expenses shall be deemed to be included in the expression "remuneration".

382 Appointment of statutory auditors – first such appointments and powers of members *vis a vis* directors

(1) The first statutory auditors of a company may be appointed by the directors at any time before the first annual general meeting of the company.

(2) Statutory auditors so appointed shall hold office until the conclusion of that first annual general meeting save that the company may, at a prior general meeting, remove any such auditors and appoint in their place as statutory auditors of the

company any other persons who have been nominated for such appointment by any member of the company.

(3) Notice of the nomination of those persons for such appointment shall have been given to the members of the company not less than 14 days before the date of the prior meeting.

(4) If the directors of the company fail to exercise their powers under *subsection (1)*, the company in general meeting may appoint the first statutory auditors of the company and, in the event of their doing so, those powers of the directors shall then cease.

(5) Statutory auditors appointed by the company in general meeting pursuant to *subsection (2)* or *(4)* shall hold office until the conclusion of the first annual general meeting of the company.

383 Subsequent appointments of statutory auditors (including provision for automatic re-appointment of auditors at annual general meetings)

(1) Subject to *subsection (2)*, a company shall at each annual general meeting appoint statutory auditors to hold office from the conclusion of that until the conclusion of the next annual general meeting.

(2) Subject to *subsection (3)*, at any annual general meeting a retiring statutory auditor, however appointed under this Part, shall be deemed to be re-appointed without any resolution being passed unless—

(a) he or she is not qualified for re-appointment, or

(b) a resolution has been passed at that meeting appointing somebody instead of him or her or providing expressly that he or she shall not be re-appointed, or

(c) he or she has given the company notice in writing, in accordance with *section 400*, of his or her unwillingness to be re-appointed.

(3) Where notice is given of an intended resolution to appoint some other person or persons in place of a retiring statutory auditor, and by reason of the death, incapacity or disqualification of that person or of all those persons, as the case may be, the resolution cannot be proceeded with, the retiring statutory auditor shall not be automatically re-appointed by virtue of *subsection (2)*.

(4) A retiring statutory auditor, however appointed under this Part, shall also be deemed to be re-appointed, as of the date on which the last member to sign it signed the resolution, in a case where the members of the company (by signing the resolution referred to in *section 175(3)*) have relieved the company of the obligation to hold an annual general meeting.

384 Appointment of statutory auditors by directors in other cases, etc.

(1) Where any casual vacancy in the office of statutory auditors arises, it shall be the duty of the directors to appoint statutory auditors to the company as soon as may be after that vacancy has arisen.

(2) Whenever by reason of circumstances arising the company is not entitled to the audit exemption in respect of the financial year concerned, it shall be the duty of

the directors of the company to appoint statutory auditors of the company as soon as may be after those circumstances arise.

(3) Statutory auditors appointed pursuant to *subsection (1)* or *(2)* shall hold office until the conclusion of the next annual general meeting of the company held after their appointment.

385 Appointment of statutory auditors: failure to appoint

(1) Where at an annual general meeting of a company no statutory auditors are appointed by the members and the company is not entitled to avail itself of the audit exemption, the Director of Corporate Enforcement may appoint one or more persons to fill the position of statutory auditors of the company.

(2) A company shall—

(a) within one week after the date on which the Director of Corporate Enforcement's power under *subsection (1)* becomes exercisable in relation to the company, give the Director of Corporate Enforcement notice in writing of that fact, and

(b) where a resolution removing the statutory auditors is passed, give notice of that fact in the prescribed form to the Registrar within 14 days after the date of the meeting at which the resolution removing the statutory auditors was passed.

(3) If a company fails to give notice as required by *subsection (2)(a)* or *(b)*, the company and any officer of it who is in default shall be guilty of a category 3 offence.

(4) Statutory auditors appointed pursuant to *subsection (1)* shall hold office until the conclusion of the next annual general meeting of the company held after their appointment.

Chapter 19
Rights, obligations and duties of statutory auditors

386 Right of access to accounting records

Statutory auditors of a company shall have a right of access at all reasonable times to the accounting records of the company.

387 Right to information and explanations concerning company

(1) Statutory auditors of a company may require from the officers of the company such information and explanations as appear to the auditors to be within the officers' knowledge or can be procured by them and which the statutory auditors think necessary for the performance of their duties.

(2) Without limiting *subsection (1)*, an officer of a company shall be guilty of a category 2 offence if the officer fails to comply—

(a) within 2 days after the date on which it is made, with a requirement made of him or her by the statutory auditors of the company to provide to those auditors any information or explanations that those auditors require as statutory auditors of the company, or

(b) within 2 days after the date on which it is made, with a requirement made of him or her by the statutory auditors of the holding company of that company to provide to those auditors any information or explanations that those auditors require as statutory auditors of the holding company,

being, in either case, information or explanations that is or are within the knowledge of, or can be procured by, the officer.

(3) In any proceedings against a person in respect of an offence under *subsection (2)*, it shall be a defence to prove that it was not reasonably possible for the person to comply with the requirement under *subsection (2)(a)* or *(b)* to which the offence relates within the time specified in that provision but that he or she complied with it as soon as was reasonably possible after the expiration of such time.

(4) In this section "officer", in relation to a company, includes any employee of the company and any shadow director and *de facto* director of it.

388 Right to information and explanations concerning subsidiary undertakings

(1) Where a company (in this section referred to as the "holding company") has a subsidiary undertaking, then—

(a) where the subsidiary undertaking is either—

(i) an existing company, a company registered under this Act or a body established in the State, or

(ii) a partnership or unincorporated body of persons having its principal place of business in the State,

it shall be the duty of the subsidiary undertaking and the statutory auditors, if any, of it to give to the statutory auditors of the holding company such information and explanations as the second-mentioned statutory auditors may reasonably require for the purposes of their duties as statutory auditors of the holding company,

(b) in any other case, it shall be the duty of the holding company, if required by its statutory auditors to do so, to take all such steps as are reasonably open to it to obtain from the subsidiary undertaking such information and explanations as are mentioned in *paragraph (a)*.

(2) If an undertaking, body or other person fails to comply, within 5 days after the date on which it is made, with a requirement made of it or him or her under *subsection (1)(a)* or *(b)*, the undertaking, body or other person, and any officer of the undertaking or body who is in default, shall be guilty of a category 2 offence.

(3) In any proceedings against a person in respect of an offence under *subsection (2)*, it shall be a defence to prove that it was not reasonably possible for the person to comply with the requirement under *subsection (1)(a)* or *(b)* to which the offence relates within the time specified in *subsection (2)* but that he or she complied with it as soon as was reasonably possible after the expiration of such time.

(4) In *subsection (2)* "officer", in relation to an undertaking or body, includes any employee of the undertaking or body and, if it is a company, any shadow director and *de facto* director of it.

389 Offence to make false statements to statutory auditors

(1) An officer of a company who knowingly makes a statement to which this section applies that is misleading or false in a material particular, or makes such a statement being reckless as to whether it is so, shall be guilty of a category 2 offence.

(2) This section applies to any statement made to the statutory auditors of a company (whether orally or in writing) which conveys, or purports to convey, any information or explanation which they require under this Act, or are entitled so to require, as statutory auditors of the company.

(3) In this section "officer", in relation to a company, includes any employee of the company and any shadow director and *de facto* director of it.

390 Obligation to act with professional integrity

Without prejudice to [Part 27][a], the one or more persons who are appointed as statutory auditors of a company shall be under a general duty to carry out the audit services concerned with professional integrity.

Amendments

a Words substituted by C(SA)A 2018, s 12 (previously: "the 2016 Audits Regulations").

---

391 Statutory auditors' report on statutory financial statements

The statutory auditors of a company shall make, in the form set out in *section 336*, a report to the members on all statutory financial statements laid before the members during their tenure of office.

392 Report to Registrar and to Director: accounting records

(1) If, at any time, the statutory auditors of a company form the opinion that the company is contravening, or has contravened, any of *sections 281* to *285* the statutory auditors shall—

(a) as soon as may be, by recorded delivery, serve a notice in writing on the company stating their opinion, and

(b) not later than 7 days after the date of service of such notice on the company, notify the Registrar in the prescribed form of the notice and the Registrar shall forthwith forward a copy of the notice to the Director.

(2) Where the statutory auditors form the opinion that the company has contravened any of *sections 281* to *285* but that, following such contravention, the directors of the company have taken the necessary steps to ensure that those provisions are complied with, *subsection (1)(b)* shall not apply.

(3) This section shall not require the statutory auditors to make the notifications referred to in *subsection (1)* if they are of the opinion that the contraventions concerned are minor or otherwise immaterial in nature.

(4) Where the statutory auditors of a company make a notification pursuant to *subsection (1)(b)*, they shall, if requested by the Director—

(a) furnish to the Director such information, including an explanation of the reasons for their opinion that the company had contravened any of *sections 281* to *285*, and

(b) give to the Director such access to documents, including facilities for inspecting and taking copies,

being information or documents in their possession or control and relating to the matter the subject of the notification, as the Director may require.

(5) Any written information given in response to a request of the Director under *subsection (4)* shall in all legal proceedings (other than proceedings for an offence) be admissible without further proof, until the contrary is shown, as evidence of the facts stated in it.

(6) No professional or legal duty to which statutory auditors are subject by virtue of their appointment as statutory auditors of a company shall be regarded as contravened by, and no liability to the company, its shareholders, creditors or other interested parties shall attach to, statutory auditors, by reason of their compliance with an obligation imposed on them by or under this section.

(7) Nothing in this section compels the disclosure by any person of any information that the person would be entitled to refuse to produce on the grounds of legal professional privilege or authorises the inspection or copying of any document containing such information that is in the person's possession.

(8) A person who fails to make the notification required by *subsection (1)(a)* or *(b)* or to comply with a request under *subsection (4)(a)* or *(b)* shall be guilty of a category 3 offence.

393 Report to Registrar and Director: category 1 and 2 offences

(1) Where, in the course of, and by virtue of, their carrying out an audit of the financial statements of the company, information comes into the possession of the statutory auditors of a company that leads them to form the opinion [there are reasonable grounds for believing that a category 1 or 2 offence may have been committed by the company or an officer or agent of it,][a] the statutory auditors shall, forthwith after having formed it, notify that opinion to the Director and provide the Director with particulars of the grounds on which they have formed that opinion.

(2) Where the statutory auditors of a company notify the Director of any matter pursuant to *subsection (1)*, they shall, in addition to performing their obligations under that subsection, if requested by the Director—

(a) furnish the Director with such further information in their possession or control relating to the matter as the Director may require, including further information relating to the particulars of the grounds on which they formed the opinion referred to in that subsection,

(b) give the Director such access to books and documents in their possession or control relating to the matter as the Director may require, and

(c) give the Director such access to facilities for the taking of copies of or extracts from those books and documents as the Director may require.

(3) Any written information given in response to a request of the Director under *subsection (2)* shall in all legal proceedings (other than proceedings for an offence) be admissible without further proof, until the contrary is shown, as evidence of the facts stated in it.

(4) No professional or legal duty to which statutory auditors are subject by virtue of their appointment as statutory auditors of a company shall be regarded as contravened by, and no liability to the company, its shareholders, creditors or other interested parties shall attach to, statutory auditors, by reason of their compliance with an obligation imposed on them by or under this section.

(5) Nothing in this section compels the disclosure by any person of any information that the person would be entitled to refuse to produce on the grounds of legal professional privilege or authorises the inspection or copying of any document containing such information that is in the person's possession.

(6) A person who contravenes *subsection (1)* or fails to comply with a request under *subsection (2)* shall be guilty of a category 3 offence.

Amendments

a Words substituted by C(A)A 2017, s 65 (previously: "there are reasonable grounds for believing that the company or an officer or agent of it has committed a category 1 or 2 offence,").

Chapter 20
Removal and resignation of statutory auditors

394 Removal of statutory auditors: general meeting

A company may, by ordinary resolution at a general meeting, remove a statutory auditor and appoint, in his or her place, any other person or persons, being a person or persons—

(a) who have been nominated for appointment by any member of the company and who are qualified by virtue of [Part 27][a] to be statutory auditors of the company, and

(b) of whose nomination notice has been given to its members,

but this is—

(i) subject to *section 395*, and

(ii) without prejudice to any rights of the statutory auditor in relation to his or her removal under this section.

Amendments

a Words substituted by C(SA)A 2018, s 13 (previously "the 2016 Audits Regulations").

395 Restrictions on removal of statutory auditor

(1) The passing of a resolution to which this section applies shall not be effective with respect to the matter it provides for unless—

(a) in case the resolution provides for the auditor's removal from office, there are good and substantial grounds for the removal related to the conduct of the auditor with regard to the performance of his or her duties as auditor of the company or otherwise, or

(b) in the case of any other resolution to which this section applies, the passing of the resolution is, in the company's opinion, in the best interests of the company,

but—

(i) for the foregoing purposes, diverging opinions on accounting treatments or audit procedures cannot constitute the basis for the passing of any such resolution, and

(ii) in *paragraph (b)* "best interests of the company" does not include any illegal or improper motive with regard to avoiding disclosures or detection of any failure by the company to comply with this Act.

(2) This section applies to—

(a) a resolution removing a statutory auditor from office,

(b) a resolution at an annual general meeting appointing somebody other than the retiring statutory auditor as statutory auditor,

(c) a resolution providing expressly that the retiring statutory auditor shall not be re-appointed.

396 Extended notice requirement in cases of certain appointments, removals, etc., of auditors

(1) Extended notice shall be required for:

(a) a resolution at an annual general meeting of a company appointing as statutory auditors any persons other than the incumbent statutory auditors or providing expressly that the incumbent statutory auditors shall not be re-appointed;

(b) a resolution at a general meeting of a company removing statutory auditors from office; and

(c) a resolution at a general meeting of a company filling a casual vacancy in the office of statutory auditor.

(2) For the purpose of this section extended notice shall comprise the following requirements:

(a) the company shall be given by the person proposing the resolution not less than 28 days' notice of the intention to move any such resolution; and

(b) on receipt of notice of such an intended resolution, the company—

(i) shall forthwith send a copy of it to the incumbent statutory auditors or the person (if any) whose ceasing to hold the office of statutory auditor of the company occasioned the casual vacancy, and

(ii) shall give its members notice of any such resolution at the same time and in the same manner as it gives notice of the meeting or, if that is not practicable, shall give them notice of it, either by advertisement in a daily newspaper circulating in the district in which the registered office of the company is situate or in any other mode allowed by this Act, not less than 21 days before the date of the meeting.

(3) If, after notice of the intention to move such a resolution has been given to the company, a meeting is called for a date 28 days or less after the date on which the notice has been given, the notice though not given within the time required by *subsection (2)* shall be deemed to have been properly given for the purposes of that subsection.

397 Right of statutory auditors to make representations where their removal or non-re-appointment proposed

(1) In this section "relevant meeting" means the meeting at which the resolution mentioned in *section 396(1)(a)* or *(b)*, as the case may be, is to be considered.

(2) Subject to *subsection (4)*, where notice is given of such an intended resolution as is mentioned in *section 396(1)(a)* or *(b)* and the statutory auditors there mentioned make, in relation to the intended resolution, representations in writing to the company (not exceeding a reasonable length) and request their notification to be sent to members of the company, the company shall, unless the representations are received by it too late for it to do so—

(a) in any notice of the resolution given to members of the company, state the fact of the representations having been made, and

(b) send a copy of the representations to every member of the company to whom notice of the relevant meeting is sent (whether before or after receipt of the representations by the company).

(3) If a copy of the representations is not sent as is mentioned in *subsection (2)* (because either they were received too late or because of the company's default) the statutory auditors concerned may (without prejudice to their right to be heard orally) require that the representations shall be read out at the relevant meeting.

(4) Copies of the representations need not be sent out and the representations need not be read out at the relevant meeting as mentioned in *subsection (2)* or *(3)* if, on the application either of the company or of any other person who claims to be aggrieved,

the court is satisfied that the rights conferred by this section are being abused to secure needless publicity for defamatory matter and orders that those things need not be done.

(5) The court may order the company's costs on such an application to be paid in whole or in part by the statutory auditors concerned notwithstanding that they are not a party to the application.

398 Statutory auditors removed from office: their rights to get notice of, attend and be heard at general meeting

(1) Statutory auditors of a company who have been removed shall be entitled to attend—

(a) the next annual general meeting of the company after their removal, and

(b) the general meeting of the company at which it is proposed to consider a resolution for the filling of the vacancy occasioned by their removal,

and to receive all notices of, and other communications relating to, any such meeting which a member of the company is entitled to receive and to be heard at any general meeting that such a member attends on any part of the business of the meeting which concerns them as former statutory auditors of the company.

(2) Subject to *subsection (4)*, where notice is given of such an intended resolution as is mentioned in *subsection (1)* and the statutory auditors there mentioned make, in relation to the intended resolution, representations in writing to the company (not exceeding a reasonable length) and request their notification to be sent to members of the company, the company shall, unless the representations are received by it too late for it to do so—

(a) in any notice of the resolution given to members of the company state the fact of the representations having been made, and

(b) send a copy of the representations to every member of the company to whom notice of the meeting is sent (whether before or after receipt of the representations by the company).

(3) If a copy of the representations is not sent as is mentioned in *subsection (2)* (because either they were received too late or because of the company's default) the statutory auditors concerned may (without prejudice to their right to be heard orally) require that the representations shall be read out at the meeting.

(4) Copies of the representations need not be sent out and the representations need not be read out at the meeting as mentioned in *subsection (2)* or *(3)* if, on the application either of the company or of any other person who claims to be aggrieved, the court is satisfied that the rights conferred by this section are being abused to secure needless publicity for defamatory matter and orders that those things need not be done.

(5) The court may order the company's costs on such an application to be paid in whole or in part by the statutory auditors concerned notwithstanding that they are not a party to the application.

399 Removal of statutory auditors: statement from statutory auditors where audit exemption availed of by company

(1) If a company, which avails itself of the audit exemption—

(a) decides that the appointment of persons as statutory auditors to the company should not be continued during the whole or part of a financial year in which the exemption is being availed of in relation to the company, and

(b) decides, accordingly, to terminate the appointment of those persons as statutory auditors to the company,

then—

(i) the statutory auditors shall, within the period of 21 days after the date of their being notified by the company of that decision, serve a notice on the company containing the statement referred to in *subsection (2)*,

(ii) unless and until the statutory auditors serve such a notice, any purported termination of their appointment as statutory auditors to the company shall not have effect.

(2) The statement to be contained in a notice under *subsection (1)(i)* shall be whichever of the following is appropriate, namely:

(a) a statement to the effect that there are no circumstances connected with the decision of the company referred to in *subsection (1)* that the statutory auditors concerned consider should be brought to the notice of the members or creditors of the company; or

(b) a statement of any such circumstances as mentioned in *paragraph (a)*.

(3) Where a notice under *subsection (1)(i)* is served on a company—

(a) the statutory auditors concerned shall, within 14 days after the date of such service, send a copy of the notice to the Registrar, and

(b) subject to *subsection (4)*, the company shall, if the notice contains a statement referred to in *subsection (2)(b)*, within 14 days after the date of such service, send a copy of the notice to every person who is entitled under *section 338* to be sent copies of the documents referred to in that section.

(4) Copies of a notice served on a company under *subsection (1)* need not be sent to the persons specified in *subsection (3)(b)*, if, on the application of the company concerned or any other person who claims to be aggrieved, the court is satisfied that the notice contains material which has been included to secure needless publicity for defamatory matter and orders that that thing need not be done.

(5) The court may order the company's costs on such an application to be paid in whole or in part by the statutory auditors concerned notwithstanding that they are not a party to the application.

(6) *Section 398* shall not apply to statutory auditors as respects their removal from office in the circumstances referred to in *subsection (1)*.

400 Resignation of statutory auditors: general

(1) Statutory auditors of a company may, by a notice in writing that complies with *subsection (3)* served on the company and stating their intention to do so, resign from the office of statutory auditors to the company.

(2) The resignation shall take effect on the date on which the notice is so served or on such later date as may be specified in the notice.

(3) A notice under *subsection (1)* shall contain either—

(a) a statement to the effect that there are no circumstances connected with the resignation to which it relates that the statutory auditors concerned consider should be brought to the notice of the members or creditors of the company, or

(b) a statement of any such circumstances as mentioned in *paragraph (a)*.

(4) Where a notice under *subsection (1)* is served on a company—

(a) the statutory auditors concerned shall, within 14 days after the date of such service, send a copy of the notice to the Registrar, and

(b) subject to *subsection (5)*, the company shall, if the notice contains a statement referred to in *subsection (3)(b)*, not later than 14 days after the date of such service, send a copy of the notice to every person who is entitled under *section 338* to be sent copies of the documents referred to in that section.

(5) Copies of a notice served on a company under *subsection (1)* need not be sent to the persons specified in *subsection (4)(b)* if, on the application of the company concerned or any other person who claims to be aggrieved, the court is satisfied that the notice contains material which has been included to secure needless publicity for defamatory matter and orders that that thing need not be done.

(6) The court may order the company's costs on such an application to be paid in whole or in part by the statutory auditors concerned notwithstanding that they are not a party to the application.

(7) This section shall also apply to a notice given by statutory auditors referred to in *section 383(2)(c)* indicating their unwillingness to be re-appointed and, accordingly, for that purpose this section shall have effect as if—

(a) the following subsection were substituted for *subsection (1)*:

> "(1) Statutory auditors of a company may, by a notice in writing that complies with *subsection (3)* and which is served on the company, indicate their unwillingness to be re-appointed as statutory auditors to the company.",

(b) *subsection (2)* were omitted, and

(c) the reference to the statutory auditors' resignation in *subsection (3)* were a reference to the indication of their unwillingness to be re-appointed.

(8) A person who fails to comply with—

(a) *subsection (3)* or *(4)(a)*, or

(b) either such provision as it applies by virtue of *subsection (7)*,

shall be guilty of a category 3 offence.

(9) If default is made in complying with *subsection (4)(b)* or that provision as it applies by virtue of *subsection (7)*, the company concerned and any officer of it who is in default shall be guilty of a category 3 offence.

(10) In *subsection (9)* "officer" includes any shadow director and *de facto* director.

401 Resignation of statutory auditor: requisition of general meeting

(1) A notice served by statutory auditors on a company under *section 400* which contains a statement in accordance with *subsection (3)(b)* of that section may also requisition the convening by the directors of the company of a general meeting of the company for the following purpose.

(2) That purpose is the purpose of receiving and considering such information and explanation of the circumstances connected with the statutory auditors' resignation from office as they may wish to give to the meeting.

(3) Where the statutory auditors make such a requisition, the directors of the company shall, within 14 days after the date of service on the company of the foregoing notice, proceed duly to convene a general meeting of the company for a day not more than 28 days after the date of such service.

(4) Subject to *subsection (5)*, where—

- (a) a notice served on a company under *section 400* contains a statement in accordance with *subsection (3)(b)* of that section, and
- (b) the statutory auditors concerned request the company to circulate to its members—
  - (i) before the next general meeting after their resignation, or
  - (ii) before any general meeting at which it is proposed to fill the vacancy caused by their resignation or convened pursuant to a requisition referred to in *subsection (1)*,

a further statement in writing prepared by the statutory auditors of circumstances connected with their resignation that the statutory auditors consider should be brought to the notice of the members, the company shall—

- (i) in any notice of the meeting given to members of the company state the fact of the statement having been made, and
- (ii) send a copy of the statement to the Registrar and to every person who is entitled under *section 338* to be sent copies of the documents referred to in that section.

(5) *Subsection (4)* need not be complied with by the company concerned if, on the application either of the company or any other person who claims to be aggrieved, the court is satisfied that the rights conferred by this section are being abused to secure needless publicity for defamatory matter and orders that that subsection need not be complied with.

(6) The court may order the company's costs on such an application to be paid in whole or in part by the statutory auditors concerned notwithstanding that they are not a party to the application.

(7) If default is made in complying with *subsection (3)* or *(4)*, the company concerned and any officer of it who is in default shall be guilty of a category 3 offence.

(8) In *subsection (7)* "officer" includes any shadow director and *de facto* director.

402 Resignation of statutory auditors: right to get notice of, attend, and be heard at general meeting

(1) Statutory auditors of a company who have resigned from the office of statutory auditors shall be permitted by the company to attend—

(a) the next annual general meeting of the company after their resignation, and

(b) any general meeting of the company at which it is proposed to fill the vacancy caused by their resignation or convened pursuant to a requisition of theirs referred to in *section 401(1)*,

and, for that purpose, the company shall—

(i) send them all notices of, and other communications relating to, any such meeting that a member of the company is entitled to receive, and

(ii) permit them to be heard at any such meeting which they attend on any part of the business of the meeting which concerns them as former statutory auditors of the company.

(2) If default is made in complying with *subsection (1)*, the company concerned and any officer of it who is in default shall be guilty of a category 3 offence.

(3) In *subsection (2)* "officer" includes any shadow director and *de facto* director.

Chapter 21

Notification to Supervisory Authority of certain matters and auditors acting while subject to disqualification order

403 Duty of auditor to notify Supervisory Authority regarding cessation of office

(1) Where, for any reason, during the period between the conclusion of the last annual general meeting and the conclusion of the next annual general meeting of a company, a statutory auditor ceases to hold office by virtue of *section 394* or *400*, the auditor shall—

(a) in such form and manner as the Supervisory Authority specifies, and

(b) within 30 days after the date of that cessation,

notify the Supervisory Authority that the auditor has ceased to hold office.

(2) That notification shall be accompanied by—

(a) in the case of resignation of the auditor, the notice served by the auditor under *section 400(1)*, or

(b) in the case of removal of the auditor at a general meeting pursuant to *section 394*, a copy of any representations in writing made to the company, pursuant to *section 397(2)*, by the outgoing auditor in relation to the intended resolution except where such representations were not sent out to the members of the company in consequence of an application to the court under *section 397(4)*.

(3) Where, in the case of resignation, the notice served under *section 400(1)* is to the effect that there are no circumstances connected with the resignation to which it relates that the auditor concerned considers should be brought to the notice of members or creditors of the company, the notification under *subsection (1)* shall also be accompanied by a statement of the reasons for the auditor's resignation.

(4) In this section—

(a) "resignation" includes an indication of unwillingness to be re-appointed at an annual general meeting; and

(b) a reference to a notice served under *section 400(1)* includes a reference to a notice given by the auditor that is referred to in *section 383(2)(c)*.

404 Duty of company to notify Supervisory Authority of auditor's cessation of office

(1) Where, for any reason, during the period between the conclusion of the last annual general meeting and the conclusion of the next annual general meeting of a company, a statutory auditor ceases to hold office by virtue of *section 394* or *400*, the company shall—

(a) in such form and manner as the Supervisory Authority specifies, and

(b) within 30 days after the date of that cessation,

notify the Supervisory Authority that the auditor has ceased to hold office.

(2) That notification shall be accompanied by—

(a) in the case of resignation of the auditor, the notice served by the auditor under *section 400(1)*, or

(b) in the case of removal of the auditor at a general meeting pursuant to *section 394*—

 (i) a copy of the resolution removing the auditor, and

 (ii) a copy of any representations in writing made to the company, pursuant to *section 397(2)*, by the outgoing auditor in relation to the intended resolution except where such representations were not sent out to the members of the company in consequence of an application to the court under *section 397(4)*.

(3) In this section—

(a) "resignation" includes an indication of unwillingness to be re-appointed at an annual general meeting; and

(b) a reference to a notice served under *section 400(1)* includes a reference to a notice given by the auditor that is referred to in *section 383(2)(c)*.

405 Prohibition on acting in relation to audit while disqualification order in force

(1) If a person who is subject or deemed to be subject to a disqualification order (within the meaning of *Chapter 4* of *Part 14*)—

(a) becomes, or remains more than 28 days after the date of the making of the order, a partner in a firm of statutory auditors,

(b) gives directions or instructions in relation to the conduct of any part of the audit of the financial statements of a company, or

(c) works in any capacity in the conduct of an audit of the financial statements of a company,

he or she shall be guilty of a category 2 offence.

(2) Where a person is convicted of an offence under *subsection (1)*, the period for which he or she was disqualified by virtue of the foregoing order shall be extended for—

(a) a further period of 10 years beginning after the date of conviction, or

(b) such other (shorter or longer) further period as the court, on the application of the prosecutor or the defendant and having regard to all the circumstances of the case, may order.

(3) *Section 847* shall not apply to a person convicted of an offence under *subsection (1)*.

Chapter 22
False statements — offence

406 False statements in returns, financial statements, etc.

If a person in any return, statement, financial statement or other document required by or for the purposes of any provision of this Part intentionally makes a statement, false in any material particular, knowing it to be so false, the person shall be guilty of a category 2 offence.

Chapter 23
Transitional

407 Transitional provision — companies accounting by reference to Sixth Schedule to Act of 1963

(1) Notwithstanding anything in this Part, the directors of an existing company may, in respect of a financial year to which this section applies, opt to prepare financial statements (and approve them) in accordance with the provisions of the Act of 1963 and the Sixth Schedule thereto.

(2) This section applies to a financial year of an existing private company that satisfies the following conditions—

(a) it begins before the commencement of this section and ends thereafter, and

(b) accounts in respect of it could, but for the repeal of the prior Companies Acts, have been prepared by the directors of the company in accordance with the provisions of the Act of 1963 and the Sixth Schedule thereto (as distinct from the Companies (Amendment) Act 1986 and the other provisions of the prior Companies Acts or regulations made under the European Communities Act 1972).

(3) All obligations and rights that arise under this Act consequent on or in respect of financial statements having been approved by the directors of a company shall likewise arise in relation to financial statements approved by directors in a case falling within *subsection (1)*.

(4) In this section—

"accounts" means accounts under the Act of 1963;

"existing private company" shall have the meaning given to it by *section 15* but with the omission of all the words appearing after *paragraphs (a)* and *(b)* of that definition in *section 15*.

PART 7
CHARGES AND DEBENTURES

Chapter 1
Interpretation

408 Definitions (*Part 7*)

(1) In this Part—

"charge", in relation to a company, means a mortgage or a charge, in an agreement (written or oral), that is created over an interest in any property of the company (and in *section 409(8)* and *sections 414* to *421* includes a judgment mortgage) but does not include a mortgage or a charge, in an agreement (written or oral), that is created over an interest in—

(a) cash,

(b) money credited to an account of a financial institution, or any other deposits,

(c) [shares, including shares in a body corporate, bonds or debt instruments,][a]

(d) units in collective investment undertakings or money market instruments, or

(e) claims and rights (such as dividends or interest) in respect of any thing referred to in any of *paragraphs (b)* to *(d)*;

"property", in relation to a company, includes any assets or undertaking of the company.

(2) Any exclusion provided in *subsection (1)* to what is defined in that subsection as constituting a "charge" may be varied by order made by the Minister if the Minister considers that it is necessary or expedient to do so in consequence of any Community act adopted after the commencement of this section relating to financial collateral arrangements.

(3) For the avoidance of doubt, in the case of a mortgage or charge created over both—

(a) an interest in anything specified in any of *paragraphs (a)* to *(e)* of *subsection (1)*; and

(b) any property, assets or undertaking not falling within any of those paragraphs,

the mortgage or charge shall, other than to the extent to which it is created over an interest in anything specified in any of the foregoing paragraphs of *subsection (1)*, be regarded as a charge within the meaning of this Part.

Amendments

a Paragraph (1)(c) substituted by C(A)A 2017, s 98(c).

Chapter 2
Registration of charges and priority

409 Registration of charges created by companies

(1) Every charge created, after the commencement of this section, by a company shall be void against the liquidator and any creditor of the company unless either the procedure set out in—

(a) *subsection (3)* — the "one-stage procedure", or

(b) *subsection (4)* — the "two-stage procedure",

with respect to the charge's registration is complied with.

(2) If, in purported compliance with the requirements of this Part as to the taking of steps in that behalf, there is received by the Registrar particulars of a charge that omit the required particulars in respect of one or more properties to which the charge relates, *subsection (1)* shall be read as operating to render void (as against the liquidator and any creditor of the company) the charge as it relates to the particular property or properties in respect of which that omission occurs but not otherwise.

(3) The procedure for registration under this subsection referred to in *subsection (1)* as the one-stage procedure consists of the taking of steps so that there is received by the Registrar, not later than 21 days after the date of the charge's creation, the prescribed particulars, in the prescribed form, of the charge.

(4) The procedure for registration under this subsection referred to in *subsection (1)* as the two–stage procedure consists of the following, namely the taking of steps:

(a) so that there is received by the Registrar a notice stating the company's intention to create the charge (being a notice in the prescribed form and containing the prescribed particulars of the charge); and

(b) so that, not later than 21 days after the date of the Registrar's receipt of the notice under *paragraph (a)* (the "first-mentioned notice"), there is received by the Registrar a notice, in the prescribed form, stating that the charge referred to in the first-mentioned notice has been created.

(5) If the requirement under *paragraph (b)* of *subsection (4)* is not complied with, within the period specified in that paragraph, the notice received under *paragraph (a)* of that subsection in relation to the charge shall be removed by the Registrar from the register.

(6) *Subsection (1)* is without prejudice to any contract or obligation for repayment of the money secured by the charge concerned and when a charge becomes void under that subsection, the money secured by it shall immediately become payable.

(7) Where a charge comprises property outside the State, the prescribed particulars, in the prescribed form (and, as the case may be, the notice under *subsection (4)(b)*) may be sent for registration under this section, notwithstanding that further proceedings may be necessary to make the charge valid or effectual according to the law of the country in which the property is situate.

(8) If there is a change among the one or more persons entitled to a charge registered under this Part, the fact of that change having occurred, and particulars of the person or persons now entitled to the charge, may be delivered, in the prescribed form, to the Registrar and registered by him or her.

(9) Nothing in this section or any other provision of this Part authorises the delivery to the Registrar of a deed, or any supplemental document to it, and this Part does not impose or confer any duty or power on the Registrar to examine any deed or any supplemental document to it.

410 Duty of company with respect to registration under *section 409* and right of others to effect registration

(1) It shall be the duty of the company that creates the charge to comply with the procedure under *section 409(3)* or *(4)* with respect to the charge's registration but this is without prejudice to *subsection (2)*.

(2) Any person interested in the charge may use the procedure under *section 409(3)* or *(4)* with respect to its registration and the person's using that procedure (and in compliance with *section 409(3)* or *(4)*) shall have the same effect as if the company had used that procedure (and in compliance with *section 409(3)* or *(4)*).

(3) Where such a person uses that procedure (and in compliance with *section 409(3)* or *(4)*), the person may recover from the company the amount of fees properly paid by that person to the Registrar in respect of the registration of the charge concerned.

411 Duty of company to register charges existing on property acquired

(1) Where a company acquires any property which is subject to a charge that, if it had been created by the company after the acquisition of the property, would have given rise to the duty under *section 409(1)* on the part of the company with respect to the charge's registration, then the company shall have the following duty.

(2) That duty is to take steps so that there is received by the Registrar, not later than 21 days after the date on which acquisition of the property concerned is completed, the prescribed particulars, in the prescribed form, of the charge.

(3) If default is made in complying with this section, the company and any officer of the company who is in default shall be guilty of a category 4 offence.

412 Priority of charges

(1) For the purposes of this section—

- (a) "relevant rule of law" means a rule of law that governs the priority of charges created by a company, and for the avoidance of doubt, any enactment governing the priority of such charges is not encompassed by that expression,
- (b) the reference in *subsection (2)* to any priority that one charge, by virtue of a person's not having notice of a matter, enjoys over another charge or charges shall be deemed to include a reference to any priority that an advance made on foot of a charge, by virtue of a person's not having notice of a matter, enjoys over a subsequent charge or charges.

(2) On and from the commencement of this section, any relevant rule of law shall stand modified in the manner specified in *subsection (3)*, but not so as to displace any priority, whether before or after that commencement, that one charge, by virtue of a person's not having notice of a matter, enjoys over another charge or charges.

(3) That modification is that, for the part of the rule that operates by reference to the time of creation of the 2 or more charges concerned, there shall be substituted a part that operates by reference to—

(a) the dates of receipt by the Registrar of the prescribed particulars of the 2 or more charges concerned, or

(b) if the date of receipt by the Registrar of the prescribed particulars of the 2 or more charges is the same, the respective times, on the date concerned, of receipt by the Registrar of those particulars.

(4) References in *subsection (3)* to the date, or time, of receipt of the prescribed particulars are references to—

(a) if the procedure under *subsection (3)* of *section 409* is complied with in relation to a particular charge, the date, or time, of receipt by the Registrar of the prescribed particulars, in the prescribed form, of the charge, or

(b) if the procedure under *subsection (4)* of *section 409* is complied with in relation to a particular charge, the date, or time, of receipt by the Registrar of the notice, in the prescribed form and containing the prescribed particulars, in relation to the charge under *paragraph (a)* of that *subsection (4)*.

(5) *Subsections (2)* and *(3)* shall not affect any agreement between persons in whose favour charges have been created in relation to the priority that those charges shall, as between them, have.

(6) Subject to *subsection (7)* in relation to particulars of a charge received by the Registrar pursuant to *section 409(3)* or *(4)*, the following provisions apply so far as those particulars consist of particulars of a negative pledge, any events that crystallise a floating charge or any restrictions on the use of any charged asset (and particulars of any such matter are referred to subsequently in this subsection as "extraneous material"):

(a) [the Registrar shall not be under any duty to enter in the register][a] under *section 414* particulars of the extraneous material pursuant to that section;

(b) the fact that the Registrar has received the particulars of the extraneous material shall have no legal effect;

but nothing in the foregoing affects the validity of the receipt by the Registrar of the other particulars of the charge.

(7) *Subsection (6)* does not apply to particulars of a negative pledge included in particulars of a floating charge granted by a company to the Central Bank for the purposes of either providing or securing collateral.

(8) In this section "negative pledge" means any agreement entered into by the company concerned and any other person or persons that—

(a) provides that the company shall not, or shall not otherwise than in specified circumstances—

(i) borrow moneys or otherwise obtain credit from any person other than that person or those persons,

(ii) create or permit to subsist any charge, lien or other encumbrance or any pledge over the whole or any part of the property of the company, or

(iii) alienate or otherwise dispose of in any manner any of the property of the company,

or

(b) contains a prohibition, either generally or in specified circumstances, on the doing by the company of one or more things referred to in one, or more than one, provision of *paragraph (a)*.

Amendments

a Words substituted by C(A)A 2017, s 66 (previously: "the Registrar shall not enter in the register").

---

413 Registration and priority of judgment mortgages

(1) If judgment is recovered against a company and that judgment is subsequently converted into a judgment mortgage affecting any property of the company, the judgment mortgage shall be void against the liquidator and any creditor of the company unless the procedure set out in *subsection (2)* with respect to the judgment mortgage's registration is complied with.

(2) The procedure for registration under this subsection consists of the taking of steps so that there is received by the Registrar, together with the relevant judgment mortgage document, the prescribed particulars, in the prescribed form, of the judgment mortgage, not later than 21 days after the following date.

(3) That date is the date on which notification by the Property Registration Authority of the judgment mortgage's creation is received by the judgment creditor.

(4) In *subsection (2)* the "relevant judgment mortgage document" means a certified copy of, as appropriate—

(a) Form 60, 60A or 60B set out in the Schedule of Forms to the Land Registration Rules 2012 (S.I. No. 483 of 2012) as amended by the Land Registration Rules 2013 (S.I. No. 389 of 2013), or

(b) Form 16 set out in the Schedule to the Registration of Deeds (No. 2) Rules 2009 (S.I. No. 457 of 2009),

used for the purposes of converting the judgment concerned into a judgment mortgage.

(5) For the purposes of this section, it shall be presumed, until the contrary is proved, that the judgment creditor received notification, of the judgment mortgage's creation,

from the Property Registration Authority on the third day after the date on which that notification is sent by it to the judgment creditor or his or her agent.

(6) If rules are made under section 126 of the Registration of Title Act 1964 or, as the case may be, section 48 of the Registration of Deeds and Title Act 2006—

(a) replacing a form that is referred to in *subsection (4)(a)* or *(b)*, as appropriate, the reference in that provision to the form shall be read as a reference to the form as so replaced, or

(b) amending a form that is so referred to, the reference in that provision to the form shall be read as a reference to the form as it stands so amended.

(7) This section shall not apply to any judgment mortgage created before the commencement of this section.

414 Register of charges

(1) The Registrar shall keep, in relation to each company, a register in the prescribed form, of the charges requiring registration under this Part, and shall, on payment of such fee as may be prescribed, enter in the register, in relation to such charges, the following particulars:

(a) without prejudice to *paragraphs (e)* and *(f)*, in the case of a charge created by the company, the date of its creation and—

(i) where the procedure for registration under *section 409(3)* is complied with, the date and time of receipt by the Registrar under that provision of the prescribed particulars, in the prescribed form, of the charge, and

(ii) where the procedure for registration under *section 409(4)* is complied with, the respective dates and times of receipt by the Registrar of the notices under *paragraphs (a)* and *(b)* of that provision in relation to the charge;

(b) without prejudice to *paragraphs (e)* and *(f)*, in the case of a charge existing on property acquired by the company, the date of the acquisition of the property by the company;

(c) without prejudice to *paragraphs (e)* and *(f)*, in the case of a judgment mortgage, the date of the mortgage's creation and the date and time, in relation to it, of receipt by the Registrar, under *section 413(2)*, of the prescribed particulars in the prescribed form together with the relevant judgment mortgage document referred to in that provision;

(d) without prejudice to *paragraphs (e)* and *(f)*, in the case of floating charge granted by the company to the Central Bank for the purposes either of providing or securing collateral, particulars of any provision of the charge that has the effect of prohibiting or restricting the company from issuing further securities that rank equally with that charge or modifying the ranking of that charge in relation to securities previously issued by the company;

(e) short particulars of the property charged; and

(f) the persons entitled to the charge.

(2) The register kept in pursuance of this section shall be open to inspection by any person on payment of such fee, if any, as may be prescribed.

415 Certificate of registration

(1) The Registrar shall give a certificate of the registration of any charge registered in pursuance of this Part.

(2) Subject to *subsection (3)*, such a certificate shall be conclusive evidence that the requirements of this Part as to the registration of the charge have been complied with.

(3) To the extent that the particulars of a charge delivered to the Registrar in purported compliance with this Part omit the required particulars in respect of one or more properties to which the charge relates, the evidential effect of the certificate provided under *subsection (2)* shall not extend to the particular property or properties in respect of which that omission occurs.

(4) Without prejudice to the generality of the definition, in *section 408*, of that expression, in *subsection (3)* "property" includes an interest in, or right over, property.

416 Entries of satisfaction and release of property from charge

(1) The Registrar may exercise the powers under *subsection (2)*, on evidence being given to his or her satisfaction with respect to any charge registered under this Part—

(a) that the debt in relation to which the charge was created has been paid or satisfied in whole or in part, or

(b) that part of the property charged has been released from the charge or has ceased to form part of the company's property,

and, where the satisfaction or release has not been signed by or on behalf of the chargee, after giving notice to the person who, for the time being, stands registered as the person entitled to such charge or to the judgment creditor, as the case may be.

(2) Those powers are to enter on the register a memorandum—

(a) of satisfaction in whole or in part, or

(b) of the fact that part of the property has been released from the charge or has ceased to form part of the company's property,

as the case may be.

(3) Where the Registrar enters such a memorandum of satisfaction in whole, he or she shall, if required, furnish the company with a copy of it.

(4) The Registrar may accept as evidence of a satisfaction or release referred to in *subsection (1)(a)* or *(b)* a statement in the prescribed form signed by a director and secretary of the company, or by 2 directors of the company, stating that the satisfaction or release has occurred.

(5) Where a person signs a statement referred to in *subsection (4)* knowing it to be false, the person shall be guilty of a category 2 offence.

(6) Where a person signs a statement referred to in *subsection (4)* and in doing so did not honestly believe on reasonable grounds that the statement was true, and the court considers that the making of that statement—

(a) contributed to the company being unable to pay its debts,

(b) prevented or impeded the orderly winding up of the company, or

(c) facilitated the defrauding of the creditors of the company,

the court, on the application of the liquidator or examiner or receiver of the property of, or any creditor or contributor of, the company, may, if it thinks it proper to do so, make the following declaration.

(7) That declaration is that that signatory shall be personally liable, without limitation of liability, for all or such part as the court may specify of the debts and other liabilities of the company.

417 Extension of time for registration of charges and rectification of register

(1) The court may grant the following relief where it is satisfied that the omission to register a charge within the time required by this Part or that the omission or misstatement of any particular with respect to any such charge or in a memorandum of satisfaction—

(a) was accidental or due to inadvertence or to some other sufficient cause, or

(b) is not of a nature to prejudice the position of creditors or shareholders of the company,

or that on other grounds it is just and equitable to grant that relief in respect of such an omission or misstatement.

(2) That relief is to order, on such terms and conditions as seem to the court just and expedient, that the time for registration shall be extended, or, as the case may be, that the omission or misstatement shall be rectified.

(3) An application for relief under this section may be made on behalf of the company or any other person interested.

418 Copies of instruments creating charges to be kept

(1) A company shall keep a copy of every instrument creating any charge in relation to it and requiring registration under this Part, including, in the case of a judgment mortgage, a copy of the relevant judgment mortgage document that was received by the Registrar.

(2) All such copies kept by the company shall be kept at the same place.

(3) *Sections 215* to *217* (rights of inspection, etc.) apply to those copies.

(4) If default is made in complying with *subsection (1)* or *(2)*, the company concerned and any officer of it who is in default shall be guilty of a category 3 offence.

419 Registration of charges created prior to commencement of this Part

(1) Notwithstanding *section 4*, sections 99 to 106, 108 to 110 and 112 of the Act of 1963 shall continue to apply to charges (within the meaning of Part IV of that Act) created before the commencement of this Part.

(2) For the avoidance of doubt, the cases in which those provisions of the Act of 1963 continue to apply include any case where, as respects a charge (within the meaning of Part IV of that Act) created before the commencement of this Part, the time allowed under those provisions for the registration of that charge under that Part IV has not expired on that commencement, and the foregoing reference to the time allowed under those provisions includes the time allowed under those provisions as extended by an order (if such has been made) under section 106 of the Act of 1963.

420 Transitional provisions in relation to priorities of charges

(1) In this section "charge to which the special transitional case applies" means a charge referred to in the case set out in *section 419(2)*.

(2) Subject to *subsection (3)*, the modification by *section 412* of any rule of law there referred to (in this section referred to as the "*section 412* rule modification") shall not apply in relation to the issue of the priority of any charge (within the meaning of Part IV of the Act of 1963), created before the commencement of this Part, as against a charge falling within this Part created on or after that commencement.

(3) The *section 412* rule modification shall apply in relation to the issue of the priority of a charge to which the special transitional case applies (as against a charge falling within this Part created on or after commencement of that Part) if the first-mentioned charge has not been registered under Part IV of the Act of 1963 before that commencement.

(4) For the purposes of the application of the *section 412* rule modification to the issue of priority falling within *subsection (3)*, references in *section 412* to the date, or time, of receipt of the prescribed particulars shall, in relation to a charge to which the special transitional case applies, be read as references to the date, or time, of delivery to, or receipt by, the Registrar (under and in compliance with Part IV of the Act of 1963, as continued by *section 419*) of the matters that are required by that Part to be so delivered or received for the purposes of registering the charge thereunder.

(5) Non-compliance with the requirement in the second sentence of section 102(1) of the Act of 1963 shall be disregarded for the purposes of *subsection (4)*.

421 Netting of Financial Contracts Act 1995 not to affect registration requirements

Nothing in section 4(1) of the Netting of Financial Contracts Act 1995 affects—

(a) the requirement to register a charge under this Part, or

(b) the consequences of failing to register a charge under this Part.

Chapter 3
Provisions as to debentures

422 Liability of trustees for debenture holders

(1) Subject to the provisions of this section, the following provision shall be void, namely, any provision contained—

(a) in a trust deed for securing an issue of debentures, or

(b) in any contract with the holders of debentures secured by a trust deed,

in so far as it would have the effect of exempting a trustee of it from, or indemnifying him or her against, liability for breach of trust where he or she fails to show the degree of care and diligence required of him or her as trustee, having regard to the provisions of the trust deed conferring on him or her any powers, authorities or discretions.

(2) *Subsection (1)* shall not invalidate—

(a) any release otherwise validly given in respect of anything done or omitted to be done by a trustee before the giving of the release, or

(b) any provision enabling such a release to be given—

(i) on the agreement to the provision of a majority of not less than three-fourths in value of the debenture holders present and voting in person or, where proxies are permitted, by proxy at a meeting summoned for the purpose, and

(ii) either with respect to specific acts or omissions or on the trustee dying or ceasing to act.

(3) *Subsection (1)* shall not operate—

(a) to invalidate any provision in force on 1 April 1964 so long as any person then entitled to the benefit of that provision or afterwards given the benefit of it under *subsection (4)*, remains a trustee of the deed in question, or

(b) to deprive any person of any exemption or right to be indemnified in respect of anything done or omitted to be done by him or her while any such provision was in force.

(4) While any trustee of a trust deed remains entitled to the benefit of a provision saved by *subsection (3)*, the benefit of that provision may be given either—

(a) to all trustees of the deed present and future, or

(b) to any named trustee or proposed trustees of the deed,

by a resolution passed by a majority of not less than three-fourths in value of the debenture holders present in person or, where proxies are permitted, by proxy at a meeting summoned for the purpose in accordance with the provisions of the deed, or if the deed makes no provision for summoning meetings, a meeting summoned for the purpose in any manner approved by the court.

423 Perpetual debentures

A condition contained in any debentures or in any deed for securing any debentures shall not be invalid by reason only that the debentures are by those means made irredeemable or redeemable only on the happening of a contingency however remote, or on the expiration of a period however long, notwithstanding any rule of law to the contrary.

424 Power to re-issue redeemed debentures

(1) Where a company has redeemed any debentures then—

- (a) unless any provision to the contrary, whether express or implied, is contained in the constitution or in any contract entered into by the company, or
- (b) unless the company has, by passing a resolution to that effect or by some other act, shown its intention that the debentures shall be cancelled,

the company shall have power to re-issue the debentures either by re-issuing the same debentures or by issuing other debentures in their place.

(2) Subject to *section 425*, on a re-issue of redeemed debentures, the person entitled to the debentures shall have the same priorities as if the debentures had never been redeemed.

(3) Where a company has deposited any of its debentures to secure advances from time to time on current account or otherwise, the debentures shall not be deemed to have been redeemed by reason only of the account of the company having ceased to be in debit whilst the debentures have remained so deposited.

425 Saving of rights of certain mortgagees in case of re-issued debentures

Where any debentures which have been redeemed before 1 April 1964 are re-issued on, or subsequently to, that date, the re-issue of the debentures shall not prejudice, and shall be deemed never to have prejudiced, any right or priority which any person would have had under or by virtue of any charge created before that date if section 104 of the Companies (Consolidation) Act 1908 had been enacted in—

- (a) the Act of 1963, or
- (b) in the case of a re-issue occurring on or after the commencement of this section, this Act,

instead of section 95 of the Act of 1963 or *section 424*, as the case may be.

426 Specific performance of contracts to subscribe for debentures

A contract with a company to take up and pay for any debentures of the company may be enforced by an order for specific performance.

Chapter 4
Prohibition on Registration of Certain Matters affecting Shareholders or Debentureholders

427 Registration against company of certain matters prohibited

(1) Subject to *subsection (3)*, the Registrar has, in relation to any company, no jurisdiction to accept receipt of, or to register in the register—

(a) an order of any authority (whether judicial or otherwise) affecting a shareholder or debentureholder of the company, or

(b) any notice of the making thereof.

(2) Any jurisdiction of an authority (whether judicial or otherwise) subsisting before the commencement of this section to make an order requiring that there be registered in the register, or that there be received by the Registrar—

(a) an order of that authority affecting a shareholder or debentureholder of a company, or

(b) a notice of the making of an order referred to in *paragraph (a)*,

shall, after that commencement, cease to be exercisable.

(3) Nothing in this section affects the jurisdiction of any authority (whether judicial or otherwise) under *Chapter 3* of *Part 13* or *Chapter 2* of *Part 14*.

PART 8
RECEIVERS

Chapter 1
Interpretation

428 Appointment of receiver under powers contained in instrument: construction of such reference

In this Part any reference to the appointment of a receiver under powers contained in any instrument includes a reference to an appointment made under powers which, by virtue of any enactment, are implied in and have effect as if contained in an instrument.

Chapter 2
Appointment of Receivers

429 Notification that receiver has been appointed

(1) Where a receiver of the property of a company has been appointed, every invoice, order for goods or business letter issued by or on behalf of the company or the receiver, being a document on or in which the name of the company appears, shall contain a statement that a receiver has been appointed.

(2) Where—

(a) a receiver of the property of a company has been appointed, and

(b) a winding up of the company is taking place (whether that winding up has commenced before or after that appointment),

every invoice, order for goods or business letter issued by or on behalf of the company or the receiver, being a document on or in which the name of the company appears, shall, in addition to the statement referred to in *subsection (1)*, contain a statement that the company is being wound up.

(3) Where a receiver of the property of a company has been appointed, then—

(a) any website of the company, and

(b) any electronic mail sent to a third party by, or on behalf of, the company,

shall contain a statement that a receiver has been appointed (and such a statement on a website shall be in a prominent and easily accessible place on it).

(4) Where—

(a) a receiver of the property of a company has been appointed, and

(b) a winding up of the company is taking place (whether that winding up has commenced before or after that appointment),

then—

(i) any website of the company, and

(ii) any electronic mail sent to a third party by, or on behalf of, the company, shall, in addition to the statement referred to in *subsection (3)*, contain a statement that the company is being wound up (and such a statement on a website shall be in a prominent and easily accessible place on it).

(5) In *subsections (3)* and *(4)*, "third party" means a person other than—

(a) an officer or employee of the company concerned, or

(b) a holding company or subsidiary of the company or an officer or employee of that holding company or subsidiary.

(6) If default is made in complying with *subsection (1)* or *(2)*—

(a) the company and any officer of the company who is in default, and

(b) any of the following persons who knowingly and intentionally authorises or permits the default, namely, any liquidator of the company and any receiver,

shall be guilty of a category 4 offence.

(7) If default is made in complying with the requirement under *subsection (3)* or *(4)* concerning the company's website, the company concerned and any officer of it who is in default shall be guilty of a category 4 offence.

(8) If default is made by a company, or any person acting on its behalf, in complying with the requirement under *subsection (3)* or *(4)* concerning electronic mail, then—

(a) in every case, the company and any officer of it who is in default, and

(b) where the default is made by a person acting on the company's behalf, that person,

shall be guilty of a category 4 offence.

430 Information to be given when receiver is appointed in certain circumstance

(1) Where a receiver of the whole, or substantially the whole, of the property of a company (referred to subsequently in this section and *sections 431* and *432* as the "receiver") is appointed on behalf of the holders of any debentures of the company secured by a floating charge, then subject to the provisions of this section and *section 431*—

(a) the receiver shall forthwith send notice to the company of his or her appointment,

(b) there shall, within 14 days after the date of receipt of the notice, or such longer period as may be allowed by the court or by the receiver, be made out and submitted to the receiver in accordance with *section 431* a statement in the prescribed form as to the affairs of the company, and

(c) the receiver shall, within 2 months after the date of receipt of that statement, send to:

(i) the Registrar;

(ii) the court;

(iii) the company;

(iv) any trustees for the debenture holders on whose behalf he or she was appointed; and

(v) so far as he or she is aware of their addresses, all such debenture holders;

a copy of the statement and of any comments he or she sees fit to make on it.

(2) In *subsection (3)* "initial period of 6 months", in relation to the receiver, means the period of 6 months falling after the date of his or her appointment.

(3) The receiver shall send to the Registrar—

(a) within 30 days after the expiration of—

(i) the initial period of 6 months, and

(ii) each subsequent period of 6 months,

and

(b) within 30 days after the date on which he or she ceases to act as receiver of the property of the company,

an abstract in the prescribed form showing—

(i) the assets of the company of which he or she has taken possession since his or her appointment, their estimated value and the proceeds of sale of any such assets since his or her appointment,

(ii) his or her receipts and payments during that period of 6 months or, where he or she ceases to act as mentioned above, during the period from the end of the period to which the last preceding abstract related up to the date of his or her so ceasing, and

(iii) the aggregate amounts of his or her receipts and of his or her payments during all preceding periods since his or her appointment.

(4) Where a receiver ceases to act as receiver of the property of the company, the abstract under *subsection (3)* shall be accompanied by a statement from the receiver of his or her opinion as to whether or not the company is solvent and the Registrar shall, on receiving the statement, forward a copy of it to the Director of Corporate Enforcement.

(5) Where a receiver is appointed under the powers contained in any instrument, this section shall have effect with the omission of the references to the court in *subsection (1)*, and in any other case, references to the court shall be taken as referring to the court by which the receiver was appointed.

(6) *Subsection (1)* shall not apply in relation to the appointment of a receiver to act with an existing receiver or in place of a receiver dying or ceasing to act, except that, where that subsection applies to a receiver who dies or ceases to act before it has been fully complied with, the references in *paragraphs (b)* and *(c)* of it to the receiver shall (subject to *subsection (7)*) include references to his or her successor and to any continuing receiver. Nothing in this subsection shall be taken as limiting the meaning of the "receiver" where used in or in relation to *subsection (3)*.

(7) This section and *section 431*, where the company is being wound up, shall apply notwithstanding that the receiver and the liquidator are the same person, but with any necessary modifications arising from that fact.

(8) Nothing in *subsection (3)* shall be taken to prejudice the duty of the receiver to render proper accounts of his or her receipts and payments to the persons to whom, and at the times at which, he or she may be required to do so apart from that subsection.

(9) Where the Registrar becomes aware of the appointment of a receiver referred to in this section, he or she shall forthwith inform the Director of Corporate Enforcement of the appointment.

(10) If the receiver makes default in complying with this section, he or she shall be guilty of a category 4 offence.

431 Contents of statement to be submitted to receiver

(1) The statement as to the affairs of a company required by *section 430* (the "statement") to be submitted to the receiver (or his or her successor) shall show as at the date of the receiver's appointment—

(a) particulars of the company's assets, debts and liabilities,

(b) the names and residences of its creditors,

(c) the securities held by those creditors respectively,

(d) the dates when those securities were respectively given, and

(e) such further or other information as may be prescribed.

(2) The statement shall be submitted by, and be verified by affidavit of, one or more of the persons who are, at the date of the receiver's appointment, the directors of the company, or by such of the persons referred to subsequently in this subsection as the receiver (or his or her successor) may require to submit and verify the statement, that is, persons—

(a) who are or have been officers of the company,

(b) who have taken part in the formation of the company at any time within one year before the date of the receiver's appointment,

(c) who are in the employment of the company or have been in the employment of the company within that year, and are, in the opinion of the receiver, capable of giving the information required,

(d) who are or have been within that year, officers of or in the employment of a company which is, or within that year was, an officer of the company to which the statement relates.

(3) Any person making the statement and affidavit shall be allowed, and shall be paid by the receiver (or his or her successor) out of his or her receipts, such costs and expenses incurred in and about the preparation and making of the statement and affidavit as the receiver (or his or her successor) may consider reasonable, subject to an appeal to the court.

(4) Where the receiver is appointed under the powers contained in any instrument, this section shall have effect with the substitution, for references to an affidavit, of references to a statutory declaration; and in any other case, references to the court shall be taken to refer to the court by which the receiver was appointed.

(5) If any person to whom *subsection (2)* applies makes default in complying with the requirements of this section, he or she shall, unless he or she can prove to the satisfaction of the court that it was not possible for him or her to comply with the requirements of this section, be guilty of a category 3 offence.

(6) References in this section to the receiver's successor include references to a continuing receiver.

432 Consequences of contravention of *section 430(1)(b)* or *431*

Where, in contravention of *sections 430(1)(b)* and *431*, a statement of affairs is not submitted to the receiver as required by those provisions, the court may, on the application of the receiver or any creditor of the company, and notwithstanding *section 431(5)*, make whatever order it thinks fit, including an order compelling compliance with *sections 430* and *431*.

433 Disqualification for appointment as receiver

(1) None of the following persons shall be qualified for appointment as receiver of the property of a company:

(a) an undischarged bankrupt;

(b) a person who is, or who has, within the period of 12 months before the date of commencement of the receivership been, an officer or employee of the company;

(c) a parent, spouse, civil partner, brother, sister or child of an officer of the company;

(d) a person who is a partner of, or in the employment of, an officer or employee of the company;

(e) a person who is not qualified by virtue of this subsection for appointment as receiver of the property of any other body corporate which is that company's subsidiary or holding company or a subsidiary of that company's holding company, or would be so disqualified if the body corporate were a company;

(f) a body corporate.

(2) References in *subsection (1)* to—

(a) a child of an officer shall be deemed to include a child of the officer's civil partner who is ordinarily resident with the officer and the civil partner,

(b) an officer or employee of the company include a statutory auditor.

(3) If a receiver of the property of a company becomes disqualified by virtue of this section, he or she shall thereupon vacate his or her office and give notice in writing within 14 days after the date of vacation to—

(a) the company,

(b) the Registrar,

(c) (i) the debenture-holder, if the receiver was appointed by a debenture-holder, or

(ii) the court, if the receiver was appointed by the court,

that he or she has vacated it by reason of such disqualification.

(4) *Subsection (3)* is without prejudice to *sections 430(3)*, *436* and *441*.

(5) Nothing in this section shall require a receiver appointed before 1 August 1991 to vacate the office to which he or she was so appointed.

(6) Any person who acts as a receiver when disqualified by this section from so doing or who fails to comply with *subsection (3)*, if that subsection applies to him or her, shall be guilty of a category 2 offence.

434 Resignation of receiver

(1) A receiver of the property of a company appointed under the powers contained in any instrument may resign, provided he or she has given at least 30 days' prior notice of the date on which the resignation will take effect to—

(a) the holders of charges (whether fixed or floating) over all or any part of the property of the company, and

(b) the company or its liquidator.

(2) A receiver appointed by the court may resign only with the authority of the court and on such terms and conditions, if any, as may be specified by the court.

(3) If a person makes default in complying with *subsection (1)* or *(2)*, he or she shall be guilty of a category 4 offence.

435 Removal of receiver

(1) The court may, on cause shown, remove a receiver of the property of a company and appoint another receiver.

(2) Notice of proceedings in which such removal is sought shall be served on the receiver and on the person who appointed him or her not less than 7 days before the date of the hearing of such proceedings and, in any such proceedings, the receiver and the person who appointed him or her may appear and be heard.

436 Notice to Registrar of appointment of receiver, and of receiver ceasing to act

(1) If any person obtains an order for the appointment of a receiver of the property of a company or appoints such a receiver under any powers contained in any instrument, he or she—

(a) shall cause to be published in *Iris Oifigiúil*, and

(b) shall deliver to the Registrar,

within 7 days after the date of the order or of the appointment, a notice in the prescribed form.

(2) When any person appointed receiver of the property of a company ceases to act as such receiver, he or she shall, on so ceasing, deliver to the Registrar a notice in the prescribed form.

(3) If a person makes default in complying with *subsection (1)* or *(2)*, he or she shall be guilty of a category 4 offence.

Chapter 3
Powers and Duties of Receivers

437 Powers of receiver

(1) Subject to the provisions of this section, a receiver of the property of a company has power to do, in the State and elsewhere, all things necessary or convenient to be done for or in connection with, or as incidental to, the attainment of the objectives for which the receiver was appointed.

(2) Without limiting the generality of *subsection (1)* but subject to *subsection (4)*, a receiver of the property of a company has (in addition to any powers conferred by the order or instrument referred to in *subsection (4)* or by any other law) power to do one or more of the following things for the purpose of attaining the objectives for which he or she was appointed.

(3) Those things are:

(a) to enter into possession and take control of property of the company in accordance with the terms of the order or instrument referred to in *subsection (4)*;

(b) to lease, let on hire or dispose of property of the company;

(c) to grant options over property of the company on such conditions as the receiver thinks fit;

(d) to borrow money on the security of property of the company;

(e) to insure property of the company;

(f) to repair, renew or enlarge property of the company;

(g) to convert property of the company into money;

(h) to carry on any business of the company;

(i) to take on lease or on hire, or to acquire, any property necessary or convenient in connection with the carrying on of a business of the company;

(j) to execute any document, bring or defend any proceedings or do any other act or thing in the name of and on behalf of the company;

(k) to draw, accept, make and endorse a bill of exchange or promissory note;

(l) to use a seal of the company;

(m) to engage or discharge employees on behalf of the company;

(n) to appoint a solicitor, accountant or other professionally qualified person to assist the receiver;

(o) to appoint an agent to do any business that the receiver is unable to do, or that it is unreasonable to expect the receiver to do, in person;

(p) where a debt or liability is owed to the company, to prove the debt or liability in a bankruptcy, insolvency or winding up and, in connection therewith, to receive dividends and to assent to a proposal for a composition or a scheme of arrangement;

(q) if the receiver was appointed under an instrument that created a charge on uncalled share capital of the company—

(i) to make a call in the name of the company for the payment of money unpaid on the company's shares, or

(ii) on giving a proper indemnity to a liquidator of the company, to make a call in the liquidator's name for the payment of money unpaid on the company's shares;

(r) to enforce payment of any call that is due and unpaid, whether the calls were made by the receiver or otherwise;

(s) to make or defend an application for the winding up of the company;

(t) to refer to arbitration or mediation, any question affecting the company.

(4) *Subsections (1)* and *(2)* are subject to any provision of the order of the court by which, or the instrument under which, the receiver was appointed, being a provision that limits the receiver's powers in any way.

(5) The conferral on a receiver, by this section, of powers in relation to property of a company does not affect any rights in relation to that property of any other person other than the company.

(6) In *subsections (3)* and *(5)* a reference, in relation to a receiver, to property of a company is a reference to the property of the company in relation to which the receiver was appointed; this subsection is in addition to *section 2(9)* providing for construction of references to a receiver of property of a company.

438 Power of receiver and certain others to apply to court for directions and receiver's liability on contracts

(1) Where a receiver of the property of a company is appointed under the powers contained in any instrument, any of the following persons may apply to the court for directions in relation to any matter in connection with the performance or otherwise, by the receiver, of his or her functions, that is to say:

(a) (i) the receiver;

(ii) an officer of the company;

(iii) a member of the company;

(iv) employees of the company comprising at least half in number of the persons employed in a permanent capacity by the company;

(v) a creditor of the company;

and

(b) (i) a liquidator;

(ii) a contributory;

and, on any such application, the court may give such directions, or make such order declaring the rights of persons before the court or otherwise, as the court thinks just.

(2) An application to the court under *subsection (1)*, except an application under that subsection by the receiver, shall be supported by such evidence that the applicant is being unfairly prejudiced by any actual or proposed act or omission of the receiver as the court may require.

(3) For the purposes of *subsection (1)*, "creditor" means one or more creditors to whom the company is indebted by more, in aggregate, than €13,000.

(4) A receiver of the property of a company shall be personally liable on any contract entered into by him or her in the performance of his or her functions (whether such contract is entered into by the receiver in the name of such company or in his or her own name as receiver or otherwise) unless the contract provides that he or she is not to be personally liable on such contract.

(5) In those circumstances, the receiver shall be entitled in respect of that liability to indemnity out of the assets of the company; but nothing in *subsection (4)* or this subsection shall be taken as—

(a) limiting any right to indemnity which the receiver would have apart from this subsection, or

(b) limiting the receiver's liability on contracts entered into without authority or as conferring any right to indemnity in respect of that liability.

(6) *Subsection (7)* applies where a receiver of the property of a company has been appointed or purported to be appointed and it is subsequently discovered that the charge or purported charge in respect of which he or she was so appointed or purported to be appointed was not effective as a charge on such property or on some part of such property.

(7) Where this subsection applies, the court may, if it thinks fit, on the application of the receiver referred to in *subsection (6)*, order that he or she be relieved wholly, or to such extent as the court shall think fit, from personal liability in respect of anything done or omitted by him or her in relation to any property purporting to be comprised in the charge by virtue of which he or she was appointed or purported to be appointed which, if such property had been effectively included in such charge or purported charge, would have been properly done or omitted by him or her and he or she shall be relieved from personal liability accordingly.

(8) In the event of such an order being made, the person by whom such receiver was appointed or purported to be appointed shall be personally liable for everything for which, but for such order, such receiver would have been liable.

439 Duty of receiver selling property to get best price reasonably obtainable, etc.

(1) A receiver of the property of a company shall, in selling property of the company, exercise all reasonable care to obtain the best price reasonably obtainable for the property as at the time of sale.

(2) Notwithstanding the provisions of any instrument and, in the case of *paragraph (b), section 438(4)* and *(5)*—

(a) it shall not be a defence to any action or proceeding brought against a receiver in respect of a breach of his or her duty under *subsection (1)* that the receiver was acting as the agent of the company or under a power of attorney given by the company, and

(b) a receiver shall not be entitled to be compensated or indemnified by the company for any liability he or she may incur as a result of a breach of his or her duty under that subsection.

(3) A receiver shall not sell by private contract a non-cash asset of the requisite value to a person who is, or who, within 3 years prior to the date of appointment of the receiver, has been, an officer of the company unless the receiver has given at least 14 days' notice of his or her intention to do so to all creditors of the company who are known to the receiver or who have been intimated to the receiver.

(4) In this section—

"non-cash asset" and "requisite value" have the meanings given to them by *section 238*;

"officer" includes a person connected (within the meaning of *section 220*) with—

(a) a director of the company,

(b) a shadow director of it, or

(c) a *de facto* director of it.

440 Preferential payments when receiver is appointed under floating charge

(1) Where either—

(a) a receiver of the property of a company is appointed on behalf of the holders of any debentures of the company secured by [any charge created as a floating charge by the company][a], or

(b) possession is taken by or on behalf of those debenture holders of any property comprised in or subject to the charge,

then, if the company is not at the time in the course of being wound up, the debts which in every winding up are, under the provisions of *Part 11* relating to preferential payments, to be paid in priority to all other debts, shall be paid out of any assets coming to the hands of the receiver or other person taking possession as mentioned above in priority to any claim for principal or interest in respect of the debentures.

(2) In the application of the foregoing provisions, *section 621(2)(c)* shall be read as if the provision for payment of accrued holiday remuneration becoming payable on the termination of employment before or by the effect of the winding-up order or

resolution were a provision for payment of such remuneration becoming payable on the termination of employment before or by the effect of the appointment of the receiver or possession being taken as mentioned above.

(3) For the purposes of this section, the periods of time mentioned in the foregoing provisions of *Part 11* shall be reckoned as beginning after the date of the appointment of the receiver or of possession being taken as mentioned above, as the case may be.

(4) Any payments made under this section shall be recouped so far as may be out of the assets of the company available for payment of general creditors.

Amendments

a Words substituted by C(A)A 2017, s 98(d) (previously: "a floating charge").

---

441 Delivery to Registrar of accounts of receivers

(1) In this section "initial period of 6 months", in relation to a receiver, means the period of 6 months falling after the date of his or her appointment.

(2) Except where *section 430(3)* applies, a receiver of the property of a company shall send to the Registrar—

(a) within 30 days after the expiration of—

(i) the initial period of 6 months, and

(ii) each subsequent period of 6 months,

and

(b) within 30 days after the date on which he or she ceases to act as receiver of the property of the company,

an abstract in the prescribed form showing—

(i) the assets of the company of which he or she has taken possession since his or her appointment, their estimated value and the proceeds of sale of any such assets since his or her appointment,

(ii) his or her receipts and payments during that period of 6 months or, where he or she ceases to act as mentioned above, during the period from the end of the period to which the last preceding abstract related up to the date of his or her so ceasing, and

(iii) the aggregate amounts of his or her receipts and of his or her payments during all preceding periods since his or her appointment.

(3) A receiver who makes default in complying with *subsection (2)* shall be guilty of a category 4 offence.

Chapter 4
Regulation of Receivers and Enforcement of their Duties

442 Enforcement of duty of receivers to make returns

(1) *Subsection (2)* applies if a receiver of the property of a company—

(a) having made default in filing, delivering or making any return, account or other document, or in giving any notice, which a receiver is by law required to file, deliver, make or give, fails to make good the default within 14 days after the date of service on him or her of a notice requiring him or her to do so, or

(b) having been appointed under the powers contained in any instrument, has, after being required at any time by the liquidator of the company to do so, failed to render proper accounts of his or her receipts and payments and to vouch those receipts and payments and to pay over to the liquidator the amount properly payable to him or her.

(2) Where this subsection applies, the court may, on an application made for the purpose, make an order directing the receiver to make good the default within such time as may be specified in the order.

(3) In the case of any such default as is mentioned in *subsection (1)(a)*, any member or creditor of the company or the Registrar may make an application for the purposes of this section.

(4) In the case of any such default as is mentioned in *subsection (1)(b)*, the liquidator of the company is alone entitled to make an application for the purposes of this section.

(5) In either of the foregoing cases, the order under this section may provide that all costs of and incidental to the application shall be borne by the receiver.

(6) Nothing in this section shall be taken to prejudice the operation of any enactments imposing penalties on receivers in respect of any such default as is mentioned in *subsection (1)*.

443 Power of court to order the return of assets improperly transferred

(1) Where a receiver of the property of a company is appointed and, on the application of the receiver or any creditor or member of the company, it can be shown to the satisfaction of the court that—

(a) any property of the company of any kind whatsoever was disposed of either by way of conveyance, transfer, mortgage, security, loan, or in any way whatsoever whether by act or omission, direct or indirect, and

(b) the effect of such disposal was to perpetrate a fraud on the company, its creditors or members,

the court may, if it deems it just and equitable to do so, make the following order.

(2) That order of the court is one requiring any person who appears to have the use, control or possession of such property or the proceeds of the sale or development of it

to deliver it or pay a sum in respect of it to the receiver on such terms or conditions as the court sees fit.

(3) *Subsection (1)* shall not apply to any conveyance, mortgage, delivery of goods, payment, execution or other act relating to property made or done by or against a company to which *section 604* applies.

(4) In deciding whether it is just and equitable to make an order under this section, the court shall have regard to the rights of persons who have *bona fide* and for value acquired an interest in the property the subject of the application.

444 Power of court to fix remuneration of receiver

(1) Where a person has, under the powers contained in any instrument, been appointed as receiver of the property of a company the court may, on an application made by the liquidator of a company or by any creditor or member of the company, make the following order.

(2) That order of the court is one fixing the amount to be paid by way of remuneration to that receiver and such an order may be made notwithstanding that his or her remuneration has been fixed by or under that instrument.

(3) Subject to *subsection (4)*, the power of the court under *subsection (1)* shall, where no previous order has been made in relation to the matter concerned under that subsection—

- (a) extend to fixing the remuneration for any period before the making of the order or the application for it,
- (b) be exercisable notwithstanding that the receiver has died or ceased to act before the making of the order or the application for it, and
- (c) if the receiver has been paid or has retained for his or her remuneration for any period before the making of the order any amount in excess of that fixed by the court for that period, extend to requiring him or her or his or her personal representatives to account for the excess or such part of it as may be specified in the order.

(4) The power conferred by *subsection (3)(c)* shall not be exercised in relation to any period before the making of the application for the order unless, in the opinion of the court, there are special circumstances making it proper for the power to be so exercised.

(5) The court may from time to time, on an application made by the liquidator or by any creditor or member of the company or by the receiver, vary or amend an order made under *subsection (1)*.

(6) Nothing in this section shall affect a receiver's right to indemnity out of the assets of the company provided by *section 438*.

445 Court may end or limit receivership on application of liquidator

(1) On the application of the liquidator of a company that is being wound up (other than by means of a members' voluntary winding up) and in respect of the property of which a receiver has been appointed (whether before or after the commencement of the winding up), the court may make the following order.

(2) That order of the court is one—

(a) that the receiver shall cease to act as such from a date specified by the court, and prohibiting the appointment of any other receiver, or

(b) that the receiver shall, from a date specified by the court, act as such only in respect of certain assets specified by the court.

(3) An order under *subsection (1)* may be made on such terms and conditions as the court thinks fit.

(4) The court may from time to time, on an application made either by the liquidator or by the receiver, discharge or amend an order made under *subsection (1)*.

(5) A copy of an application made under this section shall be served on the receiver and on the person who appointed him or her not less than 7 days before the date of the hearing of the application, and the receiver and any such person may appear before and be heard by the court in respect of the application.

(6) Except as provided in *subsection (2)*, no order made under this section shall affect any security or charge over the undertaking or property of the company.

446 Director of Corporate Enforcement may request production of receiver's books

(1) The Director of Corporate Enforcement may, where he or she considers it necessary or appropriate, make the following request of the receiver of the property of a company or companies (specifying the reason why the request is being made).

(2) That request is that the receiver produce to the Director the receiver's books for examination, either in regard to a particular receivership or to all receiverships undertaken by the receiver.

(3) The receiver of whom a request under *subsection (1)* is made shall—

(a) furnish the books to the Director of Corporate Enforcement,

(b) answer any questions concerning the content of the books and the conduct of the particular receivership or receiverships, and

(c) give to the Director of Corporate Enforcement all assistance in the matter as the receiver is reasonably able to give.

(4) A request under *subsection (1)* may not be made in respect of books relating to a receivership that has concluded more than 6 years prior to the date of the request.

(5) If a receiver fails to comply with a request under *subsection (1)* or do any of the things referred to in *subsection (3)(b)* and *(c)*, he or she shall be guilty of a category 3 offence.

447 Prosecution of offences committed by officers and members of company

(1) If it appears to the receiver of the property of a company, in the course of the receivership, that any past or present officer, or any member, of the company has been guilty of any offence in relation to the company, the receiver shall forthwith report the matter to the Director of Public Prosecutions.

(2) Where the receiver reports a matter under *subsection (1)* to the Director of Public Prosecutions, the receiver shall—

(a) provide to the Director of Public Prosecutions such information, relating to the matter in question, as he or she may require, and

(b) give to him or her such access to, and facilities for, inspecting and taking copies of such documents, being documents in the possession or under the control of the receiver and relating to the matter in question, as he or she may require.

(3) Where a foregoing report is made by the receiver, the receiver shall also report the matter to the Director of Corporate Enforcement.

(4) Where a matter is reported by the receiver under *subsection (3)* to the Director of Corporate Enforcement, the receiver shall—

(a) provide to the Director of Corporate Enforcement such information, relating to the matter in question, as he or she may require, and

(b) give to him or her such access to, and facilities for, inspecting and taking copies of such documents, being documents in the possession or under the control of the receiver and relating to the matter in question, as he or she may require.

(5) If, where any matter is reported under *subsection (1)* or *(3)* to—

(a) the Director of Public Prosecutions, or

(b) the Director of Corporate Enforcement,

the Director of Public Prosecutions or, as the case may be, the Director of Corporate Enforcement considers that the case is one in which a prosecution ought to be instituted and institutes proceedings accordingly, it shall be the duty of each of the following to give all assistance in connection with the prosecution which he or she is reasonably able to give.

(6) The persons referred to in *subsection (5)* are the receiver of the company and—

(a) every officer (past or present) of the company, and

(b) every agent (past or present) of the company,

other than the defendant in the proceedings.

(7) For the purposes of *subsection (6)*, "agent", in relation to a company, includes—

(a) the bankers and solicitors of the company, and

(b) any persons employed by the company as auditors, accountants, book-keepers or taxation advisers, or other persons employed by it in a professional, consultancy or similar capacity, whether those persons are (or were) or are not (or were not) officers of the company.

(8) If any person fails or neglects to give assistance in the manner required by *subsection (5)*, the court may, on the application of the Director of Public Prosecutions or, as the case may be, the Director of Corporate Enforcement, direct that person to comply with the requirements of that subsection.

(9) Where any such application is made in relation to a receiver, the court may, unless it appears that the failure or neglect to comply was due to the receiver not having in his or her hands sufficient assets of the company to enable him or her so to do, direct that the costs of the application shall be borne by the receiver personally.

448 Reporting to Director of Corporate Enforcement of misconduct by receivers

(1) Where a disciplinary committee or tribunal (however called) of a prescribed professional body—

(a) finds that a member of that body who is conducting or has conducted a receivership has not maintained appropriate records in relation to that activity, or

(b) has reasonable grounds for believing that such a member has committed a category 1 or 2 offence during the course of conducting a receivership,

the professional body shall report the matter, giving details of the finding or, as the case may be, of the alleged offence, to the Director of Corporate Enforcement forthwith.

(2) If a professional body fails to comply with this section, it, and any officer of the body to whom the failure is attributable, shall be guilty of a category 3 offence.

PART 9
REORGANISATIONS, ACQUISITIONS, MERGERS AND DIVISIONS

Chapter 1
Schemes of Arrangement

449 Interpretation (*Chapter 1*)

(1) In this Chapter—

"arrangement", in relation to a company, includes a reorganisation of the share capital of the company by the consolidation of shares of different classes or by the division of shares into shares of different classes or by both those methods;

"debenture trustees", in relation to a company, means the trustees of a deed securing the issue of debentures by the company;

"new company" shall be read in accordance with *section 455(1)(b)(ii)*;

"old company" shall be read in accordance with *section 455(1)(b)(ii)*;

"scheme circular" shall be read in accordance with *section 452(1)(a)*;

"scheme meeting" means a meeting of creditors (or any class of creditors) or of members (or any class of members) for the purpose of their considering, and voting on, a resolution proposing that the compromise or arrangement concerned be agreed to;

"scheme order" means an order of the court under *section 453(2)(c)* sanctioning a compromise or arrangement referred to in *section 450*;

"special majority" means a majority in number representing at least 75 per cent in value of the creditors or class of creditors or members or class of members, as the case may be, present and voting either in person or by proxy at the scheme meeting.

(2) A reference in this Chapter to a compromise or arrangement that is proposed between a company and its creditors (or any class of them) or its members (or any class of them) includes a reference to circumstances in which a compromise or arrangement is proposed between a company and both—

(a) its creditors (or any class of them), and

(b) its members (or any class of them),

and, accordingly, the powers under this Chapter are exercisable, and the duties under this Chapter are to be carried out, in the latter circumstances as in the former.

450 Scheme meetings — convening of such by directors and court's power to summon such meetings

(1) Where a compromise or arrangement is proposed between a company and—

(a) its creditors or any class of them, or

(b) its members or any class of them,

the directors of the company may convene—

(i) the appropriate scheme meetings of the creditors or the class concerned of them, or

(ii) the appropriate scheme meetings of the members or the class concerned of them.

(2) References in *subsections (1)* and *(5)* to the appropriate scheme meetings of creditors or members, as the case may be, are references to either—

(a) separate scheme meetings of the particular creditors or members (as appropriate) who fall into the separate classes that, under the general law, are required to be constituted for the purpose of voting on the proposals for the compromise or arrangement, or

(b) where, under the general law, no such separate classes are required to be constituted for that purpose, a single scheme meeting of the creditors or members (as appropriate).

(3) Where a compromise or arrangement referred to in *subsection (1)* is proposed and the directors of the company do not exercise the powers under that subsection, the court may, on the application, at any time, of any of the following persons, order a scheme meeting or scheme meetings of the creditors or members (or, as the case may be, the class of either of them concerned) to be summoned in such manner as the court directs.

(4) The persons referred to in *subsection (3)* are:

(a) the company;

(b) any creditor or member of the company;

(c) in the case of a company being wound up, the liquidator.

(5) Without prejudice to the court's jurisdiction under *section 453(2)(c)* to determine whether the scheme meetings that have been held comply with the general law referred to in *subsection (2)*, the court, in exercising its jurisdiction to summon meetings under *subsection (3)*, may, in its discretion, where it considers just and convenient to do so, give directions as to what are the appropriate scheme meetings that must be held in the circumstances concerned.

(6) If the compromise or arrangement is proposed between the company and a class of its creditors or members, then—

(a) the reference in *subsection (2)* to creditors or members, where it first occurs, is a reference to that class of creditors or members, as appropriate (the "predicate class"), and

(b) the references in *paragraphs (a)* and *(b)* of that subsection to separate classes of creditors or members are references to separate classes of creditors or members, as appropriate, who fall within the predicate class.

451 Court's power to stay proceedings or restrain further proceedings

(1) This section applies where one or more scheme meetings is convened under *section 450(1)* or an application is made under *section 450(3)* in relation to a company.

(2) Where this section applies the court may, on the application of any of the following persons, on such terms as seem just, stay all proceedings or restrain further proceedings against the company for such period as the court sees fit.

(3) The persons referred to in *subsection (2)* are:

(a) the company;

(b) the directors of the company;

(c) any creditor or member of the company;

(d) in the case of a company being wound up, the liquidator.

452 Information as to compromises or arrangements with members and creditors

(1) Where a scheme meeting is convened or summoned under *section 450* there shall—

(a) with every notice convening or summoning the meeting which is sent to a creditor or member of the company concerned, be sent also a circular (in this section referred to as a "scheme circular")—

(i) explaining the effect of the compromise or arrangement,

(ii) stating any material interests of the directors of the company, whether as directors or as members or as creditors of the company or otherwise, and the effect thereon of the compromise or arrangement, in so far as it is different from the effect on the like interests of other persons,

(iii) where the compromise or arrangement affects the rights of debenture holders of the company, giving the like explanation in relation to the debenture trustees as it is required under *subparagraph (ii)* to give in relation to the company's directors,

(b) in every notice convening or summoning the meeting which is given by advertisement, be included the scheme circular or a notification of the place at which and the manner in which creditors or members entitled to attend the meeting may obtain copies of the scheme circular.

(2) Where a notice given by advertisement includes a notification that copies of the scheme circular can be obtained by creditors or members entitled to attend the scheme meeting, every such creditor or member shall, on making application in the manner indicated by the notice, be furnished by the company free of charge with a copy of the scheme circular.

(3) Each director and debenture trustee shall provide the company in writing with the information concerning such director or debenture trustee, as the case may be, that is required for the scheme circular.

(4) Subject to *subsection (6)*, if a company fails to comply with any requirement of this section, the company and any officer of it who is in default shall be guilty of a category 3 offence.

(5) For the purpose of *subsection (4)*, any liquidator of the company and any debenture trustee of the company shall be deemed to be an officer of the company.

(6) In any proceedings against a person in respect of an offence under *subsection (4)*, it shall be a defence to prove that the default was due to the refusal of any other person, being a director or debenture trustee, to supply the necessary particulars as to his or her interests.

(7) References in this section to directors include references to shadow directors and to *de facto* directors.

453 Circumstances in which compromise or arrangement becomes binding on creditors or members concerned

(1) If the following conditions are satisfied, a compromise or arrangement shall be binding, with effect from the date of delivery referred to in *section 454(1)*, on all the creditors or class of creditors referred to in *section 450(1)(a)* or all the members or class of members referred to in *section 450(1)(b)* (or both as the case may be) and also on—

(a) the company, or

(b) in the case of a company in the course of being wound up, on the liquidator and contributories of the company.

(2) The conditions referred to in *subsection (1)* are:

(a) a special majority at the scheme meeting, or, where more than one scheme meeting is held, at each of the scheme meetings, votes in favour of a resolution agreeing to the compromise or arrangement;

(b) notice—

(i) of the passing of such resolution or resolutions at the scheme meeting or scheme meetings, and

(ii) that an application will be made under *paragraph (c)* to the court in relation to the compromise or arrangement,

is advertised once in at least 2 daily newspapers circulating in the district where the registered office or principal place of business of the company is situated; and

(c) the court, on application to it, sanctions the compromise or arrangement.

(3) *Section 192* shall apply to any such resolution as is mentioned in *subsection (2)(a)* which is passed at any adjourned scheme meeting.

(4) Where a State authority is a creditor of the company, such authority shall be entitled to accept proposals under this section notwithstanding—

(a) that any claim of such authority as a creditor would be impaired under the proposals, or

(b) any other enactment.

(5) In *subsection (4)* "State authority" means the State, a Minister of the Government, a local authority or the Revenue Commissioners.

454 Supplemental provisions in relation to *section 453*

(1) Where a scheme order is made, the company shall cause a copy of it to be delivered to the Registrar within 21 days after the date of making of the order; the scheme order shall take effect immediately upon such delivery of that copy.

(2) The company shall attach to every copy of the constitution of the company issued by it after the scheme order has been made a copy of that order.

(3) If default is made in complying with *subsection (1)* or *(2)*, the company concerned and any officer of it who is in default shall be guilty of a category 3 offence.

455 Provisions to facilitate reconstruction and amalgamation of companies

(1) Where—

(a) an application is made to the court for the sanctioning of a compromise or arrangement under *section 453(2)(c)*, and

(b) it is shown to the court that—

(i) the compromise or arrangement has been proposed for the purposes of or in connection with a scheme for the reconstruction of any company or companies or the amalgamation of any 2 or more companies, and

(ii) under the scheme the whole or any part of the undertaking, assets or liabilities of any company concerned in the scheme (in this section referred to as an "old company") is to be transferred to another company (in this section referred to as the "new company"),

the court may, either by the scheme order or by any subsequent order, make provision for all or any of the matters set out in *subsection (2)*.

(2) The matters for which the court may make such provision are:

(a) the transfer to the new company of the whole or any part of the undertaking, assets or liabilities of any old company;

(b) the allotting or appropriation by the new company of any shares, debentures, policies or other like interests in that company which, under the compromise or arrangement, are to be allotted or appropriated by that company to or for any person;

(c) the continuation by or against the new company of any legal proceedings pending by or against any old company;

(d) the dissolution, with or without winding up, of any old company;

(e) the provision to be made for any persons who, within such time and in such manner as the court directs, dissent from the compromise or arrangement;

(f) such incidental, consequential and supplemental matters as are necessary to secure that the reconstruction or amalgamation shall be fully and effectively carried out.

(3) Where the scheme order or a subsequent order under this section provides for the transfer of assets or liabilities, those assets shall, by virtue of the order, be transferred to and vest in, and those liabilities shall, by virtue of the order, be

transferred to and become the liabilities of the new company, and in the case of any assets, if the order so directs, freed from any charge which is, by virtue of the compromise or arrangement, to cease to have effect.

(4) Where provision of the kind set out in *subsection (2)* is made by—

(a) the scheme order — every company in relation to which the order is made (other than the company the compromise or arrangement in relation to which has been sanctioned by the court), or

(b) a subsequent order — every company (without exception) in relation to which the order is made,

shall cause a copy of it to be delivered to the Registrar within 21 days after the date of making of the order.

(5) If default is made by a company in complying with *subsection (4)*, the company and any officer of it who is in default shall be guilty of a category 3 offence.

(6) In this section, "assets" includes property, rights and powers of every description, and "liabilities" includes duties.

Chapter 2
Acquisitions

456 Interpretation (*Chapter 2*)

(1) In this Chapter—

"assenting shareholder" means a holder of any of the shares affected in respect of which a scheme, contract or offer has become binding or been approved or accepted and *section 459(8)* supplements this definition;

"call notice" shall be read in accordance with *section 457(4)(a)*;

"dissenting shareholder" means a holder of any of the shares affected in respect of which the scheme, contract or offer has not become binding or been approved or accepted or who has failed or refused to transfer his or her shares in accordance with the scheme, contract or offer and *section 459(8)* supplements this definition;

"information notice" shall be read in accordance with *section 457(6)*;

"offeree company" shall be read in accordance with *section 457(1)*;

"offeror" shall be read in accordance with *section 457(1)*;

"relevant scheme, contract or offer" has the meaning assigned to it by *section 457(1)*;

"shares affected" means the shares the acquisition of the beneficial ownership of which by an offeror is involved in the scheme, contract or offer referred to in *section 457(1)*.

(2) The application of this Chapter is restricted, as was the position in the case of the corresponding provisions of the Act of 1963, by the regulations made under section 3 of the European Communities Act 1972 that are referred to in *paragraph 11* of *Schedule 6*.

457 Right to buy out shareholders dissenting from scheme or contract approved by majority and right of such shareholders to be bought out

(1) In this section "relevant scheme, contract or offer" means a scheme, contract or offer involving the acquisition by a person (in this Chapter referred to as the "offeror") of the beneficial ownership of all the shares (other than the shares in which the offeror already has a beneficial interest) in the capital of a company (in this section referred to as the "offeree company").

(2) This section applies where the relevant scheme, contract or offer—

(a) has become binding or been approved or accepted in respect of not less than 80 per cent in value of the shares affected, and

(b) has become so binding or been so approved or accepted not later than the date 4 months after the date of publication generally to the holders of the shares affected of the terms of such scheme, contract or offer,

but subject to *section 458* as regards the right of the offeror under *subsection (3)* (offeror's right of buy-out).

(3) Where this section applies, the offeror shall be entitled to acquire the beneficial ownership of all or any of the remaining shares affected from the dissenting shareholder or shareholders on—

(a) the same terms as have become binding or been approved or accepted as mentioned in *subsection (2)*, or

(b) where an application is made under *section 459(5)(a)*, any different terms that the court specifies,

but only if, in either case, the following conditions are satisfied.

(4) Those conditions for such acquisition of the shares of a dissenting shareholder are:

(a) the offeror, at any time before the expiration of the period of 6 months after the date of the publication referred to in *subsection (2)(b)*, gives notice in the prescribed form to the dissenting shareholder that the offeror desires to acquire the beneficial ownership of his or her shares (which notice is referred to in this section as the "call notice"); and

(b) either—

   (i) 30 days pass after the date that the call notice was given without an application being made to the court under *section 459(5)(a)* by the dissenting shareholder or, following such an application to the court by the dissenting shareholder, the court nonetheless approves such acquisition; or

   (ii) an application is made to the court under *section 459(5)(a)* by the dissenting shareholder within that period but is withdrawn.

(5) Where the scheme, contract or offer provides that an assenting shareholder may elect between 2 or more sets of terms for the acquisition by the offeror of the beneficial ownership of the shares affected—

(a) the call notice shall be accompanied by, or embody, a notice stating the alternative sets of terms between which assenting shareholders are entitled to elect and specifying which of those sets of terms shall be applicable to the dissenting shareholder if he or she does not, before the expiration of 14 days after the date of the giving of the notice, notify to the offeror in writing his or her election as between such alternative sets of terms, and

(b) the terms upon which the offeror shall under this section be entitled and bound to acquire the beneficial ownership of the shares of the dissenting shareholder shall be the set of terms which the dissenting shareholder shall so notify or, in default of such notification, the set of terms so specified as applicable, but subject, in either case, to *subsection (3)(b)*.

(6) Save where the offeror has given a call notice to the particular dissenting shareholder, the offeror shall, within 30 days after the date of the scheme, contract or offer becoming binding, approved or accepted, give notice of that fact in the prescribed manner to each of the dissenting shareholders (which notice is in this section referred to as an "information notice").

(7) The offeror shall be bound to acquire the beneficial ownership of the remaining shares affected on the same terms as have become binding or been approved or accepted (or, where an application is made under *section 459(5)(b)*, on any different terms that the court specifies) if—

(a) the offeror has become entitled to acquire the shares under *subsection (3)*, or

(b) save where *paragraph (a)* applies, the dissenting shareholder, at any time within 3 months after the date of the giving of the information notice to him or her, requires the offeror to acquire his or her shares.

(8) Where the consideration for the acquisition pursuant to *subsection (3)* or *(7)* of the share or shares of a person who is resident in the State is paid, wholly or partly, in cash by way of cheque that cheque shall, unless that person agrees otherwise, be one drawn upon an account operated with a clearing bank or such other credit institution as may be prescribed, being an account operated with that bank or other institution at a branch of it established in the State.

458 Additional requirement to be satisfied, in certain cases, for right to buy out to apply

(1) Unless the additional requirement in *subsection (3)* is satisfied, an offeror is not entitled, in the case set out in *subsection (2)*, to serve a call notice or to acquire the shares of a dissenting shareholder under *section 457(3)*; but this section does not affect the right of a dissenting shareholder under *section 457(7)* (right to be bought out).

(2) The case referred to in *subsection (1)* is one in which shares in the offeree company are, at the date of the publication mentioned in *section 457(2)(b)*, already in the beneficial ownership of the offeror to a value greater than 20 per cent of the aggregate value of those shares and the shares affected.

(3) The additional requirement referred to in *subsection (1)* is that the assenting shareholders, besides holding not less than 80 per cent in value of the shares affected, are not less than 50 per cent in number of the holders of those shares.

459 Supplementary provisions in relation to *sections 457* and *458* (including provision for applications to court)

(1) Subject to *subsections (3)* and *(4)*, a call notice and an information notice shall—

(a) be signed by or on behalf of the offeror,

(b) be given to the shareholder—

(i) by delivering it to the shareholder, or

(ii) by leaving it at the address of the shareholder as entered in the register of members of the offeree company; or

(iii) by sending it by post in a prepaid letter—

(I) to the address of the shareholder as entered in the foregoing register, or

(II) to the address, if any, within the State supplied by the shareholder in writing to the offeree company for the giving of notices to him or her;

or

(iv) if the conditions specified in *subsection (2)* are satisfied, by electronic means.

(2) The conditions referred to in *subsection (1)(b)(iv)* are—

(a) the shareholder has consented in writing to the offeror's using electronic means to give notices in relation to him or her,

(b) at the time the electronic means are used to give the notice or notices in relation to the shareholder, no notice in writing has been received by the offeror from the shareholder stating he or she has withdrawn the consent referred to in *paragraph (a)*, and

(c) the particular means used to give the notice or notices electronically are those that the shareholder has consented to.

(3) Where there are several like call notices or information notices given, one or more of which has been signed by or on behalf of the offeror (being a body corporate), the call notices or the information notices not so signed shall, for the purposes of *subsection (1)(a)*, be deemed to be so signed if such unsigned call or information notices state the name of the director who has so signed at least one of those call or, as the case may be, information notices.

(4) Call notices and information notices shall be deemed to be correctly given for the purposes of *subsection (1)(b)*—

(a) to the joint holders of a share, by giving the notice to the joint holder first named in the register of members in respect of the share,

(b) to the persons entitled to a share in consequence of the death or bankruptcy of a shareholder—

(i) by delivering it to the persons claiming to be so entitled, or

(ii) by leaving it at the address supplied to the offeree company by the persons claiming to be so entitled, or

(iii) by sending it by post in a prepaid letter to the persons claiming to be so entitled by name or by the title of representatives of the deceased or the assignee in bankruptcy or by any like description at the address supplied to the offeree company by the persons claiming to be so entitled, or

(iv) where such persons have not notified the company in writing of such death or bankruptcy—

(I) by leaving it at the address of the shareholder as entered in the register of members of the offeree company, or

(II) by sending it by post in a prepaid letter to—

(A) the address of the shareholder as entered in the foregoing register, or

(B) the address, if any, within the State supplied in writing by the shareholder to the offeree company for the giving of notices to him or her,

or

(c) to shareholders with addresses entered in the register of members of the offeree company or who have supplied in writing to the offeree company addresses for the giving of notices to them, being (in either case) addresses which are in jurisdictions outside the State whose laws regulate the communication into those jurisdictions of schemes, contracts or offers to which this Chapter applies, by advertisement published in *Iris Oifigiúil*.

(5) A dissenting shareholder may—

(a) following receipt of a call notice, apply to the court for an order permitting the shareholder to retain his or her shares or varying the terms of the scheme, contract or offer as they apply to that shareholder, or

(b) in a case where the offeror is bound to acquire his or her shares by virtue of *section 457(7)(a)*, apply to the court for an order varying the terms of the scheme, contract or offer as they apply to that dissenting shareholder,

and the court may, on such an application, make such order as it thinks fit (including one providing for a variation such as to require payment to the dissenting shareholder of a cash consideration).

(6) Where an offeror has become bound to acquire the shares of dissenting shareholders, the offeror shall, within 30 days after the date on which the offeror becomes so bound or, if an application to the court by a dissenting shareholder is then pending, as soon as may be after that application is disposed of—

(a) deliver to the offeree company—

(i) a copy of the form of any call notice or information notice given,

(ii) a list of the persons served with any call notice or information notice and the number of shares affected held by them,

(iii) an instrument of transfer of the shares of the dissenting shareholders executed—

(I) on behalf of the dissenting shareholders as transferor by any person appointed by the offeror, and

(II) by the transferee (being either the offeror or a subsidiary of the offeror or a nominee of the offeror or of such a subsidiary),

(b) pay to or vest in the offeree company the amount or other consideration representing the price payable by the offeror for the shares, the beneficial ownership of which by virtue of this Chapter the offeror is entitled to acquire.

(7) Where an offeror has complied with *subsection (6)*, the offeree company shall—

(a) thereupon register as the holder of those shares the person who executed such instrument as the transferee,

(b) pay any sums received by the offeree company under this section into a separate bank account and, for a period of 7 years after the date of such receipt, hold any such sums and any other consideration so received on trust for the several persons entitled to the shares in respect of which those sums or other consideration were respectively received,

(c) after the expiry of the foregoing period of 7 years, transfer any money standing to the credit of that bank account and any shares, other securities or other property vested in it as consideration, together with the names of the persons believed by the company to be entitled thereto to the Minister for Public Expenditure and Reform, who shall indemnify the company in respect of such sums, shares, securities or property and any claim which may be made therefor by the persons entitled thereto,

(d) for as long as shares in the offeror are vested in the offeree company (where shares in the offeror have been issued as all or part of the consideration) not be entitled to exercise any right of voting conferred by those shares except by and in accordance with instructions given by the shareholder in respect of whom those shares were so issued or his or her successor-in-title.

(8) Where the relevant scheme, contract or offer becomes binding on or is approved or accepted by a person in respect of a part only of the shares held by him or her, he or she shall be treated as an assenting shareholder as regards that part of his or her holding and as a dissenting shareholder as regards the remainder of his or her holding.

460 Construction of certain references in Chapter to beneficial ownership, application of Chapter to classes of shares, etc.

(1) In the application of this Chapter to an offeree company, the share capital of which consists of 2 or more classes of shares, references in this Chapter to the shares in the capital of the offeree company shall be read as references to the shares in its capital of a particular class.

(2) For the purposes of this Chapter—

(a) shares in the offeree company in the beneficial ownership of a subsidiary of the offeror shall be deemed to be in the beneficial ownership of the offeror, and

(b) the acquisition of the beneficial ownership of shares in the offeree company by a subsidiary of the offeror shall be deemed to be the acquisition of such beneficial ownership by the offeror.

(3) Where a person agrees to acquire shares in an offeree company, such person shall be deemed, for the purposes of this Chapter, to have acquired the beneficial interest in those shares and it shall be immaterial that any other person has any interest in those shares.

(4) For the purposes of this Chapter, shares shall not be treated as not being in the beneficial ownership of the offeror merely by reason of the fact that—

(a) those shares are or may become subject to a charge in favour of another person, or

(b) those shares are the subject of a revocable or irrevocable undertaking on the part of their holder to accept an offer if such offer is made.

Chapter 3
Mergers

461 Interpretation (*Chapter 3*)

(1) In this Chapter—

"director", in relation to a company which is being wound up, means liquidator;

"merger" means—

(a) a merger by acquisition,
(b) a merger by absorption, or
(c) a merger by formation of a new company,

within, in each case, the meaning of *section 463*;

"merging company" means—

(a) in relation to a merger by acquisition or a merger by absorption, a company that is, in relation to that merger, a transferor company or the successor company, and

(b) in relation to a merger by formation of a new company, a company that is, in relation to that merger, a transferor company;

"share exchange ratio" means the number of shares or other securities in any successor company that the common draft terms of merger provide to be allotted to members of any transferor company for a given number of their shares or other securities in the transferor company;

"successor company", in relation to a merger, means the company to which assets and liabilities are to be, or have been, transferred from the transferor company or companies, by way of that merger;

"transferor company", in relation to a merger, means a company, the assets and liabilities of which are to be, or have been, transferred to the successor company by way of that merger.

(2) References in this Chapter to the acquisition of a company are references to the acquisition of the assets and liabilities of the company by way of a merger under this Chapter.

462 Requirements for Chapter to apply

This Chapter applies only if—

(a) none of the merging companies is a public limited company, and

(b) one, at least, of the merging companies is a private company limited by shares.

463 Mergers to which Chapter applies — definitions and supplementary provision

(1) In this Chapter "merger by acquisition" means an operation in which a company acquires all the assets and liabilities of one or more other companies that is or are dissolved without going into liquidation in exchange for the issue to the members of that company or those companies of shares in the first-mentioned company, with or without any cash payment.

(2) In this Chapter "merger by absorption" means an operation whereby, on being dissolved and without going into liquidation, a company transfers all of its assets and liabilities to a company that is the holder of all the shares representing the capital of the first-mentioned company.

(3) In this Chapter "merger by formation of a new company" means an operation in which one or more companies, on being dissolved without going into liquidation, transfers all its or their assets and liabilities to a company that it or they form — the "other company"— in exchange for the issue to its or their members of shares representing the capital of the other company, with or without any cash payment.

(4) Where a company is being wound up it may become a party to a merger by acquisition, a merger by absorption or a merger by formation of a new company, provided that the distribution of its assets to its shareholders has not begun at the date, under *section 466(5)*, of the common draft terms of merger.

464 Merger may not be put into effect save in accordance with the relevant provisions of this Act

(1) A merger may not be put into effect save under and in accordance with—

(a) the Summary Approval Procedure and the appropriate provisions of this Chapter where such procedure is employed, or

(b) in the absence of the Summary Approval Procedure being employed for that purpose, the relevant provisions of this Chapter,

but this is without prejudice to the alternative of proceeding under *Chapter 1* to achieve the same or a similar result to that which can be achieved by such an operation.

(2) The reference in *subsection (3)* to a merger taking effect under this Chapter or in *section 465* to proceeding under this Chapter includes a reference to a case in which the Summary Approval Procedure and the appropriate provisions of this Chapter are employed for that purpose.

(3) A merger shall not take effect under this Chapter (or any operation to the same or similar effect under *Chapter 1*) in the absence of the approval, authorisation or other consent, if any, that is required by any other enactment or a Community act for the merger to take effect.

465 *Chapters 1* and *3*: mutually exclusive modes of proceeding to achieve merger

All the elements of the operation constituting a merger shall be effected by proceeding either under this Chapter or under *Chapter 1* and not by proceeding partly, as regards some of its elements, under one of those Chapters and partly, as regards other of its elements, under the other of those Chapters.

466 Common draft terms of merger

(1) Where a merger is proposed to be entered into, the directors of the merging companies shall draw up common draft terms of merger and approve those terms in writing.

(2) The common draft terms of merger shall state, at least:

(a) in relation to each of the transferor companies—

(i) its name,

(ii) its registered office, and

(iii) its registered number;

(b) in relation to the successor company—

(i) where the successor company is an existing company, the particulars specified in *subparagraphs (i)* to *(iii)* of *paragraph (a)*, or

(ii) where the successor company is a new company yet to be formed, what are proposed as the particulars specified in *subparagraphs (i)* and *(ii)* of that paragraph;

(c) except in the case of a merger by absorption—

(i) the proposed share exchange ratio and amount of any cash payment,

(ii) the proposed terms relating to allotment of shares or other securities in the successor company, and

(iii) the date from which the holding of shares or other securities in the successor company will entitle the holders to participate in profits and any special conditions affecting that entitlement;

(d) the date from which the transactions of the transferor company or companies are to be treated for accounting purposes as being those of the successor company;

(e) the rights, if any, to be conferred by the successor company on members of the transferor company or companies enjoying special rights or on holders of securities other than shares representing a transferor company's capital, and the measures proposed concerning them;

(f) any special advantages granted to—

(i) any director of a merging company, or

(ii) any person appointed under *section 468*;

(g) the successor company's constitution;

(h) information on the evaluation of the assets and liabilities to be transferred to the successor company; and

(i) the dates of the financial statements of every merging company which were used for the purpose of preparing the common draft terms of merger.

(3) The common draft terms of merger may include such additional terms as are not inconsistent with this Chapter.

(4) The common draft terms of merger shall not provide for any shares in the successor company to be exchanged for shares in a transferor company held either—

(a) by the successor company itself or its nominee on its behalf, or

(b) by the transferor company itself or its nominee on its behalf.

(5) The date of the common draft terms of merger shall, for the purposes of this Chapter, be the date when the common draft terms of merger are approved in writing under *subsection (1)* by the boards of directors of the merging companies; where the dates on which those terms are so approved by each of the boards of directors are not the same, then, for the foregoing purposes, the date shall be the latest date on which those terms are so approved by a board of directors.

467 Directors' explanatory report

(1) Except in the case of a merger by absorption and subject to *subsection (4)*, a separate written report (the "explanatory report") shall be prepared in respect of each of the merging companies by the directors of each such company.

(2) The explanatory report shall at least give particulars of, and explain—

(a) the common draft terms of merger, and

(b) the legal and economic grounds for and implications of the common draft terms of merger with particular reference to the proposed share exchange ratio, organisation and management structures, recent and future commercial activities and the financial interests of the holders of the shares and other securities in the company.

(3) On the explanatory report being prepared in relation to a company, the board of directors of it shall approve the report in writing.

(4) This section shall not apply if the following condition is, or (as appropriate) the following 2 conditions are, satisfied:

(a) other than in a case falling within *paragraph (b)*, all of the holders of shares conferring the right to vote at general meetings of each of the merging companies have agreed that this section shall not apply; or

(b) where a requirement for the taking effect of a vote (whether a vote generally or of the type to which this subsection applies) by holders of shares of any of the merging companies is that a holder of securities of the company has consented thereto—

(i) the agreement mentioned in *paragraph (a)* exists, and

(ii) all of the holders of securities of the company or companies in respect of which the requirement mentioned in this paragraph operates have agreed that this section shall not apply.

468 Expert's report

(1) Subject to *subsection (2)*, there shall, in accordance with this section, be appointed one or more persons to—

(a) examine the common draft terms of merger, and

(b) make a report on those terms to the shareholders of the merging companies.

(2) *Subsection (1)* shall not apply where—

(a) the merger is a merger by absorption,

(b) the merger is a merger in which the successor company (not being a company formed for the purposes of the merger) holds 90 per cent or more (but not all) of the shares carrying the right to vote at a general meeting of the transferor company or at general meetings of each of the transferor companies, or

(c) every member of every merging company agrees that such report is not necessary.

(3) The functions referred to in *subsection (1)(a)* and *(b)* shall be performed either—

(a) in relation to each merging company, by one or more persons appointed for that purpose in relation to the particular company by its directors (and the directors of each company may appoint the same person or persons for that purpose), or

(b) in relation to all the merging companies, by one or more persons appointed for that purpose by the court, on the application to it of all of the merging companies.

(4) The person so appointed, or each person so appointed, is referred to in this Chapter as an "expert" and a reference in this Chapter to a report of an expert or other action (including an opinion) of an expert shall, in a case where there are 2 or more experts, be read as reference to a joint report or joint other action (including an opinion) of or by them.

(5) A person shall not be appointed an expert unless the person is a qualified person.

(6) A person is a qualified person for the purposes of this section if the person—

(a) is a statutory auditor, and

(b) is not—

(i) a person who is or, within the period of 12 months before the date of the common draft terms of merger has been, an officer or employee of any of the merging companies,

(ii) except with the leave of the court, a parent, spouse, civil partner, brother, sister or child of an officer of any of the merging companies (and a reference in this subparagraph to a child of an officer shall be deemed to include a child of the officer's civil partner who is ordinarily resident with the officer and the civil partner), or

(iii) a person who is a partner, or in the employment, of an officer or employee of any of the merging companies.

(7) The report of the expert shall be made available not less than 30 days before the date of the passing of the resolution referred to in *section 202(1)(a)(ii)* or *473*, as the case may be, by each of the merging companies, shall be in writing and shall—

(a) state the method or methods used to arrive at the proposed share exchange ratio,

(b) give the opinion of the expert as to whether the proposed share exchange ratio is fair and reasonable,

(c) give the opinion of the expert as to the adequacy of the method or methods used in the case in question,

(d) indicate the values arrived at using each such method,

(e) give the opinion of the expert as to the relative importance attributed to such methods in arriving at the values decided on, and

(f) specify any special valuation difficulties which have arisen.

(8) The expert may—

(a) require each of the merging companies and their officers to give to the expert such information and explanations (whether oral or in writing), and

(b) make such enquiries,

as the expert thinks necessary for the purposes of making the report.

(9) If a merging company fails to give to the expert any information or explanation in the power, possession or procurement of that company, on a requirement being made of it under *subsection (8)(a)* by the expert, that company and any officer of it who is in default shall be guilty of a category 2 offence.

(10) If a merging company makes a statement (whether orally or in writing), or provides a document, to the expert that conveys or purports to convey any information or explanation the subject of a requirement made of it under *subsection (8)(a)* by the expert and—

(a) that information is false or misleading in a material particular, and

(b) the company knows it to be so false or misleading or is reckless as to whether it is so false or misleading,

the company and any officer of it who is in default shall be guilty of a category 2 offence.

(11) If a person appointed an expert under *subsection (3)(a)* or *(b)* ceases to be a qualified person, that person—

(a) shall immediately cease to hold office, and

(b) shall give notice in writing of the fact of the person's ceasing to be a qualified person to each merging company and (in the case of an appointment under *subsection (3)(b)*) to the court within 14 days after the date of that cessation,

but without prejudice to the validity of any acts done by the person under this Chapter before that cessation.

(12) A person who purports to perform the functions of an expert (in respect of the merger concerned) under this Chapter after ceasing to be a qualified person (in respect of that merger) shall be guilty of a category 2 offence.

469 Merger financial statement

(1) Where—

(a) the latest statutory financial statements of any of the merging companies relate to a financial year ended more than 6 months before the date of the common draft terms of merger, and

(b) the Summary Approval Procedure is not being employed to effect the merger,

then, subject to *subsection (6)*, if that company is availing itself of the exemption from the requirement to hold a general meeting provided by *section 473(6)*, that company shall prepare a merger financial statement in accordance with the provisions of this section.

(2) The merger financial statement shall be drawn up—

(a) in the format of the last annual balance sheet, if any, of the company and in accordance with the provisions of *Part 6*, and

(b) as at a date not earlier than the first day of the third month preceding the date of the common draft terms of merger.

(3) Valuations shown in the last annual balance sheet, if any, shall, subject to the exceptions provided for under *subsection (4)*, only be altered to reflect entries in the accounting records of the company.

(4) Notwithstanding *subsection (3)*, the following shall be taken into account in preparing the merger financial statement—

(a) interim depreciation and provisions, and

(b) material changes in actual value not shown in the accounting records.

(5) The provisions of *Part 6* relating to the statutory auditor's report on the last statutory financial statements of the company concerned shall apply, with any necessary modifications, to the merger financial statement required of the company by *subsection (1)*.

(6) This section shall not apply to a merging company if the following condition is, or (as appropriate) the following 2 conditions are, satisfied:

(a) other than in a case falling within *paragraph (b)*, all of the holders of shares conferring the right to vote at general meetings of the company have agreed that this section shall not apply; or

(b) where a requirement for the taking effect of a vote (whether a vote generally or of the type to which this subsection applies) by holders of shares of the company is that a holder of securities of the company has consented thereto—

(i) the agreement mentioned in *paragraph (a)* exists, and

(ii) all of the holders of securities in respect of which the requirement mentioned in this paragraph operates have agreed that this section shall not apply.

470 Registration and publication of documents

(1) Subject to *subsections (4)(a)* and *(5)*, each of the merging companies shall deliver to the Registrar—

(a) a copy of the common draft terms of merger as approved in writing by the boards of directors of the companies, and

(b) a notice, in the prescribed form, specifying—

(i) its name,

(ii) its registered office,

(iii) its legal form, and

(iv) its registered number.

(2) Notice of delivery of the common draft terms of merger to the Registrar shall be published—

(a) by the Registrar, in the CRO Gazette, and

(b) by each merging company, in one national daily newspaper.

(3) The notice published in accordance with *subsection (2)* shall include:

(a) the date of delivery of the documentation under *subsection (1)*;

(b) the matters specified in *subsection (1)(b)*;

(c) a statement that copies of the common draft terms of merger, the directors' explanatory report, the statutory financial statements referred to in *section 471(1)* and the expert's report (where relevant) are available for inspection by the respective members of each merging company at each company's registered office; and

(d) a statement that a copy of the common draft terms of merger can be obtained from the Registrar.

(4) With regard to *subsections (1)* and *(2)*—

(a) compliance with those subsections is not required in a case where the Summary Approval Procedure is employed to effect the merger, and

(b) subject to that, those subsections shall be complied with by each of the merging companies at least 30 days before the date of the passing of the resolution on the common draft terms of merger by each such company in accordance with *section 473*.

(5) This section shall not apply in relation to a merging company if the company—

(a) publishes, free of charge on its website for a continuous period of at least 2 months, commencing at least 30 days before the date of the general meeting which, by virtue of *section 473*, is to consider the common draft terms of merger and ending at least 30 days after that date, a copy of the common draft terms of merger, approved pursuant to *section 466(1)*, and

(b) causes to be published in the CRO Gazette and once at least in 1 daily newspaper circulating in the district in which the registered office or principal place of business of the company is situate notice of publication on its website of the common draft terms of merger.

(6) Where, in the period referred to in *subsection (5)(a)*, access to the company's website is disrupted for a continuous period of at least 24 hours or for separate periods totalling not less than 72 hours, the period referred to in *subsection (5)(a)* shall be extended for a period corresponding to the period or periods of disruption.

471 Inspection of documents

(1) Subject to *subsection (5)*, each of the merging companies shall, in accordance with *subsection (3)*, make available for inspection free of charge by any member of the company at its registered office during business hours:

(a) the common draft terms of merger;

(b) subject to *subsection (2)*, the statutory financial statements for the preceding 3 financial years of each company (audited, where required by that Part, in accordance with *Part 6*);

(c) except in the case of a merger by absorption or in any other case where such a report is not required to be prepared by that section, the explanatory report relating to each of the merging companies referred to in *section 467*;

(d) if such a report is required to be prepared by that section, the expert's report relating to each of the merging companies referred to in *section 468*; and

(e) each merger financial statement, if any, in relation to one or, as the case may be, more than one of the merging companies, required to be prepared by *section 469*.

(2) For the purposes of *paragraph (b)* of *subsection (1)*—

(a) if any of the merging companies has traded for less than 3 financial years before the date of the common draft terms of merger, then, as respects that company, that paragraph is satisfied by the statutory financial statements for those financial years for which the company has traded (audited, where required by that Part, in accordance with *Part 6*) being made available as mentioned in that subsection by each of the merging companies, or

(b) if, by reason of its recent incorporation, the obligation of any of the foregoing companies to prepare its first financial statements under *Part 6* had not arisen as of the date of the common draft terms of merger, then the reference in that paragraph to the financial statements of that company shall be disregarded.

(3) The provisions of *subsection (1)* shall apply in the case of each of the merging companies for a period of 30 days before the date of the passing of—

(a) where the Summary Approval Procedure is employed to effect the merger, the resolution referred to in *section 202(1)(a)(ii)* by each such company, and

(b) where that procedure is not employed for that purpose, the resolution on the common draft terms of merger by each such company in accordance with *section 473*.

(4) *Section 127(1)* (access to documents during business hours) shall apply in relation to *subsection (1)* as it applies in relation to the relevant provisions of *Part 4*.

(5) *Subsection (1)* shall not apply in relation to a merging company if it publishes free of charge on its website the documents specified in that subsection for a continuous period of at least 2 months, commencing at least 30 days before—

(a) where the Summary Approval Procedure is employed to effect the merger, the date of the resolution referred to in *section 202(1)(a)(ii)* of the company, and

(b) where that procedure is not employed for that purpose, the date of the general meeting of the company which, by virtue of *section 473*, is to consider the common draft terms of merger,

and ending at least 30 days after that date.

(6) Where, in the period referred to in *subsection (5)*, access to the company's website is disrupted for a continuous period of at least 24 hours or for separate periods totalling not less than 72 hours, the period referred to in *subsection (5)* shall be extended for a period corresponding to the period or periods of disruption.

(7) A reference in this section to statutory financial statements shall be deemed to include a reference to a directors' report and a reference to auditing shall, in the case of such a report, be read as a reference to the operation referred to in *section 336(5)*.

472 Non-application of subsequent provisions of Chapter where Summary Approval Procedure employed and effect of resolution referred to in *section 202(1)(a)(ii)*

(1) Without prejudice to *subsections (2)* and *(3)*, the subsequent sections of this Chapter apply unless the Summary Approval Procedure is employed by the merging companies to effect the merger.

(2) Where the Summary Approval Procedure is employed for that purpose then, as provided for in *Chapter 7* of *Part 4*, on the passing of the resolution referred to in *section 202(1)(a)(ii)* by each of the merging companies, the merger shall, in accordance with the common draft terms of merger and any supplemental document, take effect on the date specified in those terms or in that supplemental document and *section 480(3)* shall apply as regards the effects of that merger with any necessary modifications.

(3) Notwithstanding that the Summary Approval Procedure is employed by the merging companies to effect the merger, then, in addition to the application of *section 480(3)* by virtue of *subsection (2)*—

(a) *section 479* (preservation of rights of holders of securities),

(b) *section 483* (civil liability of directors and experts), and

(c) *section 484* (criminal liability for untrue statements in merger documents),

shall apply where that procedure is employed.

(4) In this section "supplemental document" means the document referred to in *section 209(1)*.

473 General meetings of merging companies

(1) In this section a reference to a general meeting, without qualification, is a reference to a general meeting referred to in *subsection (2)*.

(2) Subject to *subsection (6)*, the subsequent steps under this Chapter in relation to the merger shall not be taken unless the common draft terms of merger have been approved by a special resolution passed at a general meeting of each of the merging companies, being a meeting held not earlier than 30 days after the date of the publication by the company of the notice referred to in *section 470(2)(b)* or, as the case may be, the notice in the daily newspapers referred to in *section 470(5)(b)*.

(3) Subject to *section 474(2)*, the notice convening that meeting shall contain a statement of every shareholder's entitlement to obtain on request, free of charge, full or, if so desired, partial copies of the documents referred to in *section 471(1)* (and, accordingly, every shareholder has, subject to the foregoing provision, that entitlement).

(4) The directors of each transferor company shall inform—

(a) the general meeting of that company, and

(b) as soon as practicable, the directors of the successor company,

of any material change in the assets and liabilities of that transfer or company between the date of the common draft terms of merger and the date of that general meeting.

(5) The directors of the successor company shall inform the general meeting of that company of all changes of which they have been informed pursuant to *subsection (4)*.

(6) Approval, by means of a special resolution, of the common draft terms of merger is not required—

(a) in the case of any transferor company in a merger by absorption, or

(b) in the case of the successor company in a merger by acquisition, if the conditions specified in *subsection (7)* have been satisfied.

(7) The conditions referred to in *subsection (6)(b)* are the following:

(a) the notice required to be published under *section 470(2)(b)* was published in accordance with *section 470(2)(b)* in respect of the successor company before the commencement of the period (in this subsection referred to as the "notice period") of 30 days before the date of the passing by the transferor company of the resolution referred to in this section (or, where there is more than one transferor company and the dates on which each of them has passed such a resolution are not the same, the earliest date on which such a resolution was passed by one of them);

(b) the members of the successor company were entitled, during the notice period—

(i) to inspect, at the registered office of the successor company, during ordinary hours of business, copies of the documents referred to in *section 471(1)*, and

(ii) to obtain copies of those documents or any part of them on request;

(c) the right, conferred by *subsection (8)*, to requisition a general meeting has not been exercised during the notice period.

(8) One or more members of the successor company who hold or together hold not less than 5 per cent of the paid-up capital of the company which carries the right to vote at general meetings of the company (excluding any shares held as treasury shares) may require the convening of a general meeting of the company to consider the common draft terms of merger, and *section 178(3)* to *(7)* apply, with any necessary modifications, in relation to the requisition.

474 Electronic means of making certain information available for purposes of *section 473*

(1) For the purposes of *section 473*, but subject to *subsection (2)*, where a shareholder has consented to the use by the company of electronic means for conveying information, the copies of the documents referred to in *section 471(1)* may be provided, by electronic mail, to that shareholder by the company and the notice convening the general meeting referred to in *section 473(2)* shall contain a statement to that effect.

(2) The entitlement referred to in *section 473(3)* shall not apply where, for the period specified in *subsection (3)*, copies of the documents referred to in *section 471(1)* are

available to download and print, free of charge, from the company's website by shareholders of the company.

(3) The period referred to in *subsection (2)* is a continuous period of at least 2 months, commencing at least 30 days before the date of the general meeting which, by virtue of *section 473*, is to consider the common draft terms of merger and ending at least 30 days after that date.

475 Meetings of classes of shareholders

(1) Where the share capital of any of the merging companies is divided into shares of different classes the provisions referred to in *subsection (2)*, with the exclusions specified in *subsection (3)*, shall apply with respect to the variation of the rights attached to any such class that is entailed by the merger.

(2) Those provisions are the provisions of *Chapter 4* of *Part 3* on the variation of the rights attached to any class of shares in a company.

(3) There is excluded the following from the foregoing provisions: *sections 88(9)* and *89*.

476 Purchase of minority shares

(1) Where the special resolution referred to in *section 473* has been passed by each of the merging companies (or such of them as are required by that section to pass such a resolution), a minority shareholder in a transferor company may, not later than 15 days after the relevant date, request the successor company in writing to acquire his or her shares in the transferor company for cash.

(2) Where a request is made by a minority shareholder in accordance with *subsection (1)*, the successor company shall purchase the shares of the minority shareholder at a price determined in accordance with the share exchange ratio set out in the common draft terms of merger and the shares so purchased by the successor company shall be treated as treasury shares within the meaning of *section 106*.

(3) Nothing in this section limits the power of the court to make any order necessary for the protection of the interests of a dissenting minority in a merging company.

(4) In this Chapter—

"minority shareholder", in relation to a transferor company, means—

(a) in a case where the successor company (not being a company formed for the purpose of the merger) holds 90 per cent or more (but not all) of the shares carrying the right to vote at general meetings of the transferor company, any other shareholder in the company, or

(b) in any other case, a shareholder in the company who voted against the special resolution;

"relevant date" means—

(a) in relation to a minority shareholder referred to in *paragraph (a)* of the definition of "minority shareholder" in this subsection, the date of publication of the notice of delivery of the common draft terms of merger under *section 470(2)(b)*, or

(b) in relation to a minority shareholder referred to in *paragraph (b)* of that definition of "minority shareholder", the date on which the resolution of the transferor company was passed.

477 Application for confirmation of merger by court

(1) An application under this section to the court for an order confirming a merger shall be made jointly by all the merging companies.

(2) That application shall be accompanied by a statement of the size of the shareholding of any shareholder who has requested the purchase of his or her shares under *section 476* and of the measures which the successor company proposes to take to comply with the shareholder's request.

478 Protection of creditors

A creditor of any of the merging companies who, at the date of publication of the notice under *section 470(2)(b)* is entitled to any debt or claim against the company, shall be entitled to be heard in relation to the confirmation by the court of the merger under *section 480*.

479 Preservation of rights of holders of securities

(1) Subject to *subsection (2)*, holders of securities, other than shares, in any of the companies being acquired to which special rights are attached shall be given rights in the successor company at least equivalent to those they possessed in the company being acquired.

(2) *Subsection (1)* shall not apply—

(a) where the alteration of the rights in the acquiring company has been approved—

(i) by a majority of the holders of such securities at a meeting held for that purpose, or

(ii) by the holders of those securities individually,

or

(b) where the holders of those securities are entitled under the terms of those securities to have their securities purchased by the successor company.

480 Confirmation order

(1) Where an application is made under *section 477* to the court for an order confirming a merger this section applies.

(2) The court, on being satisfied that—

(a) the requirements of this Chapter have been complied with,

(b) proper provision has been made for—

(i) any minority shareholder in any of the merging companies who has made a request under *section 476*, and

(ii) any creditor of any of the merging companies who objects to the merger in accordance with *section 478*,

(c) the rights of holders of securities other than shares in any of the companies being acquired are safeguarded in accordance with *section 479*, and

(d) where applicable, the relevant provisions of *Chapter 4* of *Part 3* on the variation of the rights attached to any class of shares in any of the merging companies have been complied with,

may make an order confirming the merger with effect from such date as the court appoints (the "effective date").

(3) The order of the court confirming the merger shall, from the effective date, have the following effects:

(a) all the assets and liabilities of the transferor company or companies are transferred to the successor company;

(b) in the case of a merger by acquisition or a merger by formation of a new company, where no request has been made by minority shareholders under *section 476*, all remaining members of the transferor company or companies except the successor company (if it is a member of a transferor company) become members of the successor company;

(c) the transferor company or companies is or are dissolved;

(d) all legal proceedings pending by or against any transferor company shall be continued with the substitution, for the transferor company, of the successor company as a party;

(e) the successor company is obliged to make to the members of the transferor company or companies any cash payment required by the common draft terms of merger;

(f) every contract, agreement or instrument to which a transferor company is a party shall, notwithstanding anything to the contrary contained in that contract, agreement or instrument, be read and have effect as if—

(i) the successor company had been a party thereto instead of the transferor company,

(ii) for any reference (however worded and whether express or implied) to the transferor company there were substituted a reference to the successor company, and

(iii) any reference (however worded and whether express or implied) to the directors, officers, representatives or employees of the transferor company, or any of them—

(I) were, respectively, a reference to the directors, officers, representatives or employees of the successor company or to such director, officer, representative or employee of the successor company as the successor company nominates for that purpose, or

(II) in default of such nomination, were, respectively, a reference to the director, officer, representative or employee of the successor company who corresponds as nearly as may be to the first-mentioned director, officer, representative or employee;

(g) every contract, agreement or instrument to which a transferor company is a party becomes a contract, agreement or instrument between the successor company and the counterparty with the same rights, and subject to the same obligations, liabilities and incidents (including rights of set-off), as would have been applicable thereto if that contract, agreement or instrument had continued in force between the transferor company and the counterparty;

(h) any money due and owing (or payable) by or to a transferor company under or by virtue of any such contract, agreement or instrument as is mentioned in *paragraph (g)* shall become due and owing (or payable) by or to the successor company instead of the transferor company; and

(i) an offer or invitation to treat made to or by a transferor company before the effective date shall be read and have effect, respectively, as an offer or invitation to treat made to or by the successor company.

(4) The following provisions have effect for the purposes of *subsection (3)*—

(a) "instrument" in that subsection includes—

(i) a lease, conveyance, transfer, charge or any other instrument relating to real property (including chattels real); and

(ii) an instrument relating to personalty;

(b) *paragraph (f)(ii)* of that subsection applies in the case of references to the transferor company and its successors and assigns as it applies in the case of references to the transferor company personally;

(c) *paragraph (g)* of that subsection applies in the case of rights, obligations and liabilities mentioned in that paragraph whether they are expressed in the contract, agreement or instrument concerned to be personal to the transferor company or to benefit or bind (as appropriate) the transferor company and its successors and assigns.

(5) Without prejudice to *subsections (6)* and *(7)*, the successor company shall comply with registration requirements and any other special formalities required by law and as directed by the court for the transfer of the assets and liabilities of the transferor company or companies to be effective in relation to other persons.

(6) There shall be entered by the keeper of any register in the State—

(a) upon production of a certified copy of the order under *subsection (2)*; and

(b) without the necessity of there being produced any other document (and, accordingly, any provision requiring such production shall, if it would otherwise apply, not apply),

the name of the successor company in place of any transferor company in respect of the information, act, ownership or other matter in that register and any document kept in that register.

(7) Without prejudice to the generality of *subsection (6)*, the Property Registration Authority, as respects any deed (within the meaning of section 32 of the Registration of Deeds and Title Act 2006) registered by that Authority or produced for registration by

it, shall, upon production of the document referred to in *subsection (6)(a)* but without the necessity of there being produced that which is referred to in *subsection (6)(b)*, enter the name of the successor company in place of any transferor company in respect of such deed.

(8) Without prejudice to the application of *subsection (6)* to any other type of register in the State, each of the following shall be deemed to be a register in the State for the purposes of that subsection:

(a) the register of members of a company referred to in *section 169*;

(b) the register of holders of debentures of a public limited company kept pursuant to *section 1120*;

(c) the register kept by a public limited company for the purposes of *sections 1048* to *1053*;

(d) the register of charges kept by the Registrar pursuant to *section 414*;

(e) the Land Registry;

(f) any register of shipping kept under the Mercantile Marine Act 1955.

(9) If the taking effect of the merger would fall at a time (being the time ascertained by reference to the general law and without regard to this subsection) on the particular date appointed under *subsection (2)* that is a time that would not, in the opinion of the court, be suitable having regard to the need of the parties to co-ordinate various transactions, the court may, in appointing a date under *subsection (2)* with respect to when the merger takes effect, specify a time, different from the foregoing, on that date when the merger takes effect and, where such a time is so specified—

(a) the merger takes effect on that time of the date concerned, and

(b) references in this section to the effective date shall be read accordingly.

481 Certain provisions not to apply where court so orders

Where the court makes an order confirming a merger under this Chapter, the court may, if it sees fit for the purpose of enabling the merger properly to have effect, include in the order provision permitting—

(a) the giving of financial assistance which may otherwise be prohibited under *section 82*,

(b) a reduction in company capital which may otherwise be restricted under *section 84*.

482 Registration and publication of confirmation of merger

(1) If the court makes an order confirming a merger, a certified copy of the order shall forthwith be sent to the Registrar by such officer of the court as the court may direct.

(2) Where the Registrar receives a certified copy of the order of the court in accordance with *subsection (1)*, the Registrar shall—

(a) on, or as soon as practicable after, the effective date — register in the register that certified copy and the dissolution of the transferor company or companies, and

(b) within 14 days after the date of that delivery — cause to be published in the CRO Gazette notice that a copy of an order of the court confirming the merger has been delivered to him or her.

483 Civil liability of directors and experts

(1) Any shareholder of any of the merging companies who has suffered loss or damage by reason of misconduct in the preparation or implementation of the merger by a director of any such company or by the expert, if any, who has made a report under *section 468* shall be entitled to have such loss or damage made good to him or her by—

(a) in the case of misconduct by a person who was a director of that company at the date of the common draft terms of merger — that person,

(b) in the case of misconduct by any expert who made a report under *section 468* in respect of any of the merging companies — that person.

(2) Without prejudice to the generality of *subsection (1)*, any shareholder of any of the merging companies who has suffered loss or damage arising from the inclusion of any untrue statement in any of the following, namely:

(a) the common draft terms of merger;

(b) the explanatory report, if any, referred to in *section 467*;

(c) the expert's report, if any, under *section 468*;

(d) the merger financial statement, if any, prepared under *section 469*,

shall, subject to *subsections (3)* and *(4)*, be entitled to have such loss or damage made good to him or her—

(i) in the case of the document or report referred to in *paragraph (a)*, *(b)* or *(d)* — by every person who was a director of that company at the date of the common draft terms of merger, or

(ii) in the case of the report referred to in *paragraph (c)* — by the person who made that report in relation to that company.

(3) A director of a company shall not be liable under *subsection (2)* if he or she proves—

(a) that the document or report referred to in *subsection (2)(a)*, *(b)* or *(d)*, as the case may be, was issued without his or her knowledge or consent and that, on becoming aware of its issue, he or she forthwith informed the shareholders of that company that it was issued without his or her knowledge or consent, or

(b) that as regards every untrue statement he or she had reasonable grounds, having exercised all reasonable care and skill, for believing and did, up to the time the merger took effect, believe that the statement was true.

(4) A person who makes a report under *section 468* in relation to a company shall not be liable in the case of any untrue statement in the report if he or she proves—

(a) that, on becoming aware of the statement, he or she forthwith informed that company and its shareholders of the untruth, or

(b) that he or she was competent to make the statement and that he or she had reasonable grounds for believing and did up to the time the merger took effect believe that the statement was true.

484 Criminal liability for untrue statements in merger documents

(1) Where any untrue statement has been included in—

(a) the common draft terms of merger,

(b) the explanatory report, if any, referred to in *section 467*, or

(c) the merger financial statement, if any, prepared under *section 469*,

the following:

(i) each of the persons who was a director of any of the merging companies at the date of the common draft terms of merger or, in the case of the foregoing explanatory report or merger financial statement, at the time of the report's or statement's preparation; and

(ii) any person who authorised the issue of the document;

shall be guilty of a category 2 offence.

(2) Where any untrue statement has been included in the expert's report prepared under *section 468*, the expert and any person who authorised the issue of the report shall be guilty of a category 2 offence.

(3) In any proceedings against a person in respect of an offence under *subsection (1)* or *(2)*, it shall be a defence to prove that, having exercised all reasonable care and skill, the defendant had reasonable grounds for believing and did, up to the time of the issue of the document concerned, believe that the statement concerned was true.

Chapter 4
Divisions

485 Interpretation (*Chapter 4*)

(1) In this Chapter—

"director", in relation to a company which is being wound up, means liquidator;

"division" means—

(a) a division by acquisition, or

(b) a division by formation of new companies,

within, in each case, the meaning of *section 487*;

"share exchange ratio" means the number of shares or other securities in any of the successor companies that the draft terms of division provide to be allotted to members of the transferor company for a given number of their shares or other securities in the transferor company;

"successor company" shall be read in accordance with *section 487(1)*;

"transferor company" shall be read in accordance with *section 487(1)*.

(2) A reference in this Chapter to a company involved in a division shall—

(a) in the case of a division by acquisition, be read as a reference to a company that is, in relation to that division, the transferor company or a successor company (other than a new company formed for the purpose of the acquisition concerned),

(b) in the case of a division by formation of new companies, be read as a reference to a company that is, in relation to that division, the transferor company.

(3) References in this Chapter to the acquisition of a company are references to the acquisition of the assets and liabilities of the company by way of a division under this Chapter.

486 Requirements for Chapter to apply

This Chapter applies only if—

(a) none of the companies involved in the division is a public limited company, and

(b) one, at least, of the companies involved in the division is a private company limited by shares.

487 Divisions to which this Chapter applies — definitions and supplementary provisions

(1) In this Chapter "division by acquisition" means an operation consisting of the following:

(a) 2 or more companies (each of which is referred to in this Chapter as a "successor company"), of which one or more but not all may be a new company, acquire between them all the assets and liabilities of another company that is dissolved without going into liquidation (referred to in this Chapter as the "transferor company"); and

(b) such acquisition is—

(i) in exchange for the issue to the shareholders of the transferor company of shares in one or more of the successor companies, with or without any cash payment, and

(ii) with a view to the dissolution of the transferor company.

(2) In this Chapter "division by formation of new companies" means an operation consisting of the same elements as a division by acquisition (as defined in *subsection (1)*) consists of save that the successor companies have been formed for the purposes of the acquisition of the assets and liabilities referred to in that subsection.

(3) Where a company is being wound up it may become a party to a division by acquisition or a division by formation of new companies, provided that the

distribution of its assets to its shareholders has not begun at the date, under *section 490(7)*, of the common draft terms of division.

488 Division may not be put into effect save under and in accordance with this Chapter

(1) A division may not be put into effect save under and in accordance with the provisions of this Chapter but this is without prejudice to the alternative of proceeding under *Chapter 1* to achieve the same or a similar result to that which can be achieved by such an operation.

(2) A division shall not take effect under this Chapter (or any operation to the same or similar effect under *Chapter 1*) in the absence of the approval, authorisation or other consent, if any, that is required by any other enactment or a Community act for the division to take effect.

489 *Chapters 1* and *4*: mutually exclusive modes of proceeding to achieve division

All the elements of the operation constituting a division shall be effected by proceeding either under this Chapter or under *Chapter 1* and not by proceeding partly, as regards some of its elements, under one of those Chapters and partly, as regards other of its elements, under the other of those Chapters.

490 Common draft terms of division

(1) Where a division is proposed to be entered into, the directors of the companies involved in the division shall draw up common draft terms of division and approve those terms in writing.

(2) The common draft terms of division shall state, at least:

(a) in relation to the transferor company—

(i) its name,

(ii) its registered office, and

(iii) its registered number;

(b) in relation to each of the successor companies—

(i) where any of those is an existing company, the particulars specified in *subparagraphs (i)* to *(iii)* of *paragraph (a)*, or

(ii) where any of those is a new company yet to be formed, what are proposed as the particulars specified in *subparagraphs (i)* and *(ii)* of that paragraph;

(c) the proposed share exchange ratio and amount of any cash payment;

(d) the proposed terms relating to allotment of shares or other securities in the successor companies;

(e) the date from which the holding of shares or other securities in the successor companies will entitle the holders to participate in profits and any special conditions affecting that entitlement;

(f) the date from which the transactions of the transferor company are to be treated for accounting purposes as being those of any of the successor companies;

(g) the rights, if any, to be conferred by the successor companies on members of the transferor company enjoying special rights or on holders of securities other than shares representing the transferor company's capital, and the measures proposed concerning them;

(h) any special advantages granted to—

(i) any director of a company involved in a division, or

(ii) any person appointed under *section 492*;

(i) the constitution of each of the successor companies;

(j) information on the evaluation of the assets and liabilities to be transferred to successor companies; and

(k) the dates of the financial statements, if any, of every company involved in the division which were used for the purpose of preparing the common draft terms of division.

(3) The common draft terms of division may include such additional terms as are not inconsistent with this Chapter.

(4) The common draft terms of division shall not provide for any shares in any of the successor companies to be exchanged for shares in the transferor company held either—

(a) by the successor companies themselves or their nominees on their behalf, or

(b) by the transferor company or its nominee on its behalf.

(5) Without prejudice to *subsection (6)*, where—

(a) an asset of the transferor company is not allocated by the common draft terms of division, and

(b) it is not possible, by reference to an interpretation of those terms, to determine the manner in which it is to be allocated,

the asset or the consideration therefor shall be allocated to the successor companies in proportion to the share of the net assets allocated to each of those companies under the common draft terms of division.

(6) If provision is not made by the common draft terms of division for the allocation of an asset acquired by, or otherwise becoming vested in, the transferor company on or after the date of those draft terms then, subject to any provision the court may make in an order under *section 503*, the asset or the consideration therefor shall be allocated in the manner specified in *subsection (5)*.

(7) The date of the common draft terms of division shall, for the purposes of this Chapter, be the date when the common draft terms of division are approved in writing under *subsection (1)* by the boards of directors of the companies involved in the division; where the dates on which those terms are so approved by each of the

boards of directors are not the same, then, for the foregoing purposes, the date shall be the latest date on which those terms are so approved by a board of directors.

491 Directors' explanatory report

(1) Subject to *subsections (4)* and *(5)*, a separate written report (the "explanatory report") shall be prepared in respect of each of the companies involved in the division by the directors of each such company.

(2) The explanatory report shall at least give particulars of, and explain—

(a) the common draft terms of division, and

(b) the legal and economic grounds for and implications of the common draft terms of division with particular reference to the proposed share exchange ratio, organisation and management structures, recent and future commercial activities and the financial interests of holders of the shares and other securities in the company.

(3) On the explanatory report being prepared in relation to a company, the board of directors of it shall approve the report in writing.

(4) This section shall not apply if the following condition is, or (as appropriate) the following 2 conditions are, satisfied:

(a) other than in a case falling within *paragraph (b)*, all of the holders of shares conferring the right to vote at general meetings of each of the companies involved in the division have agreed that this section shall not apply; or

(b) where a requirement for the taking effect of a vote (whether a vote generally or of the type to which this subsection applies) by holders of shares of any of the companies involved in the division is that a holder of securities of the company has consented thereto—

(i) the agreement mentioned in *paragraph (a)* exists, and

(ii) all of the holders of securities of the company or companies in respect of which the requirement mentioned in this paragraph operates have agreed that this section shall not apply.

(5) This section shall not apply in relation to a company involved in a division by formation of new companies where the shares in each of the acquiring companies are allocated to the shareholders of the transferor company in proportion to their rights in the capital of that company.

492 Expert's report

(1) Subject to *subsections (2)* and *(13)*, there shall, in accordance with this section, be appointed one or more persons to—

(a) examine the common draft terms of division, and

(b) make a report on those terms to the shareholders of the companies involved in the division.

(2) *Subsection (1)* shall not apply where—

(a) the division is a division in which one of the successor companies (not being a company formed for the purposes of the division) holds 90 per cent or more (but not all) of the shares carrying the right to vote at a general meeting of the transferor company, or

(b) every member of every company involved in the division agrees that such report is not necessary.

(3) The functions referred to in *subsection (1)(a)* and *(b)* shall be performed either—

(a) in relation to each company involved in the division, by one or more persons appointed for that purpose in relation to the particular company by its directors (and the directors of each company may appoint the same person or persons for that purpose), or

(b) in relation to all the companies involved in the division, by one or more persons appointed for that purpose by the court, on the application to it of all of the companies so involved.

(4) The person so appointed, or each person so appointed, is referred to in this Chapter as an "expert" and a reference in this Chapter to a report of an expert or other action (including an opinion) of an expert shall, in a case where there are 2 or more experts, be read as reference to a joint report or joint other action (including an opinion) of or by them.

(5) A person shall not be appointed an expert unless the person is a qualified person.

(6) A person is a qualified person for the purposes of this section if the person—

(a) is a statutory auditor, and

(b) is not—

(i) a person who is or, within the period of 12 months before the date of the common draft terms of division has been, an officer or employee of any of the companies involved in the division,

(ii) except with the leave of the court, a parent, spouse, civil partner, brother, sister or child of an officer of any of the companies involved in the division (and a reference in this subparagraph to a child of an officer shall be deemed to include a child of the officer's civil partner who is ordinarily resident with the officer and the civil partner), or

(iii) a person who is a partner, or in the employment, of an officer or employee of any of the companies involved in the division.

(7) The report of the expert shall be made available not less than 30 days before the date of the passing of the resolution referred to in *section 496* by each of the companies involved in the division, shall be in writing and shall—

(a) state the method or methods used to arrive at the proposed share exchange ratio,

(b) give the opinion of the expert as to whether the proposed share exchange ratio is fair and reasonable,

(c) give the opinion of the expert as to the adequacy of the method or methods used in the case in question,

(d) indicate the values arrived at using each such method,

(e) give the opinion of the expert as to the relative importance attributed to such methods in arriving at the values decided on, and

(f) specify any special valuation difficulties which have arisen.

(8) The expert may—

(a) require each of the companies involved in the division and their officers to give to the expert such information and explanations (whether oral or in writing), and

(b) make such enquiries,

as the expert thinks necessary for the purposes of making the report.

(9) If a company involved in the division fails to give to the expert any information or explanation in the power, possession or procurement of that company, on a requirement being made of it under *subsection (8)(a)* by the expert, that company and any officer of it who is in default shall be guilty of a category 2 offence.

(10) If a company involved in the division makes a statement (whether orally or in writing), or provides a document, to the expert that conveys or purports to convey any information or explanation the subject of a requirement made of it under *subsection (8)(a)* by the expert and—

(a) that information is false or misleading in a material particular, and

(b) the company knows it to be so false or misleading or is reckless as to whether it is so false or misleading,

the company and any officer of it who is in default shall be guilty of a category 2 offence.

(11) If a person appointed an expert under *subsection (3)(a)* or *(b)* ceases to be a qualified person, that person—

(a) shall immediately cease to hold office, and

(b) shall give notice in writing of the fact of the person's ceasing to be a qualified person to each company involved in the division and (in the case of an appointment under *subsection (3)(b)*) to the court within 14 days after the date of that cessation,

but without prejudice to the validity of any acts done by the person under this Chapter before that cessation.

(12) A person who purports to perform the functions of an expert (in respect of the division concerned) under this Chapter after ceasing to be a qualified person (in respect of that division) shall be guilty of a category 2 offence.

(13) This section shall not apply in relation to a company involved in a division by formation of new companies where the shares in each of the successor companies are allocated to the shareholders of the transferor company in proportion to their rights in the capital of that company.

493 Division financial statement

(1) Subject to *subsection (6)*, where—

(a) the latest statutory financial statements of any of the companies involved in the division relate to a financial year ended more than 6 months before the date of the common draft terms of division, and

(b) that company is availing itself of the exemption from the requirement to hold a general meeting provided by *section 496(6)*,

then that company shall prepare a division financial statement in accordance with the provisions of this section.

(2) The division financial statement shall be drawn up—

(a) in the format of the last annual balance sheet, if any, of the company and in accordance with the provisions of *Part 6*, and

(b) as at a date not earlier than the first day of the third month preceding the date of the common draft terms of division.

(3) Valuations shown in the last annual balance sheet, if any, shall, subject to the exceptions provided for under *subsection (4)*, only be altered to reflect entries in the accounting records of the company.

(4) Notwithstanding *subsection (3)*, the following shall be taken into account in preparing the division financial statement—

(a) interim depreciation and provisions, and

(b) material changes in actual value not shown in the accounting records.

(5) The provisions of *Part 6* relating to the statutory auditor's report on the last statutory financial statements of the company concerned shall apply, with any necessary modifications, to the division financial statement required of the company by *subsection (1)*.

(6) This section shall not apply to a company involved in a division if the following condition is, or (as appropriate) the following 2 conditions are, satisfied:

(a) other than in a case falling within *paragraph (b)*, all of the holders of shares conferring the right to vote at general meetings of the company have agreed that this section shall not apply; or

(b) where a requirement for the taking effect of a vote (whether a vote generally or of the type to which this subsection applies) by holders of shares of the company is that a holder of securities of the company has consented thereto—

(i) the agreement mentioned in *paragraph (a)* exists, and

(ii) all of the holders of securities in respect of which the requirement mentioned in this paragraph operates have agreed that this section shall not apply.

494 Registration and publication of documents

(1) Subject to *subsection (5)*, each of the companies involved in the division shall deliver to the Registrar—

(a) a copy of the common draft terms of division as approved in writing by the board of directors of the companies, and

(b) a notice, in the prescribed form, specifying—

(i) its name,

(ii) its registered office,

(iii) its legal form, and

(iv) its registered number.

(2) Notice of delivery of the common draft terms of division to the Registrar shall be published:

(a) by the Registrar, in the CRO Gazette; and

(b) by each company involved in the division, in one national daily newspaper.

(3) The notice published in accordance with *subsection (2)* shall include:

(a) the date of delivery of the documentation under *subsection (1)*;

(b) the matters specified in *subsection (1)(b)*;

(c) a statement that copies of the common draft terms of division, the directors' explanatory report, the statutory financial statements referred to in *section 495(1)* and the expert's report (where relevant) are available for inspection by the respective members of each company involved in the division at each company's registered office; and

(d) a statement that a copy of the common draft terms of division can be obtained from the Registrar.

(4) *Subsections (1)* and *(2)* shall be complied with by each of the companies involved in the division at least 30 days before the date of the passing of the resolution on the common draft terms of division by each such company in accordance with *section 496*.

(5) This section shall not apply in relation to a company involved in the division if the company—

(a) publishes, free of charge on its website for a continuous period of at least 2 months, commencing at least 30 days before the date of the general meeting which, by virtue of *section 496*, is to consider the common draft terms of division and ending at least 30 days after that date, a copy of the common draft terms of division, as approved pursuant to *section 490(1)*, and

(b) causes to be published in the CRO Gazette and once at least in 2 daily newspapers circulating in the district in which the registered office or principal place of business of the company is situate notice of publication on its website of the common draft terms of division.

(6) Where, in the period referred to in *subsection (5)(a)*, access to the company's website is disrupted for a continuous period of at least 24 hours or for separate periods totalling not less than 72 hours, the period referred to in *subsection (5)(a)* shall be extended for a period corresponding to the period or periods of disruption.

495 Inspection of documents

(1) Subject to *subsection (5)*, each of the companies involved in the division shall, in accordance with *subsection (3)*, make available for inspection free of charge by any member of the company at its registered office during business hours:

(a) the common draft terms of division;

(b) subject to *subsection (2)*, the statutory financial statements for the preceding 3 financial years of each company (audited, where required by that Part, in accordance with *Part 6*);

(c) the explanatory report relating to each of the companies involved in the division referred to in *section 491*;

(d) if such a report is required to be prepared by that section, the expert's report relating to each of the companies involved in the division referred to in *section 492*;

(e) each division financial statement, if any, in relation to one or, as the case may be, more than one of the companies involved in the division, required to be prepared by *section 493*.

(2) For the purposes of *paragraph (b)* of *subsection (1)*—

(a) if any of the companies involved in the division has traded for less than 3 financial years before the date of the common draft terms of division, then, as respects that company, that paragraph is satisfied by the statutory financial statements for those financial years for which the company has traded (audited, where required by that Part, in accordance with *Part 6*) being made available as mentioned in that subsection by each of the companies involved in the division, or

(b) if, by reason of its recent incorporation, the obligation of any of the foregoing companies to prepare its first financial statements under *Part 6* had not arisen as of the date of the common draft terms of division, then the reference in that paragraph to the financial statements of that company shall be disregarded.

(3) The provisions of *subsection (1)* shall apply in the case of each of the companies involved in the division for a period of 30 days before the date of the passing of the resolution on the common draft terms of division by each such company in accordance with *section 496*.

(4) *Section 127(1)* (access to documents during business hours) shall apply in relation to *subsection (1)* as it applies in relation to the relevant provisions of *Part 4*.

(5) *Subsection (1)* shall not apply in relation to a company involved in a division if it publishes free of charge on its website the documents specified in that subsection for a continuous period of at least 2 months, commencing at least 30 days before the date of the general meeting which, by virtue of *section 496*, is to consider the common draft terms of division and ending at least 30 days after that date.

(6) Where, in the period referred to in *subsection (5)*, access to the company's website is disrupted for a continuous period of at least 24 hours or for separate periods totalling

not less than 72 hours, the period referred to in *subsection (5)* shall be extended for a period corresponding to the period or periods of disruption.

(7) A reference in this section to statutory financial statements shall be deemed to include a reference to a directors' report and a reference to auditing shall, in the case of such a report, be read as a reference to the operation referred to in *section 336(5)*.

496 General meetings of companies involved in a division

(1) In this section—

(a) a reference to a general meeting, without qualification, is a reference to a general meeting referred to in *subsection (2)*,

(b) a reference to a successor company does not include a reference to a new such company formed for the purposes of the division.

(2) Subject to *subsection (6)*, the subsequent steps under this Chapter in relation to the division shall not be taken unless the common draft terms of division have been approved by a special resolution passed at a general meeting of each of the companies involved in the division, being a meeting held not earlier than 30 days after the date of the publication by the company of the notice referred to in *section 494(2)(b)*.

(3) Subject to *section 497(2)*, the notice convening that meeting shall contain a statement of every shareholder's entitlement to obtain on request, free of charge, full or, if so desired, partial copies of the documents referred to in *section 495(1)* (and, accordingly, every shareholder has, subject to the foregoing provision, that entitlement).

(4) The directors of the transferor company shall inform—

(a) the general meeting of that company, and

(b) as soon as practicable, the directors of the successor companies,

of any material change in the assets and liabilities of the transferor company between the date of the common draft terms of division and the date of that general meeting.

(5) The directors of the successor companies shall inform the general meetings of those companies of all changes of which they have been informed pursuant to *subsection (4)*.

(6) Approval, by means of a special resolution, of the common draft terms of division is not required in the case of a particular successor company in a division by acquisition if the conditions specified in *subsection (7)* have been satisfied in relation to that successor company (the "particular successor company").

(7) The conditions referred to in *subsection (6)* are the following:

(a) the notice required to be published under *section 494(2)(b)* was published in accordance with *section 494(2)(b)* in respect of the particular successor company before the commencement of the period (in this subsection referred to as the "notice period") of 30 days before the date of the passing by the transferor company of the resolution referred to in this section;

(b) the members of the particular successor company were entitled, during the notice period—

(i) to inspect, at the registered office of that successor company, during ordinary hours of business, copies of the documents referred to in *section 495(1)*, and

(ii) to obtain copies of those documents or any part of them on request;

(c) the right, conferred by *subsection (8)*, to requisition a general meeting has not been exercised during the notice period.

(8) One or more members of the particular successor company who hold or together hold not less than 5 per cent of the paid-up capital of the company which carries the right to vote at general meetings of the company (excluding any shares held as treasury shares) may require the convening of a general meeting of the company to consider the common draft terms of division, and *section 178(3)* to *(7)* apply, with any necessary modifications, in relation to the requisition.

497 Electronic means of making certain information available for purposes of *section 496*

(1) For the purposes of *section 496*, but subject to *subsection (2)*, where a shareholder has consented to the use by the company of electronic means for conveying information, the copies of the documents referred to in *section 495(1)* may be provided, by electronic mail, to that shareholder by the company and the notice convening the general meeting referred to in *section 496(2)* shall contain a statement to that effect.

(2) The entitlement referred to in *section 496(3)* shall not apply where, for the period specified in *subsection (3)*, copies of the documents referred to in *section 495(1)* are available to download and print, free of charge, from the company's website by shareholders of the company.

(3) The period referred to in *subsection (2)* is a continuous period of at least 2 months, commencing at least 30 days before the date of the general meeting which, by virtue of *section 496*, is to consider the common [draft terms of division][a] and ending at least 30 days after that date.

(4) Where, in the period referred to in *subsection (3)*, access to the company's website is disrupted for a continuous period of at least 24 hours or for separate periods totalling not less than 72 hours, the period referred to in *subsection (3)* shall be extended for a period corresponding to the period or periods of disruption.

Amendments

a Words substituted by C(A)A 2017, s 98(e) (previously: "draft terms of merger").

498 Meetings of classes of shareholder

(1) Where the share capital of any of the companies involved in the division is divided into shares of different classes the provisions referred to in *subsection (2)*, with the exclusions specified in *subsection (3)*, shall apply with respect to the variation of the rights attached to any such class that is entailed by the division.

(2) Those provisions are the provisions of *Chapter 4* of *Part 3* on the variation of the rights attached to any class of shares in a company.

(3) There is excluded the following from the foregoing provisions: *sections 88(9)* and *89*.

499 Purchase of minority shares

(1) Where the special resolution referred to in *section 496* has been passed by each of the companies involved in the division (or such of them as are required by that section to pass such a resolution), a minority shareholder in the transferor company may, not later than 15 days after the relevant date, request the successor companies in writing to acquire his or her shares in the transferor company for cash.

(2) Where a request is made by a minority shareholder in accordance with *subsection (1)*, the successor companies (or such one, or more than one of them, as they may agree among themselves) shall purchase the shares of the minority shareholder at a price determined in accordance with the share exchange ratio set out in the common draft terms of division and the shares so purchased by any successor company shall be treated as treasury shares within the meaning of *section 106*.

(3) Nothing in this section limits the power of the court to make any order necessary for the protection of the interests of a dissenting minority in a company involved in a division.

(4) In this Chapter—

"minority shareholder", in relation to the transferor company, means—

(a) in a case where a successor company (not being a company formed for the purpose of the division) holds 90 per cent or more (but not all) of the shares carrying the right to vote at general meetings of the transferor company, any other shareholder in the company, or

(b) in any other case, a shareholder in the company who voted against the special resolution;

"relevant date" means—

(a) in relation to a minority shareholder referred to in *paragraph (a)* of the definition of "minority shareholder" in this subsection, the date of publication of the notice of delivery of the common draft terms of division under *section 494(2)(b)*, or

(b) in relation to a minority shareholder referred to in *paragraph (b)* of that definition of "minority shareholder", the date on which the resolution of the transferor company was passed.

500 Application for confirmation of division by court

(1) An application under this section to the court for an order confirming a division shall be made jointly by all the companies involved in the division.

(2) The application shall be accompanied by a statement of the size of the shareholding of any shareholder who has requested the purchase of his or her shares under *section 499* and of the measures which the successor companies propose to take to comply with the shareholder's request.

501 Protection of creditors and allocation of liabilities

(1) A creditor of any of the companies involved in a division who, at the date of publication of the notice under *section 494(2)(b)* is entitled to any debt or claim against the company, shall be entitled to be heard in relation to the confirmation by the court of the division under *section 503*.

(2) Without prejudice to *subsection (3)*, where—

- (a) a liability of the transferor company is not allocated by the common draft terms of division, and
- (b) it is not possible, by reference to an interpretation of those terms, to determine the manner in which it is to be allocated,

the liability shall become, jointly and severally, the liability of the successor companies.

(3) If provision is not made by the common draft terms of division for the allocation of a liability incurred by, or which otherwise becomes attached to, the transferor company on or after the date of those draft terms then, subject to any provision the court may make in an order under *section 503*, the liability shall become, jointly and severally, the liability of the successor companies.

502 Preservation of rights of holders of securities

(1) Subject to *subsection (2)*, holders of securities, other than shares, in the transferor company to which special rights are attached shall be given rights in one or more of the successor companies at least equivalent to those they possessed in the transferor company.

(2) *Subsection (1)* shall not apply—

- (a) where the alteration of the rights in a successor company has been approved—
  - (i) by a majority of the holders of such securities at a meeting held for that purpose, or
  - (ii) by the holders of those securities individually,

  or
- (b) where the holders of those securities are entitled under the terms of those securities to have their securities purchased by a successor company.

503 Confirmation order

(1) Where an application is made under *section 500* to the court for an order confirming a division this section applies.

(2) The court, on being satisfied that—

(a) the requirements of this Chapter have been complied with,

(b) proper provision has been made for—

(i) any minority shareholder in any of the companies involved in the division who has made a request under *section 499*, and

(ii) any creditor of any of the companies who objects to the division in accordance with *section 501*,

(c) the rights of holders of securities other than shares in the transferor company are safeguarded in accordance with *section 502*, and

(d) where applicable, the relevant provisions of *Chapter 4* of *Part 3* on the variation of the rights attached to any class of shares in any of the companies involved in the division have been complied with,

may make an order confirming the division with effect from such date as the court appoints (the "effective date").

(3) In the case of an asset or liability (including any contractual right or obligation or the obligation to make any cash payment), references in subsequent provisions of this section to the relevant successor company or companies are references to such one or (as the case may be) more than one of the successor companies—

(a) as provided for in respect of the matter concerned by the common draft terms of division, or

(b) in the cases or circumstances specified in whichever of the following is applicable, namely, *section 490(5)* or *(6)* or *section 501(2)* or *(3)*—

(i) subject to where it permits such provision by an order of the court, as provided for in that applicable provision (including, where relevant, as regards the nature of the joint liability), or

(ii) as provided for in an order of the court under this section.

(4) The order of the court confirming the division shall, from the effective date, have the following effects:

(a) each asset and liability of the transferor company is transferred to the relevant successor company or companies;

(b) where no request has been made by minority shareholders under *section 499*, all remaining members of the transferor company except any successor company (if it is a member of the transferor company) become members of the successor companies or any of them as provided by the common draft terms of division;

(c) the transferor company is dissolved;

(d) all legal proceedings pending by or against the transferor company shall be continued with the substitution, for the transferor company, of the successor companies or such of them as the court before which the proceedings have been brought may order;

(e) the relevant successor company or companies is or are obliged to make to the members of the transferor company any cash payment required by the common draft terms of division;

(f) every contract, agreement or instrument to which the transferor company is a party shall, notwithstanding anything to the contrary contained in that contract, agreement or instrument, be read and have effect as if—

(i) the relevant successor company or companies had been a party or parties thereto instead of the transferor company,

(ii) for any reference (however worded and whether express or implied) to the transferor company there were substituted a reference to the relevant successor company or companies, and

(iii) any reference (however worded and whether express or implied) to the directors, officers, representatives or employees of the transferor company, or any of them—

(I) were, respectively, a reference to the directors, officers, representatives or employees of the relevant successor company or companies or to such director, officer, representative or employee of that company or those companies as that company nominates or, as the case may be, those companies nominate for that purpose, or

(II) in default of such nomination, were, respectively, a reference to the director, officer, representative or employee of the relevant successor company or companies who corresponds as nearly as may be to the first-mentioned director, officer, representative or employee;

(g) every contract, agreement or instrument to which the transferor company is a party becomes a contract, agreement or instrument between the relevant successor company or companies and the counterparty with the same rights, and subject to the same obligations, liabilities and incidents (including rights of set-off), as would have been applicable thereto if that contract, agreement or instrument had continued in force between the transferor company and the counterparty;

(h) any money due and owing (or payable) by or to the transferor company under or by virtue of any such contract, agreement or instrument as is mentioned in *paragraph (g)* shall become due and owing (or payable) by or to the relevant successor company or companies instead of the transferor company; and

(i) an offer or invitation to treat made to or by the transferor company before the effective date shall be read and have effect, respectively, as an offer or invitation to treat made to or by the relevant successor company or companies.

(5) The following provisions have effect for the purposes of *subsection (4)*—

(a) "instrument" in that subsection includes—

(i) a lease, conveyance, transfer or charge or any other instrument relating to real property (including chattels real); and

(ii) an instrument relating to personalty;

(b) *paragraph (f)(ii)* of that subsection applies in the case of references to the transferor company and its successors and assigns as it applies in the case of references to the transferor company personally;

(c) *paragraph (g)* of that subsection applies in the case of rights, obligations and liabilities mentioned in that paragraph whether they are expressed in the contract, agreement or instrument concerned to be personal to the transferor company or to benefit or bind (as appropriate) the transferor company and its successors and assigns.

(6) Without prejudice to *subsections (7)* and *(8)*, such of the successor companies as is or are appropriate shall comply with registration requirements and any other special formalities required by law and as directed by the court for the transfer of the assets and liabilities of the transferor company to be effective in relation to other persons.

(7) There shall be entered by the keeper of any register in the State—

(a) upon production of a certified copy of the order under *subsection (2)*; and

(b) without the necessity of there being produced any other document (and, accordingly, any provision requiring such production shall, if it would otherwise apply, not apply),

the name of the relevant successor company (or, as appropriate, the names of the relevant successor companies) in place of the transferor company in respect of the information, act, ownership or other matter in that register and any document kept in that register.

(8) Without prejudice to the generality of *subsection (7)*, the Property Registration Authority, as respects any deed (within the meaning of section 32 of the Registration of Deeds and Title Act 2006) registered by that Authority or produced for registration by it, shall, upon production of the document referred to in *subsection (7)(a)* but without the necessity of there being produced that which is referred to in *subsection (7)(b)*, enter the name of the relevant successor company (or, as appropriate, the names of the relevant successor companies) in place of the transferor company in respect of such deed.

(9) Without prejudice to the application of *subsection (7)* to any other type of register in the State, each of the following shall be deemed to be a register in the State for the purposes of that subsection:

(a) the register of members of a company referred to in *section 169*;

(b) the register of holders of debentures of a public limited company kept pursuant to *section 1120*;

(c) the register kept by a public limited company for the purposes of *sections 1048* to *1053*;

(d) the register of charges kept by the Registrar pursuant to *section 414*;

(e) the Land Registry;

(f) any register of shipping kept under the Mercantile Marine Act 1955.

(10) If the taking effect of the division would fall at a time (being the time ascertained by reference to the general law and without regard to this subsection) on the particular date appointed under *subsection (2)* that is a time that would not, in the opinion of the court, be suitable having regard to the need of the parties to co-ordinate various transactions, the court may, in appointing a date under *subsection (2)* with respect to when the division takes effect, specify a time, different from the foregoing, on that date when the division takes effect and, where such a time is so specified—

(a) the division takes effect on that time of the date concerned, and

(b) references in this section to the effective date shall be read accordingly.

504 Certain provisions not to apply where court so orders

Where the court makes an order confirming a division under this Chapter, the court may, if it sees fit for the purpose of enabling the division properly to have effect, include in the order provision permitting—

(a) the giving of financial assistance which may otherwise be prohibited under *section 82*,

(b) a reduction in company capital which may otherwise be restricted under *section 84*.

505 Registration and publication of confirmation of division

(1) If the court makes an order confirming a division, a certified copy of the order shall forthwith be sent to the Registrar by such officer of the court as the court may direct.

(2) Where the Registrar receives a certified copy of the order of the court in accordance with *subsection (1)*, the Registrar shall—

(a) on, or as soon as practicable after, the effective date — register that certified copy and the dissolution of the transferor company, and

(b) within 14 days after the date of that delivery — cause to be published in the CRO Gazette notice that a copy of an order of the court confirming the division has been delivered to him or her.

506 Civil liability of directors and experts

(1) Any shareholder of any of the companies involved in the division who has suffered loss or damage by reason of misconduct in the preparation or implementation of the division by a director of any such company or by the expert, if any, who has made a report under *section 492* shall be entitled to have such loss or damage made good to him or her by—

(a) in the case of misconduct by a person who was a director of that company at the date of the common draft terms of division — that person,

(b) in the case of misconduct by any expert who made a report under *section 492* in respect of any of the companies involved in the division — that person.

(2) Without prejudice to the generality of *subsection (1)*, any shareholder of any of the companies involved in the division who has suffered loss or damage arising from the inclusion of any untrue statement in any of the following, namely:

(a) the common draft terms of division;

(b) the explanatory report referred to in *section 491*;

(c) the expert's report, if any, under *section 492*;

(d) the division financial statement, if any, prepared under *section 493*,

shall, subject to *subsections (3)* and *(4)*, be entitled to have such loss or damage made good to him or her—

(i) in the case of the document or report referred to in *paragraph (a)*, *(b)* or *(d)* — by every person who was a director of that company at the date of the common draft terms of division, or

(ii) in the case of the report referred to in *paragraph (c)* — by the person who made that report in relation to that company.

(3) A director of a company shall not be liable under *subsection (2)* if he or she proves—

(a) that the document or report referred to in *subsection (2)(a)*, *(b)* or *(d)*, as the case may be, was issued without his or her knowledge or consent and that, on becoming aware of its issue, he or she forthwith informed the shareholders of that company that it was issued without his or her knowledge or consent, or

(b) that as regards every untrue statement he or she had reasonable grounds, having exercised all reasonable care and skill, for believing and did, up to the time the division took effect, believe that the statement was true.

(4) A person who makes a report under *section 492* in relation to a company shall not be liable in the case of any untrue statement in the report if he or she proves—

(a) that, on becoming aware of the statement, he or she forthwith informed that company and its shareholders of the untruth, or

(b) that he or she was competent to make the statement and that he or she had reasonable grounds for believing and did up to the time the division took effect believe that the statement was true.

507 Criminal liability for untrue statements in division documents

(1) Where any untrue statement has been included in—

(a) the common draft terms of division,

(b) the explanatory report referred to in *section 491*, or

(c) the division financial statement, if any, prepared under *section 493*, the following:

(i) each of the persons who was a director of any of the companies involved in the division at the date of the common draft terms of division or, in the case of the foregoing explanatory report or division financial statement, at the time of the report's or statement's preparation; and

(ii) any person who authorised the issue of the document,

shall be guilty of a category 2 offence.

(2) Where any untrue statement has been included in the expert's report prepared under *section 492*, the expert and any person who authorised the issue of the report shall be guilty of a category 2 offence.

(3) In any proceedings against a person in respect of an offence under *subsection (1)* or *(2)*, it shall be a defence to prove that, having exercised all reasonable care and skill, the defendant had reasonable grounds for believing and did, up to the time of the issue of the document concerned, believe that the statement concerned was true.

PART 10
EXAMINERSHIPS

Chapter 1
Interpretation

508 Interpretation (*Part 10*)

(1) In this Part—

"court" shall be read in accordance with *section 509(7)*;

"director" includes a shadow director;

"examiner" means an examiner appointed under *section 509*;

"independent expert" shall be read in accordance with *section 511(2)*;

"insurer" has the same meaning as it has in the Insurance Act 1989;

"interested party", in relation to a company to which *section 509* relates, means—

(a) a creditor of the company, or

(b) a member of the company;

"petition" means a petition referred to in *section 509(1)* (and, for the purposes of the Circuit Court's jurisdiction under this Part, "petition" includes any originating process specified by rules of court for those purposes) and references to the presentation of a petition are references to its presentation under *section 509(1)*.

(2) This Part is subject to the Insolvency Regulation.

(3) The provisions of *Chapter 15* of *Part 11* apply to proceedings under this Part with the substitution of references to "examiner" for references to "liquidator" and any other necessary modifications.

Chapter 2
Appointment of examiner

509 Power of court to appoint examiner

(1) Subject to *subsection (2)*, where it appears to the court that—

(a) a company is, or is likely to be, unable to pay its debts,

(b) no resolution subsists for the winding up of the company, and

(c) no order has been made for the winding up of the company,

the court may, on application by petition presented, appoint an examiner to the company for the purpose of examining the state of the company's affairs and performing such functions in relation to the company as may be conferred by or under this Part.

(2) The court shall not make an order under this section unless it is satisfied that there is a reasonable prospect of the survival of the company and the whole or any part of its undertaking as a going concern.

(3) For the purposes of this section, a company is unable to pay its debts if—

(a) it is unable to pay its debts as they fall due,

(b) the value of its assets is less than the amount of its liabilities, taking into account its contingent and prospective liabilities, or

(c) the circumstances set out in *section 570(a)*, *(b)* or *(c)* are applicable to the company.

(4) In deciding whether to make an order under this section, the court may also have regard to whether the company has sought from its creditors significant extensions of time for the payment of its debts, from which it could reasonably be inferred that the company was likely to be unable to pay its debts.

(5) The court shall not make an order under this section unless—

(a) the court is satisfied that the company has no obligations in relation to a bank asset that has been transferred to the National Asset Management Agency or a NAMA group entity, or

(b) if the company has any such obligation—

(i) a copy of the petition has been served on that Agency, and

(ii) the court has heard that Agency in relation to the making of the order.

(6) In *subsection (5)* "bank asset" and "NAMA group entity" have the same respective meanings as in the National Asset Management Agency Act 2009.

(7) In this section "court" means—

(a) in the case of any company (including one referred to in *paragraph (b)*), the High Court; or

(b) in the case of a company that, in respect of the latest financial year of the company that has ended prior to the date of the presentation of the petition, fell to be treated as a small company by virtue of [*sections 280A* or *280B*][a], the Circuit Court,

and—

(i) subject to *subsection (9)*, all subsequent references to the court in this Part shall, as respects the powers and jurisdiction of the court with respect to an examinership on foot of an appointment made under this section by the Circuit Court, be read accordingly; and

(ii) the jurisdiction under *section 512(7)* to appoint an examiner on an interim basis, and the jurisdiction to do the things referred to in *section 513*, are likewise available to the Circuit Court in the case of a company specified in *paragraph (b)*.

(8) For the purpose of *paragraph (b)* of *subsection (7)*, if the latest financial year of the company concerned ended within 3 months prior to the date of the presentation of the petition, the reference in that paragraph to the latest financial year of the company shall be read as a reference to the financial year of the company that preceded its latest financial year (but that reference shall only be so read if that preceding financial

year ended no more than 15 months prior to the date of the presentation of the petition).

(9) *Subsection (7)* does not confer on the Circuit Court any jurisdiction that is provided under this Part to hear a petition for the winding up of, or to wind up, a company.

(10) The jurisdiction of the Circuit Court under this Part in relation to a company shall be exercisable by the judge of the Circuit Court—

(a) for the circuit in which the registered office of the company is situated at the time of the presentation of the petition or in which it has, at that time, its principal place of business, or

(b) if, at that time, there is no registered office of the company and its principal place of business is outside the State, for the Dublin Circuit.

(11) On the making of an order appointing an examiner to a company, the proper officer of the Central Office of the High Court or, as the case may be, the county registrar shall, on request and payment of the prescribed fee and subject to any conditions that may be specified in rules of court, give to the examiner concerned—

(a) a copy of the order, certified by the officer to be a true copy, and

(b) any other prescribed particulars.

Amendments

a Words substituted by C(A)A 2017, s 88(b)(i) (previously: "*section 350*").

---

510 Petition for court

(1) Subject to *subsections (2)* and *(3)*, a petition in relation to a company may be presented by all or any of the following (separately or together):

(a) the company;

(b) the directors of the company;

(c) a creditor, or a contingent or prospective creditor (including an employee), of the company;

(d) a member or members of the company holding at the date of the presentation of the petition not less than one tenth of such of the paid-up share capital of the company as carries at that date the right of voting at general meetings of the company.

(2) Where the company referred to in *section 509* is the holding company of an insurer, a petition may be presented only by the Central Bank, and *subsection (1)* shall not apply to the company.

(3) Where the company referred to in *section 509* is—

(a) the holding company of a credit institution, or

(b) a company which one or more trustee savings banks have been reorganised into pursuant to an order under section 57 of the Trustee Savings Banks Act 1989,

a petition may be presented only by the Central Bank, and *subsection (1)* shall not apply to the company.

(4) Where the company referred to in *section 509* is a *Schedule 5* company, the following provisions shall apply:

(a) a petition may be presented by—

(i) any of the persons referred to in *paragraph (a)*, *(b)*, *(c)* or *(d)* of *subsection (1)* (including by one or more of such persons acting together);

(ii) the Central Bank; or

(iii) one or more of such persons and the Central Bank acting together;

(b) if the Central Bank does not present a petition—

(i) the petitioner shall, before he or she presents the petition at the office of the court, cause to be received by the Central Bank a notice in writing of his or her intention to present the petition, and shall serve a copy of the petition on the Central Bank as soon as may be after the presentation of it at that office;

(ii) the Central Bank shall be entitled to appear and be heard at any hearing relating to the petition.

(5) In this section "*Schedule 5* company" means a company falling within any provision (in so far as applicable to a private company limited by shares) of *Schedule 5*.

511 Independent expert's report

(1) In addition to the matters specified in *section 512*, a petition shall be accompanied by a report in relation to the company prepared by a person who is either the statutory auditor of the company or a person who is qualified to be appointed as an examiner of the company.

(2) The person who undertakes the preparation of that report is referred to in this Part as the "independent expert".

(3) The report of the independent expert shall comprise the following:

(a) the names and addresses of the officers of the company;

(b) the names of any other bodies corporate of which the directors of the company are also directors;

(c) a statement as to the affairs of the company, showing in so far as it is reasonably possible to do so, particulars of the company's assets and liabilities (including contingent and prospective liabilities) as at the latest practicable date, the names and addresses of its creditors, the securities held by each of them and the dates when the securities were given to each of them;

(d) his or her opinion as to whether any deficiency between the assets and liabilities of the company has been satisfactorily accounted for or, if not, as to whether there is evidence of a substantial disappearance of property that is not adequately accounted for;

(e) his or her opinion as to whether the company, and the whole or any part of its undertaking, would have a reasonable prospect of survival as a going concern and a statement of the conditions which he or she considers are essential to ensure such survival, whether as regards the internal management and controls of the company or otherwise;

(f) his or her opinion as to whether the formulation, acceptance and confirmation of proposals for a compromise or scheme of arrangement would offer a reasonable prospect of the survival of the company, and the whole or any part of its undertaking, as a going concern;

(g) his or her opinion as to whether an attempt to continue the whole or any part of the undertaking would be likely to be more advantageous to the members as a whole and the creditors as a whole than a winding-up of the company;

(h) recommendations as to the course he or she thinks should be taken in relation to the company including, if warranted, draft proposals for a compromise or scheme of arrangement;

(i) his or her opinion as to whether the facts disclosed would warrant further inquiries with a view to proceedings under *sections 610* and *611* or *section 722*;

(j) details of the extent of the funding required to enable the company to continue trading during the period of protection and the sources of that funding;

(k) his or her recommendations as to which liabilities incurred before the presentation of the petition should be paid;

(l) his or her opinion as to whether the work of the examiner would be assisted by a direction of the court in relation to the role or membership of any creditor's committee referred to in *section 538*; and

(m) such other matters as he or she thinks relevant.

512 Supplemental provisions in relation to *sections 510* and *511* — other matters to be mentioned in petition, hearing of petition, etc.

(1) A petition shall nominate a person to be appointed as examiner.

(2) A petition shall be accompanied—

(a) by a consent signed by the person nominated to be examiner, and

(b) if proposals for a compromise or scheme of arrangement in relation to the company's affairs have been prepared for submission to interested parties for their approval, by a copy of the proposals.

(3) The court shall not give a hearing to a petition presented by a contingent or prospective creditor until such security for costs has been given as the court thinks reasonable.

(4) The court shall not give a hearing to a petition if a receiver stands appointed to the whole or any part of the property or undertaking of the company the subject of the petition and such receiver has stood so appointed for a continuous period of at least 3 days prior to the date of the presentation of the petition.

(5) On hearing a petition the court may dismiss it, or adjourn the hearing conditionally or unconditionally, or make any interim order, or any other order it thinks fit.

(6) Without prejudice to the generality of *subsection (5)*, an interim order under that subsection may restrict the exercise of any powers of the directors or of the company (whether by reference to the consent of the court or otherwise).

(7) Without limiting *subsection (5)* or *(6)*, on or after the presentation of a petition, the court may, on application to it, appoint an examiner to the company on an interim basis.

513 Cases in which independent expert's report not available at required time: powers of court

(1) If a petition is presented and the court is satisfied—

(a) that, by reason of exceptional circumstances outside the control of the petitioner, the report of the independent expert is not available in time to accompany the petition, and

(b) that the petitioner could not reasonably have anticipated the circumstances referred to in *paragraph (a)*,

and, accordingly, the court is unable to consider the making of an order under *section 509*, the court may make an order under this section placing the company concerned under the protection of the court for such period as the court thinks appropriate in order to allow for the submission of the independent expert's report.

(2) That period shall be a period that expires not later than the 10th day after the date of the making of the order concerned or, if the 10th day after that date would fall on a Saturday, Sunday or public holiday, the first following day that is not a Saturday, Sunday or public holiday.

(3) For the avoidance of doubt, the fact that a receiver stands appointed to the whole or any part of the property or undertaking of the company at the time of the presentation of a petition in relation to the company shall not, in itself, constitute, for the purposes of *subsection (1)*, exceptional circumstances outside the control of the petitioner.

(4) If the petition concerned has been presented by any of the persons referred to in *section 510(1)(c)* or *(d)* and an order under *subsection (1)* is made in relation to the company concerned, the directors of the company shall co-operate in the preparation of the report of the independent expert, particularly in relation to the matters specified in *section 511(3)(a)* to *(c)*.

(5) If the directors of the company concerned fail to comply with *subsection (4)*, the petitioner concerned or the independent expert may apply to the court for an order requiring the directors to do specified things by way of compliance with *subsection (4)* and the court may, as it thinks fit, grant such an order accordingly.

(6) If the report of the independent expert is submitted to the court before the expiry of the period of protection specified in an order under *subsection (1)*, the court shall proceed to consider the petition together with the report as if they were presented in accordance with *section 509.*

(7) If the report of the independent expert is not submitted to the court before the expiry of the period of protection specified in an order under *subsection (1)*, then, at the expiry of that period, the company concerned shall cease to be under the protection of the court, but without prejudice to the presentation of a further petition.

514 Certain liabilities may not be certified under *section 529(2)*

Any liabilities incurred by the company concerned during the period of protection specified in an order under *section 513(1)* may not be the subject of a certificate under *section 529(2).*

515 Creditors to be heard

(1) The court shall not make an order dismissing a petition presented to it or an order appointing an examiner to a company without having afforded each creditor of the company who has indicated to the court his or her desire to be heard in the matter an opportunity to be so heard.

(2) Nothing in this section shall affect the power of the court under *section 512(5)* or *(7)* to make an interim order, including the appointment of an examiner on an interim basis, in the matter.

516 Availability of independent expert's report

(1) The independent expert shall supply a copy of the report prepared by him or her under *section 511* to the company concerned or any interested party on written application being made to the independent expert in that behalf.

(2) If the court, on application to it in that behalf, directs that that supply may be the subject of such omission, there may be omitted from any copy of the report supplied to the company or an interested party such parts of it as are specified in the direction of the court.

(3) The court may, in particular, on such an application, direct that there may be omitted from such a supply of a copy of the report any information the inclusion of which in such a copy would be likely to prejudice the survival of the company or the whole or any part of its undertaking as a going concern.

(4) If—

- (a) the company concerned is a company referred to in *section 509(4)*, and
- (b) the Central Bank does not propose to present, or has not presented, (whether alone or acting together with other persons) a petition in relation to the company,

the independent expert shall, as soon as may be after it is prepared, supply a copy of the report prepared by him or her under *section 511* to the Central Bank and *subsections (2)* and *(3)* shall not apply to such a copy.

517 Related companies

(1) Subject to *subsections (2), (3), (6)* and *(8)*, where the court appoints an examiner to a company, it may, at the same or any time thereafter, make an order—

(a) appointing the examiner to be examiner for the purposes of this Act to a related company; or

(b) conferring on the examiner, in relation to such company, all or any of the functions conferred on him or her in relation to the first-mentioned company.

(2) In deciding whether to make an order under *subsection (1)*, the court shall have regard to whether the making of the order would be likely to facilitate the survival of the company, or of the related company, or both, and the whole or any part of its or their undertaking, as a going concern.

(3) However, the court shall not, in any case, make such an order unless it is satisfied that there is a reasonable prospect of the survival of the related company, and the whole or any part of its undertaking, as a going concern.

(4) A related company to which an examiner is appointed by an order under *subsection (1)* shall be deemed to be under the protection of the court for the period beginning on the date of the making of the order and continuing for the period during which the company to which it is related is under such protection.

(5) Where an examiner stands appointed to 2 or more related companies, he or she shall have the same functions in relation to each company, taken separately, unless the court otherwise directs.

(6) The court shall not make an order under this section unless—

(a) the court is satisfied that the related company has no obligations in relation to a bank asset that has been transferred to the National Asset Management Agency or a NAMA group entity, or

(b) if the related company has any such obligation—

(i) a copy of the application for the order has been served on that Agency, and

(ii) the court has heard that Agency in relation to the making of the order.

(7) In *subsection (6)* "bank asset" and "NAMA group entity" have the same respective meanings as in the National Asset Management Agency Act 2009.

(8) The Circuit Court shall only have jurisdiction to make an order referred to in *subsection (1)(a)* or *(b)* if the related company is a company that, in respect of the latest financial year of it that has ended prior to the relevant time referred to in *subsection (1)*, fell to be treated as a small company by virtue of [*sections 280A* or *280B*][a].

(9) For the purposes of *subsection (8)*, if the latest financial year of the company concerned ended within 3 months prior to the relevant time referred to in *subsection (1)*, the reference in *subsection (8)* to the latest financial year of the company shall be read as a reference to the financial year of the company that preceded its latest financial year (but that reference shall only be so read if that preceding financial year ended no more than 15 months prior to the relevant time referred to in *subsection (1)*).

Amendments

a Words substituted by C(A)A 2017, s 88(b)(ii) (previously: "*section 350*").

518 Duty to act in utmost good faith

The court may decline to hear a petition presented to it or, as the case may be, may decline to continue hearing such a petition if it appears to the court that, in the preparation or presentation of the petition or in the preparation of the report of the independent expert, the petitioner or independent expert—

- (a) has failed to disclose any information available to him or her which is material to the exercise by the court of its powers under this Part; or
- (b) has in any other way failed to exercise utmost good faith.

519 Qualification of examiners

(1) A person shall not be qualified to be appointed or act as an examiner of a company unless he or she would be qualified to act as its liquidator (but disregarding for this purpose the requirements of *section 634* concerning professional indemnity cover).

(2) A person who acts as examiner of a company when he or she is not qualified to do so under *subsection (1)* shall be guilty of a category 2 offence.

520 Effect of petition to appoint examiner on creditors and others

(1) Subject to *section 513*, a company is, for the purposes of this Part, under the protection of the court during the following period.

(2) That period is one—

- (a) beginning with the date of the presentation of a petition in relation to the company, and
- (b) (subject to *section 534(3)* and *(4)*) ending on—
  - (i) the expiry of 70 days after that date, or
  - (ii) the withdrawal of, or refusal by the court of, the petition,

whichever first happens.

(3) The reference in *subsection (2)* to the refusal by the court of the petition shall be deemed to include a reference to its deciding to decline to hear, or to continue to hear, the petition under *section 518*.

(4) For so long as a company is under the protection of the court in a case under this Part, the following provisions shall have effect:

- (a) no proceedings for the winding up of the company may be commenced or resolution for winding up passed in relation to the company and any resolution so passed shall have no effect;

(b) no receiver over any part of the property or undertaking of the company shall be appointed, or, if so appointed before the presentation of a petition shall, subject to *section 522*, be able to act;

(c) no attachment, sequestration, distress or execution shall be put into force against the property or effects of the company, except with the consent of the examiner;

(d) where any claim against the company is secured by a mortgage, charge, lien or other encumbrance or a pledge of, on or affecting the whole or any part of the property, effects or income of the company, no action may be taken to realise the whole or any part of that security, except with the consent of the examiner;

(e) no steps may be taken to repossess goods in the company's possession under any hire-purchase agreement (within the meaning of *section 530*), except with the consent of the examiner;

(f) where, under any enactment, rule of law or otherwise, any person other than the company is liable to pay all or any part of the debts of the company—

(i) no attachment, sequestration, distress or execution shall be put into force against the property or effects of such person in respect of the debts of the company; and

(ii) no proceedings of any sort may be commenced against such person in respect of the debts of the company;

(g) no order for relief shall be made under *section 212* against the company in respect of complaints as to the conduct of the affairs of the company or the exercise of the powers of the directors prior to the presentation of the petition.

(5) Subject to *subsection (4)*, no other proceedings in relation to the company may be commenced except by leave of the court and subject to such terms as the court may impose and the court may, on the application of the examiner, make such order as it thinks proper in relation to any existing proceedings including an order to stay such proceedings.

(6) Complaints concerning the conduct of the affairs of the company while it is under the protection of the court shall not constitute a basis for the making of an order for relief under *section 212*.

521 Restriction on payment of pre-petition debts

(1) No payment may be made by a company, during the period it is under the protection of the court, by way of satisfaction or discharge of the whole or a part of a liability incurred by the company before the date of the presentation of the petition in relation to it unless—

(a) the report of the independent expert contains a recommendation that the whole or, as the case may be, the part of that liability should be discharged or satisfied, or

(b) the court authorises such payment under *subsection (2)*.

(2) The court may, on application being made to it in that behalf by the examiner or any interested party, authorise the discharge or satisfaction, in whole or in part, by the company concerned of a liability referred to in *subsection (1)* if it is satisfied that a failure to discharge or satisfy, in whole or in part, that liability would considerably reduce the prospects of the company or the whole or any part of its undertaking surviving as a going concern.

522 Effect on receiver or provisional liquidator of order appointing examiner

(1) Where, at the date of the presentation of a petition in relation to a company, a receiver stands appointed to the whole or any part of the property or undertaking of that company the court may make such order as it thinks fit, including an order as to any or all of the following matters:

(a) that the receiver shall cease to act as such from a date specified by the court;

(b) that the receiver shall, from a date specified by the court, act as such only in respect of certain assets specified by the court;

(c) directing the receiver to deliver all books, papers and other records, which relate to the property or undertaking of the company (or any part of it) and are in his or her possession or control, to the examiner within a period to be specified by the court;

(d) directing the receiver to give the examiner full particulars of all his or her dealings with the property or undertaking of the company.

(2) Where, at the date of the presentation of a petition in relation to a company, a provisional liquidator stands appointed to that company, the court may make such order as it thinks fit, including an order as to any or all of the following matters:

(a) that the provisional liquidator be appointed as examiner of the company;

(b) appointing some other person as examiner of the company;

(c) that the provisional liquidator shall cease to act as such from a date specified by the court;

(d) directing the provisional liquidator to deliver all books, papers and other records, which relate to the property or undertaking of the company (or any part of it) and are in his or her possession or control, to the examiner within a period to be specified by the court;

(e) directing the provisional liquidator to give the examiner full particulars of all his or her dealings with the property or undertaking of the company.

(3) The court shall not make an order under *subsection (1)(a)* or *(b)* or *subsection (2)(c)* unless the court is satisfied that there is a reasonable prospect of the survival of the company, and the whole or any part of its undertaking, as a going concern; this subsection is in addition to *sections 509(2)* and *517(3)*.

(4) Where the court makes an order under *subsection (1)* or *(2)*, it may, for the purpose of giving full effect to the order, include such conditions in the order and make such ancillary or other orders as it deems fit.

(5) Where a petition is presented in respect of a company at a date subsequent to the presentation of a petition for the winding up of that company, but before a provisional liquidator has been appointed or an order made for its winding up, both petitions shall be heard together.

523 Disapplication of *section 440* to receivers in certain circumstances

(1) This section applies where either—

(a) an examiner has been appointed to a company, or

(b) an examiner has not been appointed to a company but, in the opinion of the court, such an appointment may yet be made.

(2) Where this section applies, on application being made to it in that behalf, the court may, subject to *subsections (4)* and *(5)*, make, in relation to a receiver who stands appointed to the whole or any part of the property or undertaking of the company referred to in *subsection (1)*, the following order.

(3) That order of the court is one providing that *section 440* shall not apply as respects payments made by the receiver out of assets coming into his or her hands as such receiver.

(4) The court shall only make such an order if it would, in the opinion of the court, be likely to facilitate the survival of the company, and the whole or any part of its undertaking, as a going concern.

(5) An order referred to in *subsection (2)* shall not be made without each creditor of the company of the following class being afforded an opportunity to be heard, namely a creditor any of the debts owed to whom by the company are debts which in a winding up are (by virtue of the provisions of *Part 11* relating to preferential payments) required to be paid in priority to all other debts.

(6) *Subsection (2)* is without prejudice to the generality of *section 522(1)*.

Chapter 3
Powers of examiner

524 Powers of an examiner

(1) Any provision of this Act relating to the rights and powers of a statutory auditor of a company and the supplying of information to and co-operation with such auditor shall, with the necessary modifications, apply to an examiner.

(2) Notwithstanding any provision of this Act relating to notice of general meetings, an examiner shall have power to convene, set the agenda for, and preside at meetings of the board of directors and general meetings of the company to which he or she is appointed and to propose motions or resolutions and to give reports to such meetings.

(3) An examiner shall be entitled to reasonable notice of, to attend and be heard at, all meetings of the board of directors of a company and all general meetings of the company to which he or she is appointed.

(4) For the purpose of *subsection (3)* "reasonable notice" shall be deemed to include a description of the business to be transacted at any such meeting.

(5) An examiner has the power referred to in *subsection (6)* where he or she becomes aware of any actual or proposed act, omission, course of conduct, decision or contract, by or on behalf of—

(a) the company to which he or she has been appointed,

(b) that company's officers, employees, members or creditors, or

(c) any other person,

in relation to the income, assets or liabilities of the company which, in the examiner's opinion, is or is likely to be to the detriment of the company, or any interested party.

(6) That power of the examiner is to take whatever steps are necessary, subject to the right of parties acquiring an interest in good faith and for value in such income, assets or liabilities, to halt, prevent or rectify the effects of such act, omission, course of conduct, decision or contract.

(7) The examiner may apply to the court—

(a) to determine any question arising in the course of his or her office, or

(b) for the exercise in relation to the company of all or any of the following powers which the court may exercise under this Act, namely those exercisable by it upon the application of any member, contributory, creditor or director of a company.

(8) The examiner shall, if so directed by the court, have power to ascertain and agree claims against the company to which he or she has been appointed.

(9) No professional or legal duty to which an examiner is subject by virtue of his or her appointment as such to a company shall be regarded as contravened by, and no liability to the company, its shareholders, creditors or other interested parties shall attach to, an examiner by reason of his or her compliance with an obligation imposed on the examiner by or under this section.

525 Repudiation by examiner of contracts made before period of protection and of negative pledge clauses whenever made: prohibitions and restrictions

(1) Without prejudice to *subsection (2)*, nothing in *section 524* shall enable an examiner to repudiate a contract that has been entered into by the company to which he or she has been appointed prior to the period during which the company is under the protection of the court.

(2) A provision referred to in *subsection (4)* shall not be binding on the company at any time after the service of the notice under *subsection (3)(b)* and before the expiration of the period during which the company is under the protection of the court if the following 2 conditions are satisfied.

(3) Those conditions are—

(a) the examiner is of the opinion that the provision, were it to be enforced, would be likely to prejudice the survival of the company or the whole or any part of its undertaking as a going concern; and

(b) the examiner serves a notice on the other party or parties to the agreement in which the provision is contained informing the party or parties of that opinion.

(4) The provision referred to in *subsection (2)* is a provision of an agreement entered into by the company concerned and any other person or persons at any time (including a time that is prior to the period during which the company is under the protection of the court) that provides that the company shall not, or shall not otherwise than in specified circumstances—

(a) borrow moneys or otherwise obtain credit from any person other than that person or those persons; or

(b) create or permit to subsist any mortgage, charge, lien or other encumbrance or any pledge over the whole or any part of the property or undertaking of the company.

526 Production of documents and evidence

(1) It shall be the duty of the officers and agents of a company or a related company to which an examiner has been appointed to—

(a) produce to the examiner all books and documents of, or relating to, any such company which are in their custody or power,

(b) attend before the examiner when required by the examiner so to do, and

(c) otherwise give to the examiner all assistance in connection with the examiner's functions which they are reasonably able to give.

(2) If the examiner considers that a person, other than an officer or agent of any foregoing company, is or may be in possession of any information concerning the company's affairs, the examiner may require that person to—

(a) produce to the examiner any books or documents in his or her custody or power relating to the company,

(b) attend before the examiner, and

(c) otherwise give to the examiner all assistance in connection with the examiner's functions which that person is reasonably able to give,

and it shall be the duty of that person to comply with the requirement.

(3) If the examiner has reasonable grounds for believing that a director of any foregoing company maintains or has maintained a bank account of any description, whether alone or jointly with another person and whether in the State or elsewhere, into or out of which there has been paid—

(a) any money which has resulted from or been used in the financing of any transaction, arrangement or agreement particulars of which have not been disclosed in the financial statements of any company for any financial year as required by this Act, or

(b) any money which has been in any way connected with any act or omission, or series of acts or omissions, which, on the part of that director, constituted misconduct (whether fraudulent or not) towards that company or its members, the examiner may require the director to produce to the examiner all documents in the director's possession, or under his or her control, relating to that bank account and it shall be the duty of the director to comply with the requirement.

(4) In *subsection (3)*—

"bank account" includes an account with any person exempt by virtue of section 7(4) of the Central Bank Act 1971 from the requirement of holding a licence under section 9 of that Act;

"director" means—

(a) any present or past director (including any present or past shadow director); and

(b) any person connected, within the meaning of *section 220*, with such a director.

(5) An examiner may examine on oath, either by word of mouth or on written interrogatories, the officers and agents of any such company or other person as is mentioned in *subsection (1)* or *(2)* in relation to that company's affairs and may—

(a) administer an oath accordingly, or

(b) reduce the answers of such person to writing and require him or her to sign them.

(6) If any officer or agent of a foregoing company or other such person—

(a) refuses to produce to the examiner any book or document which it is his or her duty under this section to produce,

(b) refuses to attend before the examiner when requested by the examiner to do so, or

(c) refuses to answer any question which is put to him or her by the examiner with respect to the affairs of the company,

the examiner may provide a certificate under his or her hand to the court stating that such a refusal has occurred.

(7) On such a certificate being provided to it, the court may enquire into the case and, after hearing any witnesses who may be produced against or on behalf of the officer, agent or other person to whom the certificate relates or any statement which may be offered in defence, make any order or direction it thinks fit.

(8) Without prejudice to the generality of *subsection (7)*, the court may, after a hearing under that subsection, make a direction—

(a) to the person concerned to attend or re-attend before the examiner or produce particular books or documents or answer particular questions put to him or her by the examiner, or

(b) that the person concerned need not produce a particular book or document or answer a particular question put to him or her by the examiner.

(9) *Section 795* shall apply for the purposes of this section as it applies for the purposes of *Part 13* and, accordingly, for the purpose of this section, references in *section 795* to *Part 13*, or relevant provisions of that Part, shall be read as references to this section.

(10) In this section—

(a) any reference to officers or to agents includes a reference to past, as well as present, officers or agents, as the case may be; and

(b) "agents", in relation to a company, includes—

(i) the bankers and solicitors of the company; and

(ii) any persons employed by the company as auditors, accountants, book-keepers or taxation advisers, or other persons employed by it in a professional, consultancy or similar capacity, whether those persons are (or were) or are not (or were not) officers of the company.

527 No lien over company's books, records, etc.

(1) Without prejudice to *subsections (2)* and *(3)*, where the court has appointed an examiner to a company or a company is under the protection of the court, no person shall be entitled as against the examiner to—

(a) withhold possession of—

(i) any deed, instrument, or other document belonging to the company, or

(ii) any accounting records, receipts, bills, invoices, or other papers of a like nature relating to the accounts or trade, dealings or business of the company,

or

(b) claim any lien on any document or paper referred to in *paragraph (a)*.

(2) Where a mortgage, charge or pledge has been created by the deposit of any such document or paper with a person, the production of the document or paper to the examiner by the person shall not operate to prejudice the person's rights under the mortgage, charge or pledge (other than any right to possession of the document or paper).

(3) Where by virtue of this section an examiner has possession of—

(a) any document or papers of a receiver, or

(b) any documents or papers that a receiver is entitled to examine,

the examiner shall, unless the court otherwise orders, make the document or papers available for inspection by the receiver at all reasonable times.

528 Further powers of court

(1) Where it appears to the court, on the application of the examiner, that, having regard to the matters referred to in *subsection (2)*, it is just and equitable to do so, it may make an order that all or any of the functions which are vested in the directors (whether by virtue of the constitution of the company or by law or otherwise) shall be performable only by the examiner.

(2) The matters to which the court is to have regard for the purpose of *subsection (1)* are:

(a) that the affairs of the company are being conducted, or are likely to be conducted, in a manner which is calculated or likely to prejudice the interests of the company or of its employees or of its creditors as a whole; or

(b) that it is expedient, for the purpose of preserving the assets of the company or of safeguarding the interests of the company or of its employees or of its creditors as a whole, that the carrying on of the business of the company by, or the performance of the functions of, its directors or management should be curtailed or regulated in any particular respect; or

(c) that the company, or its directors, have resolved that such an order should be sought; or

(d) any other matter in relation to the company the court thinks relevant.

(3) Where the court makes an order under *subsection (1)*, it may, for the purpose of giving full effect to the order, include such conditions in the order and make such ancillary or other orders as it sees fit.

(4) On an application under *subsection (1)*, in addition to the powers under that subsection and *subsection (3)*, the court may, having regard to the matters referred to in *subsection (2)*, provide, by an order under *subsection (1)* or by a further order, that the examiner shall have all or any of the powers that he or she would have if he or she were a liquidator appointed by the court in respect of the company.

(5) Where such an order so provides, the court shall have all the powers that it would have if it had made a winding-up order and appointed a liquidator in respect of the company concerned.

529 Incurring of certain liabilities by examiner

(1) Any liabilities incurred by the company during the protection period which are specified in *subsection (2)* shall be treated as expenses properly incurred, for the purpose of *section 554*, by the examiner.

(2) The liabilities referred to in *subsection (1)* are those certified in writing by the examiner, at the time they are incurred, to have been incurred in circumstances where, in the opinion of the examiner, the survival of the company as a going concern during the protection period would otherwise be seriously prejudiced.

(3) In this section "protection period" means the period, beginning with the appointment of an examiner, during which the company is under the protection of the court.

530 Power to deal with charged property, etc.

(1) Where, on an application by the examiner, the court is satisfied that—

(a) the disposal (with or without other assets) of any property of the company concerned which is subject to a security which, as created, was a floating charge, or

(b) the exercise by the examiner of his or her powers in relation to such property,

would be likely to facilitate the survival of the whole or any part of the company as a going concern, the court may by order authorise the examiner to dispose of the property, or exercise his or her powers in relation to it, as the case may be, as if it were not subject to the security.

(2) Where, on an application by the examiner, the court is satisfied that the disposal (with or without other assets) of—

(a) any property of the company concerned subject to a security other than a security to which *subsection (1)* applies, or

(b) any goods in the possession of the company concerned under a hire-purchase agreement,

would be likely to facilitate the survival of the whole or any part of the company as a going concern, the court may by order authorise the examiner to dispose of the property as if it were not subject to the security or to dispose of the goods as if all rights of the owner under the hire-purchase agreement were vested in the company.

(3) Where property is disposed of under *subsection (1)*, the holder of the security shall have the same priority in respect of any property of the company directly or indirectly representing the property disposed of as he or she would have had in respect of the property subject to the security.

(4) An order under *subsection (2)* shall include a condition that—

(a) the net proceeds of the disposal of the property or goods concerned; and

(b) where those proceeds are less than such amount as may be determined by the court to be the net amount which would be realised on a sale of the property or goods concerned in the open market by a willing vendor, such sums as may be required to make good the deficiency,

shall be applied towards discharging the sums secured by the security or payable under the hire-purchase agreement.

(5) Where a condition imposed in pursuance of *subsection (4)* relates to 2 or more securities, that condition operates to require the net proceeds of the disposal and, where *paragraph (b)* of that subsection applies, the sums mentioned in that paragraph to be applied towards discharging the sums secured by those securities in the order of their priorities.

(6) A certified copy of an order under *subsection (1)* or *(2)* in relation to a security shall, within 7 days after the date of the making of the order, be delivered by the examiner to the Registrar.

(7) If the examiner, without reasonable excuse, fails to comply with *subsection (6)*, he or she shall be guilty of a category 4 offence.

(8) References in this section to a hire-purchase agreement include references to—

(a) a conditional sale agreement;

(b) a retention of title agreement; and

(c) an agreement for the bailment of goods which is capable of subsisting for more than 3 months.

531 Notification of appointment of examiner

(1) Where a petition has been presented, notice of the petition in the prescribed form shall, within 3 days after the date of its presentation, be delivered by the petitioner to the Registrar.

(2) An examiner shall, within the respective periods specified in *subsection (3)*, cause to be published in *Iris Oifigiúil* and in at least 2 daily newspapers circulating in the district in which the registered office or principal place of business of the company is situated a notice of his or her appointment and the date of that appointment.

(3) The periods referred to in *subsection (2)* are—

(a) 21 days after the date of the examiner's appointment — in the case of *Iris Oifigiúil*, and

(b) 3 days after the date of the examiner's appointment — in the other case referred to in that subsection.

(4) An examiner shall, within 3 days after the date of his or her appointment, deliver to the Registrar a copy of the order appointing him or her.

(5) Where a company is (by virtue of *section 520*) under, for the purposes of this Part, the protection of the court, every invoice, order for goods or business letter issued by or on behalf of the company, being a document on or in which the name of the company appears, shall, immediately after the mention of that name, include the words "*in examination under Part 10 of the Companies Act 2014*".

(6) A website of a company that is (by virtue of *section 520*) under, for the purposes of this Part, the protection of the court, and any electronic mail sent to a third party by, or on behalf of, such a company, shall contain a statement that the company is in examination under this Part (and such a statement on a website shall be in a prominent and easily accessible place on it).

(7) In *subsection (6)* "third party" means a person other than—

(a) an officer or employee of the company concerned, or

(b) a holding company or subsidiary of the company or an officer or employee of that holding company or subsidiary.

(8) A person who fails to comply with *subsection (1)*, *(2)*, *(4)* or *(5)* shall be guilty of a category 4 offence.

(9) If default is made in complying with the requirement under *subsection (6)* concerning the company's website, the company concerned and any officer of it who is in default shall be guilty of a category 4 offence.

(10) If default is made by a company, or any person acting on its behalf, in complying with the requirement under *subsection (6)* concerning electronic mail, then—

(a) in every case, the company and any officer of it who is in default, and

(b) where the default is made by a person acting on the company's behalf, that person,

shall be guilty of a category 4 offence.

532 General provisions as to examiners — resignation, filling of vacancy, etc.

(1) An examiner may resign or, on cause shown, be removed by the court.

(2) If, for any reason, a vacancy occurs in the office of examiner, the court, on application to it, may by order fill the vacancy.

(3) An application for an order under *subsection (2)* may be made by—

(a) any committee of creditors established under *section 538* in relation to the company concerned, or

(b) the company concerned, or

(c) any interested party.

(4) An examiner shall be described by the style of "the examiner" of the particular company in respect of which he or she is appointed and not by his or her name.

(5) The acts of an examiner shall be valid notwithstanding any defects that may afterwards be discovered in his or her appointment or qualification.

(6) An examiner shall be personally liable on any contract entered into by him or her in the performance of his or her functions (whether such contract is entered into by the examiner in the name of the company concerned or in his or her own name as examiner or otherwise) unless the contract provides that he or she is not to be personally liable on such contract.

(7) The examiner shall, in respect of that personal liability, be entitled to indemnity out of the assets of the company concerned.

(8) Nothing in *subsection (6)* or *(7)* shall be taken as limiting any right to indemnity which the examiner would have apart from either subsection, or as limiting the examiner's liability on contracts entered into without authority or as conferring any right to indemnity in respect of that liability.

(9) A company to which an examiner has been appointed or an interested party may apply to the court for the determination of any question arising out of the performance or otherwise by the examiner of his or her functions.

533 Hearing regarding irregularities

(1) Where, arising out of the presentation to it of the report of the independent expert or otherwise, it appears to the court that there is evidence of a substantial disappearance of property of the company concerned that is not adequately accounted for, or of other serious irregularities in relation to the company's affairs having occurred, the court shall, as soon as it is practicable, hold a hearing to consider that evidence.

(2) If, before the hearing referred to in *subsection (1)* is held, the court directs the examiner to do so, the examiner shall prepare a report setting out any matters which the examiner considers will assist the court in considering the evidence concerned on that hearing.

(3) The examiner shall supply a copy of a report prepared by him or her under *subsection (2)* to the company concerned on the same day as he or she causes the report to be delivered to the office of the court.

(4) The examiner shall also supply a copy of a report prepared by him or her under *subsection (2)* to each person who is mentioned in the report and any interested party on written application being made to him or her in that behalf.

(5) If the court, on application to it in that behalf, directs that that supply may be the subject of such omission, there may be omitted from any copy of the report supplied to a person referred to in *subsection (4)* or an interested party such parts of it as are specified in the direction of the court.

(6) The court may, in particular, on such an application, direct that there may be omitted from such a supply of a copy of the report any information the inclusion of which in such a copy would be likely to prejudice the survival of the company or the whole or any part of its undertaking as a going concern.

(7) If the company concerned is a company referred to in *section 510(2)*, *(3)* or *(4)*, the examiner shall, as soon as may be after it is prepared, supply a copy of the report prepared by him or her under *subsection (2)* to the Central Bank, and *subsections (5)* and *(6)* shall not apply to such a copy.

(8) The following persons shall be entitled to appear and be heard at a hearing under this section:

(a) the examiner;

(b) if the court decided to hold a hearing under this section because of matters contained in the report of the independent expert, the independent expert;

(c) the company concerned;

(d) any interested party;

(e) any person who is referred to in the report of the independent expert or the report prepared under *subsection (2)*;

(f) if the company concerned is a company referred to in *section 510(2)*, *(3)* or *(4)* — the Central Bank;

(g) irrespective of whether it constitutes any of the foregoing kinds of company — the Director of Corporate Enforcement.

(9) The court may, on a hearing under this section, make such order or orders as it deems fit (including, where appropriate, an order for the trial of any issue relating to the matter concerned).

(10) The court may, if it considers it appropriate to do so, direct that a certified copy of an order under *subsection (9)* shall be delivered to the Registrar by the examiner or such other person as it may specify.

534 Report by examiner

(1) An examiner shall—

(a) as soon as practicable after he or she is appointed, formulate proposals for a compromise or scheme of arrangement in relation to the company concerned,

(b) without prejudice to any other provision of this Act, perform such other functions as the court may direct the examiner to perform.

(2) Notwithstanding any provision of *Part 4* relating to notice of general meetings (but subject to notice of not less than 3 days in any case) the examiner shall—

(a) convene and preside at such meetings of members and creditors as he or she thinks proper for the purpose of *section 540*, and

(b) in accordance with *section 536*, report on those proposals to the court, within 35 days after the date of his or her appointment or such longer period as the court may allow.

(3) Where, on the application of the examiner, the court is satisfied that the examiner would be unable to report under *subsection (2)* to the court within the period of 70 days referred to in *section 520(2)* but that he or she would be able to report under that subsection to the court if that period were extended, the court may by order extend that period by not more than 30 days to enable him or her to do so.

(4) Where the examiner has submitted a report under this section to the court and, but for this subsection, the period mentioned in *section 520(2)* (and any extended period allowed under *subsection (3)*) would expire, the court may, of its own motion or on the application of the examiner, extend the period concerned by such period as the court considers necessary to enable it to take a decision under *section 541*.

(5) The examiner shall supply a copy of his or her report under this section—

(a) to the company concerned on the same day as he or she causes the report to be delivered to the office of the court, and

(b) to any interested party on written application being made to him or her in that behalf.

(6) The examiner shall, as soon as may be after it is prepared, supply a copy of his or her report under this section to—

(a) if the company concerned is a company referred to in *section 510(2)*, *(3)* or *(4)* — the Central Bank, and

(b) irrespective of whether it constitutes any of the foregoing kinds of company — the Director of Corporate Enforcement.

(7) If the court, on application to it in that behalf, directs that that supply may be the subject of such omission, there may be omitted from any copy of the report supplied under *subsection (5)(b)* to an interested party such parts of it as are specified in the direction of the court.

(8) The court may, in particular, on such an application, direct that there may be omitted from such a supply of a copy of the report any information the inclusion of which in

such a copy would be likely to prejudice the survival of the company or the whole or any part of its undertaking as a going concern.

535 Procedure where examiner unable to secure agreement or formulate proposals for compromise or scheme of arrangement

(1) If the examiner is not able to—

(a) enter into an agreement with the interested parties and any other persons concerned in the matter, or

(b) formulate proposals for a compromise or scheme of arrangement in relation to the company concerned,

the examiner may apply to the court for the grant of directions in the matter.

(2) The court may, on such an application, give such directions or make such order as it deems fit, including, if it considers it just and equitable to do so, an order for the winding up of the company.

536 Content of examiner's report

An examiner's report under *section 534* shall include:

(a) the proposals placed before the required meetings;

(b) any modification of those proposals adopted at any of those meetings;

(c) the outcome of each of the required meetings;

(d) the recommendation of the committee of creditors, if any;

(e) a statement of the assets and liabilities (including contingent and prospective liabilities) of the company as at the date of his or her report;

(f) a list of the creditors of the company, the amount owing to each such creditor, the nature and value of any security held by any such creditor, and the priority accorded under *sections 621* and *622* to any such creditor or any other statutory provision or rule of law;

(g) a list of the officers of the company;

(h) the examiner's recommendations;

(i) such other matters as the examiner deems appropriate or the court directs.

537 Repudiation of certain contracts

(1) Where proposals for a compromise or scheme of arrangement are to be formulated in relation to a company, the company may, subject to the approval of the court, affirm or repudiate any contract under which some element of performance other than payment remains to be rendered both by the company and the other contracting party or parties.

(2) Any person who suffers loss or damage as a result of such repudiation shall stand as an unsecured creditor for the amount of such loss or damage.

(3) In order to facilitate the formulation, consideration or confirmation of a compromise or scheme of arrangement, the court may hold a hearing and make an order determining the amount of any such loss or damage mentioned in *subsection (2)*

and the amount so determined shall be due by the company to the creditor as a judgment debt.

(4) Where the examiner is not a party to an application to the court for the purposes of *subsection (1)*, the company shall serve notice of such application on the examiner and the examiner may appear and be heard on the hearing of any such application.

(5) Where the court approves the affirmation or repudiation of a contract under this section, it may, in giving such approval, make such orders as it thinks fit for the purposes of giving full effect to its approval, including orders as to notice to, or declaring the rights of, any party affected by such affirmation or repudiation.

538 Appointment of creditors' committee

(1) An examiner may, and if so directed by the court shall, appoint a committee of creditors to assist the examiner in the performance of his or her functions.

(2) Save as otherwise directed by the court, a committee appointed under *subsection (1)* shall consist of not more than 5 members and shall include the holders of the 3 largest unsecured claims who are willing to serve.

(3) The examiner shall provide such a committee with a copy of any proposals for a compromise or scheme of arrangement and the committee may express an opinion on the proposals on its own behalf or on behalf of the creditors or classes of creditors represented on the committee.

(4) As soon as practicable after the appointment of a committee under *subsection (1)*, the examiner shall meet with the committee to transact such business as may be necessary.

539 Proposals for compromise or scheme of arrangement

(1) Proposals for a compromise or scheme of arrangement under this Part in relation to a company shall—

(a) specify each class of members and creditors of the company,

(b) specify any class of members and creditors whose interests or claims will not be impaired by the proposals,

(c) specify any class of members and creditors whose interests or claims will be impaired by the proposals,

(d) provide equal treatment for each claim or interest of a particular class unless the holder of a particular claim or interest agrees to less favourable treatment,

(e) provide for the implementation of the proposals,

(f) if the examiner considers it necessary or desirable to do so to facilitate the survival of the company, and the whole or any part of its undertaking, as a going concern, specify whatever changes should be made in relation to the management or direction of the company,

(g) if the examiner considers it necessary or desirable to do so to facilitate such survival, specify any changes he or she considers should be made in the constitution of the company, whether as regards the management or direction of the company or otherwise,

(h) include such other matters as the examiner deems appropriate.

(2) A statement of the assets and liabilities (including contingent and prospective liabilities) of the company as at the date of the proposals shall be attached to each copy of the proposals to be submitted to meetings of members and creditors under *section 540*.

(3) There shall also be attached to each such copy of the proposals a description of the estimated financial outcome of a winding up of the company for each class of members and creditors.

(4) The court may direct that the proposals include whatever other provisions it deems fit.

(5) For the purposes of this section and *sections 541* to *543*, a creditor's claim against a company is impaired if the creditor receives less in payment of his or her claim than the full amount due in respect of the claim at the date of presentation of the petition for the appointment of the examiner.

(6) For the purposes of this section and *sections 541* to *543*, the interest of a member of a company in the company is impaired if—

(a) the nominal value of his or her shareholding in the company is reduced, or

(b) where the member is entitled to a fixed dividend in respect of his or her shareholding in the company, the amount of that dividend is reduced, or

(c) the member is deprived of all or any part of the rights accruing to him or her by virtue of his or her shareholding in the company, or

(d) the percentage of his or her interest in the total issued share capital of the company is reduced, or

(e) the member is deprived of his or her shareholding in the company.

540 Consideration by members and creditors of proposals

(1) This section applies to a meeting of members or creditors or any class of members or creditors summoned to consider proposals for a compromise or scheme of arrangement in relation to a company to which an examiner has been appointed.

(2) Save where expressly provided otherwise in this section, this section shall not authorise, at such a meeting, anything to be done in relation to such proposals by any member or creditor.

(3) At a meeting to which this section applies a modification of the proposals may be put to the meeting but may only be accepted with the consent of the examiner.

(4) Proposals shall be deemed to have been accepted by a meeting of creditors or of a class of creditors when a majority in number representing a majority in value of the claims represented at that meeting have voted, either in person or by proxy, in favour of the resolution for the proposals.

(5) Nothing in *subsection (4)* shall, in the case of a creditor who abstains from voting, or otherwise fails to cast a vote, in respect of the proposals, be read as permitting such an abstention or failure to be regarded as a casting by that person of a vote against the proposals.

(6) Where a State authority is a creditor of the company, such authority shall be entitled to accept proposals under this section notwithstanding—

(a) that any claim of such authority as a creditor would be impaired under the proposals, or

(b) any other enactment.

(7) In *subsection (6)* "State authority" means the State, a Minister of the Government, a local authority or the Revenue Commissioners.

(8) *Section 192* shall apply to any resolution to which *subsection (4)* relates which is passed at any adjourned meeting.

(9) *Subsection (1)(a)(iii)* and *(b)*, and *subsections (2)* to *(7)*, of *section 452* shall apply to meetings under this section with the modifications specified in *subsection (10)* and any other necessary modifications.

(10) The modifications mentioned in *subsection (9)* are—

(a) the reference in *paragraph (a)(iii)* of *section 452(1)* to the explanation required to be given under *paragraph (a)(ii)* of *section 452(1)* in relation to the company's directors shall be read as a reference to the explanation required to be given under *subsection (11)* of this section in relation to those directors, and

(b) the reference in *section 452(5)* to a liquidator of the company shall be read as a reference to the examiner of the company.

(11) With every notice summoning a meeting to which this section applies which is sent to a creditor or member, there shall be sent also a statement explaining the effect of the compromise or scheme of arrangement and in particular stating any material interests of the directors of the company, whether as directors or as members or as creditors of the company or otherwise and the effect thereon of the compromise or arrangement, in so far as it is different from the effect on the like interest of other persons.

(12) Without prejudice to *subsections (1)* to *(11)*, in the case of a company referred to in *section 510(3)* or *(4)*, the examiner shall also afford the Central Bank an opportunity to consider the proposals for a compromise or scheme of arrangement and, for this purpose, shall furnish to the Central Bank a statement containing the like information to that referred to in *subsection (11)*.

541 Confirmation of proposals

(1) The report of the examiner under *section 534* shall be set down for consideration by the court as soon as may be after receipt of the report by the court.

(2) The following persons may appear and be heard at a hearing under *subsection (1)*:

(a) the company concerned;

(b) the examiner;

(c) any creditor or member whose claim or interest would be impaired if the proposals were implemented;

(d) the directors of the company;

(e) if the company concerned is a company referred to in *section 510(2)*, *(3)* or *(4)* — the Central Bank.

(3) At a hearing under *subsection (1)*, the court may, as it thinks proper, subject to the provisions of this section and *sections 542* and *543*—

(a) confirm,

(b) confirm subject to modifications, or

(c) refuse to confirm,

the proposals for the compromise or arrangement concerned (referred to subsequently in this section as "proposals").

(4) The court shall not confirm any proposals unless—

(a) at least one class of creditors whose interests or claims would be impaired by implementation of the proposals has accepted the proposals, and

(b) the court is satisfied that—

(i) the proposals are fair and equitable in relation to any class of members or creditors that has not accepted the proposals and whose interests or claims would be impaired by implementation, and

(ii) the proposals are not unfairly prejudicial to the interests of any interested party,

and in any case shall not confirm any proposals if the sole or primary purpose of them is the avoidance of payment of tax due.

(5) Without prejudice to *subsection (4)*, the court shall not confirm any proposals in respect of a company to which an examiner has been appointed under *section 517* if the proposals would have the effect of impairing the interests of the creditors of the company in such a manner as to unfairly favour the interests of the creditors or members of any company to which it is related, being a company to which that examiner has been appointed examiner under *section 509* or, as the case may be, *517*.

(6) Where the court confirms proposals (with or without modification), the proposals shall be binding on all the members or class or classes of members, as the case may be, affected by the proposal and also on the company.

(7) Where the court confirms proposals (with or without modification), the proposals shall, notwithstanding any other enactment, be binding on all the creditors or the class or classes of creditors, as the case may be, affected by the proposals in respect of any claim or claims against the company and any person other than the company who, under any enactment, rule of law or otherwise, is liable for all or any part of the debts of the company.

542 Supplemental provisions in relation to *section 541*

(1) Any amendments of the constitution of the company concerned which are specified in the relevant proposals shall, after confirmation of the proposals by the court under *section 541* and notwithstanding any other provisions of this Act, take effect from a date fixed by the court.

(2) Where the court confirms proposals under *section 541* it may make such orders for the implementation of its decision as it deems fit.

(3) A compromise or scheme of arrangement, proposals for which have been confirmed under *section 541*, shall come into effect from a date fixed by the court, which date (unless the court deems it appropriate to fix a later one) shall be a date falling no later than 21 days after the date of the proposals' confirmation.

(4) On the confirmation of proposals, a certified copy of any order made by the court under *section 541* shall be delivered by the examiner, or by such person as the court may direct, to the Registrar.

(5) Where—

(a) the court refuses to confirm proposals under *section 541*, or

(b) the report of an examiner under *section 534* concludes that, following the required meetings of creditors of a company under this Part, it has not been possible to reach agreement on a compromise or scheme of arrangement,

the court may, if it considers it just and equitable to do so, make an order for the winding up of the company, or any other order as it deems fit.

(6) Notwithstanding—

(a) *subsection (4)*, or any other provision of this Part, nothing in this Part shall prevent the examiner from including in a report under *section 534* proposals which will not involve the impairment of the interests of members or creditors of the company nor the court from confirming any such proposals, or

(b) any foregoing provision of this Part or any provision of *Part 3*, nothing in this Part or *Part 3* shall prevent the examiner from including in a report under *section 534* proposals which provide for a reduction of the company's company capital nor, subject to *subsection (7)*, the court from confirming any such proposals.

(7) If the extent of the reduction of the company's company capital provided for in the proposals as referred to in *subsection (6)(b)* would, in the opinion of the court, and having regard to—

(a) the scale and nature of the business that the company carries on, and

(b) the likely liabilities it will incur on an on-going basis after the period of protection has expired,

result in the company's having an amount of company capital that is manifestly inadequate, the court shall not confirm the proposals or, where appropriate, shall confirm the proposals subject to a modification that a lower level of reduction, as determined by the court, of the company's company capital shall have effect under the compromise or scheme of arrangement.

(8) References in *section 541* or any other provision of this Part to acceptance by a class of creditors or members of proposals are references to the proposals' acceptance at the relevant meeting held under *section 540*, that is to say acceptance signified by a resolution passed, at that meeting, by the requisite majority referred to in (in the case of creditors) *section 540(4)* or (in the case of members) *section 191(1)*.

543 Objection to confirmation by court of proposals

(1) At a hearing under *section 541* in relation to proposals referred to in that section, a member or creditor whose interest or claim would be impaired by the proposals may object in particular to their confirmation by the court on any of the following grounds—

(a) that there was some material irregularity at or in relation to a meeting to which *section 540* applies;

(b) that acceptance of the proposals by the meeting was obtained by improper means;

(c) that the proposals were put forward for an improper purpose;

(d) that the proposals unfairly prejudice the interests of the objector.

(2) Any person who voted to accept the proposals referred to in *section 541* may not object to their confirmation by the court except on the grounds—

(a) that such acceptance was obtained by improper means; or

(b) that after voting to accept the proposals the person became aware that the proposals were put forward for an improper purpose.

(3) Where the court upholds an objection under this section, the court may make such order as it deems fit, including an order that the decision of any meeting be set aside and an order that any meeting be reconvened.

544 Provisions with respect to leases

(1) Subject to *subsection (3)*, proposals for a compromise or scheme of arrangement shall not contain, nor shall any modification by the court under *section 541* of such proposals result in their containing, a provision providing for either or both—

(a) a reduction in the amount of any rent or other periodical payment reserved under a lease of land that falls to be paid after the date from which the compromise or scheme of arrangement would come into effect under *section 542(3)* or the complete extinguishment of the right of the lessor to any such payments;

(b) as respects a failure—

(i) to pay an amount of rent or make any periodical payment reserved under a lease of land; or

(ii) to comply with any other covenant or obligation of such a lease, that falls to be paid or complied with after the date referred to in *paragraph (a)*, a requirement that the lessor under such a lease shall not exercise, or shall only exercise in specified circumstances, any right, whether under the lease or otherwise, to—

(I) recover possession of the land concerned;

(II) effect a forfeiture of the lease or otherwise enter on the land;

(III) recover the amount of such rent or other payment; or

(IV) claim damages or other relief in respect of the failure to comply with such a covenant or obligation.

(2) Subject to *subsection (3)*, proposals for a compromise or scheme of arrangement in relation to a company shall not be held by the court to satisfy the condition specified in *section 541(4)(b)(ii)* if the proposals contain a provision relating to a lease of, or any hiring agreement in relation to, property other than land and, in the opinion of the court—

(a) the value of that property is substantial; and

(b) that provision is of like effect to a provision referred to in *subsection (1)(a)* or *(b)*.

(3) *Subsection (1)* or *(2)* shall not apply if the lessor or owner of the property concerned has consented in writing to the inclusion of the provision referred to in *subsection (1)* or *(2)* in the proposals for the compromise or scheme of arrangement.

(4) In deciding, for the purposes of *subsection (2)*, whether the value of the property concerned is substantial, the matters to which the court shall have regard shall include the length of the unexpired term of the lease or hiring agreement concerned.

Chapter 4

Liability of third parties for debts of a company in examination

545 What this Chapter contains

This Chapter contains provisions—

(a) specifying the effect on the liability of a person (under a guarantee or otherwise) to another person in respect of a debt of a company in examination under this Part where a compromise or scheme of arrangement takes effect in relation to the latter;

(b) restricting the enforcement of that liability by that other person unless a certain procedure is employed; and

(c) providing for other matters relating to the foregoing (including a saver for cases falling within *section 520(4)(f)* or where, by operation of any rule of law, a discharge or release of the first-mentioned person's liability occurs).

546 Definitions (*Chapter 4*)

In this Chapter—

"creditor" shall be read in accordance with *section 547*;

"debt" shall be read in accordance with *section 547*;

"liability" shall be read in accordance with *section 547*;

"third person" shall be read in accordance with *section 547*.

547 Circumstances in relation to which subsequent provisions of this Chapter have effect

Subject to *section 548(2)*, the subsequent sections of this Chapter have effect in relation to the following liability (the "liability"), namely the liability—

(a) of any person (the "third person") whether under a guarantee or otherwise;

(b) in respect of a debt (the "debt") of a company to which an examiner has been appointed that is owed to another (the "creditor").

548 General rule: liability of third person not affected by compromise or scheme of arrangement

(1) Notwithstanding *section 541(7)*, the liability shall not be affected by the fact that the debt is the subject of a compromise or scheme of arrangement that has taken effect under *section 542(3)*, but this is subject to *subsections (2)* and *(3)*.

(2) The third person and the creditor may provide in an agreement between them that the liability shall be so affected.

(3) Neither *subsection (1)* nor any of the subsequent provisions of this Chapter shall apply if the third person is a company to which an examiner has been appointed.

549 Enforcement by creditor of liability: restrictions in that regard unless certain procedure employed to the benefit of third person

(1) If the creditor proposes to enforce, by legal proceedings or otherwise, the obligation of the third person in respect of the liability, then he or she shall—

(a) if 14 days or more notice is given of such meeting, at least 14 days before the day on which the meeting concerned under *section 540* to consider the proposals is held, or

(b) if less than 14 days' notice is given of such meeting, not more than 48 hours after he or she has received notice of such meeting,

serve a notice on the third person containing the following offer.

(2) That offer is an offer in writing by the creditor to transfer to the third person (which the creditor is, by virtue of this section, empowered to do) any rights, so far as they relate to the debt, he or she may have under *section 540* to vote in respect of proposals for a compromise or scheme of arrangement in relation to the company.

(3) If that offer is accepted by the third person, that offer shall, if the third person furnishes to the examiner at the meeting concerned, a copy of the offer and informs the examiner of his or her having accepted it, operate, without the necessity for any assignment or the execution of any other instrument, to entitle the third person to exercise the rights referred to in *subsection (2)*.

(4) However neither that transfer nor any vote cast by the third person on foot of the transfer shall operate to prejudice the right of the creditor to object to the proposals under *section 543*.

(5) If the creditor fails to make the offer referred to in *subsection (1)* in accordance with that subsection, then, subject to *subsection (6)*, the creditor may not enforce by legal proceedings or otherwise the obligation of the third person in respect of the liability.

(6) *Subsection (5)* shall not apply if—

(a) a compromise or scheme of arrangement in relation to the company is not entered into or does not take effect under *section 542(3)*; and

(b) in either of those cases, the creditor has obtained the leave of the court to enforce the obligation of the third person in respect of the liability.

550 Payment by third person to creditor post period of protection — statutory subrogation in favour of third person in certain circumstances

(1) This section applies where the third person makes a payment to the creditor in respect of the liability after the period of protection in relation to the company concerned has expired.

(2) Where this section applies any amount that would, but for the foregoing payment, be payable to the creditor in respect of the debt under a compromise or scheme of arrangement that has taken effect under *section 542(3)* in relation to the company shall become and be payable to the third person upon and subject to the same terms and conditions as the compromise or scheme of arrangement provided that it was to be payable to the creditor.

551 Saving for cases falling within *section 520(4)(f)* and cases where third person discharged or released from liability

Nothing in this Chapter shall affect the operation of—

(a) *section 520(4)(f)*; or

(b) any rule of law whereby any act done by the creditor results in the third person being discharged or released from his or her obligation in respect of the liability.

Chapter 5
Conclusion of examinership

552 Cessation of protection of company and termination of appointment of examiner

(1) Subject to the provisions of that section, the protection granted by virtue of *section 520* to a company shall cease—

(a) on the coming into effect of a compromise or scheme of arrangement under this Part in relation to the company; or

(b) on such earlier date as the court may direct.

(2) Where a company ceases to be under the protection of the court, the appointment of the examiner shall terminate on the date of such cessation.

553 Revocation

(1) The company or any interested party may, within 180 days after the date of confirmation by the court, under *section 541*, of the proposals in relation to the company, apply to the court for revocation of that confirmation on the grounds that it was procured by fraud.

(2) On such an application, the court, if satisfied that that confirmation was procured by fraud, may revoke the confirmation on such terms and conditions, particularly with regard to the protection of the rights of parties acquiring interests or property in good faith and for value in reliance on that confirmation, as it deems fit.

(3) As soon as practicable after the revocation under this section of such a confirmation, a certified copy of the order made by the court shall be delivered to—

(a) the Registrar;

(b) if the company to which the order relates is a company referred to in *section 510(2)*, *(3)* or *(4)* — the Central Bank;

(c) irrespective of whether it constitutes any of the foregoing kinds of company — the Director of Corporate Enforcement,

by such person as the court may direct.

554 Costs and remuneration of examiners

(1) The court may from time to time make such orders as it thinks proper for payment of the remuneration and costs of, and reasonable expenses properly incurred by, an examiner.

(2) Unless the court otherwise orders, the remuneration, costs and expenses of an examiner shall be paid and the examiner shall be entitled to be indemnified in respect thereof out of the revenue of the business of the company to which he or she has been appointed, or the proceeds of realisation of the assets (including investments).

(3) The remuneration, costs and expenses of an examiner which have been sanctioned by order of the court (other than the expenses referred to in *subsection (4)*) shall be paid in full and shall be paid before any other claim, secured or unsecured, under any compromise or scheme of arrangement or in any receivership or winding up of the company to which he or she has been appointed.

(4) Liabilities incurred by the company to which an examiner has been appointed that, by virtue of *section 529*, are treated as expenses properly incurred by the examiner shall be paid in full and shall be paid before any other claim (including a claim secured by a floating charge), but after any claim secured by a mortgage, charge, lien or other encumbrance of a fixed nature or a pledge, under any compromise or scheme of arrangement or in any receivership or winding up of the company.

(5) In *subsections (3)* and *(4)*, references to a claim shall be deemed to include references to any payment in a winding up of the company in respect of the costs, charges and expenses of that winding up (including the remuneration of any liquidator).

(6) Subject to *subsection (7)*, the functions of an examiner may be performed by him or her with the assistance of persons appointed or employed by him or her for that purpose.

(7) An examiner shall, in so far as is reasonably possible, make use of the services of the staff and facilities of the company to which the examiner has been appointed to assist the examiner in the performance of his or her functions.

(8) In considering any matter relating to the costs, expenses and remuneration of an examiner the court shall have particular regard to *subsection (7)*.

555 Publicity

(1) An examiner or, where appropriate, such other person as the court may direct, shall, within 14 days after the date of delivery to the Registrar of every order made under *section 533*, *541* or *553*, cause to be published in the CRO Gazette notice of such delivery.

(2) Where a person fails to comply with this section, that person and, where that person is a company, the company and any officer of it who is in default, shall be guilty of a category 4 offence.

556 Hearing of proceedings otherwise than in public

The whole or part of any proceedings under this Part may be heard otherwise than in public if the court, in the interests of justice, considers that the interests of the company concerned or of its creditors as a whole so require.

557 Power of court to order the return of assets which have been improperly transferred

(1) Where, on the application of an examiner of a company that is under the protection of the court it can be shown to the satisfaction of the court that—

(a) any property of the company of any kind whatsoever was disposed of either by way of conveyance, transfer, mortgage, security, loan, or in any way whatsoever whether by act or omission, direct or indirect; and

(b) the effect of such disposal was to perpetrate a fraud on the company, its creditors or members,

the court may, if it deems it just and equitable to do so, make the following order.

(2) That order of the court is one requiring any person who appears to have the use, control or possession of such property or the proceeds of the sale or development of it to deliver it or pay a sum in respect of it to the examiner on such terms or conditions as the court sees fit.

(3) *Subsection (1)* shall not apply to any conveyance, mortgage, delivery of goods, payment, execution or other act relating to property made or done by or against a company to which *section 604* applies.

(4) In deciding whether it is just and equitable to make an order under this section, the court shall have regard to the rights of persons who have *bona fide* and for value acquired an interest in the property the subject of the application.

558 Reporting to Director of Corporate Enforcement of misconduct by examiners

(1) Where a disciplinary committee or tribunal (however called) of a prescribed professional body—

(a) finds that a member of that body who is conducting or has conducted an examinership has not maintained appropriate records in relation to that activity; or

(b) has reasonable grounds for believing that such a member has committed a category 1 or 2 offence during the course of conducting an examinership,

the professional body shall report the matter, giving details of the finding or, as the case may be, of the alleged offence, to the Director of Corporate Enforcement forthwith.

(2) If a professional body fails to comply with this section, it, and any officer of the body to whom the failure is attributable, shall be guilty of a category 3 offence.

PART 11
WINDING UP

Chapter 1
Preliminary and interpretation

559 Interpretation (*Part 11*)

(1) In this Part—

"connected person" means a person who, at the time the transaction in relation to the company concerned was carried out, was—

(a) a director of the company;

(b) a shadow director of the company;

(c) a person connected, within the meaning of *section 220*, with a director of the company;

(d) a related company; or

(e) any trustee of, or surety or guarantor for the debt due, to any person referred to in *paragraph (a)*, *(b)*, *(c)* or *(d)*;

"contributory" means every person liable to contribute to the assets of a company in the event of its being wound up, and *subsection (2)* supplements this definition;

"creditors' voluntary winding up" means a voluntary winding up in the circumstances specified in *section 562(1)(b)*;

"members' voluntary winding up" means a voluntary winding up in the circumstances specified in *section 562(1)(a)* or *(2)*;

"property" means all real and personal property, and includes any right of action by the company or liquidator under the provisions of this Act or any other enactment;

"provisional liquidator" means a liquidator appointed provisionally under *section 573*, and *subsections (3)* to *(5)* contain provisions as to the construction of references in this Part to liquidator so far as concerns the immediate expression;

"winding-up petition" means a petition presented under this Act to wind up a company.

(2) For the purposes of—

(a) all proceedings for determining; and

(b) all proceedings prior to the final determination of,

the issue as to whether a particular person is a contributory for the purposes of this Part, "contributory" in this Part includes any person alleged to be a contributory.

(3) *Subsections (4)* and *(5)* apply save where the terms of the provision concerned make express reference to a provisional liquidator or otherwise provide for the construction of the expression "provisional liquidator".

(4) Where a provision of this Part is capable of being applied in the period before the making of a winding-up order (including a provision that makes provision by reference to anything that has happened in such period), then "liquidator" in that

provision, to the extent that it is capable of such application or makes such provision, includes a provisional liquidator.

(5) Where the court confers any power on a provisional liquidator and the power conferred corresponds to any power express provision for which is made by a provision of this Part then, to the extent that that latter provision is capable of being applied in the period before the making of a winding-up order, "liquidator" in that provision includes a provisional liquidator.

560 Restriction of this Part

This Part is subject to Chapters I (general provisions) and III (secondary insolvency proceedings) of the Insolvency Regulation.

561 Modes of winding up — general statement as to position under Act

The winding up of a company may be—

(a) by the court; or

(b) voluntary.

562 Types of voluntary winding up — general statement as to position under Act

(1) The voluntary winding up of a company—

(a) may, in accordance with the Summary Approval Procedure or (where *section 579(3)* permits) in accordance with *section 580*, be a members' voluntary winding up unless—

(i) there is default in the making of a declaration referred to in *section 207* or *580(2)* in accordance with the relevant provisions of this Act; or

(ii) the court makes an order under *section 582(2)* in relation to the company; or

(iii) a creditors' meeting is held in accordance with *section 584* in relation to the company,

(each of which is referred to in *paragraph (b)* as a "bar to a members' winding up"); or

(b) shall, where there is a bar to a members' winding up or the procedure under *section 586(2)* is employed, be a creditors' voluntary winding up.

(2) *Subsection (1)(a)* is in addition to the jurisdiction of the court under *section 572(4)* to order that a company be wound up as a members' voluntary winding up.

(3) Nothing in *subsection (1)* shall be read as affecting the operation of—

(a) in the case of the Summary Approval Procedure being employed for the purpose — *section 201(3)*, or

(b) in the case of *section 580* being employed for the purpose — *section 580(6)*.

563 Provisions apply to either mode of winding up unless the contrary appears

The provisions of this Part relating to winding up apply, unless the contrary appears, to the winding up of a company in either of the modes mentioned in *section 561*.

564 Jurisdiction to wind up companies and rules of court

(1) The court shall have jurisdiction to wind up a company.

(2) In *subsections (3)* to *(6)* the "rule making authority" means the powers under section 36 of the Courts of Justice Act 1924 and section 68 of the Courts of Justice Act 1936, and all the other powers of that Committee in that behalf, of the Superior Courts Rules Committee to make rules regulating the practice and procedure of the court.

(3) The extension of the rule making authority made by section 312 of the Act of 1963 shall continue in being.

(4) As soon as may be after the passing of this Act, the rule making authority shall be exercised so as to secure that the rules of court in force before such passing in relation to windings up are altered in a manner that brings them into conformity with this Part.

(5) In particular the rule making authority shall be so exercised so as to remove those of the functions of the court officer known as "the Examiner" as are stated in those rules to be performable for the purposes of a winding up.

(6) *Subsections (4)* and *(5)* are without prejudice to the exercise generally of the rule making authority on and from the passing of this Act, whether for any purpose of this Act or any other purpose.

565 Powers of court cumulative

Any powers conferred on the court by this Act are in addition to, and not in restriction of, any existing powers of instituting proceedings against any contributory or debtor of the company or the estate of any contributory or debtor, for the recovery of any call or other sums.

566 Court may have regard to wishes of creditors or contributories

(1) The court may, as to all matters relating to the winding up of a company, have regard to the wishes of the creditors or contributories of the company, as proved to it by any sufficient evidence.

(2) For the purpose of ascertaining those wishes, the court may, if it thinks fit—

(a) direct meetings of the creditors or contributories to be called, held and conducted in such manner as the court directs, and

(b) appoint a person to act as chairperson of any such meeting and report the result of the meeting to the court.

(3) In the case of creditors, regard shall be had to the value of each creditor's debt.

(4) In the case of contributories, regard shall be had to the number of votes conferred on each contributory by this Act or the constitution of the company.

567 Application of certain provisions to companies not in liquidation

(1) This section applies in relation to a company that is not being wound up where—

(a) execution or other process issued on a judgment, decree or order of any court in favour of a creditor of the company is returned unsatisfied in whole or in part, or

(b) it is proved to the satisfaction of the court that the company is unable to pay its debts, taking into account the contingent and prospective liabilities of the company,

and, in either case, it appears to the court that the reason or the principal reason for its not being wound up is the insufficiency of its assets.

(2) The sections specified in the Table to this section apply, with the necessary modifications, to a company to which this section applies, notwithstanding that it is not being wound up; accordingly, a person who would have standing otherwise to apply for an order or judgment under a section so specified shall have such standing to make an application under that section as so applied, but this does not affect the Director's power under *subsection (3)*.

(3) The Director may apply to the court pursuant to this subsection for an order or judgment, as the case may be, under any of the sections which apply to a company to which this section applies.

(4) References in the sections specified in the Table to this section to—

(a) the commencement of the winding up of a company,

(b) the appointment of a provisional liquidator,

(c) the making of a winding-up order, or

(d) the relevant date,

shall, for the purposes of this section, be read as references to the date—

(i) of the judgment, decree or order mentioned in *subsection (1)(a)*, or

(ii) on which the court determines that the company is unable to pay its debts.

(5) Where, by virtue of this section, proceedings are instituted under *section 599*, *608*, *609*, *610*, *612* or *672*, *sections 610(6)* and *611* shall apply in relation to any order made as a result of those proceedings except that an order made as a result of an application by the Director pursuant to *subsection (3)* shall not be made in favour of the Director, otherwise than as to his or her costs and expenses.

(6) Subject to *subsection (7)*, a person having a claim against the company may apply to the court for such order as is appropriate by way of enforcement of any right the court on the application finds to arise on the person's part to payment of a share of any sums or assets recovered or available following a successful application by the Director pursuant to *subsection (3)*, and, on the hearing of an application under this subsection, the court may make such an order accordingly.

(7) An application under *subsection (6)* shall be made within a period of 30 days after the date of judgment or order given on behalf or in favour of the Director pursuant to *subsection (3)*.

(8) Where *section 721* applies by virtue of this section, it shall so apply as if the words "which is subsequently ordered to be wound up by the court or subsequently passes a resolution for voluntary winding up" were deleted from it.

Table

Sections to which this section applies

Section	Subject
Section 286(3)	Particular case of category 1 offence arising where adequate accounting records not kept, etc.
Section 599	Related company may be required to contribute to debts of company being wound up
Section 608	Power of court to order return of assets which have been improperly transferred
Section 609	Personal liability of officers of company where adequate accounting records not kept
Sections 610 and 611	Civil liability for fraudulent trading
Section 612	Power of court to assess damages against certain persons
Section 613	Directors of holding company: power of court to assess damages against them
Section 671	Power of court to summon persons for examination
Section 672	Order for payment or delivery of property against person examined under *section 671*
Section 675	Order for arrest and seizure, etc.
Section 684	Inspection of books by creditors and contributories
Section 721	Other frauds by officers of companies which have gone into liquidation: offence
Section 722	Fraudulent trading of company: offence
Section 751	Order for inspection of books or documents of company in liquidation
Section 818	Interpretation and application (*Chapter 3* of *Part 14*)

Chapter 2
Winding up by court

568 Application of Chapter

Save to the extent that the provision expressly provides otherwise, each provision of this Chapter applies only to a winding up that is ordered by the court.

569 Circumstances in which company may be wound up by the court

(1) A company may be wound up by the court—

(a) if the company has by special resolution resolved that the company be wound up by the court,

(b) if the company does not commence its business within a year after the date of its incorporation or suspends its business for a continuous period of 12 months,

(c) if the members of the company are all deceased or no longer exist,

(d) if the company is unable to pay its debts,

(e) if the court is of the opinion that it is just and equitable that the company should be wound up,

(f) if the court is satisfied that the company's affairs are being conducted, or the powers of the directors are being exercised, in a manner oppressive to any member or in disregard of his or her interests as a member and that, despite the existence of an alternative remedy, winding up would be justified in the general circumstances of the case but this paragraph is subject to *subsection (2)*,

(g) if the court is satisfied, on a petition of the Director, that it is in the public interest that the company should be wound up, or

(h) in the circumstances referred to in *section 535(2)* or *542(5)*.

(2) The court may dismiss a petition to wind up a company under *subsection (1)(f)* if it is of the opinion that proceedings under *section 212* would, in all the circumstances, be more appropriate.

(3) *Subsection (1)* is in addition to the special cases (namely those provided under *sections 455(2)(d), 760* and *761)* in which a company may be wound up by the court.

570 Circumstances in which company deemed to be unable to pay its debts

For the purposes of this Act, a company shall be deemed to be unable to pay its debts—

(a) if—

(i) a creditor, by assignment or otherwise, to whom the company is indebted in a sum exceeding €10,000 then due, has served on the company (by leaving it at the registered office of the company) a demand in writing requiring the company to pay the sum so due, and

(ii) the company has, for 21 days after the date of the service of that demand, neglected to pay the sum or to secure or compound for it to the reasonable satisfaction of the creditor,

or

(b) if—

(i) 2 or more creditors, by assignment or otherwise, to whom, in aggregate, the company is indebted in a sum exceeding €20,000 then due, have served on the company (by leaving it at the registered office of the company) a demand in writing requiring the company to pay the sum so due, and

(ii) the company has, for 21 days after the date of the service of that demand, neglected to pay the sum or to secure or compound for it to the reasonable satisfaction of each of the creditors,

or

(c) if execution or other process issued on a judgment, decree or order of any court in favour of a creditor of the company is returned unsatisfied in whole or in part, or

(d) if it is proved to the satisfaction of the court that the company is unable to pay its debts, and in determining whether a company is unable to pay its debts, the court shall take into account the contingent and prospective liabilities of the company.

571 Provisions as to applications for winding up

(1) An application to the court for the winding up of a company shall be by petition presented either by—

(a) the company, or

(b) any creditor or creditors (including any contingent or prospective creditor or creditors) of the company, or

(c) any contributory or contributories of the company,

or by all or any of those parties, together or separately, but this is subject to the following provisions.

(2) The court shall not give a hearing to a winding-up petition presented by a contingent or prospective creditor until such security for costs has been given as the court thinks reasonable, and until a *prima facie* case for winding up has been established to the satisfaction of the court.

(3) A winding-up petition on the grounds mentioned in *section 569(1)(f)* may be presented by any person entitled to bring proceedings for an order under *section 212* in relation to the company concerned.

(4) In a case falling within *section 569(1)(g)* a winding-up petition may be presented by the Director.

(5) A contributory shall not be entitled to present a winding-up petition unless the shares in respect of which the person is a contributory, or some of them, either—

(a) were originally allotted to the person or have been held by the person, and registered in the person's name, for at least 6 months during the 18 months before the commencement of the winding up, or

(b) have devolved on the person through the death of a former holder.

572 Powers of court on hearing petition

(1) On the hearing of a winding-up petition, the court may—

(a) dismiss the petition, or

(b) adjourn the hearing conditionally or unconditionally, or

(c) make any interim order, or any other order that it thinks fit, but the court shall not refuse to make a winding-up order on the ground only that the assets of the company have been mortgaged to an amount equal to or in excess of those assets, or that the company has no assets.

(2) The court shall not make an order for the winding up of a company unless—

(a) the court is satisfied that the company has no obligations in relation to a bank asset that has been transferred to the National Asset Management Agency or a NAMA group entity, or

(b) if the company has any such obligation—

(i) a copy of the petition has been served on that Agency, and

(ii) the court has heard that Agency in relation to the making of the order.

(3) In *subsection (2)* “bank asset” and “NAMA group entity” have the same respective meanings as in the National Asset Management Agency Act 2009.

(4) Upon the making of an order to wind up a company, based on a ground referred to in *paragraph (a)*, *(b)*, *(c)*, *(e)* or *(f)* of *section 569(1)*, the court may order that the company be wound up as if it were a members’ voluntary winding up and, in such event, the provisions of this Part shall apply as if the company were being so wound up.

(5) Where a petitioner does not proceed with his or her winding-up petition, the court may, upon such terms as it shall deem just, substitute as petitioner any person who would have a right to present a petition in relation to the company, and who wishes to proceed with the petition.

573 Appointment of provisional liquidator

The court may appoint a liquidator provisionally at any time after the presentation of a winding-up petition and before the first appointment of a liquidator.

574 Power to stay or restrain proceedings against company

At any time after the presentation of a winding-up petition, and before a winding-up order has been made, the company or any creditor or contributory may—

(a) where any action or proceeding against the company is pending in the High Court or on appeal in the Supreme Court, apply to the court in which the action or proceeding is pending for a stay of proceedings therein, and

(b) where any other action or proceeding is pending against the company, apply to the High Court to restrain further proceedings in the action or proceeding,

and the court to which application is so made may, as the case may be, stay or restrain the proceedings accordingly on such terms and for such period as it thinks fit.

575 Appointment of liquidator by the court

For the purpose of conducting the proceedings in winding up a company, the court may appoint a liquidator or liquidators.

576 Effect of winding-up order

An order for winding up a company shall operate in favour of all the creditors and of all the contributories of the company, as if made on the joint petition of a creditor and of a contributory.

577 Saving for rights of creditors and contributories

The voluntary winding up of a company shall not bar the right of any creditor or contributory to have it wound up by the court; but in the case of an application by a contributory the court must be satisfied that the rights of the contributories will be prejudiced by a voluntary winding up.

Chapter 3
Members' voluntary winding up

578 Application of Chapter

Save to the extent that the provision expressly provides otherwise, each provision of this Chapter applies only to a members' voluntary winding up.

579 Procedure for and commencement of members' voluntary winding up

(1) A company may be wound up voluntarily as a members' voluntary winding up.

(2) In all cases, save for a case falling within *subsection (3)*, a members' voluntary winding up shall be commenced in accordance with the Summary Approval Procedure.

(3) In either of the following cases, namely:

- (a) on the expiry of the period, if any, that is fixed for the duration of a company by its constitution; or
- (b) should such happen, when the event occurs on the occurrence of which a company's constitution provides that the company is to be dissolved;

a members' voluntary winding up of the company may, alternatively to the employment of the Summary Approval Procedure for that purpose, be commenced in accordance with *section 580*.

580 Companies of fixed duration, etc.: alternative means of commencing members' voluntary winding up

(1) In a case falling with *paragraph (a)* or *(b)* of *section 579(3)*, a members' voluntary winding up of a company may be commenced if the company in general meeting has passed a resolution (whether before or after expiry of the period referred to in that *paragraph (a)* or the happening of the event referred to in that *paragraph (b)*) that the company be wound up voluntarily and *subsections (2)* to *(4)* are complied with.

(2) Where, in either of the cases mentioned in *subsection (1)*, it is proposed to wind up a company voluntarily, the directors of the company or, in the case of a company having more than 2 directors, the majority of the directors may, at a meeting of the directors, make a declaration to the effect that they have made a full inquiry into the affairs of the company, and that having done so, they have formed the opinion that the company

will be able to pay or discharge its debts and other liabilities in full within such period not exceeding 12 months after the commencement of the winding up as may be specified in the declaration.

(3) Such a declaration shall have no effect for the purposes of this Part unless—

(a) it is made at a meeting of the directors held not earlier than 30 days before—

(i) the date of the meeting referred to in *subsection (1)*, or

(ii) if the resolution referred to in that subsection is passed by the means provided under *section 193* or *194*, the date of the signing of the resolution by the last member to sign,

(b) it states the total amount of the company's assets and liabilities as at the latest practicable date before the date of making of the declaration and in any event at a date not more than 3 months before the date of that making,

(c) a report made, in accordance with the provisions of that subsection, by a person referred to in *subsection (4)* is attached to it, and

(d) either—

(i) the company has forwarded with each notice of the meeting at which the resolution is to be considered, or

(ii) if the means referred to in *section 193* or *194* for passing the resolution is followed, the company has appended to the resolution,

a copy of the declaration.

(4) The report referred to in *subsection (3)(c)* is a report drawn up, [in the form prescribed by the Minister][a], by a person qualified at the time of the report to be appointed, or to continue to be, the statutory auditor of the company and stating whether, in the opinion of that person, the declaration is not unreasonable.

(5) The company shall deliver, within 14 days after the commencement of the members' voluntary winding up under this section, a copy of the foregoing declaration to the Registrar.

(6) The provisions of this section shall be read and shall operate so that a members' voluntary winding up under this section may be carried on at a time falling before compliance with the requirement of *subsection (5)* that a copy of the declaration there referred to be delivered to the Registrar; however – should a failure to comply with that requirement occur – that failure then invalidates the carrying on of that activity, but this is without prejudice to the power of validation conferred on the court by *subsection (7)*.

(7) On application to it by any interested party, the court may, in any case where there has been a failure to comply with *subsection (5)*, declare that the carrying on of the members' voluntary winding up shall be valid for all purposes if the court is satisfied that it would be just and equitable to do so.

Amendments

a Words substituted by C(A)A 2017, s 98(f) (previously: "in the prescribed form").

581 Publication of resolution to wind up voluntarily

(1) Where a company has passed a resolution for its voluntary winding up, whether—

(a) the special resolution referred to in *section 202(1)(a)(i)* — in a case where the Summary Approval Procedure is employed, or

(b) the resolution referred to in *section 580(1)* — where the procedure there mentioned is employed,

it shall, within 14 days after the date of the passing of the resolution, give notice of the resolution by advertisement in *Iris Oifigiúil*.

(2) If default is made in complying with this section, the company concerned and any officer of it who is in default shall be guilty of a category 3 offence.

(3) For the purposes of *subsection (2)*, the liquidator of the company shall be deemed to be an officer of the company.

582 Protections and remedies for creditors in cases where declaration of solvency made

(1) This section applies where a company has passed a resolution to wind up voluntarily.

(2) If, on application to it by a creditor of the company in accordance with *subsection (3)*, the court—

(a) is satisfied that such creditor, together with any creditors supporting him or her in the application, represents one-fifth at least in number or value of the creditors of the company, and

(b) is of opinion that it is unlikely that the company will be able to pay or discharge its debts and other liabilities within the period specified in the declaration concerned referred to in *section 207* or *580(2)*,

the court may order that all the provisions of this Act relating to a creditors' voluntary winding up shall apply to the winding up of the company.

(3) An application under *subsection (2)* shall be made within 30 days after the date on which the resolution for voluntary winding up of the company has been advertised under *section 581(1)*.

(4) If (in a case where the Summary Approval Procedure is employed) an application is made by one or more members of the company in accordance with *section 211* to cancel the special resolution referred to in *section 202(1)(a)(i)*, the court may direct that that application and an application that is made under *subsection (2)* shall be heard together or may give such other direction in the matter as it thinks just.

(5) If the court makes an order of the kind referred to in *subsection (2)*—

(a) the person who held the office of liquidator immediately prior to the making of the order, or

(b) if no liquidator is acting, the company to which the order relates,

shall, within 21 days after the date of the making of the order, deliver a certified copy of such order to the Registrar.

(6) If default is made in complying with *subsection (5)*, the person referred to in *paragraph (a)* of it or, as the case may be, the company concerned and any officer of it who is in default shall be guilty of a category 4 offence.

(7) *Section 210* (civil sanctions where opinion as to solvency stated in declaration without reasonable grounds) shall apply in relation to a declaration referred to in *section 580(2)* and, for this purpose, references in *section 210* to the opinion referred to in *section 203(1)(f)*, *204(1)(f)*, *205(1)(c)*, *206(1)(b)* or *207(1)(b)* shall be read as references to the opinion referred to in *section 580(2)*.

583 Power of company to appoint liquidators

The company in general meeting shall appoint one or more liquidators for the purpose of winding up the affairs and distributing the assets of the company.

584 Duty of liquidator to call creditors' meeting if of opinion that company unable to pay its debts

(1) If the liquidator is at any time of the opinion that the company will not be able to pay or discharge its debts and other liabilities in full within the period stated in the declaration concerned referred to in *section 207* or *580(2)*, as the case may be, the liquidator shall—

(a) summon a meeting of creditors for a day not later than the 14th day after the day on which he or she formed that opinion,

(b) send notices of the creditors' meeting to the creditors by post not less than 10 days before the day on which that meeting is to be held,

(c) cause notice of the creditors' meeting to be advertised, at least 10 days before the date of the meeting, once in *Iris Oifigiúil* and once at least in 2 daily newspapers circulating in the locality in which the company's principal place of business in the State was situated during the relevant period, and

(d) during the period before the day on which the creditors' meeting is to be held, furnish creditors free of charge with such information concerning the affairs of the company as they may reasonably require,

and the notice of the creditors' meeting shall state the duty imposed by *paragraph (d)*.

(2) The liquidator shall also—

(a) make out a statement in the prescribed form as to the affairs of the company, including a statement of the company's assets and liabilities, a list of the outstanding creditors and the estimated amount of their claims,

(b) lay that statement before the creditors' meeting, and

(c) attend and preside at that meeting.

(3) As from the day on which the creditors' meeting is held under this section, this Act shall have effect as if—

(a) without prejudice to the powers of the court under *section 582(2)*, the directors' declaration referred to in *section 207* or *580(2)*, as the case may be, had not been made, and

(b) the creditors' meeting and the company meetings at which it was resolved that the company be wound up voluntarily were the meetings mentioned in *section 587*,

and, accordingly, the winding up shall become a creditors' voluntary winding up and any appointment made or committee established by the creditors' meeting shall be deemed to have been made or established by the creditors' meeting so mentioned.

(4) The appointment of a liquidator at a meeting called under this section shall not, subject to *subsection (5)*, affect the validity of any action previously taken by the liquidator appointed by the members of the company.

(5) Where—

(a) the creditors appoint a liquidator at a meeting called under this section, and

(b) there is a dispute as to any or all of the costs, charges or expenses incurred by, the liquidator appointed by the members of the company,

the liquidator appointed by the creditors, or any creditor, may apply to the court to determine the dispute and the court may, on such application, make such order as it thinks fit.

(6) Nothing in this section shall read as taking away any right in this Act of any person to present a petition to the court for the winding up of a company.

(7) If the liquidator fails to comply with *subsection (1)*, he or she shall be guilty of a category 3 offence.

(8) In this section "relevant period" means the period of 6 months immediately preceding the day on which were sent the notices summoning the company meeting at which it was resolved that the company be wound up voluntarily.

Chapter 4
Creditors' voluntary winding up

585 Application of Chapter

Save to the extent that the provision expressly provides otherwise, each provision of this Chapter applies only to a creditors' voluntary winding up.

586 Resolution for and commencement of creditors' voluntary winding up

(1) A company may be wound up voluntarily as a creditors' voluntary winding up.

(2) A winding up of a company as a creditors' voluntary winding up pursuant to *subsection (1)* may be initiated by the company in general meeting resolving that it cannot by reason of its liabilities continue its business, and that it be wound up as a creditors' voluntary winding up.

(3) A company shall be wound up as a creditors' voluntary winding up—

(a) if a creditors' meeting is held in accordance with *section 584* in relation to the company, or

(b) if the court makes an order under *section 582(2)* in relation to the company, or

(c) if, in a case in which—

(i) a special resolution referred to in *section 202(1)(a)(i)* — where the Summary Approval Procedure is purported to be employed, or

(ii) the resolution referred to in *section 580(1)* — where the procedure there mentioned is purported to be employed,

is purported to be passed, the declaration referred to in *section 207* or *580(2)* is not made in accordance with the relevant provisions of *Chapter 7* of *Part 4* or *section 580*, as the case may be.

(4) Where a company has passed a resolution for it to be wound up as a creditors' voluntary winding up, it shall, within 14 days after the date of the passing of the resolution, give notice of the resolution by advertisement in *Iris Oifigiúil*.

(5) If default is made in complying with *subsection (4)*, the company concerned and any officer of it who is in default shall be guilty of a category 3 offence.

(6) For the purposes of *subsection (5)*, the liquidator of the company shall be deemed to be an officer of the company.

587 Meeting of creditors

(1) The company shall cause a meeting of the creditors of the company (the "creditors' meeting") to be summoned for the day, or the day next following the day, on which there is to be held the meeting at which the resolution for a creditors' voluntary winding up is to be proposed.

(2) For that purpose, the company shall send to each creditor, at least 10 days before the date of the creditors' meeting, notice in writing of such meeting.

(3) The notice required by *subsection (2)* shall—

(a) state the date, time and location of the creditors' meeting,

(b) state the name and address of the person at that time proposed for appointment as liquidator, if any, and

(c) either—

(i) attach a list of the creditors of the company, or

(ii) notify the recipient of his or her rights under *subsection (4)*, together with details of the location at which the list of creditors of the company may be inspected.

(4) A creditor who has not been provided with a copy of the list of the creditors of the company under *subsection (3)(c)(i)* may, at any time prior to the holding of the creditors' meeting—

(a) having given the company 24 hours notice in writing of his or her intention to do so, inspect during business hours the list of creditors of the company at the registered office of the company, or

(b) request the company in writing to deliver a copy of the list of creditors of the company to him or her, and such a request shall be complied with by the company.

(5) That copy may be delivered by the company to the requesting person by post or, with the consent of the requesting person, in any other manner.

(6) The company shall cause notice of the creditors' meeting to be advertised, at least 10 days before the date of the meeting, once at least in 2 daily newspapers circulating in the district where the registered office or principal place of business of the company is situate; such notice is not required to include the list of creditors attached, pursuant to *subsection (3)(c)(i)*, to the notice required by *subsection (2)*.

(7) The directors of the company shall—

(a) cause a full statement of the position of the company's affairs, together with a list of the creditors of the company and the estimated amount of their claims, to be laid before the creditors' meeting, and

(b) appoint one of their number to preside at that meeting and it shall be the duty of the director so appointed to attend the creditors' meeting and preside at it.

(8) In the case of a company having a sole director, *subsection (7)(b)* shall be read as imposing the duty there provided on that director.

(9) If the meeting of the company at which the resolution for voluntary winding up is to be proposed is adjourned and the resolution is passed at an adjourned meeting, any resolution passed at the creditors' meeting shall have effect as if it had been passed immediately after the passing of the resolution for winding up the company.

(10) If default is made by the company—

(a) in complying with *subsection (1)*, *(2)*, *(3)* or *(6)*, or

(b) in permitting an inspection under *subsection (4)(a)*, or

(c) in complying with a request under *subsection (4)(b)*,

the company and any officer of it who is in default shall be guilty of a category 3 offence.

(11) If default is made by the directors of the company in complying with *subsection (7)* or by any director in complying with his or her duty under that subsection, the directors or director, as the case may be, shall be guilty of a category 3 offence.

588 Appointment of liquidator

(1) The creditors and the company at their respective meetings mentioned in *section 587* may nominate a person to be liquidator for the purpose of winding up the company.

(2) Subject to *subsection (4)*, if—

(a) the creditors and the company nominate different persons, the person nominated by the creditors shall be liquidator, and

(b) if no person is nominated by the creditors, the person, if any, nominated by the company shall be liquidator.

(3) Where a person nominated by the company to be liquidator takes office before the creditors make their nomination and a different person is nominated by the creditors, the first-mentioned person shall, by virtue of *subsection (2)(a)*, vacate office on the second-mentioned person's being nominated but—

(a) this is without prejudice to *subsection (4)*; and

(b) for the period before the holding of the creditors' meeting under *section 587*, the first-mentioned person's powers as liquidator are restricted as provided for in *section 630(2)*.

(4) Where different persons are nominated as liquidator, any director, member or creditor of the company may, within 14 days after the date on which the nomination was made by the creditors, apply to the court for the following order.

(5) That order is an order either—

(a) directing that the person nominated as liquidator by the company shall be liquidator instead of or jointly with the person nominated by the creditors, or

(b) appointing some other person to be liquidator instead of the person nominated by the creditors,

and the court, on the making of an application under *subsection (4)*, may make such an order accordingly.

(6) If at a meeting of creditors mentioned in *section 587* a resolution as to the creditors' nominee as liquidator is proposed, it shall be deemed to be passed when a majority, in value only, of the creditors present personally or by proxy and voting on the resolution have voted in favour of the resolution.

Chapter 5
Conduct of winding up

589 Commencement of court ordered winding up

(1) Save in a case falling within *subsection (2)*, the winding up of a company by the court shall be deemed to commence at the time of the presentation of the winding-up petition in respect of the company.

(2) Where, before the presentation of a winding-up petition in respect of a company, a resolution has been passed by the company for voluntary winding up, then, despite the fact that that petition is granted, the winding up of the company shall be deemed to have commenced at the time of the passing of the resolution.

(3) In a case falling within *subsection (2)*, unless the court, on proof of fraud or mistake, thinks fit to direct otherwise, all proceedings taken in the voluntary winding up shall be deemed to have been validly taken.

590 Commencement of voluntary winding up

A voluntary winding up shall be deemed to commence at the time of the passing of the resolution for voluntary winding up.

591 Copy of order for winding up or appointment to be forwarded to Registrar

(1) On the making of a winding-up order—

(a) such officer of the court as may be prescribed or directed by the court shall forthwith cause the Registrar to be furnished with such particulars as may be prescribed of the order, and

(b) a copy of the order shall, save where the company is the petitioner, be served by the petitioner, or such other person as the court may direct, upon the company at its registered office (if any) or, if there is no registered office or notice has not been given to the Registrar of such office, at its principal or last known principal place of business or upon such other person or persons or in such other manner as the court may direct.

(2) In a winding up by the court, on the making of an order appointing a liquidator (other than a provisional liquidator), such officer of the court as may be prescribed shall forthwith cause the Registrar to be furnished with such particulars as may be prescribed of the order.

592 Notice by voluntary liquidator of his or her appointment

(1) In a voluntary winding up, the liquidator of the company shall, within 14 days after the date of his or her appointment, deliver to the Registrar a notice of his or her appointment.

(2) *Subsection (1)* does not apply in the case of an appointment to which *section 636* or *637* (subsequent appointments of liquidator) applies; *section 643* governs notifications and filings of subsequent such appointments.

(3) The Registrar shall forward a copy of that notice of appointment to the Director.

(4) If a liquidator of a company fails to comply with *subsection (1)*, he or she shall be guilty of a category 4 offence.

593 Statement of company's affairs

(1) Where the court has made a winding-up order or appointed a provisional liquidator in relation to a company, there shall, unless the court thinks fit to order otherwise and so orders, be made out and filed in the court a statement as to the affairs of the company (the "statement") in the prescribed form, verified by affidavit.

(2) The statement shall show—

(a) particulars of the company's assets, debts and liabilities,

(b) the names, residences and occupations of the company's creditors,

(c) the securities held by those creditors respectively,

(d) the dates when those securities were respectively given, and

(e) such further or other information as may be prescribed or as the court may require.

(3) The statement shall be so filed and verified by—

(a) subject to *paragraph (b)*, one or more of the persons who are at the relevant date the directors of the company, or

(b) such of the persons mentioned in *subsection (4)* as the court may require to so file and verify the statement.

(4) The persons referred to in *subsection (3)(b)* are persons—

(a) who are or have been officers of the company,

(b) who have taken part in the formation of the company at any time within 12 months before the relevant date,

(c) who are in the employment of the company, or have been in the employment of the company within that period of 12 months, and are, in the opinion of the court, capable of giving the information required,

(d) who are or have been within that period of 12 months officers of or in the employment of a company which is, or within that period of 12 months was, an officer of the company to which the statement relates.

(5) The statement shall be so filed within 21 days after the relevant date or within such extended time as the court may for special reasons appoint.

(6) Subject to *section 594(7)*, any person making or concurring in making the statement and affidavit required by this section shall be allowed, and shall be paid out of the assets of the company, such costs and expenses incurred in and about the preparation and making of the statement and affidavit as the court may allow.

594 Supplemental provisions in relation to *section 593*

(1) In *section 593* and this section the "relevant date" means—

(a) in a case where a provisional liquidator is appointed to the company, the date of his or her appointment, and

(b) in a case where no such appointment is made, the date of the winding-up order in respect of the company.

(2) The one or more persons who have made the statement of affairs of a company under *section 593* (the "statement") shall serve a copy of the statement on the liquidator (or the provisional liquidator, as the case may be) of the company as soon as may be after it is prepared and in any case not later than the expiry of 21 days after the relevant date or such extended time as the court may appoint under *section 593(5)*.

(3) The one or more persons who have made the statement shall—

(a) at the liquidator's request, provide to the liquidator such information in relation to the company as the liquidator may reasonably require, and

(b) provide such assistance, as they are in a position to give, to the liquidator during the course, and for the purpose, of the liquidator's examining (following his or her receipt of the statement) the company's affairs as he or she may reasonably require.

(4) Where any person fails to comply with the request of a liquidator made in accordance with *subsection (3)*, the court may, on the application of the liquidator, direct the person to comply with such request.

(5) In *subsections (3)* and *(4)*, "liquidator" does not include a provisional liquidator.

(6) A person who is required to make or concur in making any statement of affairs of a company shall, before incurring any costs or expenses in and about the preparation and making of the statement, apply—

(a) to the liquidator for his or her sanction and submit to the liquidator a statement of the estimated costs and expenses which the person intends to incur, or

(b) if there is no liquidator, to the court for its sanction.

(7) Except by order of the court, no person shall be allowed out of the assets of the company any costs or expenses in and about the preparation of a statement of affairs which have not, before being incurred, been sanctioned by the liquidator or the court.

(8) If any person, without reasonable excuse, makes default in complying with any of the requirements of *section 593* or with any of the preceding requirements of this section, he or she shall be guilty of a category 3 offence.

(9) Any person who states in writing that the person is a creditor or contributory of the company shall, on payment of the prescribed fee, be entitled personally, or by his or her agent—

(a) to inspect, at all reasonable times, the statement registered in pursuance of *section 593*, and

(b) to be furnished with a copy of, or an extract from, it.

(10) Any person, not being a creditor or contributory of a company, who fraudulently states himself or herself to be a creditor or contributory of the company for the purpose of seeking to avail himself or herself of the provisions of *subsection (9)* shall be guilty of a category 3 offence.

595 Notification that a company is in liquidation, etc.

(1) Every invoice, order for goods or business letter issued by or on behalf of—

(a) a company that is being wound up, or

(b) a liquidator of such a company,

being a document on or in which the name of the company appears, shall contain a statement that the company is being wound up.

(2) *Subsection (1)* is in addition (in cases where a company is in receivership) to the obligations of the receiver of the property of the company under *section 429*.

(3) Every invoice, order for goods or business letter issued by or on behalf of—

(a) a company to which a provisional liquidator has been appointed,

(b) a provisional liquidator of the company, or

(c) a receiver of the property of such a company,

being a document—

(i) on or in which the name of the company appears, and

(ii) issued during the period of office of the provisional liquidator as such provisional liquidator,

shall contain a statement that a provisional liquidator has been appointed to the company.

(4) Any website of a company that is being wound up, and any electronic mail sent to a third party by, or on behalf of, such a company, shall contain a statement that the company is being wound up (and such a statement on a website shall be in a prominent and easily accessible place on it).

(5) Where the winding up of a company commences within one year after the date on which the company has changed its name in accordance with this Act, the former name as well as the existing name of the company shall appear on all notices and advertisements in relation to the winding up and in any website of the company and in any electronic mail sent to a third party by, or on behalf of, it.

(6) If default is made in complying with *subsection (1)*, *(3)* or (other than a case dealt with by *subsection (7)*) *(5)*—

(a) the company concerned and any officer of it who is in default, and

(b) any of the following persons who knowingly and intentionally authorises or permits the default, namely, any liquidator of the company and any receiver,

shall be guilty of a category 3 offence.

(7) If default is made in complying with the requirement under *subsection (4)* or *(5)* concerning the company's website, the company concerned and any officer of it who is in default shall be guilty of a category 3 offence.

(8) If default is made by a company, or any person acting on its behalf, in complying with the requirement under *subsection (4)* or *(5)* concerning electronic mail, then—

(a) in every case, the company and any officer of it who is in default, and

(b) where the default is made by a person acting on the company's behalf, that person,

shall be guilty of a category 3 offence.

(9) In this section "third party" means a person other than—

(a) an officer or employee of the company concerned, or

(b) a holding company or subsidiary of the company or an officer or employee of that holding company or subsidiary.

Chapter 6
Realisation of assets and related matters

596 Custody of company's property

(1) Upon the appointment of a liquidator to a company, the liquidator shall take into his or her custody or under his or her control the seal, books and records of the company, and all the property to which the company is or appears to be entitled.

(2) A person who, without lawful entitlement or authority, has—

(a) at the date of the appointment of a liquidator to a company, possession or control of the books, records or other property of the company, or

(b) subsequent to such date comes into such possession or control,

shall surrender immediately to the liquidator such books, records or other property, as the case may be.

(3) In this section "liquidator" does not include a provisional liquidator.

597 Circumstances in which floating charge is invalid

(1) Where a company is being wound up, a floating charge on the undertaking or property of the company created within 12 months before the date of commencement of the winding up shall, unless it is proved that the company immediately after the creation of the charge was solvent, be invalid.

(2) *Subsection (1)* does not apply to—

(a) money actually advanced or paid, or the actual price or value of goods or services sold or supplied, to the company at the time of or subsequently to the creation of, and in consideration for, the charge, nor

(b) interest on that amount at the appropriate rate.

(3) For the purposes of *subsection (2)*, the value of any goods or services sold or supplied by way of consideration for a floating charge is the amount in money which at the time they were sold or supplied could reasonably have been expected to be obtained for the goods or services in the ordinary course of business and on the same terms (apart from the consideration) as those on which they were sold or supplied to the company.

(4) Where a floating charge on the undertaking or property of a company is created in favour of a connected person, *subsection (1)* shall apply to such a charge as if the period of 12 months mentioned in that subsection were a period of 2 years.

598 Other circumstances in which floating charge is invalid

(1) Where—

(a) a company is being wound up,

(b) the company was, within 12 months before the date of commencement of the winding up, indebted to any officer of the company or a connected person,

(c) such indebtedness was discharged whether wholly or partly by the company or by any other person, and

(d) the company created a floating charge on any of its assets or property within 12 months before the date of commencement of the winding up in favour of the officer or connected person to whom such company was indebted,

then (without prejudice to any rights or liabilities arising apart from this section) such charge shall be invalid to the extent of the repayment referred to in *paragraph (c)* unless it is proved that the company immediately after the creation of the charge was solvent.

(2) In this section, "officer" includes a spouse, civil partner, child or nominee of an officer and the reference in this subsection to a child of an officer shall be deemed to include a child of the officer's civil partner who is ordinarily resident with the officer and the civil partner.

599 Related company may be required to contribute to debts of company being wound up

(1) On the application of the liquidator or any creditor or contributory of a company that is being wound up, the court, if it is satisfied that it is just and equitable to do so, may make the following order.

(2) That order is one that any company that is or has been related to the company being wound up shall pay to the liquidator of that company an amount equivalent to the whole or part of all or any of the debts provable in that winding up.

(3) The court may specify that that order shall be subject to such terms and conditions as the court thinks fit.

(4) In deciding whether it is just and equitable to make an order under this section the court shall have regard to the following matters:

- (a) the extent to which the related company took part in the management of the company being wound up;
- (b) the conduct of the related company towards the creditors of the company being wound up;
- (c) the effect which such order would be likely to have on the creditors of the related company concerned.

(5) No order shall be made under this section unless the court is satisfied that the circumstances that gave rise to the winding up of the company are attributable to the acts or omissions of the related company.

(6) Notwithstanding any other provision, it shall not be just and equitable to make an order under this section if the only ground for making the order is—

- (a) the fact that a company is related to another company, or
- (b) that creditors of the company being wound up have relied on the fact that another company is or has been related to the first-mentioned company.

(7) For the purposes of this section—

"company" includes any company, and any other body, which is liable to be wound up under this Act;

"creditor" means a creditor, by assignment or otherwise, to whom the company is indebted in a sum exceeding €10,000 or 2 or more creditors, by assignment or otherwise, to whom in aggregate the company is indebted in a sum exceeding €20,000.

(8) Where an application for an order under this section seeks to require a credit institution to contribute to the debts of a related company, a copy of every such application shall be sent by the applicant to the Central Bank which shall be entitled to be heard by the court before an order is made.

600 Pooling of assets of related companies

(1) Where 2 or more related companies are being wound up and the court, on the application of the liquidator, or any creditor or contributor, of any of the companies, is satisfied that it is just and equitable to do so, it may make the following order.

(2) That order is one that, to the extent specified in the order, the companies shall be wound up together as if they were one company, and if such an order is made, it shall, subject to the provisions of this section, have effect and all the relevant provisions of this Part shall apply accordingly.

(3) The court may specify that that order shall be subject to such terms and conditions as the court thinks fit.

(4) In determining those terms and conditions, the court shall have particular regard to the interests of those persons who are members of some, but not all, of the companies.

(5) Where the court makes an order under this section—

- (a) the court may remove any liquidator of any of the companies, and appoint any person to act as liquidator of any one or more of the companies,
- (b) the court may give such directions as it thinks fit for the purpose of giving effect to the order,
- (c) nothing in this section or the order shall affect the rights of any secured creditor of any of the companies,
- (d) debts of a company that are to be paid in priority to all other debts of the company pursuant to *sections 621* and *622* shall, to the extent that they are not paid out of the assets of that company, be subject to the claims of holders of debentures under any floating charge created by any of the other companies,
- (e) unless the court otherwise orders, the claims of all unsecured creditors of the companies shall rank equally among themselves.

(6) In deciding whether it is just and equitable to make an order under this section, the court shall have regard to the following matters:

- (a) the extent to which any of the companies took part in the management of any of the other companies;
- (b) the conduct of any of the companies towards the creditors of any of the other companies;
- (c) the extent to which the circumstances that gave rise to the winding up of any of the companies is attributable to the acts or omissions of any of the other companies;
- (d) the extent to which the businesses of the companies have been intermingled.

(7) Notwithstanding any other provision, it shall not be just and equitable to make an order under this section if the only ground for making the order is—

- (a) the fact that a company is related to another company, or
- (b) that creditors of a company being wound up have relied on the fact that another company is or has been related to the first-mentioned company.

(8) Notice of an application to the court for the purposes of this section shall be served on every company specified in the application, and on such other persons as the court may direct, not later than the end of the 8th day before the day the application is heard.

(9) Without prejudice to *subsection (8)*, where a related company, the subject of an application for an order under this section, is a credit institution, a copy of the application shall be sent by the applicant to the Central Bank which shall be entitled to be heard by the court before an order is made.

601 Power of liquidator to accept shares as consideration for sale of property of company

(1) This section applies where a company is proposed to be, or is in course of being, wound up as a members' voluntary winding up, and the whole or part of its business or property is proposed to be transferred or sold to another company, whether a company registered under this Act, an existing company or any other type of company or undertaking (in this section referred to as the "transferee company").

(2) Where this section applies, the liquidator of the first-mentioned company in *subsection (1)* (in this section referred to as the "transferor company") may, subject to *subsection (3)*—

(a) in compensation or part compensation for the foregoing transfer or sale, receive shares, policies or other like interests in the transferee company for distribution among the members of the transferor company, or

(b) enter into any other arrangement whereby the members of the transferor company may, in lieu of receiving cash, shares, policies or other like interests, or in addition to them, participate in the profits of, or receive any other benefit from, the transferee company.

(3) The powers of the liquidator under *subsection (2)* are not exercisable unless a special resolution of the company sanctions the exercise of those powers by the liquidator, whether generally or with regard to the particular arrangement concerned, but this subsection is without prejudice to *subsections (5)* and *(8)*.

(4) Any sale or arrangement in pursuance of this section shall be binding on the members of the transferor company.

(5) If—

(a) the voting rights conferred by any shares in the transferor company were not cast in favour of the resolution concerned referred to in *subsection (3)* conferring the sanction there mentioned on the liquidator, and

(b) the holder of those shares expresses his or her dissent from such sanction in writing addressed to the liquidator and left at the registered office of the company within 7 days after the date of passing of the resolution, that holder may require the liquidator either to—

(i) abstain from carrying the resolution into effect, or

(ii) purchase that part of his or her interest which those shares represent at a price to be determined by agreement, or by arbitration in accordance with *subsections (9)* and *(10)*.

(6) If the liquidator elects to purchase that holder's interest, the purchase money shall be paid before the company is dissolved and, unless otherwise provided for, shall be deemed to be, and shall be paid as part of, the costs, charges and expenses of the winding up.

(7) A resolution referred to in *subsection (3)* shall not be invalid for the purposes of this section by reason that it was obtained before or concurrently—

(a) with the passing of—

  (i) the special resolution referred to in *section 202(1)(a)(i)* — in a case where the Summary Approval Procedure is employed, or

  (ii) the resolution referred to in *section 580(1)* — where the procedure there mentioned is employed,

  or

(b) with the passing of a resolution for appointing a liquidator or liquidators in that winding up.

(8) However a resolution referred to in *subsection (3)* shall not be effective to confer the sanction there mentioned if an order is made, within a year after the date of the resolution's passing, for winding up the company by the court, unless the resolution is confirmed by the court.

(9) An arbitration referred to in *subsection (5)(ii)* shall be conducted by a single arbitrator appointed by agreement in writing between the holder of shares referred to in *subsection (5)* and the liquidator or, in the absence of such agreement, by 2 arbitrators, one of whom shall be appointed in writing by each party to the arbitration.

(10) The provisions of the Arbitration Act 2010 applicable to arbitrations referred to in section 29 of that Act shall apply to an arbitration referred to in *subsection (5)*.

602 Voidance of dispositions of property, etc. after commencement of winding up

(1) This section applies to each of the following acts in any winding up of a company:

(a) any disposition of the property of the company;

(b) any transfer of shares in the company; or

(c) any alteration in the status of the members of the company,

made after the commencement of the winding up.

(2) Without prejudice to *subsection (3)*, an act to which this section applies that is done without the sanction of—

(a) the liquidator of the company, or

(b) a director of the company who has, by virtue of *section 677(3)* retained the power to do such act,

shall, unless the court otherwise orders, be void.

(3) Nothing in this section makes a person who does an act rendered void by this section liable for doing such act, being an act that was done by the person at the request of the company, unless it is proved that, prior to the person's doing the act, the person had actual notice that the company was being wound up.

(4) If a company that is being wound up makes a request of a person to do an act referred to in *subsection (3)* and does not, at or before the time of making the request, inform the person that it is being wound up, the company and any officer of it who is in default shall be guilty of a category 2 offence.

(5) Nothing in *subsection (4)* shall be read as limiting any liability, civil or criminal, that, apart from this section, may attach to a company, or any officer of it, for making a request of the kind referred to in that subsection, irrespective of the consideration that the relevant facts have been communicated to the person concerned or that those facts are otherwise in the knowledge of that person.

603 Voidance of executions against property of company

Unless the court orders otherwise, where a company is being wound up, each of the following shall be void, namely, any—

(a) attachment,

(b) sequestration,

(c) distress, or

(d) execution,

put in force against the property or effects of the company after the commencement of the winding up.

604 Unfair preference: effect of winding up on antecedent and other transactions

(1) *Subsection (2)* applies to each of the following acts, namely, any:

(a) conveyance;

(b) mortgage; or

(c) delivery of goods, payment, execution or other act,

relating to property made or done by or against a company, which is unable to pay its debts as they become due, in favour of—

(i) any creditor of the company, or

(ii) any person on trust for any such creditor.

(2) An act to which this subsection applies, that is done with a view to giving the creditor referred to in [*subsection (1)(i)* or *(ii)*][a], or any surety or guarantor for the debt due to such creditor, a preference over the other creditors of the company, shall be deemed an unfair preference of its creditors and be invalid accordingly if—

(a) a winding up of the company commences within 6 months after the date of the doing of the act, and

(b) the company is, at the time of the commencement of the winding up, unable to pay its debts (taking into account the contingent and prospective liabilities).

(3) Any conveyance or assignment by a company of all its property to trustees for the benefit of all its creditors shall be void.

(4) An act to which *subsection (2)* applies in favour of a connected person which was done within 2 years before the commencement of the winding up of the company shall, unless the contrary is shown, be deemed in the event of the company being wound up—

(a) to have been done with a view to giving such person a preference over the other creditors, and

(b) to be an unfair preference, and be invalid accordingly.

(5) *Subsections (2)* and *(4)* shall not affect the rights of any person making title in good faith and for valuable consideration through or under a creditor of the company.

Amendments

a Words substituted by C(A)A 2017, s 98(g) (previously: "*subsection (1)(i)*,").

---

605 Liabilities and rights of persons who have been unfairly preferred

(1) Where—

(a) a company is being wound up, and

(b) any act done is void under *section 604* as an unfair preference of a person interested in property mortgaged or charged to secure the company's debt,

then (without prejudice to any rights or liabilities arising apart from this section) the person preferred shall be subject to the same liabilities and shall have the same rights as if he or she had undertaken to be personally liable as surety for the debt to the extent of the charge on the property or the value of his or her interest, whichever is the less.

(2) The value of the foregoing person's interest shall be determined as at the date of the act constituting the unfair preference, and shall be determined as if the interest were free of all encumbrances other than those to which the charge for the company's debt was then subject.

(3) On any application made to the court in relation to any payment on the ground that the payment was an unfair preference of a surety or guarantor, the court—

(a) may determine any questions relating to the payment arising between the person to whom the payment was made and the surety or guarantor and grant relief in respect thereof, and

(b) for that purpose, may give leave to bring in the surety or guarantor as a third party as in the case of an action for the recovery of the sum paid,

and jurisdiction to do any of those things may be exercised notwithstanding that it is not necessary to exercise such jurisdiction for the purposes of the winding up.

(4) *Subsection (3)* shall apply, with the necessary modifications, in relation to transactions other than the payment of money as it applies to payments.

606 Restriction of rights of creditor as to execution or attachment in case of company being wound up

(1) Subject to *subsections (2)* to *(4)*, where a creditor has—

(a) issued execution against the goods or lands of a company, or

(b) attached any debt due to the company,

and the company is subsequently wound up, the creditor shall not be entitled to retain the benefit of the execution or attachment against the liquidator in the winding up of the company unless the creditor has completed the execution or attachment before the commencement of the winding up.

(2) In a case where a creditor has had notice of a meeting having been called at which a resolution for voluntary winding up of the company concerned is to be proposed, then, for the purposes of *subsection (1)*, the date on which the creditor so had notice shall be substituted for the date of the commencement of the winding up.

(3) A person who purchases in good faith, under a sale by a sheriff, any goods of a company on which an execution has been levied shall, in all cases, acquire a good title to them against the liquidator.

(4) Notwithstanding *subsection (1)*, the rights conferred by that subsection on the liquidator may be set aside by the court in favour of the creditor to such extent and subject to such terms as the court thinks fit.

(5) For the purposes of this section—

(a) an execution against goods shall be deemed to be completed by seizure and sale,

(b) an attachment of a debt shall be deemed to be completed by receipt of the debt,

(c) an execution against land shall be deemed to be completed by seizure, and

(d) an execution in the case of an equitable interest shall be deemed to be completed by the appointment of a receiver.

(6) Nothing in this section shall give any validity to any payment constituting an unfair preference.

(7) In this section—

"goods" includes all chattels personal;

"sheriff" includes any officer charged with the execution of a writ or other process.

607 Duties of sheriff as to goods taken in execution

(1) Subject to *subsection (5)*, where any goods of a company are taken in execution and, before the sale of them or the completion of the execution by the receipt or recovery of the full amount of the levy, notice is served on the sheriff that, in relation to the company—

(a) a provisional liquidator has been appointed, or

(b) a winding-up order has been made, or

(c) a resolution for voluntary winding up has been passed,

the sheriff shall, on being required to do so by the liquidator, deliver to the liquidator the goods and any money seized or received in part satisfaction of the execution.

(2) However, in the foregoing case, the costs of the execution shall be a first charge on the goods or the money so delivered, and the liquidator may sell the goods or a sufficient part of them for the purpose of satisfying that charge.

(3) Subject to *subsection (5)*, where under an execution in respect of a judgment for a sum exceeding €1,000 the goods of a company are sold or money is paid in order to avoid sale, the following procedures shall be adopted by the sheriff, namely, he or she shall—

(a) deduct the costs of the execution from the proceeds of the sale or the money paid,

(b) retain the balance for a period of 14 days after the date of the sale or the payment of the money,

and, if the events referred to in *subsection (4)(a)* and *(b)* occur, the sheriff shall pay the balance to the liquidator of the company who shall be entitled to retain it as against the execution creditor.

(4) The events mentioned in *subsection (3)* are—

(a) within the period referred to in *subsection (3)(b)*, notice is served on the sheriff of a petition for the winding up of the company having been presented or of a meeting having been called at which there is to be proposed a resolution for the voluntary winding up of the company, and

(b) an order is made or a resolution is passed, as the case may be, for the winding up of the company.

(5) Notwithstanding *subsection (1)* or *(3)*, the rights conferred by either subsection on the liquidator may be set aside by the court in favour of the creditor to such extent and subject to such terms as the court thinks fit.

(6) The notice referred to in *subsection (1)* or *(4)* shall be in writing and addressed to the sheriff and may be served by being delivered by hand, or by pre-paid registered post, at his or her office.

(7) In this section "goods" and "sheriff" have the same meaning as they have in *section 606*.

608 Power of the court to order return of assets which have been improperly transferred

(1) The court has the following power where, on the application of a liquidator, creditor or contributory of a company which is being wound up, it can be shown to the satisfaction of the court that—

(a) any property of the company of any kind whatsoever was disposed of either by way of conveyance, transfer, mortgage, security, loan, or in any way whatsoever whether by act or omission, direct or indirect, and

(b) the effect of such disposal was to perpetrate a fraud on the company, its creditors or members.

(2) That power of the court is to order, if it deems it just and equitable to do so, any person who appears to have—

(a) the use, control or possession of the property concerned, or

(b) the proceeds of the sale or development of that property,

to deliver it or them, or pay a sum in respect thereof, to the liquidator on such terms or conditions as the court thinks fit.

(3) This section shall not apply to any conveyance, mortgage, delivery of goods, payment, execution or other act relating to property made or done by or against a company to which *section 604* applies.

(4) In deciding whether it is just and equitable to make an order under this section, the court shall have regard to the rights of persons who have *bona fide* and for value acquired an interest in the property the subject of the application.

(5) This section is in addition to, and not in substitution for, any restitutionary or other relief by way of recovery (including the remedy of tracing) that is available to a liquidator or any other person.

609 Personal liability of officers of company where adequate accounting records not kept

(1) Subject to *subsection (2)*, if—

(a) a company that is being wound up and that is unable to pay all of its debts has contravened any of *sections 281* to *285*, and

(b) the court considers that such contravention has—

(i) contributed to the company's inability to pay all of its debts, or

(ii) resulted in substantial uncertainty as to the assets and liabilities of the company, or

(iii) substantially impeded the orderly winding up of the company,

the court, on the application of the liquidator or any creditor or contributory of the company, has the following power.

(2) That power of the court is to declare, if it thinks it proper to do so, that any one or more of the officers and former officers of the company who, with respect to the contravention, is or are in default shall be personally liable, without any limitation of

liability, for all, or such part as may be specified by the court, of the debts and other liabilities of the company.

(3) On the hearing of an application under this section, the person bringing the application may himself or herself give evidence or call witnesses.

(4) Where the court makes a declaration under this section, it may give such directions as it thinks proper for the purpose of giving effect to the declaration.

(5) In particular, and without limiting *subsection (4)*, the order providing for a declaration under this section, or a supplemental order, may include provision for making the liability of any person under the declaration (the "respondent") a charge on—

(a) any debt or obligation due from the company to the respondent, or

(b) any mortgage or charge, or any interest in any mortgage or charge, on any assets of the company held by or vested in—

  (i) the respondent or any company or other person on the respondent's behalf, or

  (ii) any person claiming as assignee from or through the respondent or any company or other person acting on behalf of the first-mentioned person in this subparagraph.

(6) The court may from time to time make such further order as may be necessary for the purpose of enforcing any charge imposed under *subsection (5)*.

(7) In *subsection (5)(b)(ii)* "assignee" includes any person to whom or in whose favour, by the directions of the person liable under the declaration, the debt, obligation, mortgage or charge was created, issued or transferred or the interest created; however the expression does not include an assignee for valuable consideration (not including consideration by way of marriage) given in good faith and without notice of any of the matters on the ground of which the declaration is made.

(8) The court shall not make a declaration under this section in respect of a person if it considers that—

(a) the person took all reasonable steps to secure compliance by the company with *sections 281* to *285*, or

(b) the person had reasonable grounds for believing and did believe that a competent and reliable person, acting under the supervision or control of a director of the company who has been formally allocated such responsibility, was—

  (i) charged with the duty of ensuring that those sections were complied with, and

  (ii) in a position to discharge that duty.

(9) This section shall have effect notwithstanding that the person concerned may be criminally liable in respect of the matters on the ground of which the declaration is to be made.

(10) In this section "officer", in relation to a company, includes a person who has been convicted of an offence under *section 389*, *392*, *393*, *406* or *876* concerning accounting records of the company or, as the case may be, a statement made to statutory auditors concerning such records.

610 Civil liability for fraudulent or reckless trading of company

(1) If in the course of the winding up of a company or in the course of proceedings under *Part 10* in relation to a company, it appears that—

(a) any person was, while an officer of the company, knowingly a party to the carrying on of any business of the company in a reckless manner, or

(b) any person was knowingly a party to the carrying on of any business of the company with intent to defraud creditors of the company, or creditors of any other person or for any fraudulent purpose,

the court, on the application of the liquidator or examiner of the company, a receiver of property of the company or any creditor or contributory of it, has the following power.

(2) That power of the court is to declare, if it thinks it proper to do so, that the person first-mentioned in *paragraph (a)* or *(b)* of *subsection (1)* shall be personally responsible, without any limitation of liability, for all or any part of the debts or other liabilities of the company as the court may direct.

(3) Without prejudice to the generality of *subsection (1)(a)*, an officer of a company shall be deemed to have been knowingly a party to the carrying on of any business of the company in a reckless manner if—

(a) the person was a party to the carrying on of such business and, having regard to the general knowledge, skill and experience that may reasonably be expected of a person in his or her position, the person ought to have known that his or her actions or those of the company would cause loss to the creditors of the company, or any of them, or

(b) the person was a party to the contracting of a debt by the company and did not honestly believe on reasonable grounds that the company would be able to pay the debt when it fell due for payment as well as all its other debts (taking into account the contingent and prospective liabilities).

(4) Notwithstanding anything contained in *subsection (2)*, the court may grant a declaration on the grounds set out in *subsection (1)(a)* only if—

(a) *paragraph (a)*, *(b)*, *(c)* or *(d)* of *section 570* applies to the company concerned, and

(b) an applicant for such a declaration, being a creditor or contributory of the company or any person on whose behalf such application is made, suffered loss or damage as a consequence of any behaviour mentioned in *subsection (1)*.

(5) In deciding whether it is proper to make a declaration on the ground set out in *subsection (3)(b)*, the court shall have regard to whether the creditor in question was, at the time the debt was incurred, aware of the company's financial state of affairs

and, notwithstanding such awareness, nevertheless assented to the incurring of the debt.

(6) Where the court makes a declaration under this section, it may provide that sums recovered under this section shall be paid to such person or classes of persons, for such purposes, in such amounts or proportions at such time or times and in such respective priorities among themselves as such declaration may specify.

(7) On the hearing of an application under this section, the applicant may himself or herself give evidence or call witnesses.

(8) Where it appears to the court that any person in respect of whom a declaration has been sought on the grounds set out in *subsection (1)(a)* has acted honestly and responsibly in relation to the conduct of the affairs of the company or any matter or matters on the ground of which such declaration is sought to be made, the court may, having regard to all the circumstances of the case, relieve him or her either wholly or in part, from personal liability on such terms as it may think fit.

611 Supplemental provisions in relation to *section 610*

(1) Where the court makes a declaration under *section 610*, it may give such directions as it thinks proper for the purpose of giving effect to the declaration.

(2) In particular, and without limiting *subsection (1)* or *section 610(6)*, the order providing for a declaration under *section 610*, or a supplemental order, may include provision for making the liability of any person under the declaration (the "respondent") a charge on—

(a) any debt or obligation due from the company to the respondent, or

(b) any mortgage or charge, or any interest in any mortgage or charge, on any assets of the company held by or vested in—

 (i) the respondent or any company or other person on the respondent's behalf, or

 (ii) any person claiming as assignee from or through the respondent or any company or other person acting on behalf of the first-mentioned person in this subparagraph.

(3) Where a charge is imposed as mentioned in *subsection (2)*, the court may from time to time make such further order as may be necessary for the purpose of enforcing that charge.

(4) *Section 610(1)(a)* shall not apply in relation to the carrying on of the business of a company during a period when the company is under the protection of the court.

(5) *Section 610* and this section shall have effect notwithstanding that—

(a) the person in respect of whom the declaration has been sought under *section 610* may be criminally liable in respect of the matters on the ground of which such declaration is to be made, or

(b) any matter or matters on the ground of which the declaration under *section 610* is to be made have occurred outside the State.

(6) In *section 610* "officer", in relation to a company, includes a statutory auditor or liquidator or provisional liquidator of the company, a receiver of property of the company and a shadow director of it.

(7) In *subsection (2)(b)(ii)* "assignee" includes any person to whom or in whose favour, by the directions of the person liable, the debt, obligation, mortgage or charge was created, issued or transferred or the interest created, but does not include an assignee for valuable consideration (not including consideration by way of marriage) given in good faith and without notice of any of the matters on the ground of which the declaration is made.

612 Power of court to assess damages against certain persons

(1) *Subsection (2)* applies if in the course of winding up a company it appears that—

(a) any person who has taken part in the formation or promotion of the company, or

(b) any past or present officer, liquidator, provisional liquidator or examiner of the company, or receiver of the property of the company,

has misapplied or retained or become liable or accountable for any money or property of the company, or has been guilty of any misfeasance or other breach of duty or trust in relation to the company.

(2) The court may, on the application of the Director or the liquidator or any creditor or contributory of the company, examine into the conduct of the promoter, officer, liquidator, examiner or receiver, and compel him or her—

(a) to repay or restore the money or property or any part of it respectively with interest at such rate as the court thinks just, or

(b) to contribute such sum to the assets of the company by way of compensation in respect of the misapplication, retainer, misfeasance or other breach of duty or trust as the court thinks just.

(3) This section shall have effect notwithstanding that the person in respect of whom an order has been sought under it may be criminally liable in respect of the matters on the ground of which the order is to be made.

613 Directors of holding company: power of court to assess damages against them

(1) *Subsection (2)* applies if, in the course of winding up a company which is a subsidiary of another company, it appears that any director of the subsidiary's holding company has—

(a) misapplied or retained or become liable or accountable for any money or property of the subsidiary, or

(b) been guilty of any misfeasance or other breach of duty or trust in relation to the subsidiary.

(2) The court may, on the application of the liquidator or any creditor, contributory or member of the subsidiary, examine into the conduct of the director concerned and compel him or her—

(a) to repay or restore the money or property or any part of it respectively with interest at such rate as the court thinks just, or

(b) to contribute such sum to the assets of the subsidiary by way of compensation in respect of the misapplication, retainer, misfeasance or other breach of duty or trust as the court thinks just.

(3) This section—

(a) shall have effect notwithstanding that the person in respect of whom an order has been sought under it may be criminally liable in respect of the matters on the ground of which the order is to be made, and

(b) is without prejudice to any other basis for imposing liability on any person (whether related to the company or not) in respect of the person's acts or defaults in relation to the company or its property.

614 Vesting of property of company in liquidator

(1) Where a company is being wound up, the court may, on the application of the liquidator, by order, direct that all or any part of the property of whatsoever description belonging to the company or held by trustees on its behalf shall vest in the liquidator by his or her official name.

(2) On such an order being made—

(a) the property to which the order relates shall vest accordingly in the liquidator, and

(b) the liquidator may, after giving such indemnity, if any, as the court may direct, bring or defend in his or her official name any action or other legal proceeding which relates to that property or which it is necessary to bring or defend for the purpose of effectually winding up the company and recovering its property.

615 Disclaimer of onerous property in case of company being wound up

(1) In this section "onerous property" means property (whether tangible or intangible) that is property of a company which is being wound up and that falls into one or more of the following categories:

(a) land of whatsoever kind burdened with onerous covenants;

(b) shares or stock in any company or undertaking;

(c) an unprofitable contract;

(d) any other property which is unsaleable or not readily saleable by reason of its binding the possessor of it to the performance of any onerous act or to the payment of any sum of money.

(2) Subject to *subsections (4)* and *(7)*, the liquidator of the company concerned may, with the leave of the court and subject to the provisions of this section, by writing signed by him or her, at any time within the relevant period, disclaim onerous property; such leave may be granted by the court and the property disclaimed notwithstanding that the liquidator—

(a) has endeavoured to sell or has taken possession of the property, or

(b) has exercised any act of ownership in relation to it.

(3) In *subsection (2)* "relevant period" means the period of 12 months after the date of the commencement of the winding up of the company or such extended period as may be allowed by the court.

(4) Where the existence of onerous property has not come to the knowledge of the liquidator of the company concerned within one month after the date of the commencement of the winding up, the power under this section of disclaiming the property may be exercised at any time within 12 months after the date on which the liquidator has become aware thereof or such extended period as may be allowed by the court.

(5) The disclaimer shall operate to determine, as from the date of disclaimer, the rights, interests and liabilities of the company, and the property of the company, in or in respect of the property disclaimed; however it shall not, except so far as is necessary for the purpose of releasing the company and the property of the company from liability, affect the rights or liabilities of any other person.

(6) The court, before or on granting leave to disclaim, may require such notices to be given to persons interested and impose such terms as a condition of granting leave, and make such other order in the matter as the court thinks just.

(7) The liquidator shall not be entitled to disclaim any property under this section in any case where—

(a) an application in writing has been made to the liquidator by any person interested in the property requiring the liquidator to decide whether he or she will or will not disclaim, and

(b) the liquidator has not, within a period of 28 days after the date of receipt of the application or such further period as may be allowed by the court, given notice to the applicant that he or she intends to apply to the court for leave to disclaim.

(8) Any person damaged by the operation of a disclaimer under this section shall be deemed to be a creditor of the company concerned to the amount of the damages, and may accordingly prove the amount as a debt in the winding up.

616 Rescission of certain contracts and provisions supplemental to *section 615*

(1) The court may, on the application of any person who is, as against the liquidator, entitled to the benefit or subject to the burden of a contract made with the company, make an order rescinding the contract on such terms as to payment by or to either party of damages for the non-performance of the contract, or otherwise as the court thinks just.

(2) Any damages payable under such an order to any such person shall be deemed to be a debt proved and admitted in the winding up.

(3) Subject to *subsection (6)*, the court, on an application by any person who either claims any interest in any property disclaimed under *section 615* or is under any

liability not discharged by this Act in respect of any property so disclaimed, has, on hearing any such persons as it thinks fit, the following power.

(4) That power of the court is to make an order for the vesting of the property in, or the delivery of the property to, any person entitled to it, or to whom it may seem just that the property should be delivered by way of compensation for any liability of the foregoing kind, or a trustee for him or her, and on such terms as the court may think just.

(5) On any such vesting order being made, the property comprised therein shall vest accordingly in the person named in the order in that behalf without any conveyance or assignment for the purpose.

(6) Where the property disclaimed under *section 615* is of a leasehold nature, the court shall not make a vesting order under this section in favour of any person claiming under the company, whether as under-lessee or as mortgagee by demise, except upon the terms of making that person—

(a) subject to the same liabilities and obligations as those to which the company was subject under the lease in respect of the property at the commencement of the winding up, or

(b) if the court thinks fit, subject only to the same liabilities and obligations as if the lease had been assigned to that person at that date,

and in either event (if the case so requires), as if the lease had comprised only the property comprised in the vesting order.

(7) Any mortgagee or under-lessee declining to accept the making of a vesting order upon such terms as are referred to in *subsection (6)* shall be excluded from all interest in and security upon the property concerned.

(8) If there is no person claiming under the company who is willing to accept the making of an order upon such terms as are referred to in *subsection (6)*, the court shall have power to vest the estate and interest of the company in the property concerned in any person liable either personally or in a representative character, and either alone or jointly with the company, to perform the lessee's covenants in the lease, freed and discharged from all estates, encumbrances and interests created therein by the company.

Chapter 7
Distribution

617 Costs, etc. in winding up

(1) All costs, charges and expenses properly incurred in the winding up of a company, including the remuneration of the liquidator, remaining after payment of—

(a) the fees and expenses properly incurred in preserving, realising or getting in the assets, and

(b) where the company has previously commenced to be wound up voluntarily, such remuneration, costs and expenses as the court may allow to a liquidator appointed in such voluntary winding up, shall be payable out of the property of the company in priority to all other claims, and shall be paid or discharged in the order of priority set out in *subsection (2)*.

(2) The costs, charges and expenses referred to in *subsection (1)* shall, subject to any order made by the court in a winding up by it, be liable to the following payments which shall be made in the following order of priority, namely:

(a) First — In the case of a winding up by the court, the costs of the petition, including the costs of any person appearing on the petition whose costs are allowed by the court;

(b) Next — Any costs and expenses necessarily incurred in connection with the summoning, advertisement and holding of a creditors' meeting under *section 587*;

(c) Next — The costs and expenses necessarily incurred in and about the preparation and making of, or concurring in the making of, the statement of the company's affairs and the accompanying list of creditors and the amounts due to them as required by *section 587(7)*;

(d) Next — The necessary disbursements of the liquidator, other than expenses properly incurred in preserving, realising or getting in the assets as provided for in *subsection (1)*;

(e) Next — The costs payable to the solicitor for the liquidator;

(f) Next — The remuneration of the liquidator;

(g) Next — The out-of-pocket expenses necessarily incurred by the committee of inspection (if any).

(3) *Subsection (4)* applies in relation to a person who has provided funds to discharge any such costs, charges or expenses (other than costs or expenses referred to in *subsection (2)(b)* or *(c)*) as are referred to in *subsection (1)*.

(4) Such person shall be entitled to be reimbursed to the extent of the funds so provided by him or her in the same order of priority as to payment out of the property of the company as would otherwise have applied to the costs, charges or expenses concerned.

618 Distribution of property of company

(1) Subject to the provisions of this Act as to preferential payments, the property of a company on its winding up—

(a) shall, subject to *subsection (2)*, be applied in satisfaction of its liabilities *pari passu*, and

(b) shall, subject to such application, and unless the constitution of the company otherwise provides, be distributed among the members according to their rights and interests in the company.

(2) Nothing in *subsection (1)(a)* shall in any way affect any rights or obligations of the company or any other person arising as a result of any agreement entered into by any person under which any particular liability of the company to any general creditor is

postponed in favour of or subordinated to the rights or claims of any other person to whom the company may be in any way liable.

(3) Subject to the provisions of this Part, in the case of a members' voluntary winding up, the liquidator may, with the sanction of a special resolution of the company and any other sanction required by this Act, divide among the members, *in specie* or kind, the whole or any part of the property of the company (whether they shall consist of property of the same kind or not) and may, for such purpose—

(a) set such value as he or she deems fair upon any property to be divided in that manner, and

(b) determine how such division shall be carried out as between the members or different classes of members,

but so that no member shall be compelled to accept any shares or other securities on which there is any liability.

(4) In the case of such a voluntary winding up, the liquidator may, subject to the provisions of this Part and with the like sanction, vest the whole or any part of such property in trustees upon such trusts for the benefit of the members as the liquidator, with the like sanction, shall think fit, but so that no member shall be compelled to accept any shares or other securities on which there is any liability.

(5) In *subsection (2)*—

"liability" includes a contingent liability;

"person" includes a class of persons.

619 Application of bankruptcy rules in winding up of insolvent companies

(1) In the winding up of an insolvent company the same rules shall prevail and be observed relating to—

(a) the respective rights of secured and unsecured creditors,

(b) debts provable, and

(c) the valuation of annuities and future and contingent liabilities,

as are in force for the time being under the law of bankruptcy relating to the estates of persons adjudicated bankrupt.

(2) In particular, all persons who in any such case would be entitled to prove for and receive dividends out of the property of the company may come in under the winding up and make such claims against the company as they respectively are entitled to by virtue of this section.

(3) Subsection (1) of section 51 of the Bankruptcy Act 1988 shall apply in the winding up of an insolvent company and, accordingly, the reference in that subsection to the date of adjudication shall be read as—

(a) subject to *paragraph (b)*, a reference to, as the case may be—

(i) the presentation of a petition for the winding up of the company by the court, or

(ii) the passing of a resolution for voluntary winding up,

and

(b) where, before the presentation of a petition for the winding up of the company by the court, a resolution has been passed by the company for voluntary winding up, a reference to the passing of the resolution.

620 Debts which may be proved

(1) Subject to the provisions of this section, in a winding up (subject, in the case of insolvent companies, to the application in accordance with the provisions of this Act of the law of bankruptcy) the following shall be admissible to proof against the company:

(a) all debts payable on a contingency; and

(b) all claims against the company, present or future, certain or contingent, ascertained or sounding only in damages;

a just estimate being made, so far as possible, of the value of such debts or claims which may be subject to any contingency or which sound only in damages, or for some other reason do not bear a certain value.

(2) The value of such debts and claims as are made admissible to proof by *subsection (1)* shall, as far as possible, be estimated according to the value thereof at the date on which the winding up shall be deemed to have commenced by virtue of *section 589* or *590*, as the case may be (referred to subsequently in this section as the "commencement date").

(3) When any rent or other payment falls due at stated times and the order or resolution to wind up is made at any time other than at one of those times, the persons entitled to the rent or payment may prove for a proportionate part of it up to the commencement date as if the rent or payment accrued due from day to day but this is subject to *subsection (4)*.

(4) Where the liquidator remains in occupation of premises demised to a company which is being wound up, nothing in *subsection (3)* shall affect the right of the landlord of such premises to claim payment of rent during the period of the company's occupation after the commencement of the winding up.

(5) *Subsection (6)* applies to a debt or sum if all of the following conditions are satisfied in respect of it:

(a) it is a debt or sum certain;

(b) it is payable at a certain time or otherwise;

(c) interest on it is not reserved or agreed for; and

(d) it is overdue at the commencement date.

(6) The creditor may prove for interest on a debt or sum to which this subsection applies at a rate, not exceeding the appropriate rate, for the period up to the commencement date and beginning—

(a) if the debt or sum is payable by virtue of a written instrument at a certain time— at the time when the debt or sum was so payable, and

(b) if the debt or sum is payable otherwise — at the making of a demand in writing in respect of it, being a demand giving notice that interest will be claimed from the date of the demand until the time of payment.

(7) A creditor may prove for a debt not payable at the commencement date as if it were payable presently, and may receive dividends equally with the other creditors, deducting only thereout a rebate of interest at the appropriate rate computed from the declaration of a dividend to the time when the debt would have become payable according to the terms on which it was contracted.

(8) Unless the company's constitution or the conditions of issue of the shares in question provide otherwise, dividends declared by a company more than 6 years preceding the commencement date, being dividends which have not been claimed within that period of 6 years, shall not be a claim admissible to proof against the company for the purposes of the winding up.

621 Preferential payments in a winding up

(1) In this section the "relevant date" means—

(a) where the company is ordered to be wound up, the date of the appointment (or first appointment) of a provisional liquidator or, if no such appointment was made, the date of the winding-up order, unless, in either case, the company had commenced to be wound up voluntarily before that date, and

(b) where *paragraph (a)* does not apply, the date of the passing of the resolution for the winding up of the company.

(2) In a winding up there shall be paid in priority to all other debts—

(a) the following rates and taxes:

(i) all local rates due from the company at the relevant date and having become due and payable within the period of 12 months before that date;

(ii) each tax assessable on, in relation to, or by the company under the Taxes Consolidation Act 1997 in respect of, or apportioned on a time basis to, a period ending on or before the relevant date, for which the tax concerned is due and payable, but the particular period (in respect of which priority under this subparagraph for the tax concerned is claimed) shall not be of more than 12 months' duration;

(iii) any amount due at the relevant date in respect of sums which an employer is liable under Part 18D or Chapter 4 of Part 42 of the Taxes Consolidation Act 1997 and regulations thereunder to deduct from emoluments to which that Part or Chapter applies paid by that employer during the period of 12 months next ended on or before the relevant date reduced by any amount which that employer was under that Part or Chapter and regulations thereunder liable to repay during that period, with the addition of interest payable under section 991 of that Act;

(iv) any tax and interest for which the company is liable under the Value-Added Tax Consolidation Act 2010 in relation to taxable periods which shall have ended within the period of 12 months next ended before the relevant date;

(v) any local property tax that the company is liable to remit to the Revenue Commissioners under section 74 of the Finance (Local Property Tax) Act 2012 during the period of 12 months next ended before the relevant date and any interest payable in relation to that tax under section 149 of that Act;

(vi) an amount of local property tax payable, under section 16 of the Finance (Local Property Tax) Act 2012, by the company at the relevant date to the extent that such tax is payable in respect of any one liability date (within the meaning of section 2 of that Act) falling before the relevant date and any interest payable in relation to that tax under section 149 of that Act,

(b) all wages or salary—

(i) whether or not earned wholly or in part by way of commission, or

(ii) whether payable for time or for piece work,

of any employee in respect of services rendered to the company during the period of 4 months before the relevant date,

(c) all accrued holiday remuneration becoming payable to any employee (or, in the case of the person's death, to any other person in his or her right) on the termination of the employee's employment before or by the effect of the winding up order or resolution,

(d) unless the company is being wound up voluntarily merely for the purposes of reconstruction or of amalgamation with another company—

(i) all amounts due in respect of contributions which are payable during the 12 months before the relevant date by the company as the employer of any persons under the Social Welfare Acts, and

(ii) all amounts due in respect of contributions which would have been payable under the provisions of section 13(2)(d) of the Social Welfare Consolidation Act 2005 by the company as the employer of any persons in respect of any remuneration in respect of any period of employment during the 12 months before the relevant date even if such remuneration is paid after the relevant date,

(e) unless the company is being wound up voluntarily merely for the purposes of reconstruction or of amalgamation with another company, all amounts due from the company in respect of damages and costs or liability for damages and costs, payable to a person employed by it in connection with an accident, being an accident occurring—

(i) before the relevant date, and

(ii) in the course of the person's employment with the company, [to the extent that the company][a] is not effectively indemnified by insurers against such damages and costs,

(f) all sums due to any employee pursuant to any scheme or arrangement for the provision of payments to the employee while he or she is absent from employment due to ill health,

(g) any payments due at any time by the company pursuant to any scheme or arrangement for the provision of superannuation benefits to or in respect of employees of the company whether such payments are due—

(i) in respect of the company's contribution to that scheme or under that arrangement, or

(ii) in respect of such contributions payable by the employees to the company under that scheme or arrangement which have been deducted from the wages or salaries of [employees,][b]

[(h) where the company being wound up has been the subject of a resolution action pursuant to the Bank Recovery and Resolution Regulations, any reasonable expenses properly incurred by the resolution authority in connection with the use of the resolution tools or powers under those Regulations,

(i) the—

(i) part of eligible deposits up to the coverage level in Article 6 of Directive 2014/49/EU of the European Parliament and of the Council of 16 April 2014, and

(ii) deposit guarantee scheme where it is subrogating to the rights and obligations of the part of the eligible deposits referred to in subparagraph (i).][c]

[(2A) In a winding up there shall be paid in priority to all other debts, but after those listed in *subsection (2)*—

(a) the part of eligible deposits from natural persons and micro, small and medium-sized enterprises which exceed the coverage level in Article 6(1) of Directive 2014/49/EU of the European Parliament and of the Council of 16 April 2014, and

(b) deposits that would be eligible deposits from natural persons, micro, small and medium-sized enterprises were they not made through branches located outside the Union of institutions established within the Union.

(2B) For the purposes of *subsections (2)(i)* and *(2A)* the following definitions shall apply:

(a) "eligible deposits" has the meaning given to it in the Bank Recovery and Resolution Regulations and shall include a share account held with a building society or credit union;

(b) "deposit guarantee scheme" has the meaning given to it in the Bank Recovery and Resolution Regulations;

(c) "micro, small and medium-sized enterprises" has the meaning given to it in the Bank Recovery and Resolution Regulations;

(d) "institution" has the meaning given to it in the Bank Recovery and Resolution Regulations.][d]

(3) *Subsection (2)* is in addition to any other enactment providing for the priority of a particular debt or sum in a winding up.

(4) Subject to *subsection (5)*, and notwithstanding anything in *subsection (2)(b)*, the sum to which priority is to be given under *subsection (2)(b)* shall not, in the case of any one claimant, exceed €10,000.

(5) Where a claimant under *subsection (2)(b)* is a farm labourer who has entered into a contract for payment of a portion of his or her wages in a lump sum at the end of the year of hiring, he or she shall have priority in respect of the whole of such sum, or such part thereof as the court may decide to be due under the contract, proportionate to the time of service up to the relevant date.

(6) Where any payment has been made—

(a) to any employee of a company, on account of wages or salary, or

(b) to any employee or, in the case of his or her death, to any other person in his or her right, on account of accrued holiday remuneration, or

(c) to any employee while he or she is absent from employment due to ill health or pursuant to any scheme or arrangement for the provision of superannuation benefit to or in respect of him or her,

out of money advanced by some person for that purpose, the person by whom the money was advanced shall, in a winding up, have a right of priority in respect of the money so advanced and paid up to the amount by which the sum, in respect of which the employee or other person in his or her right, would have been entitled to priority in the winding up has been diminished by reason of the payment having been made.

(7) [Subject to subsection (2A), the foregoing][e] debts shall—

(a) rank equally among themselves and be paid in full, unless the assets are insufficient to meet them, in which case they shall abate in equal proportions, and

(b) so far as the assets of the company available for payment of general creditors are insufficient to meet them, have priority over the claims of holders of debentures [any charge created as a floating charge by the company][f], and be paid accordingly out of any property comprised in or subject to that charge.

(8) Subject to the retention of such sums as may be necessary for the costs and expenses of the winding up, the foregoing debts shall be discharged forthwith so far as the assets are sufficient to meet them, and in the case of debts to which priority is given by *subsection (2)(d)*, formal proof of them shall not be required except in so far as is otherwise provided by rules of court.

Amendments

a Words substituted by C(A)A 2017, s 92(a) (previously: "save to the extent that the company").

b "employees," substituted for "employees." by European Union (Bank Recovery and Resolution) Regulations 2015, reg 189(4)(a)(i), with effect from 15 July 2015.

c Paragraphs (2)(h) and (2)(i) inserted by the European Union (Bank Recovery and Resolution) Regulations 2015 (SI 289/2015), reg 189(4)(a)(ii), with effect from 15 July 2015.

d Subsections (2A) and (2B) inserted by the European Union (Bank Recovery and Resolution) Regulations 2015 (SI 289/2015), reg 189(4)(b), with effect from 15 July 2015.

e "Subject to subsection (2A), the foregoing" substituted for "The foregoing" by European Union (Bank Recovery and Resolution) Regulations 2015, reg 189(4)(c), with effect from 15 July 2015.

f Words substituted by C(A)A 2017, s 92(b) (previously: "any floating charge created by the company").

622 Supplemental provisions in relation to *section 621*

(1) Subject to *subsection (2)*, in the event of a landlord or other person distraining or having distrained on any goods or effects of a company within the period of 3 months before the relevant date, the debts to which priority is given by *section 621* shall be a first charge on the goods or effects so distrained on, or the proceeds of the sale thereof.

(2) In respect of any money paid under any such charge as is referred to in *subsection (1)*, the landlord or other person shall have the same rights of priority as the person to whom the payment is made.

(3) For the purpose of *section 621* any remuneration in respect of a period of holiday, or absence from work through good cause, shall be deemed to be wages in respect of services rendered to a company during that period.

(4) Subject to *subsection (5)*, the Minister may by order alter the amount specified in *section 621(4)*.

(5) An order under *subsection (4)* may only be made, at a particular time (the "relevant time"), if it appears to the Minister to be appropriate to do so having regard to the changes in the value of money generally in the State that have occurred during the period beginning—

(a) on this Act's passing, or

(b) if the powers under *subsection (4)* have previously been exercised, immediately after their last previous exercise,

and ending at the relevant time.

(6) The priority conferred by [*section 621(2) and (2A)*][a] shall apply only to those debts which, within the period of 6 months after the date of the advertisement by the liquidator for claims in at least 2 daily newspapers circulating in the district where the registered office of the company concerned is situated, either—

(a) have been notified to the liquidator, or

(b) have become known to the liquidator.

(7) In this section "relevant date" has the same meaning as it has in *section 621*.

Amendments

a "section 621(2) and (2A)" substituted for "section 621(2)" by European Union (Bank Recovery and Resolution) Regulations 2015, reg 189(5), with effect from 15 July 2015.

623 Unclaimed dividends and balances to be paid into a particular account

(1) Where a company has been wound up, and is about to be dissolved, the liquidator shall, in such manner as may be prescribed, lodge to such account as is prescribed by the Minister the whole unclaimed dividends admissible to proof and unapplied or undistributable balances.

(2) An application to the court by a person claiming to be entitled to any dividend or payment out of a lodgment made in pursuance of *subsection (1)*, and any payment out of such lodgment in satisfaction of such claim, shall be made in the prescribed manner.

(3) At the expiration of 7 years after the date of any lodgment made in pursuance of *subsection (1)*, the amount of the lodgment remaining unclaimed shall be paid into the Exchequer, but where the court is satisfied that any person claiming is entitled to any dividend or payment out of the moneys paid into the Exchequer, it may order that that dividend or payment be made and the Minister for Finance shall issue such sum as may be necessary to provide for that payment.

(4) Where moneys invested or deposited at interest by a liquidator form part of the amount required to be lodged, pursuant to *subsection (1)*, to the account referred to in that subsection, the liquidator shall realise the investment or withdraw the deposit and shall pay the proceeds into that account.

Chapter 8
Liquidators

624 Duty of liquidator to administer, distribute, etc., property of company

(1) Subject to *subsection (3)*, it shall be the duty of a liquidator to administer the property of the company to which he or she is appointed.

(2) For the purpose of *subsection (1)* "administer the property of the company" includes ascertaining the extent of the property of the company and, as appropriate:

(a) the collection and gathering in of the company's property;

(b) the realisation of such property; and

(c) the distribution of such property;

in accordance with law.

(3) Subject to *section 559(3)* to *(5)*, the duties of a provisional liquidator shall be those duties provided in the order appointing him or her or any subsequent order of the court.

625 How liquidator is to be described and validity of acts

(1) A liquidator shall be described by the style of "the liquidator" (or, in the case of a provisional liquidator, "the provisional liquidator") of the particular company in respect of which he or she is appointed and not by his or her individual name.

(2) Subject to *section 621*, the acts of a liquidator shall be valid notwithstanding any defects that may afterwards be discovered in his or her appointment or qualification.

626 Powers of provisional liquidators

(1) Where a provisional liquidator is appointed by the court, then, subject to *section 559(3)* to *(5)*, the provisional liquidator has such powers as the court orders.

(2) Where a provisional liquidator is appointed by the court, the court may place such limitations and restrictions upon the powers of any other officers of the company as it thinks fit.

627 Liquidator's powers

The liquidator shall have the powers set out in each of the paragraphs of the Table to this section.

Table

Legal proceedings, carrying on company's business, etc.

1. Power to—

   (a) bring any action or other legal proceeding in the name and on behalf of the company;

   (b) defend any action or other legal proceeding in the name and on behalf of the company;

   (c) recommence and carry on the business of the company so far as may be necessary for the beneficial winding up thereof, where such business was not continuing at the date of the appointment of the liquidator or had ceased after such appointment;

   (d) continue to carry on the business of a company so far as may be necessary for the beneficial winding up thereof, where such business was continuing at the date of the appointment of the liquidator and had not subsequently ceased;

   (e) appoint a legal practitioner to assist the liquidator in the performance of his or her duties.

Payment of certain creditors, compromise of certain claims, etc.

2. Power to—

(a) pay any classes of creditors in full;

(b) make any compromise or arrangement with creditors or persons claiming to be creditors or having or alleging themselves to have any claim present or future, certain or contingent, ascertained or sounding only in damages against the company, or whereby the company may be rendered liable;

(c) compromise—

(i) all calls and liabilities to calls, debts and liabilities capable of resulting in debts, and all claims, present or future, certain or contingent, ascertained or sounding only in damages, subsisting or supposed to subsist between the company and a contributory or alleged contributory or other debtor or person apprehending liability to the company; and

(ii) all questions in any way relating to or affecting the assets or winding up of the company,

on such terms as may be agreed, and take any security for the discharge of any such call, debt, liability or claim and give a complete discharge in respect of it.

Ascertainment of debts and liabilities, sale of property, etc

3. Power to—

(a) ascertain the debts and liabilities of the company;

(b) sell the property of the company by public auction or private contract, with, for the purposes of this subparagraph, power to—

(i) transfer the whole of the property to any company or other person;

(ii) sell the property in lots,

and, for the purpose of selling the company's land or any part of it, to carry out such sales by grant, conveyance, transfer, lease, sublease, or otherwise, and to sell any rent reserved on any such grant or any reversion expectant upon the determination of any such lease.

Execution of certain documents, drawing of negotiable instruments, etc

4. Power to—

(a) do all acts and to execute, in the name and on behalf of the company, all deeds, receipts and other documents, and for that purpose to use, when necessary, the company's seal;

(b) draw, accept, make and endorse any bill of exchange or promissory note in the name and on behalf of the company, with the same effect with respect to the liability of the company as if the bill or note had been drawn, accepted, made or endorsed by or on behalf of the company in the course of its business.

Proving claim in the case of contributory's bankruptcy, etc.

5. Where any contributory has been adjudicated bankrupt or has presented a petition for arrangement with his or her creditors in pursuance of the Bankruptcy Act 1988, power to—

(a) prove, rank and claim in the bankruptcy or arrangement for any balance against the contributory's estate; and

(b) receive dividends in the bankruptcy or arrangement in respect of that balance,

as a separate debt due from the bankrupt or arranging debtor, and rateably with the other separate creditors.

Obtaining of credit.

6. Power to obtain credit, whether on the security of the property of the company or otherwise.

Taking out letters of administration, otherwise obtaining payment from contributory or debtor, etc.

7. Power to—

(a) take out in the liquidator's name (that is the liquidator's name as it is to be styled under *section 625*) letters of administration to any deceased contributory or debtor; and

(b) do in the liquidator's name (that is the liquidator's name as it is to be so styled) any other act necessary for obtaining payment of any money due from a contributory or debtor or his or her estate which cannot be conveniently done in the name of the company,

and, in all such cases, the money due shall, for the purpose of enabling the liquidator to take out the letters of administration or recover the money, be deemed to be due to the liquidator himself or herself.

Security for costs and appointment of agents.

8. Power to—

(a) give security for costs in any proceedings commenced by the company or by the liquidator in the name of the company;

(b) appoint an agent to do any business which the liquidator is unable to do or that it is unreasonable to expect the liquidator to do, in person.

Custody and control of property and disposal of perishables, etc.

9. Power to—

(a) take into his or her custody or under his or her control all the property to which the company is or appears to be entitled;

(b) dispose of perishable goods and other goods the value of which is likely to diminish if they are not immediately disposed of;

(c) do all such other things as may be necessary for the protection of the company's property.

Residual power

10. Power to do all such other things as may be necessary for winding up the affairs of the company and distributing its property.

628 Summoning general meetings of the company, etc.

The liquidator may summon—

(a) general meetings of the company,

(b) meetings of the creditors of the company, or

(c) if there is a committee of inspection, meetings of that committee,

for the purpose of—

(i) obtaining the sanction by resolution of members, creditors or the committee of inspection, or

(ii) any other case in which he or she thinks fit to convene such a meeting (and provision for the convening of which by the liquidator is not specifically made otherwise by this Act).

629 Notice to be given with respect to exercise of powers, restrictions on self-dealing, etc.

(1) Subject to *subsection (2)*, where a liquidator exercises any power specified in *paragraph 1* or *2* of the Table to *section 627*, he or she shall, within 14 days after the date of such exercise, give notice of such exercise—

(a) in the case of a winding up by the court or a creditors' voluntary winding up, to the committee of inspection or, if there is no such committee, to all of the creditors of the company who are known to the liquidator or who have been intimated to the liquidator, or

(b) in the case of a members' voluntary winding up, to the members of the company.

(2) In relation to the exercise of a power specified in *paragraph 2(b)* or *(c)* of the Table to *section 627*, *subsection (1)* shall not apply if the amount of the claim or call to which the exercise of the power relates does not exceed €500.

(3) Subject to *subsection (9)*, the liquidator of a company shall not sell, by private contract, a non-cash asset of the requisite value to a person who is, or who, within 3 years prior to the date of commencement of the winding up, has been, an officer of the company unless the liquidator has given the following notice.

(4) That notice is at least 14 days' notice of the liquidator's intention to do so to all creditors of the company who are known to the liquidator or who have been intimated to the liquidator.

(5) In *subsection (3)*—

"officer", in relation to a company, includes—

(a) a person connected, within the meaning of *section 220*, with a director of the company, and

(b) a shadow director of the company;

"non-cash asset" and "requisite value" have the meanings given to them by *section 238*.

(6) Subject to *subsection (9)*, the liquidator or any member of the committee of inspection of a company shall not, while acting as liquidator or member of such committee, either directly or indirectly, by himself or herself or any employer, partner, agent or employee, become purchaser of any part of the company's property.

(7) Subject to *subsection (9)*, where the liquidator carries on (in either of the 2 cases set out in *paragraph 1* of the Table to *section 627*) the business of the company, the liquidator shall not purchase goods for the carrying on of such business from any person whose connection with the liquidator is of such a nature as would result in the liquidator's obtaining any portion of the profit (if any) arising out of the transaction.

(8) Subject to *subsection (9)*, any purchase made in contravention of *subsection (3)*, *(6)* or *(7)* may, on the application of any creditor or contributory of the company, be set aside by the court.

(9) *Subsection (3)*, *(6)*, *(7)* or *(8)*, as the case may be, does not apply if, prior to the sale or, as appropriate, the making of the purchase, there has been obtained for it the express sanction—

(a) in the case of a winding up by the court or a creditors' voluntary winding up, of the committee of inspection or, if there is no such committee, a majority in number and value of the creditors of the company who are known to the liquidator or, as the case may be, the officer, former officer or member making the purchase concerned or who have been intimated to the liquidator or, as the case may be, such officer, former officer or member, or

(b) in the case of a members' voluntary winding up, of a majority in number and value of the members of the company.

(10) The costs and expenses of obtaining the sanction referred to in *subsection (9)* shall be borne by the person in whose interest such sanction is sought and shall not be payable out of the company's property.

(11) Without prejudice to the generality of *section 559(4)* and *(5)*, where a provisional liquidator has been conferred by an order of the court with any of the powers specified in the Table to *section 627*, being a power referred to (whether by express reference to that Table or otherwise) in a preceding subsection of this section, then "liquidator" in that particular subsection includes a provisional liquidator.

630 Restrictions in creditors' voluntary winding up and procedures in case of certain defaults

(1) This section applies where, in the case of a creditors' voluntary winding up, a liquidator has been nominated by the company.

(2) Subject to *subsection (3)*, the powers conferred on the liquidator by *section 627* shall not be exercised, except with sanction of the court, during the period before the holding of the creditors' meeting under *section 587*.

(3) *Subsection (2)* does not apply in relation to the exercise of a power specified in *paragraph 9* of the Table to *section 627*.

(4) The liquidator shall attend the creditors' meeting held under *section 587* and shall report to the meeting on any exercise by him or her of the powers under *section 627* or *631*.

(5) If default is made—

(a) by the company in complying with *section 587(1)*, *(2)* or *(6)*, or

(b) by the directors of the company in complying with *section 587(7)*,

the liquidator shall, within 14 days after the relevant day, apply to the court for directions as to the manner in which that default is to be remedied.

(6) In *subsection (5)*, the "relevant day" means the day on which the liquidator was nominated by the company or the day on which he or she first became aware of the default, whichever is the later.

(7) If a liquidator, without reasonable excuse, fails to comply with any provision of this section, he or she shall be guilty of a category 3 offence.

631 Power to apply to court for determination of questions or concerning exercise of powers

(1) Each of the following:

(a) the liquidator or the provisional liquidator;

(b) any contributory or creditor of the company;

(c) the Director;

may apply to the court to determine any question arising in the winding up of a company (including any question in relation to any exercise or proposed exercise of any of the powers of the liquidator).

(2) The court, if satisfied that the determination of the question will be just and beneficial, may accede wholly or partially to such an application on such terms and conditions as it thinks fit or may make such other order on the application as it thinks just.

(3) A certified copy of an order made by virtue of this section—

(a) annulling a resolution to wind up, or

(b) staying the proceedings in a winding up,

each of which orders the court is empowered by this section to make, shall forthwith be forwarded by the company concerned to the Registrar.

(4) If a company fails to comply with *subsection (3)*, the company and any officer of it who is in default shall be guilty of a category 4 offence.

632 No lien over company's books, records, etc.

(1) Without prejudice to *subsections (2)* and *(3)*, no person shall be entitled as against the liquidator or provisional liquidator of a company to—

(a) withhold possession of any deed, instrument, or other document belonging to the company, or the accounting records, receipts, bills, invoices, or other papers of a like nature relating to the financial statements or trade, dealings or business of the company, or

(b) claim any lien on a document or any other thing referred to in *paragraph (a)*.

(2) Where a mortgage, charge or pledge has been created by the deposit with a person of any such document or other paper as is referred to in *subsection (1)*, the production of the document or paper to the liquidator or provisional liquidator by the person shall be without prejudice to the person's rights under the mortgage, charge or pledge (other than any right to possession of the document or paper).

(3) Where, by virtue of this section, a liquidator or provisional liquidator has possession of any document or papers of a receiver of the property of the company concerned or that such a receiver is entitled to examine, the liquidator or provisional liquidator shall, unless the court otherwise orders, make the document or papers available for inspection by the receiver at all reasonable times.

(4) Any person who, without just cause, withholds possession, in contravention of *subsection (1)*, of any such document or other paper as is referred to in that subsection shall be guilty of a category 3 offence.

633 Qualifications for appointment as liquidator or provisional liquidator — general

(1) Subject to *sections 634* and *635*, a person shall not be qualified for appointment as a liquidator of a company unless he or she falls within a paragraph of the Table to this section.

(2) Nothing in this section shall prevent a person who—

(a) does not fall within *paragraph 1*, *2*, *3* or *4* of the Table to this section, and

(b) has made an application to the Supervisory Authority under and in accordance with *paragraph 5* of that Table (in *subsection (3)* referred to as a "relevant applicant"),

from acting as a liquidator pending the determination of that application.

(3) In addition to *subsection (2)*, nothing in this section shall prevent a relevant applicant from continuing to act as a liquidator in a winding up in relation to which he or she was appointed liquidator before the commencement of this section notwithstanding that the Supervisory Authority has refused his or her application made under and in accordance with *paragraph 5* of the Table to this section.

[(4) In this section—

'liquidator' includes provisional liquidator;

'prescribed fee' means a fee prescribed by regulations made by the Supervisory Authority with the consent of the Minister; .

'prescribed form' means a form prescribed by regulations made by the Supervisory Authority.][a]

Table

First category — member of a prescribed accountancy body.
1. The person is a member of a prescribed accountancy body, within the meaning of *Part 15*, being a person who— (a) holds a current practising certificate issued by that body; and (b) is not prohibited by virtue of rules of that body or a direction, ruling or decision of that body, or any disciplinary or professional practice committee of it, from acting as a liquidator.
Second category — practising solicitor.
2. The person is a solicitor, being a solicitor who— (a) holds a current practising certificate issued by the Law Society of Ireland under the Solicitors Acts 1954 to 2002; and (b) is not prohibited by virtue of regulations made by the Law Society of Ireland, or a decision or order made by the Solicitors Disciplinary Tribunal or the court, under those Acts from acting as a liquidator.
Third category — member of other professional body recognised by Supervisory Authority.
3. The person is a member of such professional body as the Supervisory Authority may from time to time recognise for the purposes of this section, being a person who— (a) is authorised for the time being by that professional body to pursue the particular activities that that body aims to promote or foster or as respects the pursuit of which by its members that body has been established to represent; and (b) is not prohibited by virtue of rules of that body or a direction, ruling or decision of that body, or any disciplinary or professional practice committee of it, from acting as a liquidator.
Fourth category — person qualified under the laws of another EEA state.
4. The person is entitled under the laws of an EEA state (not being the State) to act as a liquidator in insolvency proceedings and the qualifications held by, or the circumstances otherwise relating to the person, that entitle him or her so to act are ones that, by virtue of any Community act, entitle him or her to act as a liquidator in the State.

Fifth (and limited) category — person with practical experience of windings-up and knowledge of relevant law.

5. The person—

(a) having made application in that behalf to the Supervisory Authority in the prescribed form [within 30 months after][b] the commencement of this section; and

(b) paid the prescribed fee to the Supervisory Authority,

stands authorised for the time being by the Supervisory Authority (which authorisation the Supervisory Authority is, by virtue of this section, empowered to grant) to be so appointed, such authorisation having been granted on the grounds that each of the following is satisfied—

(i) the person has, prior to the commencement of this section, obtained adequate relevant experience of the winding up of companies and knowledge of the law applicable thereto by virtue of the person's either—

(I) having been—

(A) employed in relevant work by a person who at the relevant time fell (or, if this section had been in operation at that time, who would have fallen) within *paragraph 1, 2* or *3*; or

(B) engaged on his or her own account in relevant work;

or

(II) having practised in an EEA state (not being the State) as a liquidator;

(ii) the person is, in the opinion of the Supervisory Authority, after consultation with the Director, a fit and proper person to act as a liquidator; and

(iii) the person does not fall within *paragraph 1, 2, 3* or *4*.

Amendments

a Subsection substituted by C(A)A 2017, s 93(a).

b Words substituted by C(A)A 2017, s 93(b) (previously: "within 2 years after").

634 Supplemental provisions in relation to *section 633* (including requirements for professional indemnity cover)

(1) Subject to the preceding section, *subsection (3)* and *section 635*, a person shall not be qualified for appointment as a liquidator of a company unless there is in place in relation to the person an indemnity, in such amount and on such terms as may from time to time be prescribed by regulations made by the Supervisory Authority, against

losses and claims arising in respect of civil liability incurred by the person in respect of any act or omission by—

(a) the person,

(b) any servant or agent of the person, or

(c) both of them,

in the conduct of the winding up of the company concerned.

(2) The reference in *subsection (1)* to an indemnity being in place in relation to a person is a reference to an indemnity being provided (against the losses and claims referred to in that subsection) by either of the following means:

(a) a policy of indemnity insurance being effected and maintained by the person with an insurance undertaking; or

(b) the person's participating, in a manner legally enforceable by the person, in an indemnity fund of a mutual nature that is recognised by the Supervisory Authority for the time being for the purposes of this section.

(3) *Subsection (1)* does not apply to a person as respects any winding up in relation to which he or she has been appointed liquidator before the commencement of this section.

(4) A person shall not act as liquidator of a company at a time when he or she is not qualified under *section 633* or this section for appointment to that office.

(5) If, while acting as liquidator of a company, a person ceases to be qualified under *section 633* or this section for appointment to that office, the person shall thereupon vacate his or her office.

(6) On vacating such office by reason of those circumstances, the person shall give notice in writing that he or she has vacated such office (by reason of those circumstances)—

(a) within 2 days after the date of vacating office, to—

(i) the Registrar,

(ii) the Director, and

(iii) if the person had been authorised pursuant to *paragraph 5* of the Table to *section 633* to be appointed as a liquidator — the Supervisory Authority,

and

(b) within 14 days after the date of vacating office, to—

(i) in the case of a winding up by the court, the court and—

(I) if a committee of inspection has been appointed — the members of that committee, or

(II) if no committee of inspection has been appointed — the creditors of the company,

(ii) in the case of a creditors' voluntary winding up—

(I) if a committee of inspection has been appointed — the members of that committee, or

(II) if no committee of inspection has been appointed — the creditors of the company,

or

(iii) in the case of a members' voluntary winding up — the members of the company.

(7) A person who contravenes *subsection (4)* or *(5)* shall be guilty of a category 2 offence.

(8) A person who contravenes *subsection (6)* shall be guilty of a category 3 offence.

(9) As respects a person who has been authorised under *paragraph 5* of the Table to *section 633* to be appointed a liquidator—

(a) if the person becomes qualified for appointment as a liquidator of a company by reason of another provision of that Table, the person's authorisation under that *paragraph 5* shall thereupon cease to have effect,

(b) the Supervisory Authority may withdraw or suspend (for such period and on such terms as it thinks fit) the person's authorisation under that *paragraph 5* if it is satisfied that the person is no longer sufficiently capable of acting as a liquidator or is no longer a fit and proper person to act as a liquidator.

[(9A)(a) As respects a person who has been authorised under *paragraph 5* of the *Table* to *section 633* to be appointed a liquidator, the Supervisory Authority may—

(i) at the time of a grant of authorisation under that *paragraph 5*, or

(ii) at any time during the currency of an authorisation so granted, by notice in writing to the person, attach to the authorisation such terms and conditions as it thinks necessary or expedient, which said terms and conditions shall be specified in the notice.

(b) The Supervisory Authority may, where it thinks it necessary or expedient to do so, by notice in writing to the person concerned, amend one or more of the terms and conditions attached to an authorisation pursuant to *paragraph (a)*.

(c) The Supervisory Authority may, at any time upon request in writing in that behalf by a person who has been authorised under *paragraph 5* of the *Table* to *section 633* to be appointed a liquidator, withdraw the person's authorisation.][a]

(10) The Supervisory Authority may, to meet the cost of conducting such inquiries as may be necessary to be conducted for the purposes of its exercising the powers under *subsection (9)(b)*, levy, not more frequently than annually, such periodic charge as may be reasonable on any person acting as a liquidator, being a person who so acts by virtue of the person's being authorised under *paragraph 5* of the Table to *section 633*.

(11) In this section—

"insurance undertaking" means the holder of an authorisation under the European Communities (Non-Life Insurance) Regulations 1976 (S.I. No. 115 of 1976);

"liquidator" includes a provisional liquidator.

Amendments

a Subsection (9A) inserted by C(A)A 2017, s 67.

635 Specific disqualification from appointment as liquidator or provisional liquidator

(1) None of the following persons shall be qualified to be appointed or act as liquidator of a company:

(a) a person who is, or who within the period of 24 months before the date of the commencement of the winding up has been, an officer or employee of the company;

(b) except with the leave of the court, a parent, spouse, civil partner, brother, sister or child of an officer of the company;

(c) a person who is a partner or in the employment of an officer or employee of the company;

(d) a person who is an undischarged bankrupt;

(e) a person who is not qualified by virtue of a preceding provision of this subsection for appointment as liquidator of any other body corporate which is that company's subsidiary or holding company or a subsidiary of that company's holding company, or would be so disqualified if the body corporate were a company.

(2) References in *subsection (1)* to—

(a) a child of an officer shall be deemed to include a child of the officer's civil partner who is ordinarily resident with the officer and the civil partner,

(b) an officer or employee of the company include a statutory auditor of the company.

(3) An application for leave under *subsection (1)(b)* shall be supported by such evidence as the court may require.

(4) If, while acting as liquidator of a company, a person ceases to be qualified to so act by virtue of *subsection (1)*, the person shall thereupon vacate his or her office.

(5) On vacating such office by reason of those circumstances, the person shall give notice in writing that he or she has vacated such office (by reason of those circumstances)—

(a) within 2 days after the date of vacating office, to—

(i) the Registrar,

(ii) the Director, and

(iii) if the person had been authorised pursuant to *paragraph 5* of the Table to *section 633* to be appointed as a liquidator — the Supervisory Authority,

and

(b) within 14 days after the date of vacating office, to—

(i) in the case of a winding up by the court, the court and—

(I) if a committee of inspection has been appointed — the members of that committee, or

(II) if no committee of inspection has been appointed — the creditors of the company,

(ii) in the case of a creditors' voluntary winding up—

(I) if a committee of inspection has been appointed — the members of that committee, or

(II) if no committee of inspection has been appointed — the creditors of the company,

or

(iii) in the case of a members' voluntary winding up — the members of the company.

(6) A person who—

(a) acts as a liquidator of a company when he or she is not qualified by virtue of *subsection (1)* to so act, or

(b) contravenes *subsection (4)*,

shall be guilty of a category 2 offence.

(7) A person who contravenes *subsection (5)* shall be guilty of a category 3 offence.

(8) *Subsections (1)* to *(7)* shall not apply to a winding up commenced before 1 August 1991.

(9) In this section "liquidator" includes a provisional liquidator.

636 Appointment and removal in a members' voluntary winding up

(1) In *paragraphs (a)* to *(c)* of *subsection (2)* "liquidator" shall be deemed to include the one or more liquidators appointed by the company in exercise of the powers under any such paragraph.

(2) Subsequent to the appointment of a liquidator of a company under *section 583* in a members' voluntary winding up, the company, in general meeting, may, at a meeting convened for that purpose—

(a) remove the liquidator,

(b) appoint a liquidator to replace or act with the existing liquidator, or

(c) appoint a liquidator to fill a vacancy in the office of liquidator.

(3) Notwithstanding anything in *Part 4*, a general meeting of the company for the purpose of—

(a) *subsection (2)(a)* or *(b)*, may be convened, on 10 days' notice to the members of it, by—

(i) any member of it with the written authority of not less than one-tenth in number of the members, or

(ii) an existing liquidator,

or

(b) *subsection (2)(c)* may be convened, on 10 days' notice to the members of it, by—

(i) any member of it with the foregoing written authority,

(ii) an existing liquidator, or

(iii) any contributory.

(4) The powers conferred on the company by *subsection (2)* shall be subject to any order the court may make with regard to the matter on application to it by any contributory or an existing liquidator.

(5) *Section 218* (service of notices) shall apply to a notice of a meeting given by a member, liquidator or contributory under *subsection (3)* as it applies to a notice by a company or any of its officers to its members.

(6) The meeting shall be held in a manner provided by this Act or the company's constitution or in such manner as may, on application by any contributory, member or any existing liquidator, be determined by the court.

637 Appointment and removal in a creditors' voluntary winding up

(1) This section applies at any time subsequent to the appointment of a liquidator of a company under *section 588* in a creditors' voluntary winding up.

(2) In *paragraphs (a)* to *(c)* of *subsection (4)* "liquidator"—

(a) does not include a person whom the court has directed to be, or whom the court has appointed to be, liquidator of the company under *section 588(5)*,

(b) shall be deemed to include the one or more liquidators appointed by the creditors in exercise of the powers under any such paragraph.

(3) Where this section applies, the creditors may, at a meeting convened for that purpose, by resolution of a majority, in value only, of the creditors present personally or by proxy and voting on the resolution, exercise the following powers.

(4) Those powers of the creditors are to—

(a) remove the liquidator,

(b) appoint a liquidator to replace or act with the existing liquidator, or

(c) appoint a liquidator to fill a vacancy in the office of liquidator.

(5) A meeting of the creditors of the company for the purpose of *subsection (3)* may be convened, on 10 days' notice to the creditors, by—

(a) any creditor of it with the written authority of not less than one-tenth in value of the creditors, or

(b) an existing liquidator.

(6) The powers conferred on the creditors by *subsection (3)* shall be subject to any order the court may make with regard to the matter on application to it by any creditor or an existing liquidator.

638 Appointment and removal by the court

(1) In any winding up, the court may, on the application by a member, creditor, liquidator or the Director or on its own motion—

(a) appoint a liquidator if from any cause whatever there is no liquidator acting, or

(b) on cause shown, remove a liquidator and appoint another liquidator.

(2) Where the court makes an order under *subsection (1)*, it may give such consequential directions, including directions as to the delivery and transfer of the seal, books, records and any property of the company, as it thinks fit.

639 Consent to act

(1) The appointment of a liquidator (other than a provisional liquidator) shall be of no effect unless the person nominated has, prior to his or her appointment, signified his or her written consent to the appointment.

(2) A provisional liquidator shall not be appointed unless the court is satisfied that the person nominated for such appointment has, prior to his or her appointment, signified his or her consent to the appointment.

640 Position when there is more than one liquidator

(1) If more than one liquidator is appointed, the court or meeting appointing those liquidators, shall declare or resolve whether any thing by this Act required or authorised to be done by the liquidators is to be done by all or any one or more of the persons appointed.

(2) In default of such declaration or resolution, those things may be performed by any number of the liquidators but, in any case, by not less than 2 of them.

641 Resignation of liquidator

(1) In any winding up, a liquidator may resign from office.

(2) Where a liquidator resigns, he or she shall give notice in writing of that fact, within 2 days after the date of resigning, to the Registrar and the Director and, within 14 days after the date of resigning—

(a) in the case of a winding up by the court, to the court and—

  (i) if a committee of inspection has been appointed — to the members of that committee, or

  (ii) if no committee of inspection has been appointed — to the creditors of the company,

(b) in the case of a creditors' voluntary winding up—

  (i) if a committee of inspection has been appointed — to the members of that committee, or

(ii) if no committee of inspection has been appointed — to the creditors of the company,

or

(c) in the case of a members' voluntary winding up — to the members of the company.

(3) If a liquidator fails, without reasonable excuse, to comply with *subsection (2)* he or she shall be guilty of a category 3 offence.

642 Prohibition on rewards for appointment

Any person who gives or agrees or offers to give to any member or creditor of a company any valuable consideration with a view to—

(a) securing his or her own appointment or nomination as the company's liquidator, or

(b) securing or preventing the appointment or nomination of some person other than himself or herself as the company's liquidator,

shall be guilty of a category 2 offence.

643 Notifications and filings of appointments and removals

(1) The chairperson of any meeting at which a liquidator is appointed or removed shall, following the meeting, forthwith deliver to the liquidator notice in writing of the liquidator's appointment or removal, unless the liquidator or his or her duly authorised representative is present at the meeting where the resolution concerned was passed.

(2) In default of election of a chairperson by the meeting referred to in *subsection (1)*, the person who shall be chairperson of that meeting shall be the person who was the signatory or the first signatory, as the case may be, on the notice by which the meeting was called.

(3) The chairperson of a meeting referred to in *subsection (1)* at which a liquidator is removed shall, following the meeting, forthwith deliver to the Registrar notice of the removal in the prescribed form.

(4) *Subsections (5)* to *(9)* have effect in respect of—

(a) an appointment of a liquidator in a winding up other than the initial appointment of a liquidator in a winding up, and

(b) a removal of a liquidator that the court orders in any winding up.

(5) The liquidator, following receipt of notice of his or her appointment (other than an appointment made by the court), shall forthwith deliver to the Registrar notice of his or her appointment in the prescribed form.

(6) The Registrar shall forward a copy of such notice to the Director.

(7) Where an order is made appointing or removing a liquidator—

(a) the applicant for the order, or

(b) in a case where the order is made by the court of its own motion, such officer of the court as may be prescribed,

shall, following the making of the order, forthwith deliver or cause to be delivered to the liquidator notice in writing of the liquidator's appointment or removal, unless the liquidator or his or her duly authorised representative is present in court when the order is made.

(8) Where an order is made appointing or removing a liquidator, such officer of the court as may be prescribed shall, following the making of the order, forthwith cause the Registrar to be furnished with such particulars of the order as may be prescribed.

(9) The Registrar shall forward a copy of such particulars to the Director.

(10) Subject to *subsection (11)*, a person who fails to comply with a provision of this section shall be guilty of a category 3 offence.

(11) *Subsection (10)* shall not apply to the Registrar or any officer of the court prescribed for the purposes of *subsection (7)* or *(8)*.

644 Custody of books and property upon vacation of office

(1) This section applies where a person vacates the position of liquidator of a company (the "former liquidator") whether such vacation is by reason of his or her having—

(a) ceased to be qualified to act as a liquidator of the company,

(b) been removed as liquidator, or

(c) resigned as liquidator.

(2) Where this section applies and no person remains appointed to act as liquidator of the company, the former liquidator shall retain custody of—

(a) the seal, books, records, and any property of the company in his or her possession or control, and

(b) the books and records kept by him or her as liquidator,

(which seal, property, documents or other things are referred to in this section as the "relevant items") until—

(i) a new liquidator is appointed to the company — whereupon the former liquidator shall deliver custody of the relevant items to the new liquidator, or

(ii) directed by the court, upon the application of the former liquidator, the Director of Corporate Enforcement or a member or creditor of the company, to effect delivery or disposal of the relevant items as the court thinks fit.

(3) The delivery of any of the relevant items pursuant to *subsection (2)* shall not prejudice any lien which a liquidator may have over it.

(4) A person who fails to comply with this section without lawful excuse shall be guilty of a category 3 offence.

645 Provisional liquidator's remuneration

(1) A provisional liquidator is entitled to receive such remuneration as is fixed by the court.

(2) *Section 648* applies with respect to the fixing of such remuneration and otherwise supplements this section.

646 Liquidator's remuneration — procedure for fixing liquidator's entitlement thereto

(1) A liquidator, other than a provisional liquidator, has an entitlement to remuneration upon the terms agreed, fixed or otherwise set in the manner specified in *subsection (2)* and the terms upon which the liquidator has, in accordance with that subsection, such an entitlement may be expressed to be—

(a) by way of a relevant percentage,

(b) by reference to time expended in the conduct of the winding up, or

(c) otherwise by reference to any method or thing.

(2) The terms upon which the liquidator has an entitlement to remuneration shall be—

(a) where there is a committee of inspection, such terms as have been agreed in writing between the liquidator and the committee of inspection, or

(b) in a winding up by the court or a creditors' voluntary winding up, where—

(i) there is no committee of inspection, or

(ii) the liquidator and the committee of inspection fail to agree,

such terms as have been approved by resolution of the creditors, or

(c) in a members' voluntary winding up, such terms as have been approved by resolution of the members of the company in general meeting, or

(d) where the creditors or members, as the case may be — having been requested to do so by the liquidator — fail to pass a resolution in accordance with *paragraph (b)* or *(c)*, such terms as have been fixed by the court.

(3) Before the terms upon which a liquidator has an entitlement to remuneration have been agreed, approved or fixed, as the case may be, in accordance with *subsection (2)*, the liquidator shall, as appropriate—

(a) cause particulars in writing of the terms upon which he or she seeks such entitlement to be furnished—

(i) in a case to which *subsection (2)(a)* applies, to the committee of inspection,

(ii) in a case to which *subsection (2)(b)* applies, to the creditors,

(iii) in a case to which *subsection (2)(c)* applies, to the members of the company,

or

(b) in a case to which *subsection (2)(d)* applies, include, as part of his or her application to the court, particulars of the terms upon which he or she seeks such an entitlement.

(4) A liquidator shall, as soon as is practicable after his or her appointment and in accordance with *subsection (2)*, seek the agreement or, as the case may be, approval (or, as the case may require, the fixing) of the terms upon which he or she has an entitlement to remuneration.

(5) Subject to *subsection (6)*, the terms upon which a liquidator has an entitlement to remuneration may be varied by—

(a) a subsequent agreement between the liquidator and the committee of inspection,

(b) approval thereto (given by the means referred to in *subsection (2)(b)* or *(c)*, as appropriate) of the creditors or members, or

(c) a subsequent order made by the court on application to it by the liquidator,

as the case may be.

(6) No such variation may, without the consent of the liquidator, reduce the entitlement of the liquidator to remuneration for work that has already been performed.

(7) This section is subject to *sections 647* and *648*.

647 Liquidator's entitlement to receive payment where entitlement to remuneration exists

(1) This section—

(a) applies where the liquidator's entitlement to remuneration exists by virtue of the terms in respect thereof having been agreed, fixed or otherwise set in the manner specified in *section 646*, and

(b) is subject to *section 648*.

(2) A liquidator shall be entitled to receive payment in respect of his or her remuneration (whether for the entire or any portion of his or her services in the winding up, or by way of a payment on account) provided the amount sought to be received in that behalf has—

(a) where there is a committee of inspection, been approved by the committee of inspection, or

(b) in a winding up by the court or a creditors' voluntary winding up, where—

(i) there is no committee of inspection, or

(ii) the committee of inspection does not approve the amount,

been approved by resolution of the creditors, or

(c) in a members' voluntary winding up, been approved by resolution of the members of the company in general meeting, or

(d) where the creditors or members, as the case may be — having been requested to do so by the liquidator — fail to pass a resolution in accordance with *paragraph (b)* or *(c)*, been fixed by the court or such person as the court may designate for that purpose.

(3) Before the amount of remuneration sought to be received has been agreed, approved or fixed, as the case may be, in accordance with *subsection (2)*, the liquidator shall, as appropriate—

(a) cause the prescribed particulars in respect of that amount to be furnished—

(i) in a case to which *subsection (2)(a)* applies, to the committee of inspection,

(ii) in a case to which *subsection (2)(b)* applies, to the creditors,

(iii) in a case to which *subsection (2)(c)* applies, to the members of the company,

or

(b) in a case to which *subsection (2)(d)* applies, include, as part of his or her application to the court, prescribed particulars in respect of that amount.

648 Supplemental provisions in relation to *sections 646* and *647*

(1) The terms upon which a liquidator has an entitlement to remuneration, as agreed, fixed or otherwise set in accordance with *section 646*, may include provision for reference to arbitration of any dispute that may arise as to the amount of remuneration to which the liquidator is thereby entitled under *section 647*.

(2) If the foregoing terms do not include a provision of the foregoing kind, the liquidator and—

(a) where the case is one of a winding up by the court or a creditors' voluntary winding up, the creditors acting by resolution passed at a meeting of the creditors for the purpose, or

(b) where the case is one of a members' voluntary winding up, the members of the company acting by resolution passed at a meeting of the company for the purpose,

may agree to refer to arbitration any dispute as to the amount of remuneration to which the liquidator is entitled under *section 647*.

(3) In an arbitration of a dispute as to the amount of remuneration to which a liquidator is entitled under *section 647*, the matters specified in *subsection (9)* shall be taken into account by the arbitrator.

(4) Not later than 28 days after—

(a) the date on which an agreement or approval has been made or given in accordance with *section 646(2)(a)*, *(b)* or *(c)*, as the case may be, in respect of such terms, or

(b) the date on which any variation referred to in *section 646(5)* has been made of such terms,

any creditor or member of the company concerned may apply to the court to review the terms upon which the liquidator has an entitlement to remuneration as so agreed, approved or varied, and, on the making of such an application, the court may, as it thinks fit—

(i) confirm the terms as so agreed, approved or varied, or

(ii) alter those terms.

(5) Not later than 28 days after the date on which an agreement or approval has been made or given in accordance with *section 647(2)(a)*, *(b)* or *(c)*, as the case may be, in respect of an amount of remuneration of a liquidator, any creditor or member of the company concerned may apply to the court to review that amount as so agreed or approved and, on the making of such an application, the court may, as it thinks fit—

(a) confirm that amount as so agreed or approved, or

(b) alter that amount.

(6) If, on an application under *subsection (4)* or *(5)*—

(a) the court does not vary, in a manner less favourable to the liquidator, the terms of the liquidator's entitlement to remuneration or, as the case may be, reduce an amount of his or her remuneration, the applicant shall bear the costs, fees and expenses of the application, or

(b) the court does vary, in a manner less favourable to the liquidator, the terms of the liquidator's entitlement to remuneration or, as the case may be, reduce an amount of his or her remuneration, the court may make such order as it deems fit as to the costs, fees and expenses of the application.

(7) For the purpose of holding a meeting in accordance with *section 646* or *647* or this section, the liquidator may convene a meeting of the creditors of the company, the members of the company or the committee of inspection, as the case may be.

(8) Where a company is ordered to be wound up by the court upon grounds other than those specified in *section 569(1)(d)* (company unable to pay its debts) then, upon it being established to the satisfaction of the court that the company is not insolvent, the provisions of *sections 646* and *647* and this section that are applicable to a members' voluntary winding up shall, where the court so directs, apply to that company.

(9) In—

(a) fixing the amount of a provisional liquidator's remuneration under *section 645*; or

(b) the agreeing, approval, fixing or review under *section 646* or *647* or this section, as the case may be, of—

(i) the terms of a liquidator's entitlement to remuneration, or

(ii) the amount of a liquidator's remuneration,

the following shall be taken into account by the court, the committee of inspection, the creditors or, as the case may be, the members:

(i) the time properly required to be given by the person as liquidator and by his or her assistants in attending to the company's affairs;

(ii) the complexity (or otherwise) of the case;

(iii) any respects in which, in connection with the company's affairs, there falls on the liquidator any responsibility of an exceptional kind or degree;

(iv) the effectiveness with which the liquidator appears to be carrying out, or to have carried out, his or her duties; and

(v) the value and nature of the property with which the liquidator has to deal.

(10) In *sections 645* to *647* and this section "remuneration" includes remuneration for services in the winding up performed by the liquidator personally and by his or her assistants on his or her authority.

649 Disclosure of interest by creditors etc. at creditors' meeting

(1) Where, at a meeting of creditors, a resolution is proposed for the appointment of a liquidator, any creditor who has a connection with the proposed liquidator shall, before the resolution is put, make such connection known to the chairperson of the meeting who shall disclose that fact to the meeting, together with particulars thereof.

(2) *Subsection (1)* shall also apply to any person at the meeting, being a representative of a creditor and entitled to vote on the resolution on his or her behalf.

(3) Where the chairperson of a meeting of creditors has any such connection as is mentioned in *subsection (1)*, he or she shall disclose that fact to the meeting, together with particulars thereof.

(4) For the purposes of this section, a person has a connection with a proposed liquidator if he or she is—

(a) a parent, spouse, civil partner, brother, sister or child of, or

(b) employed by, or a partner of,

the proposed liquidator.

(5) A person who fails to comply with this section shall be guilty of a category 3 offence.

(6) In *subsection (4)* the reference to a child of the proposed liquidator shall be deemed to include a reference to a child of the proposed liquidator's civil partner who is ordinarily resident with the proposed liquidator and the civil partner.

(7) In exercising its jurisdiction under *section 588* or *638* (which relate to the appointment or removal of a liquidator), the court may have regard to any failure to comply with this section.

650 Duty of liquidators to include certain information in returns, etc.

(1) In this section "periodic return" includes a periodic account, a periodic abstract and a periodic statement.

(2) Where a liquidator of a company is obliged by or under this Act to make a periodic return in relation to his or her activities as liquidator, he or she shall incorporate in such return a report as to whether, at the date of such return, any past or present director or other officer, or any member, of the company is a person—

(a) in respect of whom a declaration has been made under any provision of this Act that he or she should be personally liable for all or any part of the debts of a company, or

(b) who is, or is deemed to be, subject to a disqualification order under *Part 14* or a declaration of restriction under *Chapter 3* of that Part.

(3) A liquidator who contravenes *subsection (2)* shall be guilty of a category 3 offence.

651 Penalty for default of liquidator in making certain accounts and returns

Where a liquidator is in default in relation to the making or filing of a periodic account, abstract, statement or return in pursuance of any provision of this Act he or she shall be guilty of a category 4 offence.

652 Enforcement of duty of liquidator to make returns

(1) *Subsection (2)* applies if a liquidator of a company, having made default in filing, delivering or making any return, account or other document, or in giving any notice which a liquidator is by law required to file, deliver, make or give, fails to make good the default within 14 days after the date of service on him or her of a notice requiring him or her to do so or such greater period of time as may be specified in the notice.

(2) Where this subsection applies, the court may, on an application made for the purpose, make an order directing the liquidator to make good the default within such time as may be specified in the order.

(3) Any contributory or creditor of the company, the Director or the Registrar may make an application for the purposes of this section.

(4) The order under this section may provide that all costs of and incidental to the application shall be borne by the liquidator.

(5) Nothing in this section shall be taken to prejudice the operation of any enactments imposing penalties on liquidators in respect of any such default as is mentioned in *subsection (1)*.

653 Director's power to examine books and records

(1) In this section—

"appropriate person", in relation to the company referred to in *subsection (3)*, means any of the following:

(a) the company;

(b) irrespective of the time at which he or she holds or held such status (but subject, in the case of *subparagraph (iii)*, to *subsection (2)*)—

(i) a liquidator of the company,

(ii) an officer or statutory auditor of the company, or

(iii) a receiver appointed to any property of the company;

"books and records" means the books and records of the company and, in addition, in the case of a request under *subsection (3)* made of a liquidator, statutory auditor or receiver, the books and records of the liquidator, statutory auditor or receiver;

"liquidator" includes a provisional liquidator.

(2) For the avoidance of doubt, the powers under this section do not extend to a case in which a receivership alone has been conducted in relation to any property of the

company (which case is governed by *section 446* (Director may request production of receiver's books)).

(3) Where a company is being wound up or has been dissolved, the Director may—

(a) on his or her own motion, or

(b) where a complaint is made to the Director by a member, contributory or creditor of the company,

request (specifying the reason why the request is being made) an appropriate person to produce to the Director the books and records for examination, and the appropriate person shall comply with the request.

(4) In the case of a request of a liquidator or a receiver under *subsection (3)*, the request may relate to a particular winding up or receivership process or to all windings up or receiverships conducted by the liquidator or receiver.

(5) An appropriate person shall—

(a) answer any questions of the Director concerning the content of the books and records requested to be produced under *subsection (3)*,

(b) if he or she is a liquidator or receiver, answer any questions of the Director concerning the conduct of a particular winding up or receivership, or all windings up or receiverships conducted by the appropriate person, as the case may be, and

(c) give to the Director such assistance in the matter as the appropriate person is reasonably able to give.

(6) An appropriate person shall give to the Director such access and facilities as are necessary for inspecting and taking copies of books and records requested to be produced by him or her under *subsection (3)*.

(7) A request under *subsection (3)* may not be made in respect of books and records relating to a winding up or receivership that has concluded more than 6 years prior to the date of the request but nothing in this subsection is to be read as requiring a liquidator to keep any books or records for a period longer than that specified in *section 696(2)*.

(8) An appropriate person who—

(a) fails to comply with a request under *subsection (3)*,

(b) fails to answer any question under *subsection (5)(a)* or *(b)*,

(c) fails to give the Director the assistance referred to in *subsection (5)(c)*, or

(d) without lawful excuse, fails to give the Director the access or facilities referred to in *subsection (6)*,

shall be guilty of a category 2 offence.

(9) Nothing in this section shall be taken as excluding or restricting any statutory rights of the Government, a Minister of the Government or a person acting under the authority of the Government or a Minister of the Government, or the powers of any person under *Part 13*.

Chapter 9
Contributories

654 Liability of contributory

(1) The liability of a contributory shall create a debt accruing due from him or her at the time when his or her liability commenced, but payable at the times when calls are made for enforcing the liability.

(2) An action to recover a debt created by this section shall not be brought after the expiration of 12 years after the date on which the cause of action accrued.

655 Liability as contributories of past and present members

(1) Subject to *subsection (2)*, in the event of a company being wound up, every present and past member shall be liable to contribute to the assets of the company to an amount sufficient for payment of its debts and liabilities, and the costs, charges and expenses of the winding up, and for the adjustment of the rights of the contributories among themselves.

(2) The following qualifications apply in relation to *subsection (1)*:

(a) no contribution shall be required from any member exceeding the amount, if any, unpaid on the shares in respect of which he or she is liable as a present or past member;

(b) a past member shall not be liable to contribute if he or she has ceased to be a member for one year or more before the commencement of the winding up;

(c) a past member shall not be liable to contribute in respect of any debt or liability of the company contracted after he or she ceased to be a member;

(d) a past member shall not be liable to contribute unless it appears to the court that the existing members are unable to satisfy the contributions required to be made by them in pursuance of this Act;

(e) a sum due to any member of the company, in his or her character of a member, by way of dividends, profits or otherwise, shall not be deemed to be a debt of the company, payable to that member in a case of competition between himself or herself and any other creditor not a member of the company, but any such sum may be taken into account for the purpose of the final adjustment of the rights of the contributories among themselves.

656 Settlement of list of contributories

(1) Subject to *subsection (3)*, in the event of a company being wound up, the liquidator shall, as soon as is reasonably practicable, settle a list of contributories.

(2) In a winding up the court shall, for the purpose of the foregoing function of the liquidator or any other relevant purpose of this Part, have the same power as it has under *section 173*, in the circumstances generally of a company, to rectify the register of members.

(3) Where it appears to the liquidator that it will not be necessary to make calls on or adjust the rights of contributories, the liquidator may dispense with the settlement of a list of contributories.

(4) In settling the list of contributories, the liquidator shall distinguish between persons who are contributories in their own right and persons who are contributories as being representatives of or liable for the debts of others.

657 Power to make calls

(1) The liquidator may, either before or after he or she has ascertained the sufficiency of the assets of the company, make calls on all or any of the contributories for the time being on the list of contributories to the extent of their liability, for payment of any money which the liquidator considers necessary—

(a) to satisfy the debts and liabilities of the company,

(b) to satisfy the costs, charges and expenses of the winding up, and

(c) for the adjustment of the rights of the contributories among themselves,

and may make a demand for payment of any calls so made.

(2) Without derogating from the power of the liquidator under *subsection (1)* to make such calls, the court, upon the application of the liquidator made on notice to the contributory or contributories concerned, may, either before or after it has ascertained the sufficiency of the assets of the company, exercise the following power in relation to calls.

(3) That power is to make calls on all or any of the contributories for the time being on the list of contributories to the extent of their liability, for payment of any money which the court considers necessary—

(a) to satisfy the debts and liabilities of the company,

(b) to satisfy the costs, charges and expenses of the winding up, and

(c) for the adjustment of the rights of the contributories among themselves,

and may make an order for payment of any calls so made.

(4) In making a call under this section, the court or liquidator may take into consideration that some of the contributories may partly or wholly fail to pay the call.

658 Adjustment of rights of contributories

The liquidator shall adjust the rights of the contributories among themselves and distribute any surplus among the persons entitled thereto.

659 Payment of debts due by contributory to the company and extent to which set-off allowed

(1) The court may make an order requiring any contributory for the time being on the list of contributories to pay, in a manner directed by the order, any money due from him or her or from the estate of the person whom he or she represents to the company, exclusive of any money payable by him or her or the estate by virtue of any call in pursuance of this Act.

(2) When all the creditors are paid in full, any money due on any account whatever to a contributory from the company may be allowed to him or her by way of set-off against any subsequent call.

660 Order in relation to contributory to be conclusive evidence

(1) An order made by the court in relation to a contributory shall, subject to any right of appeal, be conclusive evidence that the money, if any, thereby appearing to be due or ordered to be paid is due.

(2) All other relevant matters stated in such an order shall be taken to be truly stated as against all persons and in all proceedings.

661 Liability in case of death of contributory

(1) If a contributory dies, either before or after he or she has been placed on the list of contributories, his or her personal representatives shall be liable in due course of administration to contribute to the assets of the company in discharge of his or her liability and shall be contributories accordingly.

(2) If the personal representatives make default in paying any money ordered to be paid by them, proceedings may be taken for the administration of the estate of the deceased contributory or otherwise for compelling payment thereout of the money due.

662 Civil Liability Act 1961 not affected

Nothing in *section 661* or any other provision of this Part affects any restriction under the Civil Liability Act 1961 as to the time within which proceedings are maintainable against the estate of a deceased person.

663 Bankruptcy of contributory

(1) If a contributory becomes bankrupt, either before or after he or she has been placed on the list of contributories, the following provisions apply:

(a) the assignee in bankruptcy—

  (i) shall represent the bankrupt for all the purposes of the winding up, and shall be a contributory accordingly, and

  (ii) may be called on to admit to proof against the estate of the bankrupt, or otherwise to allow to be paid out of the bankrupt's assets in due course of law, any money due from the bankrupt in respect of his or her liability to contribute to the assets of the company;

and

(b) there may be proved against the estate of the bankrupt the estimated value of his or her liability to future calls as well as calls already made.

(2) Nothing in this section affects, to the extent and under the circumstances allowable under—

(a) the general law pertaining to the application of different jurisdictions' laws and procedures,

(b) any Community act, or

(c) any enactment giving the force of law to an agreement to which the State is a party,

the enforcement, in a winding up or other insolvency proceedings outside the State, of any liability of an individual who is a contributory.

664 Corporate insolvency of contributory

(1) If a contributory is a company which is being wound up, either voluntarily or by the court (and whether its winding up commences before or after it has been placed on the list of contributories), the following provisions apply:

(a) the liquidator of the contributory company—

(i) shall represent it for all the purposes of the winding up, and shall be a contributory accordingly, and

(ii) may be called on to admit to proof in the contributory company's winding up or otherwise to allow to be paid out of its assets in due course of law, any money due from the contributory company in respect of its liability to contribute to the assets of the company;

and

(b) there may be proved against the contributory company the estimated value of its liability to future calls as well as calls already made.

(2) In *subsection (1)* the first reference to a company and each reference to a contributory company is a reference to any of the following:

(a) a private company limited by shares;

(b) a designated activity company;

(c) a public limited company;

(d) a company limited by guarantee;

(e) an unlimited company;

(f) an unregistered company.

(3) Nothing in this section affects, to the extent and under the circumstances allowable under—

(a) the general law pertaining to the application of different jurisdictions' laws and procedures,

(b) any Community act, or

(c) any enactment giving the force of law to an agreement to which the State is a party,

the enforcement, in a winding up or other insolvency proceedings outside the State, of any liability of a body or undertaking that is a contributory.

665 Winding up of company that had been an unlimited company before re-registration

In the event of the winding up of a company that had been an unlimited company before it re-registered under this Act as a private company limited by shares, the following provisions have effect:

(a) notwithstanding *section 1278(2)(a)*, a past member of the company who was a member thereof at the time of re-registration shall, if the winding up commences within the period of 3 years beginning after the day on which the company is re-registered, be liable to contribute to the assets of the company in respect of its debts and liabilities contracted before that time;

(b) where no persons who were members of the company at the time of re-registration are existing members of the company, a person who, at that time was a present or past member thereof shall, subject to *section 1278(2)(a)* and to *paragraph (a)*, but notwithstanding *section 1278(2)(c)* be liable to contribute in the foregoing manner despite the fact that the existing members have satisfied the contributions required to be made by them in pursuance of this Act; and

(c) notwithstanding *section 655(2)(a)*, there shall be no limit on the amount which a person who, at the time of re-registration, was a past or present member of the company, is liable to contribute in the foregoing manner.

Chapter 10
Committee of inspection

666 Appointment of committee of inspection in court ordered winding up

(1) When a winding-up order has been made by the court, the liquidator may and, if directed to do so by a creditor or creditors representing not less than one-tenth in value of the creditors of the company shall, summon a meeting of the creditors of the company for the purpose of determining—

(a) whether or not a committee of inspection is to be appointed, and

(b) who are to be the members of the committee if so appointed.

(2) At a meeting summoned in accordance with *subsection (1)*, the creditors may, if they think fit, appoint a committee of inspection consisting of not more than 5 persons appointed under this subsection.

(3) If such a committee is appointed the company may, at any time subsequently in general meeting, appoint not more than 3 persons to act as members of the committee, provided that the number of members of the committee shall not at any time exceed eight.

(4) The creditors may resolve that all or any of the persons appointed under *subsection (3)* by the company ought not to be members of the committee of inspection, and if the creditors so resolve, the persons mentioned in the resolution shall not, unless the court, on application to it, otherwise directs, be qualified to act as members of the committee.

(5) On an application to the court under *subsection (4)*, the court may appoint other persons to act as members of the committee of inspection in place of the persons mentioned in the resolution concerned.

(6) Where a meeting of the creditors or members of the company is being summoned under this section, the notice of the meeting shall indicate who are proposed to be appointed as the members of the committee of inspection by the meeting concerned.

667 Appointment of committee of inspection in a creditors' voluntary winding up

(1) The creditors of the company at the meeting to be held in pursuance of *section 587*, or at any subsequent meeting, may appoint a committee of inspection consisting of not more than 5 persons appointed under this subsection.

(2) If such a committee is appointed, the company may, either at the meeting at which the resolution for voluntary winding up is passed or at any time subsequently in general meeting, appoint not more than 3 persons to act as members of the committee, provided that the number of members of the committee shall not at any time exceed eight.

(3) The creditors may resolve that all or any of the persons appointed under *subsection (2)* by the company ought not to be members of the committee of inspection, and if the creditors so resolve, the persons mentioned in the resolution shall not, unless the court, on application to it, otherwise directs, be qualified to act as members of the committee.

(4) On an application to the court under *subsection (3)*, the court may appoint other persons to act as members of the committee of inspection in place of the persons mentioned in the resolution concerned.

668 Constitution and proceedings of committee of inspection

(1) A committee of inspection appointed in pursuance of this Act (the "committee") shall meet at such times as they from time to time appoint, and the liquidator or any member of the committee may also call a meeting of the committee as and when he or she thinks necessary.

(2) The committee may act by a majority of their members present at a meeting but shall not act unless a majority of the committee is present.

(3) A member of the committee may resign by notice in writing signed by him or her and delivered to the liquidator.

(4) A person's office as member of the committee becomes vacant if and upon any of the following happening:

(a) the person is adjudicated bankrupt or compounds or arranges with his or her creditors;

(b) the person is absent from 2 consecutive meetings of the committee without the leave of those persons who, together with himself or herself, were appointed as members of the committee by the creditors or, as the case may be, members of the company.

(5) A member of the committee may be removed by resolution at a meeting of—

(a) creditors of the company if he or she was appointed as member of the committee by those creditors, or

(b) the company if he or she was appointed as member of the committee by the company,

being a meeting of which 7 days' notice has been given and which notice stated the object of the meeting.

(6) Subject to *subsection (7)*, on a vacancy occurring in the committee, the liquidator shall forthwith summon a meeting of—

(a) creditors of the company, or

(b) if the person who vacated office had been appointed by the company, of the company,

to fill the vacancy, and the meeting may, by resolution, reappoint the person who vacated office or appoint another person to fill the vacancy.

(7) If the liquidator, having regard to the position in the winding up, is of the opinion that it is unnecessary for a vacancy occurring in the committee to be filled, he or she may apply to the court and the court may make an order that the vacancy shall not be filled or shall not be filled except in such circumstances as may be specified in the order.

(8) The continuing members of the committee, if not less than 2, may act notwithstanding any vacancy in the committee.

(9) A member of the committee shall not make a profit from the winding up, except with the leave of the court or the sanction of—

(a) in the case of a members' voluntary winding up, a resolution of the company, or

(b) in the case of a creditors' voluntary winding up, a resolution of the creditors of the company.

(10) At a meeting of creditors, a resolution shall, for the purposes of this section (other than *subsection (9)(b)*), be deemed to be passed when a majority in number of the creditors present personally or by proxy and voting on the resolution have voted in favour of the resolution.

Chapter 11
Court's powers

669 Power to annul order for winding up or to stay winding up

(1) At any time after an order for winding up is made, the court—

(a) on the application of the liquidator or any creditor or contributory, and

(b) on proof to the satisfaction of the court that the order for winding up ought to be annulled, may make an order annulling the order for winding up on such terms and conditions as the court thinks fit.

(2) Without prejudice to *subsection (6)*, where the court makes an order under *subsection (1)*, the applicant shall forthwith give notice of the making of the order in the prescribed form to the Registrar.

(3) At any time after an order for winding up is made, the court—

(a) on the application of the liquidator or any creditor or contributory, and

(b) on proof to the satisfaction of the court that all proceedings in relation to the winding up ought to be stayed,

may make an order staying the proceedings, either altogether or for a limited time, on such terms and conditions as the court thinks fit.

(4) Where the court makes an order under *subsection (1)* or *(3)*, it may give such directions as to the retention or disposal of the company's seal, books and papers as it thinks fit.

(5) On any application under this section the court may require the liquidator to furnish to the court a report relating to any facts or matters which are in the liquidator's opinion relevant to the application.

(6) A certified copy of an order made under *subsection (1)* or *(3)* shall forthwith, upon the perfection of the order, be forwarded by the company, or by such other person as the court may direct, to the Registrar.

(7) If the applicant referred to in *subsection (2)* makes default in complying with that subsection, the applicant shall be guilty of a category 4 offence.

(8) If a company makes default in complying with *subsection (6)*, the company and any officer of it who is in default shall be guilty of a category 4 offence.

(9) If any other person makes default in complying with *subsection (6)*, the person shall be guilty of a category 4 offence.

670 Attendance of officers of company at meetings

The court may, on the application of the Director or the liquidator, or on its own motion, make an order requiring the attendance of any officer of the company at—

(a) any meeting of creditors,

(b) any meeting of contributories,

(c) any meeting of members, or

(d) any meeting of a committee of inspection,

for the purpose of giving information as to the trade, dealings, affairs or property of the company.

671 Power of court to summon persons for examination

(1) The court may exercise the following power:

(a) of its own motion; or

(b) on the application of the Director or the liquidator or provisional liquidator;

at any time after the appointment of a provisional liquidator, the making of a winding-up order or the passing of a resolution to wind up a company voluntarily.

(2) That power of the court is to summon before it—

(a) any officer of the company,

(b) any person known or suspected to have in his or her possession any property of the company or supposed to be indebted to the company, or

(c) any person whom the court deems capable of giving information relating to the—

(i) promotion or formation,

(ii) trade or dealings, or

(iii) affairs or property,

of the company.

(3) The court may examine on oath any person so summoned concerning the matters referred to in *subsection (2)(c)(i)* to *(iii)*, either by word of mouth or on written interrogatories, and may reduce his or her answers to writing and require him or her to sign them.

(4) The court may require any person referred to in *subsection (2)* to produce any accounting records, deed, instrument, or other document or paper relating to the company that are in his or her custody or power.

(5) The court may, before the examination takes place, require any person referred to in *subsection (2)* to place before it a statement, in such form as the court may direct, of any transactions between him or her and the company of a type or class which the court may specify.

(6) If, in the opinion of the court, it is just and equitable to do so, it may direct that the costs of the examination be paid by the person examined.

(7) A person who is examined under this section shall not be entitled to refuse to answer any question put to him or her on the ground that his or her answer might incriminate him or her and any answer by the person to such a question may be used against that person in any proceedings except proceedings for the prosecution of that person for an offence (other than perjury).

(8) If a person, without reasonable excuse, fails at any time—

(a) to attend his or her examination under this section, or

(b) to comply with the requirement under *subsection (3)* as regards signing the matters there referred to or the requirement under *subsection (4)* or *(5)*,

he or she shall be guilty of contempt of court and liable to be punished accordingly.

(9) If—

(a) a person without reasonable excuse fails at any time to attend his or her examination under this section, or

(b) there are reasonable grounds for believing that a person has absconded, or is about to abscond, with a view to avoiding or delaying his or her examination under this section,

the court may cause that person to be arrested and the person's books and documents and movable personal property to be seized or secured and the person and them to be detained until such time as the court may order.

672 Order for payment or delivery of property against person examined under *section 671*

(1) If, in the course of an examination under *section 671*, it appears to the court that any person being examined—

(a) is indebted to the company, or

(b) has in his or her possession or control any money, property or books and papers of the company,

the court may, of its own motion or on the application of the Director or the liquidator, order such person—

(i) to pay to the liquidator the amount of the debt or any part of it, or

(ii) to pay, deliver, convey, surrender or transfer to the liquidator such money, property or books and papers or any part of it or them,

as the case may be, at such time and in such manner and on such terms as the court may direct.

(2) Where the court has made an order under *subsection (1)*, it may, on the application of the Director or the liquidator, make a further order permitting the applicant or another person specified in the order, accompanied (in either case) by such persons as the applicant thinks appropriate, to—

(a) enter at any time or times within 30 days after the date of issue of the order, any premises (including a dwelling) owned or occupied by the person the subject of the order under *subsection (1)* (using such force as is reasonably necessary for the purpose),

(b) search the premises so entered, and

(c) seize, in the course of such search, any money, property or books and papers of the company found on the premises.

(3) Where the court has made an order under *subsection (2)*, the applicant shall report to it as soon as may be on the outcome of any action on foot of the court's order and the court shall direct the applicant as to the disposition of anything seized on foot of the order.

(4) A direction under *subsection (3)* shall not be made in favour of the Director except in respect of the Director's costs and reasonable expenses.

(5) A person who obstructs the exercise of—

(a) a right of entry, search and seizure conferred by virtue of an order made under *subsection (2)*, or

(b) a right so conferred to take possession of anything referred to in that subsection,

shall be guilty of a category 2 offence.

(6) Proceedings on foot of an offence alleged to be committed under *subsection (5)* shall not prejudice the power of the court to issue proceedings for contempt of court for failure by a person to comply with an order under this section.

(7) In this section "liquidator" includes a provisional liquidator.

673 Delivery of property of company to liquidator

(1) In a winding up of a company, on notice in writing being given by the liquidator requiring him or her to do so, any:

(a) contributory for the time being on the list of contributories;

(b) trustee;

(c) receiver;

(d) banker; or

(e) agent or officer;

of the company shall, within such period as is specified in the notice, pay, deliver, convey, surrender or transfer to or into the hands of the liquidator any money, property, books or papers which happen to be in his or her hands for the time being and to which the company is *prima facie* entitled.

(2) The court may exercise the following power:

(a) of its own motion; or

(b) on the application of the liquidator;

at any time after the appointment of a provisional liquidator, the making of a winding-up order or the passing of a resolution to wind up a company voluntarily.

(3) That power of the court is to require a person referred to in any of *paragraphs (a)* to *(e)* of *subsection (1)* to pay, deliver, convey, surrender or transfer forthwith, or within such period as the court directs, to the liquidator any money, property or books and papers in his or her hands to which the company concerned is *prima facie* entitled.

(4) In discharging the duties imposed by *section 624*, the liquidator shall, for the purpose of acquiring or retaining possession of the property of the company, be in the same position as if he or she were a receiver of the property appointed by the court, and the court may, on the application of the liquidator, enforce such acquisition or retention accordingly.

(5) In this section "liquidator" includes a provisional liquidator.

674 Power to exclude creditors not proving in time

(1) Subject to *subsections (3)* and *(4)*, the liquidator may fix a time or times within which creditors are to prove their debts or claims or to be excluded from the benefit of any distribution made before those debts or claims are proved.

(2) The time or times so fixed by the liquidator shall be notified, in writing, by him or her to the creditors.

(3) A time shall not be fixed pursuant to *subsection (1)* which falls earlier than 28 days after the day on which creditors are notified under *subsection (2)* of the fixing of that time.

(4) The court may upon the application of a creditor, made on notice to the liquidator, extend the time fixed pursuant to *subsection (1)* within which that creditor may prove his or her debt or claim.

675 Order for arrest and seizure, etc.

(1) The court may, in either of the cases specified in *subsection (2)*—

(a) at any time after the presentation of a petition to wind up a company or the passing of a resolution to wind up a company voluntarily, and

(b) on proof of probable cause for believing that a contributory, director, shadow director, secretary or other officer of the company is about to quit the State or otherwise to abscond or to remove or conceal any of his or her property for the purpose of evading payment of calls or of avoiding examination about the affairs of the company,

cause—

(i) the contributory, director, shadow director, secretary or other officer to be arrested, and

(ii) that person's books and papers and movable personal property to be seized or secured,

and the person and them to be detained until such time as the court may order.

(2) The court may exercise the powers under *subsection (1)*—

(a) of its own motion, or

(b) on the application of the Director, a creditor of the company or any other interested person.

676 Provisions as to arrangement binding creditors

(1) Any arrangement entered into between a company about to be, or in the course of being, wound up and its creditors shall, subject to the right of appeal under this section, be binding on the company if sanctioned by a special resolution and on the creditors if acceded to by three-fourths in number and value of the creditors.

(2) Any creditor or contributory may, within 21 days after the date of completion of the arrangement, appeal to the court against it, and the court, on the hearing of the appeal, may, as it thinks just, amend, vary or confirm the arrangement.

(3) This section is in addition to the circumstances in which a compromise or arrangement in relation to a company may become binding under *Chapter 1* of *Part 9*.

Chapter 12
Provisions supplemental to conduct of winding up

677 Effect of winding up on business and status of company

(1) From the commencement of the winding up, the company shall cease to carry on its business, except so far as may be required for the beneficial winding up of it.

(2) However the corporate state and corporate powers of the company shall, notwithstanding anything to the contrary in its constitution, continue until it is dissolved.

(3) On the appointment of a liquidator, other than a provisional liquidator, all the powers of the directors of the company shall cease, except so far as—

- (a) in the case of a winding up by the court or a creditors' voluntary winding up, the committee of inspection or, if there is no such committee, the creditors, sanction (in either case, with the approval of the liquidator) the continuance of those powers, or
- (b) in the case of a members' voluntary winding up, the members in general meeting sanction the continuance of those powers.

(4) The continuance of the directors' powers by virtue of a sanction under *subsection (3)* shall not, in any case, and notwithstanding anything in *section 40*, operate to give precedence to any decision or act of the directors made or done during the course of the winding up over that made or done by the liquidator in respect of the matter concerned and, without prejudice to the foregoing, no decision or act made or done by the directors in respect of a matter falling within *section 627* shall be valid unless made or done with the prior consent of the liquidator, but this is subject to *subsection (5)*.

(5) The court may, on application to it by a person aggrieved, grant such relief as it thinks appropriate from the sanction of invalidity provided under *subsection (4)* if it is satisfied that the person (not being an officer of the company) acted in good faith in the matter.

(6) An application under *subsection (5)* shall be made on notice to the liquidator and—

- (a) each creditor who has submitted a proof of his or her debt or claim under and in accordance with this Part, and
- (b) each contributory for the time being on the list of contributories.

678 Actions against company stayed on winding-up order

(1) When in relation to a company—

- (a) a winding-up order has been made,
- (b) a provisional liquidator has been appointed, or
- (c) a resolution for voluntary winding up has been passed,

no action or proceeding shall be proceeded with or commenced against the company except by leave of the court and subject to such terms as the court may impose.

(2) *Subsection (1)* shall not apply to the taking of proceedings before the Employment Appeals Tribunal.

679 Director may direct convening of meetings

(1) Where a meeting is required to be held under this Part and such meeting is not held within the time required or in the manner required by or under this Part, the Director may—

(a) direct the liquidator of the company concerned to convene (or, as appropriate, reconvene) such meeting, and

(b) specify procedures that are to be followed in convening (or reconvening) and holding such meeting, matters that are to be dealt with at such meeting and the time and location of such meeting.

(2) The Director, or his or her authorised representative, may attend at any meeting convened or reconvened pursuant to *subsection (1)*.

(3) A liquidator who fails to comply with a direction under *subsection (1)* shall be guilty of a category 3 offence.

680 Duty of liquidator to call meeting at end of each year

(1) If a members' voluntary winding up continues for more than 12 months, then after—

(a) the first anniversary of the commencement of the winding up, and

(b) each subsequent anniversary of that commencement (and the winding up is continuing),

the liquidator has the following duty.

(2) That duty of the liquidator is to—

(a) summon, giving 7 days' notice thereof, the holding of a general meeting of the company for a day falling not later than 28 days after the anniversary concerned, and

(b) lay before that meeting an account of his or her acts and dealings and of the conduct of the winding up during the preceding year.

(3) The liquidator shall, within 7 days after the date of such meeting, send a copy of the foregoing account to the Registrar.

(4) If a winding up by the court or a creditors' voluntary winding up continues for more than 12 months, then after—

(a) the first anniversary of the commencement of the winding up, and

(b) each subsequent anniversary of that commencement (and the winding up is continuing),

the liquidator has the following duty.

(5) That duty of the liquidator is to—

(a) summon, giving 7 days' notice thereof, the holding of—

(i) if a committee of inspection has been appointed, a meeting of the committee of inspection, or

(ii) if no committee of inspection has been appointed, a meeting of the creditors of the company,

for a day falling not later than 28 days after the anniversary concerned, and

(b) lay before that meeting an account of his or her acts and dealings and of the conduct of the winding up during the preceding year.

(6) The liquidator shall, within 7 days after the date of such meeting, send a copy of the foregoing account to the Registrar.

(7) Where a meeting of the committee of inspection is held pursuant to *subsection (5)(a)*, that committee may, by resolution, direct the liquidator to convene a meeting of the creditors of the company and, where such a direction is so given, the liquidator shall cause such meeting to be convened and held no later than 21 days after the date of such resolution.

(8) Where *section 584* has effect, *subsections (4)* to *(6)* shall apply to the winding up to the exclusion of *subsections (1)* to *(3)*, as if the winding up were a creditors' voluntary winding up and not a members' voluntary winding up.

(9) If the liquidator fails to comply with any provision of this section, or a direction under it, he or she shall be guilty of a category 3 offence.

681 Information about progress of liquidation

(1) This section applies where the winding up of a company is not concluded within 12 months after the date of its commencement and is subject to *subsection (4)*.

(2) Where this section applies, the liquidator of the company shall, at the intervals specified in *subsection (3)* until the winding up is concluded, send to the Registrar a statement in the prescribed form and containing the prescribed particulars about the proceedings in, and position of, the winding up.

(3) The intervals referred to in *subsection (2)* are—

(a) as regards the first of them — the interval ending on the date of the first anniversary of the commencement of the winding up (but, for the purposes of this interval, the obligation of the liquidator under *subsection (2)* may be fulfilled at any time before the expiry of 14 days after that anniversary), and

(b) as regards subsequent intervals — intervals of 6 months, or such greater period as may be prescribed, following on from that first anniversary.

(4) The obligation under *subsection (2)* does not apply in relation to a particular winding up if and to the extent that the court specifies in a direction given by it.

(5) If a liquidator fails to comply with *subsection (2)*, he or she shall be guilty of a category 3 offence.

682 Liquidator to report on conduct of directors

(1) In this section "insolvent company" has the same meaning as it has in *Chapter 3* (restrictions on directors of insolvent companies) of *Part 14*.

(2) In a winding up of an insolvent company, the liquidator shall, within 6 months after the date of his or her appointment, and at intervals as required by the

Director thereafter, provide to the Director a report [in the form prescribed by the Minister][a].

(3) The Director may require the liquidator of an insolvent company—

(a) to answer, whether orally or in writing, any question that the Director reasonably puts to the liquidator concerning the contents of a report made by the liquidator under *subsection (2)*, the affairs of the company or the conduct of any director of the company (as that expression is to be read in accordance with *section 683(1) (b)*), and

(b) to give such other assistance (as he or she is reasonably able to give) to the Director for the purpose of the Director's appraisal of such a report or the Director's examination of any fact or allegation contained in it or which comes to the Director's knowledge by reason of an answer given under *paragraph (a)* or otherwise through the Director's performance of functions under this Act,

and the liquidator shall comply with such a requirement.

(4) The Director's powers under *subsection (3)* are in addition to the powers of the Director or any other person under any other provision of this Act.

(5) A liquidator who fails to comply with *subsection (2)* or a requirement under *subsection (3)* shall be guilty of a category 3 offence.

Amendments

a Words substituted by C(A)A 2017, s 98(h) (previously: "in the prescribed form").

683 Obligation (unless relieved) of liquidator of insolvent company to apply for restriction of directors

(1) In this section—

(a) "insolvent company" has the same meaning as it has in *Chapter 3* (restrictions on directors of insolvent companies) of *Part 14*; and

(b) a reference to a director of the insolvent company is a reference to a person who was a director or shadow director of the company at the date of, or within 12 months before, the commencement of its winding up.

(2) In a winding up of an insolvent company, where this subsection applies, the liquidator shall apply under *section 819(1)* for a declaration under that provision in respect of each of the directors of the company.

(3) As respects *subsection (2)*—

(a) that subsection applies unless the Director has relieved the liquidator of the obligation to make the application under *section 819(1)* in relation to the winding up concerned or a particular director or directors (which power to so relieve is conferred on the Director by this paragraph), and

(b) where the Director relieves the liquidator of that obligation in respect of one or more but not all of the directors, that subsection shall be read as applying to the director or directors as respects whom the liquidator has not been relieved of that obligation.

(4) An application in respect of a director under *section 819(1)*, in compliance with *subsection (2)*, shall be made not later than the expiry of—

(a) 2 months after the date on which the Director has notified the liquidator that the Director has not relieved the liquidator of the obligation to make the application in respect of the director, or

(b) such greater period of time as the Director may allow for the purposes of the application.

(5) A liquidator who fails to comply with *subsection (2)* shall be guilty of a category 3 offence.

684 Inspection of books by creditors and contributories

(1) The court may, at any time after making a winding-up order or the commencement of a voluntary winding up, make such order for inspection of the accounting records, books and papers of the company by creditors or contributories as the court thinks just.

(2) Where such an order is made, any accounting records, books and papers in the possession of the company may be inspected by creditors or contributories accordingly, but not further or otherwise.

(3) Nothing in this section shall be taken as excluding or restricting any statutory rights of the Government, a Minister of the Government or a person acting under the authority of the Government or a Minister of the Government, or the powers of any person under *Part 13*.

685 Resolutions passed at adjourned meetings of creditors and contributories

Where a resolution is passed at an adjourned meeting of any creditors or contributories of a company, the resolution shall, for all purposes, be treated as having been passed on the date on which it was in fact passed and shall not be deemed to have been passed on any earlier date.

686 Books of company to be evidence in civil proceedings

When a company is being wound up, information contained in every book and record of the company and of the liquidator and any provisional liquidator shall, as between—

(a) the members, officers and contributories of the company, and

(b) any of the persons referred to in *paragraph (a)* and the liquidator, the provisional liquidator (if any) and the Director of Corporate Enforcement,

be admissible, in all civil proceedings, as evidence of any fact therein.

687 Liquidator may have regard to wishes of creditors and contributories

(1) Subject to this Part, the liquidator may, in the administration of the property of the company and in the distribution of the property among its creditors, have regard to any directions given to him or her by resolution of the creditors or contributories at any general meeting or by the committee of inspection (if any).

(2) In case of conflict—

(a) between any directions so given by the creditors and those so given by the contributories, or

(b) between any directions so given by the creditors or the contributories and any directions given by the committee of inspection,

the directions, in the case of *paragraph (a)*, of the creditors shall override those of the contributories and the directions, in the case of *paragraph (b)*, of the creditors or contributories shall override those of the committee of inspection.

(3) The liquidator—

(a) may convene general meetings of the creditors or contributories for the purpose of ascertaining their wishes, and

(b) shall, for that purpose, convene meetings of the creditors or, as the case may be, contributories—

(i) at such times as the creditors or contributories, as the case may be, by resolution direct, or

(ii) whenever requested in writing to do so by at least one-tenth in value of the creditors or, as the case may be, by at least one-tenth in number of the contributories.

688 Reporting to Director of misconduct by liquidators

(1) Where a disciplinary committee or tribunal (however called) of a prescribed professional body—

(a) finds that a member of that body who is conducting or has conducted a winding up has not maintained appropriate records in relation to that activity, or

(b) has reasonable grounds for believing that such a member has committed a category 1 or 2 offence during the course of conducting a winding up,

the professional body shall report the matter, giving details of the finding or, as the case may be, of the alleged offence, to the Director forthwith.

(2) If a professional body fails to comply with this section, it, and any officer of the body to whom the failure is attributable, shall be guilty of a category 3 offence.

Chapter 13
General rules as to meetings of members, contributories and creditors of a company in liquidation

689 Meetings directed by the court

(1) This section shall apply to meetings in a winding up ordered by the court that are held or to be held at the direction of the court and shall have effect subject to any directions the court may give.

(2) If the court so directs, notice of a meeting may be given by advertisement in which case the object of the meeting need not be stated in the advertisement.

(3) A certified copy of the order of the court appointing a person as chairperson of a meeting shall be sufficient authority for the person so appointed to preside at such meeting.

(4) The chairperson of a meeting shall make a report of the result of the meeting in such form (if any) as the court directs.

690 Provisions as to meetings of creditors, contributories and members generally

Save where this Act otherwise provides, the provisions of *sections 691* to *703* shall apply in relation to a meeting of creditors, contributories or members held or to be held under this Part.

691 Entitlement to attend and notice

(1) Every person appearing by the company's books to be a creditor of the company shall be entitled to attend a meeting of creditors.

(2) The liquidator shall give to every person appearing by the company's books or otherwise to be a contributory of the company notice of a meeting of contributories.

(3) Every person appearing by the company's books or otherwise to be a member of the company shall be entitled to attend a meeting of members.

(4) The liquidator shall give notice in writing to every person entitled to attend a meeting of the time and place appointed for the meeting and of the subject matter of the meeting in such form as may be prescribed not less than 7 days before the day appointed for such meeting.

(5) The notice under *subsection (4)* to each creditor shall be sent to the address given in the creditor's proof, or if he or she has not proved, to the address given in the statement of affairs of the company, if any, or to such other address as may be known to the liquidator.

(6) The notice under *subsection (4)* to each contributory shall be sent to the address mentioned in the company's books as the address of such contributory or to such other address as may be known to the liquidator.

(7) The notice under *subsection (4)* to each member shall be sent to the address mentioned in the company's books as the address of such member or to such other address as may be known to the liquidator.

(8) Where a meeting of creditors, contributories or members is summoned by notice, the proceedings and resolutions of the meeting shall, unless the court otherwise orders, be valid notwithstanding that some creditors, contributories or members, as the case may be, may not have received the notice sent to them.

692 Location of meeting

(1) Every meeting shall be held at such place as is, in the opinion of the person convening the meeting, the most convenient for the majority of the creditors, contributories or members or all, as the case may be.

(2) Different times or places may be named for the meetings of creditors and for those of contributories and for those of members.

693 Costs of meetings

(1) Any person, other than the liquidator, who summons a meeting of creditors, contributories or members shall be liable for the costs of summoning the meeting and shall, before the meeting is summoned, deposit with the liquidator such sum as may be required by the liquidator as security for the payment of such costs.

(2) Those costs shall be repaid out of the assets of the company if the court shall by order so direct or if the creditors or contributories (as the case may be) shall by resolution so direct.

(3) This section shall not apply to meetings under *section 587*.

694 Chairperson

(1) At a meeting summoned by the liquidator, the liquidator or, if the liquidator is unable to act, someone nominated by him or her, shall be chairperson and at every other meeting of creditors, contributories or members the chairperson shall be such person as the meeting by resolution shall appoint.

(2) This section shall not apply to meetings under *section 587*.

695 Passing resolutions

(1) At a meeting of creditors, a resolution shall be deemed to be passed when a majority in number and value of the creditors present personally or by proxy and voting on the resolution have voted in favour of the resolution.

(2) At a meeting of the contributories a resolution shall be deemed to be passed when a majority in number and value of the contributories present personally or by proxy and voting on the resolution have voted in favour of the resolution, the value of the contributories being determined according to the number of votes conferred on each contributory by the constitution of the company.

(3) This section shall not apply to a resolution referred to in *section 588(6)*, *637(3)* or *section 668(5)* or *(6)*.

696 Registration of resolutions of creditors, contributories and members

(1) The liquidator shall forward to the Registrar a copy certified by the liquidator of every resolution of a meeting of creditors, contributories or members within 14 days after the date upon which the meeting concerned is held.

(2) If a liquidator fails to comply with *subsection (1)*, he or she shall be guilty of a category 4 offence.

697 Proceedings at the meeting

(1) The chairperson of a meeting may, with the consent of the meeting, adjourn it from time to time and from place to place but the adjourned meeting shall be held at the same place as the original meeting unless—

(a) in the resolution for adjournment another place is specified, or

(b) the court otherwise orders.

(2) Other than on the matter of election of the chairperson or an adjournment, a meeting may not act for any purpose, unless there are present or represented at the meeting—

(a) in the case of a creditors' meeting, at least 3 creditors entitled to vote or all the creditors entitled to vote if the number entitled to vote shall not exceed three, or

(b) in the case of a meeting of contributories or members, at least 2 contributories or members, as the case may be.

(3) If within 30 minutes from the time appointed for the meeting a quorum of creditors, contributories or members, as the case may be, is not present or represented, the meeting shall be adjourned to the same day in the following week at the same time and place or to such other day or time or place as the chairperson may appoint.

(4) However the day so appointed by the chairperson shall be not less than 7 nor more than 21 days after the day from which the meeting was adjourned.

698 Entitlement to vote of creditors

(1) Subject to *subsection (3)*, in the case of a meeting of creditors held pursuant to *section 666* or of an adjournment thereof, a person shall not be entitled to vote as a creditor unless he or she has duly lodged with the liquidator, not later than the time mentioned for that purpose in the notice convening the meeting or adjourned meeting, a proof of the debt which he or she claims to be due to him or her from the company.

(2) In the case of any other meeting of creditors and subject to *subsection (3)* and *subsections (5)* to *(8)*, a person shall not be entitled to vote as a creditor unless he or she has lodged with the liquidator a proof of the debt which he or she claims to be due to him or her from the company and such proof has been admitted wholly or in part before the date on which the meeting is held.

(3) Neither *subsection (1)* or *(2)* shall apply to any creditors or class of creditors who by virtue of this Act or rules of court are not required to prove their debts, and *subsection (2)* shall not apply to a meeting referred to in *section 587*.

(4) The following subsections contain exceptions to, or apply restrictions on the exercise of, a creditor's entitlement to vote at a meeting to which *subsection (2)* applies.

(5) In respect of any unliquidated or contingent debt or any debt the value of which is not ascertained, the chairperson may put upon such a debt an estimated minimum value for the purpose of entitlement to vote and admit the creditor's proof for that purpose.

(6) A creditor shall not vote in respect of any debt on or secured by a current bill of exchange or promissory note held by him or her unless he or she is willing to do each of the following, namely:

(a) to treat the liability to him or her on the bill or note of every person who is liable thereon antecedently to the company and against whom an adjudication order in bankruptcy has not been made, as a security in his or her hands;

(b) to estimate the value of that liability; and

(c) for purposes of voting but not for the purposes of dividend, to deduct that liability from his or her proof.

(7) Unless he or she surrenders his or her security, a secured creditor shall, for the purpose of voting, state:

(a) in his or her proof; or

(b) in the case of a meeting that falls within *subsection (8)*, in the statement referred to in that subsection,

the following matters:

(i) the particulars of his or her security;

(ii) the date when that security was given; and

(iii) the value at which he or she assesses that security,

and shall be entitled to vote only in respect of the balance (if any) due to him or her after deducting the value of that security.

(8) For the purpose of voting at a meeting in a voluntary winding up (not being a meeting referred to in *section 587*), a secured creditor shall, unless the secured creditor surrenders his or her security, lodge with the liquidator, before the meeting, a statement stating the matters referred to in *subsection (7)(i)* to *(iii)*.

(9) The chairperson may admit or reject a proof for the purpose of voting, but an appeal shall lie to the court against his or her decision on that matter.

(10) If the chairperson is in doubt whether a proof should be admitted or rejected the chairperson shall mark it as objected to and allow the creditor to vote subject to the vote being declared invalid in the event of the objection being sustained.

699 Provisions consequent on *section 698* regarding secured creditors: deemed surrender of security, etc.

(1) A secured creditor who, at a meeting to which *section 698(2)* applies, votes in respect of the whole debt due to him or her shall be deemed to surrender his or her security unless the court, on application to it, is satisfied that the omission to value the security has arisen from inadvertence.

(2) The liquidator may, within 28 days after the date of there being used the proof or statement referred to in *section 698(7)* or *(8)* for the purpose of voting at a meeting to which *section 698(2)* applies, require the creditor concerned to give up the security for the benefit of the creditors generally on payment to the creditor of the value estimated in that proof or statement.

(3) However the creditor concerned may, at any time before being so required to give the security up, correct the valuation so estimated by furnishing a new proof to the liquidator and may deduct the new value from the debt due to him or her.

700 Duties of chairperson

(1) The chairperson of a meeting shall cause—

(a) minutes of the proceedings at the meeting to be drawn up and entered in a book kept for that purpose and the minutes shall be signed by him or her or by the chairperson of the next ensuing meeting, and

(b) a list of creditors, contributories or members present at the meeting to be made and kept in such form as may be prescribed and such list shall be signed by him or her.

(2) If the chairperson fails to comply with *subsection (1)(a)* or *(b)*, he or she shall be guilty of a category 3 offence.

701 Proxies

(1) A creditor, a contributory or a member may vote either in person or by proxy.

(2) An instrument of proxy shall be in the prescribed form.

(3) A creditor, a contributory or a member may appoint any person a special proxy to vote at any specified meeting or adjournment thereof—

(a) for or against the appointment or continuance in office of any specified person as liquidator or member of the committee of inspection, and

(b) on all questions relating to any matter other than those referred to in *paragraph (a)* and arising at the meeting or an adjournment thereof.

(4) A creditor, a contributory or a member may appoint any person a general proxy.

(5) A general and a special form of proxy shall be sent to each of the creditors, contributories or members with the notice summoning the meeting, and neither the name nor description of the liquidator or any other person shall be printed or inserted in the body of any instrument of proxy before it is so sent.

(6) A creditor, a contributory or a member may appoint the liquidator or, if there is no liquidator, the chairperson of a meeting to act as his or her general or special proxy.

(7) No person appointed as either a general or a special proxy shall vote in favour of any resolution which would directly or indirectly place—

(a) himself or herself,

(b) a partner of him or her, or

(c) an employer of him or her,

in a position to receive any remuneration out of the assets of the company otherwise than as a creditor rateably with the other creditors of the company.

(8) However where any person holds one or more special proxies to vote for an application to the court in favour of the appointment of himself or herself as liquidator the person may use that proxy or those proxies and vote accordingly.

702 Supplemental provisions in relation to *section 701*: time for lodging proxies, etc

(1) Every instrument of proxy shall be lodged—

(a) in the case of a winding up by the court, with the liquidator,

(b) in the case of a meeting under *section 587*, with the company at its registered office, and

(c) in the case of a voluntary winding up and the meeting is not one referred to in *paragraph (b)*, with the liquidator or, if there is no liquidator, with the person named in the notice convening the meeting to receive the proxy,

not later than four o'clock in the afternoon of the day before the meeting or adjourned meeting at which it is to be used.

(2) No person who is a minor shall be appointed a general or special proxy.

(3) In the case of a creditor who is incapable of writing because of blindness or other physical infirmity, an instrument of proxy of the creditor may, subject to *subsection (4)*, be accepted if the creditor has attached his or her signature or mark to the proxy in the presence of a witness and that witness has added to the creditor's signature the witness's description and residence.

(4) *Subsection (3)* only applies if—

(a) all insertions in the instrument of proxy are in the handwriting of the witness, and

(b) the witness has certified, at the foot of the instrument of proxy, that all such insertions have been made by the witness at the request and in the presence of the creditor before the creditor attached his or her signature or mark.

(5) Where a company is a creditor, any person who is duly authorised under the seal of that company to act generally on behalf of that company at meetings of creditors, members and contributories may fill in and sign the instrument of proxy on that company's behalf and appoint himself or herself to be that company's proxy.

(6) The instrument of proxy so filled in and signed by such person shall be received and dealt with as a proxy of that company but this is without prejudice to *section 703*.

(7) In *subsection (5)* "company" means any company which is capable of being wound up under this Act and any other body corporate.

703 Representation of bodies corporate at meetings held during winding up

For the avoidance of doubt, *section 185* applies to any meeting of a company held during the course of its being wound up.

Chapter 14
Completion of winding up

704 Dissolution of company by court

(1) In a winding up by the court, the court may, on its own motion, make an order requiring the liquidator to make, at such time as the affairs of the company have been completely wound up, an application pursuant to *subsection (3)*.

(2) Unless such an order is made by the court, *section 706* shall apply to the winding up by the court as if it were a creditors' voluntary winding up.

(3) If the court makes an order under *subsection (1)* requiring the liquidator to do so, the liquidator shall, at such time as it appears to the liquidator that the affairs of the company have been completely wound up, make an application to the court for the dissolution of the company.

(4) On the making of such application, if the court is satisfied that the affairs of the company have been completely wound up, the court shall make an order that the company be dissolved from the date of the order, and the company shall be dissolved accordingly.

(5) A certified copy of an order under *subsection (4)* shall, within 21 days after the date of the making of the order, be forwarded by the liquidator to the Registrar.

(6) If the liquidator fails to comply with *subsection (3)* or *(5)*, he or she shall be guilty of a category 3 offence.

705 Final meeting and dissolution in members' voluntary winding up

(1) In a members' voluntary winding up, as soon as the affairs of the company are completely wound up, the liquidator shall prepare an account of the winding up showing how the winding up has been conducted and the property of the company has been disposed of.

(2) On that account being prepared, the liquidator shall call a general meeting of the company for the purpose of laying before it the account and giving any explanation thereof.

(3) That meeting shall be called by giving at least 28 days' written notice to the members of the company.

(4) Within 7 days after the date of that meeting, the liquidator shall—

(a) send to the Registrar a copy of the account, and

(b) make a return to the Registrar of the holding of that meeting and of its date.

(5) Subject to *subsection (6)*, if a copy of the account is not sent to the Registrar, or the return is not made to him or her, in accordance with *subsection (4)*, the liquidator shall be guilty of a category 3 offence.

(6) If a quorum is not present at the meeting referred to in *subsection (2)*, the liquidator shall, instead of making the return referred to in *paragraph (b)* of *subsection (4)*, make, within the period specified in that subsection, a return to the Registrar that the meeting was duly summoned and that no quorum was present at it, and, upon such a return being made, *subsection (4)(b)* shall be deemed to have been complied with.

(7) Subject to *subsection (8)*, the Registrar, on receiving the account, and the return referred to in *subsection (4)(b)* or *(6)*, as the case may be, shall forthwith register them, and on the expiration of 3 months after the date of registration of the return the company shall be deemed to be dissolved.

(8) The court may, on the application of the liquidator or of any other person who appears to the court to be interested, make an order deferring the date at which the dissolution of the company is to take effect for such time as the court thinks fit.

(9) A person on whose application an order under *subsection (8)* is made shall, within 14 days after the date of making of the order, deliver to the Registrar a certified copy of the order.

(10) If a person fails to comply with *subsection (9)*, he or she shall be guilty of a category 3 offence.

(11) If the liquidator fails to call a general meeting of the company as required by this section, he or she shall be guilty of a category 3 offence.

(12) Where *section 584* has effect, *section 706* shall apply to the winding up to the exclusion of this section as if the winding up were a creditors' voluntary winding up and not a members' voluntary winding up.

706 Final meeting and dissolution in creditors' voluntary winding up

(1) In a creditors' voluntary winding up, as soon as the affairs of the company are completely wound up, the liquidator shall prepare an account of the winding up showing how the winding up has been conducted and the property of the company has been disposed of.

(2) On that account being prepared, the liquidator shall call a general meeting of the company and a meeting of the creditors for the purpose of laying the account before the meetings and giving any explanation thereof.

(3) Each such meeting shall be called by giving at least 28 days' written notice to the members or creditors of the company, as the case may be.

(4) Within 7 days after the date of the meetings, or if the meetings are not held on the same date, after the date of the later meeting, the liquidator shall—

(a) send to the Registrar a copy of the account, and

(b) make a return to the Registrar of the holding of the meetings and of their dates.

(5) Subject to *subsection (6)*, if a copy of the account is not sent to the Registrar, or the return is not made to him or her, in accordance with *subsection (4)*, the liquidator shall be guilty of a category 3 offence.

(6) If a quorum is not present at a meeting referred to in *subsection (2)*, the liquidator shall, instead of making, as respects that meeting, the return referred to in *paragraph (b)* of *subsection (4)*, make, within the period specified in that subsection, a return to the Registrar that the meeting was duly summoned and that no quorum was present at it, and, upon such a return being made, *subsection (4)(b)* shall, as respects that meeting, be deemed to have been complied with.

(7) Subject to *subsection (8)*, the Registrar, on receiving the account and, in respect of each such meeting, the return referred to in *subsection (4)(b)* or *(6)*, as the case may be, shall forthwith register them, and on the expiration of 3 months after the date of registration of the returns the company shall be deemed to be dissolved.

(8) The court may, on the application of the liquidator or of any other person who appears to the court to be interested, make an order deferring the date at which the dissolution of the company is to take effect for such time as the court thinks fit.

(9) A person on whose application an order under *subsection (8)* is made shall, within 14 days after the date of making of the order, deliver to the Registrar a certified copy of the order.

(10) If a person fails to comply with *subsection (9)*, he or she shall be guilty of a category 3 offence.

(11) If the liquidator fails to call a general meeting of the company or a meeting of the creditors as required by this section, he or she shall be guilty of a category 3 offence.

707 Disposal of books and papers of company in winding up

(1) When a company has been wound up and is about to be dissolved, the seal or seals, books and papers of the company and of the liquidator may be disposed of as follows:

(a) in the case of a members' voluntary winding up, in such way as the company by special resolution directs; and

(b) in the case of a winding up by the court or a creditors' voluntary winding up, in such way as the committee of inspection or, if there is no such committee, as the creditors of the company, may direct.

(2) However, in any of the foregoing cases and notwithstanding anything in a foregoing direction, such seal or seals, books and papers shall be retained by the liquidator for a period of at least 6 years after the date of the dissolution of the company and, in the absence of a foregoing direction as to their disposal, the liquidator may then dispose of them as he or she thinks fit.

(3) If a liquidator fails to comply with the requirements of this section, he or she shall be guilty of a category 4 offence.

(4) The winding up of a company shall, for the purposes of this section and *section 681*, be deemed to be concluded—

(a) in the case of a winding up by the court (and the case is not one to which *section 704(2)* applies), on the date on which a copy of the order dissolving the company has been forwarded by the liquidator to the Registrar in accordance with *section 704(5)*,

(b) in the case of a voluntarily winding up (including a case to which *section 704(2)* applies), on the date on which the company is deemed to be dissolved, but this paragraph is subject to *subsection (5)*.

(5) If, on the date referred to in *subsection (4)(b)*, any funds or assets of the company remain unclaimed or undistributed in the hands or under the control of the liquidator or any person who has acted as liquidator, the winding up shall not be deemed to be concluded until such funds or assets have either been distributed or paid into the Companies Liquidation Account within the meaning of *section 623*.

708 Power of court to declare dissolution of company void

(1) Where a company has been dissolved, the court may—

(a) at any time within 2 years after the date of the dissolution,

(b) on an application being made for the purpose by the liquidator of the company or by any other person who appears to the court to be interested,

make an order, upon such terms as the court thinks fit, declaring the dissolution to have been void.

(2) On an order under *subsection (1)* being made, such proceedings may be taken as might have been taken if the company had not been dissolved.

(3) A person on whose application an order under *subsection (1)* is made shall, within 14 days after the date of making of the order, or such further time as the court may allow, deliver to the Registrar a certified copy of the order.

(4) If a person fails to comply with *subsection (3)*, he or she shall be guilty of a category 4 offence.

709 Disposal of documents filed with Registrar

The Registrar shall, after the expiration of 20 years after the date of the dissolution of a company, send all the documents filed in connection with the company to the National Archives.

Chapter 15
Provisions related to the Insolvency Regulation

710 Definition (*Chapter 15*)

In this Chapter "insolvency proceedings" means insolvency proceedings opened under Article 3 of the Insolvency Regulation in the State where the proceedings relate to a company.

711 Publication in relation to insolvency proceedings

(1) In this section "publication" means publication of—

(a) notice of the judgment opening the insolvency proceedings concerned;

(b) where appropriate, the decision appointing the liquidator in those proceedings;

(c) the name and business address of the liquidator; and

(d) the provision (either paragraph 1 or paragraph 2) of Article 3 of the Insolvency Regulation giving jurisdiction to open the proceedings;

in *Iris Oifigiúil* and once at least in 2 daily morning newspapers circulating in the State.

(2) Without prejudice to *section 1050(1)*, publication shall be effected by the liquidator concerned.

(3) Where the company in relation to which the insolvency proceedings are opened, has an establishment (within the meaning of Article 2(h) of the Insolvency Regulation) in the State, the liquidator or any authority mentioned in Article 21(2) of the Insolvency Regulation shall ensure that publication takes place as soon as practicable after the opening of the insolvency proceedings.

712 Confirmation of creditors' voluntary winding up

Where—

(a) a liquidator is appointed, under *section 588*, in a creditors' voluntary winding up of a company, and

(b) the centre of the company's main interests (within the meaning of the Insolvency Regulation) is situated in the State,

the Master of the High Court may, on application by the liquidator in the prescribed form and payment of the prescribed fee, confirm the creditors' voluntary winding up for the purposes of the Insolvency Regulation; where that winding up is so confirmed, the Master of the High Court shall provide a certificate of such confirmation.

713 Provision of certain documents to liquidator

On—

(a) the making of a winding-up order, or

(b) the issue of a certificate by the Master of the High Court under *section 712* in relation to the confirmation by the Master of a creditors' voluntary winding up,

the proper officer of the Central Office of the High Court shall, on request and payment of the prescribed fee and subject to any conditions that may be specified in rules of court, give to the liquidator or examiner concerned—

(i) a copy of the order or certificate, certified by the officer to be a true copy, and

(ii) any other prescribed particulars.

714 Language of claims

A claim lodged with a liquidator by a creditor referred to in Article 42(2) of the Insolvency Regulation may, if not in the Irish or the English language, be required by the liquidator to be translated, in whole or in part, into either of those languages.

Chapter 16
Offences by officers of companies in liquidation, offences of fraudulent trading and certain other offences, referrals to D.P.P., etc.

715 Application of certain provisions of Chapter and construction of certain references to company, relevant person, etc.

(1) Without prejudice to the generality of *section 563*, *sections 716* to *720* apply irrespective of the mode of winding up that is being employed (or, subsequent to the time of the doing of the act or the making of the omission concerned, is employed) and a reference in any of *sections 716* to *720* to a company is a reference to the company that is being wound up (or, subsequent to that time, is wound up).

(2) A reference in any of *sections 716* to *720* to a relevant person is a reference to a person who, at the time of the doing of the act or the making of the omission concerned, is or was an officer of the company concerned and, for the purposes of this subsection, "officer" includes any person in accordance with whose directions or instructions the directors of the company have been accustomed to act.

716 Offence for failure to make disclosure, or deliver certain things, to liquidator

(1) Subject to *section 720(2)(a)*, a relevant person who, when requested by the liquidator to make such disclosure to the liquidator, does not, to the best of the person's knowledge and belief, fully and truly disclose to the liquidator—

(a) all the property, real and personal, of the company, and

(b) how and to whom and for what consideration and when the company disposed of any part of such property (except such part as has been disposed of in the ordinary way of the business of the company),

shall be guilty of a category 2 offence.

(2) Subject to *section 720(2)(a)*, a relevant person who—

(a) does not deliver up to the liquidator, or as the liquidator directs, all such part of the real and personal property of the company as is in the person's custody or under the person's control, and which the person is required by law to deliver up, or

(b) does not deliver up to the liquidator, or as the liquidator directs, all books and papers in the person's custody or under the person's control belonging to the company and which the person is required by law to deliver up,

shall be guilty of a category 2 offence.

717 Certain fraudulent acts within 12 months preceding winding up or any time thereafter: offences

A relevant person who, within the period of 12 months ending on the commencement of the winding up or at any time thereafter—

(a) subject to *section 720(2)(a)*, conceals any part of the property of the company to the value of €20.00 or more, or conceals any debt due to or from the company,

(b) fraudulently removes any part of the property of the company to the value of €20.00 or more,

(c) subject to *section 720(2)(b)*, conceals, destroys, mutilates or falsifies any book or paper affecting or relating to the property or affairs of the company,

(d) subject to *section 720(2)(b)*, makes any false entry in any book or paper affecting or relating to the property or affairs of the company, or

(e) fraudulently parts with, alters or makes any omission in any document affecting or relating to the property or affairs of the company,

shall be guilty of a category 2 offence.

718 Other fraudulent acts (relating to obtaining credit, irregular pledges, etc.) within 12 months preceding winding up or any time thereafter: offences

A relevant person who, within the period of 12 months ending on the commencement of the winding up or at any time thereafter—

(a) has, by any false representation or other fraud, obtained any property for or on behalf of the company on credit which the company does not subsequently pay for,

(b) subject to *section 720(2)(a)*, under the false pretence that the company is carrying on its business, obtains on credit for or on behalf of the company, any property which the company does not subsequently pay for,

(c) subject to *section 720(2)(a)*, pawns, pledges or disposes of any property of the company which has been obtained on credit and has not been paid for, unless such pawning, pledging or disposing is in the ordinary way of business of the company, or

(d) makes or perpetrates any false representation or other fraud for the purpose of obtaining the consent of the creditors of the company or any of them to an agreement with reference to the affairs of the company or to the winding up,

shall be guilty of a category 2 offence.

719 Material omission in statement relating to company's affairs, failure to report false debt, etc.

(1) Subject to *section 720(2)(a)*, a relevant person who makes any material omission in any statement relating to the affairs of the company shall be guilty of a category 2 offence.

(2) A relevant person who—

(a) knowing or believing that a false debt has been proved by any person under the winding up, fails for the period of 30 days after the date of that proof to inform the liquidator thereof, or

(b) after the commencement of the winding up, subject to *section 720(2)(b)*, prevents the production of any book or paper affecting or relating to the property or affairs of the company,

shall be guilty of a category 2 offence.

(3) A relevant person who, after the commencement of the winding up or at any meeting of the creditors of the company within the period of 12 months ending on that commencement, attempts to account for any part of the property of the company by fictitious losses or expenses shall be guilty of a category 2 offence.

720 Additional offence with respect to *section 718(c)* and certain defences with respect to foregoing matters

(1) Where any person pawns, pledges or disposes of any property in circumstances which amount to an offence under *section 718(c)*, every person who takes in pawn or pledge or otherwise receives the property knowing it to be pawned, pledged or disposed of in those foregoing circumstances shall also be guilty of a category 2 offence.

(2) In any proceedings against a person in respect of—

(a) an offence under—

(i) *section 716(1)* or *(2)*;

(ii) *section 717* consisting of a contravention of *paragraph (a)* of that section;

(iii) *section 718* consisting of a contravention of *paragraph (b)* or *(c)* of that section; or

(iv) *section 719(1)*;

it shall be a defence to prove that the person had no intent to defraud; and

(b) an offence under—

(i) *section 717* consisting of a contravention of *paragraph (c)* or *(d)* of that section;

(ii) *subsection (2)* of *section 719* consisting of a contravention of *paragraph (b)* of that subsection;

it shall be a defence to prove that the person had neither an intent to conceal the state of affairs of the company nor to defeat the process of the law and, in particular, the enforcement of this Act.

721 Other frauds by officers of companies which have gone into liquidation: offence

If any person, being at the time of the commission of the alleged offence an officer of a company which is subsequently ordered to be wound up by the court or subsequently passes a resolution for voluntary winding up—

(a) has by false pretences or by means of any other fraud induced any person to give credit to the company,

(b) with intent to defraud creditors of the company, has made or caused to be made any gift or transfer of or charge on, or has caused or connived at the levying of any execution against, the property of the company, or

(c) with intent to defraud creditors of the company, has concealed or removed any part of the property of the company since, or within 2 months before, the date of any unsatisfied judgment or order for payment of money obtained against the company,

the person shall be guilty of a category 2 offence.

722 Fraudulent trading of company: offence

If any person is knowingly a party to the carrying on of the business of a company with intent to defraud creditors of the company or creditors of any other person or for any fraudulent purpose, the person shall be guilty of a category 1 offence.

723 Prosecution of offences committed by officers and members of company

(1) If it appears to the court, in the course of a winding up by the court, that any past or present officer, or any member, of the company has been guilty of an offence in relation to the company the court may, either—

(a) on the application of any person interested in the winding up, or

(b) of its own motion,

direct the liquidator to refer the matter to the Director of Public Prosecutions.

(2) Where a direction under *subsection (1)* is given by the court to the liquidator, the liquidator shall—

(a) provide to the Director of Public Prosecutions such information, relating to the matter in question, as he or she may require, and

(b) give to him or her such access to, and facilities for inspecting and taking any copies of, such documents (being documents in the possession or under the control of the liquidator and relating to the matter in question) as he or she may require.

(3) Where the court gives the foregoing direction to the liquidator, it shall also direct the liquidator to refer the matter concerned to the Director of Corporate Enforcement.

(4) Where a direction under *subsection (3)* is given by the court to the liquidator, the liquidator shall—

(a) provide to the Director of Corporate Enforcement such information, relating to the matter in question, as he or she may require, and

(b) give to him or her such access to, and facilities for inspecting and taking copies of, such documents (being documents in the possession or under the control of the liquidator and relating to the matter in question) as he or she may require.

(5) If it appears to the liquidator in the course of a voluntary winding up that any past or present officer, or any member, of the company has been guilty of an offence in

relation to the company, the liquidator shall forthwith report the matter to the Director of Public Prosecutions.

(6) Where the liquidator reports a matter under *subsection (5)* to the Director of Public Prosecutions, the liquidator shall—

(a) provide to the Director of Public Prosecutions such information, relating to the matter in question, as he or she may require, and

(b) give to him or her such access to, and facilities for inspecting and taking any copies of, such documents (being documents in the possession or under the control of the liquidator and relating to the matter in question) as he or she may require.

(7) Where a foregoing report is made by the liquidator, the liquidator shall also report the matter to the Director of Corporate Enforcement.

(8) Where a matter is reported by the liquidator under *subsection (7)* to the Director of Corporate Enforcement, the liquidator shall—

(a) provide to the Director of Corporate Enforcement such information, relating to the matter in question, as he or she may require, and

(b) give to him or her such access to, and facilities for inspecting and taking copies of, such documents (being documents in the possession or under the control of the liquidator and relating to the matter in question) as he or she may require.

(9) In a voluntary winding up, the court, on application being made to it by any person interested in the winding up, or of its own motion, may give the following direction if it appears to the court that—

(a) in the course of the winding up any past or present officer, or any member, of the company has been guilty of an offence in relation to the company, and

(b) no report relating to the matter has been made by the liquidator to the Director of Public Prosecutions under *subsection (5)* or to the Director of Corporate Enforcement under *subsection (7)*.

(10) That direction of the court is one requiring the liquidator to make the report referred to in *subsection (5)* or *(7)* (or both as appropriate) and, on such a report being accordingly made, this section and *section 724* shall have effect as though the report had been made under *subsection (5)* or *(7)*, as the case may be.

724 Supplemental provisions in relation to *section 723*: duty to provide assistance to D.P.P. and Director of Corporate Enforcement

(1) If, where any matter is referred or reported under *section 723* to—

(a) the Director of Public Prosecutions, or

(b) the Director of Corporate Enforcement,

the Director of Public Prosecutions or, as the case may be, the Director of Corporate Enforcement considers that the case is one in which a prosecution ought to be instituted and institutes proceedings accordingly, it shall be the duty of each of the following persons to give all assistance in connection with the prosecution which he or she is reasonably able to give.

(2) The persons referred to in *subsection (1)* are the liquidator of the company and—

(a) every officer (past or present) of the company, and

(b) every agent (past or present) of the company,

(other than the defendant in the proceedings).

(3) For the purposes of *subsection (2)(b)* "agent", in relation to a company, includes—

(a) the bankers and solicitors of the company,

(b) any receiver of the property of the company, and

(c) any persons employed by the company as auditors, accountants, book-keepers or taxation advisers, or other persons employed by it in a professional, consultancy or similar capacity, whether those persons are (or were) or are not (or were not) officers of the company.

(4) If any person fails or neglects to give assistance in the manner required by *subsection (1)*, the court may, on the application of the Director of Public Prosecutions or, as the case may be, the Director of Corporate Enforcement, direct that person to comply with the requirements of that subsection.

(5) Where an application is made under *subsection (4)* or *section 723(9)* in relation to a liquidator, the court may, unless it appears that the failure or neglect to comply was due to the liquidator not having in his or her hands sufficient assets of the company to enable him or her so to do, direct that the costs of the application shall be borne by the liquidator personally.

PART 12
STRIKE OFF AND RESTORATION

Chapter 1
Strike off of company

725 When Registrar may strike company off register

(1) Except in the case of an application by a company to be struck off the register, the Registrar may strike a company off the register if—

(a) there exists one or more of the grounds for striking off set out in *section 726* —

"involuntary strike off", and

(b) the Registrar has followed the procedure set out in *sections 727*, *728*, *730* and *733(1)*.

(2) In the case of an application by a company to be struck off the register, the Registrar may strike the company off the register if—

(a) the conditions for striking off set out in *section 731* have been satisfied — "voluntary strike off", and

(b) the Registrar has followed the procedure set out in *sections 732* and *733(2)*.

726 Grounds for involuntary strike off

The grounds referred to in *section 725(1)(a)* are:

(a) the company has failed to make an annual return as required by *section 343*;

(b) the Revenue Commissioners have given a notice under section 882(3) of the Taxes Consolidation Act 1997 to the Registrar of the company's failure to deliver the statement required under section 882 of that Act;

(c) the Registrar has reasonable cause to believe that *section 137(1)* is not being complied with in relation to the company;

(d) the company is being wound up and the Registrar has reasonable cause to believe that no liquidator is acting;

(e) the company is being wound up and the Registrar has reasonable cause to believe that the affairs of the company are fully wound up and that the returns required to be made by the liquidator have not been made for a period of 6 consecutive months;

(f) there are no persons recorded in the office of the Registrar as being current directors of the company.

727 Registrar's notice to company of intention to strike it off register

(1) The Registrar may give notice in accordance with *section 728* of the Registrar's intention to strike a company off the register on a ground set out in any of *paragraphs* (a) to *(f)* of *section 726*.

(2) The Registrar shall send the notice by registered post—

(a) except where *paragraph (b)* applies, to the company at its registered office,

(b) if the ground for striking off is that set out in *section 726(d)* or *(e)* and an individual is recorded in the office of the Registrar as the liquidator of the company, to the liquidator.

(3) The Registrar shall also send a copy of the foregoing notice by prepaid ordinary post to such persons, if any, as are recorded in the office of the Registrar as being current directors of the company but non-compliance with this subsection does not affect the validity of a notice that otherwise complies with *subsection (1)*; the address to which a notice under this subsection is sent shall be the usual residential address, as recorded in the office of the Registrar, of the addressee concerned.

(4) Instead of giving a notice under *subsection (1)*, the Registrar may publish a notice in the CRO Gazette containing the information required by *section 728* if—

(a) the company has not, for 20 or more consecutive years, made an annual return as required by *section 343* or the corresponding provision of the Act of 1963, and

(b) no notice of the situation of the registered office of the company has been given to the Registrar as required by *section 50* or the corresponding provision of the prior Companies Acts.

728 Contents of Registrar's notice to company

(1) The Registrar's notice under *section 727* shall—

(a) state that the issue of the notice is the first step in a process that may lead to the company being struck off the register;

(b) state the ground or grounds for striking off being invoked by the Registrar;

(c) state that the company will be dissolved if it is struck off the register;

(d) if *subsection (3)* applies, set out the information required by that subsection;

(e) specify the remedial step;

(f) specify the date on or before which the remedial step must be taken; and

(g) state that failure to take the remedial step on or before the date so specified may result in the Registrar giving public notice of an intention to strike the company off the register.

(2) The date to be specified for the purposes of *subsection (1)(f)* shall be a date falling not less than 28 days after the date of the notice.

(3) Except where the ground for striking off is that set out in *section 726(d)*, *(e)* or *(f)*, the notice shall also state that each director of the company at the date that the notice is sent is liable for disqualification under *section 842(h)* if the company is struck off the register.

729 Meaning of remedial step

For the purposes of *sections 728*, *730* and *733*, the remedial step is whichever of the following applies:

(a) in the case of the ground for striking off set out in *section 726(a)*, the delivery to the Registrar of all annual returns as required by *section 343* that the company has failed to make;

(b) in the case of the ground for striking off set out in *section 726(b)*, the delivery to the Revenue Commissioners of the statement that the company is required to deliver under section 882(3) of the Taxes Consolidation Act 1997;

(c) in the case of the ground for striking off set out in *section 726(c)*, the provision to the Registrar of evidence that *section 137(1)* is being complied with in relation to the company;

(d) in the case of the ground for striking off set out in *section 726(d)* or *(e)*, the provision to the Registrar of the details of the liquidator and of up to date periodic statements having been furnished under *section 681*;

(e) in the case of the ground for striking off set out in *section 726(f)*, the notification to the Registrar under *section 149(8)* of the appointment of a director of the company.

730 Public notice of intention to strike company off register

(1) If the Registrar has given a notice under *section 727* and the remedial step has not been taken on or before the date specified in that notice for the purposes of *section 728(1)(f)*, the Registrar may, by publishing a notice in the CRO Gazette that complies with *subsection (2)*, give public notice of the Registrar's intention to strike the company off the register.

(2) The notice shall—

(a) specify the ground for striking the company off the register;

(b) specify the remedial step;

(c) specify the date on or before which the remedial step must be taken; and

(d) state that, unless that remedial step is taken on or before the date so specified, the Registrar may strike the company off the register and, if the Registrar does so, the company will be dissolved.

(3) The date to be specified for the purposes of *subsection (2)(c)* shall be a date falling not less than 28 days after the date of publication of the notice.

731 Conditions for voluntary strike off

(1) A company may apply to the Registrar to be struck off the register if the following conditions are satisfied:

(a) the circumstances relating to the company are such as to give the Registrar reasonable cause to believe that it has never carried on business or has ceased to carry on business;

(b) the company has, within 3 months before the date of the application, by special resolution—

(i) resolved to apply to the Registrar to be struck off the register on the ground that it has never carried on business or has ceased to carry on business; and

(ii) resolved that pending the determination (or, should it sooner occur, the cancellation, at its request, of this process) of its application to be struck off, the company will not carry on any business or incur any liabilities;

(c) the company has delivered to the Registrar all annual returns required by *section 343* that are outstanding in respect of the company as at the date of the application;

(d) the company has delivered to the Registrar a certificate in the prescribed form signed by each director certifying that as at the date of the application—

(i) the amount of any assets of the company does not exceed €150;

(ii) the amount of any liabilities of the company (including contingent and prospective liabilities) does not exceed €150; and

(iii) the company is not a party to ongoing or pending litigation;

(e) the Registrar has received from the Revenue Commissioners written confirmation dated not more than 3 months before the date on which the Registrar receives the application that the Revenue Commissioners do not object to the company being struck off the register; and

(f) the company has caused an advertisement, in the prescribed form, of its intention to apply to be struck off the register to be published within 30 days before the date of the application in at least 1 daily newspaper circulating in the State.

(2) Where an application under this section by a company to be struck off the register is made within one year after the date on which the company has changed its name or its registered office (or both), then, as the case may be—

(a) the former name of the company, as well as the existing name of the company, or

(b) the former address, as well as the current address, of the company's registered office, or

(c) both its former name and the former address of its registered office, as well as the existing name of the company and the current address of its registered office,

shall be stated in the advertisement referred to in *subsection (1)(f)*.

732 Public notice in case of voluntary strike off

(1) As soon as practicable after the receipt of an application by a company to be struck off that satisfies the conditions set out in *section 731*, the Registrar shall, by publishing a notice in the CRO Gazette that complies with *subsection (2)*, give public notice of the Registrar's intention to strike the company off the register.

(2) The notice shall—

(a) state that the company has applied to be struck off the register;

(b) state—

(i) that any person may deliver to the Registrar an objection to the striking off of the company in the prescribed form; and

(ii) that any such objection must be confined to the ground that one or more of the conditions set out in *section 731* have not been satisfied;

(c) specify the period within which such an objection may be delivered to the Registrar; and

(d) state that, unless the Registrar has received—

(i) an objection to the striking-off of the company within that period, being an objection that the Registrar sustains; or

(ii) a request for the cancellation of the process of strike off in accordance with *subsection (4)*;

the Registrar may strike the company off the register and, if the Registrar does so, the company will be dissolved.

(3) The period to be specified for the purposes of *subsection (2)(c)* shall be the period ending 90 days after the date of publication of the notice.

(4) Within the period specified for the purposes of *subsection (2)(c)*, the company may request of the Registrar, by delivering to the Registrar a notice in that behalf in the prescribed form, the cancellation of the process of its being struck off the register.

733 Striking off (involuntary and voluntary cases) and dissolution

(1) If the Registrar has given a notice under *section 730* and the remedial step has not been taken on or before the date specified in that notice for the purposes of *section 730(2)(c)*, the Registrar may strike the company off the register.

(2) If the Registrar has given a notice under *section 732* and—

(a) no objection referred to in *section 732(2)(b)* has been delivered to the Registrar within the period specified in that notice for the purposes of *section 732(2)(c)* or the Registrar is of opinion that there is no reasonable basis to such an objection that has been so delivered, and

(b) the company has not requested, in accordance with *section 732(4)*, the cancellation of the process of its being struck off the register,

the Registrar may strike the company off the register.

(3) The Registrar shall publish in the CRO Gazette a notice of the striking of a company off the register.

(4) The company is dissolved on the date of publication by the Registrar of the notice in the CRO Gazette of its being struck off the register and that date is referred to subsequently in this Part as the "date of dissolution".

734 Effect of removal and dissolution

(1) The liability, if any, of a director, other officer or a member of a company that has been dissolved under *section 733(4)* shall continue and may be enforced as if the company had not been dissolved.

(2) Nothing in this section or in *section 733* shall affect the power of the court to wind up a company that has been struck off the register or dissolved under that section.

(3) For the purposes and the purposes only of—

(a) an application for the restoration of the company to the register under *section 737* or *738*, or

(b) in so far as is necessary for the making of such an application (or the doing of anything required by or under *Chapter 2* to be done consequent on the making of it),

a company shall be deemed not to have been dissolved under *section 733*.

(4) *Subsection (3)* shall not be read as authorising the dealing with, or the exercising of control over, any property that has become the property of the State pursuant to Part III of the State Property Act 1954.

735 Power of Director to obtain information

(1) Where a company has been struck off the register under *section 733(1)* on any of the grounds set out in *section 726(a)* to *(c)*, the Director may, by notice to the directors of the company, require those persons to produce to the Director a statement of affairs of the company in accordance with this section.

(2) The persons to whom a notice is sent under *subsection (1)* shall, within the period specified in the notice in that behalf, produce to the Director a statement of affairs of the company that complies with *subsection (3)*.

(3) The statement of affairs shall—

(a) be in the prescribed form (if any);

(b) be verified by an affidavit;

(c) contain the following information in respect of the company as at the date of dissolution:

(i) particulars of its assets, debts and liabilities;

(ii) the names and addresses of its creditors;

(iii) particulars of securities given by the company, including the name of the secured creditor in each case and the date on which the security was given;

(iv) such further or other information as may be prescribed or that the Director may reasonably require.

(4) On the application of the Director, the court may require a person who has made a statement under *subsection (2)* to appear before it and answer on oath any question relating to the content of the statement.

(5) A person who fails to comply with *subsection (2)* shall be guilty of a category 3 offence.

Chapter 2
Restoration of company to register

736 Application of Chapter

This Chapter applies to a company that has been struck off the register under *Chapter 1*.

737 Restoration on application to Registrar

(1) On an application by a person specified in *subsection (4)*, the Registrar may restore a company to the register if—

(a) the Registrar has reasonable cause to believe that the strike off of the company has disadvantaged the applicant,

(b) the application is made in the prescribed form,

(c) the application is received by the Registrar within the period of 12 months after the date of dissolution of the company, and

(d) the requirements of *subsection (2)* have been satisfied within the period of 15 months after the date of dissolution of the company.

(2) Subject to *subsection (3)*, the requirements referred to in *subsection (1)(d)* are the following:

(a) the Registrar has received from the company all annual returns outstanding, if any, being annual returns prepared in accordance with *Part 6*;

(b) the Registrar is satisfied that *section 137(1)* is being complied with in relation to the company; and

(c) the Registrar is satisfied that no notification required by *section 149(8)* remains outstanding in relation to the company.

(3) If the ground, or one of the grounds, on which the company had been struck off the register is that referred to in *section 726(b)*, *subsection (2)* shall have effect as if the following paragraph were inserted after *paragraph (a)* of that subsection:

"(aa) the Registrar has received written confirmation from the Revenue Commissioners that they have no objection to the company being restored to the register under this section;".

(4) The Registrar may restore a company to the register on the application of a person who was a member or an officer of the company at the date of its dissolution.

(5) On the registration of an application under this section and on payment of such fee as may be prescribed, the Registrar shall restore the company to the register and the company shall be deemed to have continued in existence as if it had not been struck off the register.

(6) Subject to any order made by the court in the matter, the restoration of a company to the register under this section shall not affect the rights and liabilities of the company in respect of any debt or obligation incurred, or any contract entered into, by, to, with or

on behalf of the company between the date of its dissolution and the date of restoration.

738 Restoration on application to court

(1) On an application in accordance with *section 739* by a person specified in *subsection (2)*, the court may order that a company that has been struck off the register be restored to the register if—

(a) the striking off of the company has disadvantaged the applicant,

(b) the application is made within the period of 20 years after the date of dissolution of the company; and

(c) it is just and equitable to do so.

(2) The court may make the order on the application of—

(a) the company;

(b) a creditor of the company;

(c) a person who was a member or an officer of the company at its date of dissolution; or

(d) a person who, at the date of its dissolution, had an entitlement (disregarding any right of the directors to decline to register the person as such) to be registered as a member of the company by virtue of—

(i) the execution, in the person's favour, of an instrument of transfer of a share; or

(ii) the transmission, by operation of law, to the person of a right to a share.

(3) Subject to a supplementary order made under *section 742(c)*, the company shall be deemed to have continued in existence as if it had not been struck off the register upon the Registrar receiving a certified copy of the order under *subsection (1)* within 28 days after the date of its perfection.

739 Requirements for application to court under *section 738*

(1) An application under *section 738* shall be made on notice to the Registrar, the Minister for Public Expenditure and Reform and the Revenue Commissioners.

(2) In the case of an application under *section 738* by a creditor, the application shall in addition be made on notice to—

(a) such officers of the company at the date of dissolution whose names are known, or ought reasonably to be known, by the creditor; and

(b) such other members or officers of the company at the date of dissolution as the Registrar, the Revenue Commissioners or the Minister for Public Expenditure and Reform, upon being notified of the application, indicate in writing should be joined as notice parties to the application.

740 Terms of court order on application under *section 738*

(1) In making an order under *section 738* on the application of a member or an officer of the company, the court shall, unless reason to the contrary is shown to the satisfaction

of the court, make it a term of the order that the order shall not have effect unless, within a specified period, there is done each of the things (save where it has already been done) that are set out in *subsection (2)*.

(2) Those things are—

(a) all outstanding annual returns in relation to the company are delivered, in accordance with *Part 6*, to the Registrar;

(b) all outstanding statements as required by section 882 of the Taxes Consolidation Act 1997 in relation to the company are delivered to the Revenue Commissioners;

(c) the company appoints a director and delivers to the Registrar the notification and consent required by *section 149(8)* and *(10)*, respectively, and—

(i) the person so appointed is resident in an EEA state; or

(ii) unless a certificate under *section 140* in relation to the company has been granted by the Registrar and is in force, the company provides the Registrar with a bond in accordance with *section 137*.

(3) For the avoidance of doubt, *subsection (1)* requires, unless reason to the contrary there mentioned is shown, the order of the court to specify that a thing set out in *subsection (2)* is to be done (save where it has already been done) notwithstanding that the ground on which the company had been struck off the register did not relate to that thing.

(4) In making an order under *section 738* on the application of a creditor of the company, the court shall direct that, within a specified period (save where the particular thing has already been done)—

(a) there is procured by one or more specified members or officers of the company the delivery by the company of all outstanding annual returns, in accordance with *Part 6*, to the Registrar;

(b) there is delivered by such specified members or officers all outstanding statements as required by section 882 of the Taxes Consolidation Act 1997 in relation to the company to the Revenue Commissioners;

(c) such specified members or officers take all reasonable steps to ensure that the company appoints a director and delivers to the Registrar the notification and consent required by *section 149(8)* and *(10)*, respectively, and either that—

(i) the person so appointed is resident in an EEA state; or

(ii) unless a certificate under *section 140* in relation to the company has been granted by the Registrar and is in force, the company provides the Registrar with a bond in accordance with *section 137*.

(5) For the avoidance of doubt, *subsection (4)* requires the order of the court to specify that a thing set out in that subsection is to be done (save where it has already been done) notwithstanding that the ground on which the company had been struck off the register did not relate to that thing.

(6) In making an order under *section 738* on the application of a creditor of the company, the court may award the applicant the costs of the application against the company.

741 Court order for restoration on application of Registrar

(1) On an application by the Registrar in accordance with *subsection (2)*, the court may order that a company that has been struck off the register be restored to the register if—

(a) the application is made within the period of 20 years after the date of dissolution of the company, and

(b) it is just and equitable to do so.

(2) An application under this section shall be made on notice to each person who, to the knowledge of the Registrar, was an officer of the company at the date of its dissolution.

(3) On the making of the order, the company shall be deemed to have continued in existence as if it had not been struck off the register.

(4) In making an order under this section, the court may award the Registrar the costs of the application against the company restored to the register.

742 Supplementary court orders

In ordering that a company be restored to the register under *section 738* or *741*, the court may—

(a) except to the extent that the court makes an order under *paragraph (c)*, give such directions as it thinks fit for placing the company and all other persons as nearly as possible in the same position as if the company had not been struck off the register;

(b) direct the company to change its name if the name of the company is too similar to the name of another company already on the register or a name that has been reserved in accordance with *section 28*;

(c) if and to the extent that it thinks fit, order that the officers of the company, or any one or more of them as specified in the order, shall be liable for a debt or liability incurred by or on behalf of the company during the period when it stood struck off the register;

(d) make any other order that it thinks fit.

743 Meaning of court

(1) For the purposes of an application under *section 738* or *741* by a creditor or the Registrar, in this Chapter "court" means either the High Court or the Circuit Court.

(2) In the case of an application under *section 738* by a creditor to the Circuit Court, the application shall be made to the judge of the Circuit Court—

(a) for the circuit in which the registered office of the company was situated immediately before the company was struck off the register, or

(b) if there was no registered office of the company at that time, for the circuit in which the creditor resides, or

(c) if there was no registered office of the company at that time and the creditor resides outside the State, for the Dublin Circuit.

(3) An application under *section 741* to the Circuit Court shall be made to the judge of the Circuit Court for the Dublin Circuit.

744 Transitional provision for companies struck off register before commencement of this Chapter

(1) Subject to *subsection (3)*, *sections 736* to *743* shall apply to a company that has been struck off the register under any former enactment relating to companies (within the meaning of *section 5*) before the commencement of this Chapter.

(2) For that purpose—

(a) references in the foregoing provisions of this Chapter to a company that has been struck off the register under *Chapter 1* shall be read as references to a company that has been struck off under the former enactment relating to companies (within the foregoing meaning),

(b) references in the foregoing provisions of this Chapter to the date of dissolution of the company shall be read as references to the date of its dissolution under the former enactment relating to companies (within the foregoing meaning), and

(c) the foregoing provisions of this Chapter shall apply with other necessary modifications.

(3) Neither *subsections (1)* and *(2)* nor any other provision of this Chapter applies if, before the date of the commencement of this Chapter, an application has been made under any former enactment relating to companies (within the foregoing meaning) to restore the company to the register and, in such a case, that former enactment shall apply notwithstanding the repeal of it by *section 4*.

Chapter 3
Miscellaneous

745 Disclosure of information by Revenue Commissioners to Registrar

(1) This section applies if the Registrar, for the purpose of exercising any of his or her powers under this Part, is required to determine whether a statement that a company has failed to deliver to the Revenue Commissioners in accordance with section 882(3) of the Taxes Consolidation Act 1997 has or has not been subsequently delivered to them.

(2) In any case to which this section applies, the Revenue Commissioners may, notwithstanding any obligations as to secrecy or other restriction upon the disclosure of information imposed by or under statute or otherwise, disclose to the Registrar any information in their possession required by the Registrar for making the determination.

PART 13
INVESTIGATIONS

Chapter 1
Preliminary

746 Interpretation (*Part 13*)

(1) Any reference in this Part to share capital or relevant share capital in relation to a company is a reference to share capital that confers the right to vote in all circumstances at a general meeting of that company, and a reference to share shall be read accordingly.

(2) Any reference in *Chapter 2* or *4* to shares or share capital of, or a shareholding or an interest in shares, in a company or a body corporate includes a reference to—

(a) membership of the company or body corporate, and

(b) the rights or obligations attaching to such membership.

Chapter 2
Investigations by court appointed inspectors

747 Investigation of company's affairs by court appointed inspectors on application of company etc.

(1) On the application of a person or persons specified in *subsection (2)*, the court may appoint one or more competent inspectors to investigate the affairs of a company in order to enquire into matters specified by the court and to report on those matters in such manner as the court directs.

(2) The court may make the appointment on the application of any of the following persons:

(a) the company;

(b) not less than 10 members of the company;

(c) a member or members holding one-tenth or more of the paid up share capital of the company (but shares held as treasury shares shall be excluded for the purposes of this paragraph);

(d) a director of the company; or

(e) a creditor of the company.

(3) The court's power of appointment under *subsection (1)* is exercisable notwithstanding that the company is in the course of being wound up.

(4) The court may require the applicant or the applicants to give security for payment of the costs of the investigation.

(5) A person who intends making an application under this section shall give not less than 14 days' notice in writing of his or her intention to apply to the Director, and the Director shall be entitled to appear and be heard on the hearing of the application.

(6) In this section "court" means—

(a) save in the case of a company referred to in *paragraph (b)*, the High Court, or

(b) in the case of a company that, in respect of the latest financial year of the company that has ended prior to the date of the making of the application under this section, fell to be treated [as a small company by virtue of *section 280A* or *280B* or a medium company by virtue of *section 280F* or *280G*][a], the Circuit Court,

and, subject to *subsection (8)*, all subsequent references to the court in this Part shall, as respects the powers and jurisdiction of the court with respect to an investigation on foot of an appointment made under this section by the Circuit Court, be read accordingly.

(7) For the purpose of *paragraph (b)* of *subsection (6)*, if the latest financial year of the company concerned ended within 3 months prior to the date of the making of the application concerned, the reference in that paragraph to the latest financial year of the company shall be read as a reference to the financial year of the company that preceded its latest financial year (but that reference shall only be so read if that preceding financial year ended no more than 15 months prior to the date of the making of the application concerned).

(8) *Subsection (6)* does not confer jurisdiction on the Circuit Court to wind up any body corporate; however, that court, in exercise of its jurisdiction under this Part, may refer an inspectors' report made to it under this Part to the High Court which shall have the same jurisdiction to wind up any body corporate concerned as if the inspectors' report had been made to it in the first instance.

(9) In the case of an application under this section by a creditor or member to the Circuit Court, the application shall be made to the judge of the Circuit Court—

(a) for the circuit in which the registered office of the company is situated at the time of the making of the application, or

(b) if there is no registered office of the company at that time, for the circuit in which the creditor or member resides, or

(c) if there is no registered office of the company at that time and the creditor or member resides outside the State, for the Dublin Circuit.

(10) In the case of an application under this section by the company or a director of it to the Circuit Court, the application shall be made to the judge of the Circuit Court—

(a) for the circuit in which the registered office of the company is situated at the time of the making of the application; or

(b) if there is no registered office of the company at that time, for the Dublin Circuit.

Amendments

a Words substituted by C(A)A 2017, s 88(c)(i) (previously: "as a small or medium company by virtue of *section 350*").

748 Investigation of company's affairs by court appointed inspectors on application of Director

(1) On the application of the Director, the court may appoint one or more competent inspectors to investigate the affairs of a company and to report on those affairs in such manner as the court directs, if the court is satisfied that there are circumstances suggesting that—

(a) the affairs of the company are being or have been conducted with intent to defraud—

(i) its creditors;

(ii) the creditors of any other person; or

(iii) its members;

(b) the affairs of the company are being or have been conducted for a fraudulent or unlawful purpose other than described in *paragraph (a)*;

(c) the affairs of the company are being or have been conducted in an unlawful manner;

(d) the affairs of the company are being or have been conducted in a manner that is unfairly prejudicial to some part of its members;

(e) the affairs of the company are being or have been conducted in a manner that is unfairly prejudicial to some or all of its creditors;

(f) any actual or proposed act or omission of the company (including an act or omission on its behalf) was, is or would be unfairly prejudicial to some part of its members;

(g) any actual or proposed act or omission of the company (including an act or omission on its behalf) was, is or would be unfairly prejudicial to some or all of its creditors;

(h) the company was formed for a fraudulent or unlawful purpose;

(i) persons connected with its formation or the management of its affairs have, in that connection, been guilty of fraud, misfeasance or other misconduct towards the company or its members; or

(j) the company's members have not been given all the information relating to its affairs which they might reasonably expect.

(2) The court's power of appointment under this section is without prejudice to its powers under *section 747* and is exercisable notwithstanding that the company is in the course of being wound up.

(3) Inspectors appointed under this section may be or include an officer or officers of the Director.

(4) A reference in *subsection (1)* to the members of a company shall have effect as if it included a reference to any person who is not a member but to whom shares in the company have been transferred or transmitted by operation of law.

(5) In this section "court" means—

(a) save in the case of a company referred to in *paragraph (b)*, the High Court, or

(b) in the case of a company that, in respect of the latest financial year of the company that has ended prior to the date of the making of the application under this section, fell to be treated [as a small company by virtue of *section 280A* or *280B* or a medium company by virtue of *section 280F* or *280G*][a], the Circuit Court,

and, subject to *subsection (7)*, all subsequent references to the court in this Part shall, as respects the powers and jurisdiction of the court with respect to an investigation on foot of an appointment made under this section by the Circuit Court, be read accordingly.

(6) For the purpose of *paragraph (b)* of *subsection (5)*, if the latest financial year of the company concerned ended within 3 months prior to the date of the making of the application concerned, the reference in that paragraph to the latest financial year of the company shall be read as a reference to the financial year of the company that preceded its latest financial year (but that reference shall only be so read if that preceding financial year ended no more than 15 months prior to the date of the making of the application concerned).

(7) *Subsection (5)* does not confer jurisdiction on the Circuit Court to wind up any body corporate; however, that court, in exercise of its jurisdiction under this Part, may refer an inspectors' report made to it under this Part to the High Court which shall have the same jurisdiction to wind up any body corporate concerned as if the inspectors' report had been made to it in the first instance.

(8) An application under this section to the Circuit Court shall be made to the judge of the Circuit Court—

(a) for the circuit in which the registered office of the company is situated at the time of the making of the application, or

(b) if there is no registered office of the company at that time, for the Dublin Circuit.

(9) Nothing in this section shall be taken as excluding or restricting any statutory rights of the Government, a Minister of the Government or a person acting under the authority of the Government or a Minister of the Government.

Amendments

a Words substituted by C(A)A 2017, s 88(c)(ii) (previously: "as a small or medium company by virtue of *section 350*").

749 Court may give directions in relation to investigation

Where the court appoints an inspector under *section 747(1)* or *748(1)*, the court may from time to time give such directions as it thinks necessary or expedient, whether to the inspector or any other person, including directions given with a view to ensuring that the investigation is carried out as quickly and inexpensively as possible.

750 Power of inspector to expand investigation into affairs of related bodies corporate

(1) Subject to *subsection (4)*, an inspector appointed under *section 747(1)* or *748(1)* may investigate the affairs of any other body corporate that is related to the company under investigation if the inspector—

(a) considers that it is necessary for the purposes of the investigation, and

(b) has first obtained the approval of the court.

(2) An inspector who investigates the affairs of a related body corporate shall report on those affairs to the extent that the inspector considers that the results of investigation of the related body corporate are relevant to the investigation of the company.

(3) Without prejudice to the application of *section 2(10)*, a body corporate that is related to a company includes, for the purposes of this section and *sections 753* and *754*, a body corporate with which the company has a commercial relationship, and a commercial relationship exists where goods or services are sold or given by one party to another.

(4) The Circuit Court shall only have jurisdiction to grant the approval referred to in *subsection (1)*, if in respect of the latest financial year of the body corporate there referred to that has ended prior to the date of the making of the application for the approval, that body fell to be treated (or, if it were a company, would have fallen to be treated) [as a small company by virtue of *section 280A* or *280B* or a medium company by virtue of *section 280F* or *280G*][a], and *subsection (7)* of *section 747* applies for the purposes of this subsection as it applies for purposes of *subsection (6)(b)* of that section.

Amendments

a Words substituted by C(A)A 2017, s 88(c)(iii) (previously: "as a small or medium company by virtue of *section 350*").

751 Order for inspection of books or documents of company in liquidation

(1) On the application of the Director, the court may make an order for the inspection by the Director of any books or documents in the possession of a company that is in the course of being wound up.

(2) The company, every officer of the company and the liquidator shall—

(a) give the Director such access to the books or documents and facilities as are necessary for inspecting or taking copies of the books or documents as the Director may require, and

(b) give all assistance to the Director as it or he or she is reasonably able to give in connection with the Director's inspection of the books or documents.

(3) Nothing in this section shall be taken as excluding or restricting any statutory rights of the Government or a Minister of the Government or a person acting under the authority of the Government or a Minister of the Government.

752 Expanded meaning of "officer" and "agent" for purposes of *sections 753* to *757*

In *sections 753* to *757*—

(a) any reference to officers and agents includes past, as well as present, officers and agents; and

(b) "agents", in relation to a company or related body corporate, includes—

(i) the bankers and solicitors of the company or other body corporate; and

(ii) any persons employed by the company or other body corporate as auditors, accountants, book-keepers or taxation advisers, or other persons employed by it in a professional, consultancy or similar capacity, whether those persons are (or were) or are not (or were not) officers of the company or other body corporate.

753 Duty of company officer or agent to produce books or documents and give assistance

(1) Every person who is an officer or agent of a company under investigation by an inspector appointed under *section 747(1)* or *748(1)* or of a related body corporate under investigation under *section 750* shall—

(a) produce to the inspector all books or documents of or relating to the company or the related body corporate, as the case may be, that are in that person's possession or under that person's control;

(b) attend before the inspector when required to do so; and

(c) otherwise give the inspector all assistance in connection with the investigation that that person is reasonably able to give.

(2) The production by a person of a book or document under this section is without prejudice to any lien that that person may claim over the book or document.

754 Inspector may require other persons to produce books or documents and give assistance

(1) This section applies if an inspector appointed under *section 747(1)* or *748(1)* considers that a person who is not an officer or agent of the company or related body corporate under investigation possesses or may possess any information concerning the affairs of the company or related body corporate, as the case may be.

(2) In any case to which this section applies, the inspector may require the person in question to—

(a) produce to the inspector all books or documents of or relating to the company or the related body corporate, as the case may be, that are in that person's possession or under that person's control;

(b) attend before the inspector when required to do so; and

(c) otherwise give the inspector all assistance in connection with the investigation that that person is reasonably able to give.

(3) A person of whom a requirement is made under *subsection (2)* shall comply with that requirement.

(4) The production by a person of a book or document under this section is without prejudice to any lien that that person may claim over the book or document.

755 Supplementary power to compel production of books or documents in relation to certain banking transactions

(1) This section applies if an inspector appointed under *section 747(1)* or *748(1)* has reasonable grounds for believing that a director (the "director") of the company or related body corporate under investigation maintains or has maintained a bank account of any description, whether alone or jointly with another person and whether in the State or elsewhere, into or out of which there has been paid money described in *subsection (2)*.

(2) The money referred to in *subsection (1)* is—

(a) any money that has resulted from, or been used in, the financing of any transaction, arrangement or agreement—

(i) particulars of which have not been disclosed in a note to the financial statements of any company for any financial year as required by *section 307*, *308* or *309*;

(ii) in respect of which any amount outstanding was not included in the aggregate amounts outstanding in respect of certain transactions, arrangements or agreements as required by *section 311* to be disclosed in a note to the financial statements of any company for any financial year;

(iii) particulars of which were not included in any register of certain transactions, arrangements and agreements as required by *section 312(1)* or *section 1120* (including the latter as it is applied by this Act to companies other than public limited companies);

or

(b) any money that has been in any way connected with any act or omission, or series of acts or omissions, that on the part of the director constituted misconduct (whether fraudulent or not) towards the company or body corporate under investigation or its members.

(3) In any case to which this section applies, the inspector may require the director to produce to the inspector all books or documents in the director's possession or under his or her control relating to the bank account referred to in *subsection (1)* and the director shall comply with that requirement.

(4) In this section—

"bank account" includes an account with any person who is exempt, by virtue of section 7(4) of the Central Bank Act 1971, from the requirement of holding a licence under section 9 of that Act;

"director" includes any present or past director or any person connected, within the meaning of *section 220*, with that director and any present or past shadow director.

756 Power of inspector to examine officers, agents and others

(1) An inspector appointed under *section 747(1)* or *748(1)* may examine the following persons on oath in relation to the affairs of the company or related body corporate under investigation:

(a) an officer or agent of the company or related body corporate; and

(b) a person referred to in *section 754*;

and an examination under this section of an officer or agent of the company may relate to the related body corporate (as well as the company) and *vice versa*.

(2) The inspector may conduct the examination orally or through written questions and for the purpose of the examination may—

(a) administer an oath; and

(b) reduce to writing the answers of the person being examined and require that person to sign them.

757 Court may make order in relation to default in production of books or documents, etc

(1) The court may make any order or give any direction it thinks fit if—

(a) an officer or agent of a company or related body corporate under investigation or a person referred to in *section 754* refuses or fails within a reasonable time to—

(i) produce to the inspectors any book or document that it is that person's duty under *sections 753* to *755* to produce;

(ii) attend before the inspectors when required to do so; or

(iii) answer a question put to that person by the inspectors with respect to the affairs of the company or other body corporate as the case may be;

(b) the inspectors have certified the refusal or failure to the court in a certificate signed by them; and

(c) the court has taken the steps set out in *subsection (2)*.

(2) The court may make an order or give a direction under *subsection (1)* if the court has—

(a) enquired into the case;

(b) heard any witnesses who may be produced against or on behalf of the person alleged to be in default; and

(c) heard any statement made in that person's defence.

(3) Without prejudice to the generality of *subsection (1)*, the court may, after a hearing under *subsection (2)*, direct that the person concerned—

(a) attend or re-attend before the inspectors or produce particular books or documents or answer particular questions put to that person by the inspectors; or

(b) need not produce a particular book or document or answer a particular question put to that person by the inspectors.

758 Report of inspectors appointed under *section 747(1)* or *748(1)*

(1) Inspectors appointed under *section 747(1)* or *748(1)* may, and if directed by the court shall, make interim reports to the court, and on conclusion of the investigation shall make a final report to the court.

(2) Notwithstanding anything in *subsection (1)*, an inspector appointed under *section 747(1)* or *748(1)* may at any time in the course of the investigation, without the necessity of making an interim report, inform the court of matters coming to his or her knowledge as a result of the investigation that tend to show that an offence has been committed.

759 Distribution of inspectors' report

(1) The court shall provide a copy of every inspectors' report to the Director.

(2) The court may—

(a) forward a copy of an inspectors' report to the registered office of the company that is the subject of the report;

(b) provide a copy of an inspectors' report on request to any of the following:

(i) a member of the company or other body corporate that is the subject of the report;

(ii) a person whose conduct is referred to in the report;

(iii) the statutory auditors of the company or other body corporate;

(iv) if other than the Director, the person or persons who applied for the appointment of the inspectors;

(v) any other person (including an employee or creditor of the company or other body corporate) whose financial interests appear to the court to be affected by the matters dealt with in the report;

(vi) the Central Bank, if the report relates, wholly or partly, to the affairs of a credit institution.

(3) The court may provide a copy of an inspectors' report to—

(a) an appropriate authority in relation to any of the matters referred to in *section 791(a)* to *(j)*; or

(b) a competent authority as defined in *section 792(2)*.

(4) The court may cause an inspectors' report to be published in such form and manner as it thinks fit.

(5) The court may direct that a particular part of an inspectors' report be omitted from a copy that is forwarded or provided under *subsection (2)* or *(3)* or a report that is printed and published under *subsection (4)*.

(6) In this section "inspectors' report" means a report made under *section 758*.

760 Court may make order after considering inspectors' report

(1) After considering a report made under *section 758*, the court may make such order as it thinks fit.

(2) An order under *subsection (1)* may include—

(a) an order of the court's own motion for the winding up of a body corporate; or

(b) an order for remedying any disability suffered by any person whose interests were adversely affected by the conduct of the affairs of the company that is the subject of the report, provided that in making such an order the court shall have regard to the interests of any other person who may be adversely affected by the order.

761 Director may present petition for winding up following consideration of report

The Director may present a petition for the winding up of a body corporate on the ground that it is just and equitable to do so if the Director considers that such a petition should be presented having regard to—

(a) a report made under *section 758* by inspectors appointed under *section 747(1)* or *748(1)*; or

(b) any information or document obtained by the Director by virtue of the performance by him or her of functions (whether under this Part or otherwise).

762 Expenses of investigation by court appointed inspector

(1) The expenses of and incidental to an investigation by an inspector appointed under *section 747(1)* or *748(1)* shall be defrayed in the first instance by the relevant authority.

(2) The court may direct that a body corporate dealt with in the report or the applicant or applicants for the appointment of the inspector shall be liable to repay the relevant authority so much of the expenses as the court directs.

(3) Without prejudice to *subsection (2)* but subject to *subsection (5)*, where a court enters a conviction or makes an order in a case set out in *subsection (4)*, the court may in the same proceedings order the person referred to in *subsection (4)* to repay the relevant authority or any person fixed with liability for expenses under *subsection (2)* so much of the expenses of and incidental to the investigation as the court directs.

(4) The cases mentioned in *subsection (3)* are—

(a) the court convicts the person on indictment of an offence on a prosecution instituted as a result of the investigation;

(b) the court orders the person to pay damages or restore any property in proceedings brought as a result of the investigation; or

(c) the court awards damages to or orders the restoration of property to the person in proceedings brought as a result of the investigation.

(5) Where a court makes an order for payment of expenses under *subsection (3)* against a person to whom *subsection (4)(c)* relates—

(a) the court shall not order payment of expenses that are more than one-tenth of the amount of the damages awarded or of the value of the property restored, as the case may be, and

(b) the order shall not be executed until the person concerned has received the damages or the property has been restored.

(6) In the light of his or her investigation, an inspector may or, if the court so directs, shall recommend in his or her report what directions (if any) he or she considers to be appropriate under *subsection (2)*.

(7) In this section "relevant authority" means—

(a) in the case of an appointment of an inspector or inspectors under *section 747(1)*, the Minister for Justice and Equality;

(b) in the case of an appointment of an inspector or inspectors under *section 748(1)*, the Director.

Chapter 3
Investigations initiated by Director

763 Investigation of share dealing by inspector appointed by Director

(1) If the Director considers that there are circumstances suggesting that a contravention of *Chapter 5* of *Part 5* has occurred in relation to shares in or debentures of a company, the Director may appoint one or more competent inspectors to—

(a) investigate whether such a contravention has occurred; and

(b) report the results of the investigation to the Director.

(2) The appointment under this section of an inspector may limit the period to which his or her investigation is to extend or confine it to shares or debentures of a particular class or both.

(3) For the purposes of an investigation under this section, *sections 752* to *756* shall apply—

(a) with the substitution, for references to any other body corporate whose affairs are investigated by virtue of *section 750*, of a reference to any other body corporate that is, or has at any relevant time been, the company's subsidiary or holding company or a subsidiary of the company's holding company, and

(b) with the necessary modification of the reference in *section 756* to the affairs of the company or other body corporate, so, however, it shall apply to members of an authorised market operator who are individuals and to officers (past and present) of members of such an authorised market operator who are bodies corporate as it applies to officers of the company or body corporate.

(4) The inspector may, and if directed by the Director, shall make interim reports to the Director, and on the conclusion of the investigation shall make a final report to the Director.

(5) An inspector's interim or final report shall be written or printed as the Director shall direct, and the Director may cause it to be published.

(6) *Sections 750*, *757*, *768* to *777*, *795* (other than *subsection (8)*) and *881(4)* shall, with any necessary modifications, apply for the purposes of this section.

(7) The expenses of an investigation under this section shall be defrayed by the Director.

(8) Where a person is convicted on indictment of an offence on a prosecution instituted as a result of an investigation under this section, the court may, on the application of the Director, order that person to pay all or part of the expenses of the investigation as the court may direct.

764 Investigation of company ownership by inspector appointed by Director

(1) Subject to *subsection (2)* and *section 800(5)*, the Director may appoint one or more competent inspectors to investigate and report on the membership of a company or on any other matter in relation to the company for the purpose of determining the true persons who are or have been—

(a) financially interested in the success or failure (real or apparent) of the company, or

(b) able to control or materially to influence the policy of the company.

(2) The Director may make an appointment under *subsection (1)* if the Director considers that it is necessary—

(a) for the effective administration of the law relating to companies,

(b) for the effective discharge by the Director of his or her functions, or

(c) in the public interest.

(3) The appointment of an inspector under this section may define the scope of his or her investigation, whether as respects the matters or the period to which it is to extend or otherwise, and in particular may limit the investigation to matters connected with particular shares or debentures.

(4) Subject to the terms of an inspector's appointment, the inspector's powers shall extend to the investigation of any circumstances suggesting the existence of an arrangement or understanding that—

(a) although not legally binding, is or was observed or was likely to be observed in practice; and

(b) is relevant to the purposes of the investigation.

765 Application of certain provisions to investigation of company ownership

(1) For the purposes of an investigation under *section 764*, *sections 750* and *752* to *759* shall, with the necessary modifications of references to the affairs of the company or to those of any other body corporate, apply in accordance with *subsections (2)* and *(3)* and subject to *subsection (4)*.

(2) The provisions referred to in *subsection (1)* shall apply in relation to the following persons in the same way that they apply to officers and agents of the company or other body corporate whose ownership is being investigated, as the case may be:

(a) all persons who are or have been, or whom the inspector has reasonable cause to believe to be or have been, financially interested in the success or failure (real or apparent) of the company or other body corporate;

(b) all persons who are able to control or materially to influence the policy of the company or the other body corporate, including persons concerned only on behalf of others;

(c) any other person whom the inspector has reasonable cause to believe has information relevant to the investigation.

(3) For the references to the court (except in *section 757*) there shall be substituted references to the Director.

(4) The Director may—

(a) where he or she considers that there is good reason for not divulging any part of a report made by virtue of this section, disclose the report with that part omitted,

(b) where he or she discloses the report with a part omitted under *paragraph (a)*, ensure that a copy of the report with that part omitted is kept by the Registrar, and

(c) where he or she discloses the report without an omission under *paragraph (a)*, ensure that a copy of the whole report is kept by the Registrar.

766 Expenses of investigation of company ownership

(1) On the application of the Director, the court may direct a company that is the subject of an investigation under *section 764* to repay to the Director so much of the expenses of and incidental to the investigation as the court directs.

(2) Without prejudice to *subsection (1)* but subject to *subsection (3)*, where a court enters a conviction or makes an order in a case set out in *subsection (3)* the court may, in the same proceedings, order the person referred to in *subsection (3)* to pay to the Director so much of the expenses of and incidental to an investigation under *section 764* as the court directs.

(3) The cases referred to in *subsection (2)* are where the court—

(a) convicts the person on indictment of an offence on a prosecution instituted as a result of the investigation;

(b) orders the person to pay damages or restore any property in proceedings brought as a result of the investigation; or

(c) awards damages to or orders the restoration of property to the person in proceedings brought as a result of the investigation.

(4) Where the court makes an order for payment of expenses under *subsection (2)* against a person to whom *subsection (3)(c)* relates—

(a) the court shall not order payment of expenses that are more than one-tenth of the amount of the damages awarded or of the value of the property restored, as the case may be, and

(b) the order shall not be executed until the person concerned has received the damages or the property has been restored.

767 Director's power to require information as to persons interested in shares or debentures

(1) This section applies if the Director considers that an investigation of the ownership of the shares in or debentures of a company is necessary for any of the reasons set out in *section 764(2)* but that it is unnecessary to appoint an inspector for the purpose.

(2) In any case to which this section applies, the Director may, subject to *section 800(5)*, require a person to give the following information to the Director if the Director has reasonable cause to believe that the person has or is able to obtain the information:

(a) any information as to the past and present interests in the shares or debentures;

(b) the names and addresses of the persons interested in the shares or debentures; or

(c) the names and addresses of the persons who act or have acted on behalf of the persons referred to in *paragraph (b)* in relation to the shares.

(3) For the purposes of this section, a person shall be deemed to have an interest in a share or debenture if—

(a) that person has any right to acquire or dispose of the share or debenture or any interest in it;

(b) that person has any right to vote in respect of the share or debenture;

(c) the consent of that person is necessary for the exercise of any of the rights of other persons interested in the share or debenture; or

(d) other persons interested in the share or debenture can be required or are accustomed to exercise their rights in accordance with that person's instructions.

(4) A person shall be guilty of a category 2 offence if that person, when required to give any information under this section—

(a) fails to give the information to the Director; or

(b) makes any statement to the Director false in a material particular knowing it to be so false or being reckless as to whether it is so false.

(5) Without prejudice to *subsection (4)*, if a person fails to give information to the Director under this section when required by the Director to do so, the court, on application by the Director, and having given the person an opportunity to be heard, may make an order requiring the person to comply with the Director's requirement.

(6) In making an order under *subsection (5)*, the court may order the third party to pay all costs of and incidental to the application.

768 Director may impose restrictions on shares

(1) Where, in connection with an investigation under *section 764* or an enquiry under *section 767*, the Director considers that there is any difficulty in finding out the relevant facts about any shares (whether issued or to be issued), the Director may, by notice in writing, direct that the shares shall, subject to further notice, be subject to the restrictions imposed by this section.

(2) The following restrictions apply to the shares referred to in *subsection (1)* for as long as the direction in respect of the shares is in force:

(a) any transfer of the shares shall be void or, if the shares are unissued, any transfer of the right to be issued with the shares shall be void and any issue of the shares shall be void;

(b) no voting rights shall be exercisable in respect of the shares;

(c) no further shares shall be issued in right of those shares or in pursuance of any offer made to the holder of the shares; and

(d) no payment shall be made of any sums due from the company on those shares, whether in respect of capital or otherwise.

(3) Where shares are subject to the restrictions imposed by *subsection (2)(a)*, any agreement—

(a) to transfer the shares shall be void, or

(b) in the case of unissued shares, to transfer the right to be issued the shares shall be void.

(4) However, *subsection (3)* shall not apply to an agreement to sell the shares under *section 769(1)(b)* or *771(2)(c)*.

(5) Where shares are subject to the restrictions imposed by *subsection (2)(c)* or *(d)*, any agreement—

(a) to transfer any right to be issued other shares in right of the shares shall be void, and

(b) to receive any payment on those shares shall be void.

(6) However, *subsection (5)* shall not apply to an agreement to transfer any right to be issued other shares on the sale of the shares under *section 771(2)(c)*.

769 Director may lift restrictions imposed on shares under *section 768*

(1) The Director may direct that the restrictions imposed upon shares under *section 768* shall cease to apply if—

(a) the Director is satisfied that the relevant facts about the shares have been disclosed to him or her, or

(b) the shares are to be sold and the court or the Director approves the sale.

(2) However, this section does not affect a direction of the Director directing that any restriction continued in force in relation to the shares under *section 775* shall cease to apply to the shares.

770 Director shall give notice of direction

As soon as practicable after giving a direction under *section 768* or *769*, the Director shall cause notice of the direction to be—

(a) sent to the company concerned at its registered office;

(b) delivered to the Registrar; and

(c) published in *Iris Oifigiúil*.

771 Court may lift restrictions imposed on shares under *section 768*

(1) Where the Director directs that shares shall be subject to the restrictions imposed under *section 768* or refuses to direct that such restrictions shall cease to apply to the shares, any person aggrieved by the direction or refusal of the Director may apply to the court for an order that the restrictions shall cease to apply to the shares.

(2) The court may make an order under *subsection (1)* if—

(a) the court is satisfied that the relevant facts about the shares have been disclosed to the company or, as the case requires, to the Director;

(b) the court is satisfied that it is otherwise equitable to lift the restrictions; or

(c) the shares are to be sold and the court approves the sale.

(3) This section does not affect an order of the court that any restriction continued in force in relation to the shares under *section 775* shall cease to apply to the shares.

772 Court may order sale of shares

(1) Where any shares are subject to the restrictions imposed under *section 768*, the court, on the application of a person specified in *subsection (2)*, may—

(a) order that the shares shall be sold, subject to the approval of the court as to sale; and

(b) also direct that the restrictions imposed under *section 768* shall cease to apply to the shares.

(2) The court may make the order under *subsection (1)* on the application of—

(a) the Director; or

(b) the company, if the company has given notice of the application to the Director.

(3) Where the court has made an order that the shares shall be sold, on the application of a person specified in *subsection (4)* the court may make any further order relating to the sale or to the transfer of the shares as it sees fit.

(4) The court may make a further order under *subsection (3)* on the application of—

(a) the Director;

(b) the company;

(c) the person appointed under the order for sale to effect the sale; or

(d) any person interested in the shares.

773 Costs of applicant for order for sale of shares

(1) Where the court makes an order under *section 772*, the court may order that the costs of the applicant shall be paid out of the proceeds of the sale of the shares.

(2) Where an order for costs is made under *subsection (1)*, the applicant shall be entitled to payment of costs out of the proceeds of sale before any person interested in the shares sold receives any part of those proceeds.

774 Proceeds of sale following court ordered sale of shares

(1) Where shares are sold pursuant to an order made by the court under *section 772*—

(a) the proceeds of sale, less the costs of sale, shall be paid into court for the benefit of the persons who are beneficially interested in the shares, and

(b) any such person may apply to the court for the whole or part of the proceeds to be paid to that person.

(2) On an application under *subsection (1)(b)*, the court shall order—

(a) if no other person was beneficially interested in the shares at the time of sale, the payment to the applicant under *subsection (1)(b)* of the whole of the proceeds of sale after deduction of the amount of any costs awarded under *section 773(1)* and any interest accrued on those proceeds, or

(b) if any other person was beneficially interested in the shares at the time of sale, the payment to the applicant under *subsection (1)(b)* of such proportion of the proceeds of sale after the deduction of the amount of any costs awarded under *section 773(1)* and any interest accrued on those proceeds as is equal to the proportion that the value of the applicant's interest in the shares bears to the total value of the shares.

775 Continuance of certain restrictions

(1) This section applies to—

(a) a direction under *section 769* or an order of the court under *section 771* expressed to be given or made with a view to permitting a transfer of the shares in question; or

(b) an order under *section 772* for the sale of the shares in question.

(2) Any direction or order to which this section applies may continue the restrictions referred to in *section 768(2)(c)* and *(d)* in whole or in part, so far as they relate to any right acquired or offer made before the transfer of the shares in question.

(3) Any such continuance provided by a foregoing direction or order may be varied or cancelled by a subsequent direction of the Director or, as the case may be, by a subsequent order of the court (power to provide for which variation or cancellation is conferred on the Director and the court, respectively, by this subsection).

776 Offences in relation to shares that are subject to restrictions

(1) A person who does any of the following shall be guilty of a category 2 offence:

(a) exercises or purports to exercise any right to dispose of—

(i) any shares that, to the person's knowledge, are for the time being subject to the restrictions imposed under *section 768*; or

(ii) any right to be issued with any such shares;

(b) votes in respect of shares that are subject to the restrictions imposed under *section 768* or appoints a proxy to vote in respect of any such shares;

(c) being the holder of shares that are subject to the restrictions imposed under *section 768*, fails to notify any other person of the restrictions where the holder knows that the other person is entitled, apart from the restrictions, to vote in respect of the shares whether as holder or proxy;

(d) being the holder of shares that are subject to the restrictions imposed under *section 768(2)(a)*, enters into an agreement that is void by virtue of *section 768(3) (a)*;

(e) being the holder of unissued shares that are subject to the restrictions imposed under *section 768(2)(a)*, enters into an agreement that is void by virtue of *section 768(3)(b)*;

(f) being the holder of the right to be issued with other shares in right of shares that are subject to the restrictions imposed under *section 768(2)(c)* and *(d)*, enters into an agreement that is void by virtue of *section 768(5) (a)*;

(g) being the holder of the right to receive payment on shares that are subject to the restrictions imposed under *section 768(2)(c)* and *(d)*, enters into an agreement that is void by virtue of *section 768(5) (b)*.

(2) Where any shares in a company are issued in contravention of the restrictions imposed under *section 768*, the company and any officer of it who is in default shall be guilty of a category 2 offence.

777 Application of *sections 768* to *776* to debentures

Sections 768 to *776* shall apply in relation to debentures as they apply in relation to shares.

Chapter 4
Miscellaneous provisions

778 Power of Director to require company to produce books or documents

Subject to *section 779*, the Director may give a direction to any company requiring it, at such time and place, and in such manner, as may be specified in the direction, to produce such books or documents as are specified in the direction.

779 When Director may exercise power to require company to produce books or documents

The Director may give the direction described in *section 778* to a company if the Director considers that there are circumstances suggesting that—

(a) it is necessary to examine the books or documents of the company with a view to determining whether an inspector should be appointed to investigate the company under this Act;

(b) the affairs of the company are being or have been conducted with intent to defraud—

  (i) its creditors;

  (ii) the creditors of any other person; or

  (iii) its members;

(c) the affairs of the company are being or have been conducted for a fraudulent or unlawful purpose other than described in *paragraph (b)*;

(d) the affairs of the company are being or have been conducted in an unlawful manner;

(e) the affairs of the company are being or have been conducted in a manner that is unfairly prejudicial to some part of its members;

(f) the affairs of the company are being or have been conducted in a manner that is unfairly prejudicial to some or all of its creditors;

(g) any actual or proposed act or omission or series of acts or omissions of the company or on behalf of the company have been, are or would be unfairly prejudicial to some part of its members;

(h) any actual or proposed act or omission of the company (including an act or omission on its behalf) was, is or would be unfairly prejudicial to some or all of its creditors;

(i) any actual or proposed act or omission or series of acts or omissions of the company or on behalf of the company by an officer of the company acting in his or her capacity as such officer have been, are or are likely to be unlawful;

(j) the company was formed for any fraudulent or unlawful purpose; or

(k) the company may be in possession of books or documents containing information relating to the books or documents of a body that comes within the terms of one or more of *paragraphs (a)* to *(j)*.

780 Power of Director to require third party to produce books or documents

(1) Where, by virtue of *sections 778* and *779*, the Director has power to require the production of any books or documents from any company, the Director shall have power to require the production of—

(a) those books or documents from any person who appears to the Director to be in possession of them;

(b) copies of any books or documents of the company from any person who appears to the Director to be in possession of them; and

(c) subject to *section 782*, other books or documents (whether the originals of them or otherwise) which may relate to any books or documents of the company from any person who appears to the Director to be in possession of such other books or documents.

(2) Any requirement under *subsection (1)* shall be made by the giving by the Director of a direction to the person of whom the requirement is being made that specifies—

(a) the books or documents to be produced by the person; and

(b) the time and place at which, and the manner in which, they are to be produced.

(3) The production by a person of a book or document under this section is without prejudice to any lien that that person may claim over the book or document.

781 Saving in relation to *section 780*, etc and corresponding amendments effected to Act of 1990 by Companies (Amendment) Act 2009

(1) In this section the "original amendments" means the amendments of section 19 of the Act of 1990 made by section 4(1) of the Companies (Amendment) Act 2009.

(2) Nothing in either—

(a) the original amendments, or

(b) *section 780* or of any other section of this Chapter that makes similar provision to that made by those amendments,

shall be read to mean that, but for the effecting of those amendments or the making of such similar provision by any of those sections, a direction given by the Director, before the passing of the Companies (Amendment) Act 2009, under section 19(3) of the Act of 1990, was limited in any way as to its effect or extent of operation or that books or documents produced on foot of it to the Director were not lawfully produced to him.

782 Restriction on power of Director to require third party to produce certain books or documents

(1) The Director shall not exercise the power under *section 780(1)(c)* to require a person (in this section and *section 783* referred to as the "third party") to produce books or documents that may relate to any books or documents of a company unless—

(a) the Director is of the opinion that there are reasonable grounds for believing that the books or documents required to be produced and the books or documents of the company are related to one another; and

(b) subject to *subsection (4)*, the Director has first taken the steps set out in *subsection (2)*.

(2) The steps referred to in *subsection (1)(b)* are the following:

(a) the Director shall notify the third party stating—

(i) that the Director proposes to require the third party to produce books or documents that may relate to books or documents of the company;

(ii) the grounds for the Director's opinion referred to in *subsection (1)(a)*; and

(iii) that the third party may make submissions to the Director within 21 days after the date of the notification as to why the third party believes the opinion of the Director is erroneous; and

(b) the Director shall have regard to those submissions before finally deciding whether to require the books or documents in question.

(3) In *subsection (1)(a)*, the grounds for the opinion of the Director may include—

(a) grounds related to the relationship between the company and the person required to produce the books or documents;

(b) a common origin of the books or documents; or

(c) other similar considerations.

(4) The Director is not required to take the steps set out in *subsection (2)* if—

(a) the Director considers that compliance with those steps could result in the concealment, falsification, destruction or disposal of the books or documents concerned; or

(b) the books or documents concerned are merely the originals of any books or documents, copies of which have previously been produced to the Director in compliance with an earlier requirement made in exercise of the power under *section 780(1)(c)*.

(5) The third party shall not be obliged to comply with a requirement to produce documents in relation to a particular book or document if the third party would be entitled, by virtue of any law or enactment, to refuse to produce the book or document in any proceedings on the ground of any privilege (whether the privilege to which *section 795* applies or not).

783 Court may order third party to comply with requirement to produce books or documents

(1) This section applies if a third party—

(a) has failed to—

(i) comply with a requirement of the Director under *section 780(1)(c)* requiring the third party to produce books or documents, or

(ii) provide an explanation, make a statement or give assistance as required by *section 784*,

and

(b) has, in either case, failed to remedy the default within 14 days after the date of service by the Director on the third party of a notice requiring the third party to remedy the default.

(2) In any case to which this section applies, the court, on the application of the Director, and having given the third party an opportunity to be heard, may order the third party to remedy the default within such time as the court specifies.

(3) In making an order under *subsection (2)*, the court may order the third party to pay all costs of and incidental to the application.

(4) Nothing in this section shall be taken to prejudice the operation of *section 785(1)* and *(2)*.

784 Powers ancillary to power to require production of books or documents

The power to require a company or other person to produce books or documents under *section 778* or *780* shall also include the following powers:

(a) if the books or documents are produced, the power to take copies of or extracts from them;

(b) if the books or documents are produced, the power to require the following persons to provide, as far as they are reasonably able to do so, an explanation of any of the books or documents, including an explanation of any apparent omissions from them or of any omission of any book or document—

(i) the person producing the books or documents;

(ii) a present or past officer of the company in question; or

(iii) a person who was or is employed by the company in question, including a person employed in a professional, consultancy or similar capacity;

(c) if the books or documents are not produced, the power to require the person who was required to produce them to state, to the best of that person's knowledge and belief, where they are; and

(d) the power to require the company or any of the persons specified in *paragraph (b)* to give all assistance to the Director as the company or the person is reasonably able to give in connection with an examination of the books or documents in question.

785 Offences in relation to requirement to produce books or documents

(1) Subject to *subsection (2)*, a person who fails to comply with a requirement under *section 778*, *780* or *784* to produce books or documents or to provide an explanation or to make a statement shall be guilty of a category 2 offence.

(2) In any proceedings against a person in respect of an offence under *subsection (1)* consisting of a failure to comply with a requirement to produce books or documents, it shall be a defence to prove both that—

(a) the books or documents were not in that person's possession or under that person's control, and

(b) it was not reasonably practicable for that person to comply with the requirement.

(3) A person who provides an explanation or makes a statement required under *section 783* that is false or misleading in a material respect knowing it to be so false or misleading shall be guilty of a category 2 offence.

(4) Notwithstanding *section 286*, a person who with notice of a direction given under *section 778* or *780* destroys, mutilates, falsifies or conceals any document that is the subject of the direction shall be guilty of a category 2 offence.

(5) A statement made or an explanation provided by an individual in compliance with a requirement under *section 784* may be used against that person in any proceedings except proceedings for the prosecution of that person (other than for an offence under *subsection (1)* or *(3)*).

786 Expenses relating to examination of books or documents

(1) On the application of the Director, the court may direct that a company that is the subject of a direction given under *section 778* shall be liable to repay the Director so much of the expenses of and incidental to the examination of books or documents produced as the court directs.

(2) Without prejudice to *subsection (1)* but subject to *subsection (4)*, where a court enters a conviction or makes an order in a case set out in *subsection (3)*, the court may, in the same proceedings, order the person concerned to repay the Director so much of the expenses of and incidental to an examination following a direction given under *section 778* as the court directs.

(3) The cases referred to in *subsection (2)* are where the court—

(a) convicts the person on indictment of an offence on a prosecution instituted as a result of the direction;

(b) orders the person to pay damages or restore any property in proceedings brought as a result of the direction; or

(c) awards damages to or orders the restoration of property to the person in proceedings brought as a result of the direction.

(4) Where a court makes an order for payment of expenses under *subsection (2)* against a person to whom *subsection (3)(c)* relates—

(a) the court shall not order payment of expenses that are more than one-tenth of the amount of the damages awarded or of the value of the property restored, as the case may be, and

(b) the order shall not be executed until the person concerned has received the damages or the property has been restored.

787 Entry and search of premises

(1) A judge of the District Court may issue a search warrant under this section if satisfied by information on oath laid by a designated officer that there are reasonable grounds for suspecting that any material information is to be found on any premises (including a dwelling).

(2) A search warrant issued under this section shall be expressed and operate to authorise a named designated officer (the "officer"), accompanied by such other persons as the officer thinks necessary, at any time or times within the period of validity of the warrant, on production of the warrant if so requested, to—

(a) enter the named premises, if necessary by force;

(b) search the premises;

(c) require any person found on the premises to—

(i) give to the officer his or her name, home address and occupation; and

(ii) produce to the officer any material information that is in the custody or possession of that person;

(d) seize and retain any material information found on the premises or in the custody or possession of any person found on the premises; and

(e) take any other steps that appear to the officer to be necessary for preserving or preventing interference with material information.

(3) Without prejudice to *subsection (4)*, where—

(a) the officer finds anything at, or in the custody or possession of any person found on, the premises named in the warrant that the officer has reasonable grounds for believing may be or may contain material information, and

(b) it is not reasonably practicable for a determination to be made on the premises—

(i) whether what he or she has found is something that he or she is entitled to seize under the warrant (whether as mentioned in *subsection (2)(d)* or *(4)*), or

(ii) the extent to which what he or she has found contains something that he or she is entitled to seize under the warrant in either of those cases,

the officer's powers of seizure under the warrant shall include power to seize so much of what he or she has found as it is necessary to remove from the premises to enable that to be determined (referred to subsequently in this section as an "extended power of seizure").

(4) Where—

(a) the officer finds anything at, or in the custody or possession of any person found on, the premises named in the warrant being a book, document or other thing constituting material information (referred to subsequently in this section as "seizable information") which he or she would be entitled to seize but for its being comprised in something else that he or she has (apart from this subsection) no power to seize, and

(b) it is not reasonably practicable for the seizable information to be separated, on those premises, from that in which it is comprised,

the officer's powers of seizure shall include power to seize both the seizable information and that from which it is not reasonably practicable to separate it (also referred to subsequently in this section as an "extended power of seizure").

(5) Where, for the purposes of *subsection (3)* or *(4)*, an issue arises as to either of the following matters, namely:

(a) whether or not it is reasonably practicable on particular premises for something to be determined; or

(b) whether or not it is reasonably practicable on particular premises for something to be separated from something else,

the issue shall be decided by reference solely to the following matters:

(i) how long it would take to carry out the determination or separation on those premises;

(ii) the number of persons that would be required to carry out that determination or separation on those premises within a reasonable period;

(iii) whether the determination or separation would (or would if carried out on those premises) involve damage to property;

(iv) the apparatus or equipment that it would be necessary or appropriate to use for the carrying out of the determination or separation;

(v) the costs of carrying out the determination or separation on those premises as against the costs of carrying out the determination or separation in another place (being a place in which the Director can show it would be appropriate to do the thing concerned and in which the Director intends to arrange, or does arrange, for the thing to be done); and

(vi) in the case of separation, whether the separation—

(I) would be likely, or

(II) if carried out by the only means that are reasonably practicable on those premises, would be likely,

to prejudice the use of some or all of the separated seizable information for a purpose for which something seized under the warrant is capable of being used.

(6) *Section 788* supplements *subsections (3)* to *(5)* and, in particular, as regards the making of arrangements for the storage of, and access to, things seized by virtue of an

exercise of the extended power of seizure and for the maintenance of confidentiality as regards any confidential matter comprised in such a thing so seized.

(7) The officer may—

(a) operate any computer at the place that is being searched or cause any such computer to be operated by a person accompanying the officer; and

(b) require any person at that place who appears to the officer to be in a position to facilitate access to the information held in any such computer or that can be accessed by the use of that computer—

(i) to give to the officer any password necessary to operate it;

(ii) otherwise to enable the officer to examine the information accessible by the computer in a form in which the information is visible and legible; and

(iii) to produce the information in a form in which it can be removed and in which it is, or can be made, visible and legible.

(8) The power to issue a warrant under this section is in addition to and not in substitution for any other power to issue a warrant for the search of any place or person.

(9) The period of validity of a warrant shall be 30 days after the date of its issue but that period of validity may be extended in accordance with *subsections (10)* and *(11)*.

(10) The officer may, during the period of validity of a warrant (including such period as previously extended under *subsection (11)*), apply to a judge of the District Court for an order extending the period of validity of the warrant and such an application shall be grounded upon information on oath laid by the officer stating, by reference to the purpose or purposes for which the warrant was issued, the reasons why he or she considers the extension to be necessary.

(11) If the judge of the District Court is satisfied that there are reasonable grounds for believing, having regard to that information so laid, that further time is needed so that the purpose or purposes for which the warrant was issued can be fulfilled, the judge may make an order extending the period of validity of the warrant by such period as, in the opinion of the judge, is appropriate and just; where such an order is made, the judge shall cause the warrant to be suitably endorsed to indicate its extended period of validity.

(12) Nothing in the preceding subsections prevents a judge of the District Court from issuing, on foot of a fresh application made under *subsection (1)*, a further search warrant under this section in relation to the same premises.

(13) In this section—

"computer" includes a personal organiser or any other electronic means of information storage or retrieval;

"computer at the place that is being searched" includes any other computer, whether at the place being searched or at any other place, that is lawfully accessible by means of that computer;

"designated officer" means the Director or a duly authorised officer of the Director;

"material information" means—

(a) any books or documents production of which has been required under—

  (i) any of the provisions applied by *section 765*, namely *sections 750* and *752* to *759*; or

  (ii) any of *sections 767* and *778* to *780*;

  and which have not been produced in compliance with that requirement; or

(b) any books, documents or other things (including a computer) which the designated officer has reasonable grounds for believing may provide evidence of or be related to the commission of an offence under this Act.

(14) Notwithstanding the repeal of section 68(2) of the Investment Funds, Companies and Miscellaneous Provisions Act 2005, the saving in that provision concerning section 20(3) of the Act of 1990 is not affected.

788 Supplemental provisions in relation to *section 787(3)* to *(5)*

(1) In this section—

"extended power of seizure" shall be read in accordance with *section 787(3)* or *(4)*, as appropriate;

"material information" has the same meaning as it has in *section 787*;

"officer" means the officer named as mentioned in *section 787(2)* in the warrant concerned;

"seizable information" shall be read in accordance with *section 787(4)*.

(2) Save where the officer is of opinion that compliance with this subsection could result in the concealment, falsification, destruction or the disposal otherwise of material information, an extended power of seizure shall not be exercised unless the officer has first made the following arrangements in relation to the thing or things, the subject of the proposed exercise of that power, namely reasonable arrangements:

(a) providing for the appropriate storage of that thing or those things;

(b) allowing reasonable access, from time to time, to that thing or those things by the owner, lawful custodian or possessor thereof (including, in the case of documents or information in non-legible form, by the making of copies or the transmission of matter by electronic means); and

(c) providing for confidentiality to be maintained as regards any confidential matter comprised in that thing or those things;

being arrangements to apply pending the making of the foregoing determination or the carrying out of the foregoing separation and the consequent return of anything to the owner, lawful custodian or possessor that is not material information.

(3) In deciding what the terms of those arrangements shall be, the officer shall have regard to any representations reasonably made on the matter by the owner, lawful custodian or possessor of the thing or things and endeavour, where practicable, to secure the agreement of that person to those terms.

(4) Where—

(a) by reason of the officer being of the opinion referred to in *subsection (2)*, the arrangements referred to in *paragraphs (a)* to *(c)* of that subsection are not made in relation to the thing or things the subject of the proposed exercise of the extended power of seizure, or

(b) circumstances arise subsequent to the exercise of the extended power of seizure that make it appropriate to vary the arrangements made under that subsection,

the officer shall, as the case may be—

(i) make, as soon as practicable after the exercise of that power of seizure, the arrangements referred to in *subsection (2)(a)* to *(c)* in relation to the thing or things concerned, or

(ii) vary the arrangements made under that subsection in a manner he or she considers appropriate.

(5) In deciding what shall be the terms of those arrangements or that variation, the officer shall have regard to any representations on the matter reasonably made by the owner, lawful custodian or possessor of the thing or things concerned and endeavour, where practicable, to secure the agreement of that person to those terms.

(6) Where an extended power of seizure is exercised, it shall be the duty of the officer—

(a) to carry out the determination or separation concerned as soon as practicable, and, in any event, subject to *subsection (7)*, within the prescribed period, after the date of its exercise, and

(b) as respects (as the case may be)—

(i) anything seized in exercise of the power found not to be material information, or

(ii) anything separated from another thing in the exercise of the power that is not material information,

to return, as soon as practicable, and, in any event, subject to *subsection (7)*, within the prescribed period, after the date of that finding or separation, the thing to its owner or the person appearing to the officer to be lawfully entitled to the custody or possession of it.

(7) On application to the court by the Director or any person affected by the exercise of an extended power of seizure, the court may, if it thinks fit and having had regard, in particular, to any submissions made on behalf of the Director with regard to the progress of any investigation being carried on by the Director for the purpose of which the powers under this section had been exercised, give one or more of the following:

(a) a direction that the doing of an act referred to in *subsection (6)(a)* or *(b)* shall be done within such lesser or greater period of time than that specified in that provision as the court determines;

(b) a direction with respect to the making, variation or operation of arrangements referred to in *subsection (2)(a)* to *(c)* in relation to a thing concerned or a direction that such arrangements as the court provides for in the direction shall have effect in place of any such arrangements that have been or were proposed to be made;

(c) a direction of any other kind that the court considers it just to give for the purpose of further securing the rights of any person affected by the exercise of an extended power of seizure, including, if the exceptional circumstances of the case warrant doing so, a direction that a thing seized be returned to its owner or the person appearing to the court to be lawfully entitled to the custody or possession of it, notwithstanding that the determination or separation concerned has not occurred.

(8) Any such direction may—

(a) relate to some or all of the things the subject of the exercise of the extended power of seizure,

(b) be expressed to operate subject to such terms and conditions as the court specifies, including, in the case of a direction under *subsection (7)(c)*, a condition that an officer of the Director be permitted, during a specified subsequent period, to re-take and retain possession of the thing returned for the purpose of carrying out the determination or separation concerned (and, retain after the expiry of that period, that which is found to be material information or is material information).

(9) An application under *subsection (7)* shall be by motion and may, if the court directs, be heard otherwise than in public.

(10) In *subsection (6)* "prescribed period" means—

(a) in the case of *paragraph (a)* of it—

(i) unless *subparagraph (ii)* applies, 3 months, or

(ii) such other period as the Minister prescribes in consequence of a review that may, from time to time, be carried out by or on behalf of the Minister of the operation and implementation of *section 787(3)* to *(5)* and this section,

(b) in the case of *paragraph (b)* of it—

(i) unless *subparagraph (ii)* applies, 7 days, or

(ii) such other period as the Minister prescribes in consequence of such a review that may, from time to time, be carried out by or on behalf of the Minister,

but no regulations made to prescribe such a period shall be read as operating to affect any direction given by the court under *subsection (7)(a)* in force on the commencement of those regulations.

(11) The Minister may make regulations providing for such supplementary, consequential and incidental matters to or in respect of *section 787(3)* to *(5)* and *subsections (2)* to *(6)* of this section as he or she considers necessary or expedient.

789 Offences in relation to entry and search of premises and provisions catering for certain contingencies concerning designated officers

(1) A person shall be guilty of a category 2 offence if that person—

(a) obstructs the exercise of a right of entry or search conferred by a search warrant issued under *section 787*;

(b) obstructs the exercise of a right conferred by a search warrant issued under *section 787* to seize and retain material information (as defined in *section 787(13)*);

(c) fails to comply with a requirement under *section 787(2)(c)* or gives a name, address or occupation that is false or misleading; or

(d) fails to comply with a requirement under *section 787(7)(b)*.

(2) If, at any time after a search warrant has been issued under *section 787*—

(a) the designated officer named therein (including any designated officer who is named therein by reason of any prior application under this subsection)—

(i) has ceased to be an officer of the Director (by reason of death, retirement, resignation, dismissal, reassignment or any other cause), or

(ii) is otherwise unable to perform his or her functions (by reason of absence from duty, illness, incapacity or any other cause),

or

(b) the Director has reasonable grounds for apprehending that any of the circumstances referred to in *paragraph (a)* is likely to arise,

then another designated officer may apply to a judge of the District Court for an order under *subsection (3)*.

(3) On the hearing of an application under *subsection (2)* the judge of the District Court may, if—

(a) the judge is satisfied that it is appropriate to do so, and

(b) the date to be specified under *paragraph (ii)* will fall during the period of validity of the warrant (including, if that is the case, such period as extended under *section 787(11)*),

make an order directing that the search warrant be endorsed so as to—

(i) substitute the name of another designated officer (the "new officer") for the name of the designated officer who was expressed to have been authorised under the search warrant immediately prior to the making of the order (the "previous officer"), and

(ii) specify the time and date from which that substitution is to take effect.

(4) Where an order under *subsection (3)* is made then, with effect from the time on the date endorsed pursuant to *paragraph (ii)* of that subsection—

(a) the search warrant shall continue in full force and effect, but shall operate to authorise the new officer to execute the warrant as fully as if he or she had been the designated officer named in the warrant when it was first issued,

(b) the search warrant shall no longer operate to authorise the previous officer to execute the warrant (but without prejudice to the validity of anything done previously thereunder by that officer), and

(c) the order shall operate to—

(i) relieve the previous officer from any duties to which he or she had been subject under *section 788(4)*, *(5)* or *(6)* (but without prejudice to the validity of anything done previously thereunder by that officer), and

(ii) impose upon the new officer any duties under *section 788(4)*, *(5)* or *(6)* that have not yet been fully discharged.

(5) If—

(a) the period of validity of a search warrant issued under *section 787* (including, if that is the case, such period as extended under *section 787(11)*) has expired, and

(b) either of the conditions specified in *subsection (2)(a)* or *(b)* is satisfied,

then a designated officer may apply to a judge of the District Court for an order providing for each of the matters referred to in *subsections (3)* and *(4)*, other than those relating to the conferral or removal of the power of execution, and, on the making of such an application, the judge of the District Court may make such an order accordingly and *subsections (3)* and *(4)* shall apply for that purpose with any necessary modifications.

(6) For the purpose of *subsection (5)*, *subsection (2)(a)* shall apply as if for "(including any designated officer who is named therein by reason of any prior application under this subsection)" there were substituted "(including any designated officer who is named therein by reason of any prior application under this subsection or *subsection (5)*)".

(7) An application under *subsection (2)* or *(5)* may, if a judge of the District Court directs, be heard otherwise than in public.

790 Restriction on disclosure of information, books or documents

(1) No information, book or document relating to a company that has been obtained under any of *sections 778* to *780*, *783* or *787* shall be published or disclosed unless—

(a) the company consents to the publication or disclosure,

(b) the publication or disclosure is, in the opinion of the Director, required under any of *section 791(a)* to *(n)*, or

(c) the publication or disclosure is made to a competent authority specified in *section 792*.

(2) A person who publishes or discloses any information, book or document in contravention of *subsection (1)* shall be guilty of a category 2 offence.

791 Information, books or documents may be disclosed for certain purposes

Any information, book or document relating to a company (the "company") that has been obtained under any of *sections 778* to *780*, *783* or *787* may be published or disclosed without the consent of the company if, in the opinion of the Director, publication or disclosure is required—

(a) with a view to the investigation or prosecution of any offence under—

(i) this Act;

(ii) the Central Bank Acts 1942 to 2010;

(iii) the Exchange Control Acts 1954 to 1990;

(iv) the Insurance Acts 1909 to 2000;

(v) the Taxes Consolidation Act 1997 or an offence under an enactment referred to in section 1078(1) of that Act; or

(vi) regulations relating to insurance made under the European Communities Act 1972;

(b) with a view to the investigation or prosecution of any offence entailing misconduct in connection with the management of the company's affairs or the misapplication or wrongful retainer of its property;

(c) for the purpose of—

(i) assessing the liability of a person in respect of a tax or duty or other payment owed or payable to—

(I) the State;

(II) a local authority and, where the context so requires, a joint body (within the meaning of the Local Government Act 2001); or

(III) the Health Services Executive;

or

(ii) collecting an amount due in respect of such tax or duty or other payment;

(d) for the purpose of the performance by a tribunal (to which the Tribunals of Inquiry (Evidence) Acts 1921 to 2004 apply) of any of its functions;

(e) for the purpose of the performance by a commission established under the Commissions of Investigation Act 2004 of any of its functions;

(f) for the purpose of assisting or facilitating the performance by any Minister of the Government of any of his or her functions;

(g) for the purpose of assisting or facilitating the performance by any accountancy or other professional organisation of its disciplinary functions with respect to any of its members;

(h) for the purpose of the performance by the Irish Takeover Panel or any authorised market operator established in the State of any of its functions in relation to the company or any other person who, in its opinion, is connected with the company;

(i) for the purpose of the performance by the Competition Authority of any of its functions;

(j) for the purpose of the performance by a committee (being a committee within the meaning of the Committees of the Houses of the Oireachtas (Compellability, Privileges and Immunities of Witnesses) Act 1997 as amended, to which sections 3 to 14 and 16 of that Act apply) of any of its functions;

(k) for the purpose of complying with the requirements of procedural fairness, to be made to—

  (i) any company in relation to which an inspector has been appointed under *section 763* or *764*;

  (ii) any person required by the Director to give any information under *section 767*;

  (iii) any company to which the Director has given a direction under *section 778*; or

  (iv) any person named in a report or other document prepared by the Director, in the ordinary course of administration, in consequence of the exercise of powers under *section 767* or *778*;

(l) for the purpose of complying with any requirement, or exercising any power, imposed or conferred by this Part with respect to reports made by inspectors who have been appointed, under this Part or that section, by the court or by the Director;

(m) with a view to the institution by the Director of proceedings for the winding up under this Act of the company or otherwise for the purposes of proceedings instituted by him or her for that purpose; or

(n) for the purpose of proceedings under *section 787* or *842*.

792 Information, books or documents may be disclosed to competent authority

(1) Any information, book or document relating to a company that has been obtained under any of *sections 778* to *780*, *783* or *787* may be disclosed to a competent authority without the consent of the company.

(2) For the purposes of *subsection (1)*, a competent authority includes—

(a) the Minister;

(b) a person authorised by the Minister;

(c) an inspector appointed under this Act;

(d) the Registrar;

(e) the Minister for Finance;

(f) an officer authorised by the Minister for Finance;

(g) the Revenue Commissioners;

(h) the Supervisory Authority;

(i) any court of competent jurisdiction;

(j) a supervisory authority within the meaning of regulations relating to insurance made under the European Communities Act 1972;

(k) the Central Bank; or

(l) any authority established outside the State in which there are vested—

(i) functions of investigating or prosecuting an offence similar to an offence referred to in *section 791(a)* or *(b)*;

(ii) functions of assessing the liability of a person in respect of a tax or duty or other payment owed or payable to the state in which it is established or any other authority established in that state;

(iii) functions of collecting an amount due in respect of a tax or duty or other payment referred to in *subparagraph (ii)*; or

(iv) functions that are similar to the functions referred to in any of *section 791(d)* to *(h)*.

793 Offence of falsifying, concealing, destroying or otherwise disposing of document or record

(1) A person shall be guilty of a category 2 offence who—

(a) knows or suspects that—

(i) an investigation by the Director into an offence under this Act is being or is likely to be carried out; and

(ii) a document or record is or would be relevant to the investigation;

and

(b) either—

(i) falsifies, conceals, destroys or otherwise disposes of that document or record; or

(ii) causes or permits the falsification, concealment, destruction or other disposal of that document or record.

(2) Subject to *subsection (3)*, where a person falsifies, conceals, destroys or otherwise disposes of a document or record, or causes or permits its falsification, concealment, destruction or other disposal, in such circumstances that it is reasonable to conclude that the person knew or suspected that—

(a) an investigation by the Director into an offence under this Act was being or was likely to be carried out; and

(b) a document or record was or would be relevant to the investigation;

that person shall be taken for the purposes of this section to have so known or suspected.

(3) *Subsection (2)* does not apply if the court or the jury, as the case may be, is satisfied, having regard to all the evidence, that there is reasonable doubt as to whether the person so knew or suspected.

794 Production and inspection of books or documents when offence suspected

(1) This section applies if, on an application to the District Court by a person specified in *subsection (3)*, there is shown to be reasonable cause to believe that—

(a) a person has, while an officer of a company, committed an offence in connection with the management of the company's affairs; and

(b) evidence of the commission of the offence is to be found in—

(i) any books or documents of or under the control of the company; or

(ii) any documents of a person carrying on the business of banking in so far as they relate to the company's affairs.

(2) In any case to which this section applies, the District Court may make an order—

(a) authorising any person named in the order to inspect the books or documents referred to in *subsection (1)(b)(i)* or *(ii)*, as the case may be, or any of them for the purpose of investigating and obtaining evidence of the offence; or

(b) in the case of books or documents referred to in *subsection (1)(b)(i)*, requiring the secretary of the company or any other officer of the company who is named in the order to produce the books or documents or any of them to a person named in the order at the place named in the order.

(3) The District Court may make the order only on the application of—

(a) the Director of Public Prosecutions;

(b) the Director; or

(c) a Superintendent of the Garda Síochána.

795 Saving for privileged information

(1) In this section—

"computer" has the same meaning as it has in *section 787*;

"customer", in relation to a person carrying on the business of banking, includes a person who has in the past availed himself or herself of one or more of the services of the person, as defined in section 149(12) of the Consumer Credit Act 1995;

"information" means information contained in a document, a computer or otherwise;

"privileged legal material" means information which, in the opinion of the court, a person is entitled to refuse to produce on the grounds of legal professional privilege.

(2) Subject to *subsection (3)*, nothing in this Part shall compel the disclosure by any person of privileged legal material or authorise the taking of privileged legal material.

(3) The disclosure of information may be compelled, or possession of it taken, pursuant to the powers in this Part, notwithstanding that it is apprehended that the information is privileged legal material provided the compelling of its disclosure or the taking of its possession is done by means whereby the confidentiality of the information can be maintained (as against the person compelling such disclosure or

taking such possession) pending the determination by the court of the issue as to whether the information is privileged legal material.

(4) Without prejudice to *subsection (5)*, where, in the circumstances referred to in *subsection (3)*, information has been disclosed or taken possession of pursuant to the powers in this Part, the person—

(a) to whom such information has been so disclosed, or

(b) who has taken possession of it,

shall (unless the person has, within the period subsequently mentioned in this subsection, been served with notice of an application under *subsection (5)* in relation to the matter concerned) apply to the court for a determination as to whether the information is privileged legal material and an application under this subsection shall be made within 7 days after the date of disclosure or the taking of possession.

(5) A person who, in the circumstances referred to in *subsection (3)*, is compelled to disclose information, or from whose possession information is taken, pursuant to the powers in this Part, may apply to the court for a determination as to whether the information is privileged legal material.

(6) Pending the making of a final determination of an application under *subsection (4)* or *(5)*, the court may give such interim or interlocutory directions as the court considers appropriate including, without prejudice to the generality of the foregoing, directions as to—

(a) the preservation of the information, in whole or in part, in a safe and secure place in any manner specified by the court,

(b) the appointment of a person with suitable legal qualifications possessing the level of experience, and the independence from any interest falling to be determined between the parties concerned, that the court considers to be appropriate for the purpose of—

(i) examining the information, and

(ii) preparing a report for the court with a view to assisting or facilitating the court in the making by the court of its determination as to whether the information is privileged legal material.

(7) An application under *subsection (4)*, *(5)* or *(6)* shall be by motion and may, if the court directs, be heard otherwise than in public.

(8) The Director shall not, under any of *sections 778* to *780*, require the production, by a person carrying on the business of banking, of a book or document relating to the affairs of a customer, or relating to the affairs of any other person, unless either—

(a) the Director considers it necessary to do so for the purposes of investigating the affairs of the person carrying on the business of banking, or

(b) the customer or other person is a person on whom a requirement has been imposed by virtue of that section.

(9) The publication, in pursuance of any provision of this Chapter, of any report, information, book or document shall be privileged.

796 Assistance to company law authority

(1) The Director may exercise the powers conferred on him or her by this Part for the purpose of assisting a company law authority if—

(a) the Director has received a request from that company law authority for assistance in connection with inquiries being carried out by it or on its behalf, and

(b) the Director is satisfied that such assistance is for the purpose of the discharge by the authority of its supervisory or regulatory functions.

(2) The Director may decline to accede to a request referred to in *subsection (1)* if—

(a) the Director considers that it is not appropriate to give assistance, or

(b) the company law authority making the request does not undertake to make such contribution to the costs attendant on the request as the Director considers appropriate.

(3) In this section, "company law authority" means—

(a) an authority outside the State that performs functions of a supervisory or regulatory nature in relation to bodies corporate or undertakings or their officers; or

(b) a person acting on behalf of such an authority.

PART 14
COMPLIANCE AND ENFORCEMENT

Chapter 1
Compliance and protective orders

797 Court may order compliance by company or officer

(1) This section applies if a company or an officer of a company—

(a) has failed to comply with a provision of this Act, and

(b) the company or officer has failed to remedy the default within 14 days (or such longer period as may be specified in the notice) after the date of service by any person referred to in *subsection (3)* on the company or officer of a notice requiring the company or officer to remedy the default.

(2) In any case to which this section applies, the court, on the application of a person specified in *subsection (3)*, may order the company or officer in default to remedy the default within such time as the court specifies.

(3) The court may make the order only on the application of one of the following:

(a) any member of the company;

(b) any creditor of the company;

(c) the Director; or

(d) the Registrar.

(4) In making an order under *subsection (2)*, the court may order that the company or the officers responsible for the default pay all costs of and incidental to the application.

(5) Subject to *subsection (6)*, no order may be made under this section in relation to a default that, in the opinion of the court, constitutes a wrong done to the company an action in respect of which, under the general law, is maintainable by the company alone, as distinct from another by derivative proceedings.

(6) *Subsection (5)* does not apply if the facts constituting the default in question amount, in the opinion of the court, to the commission of an offence.

(7) Nothing in this section shall be taken to prejudice the operation of any enactment imposing penalties (including restriction under *Chapter 3* of this Part and disqualification under *Chapter 4* of this Part) on a company or its officers in respect of the default in question.

(8) In this section, "officer" means director, shadow director, promoter, receiver, liquidator, statutory auditor or secretary.

798 Court may restrain directors and others from removing assets

(1) The court may make an order restraining a director or other officer of a company, or a company, from—

(a) removing his or her or the company's assets from the State, or

(b) reducing his or her or the company's assets within or outside the State below an amount specified in the order.

(2) The court may make the order if it is satisfied that—

(a) the applicant has a qualifying claim, and

(b) there are grounds for believing that the director or officer, or the company, may remove or dispose of his or her assets or the assets of the company with a view to evading his or her obligations or those of the company and frustrating an order of the court.

(3) The court may make the order only on the application of—

(a) the company,

(b) a director, member, liquidator, receiver or creditor of the company, or

(c) the Director.

(4) In *subsection (2)(a)*, "qualifying claim" means a claim that—

(a) is a substantive civil cause of action or right to seek a declaration of personal liability or to claim damages against the director, officer or company, and

(b) arises—

(i) under this Act, or

(ii) under the constitution of the company, or

(iii) from the holding of an office of the company.

Chapter 2
Disclosure orders

799 Interpretation (*Chapter 2*)

(1) In this Chapter—

"disclosure order" means an order under *section 800*;

"share acquisition agreement" has the meaning given to it by *section 808*.

(2) Any reference in this Chapter to share capital or relevant share capital in relation to a company is a reference to share capital that confers the right to vote in all circumstances at a general meeting of that company, and a reference to share shall be read accordingly.

800 Court may make disclosure order

(1) On the application of—

(a) any person who has a financial interest in a company, or

(b) the Director,

the court may make an order specified in *section 801* in respect of all or any of the shares in or debentures of the company.

(2) An application under this section shall be supported by such evidence as the court may require.

(3) The court may make a disclosure order only if the court considers that—

(a) it is just and equitable to do so, and

(b) in the case of an application made other than by the Director, the financial interest of the applicant is or will be prejudiced by the non-disclosure of any interest in the shares in or debentures of the company.

(4) The court may, before hearing an application under this section, require the applicant to give security for the payment of the costs of hearing the application or any consequential proceedings.

(5) If an application is made under this section by the Director then there are not available to the Director—

(a) the powers under *section 764(1)* as regards appointing one or more competent inspectors to investigate and report on any matter in so far as such investigation and reporting would relate to the same shares or debentures of the company in question, or

(b) the powers under *section 767* to require information as to persons interested in shares or debentures, being the same shares or debentures of the company in question,

as the application under this section relates to.

(6) *Section 809* confers additional powers on the court for the purposes of ensuring that disclosure of the information sought, in cases of share acquisition agreements, is achieved.

(7) For the purposes of this section, "financial interest" includes any interest as member, contributory, creditor, employee, co-adventurer, examiner, lessor, lessee, licensor, licensee, liquidator or receiver either in relation to the company in respect of whose shares or debentures the disclosure order is sought or a related company.

801 Types of disclosure order

The court may make an order under *section 800(1)*—

(a) requiring any person whom the court believes has or is able to obtain all or any of the following information to disclose to the court so much of that information that the person has or is able to obtain:

(i) the names and addresses of persons currently interested, or interested at any time during a period specified in the order, in the shares in or debentures of a company; and

(ii) the name and address of any person who acts or has acted on behalf of any of those persons in relation to the shares or debentures;

(b) requiring any person whom the court believes to be currently interested, or to have been interested at any time during a period specified in the order, in the shares in or debentures of a company—

(i) to confirm or deny that that is the case, and

(ii) if confirming, to disclose such further information as the court may require,

or

(c) requiring a person interested in the shares in or debentures of a company specified in the order to disclose in respect of those shares or debentures to the court—

(i) the information required in *paragraph (a)(i)* to *(ii)*, and

(ii) such further information as the court may require.

802 Procedure on application for disclosure order

(1) A person intending to apply for a disclosure order shall give not less than 10 days' notice of the intention to apply to—

(a) the company in respect of whose shares or debentures the order is sought, and

(b) the person to whom the order is to be directed.

(2) If, on that application, it is intended also to apply for an order under *section 809*, not less than 10 days' notice of the intention to apply for such an order shall be given by the applicant to the person to whom that order is to be directed.

(3) Without prejudice to *subsection (2)*, the applicant shall also serve on any person specified by the court such notice of the application as the court may direct.

(4) On the hearing of the application every person notified under *subsection (1)*, *(2)* or *(3)* may appear and adduce evidence.

803 Scope of disclosure order

(1) A disclosure order may require the person to whom it is addressed—

(a) to give particulars of that person's own past or present interest in shares comprised in the share capital of the company or in debentures of the company held by that person at any time during the period specified in the order,

(b) where that person's interest is a present interest and any other interest in the shares or debentures subsists, to give such particulars of that other interest that are—

(i) required by the order, and

(ii) within that person's knowledge,

(c) where another interest in the shares or debentures subsisted at any time during the period specified in the order when the person's own interest subsisted, to give such particulars of that other interest that are—

(i) required by the order, and

(ii) within that person's knowledge,

(d) where that person's interest is a past interest, to give those particulars, that are within his or her knowledge, of the person who held that interest immediately after him or her.

(2) A disclosure order shall specify the information to be given to the court under the order in respect of any person, shares or debentures to which it refers and such information shall be given in writing.

(3) *Section 807* supplements *subsection (2)* as regards particular information to be given in cases of share acquisition agreements.

(4) For the purposes of this section, and without prejudice to *sections 804* to *808*, an interest in shares in or debentures of a company includes a present or past right, or entitlement to acquire a right, to subscribe for shares or debentures if, on the basis that those shares or debentures would be, or (as the case may be) would have been, comprised in the share capital of the company or issued by it, as the case may be.

804 Interests in shares and debentures for purposes of *section 803*: general

(1) Without prejudice to the subsequent provisions of this Chapter, this section applies to the construction, for the purposes of—

(a) *section 803*, and

(b) the subsequent sections of this Chapter as they relate to any spouse, minor child, body corporate or a party to an agreement,

(in this section referred to, respectively, as the "relevant purposes" and the "relevant sections") of references to—

(i) a person's being interested in shares or debentures, or

(ii) an interest in shares or debentures.

(2) For the relevant purposes, a reference to an interest in shares or debentures in the relevant sections is to be read as including an interest of any kind whatsoever in the shares or debentures.

(3) Accordingly there are to be disregarded any restraints or restrictions to which the exercise of any right attached to the interest is or may be subject.

(4) Where property is held on trust and an interest in shares or debentures is comprised in the property, a beneficiary of the trust who, apart from this subsection, does not have an interest in the shares or debentures, as appropriate, is to be taken, for the relevant purposes, as having such an interest; but this subsection is without prejudice to the following provisions of this section.

(5) A person is taken, for the relevant purposes, to have an interest in shares or debentures if—

(a) the person enters into a contract for their purchase by him or her (whether for cash or other consideration), or

(b) in the case of shares, not being the registered holder of the shares, the person is entitled to exercise any right conferred by the holding of the shares or is entitled to control the exercise of any such right.

(6) For the purposes of *subsection (5) (b)*, a person is entitled to exercise or control the exercise of any right conferred by the holding of shares if the person—

(a) has a right (whether subject to conditions or not) the exercise of which would make him or her so entitled, or

(b) is under an obligation (whether so subject or not) the fulfilment of which would make him or her so entitled.

(7) For the relevant purposes, a person is taken to have an interest in shares or debentures if, otherwise than by virtue of having an interest under a trust, the person has a right to acquire an interest in shares or debentures, as appropriate, or is under an obligation to take an interest in shares or debentures, as appropriate, whether in any case the right or obligation is conditional or absolute.

(8) Without prejudice to *subsections (2)* and *(3)*, rights or obligations to subscribe for any shares shall not be taken for the purposes of *subsection (7)* to be rights to acquire, or obligations to take, any interest in shares.

(9) Where persons have a joint interest, each of them shall be taken, for the relevant purposes, to have that interest.

805 Family and corporate interests

(1) For the purposes of *section 803*, a person is taken to be interested in any shares or debentures in which the person's spouse or civil partner or any child (who is a minor) of the person is interested.

(2) For the purposes of *section 803* and *subsection (1)*, a person is taken to be interested in shares or debentures if a body corporate is interested in them and—

(a) that body or its directors are accustomed to act in accordance with his or her directions or instructions, or

(b) he or she is entitled to exercise or control the exercise of one-third or more of the voting power at general meetings of that body corporate.

(3) Where a person is entitled to exercise or control the exercise of one-third or more of the voting power at general meetings of a body corporate and that body corporate is entitled to exercise or control the exercise of any of the voting power at general meetings of another body corporate (the "effective voting power") then, for the purposes of *subsection (2)(b)*, the effective voting power is taken as exercisable by that person.

(4) For the purposes of *subsections (2)* and *(3)* a person is entitled to exercise or control the exercise of voting power if—

(a) the person has a right (whether subject to conditions or not) the exercise of which would make him or her so entitled, or

(b) the person is under an obligation (whether or not so subject) the fulfilment of which would make him or her so entitled.

(5) A reference in this section to a child of a person shall be deemed to include a reference to a child of the person's civil partner who is ordinarily resident with the person and the civil partner.

806 Share acquisition agreements — attribution of interests held by other parties

(1) In the case of a share acquisition agreement, each party to the agreement shall be taken, for the purposes of *section 803*, to be interested in all shares in the company in which any other party to it is interested apart from the agreement (whether or not the interest of the other party in question was acquired, or includes any interest which was acquired, in pursuance of the agreement).

(2) For those purposes, an interest of a party to such an agreement in shares in the company is an interest apart from the agreement if the party is interested in those shares otherwise than by virtue of the application of this section and *section 808* in relation to the agreement.

(3) Accordingly, any such interest of the person (apart from the agreement) includes for those purposes any interest treated as his or hers—

(a) under the preceding provisions of this Chapter, or

(b) by the application of this section (and *section 808*) in relation to any other agreement with respect to shares in the company to which he or she is a party.

807 Particulars of interests referred to in *section 806* to be given in compliance with disclosure order

In addition to the particulars (if any) to be given otherwise by the person in compliance with such order, the particulars given, in compliance with a disclosure order, with respect to his or her interest in shares in the company by a person who is, or (as the case may be) was at any time in the period specified in the order, a party to a share acquisition agreement shall—

(a) state that the person is or (as the case may be) was at a particular time a party to such an agreement,

(b) include the names and (so far as known to him or her) the addresses of the other persons who are or (as the case may be) were at a particular time parties to the agreement, identifying them as such, and

(c) state whether or not any of the shares to which the particulars given in compliance with the disclosure order relate are shares in which he or she is or (as the case may be) was interested by virtue of *sections 806* and *808* and, if so, the number of those shares.

808 "Share acquisition agreement" — meaning

(1) Subject to the following provisions of this section, "share acquisition agreement", for the purposes of this Chapter, means an agreement between 2 or more persons which includes provision for the acquisition by any one or more of the parties to the agreement of interests in shares comprised in the share capital of the company concerned but only if the following 2 conditions are satisfied.

(2) Those conditions are—

(a) the agreement also includes provisions imposing obligations or restrictions on any one or more of the parties to the agreement with respect to their use, retention or disposal of interests in that company's shares acquired in pursuance of the agreement (whether or not together with any other interests of theirs in that company's shares to which the agreement relates), and

(b) any interest in the company's shares is in fact acquired by any of the parties in pursuance of the agreement.

(3) The reference in *subsection (2)(a)* to the use of interests in shares in the company is to the exercise of any rights or of any control or influence arising from those interests (including the right to enter into any agreement for the exercise, or for control of the exercise, of any of those rights by another person).

(4) Once any interest in shares in the company has been acquired in pursuance of such an agreement as is mentioned in *subsection (1)*, the agreement continues to be a share acquisition agreement for the purposes of this Chapter irrespective of—

(a) whether or not any further acquisitions of interests in the company's shares take place in pursuance of the agreement, and

(b) any change in the persons who are for the time being parties to it, and

(c) any variation of the agreement, so long as the agreement continues to include provisions of any description mentioned in *subsection (2)(a)*.

(5) References in *subsection (4)* to the agreement include any agreement having effect (whether directly or indirectly) in substitution for the original agreement.

(6) In this section, and also in references elsewhere in this Chapter to a share acquisition agreement as defined by this section, "agreement" includes any agreement or arrangement; and references in this section to provisions of an agreement—

(a) accordingly include undertakings, expectations or understandings operative under any arrangement, and

(b) (without prejudice to the foregoing) also include any provisions, whether express or implied and whether absolute or not.

(7) An agreement which is not legally binding is not a share acquisition agreement for the purposes of this Chapter unless it involves mutuality in the undertakings, expectations or understandings of the parties to it.

809 Supplemental power of court in relation to a share acquisition agreement

(1) The court has the following power if—

(a) on the making of an application for a disclosure order, or

(b) at any time subsequent to the making of such an order (on application to the court in that behalf),

it has grounds to believe that all of the information sought to be obtained by the disclosure order will not, or may not, be obtained by reason of a person who is both—

(i) a party or former party to a share acquisition agreement, and

(ii) the person against whom the order is sought to be, or has been, made, appearing not to be in possession of all the facts relevant to the application of *section 806* as it applies, or applied, to that agreement.

(2) That power of the court is to make an order requiring any other party or former party to the share acquisition agreement to give, in writing, to the court such particulars as the court specifies, and which the party or former party is able to give, in relation to matters affecting the application of *section 806* as it applies, or applied, to that agreement and, in particular, the party's or former party's interests in shares in the company that are or were the subject of attribution to another party to that agreement by virtue of that application.

(3) An application under *subsection (1)(b)* may be made by a person having a financial interest (within the meaning of *section 800*) in the company or by the Director.

(4) A person intending to make an application under *subsection (1)(b)* shall give not less than 10 days' notice of the intention to apply to—

(a) the company in respect of whose shares the order is sought, and

(b) the person to whom the order is to be directed.

(5) An applicant under *subsection (1)(b)* shall also serve on any person specified by the court such notice of the application as the court may direct.

(6) On the hearing of an application under *subsection (1)(b)* every person notified under *subsection (4)* or *(5)* may appear and adduce evidence.

810 Court may grant exemption from requirements of disclosure order

(1) The court may, in making a disclosure order, include an exemption for any of the following persons or interests from all or part of the requirements of a disclosure order:

(a) any person, group or class of persons;

(b) any interest or class of interest in shares or debentures;

(c) any shares or group or class of shares;

(d) any debentures or group or class of debentures.

(2) The court may grant such an exemption only if it considers that—

(a) it would be just and equitable to do so, and

(b) the financial interest of the applicant for the disclosure order would not be prejudiced by the grant of the exemption.

811 Other powers of court in relation to disclosure orders

(1) The court may, on cause shown, discharge or vary a disclosure order.

(2) A disclosure order may specify a person, group or class of persons to which the order applies.

(3) Where the court makes a disclosure order, it may impose, for a specified period of time, such conditions or restrictions as it thinks fit on the rights or obligations attaching to the shares or debentures that are the subject of the order.

(4) Any person whose interests are affected by any conditions or restrictions imposed on shares or debentures under *subsection (3)* may apply to the court for relief from all or any of those conditions or restrictions, and the court may, if it considers it just and equitable to do so, grant such relief, in whole or in part, and on such terms and conditions (if any) as it sees fit.

812 Notice of disclosure order

(1) The applicant for a disclosure order shall ensure that a notice in the prescribed form of the making of the disclosure order is sent, with a copy of the order, to the following:

(a) the company (at its registered office) whose shares or debentures are the subject of the order;

(b) the Registrar;

(c) the registered holder of any of the shares or debentures that are the subject of the order where it appears to the court that that person—

(i) is not resident in the State at the date of the making of the order, and

(ii) should be notified;

and

(d) any other person as the court sees fit.

(2) The notice shall be sent—

(a) by registered post, and

(b) within 7 days after the date of the making of the order.

(3) The applicant shall ensure that notice of the making of the disclosure order is published in *Iris Oifigiúil* within 7 days after the date of the making of the order.

(4) For the purposes of *subsection (1)(c)*—

(a) the address of a registered holder of shares or debentures who is not resident in the State shall be deemed to be the address of that holder that was last delivered to the Registrar or otherwise published, as the case may be, in accordance with this Act before the date of making the order, or

(b) if no address of the non-resident registered holder has ever been duly delivered to the Registrar or otherwise so published, the requirements of *subsection (1)(c)* are complied with by sending the notice and copy of the order to the Registrar.

813 Information disclosed under order

(1) A person who is the subject of a disclosure order shall provide the information in a written notice.

(2) The notice shall identify the person providing the information and give that person's current address, and that person does not comply with the disclosure order if the requirement with respect to the person's identity and current address is not met.

(3) Where information is given to the court in compliance with a disclosure order, a prescribed officer of the court shall ensure that the information is provided to the applicant and the company unless the court directs otherwise (which may include a direction that only part of the information shall be provided).

(4) In making a direction under *subsection (3)*, the court shall have regard to whether the requirements of *section 812* have been met.

814 Court may impose restrictions on publication of information provided

Where any information is provided to the applicant or the company under *section 813(3)*, the court may impose such restrictions as it sees fit as to the publication of the information by the person to whom it has been provided.

815 Right or interest in shares or debentures unenforceable by person in default

(1) A person who is the subject of a disclosure order shall not be entitled to enforce any right or interest of any kind whatsoever in respect of any shares in or debentures of the company concerned held by that person if that person—

(a) fails to comply with the order within the period specified in the order, or

(b) in purported compliance with the order makes a statement to the court that is false knowing it to be false or being reckless as to whether it is false.

(2) In *subsection (1)*, "enforce" means enforce by action or legal proceeding, whether directly or indirectly.

816 Court may grant relief from restriction on enforceability of right or interest in shares or debentures

(1) Subject to *subsections (2)* and *(5)*, where any right or interest is restricted under *section 815*, the court, on the application of a person specified in *subsection (3)*, may grant relief from that restriction.

(2) The court may grant relief if it is satisfied that—

(a) the default was accidental or due to inadvertence or some other sufficient cause, or

(b) on other grounds it is just and equitable to do so.

(3) The court may grant relief on the application of—

(a) the person in default, or

(b) any other person affected by the restriction.

(4) The court may grant relief—

(a) generally,

(b) in relation to a particular right or interest, or

(c) subject to such terms and conditions as it sees fit.

(5) The court may not grant relief on the application of the person in default if it appears that the default has arisen as a result of a deliberate act or omission on the part of that person.

817 Dealing by agent in shares or debentures subject to disclosure order

(1) This section applies where a person (the "principal") authorises another person (the "agent") to acquire or dispose of, on the principal's behalf, interests in shares (the "shares") comprised in the share capital of a company, or in debentures (the "debentures") of the company, in respect of which a disclosure order is made.

(2) For the duration of the disclosure order, the principal shall ensure that the agent notifies the principal immediately of acquisitions or disposals of the shares or debentures effected by the agent that will or may give rise to any obligation under the order on the part of the principal to provide information in respect of the principal's interest in the shares or debentures.

Chapter 3
Restrictions on directors of insolvent companies

818 Interpretation and application (*Chapter 3*)

(1) In this Chapter—

"company", in the context of a provision that imposes a restriction on a company by reference to the fact of its having a restricted person (within the meaning of *section 826*) or otherwise makes provision in consequence of that fact, means any company referred to in *section 819(6)*;

"director of an insolvent company" means a person who was a director or shadow director of an insolvent company at the date of, or within 12 months before, the commencement of its winding up;

"insolvent company" means a company that is unable to pay its debts;

"restricted person" means a person who is subject to a restriction under a declaration made under *section 819(1)* that is in force.

(2) For the purposes of the definition of "insolvent company" in *subsection (1)*, a company is unable to pay its debts if—

(a) at the date of the commencement of its winding up it is proved to the court that it is unable to pay its debts (within the meaning of *section 570*), or

(b) at any time during the course of its winding up the liquidator certifies, or it is proved to the court, that it is unable to pay its debts (within the meaning of *section 570*).

(3) For the purpose of a restriction imposed pursuant to this Part on a person's acting as a director of a company, that restriction shall, in the case of a person who continues in office as a director of a company on the restriction taking effect (and the requirements set out in *section 819(3)* are not met in respect of the company), be deemed, without proof of anything more, to have been contravened.

(4) This Chapter shall not apply to a company that commenced to be wound up before 1 August 1991.

819 Declaration by court restricting director of insolvent company in being appointed or acting as director etc.

(1) On the application of a person referred to in *section 820(1)* and subject to *subsection (2)*, the court shall declare that a person who was a director of an insolvent company shall not, for a period of 5 years, be appointed or act in any way, directly or indirectly, as a director or secretary of a company, or be concerned in or take part in the formation or promotion of a company, unless the company meets the requirements set out in *subsection (3)*.

(2) The court shall make a declaration under *subsection (1)* unless it is satisfied that—

(a) the person concerned has acted honestly and responsibly in relation to the conduct of the affairs of the company in question, whether before or after it became an insolvent company,

(b) he or she has, when requested to do so by the liquidator of the insolvent company, cooperated as far as could reasonably be expected in relation to the conduct of the winding up of the insolvent company, and

(c) there is no other reason why it would be just and equitable that he or she should be subject to the restrictions imposed by an order under *subsection (1)*.

(3) The requirements referred to in *subsection (1)* are—

(a) the company shall have an allotted share capital of nominal value not less than—

(i) €500,000 in the case of a public limited company (other than an investment company) or a public unlimited company, or

(ii) €100,000 in the case of any other company,

(b) each allotted share shall be paid up to an aggregate amount not less than the amount referred to in *paragraph (a)*, including the whole of any premium on that share, and

(c) each allotted share and the whole of any premium on each allotted share shall be paid for in cash.

(4) In the application of *subsection (3)* to a company limited by guarantee, *paragraphs (a)* to *(c)* of it shall be disregarded and, instead, that subsection shall be read as if it set out both of the following requirements:

(a) that the company's memorandum of association specifies that the amount of the contribution on the part of the member of it, or at least one member of it, being the contribution undertaken to be made by the member as mentioned in *section 1176(2)(d)*, is not less than €100,000;

(b) that the member whose foregoing contribution is to be not less than that amount is an individual, as distinct from a body corporate.

(5) In the application of *subsection (3)* to an investment company, *paragraphs (a)* to *(c)* of it shall be disregarded and, instead, that subsection shall be read as if it set out both of the following requirements—

(a) that the value of the issued share capital of the company is not less than €100,000,

(b) that an amount of not less than €100,000 in cash has been paid in consideration for the allotment of shares in the company.

(6) Where *subsection (1)* refers to being appointed or acting as a director or secretary of a company, or taking part in the formation or promotion of a company, "company" means any of the following:

(a) a private company limited by shares;

(b) a designated activity company;

(c) a public limited company;

(d) a company limited by guarantee;

(e) an unlimited company;

(f) an unregistered company.

(7) A prescribed officer of the court shall ensure that the prescribed particulars of a declaration under this section are provided to the Registrar in the prescribed form and manner (if any).

820 Application for declaration of restriction

(1) An application for a declaration under *section 819(1)* may be made by—

(a) the Director,

(b) the liquidator of the insolvent company, or

(c) a receiver of the property of the company.

(2) The court may order that the person who is the subject of the declaration shall pay—

(a) the costs of the application, and

(b) the whole (or so much of them as the court specifies) of the costs and expenses incurred by the applicant—

(i) in investigating the matters that are the subject of the application, and

(ii) in so far as they do not fall within *paragraph (a)*, in collecting evidence in respect of those matters,

including so much of the remuneration and expenses of the applicant as are attributable to such investigation and collection.

821 Liquidator shall inform court of jeopardy to other company or its creditors

(1) This section applies if the liquidator of an insolvent company is of the opinion that—

(a) a restricted person is appointed or is acting in any way, whether directly or indirectly, as a director of, or is concerned or taking part in the formation or promotion of, another company, and

(b) the interests of that other company or its creditors may be jeopardised by the matters referred to in *paragraph (a)*.

(2) In any case to which this section applies—

(a) the liquidator shall inform the court of his or her opinion as soon as practicable, and

(b) the court, on being so informed by the liquidator, shall make whatever order it sees fit.

(3) A liquidator who, without reasonable excuse, fails to comply with *subsection (2)(a)* shall be guilty of a category 3 offence.

(4) In this section "company" means any company referred to in *section 819(6)*.

822 Court may grant restricted person relief from restrictions

(1) On the application of a restricted person, the court may, if it deems it just and equitable to do so, grant that person relief, either in whole or in part, from—

(a) any restriction under a declaration made under *section 819(1)*, or

(b) an order made under *section 821(2)(b)*.

(2) Such relief may, if the court considers it appropriate, be granted on such terms and conditions as it sees fit.

(3) A person who intends applying for relief under *subsection (1)* shall give not less than 14 days' notice in writing of his or her intention to apply to—

(a) the Director, and

(b) the liquidator of the company the insolvency of which gave rise to the application for the declaration made in respect of him or her under *section 819(1)*.

(4) On receipt of a notice under *subsection (3)*, the liquidator shall as soon as practicable notify such creditors and contributories of the company as have been notified to the liquidator or become known to the liquidator.

(5) On the hearing of an application under this section, the Director, the liquidator, or any creditor or contributory of the company may appear and give evidence.

(6) A liquidator who fails to comply with *subsection (4)* shall be guilty of a category 3 offence.

823 Register of restricted persons

(1) The Registrar shall, subject to the provisions of this section, keep a register of the particulars notified to him or her under *section 819(7)*.

(2) Where the court grants partial relief to a restricted person under *section 822(1)*—

(a) a prescribed officer of the court shall ensure that the prescribed particulars of the relief are provided to the Registrar, and

(b) the Registrar shall as soon as practicable enter those particulars on the register.

(3) Where the court grants full relief to a restricted person under *section 822(1)*—

(a) a prescribed officer of the court shall ensure that the Registrar is notified, and

(b) the Registrar shall as soon as practicable remove the particulars of that person from the register.

(4) The Registrar shall remove from the register any particulars of a restricted person on the expiry of 5 years after the date of the declaration made in respect of that person under *section 819(1)*.

(5) Nothing in this section shall prevent the Registrar from keeping the register required under this section as part of any other system of classification, whether under [*section 895*][a] or otherwise.

Amendments

a Words substituted by C(A)A 2017, s 98(i) (previously: "*section 894*").

824 Application of this Chapter to receivers

(1) Where a receiver of the property of a company is appointed, the provisions of this Chapter shall, with the modification referred to in *subsection (2)* and any other necessary modifications, apply as if references in this Chapter to the liquidator and to winding up were references to the receiver and to receivership.

(2) The modification mentioned in *subsection (1)* is that in the definition of "director of an insolvent company" in *section 818(1)* the words "director or shadow director of an insolvent company at the date of, or within 12 months before, the appointment of a receiver to the property of the company" shall be substituted for the words "director or shadow director of an insolvent company at the date of, or within 12 months before, the date of the commencement of its winding up".

825 Restricted person shall give notice to company before accepting appointment or acting as director or secretary

(1) A restricted person shall not be appointed or act in any way, whether directly or indirectly, as a director or secretary of a company unless he or she has given the company notice in writing in accordance with *subsection (2)* that he or she is a restricted person.

(2) The restricted person shall send the notice to the registered office of the company within the period of 14 days immediately before the date on which the restricted person accepts the appointment or acts in any way referred to in *subsection (1)*.

(3) A person who accepts the appointment or acts in any way referred to in *subsection (1)* without having complied with that subsection shall be guilty of a category 3 offence.

(4) In this section "company" means any company referred to in *section 819(6)*.

826 "Company that has a restricted person" — meaning of that expression in *sections 827* to *834*

In *sections 827* to *834* "company that has a restricted person" means a company—

(a) in relation to which a restricted person is appointed or acts in any way, whether directly or indirectly, as a director or secretary, or

(b) in the promotion or formation of which a restricted person is concerned or takes part.

827 Disapplication of certain provisions to company having a restricted person

(1) Subject to *subsection (2)*, the Summary Approval Procedure shall not apply to a company that has a restricted person.

(2) *Subsection (1)* does not affect the availability of that procedure so far as it relates to a members' voluntary winding up.

(3) Without prejudice to *section 247*, *sections 240* and *245* shall not apply to a company that has a restricted person.

828 Company having a restricted person may not acquire certain non-cash assets from subscribers, etc., unless particular conditions satisfied

(1) A company that has a restricted person shall not, unless the conditions specified in *subsection (3)* have been satisfied, enter into an agreement with a relevant person for the transfer by him or her of one or more non-cash assets to the company or another for a consideration to be given by the company equal in value at the time of the agreement to at least one-tenth of the nominal value of the company's share capital issued at that time.

(2) In this section—

"non-cash asset" means any property or interest in property other than cash (including foreign currency);

"relevant person", in relation to a company, means any subscriber to the constitution, any director or any person involved in the promotion or formation of the company.

(3) The conditions referred to in *subsection (1)* are that—

(a) the consideration to be received by the company (that is to say, the asset to be transferred to the company or the advantage to the company of its transfer to another person) and any consideration other than cash to be given by the company have been valued under the following provisions of this section,

(b) a report with respect to the consideration to be so received and given has been made to the company in accordance with those provisions during the 6 months immediately preceding the date of the agreement,

(c) the terms of the agreement have been approved by an ordinary resolution of the company, and

(d) not later than the giving of the notice of the meeting at which the resolution is proposed, copies of the resolution and report have been circulated to the members of the company entitled to receive that notice and, if the relevant person is not then such a member, to that person.

(4) *Subsection (1)* shall not apply to the following agreements for the transfer of an asset for a consideration to be given by the company, that is to say—

(a) where it is part of the ordinary business of the company to acquire or arrange for other persons to acquire assets of a particular description, an agreement entered into by the company in the ordinary course of its business for the transfer of an asset of that description to it or such a person, as the case may be, or

(b) an agreement entered into by the company under the supervision of the court or an officer authorised by the court for the purpose, for the transfer of an asset to the company or to another.

(5) Subject to *subsection (6)*, the valuation and report required by *subsection (3)* shall be made by an independent person, that is to say, a person qualified at the time of the report to be appointed or to continue to be statutory auditor of the company.

(6) Where it appears to the independent person referred to in *subsection (5)* to be reasonable for the valuation of the consideration, or a valuation of part of the consideration, to be made, or to accept such a valuation made, by any person who—

(a) appears to that independent person to have the requisite knowledge and experience to value the consideration or that part of the consideration, and

(b) is not—

(i) an officer or employee of the company or any other body corporate which is that company's subsidiary or holding company or a subsidiary of that company's holding company, or

(ii) a partner or employee of an officer or employee referred to in *subparagraph (i)*;

that independent person may arrange for or accept such a valuation, together with a report which will enable the independent person to make his or her own report under *subsection (3)* and provide a note in accordance with *subsection (7)*.

(7) The report of the independent person under *subsection (3)* shall—

(a) state the consideration to be received by the company, describing the asset in question, specifying the amount to be received in cash, and the consideration to be given by the company, specifying the amount to be given in cash,

(b) state the method and date of valuation,

(c) contain a note by the independent person, or be accompanied by such a note—

(i) in the case of a valuation made by another person, that it appeared to the independent person reasonable to arrange for it to be so made, or to accept a valuation so made,

(ii) whoever made the valuation, that the method of valuation was reasonable in all the circumstances, and

(iii) that it appears to the independent person that there has been no material change in the value of the consideration in question since the valuation,

and

(d) contain a note by the independent person, or be accompanied by such a note, that, on the basis of the valuation, the value of the consideration to be received by the company is not less than the value of the consideration to be given by it.

(8) Where any consideration is valued under this section by a person other than the independent person, the latter's report under *subsection (3)* shall state that fact and shall also—

(a) state the former's name and what knowledge and experience that other person has to carry out the valuation, and

(b) describe so much of the consideration as was valued by that other person, the method used to value it and state the date of valuation.

(9) If a company enters into an agreement with any relevant person in contravention of *subsection (1)* and either the relevant person has not received a report under this section or there has been some other contravention of this section which he or she knew or ought to have known amounted to a contravention, then, subject to *subsection (10)*—

(a) the company shall be entitled to recover from the relevant person any consideration given by the company under the agreement or an amount equivalent to its value at the time of the agreement, and

(b) the agreement, so far as not carried out, shall be void.

(10) Where a company enters into an agreement in contravention of *subsection (1)* and that agreement is or includes an agreement for the allotment of shares in that company—

(a) *subsection (9)* shall not apply to the agreement in so far as it is an agreement for the allotment of shares, and

(b) the following provisions shall apply in relation to the shares as if they had been allotted in contravention of *section 1028*.

(11) The provisions referred to in *subsection (10)(b)* are as follows:

(a) the allottee of the shares concerned shall be liable to pay the company an amount equal to the nominal value of the shares, together with the whole of any premium or, if the case so requires, such proportion of that amount as is treated as paid up by the consideration, and shall be liable to pay interest at the appropriate rate on the amount payable under this paragraph; and

(b) where any person becomes a holder of any shares in respect of which—

(i) there has been a contravention of this section, and

(ii) by virtue of that contravention, another is liable to pay any amount under this subsection;

the first-mentioned person in this paragraph also shall be liable to pay that amount (jointly and severally with any other person so liable) unless either that first-mentioned person is a purchaser for value and, at the time of the purchase, he or she did not have actual notice of the contravention or he or she derived title to the shares (directly or indirectly) from a person who became a holder of them after the contravention and was not so liable.

829 Supplemental provisions in relation to *section 828*

(1) Any person carrying out a valuation or making a report under *section 828* shall be entitled to require from the officers of the company such information and explanation as the person thinks necessary to enable him or her to carry out the valuation or make the report and provide the note required by that section.

(2) A company which has passed a resolution under *section 828* with respect to the transfer of an asset shall, within 15 days after the date of passing of the resolution, deliver to the Registrar a copy of the resolution together with the report required by that section and, if the company fails to do so, the company and any officer of it who is in default shall be guilty of a category 4 offence.

(3) Any reference in *section 828* or this section to consideration given for the transfer of an asset includes a reference to consideration given partly for its transfer but—

(a) the value of any consideration partly so given shall be taken to be the proportion of that consideration properly attributable to its transfer,

(b) the independent person shall carry out or arrange for such valuations of anything else as will enable him or her to determine that proportion, and

(c) his or her report under *section 828* shall state what valuation has been made by virtue of *paragraph (b)* and also the reason for and method and date of any such valuation and any other matters which may be relevant to that determination.

(4) References in *section 828* to a holder, in relation to any shares in a company, include references to any person who has an unconditional right to be included in the company's register of members in respect of those shares or to have an instrument of transfer of the shares executed in his or her favour.

830 Relief from liability under *section 828*

(1) Where any person is liable to a company under *section 828* in relation to payment in respect of any shares in the company, the person so liable may make an application to the court under this section to be exempted in whole or in part from that liability.

(2) The court may, on an application under this section, exempt the applicant from that liability if and to the extent that it appears to the court to be just and equitable to do so.

831 Offence for contravention of *section 828*

Where a company contravenes *section 828*, the company and any officer of it who is in default shall be guilty of a category 3 offence.

832 Allotment of share not fully paid up by company that has a restricted person

(1) This section applies if a company that has a restricted person allots a share that is not fully paid up as required by *section 819(3)(b)*.

(2) Subject to *subsection (3)*, in any case to which this section applies, the share shall be treated as if its nominal value together with the whole of any premium had been received by the company.

(3) The allottee of the share shall be liable to pay the company—

(a) the full amount that should have been received by the company as required by *section 819(3)(b)* less—

(i) the value of any consideration actually applied in payment up (to any extent) of the share, and

(ii) the whole of any premium on the share,

and

(b) interest at the appropriate rate on the amount payable under *paragraph (a)*.

(4) This section does not apply in relation to—

(a) a bonus share that is not fully paid up as required by *section 819(3)(b)* unless the allottee knew or ought to have known that the share was so allotted, or

(b) a share allotted under an employees' share scheme.

(5) Where any person becomes a holder of any shares in respect of which—

(a) there has been a failure to comply with *section 819(3)(b)*, and

(b) by virtue of that failure to comply, another is liable to pay any amount under this section,

the first-mentioned person in this subsection also shall be liable to pay that amount (jointly and severally with any other person so liable) unless either that first-mentioned person is a purchaser for value and, at the time of the purchase, he or she did not have actual notice of that non-compliance or he or she derived title to the shares (directly or indirectly) from a person who became a holder of them after that non-compliance and was not so liable.

(6) In this section—

(a) "employees' share scheme" has the meaning given to it by *section 64(1)*,

(b) references to a holder, in relation to any shares in a company, include references to any person who has an unconditional right to be included in the company's register of members in respect of those shares or to have an instrument of transfer of the shares executed in his or her favour.

833 Allotment of share not fully paid for in cash by company that has a restricted person

(1) This section applies if a company that has a restricted person allots a share that is not fully paid for in cash as required by *section 819(3)(c)*.

(2) In any case to which this section applies, the allottee of the share shall be liable to pay the company in cash—

(a) an amount equal to the nominal value of the share, together with the whole of any premium, and

(b) interest at the appropriate rate on the amount payable under *paragraph (a)*.

(3) Where any person becomes a holder of any shares in respect of which—

(a) there has been a failure to comply with *section 819(3)(c)*, and

(b) by virtue of that failure to comply, another is liable to pay any amount under this section,

the first-mentioned person in this subsection also shall be liable to pay that amount (jointly and severally with any other person so liable) unless either that first-mentioned person is a purchaser for value and, at the time of the purchase, he or she did not have actual notice of that non-compliance or he or she derived title to the shares (directly or indirectly) from a person who became a holder of them after that non-compliance and was not so liable.

(4) In this section references to a holder, in relation to any shares in a company, include references to any person who has an unconditional right to be included in the company's register of members in respect of those shares or to have an instrument of transfer of the shares executed in his or her favour.

834 Relief for company in respect of prohibited transaction

(1) Subject to *subsection (2)*, the court may, if it considers it just and equitable, grant relief to—

(a) any company that has a restricted person that by virtue of *section 827* has contravened any provision of this Act, or

(b) any person adversely affected by that contravention.

(2) The court shall not grant relief to a company in respect of a contravention if the restricted person concerned complied with *section 825*.

(3) The court may grant such relief, under this section, as it thinks fit, including an exemption from the provision in question, and on such terms and conditions as it thinks fit.

835 Power to vary amounts specified in *section 819(3)*

(1) Subject to *subsection (4)*, the Minister may from time to time, by order, increase any amount specified in *section 819(3)*.

(2) An increase by order made under *subsection (1)* shall not operate to effect any increase in relation to a declaration under *section 819(1)* made before the commencement of the order.

(3) The requirements set out in *section 819(3)* that shall apply in respect of a restricted person by virtue of such a declaration made before that commencement shall be those that applied at the time of the making of the order.

(4) An order under *subsection (1)* may only be made, at a particular time (the "relevant time"), if it appears to the Minister the changes in the value of money generally in the State that have occurred during the period beginning—

(a) on this Act's passing, or

(b) if the powers under that subsection have previously been exercised, immediately after their last previous exercise,

and ending at the relevant time, warrant the exercise of powers under that subsection so as to secure the continued effectiveness of *section 819* as regards the amounts specified for the time being in *subsection (3)* of it.

836 Personal liability for debts of company subject to restriction

(1) This section applies where a company—

(a) has received a notice under *section 825*,

(b) after receipt of the notice, carries on business without the requirements of *section 819(3)* being fulfilled within a reasonable period of receipt,

(c) is subsequently wound up, and

(d) at the time of commencement of the winding up is unable to pay its debts (taking into account its contingent and prospective liabilities).

(2) On the application of the liquidator or any creditor or contributory of the company, the court may declare that a person shall be personally liable, without any limitation of liability, for all or part of the debts or other liabilities of the company as the court directs if that person—

(a) was an officer of the company while it carried on business without the requirements of *section 819(3)* being fulfilled within a reasonable period of receipt of the notice referred to in *subsection (1)(a)*, and

(b) knew or ought to have known that the company had received the notice.

(3) In any proceedings against a person under this section, the court may, if, having regard to the circumstances of the case, it considers that it is just and equitable to do so, grant relief—

(a) in whole or in part from the liability of that person under this section, and

(b) subject to such conditions as the court sees fit.

Chapter 4
Disqualification generally

837 Interpretation generally (*Chapter 4*)

In this Chapter—

"company" includes every company and every body, whether corporate or unincorporated, that may be wound up under this Act;

"court", in relation to a disqualification order made by a court of its own motion under *section 842(a), (b), (c), (d)* or *(f)*, means the High Court or any other court of competent jurisdiction dealing with the person concerned in criminal or civil proceedings before it;

"default order" means an order made against any person under *section 797* by virtue of any contravention of or failure to comply with any relevant requirement (whether on that person's part or on the part of any company);

"officer", in relation to any company, includes any director, shadow director or secretary of the company;

"relevant requirement" means any provision of this Act (including any provision repealed by this Act) that requires or required any return, account or other document to be filed with, delivered or sent to, or notice of any matter to be given, to the Registrar.

838 Meaning of "disqualified" and "disqualification order"

In this Chapter—

"disqualification order" means an order of the court that a person shall be disqualified;

"disqualified", in relation to a person, means the person's being disqualified from being appointed or acting as a director or other officer, statutory auditor, receiver, liquidator or examiner or being in any way, whether directly or indirectly, concerned or taking part in the promotion, formation or management of each of the following:

(a) a company within the meaning of *section 819(6)*;

(b) any friendly society within the meaning of the Friendly Societies Acts 1896 to 2014;

(c) any society registered under the Industrial and Provident Societies Acts 1893 to 2014.

839 Automatic disqualification on conviction of certain indictable offences

(1) A person is automatically disqualified if that person is convicted on indictment of—

(a) any offence under this Act, or any other enactment as may be prescribed, in relation to a company, or

(b) any offence involving fraud or dishonesty.

(2) A person disqualified under *subsection (1)* is disqualified for a period of 5 years after the date of conviction or for such other (shorter or longer) period as the court, on the application of the prosecutor or the defendant and having regard to all the circumstances of the case, may order.

(3) A person disqualified under *subsection (1)* is deemed, for the purposes of this Act, to be subject to a disqualification order for the period of his or her disqualification.

(4) *Subsection (1)* is in addition to the other provisions of this Act providing that, upon conviction of a person for a particular offence, the person is deemed to be subject to a disqualification order.

840 Default under *section 149(8)* concerning fact of director's becoming disqualified under law of another state

(1) In this section—

"relevant change amongst its directors", in relation to a company, means the change referred to in *section 150(1)*, namely the case of a director's becoming disqualified under the law of another state (whether pursuant to an order of a judge or a tribunal or otherwise) from being appointed or acting as a director or secretary of a body corporate or an undertaking;

"relevant director" means the director of the company who has become so disqualified under the law of another state;

"statement of particulars of foreign disqualification" means the statement of particulars of disqualification that is required under *section 150(1)*.

(2) If—

(a) a company fails to comply with the requirement under *section 149(8)* to send to the Registrar the notification of the relevant change amongst its directors and that failure is by reason of a default of the relevant director, or

(b) in purported compliance with that requirement, a company sends to the Registrar the notification of the relevant change amongst its directors and, by reason of a default of the relevant director, the statement of particulars of foreign disqualification is false or misleading in a material respect,

the relevant director shall be deemed, for the purposes of this Act, to be subject to a disqualification order for the period specified in *subsection (3)*.

(3) The period of disqualification—

(a) commences—

(i) in the case of a failure referred to in *subsection (2)(a)*, on the expiry of 14 days after the date on which the relevant director has become disqualified, as mentioned in the definition of "relevant change amongst its directors" in *subsection (1)*, under the law of another state, or

(ii) in the case, as referred to in *subsection (2)(b)*, of the sending of a statement of particulars of foreign disqualification to the Registrar that is false or misleading in a material respect, when that statement is delivered to the Registrar,

and

(b) continues only for so much of—

(i) the period of foreign disqualification as remains unexpired as at the date of commencement referred to in *paragraph (a)*, or

(ii) if the person is disqualified under the law of more than one state, and the unexpired periods of disqualification in each of the states are not equal, whichever unexpired period of disqualification is the greatest.

(4) Without limiting the circumstances in which such a default can arise, a failure referred to in—

(a) *subsection (2)(a)* occurs by reason of a default of the relevant director if the latter has failed in his or her duty under *section 150(3)* to give the necessary information to the company so as to enable it to comply with the requirement under *section 149(8)* to send to the Registrar the notification of the relevant change amongst its directors, and

(b) *subsection (2)(b)* occurs by reason of a default of the relevant director if the latter, in purported compliance with the foregoing duty, has given information to the company, for the purposes of the statement of particulars of foreign disqualification, that is false or misleading in a material respect.

(5) This section shall also apply to the additional case that, by virtue of *subsection (9)* of *section 150, subsection (1)* of *section 150* applies to.

(6) For the purposes of the application of this section to the foregoing additional case, this section shall have effect subject to the following modifications:

(a) the following definition shall be substituted for the definition of "relevant change amongst its directors" in *subsection (1)*:

" 'relevant change amongst its directors', in relation to a company, means the change referred to in *subsection (1)* of *section 150* (as that subsection applies by virtue of *subsection (9)* of that section), namely the case of a person appointed a director of a company before the commencement of that section and who, subsequent to his or her appointment but before that commencement, becomes disqualified under the law of another state (whether pursuant to an order of a judge or a tribunal or otherwise) from being appointed or acting as director or secretary of a body corporate or an undertaking;";

(b) in *subsection (2)*, after "*section 149(8)*" there shall be inserted "(as that provision applies by virtue of *section 150(10)*)";

(c) in *subsection (3)(a)*, there shall be substituted the following for *subparagraph (i)*:

"(i) in the case of a failure referred to in *subsection (2)(a)*, on the expiry of 3 months after the commencement of *section 150*; or";

and

(d) in *subsection (3)(b)*, there shall be substituted the following for *subparagraph (i)*:

"(i) the period of foreign disqualification as remains unexpired as at the date that is specified in *paragraph (a)* to be the date on which the period of disqualification commences;".

841 Default under *section 23* or *150(2)* by director disqualified under law of another state

(1) This section applies to a person if the person—

(a) is disqualified under the law of another state (whether pursuant to an order of a judge or a tribunal or otherwise) from being appointed or acting as a director or secretary of a body corporate or an undertaking, and

(b) one of the following occurs:

(i) the person fails to comply with *section 23* or *150(2)*;

(ii) in purported compliance with *section 23*, the person permits the statement of first directors and secretary to be accompanied by a statement of particulars of foreign disqualification signed by him or her that is false or misleading in a material respect; or

(iii) in purported compliance with *section 150(2)*, the person permits the notification of change of director to be accompanied by a statement of particulars of foreign disqualification signed by him or her that is false or misleading in a material respect.

(2) A person to whom this section applies shall be deemed, for the purposes of this Act, to be subject to a disqualification order for the period specified in *subsection (3)*.

(3) The period of disqualification—

(a) commences—

(i) in the case of a default referred to in *subsection (1)(b)(i)*, when the statement of first directors and secretary or notification of change of director, as the case may be, is delivered to the Registrar, or

(ii) in the case of a default referred to in *subsection (1)(b)(ii)* or *(iii)*, when the statement of first directors and secretary or notification of change of director, as the case may be, accompanied by the statement of particulars of foreign disqualification is delivered to the Registrar,

and

(b) continues only for so much of—

(i) the period of foreign disqualification as remains unexpired as at the date of commencement referred to in *paragraph (a)*, or

(ii) if the person is disqualified under the law of more than one state, and the unexpired periods of disqualification in each of the states are not equal, whichever unexpired period of disqualification is the greatest.

(4) In this section—

"notification of change of director" means the notification of a change in director that is required to be sent under *section 149(8)*;

"statement of first directors and secretary" means the statement required to be delivered under *section 21(1)(a)*;

"statement of particulars of foreign disqualification" means the statement of particulars of disqualification that is required under *section 23* or *150(2)*.

842 Court may make disqualification order

On the application of a person specified in *section 844* or of its own motion, the court may make a disqualification order in respect of a person for such period as it sees fit if satisfied—

(a) that the person has been guilty, while a promoter, officer, statutory auditor, receiver, liquidator or examiner of a company, of any fraud in relation to the company, its members or creditors,

(b) that the person has been guilty, while a promoter, officer, statutory auditor, receiver, liquidator or examiner of a company, of any breach of his or her duty as such promoter, officer, auditor, receiver, liquidator or examiner,

(c) that a declaration has been granted under *section 610* in respect of the person,

(d) that the conduct of the person as promoter, officer, statutory auditor, receiver, liquidator or examiner of a company makes him or her unfit to be concerned in the management of a company,

(e) that, as disclosed in a report of inspectors appointed by the court or the Director under this Act, the conduct of the person makes him or her unfit to be concerned in the management of a company,

(f) that the person has been persistently in default in relation to the relevant requirements,

(g) that the person has been guilty of 2 or more offences under *section 286*,

(h) that the person was a director of a company when a notice was sent to the company under *section 727* and the company, following the taking of the other steps under *Chapter 1* of *Part 12* consequent on the sending of the notice, was struck off the register under *section 733*, [...][a]

(i) that—

(i) the person is disqualified under the law of another state (whether pursuant to an order of a judge or a tribunal or otherwise) from being appointed or acting as a director or secretary of a body corporate or an undertaking, and

(ii) it would have been proper to make a disqualification order against the person otherwise under this section if his or her conduct or the circumstances otherwise affecting him or her that gave rise to the foreign disqualification had occurred or arisen [in the State, or][b]

[(j) that the person has contravened section 4 or 5 of the Competition Act 2002 or Article 101 or 102 of the Treaty on the Functioning of the European Union.][c]

Amendments

a Subparagraph (h) substituted by C(A)A 2017, s 94(a).
b Words substituted by C(A)A 2017, s 94(b) (previously: "in the State.").
c Subparagraph (j) inserted by C(A)A 2017, s 94(c).

843 Provisions relating to particular grounds for disqualification

(1) In relation to *section 842(f)*, the fact that a person has been persistently in default in relation to the relevant requirements may (without prejudice to its proof in any other

manner) be conclusively proved by showing that, in the 5 years ending with the date of the application, the person has been found guilty (whether or not on the same occasion) of 3 or more defaults in relation to those requirements.

(2) For the purposes of *subsection (1)*, a person shall be treated as having been found guilty of a default in relation to a relevant requirement if he or she is convicted of any offence consisting of a contravention of a relevant requirement or a default order is made against him or her.

(3) The court shall not make a disqualification order under *section 842(h)* if the person concerned shows that—

(a) the company in question had no liabilities (whether actual, contingent or prospective) when it was struck off the register, or

(b) in a case where the company did have such liabilities when it was struck off the register, those liabilities were discharged before the date of the making of the application for the disqualification order.

(4) The court may make a disqualification order under *section 842(i)* notwithstanding that under *section 840(2)* or *841(2)* the person concerned is deemed for the purposes of this Act to be subject to a disqualification order.

(5) A disqualification order under *section 842(i)* shall express the period of disqualification to begin on the expiry of the disqualification period determined in accordance with *section 840(3)(b)* or *841(3)(b)* or such shorter disqualification period following the grant of an application for relief under *section 847*.

844 Persons who may apply for disqualification order under *section 842*

(1) The Director may make an application under any of *section 842(a)* to *(i)*.

(2) The Director of Public Prosecutions may make an application under any of *section 842(a)* to *(g)*.

(3) The Registrar may make an application under *section 842(f)*.

(4) An application under any of *section 842(a)* to *(d)* may be made by any member, contributory, officer, employee, receiver, liquidator, examiner or creditor of any company in relation to which the person who is the subject of the application—

(a) has been or is acting or is proposing to or is being proposed to act as officer, statutory auditor, receiver, liquidator or examiner, or

(b) has been or is concerned or taking part in, or is proposing to be concerned or take part in, the promotion, formation or management.

[(4A) An application under *section 842(j)* may be made by the competent authority (within the meaning of the Competition Act 2002).][a]

(5) The court may require a person who makes an application under *section 842* to provide security for some or all of the costs of the application.

Amendments

a Subsection (4A) inserted by C(A)A 2017, s 95.

845 Miscellaneous provisions relating to disqualification by court order

(1) Where it is intended to make an application under *section 842* in respect of any person, the applicant shall give not less than 10 days' notice of his or her intention to that person.

(2) A disqualification order may be made on grounds that are or include matters other than criminal convictions notwithstanding that the person who is the subject of the order may be made criminally liable in respect of those matters.

(3) On an application for a disqualification order, the court may as an alternative, if it considers that disqualification is not justified, make a declaration under *section 819*.

846 Costs and expenses of application

The court, on hearing an application under *section 842*, may order that the person disqualified or against whom a declaration under *section 819* is made as a result of the application (by virtue of *section 845(3)*) shall bear—

- (a) the costs of the application, and
- (b) in the case of an application by the Director, the Director of Public Prosecutions, a liquidator, a receiver or an examiner, the whole (or so much of them as the court specifies) of the costs and expenses that are incurred by the applicant—
  - (i) in investigating the matters that are the subject of the application, and
  - (ii) in so far as they do not fall within *paragraph (a)*, in collecting evidence in respect of those matters,

including so much of the remuneration and expenses of the applicant as are attributable to such investigation and collection.

847 Court may grant relief to person subject to disqualification order

(1) On the application by a person who is subject to a disqualification order, the court may, if it considers that it is just and equitable, grant relief from the disqualification—

- (a) in whole or in part, and
- (b) on such terms and conditions as it sees fit.

(2) Without prejudice to *subsection (3)*, in the case of an application for relief from a disqualification order made under *section 842*, the application shall be served on—

- (a) the applicant for the disqualification order, and
- (b) the Director, if different from the applicant for the disqualification order.

(3) A person who intends applying for relief under *subsection (1)* shall give not less than 14 days' notice in writing of his or her intention to apply to—

(a) the applicant for the disqualification order, and

(b) the Director, if different from the applicant for the disqualification order.

(4) If the applicant for the disqualification order was the liquidator of a company, the insolvency of which gave rise to the application for the disqualification order, then, on receipt of a notice under *subsection (3)*, the liquidator shall as soon as practicable notify such creditors and contributories of the company as have been notified to the liquidator or become known to the liquidator.

(5) On the hearing of an application under this section, the Director and the applicant for the disqualification order and, where the latter is a liquidator referred to in *subsection (4)*, any creditor or contributory of the company concerned, may appear and give evidence.

(6) A liquidator who fails to comply with *subsection (4)* shall be guilty of a category 3 offence.

848 Disqualification of restricted person following subsequent winding up

(1) This section applies where—

(a) a restricted person is or becomes a director of a company that commences to be wound up within the period of 5 years after the date of commencement of the winding up of the company whose insolvency caused that person to be a restricted person, and

(b) it appears to the liquidator of the first-mentioned company that that company is, at the date of commencement of its winding up or at any time during the course of its winding up, unable to pay its debts.

(2) In any case to which this section applies, the liquidator shall report the matters set out in *subsection (1)* to the court, and the court, if it considers that it is proper to do so, may make a disqualification order against the restricted person for such period as it thinks fit.

(3) If the liquidator fails to comply with *subsection (2)*, he or she shall be guilty of a category 3 offence.

(4) In this section—

(a) "restricted person" has the same meaning as it has in *Chapter 3*;

(b) references to a company (other than the company whose insolvency caused the person concerned to be a restricted person) are references to any company within the meaning of *section 819(6)*.

Chapter 5
Disqualification and restriction undertakings

849 Definitions (*Chapter 5*)

In this Chapter—

"disqualification" means being disqualified from being appointed or acting as a director or other officer, receiver, statutory auditor, liquidator or examiner or being in any way, whether directly or indirectly, concerned or taking part in the promotion, formation or management of each of the following:

(a) any company within the meaning of *section 819(6)*;

(b) any friendly society within the meaning of the Friendly Societies Acts 1896 to 2014;

(c) any society registered under the Industrial and Provident Societies Acts 1893 to 2014;

"disqualification acceptance document" means the document provided for by regulations under *section 854(1)* and referred to in *paragraph (a)(i)* of that provision;

"disqualification order" means an order made under *section 842*;

"disqualification undertaking", in relation to a person, means an undertaking by the person, given by the means provided in this Chapter, by which the person submits himself or herself to be subject to disqualification;

"restriction" means being restricted for a period of 5 years from being appointed or acting in any way, directly or indirectly, as a director or secretary of a company (within the meaning of *section 819(6)*) or being concerned in or taking part in the promotion or formation of a company (within that meaning) unless the company meets the requirements set out in *section 819(3)*;

"restriction acceptance document" means the document provided for by regulations under *section 854(1)* and referred to in *paragraph (a)(ii)* of that provision;

"restriction declaration" means a declaration made under *section 819*;

"restriction undertaking", in relation to a person, means an undertaking by the person, given by the means provided in this Chapter, by which the person submits himself or herself to be subject to restriction.

850 Disqualification undertaking — initiation of procedure that provides person opportunity to submit to disqualification

(1) In this section—

"disqualification period" shall be read in accordance with *subsection (3)(b)*;

"notice period" shall be read in accordance with *subsection (3)(d)*;

"person" shall be read in accordance with *subsection (2)*;

"specified date" shall be read in accordance with *subsection (3)(c)*;

"underlying facts and circumstances" shall be read in accordance with *subsection (3)(a)*.

(2) Subject to *section 851(6)*, where the Director has reasonable grounds for believing that one or more of the circumstances specified in *section 842(a)* to *(i)* applies to a person (in this section referred to as the "person"), the Director may, in his or her discretion, deliver to the person, or to the person's duly authorised agent, the following notice.

(3) That notice is a notice in the prescribed form stating—

(a) both—

(i) which of the circumstances specified in *section 842(a)* to *(i)* the Director believes apply to the person; and

(ii) particulars of the facts and allegations that have given rise to that belief;

and the circumstances so stated, and the facts and allegations that have given rise to that belief (and of which particulars are so stated), are referred to together in this section as the "underlying facts and circumstances";

(b) the period of disqualification (referred to in this section as the "disqualification period") which, in the Director's opinion, is warranted in relation to the person by the underlying facts and circumstances;

(c) the date (referred to in this section as the "specified date") that will, subject to *subsection (5)*, be the date of commencement of the disqualification period, if a disqualification undertaking is given by the person;

(d) that during—

(i) such period as may be specified in the notice (referred to in this section as the "notice period"), being a period beginning on a day falling not less than 21 days after the date of the notice and expressed to end immediately before the specified date; or

(ii) in the event of a request under *subsection (5)* by the person being acceded to, the notice period as extended in pursuance of that subsection;

the person may—

(I) notify the Director, in the prescribed form, of his or her willingness to give a disqualification undertaking for the disqualification period; and

(II) return to the Director the disqualification acceptance document duly signed;

(e) that during the notice period, or that period as so extended, the Director will refrain from making an application in respect of the person under *section 842* arising from or in connection with the underlying facts and circumstances;

(f) that if the person, within the notice period or that period as so extended, does the things referred to in *paragraph (d)(I)* and *(II)*, the Director shall not, after the expiry of that period, make an application in respect of the person under *section 842* arising from or in connection with the underlying facts and circumstances.

(4) That notice shall also state—

(a) that the person may make a request, under *subsection (5)*, for an extension of the notice period,

(b) the legal effect (for the person) of giving a disqualification undertaking for the disqualification period beginning on the specified date, and

(c) that if the person gives a disqualification undertaking—

(i) the person may seek to be relieved (whether in whole or in part) from the undertaking only by applying to the court under *section 847*, and

(ii) that, on the making of such an application, the court may grant such relief only if it considers it just and equitable to do so, and then only on the terms and conditions as it sees fit.

(5) Where a notice is delivered under *subsection (2)*, the Director may, at any time before the specified date, on the request of the person, where the Director considers it appropriate to do so for the purposes of extending the notice period (and postponing the commencement of the proposed disqualification period in consequence), substitute a later date for the specified date and, where such a date is so substituted, references in *section 851*—

(a) to the notice period shall be read as references to the notice period as extended in pursuance of this subsection, and

(b) to the specified date shall be read as references to the date that has been substituted for it in pursuance of this subsection.

851 Effect of delivery of notice under *section 850*, giving of disqualification undertaking on foot thereof and related matters

(1) Where a notice is delivered under *section 850(2)*, the Director and every person who is aware of the notice shall not, during the notice period, make an application under *section 842*, arising from or in connection with the underlying facts and circumstances, in respect of the person who is the subject of the notice.

(2) *Subsections (3)* to *(5)* apply where a person, the subject of a notice delivered under *section 850(2)*, has, within the notice period—

(a) notified the Director, in the prescribed manner, of his or her willingness to give a disqualification undertaking for the disqualification period, and

(b) returned to the Director the disqualification acceptance document duly signed.

(3) The Director shall, as soon as practicable—

(a) cause the Registrar to be furnished with the prescribed particulars of the disqualification undertaking at such time and in such form and manner as may be prescribed, and the Registrar shall enter the prescribed particulars in the register of persons kept under *section 864*, and

(b) notify the person of the prescribed particulars of the disqualification undertaking furnished to the Registrar and provide the person with a copy of the disqualification acceptance document executed by or on behalf of the Director.

(4) After the expiry of the notice period, neither the Director nor any other person shall make an application under *section 842*, arising from or in connection with the underlying facts and circumstances, in respect of the person who has given the disqualification undertaking.

(5) For the duration of the disqualification period beginning on the specified date, the person who has given the disqualification undertaking—

(a) shall not be appointed or act as a director or other officer, statutory auditor, receiver, liquidator or examiner or be in any way, whether directly or indirectly, concerned or take part in the promotion, formation or management of each of the following:

(i) any company within the meaning of *section 819(6)*;

(ii) any friendly society within the meaning of the Friendly Societies Acts 1896 to 2014;

(iii) any society registered under the Industrial and Provident Societies Acts 1893 to 2014;

and

(b) shall be deemed, for the purposes of this Act, to be subject to a disqualification order.

(6) The Director shall not exercise his or her power under *section 850(2)* in relation to a person where—

(a) in the Director's opinion, a period of disqualification, in relation to the person, that is longer than 5 years is warranted by the underlying facts and circumstances, or

(b) the Director is aware that an application under *section 842* has already been made in respect of the person arising from or in connection with the underlying facts and circumstances.

(7) Where the person who has given the disqualification undertaking (the "immediate undertaking") is already disqualified by virtue of an earlier disqualification undertaking or disqualification order, the period specified in the immediate undertaking shall run concurrently with the remaining period for which the person is already subject to disqualification.

(8) In this section—

(a) without prejudice to *section 850(5)*, "specified date" and "notice period" are to be read in accordance with *section 850(3)(c)* and *(d)*, respectively,

(b) "person", "underlying facts and circumstances" and "disqualification period" are to be read in accordance with *section 850(2)*, *(3)(a)* and *(3)(b)*, respectively.

852 Restriction undertaking — initiation of procedure that provides person opportunity to submit to restriction

(1) In this section—

"notice period" shall be read in accordance with *subsection (3)(c)*;

"person" shall be read in accordance with *subsection (2)*;

"restriction period" means the period of 5 years, as mentioned in the definition of "restriction" in *section 849*, for which the restrictions set out in that definition are to operate;

"specified date" shall be read in accordance with *subsection (3)(b)*;

"underlying facts and circumstances" shall be read in accordance with *subsection (3)(a)*.

(2) Subject to *section 853(6)*, where the Director has reasonable grounds for believing that a person falls within the description of the second-mentioned person in *section 819(1)*, namely a person who was a director of an insolvent company within the meaning of *Chapter 3* (in this section referred to as the "person"), the Director may, in his or her discretion, deliver to the person, or to the person's duly authorised agent, the following notice.

(3) That notice is a notice in the prescribed form stating—

(a) the circumstances, facts and allegations that have given rise to that belief of the Director, citing the provisions of *section 819(1)* and *section 818(1)* (and also, where appropriate, *section 824*) and stating particulars of those facts and allegations (and the circumstances so stated, and those facts and allegations, of which particulars are so stated, are referred to together in this section as the "underlying facts and circumstances"),

(b) the date (referred to in this section as the "specified date") that will, subject to *subsection (5)*, be the date of commencement of the restriction period, if a restriction undertaking is given by the person,

(c) that during—

(i) such period as may be specified in the notice (referred to in this section as the "notice period"), being a period beginning on a day falling not less than 21 days after the date of the notice and expressed to end immediately before the specified date; or

(ii) in the event of a request under *subsection (5)* by the person being acceded to, the notice period as extended under that subsection;

the person may—

(I) notify the Director, in the prescribed form, of his or her willingness to give a restriction undertaking; and

(II) return to the Director the restriction acceptance document duly signed;

(d) that during the notice period, or that period as so extended, the Director will refrain from making an application in respect of the person under *section 819* arising from or in connection with the underlying facts and circumstances;

(e) that if the person, within the notice period or that period as so extended, does the things referred to in *paragraph (c)(I)* and *(II)*, the Director shall not, after the expiry of that period, make an application in respect of the person under *section 819* arising from or in connection with the underlying facts and circumstances.

(4) That notice shall also state—

(a) that the person may make a request, under *subsection (5)*, for an extension of the notice period,

(b) the legal effect (for the person) of giving a restriction undertaking beginning on the specified date, and

(c) that if the person gives a restriction undertaking—

(i) the person may seek to be relieved (whether in whole or in part) from the undertaking only by applying to the court under *section 822*, and

(ii) that, on the making of such an application, the court may grant such relief only if it considers it just and equitable to do so, and then only on the terms and conditions as it sees fit.

(5) Where a notice is delivered under *subsection (2)*, the Director may, at any time before the specified date, on the request of the person, where the Director considers it appropriate to do so for the purposes of extending the notice period (and postponing the commencement of the restriction period in consequence), substitute a later date for the specified date and, where such a date is so substituted, references in *section 853*—

(a) to the notice period shall be read as references to the notice period as extended in pursuance of this subsection, and

(b) to the specified date shall be read as references to the date that has been substituted for it in pursuance of this subsection.

853 Effect of delivery of notice under *section 852*, giving of restriction undertaking on foot thereof and related matters

(1) Where a notice is delivered under *section 852(2)*, the Director and every person who is aware of the notice shall not, during the notice period, make an application under *section 819*, arising from or in connection with the underlying facts and circumstances, in respect of the person who is the subject of the notice.

(2) *Subsections (3)* to *(5)* apply where a person, the subject of a notice delivered under *section 852(2)*, has, within the notice period—

(a) notified the Director, in the prescribed manner, of his or her willingness to give a restriction undertaking, and

(b) returned to the Director the restriction acceptance document duly signed.

(3) The Director shall, as soon as practicable—

(a) cause the Registrar to be furnished with the prescribed particulars of the restriction undertaking at such time and in such form and manner as may be prescribed, and the Registrar shall enter the prescribed particulars in the register of persons kept under *section 823*, and

(b) notify the person of the prescribed particulars of the restriction undertaking furnished to the Registrar and provide the person with a copy of the restriction acceptance document executed by or on behalf of the Director.

(4) After the expiry of the notice period, neither the Director nor any other person shall make an application under *section 819*, arising from or in connection with the underlying facts and circumstances, in respect of the person who has given the restriction undertaking.

(5) For the duration of the restriction period beginning on the specified date, the person who has given the restriction undertaking—

(a) shall not be appointed or act in any way, directly or indirectly, as a director or secretary of a company (within the meaning of *section 819(6)*) or be concerned in or take part in the promotion or formation of a company (within that meaning) unless the company meets the requirements set out in *section 819(3)*, and

(b) shall be deemed, for the purposes of this Act, to be subject to a restriction declaration.

(6) The Director shall not exercise his or her power under *section 852(2)* in relation to a person where the Director is aware that an application under *section 819* has already been made in respect of the person arising from or in connection with the underlying facts and circumstances.

(7) Where the person who has given the restriction undertaking (the "immediate undertaking") is already restricted by virtue of an earlier restriction undertaking or restriction declaration, the period specified in the immediate undertaking shall run concurrently with the remaining period for which the person is already subject to restriction.

(8) In this section—

(a) without prejudice to *section 852(5)*, "specified date" and "notice period" are to be read in accordance with *section 852(3)(b)* and *(c)*, respectively,

(b) "restriction period", "person" and "underlying facts and circumstances" are to be read in accordance with *section 852(1)*, *(2)* and *(3)(a)*, respectively.

854 Regulations for the purposes of *sections 850* to *853*

(1) The Minister shall make regulations requiring—

(a) that a document, in a form specified in the regulations, to be known as—

(i) in the case of *sections 850* and *851*, a "disqualification acceptance document"; and

(ii) in the case of *sections 852* and *853*, a "restriction acceptance document";

(being the document by which the person to whom a notice delivered under *section 850(2)* or *852(2)*, as the case may be, relates signifies in writing (if such be the person's decision) the person's voluntary submission to disqualification or restriction, as appropriate, in accordance with this

Chapter) shall be returned by the person within the relevant notice period to the Director; and

(b) that, on receipt of that document, the Director shall execute, or cause to be executed, on his or her part the document by the affixing of his or her seal to it.

(2) Regulations under *subsection (1)* may contain such consequential and supplemental provisions for the purposes of those regulations or for the purpose of giving further effect to *sections 850* to *853* as the Minister thinks expedient, including—

(a) provision for particular procedures to be employed by the Director in relation to the delivery of a notice under *section 850(2)* or *852(2)* or any communication between the Director and the person concerned or his or her duly authorised agent consequent on the delivery of such a notice (a "post-delivery-of notice communication"), and

(b) provision for a like privilege to legal professional privilege to attach to a post-delivery-of notice communication.

(3) This section is in addition to the powers under *section 12(1)* to prescribe anything referred to in *sections 850* to *853* as prescribed or to be prescribed.

Chapter 6
Enforcement in relation to disqualification and restriction

855 Offence of contravening disqualification order or restriction

(1) A person shall be guilty of a category 2 offence who acts, in relation to any company, in a manner or a capacity which he or she is prohibited from doing by virtue of being a person—

(a) who is subject to a disqualification order, or

(b) who is subject to a declaration of restriction under *section 819.*

(2) A person convicted of an offence under *subsection (1)* shall be deemed to be subject to a disqualification order from the date of the conviction unless he or she is already subject to a disqualification order at that date.

(3) Where a person convicted of an offence under *subsection (1)* was subject to a disqualification order immediately before the date of the conviction, the period for which he or she was disqualified shall be extended for—

(a) a further period of 10 years beginning after the date of the conviction, or

(b) such other (shorter or longer) further period as the court, on the application of the prosecutor or the defendant and having regard to all the circumstances of the case, may order.

(4) *Section 847* shall not apply to a person convicted of an offence under *subsection (1).*

(5) In this section and the subsequent provisions of this Chapter—

(a) a reference to a company—

(i) shall be read as a reference to a company within the meaning of *section 819(6)*, and

(ii) in addition, where the context admits, shall be deemed to include a reference to any friendly society within the meaning of the Friendly Societies Acts 1896 to 2014 and any society registered under the Industrial and Provident Societies Acts 1893 to 2014,

(b) for the avoidance of doubt, the employment, in relation to "disqualification order", of the words "shall be deemed to be subject to", followed by the employment, in relation to another occurrence of "disqualification order", of the words "is subject to" does not limit the meaning of the latter to a case of the person's being actually subject (as distinct from being deemed to be subject) to a disqualification order.

(6) Likewise, the employment, in this or any subsequent provision of this Chapter, of the words "shall be deemed to be subject to" does not so limit the meaning of the words "is subject to" where employed in relation to "a declaration of restriction under *section 819*".

(7) If a case referred to in *subsection (1)* would also fall within *section 405* (prohibition on acting in relation to audit while disqualification order in force), then *section 405* applies to that case to the exclusion of this section.

856 Offence of acting under directions of person where directions given in contravention of this Part

(1) A person shall be guilty of a category 2 offence if he or she, while a director, acts in accordance with the directions or instructions of another person knowing that that other person, in giving the directions or instructions, is acting in contravention of any provision of this Part.

(2) A person who is convicted of an offence under *subsection (1)* shall be deemed to be subject to a disqualification order from the date of the conviction unless he or she is already subject to a disqualification order at that date.

857 Period of disqualification following conviction of offence under this Chapter

Where a person is, as a consequence of his or her conviction for an offence under *section 855(1)* or *856(1)*, deemed to be subject to a disqualification order, he or she shall be deemed to be so subject to a disqualification order for a period of 5 years beginning after the date of such conviction or such other (shorter or longer) period as the court, on the application of the prosecutor or the defendant and having regard to the circumstances of the case, may order.

858 Company may recover consideration

(1) This section applies if a person acts, in relation to a company, in a manner or a capacity which he or she is prohibited from doing by virtue of being a person who is subject to a declaration of restriction under *section 819* or who is subject to a disqualification order made under *section 842*.

(2) The company may recover from a person acting as described in *subsection (1)* any consideration (or an amount representing its value) given by or on behalf of the company for an act or service performed by that person while he or she was so acting.

(3) The company may recover the consideration or amount representing its value as a simple contract debt in any court of competent jurisdiction.

859 Person acting while disqualified or restricted liable for debts of company

(1) This section applies if—

(a) a person acts, in relation to a company, in a manner or a capacity which he or she is prohibited from doing by virtue of being a person who is subject to a declaration of restriction under *section 819* or who is subject to a disqualification order made under *section 842*,

(b) the company commences to be wound up—

  (i) while he or she is acting in such a manner or capacity, or

  (ii) within 12 months after the date of his or her so acting,

  and

(c) the company is unable to pay its debts within the meaning of *section 570.*

(2) In any case to which this section applies, the court may, on the application of the liquidator or any creditor of the company, declare that the person referred to in *subsection (1)* shall be personally liable, without any limitation of liability, for all or part of the debts or other liabilities of the company incurred in the period during which the person was acting as described in *subsection (1)(a).*

860 Person acting under directions of disqualified person liable for debts of company

A person who is convicted, on indictment, of an offence under *section 856* for acting in accordance with the directions or instructions of another in contravention of that section shall, if the court determines that it is just to so order and orders accordingly, be personally liable, without any limitation of liability, for so much as the court specifies of the debts or other liabilities of the company concerned incurred during the period that the person was so acting.

861 Relief from liability under *section 858, 859* or *860*

In any proceeding against a person under *section 858*, *859* or *860*, the court may, if, having regard to the circumstances of the case, it considers that it is just and equitable to do so, grant relief—

(a) in whole or in part from the liability of that person under the section concerned, and

(b) subject to such conditions as the court sees fit.

862 Court may require director to give certain information

(1) This section applies if—

(a) a director of a company is charged with an offence or civil proceedings are instituted against such a director, and

(b) the charge or proceedings relate to the company or involve alleged fraud or dishonesty by the director.

(2) In any case to which this section applies, the court before which the proceedings consequent on that charge or those civil proceedings are pending may, of its own motion or at the request of any party to the proceedings and if it considers that it is appropriate to do so, require the director to lodge with the office of the court a written notice—

(a) giving the names of all companies of which he or she is a director at the date of the notice,

(b) giving the names of all companies of which he or she was a director in the period—

(i) within a period commencing not earlier than 12 months before the director was charged or the proceedings were commenced against him or her, and

(ii) ending at the date of the notice,

(c) stating whether he or she is at the date of the notice or ever was subject to a disqualification order, and

(d) giving the dates and duration of each period for which he or she was disqualified.

(3) This section applies to shadow directors as it does to directors.

863 Information to be supplied to Registrar

(1) This section applies where a court—

(a) makes a disqualification order,

(b) grants or varies relief under *section 847*, or

(c) convicts a person of—

(i) an offence that has the effect that the person is deemed to be subject to a disqualification order, or

(ii) an offence under *section 855(1)* or *856(1)*.

(2) In any case to which this section applies, a prescribed officer of the court shall ensure that the Registrar is given the prescribed particulars of the order, relief or conviction at such time and in such form and manner as may be prescribed.

864 Register of disqualified persons

(1) Subject to the provisions of this section, the Registrar shall keep a register of the particulars given to him or her under *section 863*.

(2) Where the Registrar receives particulars of full relief under *section 847*, the Registrar shall—

(a) not enter the particulars on the register, and

(b) as soon as practicable remove from the register any existing particulars in respect of the person concerned.

(3) The Registrar shall remove from the register any particulars in respect of a person on the expiry of the period for which the person is subject to a disqualification

order, unless the Registrar has received a further notification in respect of that person under *section 863(1)(a)* or *(c)*.

(4) If the person is concurrently subject to 2 or more disqualification orders and the periods to which they relate do not expire at the same time, then the reference in *subsection (3)* to removal from the register of particulars is a reference only to those particulars that relate to the disqualification order or orders the period or periods of which have expired.

(5) Nothing in this section shall prevent the Registrar from keeping the register required under this section as part of any other system of classification, whether pursuant to *section 895* or otherwise.

Chapter 7
Provisions relating to offences generally

865 Summary prosecutions

(1) Summary proceedings in relation to an offence under this Act may be brought and prosecuted by:

(a) the Director of Public Prosecutions; or
(b) the Director.

(2) Without prejudice to the generality of *subsection (1)*, summary proceedings in relation to an offence under each of the following provisions may be brought and prosecuted by the Registrar:

(a) *section 30(8)*;
(b) *section 137(6)*;
(c) *section 343(11)*;
(d) *section 430(10)*, in so far as it relates to a default under *section 430(3)*;
(e) *section 441(3)*;
(f) *section 530(7)*;
(g) *section 531(8), (9)* or *(10)*;
(h) *section 555(2)*;
(i) section 592(4);
(j) *section 631(4)*;
(k) *section 651*;
(l) *section 669(8)* or *(9)*;
(m) *section 680(9)*;
(n) *section 681(5)*;
(o) [*section 704(6)*;][a]
[(p) *section 1401A(5)*;
(q) *section 1459(2)*;
(r) *section 1460(3)*;[b]][c]

[(s) *section 1487(4)*;

(t) *section 1488(3)*.][d]

Amendments

a Words substituted by C(A)A 2017, s 68(a) (previously: "*section 704(6)*.").

b Words substituted by C(SA)A 2018, s 14(a) (previously: "*section 1460(3)*.".

c Subparagraphs (p), (q) and (r) inserted by C(A)A 2017, s 68(b).

d Subparagraphs (s) and (t) inserted by C(SA)A 2018, s 14(b).

866 District court district within which summary proceedings may be brought

(1) Summary proceedings against a company or an officer of a company acting in his or her capacity as such (or a person purporting to so act) for an offence under this Act may be brought, heard and determined—

(a) before and by a judge of the District Court as provided for under section 79 or 79A of the Courts of Justice Act 1924,

(b) before and by a judge of the District Court for the time being assigned to the district court district in which the registered office of the company is situated immediately prior to the commencement of the proceedings, or

(c) where the offence is an offence under *section 343(11)* (but without prejudice to the alternative venues provided under the preceding paragraphs) before a judge of the District Court for the time being assigned to—

(i) the Dublin Metropolitan District; or

(ii) the district court district of which the district court area of Carlow forms part;

but only to the extent, in the case of the district court district referred to in *subparagraph (ii)*, that the judge so assigned is exercising jurisdiction in the district court area of Carlow so referred to.

(2) In this section "officer of a company" includes a director, shadow director, promoter, statutory auditor, receiver, liquidator or secretary of a company.

(3) For the purposes of this section, the place for the time being recorded by the Registrar as the situation of the registered office of the company shall be deemed to be the registered office of the company notwithstanding that the situation of its registered office may have changed.

867 Period within which summary proceedings may be commenced

(1) Notwithstanding (in the case of category 3 or 4 offences) section 10(4) of the Petty Sessions (Ireland) Act 1851, summary proceedings in relation to an offence under this Act may be commenced—

(a) at any time within 3 years after the date on which the offence was committed, or

(b) if, at the expiry of the period referred to in *paragraph (a)*, the person against whom the proceedings are to be brought is outside the State, within 6 months after the date on which he or she next enters the State, or

(c) at any time within 3 years after the date on which evidence that, in the opinion of the person bringing the proceedings, is sufficient to justify the bringing of the proceedings comes to that person's knowledge,

whichever is the later.

(2) For the purposes of *subsection (1)(c)*, a certificate signed by or on behalf of the person bringing the proceedings as to the date on which the evidence referred to in that provision came to his or her knowledge shall be *prima facie* evidence of that date.

(3) In any proceedings, a document purporting to be a certificate issued for the purposes of *subsection (2)* and to be signed by the person bringing the proceedings shall be—

(a) deemed to be so signed, and

(b) admitted as evidence without further proof of the signature or of the person purporting to sign the certificate.

868 Prosecution of companies on indictment

(1) The following provisions of this section apply where a company is charged, either alone or with some other person, with an indictable offence.

(2) The company may appear, at all stages of the proceedings, by a representative and the answer to any question put to a person charged with an indictable offence may be made on behalf of the company by that representative but if the company does not so appear it shall not be necessary to put the questions and the District Court may, notwithstanding its absence, send forward the company for trial and exercise any of its other powers under Part 1A of the Criminal Procedure Act 1967, including the power to take depositions.

(3) Any right of objection or election conferred upon the accused person by any enactment may be exercised on behalf of the company by its representative.

(4) Any plea that may be entered or signed by an accused person, whether before the District Court or before the trial judge, may be entered in writing on behalf of the company by its representative, and if the company does not appear by its representative or does appear but fails to enter any such plea, the trial shall proceed as though the company had duly entered a plea of not guilty.

(5) In this section, "representative" in relation to a company means a person duly appointed by the company to represent it for the purpose of doing any act or thing which the representative of a company is authorised by this section to do.

(6) A representative of a company shall not, by virtue only of being appointed for the purpose referred to in *subsection (5)*, be qualified to act on behalf of the company before any court for any other purpose.

(7) A representative for the purpose of this section need not be appointed under the seal of the company.

(8) A statement in writing purporting to be signed by a managing director of the company or some other person (by whatever name called) who manages, or is one of the persons who manage, the affairs of the company, to the effect that the person named in the statement has been appointed as the representative of the company for the purposes of this section shall be admissible without further proof as evidence that that person has been so appointed.

869 Offences by body committed with consent of its officer

(1) This section applies where an offence is committed by a body corporate under:

- (a) *section 785*;
- (b) *section 790*; [...][a]
- (c) [*section 876*;][b]
- (d) [*Part 27*][c].

(2) In any case to which this section applies, if the offence under *section 785*, *790* or *876*, [or *Part 27*][d], as the case may be, is proved to have been committed with the consent or connivance of or to be attributable to any neglect on the part of any person who is a director, manager, secretary, or other officer of the body corporate, or any person who was purporting to act in any such capacity, that person as well as the body corporate shall be guilty of an offence and shall be liable to be proceeded against and punished as if he or she were guilty of the first-mentioned offence.

(3) Where the affairs of a body corporate are managed by its members, *subsection (2)* shall apply in relation to the acts and defaults of a member in connection with his or her functions of management as if he or she were a director or manager.

Amendments

a Word "or" deleted by C(SA)A 2018, s 15(a)(i).
b Words substituted by C(SA)A 2018, s 15(a)(ii) (previously: "*section 790.*").
c Subparagraph (d) inserted by C(SA)A 2018, s 15(a)(iii).
d Words inserted by C(SA)A 2018, s 15(b).

---

870 Further offence, where contravention continued after conviction for an offence, and penalties for such offence

If the contravention in respect of which a person is convicted of an offence under this Act is continued after the conviction, the person shall be guilty of a further offence on every day on which the contravention continues and for each such offence the person shall be liable—

- (a) where the original contravention was a category 1 offence, whether prosecuted summarily or on indictment, on—
  - (i) conviction on indictment, to a fine not exceeding €5,000, or
  - (ii) summary conviction, to a class D fine,

(b) where the original contravention was a category 2 offence, whether prosecuted summarily or on indictment, on—

(i) conviction on indictment, to a fine not exceeding €1,000, or

(ii) summary conviction, to a fine not exceeding €100,

or

(c) where the original contravention was a category 3 offence or a category 4 offence, on summary conviction to a fine not exceeding €50.

871 Categories 1 to 4 offences — penalties

(1) A person guilty of an offence under this Act that is stated to be a category 1 offence shall be liable—

(a) on summary conviction, to a class A fine or imprisonment for a term not exceeding 12 months or both, or

(b) on conviction on indictment, to a fine not exceeding €500,000 or imprisonment for a term not exceeding 10 years or both.

(2) A person guilty of an offence under this Act that is stated to be a category 2 offence shall be liable—

(a) on summary conviction, to a class A fine or imprisonment for a term not exceeding 12 months or both, or

(b) on conviction on indictment, to a fine not exceeding €50,000 or imprisonment for a term not exceeding 5 years or both.

(3) A person guilty of an offence under this Act that is stated to be a category 3 offence shall be liable, on summary conviction, to a class A fine or imprisonment for a term not exceeding 6 months or both.

(4) A person guilty of an offence under this Act that is stated to be a category 4 offence shall be liable, on summary conviction, to a class A fine.

872 Court may order that convicted person remedy breach

The court in which a conviction for an offence under this Act is recorded or affirmed may order that the person convicted shall remedy the breach of this Act in respect of which that person was convicted.

873 Notice by Director to remedy default

(1) The Director may deliver a notice that complies with *subsection (2)* to a person if the Director has reasonable grounds for believing that the person has committed a category 3 or 4 offence.

(2) The notice referred to in *subsection (1)* is a notice that—

(a) is in the prescribed form,

(b) states that the person is alleged to have committed the offence,

(c) states that the person to whom the notice is delivered may during a period of 21 days beginning after the date of the notice, or such greater period as may be specified in the notice—

(i) remedy as far as practicable to the satisfaction of the Director any default that constitutes the offence, and

(ii) pay to the Director a prescribed amount which shall be accompanied by the notice,

and

(d) states that a prosecution of the person to whom the notice is delivered—

(i) will not be instituted during the period referred to in *paragraph (c)*, and

(ii) will not be instituted in any event if, within the period referred to in *paragraph (c)*, the default is remedied to the satisfaction of the Director and payment is made in accordance with the notice.

(3) Where a notice is delivered under *subsection (1)*—

(a) a person to whom it is delivered may, during the period specified in the notice, make to the Director payment of the amount specified in the notice, accompanied by the notice,

(b) the Director may receive the payment and issue a receipt for it and no payment so received shall in any circumstances be recoverable by the person who made it, and

(c) a prosecution in respect of the alleged offence shall not be instituted in the period specified in the notice and if the default is remedied to the satisfaction of the Director and payment of the amount specified in the notice is made during that period, no prosecution in respect of the alleged offence shall be instituted in any event.

(4) In a prosecution for an offence to which this section applies, the defendant shall bear the onus of showing that a payment pursuant to a notice under this section has been made.

(5) All payments made to the Director in pursuance of this section shall be paid into or disposed of for the benefit of the Exchequer in such manner as the Minister for Public Expenditure and Reform may direct.

(6) If the person mentioned in *subsection (1)* is a company, then that subsection authorises the delivery of the notice mentioned in it to an officer of the company but, where the notice is delivered to that officer, the second reference in that subsection to person, and each reference in *subsections (2)* and *(3)* to the person to whom the notice is delivered or otherwise to person, is to be read as a reference to the company.

874 Special provisions applying where default in delivery of documents to Registrar

(1) The Registrar may deliver a notice that complies with *subsection (2)* to a person if the Registrar has reasonable grounds for believing that the person is in default in the delivery, filing or making to the Registrar of a return or similar document required under this Act (being a default that constitutes a category 3 or 4 offence).

(2) The notice referred to in *subsection (1)* is a notice that—

(a) is in the prescribed form,

(b) states that the person has failed to deliver, file or make a specified return or similar document to the Registrar under a specified provision of this Act,

(c) states that the person to whom the notice is delivered may during a period of 21 days beginning after the date of the notice, or such greater period as may be specified in the notice—

(i) remedy the default, and

(ii) pay to the Registrar a prescribed amount which shall be accompanied by the notice,

and

(d) states that a prosecution of the person to whom the notice is delivered—

(i) will not be instituted during the period referred to in *paragraph (c)*, and

(ii) will not be instituted in any event if, within the period referred to in *paragraph (c)*, the default is remedied and payment is made in accordance with the notice.

(3) Where a notice is delivered under *subsection (1)*—

(a) a person to whom it is delivered may, during the period specified in the notice, make to the Registrar payment of the amount specified in the notice, accompanied by the notice,

(b) the Registrar may receive the payment and issue a receipt for it and no payment so received shall in any circumstances be recoverable by the person who made it, and

(c) a prosecution in respect of the alleged offence shall not be instituted in the period specified in the notice and if the default is remedied to the satisfaction of the Registrar and payment of the amount specified in the notice is made during that period, no prosecution in respect of the alleged offence shall be instituted in any event.

(4) In a prosecution for an offence to which this section applies, the defendant shall bear the onus of showing that a payment pursuant to a notice under this section has been made.

(5) All payments made to the Registrar in pursuance of this section shall be paid into or disposed of for the benefit of the Exchequer in such manner as the Minister for Public Expenditure and Reform may direct.

(6) If the person mentioned in *subsection (1)* is a company, then that subsection authorises the delivery of the notice mentioned in it to an officer of the company but, where the notice is delivered to that officer, the second reference in that subsection to person, and each reference in *subsections (2)* and *(3)* to the person to whom the notice is delivered or otherwise to person, is to be read as a reference to the company.

Chapter 8
Provision for enforcement of section 27(1) and additional general offences

875 Civil enforcement of prohibition on trading under misleading name

(1) On the application of the Registrar or the Director, the court may order that a person shall cease, within the time specified in the order, to carry on any trade, profession or business in contravention of *section 27(1)* if that person has—

(a) been convicted of an offence under *section 27(2)*,

(b) been served with a notice by the Registrar or Director requiring that person to cease to carry on a trade, profession or business in contravention of *section 27(1)*, and

(c) failed to comply with the notice within 14 days after the date of service of the notice, or such greater period as may be specified in the notice in that behalf.

(2) In making an order under *subsection (1)* the court may order that all costs of and incidental to the application shall be borne by the person against whom the order is made.

876 Offence of providing false information

(1) A person shall be guilty of a category 2 offence if that person—

(a) in purported compliance with a provision of this Act, answers a question, provides an explanation, makes a statement or completes, signs, produces, lodges or delivers any return, report, certificate, balance sheet or other document that is false in a material particular, and

(b) knows that it is false in a material particular or is reckless as to whether it is or not,

but this subsection is subject to *subsection (3)* which provides for greater maximum penalties in certain cases.

(2) A person shall be guilty of a category 2 offence if—

(a) the person provides false information to an electronic filing agent knowing it to be false or being reckless as to whether it is so, and

(b) that information is subsequently transmitted in a return made, on that person's behalf, to the Registrar,

but this subsection is subject to *subsection (3)* which provides for greater maximum penalties in certain cases.

(3) Where a person is convicted on indictment of an offence under *subsection (1)* or *(2)* and the court is of the opinion that any act, omission or conduct which constituted that offence has—

(a) substantially contributed to a company being unable to pay its debts,

(b) prevented or seriously impeded the orderly winding up of a company, or

(c) substantially facilitated the defrauding of the creditors of a company or creditors of any other person,

then, notwithstanding that it is a category 2 offence of which he or she has been convicted, the maximum term of imprisonment and the maximum amount of fine to which the person shall be liable for the offence shall be that as provided for in *section 871(1)(b)* in relation to a category 1 offence.

877 Offence of destruction, mutilation or falsification of book or document

(1) Subject to *subsection (2)*, an officer of a company shall be guilty of a category 2 offence who—

(a) destroys, mutilates or falsifies, or is privy to the destruction, mutilation or falsification, of any book or document affecting or relating to the property or affairs of the company, or

(b) makes or is a party to the making of a false entry in any such book or document.

(2) In any proceedings against a person in respect of an offence under *subsection (1)*, it shall be a defence to prove that, in carrying out the destruction, mutilation or other act concerned, the person had no intention to defeat the process of the law and, in particular, the enforcement of this Act.

878 Offence of fraudulently parting with, altering or making omission in book or document

An officer of a company shall be guilty of a category 2 offence who—

(a) fraudulently parts with, alters, or makes an omission in any book or document affecting or relating to the property or affairs of the company, or

(b) is a party to the fraudulent parting with, fraudulent altering or fraudulent making of an omission in any such book or document.

Chapter 9
Evidential matters

879 Proof of certificate as to overseas incorporation

(1) This section applies where in any proceedings under, or for any other purpose of, this Part or *Parts 1* to *13* or *Part 15*, the existence of a body corporate or undertaking outside the State is alleged or is otherwise in issue.

(2) In *subsection (3)* "relevant certificate" means a certificate that—

(a) is signed by any person purporting to hold the office of registrar of companies or assistant registrar of companies or any similar office in any country prescribed for the purposes of this section, and

(b) certifies that the body corporate or undertaking named in the certificate has been incorporated or registered in that country.

(3) A relevant certificate shall be *prima facie* evidence of the incorporation or registration of the named body corporate or undertaking in the country concerned

without proof of the signature of the person signing the certificate and without proof that the person signing the certificate holds the office purported to be held.

880 Proof of incorporation under overseas legislation

(1) This section applies where in any proceedings under, or for the purposes of, this Part or *Parts 1* to *13* or *Part 15* the incorporation, by virtue of any Act passed in any country, not being the State, of a corporation is alleged or is otherwise in issue.

(2) A copy of any Act by which a corporation is incorporated purporting—

(a) to be passed in any country prescribed for the purposes of this section, and

(b) to be published by the Government publishers of that country,

shall, without further proof, be *prima facie* evidence of the incorporation of the corporation.

881 Admissibility in evidence of certain matters

(1) Where an answer is given by an individual to a question put to that individual in the exercise of powers conferred by any of the provisions specified in *subsection (2)*, that answer—

(a) may be used in evidence against that individual in any civil proceedings,

(b) shall not be used in evidence against that individual in any criminal proceedings except a prosecution for perjury in respect of an answer given.

(2) The provisions referred to in *subsection (1)* are the following:

(a) *sections 753* to *757*;

(b) *sections 753*, *756* and *757* as applied by *section 765*;

(c) rules made in respect of the winding up of companies (whether by the court or voluntarily) by the rule making authority referred to in *section 564*.

(3) A statement required by *section 593*—

(a) may be used in evidence, in any civil proceedings, against any individual who makes or concurs in the making of the statement,

(b) shall not be used in evidence against that individual in any criminal proceedings except a prosecution for perjury in respect of any matter contained in the statement.

(4) A document purporting to be a copy of a report of an inspector appointed under *Part 13* shall be admissible in any civil proceedings as evidence—

(a) of the facts set out in it without further proof, unless the contrary is shown, and

(b) of the opinion of the inspector in relation to any matter contained in the report.

882 Provision of information to juries

(1) In a trial on indictment of an offence under this Act, the trial judge may order that copies of all or any of the following documents be given to the jury in any form that the judge considers appropriate:

(a) any document admitted in evidence at the trial;

(b) the transcript of the opening speeches of counsel;

(c) any charts, diagrams, graphics, schedules or summaries of evidence produced at trial;

(d) the transcript of the whole or part of the evidence given at the trial;

(e) the transcript of the trial judge's charge to the jury;

(f) any other document that in the opinion of the trial judge would assist the jury in its deliberations including, where appropriate, an affidavit by an accountant summarising, in a form that is likely to be comprehended by the jury, any transactions by the accused or other persons relevant to the offence.

(2) If the prosecutor proposes to apply to the trial judge for an order that a document referred to in *subsection (1)(f)* shall be given to the jury, the prosecutor shall give a copy of the document to the accused in advance of the trial and, on the hearing of the application, the trial judge shall take into account any representations made by or on behalf of the accused in relation to it.

(3) Where the trial judge has made an order that an affidavit referred to in *subsection (1)(f)* shall be given to the jury, the judge may in an appropriate case, with a view to assisting the jury in its deliberations, require the accountant who prepared the affidavit to explain to the jury any relevant accounting procedures or principles.

883 Certificate evidence

(1) In any legal proceedings (including proceedings relating to an offence), a certificate signed by an appropriate officer in the course of performing his or her functions is, in the absence of evidence to the contrary, proof of the following:

(a) if it certifies that the officer has examined the relevant records and that it appears from them that during a stated period an item was not received from a stated person, proof that the person did not during that period provide the item and that the item was not received;

(b) if it certifies that the officer has examined the relevant records and that it appears from them that a stated notice was not issued to a stated person, proof that the person did not receive the notice;

(c) if it certifies that the officer has examined the relevant records and that it appears from them that a stated notice was duly given to a stated person on a stated date, proof that the person received the notice on that date;

(d) if it certifies that the officer has examined the relevant records and that it appears from them that a stated notice was posted to a stated person at a stated address on a stated date, proof that the notice was received by that person at that address on a date 3 days after the date on which the document was posted;

(e) if it certifies that the officer has examined the relevant records and that it appears from them that a document was filed or registered with or delivered at a stated place, on a stated date or at a stated time, proof that the document was filed or registered with or delivered at that place, on that date or at that time.

(2) A certificate referred to in *subsection (1)* that purports to be signed by an appropriate officer is admissible in evidence in any legal proceedings without proof of the officer's signature or that the officer was the proper person to sign the certificate.

(3) In this section—

"appropriate officer" means—

(a) in respect of functions that, under this Act, are to be performed by the Minister, the Minister or an officer of the Minister;

(b) in respect of functions that, under this Act, are to be performed by the Director, the Director or an officer of the Director;

(c) in respect of functions that, under this Act, are to be performed by the inspector or inspectors appointed under *Part 13*, an inspector or, where more than one inspector is appointed, any inspector;

(d) in respect of functions that, under this Act, are to be performed by the Registrar, an assistant registrar or any other person authorised by the Minister under *section 887(9)*;

(e) in respect of functions that, under this Act, are to be performed by the Central Bank—

(i) the Head of Financial Regulation (within the meaning given by the Central Bank Act 1942); or

(ii) a person appointed by some other person to whom the Head of Financial Regulation has delegated responsibility for appointing persons for the purposes of this section;

"item" includes a document and any other thing;

"notice" includes—

(a) any request, notice, letter, demand or other document; and

(b) any form of obligation that an individual may have under this Act by reason of a demand or request made by an appropriate officer, whether communicated in writing, orally or by other means.

884 Documentary evidence

(1) A document prepared pursuant to any provision of this Act and purporting to be signed by any person is deemed, in the absence of evidence to the contrary, to have been signed by that person.

(2) A document submitted under this Act on behalf of any person is deemed to have been submitted by that person unless that person proves that it was submitted without that person's consent or knowledge.

(3) A document that purports to be a copy of, or an extract from, any document kept by or on behalf of the Director and that purports to be certified by the Director, an officer of the Director or any person authorised by the Director to be a true copy of or extract from the original document is, without proof of the official position of the person

certifying the document, admissible in evidence in all legal proceedings and of the same evidential effect as the original document.

(4) A document that purports to be a copy of, or an extract from, any document kept by the Minister and that purports to be certified by the Minister, an officer of the Minister or any person authorised by the Minister to be a true copy of or extract from the original document is, without proof of the official position of the person certifying the document, admissible in evidence in all legal proceedings and of the same evidential effect as the original document.

(5) A document that purports to be a copy of, or an extract from, any document kept by an inspector and that purports to be certified by the inspector or any person authorised by the inspector to be a true copy of or extract from the original document is, without proof of the official position of the person certifying the document, admissible in evidence in all legal proceedings and of the same evidential effect as the original document.

(6) A document that purports to be a copy of, or an extract from, any document kept by the Central Bank and certified by—

(a) the Head of Financial Regulation (within the meaning given by the Central Bank Act 1942), or

(b) a person authorised by the Head of Financial Regulation,

to be a true copy of or extract from the original document is, without proof of the official position of the person certifying the document, admissible in evidence in all legal proceedings and of the same evidential effect as the original document.

(7) For the purposes of this Act, a document that purports to have been created by a person is deemed, in the absence of evidence to the contrary, to have been created by that person, and any statement contained in the document is presumed to have been made by that person unless the document expressly attributes its making to some other person.

(8) This section, and in particular *subsection (1)*, is in addition to, and does not derogate from, any other provision of this Act that provides for the receiving in evidence of a particular document and, in particular, its being received in evidence without proof of the signature of the person who purported to sign it, or that he or she possessed or held the capacity or position concerned.

885 Saving for privileged communications in context of requirements under *section 724*

Where proceedings are brought under this Act against any person, nothing in *section 447* or *724* shall be taken to require any person who has acted as solicitor for the company to disclose any privileged communication made to him or her in that capacity.

886 Statutory declaration made in foreign place

(1) A statutory declaration made in a foreign place (in pursuance of, or for the purposes of, this Act) shall be deemed to have been validly made (in pursuance of, or for the purposes of, this Act) if—

(a) it is made in that place before a person entitled under the Solicitor's Act 1954 to practise as a solicitor in the State, or

(b) it is made before a person authorised under the law of that place to administer oaths in that place and *subsection (3)*, *(4)* or *(5)*, whichever applies, is complied with.

(2) *Subsection (1)* is—

(a) without prejudice to the circumstances set out in the Statutory Declarations Act 1938 in which a statutory declaration may be made, and

(b) in addition to, and not in substitution for, the circumstances provided under the Diplomatic and Consular Officers (Provision of Services) Act 1993 or any other enactment in which a statutory declaration made by a person outside the State is regarded as a statutory declaration validly made (whether for purposes generally or any specific purpose).

(3) In a case falling within *subsection (1)(b)*, and if the foreign place in question is situate in a state that is a contracting party to the EC Convention, then (unless that Convention does not extend to that particular place), the provisions of the EC Convention with regard to authentication shall apply in relation to the statutory declaration concerned, including the procedures for verification of any matter in circumstances where serious doubts, with good reason, arise in respect of that matter.

(4) In a case falling within *subsection (1)(b)*, and if the foreign place in question is situate in a state that is a contracting party to the Hague Convention but is not a contracting party to the EC Convention, then (unless the Hague Convention does not extend to that particular place), the provisions of the Hague Convention with regard to authentication shall apply in relation to the statutory declaration concerned, including the procedures for verification of any matter in circumstances where serious doubts, with good reason, arise in respect of that matter.

(5) In a case falling within *subsection (1)(b)* to which neither *subsection (3)* nor *(4)* applies, the following shall be authenticated in accordance with the law of the foreign place in question:

(a) the signature of the person making the declaration (the "declarer"); and

(b) to the extent that that law requires either or both of the following to be authenticated—

(i) the capacity in which the declarer has acted in making the declaration;

(ii) the seal or stamp of the person who has administered the oath to the declarer.

(6) The Registrar may, in respect of a statutory declaration that purports to have been authenticated in the manner specified in *subsection (5)* and to be made in pursuance of or for the purposes of this Act, require such proof as the Registrar considers appropriate of any particular requirements of the law referred to in *subsection (5)* .

(7) In this section—

"EC Convention" means the Convention Abolishing the Legalisation of Documents in the Member States of the European Communities of 25 May 1987;

"foreign place" means a place outside the State;

"Hague Convention" means the Convention Abolishing the Requirement of Legalisation for Foreign Public Documents done at the Hague on 5 October 1961;

"statutory declaration", in addition to the meaning assigned to it by the Interpretation Act 2005, means a declaration that conforms with the requirements of the Statutory Declarations Act 1938, except for any requirements contained in section 1 of that Act or any other provision of it, expressly or impliedly limiting—

(a) the class of persons who may take and receive a declaration; or

(b) the places in which a declaration may be taken or received.

(8) A statutory declaration made—

(a) before 24 December 2006,

(b) in a place outside the State,

(c) before—

(i) if the place is not a place in England and Wales, Northern Ireland or Scotland, a person authorised under the law of that place to administer oaths or a person entitled under the Solicitor's Act 1954 to practise as a solicitor in the State, or

(ii) if the place is a place in England and Wales, Northern Ireland or Scotland—

(I) a person entitled under the law of England and Wales, Northern Ireland or Scotland, as the case may be, to practise as a solicitor in England and Wales, Northern Ireland or Scotland, as the case may be, or to administer oaths there, or

(II) a person entitled under the Solicitor's Act 1954 to practise as a solicitor in the State,

and

(d) purporting to be made in pursuance of or for the purposes of the Companies Acts (being the collective citation, with respect to enactments concerning companies, as stood provided, for the time being, by statute),

shall, if the declaration was delivered to the Registrar before 24 December 2006, be valid and deemed always to have been valid notwithstanding anything in the Diplomatic and Consular Officers (Provision of Services) Act 1993 or any other enactment and anything done on foot of that declaration's delivery to the Registrar, including any subsequent registration of that declaration by the Registrar, shall be valid and be deemed always to have been valid notwithstanding anything in that Act or any other enactment.

(9) Nothing in *subsection (8)* affects any proceedings commenced before 24 December 2006.

PART 15
FUNCTIONS OF REGISTRAR AND OF REGULATORY AND ADVISORY BODIES

Chapter 1
Registrar of Companies

887 Registration office, "register", officers and CRO Gazette

(1) The Minister shall maintain and administer an office or offices in the State at such places as the Minister thinks fit for the purposes of—

(a) the registration of companies under this Act, and

(b) the performance of the other functions under this Act expressed to be performable by the Registrar.

(2) A reference in this Act to the register (where the context is not that of a register to be kept by a company or other body) is a reference to, as appropriate—

(a) the register to be kept by the Registrar (which the Registrar is empowered by this subsection to keep) in which notices or other documents, information or things delivered in pursuance of this Act to the Registrar are to be registered or recorded (and in which, in particular, in the case of a registration of a company, the fact of the company's incorporation is to be disclosed), or

(b) the particular register that a provision of this Act requires the Registrar to keep for a special purpose,

but any such register as is mentioned in *paragraph (b)* shall, for the purposes generally of this Act, be regarded as forming part of the first-mentioned register.

(3) The Minister may appoint a registrar (who shall be known as the "Registrar of Companies") and such assistant registrars as he or she thinks necessary for any of the purposes referred to in *subsection (1)*, and may make regulations with respect to their duties and may remove any persons so appointed.

(4) The Minister may direct a seal or seals to be prepared for the authentication of documents required for or connected with any of the purposes referred to in *subsection (1)*.

(5) A person appointed under section 368 of the Act of 1963 before the commencement of this section and who holds office immediately before such commencement (and, in particular the person mentioned in *subsection (6)*) shall continue in office for the unexpired period of his or her term unless he or she sooner retires, resigns or dies or is removed from office.

(6) The person referred to in *subsection (5)* is the person who holds the office bearing the title "Registrar of Companies" and that person shall continue to be known by that title for so long as that person continues to hold office in accordance with that subsection.

(7) The electronic gazette maintained by the Registrar before the commencement of this section and known as the "Companies Registration Office Gazette" shall continue to be maintained by the Registrar and is referred to in this Act as the "CRO Gazette".

(8) Any act referred to in subsection (4) of section 368 of the Act of 1963 which, before 21 December 1999, was done by—

(a) an assistant registrar appointed under subsection (2) of that section, or

(b) any other person employed in the office of the Registrar to perform generally duties under any enactment referred to in that subsection (4),

shall be valid and be deemed always to have been valid as if the Minister had directed under that subsection (4) that such an act was to be done to or by such an assistant registrar or such other person (including in cases where the existing registrar of joint stock companies (or his or her successor) was not absent).

(9) Any act required or authorised by—

(a) this Act,

(b) the Limited Partnerships Act 1907, or

(c) the Registration of Business Names Act 1963,

to be done to or by the Registrar, the registrar of joint stock companies or a person referred to in the enactment as "the registrar", as the case may be, may be done to or by a registrar or assistant registrar appointed under *subsection (3)*, a person continued in office by virtue of *subsection (5)* or any other person so authorised by the Minister.

888 Authentication of documents other than by signing or sealing them

A requirement of this Act that a document shall be signed or sealed shall be satisfied if the document is authenticated in the prescribed manner.

889 Fees

(1) In respect of the doing of the following (where the provision concerned does not, itself, expressly provide for the payment of a prescribed fee in that behalf), namely—

(a) the registration of a company,

(b) the registration of any notice, return or other document, or

(c) the doing of any other thing that the Registrar is required or authorised by or under this Act to do (whether, at the request or direction of, or on application of any person, or otherwise in the circumstances provided by or under this Act),

regulations may be made by the Minister requiring the payment to the Registrar of a fee, of an amount specified in the regulations, by the person concerned.

(2) The references in *subsection (1)(a)* and *(b)* to registration, and the reference in *subsection (1)(c)* to the doing of any other thing, include a reference to—

(a) a case in which, in accordance with this Act or an instrument thereunder, registration or the doing of the other thing is declined or otherwise not proceeded with by the Registrar, and

(b) a case in which the application or request for registration or the doing of the other thing is withdrawn.

(3) Where a provision of this Act expressly provides for the payment of a prescribed fee in respect of the doing of a thing referred to in *subsection (1)(a)* or *(b)*, that provision shall be read as imposing liability for payment of the fee notwithstanding that the matter eventuates in a case referred to in *subsection (2)(a)* or *(b)*.

(4) In *subsection (1)* "person concerned" means—

(a) in a case where the registration is to be effected or the other thing concerned is to be done by the Registrar at the instance of a person — that person, or

(b) in any other case — the person who is specified in the regulations to be the person concerned for the purpose of that case (and the person so specified may be such person as the Minister reasonably determines to be the person for whom the principal benefit will enure by the thing concerned being done by the Registrar).

(5) Different amounts of fees may be so specified for different classes of case in which a thing falling within any particular paragraph of *subsection (1)* is done and any such class of case may be defined in the regulations concerned by reference to such matter or matters as the Minster considers reasonable and appropriate for the purpose.

(6) Without prejudice to the generality of *subsection (5)*, a different amount of fee may be so specified in respect of the doing of a foregoing thing, where the step or steps by another person, in consequence of, or on foot of which, the thing is authorised or required to be done, have not been taken in observance of a time limit specified by or under this Act.

(7) In a case falling within *subsection (6)*, any different amount of fee that is specified may be specified by reference to the period of time that has elapsed between the latest date, in observance of the particular time limit specified by or under this Act, by which the one or more steps concerned ought to have been taken and the date on which they have been taken.

(8) Where regulations under this section require, in respect of the doing of a thing referred to in *subsection (1)*, the payment of a fee of an amount specified in them and the fee of the specified amount is not paid to the Registrar, then, subject to any special cases that the Minister may deem it expedient to provide for in the regulations, the Registrar is not obliged to do (where the Registrar would otherwise be so obliged) the thing concerned.

(9) *Subsection (7)* is in addition to, and not in derogation from, any particular provision of or under this Act that provides or the effect of which is that a fee of a prescribed amount must be paid to the Registrar as a condition, or one of the conditions, for the Registrar's doing the particular act concerned.

(10) All fees paid to the Registrar in pursuance of this Act shall be paid into or disposed of for the benefit of the Exchequer in such manner as the Minister for Public Expenditure and Reform may direct.

890 Annual report by Registrar

(1) The Registrar shall, as soon as may be, but not later than 4 months, after the end of each year, make a report in writing to the Minister of the Registrar's activities during

that year and the Minister shall cause copies of the report to be laid before each House of the Oireachtas not later than 6 months after the end of that year.

(2) The Minister may, after consultation with the Registrar, prescribe the form of a report under this section and the manner in which any matter is to be addressed in such a report.

891 Inspection and production of documents kept by Registrar

(1) On payment of the prescribed fee, any person may—

(a) inspect any document which has been received and recorded by the Registrar in pursuance of this Act,

(b) require the Registrar to certify a certificate of incorporation of any company, or

(c) require the Registrar to certify a copy of or extract from any other document or any part of any other document kept by the Registrar.

(2) A process for compelling the production of any document kept by the Registrar—

(a) shall not issue from any court except with the leave of that court, and

(b) if so issued, shall state that it is issued with the leave of the court.

(3) For the purposes of communications between registers through the system of interconnection of registers, the Registrar shall assign to each company a unique identifier which shall include elements to identify the company as a company in the State, to identify the number assigned to the company in the register and other appropriate elements to avoid identification errors.

(4) The Registrar shall make available, through the system of interconnection of registers, electronic copies of the documents and particulars of companies referred to in Article 2 of Directive 2009/101/EC.

(5) The Registrar shall ensure that any changes to those documents and particulars, other than changes to the accounting documents referred to in Article 2(f) of Directive 2009/101/EC, are entered into the register and that such entering is done (normal circumstances prevailing) within 21 days after the date of receipt of the complete documentation regarding those changes.

(6) The Registrar shall make available, as soon as practicable, through the system of interconnection of registers, information on—

(a) the opening and termination of winding up or insolvency proceedings of a company on the register;

(b) the opening and termination of a receivership applicable to a company on the register; and

(c) the striking-off of a company from the register.

(7) The Registrar shall ensure that the following particulars relating to a company on the register are available, free of charge, through the system of interconnection of registers—

(a) its name and legal form;

(b) the address of its registered office, including the fact that it is registered in the State; and

(c) its registration number on the register.

(8) The Registrar shall ensure that information is made available explaining the provisions of this Act according to which a third party can rely on the information and particulars referred to in *subsection (4)*.

892 Admissibility of certified copy or extract

(1) A copy of or extract from any document registered with and kept by the Registrar shall be admissible in evidence in all legal proceedings and be of the same evidential effect as the original document if it has been certified as a true copy under the signature of the Registrar, an assistant registrar or another officer authorised by the Minister.

(2) For the purposes of *subsection (1)* it shall not be necessary to prove the official position of the person whose signature appears on the copy concerned.

893 Certificate by Registrar admissible as evidence of facts stated

A certificate in writing and signed by the Registrar shall be admissible in all legal proceedings as evidence without further proof of any of the following facts stated in the certificate unless the contrary is shown—

(a) the contents of a register kept by the Registrar,

(b) the date on which a document was filed or registered with or delivered to the Registrar,

(c) the date on which a document was received by the Registrar, or

(d) the most recent date (if any) on which a requirement under this Act was complied with.

894 Disposal of documents filed with Registrar

(1) The Registrar may, as respects any document that has (whether pursuant to this Act or the prior Companies Acts) been received and recorded by the Registrar, destroy the document if the following conditions are satisfied—

(a) 6 or more years have elapsed after the date of its receipt by him or her, and

(b) its destruction is authorised by the Director of the National Archives under section 7 of the National Archives Act 1986,

but this is subject to *subsection (2)*.

(2) Without prejudice to *subsection (3)*, for so long as a company's existence is recorded in the register, and for a period of 20 years after the date of its dissolution, the Registrar shall keep in electronic form a copy of every document that, in relation to that company, has been received and recorded (whether pursuant to this Act or the prior Companies Acts) by the Registrar and the keeping of such copy in that form shall be such as to ensure the authenticity and accuracy of the data and that the data may be reliably accessed.

(3) On and from the expiry of 20 years after the date of its dissolution, a copy of every document kept, in relation to a company, by the Registrar under *subsection (2)*, and in the form specified therein, shall be kept and maintained by the Registrar in an

archival database comprising the records of companies, the length of the period of dissolution of which stands at 20 or more years.

(4) The means of keeping, in electronic form, the archival database referred to in *subsection (3)* shall be such as are, in the opinion of the Registrar (after consultation with the Director of the National Archives), best calculated to preserve and maintain the integrity of the data.

895 Registrar may apply system of information classification

(1) The Registrar may, as he or she considers appropriate—

(a) apply a system of classification to information to which this section applies, and

(b) assign symbols of identification to persons or classes of persons to whom any such information relates.

(2) This section applies to any information that, under this Act, is required to be delivered to the Registrar and is so received by the Registrar.

(3) The Minister may make regulations—

(a) requiring that the symbol assigned by the Registrar to a person individually or as one of a class of persons shall be entered on all documents that are required under this Act to contain the name of that person, and

(b) specifying particular persons whose duty it shall be to comply or ensure compliance with the regulations.

(4) If a person is required under a regulation made under *subsection (3)* to comply or ensure compliance with a requirement referred to in *subsection (3)(a)* and fails to do so, the person shall be guilty of a category 3 offence.

896 Delivery to Registrar of documents in legible form

(1) This section applies to the delivery under any provision of this Act of a document to the Registrar in legible form.

(2) The document shall—

(a) state in a prominent position the registered number of the company to which the document relates, and

(b) comply with regulations (if any) prescribing—

(i) the form and contents of the document,

(ii) requirements to enable the Registrar to copy the document.

(3) Regulations made for the purposes of this section may prescribe different requirements for the form and content of a document with respect to different classes of document.

(4) In this section, "document" includes any periodic account, abstract, statement or return.

897 Delivery of documents in electronic form may be made mandatory

(1) If the Minister, after consultation with the Registrar, considers that the performance by the Registrar of functions under this Act with respect to the receipt and registration of information under any particular provision of it could be more efficiently discharged if an order under this section were to be made in relation to that provision then the Minister may make such an order accordingly.

(2) The order referred to in *subsection (1)* is an order providing that the sole means to be used to deliver, under the particular provision concerned, a document (within the meaning of *section 896*) to the Registrar shall be those provided for under the Electronic Commerce Act 2000 and, accordingly, where such an order is made, those means shall, for that purpose, be used to the exclusion of any other means.

(3) An order under this section may relate to more than one, or to every, provision of this Act.

(4) In *subsection (1)* "information" shall be read in the same manner as *section 896* provides "document" in that section is to be read.

(5) In *subsection (2)* the reference to the use of the means provided for under the Electronic Commerce Act 2000 is a reference to their use in a manner that complies with any requirements of the Registrar of the kind referred to in sections 12(2)(b) and 13(2)(a) of that Act.

898 Registrar's notice that document does not comply

(1) On receipt of a non-complying document the Registrar may, in his or her discretion—

- (a) serve on the person delivering the document (or, if there is more than one such person, any of them) a notice that the document does not comply, or
- (b) neither serve such a notice nor otherwise advise or give notice to any such person that the document does not comply,

and the provision made by the following provisions of this section, in a case where the course under *paragraph (a)* is taken by the Registrar, is not to be read as implying that, in a case where the course under *paragraph (b)* is taken by the Registrar, any legal consequences arising from the fact that a non-complying document has been delivered are thereby avoided.

(2) A notice under *subsection (1)(a)* shall state in what respects the document is a non-complying document.

(3) A document referred to in *subsection (1)* shall be deemed not to have been delivered to the Registrar if—

- (a) it is the subject of a notice served under *subsection (1)(a)*, and
- (b) the Registrar has not received within 14 days after the date of service of the notice a replacement document that—
  - (i) complies with the requirements referred to in *subsection (4)(b)*, or
  - (ii) is not rejected by the Registrar for non-compliance with those requirements.

(4) In this section, a non-complying document is a document that—

(a) is required or authorised to be delivered to the Registrar under this Act, and

(b) fails to comply with—

(i) the relevant requirements of this Act (and, in particular, the provisions of any section under which the requirement to deliver the document to the Registrar arises) or regulations made under this Act, or

(ii) any requirements imposed by or under any other enactment relating to the completion of a document and its delivery to the Registrar.

899 Supplementary and clarificatory provisions for *section 898*

(1) For the purposes of any provision which—

(a) imposes a penalty for failure to deliver a document, so far as it imposes a penalty for continued contravention, or

(b) provides for the payment of a fee in respect of the registration of a document, being a fee of a greater amount than the amount provided under the provision in respect of the registration of such a document that has been delivered to the Registrar within the period specified for its delivery to him or her,

no account shall be taken of the period between the delivery of the original document referred to in *section 898(1)* and the end of the period of 14 days after the date of service of the notice under *section 898(1)(a)* in relation to it (but only if, before the end of the latter period, a replacement document that complies with the requirements referred to in *section 898(4)(b)* is delivered to the Registrar).

(2) Nothing in this section or *section 898* shall have the effect of making valid any matter which a provision of this Act or of any other enactment provides is to be void or of no effect in circumstances where a document in relation to it is not delivered to the Registrar within the period specified for the document's delivery to him or her.

[899A Function imposed on Registrar under section 930D

Section 930D makes additional provision with regard to the performance of functions by, amongst others, the Registrar.][a]

Amendments

a Section 899A inserted by C(SA)A 2018, s 16. Heading of the amending section used here in the absence of one in the amendment.

Chapter 2
Irish Auditing and Accounting Supervisory Authority

900 Interpretation (*Chapter 2*)

(1) In this Chapter—

"1993 Accounts Regulations" means the European Communities (Accounts) Regulations 1993 (S.I. No. 396 of 1993);

[...][a]

"Act of 2003" means the Companies (Auditing and Accounting) Act 2003;

"amount of turnover" has the same meaning as it has in [*section 275*][b];

["applicable provisions", in relation to a *Part 27* function and a recognised accountancy body, means, in addition to the provision of this Act that confers that function—

(a) any other provisions of this Act or of a statutory instrument made under this Act,

(b) the provisions of any *section 931* notice given to the body that are relevant to that function,

(c) the provisions of Regulation (EU) No 537/2014 that are relevant to that function, and

(d) the provisions of any rule, guideline, term or condition, relevant obligation, or direction, referred to in section 906 that are relevant to that function,

in accordance with which that function shall be performed by that body;][c]

"balance sheet total" has the same meaning as it has in [*section 275*][b];

"board" means the board of directors of the Supervisory Authority;

["CEAOB" has the meaning assigned to it by *section 905(3)(c)*;][d]

"chief executive officer" means the chief executive officer of the Supervisory Authority;

"designated body" means a body that, under *section 902(2)*, is a designated body at the relevant time;

"disciplinary committee" means any disciplinary committee or tribunal (however called) of a prescribed accountancy body;

"member", in relation to a prescribed accountancy body, means—

(a) a person; or

(b) a firm,

that is, or was at the relevant time, subject to the investigation and disciplinary procedures approved for that body under—

(i) *section 905(2)(c)*;

(ii) section 9(2)(c) of the Act of 2003; or

(iii) the Act of 1990, whether before or after the amendments of that Act that were made by section 32 of the Act of 2003;

["monetary sanction"—

(a) in relation to a specified person who falls within paragraph (a) of the definition of "specified person", means the monetary sanction referred to in section 934(8), and

(b) in relation to a specified person who falls within paragraph (b) of the definition of 'specified person', means the monetary sanction referred to in *section 934C(2)(g)*;][c]

["Part 27 function" means a function conferred on a recognised accountancy body by a provision of Part 27 or of Schedule 19 or 20;][c]

"prescribed accountancy body" means—

(a) a recognised accountancy body; or
(b) any other body of accountants that is prescribed;

["public notice of relevant sanction imposed", in relation to a specified person, means the publication in accordance with *section 934F(1)* of the specified person's particulars referred to in that section together with the other related particulars referred to in that section;][c]

["recognised accountancy body" means a body of accountants recognised under section 930 for the purposes of the relevant provisions;][c]

["Regulation (EU) No 537/2014" has the meaning assigned to it by *Part 27*;][c]

["relevant body" has the meaning assigned to it by *section 933(1)*;][c]

["relevant contravention" means—

(a) a breach of the standards of a prescribed accountancy body by a member of that body, or

(b) a contravention by a statutory auditor of a provision of—

(i) section 336 or 337,

(ii) Part 27, or

(iii) Regulation (EU) No 537/2014;][c]

["relevant decision", in relation to a specified person, means—

(a) a decision under *section 934(8)* or (9) that a specified person has committed a relevant contravention,

(b) if, in consequence of a decision referred to in paragraph (a), the Supervisory Authority decides under *section 934(8)* or *(9)* to impose a relevant sanction on the specified person, the decision to impose that sanction, or

(c) both such decisions;][c]

["relevant director" means a director or former director of a public-interest entity;][c]

["relevant provisions" means the provisions of—

(a) this Chapter,

(b) Part 27, and

(c) Regulation (EU) No 537/2014;][c]

["relevant sanction"—

(a) in relation to a specified person who falls within paragraph (a) of the definition of "specified person", means a sanction referred to in *section 934(8)*, and

(b) in relation to a specified person who falls within paragraph (b) of the definition of "specified person", means a sanction referred to in *section 934C(2)*;][c]

"reserve fund" means the fund referred to in *section 919*;

["section 931 notice" shall be read in accordance with *section 931(2)*;][c]

["section 933A agreement" shall be read in accordance with *section 933A(2)*;][c]

["section 934E agreement" shall be read in accordance with *section 934E(1)*;][c]

["specified person", in relation to a relevant contravention, means—

(a) if the relevant contravention falls within paragraph (a) of the definition of 'relevant contravention', the member or former member concerned of the prescribed accountancy body, and

(b) if the relevant contravention falls within paragraph (b) of the definition of "relevant contravention", the statutory auditor or former statutory auditor concerned;][c]

"standards", in relation to a prescribed accountancy body, means the rules, regulations and standards that body applies to its members and to which, by virtue of their membership, they are obliged to adhere;

"superannuation benefits" means pensions, gratuities and other allowances payable on resignation, retirement or death;

"Supervisory Authority" means the Irish Auditing and Accounting Supervisory Authority.

(2) In this Chapter, "material interest" is to be read in accordance with section 2(3) of the Ethics in Public Office Act 1995.

[...][f]

Amendments

a Definition of '2010 Audits Regulations' repealed by the European Union (Statutory Audits) (Directive 2006/43/EC, as amended by Directive 2014/56/EU, and Regulation (EU) No 537/2014) Regulations 2016 (SI 312/2016), reg 14(a)(i), with effect from 17 June 2016.

b Words substituted by C(A)A 2017, s 88(a)(ii) (previously: "*section 350*").

c Definitions inserted by C(SA)A 2018, s 17(ii).

d Definition of 'CEAOB' inserted by the European Union (Statutory Audits) (Directive 2006/43/EC, as amended by Directive 2014/56/EU, and Regulation (EU) No 537/2014) Regulations 2016 (SI 312/2016), reg 14(a)(iii), with effect from 17 June 2016.

e Definition substituted by C(SA)A 2018, s 17(a)(i).

f Subsection (3) deleted by C(SA)A 2018, s 17(b).

901 Continuance of designation of Irish Auditing and Accounting Supervisory Authority and other transitional matters

(1) The company, namely, the Irish Auditing and Accounting Supervisory Authority, that was designated under section 5 of the Act of 2003 before the commencement of this section as the body to perform the functions of the Supervisory Authority under that Act shall be the Supervisory Authority for the purposes of this Chapter.

(2) A person appointed to the board of the Irish Auditing and Accounting Supervisory Authority before the commencement of this section and who holds office immediately before such commencement shall continue in office for the unexpired period of his or her term unless he or she sooner retires, resigns or dies or is removed from office; this subsection applies notwithstanding the cessation of membership of that Authority effected by this Chapter of certain bodies (corporate and unincorporated) that had nominated persons for appointment to that board.

(3) Without prejudice to the generality of the preceding subsections, the enactment of this Act does not otherwise affect—

(a) the corporate existence of the Irish Auditing and Accounting Supervisory Authority, and

(b) the continuance in being of the membership of it by the bodies corporate and individuals which or who were members of it immediately before the commencement of this section,

but, as regards that membership—

(i) subject to *section 902(2)* (which effects a reduction in the number of members from that provided in the Act of 2003), and

(ii) subject (as was provided by the corresponding provisions of the Act of 2003) to the provisions of this Chapter enabling the termination, change and increase of that membership.

902 Membership of Supervisory Authority

(1) The Supervisory Authority is to consist of the following members:

(a) each prescribed accountancy body that is a body corporate;

(b) in the case of a prescribed accountancy body that is not a body corporate, an individual or body corporate nominated by that prescribed accountancy body to be a member;

(c) each designated body that is a body corporate;

(d) in the case of a designated body that is not a body corporate, an individual or body corporate nominated by that designated body to be a member.

(2) Unless a regulation under *section 943(1)(b)* provides otherwise, each of the following is, on and from the commencement of this section, a designated body for the purposes of *subsection (1)*:

(a) the Director of Corporate Enforcement;

(b) the Central Bank;

(c) the Irish Stock Exchange;

(d) the Revenue Commissioners;

(e) any body prescribed under *section 943(1)(a)* as a designated body.

903 Amendment to memorandum or articles

An amendment to the memorandum of association or articles of association of the Supervisory Authority takes effect only if the alteration is made with the Minister's prior approval.

904 Objects of Supervisory Authority

(1) The principal objects of the Supervisory Authority which are to be included in its memorandum of association are to—

(a) supervise how the prescribed accountancy bodies regulate and monitor their members,

(b) promote adherence to high professional standards in the auditing and accountancy profession,

(c) monitor whether the financial statements or accounts of certain classes of companies and other undertakings comply with this Act (or, as the case may be, this Act as applied by the 1993 Accounts Regulations) and, where applicable, Article 4 of the [IAS Regulation,][a]

(d) act as a specialist source of advice to the Minister on auditing and accounting [matters, and][b]

[(e) oversee statutory auditors and the conduct of statutory audits in accordance with the relevant provisions and perform functions under those provisions in relation to such oversight.][c]

(2) Nothing in this section prevents or restricts the inclusion in that memorandum of association of all objects and powers, consistent with this Chapter, that are reasonable, necessary or proper for, or incidental or ancillary to, the due attainment of those principal objects.

Amendments

a Words substituted by the European Union (Statutory Audits) (Directive 2006/43/EC, as amended by Directive 2014/56/EU, and Regulation (EU) No 537/2014) Regulations 2016 (SI 312/2016), reg 15(a), with effect from 17 June 2016 (previously: "IAS Regulation, and").

b Words substituted by the European Union (Statutory Audits) (Directive 2006/43/EC, as amended by Directive 2014/56/EU, and Regulation (EU) No 537/2014) Regulations 2016 (SI 312/2016), reg 15(b), with effect from 17 June 2016 (previously: "matters.").

c Paragraph (1)(e) substituted by C(SA)A 2018, s 18.

---

905 Functions of Supervisory Authority

(1) The Supervisory Authority shall do all things necessary and reasonable to further its objects.

(2) Without limiting its functions under *subsection (1)*, the functions of the Supervisory Authority are to—

[(a) grant recognition to bodies of accountants for the purposes of the relevant provisions,][a]

(b) attach under *section 931* terms and conditions to the recognition of bodies of accountants, including terms and conditions—

(i) requiring changes to, and the approval by the Supervisory Authority of, their regulatory plans, and

(ii) requiring their annual reports to the Supervisory Authority on their regulatory plans to be prepared in the manner and form directed by the Supervisory Authority,

(c) require changes to and to approve—

(i) the constitution and bye laws of each prescribed accountancy body, including its investigation and disciplinary procedures and its standards, and

(ii) any amendments to the approved constitution or bye laws of each prescribed accountancy body, including amendments to its investigation and disciplinary procedures and to its standards,

(d) conduct under *section 933* enquiries into whether a prescribed accountancy body has complied with the investigation and disciplinary procedures approved for that body under *paragraph (c)* or referred to in [*paragraph (a)(ii)* or *(iii)* or *(b)(ii)* of the definition of "approved investigation and disciplinary procedures" in *subsection (1)* of that section,][b]

[(e) impose under *section 933* sanctions on prescribed accountancy bodies in relation to enquiries referred to in paragraph (d),][c]

[(ea) conduct under *section 933* enquiries into whether a recognised accountancy body has complied with the applicable provisions in performing a *Part 27* function,

(eb) impose under *section 933* sanctions on recognised accountancy bodies in relation to enquiries referred to in paragraph (ea),][d]

(f) undertake under *section 934* investigations into possible breaches of the standards of a prescribed accountancy body [by a member of that body][e],

[(fa) undertake under *section 934* investigations into possible contraventions of a provision of *section 336 or 337, Part 27* or Regulation (EU) No 537/2014 by a statutory auditor,

(fb) impose under section 934 sanctions on members of prescribed accountancy bodies and statutory auditors for relevant contraventions committed by such members,][f] [(g) supervise how each recognised accountancy body monitors its members and statutory auditors for which the recognised accountancy body has responsibility by virtue of performing a *Part 27* function,][g]

[....][h]

[(i) monitor the effectiveness of provisions of [Part 27] and Regulation (EU) No 537/2014 relating to the independence of statutory auditors,

(ia) monitor developments in the market for audit services to public-interest entities as required by Regulation (EU) No 537/2014,][i]

(j) supervise the investigation and disciplinary procedures of each prescribed accountancy body, including by requiring access to its records and by requiring explanations about the performance of its regulatory and monitoring duties,

(k) co-operate with the prescribed accountancy bodies and other interested parties in developing auditing and accounting standards and practice notes,

[...][j]

(m) perform the functions conferred on it by transparency (regulated markets) law (within the meaning of *Chapter 4* of *Part 23*) in respect of the matters referred to in Article 24(4)(h) of the Transparency (Regulated Markets) Directive (within the meaning of that Chapter),

[(ma) adopt auditing standards for the purposes of [Part 27] and Regulation (EU) No 537/2014,][k]

(n) oversee, in accordance with [Part 27 and Regulation (EU) No 537/2014, the performance of (and, where permitted by that Part, that Regulation or any other Part of this Act (including this Part), perform)] the following functions with respect to statutory auditors:

(i) the approval and registration of statutory auditors (including the registration of Member State audit firms);

(ii) continuing education;

(iii) quality assurance systems;

(iv) investigative and administrative disciplinary systems,][l]

[(na) enable, by virtue of recognition under section 930 or a section 931 notice, functions under paragraph (n) to be performed by recognised accountancy bodies,][m]

(o) perform any other duties or discharge any other responsibilities imposed on it by this Act.

[(3) The Supervisory Authority shall—

(a) cooperate with competent authorities in other Member States to achieve the convergence of the educational qualifications required for the approval of an individual as a statutory auditor,

(b) when engaging in such operation, take into account developments in auditing and the audit profession and, in particular, convergence that has already been achieved by the profession, and

(c) cooperate with the Committee of European Auditing Oversight Bodies (in this Chapter referred to as 'CEAOB') established under Article 30 of Regulation (EU) No 537/2014 and the competent authorities referred to in Article 20 of that Regulation in so far as such convergence relates to the statutory audit of public-interest entities.

(4) The Supervisory Authority shall—

(a) cooperate within the framework of the CEAOB with a view to achieving the convergence of the requirements of the aptitude test,

(b) enhance the transparency and predictability of those requirements, and

(c) cooperate with the CEAOB and with the competent authorities referred to in Article 20 of Regulation (EU) No 537/2014 in so far as such convergence relates to statutory audits of public-interest entities.

(5) With regard to the cooperation that the State is required to engage in by virtue of Article 33 of the Audit Directive, the Supervisory Authority is assigned responsibility in that behalf.

(6) For the purpose of discharging the responsibility referred to in *subsection (5)*, the Supervisory Authority shall put in place appropriate mechanisms, including arrangements with competent authorities in other Member States.][n]

Amendments

a Paragraph (2)(a) substituted by C(SA)A 2018, s 19(a).
b Words substituted by C(SA)A 2018, s 19(b).
c Paragraph (2)(e) substituted by C(SA)A 2018, s 19(c).
d Paragraph (2)(ea) and para (2)(eb) inserted by C(SA)A 2018, s 19(d).
e Words inserted by C(SA)A 2018, s 19(e).
f Paragraph (2)(fa) and para (2)(fb) inserted by C(SA)A 2018, s 19(f).
g Paragraph (2)(g) substituted by C(SA)A 2018, s 19(g).
h Paragraph (2)(h) deleted by C(SA)A 2018, s 19(h).
i Paragraph (2)(i) substituted and para (2)(ia) inserted by the European Union (Statutory Audits) (Directive 2006/43/EC, as amended by Directive 2014/56/EU, and Regulation (EU) No 537/2014) Regulations 2016 (SI 312/2016), reg 16(a)(ii), with effect from 17 June 2016. Words "Part 27" substituted for "the 2016 Audits Regulations" by C(SA)A 2018, s 19(i).
j Paragraph (2)(l) deleted by C(SA)A 2018, s 19(j).
k Paragraph (2)(ma) inserted by the European Union (Statutory Audits) (Directive 2006/43/EC, as amended by Directive 2014/56/EU, and Regulation (EU) No 537/2014) Regulations 2016 (SI 312/2016), reg 16(a)(iii), with effect from 17 June 2016. Words "Part 27" substituted for "2016 Audits Regulations" by C(SA)A 2018, s 19(k).
l Paragraph (2)(n) substituted by the European Union (Statutory Audits) (Directive 2006/43/EC, as amended by Directive 2014/56/EU, and Regulation (EU) No 537/2014) Regulations 2016 (SI 312/2016), reg 16(a)(iii), with effect from 17 June 2016. Words "Part 27 and Regulation (EU) No 537/2014, the performance of (and, where permitted by that Part, that

Regulation or any other Part of this Act (including this Part), perform)" for "the 2016 Audits Regulations and Regulation (EU) No 537/2014, the performance of (and, where permitted by those Regulations, that Regulation or this Act, perform)" by C(SA)A 2018, s 19(l).

m Paragraph (2)(na) inserted by C(SA)A 2018, s 19(m).

n Sub-sections (3), (4), (5) and (6) inserted by the European Union (Statutory Audits) (Directive 2006/43/EC, as amended by Directive 2014/56/EU, and Regulation (EU) No 537/2014) Regulations 2016 (SI 312/2016), reg 16(b), with effect from 17 June 2016.

---

906 General powers

(1) The Supervisory Authority has the power to do anything that appears to it to be requisite, advantageous or incidental to, or to facilitate, the performance of its functions and that is not inconsistent with any enactment.

(2) A power conferred by *subsection (1)* is not to be considered to be limited merely by implication from another provision, whether of this or any other Act, that confers a power on the Supervisory Authority.

(3) The Supervisory Authority may adopt rules and issue guidelines concerning any matter that relates to its functions [(including its functions under Regulation (EU) No 537/2014)][a].

(4) The Supervisory Authority may apply to the court for an order under *section 941(6)* compelling—

(a) a prescribed accountancy body to comply with a rule adopted or guideline issued under *subsection (3)*,

(b) a recognised accountancy body to comply with a term or condition attached under section 192 of the Act of 1990 (before or after the amendment of that Act by section 32 of the Act of [2003),][b]

(c) a person on whom a relevant obligation or obligations is or are imposed to comply with that obligation or those obligations,

[(d) a recognised accountancy body to comply with a *section 931* notice that is relevant to the body's recognition under *section 930* or to the performance of a Part 27 function by the body, or

(e) a relevant body to comply with a direction given to it by the Supervisory Authority under *section 934A(2) or 934C(5)*,][c]

if, in the Authority's opinion, the body or other person concerned may fail or has failed to comply with the rule, guideline, term or condition[, obligation or obligations, notice or direction][d], as the case may be.

(5) In *subsection (4)*, the reference to a relevant obligation or obligations that is or are imposed on a person is a reference to an obligation or obligations that is or are imposed on the person by—

(a) provisions of transparency (regulated markets) law (within the meaning of *Chapter 4* of *Part 23*) that implement Article 24(4)(h) of the Transparency (Regulated Markets) Directive (within the meaning of that [Chapter),][e]

(b) rules adopted by the Supervisory Authority under *subsection (3)* concerning the matters that relate to its functions under [*section 905(2)(m)*,][f]

[(c) provisions of [*Part 27*][g] or Regulation (EU) No 537/2014, or

(d) rules adopted by the Supervisory Authority under *subsection (3)* concerning matters that relate to its functions under *section 905(2)(n)*.][h]

Amendments

a Words inserted by the European Union (Statutory Audits) (Directive 2006/43/EC, as amended by Directive 2014/56/EU, and Regulation (EU) No 537/2014) Regulations 2016 (SI 312/2016), reg 17(a), with effect from 17 June 2016.

b Words substituted by C(SA)A 2018, s 20(a)(i).

c Paragraphs (4)(d) and (e) inserted by C(SA)A 2018, s 20(a)(ii).

d Words substituted by C(SA)A 2018, s 20(a)(iii).

e Words substituted by the European Union (Statutory Audits) (Directive 2006/43/EC, as amended by Directive 2014/56/EU, and Regulation (EU) No 537/2014) Regulations 2016 (SI 312/2016), reg 17(b)(i), with effect from 17 June 2016 (previously: "Chapter), or").

f Words substituted by the European Union (Statutory Audits) (Directive 2006/43/EC, as amended by Directive 2014/56/EU, and Regulation (EU) No 537/2014) Regulations 2016 (SI 312/2016), reg 17(b)(ii), with effect from 17 June 2016 (previously: "*section 905(2)(m)*.").

g Words substituted by C(SA)A 2018, s 20(b) (previously: "the 2016 Audits Regulations").

h Paragraphs (5)(c) and (5)(d) inserted by the European Union (Statutory Audits) (Directive 2006/43/EC, as amended by Directive 2014/56/EU, and Regulation (EU) No 537/2014) Regulations 2016 (SI 312/2016), reg 17(b)(iii), with effect from 17 June 2016.

---

907 Board of directors

(1) Subject to a regulation under *section 943(1)(c)* and to *section 901(2)*, the board of directors of the Supervisory Authority is, on and from the commencement of this section, to consist of—

(a) not more than 8 directors (including the chairperson and the deputy chairperson) appointed by the Minister under *subsection (2)*, and

(b) the person holding the office of chief executive officer who, by virtue of that office, is a director.

(2) Subject to [*subsections (2A) and (2B)* and][a] a regulation under *section 943(1)(c)*, the directors appointed by the Minister shall, on and from the commencement of this section, include—

(a) subject to *paragraphs (b)* and *(c)*, 2 persons, each of whom is nominated by the prescribed accountancy bodies by a decision taken by a majority of those bodies,

(b) if there is no such decision taken by those bodies as respects the nomination, under *paragraph (a)*, of those 2 persons, 2 persons, each of whom is chosen by the Minister from amongst the persons who had been proposed by any one or more, or all, of those bodies for nomination under that paragraph,

(c) if there is such a decision taken by those bodies as respects the nomination, under *paragraph (a)*, of one, only, of those persons, 2 persons—

(i) one of whom is the person so nominated by those bodies, and

(ii) the other of whom is chosen by the Minister from amongst the persons who had been proposed by any one or more, or all, of those bodies for nomination under that paragraph,

(d) 2 persons nominated by the Minister, one of whom—

(i) is neither an officer or employee of the Minister nor a member, officer or employee of a prescribed accountancy body, and

(ii) is appointed as chairperson by the Minister,

and

(e) for each designated body, one person nominated by that body.

[(2A) On and from 17 June 2016, the Minister shall not appoint a person under *subsection (2)* as a director unless the Minister is satisfied that the person is knowledgeable in [at least one area relevant to the conduct of statutory audits as specified in Schedule 19].[b]

[(2B) On and from 17 June 2016, the Minister shall not appoint a person as a director under *subsection (2)* if the person—

(a) on the proposed date of his or her appointment as a director—

(i) carries out statutory audits,

(ii) holds voting rights in an audit firm,

(iii) is a director or member of an audit firm, or

(iv) is employed by or otherwise contracted with an audit firm,

or

(b) has, at any time during the 3 years immediately preceding the proposed date of his or her appointment as a director—

(i) carried out statutory audits,

(ii) held voting rights in an audit firm,

(iii) was a director or member of an audit firm, or

(iv) was employed by or otherwise contracted with an audit firm.][c]

(3) For the purposes of *subsection (2)*—

(a) a majority decision of the prescribed accountancy bodies is taken where a majority of those bodies signify in writing that they have nominated the particular person or persons (and the number of prescribed accountancy bodies by reference to which that majority is to be reckoned excludes any of the prescribed accountancy bodies that abstain from taking a decision on the matter), and

(b) without prejudice to the generality of *paragraphs (b)* and *(c)* of that subsection, the power of the Minister under that *paragraph (b)* or *(c)*, as the case may be, is exercisable where the prescribed accountancy bodies are evenly divided as to the decision to be taken concerning the nomination of a person.

(4) Subject to a regulation under *section 943(1)(c)*, the board shall not include at any one time more than 3 directors appointed under *subsection (2)* who are members of prescribed accountancy bodies, and of those 3 directors—

(a) two may be nominees of the prescribed accountancy bodies, and

(b) one may be a nominee of a designated body.

(5) If, at any time, more than one designated body proposes to nominate a member of a prescribed accountancy body for appointment to the board, the designated bodies proposing to do so shall decide among themselves which one of them is to nominate such a member.

(6) The directors may select the deputy chairperson from among those directors who are not members of a prescribed accountancy body.

(7) The term of office of a director appointed under *subsection (2)* shall be specified by the Minister when appointing the director and, subject to *section 908(5)*, may not be less than 3 or more than 5 years.

(8) The members of the Supervisory Authority may not instruct the directors, at any meeting of those members or by any other means, regarding the carrying out of their duties as directors of the Supervisory Authority.

Amendments

a Words inserted by the European Union (Statutory Audits) (Directive 2006/43/EC, as amended by Directive 2014/56/EU, and Regulation (EU) No 537/2014) Regulations 2016 (SI 312/2016), reg 18(a), with effect from 17 June 2016.

b Subsection (2A) inserted by the European Union (Statutory Audits) (Directive 2006/43/EC, as amended by Directive 2014/56/EU, and Regulation (EU) No 537/2014) Regulations 2016 (SI 312/2016), reg 18(b), with effect from 17 June 2016. Further amended by substitutions of words by C(SA)A 2018, s 21.

c Subsection (2B) inserted by the European Union (Statutory Audits) (Directive 2006/43/EC, as amended by Directive 2014/56/EU, and Regulation (EU) No 537/2014) Regulations 2016 (SI 312/2016), reg 18(b), with effect from 17 June 2016.

908 Supplementary provisions in relation to board of directors

(1) *Section 146* (as applied by *sections 1173* and *1198*) does not apply to the Supervisory Authority.

(2) A director may resign by letter addressed to the Minister and copied to the Supervisory Authority and the resignation takes effect on the date the Minister receives the letter.

(3) At any time, the Minister may remove for stated reasons, any director appointed under *section 907(2)*, including a director nominated under *section 907(2)(d)*.

(4) The Minister shall fill any vacancy that arises on the board as a consequence of the resignation or removal of a director by appointing a replacement nominated (or, as the case may be, chosen by the Minister) in the same manner as the replaced director.

(5) A director appointed under *subsection (4)* to replace another holds office for the remainder of the replaced director's term of office and the same terms and conditions apply to the new appointee.

(6) The directors may act despite one or more vacancies in their numbers.

(7) On and from the commencement of this section, a person is disqualified from appointment to the board for so long as he or she is—

(a) entitled under the Standing Orders of either House of the Oireachtas to sit in that House,

(b) a member of the European Parliament, or

(c) a member of a local authority.

(8) On and from the commencement of this section, a member of the board shall cease to hold office on—

(a) being nominated as a member of Seanad Éireann,

(b) being nominated as a candidate for election to either House of the Oireachtas or to the European Parliament,

(c) being regarded, pursuant to section 19 of the European Parliament Elections Act 1997, as having been elected to the European Parliament to fill a vacancy, or

(d) becoming a member of a local authority.

909 Chief executive officer (including provision of transitional nature)

(1) The directors appointed under *section 907(2)* shall appoint a person to be the chief executive officer of the Supervisory Authority (to be known and in this Act referred to as the "chief executive officer") to—

(a) carry on, manage and control generally the administration and business of the Supervisory Authority, and

(b) perform any other functions that may be determined by the board.

(2) The chief executive officer holds office on and subject to the terms and conditions (including terms and conditions relating to remuneration and allowances) that the directors appointed under *section 907(2)* may, with the approval of the Minister given with the consent of the Minister for Public Expenditure and Reform, determine.

(3) The directors appointed under *section 907(2)* may remove the chief executive officer from office at any time.

(4) Without prejudice to the generality of *section 901(2)*, the person who held the office of Chief Executive Officer of the Irish Auditing and Accounting Supervisory Authority immediately before the commencement of this section shall continue in

office for the unexpired period of his or her term unless he or she sooner retires, resigns or dies or is removed from office.

910 Work programme

(1) The Supervisory Authority shall continue to prepare and submit to the Minister, for each successive period of 3 years beginning on the day after the last day of the period covered by the preceding such programme, a work programme.

(2) For the purposes of the initial operation of *subsection (1)*, the reference in it to the preceding work programme is a reference to the work programme last prepared by the Supervisory Authority under section 13 of the Act of 2003.

(3) In preparing the work programme, the Supervisory Authority shall have regard to the need to ensure the most beneficial, effective and efficient use of its resources.

(4) The work programme shall include the following information:

(a) the key strategies and activities that the Supervisory Authority will pursue to further its objects and to perform its functions;

(b) the outputs that the Supervisory Authority aims to achieve and against which its performance will be assessed;

(c) the staff, resources and expenditure (including an annual programme of expenditure approved under *section 911*) that will be required to pursue the strategies and activities referred to in *paragraph (a)*.

(5) The Minister shall not give directions to the Supervisory Authority concerning the discharge of a work programme, including an amended or supplementary work programme.

(6) Subject to *subsection (7)*, the Minister shall ensure that a copy of each work programme (including each revised, amended or supplementary work programme) is laid before each House of the Oireachtas not later than 60 days after the date on which it was submitted to the Minister.

(7) If a revised work programme (including a revised, amended or supplementary work programme) is submitted to the Minister before the unrevised work programme is laid before the Houses of the Oireachtas as required by *subsection (6)*, only the revised work programme need be laid before the Houses.

911 Annual programme of expenditure

(1) The annual programme of expenditure referred to in *section 910(4)(c)* shall not be included in the work programme unless it has first been approved by the Minister under *subsection (3)*.

(2) The Minister shall not so approve the annual programme of expenditure unless the Minister has first—

(a) considered the views of the prescribed accountancy bodies, and

(b) obtained the consent of the Minister for Public Expenditure and Reform,

and this subsection extends to an approval by the Minister of the programme with amendments.

(3) The Minister may approve the annual programme of expenditure with or without amendment by the Minister.

(4) If the Minister approves the annual programme of expenditure with amendments, the Supervisory Authority—

(a) may revise any other part of the work programme, and

(b) if it does so, shall submit to the Minister the revised work programme, including the annual programme of expenditure as amended by the Minister.

912 Specification in annual programme of expenditure of amounts for reserve fund

In addition to capital and other expenditures, the annual programme of expenditure shall specify the portion of the revenue received or to be received under *sections 914(2)* and *916* for the financial year in question that has been set aside as mentioned in *section 919(3)*.

913 Review of work programme

(1) The Supervisory Authority may—

(a) if it considers it necessary to do so, undertake an interim review of a work programme, and

(b) may submit to the Minister, within the period covered by the work programme, an amended or supplementary work programme, including an amended or supplementary annual programme of expenditure.

(2) An amended or supplementary annual programme of expenditure shall not be included in an amended or supplementary work programme unless it has first been approved in accordance with *subsection (3)* of *section 911* and *subsection (2)* of that section applies to such an approval as it applies to the approval of an original annual programme of expenditure.

(3) If the Minister so approves with amendments the Supervisory Authority's amended or supplementary annual programme of expenditure, the powers under *section 911(4)* are equally available to the Supervisory Authority with respect to its amended or supplementary work programme under this section as they are available with respect to an original work programme and, accordingly, *section 911(4)* applies, with any necessary modifications, to that amended or supplementary work programme.

914 Funding

(1) For the purposes specified in *section 915(1)*, the Supervisory Authority in each financial year—

(a) shall be paid a grant in accordance with *subsection (2)*, and

(b) may impose [a levy under *section 916*][a].

(2) In each financial year, a grant not exceeding 40 per cent of the annual programme of expenditure approved for that year under *section 911* shall, subject to any conditions that the Minister thinks proper, be paid to the Supervisory Authority out of money provided by the Oireachtas.

Amendments

a Words substituted by C(A)A 2017, s 69 (previously: "levies under *sections 916* and *917*.").

915 Application of money received by Supervisory Authority

(1) [Subject to *subsection (3)*, the Supervisory Authority][a] shall not use the money received by it under this Chapter except for the purpose of meeting expenses properly incurred by it in performing its functions under this Chapter.

(2) The Supervisory Authority may use money set aside for or paid into the reserve fund in accordance with *section 919* only for the purpose of meeting expenses incurred by it in performing its functions under *section 933* and may not use any other money received by it for that purpose.

[(3) The Supervisory Authority may use money referred to in *subsection (2)* that comprises any part of any money paid to the Supervisory Authority pursuant to *section 934C(2)(g)* only for the purpose of meeting expenses incurred by it in undertaking an investigation under *section 934*.][b]

Amendments

a Words substituted by C(SA)A 2018, s 22(a) (previously: "The Supervisory Authority.").
b Subsection (3) inserted by C(SA)A 2018, s 22(b).

916 Supervisory Authority may levy prescribed accountancy bodies

(1) For the purpose specified in [*section 915(1)*][a] and in accordance with this section, the Supervisory Authority may impose one or more levies in each financial year of the Supervisory Authority on each prescribed accountancy body.

(2) The total amount levied in any financial year of the Supervisory Authority on all prescribed accountancy bodies under this section shall not exceed 60 per cent of the annual programme of expenditure approved for that year under *section 911*.

(3) The Supervisory Authority shall not impose a levy on a prescribed accountancy body under this section unless the Minister has—

(a) first approved—

(i) the total amount to be levied on all prescribed accountancy bodies in the relevant financial year, and

(ii) the criteria for apportioning the levy among the classes of prescribed accountancy bodies,

and

(b) consented to the levy.

(4) The Supervisory Authority shall—

(a) establish criteria for apportioning a levy among the classes of prescribed accountancy bodies,

(b) submit the criteria to the Minister for approval before imposing the levy, and

(c) specify the date on which the levy is due to be paid by those bodies.

(5) As a consequence of the apportionment of a levy according to the criteria established by the Supervisory Authority, different classes of prescribed accountancy bodies may be required to pay different amounts of the levy.

(6) Before consenting to a levy under this section, the Minister—

(a) shall consult with the prescribed accountancy bodies, and

(b) may consult with any other persons who, in the opinion of the Minister, are interested in the matter.

(7) The Supervisory Authority may recover a levy imposed under this section as a simple contract debt in any court of competent jurisdiction from the prescribed accountancy body from which the levy is due.

[(8) Levies imposed under this section on that class of prescribed accountancy bodies comprising recognised accountancy bodies may be used for the purposes of meeting expenses properly incurred by the Supervisory Authority in performing its function referred to in section 905(2)(ma).][b]

Amendments

a "section 915(1)" substituted for "section 915(2)" by Credit Guarantee (Amendment) Act 2016, s 20; subsequently substituted by C(A)A 2017, s 70.

b Subsection (8) inserted by C(SA)A 2018, s 23.

---

917 Supervisory Authority may levy certain companies and other undertakings

[...][a]

Amendments

a Section 917 repealed by C(A)A 2017, s 3(1)(f).

---

918 Funding in respect of functions of Supervisory Authority under certain regulations

[...][a]

(2) For the purposes specified in *subsection (3)*, the Supervisory Authority may impose, with the Minister's consent and subject to *subsections (4)* to *(6)*, one or more levies in each financial year of the Supervisory Authority on statutory auditors and audit firms auditing public-interest entities.

[(3) Money received by the Supervisory Authority under this section may be used only for the purposes of meeting expenses properly incurred by it in performing its functions as the competent authority under Regulation (EU) No 537/2014 or this Act (including a function under *section 905(2)(n)*) in relation to statutory auditors of public-interest entities.][b]

(4) In addition to the requirement under *subsection (2)* with regard to the Minister's consent, the total amount levied in any financial year of the Supervisory Authority on statutory auditors and audit firms shall not exceed an amount in relation to that year specified in writing by the Minister for the purposes of this subsection.

(5) The Supervisory Authority shall—

(a) establish criteria for apportioning a levy among the several statutory auditors and audit firms auditing public-interest entities,

(b) submit the criteria to the Minister for approval before imposing the levy, and

(c) specify the date on which the levy is due to be paid by the relevant statutory auditors and audit firms.

(6) As a consequence of the apportionment of the levy under *subsection (5)*, different statutory auditors and audit firms may be required to pay different amounts of the levy.

(7) Notwithstanding that the particular audit of a public-interest entity has been carried out by a statutory auditor, no levy under this section shall be imposed on the statutory auditor if he or she was designated by a statutory audit firm to carry out the audit, and the levy under this section shall, in those circumstances, be imposed on the statutory audit firm instead.

(8) The Supervisory Authority may recover, as a simple contract debt in any court of competent jurisdiction, from a statutory auditor or audit firm from which the levy is due, a levy imposed under this section.

Amendments

a Subsection (1) repealed by the European Union (Statutory Audits) (Directive 2006/43/EC, as amended by Directive 2014/56/EU, and Regulation (EU) No 537/2014) Regulations 2016 (SI 312/2016), reg 19(a), with effect from 17 June 2016.

b Subsection (3) substituted by C(SA)A 2018, s 24.

919 Reserve fund

(1) The reserve fund established under section 15(1) of the Act of 2003 shall continue in being and continue to be maintained by the Supervisory Authority but subject to any limit specified by the Minister under that provision or that limit as it may stand amended under *subsection (2)*.

(2) The Minister may amend the limit referred to in *subsection (1)*.

(3) In each financial year of the Supervisory Authority, the Supervisory Authority shall set aside for the reserve fund such portion of the revenue received or to be received under *sections 914(2)* and *916* for that financial year as it considers to be appropriate.

(4) In each financial year of the Supervisory Authority, the Supervisory Authority shall pay into the reserve fund—

(a) the amount set aside under *subsection (3)* or, if that amount is amended through an amendment under *section 911(3)* to the annual programme of expenditure, [the amended amount, and][a]

[...][b]

[(c) any amounts paid to the Supervisory Authority under *section 933(6)* or *(7)* or *934(8)* or *(10)*, and

(d) any amounts paid to the Supervisory Authority under *section 934C(2)(g)*.][c]

(5) The Supervisory Authority shall promptly inform the Minister if, in any financial year, the total amount in the reserve fund is likely to exceed any limit standing specified in relation to the fund by the Minister.

[...][d]

Amendments

a Words substituted by C(A)A 2017, s 71(a) (previously: "the amended amount,").

b Paragraph (4)(b) repealed by C(A)A 2017, s 71(b).

c Paragraphs (4)(c) and (d) substituted by C(SA)A 2018, s 25(a).

d Subsection (6) deleted by C(SA)A 2018, s 25(b).

---

920 Borrowing

For the purpose of providing for activities specified in its work programme, the Supervisory Authority may, from time to time, borrow money subject to—

(a) the consent of the Minister and the Minister for Public Expenditure and Reform, and

(b) such conditions as they may specify.

921 Excess revenue

(1) The Supervisory Authority shall apply any excess of its revenue over its expenditure in any financial year to meet its programme of expenditure approved for the subsequent year under *section 911*, and the amounts payable under *sections 914(2)*, *916* and *918* for the subsequent year shall be appropriately reduced.

(2) Money in, or set aside for, the reserve fund shall not be considered revenue for the purpose of this section.

922 Employees (including provision of a transitional nature)

(1) Subject to *subsection (2)* and to the limits of staffing numbers specified in its work programme under *section 910*, the Supervisory Authority may employ such persons as it thinks necessary.

(2) Subject to the prior approval of the Minister given with the consent of the Minister for Public Expenditure and Reform, the Supervisory Authority shall determine the numbers and grades of its employees and the terms and conditions of their employment.

(3) The Supervisory Authority may from time to time engage the services of professional and other advisers.

(4) A person who was in the employment of the Irish Auditing and Accounting Supervisory Authority immediately before the commencement of this section shall continue in the employment of the Supervisory Authority and such employment shall (subject to any determination for the time being that may be made under *subsection (2)* of a like kind as could, from time to time, have been made under section 17(2) of the Act of 2003) be on the same terms and conditions as applied to the person immediately before such commencement.

923 Director's obligations when material interest in arrangement, contract or agreement with Supervisory Authority arises

(1) A director of the Supervisory Authority who, otherwise than in his or her capacity as such director, has a material interest in a specified matter shall neither influence nor seek to influence any decision to be made by the Authority in relation to that matter.

(2) A director of the Supervisory Authority present at a meeting where a specified matter arises in which he or she has a material interest otherwise than in his or her capacity as such director shall—

(a) at the meeting, disclose the fact of the interest and its nature to the board or the committee, as the case may be,

(b) absent himself or herself from the meeting or the part of the meeting during which the matter is discussed,

(c) take no part in any deliberations of the board or committee relating to the matter, and

(d) refrain from voting on any decision relating to the matter.

(3) Where a director discloses a material interest under this section—

(a) the chairperson of the meeting shall ensure that the disclosure is recorded in the minutes of the meeting, and

(b) for as long as the matter is being dealt with by the meeting, the director shall not be counted in the quorum for the meeting.

(4) Where at a meeting a question arises as to whether or not a course of conduct, if pursued by a director, would be a contravention of *subsection (2)*—

(a) subject to *subsection (5)*, the chairperson of the meeting shall determine the question,

(b) the chairperson's determination shall be final, and

(c) the chairperson shall ensure that the particulars of the determination are recorded in the minutes of the meeting.

(5) For the purposes of *subsection (4)*, if the chairperson is the director in respect of whom the question arises, the other directors present at the moment shall choose one of themselves to be the chairperson of the meeting.

(6) *Section 231* (as applied by *section 1173*) does not apply to a director of the Supervisory Authority.

(7) Nothing in this section prejudices the operation of any rule of law restricting directors of a company from having any interest in contracts with the company.

(8) In this section—

"meeting" means a meeting of the board of the Supervisory Authority or of a committee of its directors;

"specified matter" means—

(a) an arrangement or a proposed arrangement to which the Supervisory Authority is a party; or

(b) a contract or other agreement, or proposed contract or other agreement, with the Supervisory Authority.

924 Effect of breach of director's obligations in relation to material interest

(1) If satisfied that a director of the Supervisory Authority has contravened *section 923(1)* or *(2)*, the Minister may—

(a) in the case of a director appointed by the Minister and if the Minister thinks fit, remove that director from office,

(b) in the case of a director who is the chief executive officer, recommend to the board that the board remove him or her.

(2) A director who is removed by the Minister under this section or on the recommendation of the Minister made under this section shall be disqualified for appointment as a director or chief executive of the Supervisory Authority.

925 Employee's duty of disclosure

(1) An employee of the Supervisory Authority who otherwise than in his or her capacity as such employee has a material interest in a specified matter as defined in *section 923(8)* shall—

(a) disclose to the Supervisory Authority the fact of the interest and its nature,

(b) take no part in—

(i) the negotiation of the arrangement, contract or other agreement in question, or

(ii) any deliberation by the Supervisory Authority or its employees relating to the matter,

(c) refrain from making any recommendation relating to the matter, and

(d) neither influence nor seek to influence a decision to be made in the matter.

(2) *Subsection (1)* does not apply to contracts or proposed contracts of employment between the Supervisory Authority and its employees.

(3) Where a person contravenes this section, the Supervisory Authority may—

(a) terminate that person's contract of employment, or

(b) amend the terms and conditions of that person's employment as it considers appropriate.

926 Superannuation scheme

(1) The Supervisory Authority may, if it considers it appropriate to do so, prepare and submit to the Minister a scheme or schemes for granting superannuation benefits to or in respect of one or both of the following—

(a) the chief executive officer,

(b) any employee of the Supervisory Authority.

(2) Each superannuation scheme shall fix the time and conditions of retirement for all persons to or in respect of which superannuation benefits are payable under the scheme, and different terms and conditions may be fixed in respect of different classes of persons.

(3) A superannuation scheme submitted to the Minister under this section shall, if approved by the Minister with the consent of the Minister for Public Expenditure and Reform, be carried out in accordance with its terms.

(4) A superannuation scheme may be amended or revoked by a subsequent scheme prepared, submitted and approved under this section.

(5) The Supervisory Authority may not grant, or enter into any arrangement for the provision of, any superannuation benefit to or in respect of a person referred to in *subsection (1)* except—

(a) in accordance with a superannuation scheme approved under this section, or

(b) with the approval of the Minister given with the consent of the Minister for Public Expenditure and Reform.

(6) In the case of a dispute as to the claim of any person to, or the amount of, any superannuation benefit payable under a superannuation scheme approved under this section—

(a) the dispute shall be submitted to the Minister,

(b) the Minister shall refer the dispute to the Minister for Public Expenditure and Reform for his or her determination of it, and

(c) the decision of the Minister for Public Expenditure and Reform shall be final.

(7) Every superannuation scheme approved by the Minister under this section shall be laid before each House of the Oireachtas as soon as may be after it is made and, if a resolution annulling the scheme is passed by either such House within the next 21 days on which that House has sat after the scheme is laid before it, the scheme shall be annulled accordingly but without prejudice to the validity of anything previously done thereunder.

927 Accounts and audit

(1) Without prejudice to the requirements of *Part 6* (as applied by *section 1173*) in relation to financial statements, the Supervisory Authority shall keep records of, and prepare all proper and usual accounts of—

(a) all income received by it, including records of the sources of that income,

(b) all expenditure incurred by it, and

(c) its assets and liabilities.

(2) Not later than 3 months after the end of the financial year to which the accounts relate, the Supervisory Authority shall submit the accounts prepared under this section to the Comptroller and Auditor General for audit.

(3) After the audit, the Comptroller and Auditor General shall present to the Minister the audited accounts together with the Comptroller and Auditor General's report.

(4) The Minister shall ensure that, as soon as practicable after those accounts and that report are presented to the Minister, copies of them are—

(a) laid before each House of the Oireachtas, and

(b) supplied to the prescribed accountancy bodies.

(5) The Supervisory Authority shall—

(a) at the Minister's request, permit any person appointed by the Minister to examine its accounts in respect of any financial year or other period,

(b) facilitate the examination of the accounts by the person appointed, and

(c) pay any fee that is set by the Minister for the examination.

928 Annual report

(1) As soon as practicable but in any event not later than 4 months after the end of each financial year, the Supervisory Authority shall make a written report to the Minister of its activities during that year.

(2) The annual report shall be prepared in such manner and form as the Minister may direct.

(3) The Minister shall ensure that a copy of the annual report is laid before each House of the Oireachtas not later than 6 months after the end of the financial year to which the report relates.

929 Accountability to Dáil Éireann

(1) Whenever required to do so by the Committee of Dáil Éireann established under the Standing Orders of Dáil Éireann to examine and report to Dáil Éireann on the

appropriation accounts and reports of the Comptroller and Auditor General, the chief executive officer and the chairperson of the board of the Supervisory Authority shall give evidence to that Committee in respect of the following:

(a) the regularity and propriety of the transactions recorded or to be recorded in any account that—

(i) the Supervisory Authority is required by law to prepare; and

(ii) is subject to audit by the Comptroller and Auditor General;

(b) the economy and efficiency of the Supervisory Authority in using its resources;

(c) systems, procedures and practices used by the Supervisory Authority for evaluating the effectiveness of its operations;

(d) any matter affecting the Supervisory Authority that is referred to in—

(i) a special report under section 11(2) of the Comptroller and Auditor General (Amendment) Act 1993; or

(ii) any other report of the Comptroller and Auditor General that is laid before Dáil Éireann, in so far as that report relates to a matter specified in any of *paragraphs (a)* to *(c)*.

(2) Whenever required by any other committee appointed by either House of the Oireachtas or appointed jointly by both Houses, the chief executive officer and the chairperson of the board of the Supervisory Authority shall account to the committee for the performance of the functions of the Supervisory Authority.

(3) The Supervisory Authority shall have regard to any recommendations relating to its functions that are made by a committee in response to an account given under *subsection (2)*.

(4) In giving evidence under *subsection (1)* or an account under *subsection (2)*, the chief executive officer and the chairperson of the board of the Supervisory Authority shall not question or express an opinion on the merits of—

(a) any policy of the Government or a Minister of the Government; or

(b) the objectives of such a policy.

930 Recognition of body of accountants

[(1) Subject to subsection (1A), the Supervisory Authority may grant recognition in writing to a body of accountants for the purposes of the relevant provisions but may only grant such recognition if satisfied—

(a) that the standards relating to training, qualifications and repute required by that body for the approval of a person as a statutory auditor are not less than those specified in Articles 4, 6 to 8 and 10 of the Audit Directive,

(b) as to the standards that body applies to its members in the area of ethics, codes of conduct and practice, independence, professional integrity, auditing and accounting standards, quality assurance, continuing education and investigation and disciplinary procedures,

(c) as to the capacity of the body to institute and apply effective arrangements to ensure compliance with, and the enforcement of, the standards referred to in paragraphs (a) and (b) in relation to its members having regard to the body's ongoing performance, financial soundness, staffing and other relevant resources of the body, and

(d) that the body will effectively perform the *Part 27* functions concerned (which may be all of them).

(1A) Subject to *sections 931* and *931B*, a recognised accountancy body shall not perform a *Part 27* function unless the body's recognition under this section states that the body may perform that function.][a]

(2) Each of the following:

(a) the Association of Chartered Certified Accountants;

(b) the Institute of Chartered Accountants in Ireland;

(c) the Institute of Chartered Accountants in England and Wales;

(d) the Institute of Chartered Accountants of Scotland;

(e) the Institute of Certified Public Accountants in Ireland;

(f) the Institute of Incorporated Public Accountants;

shall be deemed to have been granted recognition under this section by the Supervisory Authority for the purposes of [the relevant provisions and, subject to *sections 931* and *931B*, for such recognition to have stated that each such body may perform each of the *Part 27* functions].[b]

[(3) A body of accountants granted recognition under subsection (1) or (2) shall continue to satisfy the Supervisory Authority as referred to in subsection (1) for the duration of such recognition.

(4) A body granted recognition under subsection (1) or (2) may make a request in writing to the Supervisory Authority for the Authority to revoke its recognition under *section 931*.][c]

Amendments

a Subsection (1) substituted and subs (1A) inserted by C(SA)A 2018, s 26(a).

b Words substituted by C(SA)A 2018, s 26(b).

c Subsections (3) and (4) inserted by C(SA)A 2018, s 26(c).

[930A Designation of competent authority

(1) Subject to *subsection (2)*, the Supervisory Authority is designated as the competent authority for the oversight of statutory auditors in accordance with the Audit Directive and Regulation (EU) No 537/2014.

(2) Subject to *subsection (4)*, the Director is designated as the competent authority for the purpose of imposing relevant sanctions (within the meaning of section 957AA) on relevant directors.

(3) The Supervisory Authority is designated as the competent authority for the purposes of public oversight, quality assurance (if applicable), investigations and penalties of third-country auditors and third-country audit entities (within the meaning of *Part 27*) registered under *section 1573(1)*.

(4) (a) Subject to paragraph (b), to the extent that the Director is a competent authority by virtue of subsection (2), a reference in this Chapter (other than this section) and Part 27 to the Supervisory Authority shall include a reference to the Director.

(b) The Supervisory Authority shall perform the functions under this Chapter and Part 27 that would, but for this subsection, otherwise fall to be performed by the Director by virtue of subsection (2).

(c) The Director shall cooperate with the Supervisory Authority so as to enable the Supervisory Authority to perform the functions referred to in paragraph (b).

(5) The Supervisory Authority shall, as soon as is practicable on or after the commencement of section 27 of the Companies (Statutory Audits) Act 2018, publish on its website information on the designation of competent authorities effected by this section between the Supervisory Authority and the Director.][a]

Amendments

a Subsection 930A inserted by C(SA)A 2018, s 27.

[930B Annual audit programme and activity report

(1) The Supervisory Authority shall, not later than 6 months after the end of each financial year, prepare a report (in this Act referred to as the 'annual audit programme and activity report' or 'AAPA report') in accordance with this section on, amongst others, its oversight functions referred to in *section 930A* performed during that year.

(2) The AAPA report shall contain the following information:

(a) an activity report on the functions performed by the recognised accountancy bodies during the financial year to which the AAPA report relates;

(b) a work programme concerning the oversight functions referred to in *section 930A* that the Supervisory Authority proposes to perform during the financial year immediately following the financial year to which the AAPA report relates;

(c) an activity report regarding the functions of the Supervisory Authority under Regulation (EU) No 537/2014 during the financial year to which the AAPA report relates;

(d) a work programme regarding the functions of the Supervisory Authority under Regulation (EU) No 537/2014 that the Supervisory Authority proposes to perform during the financial year immediately following the financial year to which the AAPA report relates;

(e) a report for the financial year to which the AAPA report relates on the overall results of the quality assurance system required by *section 1494(1)*, including—

(i) information on recommendations issued, follow-up on the recommendations, supervisory measures taken and relevant sanctions (including relevant sanctions within the meaning of *section 957AA*) and public notices of relevant sanctions imposed (including public notices of relevant sanctions imposed within the meaning of *section 957AA*), and

(ii) quantitative information and other key performance information on financial resources and staffing, and the efficiency and effectiveness of the quality assurance system.

(3) The Supervisory Authority shall cause the AAPA report to be published on its website not later than 6 months after the end of the financial year to which the report relates.][a]

Amendments

a Subsection 930B inserted by C(SA)A 2018, s 27.

[930C Operation of certain provisions with regard to particular recognised accountancy bodies

(1) *Section 1461* applies to the interpretation of this section as it applies to the interpretation of *Part 27*.

(2) This section applies where the provision referred to in *subsection (3)*, *(4)*, *(5)* or *(6)* uses the expression 'recognised accountancy body' without qualification and that provision does not, by its express terms, itself indicate which recognised accountancy body is being referred to.

(3) A provision of the relevant provisions that confers a function on a recognised accountancy body in relation to a statutory auditor or audit firm shall be read as conferring that function—

(a) in the case of a statutory auditor who is not a member of a statutory audit firm, on the recognised accountancy body of which the statutory auditor is a member,

(b) in the case of a statutory auditor who is a member of a statutory audit firm, on the recognised accountancy body of which the statutory audit firm is a member, and

(c) in the case of a statutory audit firm, on the recognised accountancy body of which the statutory audit firm is a member.

(4) With regard to the function conferred by *section 1464* on a recognised accountancy body in relation to an individual or firm, *subsection (3)* applies as if, for each reference in that subsection to a statutory auditor or audit firm, as the case may be, there were substituted a reference to the individual or firm, as appropriate.

(5) A provision of the relevant provisions requiring that an act is to be done, or enabling an act to be done, by a person (other than a person referred to in subsection (6)(b)) in relation to a recognised accountancy body shall be read as requiring or enabling it to be done by the person in relation to—

(a) if the person is not a member of a statutory audit firm, the recognised accountancy body of which the person is a member,

(b) if the person is a member of a statutory audit firm, the recognised accountancy body of which the statutory audit firm is a member, and

(c) if the person is a statutory audit firm, the recognised accountancy body of which the statutory audit firm is a member.

(6) *Subsection (7)* applies in the case—

(a) of a provision of the kind referred to in *subsection (3)*, *(4)* or *(5)*, and

(b) where the provision falls to be applied to a Member State auditor, a Member State audit firm, a third-country auditor (within the meaning of *Part 27*) or any other person who is not a member of a recognised accountancy body (or, as the case may be, the firm of which the person is a member is not a member of a recognised accountancy body).

(7) The recognised accountancy body that shall perform the function concerned or, as the case may be, in relation to which the act concerned is required or enabled to be done shall be determined—

(a) by reference to arrangements in writing entered into by the recognised accountancy bodies amongst themselves for the purpose (which arrangements those bodies are empowered by this subsection to enter into), or

(b) in default of—

(i) such arrangements being entered into, or

(ii) the provision of such arrangements dealing with the particular case falling to be determined,

by the Supervisory Authority.

(8) On a determination being made by the Supervisory Authority for the purposes of *subsection (7)(b)*, a direction in writing, reflecting the terms of the determination, shall be given by it (which direction the Supervisory Authority is empowered by this subsection to give).

(9) Arrangements shall not be entered into under *subsection (7)(a)* by the recognised accountancy bodies save after consultation by them with the Supervisory Authority.

(10) Subject to *subsection (11)*, if in consequence of the operation of this section, the function of withdrawal of a particular approval of a statutory auditor or audit firm falls to be discharged by a recognised accountancy body (in this section referred to as the "first-mentioned accountancy body") that is different from the recognised accountancy body (in this section referred to as the "second-mentioned accountancy body") that granted the approval—

(a) the first-mentioned accountancy body shall notify in writing the second-mentioned accountancy body of the proposal by it to withdraw the approval, and

(b) the second-mentioned accountancy body shall provide such assistance by way of provision of information or clarification of any matter, to the first-mentioned accountancy body, as the latter considers it may require so as to inform itself better on any issue bearing on the performance of the function of withdrawal.

(11) The procedures adopted for the purposes of *subsection (10)* by the first-mentioned accountancy body and the second-mentioned accountancy body shall be such as will—

(a) avoid any unnecessary delay in the performance of the function of withdrawal, and

(b) respect the requirements of procedural fairness as concerns the auditor or audit firm concerned being able to answer any part of the case made against him or her that is informed by those procedures being employed.

(12) In a case falling within *subsections (10)* and *(11)*, if the approval concerned is withdrawn, the first-mentioned accountancy body, in addition to making the notifications required by *section 1482* and (where it applies) *section 1483*, shall notify the second-mentioned accountancy body of the withdrawal of approval.][a]

Amendments

a Subsection 930C inserted by C(SA)A 2018, s 27.

[930D Conflicts of interest to be avoided

(1) The persons to whom this subsection applies shall organise themselves in such a manner so that conflicts of interest are avoided in the performance of their respective functions under this Act.

(2) *Subsection (1)* applies to—

(a) the Supervisory Authority,

(b) the Director,

(c) the Registrar, and

(d) the recognised accountancy bodies.][a]

Amendments

a Subsection 930D inserted by C(SA)A 2018, s 27.

[931 Provisions in relation to recognition by Supervisory Authority under *section 930*

(1) This section applies at any of the following times:

(a) at the time of the grant of a recognition under *section 930* (in this section referred to as the "relevant recognition") to a body of accountants (in this section referred to as the "body concerned");

(b) at any time during the currency of the relevant recognition.

(2) The Supervisory Authority may give the body concerned a notice in writing (in this section referred to as a '*section 931* notice') providing for any, or any combination of, the following:

(a) directing the body, with regard to the relevant recognition, to take the action or actions specified in the notice regarding such matters specified in the notice as the Authority thinks necessary or expedient;

(b) attaching to the relevant recognition such terms and conditions specified in the notice as the Authority thinks necessary or expedient.

(3) The Supervisory Authority may, by a further section 931 notice given to the body concerned, amend, replace or revoke one or more than one earlier section 931 notice given to the body.

(4) The Supervisory Authority may, by notice in writing given to the body concerned, revoke, or suspend for a period specified in the notice, the relevant recognition if—

(a) the Supervisory Authority ceases to be satisfied as referred to in *section 930(1)*, or

(b) the body fails to comply with any of the provisions of a *section 931* notice.

(5) Without prejudice to the generality of *subsection (2)*, a *section 931* notice may—

(a) direct the body concerned (including a body referred to in *section 930(2)*) to cease, or again cease, performing the *Part 27* function specified in the notice, either (as specified in the notice) in all cases or in a particular case, on and from the date, or the occurrence of the event, specified in that notice,

(b) direct the body concerned to commence, or again commence, performing the *Part 27* function specified in the notice, either (as specified in the notice) in all cases or in a particular case, on and from the date, or the occurrence of the event, specified in that notice (and notwithstanding any case where the body's recognition under *section 930* does not otherwise permit it to perform that function), or

(c) attach terms and conditions to the relevant recognition that relate to the performance by the body concerned of a *Part 27* function, either (as specified in the notice) in all cases or in a particular case.

(6) (a) Subject to paragraph (b), the Supervisory Authority shall not give a *section 931* notice, or a notice under *subsection (4)*, to the body concerned unless, in the interests of procedural fairness, it has first—

(i) given the body a notice in writing stating the nature of the notice that it is minded to give the body and the reasons why it is so minded, and

(ii) given the body a reasonable opportunity, in the circumstances concerned, to make representations in writing to the Supervisory Authority on what is stated in the notice referred to in *subparagraph (i)*.

(b) *Paragraph (a)* shall not apply in any case where a *section 931* notice is giving effect to a request referred to in *section 930(4)*.

(7) The Supervisory Authority may publish information on its website regarding—

(a) a *section 931* notice given to the body concerned and the body's response (if any) thereto, or

(b) a notice under *subsection (4)* given to the body concerned and the body's response (if any) thereto.

(8) Where a disciplinary committee of the body concerned has reasonable grounds for believing that a category 1 or 2 offence may have been committed by a person while the person was a member of the body, the body shall, as soon as is practicable, provide a report to the Director giving details of the alleged offence and shall furnish the Director with such further information in relation to the matter as the Director may require.

(9) Where the body concerned fails to comply with *subsection (8)* or a requirement of the Director under that subsection, the body, and any officer of that body to whom the failure is attributable, shall be guilty of a category 3 offence.

(10) Any terms and conditions which were, immediately before the commencement of section 28 of the Companies (Statutory Audits) Act 2018, attached under this section as in force immediately before that commencement to the relevant recognition of the body concerned shall, on and from that commencement, be deemed to be terms and conditions attached to that recognition by virtue of a *section 931* notice, and *section 906(4)(d)* and the other provisions of this section (including subsection (3)) shall be read accordingly.][a]

Amendments

a Subsection 931 substituted by C(SA)A 2018, s 28.

[931A Investigation by disciplinary committees of prescribed accountancy bodies

(1) In this section—[a]

"client" has the same meaning as it has in *section 934*;

["relevant person", in relation to an investigation of a member or former member of a prescribed accountancy body, means—

(a) that member or any other member or former member of the prescribed accountancy body,

(b) a client or former client of the member,

(c) if the client or former client is a body corporate, a person who is or was an officer, employee or agent of the client or former client,

(d) the prescribed accountancy body or a person who is or was an officer, employee or agent of that body,

(e) if the member is an individual, a person who is or was an employee or agent of the member,

(f) if the member is a firm, a person who is or was an officer, member, partner, employee or agent of the firm, or

(g) any person whom the prescribed accountancy body reasonably believes has information or documents relating to the investigation other than information or documents the disclosure of which is prohibited or restricted by law.][b]

(2) For the purposes of an investigation of a possible breach of a prescribed accountancy body's standards by a member, a disciplinary committee may require a relevant person to do one or more of the following:

(a) produce to the committee all books or documents relating to the investigation that are in the relevant person's possession or control;

(b) attend before the committee;

(c) give the committee any other assistance in connection with the investigation that the relevant person is reasonably able to give.

(3) For the purposes of an investigation referred to in subsection (2), the disciplinary committee may—

(a) examine on oath, either by word of mouth or on written interrogatories, a relevant person,

(b) administer oaths, for the purpose of that examination, and

(c) record, in writing, answers of a person so examined and require that person to sign them.

(4) The disciplinary committee may certify the refusal or failure to the Court if a relevant person refuses or fails to do one or more of the following:

(a) produce to the committee any book or document that it is the person's duty under this section to produce;

(b) attend before the committee when required to do so under this section;

(c) answer a question put to the person by the committee with respect to the matter under investigation.

(5) On receiving a certificate of refusal or failure concerning a relevant person, the Court may enquire into the case and, after hearing any evidence that may be adduced, may do one or more of the following:

(a) direct that the relevant person attend or re-attend before the disciplinary committee or produce particular books or documents or answer particular questions put to him or her by the committee;

(b) direct that the relevant person need not produce a particular book or document or answer a particular question put to him or her by that committee;

(c) make any other ancillary or consequential order or give any other direction that the Court thinks fit.

(6) The production of any books or documents under this section by a person who claims a lien on them does not prejudice the lien.

(7) Any information produced or answer given by a member of a prescribed accountancy body in compliance with a requirement under this section may be used in evidence against the member in any proceedings whatsoever, save proceedings for an offence (other than perjury in respect of such an answer).]

Amendments

a Section 931A inserted by C(A)A 2017, s 96.

b Definition of "relevant person" substituted by C(SA)A 2018, s 29.

[931B Provisions that apply when recognised accountancy body is not able to perform Part 27 function

(1) In this section—

"recognised accountancy body A" means a recognised accountancy body which is not able to perform, either in all cases or in a particular case, one or more than one *Part 27* function by virtue of *section 930(1A)* or a *section 931* notice;

"recognised accountancy body B" means a recognised accountancy body which is able to perform, in all cases, the relevant *Part 27* function by virtue of its recognition under *section 930* or a *section 931* notice;

"relevant members", in relation to a relevant *Part 27* function, means the statutory auditors or potential statutory auditors of recognised accountancy body A in relation to whom that body is not able to perform that function;

"relevant Part 27 function" means that one or more than one *Part 27* function referred to in the definition of 'recognised accountancy body A'.

(2) The following provisions shall apply in the case of the relevant *Part 27* function and the relevant members:

(a) the Supervisory Authority may perform that function in relation to those members and, accordingly, the applicable provisions shall be read with any necessary modifications to take account of the fact that that function will, in relation to those members, be performed by the Supervisory Authority until such time (if any) as the Supervisory Authority gives a *section 931* notice—

(i) to recognised accountancy body A to again perform that function in relation to those members, or

(ii) to recognised accountancy body B to perform that function in relation to those members until the date, or the occurrence of the event, specified in the notice;

(b) any obligations which, by virtue of the standards referred to in *section 930(1)(a)* and *(b)*, the relevant members owed to recognised accountancy body A, in so far as such obligations relate to the relevant Part 27 function, are owed to the Supervisory Authority or, if the Supervisory Authority has given a *section 931* notice referred to in *paragraph (a)* to recognised accountancy body B, to recognised accountancy body B;

(c) subject to *subsection (3)* and *section 941(4)* and *(4A)*, the costs, as determined by the Supervisory Authority, incurred by the Supervisory Authority or recognised accountancy body B in performing the relevant *Part 27* function in relation to the relevant members shall be defrayed by recognised accountancy body A or by money received by the Supervisory Authority under *section 916*.

(3) For the purposes of *subsection (2)(c)*—

(a) the Supervisory Authority may prescribe by regulations—

(i) that specified procedures and methods of calculation shall apply in the determination of the amount of costs referred to in that subsection incurred by it or recognised accountancy body B, and

(ii) requirements otherwise as to the liability of recognised accountancy body A for, and the manner in which that body shall pay, that amount,

and

(b) in default of payment of that amount to the Supervisory Authority, the Authority may recover that amount as a simple contract debt in any court of competent jurisdiction.

(4) Where the recognition granted under *section 930* of a body of accountants is revoked under *section 931*, neither the Supervisory Authority nor a recognised accountancy body owes any obligation under this Act, in so far as this Act relates to statutory audits, to a statutory auditor who is a member of the first-mentioned body but without prejudice to any such obligation owed to that statutory auditor if the auditor is a member of another body of accountants which is recognised under *section 930*.

(5) Recognised accountancy body A may appeal to the court against a decision made by the Supervisory Authority under *subsection (2)(c)* determining an amount of costs to be paid by that body.

(6) An appeal under *subsection (5)* shall be brought within 3 months after the date on which recognised accountancy body A was notified by the Supervisory Authority of its decision.][a]

Amendments

a Section 931B inserted by C(SA)A 2018, s 30.

[932 Consultation by Supervisory Authority regarding standards and qualifications

Before granting, renewing, withdrawing, revoking, suspending or refusing a recognition of a body of accountants under *section 930* for the purposes of the relevant provisions, the Supervisory Authority may consult with any body of persons or other person as to the conditions or standards required by the body of accountants concerned in connection with membership of that body or, as the case may be, the approval of persons as statutory auditors.][a]

Amendments

a Section 932 substituted by C(SA)A 2018, s 31.

933 Intervention in disciplinary process of prescribed accountancy bodies

[(1) In this section—

"approved investigation and disciplinary procedures" means—

(a) in relation to a prescribed accountancy body that is a recognised accountancy body, the investigation and disciplinary procedures approved under—

(i) *section 905(2)(c)*,

(ii) section 9(2)(c) of the Act of 2003, or

(iii) the Act of 1990, whether before or after the amendments of that Act that were made by section 32 of the Act of 2003,

and

(b) in relation to any other prescribed accountancy body, the investigation and disciplinary procedures approved under—

(i) *section 905(2)(c)*, or

(ii) section 9(2)(c) of the Act of 2003;

"relevant body" means—

(a) in relation to an enquiry referred to in *subsection (2)*, the prescribed accountancy body the subject of the enquiry, and

(b) in relation to an enquiry referred to in *subsection (3)*, the recognised accountancy body the subject of the enquiry.

(2) Following a complaint or on its own initiative, the Supervisory Authority may, for the purpose of determining whether a prescribed accountancy body has complied with the approved investigation and disciplinary procedures, enquire into—

(a) a decision by that body not to undertake an investigation into a possible breach of its standards by a member,

(b) the conduct of an investigation by that body into a possible breach of its standards by a member, or

(c) any other decision of that body relating to a possible breach of its standards by a member, unless the matter is or has been the subject of an investigation under section 934 relating to that member.

(3) The Supervisory Authority may, for the purpose of determining whether a recognised accountancy body has complied with the applicable provisions in performing a *Part 27* function, enquire into the performance by the body of that function (including, where applicable, enquire into the conduct by that body of an investigation into the conduct of a member of that body).

(4) For the purposes of an enquiry under this section, the Supervisory Authority may—

(a) inspect and make copies of all relevant documents in the possession or control of the relevant body,

(b) if the relevant body falls within paragraph (a) of the definition of 'relevant body', require the body to explain why it reached a decision referred to in *subsection (2)(a)* or *(c)* or explain how it conducted its investigation, or

(c) if the relevant body falls within *paragraph (b)* of the definition of 'relevant body', require the body to explain how it complied (if it in fact did comply) with the applicable provisions in performing the *Part 27* function concerned (and, also, to explain how it conducted an investigation referred to in *subsection (3)* if the conduct of that investigation is, in the opinion of the Supervisory Authority, relevant to the enquiry).

(5) If at any time before completing an enquiry under this section into a matter relating to a member of a relevant body, the Supervisory Authority forms the opinion that it is appropriate or in the public interest that a matter be investigated under section 934 as regards a possible relevant contravention committed by a specified person, the Authority may apply to the court for permission to investigate the matter under that section.

(6) (a) *Paragraph (b)* applies if the Supervisory Authority is not satisfied, after completing the enquiry—

(i) if the relevant body falls within *paragraph (a)* of the definition of "relevant body", that the body complied with the approved investigation and disciplinary procedures, or

(ii) if the relevant body falls within paragraph (b) of the definition of "relevant body", that the body complied with the applicable provisions in performing the *Part 27* function.

(b) Subject to *section 941(4)* and *(4A)*, the Supervisory Authority may advise, or admonish, the relevant body or may censure it by doing one or more of the following:

(i) annulling all or part of a decision of that body relating to the matter that was the subject of the enquiry;

(ii) directing that body to conduct an investigation or a fresh investigation into the matter;

(iii) directing that body to perform the function that was the subject of the enquiry again in accordance with any directions or terms and conditions that the Supervisory Authority considers appropriate;

(iv) directing that body, where it in future performs the function that was the subject of the enquiry, to do so in accordance with any directions or terms and conditions that the Supervisory Authority considers appropriate;

(v) requiring that body to pay to the Supervisory Authority an amount not exceeding the greater of the following:

(I) €125,000;

(II) the amount prescribed under *section 943(1)(e)*.

(c) In default of payment of an amount referred to in *paragraph (b)(v)*, the Supervisory Authority may recover that amount as a simple contract debt in any court of competent jurisdiction.

(7) Subject to *subsection (14)* and *section 941(4)* and *(4A)*, where, as referred to in subsection (5), the Supervisory Authority is not satisfied as referred to in subsection (6), the relevant body concerned is, in addition to any liability or obligation to pay an amount or do a thing by virtue of *subsection (6)*, liable to pay the amount specified by the Supervisory Authority towards its costs in conducting the enquiry under this section.

(8) Where the Supervisory Authority applies under *subsection (5)* to the court for permission to investigate, under *section 934*, any matter relating to a member of a relevant body or decides to direct under *subsection (6)(b)(ii)* a relevant body to conduct an investigation or fresh investigation into any matter, the following rules apply:

(a) in the case of an application to the court to investigate a matter, any decision of that body relating to the matter is suspended if and as soon as the body is notified by the Supervisory Authority that permission has been granted under *section 941(3)*;

(b) in the case of a direction to conduct an investigation or a fresh investigation, any decision of that body relating to the matter is suspended if and as soon as the body is notified by the Supervisory Authority that the direction has been confirmed as referred to in *section 941(4A)*.

(9) The Supervisory Authority may publish on its website each decision made under *subsection (6)* or each decision made specifying an amount under *subsection (7)* and the reasons for the decision after giving the relevant body and the member (if any) thereof concerned not less than 3 months notice in writing of its intention to do so.

(10) The relevant body or the member thereof (if any) concerned may appeal to the court against a decision made by the Supervisory Authority under *subsection (6)* (which may be the decision under *subsection (6)(a)* or the decision under subsection (6)(b), or both) or a decision made by it specifying an amount under subsection (7).

(11) An appeal under *subsection (10)* shall be brought within 3 months after the date on which, as appropriate, the relevant body or the member thereof (if any) concerned was notified by the Supervisory Authority of its decision.

(12) If the Supervisory Authority is not satisfied that a relevant body has, when undertaking an investigation or fresh investigation into any matter as required by a direction under *subsection (6)(b)(ii)*—

(a) if the relevant body falls within paragraph (a) of the definition of "relevant body", complied with the approved investigation and disciplinary procedures, or

(b) if the relevant body falls within paragraph (b) of the definition of "relevant body", complied with the applicable provisions in performing the *Part 27* function,

the Supervisory Authority may appeal to the court against any decision of the relevant body relating to the matter.

(13) An appeal under *subsection (12)* shall be brought within 3 months after the date on which the Supervisory Authority was notified by the relevant body of its decision.

(14) For the purpose of *subsection (7)*—

(a) the Supervisory Authority may prescribe by regulations—

  (i) that specified procedures and methods of calculation shall apply in the determination of the amount of costs referred to in that subsection incurred by it, and

  (ii) requirements otherwise as to the liability of the relevant body for, and the manner in which that body shall pay, that amount,

and

(b) in default of payment of that amount to the Supervisory Authority, the Authority may recover that amount as a simple contract debt in any court of competent jurisdiction.

(15) Nothing in this section shall be construed to prevent the undertaking of one enquiry under this section into 2 or more matters concerning the same body of accountants where one or more than one of such matters falls within *subsection (2)* and one or more than one of such matters falls within *subsection (3)*.

(16) For the purposes of this section—

(a) any decision made or any investigation conducted by the disciplinary committee of a relevant body is considered to have been made or conducted by the relevant body, and

(b) "member", in addition to the meaning given to that expression by *section 900(1)*, includes, in relation to a relevant body that is a recognised accountancy body, an individual or firm who or which, though not a member of the recognised accountancy body, is an individual or firm in relation to whom that body may perform functions under the relevant provisions.][a]

Amendments

a Section 933 substituted by C(SA)A 2018, s 32.

[933A Resolution of suspected non-compliance by agreement – relevant body

(1) *Section 933(1)* applies to the interpretation of this section as it applies to the interpretation of *section 933*.

(2) Subject to *subsection (3)*, if the Supervisory Authority believes on reasonable grounds—

(a) if the relevant body falls within *paragraph (a)* of the definition of 'relevant body', that the body did not comply with the approved investigation and disciplinary procedures, or

(b) if the relevant body falls within *paragraph (b)* of the definition of 'relevant body', that the body did not comply with the applicable provisions in performing the *Part 27* function,

the Supervisory Authority and the relevant body may, at their absolute discretion, enter into an agreement (in this section referred to as a "*section 933A* agreement") to resolve the matters the subject of the non-compliance.

(3) The following provisions shall apply to the *section 933A* agreement:

(a) the agreement may be entered into notwithstanding that no enquiry under *section 933* into the non-compliance has been commenced;

(b) the agreement may be entered into after an enquiry under *section 933* into the non-compliance has been commenced but not, subject to *paragraph (d)*, after it has been completed;

(c) without prejudice to the generality of the terms of the agreement, such terms may include terms under which the relevant body accepts—

(i) the imposition of one or more sanctions that may be imposed under *section 933(6)(b)*, and

(ii) if an enquiry under *section 933* into the non-compliance has been commenced, the payment of costs referred to in *section 933(7)*;

(d) the agreement may be entered into after an enquiry under *section 933* has been undertaken and carried out only to the extent to determine which sanctions (if any) referred to in *paragraph (c)(i)* to impose on the relevant body;

(e) the terms of the agreement are binding on the Supervisory Authority and the relevant body.

(4) Subject to *subsection (5)*, where the relevant body with whom the Supervisory Authority has entered into the *section 933A* agreement fails to comply with one or more of the terms of the agreement, the Supervisory Authority may apply to the court for an order compelling that body to comply with those terms.

(5) In default of payment, any amount agreed to be paid to the Supervisory Authority by the relevant body under the *section 933A* agreement may be recovered by the Supervisory Authority from the body as a simple contract debt in any court of competent jurisdiction.

(6) The Supervisory Authority may, at its discretion, publish a *section 933A* agreement on its website.

(7) *Section 941* shall be disregarded for the purposes of a *section 933A* agreement.][a]

Amendments

a Section 933A inserted by C(SA)A 2018, s 33. Heading of the amending section used here in the absence of one in the amendment.

934 Investigation of possible breaches of standards of prescribed accountancy bodies

[(1) In this section—

"client" includes an individual, a body corporate, an unincorporated body of persons and a partnership;

"relevant person"—

(a) in relation to an investigation of a member or former member of a prescribed accountancy body, means—

(i) that member or any other member or former member of the prescribed accountancy body,

(ii) a client or former client of the member,

(iii) if the client or former client is a body corporate, a person who is or was an officer, employee or agent of the client or former client,

(iv) the prescribed accountancy body or a person who is or was an officer, employee or agent of that body,

(v) if the member is an individual, a person who is or was an employee or agent of the member,

(vi) if the member is a firm, a person who is or was an officer, member, partner, employee or agent of the firm, or

(vii) any person whom the Supervisory Authority reasonably believes has information or documents relating to the investigation other than information or documents the disclosure of which is prohibited or restricted by law,

and

(b) in relation to an investigation of a statutory auditor or former statutory auditor, means—

(i) that auditor and any other statutory auditor or former statutory auditor who is or was a member of the same recognised accountancy body as the first-mentioned statutory auditor,

(ii) a client or former client of the auditor,

(iii) if the client or former client is a body corporate, a person who is or was an officer, employee or agent of the client or former client,

(iv) the recognised accountancy body or a person who is or was an officer, employee or agent of that body,

(v) if the auditor is an individual, a person who is or was an employee or agent of the auditor,

(vi) if the auditor is or was an audit firm, a person who is or was an officer, member, partner, employee or agent of the auditor, or

(vii) any person whom the Supervisory Authority reasonably believes has information or documents relating to the investigation other than information or documents the disclosure of which is prohibited or restricted by law.

(2)(a) Subject to *paragraph (b)* and *subsection (3)*, the Supervisory Authority may undertake an investigation into a possible relevant contravention committed by a specified person—

(i) following a complaint, or

(ii) on its own initiative.

(b) The Supervisory Authority shall not undertake an investigation into a possible relevant contravention committed by a specified person who falls within *paragraph (a)* of the definition of 'specified person' unless the Supervisory Authority is of the opinion that it is appropriate or in the public interest to do so.

(3) An investigation shall not be undertaken into a matter that is or has been the subject of an enquiry under *section 933* relating to the specified person except with the permission of the court granted on application under *section 933(5)*.

(4) For the purposes of an investigation under this section, the Supervisory Authority may require a relevant person to do one or more of the following:

(a) produce to the Supervisory Authority all books or documents relating to the investigation that are in the relevant person's possession or control;

(b) attend before the Supervisory Authority;

(c) give the Supervisory Authority any other assistance in connection with the investigation that the relevant person is reasonably able to give.

(5) For the purposes of an investigation under this section, the Supervisory Authority may—

(a) examine on oath, either by word of mouth or on written interrogatories, a relevant person,

(b) administer oaths for the purposes of the examination, and

(c) record, in writing, the answers of a person so examined and require that person to sign them.

(6) The Supervisory Authority may certify the refusal or failure to the court if a relevant person refuses or fails to do one or more of the following:

(a) produce to the Supervisory Authority any book or document that it is the person's duty under this section to produce;

(b) attend before the Supervisory Authority when required to do so under this section;

(c) answer a question put to the person by the Supervisory Authority with respect to the matter under investigation.

(7) On receiving a certificate of refusal or failure concerning a relevant person, the court may enquire into the case and after hearing any evidence that may be adduced, may do one or more of the following:

(a) direct that the relevant person attend or re-attend before the Supervisory Authority or produce particular books or documents or answer particular questions put to him or her by the Supervisory Authority;

(b) direct that the relevant person need not produce particular books or documents or answer particular questions put to him or her by the Supervisory Authority;

(c) make any other ancillary or consequential order or give any other direction that the court thinks fit.

(8) Subject to *sections 934G* and *941(4)* and *(4A)*, if, in the case of a specified person who falls within *paragraph (a)* of the definition of 'specified person', the Supervisory Authority finds that the person committed a relevant contravention, the Supervisory Authority may impose on the person such sanction to which the person is liable under the approved constitution and bye laws of the prescribed accountancy body of which the person is a member (including a monetary sanction) as the Supervisory Authority considers appropriate after having regard to the circumstances referred to in *section 934D(2)*.

(9) Subject to *section 941(4)* and *(4A)*, if, in the case of a specified person who falls within *paragraph (b)* of the definition of 'specified person', the Supervisory Authority finds that the person has committed a relevant contravention, the Supervisory Authority may impose such relevant sanction on the person as the Supervisory Authority considers appropriate after having regard to the circumstances referred to in *section 934D(2)*.

(10) Subject to *subsection (15)* and *section 941(4)* and *(4A)*, if *subsection (8)* or *(9)* applies, the costs incurred by the Supervisory Authority in investigating and determining a matter under this section (other than any costs of or incidental to an enquiry by the court under *subsection (7)*) shall be defrayed by, in the case of a specified person who falls within *paragraph (a)* of the definition of 'specified person', the

prescribed accountancy body of which the specified person is a member and, in any other case, by the specified person.

(11) Subject to *subsection (12)*, the specified person who is the subject of a relevant decision made by the Supervisory Authority may appeal to the court against the decision.

(12) An appeal under *subsection (11)* shall be brought within 3 months after the date on which the specified person concerned was notified by the Supervisory Authority of the relevant decision.

(13) The prescribed accountancy body or specified person, as appropriate, may appeal to the court against a decision made by the Supervisory Authority specifying an amount of costs under *subsection (10)*.

(14) An appeal under *subsection (13)* shall be brought within 3 months after the date on which the prescribed accountancy body or specified person, as appropriate, was notified by the Supervisory Authority of the decision.

(15) For the purposes of *subsection (10)*—

- (a) the Supervisory Authority may prescribe by regulations—
  - (i) that specified procedures and methods of calculation shall apply in the determination of the amount of costs so incurred by it, and
  - (ii) requirements otherwise as to the liability of, as appropriate, the prescribed accountancy body or specified person for, and the manner in which that body or person shall pay, that amount,

  and
- (b) in default of payment of that amount to the Supervisory Authority, the Authority may recover that amount as a simple contract debt in any court of competent jurisdiction.

(16) The production of any books or documents under this section by a person who claims a lien on them does not prejudice the lien.

(17) Nothing in this section shall be construed to prevent the undertaking of one investigation under this section into 2 or more possible relevant contraventions committed by the same specified person where one or more of such possible contraventions fall within *paragraph (a)* of the definition of 'relevant contravention' and one or more of such possible contraventions fall within *paragraph (b)* of that definition.][a]

Amendments

a Section 934 substituted by C(SA)A 2018, s 34.

[934A Supplemental provisions to section 934 - certain specified persons

(1) This section applies to a specified person the subject of a decision under *section 934(8)* that the person has committed a relevant contravention.

(2) Where applicable, the Supervisory Authority shall direct the prescribed accountancy body of which the specified person referred to in *subsection (1)* is a member to take any necessary action on foot of the imposition of a relevant sanction on the person and that body shall comply with the direction.

(3) The Supervisory Authority shall, as soon as is practicable after imposing a relevant sanction on a specified person referred to in *subsection (1)*, notify the prescribed accountancy body of which the specified person is a member of the imposition of the sanction together with such particulars of the person, the relevant contravention concerned and the sanction as the Supervisory Authority considers appropriate.][a]

Amendments

a Section 934A inserted by C(SA)A 2018, s 35.

[934B Immediate action required to protect public

(1) This section applies if the Supervisory Authority is of the opinion that the nature or gravity of the possible relevant contravention committed by a specified person warrants, in the interest of protecting the public, a direction to the specified person prohibiting him or her from carrying out statutory audits or signing statutory auditors' reports, or both, until steps or further steps are taken under section 934 in relation to that contravention by that person.

(2) The Supervisory Authority may make an ex parte application to the court for a direction referred to in *subsection (1)* until the steps or further steps referred to in that subsection are taken.][a]

Amendments

a Section 934B inserted by C(SA)A 2018, s 35.

[934C Sanctions which Supervisory Authority may impose on statutory auditor for relevant contravention

(1) This section applies to a specified person the subject of a decision under *section 934(9)* that the person has committed a relevant contravention.

(2) Subject to *section 934D*, the Supervisory Authority may impose on the specified person one or more of the following sanctions in relation to the relevant contravention:

(a) a direction by the Supervisory Authority to the specified person that he or she cease the conduct giving rise (whether in whole or in part) to the contravention and to abstain from any repetition of that conduct;

(b) a direction by the Supervisory Authority to the specified person to remediate the conduct giving rise (whether in whole or in part) to the contravention;

(c) a reprimand or severe reprimand by the Supervisory Authority to the specified person in relation to the conduct giving rise (whether in whole or in part) to the contravention;

(d) a declaration by the Supervisory Authority that the statutory auditors' report concerned does not meet the requirements of section 336 or 337 or, where applicable, Article 10 of Regulation (EU) No 537/2014;

(e) a direction by the Supervisory Authority to the specified person (being any one or more of a statutory auditor or key audit partner (within the meaning of *Part 27*)) prohibiting him or her, for the period specified in the direction (which may be up to and including an indefinite period), from carrying out statutory audits or signing statutory auditors' reports, or both;

(f) if the specified person is an audit firm, a direction by the Supervisory Authority to the firm, or to an officer, member or partner of the firm, or to both, prohibiting the firm or, as the case may be, the officer, member or partner, for the period specified in the direction (which may be up to and including an indefinite period) from performing functions—

(i) in the case of the firm, as an audit firm, or

(ii) in the case of the officer, member or partner, in audit firms or public-interest entities;

(g) subject to *section 934G*, a direction by the Supervisory Authority to the specified person to pay an amount, as specified in the direction but not exceeding—

(i) €100,000 in the case of a specified person who is an individual, or

(ii) in the case of a specified person which is an audit firm, ?100,000 multiplied by the number of statutory auditors in the firm at the time that the relevant contravention occurred (and irrespective of whether any particular statutory auditor was or was not a party to the relevant contravention),

to the Supervisory Authority;

(h) an order excluding the specified person from having his or her particulars entered, or continuing to be entered, in the public register (within the meaning of *Part 27*) in respect of one or more recognised accountancy bodies.

(3) In default of payment of an amount referred to in *subsection (2)(g)*, the Supervisory Authority may recover that amount as a simple contract debt in any court of competent jurisdiction.

(4) A person the subject of a direction under *subsection (2)* shall comply with the direction.

(5) Where applicable, the Supervisory Authority shall direct the recognised accountancy body of which the specified person is a member to take any necessary action on foot of the imposition of a relevant sanction on the person and that body shall comply with the direction.

(6) The Supervisory Authority shall, as soon as is practicable after imposing a relevant sanction on a specified person, notify the recognised accountancy body of which the specified person is a member of the imposition of the sanction together with such particulars of the person, the relevant contravention concerned and the sanction as the Supervisory Authority considers appropriate.][a]

Amendments

a Section 934C inserted by C(SA)A 2018, s 35.

[934D Relevant circumstances to be considered in imposing relevant sanctions on specified person

(1) This section applies to a specified person the subject of a decision under *section 934(8)* or *(9)* that the person has committed a relevant contravention.

(2) In imposing a relevant sanction on a specified person, the Supervisory Authority shall consider the following circumstances:

(a) the gravity and duration of the relevant contravention;

(b) the degree of responsibility of the specified person;

(c) the financial strength of the specified person (including, in the case of a specified person who is not an individual, the total turnover of the specified person or, in the case of a specified person who is an individual, the annual income of the individual);

(d) the amount of profits gained or losses avoided by the specified person in consequence of the relevant contravention, in so far as they can be determined;

(e) the level of cooperation of the specified person with the Supervisory Authority;

(f) previous relevant contraventions committed by the specified person.][a]

Amendments

a Section 934D inserted by C(SA)A 2018, s 35.

[934E Resolution of suspected relevant contravention by agreement – specified person

(1) Subject to *subsection (2)*, if the Supervisory Authority believes on reasonable grounds that a specified person is committing, or has committed, a relevant contravention, the Supervisory Authority and the person may, at their absolute discretion, enter into an agreement (in this section referred to as a "*section 934E* agreement") to resolve the matters the subject of the contravention.

(2) The following provisions shall apply to the section 934E agreement:

(a) the agreement may be entered into notwithstanding that no investigation under *section 934* into the contravention has been commenced;

(b) the agreement may be entered into after an investigation under *section 934* into the relevant contravention has been commenced but not, subject to *paragraph (d)*, after it has been completed;

(c) without prejudice to the generality of the terms of the agreement, such terms may include terms under which the specified person accepts—

(i) the imposition of one or more relevant sanctions that may be imposed under *section 934(8)* or *(9)*, as appropriate, and

(ii) if an investigation under *section 934* into the contravention has been commenced, the payment of costs referred to in *section 934(10)*;

(d) the agreement may be entered into after an investigation under section 934 has been undertaken and carried out only to the extent to determine which sanctions (if any) referred to in *paragraph (c)(i)* to impose on the specified person;

(e) the terms of the agreement are binding on the Supervisory Authority and the specified person.

(3) Subject to subsection (6), the provisions of *sections 934C, 934D, 934F, 934G* and *934H* shall apply, with any necessary modifications, to any relevant sanctions imposed on a specified person pursuant to a section 934E agreement as those sections apply to any relevant sanctions imposed on a specified person otherwise than pursuant to a *section 934E* agreement.

(4) Subject to *subsection (5)*, where the specified person with whom the Supervisory Authority has entered into the *section 934E* agreement fails to comply with one or more of the terms of the agreement, the Supervisory Authority may apply to the court for an order compelling that person comply with those terms.

(5) In default of payment, any amount agreed to be paid to the Supervisory Authority by the specified person under the *section 934E* agreement may be recovered by the Supervisory Authority from the person as a simple contract debt in any court of competent jurisdiction.

(6) The necessary modifications referred to in *subsection (3)*, in so far as *section 934F* is concerned, include reading that section as if—

(a) the following subsection were substituted for subsection (1) of that section:

> "(1) Subject to subsection (3), the Supervisory Authority shall, in so far as a relevant decision imposes a relevant sanction on a specified person, as soon as is practicable, publish on its website particulars of the relevant contravention for which the relevant sanction was imposed, particulars of the relevant sanction imposed and particulars of the specified person on whom the relevant sanction was imposed.",

(b) *subsections (2)* and *(4)* of that section were deleted, and

(c) in *subsection (5)* of that section, the reference to "or (2)" were deleted.

(7) *Section 941* shall be disregarded for the purposes of a section 934E agreement.][a]

Amendments

a Section 934E inserted by C(SA)A 2018, s 35.

[934F Publication of relevant sanction imposed on specified person, etc.

(1) Subject to *subsections (2)* and *(3)*, the Supervisory Authority shall, in so far as a relevant decision imposes a relevant sanction on a specified person, as soon as is practicable after—

(a) that decision has been confirmed by the court as referred to in *section 941(4A)*, or

(b) a decision of the court under *section 941(2)(b)* has been made to impose a different relevant sanction on the specified person,

publish on its website particulars of the relevant contravention for which the relevant sanction was imposed, particulars of the relevant sanction imposed and particulars of the specified person on whom the relevant sanction was imposed.

(2) Subject to *subsection (4)*, if there is an appeal to the court from a confirmation referred to in *subsection (1)(a)*, or a decision referred to in *subsection (1)(b)*, the Supervisory Authority shall, as soon as may be, as it considers appropriate, publish particulars on its website of the status or outcome of the appeal.

(3) The Supervisory Authority shall publish the particulars, comprising a public notice of a relevant sanction imposed, on an anonymous basis on its website in any one or more of the following circumstances:

(a) the Supervisory Authority, following an assessment of the proportionality of the publication of those particulars in accordance with *subsection (1)* in so far as personal data are concerned, is of the opinion that, in relation to the relevant sanction imposed on a specified person who is an individual, such publication would be disproportionate;

(b) the Supervisory Authority is of the opinion that the publication of those particulars in accordance with *subsection (1)* would jeopardise the stability of financial markets or an ongoing criminal investigation;

(c) the Supervisory Authority is of the opinion that the publication of those particulars in accordance with *subsection (1)* would cause disproportionate damage to the specified person.

(4) *Subsection (2)* shall not apply in any case where *subsection (3)* applies.

(5) The Supervisory Authority shall ensure that particulars published on its website in accordance with *subsection (1)* or *(2)* remain on its website for at least 5 years.][a]

Amendments

a Section 934F inserted by C(SA)A 2018, s 35.

[934G Limitations on imposing monetary sanctions on specified person

(1) If the Supervisory Authority decides to impose a monetary sanction on a specified person, the Supervisory Authority shall not impose an amount—

(a) that would be likely to cause the specified person to cease business, or

(b) that would, if the specified person is an individual, be likely to cause the person to be adjudicated bankrupt.

(2) If the conduct engaged in by the specified person has given rise (whether in whole or in part) to 2 or more relevant contraventions, the Supervisory Authority shall not impose more than one monetary sanction on the person in respect of the same conduct.][a]

Amendments

a Section 934G inserted by C(SA)A 2018, s 35.

[934H Specified person not to be liable to be penalised twice for same relevant contravention

(1) If the Supervisory Authority imposes a monetary sanction on a specified person and the conduct engaged in by the person that has given rise (whether in whole or in part) to the relevant contravention is an offence under the law of the State, the person shall not be liable to be prosecuted or punished for the offence under that law.

(2) The Supervisory Authority shall not impose a monetary sanction on a specified person if—

(a) the person has been charged with having committed an offence under a law of the State and has either been found guilty or not guilty of having committed the offence, and

(b) the offence involves the conduct engaged in by the person that has given rise (whether in whole or in part) to the relevant contravention.][a]

Amendments

a Section 934H inserted by C(SA)A 2018, s 35.

[934I Reporting of relevant contraventions

(1) The Supervisory Authority and each recognised accountancy body shall establish effective mechanisms to encourage the reporting to it of relevant contraventions or suspected relevant contraventions.

(2) The mechanisms referred to in subsection (1) shall include at least:

(a) specific procedures (including follow-up procedures) for the receipt of reports of relevant contraventions and suspected relevant contraventions;

(b) the protection of personal data concerning both the person who reports the relevant contravention or suspected relevant contravention and the specified person concerned in compliance with the principles laid down in the Data Protection Acts 1988 to 2018 and Regulation (EU) 2016/679.

(3) A statutory auditor which is an audit firm shall, as soon as is practicable after the commencement of section 35 of the Companies (Statutory Audits) Act 2018, establish effective procedures within the firm for employees to report relevant contraventions or suspected relevant contraventions.][a]

Amendments

a Section 934I inserted by C(SA)A 2018, s 35.

[935 Supplemental provisions in relation to *section 934* (including as concerns its relationship to provisions of 2016 Audits Regulations)[a]

(1) For the avoidance of doubt, the following matters may, without prejudice to the generality of the provisions of *section 934*, be the subject of an investigation by the Supervisory Authority under that section, namely matters—

(a) in relation to which a recognised accountancy body has decided not to withdraw a person's approval under [*Part 27*][b] as a statutory auditor or audit firm, or

(b) which either—

(i) have not been considered by a recognised accountancy body as grounds for the withdrawal of a person's approval under [that Part][c] as a statutory auditor or audit firm, or

(ii) having been considered by it as such grounds, are not considered by it to disclose a *prima facie* case for proceeding further.

(2) Where—

(a) those matters are the subject of such an investigation by the Supervisory Authority, and

(b) a breach of standards is found by the Supervisory Authority,

[*section 934(7)*][d] shall be read as requiring or enabling (depending on whether the breach of standards found falls within [*Chapters 2* to *4*, or *Chapter 8*, of *Part 27*][e]) the

Supervisory Authority to withdraw the approval under [that *Part*][f] of the person concerned as a statutory auditor or audit firm.

[(3) Where such an approval is withdrawn by the Supervisory Authority, *section 1479(13)* to *(15)* or, as the case may be, *section 1480(13)* to *(15)*, shall, with all necessary modifications, apply to that withdrawal and *section 934(11)* and *(12)* shall not apply to that withdrawal.][g]

(4) *Subsection (2)* does not prejudice the imposition, in the circumstances concerned, by the Supervisory Authority of another sanction referred to in [*section 934(8)*][h] in addition to a withdrawal of approval (where withdrawal of the approval is mandatory under [Part 27][i]) or in lieu of a withdrawal of approval (where such withdrawal is not so mandatory).

(5) For the purposes of *section 934* 'member', in addition to the meaning given to that expression by *section 900(1)*, includes, in relation to a prescribed accountancy body that is a recognised accountancy body, an individual or firm who or which, though not a member of the recognised accountancy body, is an individual or firm in relation to whom that body may exercise powers under [*Part 27*].[j]]

Amendments

a Section 935 substituted by the European Union (Statutory Audits) (Directive 2006/43/EC, as amended by Directive 2014/56/EU, and Regulation (EU) No 537/2014) Regulations 2016 (SI 312/2016), reg 23, with effect from 17 June 2016.

b Words substituted by C(SA)A 2018, s 36(a)(i) (previously: "the 2016 Audits Regulations").

c Words substituted by C(SA)A 2018, s 36(a)(ii) (previously: "those Regulations").

d Words substituted by C(SA)A 2018, s 36(b)(i) (previously: "section 934(7)").

e Words substituted by C(SA)A 2018, s 36(b)(ii) (previously: "Part 4 or Chapter 2 of Part 8 of the 2016 Audits Regulations").

f Words substituted by C(SA)A 2018, s 36(b)(ii) (previously: "those Regulations").

g Subsection (3) substituted by C(SA)A 2018, s 36(c).

h Words substituted by C(SA)A 2018, s 36(d)(i) (previously: "section 934(7)").

i Words substituted by C(SA)A 2018, s 36(d)(ii) (previously: "the 2016 Audits Regulations").

i Words substituted by C(SA)A 2018, s 36(e) (previously: "the 2016 Audits Regulations").

935A Interpretation of sections 935A to 935D and 941A

[...][a]

Amendments

a Section 935A repealed by C(SA)A 2018, s 3(1).

935B Investigation of possible relevant contraventions

[...][a]

Amendments

a Section 935B repealed by C(SA)A 2018, s 3(1).

935C Sanctions which Supervisory Authority or Director of Corporate Enforcement may impose

[...][a]

Amendments

a Section 935C repealed by C(SA)A 2018, s 3(1).

935D Publication of relevant sanction imposed, etc

[...][a]

Amendments

a Section 935D repealed by C(SA)A 2018, s 3(1).

936 Review of members of recognised accountancy bodies

[...][a]

Amendments

a Section 936 repealed by C(SA)A 2018, s 3(1).

[936A Supplemental provisions in relation to section 934 – relevant directors

(1) This section applies if—

(a) either—

(i) a specified person is the subject of a decision under *section 934(9)* that he or she has committed a relevant contravention, or

(ii) the Supervisory Authority and a specified person who falls within *paragraph (b)* of the definition of 'specified person' have entered into a *section 934E* agreement in respect of a relevant contravention that the Supervisory Authority reasonably believes that the person has committed,

and

(b) that contravention relates, whether directly or indirectly, to the audit of a public-interest entity.

(2) The Supervisory Authority shall, as soon as is practicable, give the Director particulars of—

(a) the specified person,

(b) the relevant contravention, and

(c) the public-interest entity.

(3) The Supervisory Authority shall, in addition to complying with *subsection (2)*, give the Director such information and documents and assistance as the Director may reasonably require for the Director to decide whether or not—

(a) to investigate under *Part 13* a relevant director, or

(b) to impose, under *section 957B*, a relevant sanction (within the meaning of *section 957AA*) on a relevant director for engaging in conduct giving rise (whether in whole or in part) to the relevant contravention,

or both.][a]

Amendments

a Section 936A inserted by C(SA)A 2018, s 37.

[936B Communication with the CEAOB

(1) The Supervisory Authority shall immediately communicate to the CEAOB particulars of—

(a) any direction under *section 934(8)* that is equivalent to a direction referred to in *paragraph (b)*,

(b) any direction given by the Authority under *section 934C(2)(e)* or *(f)*, and

(c) any direction given by the Director under *section 957C(2)(b)*.

(2) The Supervisory Authority shall, as soon as may be after the end of a year, give to the CEAOB aggregated information in relation to—

(a) all relevant sanctions imposed by it on specified persons (being specified persons who fall within *paragraph (b)* of the definition of "specified person") during the year in accordance with this Chapter,

(b) all public notices of relevant sanctions imposed by it on specified persons (being specified persons who fall within *paragraph (b)* of the definition of "specified person") during the year in accordance with this Chapter,

(c) all relevant sanctions (within the meaning of *Chapter 9* of *Part 27*) imposed by it on specified persons (within the meaning of that Chapter) during the year in accordance with that Chapter,

(d) all public notices of relevant sanctions imposed (within the meaning of *Chapter 9* of *Part 27*) by it on specified persons (within the meaning of that Chapter) during the year in accordance with that Chapter,

(e) all relevant sanctions (within the meaning of *section 957AA*) imposed by the Director during the year in accordance with *Chapter 3*, and

(f) all public notices of relevant sanctions imposed (within the meaning of *section 957AA*) by the Director during the year in accordance with Chapter 3.

(3) A recognised accountancy body shall immediately communicate to the Supervisory Authority particulars of any temporary prohibition referred to in point (c) or (e) of Article 30a(1) of the Audit Directive imposed by the body on a relevant person.

(4) The Supervisory Authority shall immediately communicate to the CEAOB particulars which have been communicated to it under *subsection (3)*.

(5) Without prejudice to the generality of *sections 1523* and *1556*, a recognised accountancy body shall, as soon as may be after the end of a year, give to the Supervisory Authority aggregated information in relation to—

(a) all sanctions equivalent to relevant sanctions imposed by it on relevant persons during the year in accordance with *Part 27*, and

(b) all notices equivalent to public notices of the sanctions first-mentioned in *paragraph (a)* imposed by it on relevant persons during the year in accordance with *Part 27*.

(6) The Supervisory Authority shall, as soon as may be after it is given the information referred to in *subsection (5)*, give the information to the CEAOB.

(7) In this section, 'relevant person', in relation to a recognised accountancy body, means—

(a) a member of the body, or

(b) an auditor or audit firm in relation to whom, by virtue of section 930C, the body may perform functions,

who is a statutory auditor or former statutory auditor.][a]

Amendments

a Section 936B inserted by C(SA)A 2018, s 37.

937 Delegation of Supervisory Authority's functions

(1) The Supervisory Authority may delegate some or all of the functions under [*sections 933* to *934I*, *935* and *936B* and *Chapter 9* of *Part 27*][a] to a committee

established for that purpose and consisting of persons from one or more of the following categories of persons:

(a) persons who are, at the time the committee is established, directors of the Authority;

(b) other persons that the Authority considers appropriate.

(2) Where functions under a provision referred to in *subsection (1)* are delegated to a committee, any references in that provision to the Supervisory Authority shall be read as references to that committee.

(3) Subject to the regulations made under *section 938(4)*, a committee may regulate its own procedure.

[(3A) The Supervisory Authority may delegate some or all of the functions under *sections 933* to *934I*, *935* and *936B* and *Chapter 9* of *Part 27* to any of its officers or employees or any other person duly authorised by it in that behalf.][b]

(4) The Supervisory Authority may, if it reasonably considers it appropriate to do so, perform any of its other functions through or by any of its officers or employees or any other person duly authorised by it in that behalf, including the determination of whether a matter should be referred to a committee established for a purpose referred to in *subsection (1)*.

(5) A delegation under this section is revocable at will.

(6) For the avoidance of doubt, a committee that was established under section 27(1) of the Act of 2003 prior to the commencement of section 4 of the Companies (Miscellaneous Provisions) Act 2009 shall be deemed to have been properly constituted, and shall be deemed to have and to have had all the powers necessary to perform its functions notwithstanding that any of its members was a director when he or she was appointed to the committee but ceased to be such a director before the completion of the enquiry, investigation or review for which it was established.

Amendments

a Words substituted by C(SA)A 2018, s 38(a) (previously: "sections 933 to 936").

b Subsection (3A) inserted by C(SA)A 2018, s 38(b).

---

938 Hearings, privileges and procedural rules

(1) The Supervisory Authority may for the purposes of performing its functions under section *933, 934* [or *935*][a] conduct an oral hearing in accordance with regulations made under *subsection (4)*.

(2) A witness before the Supervisory Authority is entitled to the same immunities and privileges as a witness before the court.

(3) Nothing in *section 933*, *934*, *935* [or *935*][b] or *936* compels the disclosure by any person of any information that the person would be entitled to refuse to produce on the

grounds of legal professional privilege or authorises the inspection or copying of any document containing such information that is in the person's possession.

[(4) Subject to *subsection (5)*, the Supervisory Authority may make regulations respecting the procedures to be followed in conducting enquiries under section 933 and investigations under *section 934* or *935*.

(5) There is no obligation to make regulations under *subsection (4)* with respect to a particular provision referred to in that subsection.][c]

[(6) The Supervisory Authority shall, as soon as is practicable after making any regulations under *subsection (4)*, publish the regulations on its website.

(7) Any information produced or answer given by a person (howsoever described) in compliance with a requirement under section 933, 934 or 935 may be used in evidence against the person in any proceedings whatsoever, save proceedings for an offence (other than perjury in respect of such an answer).

(8) A finding or decision of the Supervisory Authority under *section 933*, *934* or *935* is not a bar to any civil or criminal proceedings against the person (howsoever described) who is the subject of the finding or decision.][d]

Amendments

a Words substituted by C(SA)A 2018, s 39(a) (previously: ", 935 or 935B".
b Words substituted by C(SA)A 2018, s 39(b) (previously: ", 935 or 935B".
c Subsections (4) and (5) substituted by C(SA)A 2018, s 39(c).
d Subsections (6), (7) and (8) inserted by C(SA)A 2018, s 39(d).

939 Supervisory Authority's seal and instruments

(1) Judicial notice shall be taken of the seal of the Supervisory Authority.

(2) Every document that appears to be an instrument made by the Supervisory Authority and to be sealed with its seal (purporting to be authenticated in accordance with its articles of association) shall be received in evidence and be deemed to be such instrument without proof, unless the contrary is shown.

940 Confidentiality of information

(1) A person shall not disclose information that—

(a) comes into the possession of the Supervisory Authority by virtue of the performance by it of any of its functions under this Act; and

(b) has not otherwise come to the notice of members of the public.

(2) *Subsection (1)* shall not apply to—

(a) person specified in *subsection (3)* or a director of the Authority in the performance by the Authority, or him or her, of any of its or his or her functions under this Act or any other enactment, being a communication the making of which was, in the Authority's or his or her opinion, appropriate for the performance of the function concerned; or

(b) the disclosure of information in a report of the Supervisory Authority or for the purpose of any legal proceedings, investigation, enquiry or review under this Act or any other enactment or pursuant to an order of a court of competent jurisdiction for the purposes of any proceedings in that court; or

(c) a disclosure made where such disclosure is required by, or in accordance with, law; or

(d) a disclosure of information which, in the opinion of the Supervisory Authority, a member of its staff, any person specified in *subsection (3)* or a director of the Authority, may relate to the commission of an offence; or

(e) a disclosure to a person prescribed by regulations made by the Supervisory Authority as a person to whom a disclosure, or a specified class of disclosure, may lawfully be made.

(3) The persons mentioned in *subsection (2)(a)* and *(d)* are any agent of the Supervisory Authority or professional or other adviser to it.

(4) A person who contravenes *subsection (1)* shall be guilty of a category 2 offence.

[(5) Nothing in this section shall operate to prevent the Supervisory Authority from complying with its obligations under the relevant provisions.][a]

Amendments

a Subsection (5) inserted by C(SA)A 2018, s 40.

941 Appeals to and orders of the court, including orders confirming decisions of Supervisory Authority

(1) In an appeal under [*section 931B(5)*, *933(10)* or *(12)* or *934(11)* or *(13)*][a], the court may consider any evidence adduced or argument made, whether or not adduced or made to the Supervisory Authority or other body whose decision is under appeal.

(2) On the hearing of such an appeal, the court may make any order or give any direction it thinks fit, including an order—

(a) confirming the decision under appeal, or

(b) modifying or annulling that decision.

(3) On application under [*section 933(5)*][b] for an order granting permission for an investigation under *section 934* into a possible [relevant contravention committed by a specified person][c], the court may—

(a) grant or refuse to grant permission, and

(b) make any ancillary or consequential order it thinks fit, including, if permission is granted, an order setting aside any decision of the body relating to [such person].[d]

[(4) *Subsection (4A)* applies to the following decisions of the Supervisory Authority:

(a) a decision under *section 931B(2)(c)*;

(b) a decision under *section 933(6)* in so far as it relates to the advisement, or admonishment, or censure referred to in that section of a relevant body;

(c) a decision under *section 933(7)*;

(d) a decision under *section 934(10)*;

(e) a relevant decision in so far as it relates to the imposition of a relevant sanction on a specified person.

(4A) A decision to which this subsection applies does not take effect until the decision is confirmed by the court either—

(a) on appeal under *section 931B(5)*, *933(10)* or *934(11)* or *(13)*, or

(b) on application by the Supervisory Authority under subsection (5).][e]

(5) On application by motion on notice by the Supervisory Authority for an order confirming a decision [to which *subsection (4A)* applies][f], the court may make an order confirming the decision or may refuse to make such an order.

(6) On application under *section 906(4)* for an order compelling compliance with—

(a) a rule adopted or guideline issued by the Supervisory Authority,

(b) a term or condition of recognition,

(c) an obligation or obligations referred to in that subsection,

(d) a *section 931* notice, or

(e) a direction under *section 934A(2)* or *934C(5)*,][g]

the court may make any order or give any direction it thinks fit.

[(7) On an application under *section 933A(4)* for an order compelling compliance with a *section 933A* agreement, the court may make any order or give any direction as it thinks fit.

(8) On an application under *section 934B(2)* for a direction referred to in section 934B(1), the court may make any order or give any direction as it thinks fit.

(9) On an application under *section 934E(4)* for an order compelling compliance with a section 934E agreement, the court may make any order or give any direction as it thinks fit.][h]

Amendments

a Words substituted by C(SA)A 2018, s 41(a) (previously: "section 933(9) or (11), 934(10) or 935B(7)").

b Words substituted by C(SA)A 2018, s 41(b)(i) (previously: "section 933(4)").

c Words substituted by C(SA)A 2018, s 41(b)(ii) (previously: "breach of a prescribed accountancy body's rules by a member").

d Words substituted by C(SA)A 2018, s 41(b)(ii) (previously: "the member").

e Subsection (4) substituted and sub-s (4A) inserted by C(SA)A 2018, s 41(c).

f Words substituted by C(SA)A 2018, s 41(d) (previously: "referred to in subsection (4)").

g Paragraphs (b) and (c) substituted and paras (d) and (e) inserted by C(SA)A 2018, s 41(e).
h Subsections (7)–(9) inserted by C(SA)A 2018, s 41(f).

941A

[...][a]

Amendments

a Section 941A repealed by C(SA)A 2018, s 3(1)(g).

942 Liability of Supervisory Authority for acts, omissions, etc.

(1) Neither the Supervisory Authority nor any person who is or was—

(a) a member or director;

(b) other officer or employee;

(c) a member of a committee; or

(d) a professional or other adviser or duly authorised agent;

of the Supervisory Authority shall be liable for damages for anything done, anything purported to be done or anything omitted to be done—

(i) by the Supervisory Authority or that person (not being such an agent) in performing their functions under this Act; or

(ii) in the case of such an agent, by the agent in doing on behalf of the Authority or other foregoing person an act that was done to enable such functions to be performed;

unless the act or omission is shown to have been in bad faith.

[...][a]

(3) Subject to any enactment or rule of law the Supervisory Authority may indemnify—

(a) any person who is or was a member or director, other officer or employee, member of a committee or a professional or other adviser of the Supervisory Authority in respect of anything done or omitted to be done by that person in good faith in carrying out duties under this Act, and

(b) any person who is or was a duly authorised agent of the Supervisory Authority in respect of anything done or omitted to be done by that person in good faith in his or her doing an act on behalf of a person referred to in *paragraph (a)* that was done to enable the latter's duties under this Act to be carried out.

(4) The power to indemnify under *subsection (3)* includes the power to indemnify a person referred to in that subsection for any liability to pay damages or costs because of anything done or omitted to be done by that person in carrying out duties under this

Act or, in the case of an agent referred to in *paragraph (b)* of that subsection, in doing an act referred to in that paragraph, where the liability—

(a) has been determined in proceedings before a court or tribunal in another state or arises by virtue of an agreement entered into in settlement of such proceedings, and

(b) would not have been determined had [*subsection (1)*][b] been applied in those proceedings or would not have been the subject of such an agreement but for that person's reliance in good faith on a legal opinion or advice that those subsections would not be applied by the court or tribunal in those proceedings.

Amendments

a Subsection (2) deleted by C(SA)A 2018, s 42(a).

b Words substituted by C(SA)A 2018, s 42(b) (previously "subsections (1) and (2)").

[942A Liability of prescribed body for acts, omissions etc.

(1) Neither a prescribed body nor any person who is or was—

(a) a member or director, or

(b) other officer or employee,

of the prescribed body shall be liable for damages for anything done, anything purported to be done or anything omitted to be done by the prescribed body or that person in performing the functions specified in subsection (2) unless the act or omission is shown to have been in bad faith.

(2) Subsection (1) applies to the issuing of accounting standards.

(3) In this section, 'prescribed body' means a body prescribed under *section 943(1)(h)*.][a]

Amendments

a Section 942A inserted by C(A)A 2017, s 97.

943 Minister's power to make regulations for purposes of Chapter, etc.

(1) Subject to *section 944* and without prejudice to the application of *section 12(1)* to this Chapter, the Minister may make regulations that are necessary or advisable for giving effect to this Chapter or the provisions hereafter mentioned of *sections 167*, *225* and *275*, including regulations—

(a) prescribing designated bodies for the purposes of *sections 902* and *907*;

(b) providing that, effective on a specified date, a body referred to in *section 902(2)* ceases to be a designated body;

(c) varying, as a consequence of a regulation under *paragraph (a)* or *(b)*, the numbers specified in *section 907(1)*, *(2)* and *(4)*, as the Minister considers necessary or expedient;

(d) [...][a];

[(e) prescribing the amount of a penalty under *section 933(6)(b)(v)*;

(f) prescribing for the purposes of *section 933(9)* the manner in which notice is to be given;][b]

(g) [exempting from *section 225*][c]—

(i) qualifying companies within the meaning of section 110 of the Taxes Consolidation Act 1997 (as inserted by section 48 of the Finance Act 2003); and

(ii) classes of other companies and other undertakings, if the extent to which or the manner in which they are or may be regulated under any enactment makes it, in the Minister's opinion, unnecessary or inappropriate to apply those provisions or that provision to them;

(h) prescribing for the purposes of the definition of "accounting standards" in *section 275(1)* one or more bodies that issue statements of accounting standards;

(i) prescribing for the purposes of the definition of "[relevant company][d]" in *section 167(1)* or for the purposes of *section 225(7)* amounts that are higher or lower than the euro amounts specified in that definition or in *section 225(7)*, as the case may be, and that apply instead of the euro amounts.

(2) On a body ceasing—

(a) to be a prescribed accountancy body because of the revocation of a regulation made under *section 12(1)*, or

(b) to be a designated body because of a regulation made under *subsection (1)(b)*,

any director who was nominated by that body under *section 907* immediately ceases to hold office.

(3) Before preparing, for the purposes of *section 944*, a draft regulation under—

(a) *section 12(1)* prescribing bodies of accountants for the purposes of the definition of "prescribed accountancy body" in *section 900(1)*, or

(b) *subsection (1)(a)*, *(d)* or *(i)*,

the Minister shall consider any recommendations that the Supervisory Authority may make.

(4) Subject to *subsection (3)*, before making a regulation under this section the Minister may consult with any persons that the Minister considers should be consulted.

(5) Regulations under this section may contain any transitional and other supplementary and incidental provisions that appear to the Minister to be appropriate.

Amendments

a Paragraph (1)(d) repealed by C(A)A 2017, s 73(a).

b Paragraphs (1)(e) and (f) substituted by C(SA)A 2018, s 43.

c Words substituted by C(A)A 2017, s 73(b) (previously: "exempting from *sections 225* and *917* (or either of those sections)").

d Words substituted by C(A)A 2017, s 73(c) (previously: "large company").

944 Prior approval by Houses of Oireachtas required for certain regulations

Where it is proposed to make a regulation under—

(a) *section 12(1)* prescribing bodies of accountants for the purposes of the definition of "prescribed accountancy body" in *section 900(1)*, or

(b) section 943(1)(a), (d), (g) or (i),

a draft of the proposed regulation shall be laid before each House of the Oireachtas and the regulation shall not be made until a resolution approving of the draft has been passed by each such House.

Chapter 3
Director of Corporate Enforcement

945 Director of Corporate Enforcement

(1) The office of Director of Corporate Enforcement established by section 7 of the Company Law Enforcement Act 2001 shall continue in being.

(2) The person holding the office of Director of Corporate Enforcement immediately before the commencement of this section shall, unless he or she resigns, dies, is removed from, or otherwise vacates, office, continue to hold office after that commencement for the remainder of the period of office for which he or she was appointed before that commencement; unless those terms or conditions are varied in accordance with this Chapter, that person shall continue to hold such office subject to the same terms and conditions as those subject to which he or she held office immediately before that commencement.

(3) Any appointment of a person to be the Director of Corporate Enforcement falling to be made after the commencement of this section shall be made by the Minister.

(4) The person to be appointed shall be a person duly selected following a competition under the Public Service Management (Recruitment and Appointments) Act 2004 and of which selection the Minister has been advised accordingly.

(5) The Director shall be a corporation sole and, notwithstanding any casual vacancy in the office from time to time, shall have perpetual succession and shall be capable in his or her corporate name of holding and disposing of real or personal property and of suing and being sued.

(6) The Director shall perform the functions conferred on him or her under this or any other Act and shall be assisted in the performance of those functions by the officers of the Director.

(7) Judicial notice shall be taken of the signature of the Director on or affixed to any document and it shall be presumed, unless the contrary is proved, that it has been duly signed or affixed.

946 Terms and conditions of appointment

(1) Subject to *subsection (3)* and *section 945(2)*, the Director shall hold office for such period not exceeding 5 years beginning on the date of his or her appointment as the Minister, with the consent of the Minister for Public Expenditure and Reform, determines.

(2) The Minister may, with the consent of the Minister for Public Expenditure and Reform, continue the appointment of the Director (including an appointment previously continued under this subsection) for such further period, not exceeding 5 years at any one time, as the Minister determines.

(3) The Director shall hold office on such terms and conditions (which shall include a scheme of superannuation under *section 950*) as the Minister, with the consent of the Minister for Public Expenditure and Reform, determines.

(4) A person appointed as the Director is, by virtue of the appointment, a civil servant within the meaning of the Civil Service Regulation Acts 1956 to 2005.

(5) The Director shall not hold any other office or employment for which remuneration is payable.

947 Removal, cessation or disqualification of Director

(1) The Minister may at any time, for stated reasons, remove the Director from office.

(2) If the Director is removed from office under *subsection (1)*, the Minister shall ensure that a statement of the reasons for the Director's removal is laid before each House of the Oireachtas.

(3) The Director shall cease to be the Director on—

- (a) being nominated as a member of Seanad Éireann,
- (b) being nominated as a candidate for election to either House of the Oireachtas or to the European Parliament,
- (c) being regarded, pursuant to section 19 of the European Parliament Elections Act 1997, as having been elected to the European Parliament to fill a vacancy, or
- (d) becoming a member of a local authority.

(4) A person is disqualified from appointment as the Director for so long as he or she is—

- (a) entitled under the Standing Orders of either House of the Oireachtas to sit in that House,
- (b) a member of the European Parliament, or

(c) a member of a local authority.

948 Acting Director of Corporate Enforcement

(1) Subject to *subsection (2)*, the Minister may appoint a person to be the Acting Director of Corporate Enforcement to perform the functions of the Director during—

(a) a period, or during all periods, when the Director is absent from duty or from the State or is, for any other reason, unable to perform the functions of the Director,

(b) any suspension from office of the Director, or

(c) a vacancy in the office of Director.

(2) A person shall not be appointed to perform the functions of the Director for a continuous period of more than 6 months during a vacancy in the office of Director.

(3) The Minister may, at any time, terminate an appointment under this section.

949 Functions of Director

(1) The functions of the Director are—

(a) to encourage compliance with this Act,

(b) to investigate—

(i) instances of suspected offences under this Act, and

(ii) instances otherwise of suspected non-compliance with this Act or with the duties and obligations to which companies and their officers are subject,

(c) to enforce this Act, including by the prosecution of offences by way of summary proceedings,

(d) at his or her discretion, to refer cases to the Director of Public Prosecutions where the Director has reasonable grounds for believing that an indictable offence under this Act has been committed,

(e) to exercise, in so far as the Director considers it necessary or appropriate, a supervisory role over the activity of liquidators and receivers in the discharge of their functions under this Act,

(f) for the purpose of ensuring the effective application and enforcement of obligations, standards and procedures to which companies and their officers are subject, to perform such other functions in respect of any matters to which this Act relates as the Minister considers appropriate and may by order confer on the Director,

(g) to act under *Chapter 2* as a member of the Supervisory Authority and, if appointed under *section 907*, act as a director of that body, and

(h) to perform such other functions for a purpose referred to in *paragraph (f)* as may be assigned to the Director under this Act or any other Act of the Oireachtas.

[(1A) *Sections 930A* and *930D* make additional provision with regard to the performance of functions by, amongst others, the Director.][a]

(2) The Director may do all such acts or things as are necessary or expedient for the performance of his or her functions under this Act or any other Act.

(3) The Director shall be independent in the performance of his or her functions.

(4) The Director may perform such of his or her functions as he or she thinks fit through an officer of the Director and in the performance of those functions the officer shall be subject to the directions of the Director only.

Amendments

a Subsection (1A) inserted by C(SA)A 2018, s 44.

950 Superannuation

(1) The Minister shall, with the consent of the Minister for Public Expenditure and Reform, if he or she considers it appropriate, make and carry out a scheme or schemes for granting superannuation benefits to or in respect of one or more of the following:

(a) the Director;

(b) the Acting Director;

(c) any officer of the Director.

(2) Each superannuation scheme shall fix the terms and conditions of retirement for all persons to or in respect of whom superannuation benefits are payable under the scheme, and different terms and conditions may be fixed in respect of different classes of persons.

(3) A superannuation scheme may be amended or revoked by a subsequent scheme made under this section with the consent of the Minister for Public Expenditure and Reform.

(4) The Minister shall not grant, or enter into any arrangement for the provision of, any superannuation benefit to or in respect of a person referred to in *subsection (1)* except—

(a) in accordance with a superannuation scheme made under this section, or

(b) with the consent of the Minister for Public Expenditure and Reform.

(5) In the case of a dispute as to the claim of any person to, or the amount of, any superannuation benefit payable under a superannuation scheme made under this section—

(a) the dispute shall be submitted to the Minister,

(b) the Minister shall refer the dispute to the Minister for Public Expenditure and Reform for his or her determination of it, and

(c) the decision of the Minister for Public Expenditure and Reform shall be final.

(6) Every superannuation scheme made by the Minister under this section shall be laid before each House of the Oireachtas as soon as may be after it is made and, if a resolution annulling the scheme is passed by either such House within the next 21 days on which that House has sat after the scheme is laid before it, the scheme shall be annulled accordingly but without prejudice to the validity of anything previously done thereunder.

951 Secondment to Director's office of member of Garda Síochána

(1) This section applies where a member of the Garda Síochána has been seconded to the office of the Director.

(2) Notwithstanding the secondment, and without prejudice to *section 949(3)* and *(4)*, the person seconded shall continue to be under the general direction and control of the Commissioner of the Garda Síochána.

(3) For the purposes of this Act and for purposes outside this Act, the person seconded—

(a) shall continue to be vested with the powers and to be subject to the duties of a member of the Garda Síochána, and

(b) may continue to exercise those powers and perform those duties.

952 Delegation by Director

(1) The Director may, in writing, delegate to an officer of the Director any of his or her powers under this or any other enactment, except this power of delegation.

(2) A power delegated under *subsection (1)* shall not be exercised by the delegate except in accordance with the instrument of delegation.

(3) A delegate shall, on request by a person affected by the exercise of a power delegated to him or her, produce the instrument of delegation under this section, or a copy of that instrument, for inspection.

(4) A delegation under this section is revocable at will and does not prevent the exercise by the Director of a power so delegated.

953 Liability of Director or officer for acts and omissions

Neither—

(a) the Director or a former Director, nor

(b) a present or former officer of the Director,

is liable for damages for anything done, anything purported to be done or anything omitted to be done by him or her in performing a function under this Act, unless the act or omission is shown to have been in bad faith.

954 Director's annual report

(1) As soon as practicable but in any event not later than 4 months after the end of each year, the Director shall report in writing to the Minister about the activities of the Director during that year.

(2) The annual report shall be prepared in such manner and form as the Minister may direct.

(3) The Minister shall ensure that copies of the annual report are laid before each House of the Oireachtas not later than 6 months after the end of the year to which the report relates.

(4) Nothing in *subsection (2)* shall be read as requiring the Director to include in the annual report information the inclusion of which would, in the Director's opinion, be likely to prejudice the performance of any of his or her functions.

955 Director shall report as required

(1) Subject to *subsection (2)*, the Director shall—

(a) provide the Minister with such information as the Minister may from time to time require about the performance of the Director's functions, and

(b) when requested, account to an appropriately established Committee of either House of the Oireachtas for the performance of his or her functions.

(2) The Director shall not be required to—

(a) provide the Minister or the Committee with information, or

(b) answer a question by the Committee,

if the provision of the information or the answering of the question would, in the Director's opinion, be likely to prejudice the performance of any of his or her functions.

956 Confidentiality of information

(1) No person shall disclose, except in accordance with law, information that—

(a) is obtained in performing the functions of the Director, and

(b) has not otherwise come to the notice of members of the public.

(2) Without limiting *subsection (1)*, the persons to whom that subsection applies include the following:

(a) the Director or a former Director;

(b) an officer of the Director.

(3) Nothing in *subsection (1)* shall prevent the disclosure of information by or under the authority of the Director if, and to the extent that, the Director considers the information is required—

(a) for a purpose or reason specified in *section 791(a)* to *(m)*,

(b) for the performance by a competent authority (as defined in *section 792*) of a function or functions by that authority, or

(c) for the performance by the Director of a function or functions of the Director.

(4) Nothing in *subsection (1)* shall prevent the disclosure of information to any member of the Garda Síochána if that information, in the opinion of the Director or an officer of the Director, may relate to the commission of an offence other than an offence under this Act.

(5) A person who contravenes this section shall be guilty of a category 2 offence.

957 Disclosure of information to Director

(1) Notwithstanding any other law—

(a) the Competition Authority;

(b) a member of the Garda Síochána;

(c) an officer of the Revenue Commissioners;

(d) the Insolvency Service of Ireland;

(e) the Irish Takeover Panel; or

(f) such other authority or other person as may be prescribed;

may disclose to the Director or an officer of the Director information that, in the opinion of the authority or other person disclosing it—

(i) relates to the commission of an offence under this Act or non-compliance otherwise with this Act or with the duties and obligations to which companies and their officers are subject; or

(ii) is information that could materially assist the Director or an officer of the Director in investigating—

(I) whether an offence under this Act has been committed or whether there has been non-compliance otherwise with this Act or with the duties and obligations to which companies and their officers are subject; or

(II) without prejudice to the generality of *clause (I)*, in a case where the making of an application for a disqualification order in relation to a particular person in accordance with *section 842(h)* is contemplated, whether and to what extent the matters mentioned in *section 843(3)* apply in the circumstances concerned.

(2) Without prejudice to the generality of *subsection (1)*, an officer of the Revenue Commissioners shall, notwithstanding any other law, be permitted to give or produce evidence relating to taxpayer information (within the meaning of section 851A (inserted by the Finance Act 2011) of the Taxes Consolidation Act 1997) in connection with any proceedings initiated under this Act.

(3) For the avoidance of doubt, the fact that particular circumstances specified in *subsection (1)(i)* or *(ii)* have been invoked by an authority or other person as the basis for disclosure by it or him or her of information under that subsection shall not prevent the Director or an officer of the Director from using the information in relation to other circumstances specified in *subsection (1)(i)* or *(ii)*.

[957A Restriction of application of certain articles of Data Protection Regulation

(1) Articles 14 (Information to be provided where personal data have not been obtained from the data subject) and 15 (Right of access by the data subject) of the Data Protection Regulation are restricted, to the extent necessary and proportionate to safeguard the effective performance by the Director of his or her functions referred to in paragraph (b) and (e) of section 949(1), where the performance of those functions give rise to the processing of personal data to which the Data Protection Regulation applies.

(2) In this section, 'Data Protection Regulation' means Regulation (EU) 2016/679 of the European Parliament and of the Council of 27 April 201647 on the protection of natural persons with regard to the processing of personal data and on the free movement of such data, and repealing Directive 95/46/EC (General Data Protection Regulation).][a]

Amendments

a Section 957A inserted by the Data Protection Act 2018, s 224.

[957AA Definitions (sections 957A to 957I)

In this section and *sections 957B to 957I*—

"court" means the High Court;

"monetary sanction", in relation to a relevant director, means the monetary sanction referred to in *section 957C(2)(c)*;

"public notice of relevant sanction imposed", in relation to a relevant director, means the publication in accordance with *section 957F(1)* of the relevant director's particulars referred to in that section together with the other related particulars referred to in that section;

"relevant contravention" has the meaning assigned to it by section 900;

"relevant decision", in relation to a relevant director, means—

(a) a decision under *section 957B(2)* that the director has engaged in conduct giving rise (whether in whole or in part) to a relevant contravention,

(b) if, in consequence of a decision referred to in *paragraph (a)*, the Director decides under *section 957B(2)* to impose a relevant sanction on the relevant director, the decision to impose that sanction, or

(c) both such decisions;

"relevant director" has the meaning assigned to it by *section 900*;

"relevant sanction", in relation to a relevant director, means a sanction referred to in *section 957C(2)*;

"*section 957E* agreement" shall be read in accordance with *section 957E(1)*;

"Supervisory Authority" has the meaning assigned to it by *section 900*.][a]

Amendments

a Section 957AA inserted by C(SA)A 2018, s 45.

[957B Provisions applicable where Director receives particulars, etc., from Supervisory Authority concerning relevant contravention and relevant director

(1) This section applies where—

(a) the Director has received from the Supervisory Authority particulars referred to in *section 936A(2)* and (where applicable) information and documents and assistance referred to in *section 936A(3)*, and

(b) in consequence thereof, the Director has investigated under *Part 13* a relevant director in order to find whether or not the relevant director has engaged in conduct giving rise (whether in whole or in part) to a relevant contravention.

(2) Subject to *section 957I(3)* and *(4)*, where the Director finds that a relevant director has engaged in conduct giving rise (whether in whole or in part) to the relevant contravention, the Director may impose such relevant sanction on the relevant director as the Director considers appropriate after having regard to the circumstances referred to in *section 957D(2)*.

(3) Subject to *subsection (4)*, the relevant director the subject of a relevant decision may appeal to the court against the decision.

(4) An appeal under *subsection (3)* shall be brought within 3 months after the date on which the relevant director was notified of the relevant decision by the Director.

(5) A finding or relevant decision of the Director under this section is not a bar to any civil or criminal proceedings against the relevant director who is the subject of the finding or relevant decision.

(6) Subject to *subsection (7)*, the Director shall, as soon as is practicable after imposing under this section a relevant sanction on a relevant director, give particulars of the relevant director and of the sanction imposed to the Supervisory Authority.

(7) The Director shall immediately communicate to the Supervisory Authority particulars of any direction given by the Director under *section 957C(2)(b)*.][a]

Amendments

a Section 957B inserted by C(SA)A 2018, s 45.

[957C Sanctions which Director may impose on relevant director for certain conduct

(1) This section applies to a relevant director the subject of a decision under *section 957B(2)* that the director has engaged in conduct giving rise (whether in whole or in part) to a relevant contravention.

(2) Subject to *section 957D*, the Director may impose on the relevant director one or more of the following sanctions in relation to the relevant contravention:

(a) a direction to the relevant director that he or she cease the conduct giving rise (whether in whole or in part) to the contravention and abstain from any repetition of that conduct;

(b) a direction to the relevant director prohibiting the director, for the period specified in the direction (being a period of not more than 3 years' duration), from performing functions in audit firms or public-interest entities;

(c) subject to *section 957G*, a direction to the director to pay an amount, as specified in the direction but not exceeding €100,000, to the Director.

(3) In default of payment of an amount referred to in *subsection (2)(c)*, the Director may recover that amount as a simple contract debt in any court of competent jurisdiction.][a]

Amendments

a Section 957C inserted by C(SA)A 2018, s 45.

[957D Relevant circumstances to be considered in imposing relevant sanctions on relevant director

(1) This section applies to a relevant director the subject of a decision under s*ection 957B(2)* that the director has engaged in conduct giving rise (whether in whole or in part) to a relevant contravention.

(2) In imposing a relevant sanction on a relevant director, the Director shall consider the following circumstances:

(a) the gravity and duration of the relevant contravention;

(b) the degree of responsibility of the relevant director;

(c) the financial strength of the relevant director (including the annual income of the director);

(d) the amount of profits gained or losses avoided by the relevant director in consequence of the contravention, in so far as they can be determined;

(e) the level of cooperation of the relevant director with the Supervisory Authority or Director, or both;

(f) previous impositions of relevant sanctions on the relevant director.][a]

Amendments

a Section 957D inserted by C(SA)A 2018, s 45.

[957E Resolution of suspected certain conduct by agreement - relevant director

(1) Subject to *subsection (2)*, if the Director believes on reasonable grounds that a relevant director has engaged in conduct (in this section referred to as the "relevant

conduct") giving rise (whether in whole or in part) to a relevant contravention referred to in *section 936A(1)*, the Director and the relevant director may, at their absolute discretion, enter into an agreement (in this section referred to as a "*section 957E* agreement") to resolve the matters relating to such conduct.

(2) The following provisions shall apply to the *section 957E* agreement:

(a) the agreement may be entered into notwithstanding that no investigation under *Part 13* into the relevant conduct has been commenced;

(b) the agreement may be entered into after an investigation under *Part 13* into the relevant conduct has been commenced but not, subject to *paragraph (d)*, after it has been completed;

(c) without prejudice to the generality of the terms of the agreement, such terms may include terms under which the relevant director accepts the imposition of one or more relevant sanctions that may be imposed under *section 957B(2)*;

(d) the agreement may be entered into after an investigation under *Part 13* has been undertaken and carried out only to the extent to determine which sanctions (if any) referred to in *paragraph (c)* to impose on the relevant director;

(e) the terms of the agreement are binding on the Director and the relevant director.

(3) Subject to *subsection (6)*, the provisions of *sections 957C, 957D, 957F, 957G* and *957H* shall apply, with any necessary modifications, to any relevant sanctions imposed on a relevant director pursuant to a *section 957E* agreement as those sections apply to any relevant sanctions imposed on a relevant director otherwise than pursuant to a *section 957E* agreement.

(4) Subject to *subsection (5)*, where the relevant director with whom the Director has entered into the *section 957E* agreement fails to comply with one or more of the terms of the agreement, the Director may apply to the court for an order compelling that relevant director to comply with those terms.

(5) In default of payment, any amount agreed to be paid to the Director by the relevant director under the *section 957E* agreement may be recovered by the Director from the relevant director as a simple contract debt in any court of competent jurisdiction.

(6) The necessary modifications referred to in subsection (3), in so far as *section 957F* is concerned, include reading that section as if—

(a) the following subsection were substituted for subsection (1) of that section:

> '(1) Subject to subsection (3), the Director shall, in so far as a relevant decision imposes a relevant sanction on a relevant director, as soon as is practicable, publish on his or her website particulars of the relevant contravention to which the relevant sanction relates, particulars of the relevant conduct, particulars of the relevant sanction imposed and particulars of the relevant director on whom the relevant sanction was imposed.',

(b) *subsections (2)* and *(4)* of that section were deleted, and

(c) in *subsection (5)* of that section, the reference to "or (2)" were deleted.

(7) *Section 957I* shall be disregarded for the purposes of a *section 957E* agreement.][a]

Amendments

a Section 957E inserted by C(SA)A 2018, s 45.

[957F Publication of relevant sanction imposed on relevant director

(1) Subject to *subsections (2)* and *(3)*, the Director shall, in so far as a relevant decision imposes a relevant sanction on a relevant director, as soon as is practicable after—

(a) that decision has been confirmed by the court as referred to in *section 957I(4)*, or

(b) a decision of the court under *section 957I(2)(b)* has been made to impose a different relevant sanction on the relevant director,

publish on his or her website particulars of the relevant contravention to which the relevant sanction relates, particulars of the relevant conduct, particulars of the relevant sanction imposed and particulars of the relevant director on whom the relevant sanction was imposed.

(2) Subject to *subsection (4)*, if there is an appeal to the court from a confirmation referred to in *subsection (1)(a)*, or a decision referred to in *subsection (1)(b)*, the Director shall, as soon as may be, as he or she considers appropriate, publish particulars on his or her website of the status or outcome of the appeal.

(3) The Director shall publish the particulars, comprising a public notice of a relevant sanction imposed, on an anonymous basis on the Director's website in any one or more of the following circumstances:

(a) the Director, following an assessment of the proportionality of the publication of those particulars in accordance with *subsection (1)* in so far as personal data are concerned, is of the opinion that, in relation to the relevant sanction imposed on the relevant director, such publication would be disproportionate;

(b) the Director is of the opinion that the publication of those particulars in accordance with *subsection (1)* would jeopardise the stability of financial markets or an ongoing criminal investigation;

(c) the Director is of the opinion that the publication of those particulars in accordance with *subsection (1)* would cause disproportionate damage to the relevant director.

(4) Subsection (2) shall not apply in any case where *subsection (3)* applies.

(5) The Director shall ensure that particulars published on his or her website in accordance with *subsection (1)* or *(2)* remain on his or her website for at least 5 years.

(6) The Director shall, as soon as is practicable after publishing a public notice of a relevant sanction imposed in relation to a relevant director, give particulars of the relevant director and of the relevant sanction imposed to the Supervisory Authority.][a]

Amendments

a Section 957F inserted by C(SA)A 2018, s 45.

[957G Relevant director not to be liable to be penalised twice for same conduct

(1) If the Director decides to impose a monetary sanction on a relevant director, the Director shall not impose an amount that would be likely to cause the relevant director to be adjudicated bankrupt.

(2) If the conduct engaged in by the relevant director has given rise (whether in whole or in part) to 2 or more relevant contraventions, the Director shall not impose more than one monetary sanction on the relevant director in respect of the same conduct.][a]

Amendments

a Section 957G inserted by C(SA)A 2018, s 45.

[957H Relevant director not to be liable to be penalised twice for same conduct

(1) If the Director imposes a monetary sanction on a relevant director and the conduct engaged in by the relevant director that has given rise (whether in whole or in part) to the relevant contravention is an offence under the law of the State, the relevant director shall not be liable to be prosecuted or punished for the offence under that law.

(2) The Director shall not impose a monetary sanction on a relevant director if—

(a) the relevant director has been charged with having committed an offence under a law of the State and has either been found guilty or not guilty of having committed the offence, and

(b) the offence involves the conduct engaged in by the relevant director that has given rise (whether in whole or in part) to the relevant contravention.][a]

Amendments

a Section 957H inserted by C(SA)A 2018, s 45.

[957I Appeals to and orders of court, including orders confirming decisions of Director

(1) In an appeal under *section 957B(3)*, the court may consider any evidence adduced or argument made, whether or not adduced or made to the Director.

(2) On the hearing of such an appeal, the court may make any order or give any direction it thinks fit, including an order—

(a) confirming the decision under appeal, or

(b) modifying or annulling that decision.

(3) A relevant decision, in so far as it relates to the imposition of a relevant sanction on a relevant director, does not take effect until that decision is confirmed by the court either—

(a) on appeal under *section 957B(3)*, or

(b) on application by the Director under *subsection (4)*.

(4) On application by motion on notice by the Director for an order confirming a decision referred to in *subsection (3)*, the court may make an order confirming the decision or may refuse to make such an order.

(5) On an application under *section 957E(4)* for an order compelling compliance with a *section 957E* agreement, the court may make any order or give any direction as it thinks fit.][a]

Amendments

a Section 957H inserted by C(SA)A 2018, s 45.

Chapter 4
Company Law Review Group

958 Company Law Review Group

(1) The Company Law Review Group, established by section 67 of the Company Law Enforcement Act 2001, shall continue in being.

(2) That Group is referred to in this Chapter as the "Review Group".

959 Functions of Review Group

(1) The Review Group shall monitor, review and advise the Minister on matters concerning—

(a) the implementation of this Act,

(b) the amendment of this Act,

(c) where subsequent enactments amend this Act, the consolidation of those enactments and this Act or the preparation of a restatement under the Statute Law (Restatement) Act 2002 in respect of them,

(d) the introduction of new legislation relating to the operation of companies and commercial practices in Ireland,

(e) the Rules of the Superior Courts and judgments of courts relating to companies,

(f) issues arising from the State's membership of the European Union in so far as they affect the operation of this Act,

(g) international developments in company law in so far as they provide lessons for improved State practice, and

(h) other related matters or issues, including issues submitted by the Minister to the Review Group for consideration.

(2) In advising the Minister the Review Group shall seek to promote enterprise, facilitate commerce, simplify the operation of this Act, enhance corporate governance and encourage commercial probity.

960 Membership of Review Group

(1) The Review Group shall consist of the persons appointed by the Minister to be members of it.

(2) The Minister shall appoint a member of the Review Group to be its chairperson.

(3) Members of the Review Group shall be paid such remuneration and allowances for expenses as the Minister, with the consent of the Minister for Public Expenditure and Reform, may determine.

(4) A member of the Review Group may at any time resign his or her membership by letter addressed to the Minister.

(5) The Minister may at any time, for stated reasons, terminate a person's membership of the Review Group.

(6) Any appointment of a person as a member of the Review Group, or of a member of it as chairperson, made before the commencement of this section shall continue in being in accordance with its terms.

961 Meetings and business of Review Group

(1) The Minister shall, at least once in every 2 years, after consultation with the Review Group, determine the programme of work to be undertaken by the Review Group over the ensuing specified period.

(2) A work programme determined by the Minister under section 70(1) of the Company Law Enforcement Act 2001 before the commencement of this section shall, for the unexpired portion of the period to which it relates, continue to be undertaken by the Review Group.

(3) Notwithstanding *subsection (1)*, the Minister may, from time to time, amend the Review Group's work programme, including the period to which it relates.

(4) The Review Group shall hold such and so many meetings as may be necessary for the performance of its functions and the achievement of its work programme and may regulate the procedure of those meetings (including by the establishment of subcommittees and fixing a quorum) as it considers appropriate.

(5) The members shall elect one of themselves as chairperson for any meeting from which the chairperson of the Review Group is absent.

(6) A member of the Review Group, but not the chairperson, may nominate a deputy to attend in his or her place any meeting that the member is unable to attend.

962 Annual report and provision of information to Minister

(1) Not later than 3 months after the end of each year, the Review Group shall make a report to the Minister on its activities during that year and the Minister shall ensure that copies of the report are laid before each House of the Oireachtas within 2 months after the date of receipt of the report.

(2) The report shall include information in such form and regarding such matters as the Minister may direct.

(3) The Review Group shall, if so requested by the Minister, provide a report to the Minister on any matter—

(a) concerning the functions or activities of the Review Group, or

(b) referred by the Minister to the Review Group for its advice.

PART 16
DESIGNATED ACTIVITY COMPANIES

Chapter 1
Preliminary and definitions

963 Definitions (*Part 16*)

In this Part—

"constitution" shall be read in accordance with *section 967(1)*;

"DAC limited by guarantee" means a DAC falling within *paragraph (b)* of the definition of "designated activity company" in this section;

"DAC limited by shares" means a DAC falling within *paragraph (a)* of the definition of "designated activity company" in this section;

"designated activity company" or "DAC" means a company that, as provided under *section 965(2)*, has either—

(a) the status of a private company limited by shares registered under this Part (as distinct from a private company limited by shares registered under *Part 2*); or

(b) the status of a private company limited by guarantee, and having a share capital.

964 Application of *Parts 1* to *14* to DACs

(1) The provisions of *Parts 1* to *14* apply to a DAC except to the extent that they are disapplied or modified by—

(a) this section; or

(b) any other provision of this Part.

(2) For the purposes of that application, *section 10(1)* shall have effect as if it read:

> "(1) Unless expressly provided otherwise, a reference in *Parts 2* to *14* to a company is a reference to a DAC.".

(3) Subject to *subsection (4)*, the provisions of this Act specified in the Table to this section shall not apply to a DAC.

(4) In relation to a DAC limited by guarantee the non-application of *section 32(1)* is provided for by *section 976* and, accordingly, the entry of that provision in the Table to this section shall (so far as it relates to that type of DAC) be disregarded.

(5) The specification in the foregoing Table of a provision (a "specified provision") of *Parts 1* to *14* also operates to disapply to a DAC any other provision of those Parts (notwithstanding that it is not specified in that Table) that makes consequential, incidental or supplemental provision on, or in relation to, the specified provision.

Table
Provisions disapplied to DACs

Subject matter	Provision disapplied
Way of forming a private company limited by shares	*Section 17*
Company to carry on activity in the State and prohibition of certain activities	*Section 18*
Form of the constitution	*Section 19*
Certificate of incorporation to state that company is a private company limited by shares	*Section 25(3)*
Provisions as to names of companies	*Section 26(1) to (4)*
Trading under a misleading name	*Section 27*
Amendment of constitution by special resolution	*Section 32(1)*
Capacity of private company limited by shares	*Section 38*
Variation of rights attached to special classes of shares	*Section 88*
Directors	*Section 128*
Share qualifications of directors	*Section 136*
Liability as contributories of past and present members	*Section 655*

Chapter 2
Incorporation and consequential matters

965 Way of forming a DAC and the 2 types of DAC

(1) A DAC may be formed for any lawful purpose by any person or persons subscribing to a constitution and complying with the relevant provisions of—

(a) *Chapter 2* of *Part 2*, as applied by this Part, and

(b) this Part,

in relation to registration of a DAC.

(2) If the memorandum of the DAC contains the statement referred to in—

(a) *section 967(2)(b)(i)*, the DAC shall have the status of a private company limited by shares registered under this Part (as distinct from a private company limited by shares registered under *Part 2*), or

(b) *section 967(2)(b)(ii)*, the DAC shall have the status of a private company limited by guarantee, and having a share capital.

(3) Without prejudice to the means by which a DAC may be formed under the relevant provisions referred to in *subsection (1)*, a company may be registered as a DAC by means of—

(a) re-registration as a DAC (but only as one limited by shares) pursuant to *Chapter 6* of *Part 2*,

(b) the re-registration, or registration, as a DAC of a body corporate pursuant to *Part 20* or *Part 22*,

(c) the merger of 2 or more companies pursuant to *Chapter 3* of *Part 9*,

(d) the division of a company pursuant to *Chapter 4* of *Part 9*, or

(e) the merger operation provided for by the European Communities (Cross-Border Mergers) Regulations 2008 (S.I. No. 157 of 2008).

(4) The liability of a member of a DAC at any time shall be limited—

(a) in the case of a DAC limited by shares, to the amount, if any, unpaid on the shares registered in the member's name at that time,

(b) in the case of a DAC limited by guarantee, to—

(i) the amount undertaken, as mentioned in *section 967(2)(f)*, to be contributed by him or her to the assets of the DAC in the event of its being wound up, and

(ii) the amount, if any, unpaid on the shares registered in the member's name at that time.

(5) *Subsection (4)* is without prejudice to any other liability to which a member may be subject as provided by this Act.

(6) The number of members of a DAC shall not exceed 149 but, in reckoning that limit, there shall be disregarded any of the following persons.

(7) Those persons are—

(a) a person in the employment of the DAC who is a member of it,

(b) a person who, having been formerly in the employment of the DAC, was, while in that employment, and has continued after the termination of the employment to be, a member of it.

(8) Where 2 or more persons hold one or more shares in a DAC jointly, they shall, for the purposes of this section, be treated as a single member.

(9) Any registration of a person as a member of a DAC in excess of the limit provided by *subsection (6)* shall be void.

(10) The certificate of incorporation issued under *section 25(1)* shall state that the company is a designated activity company limited by shares or, as the case may be, a designated activity company limited by guarantee.

966 DAC to carry on activity in the State

A DAC shall not be formed and registered unless it appears to the Registrar that the DAC, when registered, will carry on an activity in the State, being an activity that is mentioned in its memorandum.

967 The form of a DAC's constitution

(1) Subject to *subsection (3)*, the constitution of a DAC shall be in the form of a memorandum of association and articles of association which together are referred to in this Part as a "constitution".

(2) The memorandum of association of a DAC shall state—

(a) its name,

(b) that it is a designated activity company having the status, as the case may be, of—

(i) a private company limited by shares, or

(ii) a private company limited by guarantee, and having a share capital,

registered under this Part,

(c) its objects,

(d) that the liability of its members is limited,

(e) in the case of a DAC limited by shares, the amount of share capital with which the DAC proposes to be registered and the division thereof into shares of a fixed amount,

(f) in the case of a DAC limited by guarantee — in addition to the matter set out in the preceding paragraph — that each member undertakes that, if the company is wound up while he or she is a member, or within one year after the date on which he or she ceases to be a member, he or she will contribute to the assets of the company such amount as may be required for—

(i) payment of the debts and liabilities of the company contracted before he or she ceases to be a member,

(ii) payment of the costs, charges and expenses of winding up, and

(iii) adjustment of the rights of contributories among themselves,

not exceeding an amount specified in the memorandum.

(3) The constitution of a DAC shall—

(a) in addition to the matters specified in *subsection (2)*, state the number of shares (which shall not be less than one) taken by each subscriber to the constitution,

(b) be in accordance with the form set out in—

(i) *Schedule 7* — in the case of a DAC limited by shares, or

(ii) *Schedule 8* — in the case of a DAC limited by guarantee,

or, in either case, as near thereto as circumstances permit,

(c) be printed in an entire format, that is to say the memorandum and articles shall be contained in the one document, being a document either in legible form or (as long as it is capable of being reproduced in legible form) in non-legible form, and

(d) either—

(i) be signed by each subscriber in the presence of at least one witness who shall attest the signature, or

(ii) be authenticated in the manner referred to in *section 888*.

(4) Where, subsequent to the registration of the constitution, an amendment of the memorandum of association is made affecting the matter of share capital, or another matter, referred to in *subsection (2)*, that subsection shall be read as requiring the memorandum to state the matter as it stands in consequence of that amendment.

968 Supplemental provisions in relation to constitution

(1) This section—

(a) contains provisions as to the articles of a DAC, and

(b) provides that, in certain circumstances, a default position shall obtain in relation to the articles of a DAC.

(2) In this section—

"mandatory provision" means a provision of any of *Parts 1* to *14* (as applied by this Part) or of this Part that is not an optional provision;

"optional provision" means a provision of any of *Parts 1* to *14* (as applied by this Part) or of this Part that—

(a) contains a statement to the effect, or is governed by provision elsewhere to the effect, that the provision applies save to the extent that the constitution provides otherwise or unless the constitution states otherwise; or

(b) is otherwise of such import.

(3) The articles of a DAC may contain regulations in relation to the DAC.

(4) So far as the articles of a DAC do not exclude or modify an optional provision, that optional provision shall apply in relation to the DAC.

(5) Articles, instead of containing any regulations in relation to the DAC, may consist solely of a statement to the effect that the provisions of the *Companies Act 2014* are adopted and, if the articles consist solely of such a statement, *subsection (4)* shall apply.

969 Provisions as to names of DACs

(1) The name of a DAC shall end with one of the following:

— designated activity company;

— cuideachta ghníomhaíochta ainmnithe.

(2) The words "designated activity company" may be abbreviated to "d.a.c." or "dac" (including either such abbreviation in capitalised form) in any usage after the company's registration by any person including the DAC.

(3) The words "cuideachta ghníomhaíochta ainmnithe" may be abbreviated to "c.g.a." or "cga" (including either such abbreviation in capitalised form) in any usage after the company's registration by any person including the DAC.

(4) A DAC carrying on business under a name other than its corporate name shall register in the manner directed by law for the registration of business names but the use of the abbreviations set out in *subsection (2)* or *(3)* shall not of itself render such registration necessary.

970 Trading under a misleading name

(1) Subject to *subsection (6)*, neither a body that is not a DAC nor an individual shall carry on any trade, profession or business under a name which includes, as its last

part, the words "designated activity company", or "cuideachta ghníomhaíochta ainmnithe" or abbreviations of those words.

(2) If a body or individual contravenes *subsection (1)*, the body or individual and, in the case of a body, any officer of it who is in default, shall be guilty of a category 3 offence.

(3) A DAC shall not, in the following circumstances, use a name which may reasonably be expected to give the impression that it is any type of a company other than a DAC or that it is any other form of body corporate.

(4) Those circumstances are circumstances in which the fact that it is a DAC is likely to be material to any person.

(5) If a DAC contravenes *subsection (3)*, the DAC and any officer of it who is in default shall be guilty of a category 3 offence.

(6) *Subsection (1)* shall not apply to any company—

(a) to which *Part 21* applies, and

(b) which has provisions in its constitution that would entitle it to rank as a DAC if it had been registered in the State.

971 Power to dispense with "designated activity company" or Irish equivalent in name of charitable and other companies

(1) A DAC shall, notwithstanding its registration as a company with limited liability, be exempt from the provisions of this Act relating to the use of the words "designated activity company" or "cuideachta ghníomhaíochta ainmnithe" as part of its name and the publishing of its name, but shall enjoy all the privileges and shall (subject to this section) be subject to all the obligations of a DAC, where—

(a) its objects are the promotion of commerce, art, science, education, religion, charity or any other prescribed object, and

(b) its constitution—

(i) requires its profits (if any) or other income to be applied to the promotion of its objects,

(ii) prohibits the making of distributions to its members, and

(iii) requires all the assets which would otherwise be available to its members to be transferred on its winding up to another company whose objects comply with *paragraph (a)* and which meets the requirements of this paragraph,

and

(c) a director or secretary of the company (or, in the case of an association about to be formed as a limited company, one of the persons who are to be the first directors or the person who is to be the first secretary of the company) has delivered to the Registrar a statement in the prescribed form that the company complies or, where applicable, will comply with the requirements of *paragraphs (a)* and *(b)*.

(2) The Registrar shall refuse to register as a DAC any association about to be formed as a DAC by a name which does not include the words "designated activity company" or

"cuideachta ghníomhaíochta ainmnithe" unless a statement, as provided for under *subsection (1)(c)*, has been delivered to the Registrar.

(3) An application by a company registered as a DAC for a change of name, being a change that includes or consists of the omission of the words "designated activity company" or "cuideachta ghníomhaíochta ainmnithe", shall be made in accordance with *section 30* and the Registrar shall refuse to accede to the application unless a statement, as provided for under *subsection (1)(c)*, has been delivered to the Registrar.

(4) A DAC which is exempt under *subsection (1)* and which is permitted to omit the words "designated activity company" or "cuideachta ghníomhaíochta ainmnithe" from its name shall not alter its constitution so that it ceases to comply with the requirements of that subsection.

(5) If it appears to the Registrar that a DAC which is registered under a name not including the words "designated activity company" or "cuideachta ghníomhaíochta ainmnithe"—

(a) has carried on any business other than the promotion of any of the objects mentioned in *subsection (1)(a)*,

(b) has applied any of its profits or other income otherwise than in promoting such objects, or

(c) has made a distribution to any of its members,

the Registrar may, in writing, direct the DAC to change its name within such period as may be specified in the direction so that its name ends with the words "designated activity company" or "cuideachta ghníomhaíochta ainmnithe", and the change of name shall be made in accordance with *section 30*.

(6) A DAC which has received a direction under *subsection (5)* shall not thereafter be registered by a name which does not include the words "designated activity company" or "cuideachta ghníomhaíochta ainmnithe" without the approval of the Registrar.

(7) A person who—

(a) alters the constitution of a DAC in contravention of *subsection (4)*, or

(b) fails to comply with a direction from the Registrar under *subsection (5)*,

shall be guilty of a category 3 offence.

(8) *Subsections (9)* to *(12)* have effect notwithstanding—

(a) the repeal by the Act of 2001 of section 24, as originally enacted, of the Act of 1963 (the "original section 24"), or

(b) the repeal by this Act of section 24, inserted by section 88(1) of the Act of 2001, of the Act of 1963 (the "substituted section 24") or of the Act of 2001.

(9) A licence that—

(a) had been granted by the Minister pursuant to subsection (1) or (2) of the original section 24 to a private company limited by shares (being a company that has re-registered as a DAC pursuant to *Chapter 6* of *Part 2*), and

(b) is in force immediately before the commencement of this section, shall continue to have effect but with the modification that it shall operate to exempt the company from the use of the words "designated activity company" or "cuideachta ghníomhaíochta ainmnithe" as part of its name and the publishing of its name.

(10) Subsections (4) to (7) of the original section 24 shall continue in force in relation to the foregoing licence as if that section 24 had never been repealed, except that references in those subsections to the Minister, wherever occurring, shall be read as references to the Registrar.

(11) An exemption that immediately before the repeal of the Act of 2001 operated, by virtue of the substituted section 24, in favour of a private company limited by shares (being a company that has re-registered as a DAC pursuant to *Chapter 6* of *Part 2*) shall continue to have effect but—

(a) with the modification that it shall operate to exempt the company from the use of the words "designated activity company" or "cuideachta ghníomhaíochta ainmnithe" as part of its name and the publishing of its name, and

(b) subject to *subsection (12)*.

(12) *Subsections (4)* to *(7)* shall, with the necessary modifications, apply to a foregoing exemption as they apply to an exemption under *subsection (1)*.

(13) In relation to a DAC that avails itself of the exemption under *subsection (1)*, or continues to avail itself of a licence or exemption referred to in *subsection (9)* or *(11)*, *section 151* shall have effect as if, in addition to the particulars specified in *subsection (2)(a)* to *(c)* of that section to be included on all business letters and order forms of the DAC, there were specified in that subsection the fact of the DAC being a limited company.

(14) In this section "Act of 2001" means the Company Law Enforcement Act 2001.

972 Capacity of a DAC

(1) A DAC shall have the capacity to do any act or thing stated in the objects set out in its memorandum.

(2) For the purposes of *subsection (1)*—

(a) the reference in it to an object includes a reference to anything stated in the memorandum to be a power to do any act or thing (whether the word "power" is used or not),

(b) if an object is stated in the DAC's memorandum without the following also being stated in relation to it, the capacity of the DAC extends to doing any act or thing that appears to it to be requisite, advantageous or incidental to, or to facilitate, the attainment of that object and that is not inconsistent with any enactment,

and a subsequent reference in this Part to an object of a DAC shall be read accordingly.

973 Capacity not limited by a DAC's constitution

(1) The validity of an act done by a DAC shall not be called into question on the ground of lack of capacity by reason of anything contained in the DAC's objects.

(2) A member of a DAC may bring proceedings to restrain the doing of an act which, but for *subsection (1)*, would be beyond the DAC's capacity but no such proceedings shall lie in respect of any act to be done in fulfilment of a legal obligation arising from a previous act of the DAC.

(3) Notwithstanding the enactment of *subsection (1)*, it remains the duty of the directors to observe any limitations on their powers flowing from the DAC's objects and action by the directors which, but for *subsection (1)*, would be beyond the DAC's capacity may only be ratified by the DAC by special resolution.

(4) A resolution ratifying such action shall not affect any liability incurred by the directors or any other person; if relief from any such liability is to be conferred by the DAC it must be agreed to separately by a special resolution of it.

(5) A party to a transaction with a DAC is not bound to enquire as to whether it is permitted by the DAC's objects.

974 Alteration of objects clause by special resolution

(1) Subject to *subsection (2)*, a DAC may, by special resolution, alter the provisions of its memorandum of association by abandoning, restricting or amending any existing object or by adopting a new object and any alteration so made shall be as valid as if originally contained therein, and be subject to alteration in like manner.

(2) If an application is made to the court in accordance with this section for the alteration to be cancelled, it shall not have effect except in so far as it is confirmed by the court.

(3) Subject to *subsection (4)*, an application under this section may be made—

- (a) by the holders of not less, in the aggregate, than 15 per cent in nominal value of the DAC's issued share capital or any class thereof, or
- (b) by the holders of not less than 15 per cent of the DAC's debentures, entitling the holders to object to alterations of its objects.

(4) An application shall not be made under this section by any person who has consented to or voted in favour of the alteration.

(5) An application under this section shall be made within 21 days after the date on which the resolution altering the DAC's objects was passed and may be made on behalf of the persons entitled to make the application by such one or more of their number as they may appoint in writing for the purpose.

(6) On an application under this section, the court may—

- (a) make an order cancelling the alteration or confirming the alteration, either wholly or in part, and on such terms and conditions as it thinks fit, and
- (b) if it thinks fit, adjourn the proceedings in order that an arrangement may be made to the satisfaction of the court for the purchase of the interests of dissenting members and may give such directions and make such orders as it may think expedient for facilitating or carrying into effect any such arrangement.

(7) An order under this section may, if the court thinks fit, provide for the purchase by the DAC of the shares of any members of the DAC and for the reduction accordingly of the DAC's company capital and may make such alterations in the constitution of the DAC as may be required in consequence of that provision; and such a purchase may be so ordered notwithstanding anything in *section 102*.

975 Supplemental provisions in relation to *section 974*

(1) Where an order under *section 974* requires the DAC not to make any, or any specified, alteration in its constitution, then, notwithstanding anything in this Act, but subject to the provisions of the order, the DAC shall not have power, without the leave of the court, to make any such alteration in contravention of that requirement.

(2) Any alteration in the constitution of a DAC made by virtue of an order under *section 974*, other than one made by resolution of the DAC, shall be of the same effect as if duly made by resolution of the DAC and the provisions of this Act shall apply to the constitution as so altered accordingly.

(3) Notice of the meeting at which the special resolution altering a DAC's objects is intended to be proposed shall be given to any holders of the DAC's debentures that entitle the holders to object to alterations of its objects; that notice shall be the same as that given to members of the DAC, so however that not less than 10 days' notice shall be given to the holders of any such debentures.

(4) If the written resolution procedure is used in the matter, notice, which shall not be less than 10 days, of the proposed use of that procedure shall, together with a copy of the proposed text of the resolution, be given to the debenture holders referred to in *subsection (3)*.

(5) In default of any provisions in the DAC's constitution regulating the giving to the foregoing debenture holders of notice referred to in *subsection (3)* or *(4)*, the provisions of *Part 4* or, as the case may be, of the DAC's constitution regulating the giving of notice to members shall apply.

(6) Without prejudice to *subsections (3)* and *(4)*, in the case of a DAC which is, by virtue of *section 971*, permitted to omit the words "designated activity company" or "cuideachta ghníomhaíochta ainmnithe" from its name, notice of—

(a) the meeting at which the special resolution altering a DAC's objects is intended to be proposed, or

(b) if the written resolution procedure is used in the matter, notice of the proposed use of that procedure, together with a copy of the proposed text of the resolution,

shall be given to the Registrar and *subsections (3)* to *(5)* shall apply as respects such notice as they apply as respects notice of the meeting or resolution to debenture holders.

(7) Where a DAC passes a resolution altering its objects—

(a) if no application is made under *section 974* with respect to the alteration, it shall, within 15 days after the end of the period for making such an application, deliver to the Registrar a copy of its memorandum of association as altered, and

(b) if such an application is made, it shall—

(i) forthwith give notice of that fact to the Registrar, and

(ii) within 15 days after the date of any order cancelling or confirming the alteration, deliver to the Registrar a certified copy of the order and, in the case of an order confirming the alteration, a copy of the memorandum as altered.

(8) The court may by order at any time extend the time for delivery of documents to the Registrar under *subsection (7)(b)* for such period as the court may think proper.

(9) If a DAC makes default in giving notice or delivering any document to the Registrar as required by *subsection (7)*, the DAC and any officer of it who is in default shall be guilty of a category 4 offence.

976 Restriction of *section 32(1)* in relation to a DAC limited by guarantee

(1) Other than in respect of making an amendment of the type specified in *subsection (2)*, *section 32(1)* shall not apply in relation to a DAC limited by guarantee.

(2) The amendment referred to in *subsection (1)* is an amendment of the amount referred to in *section 967(2)(f)* that is specified in the memorandum of the DAC limited by guarantee.

977 Alteration of articles by special resolution

(1) Subject to the provisions of this Act and to the conditions contained in its memorandum, a DAC may, by special resolution, alter or add to its articles.

(2) Any alteration or addition so made in the articles shall, subject to the provisions of this Act, be as valid as if originally contained therein and be subject in like manner to alteration by special resolution.

978 Power to alter provisions in memorandum which could have been contained in articles

(1) Subject to *subsection (2)*, *sections 32(4)* and *(5)* and *212*, any provision contained in a DAC's memorandum which could lawfully have been contained in articles instead of in the memorandum may, subject to the provisions of this section, be altered by the DAC by special resolution.

(2) If an application is made to the court for the alteration to be cancelled, it shall not have effect except in so far as it is confirmed by the court.

(3) This section shall not apply where the memorandum itself provides for or prohibits the alteration of all or any of the foregoing provisions, and shall not authorise any variation or abrogation of the special rights of any class of members.

(4) *Section 974(3)* to *(7)* (other than *subsection (3)(b)*) and *section 975* (other than *subsections (3)* to *(6)*) shall apply in relation to any alteration and to any application made under this section as they apply in relation to alterations and to applications made under those sections.

Chapter 3
Share capital

979 Status of existing guarantee company, having a share capital

(1) This section—

(a) makes provision as to the status of an existing guarantee company, having a share capital; and

(b) continues in force the memorandum and articles of such a company.

(2) In this section—

"existing guarantee company, having a share capital" means a private company limited by guarantee, having a share capital, which—

(a) was incorporated under any former enactment relating to companies (within the meaning of *section 5*); and

(b) is in existence immediately before the commencement of this section;

"mandatory provision" means a provision of any of *Parts 1* to *14* (as applied by this Part) or of this Part that is not an optional provision;

"optional provision" means a provision of any of *Parts 1* to *14* (as applied by this Part) or of this Part that—

(a) contains a statement to the effect, or is governed by provision elsewhere to the effect, that the provision applies save to the extent that the constitution provides otherwise or unless the constitution states otherwise; or

(b) is otherwise of such import.

(3) An existing guarantee company, having a share capital shall, on and from the commencement of this section, continue in existence and be deemed to be a DAC limited by guarantee to which this Part applies.

(4) *Section 980* contains provisions—

(a) for enabling such a company to continue to use, for a limited period, "limited" or "teoranta" in its name despite the foregoing status that it has assumed; and

(b) deeming the name of such a company, after a specified period and in default of its having changed its name in that fashion, to be altered by the replacement of—

(i) "designated activity company" for "limited" at the end thereof; or

(ii) "cuideachta ghníomhaíochta ainmnithe" for "teoranta" at the end thereof;

as the case may be.

(5) Reference, express or implied, in this Act to the date of registration of a company mentioned in a preceding subsection shall be read as a reference to the date on which the company was registered under the Joint Stock Companies Act 1862, the Companies (Consolidation) Act 1908 or the prior Companies Acts, as the case may be.

(6) The memorandum and articles of an existing guarantee company, having a share capital shall—

(a) save to the extent that they are inconsistent with a mandatory provision, and

(b) in the case of the memorandum, subject to *section 980(6)*,

continue in force but may be altered or added to under and in accordance with the conditions under which memorandums or articles, whenever registered, are permitted by this Act to be altered or added to.

(7) References in the provisions of a memorandum or articles so continued in force to any provision of the prior Companies Acts shall be read as references to the corresponding provision of this Act.

(8) To the extent that an existing guarantee company, having a share capital was, immediately before the commencement of this section, governed by—

(a) the regulations of Table D in the First Schedule to the Act of 1963, or

(b) the regulations of any Table referred to in section 3(9)(b), (c) or (d) of the Act of 1963,

it shall, after that commencement, continue to be governed by those regulations but—

(i) this is save to the extent that those regulations are inconsistent with a mandatory provision,

(ii) those regulations may be altered or added to under and in accordance with the conditions under which articles, whenever registered, are permitted by this Act to be altered or added to, and

(iii) references in the regulations to any provision of the prior Companies Acts shall be read as references to the corresponding provision of this Act.

980 Transitional provision — use of "limited" or "teoranta" by existing guarantee company, having a share capital

(1) In this section—

"existing guarantee company, having a share capital" has the same meaning as it has in *section 979*;

"new provisions" means the provisions of this Part (and the relevant provisions of *Part 2* as applied by this Part) relating to the use of either of the required sets of words (or their abbreviations) set out in *subsection (2)*;

"transition period" means the period of 18 months beginning after the commencement of this section.

(2) For the purposes of this section, each of the following is a required set of words—

(a) "designated activity company";

(b) "cuideachta ghníomhaíochta ainmnithe".

(3) The reference—

(a) in the preceding definition of "new provisions", and

(b) in *subsection (4)*,

to provisions relating to the use of any words includes a reference to provisions conferring an exemption from the use of those words.

(4) During—

(a) the transition period, or

(b) if before the expiry of that period the company has changed its name to include either of the required sets of words, the period preceding the making of that change,

the provisions of the prior Companies Acts relating to the use of limited or teoranta (or their abbreviations) shall apply as respects the name of an existing guarantee company, having a share capital in place of the new provisions.

(5) On and from—

(a) the expiry of the transition period, or

(b) the company changing its name to include either of the required sets of words,

whichever happens first, the new provisions shall apply as respects the name of an existing guarantee company, having a share capital.

(6) Without prejudice to the generality of *subsection (5)*, on the expiry of the transition period (and the company has not changed its name before then to include either of the required sets of words), the name of an existing guarantee company, having a share capital, as set out in its memorandum, shall be deemed to be altered by the replacement of—

(a) "designated activity company" for "limited" at the end thereof, or

(b) "cuideachta ghníomhaíochta ainmnithe" for "teoranta" at the end thereof,

as the case may be.

(7) Where the name, as set out in its memorandum, of an existing guarantee company, having a share capital is altered by virtue of *subsection (6)*, the Registrar shall issue to the company a fresh certificate of incorporation in respect of it, being a certificate of incorporation that is altered to meet the circumstances of the case.

981 Limitation on offers by DACs of securities to the public

Section 68 shall apply to a DAC as if the following subsection were substituted for *subsection (2)*:

"(2) A company shall—

(a) neither apply to have securities (or interests in them) admitted to trading or to be listed on, nor

(b) have securities (or interests in them) admitted to trading or listed on,

any market, whether a regulated market or not, in the State or elsewhere; however nothing in this subsection prohibits the admission to trading or listing (or an application being made therefor) on any market of debentures (or interests in them) for the purposes of any of *paragraphs (a)* to *(e)* of *subsection (3)*.".

982 Variation of rights attached to special classes of shares

(1) This section shall have effect with respect to the variation of the rights attached to any class of shares in a DAC whose share capital is divided into shares of different classes, whether or not the DAC is being wound up.

(2) Where the rights are attached to a class of shares in the DAC otherwise than by the memorandum, and the articles of the DAC do not contain provision with respect to the variation of the rights, those rights may be varied if, but only if—

- (a) the holders of 75 per cent, in nominal value, of the issued shares of that class, consent in writing to the variation, or
- (b) a special resolution, passed at a separate general meeting of the holders of that class, sanctions the variation,

and any requirement (however it is imposed) in relation to the variation of those rights is complied with, to the extent that it is not comprised in the requirements in *paragraphs (a)* and *(b)*.

(3) Where—

- (a) the rights are attached to a class of shares in the DAC by the memorandum or otherwise,
- (b) the memorandum or articles contain provision for the variation of those rights, and
- (c) the variation of those rights is connected with the giving, variation, revocation or renewal of an authority for the purposes of *section 69(1)* or with a reduction of the company's company capital by either of the means referred to in *section 84*,

those rights shall not be varied unless—

- (i) the requirement in *subsection (2)(a)* or *(b)* is satisfied, and
- (ii) any requirement of the memorandum or articles in relation to the variation of rights of that class is complied with to the extent that it is not comprised in the requirement in *subsection (2)(a)* or *(b)*.

(4) Where the rights are attached to a class of shares in the DAC by the memorandum or otherwise and—

- (a) where they are so attached by the memorandum, the articles contain provision with respect to their variation which had been included in the articles at the time of the DAC's original incorporation, or
- (b) where they are so attached otherwise, the articles contain such provision (whenever first so included),

and in either case the variation is not connected as mentioned in *subsection (3)(c)*, those rights may only be varied in accordance with that provision of the articles.

(5) Where the rights are attached to a class of shares in the DAC by the memorandum and the memorandum and articles do not contain provisions with respect to the variation of the rights, those rights may be varied if all the members of the DAC agree to the variation.

(6) The provisions of *sections 180* and *181* and the provisions of the DAC's articles relating to general meetings shall, so far as applicable, apply in relation to any meeting of shareholders required by this section or otherwise to take place in connection with the variation of the rights attached to a class of shares and shall so apply with the necessary modifications and subject to the following provisions, namely:

(a) the necessary quorum at any such meeting, other than an adjourned meeting, shall be 2 persons holding or representing by proxy at least one-third in nominal value of the issued shares of the class in question and at an adjourned meeting one person holding shares of the class in question or his or her proxy;

(b) any holder of shares of the class in question present in person or by proxy may demand a poll.

(7) Any amendment of a provision contained in the articles of a DAC for the variation of the rights attached to a class of shares or the insertion of any such provision into the DAC's articles shall itself be treated as a variation of those rights.

(8) *Section 89* shall apply in relation to a variation, pursuant to this section, of rights attached to any class of shares as it applies in relation to a variation, pursuant to *section 88*, of such rights.

(9) References to the variation of the rights attached to a class of shares in—

(a) this section, and

(b) except where the context otherwise requires, in any provision for the variation of the rights attached to a class of shares contained in the DAC's memorandum or articles,

shall include references to their abrogation.

(10) Nothing in *subsections (2)* to *(5)* shall be read as derogating from the powers of the court under *section 1287* or any of the following sections, that is to say, *sections 212*, *453*, *455*, *974* and *975*.

983 Application of *section 114* in relation to DACs

In its application to this Part, *section 114* shall apply as if each reference in it to the acquisition and holding of shares in a company included, in a case where the holding company is a DAC limited by guarantee, a reference to becoming, and being, a member of the company otherwise than by means of acquiring and holding shares.

984 Uncertificated transfer of securities

Sections 1085 to *1087* shall apply to securities of a DAC as they apply to securities of a PLC.

Chapter 4
Corporate governance

985 Directors

(1) A DAC shall have at least 2 directors.

(2) Nothing in *Parts 1* to *14* that makes provision in the case of a company having a sole director shall apply to a DAC.

986 Limitation on number of directorships

For the purposes of this Part *section 142* shall apply as if the following subsection were substituted for *subsection (1)*:

"(1) A person shall not, at a particular time, be a director of more than—

(a) 25 designated activity companies, or

(b) 25 companies, one, or more than one, of which is a designated activity company and one, or more than one, of which is any other type of company capable of being wound up under this Act.".

987 Membership of DAC limited by guarantee confined to shareholders

For the avoidance of doubt, no person, other than a subscriber to its memorandum or a person who is subsequently allotted a share in it and entered on its register of members, may be a member of a DAC limited by guarantee.

988 DAC, with 2 or more members, may not dispense with holding of a.g.m.

Section 175(3) and *(4)* (which relate to dispensing with the holding of an annual general meeting) shall not apply to a DAC if it has more than one member.

989 Application of *section 193* in relation to a DAC

Section 193 shall apply to a DAC as if, in *subsection (1)*, after "Notwithstanding any provision to the contrary in this Act", there were inserted "and unless the constitution provides otherwise".

990 Application of *section 194* in relation to a DAC

Section 194 shall apply to a DAC as if after "Notwithstanding any provision to the contrary in this Act,", in each place where it occurs in *subsections (1)* and *(4)* there were inserted "and unless the constitution provides otherwise,".

Chapter 5

Financial statements, annual return and audit

991 Non-application of *Part 6* to DACs that are credit institutions or insurance undertakings

Part 6 shall not apply to a DAC that is a credit institution or an insurance undertaking—

(a) to the extent provided by regulations made under section 3 of the European Communities Act 1972 to give effect to Community acts on accounts of credit institutions and insurance undertakings, respectively; or

(b) to the extent provided by any other enactment.

992 Requirement for corporate governance statement and modification of certain provisions of *Parts 5* and *6* as they apply to DACs

Chapter 3 of *Part 23* has effect in relation to, amongst other companies, a DAC that has debentures admitted to trading on a regulated market in an EEA state.

993 Modification of definition of "IAS Regulation" in the case of DACs

Section 1116 (modification of definition of "IAS Regulation") shall apply in the case of a DAC as it applies in the case of PLC.

994 Application of *sections 297, 350* and *362* to a DAC

[...][a]

Amendments

a Section 994 repealed by C(A)A 2017, s 3(1)(g).

---

995 Disclosures by DAC that is a credit institution

In addition to its having effect in relation to a public limited company, *section 1120* shall have effect in relation to a DAC.

996 Exemption from filing with Registrar financial statements, etc.

(1) *Sections 347* and *348* shall not apply to a DAC if it satisfies the following conditions:

(a) it has been formed for charitable purposes, and

(b) it stands exempted from those sections by an order made by the relevant authority (which order the relevant authority is, by virtue of this section, empowered to make),

and the exemption provided by that order may, as the relevant authority considers appropriate, be either for an indefinite or a limited period.

(2) The following provisions have effect in relation to a DAC referred to in *subsection (1)*:

(a) unless the DAC is entitled to and has availed itself of the audit exemption conferred by *Chapter 15* or *16* of *Part 6*, the statutory auditors of the DAC shall prepare a separate report to the directors which—

(i) confirms that they audited the relevant statutory financial statements for the relevant financial year; and

(ii) includes within it the report made to the members of the DAC pursuant to *section 391*;

and

(b) a copy of the report prepared under *paragraph (a)* shall be annexed to the annual return delivered by the DAC to the Registrar.

(3) The reference in *subsection (2)* to a copy of the report prepared under *paragraph (a)* of it is a reference to a copy that satisfies the following conditions:

(a) it is a true copy of the original save for the difference that the signature or signatures on the original, and any date or dates thereon, shall appear in typeset form on the copy; and

(b) it is accompanied by a certificate of a director and the secretary of the company, that bears the signature of the director and the secretary in electronic or written form, stating that the copy is a true copy of the original (and the foregoing statement need not be qualified on account of the difference permitted by *paragraph (a)* as to the form of a signature or of a date).

[...][a]

(6) In this section "relevant authority" means—

(a) before the establishment day (within the meaning of the Charities Act 2009), the Commissioners of Charitable Donations and Bequests for Ireland, and

(b) on or after the foregoing day, the Charities Regulatory Authority.

Amendments

a Subsections (4) and (5) repealed by C(SA)A 2018, s 3(1)(h).

Chapter 6
Liability of contributories in winding up

997 Liability as contributories of past and present members and provision concerning winding up after certain re-registration

(1) Subject to *subsection (2)*, in the event of a DAC being wound up, every present and past member shall be liable to contribute to the assets of the DAC to an amount sufficient for payment of its debts and liabilities, and the costs, charges and expenses of the winding up, and for the adjustment of the rights of the contributories among themselves.

(2) The following qualifications apply in relation to *subsection (1)*:

(a) in the case of a DAC limited by shares, no contribution shall be required from any member exceeding the amount, if any, unpaid on the shares in respect of which he or she is liable as a present or past member;

(b) in the case of a DAC limited by guarantee, no contribution shall, subject to *subsection (3)*, be required from any member exceeding the amount undertaken to be contributed by him or her to the assets of the DAC in the event of its being wound up;

(c) a past member shall not be liable to contribute if he or she has ceased to be a member for one year or more before the commencement of the winding up;

(d) a past member shall not be liable to contribute in respect of any debt or liability of the DAC contracted after he or she ceased to be a member;

(e) a past member shall not be liable to contribute unless it appears to the court that the existing members are unable to satisfy the contributions required to be made by them in pursuance of this Act;

(f) nothing in this Act shall invalidate any provision contained in any policy of insurance or other contract whereby the liability of individual members on the policy or contract is restricted, or whereby the funds of the DAC are alone made liable in respect of the policy or contract;

(g) a sum due to any member of the DAC, in his or her character of a member, by way of dividends, profits or otherwise, shall not be deemed to be a debt of the company, payable to that member in a case of competition between himself or herself and any other creditor not a member of the DAC, but any such sum may be taken into account for the purpose of the final adjustment of the rights of the contributories among themselves.

(3) In a winding up of a DAC limited by guarantee, every member of the DAC shall be liable, in addition to the amount undertaken to be contributed by him or her to the assets of the DAC in the event of its being wound up, to contribute to the extent of any sums unpaid on any shares held by him or her.

(4) Without prejudice to the application of that section to a DAC, and its adaptation generally, by *section 964* of *section 665* (winding up of company that had been an unlimited company before re-registration), *paragraph (c)* of *section 665* shall apply as if the reference in it to *section 655(2)(a)* were—

(a) in the case of a DAC limited by shares, a reference to *subsection (2)(a)* of this section,

(b) in the case of a DAC limited by guarantee, a reference to *subsections (2)(b)* and *(3)* of this section.

Chapter 7
Examinerships

998 Petitions for examinerships

Section 510 shall apply to a DAC as if the following subsections were substituted for *subsections (2)* and *(3)*:

"(2) Where the company referred to in *section 509* is an insurer or the holding company of an insurer, a petition may be presented only by the Central Bank, and *subsection (1)* shall not apply to the company.

(3) Where the company referred to in *section 509* is—

(a) a credit institution or the holding company of a credit institution;

(b) a company which one or more trustee savings banks have been reorganised into pursuant to an order under section 57 of the Trustee Savings Banks Act 1989; or

(c) a company which a building society has converted itself into under Part XI of the Building Societies Act 1989,

a petition may be presented only by the Central Bank, and *subsection (1)* shall not apply to the company.".

Chapter 8
Public offers of securities, prevention of market abuse, etc.

999 Application of *Chapters 1, 2* and *4* of *Part 23* to DACs

Chapters 1, 2 and *4* of *Part 23*, so far as they are applicable to companies other than public limited companies, shall apply to a DAC.

PART 17
PUBLIC LIMITED COMPANIES

Chapter 1
Preliminary and definitions

1000 Interpretation (*Part 17*)

(1) In this Part—

"authorised minimum" means—

(a) subject to *paragraph (b)*, €25,000; or

(b) such greater sum as may be specified by order made by the Minister under *subsection (2)*;

"authorised share capital" shall be read in accordance with *section 1006(2)(e)*;

"constitution" shall be read in accordance with *section 1006(1)*;

"public limited company" or "PLC" means a company limited by shares and having a share capital, being a company—

(a) the constitution of which states that the company is to be a public limited company; and

(b) in relation to which the provisions of this Act as to the registration (or re-registration or registration under *Part 20* or *Part 22* of a body corporate) as a public limited company have been complied with;

and *section 1001(2)* supplements this definition with regard to restricting the scope of that expression, as it occurs in this Part, to public limited companies that are not investment companies (as defined in *Part 24*);

"regulated market" has the meaning given to it by point 14 of Article 4(1) of Directive 2004/39/EC of the European Parliament and of the Council of 21 April 2004 on markets in financial instruments;

"securities" means transferable securities as defined in point 18 of Article 4(1) of Directive 2004/39/EC of the European Parliament and of the Council of 21 April 2004 on markets in financial instruments, with the exception of money market instruments as defined in point 19 of Article 4(1) of that Directive, having a maturity of less than 12 months.

(2) The Minister may, by order, specify that the authorised minimum for the purposes of this Part shall be an amount greater than €25,000 and such an order may—

(a) require any PLC, having an allotted share capital of which the nominal value is less than the amount specified in the order as the authorised minimum, to increase that value to not less than that amount or make an application to be re-registered as another form of company,

(b) make, in connection with any such requirement, provision for any of the matters for which provision is made by any provision of this Act relating to a PLC's registration, re-registration or change of name, payment for any share comprised in a company's capital and offers of shares in, or debentures of, a company to the public, including provision as to the consequences (whether in criminal law or otherwise) of a failure to comply with any requirement of the order, and

(c) contain such supplemental and transitional provision as the Minister thinks appropriate, make different provision for different cases and, in particular, provide for any provision of the order to come into operation on different days for different purposes.

(3) Provision in an order under *subsection (2)(b)* as to the consequences in criminal law of a failure to comply with any requirement of the order shall consist only of any adaptation of an offence under this Act that may be necessary with respect to the amount mentioned therein (not being a penalty).

1001 Investment company to be a PLC but non-application of this Part to that company type

(1) Public limited companies shall comprise 2 types—

(a) those that are not investment companies (as defined in *Part 24*), and

(b) those that are such companies.

(2) This Part applies only to public limited companies that are not investment companies (as so defined) and, accordingly, a reference in this Part to a public limited company does not include a reference to an investment company (as so defined).

(3) The law in this Act in relation to investment companies is to be found in *Part 24* (which makes provision for such companies by, *inter alia*, applying or adapting provisions of this Part and *Parts 1* to *14*) and certain associated provisions of this Act.

1002 Application of *Parts 1* to *14* to PLCs

(1) The provisions of *Parts 1* to *14* apply to a PLC except to the extent that they are disapplied or modified by—

(a) this section, or

(b) any other provision of this Part.

(2) For the purposes of that application, *section 10(1)* shall have effect as if it read:

"(1) Unless expressly provided otherwise, a reference in *Parts 2* to *14* to a company is a reference to a PLC.".

(3) The provisions of this Act specified in the Table to this section shall not apply to a PLC.

(4) The specification in the foregoing Table of a provision (a "specified provision") of *Parts 1* to *14* also operates to disapply to a PLC any other provision of those Parts (notwithstanding that it is not specified in that Table) that makes consequential, incidental or supplemental provision on, or in relation to, the specified provision.

Table

Subject matter	Provision disapplied
Way of forming a private company limited by shares	*Section 17*
Company to carry on activity in the State and prohibition of certain activities	*Section 18*
Form of the constitution	*Section 19*
Certificate of incorporation to state that the company is a private company limited by shares	*Section 25(3)*
Provisions as to names of companies	*Section 26(1) to (4)*
Trading under a misleading name	*Section 27*
Amendment of constitution by special resolution	*Section 32(1)*
Capacity of private company limited by shares	*Section 38*
Conversion of existing private company to private company limited by shares to which *Parts 1* to *14* apply	*Chapter 6 of Part 2*
Limitation on offers of securities to the public	*Section 68*
Allotment of shares	*Section 69*
Supplemental and additional provisions as regards allotments	*Section 70*
Reduction in company capital — use of Summary Approval Procedure therefor	*Section 84(2)(a) and (3)*
Variation of rights attached to special classes of shares	*Section 88*
Variation of company capital on reorganisation — use of Summary Approval Procedure therefor	*Section 91(4)(a)*
Directors	*Section 128*
Directors' duty as regards certain matters in appointing secretary	*Section 129(4)*
Removal of directors	*Section 146(2)*
Remuneration of directors	*Section 155*
Voting by director in respect of contract, etc. in which director is interested	*Section 161(7)*
Majority written resolutions	*Section 194*
Supplemental provisions in relation to *section 194*	*Section 195*
Summary Approval Procedure	*Chapter 7* of *Part 4* (save as it applies to— (a) a members' voluntary winding up under *section 579*;

Subject matter	Provision disapplied
Summary Approval Procedure	(b) an activity specified in *section 118* (prohibition on pre-acquisition profits or losses being treated in holding company's financial statements as profits available for distribution); or (c) the making of a loan or quasi-loan or the doing of any other thing referred to in *section 239*).
Directors' compliance statement and related statement—exemption for companies below a particular size	The words "to which this section applies" in *section 225(2)*, and *section 225(7)*
[Qualification of company based on size of company	*Sections 280A* to *280G*][a]
Exemption from consolidation: size of group	[...][b]
Statutory financial statements must be audited (unless audit exemption availed of)	*Section 333*
Exclusions, exemptions and special arrangements with regard to public disclosure of financial information	*Chapter 14 of Part 6*
Audit exemption	*Chapter 15 of Part 6*
Special audit exemption for dormant companies	*Chapter 16 of Part 6*
Small and medium companies	*Section 377*
Mergers and divisions of companies	*Chapters 3 and 4 of Part 9*
Disclosure orders	*Chapter 2 of Part 14*

Amendments

a Entry inserted by C(A)A 2017, s 74.

b Words repealed by C(A)A 2017, s 88(f)(i).

1003 Societas Europaea to be regarded as PLC

A Societas Europaea which is registered with the Registrar shall be regarded as a PLC for the purposes of this Part (but not as an investment company as defined in *Part 24*).

Chapter 2
Incorporation and consequential matters

1004 Way of forming a PLC

(1) A PLC may be formed for any lawful purpose by any person or persons subscribing to a constitution and complying with the relevant provisions of—

(a) *Chapter 2* of *Part 2*, as applied by this Part, and

(b) this Part,

in relation to registration of a PLC.

(2) Without prejudice to the means by which a PLC may be formed under the relevant provisions referred to in *subsection (1)*, a company may be registered as a PLC by means of—

(a) the re-registration, or registration, as a PLC of a body corporate pursuant to *Part 20* or *22*,

(b) the merger of 2 or more bodies corporate pursuant to *Chapter 16*,

(c) the division of a body corporate pursuant to *Chapter 17*, or

(d) the merger operation provided for by the European Communities (Cross-Border Mergers) Regulations 2008 (S.I. No. 157 of 2008).

(3) The liability of a member of a PLC at any time shall be limited to the amount, if any, unpaid on the shares registered in the member's name at that time.

(4) *Subsection (3)* is without prejudice to any other liability to which a member may be subject as provided by this Act.

(5) The certificate of incorporation issued under *section 25(1)* shall state that the company is a public limited company.

1005 PLC to carry on activity in the State

A PLC shall not be formed and registered unless it appears to the Registrar that the company, when registered, will carry on an activity in the State, being an activity that is mentioned in its memorandum.

1006 The form of a PLC's constitution

(1) Subject to *subsection (3)*, the constitution of a PLC shall be in the form of a memorandum of association and articles of association which together are referred to in this Part as a "constitution".

(2) The memorandum of association of a PLC shall state—

(a) its name,

(b) that it is a public limited company registered under this Part,

(c) its objects,

(d) that the liability of its members is limited, and

(e) its authorised share capital, being the amount of share capital with which the PLC proposes to be registered which shall not be less than the authorised minimum, and the division thereof into shares of a fixed amount.

(3) The constitution of a PLC shall—

(a) in addition to the matters specified in *subsection (2)*, state the number of shares (which shall not be less than one) taken by each subscriber to the constitution,

(b) be in accordance with the form set out in *Schedule 9* or as near thereto as circumstances permit,

(c) be printed in an entire format, that is to say the memorandum and articles shall be contained in the one document, being a document either in legible form or (as long as it is capable of being reproduced in legible form) in non-legible form, and

(d) either—

(i) be signed by each subscriber in the presence of at least one witness who shall attest the signature, or

(ii) be authenticated in the manner referred to in *section 888.*

(4) Where, subsequent to the registration of the constitution, an amendment of the memorandum of association is made affecting the matter of share capital, or another matter, referred to in *subsection (2)*, that subsection shall be read as requiring the memorandum to state the matter as it stands in consequence of that amendment.

1007 Supplemental provisions in relation to constitution and continuance in force of existing memorandum and articles

(1) This section—

(a) contains provisions as to the articles of a PLC,

(b) provides that, in certain circumstances, a default position shall obtain in relation to the articles of a PLC, and

(c) continues in force the memorandum and articles of a PLC registered under the prior Companies Acts.

(2) In this section—

"mandatory provision" means a provision of any of *Parts 1* to *14* (as applied by this Part) or of this Part that is not an optional provision;

"optional provision" means a provision of any of *Parts 1* to *14* (as applied by this Part) or of this Part that—

(a) contains a statement to the effect, or is governed by provision elsewhere to the effect, that the provision applies save to the extent that the constitution provides otherwise or unless the constitution states otherwise, or

(b) is otherwise of such import.

(3) The articles of a PLC may contain regulations in relation to the PLC.

(4) So far as the articles of a PLC do not exclude or modify an optional provision, that optional provision shall apply in relation to the PLC.

(5) Articles, instead of containing any regulations in relation to the PLC, may consist solely of a statement to the effect that the provisions of the *Companies Act 2014* are adopted and, if the articles consist solely of such a statement, *subsection (4)* shall apply.

(6) The memorandum and articles of a PLC registered before the commencement of this section shall, save to the extent that they are inconsistent with a mandatory provision, continue in force but may be altered or added to under and in accordance with the conditions under which memorandums or articles, whenever registered, are permitted by this Act to be altered or added to.

(7) References in the provisions of a memorandum or articles so continued in force to any provision of the prior Companies Acts shall be read as references to the corresponding provision of this Act.

(8) To the extent that a PLC registered before the commencement of this section was, immediately before that commencement, governed by—

- (a) the regulations of Part I of Table A in the First Schedule to the Act of 1963, or
- (b) the regulations of any Table referred to in section 3(9)(b), (c) or (d) of the Act of 1963,

it shall, after that commencement, continue to be governed by those regulations but—

- (i) this is save to the extent that those regulations are inconsistent with a mandatory provision,
- (ii) those regulations may be altered or added to under and in accordance with the conditions under which articles, whenever registered, are permitted by this Act to be altered or added to, and
- (iii) references in the regulations to any provision of the prior Companies Acts shall be read as references to the corresponding provision of this Act.

1008 Provisions as to names of PLCs

(1) The name of a PLC shall end with one of the following:

- — public limited company;
- — cuideachta phoiblí theoranta.

(2) The words "public limited company" may be abbreviated to "p.l.c." or "plc" (including either such abbreviation in capitalised form) in any usage after the company's registration by any person including the PLC.

(3) The words "cuideachta phoiblí theoranta" may be abbreviated to "c.p.t." or "cpt" (including either such abbreviation in capitalised form) in any usage after the company's registration by any person including the PLC.

(4) A PLC carrying on business under a name other than its corporate name shall register in the manner directed by law for the registration of business names but the use

of the abbreviations set out in *subsection (2)* or *(3)* shall not of itself render such registration necessary.

1009 Trading under a misleading name

(1) Subject to *subsection (6)*, neither a body that is not a PLC nor an individual shall carry on any trade, profession or business under a name which includes, as its last part, the words "public limited company", or "cuideachta phoiblí theoranta" or abbreviations of those words.

(2) If a body or individual contravenes *subsection (1)*, the body or individual and, in the case of a body, any officer of it who is in default, shall be guilty of a category 3 offence.

(3) A PLC shall not, in the following circumstances, use a name which may reasonably be expected to give the impression that it is any type of a company other than a PLC or that it is any other form of body corporate.

(4) Those circumstances are circumstances in which the fact that it is a PLC is likely to be material to any person.

(5) If a PLC contravenes *subsection (3)*, the PLC and any officer of it who is in default shall be guilty of a category 3 offence.

(6) *Subsection (1)* shall not apply to any company—

(a) to which *Part 21* applies, and

(b) which has provisions in its constitution that would entitle it to rank as a PLC if it had been registered in the State.

1010 Restriction on commencement of business by a PLC

(1) A company registered as a PLC on its original incorporation or pursuant to a merger or division shall not do business or exercise any borrowing powers unless the Registrar has issued to it a certificate under this section or the PLC is re-registered as another type of company.

(2) The Registrar shall issue to a PLC a certificate under this section if, on an application made to him or her in the prescribed form by the PLC, the Registrar is satisfied that the nominal value of the PLC's allotted share capital is not less than the authorised minimum and there is delivered to the Registrar a declaration complying with *subsection (3)*.

(3) The declaration mentioned in *subsection (2)* shall be in the prescribed form and signed by a director or secretary of the PLC and shall state—

(a) that the nominal value of the PLC's allotted share capital is not less than the authorised minimum,

(b) the amount paid up, at the time of the application, on the PLC's allotted share capital,

(c) the amount, or estimated amount, of the preliminary expenses of the PLC and the persons by whom any of those expenses have been paid or are payable, and

(d) any amount or benefit paid or given or intended to be paid or given to any promoter of the PLC, and the consideration for the payment or benefit.

(4) For the purposes of *subsection (2)*, a share allotted in pursuance of an employees' share scheme may not be taken into account in determining the nominal value of the PLC's allotted share capital unless it is paid up at least as to one-quarter of the nominal value of the share and the whole of any premium on the share.

(5) The Registrar may accept a declaration delivered to him or her under *subsection (2)* as sufficient evidence of the matters stated therein.

(6) A certificate under this section in respect of any PLC shall be conclusive evidence that the PLC is entitled to do business and exercise any borrowing powers.

(7) If a PLC does business or exercises borrowing powers in contravention of this section, the PLC and any officer of it who is in default shall be guilty of a category 3 offence.

(8) Subject to *subsection (9)*, the provisions of this section are without prejudice to the validity of any transaction entered into by a PLC.

(9) If a PLC enters into a transaction in contravention of those provisions and fails to comply with its obligations in connection with them within 21 days after the date on which it is called upon to do so, the directors of the PLC shall be jointly and severally liable to indemnify the other party to the transaction in respect of any loss or damage suffered by that party by reason of the failure of the PLC to comply with those obligations.

1011 Capacity of a PLC

(1) A PLC shall have the capacity to do any act or thing stated in the objects set out in its memorandum.

(2) For the purposes of *subsection (1)*—

(a) the reference in it to an object includes a reference to anything stated in the memorandum to be a power to do any act or thing (whether the word "power" is used or not),

(b) if an object is stated in the PLC's memorandum without the following also being stated in relation to it, the capacity of the PLC extends to doing any act or thing that appears to it to be requisite, advantageous or incidental to, or to facilitate, the attainment of that object and that is not inconsistent with any enactment,

and a subsequent reference in this Part to an object of a PLC shall be read accordingly.

1012 Capacity not limited by a PLC's constitution

(1) The validity of an act done by a PLC shall not be called into question on the ground of lack of capacity by reason of anything contained in the PLC's objects.

(2) A member of a PLC may bring proceedings to restrain the doing of an act which, but for *subsection (1)*, would be beyond the PLC's capacity but no such proceedings

shall lie in respect of any act to be done in fulfilment of a legal obligation arising from a previous act of the PLC.

(3) Notwithstanding the enactment of *subsection (1)*, it remains the duty of the directors to observe any limitations on their powers flowing from the PLC's objects and action by the directors which, but for *subsection (1)*, would be beyond the PLC's capacity may only be ratified by the company by special resolution.

(4) A resolution ratifying such action shall not affect any liability incurred by the directors or any other person; if relief from any such liability is to be conferred by the company it must be agreed to separately by a special resolution of it.

(5) A party to a transaction with a PLC is not bound to enquire as to whether it is permitted by the PLC's objects.

1013 Alteration of objects clause by special resolution

(1) Subject to *subsection (2)*, a PLC may, by special resolution, alter the provisions of its memorandum of association by abandoning, restricting or amending any existing object or by adopting a new object and any alteration so made shall be as valid as if originally contained therein, and be subject to alteration in like manner.

(2) If an application is made to the court in accordance with this section for the alteration to be cancelled, it shall not have effect except in so far as it is confirmed by the court.

(3) Subject to *subsection (4)*, an application under this section may be made—

- (a) by the holders of not less, in the aggregate, than 15 per cent in nominal value of the PLC's issued share capital or any class thereof, or
- (b) by the holders of not less than 15 per cent of the PLC's debentures, entitling the holders to object to alterations of its objects.

(4) An application shall not be made under this section by any person who has consented to or voted in favour of the alteration.

(5) An application under this section shall be made within 21 days after the date on which the resolution altering the PLC's objects was passed and may be made on behalf of the persons entitled to make the application by such one or more of their number as they may appoint in writing for the purpose.

(6) On an application under this section, the court may—

- (a) make an order cancelling the alteration or confirming the alteration, either wholly or in part, and on such terms and conditions as it thinks fit, and
- (b) if it thinks fit, adjourn the proceedings in order that an arrangement may be made to the satisfaction of the court for the purchase of the interests of dissenting members and may give such directions and make such orders as it may think expedient for facilitating or carrying into effect any such arrangement.

(7) An order under this section may, if the court thinks fit, provide for the purchase by the PLC of the shares of any members of the PLC and for the reduction accordingly of the PLC's company capital and may make such alterations in the constitution of the

PLC as may be required in consequence of that provision; and such a purchase may be so ordered notwithstanding anything in *section 102*.

1014 Supplemental provisions in relation to *section 1013*

(1) Where an order under *section 1013* requires the PLC not to make any, or any specified, alteration in its constitution, then, notwithstanding anything in this Act, but subject to the provisions of the order, the PLC shall not have power, without the leave of the court, to make any such alteration in contravention of that requirement.

(2) Any alteration in the constitution of a PLC made by virtue of an order under *section 1013*, other than one made by resolution of the PLC, shall be of the same effect as if duly made by resolution of the PLC and the provisions of this Act shall apply to the constitution as so altered accordingly.

(3) Notice of the meeting at which the special resolution altering a PLC's objects is intended to be proposed shall be given to any holders of the PLC's debentures that entitle the holders to object to alterations of its objects; that notice shall be the same as that given to members of the PLC, so however that not less than 10 days' notice shall be given to the holders of any such debentures.

(4) If the written resolution procedure is used in the matter, notice, which shall not be less than 10 days, of the proposed use of that procedure shall, together with a copy of the proposed text of the resolution, be given to the debenture holders referred to in *subsection (3)*.

(5) In default of any provisions in the PLC's constitution regulating the giving to the foregoing debenture holders of notice referred to in *subsection (3)* or *(4)*, the provisions of *Part 4* or, as the case may be, of the PLC's constitution regulating the giving of notice to members shall apply.

(6) Where a PLC passes a resolution altering its objects—

- (a) if no application is made under *section 1013* with respect to the alteration, it shall, within 15 days after the end of the period for making such an application, deliver to the Registrar a copy of its memorandum of association as altered, and
- (b) if such an application is made, it shall—
  - (i) forthwith give notice of that fact to the Registrar, and
  - (ii) within 15 days after the date of any order cancelling or confirming the alteration, deliver to the Registrar a certified copy of the order and, in the case of an order confirming the alteration, a copy of the memorandum as altered.

(7) The court may, by order, at any time extend the time for delivery of documents to the Registrar under *subsection (6)(b)* for such period as the court may think proper.

(8) If a PLC makes default in giving notice or delivering any document to the Registrar as required by *subsection (6)*, the PLC and any officer of it who is in default shall be guilty of a category 4 offence.

1015 Alteration of articles by special resolution

(1) Subject to the provisions of this Act and to the conditions contained in its memorandum, a PLC may, by special resolution, alter or add to its articles.

(2) Any alteration or addition so made in the articles shall, subject to the provisions of this Act, be as valid as if originally contained therein and be subject in like manner to alteration by special resolution.

1016 Power to alter provisions in memorandum which could have been contained in articles

(1) Subject to *subsection (2)*, *sections 32(4)* and *(5)* and *212*, any provision contained in a PLC's memorandum which could lawfully have been contained in articles instead of in the memorandum may, subject to the provisions of this section, be altered by the PLC by special resolution.

(2) If an application is made to the court for the alteration to be cancelled, it shall not have effect except in so far as it is confirmed by the court.

(3) This section shall not apply where the memorandum itself provides for or prohibits the alteration of all or any of the foregoing provisions, and shall not authorise any variation or abrogation of the special rights of any class of members.

(4) *Section 1013(3)* to *(7)* (other than *subsection (3)(b)*) and *section 1014* (other than *subsections (3)* to *(5)*) shall apply in relation to any alteration and to any application made under this section as they apply in relation to alterations and to applications made under those sections.

1017 Official seal for sealing securities

(1) A PLC may have for use, for sealing—

(a) securities issued by the company, and

(b) documents creating or evidencing securities so issued,

an official seal which is a facsimile of the common seal of the company with the addition on its face of the word "Securities" or the word "Urrúis".

(2) Where a company was incorporated before 3 April 1978 and which has such an official seal as is mentioned in *subsection (1)*, the following provisions apply:

(a) the company may use the seal for sealing such securities and documents as are mentioned in that subsection notwithstanding anything in any instrument constituting or regulating the company or in any instrument made before 3 April 1978 which relates to any securities issued by the company; and

(b) any provision of an instrument referred to in *paragraph (a)* which requires any such securities or documents to be signed shall not apply to the securities or documents if they are sealed with that seal.

(3) Where a company has such an official seal as is mentioned in *subsection (1)* then *section 99(1)* shall apply to the company as if after "common seal of the company" there were inserted "or the seal kept by the company by virtue of *section 1017*".

1018 Status of existing PLC

(1) A public limited company incorporated under the prior Companies Acts and in existence immediately before the commencement of this section shall continue in existence and be deemed to be a PLC to which this Part applies.

(2) In *subsection (1)* "public limited company incorporated under the prior Companies Acts" includes an old public limited company (within the meaning of the Companies (Amendment) Act 1983) that re-registered as a public limited company under that Act as well as a public limited company that any company re-registered as under the prior Companies Acts.

(3) Reference, express or implied, in this Act to the date of registration of a company mentioned in a preceding subsection shall be read as a reference to the date on which the company was registered under the Joint Stock Companies Act 1862, the Companies (Consolidation) Act 1908 or the prior Companies Acts, as the case may be.

Chapter 3
Share capital

1019 Provisions as to shares transferable by delivery (general prohibition and provision for certain letters of allotment)

(1) The provisions of this section shall, in relation to a PLC, have effect in place of *subsections (8)* to *(10)* of *section 66.*

(2) In this section—

"bearer instrument" means an instrument, in relation to shares of a PLC, which entitles or purports to entitle the bearer thereof to transfer the shares that are specified in the instrument by delivery of the instrument, and includes a share warrant as that expression was defined by section 88 of the Act of 1963;

"expiry date", in relation to a permissible letter of allotment, means a date no later than 30 days after the date of the instrument;

"permissible letter of allotment" means a letter of allotment by a PLC to a member of it of—

(a) bonus shares of the PLC, credited as fully paid;

(b) shares of the PLC, in lieu of a dividend, credited as fully paid; or

(c) shares of the PLC allotted provisionally, on which no amount has been paid or which are shares partly paid up, where the shares are allotted in connection with a rights issue or open offer in favour of members and the shares are issued proportionately (or as nearly as may be) to the respective number of shares held by the members of the PLC, there being disregarded for this purpose any exceptions to such proportionality, or arrangements for a deviation from such proportionality, as the directors of the PLC may deem necessary or expedient to make for the purposes of dealing with—

(i) fractional entitlements; or

(ii) problems of a legal or practical nature arising under the laws of any territory or requirements imposed by any recognised regulatory body in any territory,

which letter is expressed to be transferable by delivery during a period expiring on its expiry date.

(3) Save as provided by this section, a PLC shall not have power to issue any bearer instrument.

(4) If a PLC purports to issue a bearer instrument in contravention of *subsection (3)*, the shares that are specified in the instrument shall be deemed not to have been allotted or issued, and the amount subscribed therefor (and in the case of a non-cash asset subscribed therefor, the cash value of that asset) shall be due as a debt of the PLC to the purported subscriber thereof.

(5) *Subsection (3)* shall not apply to an instrument falling within the definition of "permissible letter of allotment" in this section.

(6) Shares comprised in a permissible letter of allotment shall, until its expiry date, be transferable by renunciation and delivery of the letter, but subject to compliance with such conditions (if any) as may be specified in the letter.

(7) Where, on the commencement of this section, a PLC has in issue a bearer instrument in relation to shares of the PLC, other than a permissible letter of allotment—

(a) the PLC shall procure the entry in its register of members of the name of the holder or holders of those shares no later than the expiry of 18 months after that commencement;

(b) if and to the extent that *paragraph (a)* is not complied with, the PLC shall enter in its register of members the Minister for Finance as the person entitled to the share or shares concerned and thereupon the Minister for Finance shall become and be the full beneficial owner of that share or those shares.

(8) Subject to *subsection (7)*, where on the commencement of this section a person has or is entitled to possession of a bearer instrument (other than a permissible letter of allotment), whether as owner or as encumbrancer, nothing in this section shall affect any rights which such person has by virtue of such entitlement or possession, provided that any right to transfer the shares that are specified in it by delivery of the instrument shall cease 21 days before the expiry of the period referred to in *subsection (7)(a)*.

1020 Capacity to make public offers of securities

Save to the extent prohibited by its constitution, a PLC shall have the capacity to offer, allot and issue securities (as defined in *Part 3*) to the public subject to compliance, where applicable, with *Part 23*.

1021 Allotment of shares and other securities

(1) No relevant securities may be allotted by a PLC unless the allotment is authorised, either specifically or pursuant to a general authority, by ordinary resolution or by the constitution of the PLC.

(2) Without prejudice to *subsection (1)*, no shares may be allotted by a PLC unless those shares are comprised in the authorised but unissued share capital of the PLC.

(3) Any such authority as is referred to in *subsection (1)* shall state the maximum amount of relevant securities that may be allotted under it and the date on which the authority will expire, which shall be not more than 5 years after whichever is relevant of the following dates:

(a) in the case of an authority contained at the time of the original incorporation of the PLC in the articles of the PLC, the date of that incorporation, and

(b) in any other case, the date on which the resolution is passed by virtue of which that authority is given,

but any such authority (including an authority contained in the articles of the PLC) may be previously revoked or varied by the PLC in general meeting.

(4) Any such authority (whether or not it has been previously renewed under this subsection) may be renewed by the PLC in general meeting for a further period not exceeding 5 years; but the resolution must state (or restate) the amount of relevant securities which may be allotted under the authority or, as the case may be, the amount remaining to be allotted thereunder, and must specify the date on which the renewed authority will expire.

(5) Notwithstanding that any authorisation conferred by a resolution or the constitution such as is mentioned in *subsection (1)* has expired, the directors of a PLC may allot relevant securities in pursuance of an offer or agreement previously made by the PLC, if that authorisation enabled the PLC to make an offer or agreement which would or might require relevant securities to be allotted after the authorisation's expiry.

(6) A resolution of a PLC to give, vary, revoke or renew such an authority may, notwithstanding that it alters the articles of association of the PLC, be an ordinary resolution.

(7) Where a PLC allots shares, the shares shall be taken, for the purposes of this Act, to be allotted when a person acquires the unconditional right to be included in the PLC's register of members in respect of those shares.

(8) Any director of a PLC who knowingly contravenes, or knowingly permits or authorises a contravention of, a preceding provision of this section shall be guilty of a category 3 offence.

(9) Where a PLC allots shares, it shall, within 30 days after the date of allotment, deliver particulars of the allotment in the prescribed form to the Registrar.

(10) If a PLC fails to comply with *subsection (9)*, the PLC and any officer of it who is in default shall be guilty of a category 4 offence.

(11) Nothing in this section shall affect the validity of any allotment of relevant securities.

(12) In this section "relevant securities" means, in relation to a PLC—

(a) shares in the PLC other than shares shown in the memorandum to have been taken by the subscribers thereto or shares allotted in pursuance of an employees' share scheme, and

(b) any right to subscribe for, or to convert any security into, shares in the PLC other than shares so allotted,

and any reference in this section to the allotment of relevant securities includes a reference to the grant of such a right but does not include any reference to the allotment of shares pursuant to such a right.

1022 Pre-emption rights

(1) Subject to the provisions of this section and *section 1023*, a PLC proposing to allot any equity securities—

(a) shall not allot any of those securities, on any terms—

(i) to any non-member, unless it has made an offer to each person who holds relevant shares or relevant employee shares in the PLC to allot to him or her, on the same or more favourable terms, a proportion of those securities which is, as nearly as practicable, equal to the proportion in nominal value held by him or her of the aggregate of the relevant shares and relevant employee shares, or

(ii) to any person who holds relevant shares or relevant employee shares in the PLC, unless it has made an offer to each person who holds relevant shares or relevant employee shares in the PLC to allot to him or her, on the same or more favourable terms, a proportion of those securities which is, as nearly as practicable, equal to the proportion in nominal value held by him or her of the aggregate of the relevant shares and relevant employee shares,

and

(b) shall not allot any of those securities to any person unless the period during which any such offer may be accepted has expired or the PLC has received notice of the acceptance or refusal of every offer so made.

(2) In *subsection (1)(a)(i)* "non-member" means a person who is not a holder of shares (as that expression is to be read by virtue of *subsection (11)*) in the PLC.

(3) *Subsection (4)* applies to any provision of the memorandum or articles of a PLC which requires the PLC, when proposing to allot equity securities consisting of relevant shares of any particular class, not to allot those securities on any terms unless it has complied with the condition that it makes such an offer as is described in *subsection (1)* to each person who holds relevant shares or relevant employee shares of that class.

(4) If, in accordance with a provision to which this subsection applies—

(a) a PLC makes an offer to allot any securities to such a holder, and

(b) that holder or anyone in whose favour that holder has renounced his or her right to their allotment accepts the offer,

subsection (1) shall not apply to the allotment of those securities and the PLC may allot them accordingly; but this subsection is without prejudice to the application of *subsection (1)* in any other case.

(5) *Subsection (1)* shall not apply in relation to a particular allotment of equity securities if the securities are, or are to be, wholly or partly paid up otherwise than in cash.

(6) Securities which a PLC has offered to allot to a holder of relevant shares or relevant employee shares may be allotted to that holder or anyone in whose favour that holder has renounced his or her right to their allotment without contravening *subsection (1)(b)*.

(7) *Subsection (1)* shall not apply in relation to the allotment of any securities which would, apart from a renunciation or assignment of the right to their allotment, be held under an employees' share scheme.

(8) An offer which is required by *subsection (1)* or by any provision to which *subsection (4)* applies to be made to any person shall be made by serving it on him or her in the same manner in which notices are authorised to be given by *sections 180, 181* and *218*.

(9) Any such offer as is mentioned in *subsection (8)* shall state a period of not less than 14 days during which the offer may be accepted; and the offer shall not be withdrawn before the end of that period.

(10) *Subsections (8)* and *(9)* shall not invalidate a provision to which *subsection (4)* applies by reason that that provision requires or authorises an offer thereunder to be made in contravention of one or both of those subsections, but, to the extent that the provision requires or authorises such an offer to be so made, it shall be of no effect.

(11) In relation to any offer to allot any securities required by *subsection (1)* or by any provision to which *subsection (4)* applies, references in this section (however expressed) to the holder of shares of any description shall be read as including references to any person who held shares of that description on any day within the period of 28 days ending with the day immediately preceding the date of the offer which is specified by the directors of the PLC concerned as being the record date for the purposes of the offer.

(12) Where there is a contravention of *subsection (1)*, *(8)* or *(9)* or a provision to which *subsection (4)* applies, the PLC and every officer of the PLC who knowingly authorised or permitted the contravention, shall be jointly and severally liable to compensate any person to whom an offer should have been made under the subsection or provision contravened for any loss, damage, costs or expenses which that person has sustained or incurred by reason of the contravention.

(13) No proceedings to recover any such loss, damage, costs or expenses shall be commenced after the expiration of 2 years after the date of the delivery to the Registrar of the return of allotments in question or, where equity securities other than shares are granted, after the date of the grant.

1023 Interpretation and supplemental provisions in relation to *section 1022*

(1) In *section 1022* and this section—

"equity security", in relation to a PLC, means a relevant share in the PLC (other than a share shown in the memorandum to have been taken by a subscriber thereto or a bonus share) or a right to subscribe for, or to convert any securities into, relevant shares in the PLC, and references to the allotment of equity securities or of equity securities consisting of relevant shares of a particular class include references to the grant of a right to subscribe for, or to convert any securities into, relevant shares in the company or, as the case may be, relevant shares of a particular class, but does not include references to the allotment of any relevant shares pursuant to such a right;

"relevant employee shares", in relation to a PLC, means shares of the PLC which would be relevant shares in the PLC but for the fact that they are held by a person who acquired them in pursuance of an employees' share scheme;

"relevant shares", in relation to a PLC, means shares in the PLC other than—

(a) shares which as respects dividends and capital carry a right to participate only up to a specified amount in a distribution, and

(b) shares which are held by a person who acquired them in pursuance of an employees' share scheme, or, in the case of shares which have not been allotted, are to be allotted in pursuance of such a scheme.

(2) Any reference in *section 1022* or this section to a class of shares shall be read as a reference to shares to which the same rights are attached as to voting and as to participation, both as respects dividends and as respects capital, in a distribution.

(3) Where the directors of a PLC are generally authorised for the purposes of *section 1021*, they may be given power by the articles or by a special resolution of the PLC to allot equity securities pursuant to that authority as if—

(a) *subsection (1)* of *section 1022* did not apply to the allotment; or

(b) that subsection applied to the allotment with such modifications as the directors may determine;

and where the directors make an allotment under this subsection, *section 1022* shall have effect accordingly.

(4) Where the directors of a PLC are authorised for the purposes of *section 1021* (whether generally or otherwise), the PLC may by special resolution resolve either—

(a) that *subsection (1)* of *section 1022* shall not apply to a specified allotment of equity securities to be made pursuant to that authority; or

(b) that that subsection shall apply to the allotment with such modifications as may be specified in the resolution;

and where such a resolution is passed *section 1022* shall have effect accordingly.

(5) A power conferred by virtue of *subsection (3)* or a special resolution under *subsection (4)* shall cease to have effect when the authority to which it relates is revoked or would, if not renewed, expire, but if that authority is renewed, the power or, as the case may be, the resolution may also be renewed, for a period not longer than that for which the authority is renewed, by a special resolution of the company.

(6) Notwithstanding that any such power or resolution has expired, the directors may allot equity securities in pursuance of an offer or agreement previously made by the PLC, if the power or resolution enabled the PLC to make an offer or agreement which would or might require equity securities to be allotted after it expired.

(7) A special resolution under *subsection (4)*, or a special resolution to renew such a resolution, shall not be proposed unless it is recommended by the directors and there has been circulated, with the notice of the meeting at which the resolution is proposed, to the members entitled to have that notice a written statement by the directors setting out—

(a) their reasons for making the recommendation;

(b) the amount to be paid to the PLC in respect of the equity securities to be allotted; and

(c) the directors' justification of that amount.

(8) A person who authorises or permits the inclusion in a statement circulated under *subsection (7)* of any matter which is false or misleading in a material particular knowing it to be so false or misleading or being reckless as to whether it is so false or misleading shall be guilty of a category 3 offence.

[(9) Section 1022 and this section shall not have effect in respect of a company to which the resolution tools, powers or mechanisms provided for in Part 4 of the Bank Recovery and Resolution Regulations are applied or exercised.][a]

Amendments

a Subsection (9) inserted by European Union (Bank Recovery and Resolution) Regulations 2015, reg 189(6), with effect from 15 July 2015.

1024 Status of authority to allot shares conferred prior to company's re-registration as a PLC

Any authority of directors to allot shares under *section 69* conferred by ordinary resolution passed by a company prior to its re-registration as a PLC shall lapse at the conclusion of its annual general meeting next held after its re-registration as a PLC.

1025 Subscription of share capital

(1) A PLC shall not accept at any time, in payment up of its shares or any premium on them, an undertaking given by any person that he or she or another should do work or perform services for the PLC or any other person.

(2) Where a PLC accepts such an undertaking as payment up of its shares or any premium payable on them, the holder of the shares when they or the premium are treated as paid up, in whole or in part, by the undertaking—

(a) shall be liable to pay the PLC in respect of those shares, an amount equal to their nominal value, together with the whole of any premium or, if the case so requires, such proportion of that amount as is treated as paid up by the undertaking, and

(b) shall be liable to pay interest at the appropriate rate on the amount payable under *paragraph (a)*.

(3) Where any person becomes a holder of any shares in respect of which—

(a) there has been a contravention of this section, and

(b) by virtue of that contravention, another is liable to pay any amount under this section,

the first-mentioned person in this subsection also shall be liable to pay that amount (jointly and severally with any other person so liable) unless either that first-mentioned person is a purchaser for value and, at the time of the purchase, he or she did not have actual notice of the contravention or he or she derived title to the shares (directly or indirectly) from a person who became a holder of them after the contravention and was not so liable.

(4) References in this section to a holder, in relation to any shares in a PLC, include references to any person who has an unconditional right to be included in the PLC's register of members in respect of those shares or to have an instrument of transfer of the shares executed in his or her favour.

(5) Where a PLC contravenes any of the provisions of this section, the PLC and any officer of it who is in default shall be guilty of a category 3 offence.

1026 Payment for allotted shares

(1) Subject to *subsection (4)*, a PLC shall not allot a share except as paid up at least as to one-quarter of the nominal value of the share and the whole of any premium on it.

(2) Where a PLC allots a share in contravention of *subsection (1)*, the share shall be treated as if one-quarter of its nominal value together with the whole of any premium had been received, but the allottee shall be liable to pay the PLC the minimum amount which should have been received in respect of the share under that subsection less the value of any consideration actually applied in payment up (to any extent) of the share and any premium on it, and interest at the appropriate rate on the amount payable under this subsection.

(3) *Subsection (2)* shall not apply in relation to the allotment of a bonus share in contravention of *subsection (1)* unless the allottee knew or ought to have known the share was so allotted.

(4) *Subsections (1)* to *(3)* shall not apply to shares allotted in pursuance of an employees' share scheme.

(5) *Subsection (3)* of *section 1025* shall apply for the purposes of this section as it applies for the purposes of *section 1025*.

(6) Where a PLC contravenes any of the provisions of this section, the PLC and any officer of it who is in default shall be guilty of a category 3 offence.

1027 Payment of non-cash consideration

(1) A PLC shall not allot shares as fully or partly paid up (as to their nominal value or any premium payable on them) otherwise than in cash if the consideration for the allotment is or includes an undertaking which is to be or may be performed more than 5 years after the date of the allotment.

(2) Where a PLC allots shares in contravention of *subsection (1)*, the allottee of the shares shall be liable to pay the PLC an amount equal to their nominal value, together with the whole of any premium, or if the case so requires, such proportion of that amount as is treated as paid up by the undertaking and shall be liable to pay interest at the appropriate rate on the amount payable under this subsection.

(3) Where a contract for the allotment of shares does not contravene *subsection (1)*, any variation of the contract which has the effect that the contract would have contravened that subsection if the terms of the contract as varied had been its original terms shall be void.

(4) *Subsection (3)* shall apply to the variation by a PLC of the terms of a contract entered into before the company was registered or re-registered as a PLC.

(5) Where a PLC allots shares for a consideration which consists of or includes (in accordance with *subsection (1)*) an undertaking which is to be performed within 5 years after the date of the allotment but that undertaking is not performed within the period allowed by the contract for the allotment of the shares, the following subsection applies.

(6) The allottee of the shares in question shall be liable to pay the PLC at the end of the period secondly referred to in *subsection (5)* the following:

(a) an amount equal to the nominal value of the shares, together with the whole of any premium, or if the case so requires, such proportion of that amount as is treated as paid up by the undertaking; and

(b) interest at the appropriate rate on the amount payable under *paragraph (a)*.

(7) *Subsection (3)* of *section 1025* shall apply in relation to a contravention of this section and to a failure to carry out a term of a contract as mentioned in *subsection (5)* as it applies in relation to a contravention of *section 1025*.

(8) Any reference in this section to a contract for the allotment of shares includes a reference to an ancillary contract relating to payment in respect of those shares.

(9) Where a PLC contravenes any of the provisions of this section, the PLC and any officer of it who is in default shall be guilty of a category 3 offence.

1028 Expert's report on non-cash consideration before allotment of shares

(1) Subject to *subsection (2)* and *sections 1029* and *1031* to *1033*, a PLC shall not allot shares as fully or partly paid up (as to their nominal value or any premium payable on them) otherwise than in cash unless—

(a) the consideration for the allotment has been valued in accordance with the following provisions of this section;

(b) a report with respect to its value has been made to the PLC by a person appointed by the PLC in accordance with those provisions during the 6 months immediately preceding the date of the allotment of the shares; and

(c) a copy of the report has been sent to the proposed allottee of the shares.

(2) Subject to *subsection (3), subsection (1)* shall not apply to the allotment of shares by a PLC in connection with an arrangement providing for the allotment of shares in that PLC on terms that the whole or part of the consideration for the shares allotted is to be provided by the transfer to that PLC or the cancellation of all or some of the shares, or of all or some of the shares of a particular class, in another company (with or without the issue to that PLC of shares, or of shares of any particular class, in that other company).

(3) *Subsection (2)* does not exclude the application of *subsection (1)* to the allotment of shares by a PLC in connection with any such arrangement as is there mentioned unless the following condition is satisfied, namely, it is open to all the holders of the shares in the other company in question or, where the arrangement applies only to shares of a particular class, to all the holders of shares in that other company of that class, to take part in the arrangement.

(4) In determining whether the foregoing condition is satisfied, shares held by, or by a nominee of, the PLC proposing to allot the shares in connection with the arrangement, or by, or by a nominee of, a company which is that PLC's holding company or subsidiary or a company which is a subsidiary of that PLC's holding company, shall be disregarded.

(5) Subject to *subsections (6)* and *(7)*, the valuation and report required by *subsection (1)* shall be made by an independent person, that is to say, a person qualified at the time of the report to be appointed or to continue to be the statutory auditor of the PLC.

(6) Where it appears to the independent person referred to in *subsection (5)* to be reasonable for the valuation of the consideration, or a valuation of part of the consideration, to be made, or to accept such a valuation made, by any person who—

(a) appears to that independent person to have the requisite knowledge and experience to value the consideration or that part of the consideration; and

(b) is not—

(i) an officer or employee of the PLC or any other body corporate which is that PLC's subsidiary or holding company or a subsidiary of that PLC's holding company;

(ii) a partner or employee of an officer or employee referred to in *subparagraph (i)*; or

(iii) a person otherwise connected (within the meaning of *section 220* as adapted by *section 1029(7)*) with an officer or employee referred to in *subparagraph (i)*;

that independent person may arrange for or accept such a valuation, together with a report which will enable the independent person to make his or her own report under *subsection (1)* and provide a note in accordance with *subsection (11)*.

(7) Where the allotment of shares by a PLC is in connection with—

(a) a proposed merger, where that company was formed as a successor company for the purpose of the proposed merger, the merger being a merger by formation of a new company within the meaning of *Chapter 16* or the European Communities (Cross-Border Mergers) Regulations 2008 (S.I. No. 157 of 2008);

(b) a proposed merger of that company with another company; or

(c) a proposed division of that company;

the valuation and report required by *subsection (1)* may be made by the person appointed pursuant to *section 1133* or *1155* or an expert within the meaning of Regulation 7 of the foregoing Regulations, in which case the person so appointed shall be deemed to be an independent person for the purposes of *subsection (5)*.

(8) For the purposes of *subsection (7)* there is a proposed merger of a PLC with a company when one of them proposes to acquire all the assets and liabilities of the other in exchange for the issue of shares or other securities in that one to shareholders of the other, with or without any cash payment to those shareholders.

(9) The report of the independent person under *subsection (1)* shall state—

(a) the nominal value of the shares to be wholly or partly paid for by the consideration in question;

(b) the amount of any premium payable on those shares;

(c) the description of the consideration and, as respects so much of the consideration as the independent person himself or herself has valued, a description of that part of the consideration, the method used to value it and the date of the valuation; and

(d) the extent to which the nominal value of the shares and any premium are to be treated as paid up—

(i) by the consideration;

(ii) in cash.

(10) Where any consideration is valued under this section by a person other than the independent person, the latter's report under *subsection (1)* shall state that fact and shall also—

(a) state the former's name and what knowledge and experience that other person has to carry out the valuation; and

(b) describe so much of the consideration as was valued by that other person, the method used to value it and state the date of valuation.

(11) The report of the independent person made under *subsection (1)* shall contain a note by the independent person, or be accompanied by such a note—

(a) in the case of a valuation made by another person, that it appeared to the independent person reasonable to arrange for it to be so made, or to accept a valuation so made;

(b) irrespective of whether the valuation has been by that person or the independent person, that the method of valuation was reasonable in all the circumstances;

(c) that it appears to the independent person that there has been no material change in the value of the consideration in question since the valuation; and

(d) that on the basis of the valuation the value of the consideration, together with any cash by which the nominal value of the shares or any premium payable on them is to be paid up, is not less than so much of the aggregate of the nominal value and the whole of any such premium as is treated as paid up by the consideration and any such cash.

1029 Supplemental provisions in relation to *section 1028*

(1) *Subsection (2)* applies where a PLC allots any share in contravention of *section 1028(1)* and either—

(a) the allottee has not received a report under *section 1028*; or

(b) there has been some other contravention of that section and the allottee knew or ought to have known that it amounted to a contravention.

(2) Where this subsection applies, the allottee shall be liable to pay the PLC an amount equal to the nominal value of the shares, together with the whole of any premium or if the case so requires, such proportion of that amount as is treated as paid up by the consideration, and shall be liable to pay interest at the appropriate rate on the amount payable under this subsection.

(3) *Subsection (3)* of *section 1025* shall apply for the purposes of *section 1028* as it applies for the purposes of *section 1025*.

(4) Where the consideration referred to in *section 1028* is accepted partly in payment up of the nominal value of the shares and any premium and partly for some other consideration given by the company, the provisions of that section and this section shall apply as if references to the consideration accepted by the PLC included references to the proportion of that consideration which is properly attributable to the payment up of that value and any premium; and—

(a) the independent person shall carry out or arrange for such other valuations as will enable him or her to determine that proportion, and

(b) the independent person's report under *section 1028(1)* shall state what valuations have been made by virtue of this subsection and also the reason for and method and date of any such valuation and any other matters which may be relevant to that determination.

(5) It is declared for the avoidance of doubt that *section 1028(1)* does not apply by reference to the application of an amount for the time being standing to the credit of any of the PLC's reserve accounts or to the credit of its profit and loss account in paying up (to any extent) any shares allotted to members of the PLC or any premiums on any shares so allotted; and in relation to any such allotment references in *section 1028* or this section to the consideration for the allotment do not include any such amount so applied.

(6) In *section 1028* and this section—

(a) "arrangement" means any agreement, scheme or arrangement (including an arrangement sanctioned in accordance with *section 453, 541* or *601*),

(b) any reference to a company, except where it is or is to be read as a reference to a PLC, includes a reference to any body corporate and any body to which letters patent have been issued under the Chartered Companies Act 1837, and

(c) any reference to an officer or employee shall not include a reference to a statutory auditor.

(7) For the purposes of the provision made by *section 1028(6)(b)(iii)* concerning a person's being connected with an officer or employee there referred to (which officer or employee is, in this subsection, subsequently referred to as the "relevant person"), *section 220* applies as if—

(a) for each reference in *subsections (1)*, *(2)*, *(3)* and *(8)* to a director of a company there were substituted a reference to the relevant person;

(b) for the first reference and the third reference in *subsection (5)* to a director of a company there were substituted a reference to the relevant person;

(c) the references in *subsection (5)* to another director or directors included references to one or more other relevant persons; and

(d) the reference in *subsection (6)(b)* to a director included a reference to a relevant person.

(8) Where a PLC contravenes any of the provisions of *section 1028* or this section, the PLC and any officer of it who is in default shall be guilty of a category 3 offence.

[(9) Section 1028 and this section shall not have effect in respect of a company to which the resolution tools, powers or mechanisms provided for in Part 4 of the Bank Recovery and Resolution Regulations are applied or exercised.][a]

Amendments

a Subsection (9) inserted by European Union (Bank Recovery and Resolution) Regulations 2015, reg 189(7), with effect from 15 July 2015.

1030 Expert's report: supplemental provisions in relation to *section 1028*

(1) Any person carrying out a valuation or making a report under *section 1028* with respect to any consideration proposed to be accepted or given by a PLC shall be entitled to require from the officers of the PLC such information and explanation as the person thinks necessary to enable him or her to carry out the valuation or to make the report and provide a note required by that section.

(2) A PLC to which such a report is made as to the value of any consideration for which, or partly for which, it proposes to allot shares shall deliver a copy of the report to the Registrar at the same time that it delivers particulars of the allotments of those shares under *section 1021(9)*.

(3) *Section 1021(10)* shall apply to a default in complying with *subsection (2)* as it applies to a default in complying with *section 1021(9)*.

(4) Any person who makes a statement—

(a) that is a statement to which this subsection applies; and

(b) which is false or misleading in a material particular;

knowing it to be so false or misleading or being reckless as to whether it is so false or misleading, shall be guilty of a category 2 offence.

(5) *Subsection (4)* applies to any statement made (whether orally or in writing) to any person carrying out a valuation or making a report under *section 1028*, being a statement which conveys or purports to convey any information or explanation which that person requires, or is entitled to require, under *subsection (1)*.

1031 Dispensation from *section 1028* — certain securities or money-market instruments constituting consideration for allotment

(1) In this section—

"relevant assets" means securities or instruments (or, as the case may be, both) referred to in the definition of "securities based consideration" in this subsection;

"securities based consideration" means consideration consisting of—

(a) transferable securities as defined in point 18 of Article 4(1) of Directive 2004/39/EC of the European Parliament and of the Council of 21 April 2004 on markets in financial instruments;

(b) money-market instruments as defined in point 19 of Article 4(1) of that Directive; or

(c) both such transferable securities and such money-market instruments.

(2) Where this section applies then either—

(a) the requirements of *section 1028* do not apply; or

(b) those requirements only apply if the contingency specified in *subsection (4)(b)* arises.

(3) This section applies where the consideration for the allotment of the shares consists wholly, or together with cash consideration, of securities based consideration and—

(a) the conditions specified in *subsection (4)* are satisfied with respect to the securities based consideration; and

(b) the value of the securities based consideration is not less than the value of the relevant assets as determined in accordance with *paragraph (a)* of that subsection.

(4) The following are the conditions with respect to the securities based consideration—

(a) the relevant assets are valued at the weighted average price at which they have been traded on one or more regulated markets during a period of 5 consecutive days (any break arising on account of closure of such market on one or more days being disregarded) immediately preceding the date on which those assets are treated as consideration given for the allotment of the shares in question; and

(b) the foregoing price has not been affected by exceptional circumstances that would significantly change the value of the asset at the foregoing date, including situations where the market for the securities or instruments concerned has become illiquid.

(5) If exceptional circumstances or a situation as mentioned in *subsection (4)(b)* arise, a valuation under *section 1028* of the relevant assets shall be caused to be carried out by the PLC and the relevant provisions of *sections 1028* to *1030* shall apply accordingly.

(6) Where this section applies and shares are proposed to be allotted by a PLC without a report of an independent expert as otherwise required by *sections 1028* to *1030*, the PLC shall, no later than the date of allotment, deliver, in the prescribed form, notice of the proposed allotment to the Registrar, which notice shall contain—

(a) a description of the consideration other than in cash at issue;

(b) the value of that consideration, the source of its valuation and, where appropriate, the method of valuation;

(c) a statement whether the value arrived at corresponds at least to the number and nominal value of, and (where appropriate) to the premium on, the shares to be issued for that consideration.

(7) Where shares have been allotted as mentioned in *subsection (6)*, the notice of the allotment delivered under *section 1021(9)* to the Registrar in respect of those shares shall—

(a) contain—

(i) a description of the consideration other than in cash at issue;

(ii) the value of that consideration, the source of its valuation and, where appropriate, the method of valuation; and

(iii) a statement whether the value arrived at corresponds at least to the number and nominal value of, and (where appropriate) to the premium on, the shares issued for that consideration;

which may be by reference to the particulars delivered in accordance with *subsection (6)*; and

(b) contain a statement that no exceptional circumstances or a situation as mentioned in *subsection (4)(b)* with regard to the original valuation arose prior to the allotment.

1032 Dispensation from *section 1028* — consideration for allotment other than securities and money-market instruments referred to in *section 1031*

(1) In this section—

"non-securities based consideration" means consideration other than that falling within the definition of "securities based consideration" in *section 1031(1)*;

"relevant assets" means assets other than those falling within that definition of "securities based consideration".

(2) Where this section applies then either—

(a) the requirements of *section 1028* do not apply; or

(b) those requirements only apply if—

(i) the contingency specified in *subsection (4)(e)* arises; or

(ii) a request of the kind referred to in *subsection (6)* is made by one or more members of the PLC, being a request that, as provided therein, must be acceded to by the PLC.

(3) This section applies where the consideration for the allotment of the shares consists wholly, or together with cash consideration, of non-securities based consideration and—

(a) the conditions specified in *subsection (4)* are satisfied with respect to the non-securities based consideration; and

(b) the value of the non-securities based consideration is not less than the value of the relevant assets as determined in accordance with *paragraph (a)* of that subsection.

(4) The following are the conditions with respect to the non-securities based consideration:

(a) the relevant assets are valued by reference to an opinion as to their fair value by an expert who, in the opinion of the PLC, possesses the requisite degree of independence from the interests concerned in the transaction and holds an appropriate qualification;

(b) that fair value was determined for a date not more than 6 months before the date on which the relevant assets are treated as consideration given for the allotment of the shares in question;

(c) that valuation as to fair value has been performed in accordance with generally accepted valuation standards and principles in the State (or such standards and principles in another Member State as are equivalent to them) and, in either case, which are applicable to the class of assets concerned;

(d) the giving of such consideration is approved—

(i) by ordinary resolution of the PLC; or

(ii) following 14 days' notice by the board of directors (of the PLC's intention to give that consideration) to the members, by a resolution of the board of directors of the PLC,

and, in either case, that approval is granted not more than 30 days before the date on which the agreement to allot the shares in question is entered into or, where such agreement is subject to conditions that required fulfilment before the agreement can be carried into effect, on the date of those conditions' fulfilment;

(e) no exceptional circumstances arise that would significantly change the fair value of the asset at the date secondly referred to in *paragraph (b)*; and

(f) in a case where *paragraph (d)(ii)* applies, the resolution there referred to includes a statement by the board of directors that they are satisfied that there are no exceptional circumstances known to them that, in their opinion, have significantly changed the fair value of the assets at the date secondly referred to in *paragraph (b)*.

(5) If either—

(a) exceptional circumstances as mentioned in *paragraph (e)* of *subsection (4)* arise; or

(b) notwithstanding that the conditions specified in that subsection are satisfied, a request of the kind referred to in *subsection (6)* is made by one or more members of the PLC, being a request that, as provided therein, must be acceded to by the PLC;

a valuation under *section 1028* of the relevant assets shall be caused to be carried out by the PLC and the relevant provisions of *sections 1028* to *1030* shall apply accordingly.

(6) One or more members who hold, or together hold, not less than 5 per cent of the issued shares of the PLC on the date of the passing of the ordinary resolution or the notification by the directors, as the case may be, referred to in *subsection (4)(d)* may, by notice in writing served on the PLC before the date secondly referred to in *subsection (4)(b)*, request a valuation under *section 1028* of the relevant assets to be carried out; unless, on the date of service of that notice, the percentage of the issued shares of the PLC held by the requester or, as appropriate, the requesters has fallen below 5 per cent, the request shall be acceded to by the PLC.

(7) Where this section applies and shares are proposed to be allotted by a PLC without a report of an independent expert as otherwise required by *sections 1028* to *1030*, the PLC shall, no later than the earliest of the dates specified in *subsection (8)*, deliver, in the prescribed form, notice of the proposed allotment to the Registrar, which notice shall contain—

(a) a description of the consideration other than in cash at issue;

(b) the value of that consideration, the source of its valuation and, where appropriate, the method of valuation; and

(c) a statement whether the value arrived at corresponds at least to the number and nominal value of, and (where appropriate) to the premium on, the shares to be issued for that consideration.

(8) The dates referred to in *subsection (7)* are—

(a) the date of the allotment;

(b) where the allotment is to be authorised by ordinary resolution, as appropriate—

(i) the date of the notice of the general meeting at which the ordinary resolution is to be passed; or

(ii) where the ordinary resolution is to be passed by written resolution, the date on which the written resolution is deemed to be passed;

(c) where the allotment is to be authorised by the board of directors only, the date of the notification by the directors referred to in *subsection (4)(d)*.

(9) Where shares have been allotted as mentioned in *subsection (7)*, the notice of the allotment delivered under *section 1021(9)* to the Registrar in respect of those shares shall—

(a) contain—

(i) a description of the consideration other than in cash at issue;

(ii) the value of that consideration, the source of its valuation and, where appropriate, the method of valuation; and

(iii) a statement whether the value arrived at corresponds at least to the number and nominal value of, and (where appropriate) to the premium on, the shares issued for that consideration;

which may be by reference to the particulars delivered in accordance with *subsection (7)*; and

(b) contain a statement that no exceptional circumstances with regard to the original valuation arose prior to the allotment.

1033 Dispensation from *section 1028*: cases in which consideration for allotment falls into both *section 1031* and *section 1032*

(1) If the consideration for the allotment of the shares consists of both—

(a) securities based consideration; and

(b) non-securities based consideration;

(whether in addition to cash or not), the provisions of *sections 1031* and *1032* shall apply, respectively, to the securities based consideration and the non-securities based consideration, but with the modification that the notice of the proposed allotment, as provided for in *sections 1031(6)* and *1032(7)*, may be combined in the one document as long as that document is delivered to the Registrar no later than the earliest of the dates specified in *section 1032(8)*.

(2) In this section—

"non-securities based consideration" has the same meaning as it has in *section 1032*;

"securities based consideration" has the same meaning as it has in *section 1031*.

1034 Expert's report on non-cash assets acquired from subscribers, etc.

(1) A PLC shall not, unless the conditions specified in *subsection (3)* have been satisfied, enter into an agreement with a relevant person for the transfer by him or her, during the initial period, of one or more non-cash assets to the PLC or another for a consideration to be given by the PLC equal in value at the time of the agreement to at least one-tenth of the nominal value of the PLC's share capital issued at that time.

(2) In this section—

(a) in relation to a company formed as a PLC—

(i) "relevant person" means any subscriber to the memorandum of the company; and

(ii) "initial period" means the period of 2 years beginning after the date on which the company is issued with a certificate under *section 1010* that it is entitled to do business;

(b) in relation to a company re-registered or registered in accordance with *Part 20* or *22* as a PLC—

(i) "relevant person" means any person who was a member of the company on the date of the re-registration or registration; and

(ii) "initial period" means the period of 2 years beginning after that date.

(3) The conditions referred to in *subsection (1)* are that—

(a) the consideration to be received by the PLC (that is to say, the asset to be transferred to the PLC or the advantage to the PLC of its transfer to another person) and any consideration other than cash to be given by the PLC have been valued under the following provisions of this section (without prejudice to any requirement to value any consideration under *sections 1028* to *1030*);

(b) a report with respect to the consideration to be so received and given has been made to the PLC in accordance with those provisions during the 6 months immediately preceding the date of the agreement;

(c) the terms of the agreement have been approved by an ordinary resolution of the PLC; and

(d) not later than—

(i) the date of the giving of the notice of the meeting at which the resolution is proposed; or

(ii) where the means under *section 193* (unanimous written resolutions) for passing the resolution is used, 21 days before the date of the signing of the resolution by the last member to sign;

copies of the resolution and report have been circulated to the members of the PLC entitled to receive that notice or sign the resolution and, if the relevant person is not then such a member, to that person, but, in a case falling within *subparagraph (ii)*, compliance with this paragraph may be waived in writing by such members and the relevant person.

(4) *Subsection (1)* shall not apply to the following agreements for the transfer of an asset for a consideration to be given by the PLC, that is to say—

(a) where it is part of the ordinary business of the PLC to acquire or arrange for other persons to acquire assets of a particular description, an agreement entered into by the PLC in the ordinary course of its business for the transfer of an asset of that description to it or such a person, as the case may be; or

(b) an agreement entered into by the PLC under the supervision of the court, or an officer authorised by the court for the purpose, for the transfer of an asset to the PLC or to another.

(5) *Subsections (5)*, *(6)* and *(10)* of *section 1028* shall apply to a valuation and report of any consideration under this section as those subsections apply to a valuation of and report on any consideration under *subsection (1)* of *section 1028*.

(6) The report of the independent person under this section shall—

(a) state the consideration to be received by the PLC, describing the asset in question, specifying the amount to be received in cash and the consideration to be given by the PLC, specifying the amount to be given in cash;

(b) state the method and date of valuation;

(c) contain a note by the independent person, or be accompanied by such a note, as to the matters mentioned in *section 1028(11)(a)* to *(c)*; and

(d) contain a note by the independent person, or be accompanied by such a note, that, on the basis of the valuation, the value of the consideration to be received by the PLC is not less than the value of the consideration to be given by it.

(7) If a PLC enters into an agreement with any relevant person in contravention of *subsection (1)* and either the relevant person has not received a report under this section or there has been some other contravention of this section or *section 1028(5)*, *(6)* or *(10)* which he or she knew or ought to have known amounted to a contravention, then, subject to *subsection (8)*—

(a) the PLC shall be entitled to recover from the relevant person, any consideration given by the PLC under the agreement or an amount equivalent to its value at the time of the agreement; and

(b) the agreement, so far as not carried out, shall be void.

(8) Where a PLC enters into an agreement in contravention of *subsection (1)* and that agreement is or includes an agreement for the allotment of shares in that PLC, then whether or not the agreement also contravenes *section 1028*—

(a) *subsection (7)* shall not apply to the agreement in so far as it is an agreement for the allotment of shares; and

(b) *sections 1025(3)* and *1029(2)* shall apply in relation to the shares as if they had been allotted in contravention of *section 1028*.

(9) Where a PLC contravenes any of the provisions of this section, the PLC and any officer of it who is in default shall be guilty of a category 3 offence.

1035 Supplemental provisions in relation to *section 1034*

(1) Any person carrying out a valuation or making a report under *section 1034* shall be entitled to require from the officers of the PLC such information and explanation as the person thinks necessary to enable him or her to carry out the valuation or make the report and provide the note required by that section.

(2) *Section 1030(4)* shall apply in relation to any such valuation and report as it applies in relation to a valuation and report under *section 1028* with the substitution of a reference to this subsection for the reference in *section 1030(5)* to *section 1030(1)*.

(3) A PLC which has passed a resolution under *section 1034* with respect to the transfer of an asset shall, within 15 days after the date of the passing of the resolution, deliver to the Registrar a copy of the resolution together with the report required by that section and, if the PLC fails to do so, the PLC and any officer of it who is in default shall be guilty of a category 4 offence.

(4) Any reference in *section 1034* or this section to consideration given for the transfer of an asset includes a reference to consideration given partly for its transfer but—

(a) the value of any consideration partly so given shall be taken to be the proportion of that consideration properly attributable to its transfer;

(b) the independent person shall carry out or arrange for such valuations of anything else as will enable him or her to determine that proportion; and

(c) his or her report under *section 1034* shall state what valuation has been made by virtue of *paragraph (b)* and also the reason for and method and date of any such valuation and any other matters which may be relevant to that determination.

[(5) Section 1034 and this section shall not have effect in respect of a company to which the resolution tools, powers or mechanisms provided for in Part 4 of the Bank Recovery and Resolution Regulations are applied or exercised.][a]

Amendments

a Subsection (5) inserted by European Union (Bank Recovery and Resolution) Regulations 2015, reg 189(8), with effect from 15 July 2015.

1036 Relief

(1) Where any person is liable to a PLC under *section 1025*, *1027*, *1028*, *1029* or *1034* in relation to payment in respect of any shares in the PLC or is liable by virtue of any undertaking given to the PLC in, or in connection with, payment for any such shares,

the person so liable may make an application to the court under this subsection to be exempted in whole or in part from that liability.

(2) Where the liability mentioned in *subsection (1)* arises under any of the foregoing sections in relation to payment in respect of any shares, the court may, on an application under that subsection, exempt the applicant from that liability only—

(a) if and to the extent that it appears to the court just and equitable to do so having regard to the following, namely:

(i) whether the applicant has paid, or is liable to pay, any amount in respect of any other liability arising in relation to those shares under any of the foregoing sections or of any liability arising by virtue of any undertaking given in or in connection with payment for those shares;

(ii) whether any person other than the applicant has paid or is likely to pay (whether in pursuance of an order of the court or otherwise) any such amount; and

(iii) whether the applicant or any other person has performed, in whole or in part, or is likely so to perform any such undertaking or has done or is likely to do any other thing in payment or part payment in respect of those shares;

(b) if and to the extent that it appears to the court just and equitable to do so in respect of any interest which he or she is liable to pay to the PLC under any of the foregoing sections.

(3) Where the liability mentioned in *subsection (1)* arises by virtue of an undertaking given to the PLC in or in connection with, payment for any shares in the PLC, the court may, on an application under that subsection, exempt the applicant from that liability only if and to the extent that it appears to the court just and equitable to do so having regard to the following, namely:

(a) whether the applicant has paid or is liable to pay any amount in respect of any liability arising in relation to those shares under *section 1025*, *1027*, *1028*, *1029* or *1034*; and

(b) whether any person other than the applicant has paid or is likely to pay (whether in pursuance of an order of the court or otherwise) any such amount.

(4) In determining in pursuance of an application under *subsection (1)* whether it should exempt the applicant in whole or in part from any liability, the court shall have regard to the following overriding principles, namely:

(a) that a PLC which has allotted shares should receive money or money's worth at least equal in value to the aggregate of the nominal value of those shares and the whole of any premium or, if the case so requires, so much of that aggregate as is treated as paid up; and

(b) subject to *paragraph (a)*, that where such a PLC would, if the court did not grant that exemption, have more than one remedy against a particular person, it should be for the PLC to decide which remedy it should remain entitled to pursue.

(5) Where a person brings any proceedings against another (the "contributor") for a contribution in respect of any liability to a company arising under any of *sections 1025* to *1029* and *1034* and it appears to the court that the contributor is liable to make such a contribution, the court may, if and to the extent that it appears to the court, having regard to the respective culpability in respect of the liability to the PLC of the contributor and the person bringing the proceedings, that it is just and equitable to do so—

(a) exempt the contributor in whole or in part from his or her liability to make such a contribution, or

(b) order the contributor to make a larger contribution than, but for this subsection, he or she would be liable to make.

(6) Where a person is liable to a PLC by virtue of *subsection (7)(a)* of *section 1034* the court may, on an application under this subsection, exempt that person in whole or in part from that liability if and to the extent that it appears to the court just and equitable to do so having regard to any benefit accruing to the PLC by virtue of anything done by that person towards the carrying out of the agreement mentioned in that *subsection (7)(a)*.

[(7) This section shall not have effect in respect of a company to which the resolution tools, powers or mechanisms provided for in Part 4 of the Bank Recovery and Resolution Regulations are applied or exercised.][a]

Amendments

a Subsection (7) inserted by European Union (Bank Recovery and Resolution) Regulations 2015, reg 189(9), with effect from 15 July 2015.

1037 Special provisions as to issue of shares to subscribers

(1) Any shares taken by a subscriber to the constitution of a PLC in pursuance of an undertaking of his or hers in the constitution and any premium on the shares shall be paid up in cash.

(2) If a PLC permits any such share to be paid up otherwise than in cash, the PLC and any officer of it who is in default shall be guilty of a category 3 offence.

1038 Enforceability of undertakings made in contravention of certain provisions of Chapter

Subject to *section 1036*—

(a) an undertaking given by any person in or in connection with payment for shares in a PLC to do work or perform services or to do any other thing shall, if it is enforceable by the PLC apart from this Part, be so enforceable notwithstanding that there has been a contravention in relation thereto of *section 1025*, *1027*, *1028* or *1029*; and

(b) where such an undertaking is given in contravention of *section 1034* or *1035* in respect of the allotment of any shares it shall be so enforceable notwithstanding that contravention.

1039 Adaptation of *section 102(1)* and *(2)* in relation to a PLC

Section 102(1) and *(2)* shall apply in relation to a PLC as if references in them to *Chapter 3* or *4* of *Part 9* were references to *Chapter 16* or, as the case may be, *Chapter 17* of this Part.

1040 Treatment of own shares held by or on behalf of a PLC

(1) Subject to *section 1041(5)*, this section applies to a PLC—

(a) where shares in the PLC are forfeited, or are surrendered to the PLC in lieu of forfeiture, in pursuance of *Part 3* or its constitution for failure to pay any sum payable in respect of those shares,

(b) where shares in the PLC are acquired by the PLC otherwise than by any of the methods mentioned in *section 102(1)* and the company has a beneficial interest in those shares,

(c) where the nominee of the PLC acquires shares in the PLC from a third person without financial assistance being given directly or indirectly by the PLC and the PLC has a beneficial interest in those shares, or

(d) where any person acquires shares in the PLC with financial assistance given to him or her directly or indirectly by the PLC for the purpose of the acquisition and the PLC has a beneficial interest in those shares.

(2) In determining for the purposes of *subsection (1)(b)* or *(c)* whether a PLC has a beneficial interest in any shares, there shall be disregarded, in any case where the PLC is a trustee (whether as personal representative or otherwise), any right of the PLC (as trustee) to recover its expenses or be remunerated out of the trust property.

(3) Unless the shares or any interest of the PLC in them are previously disposed of, the PLC shall, not later than the end of the relevant period after the date of their forfeiture or surrender or, in a case to which *subsection (1)(b)*, *(c)* or *(d)* applies, their acquisition—

(a) cancel them and reduce the amount of the share capital by the nominal value of the shares, and

(b) where the effect of cancelling the shares will be that the nominal value of the PLC's allotted share capital is brought below the authorised minimum, apply for re-registration as another type of company, stating the effect of the cancellation,

and the directors may take such steps as are requisite to enable the PLC to carry out its obligations under this subsection without complying with *sections 84* and *85*, including passing a resolution in accordance with *subsection (5)*.

(4) The PLC and, in a case falling within *subsection (1)(c)* or *(d)*, the PLC's nominee or, as the case may be, the other shareholder, shall not exercise any voting rights in respect of the shares and any purported exercise of those rights shall be void.

(5) The resolution authorised by *subsection (3)* may alter the PLC's constitution so that it no longer states that the company is to be a PLC and may make such other alterations in the constitution as are requisite in the circumstances.

(6) Without prejudice to the generality of *subsection (5)*, where the resultant company type is a private company limited by shares, the alteration referred to in that subsection shall include the replacement of the memorandum and articles of the re-registering company by a constitution in conformity with *section 19* and *Schedule 1* (but nothing in this section authorises the alteration of the rights and obligations of members of the re-registering company, or of other persons, as set out in its memorandum and articles and, accordingly, where necessary, the foregoing replacement constitution shall include such supplemental regulations as will secure those rights and obligations).

(7) The application for re-registration required by *subsection (3)(b)* shall be in the prescribed form and signed by a director or secretary of the PLC and shall be delivered to the Registrar together with a copy of the constitution of the PLC as altered by the resolution.

(8) If a PLC required to apply to be re-registered as another type of company under this section, fails to do so before the end of the relevant period, *section 68* shall apply to it as if it were a private company limited by shares, but, subject to that, the company shall continue to be treated for the purposes of this Act as a PLC until it is re-registered as another form of company.

(9) If a PLC, when required to do so by *subsection (3)*, fails to cancel any shares in accordance with *paragraph (a)* of that subsection or to make an application for re-registration in accordance with *paragraph (b)* of that subsection, the PLC and any officer of it who is in default shall be guilty of a category 3 offence.

(10) In addition to the resolutions which *subsection (4)* of that section provides that that section applies to, *section 198* shall apply to resolutions of the directors of a PLC passed by virtue of *subsection (3)*.

1041 Supplemental provisions in relation to *section 1040* (including definition of "relevant period")

(1) If the Registrar is satisfied that a PLC is required to be re-registered in accordance with *section 1040*, the Registrar shall—

(a) retain the application and other documents delivered to him or her under *subsection (7)* of that section; and

(b) issue to the company an appropriate certificate of incorporation.

(2) Upon the issue of a certificate of incorporation under *subsection (1)*—

(a) the company shall, by virtue of the issue of that certificate, become the type of company stated in the certificate; and

(b) the alterations in the constitution set out in the resolution shall take effect accordingly.

(3) A certificate of incorporation issued to a company under *subsection (1)* shall be conclusive evidence—

(a) that the requirements of *section 1040* and this section in respect of re-registration and of matters precedent and incidental thereto have been complied with; and

(b) that the company is the type of company stated in the certificate.

(4) *Section 1285(9)* shall apply to a re-registration pursuant to *section 1040* as it applies to a re-registration pursuant to *Part 20*.

(5) Where, after shares in a company—

(a) are forfeited, or are surrendered to the company in lieu of forfeiture, in pursuance of *Part 3* or its constitution or are otherwise acquired by the company;

(b) are acquired by a nominee of the company in the circumstances mentioned in *section 1040(1)(c)* (and the references in that provision to a PLC shall, for the purposes of this paragraph, be read as references to a company); or

(c) are acquired by any person in the circumstances mentioned in *section 1040(1)(d)* (and the references in that provision to a PLC shall, for the purposes of this paragraph, be read as references to a company);

the company is re-registered as a PLC, *section 1040* and the foregoing provisions of this section shall apply to the company as if it had been a PLC at the time of the forfeiture, surrender or acquisition and as if for any reference to the relevant period after the date of the forfeiture, surrender or acquisition there were substituted a reference to the relevant period after the date of the re-registration of the company as a PLC.

(6) *Section 104(1)* shall not apply to shares acquired otherwise than by subscription by a nominee of a PLC in a case falling within *section 1040(1)(d)*.

(7) In *section 1040* and this section "relevant period", in relation to any shares, means—

(a) in the case of shares forfeited or surrendered to the company in lieu of forfeiture or acquired as mentioned in *section 1040(1)(b)* or *(c)* — 3 years;

(b) in the case of shares acquired as mentioned in *section 1040(1)(d)* — one year.

1042 Charges taken by PLC on own shares

(1) A mortgage, charge, lien or pledge of a PLC on its own shares (whether taken expressly or otherwise), except a mortgage or charge permitted by *subsection (2)*, is void.

(2) The following are permitted mortgages and charges, that is to say:

(a) in the case of every description of PLC, a mortgage or charge on its own shares (not being fully paid) for any amount payable in respect of the shares;

(b) in the case of a PLC whose ordinary business includes the lending of money or consists of the provision of credit or the bailment or hiring of goods under a hire-purchase agreement, or both, a mortgage or charge of the PLC on its own shares (whether fully paid or not) which arises in connection with a transaction entered into by the company in the ordinary course of its business;

(c) in the case of a company which is re-registered under *Part 20* as a PLC, a mortgage or charge on its own shares which was in existence immediately before its application for re-registration.

1043 Application of certain provisions of *section 82(6)* in relation to PLCs

(1) Without prejudice to *subsections (2)* to *(4)*, in its application to a PLC giving financial assistance, *section 82(6)* shall apply—

(a) as if, in *paragraph (k)*, "of it or its holding company" were substituted for "of its holding company";

(b) as if, in *paragraph (m)*, "by an offeree (within the meaning of the Irish Takeover Panel Act 1997) or a private limited subsidiary of an offeree" were substituted for "by a private limited subsidiary of an offeree (within the meaning of the Irish Takeover Panel Act 1997)"; and

(c) as if the following paragraph were substituted for *paragraph (n)*:

> "(n) in connection with an allotment of shares by a company or its holding company, the payment by the company of commissions, not exceeding 10 per cent of the money received in respect of such allotment, to intermediaries, and the payment by the company of professional fees;".

(2) Subject to *subsection (3)*, *section 82(6)(a)* shall not apply to a PLC.

(3) In either of the following 2 cases, namely:

(a) a case in which the giving of particular financial assistance by a company (not being a PLC) has been authorised by the company's use of the Summary Approval Procedure; or

(b) a case in which, before the commencement of this section, the giving of particular financial assistance by an existing company (not being a PLC) has been authorised by the company's use of the procedure contained in subsection (2) of section 60 of the Act of 1963 (and that subsection and subsections (3) to (11) of that section shall remain in force for the purposes of the particular transaction and for the purposes of, and incidental to, the court's jurisdiction to cancel the special resolution concerned);

and—

(i) following such authorisation, the company has applied to re-register, and has re-registered (whether under the prior Companies Acts or *Part 20*), as a PLC; and

(ii) save where, by reason of the operation of *Chapter 7* of *Part 4* or, as the case may be, the foregoing subsections (3) to (11), the particular transaction may not be proceeded with;

then the giving by the PLC of the financial assistance (pursuant to the foregoing authority) shall be lawful.

(4) A PLC may, in accordance with *paragraph (e)*, *(f)* or *(g)* of *section 82(6)*, give financial assistance to any person only if the PLC's net assets are not thereby reduced or, to the extent that those assets are thereby reduced, if the financial assistance is provided out of profits which are available for distribution.

(5) In *subsection (4)* "net assets" means the aggregate of the PLC's assets less the aggregate of its liabilities; and "liabilities" includes—

(a) where the PLC prepares Companies Act entity financial statements, any provision for liabilities (within the meaning of [*paragraph 80* of *Schedule 3* or *paragraph 65* of *Schedule 3A*, as the case may be][a]) that is made in those financial statements;

(b) where the PLC prepares IFRS entity financial statements, any provision that is made in those financial statements;

except to the extent that that provision is taken into account in calculating the value of any asset to the PLC.

Amendments

a Words substituted by C(A)A 2017, s 90(f) (previously: "*paragraph 82* of *Schedule 3*").

1044 Variation of rights attached to special classes of shares

Section 982 shall apply to a PLC as if—

(a) each reference in it to a DAC were a reference to a PLC; and

(b) in *subsection (3)(c)*—

(i) the reference to the giving, variation, revocation or renewal of an authority for the purposes of *section 69(1)* were a reference to the giving, variation, revocation or renewal of an authority for the purposes of *section 1021(1)*; and

(ii) "by the means referred to in *section 84(2)(b)*" were substituted for "by either of the means referred to in *section 84*".

1045 Restriction on transfer of shares

Section 95(2) shall not apply in respect of a transfer of shares in a PLC where those shares fall within a class of securities the evidencing and transfer of title to which is for the time being governed by, as appropriate—

(a) regulations under *section 1086*, or

(b) for so long as they remain in force (including for any period as they may stand amended by regulations under *section 1086*), the Companies Act 1990 (Uncertificated Securities) Regulations 1996 (S.I. No. 68 of 1996).

Chapter 4
Interests in shares: disclosure of individual and group acquisitions

1046 Purpose of Chapter

The purpose of this Chapter is to require the disclosure to a PLC (and the keeping of a register by the PLC as to the matters disclosed) of the following facts, and certain associated particulars, namely:

(a) the fact of there being acquired an interest in shares of the PLC (being shares with full voting rights) of an amount that is equal to or above a specified percentage — see, principally, *sections 1048* and *1049*;

(b) the fact of there no longer being held an interest in shares of the PLC (of the foregoing kind) of an amount that is equal to or above a specified percentage — see, principally, *sections 1048* and *1049*;

(c) the fact of there being acquired, or there no longer being held, an interest in shares of the PLC (of the foregoing kind) where, in consequence of either such event, the percentage levels of the interest (in terms of whole number of percentages) in the shares before and immediately after that event are not the same — see, principally, *sections 1048* and *1049*; and

(d) facts relevant to the application of the provisions of this Chapter as they require a disclosure of the kind described in a preceding paragraph, for example, the fact that full voting rights have, by virtue of a condition being satisfied, become attached to the shares in which the interests concerned exist – see, principally, *sections 1048* and *1050*;

and this Chapter—

(i) includes provisions for reckoning the interest of a spouse, civil partner or child of the person concerned, or a body corporate controlled by any of them, as an interest of that person and for reckoning, as an interest of the person concerned, the interest of another who is party with that person to a particular type of agreement;

(ii) may limit the duty of disclosure to circumstances in which the person concerned has become aware of the relevant facts; and

(iii) in addition to the various foregoing requirements, enables or, in certain cases requires, a PLC to conduct an investigation into whether interests are, or within a certain period have been, held in its shares that carry full voting rights.

1047 Interpretation and supplemental (Chapter 4)

(1) In this Chapter—

"child" does not include a person who has attained the age of majority;

"duty of disclosure" shall be read in accordance with *section 1048* or *1050(1)*, as appropriate;

"notifiable percentage" has the meaning given to it by *section 1052*;

"relevant share capital", in relation to a PLC, means the PLC's issued share capital of a class carrying rights to vote in all circumstances at general meetings of the PLC.

(2) It is declared for the avoidance of doubt that—

(a) where a PLC's relevant share capital is divided into different classes of shares, references in this Chapter to a percentage of the nominal value of its relevant share capital are references to a percentage of the nominal value of the issued shares comprised in each of the classes taken separately, and

(b) the temporary suspension of voting rights in respect of shares comprised in issued share capital of a PLC of any such class does not affect the application of this Chapter in relation to interests in those or any other shares comprised in that class.

(3) The application of this Chapter is restricted, as was the position in the case of the corresponding provisions of the Act of 1990, by the regulations made under section 20 of the Investment Funds, Companies and Miscellaneous Provisions Act 2006 that are referred to in *paragraph 11* of *Schedule 6*.

1048 Duty of disclosure — first class of case in which duty arises

Where a person either—

(a) to the person's knowledge acquires an interest in shares comprised in a PLC's relevant share capital, or ceases to be interested in shares so comprised (whether or not retaining an interest in other shares so comprised), or

(b) becomes aware that he or she has acquired an interest in shares so comprised or that he or she has ceased to be interested in shares so comprised in which he or she was previously interested,

then, if—

(i) the interest in the shares is a notifiable interest as provided for in *section 1049(2)*, and

(ii) the case concerned falls within *section 1049(4)* or *(5)*,

the person shall be under a duty (in this Chapter referred to as the "duty of disclosure") to make notification to the PLC of the interests which the person has, or had, in its shares.

1049 Notifiable interest

(1) For the purposes of the duty of disclosure, the interests to be taken into account are those in relevant share capital of the PLC concerned; *section 1059* has effect (by means of its applying certain provisions of *Chapter 5* of *Part 5*) for the purpose of determining whether a particular interest in shares is an interest in shares that is to be reckoned in applying the next following subsection.

(2) For the purposes of this Chapter, a person has a notifiable interest at any time when the person is interested in shares comprised in that share capital of an aggregate nominal value equal to or more than the percentage of the nominal value of that share capital which is for the time being the notifiable percentage.

(3) All facts relevant to determining whether a person has a notifiable interest at any time (or the percentage level of the person's interest) are taken to be what he or she knows the facts to be at that time.

(4) The duty of disclosure arises under *section 1048* where the person has a notifiable interest immediately after the relevant time, but did not have such an interest immediately before that time.

(5) The duty of disclosure also arises under *section 1048* where—

(a) the person had a notifiable interest immediately before the relevant time, but does not have such an interest immediately after it, or

(b) the person had a notifiable interest immediately before that time, and has such an interest immediately after it, but the percentage levels of his or her interest immediately before and immediately after that time are not the same.

(6) For the purposes of this section, the "relevant time" means—

(a) in a case falling within *section 1048(a)* — the time of the event there mentioned, and

(b) in a case falling within *section 1048(b)* — the time at which the person became aware of the facts in question.

1050 Duty of disclosure — second class of case in which duty arises

(1) Where, otherwise than in circumstances falling within *section 1048*, a person—

(a) is aware at the time when it occurs of any change of circumstances affecting facts relevant to the application of *section 1049(2)* to an existing interest of his or hers in shares comprised in a PLC's share capital of any description, or

(b) otherwise becomes aware of any such facts (whether or not arising from any such change of circumstances),

then, if the case concerned falls within *subsection (2)*, the person shall be under a duty (in this Chapter also referred to as the "duty of disclosure") to make notification to the PLC of those circumstances or facts.

(2) The duty of disclosure arises under this section where the person has a notifiable interest immediately after the relevant time, but did not have such an interest immediately before that time.

(3) For the purposes of this section, the "relevant time" means—

(a) in a case falling within *subsection (1)(a)* — the time of the change of circumstances there mentioned, and

(b) in a case falling within *subsection (1)(b)* — the time at which the person became aware of the facts in question.

1051 "Percentage level" in relation to notifiable interests

(1) Subject to *subsection (2)*, in this Chapter "percentage level" means the percentage figure found by expressing the aggregate nominal value of all the shares comprised in the share capital concerned in which the person is interested immediately before or (as the case may be) immediately after the relevant time as a percentage of the

nominal value of that share capital and rounding that figure down, if it is not a whole number, to the next whole number.

(2) Where the nominal value of the share capital is greater immediately after the relevant time than it was immediately before, the percentage level of the person's interest immediately before (as well as immediately after) that time is determined by reference to the larger amount.

1052 The notifiable percentage

(1) In this Chapter "notifiable percentage" means—

(a) subject to *paragraph (b)*, 3 per cent; or

(b) such other rate as may be specified by order made by the Minister under *subsection (2)*.

(2) The Minister may, by order, specify the percentage to apply in determining whether a person's interest in a PLC's shares is notifiable under this Chapter; and different percentages may be so specified in relation to public limited companies of different classes or descriptions.

(3) Where — in consequence of a reduction specified under this section in the percentage made by such order — a person's interest in a PLC's shares becomes notifiable, the person shall then come under the duty of disclosure in respect of it; and the duty shall be performed within the period of 10 days after the day on which it arises.

1053 Particulars to be contained in notification

(1) Subject to *section 1052(3)*, a person's duty to make a notification under *section 1048* or *1050* shall be performed within the period of 5 days after the day on which the duty arises; and the notification shall be in writing to the PLC.

(2) The notification shall specify the share capital to which it relates, and shall also—

(a) state the number of shares comprised in that share capital in which the person making the notification knows he or she was interested immediately after the time when the duty arose, or

(b) in a case where the person no longer has a notifiable interest in shares comprised in that share capital, state that he or she no longer has that interest.

(3) A notification with respect to a person's interest in a PLC's relevant share capital (other than one stating that he or she no longer has a notifiable interest in shares comprised in that share capital) shall include particulars of—

(a) the identity of each registered holder of shares to which the notification relates, and

(b) the number of those shares held by each such registered holder,

so far as known to the person making the notification at the date when the notification is made.

(4) A person who has an interest in shares comprised in a PLC's relevant share capital, that interest being notifiable, is under a duty to notify the PLC in writing—

(a) of any particulars in relation to those shares which are specified in *subsection (3)*, and

(b) of any change in those particulars,

of which, in either case, the person becomes aware at any time after any interest notification date and before the first occasion following that date on which the person comes under any further duty of disclosure with respect to his or her interest in shares comprised in that share capital.

(5) A duty arising under *subsection (4)* shall be performed within the period of 5 days after the day on which it arises.

(6) The reference in *subsection (4)* to an interest notification date, in relation to a person's interest in shares comprised in a PLC's relevant share capital, is to either of the following:

(a) the date of any notification made by the person with respect to his or her interest under this Chapter; or

(b) where the person has failed to make a notification, the date on which the period allowed for making it came to an end.

(7) A person who at any time has an interest in shares which is notifiable is to be regarded under *subsection (4)* as continuing to have a notifiable interest in them unless and until the person comes under a duty to make a notification stating that he or she no longer has such an interest in those shares.

1054 Notification of family and corporate interests

(1) For the purposes of *sections 1047* to *1053*, a person is taken to be interested in any shares in which the person's spouse or civil partner or any child of the person is interested.

(2) For the purposes of *sections 1047* to *1053* and *subsection (1)*, a person is taken to be interested in shares if a body corporate is interested in them and—

(a) that body or its directors are accustomed to act in accordance with his or her directions or instructions, or

(b) he or she is entitled to exercise or control the exercise of one-third or more of the voting power at general meetings of that body corporate.

(3) Where a person is entitled to exercise or control the exercise of one-third or more of the voting power at general meetings of a body corporate and that body corporate is entitled to exercise or control the exercise of any of the voting power at general meetings of another body corporate (the "effective voting power") then, for the purposes of *subsection (2)(b)*, the effective voting power is taken as exercisable by that person.

(4) For the purposes of *subsections (2)* and *(3)* a person is entitled to exercise or control the exercise of voting power if—

(a) the person has a right (whether subject to conditions or not) the exercise of which would make him or her so entitled, or

(b) the person is under an obligation (whether or not so subject) the fulfilment of which would make him or her so entitled.

(5) A reference in this section to a child of a person shall be deemed to include a reference to a child of the person's civil partner who is ordinarily resident with the person and the civil partner.

1055 "Share acquisition agreement" — meaning

(1) Subject to the following provisions of this section, "share acquisition agreement", for the purposes of this Chapter, means an agreement between 2 or more persons which includes provision for the acquisition by any one or more of the parties to the agreement of interests in shares comprised in relevant share capital of a particular PLC (the "target company") but only if the following 2 conditions are satisfied.

(2) Those conditions are—

(a) the agreement also includes provisions imposing obligations or restrictions on any one or more of the parties to the agreement with respect to their use, retention or disposal of interests in that company's shares acquired in pursuance of the agreement (whether or not together with any other interests of theirs in that company's shares to which the agreement relates); and

(b) any interest in the company's shares is in fact acquired by any of the parties in pursuance of the agreement.

(3) In relation to such an agreement references in this section and in *sections 1056* and *1057* to the target company are to the company which is the target company for that agreement in accordance with this section.

(4) The reference in *subsection (2)(a)* to the use of interests in shares in the target company is to the exercise of any rights or of any control or influence arising from those interests (including the right to enter into any agreement for the exercise, or for control of the exercise, of any of those rights by another person).

(5) Once any interest in shares in the target company has been acquired in pursuance of such an agreement as is mentioned in *subsection (1)*, the agreement continues to be a share acquisition agreement for the purposes of this Chapter irrespective of—

(a) whether or not any further acquisitions of interests in the company's shares take place in pursuance of the agreement; and

(b) any change in the persons who are for the time being parties to it; and

(c) any variation of the agreement, so long as the agreement continues to include provisions of any description mentioned in *subsection (2)(a)*.

(6) References in *subsection (5)* to the agreement include any agreement having effect (whether directly or indirectly) in substitution for the original agreement.

(7) In this section, and also in references elsewhere in this Chapter to a share acquisition agreement as defined by this section, "agreement" includes any agreement or arrangement; and references in this section to provisions of an agreement—

(a) accordingly include undertakings, expectations or understandings operative under any arrangement; and

(b) (without prejudice to the foregoing) also include any provisions, whether express or implied and whether absolute or not.

(8) Neither of the following is a share acquisition agreement for the purposes of this Chapter:

(a) an agreement which is not legally binding unless it involves mutuality in the undertakings, expectations or understandings of the parties to it;

(b) an agreement to underwrite or sub-underwrite any offer of shares in a company, provided the agreement is confined to that purpose and any matters incidental to it.

1056 Duties of disclosure arising in consequence of *section 1055*

(1) In the case of a share acquisition agreement, each party to the agreement shall be taken (for purposes of the duty of disclosure) to be interested in all shares in the target company in which any other party to it is interested apart from the agreement (whether or not the interest of the other party in question was acquired, or includes any interest which was acquired, in pursuance of the agreement).

(2) For those purposes, and also for those of *section 1057*, an interest of a party to such an agreement in shares in the target company is an interest apart from the agreement if the party is interested in those shares otherwise than by virtue of the application of *section 1055* and this section in relation to the agreement.

(3) Accordingly, any such interest of the person (apart from the agreement) includes for those purposes any interest treated as his or hers under *section 1054* or by the application of *section 1055* and this section in relation to any other agreement with respect to shares in the target company to which he or she is a party.

(4) A notification with respect to his or her interest in shares in the target company made to that company under this Chapter by a person who is for the time being a party to a share acquisition agreement shall—

(a) state that the person making the notification is a party to such an agreement;

(b) include the names and (so far as known to the person) the addresses of the other parties to the agreement, identifying them as such; and

(c) state whether or not any of the shares to which the notification relates are shares in which the person is interested by virtue of *section 1055* and this section and, if so, the number of those shares.

(5) Where a person makes a notification to a PLC under this Chapter in consequence of ceasing to be interested in any shares of that PLC by virtue of the fact that he or she or any other person has ceased to be a party to a share acquisition agreement, the notification shall include a statement that he or she or that other person has ceased to be a party to the agreement (as the case may require) and also (in the latter case) the name and (if known to him or her) the address of that other.

1057 Duty of persons acting together to keep each other informed

(1) A person who is a party to a share acquisition agreement shall be subject to the requirements of this section at any time when—

(a) the target company is a PLC, and the person knows it to be so; and
(b) the shares in that company to which the agreement relates consist of or include shares comprised in relevant share capital of the company, and the person knows that to be the case; and
(c) the person knows the facts which make the agreement a share acquisition agreement.

(2) Such a person shall be under a duty to notify every other party to the agreement, in writing, of the relevant particulars of his or her interest (if any) apart from the agreement in shares comprised in relevant share capital of the target company—

(a) on the person's first becoming subject to the requirements of this section; and
(b) on each occurrence after that time while the person is still subject to those requirements of any event or circumstances within *section 1048* or *1050* (as it applies to the person's case otherwise than by reference to interests treated as his or hers under *section 1056* as applying to that agreement).

(3) The relevant particulars to be notified under *subsection (2)* are—

(a) the number of shares (if any) comprised in the target company's relevant share capital in which the person giving the notice would be required to state his or her interest if he or she were under the duty of disclosure with respect to that interest (apart from the agreement) immediately after the time when the obligation to give notice under *subsection (2)* arose; and
(b) the relevant particulars with respect to the registered ownership of those shares, so far as known to the person at the date of the notice.

(4) A person who is for the time being subject to the requirements of this section shall be under a duty to notify every other party to the agreement, in writing—

(a) of any relevant particulars with respect to the registered ownership of any shares comprised in relevant share capital of the target company in which he or she is interested apart from the agreement, and
(b) of any change in those particulars,

of which, in either case, the person becomes aware at any time after any interest notification date and before the first occasion following that date on which the person becomes subject to any further duty to give notice under *subsection (2)* with respect to his or her interest in shares comprised in that share capital.

(5) The reference in *subsection (4)* to an interest notification date, in relation to a person's interest in shares comprised in the target company's relevant share capital, is to either of the following:

(a) the date of any notice given by the person with respect to his or her interest under *subsection (2)*; and

(b) where the person has failed to give that notice, the date on which the period allowed by this section for giving the notice came to an end.

(6) A person who is a party to a share acquisition agreement shall be under a duty to notify each other party to the agreement, in writing, of his or her current address—

(a) on the person's first becoming subject to the requirements of this section, and

(b) on any change in his or her address occurring after that time and while he or she is still subject to those requirements.

(7) A reference in this section to the relevant particulars with respect to the registered ownership of shares is a reference to such particulars in relation to those shares as are mentioned in *section 1053(3)(a)* or *(b)*.

(8) A person's duty to give any notice required by this section to any other person shall be performed within the period of 5 days after the day on which that duty arose.

1058 Interest in shares by attribution

(1) Where *section 1048* refers to a person acquiring an interest in shares or ceasing to be interested in shares, that reference in certain cases includes the person's becoming or ceasing to be interested in those shares by virtue of another person's interest.

(2) This section applies where the person (the "first-mentioned person") becomes or ceases to be interested by virtue of *section 1054* or (as the case may be) *section 1056* whether—

(a) by virtue of the fact that the person who is interested in the shares becomes or ceases to be a person whose interests (if any) fall by virtue of either section to be treated as the first-mentioned person's; or

(b) in consequence of the fact that such a person has become or ceased to be interested in the shares; or

(c) in consequence of the fact that the first-mentioned person himself or herself becomes or ceases to be a party to a share acquisition agreement to which the person interested in the shares is for the time being a party; or

(d) in consequence of the fact that an agreement to which both the first-mentioned person and that person are parties becomes or ceases to be a share acquisition agreement.

(3) The person shall be treated under *section 1048* as knowing he or she has acquired an interest in the shares or (as the case may be) that he or she has ceased to be interested in them, if and when the person knows both—

(a) the relevant facts with respect to the other person's interest in the shares; and

(b) the relevant facts by virtue of which the person himself or herself has become or ceased to be interested in them in accordance with *section 1054* or *1056*.

(4) The person shall be deemed to know the relevant facts referred to in *subsection (3)(a)* if the person knows (whether contemporaneously or not) either of the subsistence of the other person's interest at any material time or of the fact that the other has become or ceased to be interested in the shares at any such time; and in this

subsection "material time" means any time at which the other's interests (if any) fall or fell to be treated as his or hers under *section 1054* or *1056*.

(5) A person shall be regarded as knowing of the subsistence of another's interest in shares or (as the case may be) that another has become or ceased to be interested in shares if the person has been notified under *section 1057* of facts with respect to the other's interest which indicate that he or she is or has become or ceased to be interested in the shares (whether on his or her own account or by virtue of a third party's interest in them).

1059 Interest in shares that are notifiable interests for purposes of Chapter

(1) *Sections 257* to *260* shall, with the adaptations and modifications in this section, apply for the purposes of determining whether a particular interest in shares is an interest that is notifiable under this Chapter and, for the purpose of those adaptations, the expression "reckonable interest" means such an interest that is so notifiable.

(2) The adaptations of *sections 257* to *260* are—

(a) for each reference in them to disclosable interest there shall be substituted a reference to reckonable interest,

(b) references in them to debentures shall be disregarded.

(3) *Section 260* shall have effect as if—

(a) the existing section were re-numbered as *subsection (1)* thereof,

(b) the following paragraphs were substituted for *paragraph (h)* of that subsection:

"(h) an exempt security interest;

(i) an interest of the President of the High Court subsisting by virtue of section 13 of the Succession Act 1965;

(j) an interest of the Accountant of the High Court in shares held by him or her in accordance with rules of court;

(k) such interests, or interests of such a class, as may be prescribed for purposes of this section.";

and

(c) the following subsection were added:

"(2) An interest in shares is an exempt security interest for the purposes of *subsection (1)(h)* if—

(a) it is held by—

(i) a credit institution, or an insurance undertaking within the meaning of *Part 6*;

(ii) a trustee savings bank (within the meaning of the (Trustee Savings Banks Act 1989)) or a Post Office Savings Bank within the meaning of the Post Office Savings Bank Acts 1861 to 1958; or

(iii) a member of an authorised market operator carrying on business as a stockbroker;

and

(b) it is held by way of security only for the purposes of a transaction entered into by the body or other person concerned in the ordinary course of business of such body or other person.".

1060 Enforcement of notification obligation

(1) Where a person authorises any other person (the "agent") to acquire or dispose of, on his or her behalf, interests in shares comprised in relevant share capital of a PLC, the person shall secure that the agent notifies him or her immediately of acquisitions or disposals of interests in shares so comprised effected by the agent which will or may give rise to any duty on the person's part to make a notification under this Chapter with respect to his or her interest in that share capital.

(2) An obligation to make any notification imposed on any person by this Chapter shall be treated as not being fulfilled unless the notice by means of which it purports to be fulfilled identifies the person and gives his or her address, and in a case where the person is a director or secretary of the PLC, is expressed to be given in fulfilment of that obligation.

(3) Subject to the subsequent provisions of this section, where a person fails to fulfil, within the period specified by this Chapter in that behalf, a duty to which he or she is, by virtue of *section 1048*, *1050* or *1057*, subject, no right or interest of any kind whatsoever in respect of any shares in the PLC concerned, held by the person, shall be enforceable by the person, whether directly or indirectly, by action or legal proceeding.

(4) Where any right or interest is restricted under *subsection (3)*—

(a) any person in default as is mentioned in that subsection or any other person affected by such restriction may apply to the court for relief against a disability imposed by or arising out of that subsection;

(b) the court, on being satisfied that the default was accidental or due to inadvertence or some other sufficient cause or that on other grounds it is just and equitable to grant relief, may grant such relief either generally or as respects any particular right or interest, on such terms and conditions as it sees fit;

(c) where an applicant for relief under this subsection is a person referred to in *subsection (3)*, the court may not grant such relief if it appears that the default has arisen as a result of any deliberate act or omission on the part of the applicant.

(5) *Subsection (3)* shall not apply to a duty relating to a person ceasing to be interested in shares in any PLC.

(6) A person who fails without reasonable excuse to comply with *subsection (1)* shall be guilty of a category 3 offence.

(7) A person who fails to fulfil, within the period specified by this Chapter in that behalf, a duty to which he or she is, by virtue of *section 1048*, *1050* or *1057*, subject, shall be guilty of a category 3 offence.

(8) In any proceedings in respect of an offence under *subsection (7)* consisting of a failure by a person to fulfil, within the period specified by this Chapter in that behalf, a duty to which the person is, by virtue of *section 1057*, subject, it shall be a defence to prove that it was not possible for the person to give the notice to the other person concerned required by that section within that period, and either—

(a) that it has not since become possible for him or her to give the notice so required; or

(b) that he or she gave that notice as soon after the end of that period as it became possible for him or her to do so.

1061 Individual and group acquisitions register

(1) A PLC shall keep a register (the "individual and group acquisitions register") for the purposes of *sections 1048* to *1053*.

(2) Whenever the PLC receives information from a person in consequence of the fulfilment of a duty to which he or she is, by virtue of any of those sections, subject, the PLC shall enter in the individual and group acquisitions register, against that person's name, that information and the date of the entry.

(3) Without prejudice to *subsection (2)*, where a PLC receives a notification under any of *sections 1048* to *1053* which includes a statement that the person making the notification, or any other person, has ceased to be a party to a share acquisition agreement, the PLC shall record that information against the name of that person in every place where the person's name appears in the individual and group acquisitions register as a party to that agreement (including any entry relating to that person made against another person's name).

(4) An obligation imposed by *subsection (2)* or *(3)* on a PLC shall be fulfilled within the period of 3 days after the day on which it arises.

(5) The nature and extent of an interest recorded in the individual and group acquisitions register of a person in any shares shall, if he or she so requires, be recorded in that register.

(6) A PLC shall not, by virtue of anything done for the purposes of this section, be affected with notice of, or put upon enquiry as to, the rights of any person in relation to any shares.

(7) The individual and group acquisitions register shall be so made up that the entries in it against the several names inscribed in it appear in chronological order.

(8) Unless the forgoing register is in such form as to constitute in itself an index, the PLC shall keep an index of the names entered in it which shall, in respect of each name, contain a sufficient indication to enable the information inscribed against it to be readily found; and the PLC shall, within 10 days after the date on which a name is entered in the register, make any necessary alteration in the index.

(9) If the PLC ceases to be a PLC it shall continue to keep the individual and group acquisitions register and any associated index until the end of the period of 6 years beginning after the date on which it ceases to be a PLC.

(10) If default is made by a PLC (or, in the case of *subsection (9)* by the company that it has re-registered as) in complying with any of the provisions of this section, the PLC (or the other company, as the case may be) and any officer of it who is in default shall be guilty of a category 3 offence.

1062 Company investigations concerning interests in shares

(1) A PLC may, by notice in writing, require a person whom the PLC knows or has reasonable cause to believe to be, or at any time during the 3 years immediately preceding the date on which the notice is issued, to have been, interested in shares comprised in the PLC's relevant share capital—

(a) to confirm that fact or (as the case may be) to indicate whether or not it is the case; and

(b) where he or she holds or has during that time held an interest in shares so comprised, to give such further information as may be required in accordance with *subsection (2)*.

(2) A notice under this section may require the person to whom it is addressed—

(a) to give particulars of the person's own past or present interest in shares comprised in relevant share capital of the PLC (held by him or her at any time during the 3 year period mentioned in *subsection (1)*);

(b) where—

(i) the interest is a present interest and any other interest in the shares subsists;

or

(ii) in any case, where another interest in the shares subsisted during that 3 year period at any time when the person's own interest subsisted;

to give (so far as lies within his or her knowledge) such particulars with respect to that other interest as may be required by the notice;

(c) where the person's interest is a past interest, to give (so far as lies within his or her knowledge) particulars of the identity of the person who held that interest immediately upon his or her ceasing to hold it.

(3) The particulars referred to in *subsection (2)(a)* and *(b)* include particulars of the identity of persons interested in the shares in question and of whether persons interested in the same shares are or were parties to a share acquisition agreement or to any agreement or arrangement relating to the exercise of any rights conferred by the holding of the shares.

(4) A notice under this section shall require any information given in response to the notice to be given in writing within such reasonable time as may be specified in the notice.

(5) *Sections 257* to *259* (as adapted by *section 1059*) apply for the purpose of construing references in this section to persons interested in shares and to interests in shares respectively, as they apply for the purposes mentioned in *section 1059* (but with the omission of any reference to *section 260*).

(6) This section applies in relation to a person who has or previously had, or is or was entitled to acquire, a right to subscribe for shares in a PLC which would on issue be comprised in relevant share capital of that PLC as it applies in relation to a person who is or was interested in shares so comprised; and references in this section to an interest in shares so comprised and to shares so comprised are to be read accordingly in any such case as including, respectively, any such right and shares which would on issue be so comprised.

1063 Registration of interest disclosed under *section 1062*

(1) Whenever, in pursuance of a requirement imposed on a person under *section 1062*, a PLC receives information to which this section applies relating to shares comprised in its relevant share capital, the PLC shall enter against the name of the registered holder of those shares, in a separate part of the register kept by it under *section 1061*—

(a) the fact that the requirement was imposed and the date on which it was imposed, and

(b) any information to which this section applies received in pursuance of the requirement.

(2) This section applies to any information received in pursuance of a requirement imposed by *section 1062* which relates to the present interests held by any persons in shares comprised in relevant share capital of the PLC in question.

(3) *Subsections (4)* to *(10)* of *section 1061* apply in relation to any part of the register maintained in accordance with *subsection (1)* of this section, reading references to *subsection (2)* of that section to include *subsection (1)* of this section.

1064 Company investigations on requisition by members

(1) A PLC may be required to exercise its powers under *section 1062* on the requisition of members of the PLC holding at the date of the deposit of the requisition not less than one-tenth of such of the paid-up capital of the company as carries at that date the right of voting at general meetings of the company.

(2) The requisition shall—

(a) state that the requisitionists are requiring the PLC to exercise its powers under *section 1062*;

(b) specify the manner in which they require those powers to be exercised; and

(c) give reasonable grounds for requiring the PLC to exercise those powers in the manner specified;

and shall be signed by the requisitionists and deposited at the PLC's registered office.

(3) The requisition may consist of several documents in like form each signed by one or more requisitionists.

(4) On the deposit of a requisition complying with this section, the PLC shall exercise its powers under *section 1062* in the manner specified in the requisition.

(5) If default is made in complying with *subsection (4)*, the court may, on the application of the requisitionists, or any of them, and on being satisfied that it is

reasonable to do so, require the PLC to exercise its powers under *section 1062* in a manner specified in the order of the court.

1065 Company reports on investigation

(1) On the conclusion of an investigation carried out by a PLC in pursuance of a requisition under *section 1064*, the PLC shall cause a report of the information received in pursuance of that investigation to be prepared.

(2) Where—

(a) a PLC undertakes an investigation in pursuance of a requisition under *section 1064*, and

(b) the investigation is not concluded before the end of the period of 3 months falling after the date of the deposit of the requisition,

the PLC shall cause to be prepared, in respect of that period and each successive period of 3 months ending before the conclusion of the investigation, an interim report of the information received during that period in pursuance of the investigation.

(3) The PLC shall, within 3 days after the date of making any report prepared under this section available for inspection in accordance with *Chapter 10* of *Part 4* (as adapted by *section 1069*), notify the requisitionists that the report is so available.

(4) An investigation carried out by a company in pursuance of a requisition under *section 1064* shall be regarded for the purposes of this section as concluded when—

(a) the PLC has made all such inquiries as are necessary or expedient for the purposes of the requisition; and

(b) in the case of each such inquiry—

(i) a response has been received by the PLC; or

(ii) the time allowed for a response has elapsed.

(5) If default is made by a PLC in complying with *subsection (1)*, *(2)* or *(3)*, the PLC and any officer of it who is in default shall be guilty of a category 3 offence.

1066 Penalty for failure to provide information

(1) Where notice is served by a PLC under *section 1062* on a person who is or was interested in shares of the PLC and that person fails to give the PLC any information required by the notice within the time specified in it, the PLC may apply to the court for an order directing that the shares in question be subject to restrictions under *section 768.*

(2) Such an order may be made by the court notwithstanding any power contained in the applicant PLC's constitution enabling the company itself to impose similar restrictions on the shares in question.

(3) Subject to the following subsections, a person who fails to comply with a notice under *section 1062* shall be guilty of a category 3 offence.

(4) A person shall not be guilty of an offence by virtue of failing to comply with a notice under *section 1062* if he or she proves that the requirement to give the information was frivolous or vexatious.

(5) Where an order is made under this section directing that shares shall be subject to restrictions under *section 768*, the PLC or any person aggrieved by the order may apply to the court for an order directing that the shares shall cease to be subject thereto.

(6) *Sections 769* to *776* shall apply in relation to any shares subject to the restrictions imposed by *section 768* by virtue of an order under this section but with the omission in *sections 769* to *775* of any reference to the Director.

1067 Removal of entries from register

(1) A PLC may remove an entry against a person's name from the register required to be kept by it under *section 1061* (the "register") if more than 6 years have elapsed after the date of the entry being made, and either—

(a) that entry recorded the fact that the person in question had ceased to have an interest notifiable under *sections 1048* to *1053* in relevant share capital of the PLC, or

(b) it has been superseded by a later entry made under *section 1061* against the same person's name,

and, in a case falling within *paragraph (a)*, the PLC may also remove that person's name from the register.

(2) If a person, in pursuance of an obligation imposed on him or her by any of *sections 1048* to *1053*, gives to a PLC the name and address of another person as being interested in shares in the PLC, the PLC shall, within 15 days after the date on which it was given that information, notify the other person that he or she has been so named and shall include in that notification—

(a) particulars of any entry relating to the person made, in consequence of its being given that information, by the PLC in the register; and

(b) a statement informing the person of his or her right to apply to have the entry removed in accordance with the following provisions of this section.

(3) A person who has been notified by a PLC in pursuance of *subsection (2)* that an entry relating to him or her has been made in the register, may apply in writing to the PLC for the removal of that entry from the register, and the PLC shall remove the entry if satisfied that the information in pursuance of which the entry was made was incorrect.

(4) If a person who is identified in the register as being a party to a share acquisition agreement (whether by an entry against the person's own name or by an entry relating to him or her made against another person's name as mentioned in *subsection (2)(a)*) ceases to be a party to that agreement, the person may apply in writing to the PLC for the inclusion of that information in the register.

(5) If the PLC is satisfied that the first-mentioned person in *subsection (4)* has ceased to be a party to the agreement concerned, it shall record that information (if not already recorded) in every place where that person's name appears as a party to that agreement in the register.

(6) If an application under—

(a) *subsection (3)* is refused, or

(b) *subsection (4)* is refused otherwise than on the ground that the information has already been recorded,

the applicant may apply to the court for an order directing the PLC to remove the entry in question from the register or (as the case may be) to include the information in question in the register; and the court may, if it thinks fit, make such an order.

(7) Where a name is removed from the register pursuant to *subsection (1)* or *(3)* or an order under *subsection (6)*, the PLC shall, within 14 days after the date of that removal, make any necessary alterations in any associated index.

(8) If default is made by a PLC in complying with *subsection (2)* or *(7)*, the PLC and any officer of it who is in default shall be guilty of a category 3 offence.

1068 Entries, when not to be removed

(1) Entries in the register kept by a PLC under *section 1061* shall not be deleted except in accordance with *section 1067*.

(2) If an entry is deleted from that register in contravention of *subsection (1)*, the PLC shall restore that entry to the register as soon as is reasonable and practicable.

(3) If default is made by a PLC in complying with *subsection (1)* or *(2)*, the PLC and any officer of it who is in default shall be guilty of a category 3 offence.

1069 Where register to be kept, inspection of register, inspection of reports, etc

(1) *Chapter 10* of *Part 4*, as adapted by this section, shall apply in relation to—

(a) the register under *section 1061*; and

(b) any report referred to in *section 1065*.

(2) For the purposes of this section, *Chapter 10* of *Part 4* is adapted as follows:

(a) in *section 215(a)*, there shall be added the following definitions:

> " 'individual and group acquisitions register' means the register kept by the company pursuant to section 1061(1);
>
> 'share interest investigation report' means any report referred to in section 1065 caused to be prepared by the company;";

(b) *section 216(1)* shall have effect as if, in addition to the registers and documents specified in that provision as being registers and documents to which *section 216* applies, that provision specified the individual and group acquisitions register and the share interest investigation report as being, respectively, a register and a document to which that section applies; and

(c) each of *subsections (9)*, *(11)* and *(12)* of *section 216* shall have effect as if, in addition to the registers or documents specified in the particular subsection, there were specified in the particular subsection the individual and group acquisitions register and the share interest investigation report.

(3) The register under *section 1061* shall also be and remain open and accessible to any person attending the PLC's annual general meeting at least one quarter hour

before the appointed time for the commencement of the meeting and during the continuance of the meeting.

(4) A report referred to in *section 1065(1)* shall be made available for inspection in accordance with *Chapter 10* of *Part 4* (as so adapted) within a reasonable period (not more than 15 days) after the date of conclusion of the investigation concerned.

(5) Each report referred to in *section 1065(2)* shall be made available for inspection in accordance with *Chapter 10* of *Part 4* (as so adapted) within a reasonable period (not more than 15 days) after the end of the period to which it relates.

(6) Such a report (that is a report whether referred to in *section 1065(1)* or *(2)*) shall continue to be so made available for inspection for a period that expires 6 years beginning on the day after the first day that it is made available for inspection in accordance with the foregoing provisions.

(7) *Section 127(1)* (access to documents during business hours) shall apply for the purposes of *Chapter 10* of *Part 4*, as that Chapter is adapted for the purposes of this section, as it applies in relation to the relevant provisions of *Part 4*.

1070 Duty of PLC to notify authorised market operator

(1) In this section "relevant PLC" means a PLC dealing facilities in respect of the shares or debentures of which are provided by an authorised market operator.

(2) If—

(a) a relevant PLC is notified of any matter by a director or secretary in consequence of the fulfilment of a duty imposed on him or her by *Chapter 5* of *Part 5*, and

(b) the matter relates to shares or debentures for which the dealing facilities referred to in *subsection (1)* are provided,

the PLC shall be under an obligation to notify the market operator referred to in that subsection of the matter.

(3) That market operator may publish, in such manner as it may determine, any information received by it under *subsection (2)*.

(4) An obligation imposed by *subsection (2)* shall be fulfilled before the end of the day after that on which it arises.

(5) If default is made in complying with this section, the PLC and any officer of it who is in default shall be guilty of a category 3 offence.

Chapter 5

Acquisition of own shares and certain acquisitions by subsidiaries

1071 Additional (general) provisions relating to acquisition by PLCs of own shares

(1) In addition to the requirements set out in *sections 105* and *106*—

(a) an acquisition by a PLC of its own shares, in so far as the consideration therefor is profits available for distribution, shall be in compliance with the restriction on the distribution of assets specified in *section 1082*; and

(b) a PLC shall not purchase any of its shares if as a result of such purchase the nominal value of its issued share capital which is not redeemable would be less than one-tenth of the nominal value of the total issued share capital of the PLC.

(2) With regard to the purchase by a PLC of its own shares, the requirements of *sections 105* and *106* and the preceding subsection shall have effect without prejudice to—

(a) the principle of equal treatment of all shareholders who are in the same position; and

(b) *Chapter 2* of *Part 23* and regulations thereunder.

1072 "Market purchase", "overseas market purchase" and "off-market purchase"

(1) For the purposes of *sections 1073* to *1081*, a purchase by a PLC of its own shares is—

(a) an "off-market purchase" if the shares are purchased either—

(i) otherwise than on a securities market; or

(ii) on a securities market but are not subject to a marketing arrangement on that market;

(b) a "market purchase" if the shares are purchased on a securities market within the State and are subject to a marketing arrangement.

(2) For the purposes of *sections 1073* to *1081*, a purchase by a PLC that issues shares, or by a subsidiary of that PLC, of the first-mentioned company's shares, is an "overseas market purchase" if the shares—

(a) are purchased on—

(i) a regulated market; or

(ii) another market recognised for the purposes of this section;

being, in either case, a market outside the State; and

(b) are subject to a marketing arrangement.

(3) For the purposes of *subsections (1)* and *(2)*, a PLC's shares are subject to a marketing arrangement on a securities market or, in the case of *subsection (2)(a)*, a regulated market or another market recognised for the purposes of this section, if either—

(a) they are listed or admitted to trading on that market; or

(b) the PLC has been afforded facilities for dealings in those shares to take place on that market without prior permission for individual transactions from the—

(i) authorised market operator concerned; or

(ii) in the case of *subsection (2)(a)*, the authority in the state concerned that governs the market;

and without limit as to the time during which those facilities are to be available.

(4) *Sections 1073* to *1081* shall apply to American depositary receipts as those sections apply to shares.

(5) In this section—

"American depositary receipt" means an instrument—

(a) which acknowledges—

(i) that a depositary or a nominee acting on his or her behalf, holds stocks or marketable securities which are dealt in and quoted on a market recognised for the purposes of this section; and

(ii) that the holder of the instrument has rights in or in relation to such stocks or marketable securities, including the right to receive such stocks or marketable securities from the depositary or his or her nominee;

and

(b) which—

(i) is dealt in and quoted on a market recognised for the purposes of this section, being a market which is situated in the United States of America; or

(ii) represents stocks or marketable securities which are so dealt in and quoted;

"recognised for the purposes of this section", in relation to a market, means recognised by order made by the Minister (and such an order may provide for different markets to be recognised for the purposes of different provisions of this section);

"securities market" means—

(a) a regulated market;

(b) a multilateral trading facility (within the meaning of Article 4(1), point (15) of Directive 2004/39/EC of the European Parliament and of the Council of 21 April 2004); or

(c) such other securities market as may be prescribed.

1073 Authority for PLC's purchase of own shares

Neither *paragraph (a)* or *(b)* of *section 105(4)* shall be regarded as conferring authority for a purchase by a PLC of its own shares and accordingly such purchase shall be required to have the authority of—

(a) in a case falling within *section 1074* — an ordinary resolution of the PLC;

(b) in a case falling within *section 1075* — a special resolution of the PLC.

1074 Market purchase of own shares

(1) A PLC shall not make a market purchase or overseas market purchase of its own shares unless the purchase has first been authorised by the PLC by ordinary resolution and any such authority may be varied, revoked or from time to time renewed by the PLC by ordinary resolution.

(2) *Subsection (1)* shall not be read as requiring any particular contract for the market purchase or overseas market purchase of shares to be authorised by the PLC in general meeting and, for the purposes of this Part, where a market purchase or overseas market purchase of shares has been authorised in accordance with this section any contract entered into pursuant to that authority in respect of such a purchase shall be deemed also to be so authorised.

(3) *Section 198* shall apply to a resolution under *subsection (1).*

(4) The authority granted under *subsection (1)* shall—

(a) specify the maximum number of shares authorised to be acquired;

(b) determine both the maximum and minimum prices which may be paid for the shares, either by—

(i) specifying a particular sum; or

(ii) providing a basis or formula for calculating the amount of the price in question without reference to any person's discretion or opinion;

(c) specify the date on which the authority is to expire which shall not be later than 5 years after the date on which the ordinary resolution granting the authority is passed.

(5) A PLC may make a purchase referred to in *subsection (1)* after the expiry of any time limit imposed by virtue of *subsection (4)(c)* in any case where the contract of purchase was concluded before the authority conferred on it expired and the terms of that authority permit the PLC to make a contract of purchase which would or might be executed wholly or partly after the authority expired.

1075 Off-market purchase of own shares

(1) A PLC shall not make an off-market purchase of its own shares otherwise than in pursuance of a contract authorised in advance by a special resolution of the PLC.

(2) Any such authority may be varied, revoked or from time to time renewed by the PLC by special resolution.

(3) *Section 105(5)*, *(7)*, *(8)* and *(10)* to *(12)* apply to a special resolution referred to in *subsection (1)* or *(2)* as they apply to a special resolution of a private company limited by shares authorising the acquisition by it of its own shares but *subsections (4)* and *(5)* of this section supplement those provisions.

(4) Any authority granted under *subsection (1)* or *(2)* shall specify the date on which the authority is to expire which shall not be later than 18 months after the date on which the special resolution granting the authority is passed.

(5) A PLC may make a purchase referred to in *subsection (1)* after the expiry of any time limit imposed by virtue of *subsection (4)* in any case where the contract of purchase was concluded before the authority conferred on it expired and the terms of that authority permit the PLC to make a contract of purchase which would or might be executed wholly or partly after the authority expired.

1076 Assignment or release of company's right to purchase own shares

(1) Any purported assignment of the rights of a PLC under any contract authorised under *section 1074* or *1075* shall be void.

(2) Nothing in *subsection (1)* shall prevent a PLC from releasing its right under any contract authorised under *section 1074* or *1075* provided that the release has been authorised by—

(a) in the case of *section 1074* — an ordinary resolution of the PLC;

(b) in the case of *section 1075* — a special resolution of the PLC,

before the release is entered into, and any such purported release by a PLC which has not been authorised in that manner shall be void.

(3) *Subsections (5)*, *(7)* and *(8)* of *section 105* shall apply to a resolution under *subsection* (*2)* and, for the purposes of this subsection, *subsection (8)* of *section 105* shall have effect as if the references in it to the contract of purchase were references to the release concerned.

1077 Relationship of certain acquisition provisions to those in *Part 3*

(1) For the avoidance of doubt, the provisions of *Part 3* that make consequential or supplementary provision in respect of an acquisition by a company under *section 105* of its own shares (and, in particular, the provisions referred to in *subsection (2)*) apply to an acquisition by a PLC of its own shares referred to in *sections 1071* to *1076*, and the authorisation of any contract thereunder, unless a contrary intention is indicated in one of those latter sections.

(2) The particular provisions mentioned in *subsection (1)* are those that contain reference, however expressed, to a contract authorised under *section 105*.

1078 Off-market re-allotment of treasury shares by PLC

(1) The maximum and minimum prices at which treasury shares may be re-allotted off-market (the "re-allotment price range") by a PLC shall be determined in advance by the PLC in general meeting in accordance with *subsections (2)* to *(4)* and such determination may fix different maximum and minimum prices for different shares.

(2) Where the treasury shares to be re-allotted are derived in whole or in part from shares purchased by the PLC in accordance with the provisions of *Part 3* (as applied by this Part) the re-allotment price range of the whole or such part (as the case may be) of those shares shall be determined by special resolution of the PLC passed at the meeting at which the resolution authorising that purchase has been passed and such determination shall, for the purposes of this section, remain effective with respect to those shares for the requisite period.

(3) Where the treasury shares to be re-allotted are derived in whole or in part from shares redeemed by the PLC in accordance with the provisions of *Part 3* (as applied by this Part) the re-allotment price range of the whole or such part (as the case may be) of those shares shall be determined by special resolution of the PLC passed before any contract for the re-allotment of those shares is entered into and such determination shall, for the purposes of this section, remain effective with respect to those shares for the requisite period.

(4) The PLC may from time to time by special resolution vary or renew a determination of re-allotment price range under *subsection (2)* or *(3)* with respect to particular treasury shares before any contract for re-allotment of those shares is entered into and any such variation or renewal shall, for the purposes of this section, remain effective as a determination of the re-allotment price range of those shares for the requisite period.

(5) A re-allotment by a PLC of treasury shares in contravention of *subsection (2)*, *(3)* or *(4)* shall be unlawful.

(6) For the purposes of determining in this section whether treasury shares are re-allotted off-market, the provisions of *section 1072* shall have effect with the substitution of the words "re-allotment", "off-market re-allotment" and "re-allotted" respectively for the words "purchase", "off-market purchase" and "purchased" in *subsection (1)(a)* of that section.

(7) In this section, the "requisite period" means the period of 18 months after the date of the passing of the resolution determining the re-allotment price range or varying or renewing (as the case may be) such determination or such lesser period of time as the resolution may specify.

1079 Return to be made to Registrar under *section 116(1)*

(1) In its application to shares, the subject of an overseas market purchase by a PLC, *section 116(1)* shall apply as if "3 days" were substituted for "30 days".

(2) In addition to the requirements of *section 116*, the return required to be made by a PLC under that section shall state—

(a) the aggregate amount paid by the PLC for the shares; and

(b) the maximum and minimum prices paid in respect of each class purchased.

(3) Where *subsection (2)* applies, then the following subsection shall be substituted for *subsection (2)* of *section 116*:

> "(2) Particulars of shares delivered to the company on different dates and under different contracts may be included in a single return to the Registrar, and in such a case the amount required to be stated under *section 1079(2)(a)* shall be the aggregate amount paid by the company for all the shares to which the return relates.".

1080 Duty of PLC to publish particulars of overseas market purchase

(1) Whenever shares for which dealing facilities are provided on a regulated market or other market referred to in *section 1072(2)(a)* are the subject of an overseas market

purchase either by the PLC which issued the shares or by a company which is that PLC's subsidiary, the PLC which issued the shares has the following duty.

(2) That duty of the PLC is to publish—

(a) on its website; or

(b) in any other prescribed manner;

for a continuous period of not less than 28 days beginning on the day that next follows the overseas market purchase concerned and is a day on which the market concerned is open for business the following information for total purchases on the market concerned on each such day—

(i) the date, in the place outside the State where the market concerned is located, of the overseas market purchase;

(ii) the purchase price at which the shares were purchased, or the highest such price and lowest such price paid by the PLC or the subsidiary;

(iii) the number of shares which were purchased; and

(iv) the market on which the shares were purchased.

(3) If a PLC fails to fulfil its duty under *subsection (1)*, the PLC and any officer of it who is in default shall be guilty of a category 3 offence.

1081 Duty of PLC to notify authorised market operator

(1) Whenever shares for which dealing facilities are provided on a regulated market have been purchased, either by the PLC which issued the shares or by a company which is that PLC's subsidiary, then, save where the purchase was an overseas market purchase, the PLC whose shares have been purchased has the following duty.

(2) That duty of the PLC is to notify the authorised market operator concerned of the fact of that purchase; that operator may publish, in such manner as it may determine, any information received by it under this subsection.

(3) That duty shall be fulfilled before the end of the day after that on which the purchase concerned has taken place.

(4) If a PLC fails to fulfil its duty under *subsection (1)*, the PLC and any officer of it who is in default shall be guilty of a category 3 offence.

Chapter 6
Distribution by a PLC

1082 Restriction on distribution of assets

(1) A PLC may only make a distribution at any time—

(a) if at that time the amount of its net assets is not less than the aggregate of the PLC's called-up share capital and its undistributable reserves; and

(b) if, and to the extent that, the distribution does not reduce the amount of those assets to less than that aggregate.

(2) For the purposes of this section the undistributable reserves of a PLC are—

(a) the PLC's undenominated capital;

(b) the amount by which the PLC's accumulated, unrealised profits, so far as not previously utilised by any capitalisation, exceed its accumulated, unrealised losses, so far as not previously written off in a reduction or reorganisation of capital duly made; and

(c) any other reserve which the PLC is prohibited from distributing by any enactment, other than one contained in this Part, or by its constitution.

(3) *Subsections (4)* to *(8)* of *section 117* shall apply for the purposes of this section as they apply for the purposes of that section.

(4) A PLC shall not include any uncalled share capital as an asset in any financial statement relevant for the purposes of this section.

1083 Relevant financial statements in the case of distribution by PLC

(1) In addition to its application for the purpose of determining whether a distribution may be made by a PLC without contravening *section 117*, and the amount of any distribution which may be so made, *section 121* shall apply for the purpose of determining whether a distribution may be made by a PLC without contravening *section 1082*, and the amount of any distribution which may be so made.

(2) Accordingly *section 1082* shall be treated as contravened in the case of a distribution unless the requirements of *section 121* in relation to the financial statements mentioned therein are complied with in the case of that distribution.

(3) For the purposes of the application of *section 121*, by virtue of *subsection (1)*, to a distribution (and without prejudice to that section's application otherwise to a distribution by a PLC)—

(a) there shall, in *section 121(2)(b)*, be substituted "if that distribution would be found to contravene *section 1082*" for "if that distribution would be found to contravene *section 117*"; and

(b) there shall, in *section 121(3)(a)* and *(c)*, be substituted "whether that distribution would be in contravention of *section 1082*" for "whether that distribution would be in contravention of *section 117*".

(4) In addition to the foregoing provisions as regards *section 121*'s application, *subsections (5)* to *(8)* contain provisions supplementing *section 121*'s application in the case of a distribution by a PLC and that section shall have effect accordingly.

(5) The following requirements apply to interim financial statements, as referred to in *section 121*, that are prepared for a proposed distribution by a PLC, that is to say:

(a) the financial statements shall have been properly prepared or have been so prepared subject only to matters which are not material for the purpose of determining, by reference to the relevant items as stated in those statements, whether that distribution would be in contravention of *section 117* or *1082*, as the case may be;

(b) a copy of those financial statements shall have been delivered to the Registrar;

(c) if the financial statements are in a language other than the English or Irish language, a translation into English or Irish of the statements which has been certified in the prescribed manner to be a correct translation, shall also have been delivered to the Registrar.

(6) The following requirements apply to initial financial statements, as referred to in *section 121*, that are prepared for a proposed distribution by a PLC, that is to say:

(a) the financial statements shall have been properly prepared or have been so prepared subject only to matters which are not material for the purpose of determining, by reference to the relevant items as stated in those statements, whether that distribution would be in contravention of *section 117* or *1082*, as the case may be;

(b) the statutory auditors of the PLC shall have made a report stating whether, in their opinion, the financial statements have been properly prepared;

(c) if, by virtue of anything referred to in that report, the report is not an unqualified report, the statutory auditors shall also have stated in writing whether, in their opinion, that thing is material for the purpose of determining, by reference to the relevant items as stated in those financial statements, whether that distribution would be in contravention of *section 117* or *1082*, as the case may be;

(d) a copy of those financial statements, of the report made under *paragraph (b)* and of any such statement shall have been delivered to the Registrar; and

(e) if the financial statements are, or that report or statement is, in a language other than the English or Irish language, a translation into English or Irish of the financial statements, the report or statement, as the case may be, which has been certified in the prescribed manner to be a correct translation, shall also have been delivered to the Registrar.

(7) For the purposes of this section, *section 121(6)* shall apply as if "Where *subsection (3)(a)* or *section 1083(5)(a)* or *1083(6)(a)* applies to the relevant financial statements" were substituted for "Where *subsection (3)(a)* applies to the relevant entity financial statements".

(8) The reference in the definition of "properly prepared" in *section 121(7)* to financial statements includes a reference to interim or initial financial statements referred to in *subsection (5)* or *(6)* and, for the purpose of that definition as it relates to either such type of statement, *section 290* and *section 291* or *292* as appropriate, and, where applicable, [*Schedule 3* or *3A*, as the case may be][a] shall be deemed to have effect in relation to interim and initial financial statements with such modifications as are necessary by reason of the fact that the financial statements are prepared otherwise than in respect of a financial year.

Amendments

a Words substituted by C(A)A 2017, s 90(g) (previously: "*Schedule 3*").

1084 Limitation on reduction by a PLC of its company capital

A PLC may not reduce its company capital below the authorised minimum and *section 84* shall be read accordingly.

Chapter 7
Uncertificated securities

1085 Transfer in writing

The following:

(a) section 6 of the Statute of Frauds 1695;

(b) section 28(6) of the Supreme Court of Judicature (Ireland) Act 1877;

(c) *section 94(4)*; and

(d) any other enactment or rule of law requiring the execution, under hand or seal, of a document in writing for the transfer of property,

shall not apply (if they would otherwise do so) to any transfer of title to securities pursuant to—

(i) section 12 of the Electronic Commerce Act 2000; or

(ii) procedures authorised or required pursuant to regulations made by the Minister under *section 1086*.

1086 Power to make regulations for the transfer of securities

(1) The Minister may make provision by regulations for enabling or requiring title to securities or any class of securities to be evidenced and transferred without a written instrument.

(2) Subject to any exceptions that may be specified in the regulations, the regulations may, in respect of—

(a) securities of public limited companies admitted to trading on a regulated market,

(b) securities of public limited companies admitted to trading on a market other than a regulated market, or

(c) securities of public limited companies of a specified class,

provide that the means provided by the regulations for evidencing and transferring title to such securities shall constitute the sole and exclusive means for doing so (and accordingly, that any purported transfer of such securities otherwise than by those means shall be void).

(3) In this section—

(a) "securities" means transferable securities as defined by Directive 2004/39/EC of the European Parliament and the Council of 21 April 2004;

(b) references to title to securities include any legal or equitable interest in securities; and

(c) references to a transfer of title include a transfer by way of security.

(4) The regulations may make provision—

(a) for procedures for recording and transferring title to securities; and

(b) for the regulation of those procedures and the persons responsible for or involved in their operation; and

(c) for dispensing with the obligations of a company under *section 99* to issue certificates and providing for alternative procedures.

(5) The regulations shall contain such safeguards as appear to the Minister appropriate for the protection of investors and for ensuring that competition is not restricted, distorted or prevented.

(6) The regulations may, for the purpose of enabling or facilitating the operation of the new procedures, make provision with respect to the rights and obligations of persons in relation to securities dealt with under the procedures.

(7) The regulations shall be framed so as to secure that the rights and obligations in relation to securities dealt with under the new procedures correspond, so far as practicable, with those which would arise apart from any regulations under this section.

(8) The regulations may—

(a) require the provision of statements by a company to holders of securities (at specified intervals or on specified occasions) of the securities held in their name;

(b) make provision removing any requirement for the holders of securities to surrender existing share certificates to issuers; and

(c) make provision that the requirements of the regulations supersede any existing requirements in the articles of association of a company which would be incompatible with the requirements of the regulations.

1087 Supplemental provisions in relation to *section 1086*

(1) Without prejudice to the generality of *subsections (5)* to *(8)* of *section 1086*, regulations under that section shall not contain provisions that would result in a person who, but for the regulations, would be entitled—

(a) to have his or her name entered in the register of members of a company, or

(b) to give instructions in respect of any securities,

ceasing to be so entitled.

(2) Regulations under *section 1086* may include such supplementary, incidental and transitional provisions as appear to the Minister to be necessary or expedient.

(3) In particular, provision may be made for the purpose of giving effect to—

(a) the transmission of title of securities by operation of law;

(b) any restriction on the transfer of title to securities arising by virtue of the provisions of any enactment or instrument, court order or agreement;

(c) any power conferred by any such provision on a person to deal with securities on behalf of the person entitled.

(4) Regulations under *section 1086* may, for the purposes mentioned in that section and this section, make provision with respect to the persons who are to be responsible for the operation of the new procedures and for those purposes may empower the Minister to delegate to any person willing and able to discharge them, any functions of the Minister under the regulations.

(5) Regulations under *section 1086* may make different provision for different cases.

Chapter 8
Corporate governance

1088 Number of directors of a PLC

(1) A PLC shall have at least 2 directors.

(2) Nothing in *Parts 1* to *14* that makes provision in the case of a company having a sole director shall apply to a PLC.

1089 PLC, with 2 or more members, may not dispense with holding of a.g.m.

Section 175(3) and *(4)* (which relate to dispensing with the holding of an annual general meeting) shall not apply to a PLC if it has more than one member.

1090 Rotation of directors

(1) Each provision of this section applies save to the extent that the PLC's constitution provides otherwise.

(2) At the first annual general meeting of the PLC all the directors shall retire from office.

(3) At the annual general meeting in every subsequent year, one-third of the directors for the time being, or, if their number is not 3 or a multiple of 3, then the number nearest one-third shall retire from office.

(4) The directors to retire in every year shall be those who have been longest in office since their last election but as between persons who became directors on the same day, those to retire shall (unless they otherwise agree among themselves) be determined by lot.

(5) A retiring director shall be eligible for re-election.

(6) The PLC, at the meeting at which a director retires in any of the foregoing instances, may fill the vacated office by electing a person to it.

(7) In default of the PLC doing so, the retiring director shall, if offering himself or herself for re-election, be deemed to have been re-elected, unless—

(a) at such meeting it is expressly resolved not to fill such vacated office, or

(b) a resolution for the re-election of such director has been put to the meeting and lost.

1091 Modification of *section 149(8)*'s operation where public or local offer co-incides with change among directors

Where—

(a) a change among a PLC's directors occurs, and

(b) prior to the end of the period referred to in *section 149(8)* (as that provision operates apart from this section) for the sending to the Registrar of the notification required by that provision of the change, the PLC issues a prospectus or, in the case of a local offer (within the meaning of *Chapter 1* of *Part 23*), a document for the purposes of making such an offer,

then, notwithstanding that the foregoing period has not expired, the PLC shall send that notification to the Registrar no later than the time of issue of such prospectus or document, and *section 149(8)* shall be read and operate accordingly.

1092 Remuneration of directors

(1) Each provision of this section applies save to the extent that the PLC's constitution provides otherwise.

(2) The remuneration of the directors of a PLC shall be such as is determined, from time to time, by the PLC in general meeting and such remuneration shall be deemed to accrue from day to day.

(3) The directors of a PLC may also be paid all travelling, hotel and other expenses properly incurred by them—

(a) in attending and returning from—

(i) meetings of the directors or any committee referred to in *section 160(9)*, or

(ii) general meetings of the PLC,

or

(b) otherwise in connection with the business of the PLC.

1093 Application of *section 193* in relation to PLC

Section 193 shall apply to a PLC as if, in *subsection (1)*, after "Notwithstanding any provision to the contrary in this Act", there were inserted "and unless the constitution provides otherwise".

1094 Provisions consequent on participation by PLC in system for uncertificated transfer of securities

(1) *Sections 1095* and *1096* have effect where a PLC is a participating issuer.

(2) *Sections 1095* and *1096* are without prejudice to *sections 1099* to *1110*.

(3) In this section and *sections 1095* and *1096* "participating issuer" has the meaning given to it by—

(a) the Companies Act 1990 (Uncertificated Securities) Regulations 1996 (S.I. No. 68 of 1996) which regulations are continued in force by *Schedule 6*; or

(b) if regulations under *section 1086* are made and those regulations—

(i) replace the regulations referred to in *paragraph (a)* — those replacement regulations; or

(ii) amend the regulations referred to in *paragraph (a)* — the latter regulations as they stand so amended.

1095 Attendance and voting at meetings

(1) For the purposes of determining which persons are entitled to attend or vote at a meeting, and how many votes such persons may cast, a PLC that is a participating issuer may specify in the notice of the meeting a time, not more than 48 hours before the time fixed for the meeting, by which a person must be entered on the relevant register of securities in order to have the right to attend or vote at the meeting.

(2) Changes to entries on the relevant register of securities after the time specified by virtue of *subsection (1)* shall be disregarded in determining the rights of any person to attend or vote at the meeting, notwithstanding any provisions in any enactment, articles of association or other instrument to the contrary.

(3) In this section, "register of securities" has the meaning given to it by—

(a) the Companies Act 1990 (Uncertificated Securities) Regulations 1996 (S.I. No. 68 of 1996) which regulations are continued in force by *Schedule 6*; or

(b) if regulations under *section 1086* are made and those regulations—

(i) replace the regulations referred to in *paragraph (a)* — those replacement regulations; or

(ii) amend the regulations referred to in *paragraph (a)* — the latter regulations as they stand so amended.

1096 Notice of meetings

(1) For the purposes of serving notices of meetings, whether under *section 218*, any other enactment, a provision in the articles or any other instrument, a participating issuer may determine that persons entitled to receive such notices are those persons entered on the relevant register of securities at the close of business on a day determined by the participating issuer.

(2) The day determined by a participating issuer under *subsection (1)* may not be more than 7 days before the day that the notices of the meeting are sent.

(3) In this section "register of securities" has the same meaning as *subsection (3)* of *section 1095* provides it is to have in that section.

1097 Application of *section 167* to PLC that is not a public-interest entity under S.I No 220 of 2010

Section 167 shall apply to a PLC that does not fall within [*section 1551* (which relates to an obligation of a public-interest entity to establish an audit committee)][a] and, for the avoidance of doubt, that section shall apply irrespective of the balance sheet amount or the amount of turnover of the PLC for any financial year.

Amendments

a Words substituted by C(SA)A 2018, s 46 (previously "Regulation 115 (which relates to an obligation of a public-interest entity to establish an audit committee) of the 2016 Audits Regulations").

1098 Length of notice of general meetings to be given

Subject to *section 1102*, in its application to a PLC, *section 181(1)* shall apply as if the following paragraph were substituted for *paragraph (b)*:

"(b) in the case of any other extraordinary general meeting, by not less than 14 days' notice.".

1099 Additional rights of shareholders in certain PLCs (provisions implementing Shareholders' Rights Directive 2007/36/EC)

(1) *Sections 1100* to *1110* have effect in relation to—

(a) a notice of a general meeting given by a PLC, and

(b) otherwise in relation to a general meeting of a PLC,

being a PLC whose shares are admitted to trading on a regulated market in any Member State (in *sections 1100* to *1110* referred to as a "traded PLC").

(2) *Sections 1100* to *1110* have effect notwithstanding anything in the PLC's constitution.

[(3) *Sections 1100 to 1110* shall not have effect in respect of a company to which the resolution tools, powers or mechanisms provided for in Part 4 of the Bank Recovery and Resolution Regulations are applied or exercised.][a]

Amendments

a Subsection (3) inserted by European Union (Bank Recovery and Resolution) Regulations 2015, reg 189(10), with effect from 15 July 2015.

1100 Equality of treatment of shareholders

In addition to any provisions of *Part 4* imposing requirements on the company in that behalf, a traded PLC shall ensure equal treatment for all members who are in the same position with regard to the exercise of voting rights and participation in a general meeting of the company.

1101 Requisitioning of general meeting by members — modification of *section 178(3)*

In its application to a traded PLC, *section 178* shall apply as if the following subsection were substituted for *subsection (3)*:

> "(3) The directors of a company shall, on the requisition of one or more members holding, or together holding, at the date of the deposit of the requisition, not less than 5 per cent of the paid up share capital of the company, as at the date of the deposit carries the right of voting at general meetings of the company, forthwith proceed duly to convene an extraordinary general meeting of the company.".

1102 Length of notice of general meetings to be given by traded PLC

(1) In its application to a PLC which is a traded PLC, *section 181* shall apply as if—

(a) the following subsection were substituted for *subsection (1)*:

> "(1) Subject to *section 1102(2)*, a general meeting of a company (whether an annual general meeting or an extraordinary general meeting), other than an adjourned meeting, shall be called by not less than 21 days' notice.";

and

(b) *subsection (2)* were omitted.

(2) Notwithstanding *section 181(1)* as it applies by virtue of *subsection (1)* of this section, a general meeting of a PLC which is a traded PLC (other than an annual general meeting or an extraordinary general meeting for the passing of a special resolution) may be called by not less than 14 days' notice if—

(a) the PLC offers the facility for members to vote by electronic means accessible to all members who hold shares that carry rights to vote at general meetings; and

(b) a special resolution reducing the period of notice to 14 days has been passed at the immediately preceding annual general meeting, or at a general meeting held since that meeting.

[(3) Notwithstanding section 181(1) as it applies by virtue of subsections (1) and (2), for the purposes of the Bank Recovery and Resolution Regulations a general meeting of a company may, by a majority of two-thirds of the votes validly cast, issue a notice requiring a general meeting (or modify its constitution to prescribe that a notice requiring a general meeting is issued) at shorter notice than as set out in paragraph (1) to decide on a capital increase, provided that—

(a) the meeting does not take place within 10 calendar days of the issue of the relevant notice,

(b) the conditions of Regulation 39 or Chapter 3 of Part 3 of the Bank Recovery and Resolution Regulations are met, and

(c) the capital increase is necessary to avoid the occurrence of the conditions laid down in Regulations 62 and 63 of the Bank Recovery and Resolution Regulations arising.

(4) For the purposes of subsection (3)—

(a) the notice obligations in section 1104(2) and (3), and

(b) the requirement regarding entry of a person by the record date in section 1105(2),

do not apply.][a]

Amendments

a Subsections (3) and (4) inserted by European Union (Bank Recovery and Resolution) Regulations 2015, reg 189(11), with effect from 15 July 2015.

1103 Additional provisions concerning notice under *section 181* by a traded PLC

(1) In addition to the requirements of *section 181*, a notice, under that section, by a traded PLC of a general meeting, whether—

(a) an annual general meeting; or

(b) an extraordinary general meeting;

shall be issued, free of charge, in a manner ensuring fast access to the notice on a non-discriminatory basis, using such media as may reasonably be relied upon for the effective dissemination of information to the public throughout the Member States.

(2) Notice of a general meeting shall set out—

(a) when and where the meeting is to take place and the proposed agenda for the meeting;

(b) a clear and precise statement of any procedures a member shall comply with in order to participate and vote in the meeting, including—

(i) the right of a member to put items on the agenda of a general meeting and to table draft resolutions pursuant to *section 1104* and to ask questions relating to items on the agenda pursuant to *section 1107*, and the time limits applicable to the exercise of any of those rights;

(ii) the right of a member entitled to attend, speak, ask questions and vote, to appoint, pursuant to *section 183* as it applies by virtue of *section 1108*, by electronic means or otherwise—

(I) a proxy; or

(II) in any of the cases set out in those sections, more than one proxy;

to attend, speak, ask questions and vote instead of the member and that any such proxy need not be a member;

(iii) the procedure for voting by proxy pursuant to *section 183* as so applied, including the forms to be used and the means by which the company is prepared to accept electronic notification of the appointment of a proxy; and

(iv) the procedure (where applicable) to be followed pursuant to *sections 1106* and *1109* for voting electronically or by correspondence respectively;

(c) the record date for eligibility for voting as defined in *section 1105* and state that only members registered on the record date shall have the right to participate and vote in the general meeting;

(d) where and how the full, unabridged text of the documents and draft resolutions referred to in *subsection (3)(c)* and *(d)* may be obtained; and

(e) the website at which the information contained in *subsection (3)* shall be made available.

(3) A traded PLC shall make available to its members on its website, for a continuous period beginning not later than 21 days before a general meeting (inclusive of the day of the meeting), the following:

(a) the notice under *section 181*;

(b) the total number of shares and voting rights at the date of the giving of the notice (including separate totals for each class of shares where the company's capital is divided into 2 or more classes of shares);

(c) the documents to be submitted to the meeting;

(d) a copy of any draft resolution or, where no such resolution is proposed to be adopted, a comment from the board of directors on each item of the proposed agenda of the meeting;

(e) a copy of forms to be used to vote by proxy and to vote by correspondence unless these forms are sent directly to each member.

(4) The traded PLC shall make available, on its website as soon as possible following their receipt, draft resolutions tabled by members.

(5) Where the forms referred to in *subsection (3)(e)* cannot be made available on the traded PLC's website for technical reasons, the PLC shall indicate on its website how the forms may be obtained in hard copy form and the PLC shall send the forms by post, free of charge, to every member who requests them.

(6) Where notice of a general meeting is issued later than on the twenty first day before the meeting pursuant to *section 1102(2)* or Article 9(4) or 11(4) of Directive 2004/25/EC, the period specified in *subsection (3)* shall be reduced accordingly.

1104 Right to put items on the agenda of the general meeting and to table draft resolutions

(1) One or more members of a traded PLC shall have the right, by electronic or postal means, at an address specified by the PLC, to—

(a) put an item on the agenda of an annual general meeting, provided that each such item is accompanied by—

(i) stated grounds justifying its inclusion; or

(ii) a draft resolution to be adopted at the general meeting;

and

(b) table a draft resolution for an item on the agenda of a general meeting (whether an annual general meeting or not);

subject to the member or members concerned holding 3 per cent of the issued share capital of the PLC, representing at least 3 per cent of the total voting rights of all the members who have a right to vote at the meeting to which the request for inclusion of the item relates.

(2) A request by a member to put an item on the agenda or to table a draft resolution under *subsection (1)(a)* shall be received by the traded PLC in written or electronic form at least 42 days before the date of the meeting to which it relates.

(3) Where the exercise of the right conferred by *subsection (1)(a)* involves a modification of the agenda for the annual general meeting, in situations where the agenda has already been communicated to the members, and only in such situations, the traded PLC shall make available a revised agenda in the same manner as the previous agenda—

(a) in advance of the applicable record date (as defined in *section 1105*) of share-ownership for purposes of entitlement to vote, or

(b) if no such record date applies, sufficiently in advance of the date of the annual general meeting so as to enable other members to appoint a proxy or, where applicable, to vote by correspondence.

(4) In order to facilitate a member to avail of *subsection (1)(a)*, the traded PLC shall ensure that the date of the next annual general meeting is placed on its website by—

(a) the end of the previous financial year, or

(b) not later than 70 days prior to the date of the annual general meeting,

whichever is the earlier.

1105 Requirements for participation and voting in general meeting

(1) In this section—

"record date" means a date not more than 48 hours before the general meeting to which it relates;

"register of securities" has the same meaning as *subsection (3)* of *section 1095* provides it is to have in that section.

(2) A person shall be entered on the relevant register of securities by the record date in order to exercise the right of a member to participate and vote at a general meeting and any change to an entry on the relevant register of securities after the record date shall be disregarded in determining the right of any person to attend and vote at the meeting.

(3) The right of a member to participate in a general meeting and to vote in respect of his or her shares shall not be subject to any requirement that the shares be deposited with, or transferred to, or registered in the name of another person before the general meeting.

(4) Unless that right is otherwise subject to such a restriction, a member shall have the right to sell or otherwise transfer shares in the traded PLC at any time between the record date and the general meeting to which it applies.

(5) In relation to the subjecting by a traded PLC of a person to proof of the person's qualification as a member, that person may be made subject only to such requirements—

(a) as are necessary to ensure the identification of the person as a member, and

(b) then only to the extent that such requirements are proportionate to the achievement of that objective.

1106 Participation in general meeting by electronic means

(1) A traded PLC may provide for participation in a general meeting by electronic means including—

(a) a mechanism for casting votes, whether before or during the meeting, and the mechanism adopted shall not require the member to be physically present at the meeting or require the member to appoint a proxy who is physically present at the meeting;

(b) real time transmission of the meeting;

(c) real time two way communication enabling members to address the meeting from a remote location.

(2) The use of electronic means pursuant to *subsection (1)* may be made subject only to such requirements and restrictions as are necessary to ensure the identification of those taking part and the security of the electronic communication, to the extent that such requirements and restrictions are proportionate to the achievement of those objectives.

(3) Members shall be informed of any requirements or restrictions which a traded PLC puts in place pursuant to *subsection (2)*.

(4) A traded PLC that provides electronic means for participation at a general meeting by a member shall ensure, as far as practicable, that—

(a) such means—

(i) guarantee the security of any electronic communication by the member;

(ii) minimise the risk of data corruption and unauthorised access;

(iii) provide certainty as to the source of the electronic communication;

and

(b) in the case of any failure or disruption of such means, that failure or disruption is remedied as soon as practicable.

1107 Right to ask questions

(1) A member of a traded PLC has the right to ask questions related to items on the agenda of a general meeting and to have such questions answered by the PLC subject to any reasonable measures the PLC may take to ensure the identification of the member.

(2) An answer to a question asked pursuant to *subsection (1)* is not required where—

(a) to give an answer would interfere unduly with the preparation for the meeting or the confidentiality and business interests of the PLC;

(b) the answer has already been given on the PLC's website by means of what is commonly known as "a question and answer forum"; or

(c) it appears to the chairperson of the meeting that it is undesirable in the interests of good order of the meeting that the question be answered.

1108 Provisions concerning appointment of proxies

(1) In the case of a traded PLC, *section 183* shall have effect subject to the following subsections.

(2) *Section 183* shall apply as if the following subsection were substituted for *subsection (3)*:

"(3) Unless the company's constitution otherwise provides, a member of a company shall not be entitled to appoint more than one proxy to attend on the same occasion, but this is subject to *section 1108(3)*.".

(3) Notwithstanding anything in *section 183(3)*, as applied by *subsection (2)*, or in the traded PLC's constitution—

(a) no limitation may be placed on the right of a member to appoint more than one proxy to attend on the same occasion in respect of shares held in different securities accounts, and

(b) a member (being an individual or a body corporate) acting as an intermediary on behalf of one or more clients shall not be prohibited from granting a proxy to each of his or her clients or to any third party designated by such a client,

and an intermediary referred to in *paragraph (b)* shall be permitted to cast votes attaching to some of the shares differently from others.

(4) Without prejudice to the member's general entitlements in that regard under *section 183(7)*, a member shall be entitled to—

(a) appoint a proxy by electronic means, to an address specified by the traded PLC;

(b) have the electronic notification of such appointment accepted by the traded PLC; and

(c) have at least one effective method of notification of a proxy by electronic means offered to it by the traded PLC.

(5) The appointment and notification of appointment of a proxy to a traded PLC and the issuing of voting instructions to a proxy may be subject only to such formal

requirements as are necessary to ensure identification of a member or the proxy, or the possibility of verifying the content of voting instructions, if any, and only to the extent that those requirements are proportionate to achieving those objectives.

(6) *Subsections (4)* and *(6)* apply with the necessary modifications to the revocation of the appointment of a proxy.

(7) Any provision contained in the constitution of a traded PLC (other than a requirement that a person appointed as a proxy shall possess legal capacity) shall be void in so far as it would have the effect of restricting the eligibility of a person to be appointed as a proxy.

1109 Traded PLC may permit vote to be cast in advance by correspondence

(1) A traded PLC may permit, by appropriate arrangements, a vote to be exercised for the purpose of a poll (that is to be taken at a general meeting) by means of the vote being cast in advance by correspondence.

(2) Any such arrangements may be made subject only to such requirements and restrictions as are—

(a) necessary to ensure the identification of the person voting, and

(b) proportionate to the achievement of that objective.

(3) A traded PLC shall not be required to count votes cast in advance by correspondence pursuant to *subsection (1)* unless such votes are received before the date and time specified by the PLC; however, for that purpose, the PLC may not specify a date and time that is more than 24 hours before the time at which the vote is to be concluded.

1110 Voting results

(1) Where a member requests a full account of a vote before or on the declaration of the result of a vote at a general meeting, then with respect to each resolution proposed at a general meeting the traded PLC shall establish—

(a) the number of shares for which votes have been validly cast;

(b) the proportion of the company's issued share capital at close of business on the day before the meeting represented by those votes;

(c) the total number of votes validly cast; and

(d) the number of votes cast in favour of and against each resolution and, if counted, the number of abstentions.

(2) Where no member requests a full account of the voting before or on the declaration of the result of a vote at a general meeting, it shall be sufficient for the traded PLC to establish the voting results only to the extent necessary to ensure that the required majority is reached for each resolution.

(3) A traded PLC shall ensure that a voting result established in accordance with this section is published on its website not later than the expiry of 15 days after the date of the meeting at which the voting result was obtained.

Chapter 9
Duties of directors and other officers

1111 Obligation to convene extraordinary general meeting in event of serious loss of capital

(1) Where the net assets of a PLC are half or less of the amount of the PLC's called-up share capital, the directors of the PLC shall, not later than 28 days after the earliest day on which that fact is known to a director of the PLC (the "relevant day"), duly convene an extraordinary general meeting of the PLC.

(2) That extraordinary general meeting shall be convened—

(a) for the purpose of considering whether any, and if so what, measures should be taken to deal with the situation; and

(b) for a date not later than 56 days after the relevant day.

(3) If there is a failure to convene an extraordinary general meeting of a PLC as required by *subsections (1)* and *(2)*, each of the directors of the PLC who—

(a) knowingly and intentionally authorises or permits that failure, or

(b) after the expiry of the period during which that meeting should have been convened, knowingly and intentionally authorises or permits that failure to continue,

shall be guilty of a category 3 offence.

(4) Nothing in this section shall be taken as authorising the consideration, at an extraordinary general meeting convened in pursuance of this section, of any matter which could not have been considered at that meeting apart from this section.

[(5) This section shall not have effect in respect of a company to which the resolution tools, powers or mechanisms provided for in Part 4 of the Bank Recovery and Resolution Regulations are applied or exercised.][a]

Amendments

a Subsection (5) inserted by European Union (Bank Recovery and Resolution) Regulations 2015, reg 189(12), with effect from 15 July 2015.

1112 Qualifications of secretary of a PLC

(1) The directors of a PLC shall have a duty to ensure that the person appointed as secretary has the skills or resources necessary to discharge his or her statutory and other duties and that the person complies with one, or more than one, of the following 3 conditions.

(2) Those conditions are—

(a) the person, for at least 3 years of the 5 years immediately preceding his or her appointment as secretary, held the office of secretary of a company;

(b) the person is a member of a body for the time being recognised for the purposes of this section by the Minister;

(c) the person is a person who, by virtue of his or her—

(i) holding or having held any other position; or

(ii) his or her being a member of any other body;

appears to the directors of the PLC to be capable of discharging the duties referred to in *subsection (1)*.

(3) *Section 226* shall apply, in relation to a PLC, as if, in *subsection (2)*, "Without prejudice to the generality of *section 1112(1)* and *(2)*" were substituted for "Without prejudice to the generality of *section 129(4)*".

1113 Voting by director in respect of certain matters: prohibition and exceptions thereto

Save to the extent that the PLC's constitution provides otherwise, a director of a PLC shall not vote in respect of any contract or arrangement in which the director is interested, and if the director does so vote, the director's vote shall not be counted, nor shall he or she be counted in the quorum present at the meeting, but neither of those prohibitions shall apply to:

(a) any arrangement for giving any director any security or indemnity in respect of money lent by the director to or obligations undertaken by the director for the benefit of the PLC; or

(b) any arrangement for the giving by the PLC of any security to a third party in respect of a debt or obligation of the PLC for which the director himself or herself has assumed responsibility in whole or in part under a guarantee or indemnity or by the deposit of security; or

(c) any contract by the director to subscribe for or underwrite shares or debentures of the PLC; or

(d) any contract or arrangement with any other company in which the director is interested only as an officer of such other company or as a holder of shares or other securities in such other company,

and the operation of those prohibitions may at any time be suspended or limited to any extent and either generally or in respect of any particular contract, arrangement or transaction by the PLC in general meeting.

Chapter 10
Financial statements, annual return and audit

1114 Non-application of *Part 6* to PLCs that are credit institutions or insurance undertakings

Part 6 shall not apply to a PLC that is a credit institution or an insurance undertaking—

(a) to the extent provided by regulations made under section 3 of the European Communities Act 1972 to give effect to Community acts on accounts of credit institutions and insurance undertakings, respectively; or

(b) to the extent provided by any other enactment.

1115 Requirement for corporate governance statement and modification of certain provisions of *Parts 5* and *6* as they apply to PLCs

Chapter 3 of *Part 23* has effect in relation to, amongst other companies, a PLC that has shares or debentures admitted to trading on a regulated market in an EEA state.

1116 Modification of definition of "IAS Regulation" in the case of PLCs

The definition of "IAS Regulation" in *section 274(1)* shall apply in the case of PLC as if "and a reference to Article 4 of that Regulation is, where the financial statements concerned are entity financial statements or the company concerned is not a traded company (within the meaning of *section 1372*), a reference to Article 5 of that Regulation" were substituted for "and a reference to Article 4 of that Regulation is, in the case of a private company limited by shares, a reference to Article 5 of that Regulation".

[1116A Modification of definition of "ineligible entities" in the case of PLCs

The definition of 'ineligible entities' in *section 275(1)* shall apply to a PLC as if—

(a) in *paragraph (c)*, 'undertakings,' were substituted for 'undertakings, or',

(b) in *paragraph (d)(ii)*, 'shall be read accordingly, or' were substituted for 'shall be read accordingly;', and

(c) the following paragraph were inserted after *paragraph (d)*:

(e) are PLCs;'.][a]

Amendments

a Section 1116A inserted by C(A)A 2017, s 75.

1117 Obligation for a PLC's statutory financial statements to be audited

The directors of a PLC shall arrange for the statutory financial statements of the PLC for a financial year to be audited by statutory auditors.

1118 Statutory auditors' report on revised financial statements and revised report

Section 370 shall apply to a PLC as if, in *subsection (1)*, "Subject to *subsection (3)*" were substituted for "Subject to *section 371* and *subsection (3)*".

1119 Summary financial statements and circulation of them to members in lieu of full financial statements

(1) The directors of a PLC may prepare in respect of each financial year a summary financial statement for that financial year derived from the statutory financial statements and the directors' report for that period, giving a fair and accurate summary account of the PLC's financial development during that financial year and financial position at the end of that year.

(2) The summary financial statement shall be approved by the board of directors and shall be signed by them or, if there are more than 2 directors, shall be signed on their behalf by 2 of them.

(3) Where the PLC has subsidiary undertakings or undertakings of substantial interest (within the meaning of *section 314*), the statement shall (so far as they are dealt with in the group financial statements) give an account of the financial development and position of the PLC and its subsidiary undertakings and other such undertakings.

(4) Every summary financial statement shall include a statement of the statutory auditors' opinion as to its consistency with the statutory financial statements of the PLC and the directors' report and its conformity with the requirements of this section.

(5) Not later than the day specified in *subsection (6)*, a copy of—

(a) the summary financial statement, and

(b) where it includes a qualification, the statutory auditors' report under *section 391*,

may, in lieu of the documents specified in *section 338(2)*, be sent by the PLC to every member who is entitled to notice of the meeting referred to in *subsection (6)* and to the Registrar.

(6) The day referred to in *subsection (5)* is the 21st day before the date of the annual general meeting at which the statutory financial statements and directors' report of the PLC are to be considered.

(7) Every summary financial statement shall also include statements to the effect that—

(a) it is only a summary of information in the statutory financial statements and directors' report;

(b) the statutory financial statements have been audited; and

(c) copies of the statutory financial statements, statutory auditors' report and directors' report will be available to members upon request;

and copies of those documents will, accordingly, be made available by the PLC to any member upon request.

(8) For the avoidance of doubt, the reference, in relation to non-statutory financial statements, in *section 340(4)* to publication does not include the sending of a summary financial statement to a member in accordance with *subsection (5)*.

(9) *Section 347(2)* applies for the purpose of the construction of the reference to a copy of a document in *subsection (5)* of this section (in so far as the reference is to a copy to be sent to the Registrar) as it applies for the purpose of the construction of the reference to a copy of a document in *section 347(1)*.

1120 Application of *sections 310* to *313*

(1) For the purposes of this Part, *sections 310* to *313* shall apply as if, in those sections, there were substituted for the references to a holding company of a credit institution preparing financial statements references to a PLC that is a credit institution preparing

financial statements; but this adaptation does not displace those sections' application in cases where—

(a) the holding company of the company concerned is a PLC that is a credit institution, or

(b) both the holding company and the company concerned are credit institutions.

(2) In particular, that adaptation does not limit the provisions of *sections 310* to *313* that operate by reference to something that has been done to or in relation to a person connected with a director of a holding company of another company.

(3) Accordingly any exemption conferred, or requirement imposed, by any of those sections applies in respect of a transaction, arrangement or agreement (being a transaction, arrangement or agreement to which the PLC hereafter mentioned is a party) that is entered into or made with or for—

(a) a person connected with a director of a holding company of a PLC which PLC is a credit institution, or

(b) an officer of such a PLC,

as it applies in respect of a transaction, arrangement or agreement (being a transaction, arrangement or agreement to which such a PLC is a party) entered into or made with or for—

(i) a person connected with a director of such a PLC, or

(ii) an officer of such a PLC.

(4) *Section 312(3)* to *(6)* shall not apply to a credit institution which is the wholly owned subsidiary of a company incorporated in the State.

Chapter 11
Debentures

1121 Provisions as to register of debenture holders

(1) A PLC shall keep a register of holders of debentures (the "debenture holders' register") of the PLC and enter therein the names and addresses of the debenture holders and the amount of debentures currently held by each.

(2) For the purposes of *subsection (1)*, debentures do not include any debenture which does not form part of a series ranking *pari passu* nor any debenture which is transferable by delivery.

(3) *Chapter 10* of *Part 4*, as adapted by *subsection (4)*, shall apply in relation to the debenture holders' register.

(4) For the purposes of this section, *Chapter 10* of *Part 4* is adapted as follows:

(a) in *section 215(a)*, there shall be added the following definition:

" 'debenture holders' register' means the register kept by the company pursuant to *section 1121(1)*;";

(b) *section 216(1)* shall have effect as if, in addition to the registers specified in that provision as being registers to which *section 216* applies, that provision specified the debenture holders' register as being a register to which that section applies;

(c) *subsection (7)* of *section 216* shall have effect as if after "it is closed under *section 174*" there were inserted "and, in the case of the debenture holders' register, when it is deemed to be closed under *section 1121(6)*"; and

(d) each of *subsections (9)*, *(11)* and *(12)* of *section 216* shall have effect as if, in addition to the registers specified in the particular subsection, there were specified in the particular subsection the debenture holders' register.

(5) *Section 127(1)* (access to documents during business hours) shall apply for the purposes of *Chapter 10* of *Part 4*, as that Chapter is adapted for the purposes of this section, as it applies in relation to the relevant provisions of *Part 4*.

(6) For the purposes of *section 216(7)*, as adapted by *subsection (4)*, the debenture holders' register shall be deemed to be closed if closed in accordance with provisions contained in—

(a) the articles of the PLC; or

(b) the debentures, or in the case of debenture stock, in the stock certificates; or

(c) the trust deed or other document securing the debentures or debenture stock;

during such period or periods, not exceeding in the whole 30 days in any year, as may be specified in the document referred to in *paragraph (a)*, *(b)* or *(c)*.

(7) A copy of any trust deed for securing any issue of debentures shall be forwarded to every holder of any such debentures, at his or her request, by the PLC on payment to it of a fee of €10.00 or such less sum as may be determined by the PLC.

(8) If a copy of a trust deed referred to in *subsection (7)* is not forwarded by the PLC in accordance with that subsection, the PLC and any officer of it who is in default shall be guilty of a category 3 offence.

(9) In the case of a failure to comply with *subsection (7)*, the court may, on application being made to it, make an order directing that the copy requested be forwarded to the person requesting it.

Chapter 12
Examinerships

1122 Petitions for examinerships

Section 510 shall apply to a PLC as if the following subsections were substituted for *subsections (2)* and *(3)*:

"(2) Where the company referred to in *section 509* is an insurer or the holding company of an insurer, a petition may be presented only by the Central Bank, and *subsection (1)* shall not apply to the company.

(3) Where the company referred to in *section 509* is—

(a) a credit institution or the holding company of a credit institution;

(b) a company which one or more trustee savings banks have been reorganised into pursuant to an order under section 57 of the Trustee Savings Banks Act 1989; or

(c) a company which a building society has converted itself into under Part XI of the Building Societies Act 1989,

a petition may be presented only by the Central Bank, and *subsection (1)* shall not apply to the company.".

Chapter 13
Reorganisations

1123 Acquisitions of uncertificated securities from dissenting shareholders

(1) In this section—

"dissenting security holder" has the meaning given to it by Part 5 of the European Communities (Takeover Bids (Directive 2004/25/EC)) Regulations 2006 (S.I. No. 255 of 2006);

"dissenting shareholder" has the meaning given to it by *Chapter 2* of *Part 9*;

"relevant offeree" means an offeree company within the meaning of—

(a) *Chapter 2* of *Part 9*; or

(b) Part 5 of the European Communities (Takeover Bids (Directive 2004/25/EC)) Regulations 2006;

which is a participating issuer;

"relevant offeror" means an offeror within the meaning of—

(a) *Chapter 2* of *Part 9*; or

(b) Part 5 of the European Communities (Takeover Bids (Directive 2004/25/EC)) Regulations 2006;

"relevant regulations" means—

(a) the Companies Act 1990 (Uncertificated Securities) Regulations 1996 (S.I. No. 68 of 1996) which regulations are continued in force by *Schedule 6*; or

(b) if regulations under *section 1086* are made and those regulations—

(i) replace the regulations referred to in *paragraph (a)* — those replacement regulations; or

(ii) amend the regulations referred to in *paragraph (a)* — the latter regulations as they stand so amended.

(2) In this section each of the following:

(i) "issuer-instruction";

(ii) "operator";

(iii) "operator-instruction";

(iv) "participating issuer";

(v) "register of securities";

(vi) "system-member";

(vii) "uncertificated securities";

(viii) "unit of a security";

has the meaning given to it by the relevant regulations.

(3) Where a relevant offeror has become bound to acquire under, as the case may be—

(a) *Chapter 2* of *Part 9*; or

(b) Part 5 of the European Communities (Takeover Bids (Directive 2004/25/EC)) Regulations 2006;

the shares or securities of a dissenting shareholder or dissenting security holder then, *subsection (4)* applies, in lieu of the relevant procedures specified in *section 459* or Regulation 25 of the foregoing Regulations, with respect to effecting the transfer and a reference in *subsection (4)* to securities includes shares.

(4) The relevant offeree shall enter the relevant offeror in its register of securities as the holder of the uncertificated units of the securities concerned in place of the system-member who was, immediately prior to such entry, registered as the holder of such units as if it had received an operator-instruction requiring it to amend its register of securities in such manner.

(5) A company which amends its register of securities in accordance with *subsection (4)* shall forthwith notify the operator by issuer-instruction of the amendment.

Chapter 14
Strike off and restoration

1124 Power of Registrar to strike PLC off register

(1) In addition to the cases mentioned in *section 725*, a PLC may be struck off the register in the circumstances and under the conditions specified in the following provisions.

(2) Where a PLC, registered as such on its original incorporation, has not been issued with a certificate under *section 1010* within one year after the date on which it was registered, the Registrar may employ the following procedure.

(3) That procedure consists of there being sent by the Registrar, by registered post, the notice referred to in *subsection (5)* to the PLC at its registered office.

(4) The Registrar shall also send a copy of the foregoing notice by prepaid ordinary post to such persons, if any, as are recorded in the office of the Registrar as being current directors of the PLC but non-compliance with this subsection does not affect the validity of a notice that otherwise complies with *subsection (3)*; the address to which a notice under this subsection is sent shall be the usual residential address, as recorded in the office of the Registrar, of the addressee concerned.

(5) The Registrar's notice referred to in *subsections (3)* and *(4)* shall—

(a) state that the issue of the notice is the first step in a process that may lead to the PLC being struck off the register;

(b) state the ground for striking off being invoked by the Registrar, namely, that the PLC has not been issued with a certificate under *section 1010* within one year after the date on which it was registered;

(c) state that the PLC will be dissolved if it is struck off the register;

(d) specify the remedial step, namely the procuring by the PLC of the issue to it of a certificate under *section 1010*;

(e) specify the date on or before which that certificate must be issued to the PLC; and

(f) state that failure to have that certificate issued to it on or before the date so specified may result in the Registrar giving public notice of an intention to strike the PLC off the register.

(6) The date to be specified for the purposes of *subsection (5)(e)* shall be a date falling not less than 28 days after the date of the notice.

(7) If the Registrar has given a notice under *subsection (3)* and the remedial step referred to in *subsection (5)(d)* has not been taken on or before the date specified in that notice for the purposes of *subsection (5)(e)*, the Registrar may, by publishing a notice in the CRO Gazette that complies with *subsection (8)*, give public notice of the Registrar's intention to strike the PLC off the register.

(8) The notice referred to in *subsection (7)* shall—

(a) specify the ground for striking the PLC off the register, namely, that the PLC has not been issued with a certificate under *section 1010* within one year after the date on which it was registered;

(b) specify the remedial step, namely the procuring by the PLC of the issue to it of a certificate under *section 1010*;

(c) specify the date on or before which that remedial step must be taken; and

(d) state that unless that remedial step is taken on or before the date so specified the Registrar may strike the PLC off the register and, if the Registrar does so, the PLC will be dissolved.

(9) The date to be specified for the purposes of *subsection (8)(c)* shall be a date falling not less than 28 days after the date of publication of the notice.

(10) If the Registrar has given a notice referred to in *subsection (8)* and the remedial step referred to in *paragraph (b)* of that subsection has not been taken on or before the date specified in that notice for the purposes of *paragraph (c)* of that subsection, the Registrar may strike the PLC off the register.

(11) *Section 733(3)* and *(4)*, *section 734* and *sections 738* to *743* shall apply to a PLC which has been struck off the register in accordance with *subsection (10)* as those provisions apply to a company struck off the register in accordance with *section 733(1)*.

1125 Reinstatement as PLC confined to company which had such status before dissolution

Where a company has been dissolved under this Act or under any of the prior Companies Acts, it may not be restored to the register as a PLC unless it was a PLC immediately before such dissolution.

Chapter 15
Investigations

1126 Inspectors — minimum number of members that may apply for their appointment in the case of a PLC

Section 747(2) shall apply to a PLC as if the following paragraph were substituted for *paragraph (b)*:

"(b) not less than 100 members of the company;".

Chapter 16
Mergers

1127 Interpretation (*Chapter 16*)

(1) In this Chapter—

"company" includes a body corporate to which *section 1312(1)* (application of certain provisions of Act to unregistered companies) relates;

"director", in relation to a company which is being wound up, means liquidator;

"merger" means—

(a) a merger by acquisition;

(b) a merger by absorption; or

(c) a merger by formation of a new company;

within, in each case, the meaning of *section 1129*;

"merging company" means—

(a) in relation to a merger by acquisition or a merger by absorption, a company that is, in relation to that merger, a transferor company or the successor company; and

(b) in relation to a merger by formation of a new company, a company that is, in relation to that merger, a transferor company;

"share exchange ratio" means the number of shares or other securities in the successor company that the common draft terms of merger provide to be allotted to members of any transferor company for a given number of their shares or other securities in the transferor company;

"successor company" shall be read in accordance with *section 1129*;

"transferor company", in relation to a merger, means a company, the assets and liabilities of which are to be, or have been, transferred to the successor company by way of that merger.

(2) References in this Chapter to the acquisition of a company are references to the acquisition of the assets and liabilities of the company by way of a merger under this Chapter.

1128 Requirement for Chapter to apply

[(1) Subject to *subsection (2)*, this Chapter applies only if each of the merging companies, or, one at least, of them, is a PLC.

(2) This Chapter shall not apply if each of the merging companies is—

(a) a PLC, or

(b) any other company to which Directive 2011/35/EU of the European Parliament and of the Council of 5 April 2011 applies,

any of which is the subject of the use of resolution tools, powers and mechanisms provided for in Title IV of Directive 2014/59/EU of the European Parliament and of the Council.][a]

Amendments

a Section 1128 substituted by European Union (Bank Recovery and Resolution) Regulations 2015, reg 189(13), with effect from 15 July 2015.

1129 Mergers to which Chapter applies — definitions and supplementary provision

(1) In this Chapter "merger by acquisition" means an operation in which a company (the "successor company") acquires all the assets and liabilities of one or more other companies that is or are dissolved without going into liquidation in exchange for the issue to the members of that company or those companies of shares in the first-mentioned company, with or without any cash payment.

(2) In this Chapter "merger by absorption" means an operation whereby, on being dissolved and without going into liquidation, a company transfers all of its assets and liabilities to a company that is the holder of all the shares representing the capital of the first-mentioned company.

(3) The reference in *subsection (2)* to a company (the "second-mentioned company") that is the holder of all the shares representing the capital of the first-mentioned company in that subsection includes a reference to either of the following cases:

(a) a case where all of those shares are held by other persons in their own names but on behalf of the second-mentioned company;

(b) a case where the shares representing the capital of the first-mentioned company held by the second-mentioned company and by other persons in their own names but on behalf of the second-mentioned company amount, in aggregate, to all of the shares representing the foregoing capital.

(4) In this Chapter "merger by formation of a new company" means an operation in which 2 or more companies, on being dissolved without going into liquidation, transfer all their assets and liabilities to a company that they form — the "other company"— in exchange for the issue to their members of shares representing the capital of the other company, with or without any cash payment.

(5) Where a company is being wound up it may—

(a) become a party to a merger by acquisition, a merger by absorption or a merger by formation of a new company, provided that the distribution of its assets to its shareholders has not begun at the date, under *section 1131(6)*, of the common draft terms of merger; or

(b) opt to avail itself of the provisions of *Chapters 1* and *2* of *Part 9* or *section 601.*

(6) Subject to *subsection (5)*, the provisions of *Chapters 1* and *2* of *Part 9* and *section 601* shall not apply to a merger by acquisition, a merger by absorption or a merger by formation of a new company.

1130 Merger may not be put into effect save in accordance with this Chapter

(1) A merger may not be put into effect save under and in accordance with the provisions of this Chapter.

(2) A merger shall not take effect under this Chapter in the absence of the approval, authorisation or other consent, if any, that is required by any other enactment or a Community act for the merger to take effect.

1131 Common draft terms of merger

(1) Where a merger is proposed to be entered into, the directors of the merging companies shall draw up common draft terms of the merger in writing and approve those terms in writing.

(2) The common draft terms of merger shall state, at least—

(a) the name and registered office of each of the merging companies;

(b) as to each of the merging companies, whether it is a PLC, another type of company as defined in *section 2(1)* or a body corporate to which *section 1312(1)* relates;

(c) save in the case of a merger by absorption, the proposed share exchange ratio and the amount of any cash payment;

(d) save in the case of a merger by absorption, the proposed terms relating to allotment of shares in the successor company;

(e) save in the case of a merger by absorption, the date from which holders of such shares will become entitled to participate in the profits of the successor company;

(f) the date from which the transactions of the company or companies being acquired are to be treated for accounting purposes as being those of the successor company;

(g) any special conditions, including special rights or restrictions, whether in regard to voting, participation in profits, share capital or otherwise, which will apply to shares issued by the successor company in exchange for shares in the company or companies being acquired;

(h) any payment or benefit in cash or otherwise, paid or given or intended to be paid or given to any expert referred to in *section 1133* and to any director of any of the merging companies in so far as it differs from the payment or benefit paid or given to other persons in respect of the merger and the consideration, if any, for any such payment or benefit.

(3) The common draft terms of merger shall not provide for any shares in the successor company to be exchanged for shares in a company being acquired that are held either—

(a) by the successor company itself or its nominee on its behalf; or

(b) by the company being acquired itself or its nominee on its behalf.

(4) Where the merger is a merger by formation of a new company the common draft terms of merger shall include or be accompanied by the constitution or draft constitution of the new company.

(5) The common draft terms of merger, as approved under *subsection (1)*, shall be signed, on the same date, on behalf of each of the merging companies by 2 directors of each such company (or, in the case of each of one or more of them having a sole director, by the sole director); the common draft terms shall bear the date of such signing.

(6) That date shall, for the purposes of this Chapter, be the date of the common draft terms of merger.

1132 Directors' explanatory report

(1) Except in the case of a merger by absorption and subject to *subsections (4)* and *(5)*, a separate written report (the "explanatory report") shall be prepared in respect of each of the merging companies by the directors of each such company.

(2) The explanatory report shall at least give particulars of, and explain—

(a) the common draft terms of merger;

(b) the legal and economic grounds for and implications of the common draft terms of merger with particular reference to the proposed share exchange ratio, organisation and management structures, recent and future commercial activities and the financial interests of the holders of the shares and other securities in the company;

(c) the methods used to arrive at the proposed share exchange ratio and the reasons for the use of these methods; and

(d) any special valuation difficulties which have arisen.

(3) The explanatory report shall be signed, on the same date, on behalf of each of the merging companies by 2 directors of each such company (or, in the case of each

of one or more of them having a sole director, by the sole director); the report shall bear the date of such signing.

(4) This section is subject to *section 1137(11)* (which provides for an exemption from its requirements in relation to a particular type of merger operation).

(5) This section shall not apply if the following condition is, or (as appropriate) the following 2 conditions are, satisfied:

(a) other than in a case falling within *paragraph (b)*, all of the holders of shares conferring the right to vote at general meetings of each of the merging companies have agreed that this section shall not apply; or

(b) where a requirement for the taking effect of a vote (whether a vote generally or of the type to which this subsection applies) by holders of shares of any of the merging companies is that a holder of securities of the company has consented thereto—

(i) the agreement mentioned in *paragraph (a)* exists; and

(ii) all of the holders of securities of the company or companies in respect of which requirement mentioned in this paragraph operates have agreed that this section shall not apply.

1133 Expert's report

(1) Subject to *subsections (2)*, *(13)* and *(14)*, there shall, in accordance with this section, be appointed one or more persons to—

(a) examine the common draft terms of merger; and

(b) make a report on those terms to the shareholders of the merging companies.

(2) *Subsection (1)* shall not apply where the merger is a merger by absorption.

(3) The functions referred to in *subsection (1)(a)* and *(b)* shall be performed either—

(a) in relation to each merging company, by one or more persons appointed for that purpose in relation to the particular company by its directors and—

(i) no person may be appointed under this paragraph unless the person's appointment has first been approved by the court on the application to it of the company concerned;

(ii) the directors of each company may appoint the same person or persons for that purpose;

or

(b) in relation to all the merging companies, by one or more persons appointed for that purpose by the court, on the application to it of all of the merging companies.

(4) The person so appointed, or each person so appointed, is referred to in this Chapter as an "expert" and a reference in this Chapter to a report of an expert or other action (including an opinion) of an expert shall, in a case where there are 2 or more experts, be read as reference to a joint report or joint other action (including an opinion) of or by them.

(5) A person shall not be appointed an expert unless the person is a qualified person.

(6) A person is a qualified person for the purposes of this section if the person—

(a) is a statutory auditor; and

(b) is not—

(i) a person who is or, within the period of 12 months before the date of the common draft terms of merger has been, an officer or employee of any of the merging companies;

(ii) except with the leave of the court, a parent, spouse, civil partner, brother, sister or child of an officer of any of the merging companies (and a reference in this subparagraph to a child of an officer shall be deemed to include a child of the officer's civil partner who is ordinarily resident with the officer and the civil partner); or

(iii) a person who is a partner, or in the employment, of an officer or employee of any of the merging companies.

(7) The report of the expert shall be in writing and shall—

(a) state the method or methods used to arrive at the proposed share exchange ratio;

(b) give the opinion of the expert as to whether the proposed share exchange ratio is fair and reasonable;

(c) give the opinion of the expert as to the adequacy of the method or methods used in the case in question;

(d) indicate the values arrived at using each such method;

(e) give the opinion of the expert as to the relative importance attributed to such methods in arriving at the values decided on; and

(f) specify any special valuation difficulties which have arisen.

(8) The expert may—

(a) require each of the merging companies and their officers to give to the expert such information and explanations (whether oral or in writing); and

(b) make such enquiries;

as the expert thinks necessary for the purposes of making the report.

(9) If a merging company fails to give to the expert any information or explanation in the power, possession or procurement of that company, on a requirement being made of it under *subsection (8)(a)* by the expert, that company and any officer of it who is in default shall be guilty of a category 2 offence.

(10) If a merging company makes a statement (whether orally or in writing), or provides a document, to the expert that conveys or purports to convey any information or explanation the subject of a requirement made of it under *subsection (8)(a)* by the expert and—

(a) that information is false or misleading in a material particular, and

(b) the company knows it to be so false or misleading or is reckless as to whether it is so false or misleading, the company and any officer of it who is in default shall be guilty of a category 2 offence.

(11) If a person appointed an expert under *subsection (3)(a)* or *(b)* ceases to be a qualified person, that person—

(a) shall immediately cease to hold office, and

(b) shall give notice in writing of the fact of the person's ceasing to be a qualified person to each merging company and (in the case of an appointment under *subsection (3)(b)*) to the court within 14 days after the date of that cessation,

but without prejudice to the validity of any acts done by the person under this Chapter before that cessation.

(12) A person who purports to perform the functions of an expert (in respect of the merger concerned) under this Chapter after ceasing to be a qualified person (in respect of that merger) shall be guilty of a category 2 offence.

(13) This section is subject to *section 1137(11)* (which provides for an exemption from its requirements in relation to a particular type of merger operation).

(14) This section shall not apply if the following condition is, or (as appropriate) the following 2 conditions are, satisfied:

(a) other than in a case falling within *paragraph (b)*, all of the holders of shares conferring the right to vote at general meetings of each of the merging companies have agreed that this section shall not apply; or

(b) where a requirement for the taking effect of a vote (whether a vote generally or of the type to which this subsection applies) by holders of shares of any of the merging companies is that a holder of securities of the company has consented thereto—

(i) the agreement mentioned in *paragraph (a)* exists; and

(ii) all of the holders of securities of the company or companies in respect of which the requirement mentioned in this paragraph operates have agreed that this section shall not apply.

1134 Merger financial statement

(1) Subject to *subsections (6)* and *(8)*, where the latest statutory financial statements of any of the merging companies relate to a financial year ended more than 6 months before the date of the common draft terms of merger, that company shall prepare a merger financial statement in accordance with the provisions of this section.

(2) The merger financial statement shall be drawn up—

(a) in the format of the last annual balance sheet, if any, of the company and in accordance with the provisions of *Part 6*, and

(b) as at a date not earlier than the first day of the third month preceding the date of the common draft terms of merger.

(3) Valuations shown in the last annual balance sheet, if any, shall, subject to the exceptions provided for under *subsection (4)*, only be altered to reflect entries in the accounting records of the company.

(4) Notwithstanding *subsection (3)*, the following shall be taken into account in preparing the merger financial statement:

(a) interim depreciation and provisions; and

(b) material changes in actual value not shown in the accounting records.

(5) The provisions of *Part 6* relating to the statutory auditor's report on the last statutory financial statements of the company concerned shall apply, with any necessary modifications, to the merger financial statement required of the company by *subsection (1)*.

(6) This section shall not apply in relation to a merging company which makes public a half-yearly financial report covering the first 6 months of its financial year pursuant to the provision referred to in *subsection (7)* if that company makes that report available for inspection pursuant to *section 1136*.

(7) The provision referred to in *subsection (6)* is, as appropriate—

(a) Regulation 6 of the Transparency (Directive 2004/109/EC) Regulations 2007 (S.I. No. 277 of 2007) which regulations are continued in force by *Schedule 6*; or

(b) if regulations under *section 1380* are made and those regulations—

(i) replace the regulations referred to in *paragraph (a)* — the provision of those replacement regulations corresponding to the foregoing Regulation 6; or

(ii) amend the foregoing Regulation 6 — that Regulation as it stands so amended.

(8) This section shall not apply to a merging company if the following condition is, or (as appropriate) the following 2 conditions are, satisfied:

(a) other than in a case falling within *paragraph (b)*, all of the holders of shares conferring the right to vote at general meetings of the company have agreed that this section shall not apply; or

(b) where a requirement for the taking effect of a vote (whether a vote generally or of the type to which this subsection applies) by holders of shares of the company is that a holder of securities of the company has consented thereto—

(i) the agreement mentioned in *paragraph (a)* exists; and

(ii) all of the holders of securities in respect of which the requirement mentioned in this paragraph operates have agreed that this section shall not apply.

1135 Registration and publication of documents

(1) Subject to *subsection (3)*, each of the merging companies shall—

(a) deliver to the Registrar a copy of the common draft terms of merger, signed and dated as required by *section 1131(5)*;

(b) cause to be published in the CRO Gazette notice of delivery to the Registrar of the common draft terms of merger.

(2) The requirements of *subsection (1)* shall be fulfilled by each of the merging companies at least 30 days before the date of the general meeting of each such company which, by virtue of *section 1137*, is held to consider the common draft terms of merger.

(3) This section shall not apply in relation to a merging company if the company—

(a) publishes, free of charge on its website for a continuous period of at least 2 months, commencing at least 30 days before the date of the general meeting which, by virtue of *section 1137*, is to consider the common draft terms of merger and ending at least 30 days after that date, a copy of the common draft terms of merger, signed and dated pursuant to *section 1131(5)*, and

(b) causes to be published in the CRO Gazette and once at least in 2 daily newspapers circulating in the district in which the registered office or principal place of business of the company is situate notice of publication on its website of the common draft terms of merger.

(4) Where, in the period referred to in *subsection (3)(a)*, access to the company's website is disrupted for a continuous period of at least 24 hours or for separate periods totalling not less than 72 hours, the period referred to in *subsection (3)(a)* shall be extended for a period corresponding to the period or periods of disruption.

1136 Inspection of documents

(1) Subject to *subsections (5)* and *(9)*, each of the merging companies shall, in accordance with *subsection (3)*, make available for inspection free of charge by any member of the company at its registered office during business hours—

(a) the common draft terms of merger;

(b) subject to *subsection (2)*, the statutory financial statements for the preceding 3 financial years of each company (audited, where required by that Part, in accordance with *Part 6*);

(c) if such a report is required to be prepared by that section, each explanatory report in relation to the merging companies referred to in *section 1132*;

(d) if such a report is required to be prepared by that section, the expert's report relating to each of the merging companies referred to in *section 1133*; and

(e) each merger financial statement, if any, in relation to one or, as the case may be, more than one of the merging companies, required to be prepared by *section 1134* or, as appropriate, its half-yearly financial report referred to in *subsection (6)* of that section.

(2) For the purposes of *paragraph (b)* of *subsection (1)*—

(a) if any of the merging companies has traded for less than 3 financial years before the date of the common draft terms of merger, then, as respects that company, that paragraph is satisfied by the statutory financial statements for those financial years for which the company has traded (audited, where required by that Part, in accordance with *Part 6*) being made available as mentioned in that subsection by each of the merging companies; or

(b) if, by reason of its recent incorporation, the obligation of any of the foregoing companies to prepare its first financial statements under *Part 6* had not arisen as of the date of the common draft terms of merger, then the reference in that paragraph to the financial statements of that company shall be disregarded.

(3) The provisions of *subsection (1)* shall apply in the case of each of the merging companies for a period of 30 days before the date of the meeting of each such company which, by virtue of *section 1137*, is held to consider the common draft terms of merger.

(4) *Section 127(1)* (access to documents during business hours) shall apply in relation to *subsection (1)* as it applies in relation to the relevant provisions of *Part 4*.

(5) Subject to *subsection (6)*, *subsection (1)* shall not apply in relation to a merging company if it publishes free of charge on its website the documents specified in that subsection for a continuous period of at least 2 months, commencing at least 30 days before the date of the general meeting which, by virtue of *section 1137*, is to consider the common draft terms of merger and ending at least 30 days after that date.

(6) *Subsection (5)* shall not apply where the entitlement referred to in *section 1137(4)* does not apply in consequence of the application of *section 1138(2)*.

(7) Where, in the period referred to in *subsection (5)*, access to the company's website is disrupted for a continuous period of at least 24 hours or for separate periods totalling not less than 72 hours, the period referred to in *subsection (5)* shall be extended for a period corresponding to the period or periods of disruption.

(8) A reference in this section to statutory financial statements shall be deemed to include a reference to a directors' report and a reference to auditing shall, in the case of such a report, be read as a reference to the operation referred to in *section 336(5)*.

(9) This section is subject to *section 1137(11)* (which provides for an exemption from its requirements in relation to a particular type of merger operation).

1137 General meetings of merging companies

(1) In this section a reference to a general meeting, without qualification, is a reference to a general meeting referred to in *subsection (2)*.

(2) Subject to *subsection (7)* and without prejudice to *section 1139*, the subsequent steps under this Chapter in relation to the merger shall not be taken unless the

common draft terms of merger have been approved by a special resolution passed at a general meeting of each of the merging companies.

(3) In addition, where the merger is a merger by formation of a new company, those subsequent steps shall not be taken unless the constitution or draft constitution of the new company has been approved by a special resolution of each of the companies being acquired.

(4) Subject to *section 1138(2)*, the notice convening the general meeting referred to in *subsection (2)* shall contain a statement of every shareholder's entitlement to obtain on request, free of charge, full or, if so desired, partial copies of the documents referred to in *section 1136(1)* (and, accordingly, every shareholder has, subject to the foregoing provision, that entitlement).

(5) The directors of each of the companies involved in a merger shall inform—

(a) the general meeting of that company; and

(b) the directors of each of the other companies involved in the merger;

of any material change in the assets and liabilities of that company that occurs between the date of the common draft terms of merger and the date of such general meeting.

(6) On being so informed of them, the directors of each such other company involved in the merger shall inform the general meeting of that company of the matters referred to in *subsection (5)*.

(7) Where the merger is—

(a) a merger by acquisition (not falling within *paragraph (b)*); or

(b) a merger by acquisition carried out by a company which holds 90 per cent or more, but not all, of the shares conferring the right to vote at general meetings (excluding any shares held as treasury shares) of the company or companies being acquired; or

(c) a merger by absorption;

approval, by means of a special resolution, of the common draft terms of merger is not required in the case of the successor company if the conditions specified in *subsection (8)* are satisfied.

(8) The conditions referred to in *subsection (7)* are the following:

(a) the provisions of *sections 1135* and *1136* are complied with at least 30 days before the date of the general meeting of each of the companies being acquired; and

(b) the right, conferred by *subsection (9)*, to requisition a general meeting has not been exercised during that period of 30 days.

(9) One or more members of the successor company who hold or together hold not less than 5 per cent of the paid-up capital of the company which carries the right to vote at general meetings of the company (excluding any shares held as treasury shares) may require the convening of a general meeting of the company to consider the common draft terms of merger, and *section 178(3)* to *(7)* apply, with any necessary modifications, in relation to the requisition.

(10) The reference in *subsection (7)(b)* to a percentage of shares (the "specified percentage") being held by the company carrying out the acquisition includes a reference to either of the following cases:

(a) a case where the specified percentage of shares are held by other persons in their own names but on behalf of that company;

(b) a case where the percentages of—

(i) shares held by that company; and

(ii) shares held by other persons in the manner referred to in *paragraph (a)*;

amount, in aggregate, to the specified percentage.

(11) *Sections 1132*, *1133* and *1136* shall not apply to an operation referred to in *subsection (7)(b)* if—

(a) any shareholder in any of the merging companies indicates to the successor company that the shareholder will not vote in favour of the special resolution concerning the common draft terms of merger and requests, in writing, that company to purchase his or her shares in the company concerned for cash (which request such a shareholder is empowered by this subsection to make), and

(b) within 15 days after the date of that request, the successor company purchases those shares of that shareholder at the market sale price.

1138 Electronic means of making certain information available for purposes of *section 1137*

(1) For the purposes of *section 1137*, but subject to *subsection (2)*, where a shareholder has consented to the use by the company of electronic means for conveying information, the copies of the documents referred to in *section 1136(1)* may be provided, by electronic mail, to that shareholder by the company and the notice convening the general meeting referred to in *section 1137(2)* shall contain a statement to that effect.

(2) The entitlement referred to in *section 1137(4)* shall not apply where, for the period specified in *subsection (3)*, copies of the documents referred to in *section 1136(1)* are available to download and print, free of charge, from the company's website by shareholders of the company.

(3) The period referred to in *subsection (2)* is a continuous period of at least 2 months, commencing at least 30 days before the date of the general meeting which, by virtue of *section 1137*, is to consider the common draft terms of merger and ending at least 30 days after that date.

(4) Where, in the period referred to in *subsection (3)*, access to the company's website is disrupted for a continuous period of at least 24 hours or for separate periods totalling not less than 72 hours, the period referred to in *subsection (3)* shall be extended for a period corresponding to the period or periods of disruption.

1139 Meetings of classes of shareholders

(1) Where the share capital of any of the merging companies is divided into shares of different classes the provisions referred to in *subsection (2)*, with the exclusions specified in *subsection (3)*, shall apply with respect to the variation of the rights attached to any such class that is entailed by the merger.

(2) Those provisions are—

(a) if the merging company is not a private company limited by shares, as appropriate—

(i) *section 982*;

(ii) *section 1044*;

(iii) *section 1250*;

or

(b) if the merging company is a private company limited by shares, the provisions of *Chapter 4* of *Part 3* on the variation of the rights attached to any class of shares in a company.

(3) There is excluded the following from the foregoing provisions:

(a) *section 88(9)*;

(b) *section 982(10)* (including as it applies to a company other than a DAC);

(c) *section 89* (including as it applies to a company other than a private company limited by shares).

1140 Purchase of minority shares

(1) Any person being—

(a) a shareholder in any of the merging companies who voted against the special resolution of the company concerned relating to the common draft terms of merger, or

(b) in a case to which *section 1137(7)(b)* relates, any shareholder other than the successor company,

may, not later than 15 days after the relevant date, request the successor company in writing to acquire his or her shares for cash.

(2) Where a request is made by a shareholder in accordance with *subsection (1)*, the successor company shall purchase the shares of the shareholder at a price determined in accordance with the share exchange ratio set out in the common draft terms of merger and the shares so purchased by the successor company shall be treated as treasury shares within the meaning of *section 106*.

(3) In this section the "relevant date" means, in relation to the particular merging company to which *subsection (1)(a)* or *(b)* relates, the date on which the latest general meeting of that company to consider the draft terms of merger, or of any class of the holders of shares or other securities of such company, as required by this Chapter, is held.

(4) Nothing in this section shall prejudice the power of the court to make any order necessary for the protection of the interests of a dissenting minority in a merging company.

1141 Application for confirmation of merger by court

(1) An application under this section to the court for an order confirming a merger shall be made jointly by all the merging companies.

(2) That application shall be accompanied by a statement of the size of the shareholding of any shareholder who has requested the purchase of his or her shares under *section 1140* and of the measures which the successor company proposes to take to comply with the shareholder's request.

1142 Protection of creditors

(1) A creditor of any of the merging companies who—

(a) at the date of publication of the notice under *section 1135(1)(b)* is entitled to any debt or claim against the company, and

(b) can credibly demonstrate that the proposed merger would be likely to put the satisfaction of that debt or claim at risk, and that no adequate safeguards have been obtained from the company or the acquiring company,

shall be entitled to object to the confirmation by the court of the merger.

(2) If the court deems it necessary in order to secure the adequate protection of creditors of any of the merging companies it may—

(a) determine a list of creditors entitled to object and the nature and amount of their debts or claims, and may publish notices fixing a day or days within which creditors not entered on the list are to claim to be so entered or are to be excluded from the right of objecting to the confirmation;

(b) where a creditor entered on the list whose debt or claim is not discharged or has not terminated does not consent to the confirmation, the court may, if it thinks fit, dispense with the consent of that creditor, on either—

(i) the company securing payment of his or her debt or claim by appropriating, as the court may direct, the following amount—

(I) if the company admits the full amount of the debt or claim, or, though not admitting it, is willing to provide for it, then the full amount of the debt or claim;

(II) if the company does not admit and is not willing to provide for the full amount of the debt or claim, or, if the amount is contingent or not ascertained, then an amount fixed by the court after the like inquiry and adjudication as if the company were being wound up by the court;

(ii) the successor company, on behalf of the company liable for the debt or claim, securing payment of the debt or claim.

(3) If, having regard to any special circumstances of the case it thinks proper so to do, the court may direct that *subsection (2)* shall not apply as regards any class of creditors.

(4) References in this section to a debt or claim having terminated are references to the debt or claim ceasing to be enforceable or to its otherwise determining.

1143 Preservation of rights of holders of securities

(1) Subject to *subsection (2)*, holders of securities, other than shares, in any of the companies being acquired to which special rights are attached shall be given rights in the successor company at least equivalent to those they possessed in the company being acquired.

(2) *Subsection (1)* shall not apply—

(a) where the alteration of the rights in the successor company has been approved—

(i) by a majority of the holders of such securities at a meeting held for that purpose, or

(ii) by the holders of those securities individually,

or

(b) where the holders of those securities are entitled under the terms of those securities to have their securities purchased by the successor company.

1144 Confirmation order

(1) Where an application is made under *section 1141* to the court for an order confirming a merger this section applies.

(2) The court, on being satisfied that—

(a) the requirements of this Chapter have been complied with;

(b) proper provision has been made for—

(i) any shareholder in any of the merging companies who has made a request under *section 1140*; and

(ii) any creditor of any of the merging companies who objects to the merger in accordance with *section 1142*;

(c) the rights of holders of securities other than shares in any of the companies being acquired are safeguarded in accordance with *section 1143*; and

(d) where applicable, the relevant provisions referred to in *section 1139(2)* on the variation of the rights attached to any class of shares in any of the merging companies have been complied with;

may make an order confirming the merger with effect from such date as the court appoints (the "effective date").

(3) The order of the court confirming the merger shall, from the effective date, have the following effects:

(a) all the assets and liabilities of the company or companies being acquired are transferred to the successor company;

(b) in the case of a merger by acquisition or a merger by formation of a new company, where no request has been made by shareholders under *section 1140*, all remaining members of the transferor company or companies except the successor company (if it is a member of a transferor company) become members of the successor company;

(c) the transferor company or companies is or are dissolved;

(d) all legal proceedings pending by or against any transferor company shall be continued with the substitution, for the transferor company, of the successor company as a party;

(e) the successor company is obliged to make to the members of the transferor company or companies any cash payment required by the common draft terms of merger;

(f) every contract, agreement or instrument to which a transferor company is a party shall, notwithstanding anything to the contrary contained in that contract, agreement or instrument, be read and have effect as if—

(i) the successor company had been a party thereto instead of the transferor company;

(ii) for any reference (however worded and whether express or implied) to the transferor company there were substituted a reference to the successor company; and

(iii) any reference (however worded and whether express or implied) to the directors, officers, representatives or employees of the transferor company, or any of them—

(I) were, respectively, a reference to the directors, officers, representatives or employees of the successor company or to such director, officer, representative or employee of the successor company as the successor company nominates for that purpose; or

(II) in default of such nomination, were, respectively, a reference to the director, officer, representative or employee of the successor company who corresponds as nearly as may be to the first-mentioned director, officer, representative or employee;

(g) every contract, agreement or instrument to which a transferor company is a party becomes a contract, agreement or instrument between the successor company and the counterparty with the same rights, and subject to the same obligations, liabilities and incidents (including rights of set-off), as would have been applicable thereto if that contract, agreement or instrument had continued in force between the transferor company and the counterparty;

(h) any money due and owing (or payable) by or to a transferor company under or by virtue of any such contract, agreement or instrument as is mentioned in *paragraph (g)* shall become due and owing (or payable) by or to the successor company instead of the transferor company; and

(i) an offer or invitation to treat made to or by a transferor company before the effective date shall be read and have effect, respectively, as an offer or invitation to treat made to or by the successor company.

(4) The following provisions have effect for the purposes of *subsection (3)*—

(a) "instrument" in that subsection includes—

(i) a lease, conveyance, transfer or charge or any other instrument relating to real property (including chattels real); and

(ii) an instrument relating to personalty;

(b) *paragraph (f)(ii)* of that subsection applies in the case of references to the transferor company and its successors and assigns as it applies in the case of references to the transferor company personally;

(c) *paragraph (g)* of that subsection applies in the case of rights, obligations and liabilities mentioned in that paragraph whether they are expressed in the contract, agreement or instrument concerned to be personal to the transferor company or to benefit or bind (as appropriate) the transferor company and its successors and assigns.

(5) Without prejudice to *subsections (6)* and *(7)*, the successor company shall comply with registration requirements and any other special formalities required by law and as directed by the court for the transfer of the assets and liabilities of the transferor company or companies to be effective in relation to other persons.

(6) There shall be entered by the keeper of any register in the State—

(a) upon production of a certified copy of the order under *subsection (2)*; and

(b) without the necessity of there being produced any other document (and, accordingly, any provision requiring such production shall, if it would otherwise apply, not apply),

the name of the successor company in place of any transferor company in respect of the information, act, ownership or other matter in that register and any document kept in that register.

(7) Without prejudice to the generality of *subsection (6)*, the Property Registration Authority, as respects any deed (within the meaning of section 32 of the Registration of Deeds and Title Act 2006) registered by that Authority or produced for registration by it, shall, upon production of the document referred to in *subsection (6)(a)* but without the necessity of there being produced that which is referred to in *subsection (6)(b)*, enter the name of the successor company in place of any transferor company in respect of such deed.

(8) Without prejudice to the application of *subsection (6)* to any other type of register in the State, each of the following shall be deemed to be a register in the State for the purposes of that subsection:

(a) the register of members of a company referred to in *section 169*;

(b) the register of holders of debentures of a public limited company kept pursuant to *section 1121*;

(c) the register kept by a public limited company for the purposes of *sections 1048* to *1053*;

(d) the register of charges kept by the Registrar pursuant to *section 414*;

(e) the Land Registry;

(f) any register of shipping kept under the Mercantile Marine Act 1955.

(9) The court may, either by the order confirming the merger or by a separate order, make provision for such matters as the court considers necessary to secure that the merger shall be fully and effectively carried out.

(10) If the taking effect of the merger would fall at a time (being the time ascertained by reference to the general law and without regard to this subsection) on the particular date appointed under *subsection (2)* that is a time that would not, in the opinion of the court, be suitable having regard to the need of the parties to co-ordinate various transactions, the court may, in appointing a date under *subsection (2)* with respect to when the merger takes effect, specify a time, different from the foregoing, on that date when the merger takes effect and, where such a time is so specified—

(a) the merger takes effect on that time of the date concerned; and

(b) references in this section to the effective date shall be read accordingly.

1145 Certain provisions not to apply where court so orders

Where the court makes an order confirming a merger under this Chapter, the court may, if it sees fit for the purpose of enabling the merger properly to have effect, include in the order provision permitting—

(a) the giving of financial assistance which may otherwise be prohibited under *section 82*;

(b) a reduction in company capital which may otherwise be restricted under *section 84*.

1146 Registration and publication of confirmation of merger

(1) If the court makes an order confirming a merger, a certified copy of the order shall forthwith be sent to the Registrar by such officer of the court as the court may direct.

(2) Where the Registrar receives a certified copy of the order of the court in accordance with *subsection (1)*, the Registrar shall—

(a) on, or as soon as practicable after, the effective date — register in the register that certified copy and the dissolution of the transferor company or companies; and

(b) within 14 days after the date of that delivery — cause to be published in the CRO Gazette notice that a copy of an order of the court confirming the merger has been delivered to him or her.

1147 Civil liability of directors and experts

(1) Subject to *subsection (5)*, any shareholder of any of the merging companies who has suffered loss or damage by reason of misconduct in the preparation or implementation of the merger by a director of any such company or by the expert, if any, who has made a report under *section 1133* shall be entitled to have such loss or damage made good to him or her by—

- (a) in the case of misconduct by a person who was a director of that company at the date of the common draft terms of merger — that person;
- (b) in the case of misconduct by any expert who made a report under *section 1133* in respect of any of the merging companies — that person.

(2) Without prejudice to the generality of *subsection (1)*, any shareholder of any of the merging companies who has suffered loss or damage arising from the inclusion of any untrue statement in any of the following, namely:

- (a) the common draft terms of merger;
- (b) the explanatory report, if any, referred to in *section 1132*;
- (c) the expert's report, if any, under *section 1133*;
- (d) the merger financial statement, if any, prepared under *section 1134*;

shall, subject to *subsections (3)* to *(5)*, be entitled to have such loss or damage made good to him or her—

- (i) in the case of the document or report referred to in *paragraph (a)*, *(b)* or *(d)* — by every person who was a director of that company at the date of the common draft terms of merger; or
- (ii) in the case of the report referred to in *paragraph (c)* — by the person who made that report in relation to that company.

(3) A director of a company shall not be liable under *subsection (2)* if he or she proves—

- (a) that the document or report referred to in *subsection (2)(a)*, *(b)* or *(d)*, as the case may be, was issued without his or her knowledge or consent and that, on becoming aware of its issue, he or she forthwith informed the shareholders of that company that it was issued without his or her knowledge or consent; or
- (b) that as regards every untrue statement he or she had reasonable grounds, having exercised all reasonable care and skill, for believing and did, up to the time the merger took effect, believe that the statement was true.

(4) A person who makes a report under *section 1133* in relation to a company shall not be liable in the case of any untrue statement in the report if he or she proves—

- (a) that, on becoming aware of the statement, he or she forthwith informed that company and its shareholders of the untruth; or
- (b) that he or she was competent to make the statement and that he or she had reasonable grounds for believing and did up to the time the merger took effect believe that the statement was true.

(5) This section shall not apply to a merger by absorption.

1148 Criminal liability for untrue statements in merger documents

(1) Where any untrue statement has been included in—

(a) the common draft terms of merger;

(b) the explanatory report, if any, referred to in *section 1132*; or

(c) the merger financial statement, if any, prepared under *section 1134*;

the following:

(i) each of the persons who was a director of any of the merging companies at the date of the common draft terms of merger or, in the case of the foregoing explanatory report or merger financial statement, at the time of the report's or statement's preparation; and

(ii) any person who authorised the issue of the document;

shall be guilty of a category 2 offence.

(2) Where any untrue statement has been included in the expert's report prepared under *section 1133*, the expert and any person who authorised the issue of the report shall be guilty of a category 2 offence.

(3) In any proceedings against a person in respect of an offence under *subsection (1)* or *(2)*, it shall be a defence to prove that, having exercised all reasonable care and skill, the defendant had reasonable grounds for believing and did, up to the time of the issue of the document concerned, believe that the statement concerned was true.

Chapter 17
Divisions

1149 Interpretation (*Chapter 17*)

(1) In this Chapter—

"company" includes a body corporate to which *section 1312(1)* (application of certain provisions of Act to unregistered companies) relates;

"director", in relation to a company which is being wound up, means liquidator;

"division" means—

(a) a division by acquisition; or

(b) a division by formation of new companies;

within, in each case, the meaning of *section 1151*;

"share exchange ratio" means the number of shares or other securities in any of the successor companies that the draft terms of division provide to be allotted to members of the transferor company for a given number of their shares or other securities in the transferor company;

"successor company" shall be read in accordance with *section 1151(1)*;

"transferor company" shall be read in accordance with *section 1151(1)*.

(2) A reference in this Chapter to a company involved in a division shall—

(a) in the case of a division by acquisition, be read as a reference to a company that is, in relation to that division, the transferor company or a successor company (other than a new company formed for the purpose of the acquisition concerned);

(b) in the case of a division by formation of new companies, be read as a reference to a company that is, in relation to that division, the transferor company.

(3) References in this Chapter to the acquisition of a company are references to the acquisition of the assets and liabilities of the company by way of a division under this Chapter.

1150 Requirements for Chapter to apply

This Chapter applies only if each of the companies involved in the division, or, one at least, of them, is a PLC.

1151 Divisions to which this Chapter applies — definitions and supplementary provisions

(1) In this Chapter "division by acquisition" means an operation consisting of the following:

(a) 2 or more companies (each of which is referred to in this Chapter as a "successor company"), of which one or more but not all may be a new company, acquire between them all the assets and liabilities of another company that is dissolved without going into liquidation (referred to in this Chapter as the "transferor company"); and

(b) such acquisition is—

(i) in exchange for the issue to the shareholders of the transferor company of shares in one or more of the successor companies, with or without any cash payment; and

(ii) with a view to the dissolution of the transferor company.

(2) In this Chapter "division by formation of new companies" means an operation consisting of the same elements as a division by acquisition (as defined in *subsection (1)*) consists of save that the successor companies have been formed for the purposes of the acquisition of the assets and liabilities referred to in that subsection.

(3) Where a company is being wound up it may—

(a) become a party to a division by acquisition or a division by formation of new companies, provided that the distribution of its assets to its shareholders has not begun at the date, under *section 1153(8)*, of the common draft terms of division; or

(b) opt to avail itself of the provisions of *Chapters 1* and *2* of *Part 9* or *section 601*.

(4) Subject to *subsection (3)*, the provisions of *Chapters 1* and *2* of *Part 9* and *section 601* shall not apply to a division by acquisition or a division by formation of new companies.

1152 Division may not be put into effect save under and in accordance with this Chapter

(1) A division may not be put into effect save under and in accordance with the provisions of this Chapter.

(2) A division shall not take effect under this Chapter in the absence of the approval, authorisation or other consent, if any, that is required by any other enactment or a Community act for the division to take effect.

1153 Common draft terms of division

(1) Where a division is proposed to be entered into, the directors of the companies involved in the division shall draw up common draft terms of division and approve those terms in writing.

(2) The common draft terms of division shall state, at least—

(a) in relation to the transferor company—

(i) its name;

(ii) its registered office; and

(iii) its registered number;

(b) in relation to each of the successor companies—

(i) where any of those is an existing company, the particulars specified in *subparagraphs (i)* to *(iii)* of *paragraph (a)*; or

(ii) where any of those is a new company yet to be formed, what is proposed as the particulars specified in *subparagraphs (i)* and *(ii)* of that paragraph;

(c) as to each of the companies involved in the division, whether it is a PLC, another type of company as defined in *section 2(1)* or a body corporate to which *section 1312(1)* relates;

(d) the proposed share exchange ratio and amount of any cash payment;

(e) the proposed terms relating to allotment of shares or other securities in the successor companies;

(f) the date from which the holding of shares or other securities in the successor companies will entitle the holders to participate in profits and any special conditions affecting that entitlement;

(g) the date from which the transactions of the transferor company are to be treated for accounting purposes as being those of any of the successor companies;

(h) the rights, if any, to be conferred by the successor companies on members of the transferor company enjoying special rights or on holders of securities other than shares representing the transferor company's capital, and the measures proposed concerning them;

(i) any special advantages granted to—

(i) any director of a company involved in the division; or

(ii) any person appointed under *section 1155*;

(j) the precise description and allocation of the assets and liabilities of the company being acquired that are to be transferred to each of the successor companies;

(k) the allocation of shares in the successor companies to the shareholders of the transferor company and the criteria on which such allocation is based;

(l) the dates of the financial statements, if any, of every company involved in the division which were used for the purpose of preparing the common draft terms of division.

(3) Where the division involves the formation of one or more new companies the common draft terms of division shall include or be accompanied by the constitution or draft constitution of each of the new companies.

(4) The common draft terms of division shall not provide for any shares in any of the successor companies to be exchanged for shares in the transferor company held either—

(a) by the successor companies themselves or their nominees on their behalf; or

(b) by the transferor company or its nominee on its behalf.

(5) Without prejudice to *subsection (6)*, where—

(a) an asset of the transferor company is not allocated by the common draft terms of division, and

(b) it is not possible, by reference to an interpretation of those terms, to determine the manner in which it is to be allocated,

the asset or the consideration therefor shall be allocated to the successor companies in proportion to the share of the net assets allocated to each of those companies under the common draft terms of division.

(6) If provision is not made by the common draft terms of division for the allocation of an asset acquired by, or otherwise becoming vested in, the transferor company on or after the date of those draft terms then, subject to any provision the court may make in an order under *section 1166*, the asset or the consideration therefor shall be allocated in the manner specified in *subsection (5)*.

(7) The common draft terms of division, as approved under *subsection (1)*, shall be signed, on the same date, on behalf of each of the companies involved in the division by 2 directors of each such company (or, in the case of each of one or more of them having a sole director, by the sole director); the common draft terms shall bear the date of such signing.

(8) That date shall, for the purposes of this Chapter, be the date of the common draft terms of division.

1154 Directors' explanatory report

(1) Subject to *subsections (5)* and *(6)*, a separate written report (the "explanatory report") shall be prepared in respect of each of the companies involved in the division by the directors of each such company.

(2) The explanatory report shall at least give particulars of, and explain—

(a) the common draft terms of division;

(b) the legal and economic grounds for and implications of the common draft terms of division with particular reference to the proposed share exchange ratio, organisation and management structures, recent and future commercial activities and the financial interests of holders of the shares and other securities in the company;

(c) the methods used to arrive at the proposed share exchange ratio and the reasons for the use of these methods; and

(d) any special valuation difficulties which have arisen.

(3) Where it is proposed that any of the successor companies (being a company that is a PLC) will allot shares for a consideration other than in cash, the explanatory report shall also state—

(a) whether a report has been made to that successor company under *section 1028* in relation to that consideration; and

(b) if so, whether that report has been delivered to the Registrar.

(4) The explanatory report shall be signed on behalf of each of the companies involved in the division by 2 directors of each such company (or, in the case of each of one or more of them having a sole director, by the sole director) and shall bear the date of such signing.

(5) This section shall not apply if the following condition is, or (as appropriate) the following 2 conditions are, satisfied:

(a) other than in a case falling within *paragraph (b)*, all of the holders of shares conferring the right to vote at general meetings of each of the companies involved in the division have agreed that this section shall not apply; or

(b) where a requirement for the taking effect of a vote (whether a vote generally or of the type to which this subsection applies) by holders of shares of any of the companies involved in the division is that a holder of securities of the company has consented thereto—

(i) the agreement mentioned in *paragraph (a)* exists; and

(ii) all of the holders of securities of the company or companies in respect of which the requirement mentioned in this paragraph operates have agreed that this section shall not apply.

(6) This section shall not apply in relation to a company involved in a division by formation of new companies where the shares in each of the acquiring companies are allocated to the shareholders of the transferor company in proportion to their rights in the capital of that company.

1155 Expert's report

(1) Subject to *subsections (12)* and *(13)*, there shall, in accordance with this section, be appointed one or more persons to—

(a) examine the common draft terms of division; and

(b) make a report on those terms to the shareholders of the companies involved in the division.

(2) The functions referred to in *subsection (1)(a)* and *(b)* shall be performed either—

(a) in relation to each company involved in the division, by one or more persons appointed for that purpose in relation to the particular company by its directors and—

(i) no person may be appointed under this paragraph unless the person's appointment has first been approved by the court on the application to it of the company concerned;

(ii) the directors of each company may appoint the same person or persons for that purpose;

or

(b) in relation to all the companies involved in the division, by one or more persons appointed for that purpose by the court, on the application to it of all of the companies so involved.

(3) The person so appointed, or each person so appointed, is referred to in this Chapter as an "expert" and a reference in this Chapter to a report of an expert or other action (including an opinion) of an expert shall, in a case where there are 2 or more experts, be read as reference to a joint report or joint other action (including an opinion) of or by them.

(4) A person shall not be appointed an expert unless the person is a qualified person.

(5) A person is a qualified person for the purposes of this section if the person—

(a) is a statutory auditor; and

(b) is not—

(i) a person who is or, within the period of 12 months before the date of the common draft terms of division has been, an officer or employee of any of the companies involved in the division;

(ii) except with the leave of the court, a parent, spouse, civil partner, brother, sister or child of an officer of any of the companies involved in the division (and a reference in this subparagraph to a child of an officer shall be deemed to include a child of the officer's civil partner who is ordinarily resident with the officer and the civil partner); or

(iii) a person who is a partner, or in the employment, of an officer or employee of any of the companies involved in the division.

(6) The report of the expert shall be made available not less than 30 days before the date of the passing of the resolution referred to in *section 1159* by each of the companies involved in the division, shall be in writing and shall—

(a) state the method or methods used to arrive at the proposed share exchange ratio;

(b) give the opinion of the expert as to whether the proposed share exchange ratio is fair and reasonable;

(c) give the opinion of the expert as to the adequacy of the method or methods used in the case in question;

(d) indicate the values arrived at using each such method;

(e) give the opinion of the expert as to the relative importance attributed to such methods in arriving at the values decided on; and

(f) specify any special valuation difficulties which have arisen.

(7) The expert may—

(a) require each of the companies involved in the division and their officers to give to the expert such information and explanations (whether oral or in writing), and

(b) make such enquiries,

as the expert thinks necessary for the purposes of making the report.

(8) If a company involved in the division fails to give to the expert any information or explanation in the power, possession or procurement of that company, on a requirement being made of it under *subsection (7)(a)* by the expert, that company and any officer of it who is in default shall be guilty of a category 2 offence.

(9) If a company involved in the division makes a statement (whether orally or in writing), or provides a document, to the expert that conveys or purports to convey any information or explanation the subject of a requirement made of it under *subsection (7)(a)* by the expert and—

(a) that information is false or misleading in a material particular, and

(b) the company knows it to be so false or misleading or is reckless as to whether it is so false or misleading,

the company and any officer of it who is in default shall be guilty of a category 2 offence.

(10) If a person appointed an expert under *subsection (2)(a)* or *(b)* ceases to be a qualified person, that person—

(a) shall immediately cease to hold office; and

(b) shall give notice in writing of the fact of the person's ceasing to be a qualified person to each company involved in the division and (in the case of an appointment under *subsection (2)(b)*) to the court within 14 days after the date of that cessation,

but without prejudice to the validity of any acts done by the person under this Chapter before that cessation.

(11) A person who purports to perform the functions of an expert (in respect of the division concerned) under this Chapter after ceasing to be a qualified person (in respect of that division) shall be guilty of a category 2 offence.

(12) This section shall not apply if the following condition is, or (as appropriate) the following 2 conditions are, satisfied:

(a) other than in a case falling within *paragraph (b)*, all of the holders of shares conferring the right to vote at general meetings of each of the companies involved in the division have agreed that this section shall not apply; or

(b) where a requirement for the taking effect of a vote (whether a vote generally or of the type to which this subsection applies) by holders of shares of any of the companies involved in the division is that a holder of securities of the company has consented thereto—

(i) the agreement mentioned in *paragraph (a)* exists; and

(ii) all of the holders of securities of the company or companies in respect of which the requirement mentioned in this paragraph operates have agreed that this section shall not apply.

(13) This section shall not apply in relation to a company involved in a division by formation of new companies where the shares in each of the successor companies are allocated to the shareholders of the transferor company in proportion to their rights in the capital of that company.

1156 Division financial statement

(1) Subject to *subsections (6)* and *(8)*, where the latest statutory financial statements of any of the companies involved in the division relate to a financial year ended more than 6 months before the date of the common draft terms of division then that company shall prepare a division financial statement in accordance with the provisions of this section.

(2) The division financial statement shall be drawn up—

(a) in the format of the last annual balance sheet, if any, of the company and in accordance with the provisions of *Part 6*; and

(b) as at a date not earlier than the first day of the third month preceding the date of the common draft terms of division.

(3) Valuations shown in the last annual balance sheet, if any, shall, subject to the exceptions provided for under *subsection (4)*, only be altered to reflect entries in the accounting records of the company.

(4) Notwithstanding *subsection (3)*, the following shall be taken into account in preparing the division financial statement—

(a) interim depreciation and provisions; and

(b) material changes in actual value not shown in the accounting records.

(5) The provisions of *Part 6* relating to the statutory auditor's report on the last statutory financial statements of the company concerned shall apply, with any necessary

modifications, to the division financial statement required of the company by *subsection (1)*.

(6) This section shall not apply in relation to a company involved in a division which makes public a half-yearly financial report covering the first 6 months of its financial year pursuant to the provision referred to in *subsection (7)* if that company makes that report available for inspection pursuant to *section 1158*.

(7) The provision referred to in *subsection (6)* is, as appropriate—

(a) Regulation 6 of the Transparency (Directive 2004/109/EC) Regulations 2007 (S.I. No. 277 of 2007) which regulations are continued in force by *Schedule 6*; or

(b) if regulations under *section 1380* are made and those regulations—

(i) replace the regulations referred to in *paragraph (a)* — the provision of those replacement regulations corresponding to the foregoing Regulation 6; or

(ii) amend the foregoing Regulation 6 — that Regulation as it stands so amended.

(8) This section shall not apply to a company involved in a division if the following condition is, or (as appropriate) the following 2 conditions are, satisfied:

(a) other than in a case falling within *paragraph (b)*, all of the holders of shares conferring the right to vote at general meetings of the company have agreed that this section shall not apply; or

(b) where a requirement for the taking effect of a vote (whether a vote generally or of the type to which this subsection applies) by holders of shares of the company is that a holder of securities of the company has consented thereto—

(i) the agreement mentioned in *paragraph (a)* exists; and

(ii) all of the holders of securities in respect of which the requirement mentioned in this paragraph operates have agreed that this section shall not apply.

1157 Registration and publication of documents

(1) Subject to *subsection (3)*, each of the companies involved in the division shall—

(a) deliver to the Registrar a copy of the common draft terms of division, signed and dated as required by *section 1153(7)*;

(b) cause to be published in the CRO Gazette notice of delivery to the Registrar of the common draft terms of division.

(2) The requirements of *subsection (1)* shall be fulfilled by each of the companies involved in the division at least 30 days before the date of the general meeting of each such company which, by virtue of *section 1159*, is held to consider the common draft terms of division.

(3) This section shall not apply in relation to a company involved in the division if the company—

(a) publishes, free of charge on its website for a continuous period of at least 2 months, commencing at least 30 days before the date of the general meeting which, by virtue of *section 1159*, is to consider the common draft terms of division and ending at least 30 days after that date, a copy of the common draft terms of division, signed and dated pursuant to *section 1153(7)*; and

(b) causes to be published in the CRO Gazette and once at least in 2 daily newspapers circulating in the district in which the registered office or principal place of business of the company is situate notice of publication on its website of the common draft terms of division.

(4) Where, in the period referred to in *subsection (3)(a)*, access to the company's website is disrupted for a continuous period of at least 24 hours or for separate periods totalling not less than 72 hours, the period referred to in *subsection (3)(a)* shall be extended for a period corresponding to the period or periods of disruption.

1158 Inspection of documents

(1) Subject to *subsections (5)* and *(6)*, each of the companies involved in the division shall, in accordance with *subsection (3)*, make available for inspection free of charge by any member of the company at its registered office during business hours—

(a) the common draft terms of division;

(b) subject to *subsection (2)*, the statutory financial statements for the preceding 3 financial years of each company (audited, where required by that Part, in accordance with *Part 6*);

(c) if such a report is required to be prepared by that section, each explanatory report in relation to the companies involved in the division referred to in *section 1154*;

(d) if such a report is required to be prepared by that section, the expert's report relating to each of the companies involved in the division referred to in *section 1155*;

(e) each division financial statement, if any, in relation to one or, as the case may be, more than one of the companies involved in the division, required to be prepared by *section 1156* or, as appropriate, its half-yearly financial report referred to in *subsection (6)* of that section.

(2) For the purposes of *paragraph (b)* of *subsection (1)*—

(a) if any of the companies involved in the division has traded for less than 3 financial years before the date of the common draft terms of division, then, as respects that company, that paragraph is satisfied by the statutory financial statements for those financial years for which the company has traded (audited, where required by that Part, in accordance with *Part 6*) being made available as mentioned in that subsection by each of the companies involved in the division, or

(b) if, by reason of its recent incorporation, the obligation of any of the foregoing companies to prepare its first financial statements under *Part 6* had not arisen as of the date of the common draft terms of division, then the reference in that paragraph to the financial statements of that company shall be disregarded.

(3) The provisions of *subsection (1)* shall apply in the case of each of the companies involved in the division for a period of 30 days before the date of the meeting of each such company which, by virtue of *section 1159*, is held to consider the common draft terms of division.

(4) *Section 127(1)* (access to documents during business hours) shall apply in relation to *subsection (1)* as it applies in relation to the relevant provisions of *Part 4*.

(5) *Subsection (1)(e)* shall not apply in relation to a company involved in a division by formation of new companies where the shares in each of the successor companies are allocated to the shareholders of the transferor company in proportion to their rights in the capital of that company.

(6) Subject to *subsection (7)*, *subsection (1)* shall not apply in relation to a company involved in a division if it publishes free of charge on its website the documents specified in that subsection for a continuous period of at least 2 months, commencing at least 30 days before the date of the general meeting which, by virtue of *section 1159*, is to consider the common draft terms of division and ending at least 30 days after that date.

(7) *Subsection (6)* shall not apply where the entitlement referred to in *section 1159(4)* does not apply in consequence of the application of *section 1160(2)*.

(8) Where, in the period referred to in *subsection (6)*, access to the company's website is disrupted for a continuous period of at least 24 hours or for separate periods totalling not less than 72 hours, the period referred to in *subsection (6)* shall be extended for a period corresponding to the period or periods of disruption.

(9) A reference in this section to statutory financial statements shall be deemed to include a reference to a directors' report and a reference to auditing shall, in the case of such a report, be read as a reference to the operation referred to in *section 336(5)*.

1159 General meetings of companies involved in a division

(1) In this section a reference to a general meeting, without qualification, is a reference to a general meeting referred to in *subsection (2)*.

(2) Subject to *subsections (7)* and *(10)* and without prejudice to *section 1161*, the subsequent steps under this Chapter in relation to the division shall not be taken unless the common draft terms of division have been approved by a special resolution passed at a general meeting of each of the companies involved in the division.

(3) In addition, where the division is a division by formation of new companies, those subsequent steps shall not be taken unless the constitution or draft constitution of each of the new companies has been approved by a special resolution of the transferor company.

(4) Subject to *section 1160(2)*, the notice convening the general meeting referred to in *subsection (2)* shall contain a statement of every shareholder's entitlement to obtain on request, free of charge, full or, if so desired, partial copies of the documents

referred to in *section 1158(1)* (and, accordingly, every shareholder has, subject to the foregoing provision, that entitlement).

(5) The directors of the transferor company shall inform—

(a) the general meeting of that company, and

(b) the directors of the successor companies,

of any material change in the assets and liabilities of the transferor company that occurs between the date of the common draft terms of division and the date of that general meeting.

(6) On being so informed of them, the directors of each such other company involved in the division shall inform the general meeting of that company of the matters referred to in *subsection (5)*; this and the preceding subsection operate subject to *subsections (10)(c)* and *(11)*.

(7) Approval, by means of a special resolution, of the common draft terms of division is not required in the case of a successor company (in *subsections (8)* and *(9)* referred to as the "particular successor company") if the conditions specified in *subsection (8)* have been satisfied.

(8) The conditions referred to in *subsection (7)* are the following:

(a) the provisions of *sections 1157* and *1158* are complied with at least 30 days before the date of the general meeting of the transferor company; and

(b) the right, conferred by *subsection (9)*, to requisition a general meeting of the particular successor company has not been exercised during that period of 30 days.

(9) One or more members of the particular successor company who hold or together hold not less than 5 per cent of the paid-up capital of the company which carries the right to vote at general meetings of the company (excluding any shares held as treasury shares) may require the convening of a general meeting of the company to consider the common draft terms of division, and *section 178(3)* to *(7)* apply, with any necessary modifications, in relation to the requisition.

(10) Approval, by means of a special resolution, of the common draft terms of division is not required in the case of the transferor company if the following conditions have been satisfied:

(a) the successor companies together hold all of the shares carrying the right to vote at general meetings of the transferor company;

(b) the companies involved in the division comply with the provisions of *sections 1157* and *1158* at least 30 days before the earlier of the dates specified in *paragraphs (f)* and *(g)* of *section 1153(2)*; and

(c) the condition specified in *subsection (11)*.

(11) The condition referred to in *subsection (10)(c)* is that the directors of the transferor company shall inform—

(a) the members of that company, and

(b) the directors of the successor companies,

of any material change in the assets and liabilities of the transferor company that has occurred since the date of the common draft terms of division and *subsection (6)* shall be read, as regards the information to which it applies, as referring to the foregoing information.

1160 Electronic means of making certain information available for purposes of *section 1159*

(1) For the purposes of *section 1159*, but subject to *subsection (2)*, where a shareholder has consented to the use by the company of electronic means for conveying information, the copies of the documents referred to in *section 1158(1)* may be provided, by electronic mail, to that shareholder by the company and the notice convening the general meeting referred to in *section 1159(2)* shall contain a statement to that effect.

(2) The entitlement referred to in *section 1159(4)* shall not apply where, for the period specified in *subsection (3)*, copies of the documents referred to in *section 1158(1)* are available to download and print, free of charge, from the company's website by shareholders of the company.

(3) The period referred to in *subsection (2)* is a continuous period of at least 2 months, commencing at least 30 days before the date of the general meeting which, by virtue of *section 1159*, is to consider the common draft terms of merger and ending at least 30 days after that date.

(4) Where, in the period referred to in *subsection (3)*, access to the company's website is disrupted for a continuous period of at least 24 hours or for separate periods totalling not less than 72 hours, the period referred to in *subsection (3)* shall be extended for a period corresponding to the period or periods of disruption.

1161 Meetings of classes of shareholders

(1) Where the share capital of any of the companies involved in the division is divided into shares of different classes the provisions referred to in *subsection (2)*, with the exclusions specified in *subsection (3)*, shall apply with respect to the variation of the rights attached to any such class that is entailed by the division.

(2) Those provisions are:

(a) if the particular company involved in the division is not a private company limited by shares, as appropriate—

(i) *section 982*;

(ii) *section 1044*;

(iii) *section 1250*;

or

(b) if the particular company involved in the division is a private company limited by shares, the provisions of *Chapter 4* of *Part 3* on the variation of the rights attached to any class of shares in a company.

(3) There is excluded the following from the foregoing provisions:

(a) *section 88(9)*;

(b) *section 982(10)* (including as it applies to a company other than a DAC);

(c) *section 89* (including as it applies to a company other than a private company limited by shares).

1162 Purchase of minority shares

(1) Subject to *subsection (5)*, any person being—

(a) a shareholder in any of the companies involved in the division who voted against the special resolution of the company concerned relating to the common draft terms of division, or

(b) in a case to which *subsection (2)* relates, any shareholder in the transferor company other than the successor company there referred to,

may, not later than 15 days after the relevant date, request the successor companies in writing to acquire his or her shares for cash.

(2) This subsection relates to a case where a successor company (not being a company formed for the purpose of the division) holds 90 per cent or more (but not all) of the shares carrying the right to vote at general meetings of the transferor company.

(3) Where a request is made by a shareholder in accordance with *subsection (1)*, the successor companies (or such one, or more than one of them, as they may agree among themselves) shall purchase the shares of the shareholder at a price determined in accordance with the share exchange ratio set out in the common draft terms of division and the shares so purchased by any successor company shall be treated as treasury shares within the meaning of *section 106*.

(4) Nothing in the preceding subsections limits the power of the court to make any order necessary for the protection of the interests of a dissenting minority in a company involved in a division.

(5) This section shall not apply where the shares in each of the successor companies are allocated to the shareholders of the transferor company in proportion to their rights in the capital of that company.

(6) In this section "relevant date" means—

(a) in relation to a shareholder referred to in *subsection (1)(a)* — the date on which the resolution of the transferor company was passed;

(b) in relation to a shareholder referred to in *subsection (1)(b)* — the date of publication of the notice of delivery of the common draft terms of division under *section 1157(1)(b)*.

1163 Application for confirmation of division by court

(1) An application under this section to the court for an order confirming a division shall be made jointly by all the companies involved in the division.

(2) The application shall be accompanied by a statement of the size of the shareholding of any shareholder who has requested the purchase of his or her shares under *section*

1162 and of the measures which the successor companies propose to take to comply with the shareholder's request.

1164 Protection of creditors and allocation of liabilities

(1) A creditor of any of the companies involved in a division who—

(a) at the date of publication of the notice under *section 1157(1)(b)* is entitled to any debt or claim against the company, and

(b) can credibly demonstrate that the proposed division would be likely to put the satisfaction of that debt or claim at risk and that no adequate safe-guards have been obtained from the company or a successor company,

shall be entitled to object to the confirmation by the court of the division.

(2) If the court deems it necessary in order to secure the adequate protection of creditors of any of the companies involved in the division it may—

(a) determine a list of creditors entitled to object and the nature and amount of their debts or claims, and may publish notices fixing a day or days within which creditors not entered on the list are to claim to be so entered or are to be excluded from the right of objecting to the confirmation,

(b) where a creditor entered on the list whose debt or claim is not discharged or has not terminated does not consent to the confirmation, the court may, if it thinks fit, dispense with the consent of that creditor, on either—

(i) the company securing payment of his or her debt or claim by appropriating, as the court may direct, the following amount:

(I) if the company admits the full amount of the debt or claim, or, though not admitting it, is willing to provide for it, then the full amount of the debt or claim;

(II) if the company does not admit and is not willing to provide for the full amount of the debt or claim, or, if the amount is contingent or not ascertained, then an amount fixed by the court after the like inquiry and adjudication as if the company were being wound up by the court;

(ii) a successor company, on behalf of the company liable for the debt or claim, securing payment of the debt or claim.

(3) If, having regard to any special circumstances of the case it thinks proper so to do, the court may direct that *subsection (2)* shall not apply as regards any class of creditors.

(4) Without prejudice to *subsection (5)*, where—

(a) a liability of the transferor company is not allocated by the common draft terms of division, and

(b) it is not possible, by reference to an interpretation of those terms, to determine the manner in which it is to be allocated,

the liability shall become, jointly and severally, the liability of the successor companies.

(5) If provision is not made by the common draft terms of division for the allocation of a liability incurred by, or which otherwise becomes attached to, the transferor company on or after the date of those draft terms then, subject to any provision the court may make in an order under *section 1166*, the liability shall become, jointly and severally, the liability of the successor companies.

(6) References in this section to a debt or claim having terminated are references to the debt or claim ceasing to be enforceable or to its otherwise determining.

1165 Preservation of rights of holders of securities

(1) Subject to *subsection (2)*, holders of securities, other than shares, in the transferor company to which special rights are attached shall be given rights in one or more of the successor companies at least equivalent to those they possessed in the transferor company.

(2) *Subsection (1)* shall not apply—

(a) where the alteration of the rights in a successor company has been approved—

(i) by a majority of the holders of such securities at a meeting held for that purpose, or

(ii) by the holders of those securities individually,

or

(b) where the holders of those securities are entitled under the terms of those securities to have their securities purchased by a successor company.

1166 Confirmation order

(1) Where an application is made under *section 1163* to the court for an order confirming a division this section applies.

(2) The court, on being satisfied that—

(a) the requirements of this Chapter have been complied with,

(b) proper provision has been made for—

(i) any shareholder in any of the companies involved in the division who has made a request under *section 1162*, and

(ii) any creditor of any of the companies who objects to the division in accordance with *section 1164*,

(c) the rights of holders of securities other than shares in the transferor company are safeguarded in accordance with *section 1165*, and

(d) where applicable, the relevant provisions referred to in *section 1161(2)* on the variation of the rights attached to any class of shares in any of the companies involved in the division have been complied with,

may make an order confirming the division with effect from such date as the court appoints (the "effective date").

(3) In the case of an asset or liability (including any contractual right or obligation or the obligation to make any cash payment), references in subsequent provisions of

this section to the relevant successor company or companies are references to such one or (as the case may be) more than one of the successor companies—

(a) as provided for in respect of the matter concerned by the common draft terms of division, or

(b) in the cases or circumstances specified in whichever of the following is applicable, namely, *section 1153(5)* or *(6)* or *section 1164(4)* or *(5)*—

(i) subject to where it permits such provision by an order of the court, as provided for in that applicable provision (including, where relevant, as regards the nature of the joint liability), or

(ii) as provided for in an order of the court under this section.

(4) The order of the court confirming the division shall, from the effective date, have the following effects:

(a) each asset and liability of the transferor company is transferred to the relevant successor company or companies;

(b) where no request has been made by shareholders under *section 1162*, all remaining members of the transferor company except any successor company (if it is a member of the transferor company) become members of the successor companies or any of them as provided by the common draft terms of division;

(c) the transferor company is dissolved;

(d) all legal proceedings pending by or against the transferor company shall be continued with the substitution, for the transferor company, of the successor companies or such of them as the court before which the proceedings have been brought may order;

(e) the relevant successor company or companies is or are obliged to make to the members of the transferor company any cash payment required by the common draft terms of division;

(f) every contract, agreement or instrument to which the transferor company is a party shall, notwithstanding anything to the contrary contained in that contract, agreement or instrument, be read and have effect as if—

(i) the relevant successor company or companies had been a party or parties thereto instead of the transferor company,

(ii) for any reference (however worded and whether express or implied) to the transferor company there were substituted a reference to the relevant successor company or companies, and

(iii) any reference (however worded and whether express or implied) to the directors, officers, representatives or employees of the transferor company, or any of them—

(I) were, respectively, a reference to the directors, officers, representatives or employees of the relevant successor company or companies or to such director, officer, representative or employee of that company or those companies as that company nominates or, as the case may be, those companies nominate for that purpose, or

(II) in default of such nomination, were, respectively, a reference to the director, officer, representative or employee of the relevant successor company or companies who corresponds as nearly as may be to the first-mentioned director, officer, representative or employee;

(g) every contract, agreement or instrument to which the transferor company is a party becomes a contract, agreement or instrument between the relevant successor company or companies and the counterparty with the same rights, and subject to the same obligations, liabilities and incidents (including rights of set-off), as would have been applicable thereto if that contract, agreement or instrument had continued in force between the transferor company and the counterparty;

(h) any money due and owing (or payable) by or to the transferor company under or by virtue of any such contract, agreement or instrument as is mentioned in *paragraph (g)* shall become due and owing (or payable) by or to the relevant successor company or companies instead of the transferor company; and

(i) an offer or invitation to treat made to or by the transferor company before the effective date shall be read and have effect, respectively, as an offer or invitation to treat made to or by the relevant successor company or companies.

(5) The following provisions have effect for the purposes of *subsection (4)*—

(a) "instrument" in that subsection includes—

(i) a lease, conveyance, transfer or charge or any other instrument relating to real property (including chattels real); and

(ii) an instrument relating to personalty;

(b) *paragraph (f)(ii)* of that subsection applies in the case of references to the transferor company and its successors and assigns as it applies in the case of references to the transferor company personally;

(c) *paragraph (g)* of that subsection applies in the case of rights, obligations and liabilities mentioned in that paragraph whether they are expressed in the contract, agreement or instrument concerned to be personal to the transferor company or to benefit or bind (as appropriate) the transferor company and its successors and assigns.

(6) Without prejudice to *subsections (7)* and *(8)*, such of the successor companies as is or are appropriate shall comply with registration requirements and any other special formalities required by law and as directed by the court for the transfer of the assets and liabilities of the transferor company to be effective in relation to other persons.

(7) There shall be entered by the keeper of any register in the State—

(a) upon production of a certified copy of the order under *subsection (2)*; and

(b) without the necessity of there being produced any other document (and, accordingly, any provision requiring such production shall, if it would otherwise apply, not apply),

the name of the relevant successor company (or, as appropriate, the names of the relevant successor companies) in place of the transferor company in respect of the information, act, ownership or other matter in that register and any document kept in that register.

(8) Without prejudice to the generality of *subsection (7)*, the Property Registration Authority, as respects any deed (within the meaning of section 32 of the Registration of Deeds and Title Act 2006) registered by that Authority or produced for registration by it, shall, upon production of the document referred to in *subsection (7)(a)* but without the necessity of there being produced that which is referred to in *subsection (7)(b)*, enter the name of the relevant successor company (or, as appropriate, the names of the relevant successor companies) in place of the transferor company in respect of such deed.

(9) Without prejudice to the application of *subsection (7)* to any other type of register in the State, each of the following shall be deemed to be a register in the State for the purposes of that subsection:

(a) the register of members of a company referred to in *section 169*;

(b) the register of holders of debentures of a public limited company kept pursuant to *section 1121*;

(c) the register kept by a public limited company for the purposes of *sections 1048* to *1053*;

(d) the register of charges kept by the Registrar pursuant to *section 414*;

(e) the Land Registry;

(f) any register of shipping kept under the Mercantile Marine Act 1955.

(10) The court may, either by the order confirming the division or by a separate order, make provision for such matters as the court considers necessary to secure that the division shall be fully and effectively carried out.

(11) If the taking effect of the division would fall at a time (being the time ascertained by reference to the general law and without regard to this subsection) on the particular date appointed under *subsection (2)* that is a time that would not, in the opinion of the court, be suitable having regard to the need of the parties to co-ordinate various transactions, the court may, in appointing a date under *subsection (2)* with respect to when the division takes effect, specify a time, different from the foregoing, on that date when the division takes effect and, where such a time is so specified—

(a) the division takes effect on that time of the date concerned, and

(b) references in this section to the effective date shall be read accordingly.

1167 Certain provisions not to apply where court so orders

[(1)][a] Where the court makes an order confirming a division under this Chapter, the court may, if it sees fit for the purpose of enabling the division properly to have effect, include in the order provision permitting—

(a) the giving of financial assistance which may otherwise be prohibited under *section 82*,

(b) a reduction in company capital which may otherwise be restricted under *section 84*.

[(2) *Section 84* and *subsection (1)(b)* shall not have effect in respect of a company to which the resolution tools, powers or mechanisms provided for in Part 4 of the Bank Recovery and Resolution Regulations are applied or exercised.][b]

Amendments

a Renumbered as subsection (1) by European Union (Bank Recovery and Resolution) Regulations 2015, reg 189(14), with effect from 15 July 2015.

b Subsection (2) inserted by European Union (Bank Recovery and Resolution) Regulations 2015, reg 189(14), with effect from 15 July 2015.

1168 Registration and publication of confirmation of division

(1) If the court makes an order confirming a division, a certified copy of the order shall forthwith be sent to the Registrar by such officer of the court as the court may direct.

(2) Where the Registrar receives a certified copy of the order of the court in accordance with *subsection (1)*, the Registrar shall—

(a) on, or as soon as practicable after, the effective date — register that certified copy and the dissolution of the transferor company, and

(b) within 14 days after the date of that delivery — cause to be published in the CRO Gazette notice that a copy of an order of the court confirming the division has been delivered to him or her.

1169 Civil liability of directors and experts

(1) Any shareholder of any of the companies involved in the division who has suffered loss or damage by reason of misconduct in the preparation or implementation of the division by a director of any such company or by the expert, if any, who has made a report under *section 1155* shall be entitled to have such loss or damage made good to him or her by—

(a) in the case of misconduct by a person who was a director of that company at the date of the common draft terms of division — that person;

(b) in the case of misconduct by any expert who made a report under *section 1155* in respect of any of the companies involved in the division — that person.

(2) Without prejudice to the generality of *subsection (1)*, any shareholder of any of the companies involved in the division who has suffered loss or damage arising from the inclusion of any untrue statement in any of the following, namely:

(a) the common draft terms of division;

(b) the explanatory report, if any, referred to in *section 1154*;

(c) the expert's report, if any, under *section 1155*;

(d) the division financial statement, if any, prepared under *section 1156*;

shall, subject to *subsections (3)* and *(4)*, be entitled to have such loss or damage made good to him or her—

(i) in the case of the document or report referred to in *paragraph (a)*, *(b)* or *(d)* — by every person who was a director of that company at the date of the common draft terms of division, or

(ii) in the case of the report referred to in *paragraph (c)* — by the person who made that report in relation to that company.

(3) A director of a company shall not be liable under *subsection (2)* if he or she proves—

(a) that the document or report referred to in *subsection (2)(a)*, *(b)* or *(d)*, as the case may be, was issued without his or her knowledge or consent and that, on becoming aware of its issue, he or she forthwith informed the shareholders of that company that it was issued without his or her knowledge or consent, or

(b) that as regards every untrue statement he or she had reasonable grounds, having exercised all reasonable care and skill, for believing and did, up to the time the division took effect, believe that the statement was true.

(4) A person who makes a report under *section 1155* in relation to a company shall not be liable in the case of any untrue statement in the report if he or she proves—

(a) that, on becoming aware of the statement, he or she forthwith informed that company and its shareholders of the untruth, or

(b) that he or she was competent to make the statement and that he or she had reasonable grounds for believing and did up to the time the division took effect believe that the statement was true.

1170 Criminal liability for untrue statements in division documents

(1) Where any untrue statement has been included in—

(a) the common draft terms of division,

(b) the explanatory report, if any, referred to in *section 1154*, or

(c) the division financial statement, if any, prepared under *section 1156*,

the following:

(i) each of the persons who was a director of any of the companies involved in the division at the date of the common draft terms of division or, in the case of the foregoing explanatory report or division financial statement, at the time of the report's or statement's preparation; and

(ii) any person who authorised the issue of the document;

shall be guilty of a category 2 offence.

(2) Where any untrue statement has been included in the expert's report prepared under *section 1155*, the expert and any person who authorised the issue of the report shall be guilty of a category 2 offence.

(3) In any proceedings against a person in respect of an offence under *subsection (1)* or *(2)*, it shall be a defence to prove that, having exercised all reasonable care and skill, the defendant had reasonable grounds for believing and did, up to the time of the issue of the document concerned, believe that the statement concerned was true.

Chapter 18
Public offers of securities, prevention of market abuse, etc.

1171 Application of *Chapters 1, 2* and *4* of *Part 23* to PLCs

Chapters 1, 2 and *4* of *Part 23* shall apply to a PLC.

PART 18
GUARANTEE COMPANIES

Chapter 1
Preliminary and definitions

1172 Definitions (*Part 18*)

In this Part—

"company limited by guarantee" or "CLG" means a company which does not have a share capital and which, as provided under *section 1176(2)(e)*, has the liability of its members limited by the constitution to such amount as the members may respectively thereby undertake to contribute to the assets of the company in the event of its being wound up;

"constitution" shall be read in accordance with *section 1176(1)*.

1173 Application of *Parts 1* to *14* to CLGs

(1) The provisions of *Parts 1* to *14* apply to a CLG except to the extent that they are disapplied or modified by—

(a) this section, or

(b) any other provision of this Part.

(2) For the purposes of that application, *section 10(1)* shall have effect as if it read—

> "(1) Unless expressly provided otherwise, a reference in *Parts 2* to *14* to a company is a reference to a CLG.".

(3) Any of *Parts 1* to *14* that makes provision by reference to—

(a) membership arising by virtue of a shareholding, or

(b) right or incidents of membership, including the right to vote or receive a distribution, arising by virtue of a shareholding,

shall be read, in the case of a CLG, as making such provision in the analogous context in which membership, or rights or incidents of membership, may arise in the case of a CLG.

(4) *Subsection (3)* is without prejudice to the generality of the application and adaptation of *Parts 1* to *14* provided by *subsections (1)* and *(2)* or any specific adaptation provided by a subsequent section of this Part.

(5) The provisions of this Act specified in the Table to this section shall not apply to a CLG.

(6) The specification in the foregoing Table of a provision (a "specified provision") of *Parts 1* to *14* also operates to disapply to a CLG any other provision of those Parts (notwithstanding that it is not specified in that Table) that makes consequential, incidental or supplemental provision on, or in relation to, the specified provision.

Table

Subject matter	Provision disapplied
Way of forming a private company limited by shares	*Section 17*
Company to carry on activity in the State and prohibition of certain activities	*Section 18*
Form of the constitution	*Section 19*
Certificate of incorporation to state that company is a private company limited by shares	*Section 25(3)*
Provisions as to names of companies	*Section 26(1) to (4)*
Trading under a misleading name	*Section 27*
Capacity of private company limited by shares	*Section 38*
Conversion of existing private company to private company limited by shares to which *Parts 1* to *15* apply	*Chapter 6 of Part 2*
Power to convert shares into stock, etc.	*Section 65*
Shares	*Section 66*
Numbering of shares	*Section 67*
Allotment of shares and variation in capital	*Chapters 3 and 4 of Part 3*
Transfer of shares	*Chapter 5 of Part 3* (save *section 94* in so far as it relates to debentures)
Acquisition of own shares	*Chapter 6* of *Part 3* (save *sections 113* to *116*)
Procedures for declarations, payments, etc., of dividends and other things	*Section 124*
Supplemental provisions in relation to *section 124*	*Section 125*
Bonus issues	*Section 126*
Directors	*Section 128*
Share qualifications of directors	*Section 136*
Director voting on contract, etc., in which director is interested	*Section 161(7)*
Holding of any other office or place of profit under the company by a director	*Section 162*
Majority written resolutions	*Section 194*
Supplemental provisions in relation to *section 194*	*Section 195*
Holding of own shares	*Section 320(1)*
Directors' report as it relates to dividends	*Section 326(1)(d)*
Acquisition of shares	*Chapter 2 of Part 9*
Liability as contributories of past and present members	*Section 655*

Chapter 2
Incorporation and consequential matters

1174 Way of forming a CLG

(1) A CLG may be formed for any lawful purpose by any person or persons subscribing to a constitution and complying with the relevant provisions of—

(a) *Chapter 2* of *Part 2*, as applied by this Part, and

(b) this Part,

in relation to registration of a CLG.

(2) Without prejudice to the means by which a CLG may be formed under the relevant provisions referred to in *subsection (1)*, a company may be registered as a CLG by means of—

(a) the re-registration or registration as a CLG of a body corporate pursuant to *Part 20* or *22*,

(b) the merger of 2 or more companies pursuant to *Chapter 3* of *Part 9*, or

(c) the division of a company pursuant to *Chapter 4* of *Part 9*.

(3) The certificate of incorporation issued under *section 25(1)* shall state that the company is a company limited by guarantee.

1175 CLG to carry on activity in the State

A CLG shall not be formed and registered unless it appears to the Registrar that the CLG, when registered, will carry on an activity in the State, being an activity that is mentioned in its memorandum.

1176 The form of a CLG's constitution

(1) Subject to *subsection (3)*, the constitution of a CLG shall be in the form of a memorandum of association and articles of association which together are referred to in this Part as a "constitution".

(2) The memorandum of association of a CLG shall state—

(a) its name,

(b) that it is a company limited by guarantee registered under this Part,

(c) its objects,

(d) that the liability of its members is limited, and

(e) that each member undertakes that, if the company is wound up while he or she is a member, or within one year after the date on which he or she ceases to be a member, he or she will contribute to the assets of the company such amount as may be required for—

(i) payment of the debts and liabilities of the company contracted before he or she ceases to be a member,

(ii) payment of the costs, charges and expenses of winding up, and

(iii) adjustment of the rights of contributories among themselves,

not exceeding an amount specified in the memorandum.

(3) The constitution of a CLG shall—

(a) be in accordance with the form set out in *Schedule 10* or as near thereto as circumstances permit,

(b) be printed in an entire format, that is to say the memorandum and articles shall be contained in the one document, being a document either in legible form or (as long as it is capable of being reproduced in legible form) in non-legible form, and

(c) either—

(i) be signed by each subscriber in the presence of at least one witness who shall attest the signature, or

(ii) be authenticated in the manner referred to in *section 888*.

(4) Where, subsequent to the registration of the constitution, an amendment of the memorandum of association is made affecting a matter referred to in *subsection (2)*, that subsection shall be read as requiring the memorandum to state the matter as it stands in consequence of that amendment.

1177 Supplemental provisions in relation to constitution and continuance in force of existing memorandum and articles

(1) This section—

(a) contains provisions as to the articles of a CLG,

(b) provides that, in certain circumstances, a default position shall obtain in relation to the articles of a CLG, and

(c) continues in force the memorandum and articles of a company limited by guarantee registered under the prior Companies Acts.

(2) In this section—

"mandatory provision" means a provision of any of *Parts 1* to *14* (as applied by this Part) or of this Part that is not an optional provision;

"optional provision" means a provision of any of *Parts 1* to *14* (as applied by this Part) or of this Part that—

(a) contains a statement to the effect, or is governed by provision elsewhere to the effect, that the provision applies save to the extent that the constitution provides otherwise or unless the constitution states otherwise, or

(b) is otherwise of such import.

(3) The articles of a CLG may contain regulations in relation to the CLG.

(4) So far as the articles of a CLG do not exclude or modify an optional provision, that optional provision shall apply in relation to the CLG.

(5) Subject to their compliance with *section 1199(3)* (articles must state the number of members with which the company proposes to be registered), articles may otherwise consist solely of a statement to the effect that the provisions of the *Companies Act 2014* are adopted and, if the articles contain such a statement, *subsection (4)* shall apply.

(6) The memorandum and articles of a company limited by guarantee registered before the commencement of this section shall—

(a) save to the extent that they are inconsistent with a mandatory provision, and

(b) in the case of the memorandum, subject to *section 1190(6)*,

continue in force but may be altered or added to under and in accordance with the conditions under which memorandums or articles, whenever registered, are permitted by this Act to be altered or added to.

(7) References in the provisions of a memorandum or articles so continued in force to any provision of the prior Companies Acts shall be read as references to the corresponding provision of this Act.

(8) To the extent that a company limited by guarantee registered before the commencement of this section was, immediately before that commencement, governed by—

(a) the regulations of Table C in the First Schedule to the Act of 1963, or

(b) the regulations of any Table referred to in section 3(9)(b), (c) or (d) of the Act of 1963,

it shall, after that commencement, continue to be governed by those regulations but—

(i) this is save to the extent that those regulations are inconsistent with a mandatory provision,

(ii) those regulations may be altered or added to under and in accordance with the conditions under which articles, whenever registered, are permitted by this Act to be altered or added to, and

(iii) references in the regulations to any provision of the prior Companies Acts shall be read as references to the corresponding provision of this Act.

1178 Provisions as to names of CLGs

(1) The name of a CLG shall end with one of the following:

— company limited by guarantee;

— cuideachta faoi theorainn ráthaíochta.

(2) The words "company limited by guarantee" may be abbreviated to "c.l.g." or "clg" (including either such abbreviation in capitalised form) in any usage after the company's registration by any person including the CLG.

(3) The words "cuideachta faoi theorainn ráthaíochta" may be abbreviated to "c.t.r." or "ctr" (including either such abbreviation in capitalised form) in any usage after the company's registration by any person including the CLG.

(4) A CLG carrying on business under a name other than its corporate name shall register in the manner directed by law for the registration of business names but the use of the abbreviations set out in *subsection (2)* or *(3)* shall not of itself render such registration necessary.

(5) This section is subject to [*section 1190*][a] (which makes transitional provision for an existing guarantee company as regards its name).

Amendments

a Words substituted by C(A)A 2017, s 98(j) (previously: "*section 1189*").

1179 Trading under a misleading name

(1) Subject to *subsection (5)*, neither a body that is not a CLG nor an individual shall carry on any trade, profession or business under a name which includes, as its last part, the words "company limited by guarantee", or "cuideachta faoi theorainn ráthaíochta" or abbreviations of those words.

(2) If a body or individual contravenes *subsection (1)*, the body or individual and, in the case of a body, any officer of it who is in default, shall be guilty of a category 3 offence.

(3) A CLG shall not, in the following circumstances, use a name which may reasonably be expected to give the impression that it is any type of a company other than a CLG or that it is any other form of body corporate.

(4) Those circumstances are circumstances in which the fact that it is a CLG is likely to be material to any person.

(5) If a CLG contravenes *subsection (3)*, the CLG and any officer of it who is in default shall be guilty of a category 3 offence.

(6) *Subsection (1)* shall not apply to any company—

(a) to which *Part 21* applies, and

(b) which has provisions in its constitution that would entitle it to rank as a CLG if it had been registered in the State.

1180 Power to dispense with "company limited by guarantee" or Irish equivalent in name of charitable and other companies

(1) A CLG shall, notwithstanding its registration as a company with limited liability, be exempt from the provisions of this Act relating to the use of the words "company limited by guarantee" or "cuideachta faoi theorainn ráthaíochta" as part of its name and the publishing of its name, but shall enjoy all the privileges and shall (subject to this section) be subject to all the obligations of a CLG, where—

(a) its objects are the promotion of commerce, art, science, education, religion, charity or any other prescribed object, and

(b) its constitution—

(i) requires its profits (if any) or other income to be applied to the promotion of its objects,

(ii) prohibits the making of distributions to its members, and

(iii) requires all the assets which would otherwise be available to its members to be transferred on its winding up to another company whose objects comply with *paragraph (a)* and which meets the requirements of this paragraph,

and

(c) a director or secretary of the company (or, in the case of an association about to be formed as a limited company, one of the persons who are to be the first directors or the person who is to be the first secretary of the company) has delivered to the Registrar a statement in the prescribed form that the company complies or, where applicable, will comply with the requirements of *paragraphs (a)* and *(b)*.

(2) The Registrar shall refuse to register as a CLG any association about to be formed as a CLG by a name which does not include the words "company limited by guarantee" or "cuideachta faoi theorainn ráthaíochta" unless a statement, as provided for under *subsection (1)(c)*, has been delivered to the Registrar.

(3) An application by a company registered as a CLG for a change of name, being a change that includes or consists of the omission of the words "company limited by guarantee" or "cuideachta faoi theorainn ráthaíochta", shall be made in accordance with *section 30* and the Registrar shall refuse to accede to the application unless a statement, as provided for under *subsection (1)(c)*, has been delivered to the Registrar.

(4) A CLG which is exempt under *subsection (1)* and which is permitted to omit the words "company limited by guarantee" or "cuideachta faoi theorainn ráthaíochta" from its name shall not alter its constitution so that it ceases to comply with the requirements of that subsection.

(5) If it appears to the Registrar that a CLG which is registered under a name not including the words "company limited by guarantee" or "cuideachta faoi theorainn ráthaíochta"—

(a) has carried on any business other than the promotion of any of the objects mentioned in *subsection (1)(a)*,

(b) has applied any of its profits or other income otherwise than in promoting such objects, or

(c) has made a distribution to any of its members,

the Registrar may, in writing, direct the CLG to change its name within such period as may be specified in the direction so that its name ends with the words "company limited by guarantee" or "cuideachta faoi theorainn ráthaíochta", and the change of name shall be made in accordance with *section 30*.

(6) A CLG which has received a direction under *subsection (5)* shall not thereafter be registered by a name which does not include the words "company limited by guarantee" or "cuideachta faoi theorainn ráthaíochta" without the approval of the Registrar.

(7) A person who—

(a) alters the constitution of a CLG in contravention of *subsection (4)*, or

(b) fails to comply with a direction from the Registrar under *subsection (5)*,

shall be guilty of a category 3 offence.

(8) *Subsections (9)* to *(12)* have effect notwithstanding—

(a) the repeal by the Act of 2001 of section 24, as originally enacted, of the Act of 1963 (the "original section 24"), or

(b) the repeal by this Act of section 24, inserted by section 88(1) of the Act of 2001, of the Act of 1963 (the "substituted section 24") or of the Act of 2001.

(9) A licence that—

(a) had been granted by the Minister pursuant to subsection (1) or (2) of the original section 24 to a company limited by guarantee, and

(b) is in force immediately before the commencement of this section,

shall, on and from whichever thing referred to in *section 1190(5)(a)* or *(b)* happens first, continue to have effect but with the modification that it shall operate to exempt the company from the use of the words "company limited by guarantee" or "cuideachta faoi theorainn ráthaíochta" as part of its name and the publishing of its name.

(10) Subsections (4) to (7) of the original section 24 shall continue in force in relation to the foregoing licence as if that section 24 had never been repealed, except that references in those subsections to the Minister, wherever occurring, shall be read as references to the Registrar.

(11) An exemption that immediately before the repeal of the Act of 2001 operated, by virtue of the substituted section 24, in favour of a company limited by guarantee shall, on and from whichever thing referred to in *section 1190(5)(a)* or *(b)* happens first, continue to have effect but—

(a) with the modification that it shall operate to exempt the company from the use of the words "company limited by guarantee" or "cuideachta faoi theorainn ráthaíochta" as part of its name and the publishing of its name; and

(b) subject to *subsection (12)*.

(12) *Subsections (4)* to *(7)* shall, with the necessary modifications, apply to a foregoing exemption as they apply to an exemption under *subsection (1)*.

(13) *Subsections (9)* to *(12)* are without prejudice to *section 1190(4)* (which saves for a limited period the effect of provisions of the prior Companies Acts (including section 88(2) of the Act of 2001) that impose a requirement, or confer an exemption from a requirement, with regard to the use of "limited" or "teoranta" or their abbreviations).

(14) In relation to—

(a) a CLG that avails itself of the exemption under *subsection (1)* or continues to avail itself of a licence or exemption referred to in *subsection (9)* or *(11)*, and

(b) an existing guarantee company (within the meaning of *section 1189*) that avails itself, during the period specified in *section 1190(4)*, of an exemption conferred by a provision of the prior Companies Acts with regard to the use of "limited" or "teoranta" or their abbreviations,

section 151 shall have effect as if, in addition to the particulars specified in *subsection (2)(a)* to *(c)* of that section to be included on all business letters and order forms of the

CLG, there were specified in that subsection the fact of the CLG being a limited company.

(15) In this section "Act of 2001" means the Company Law Enforcement Act 2001.

1181 Prohibition on certain provisions in constitution, etc and issuing of shares

(1) Any provision in the memorandum or articles of a CLG, or in any resolution of a CLG, purporting to give any person a right to participate in the divisible profits of the company, otherwise than as a member, shall be void.

(2) Nothing in *subsection (1)* invalidates any distribution by a company limited by guarantee registered before 1 January 1901, on foot of a provision or resolution referred to in that subsection, if the distribution was made before the commencement of this section.

(3) For the purposes of the provisions of this Part stipulating that a characteristic of a CLG is that it does not have a share capital and of this section, the following has effect—

- (a) every provision in the constitution, or in any resolution, of a CLG purporting to divide the undertaking of the CLG into shares or interests, shall be treated as a provision for a share capital, notwithstanding that the nominal amount or number of the shares or interests is not specified thereby, and
- (b) every such provision or resolution shall be void.

(4) A CLG shall not purport to issue shares.

(5) If a CLG contravenes *subsection (4)*, the CLG and any officer of it who is in default shall be guilty of a category 3 offence.

1182 Capacity of a CLG

(1) A CLG shall have the capacity to do any act or thing stated in the objects set out in its memorandum.

(2) For the purposes of *subsection (1)*—

- (a) the reference in it to an object includes a reference to anything stated in the memorandum as being a power to do any act or thing (whether the word "power" is used or not),
- (b) if an object is stated in the CLG's memorandum without the following also being stated in relation to it, the capacity of the CLG extends to doing any act or thing that appears to it to be requisite, advantageous or incidental to, or to facilitate, the attainment of that object and that is not inconsistent with any enactment,

and a subsequent reference in this Part to an object of a CLG shall be read accordingly.

1183 Capacity not limited by a CLG's constitution

(1) The validity of an act done by a CLG shall not be called into question on the ground of lack of capacity by reason of anything contained in the CLG's objects.

(2) A member of a CLG may bring proceedings to restrain the doing of an act which, but for *subsection (1)*, would be beyond the CLG's capacity but no such proceedings shall lie in respect of any act to be done in fulfilment of a legal obligation arising from a previous act of the CLG.

(3) Notwithstanding the enactment of *subsection (1)*, it remains the duty of the directors to observe any limitations on their powers flowing from the CLG's objects and action by the directors which, but for *subsection (1)*, would be beyond the CLG's capacity may only be ratified by the CLG by special resolution.

(4) A resolution ratifying such action shall not affect any liability incurred by the directors or any other person; if relief from any such liability is to be conferred by the CLG it must be agreed to separately by a special resolution of it.

(5) A party to a transaction with a CLG is not bound to enquire as to whether it is permitted by the CLG's objects.

1184 Alteration of objects clause by special resolution

(1) Subject to *subsection (2)*, a CLG may, by special resolution, alter the provisions of its memorandum of association by abandoning, restricting or amending any existing object or by adopting a new object and any alteration so made shall be as valid as if originally contained therein, and be subject to alteration in like manner.

(2) If an application is made to the court in accordance with this section for the alteration to be cancelled, it shall not have effect except in so far as it is confirmed by the court.

(3) Subject to *subsection (4)*, an application under this section may be made—

(a) by not less than 15 per cent of the CLG's members, or

(b) by the holders of not less than 15 per cent of the CLG's debentures, entitling the holders to object to alterations of its objects.

(4) An application shall not be made under this section by any person who has consented to or voted in favour of the alteration.

(5) An application under this section shall be made within 21 days after the date on which the resolution altering the CLG's objects was passed and may be made on behalf of the persons entitled to make the application by such one or more of their number as they may appoint in writing for the purpose.

(6) On an application under this section, the court may—

(a) make an order cancelling the alteration or confirming the alteration, either wholly or in part, and on such terms and conditions as it thinks fit, and

(b) if it thinks fit, adjourn the proceedings in order that an arrangement may be made to the satisfaction of the court for the purchase of the interests of dissenting members and may give such directions and make such orders as it may think expedient for facilitating or carrying into effect any such arrangement.

1185 Supplemental provisions in relation to section 1184

(1) Where an order under *section 1184* requires the CLG not to make any, or any specified, alteration in its constitution, then, notwithstanding anything in this Act, but subject to the provisions of the order, the CLG shall not have power, without the leave of the court, to make any such alteration in contravention of that requirement.

(2) Any alteration in the constitution of a CLG made by virtue of an order under *section 1184*, other than one made by resolution of the CLG, shall be of the same effect as if duly made by resolution of the CLG and the provisions of this Act shall apply to the constitution as so altered accordingly.

(3) Notice of the meeting at which the special resolution altering a CLG's objects is intended to be proposed shall be given to any holders of the CLG's debentures that entitle the holders to object to alterations of its objects; that notice shall be the same as that given to members of the CLG, so however that not less than 10 days' notice shall be given to the holders of any such debentures.

(4) If the written resolution procedure is used in the matter, notice, which shall not be less than 10 days, of the proposed use of that procedure shall, together with a copy of the proposed text of the resolution, be given to the debenture holders referred to in *subsection (3)*.

(5) In default of any provisions in the CLG's constitution regulating the giving to the foregoing debenture holders of notice referred to in *subsection (3)* or *(4)*, the provisions of *Part 4* or, as the case may be, of the CLG's constitution regulating the giving of notice to members shall apply.

(6) Without prejudice to *subsections (3)* and *(4)*, in the case of a CLG which is, by virtue of *section 1180*, permitted to omit the words "company limited by guarantee" or "cuideachta faoi theorainn ráthaíochta" from its name, notice of—

(a) the meeting at which the special resolution altering a CLG's objects is intended to be proposed; or

(b) if the written resolution procedure is used in the matter, notice of the proposed use of that procedure, together with a copy of the proposed text of the resolution,

shall be given to the Registrar and *subsections (3)* to *(5)* shall apply as respects such notice as they apply as respects notice of the meeting or resolution to debenture holders.

(7) Where a CLG passes a resolution altering its objects—

(a) if no application is made under *section 1184* with respect to the alteration, it shall, within 15 days after the end of the period for making such an application, deliver to the Registrar a copy of its memorandum of association as altered, and

(b) if such an application is made, it shall—

(i) forthwith give notice of that fact to the Registrar, and

(ii) within 15 days after the date of any order cancelling or confirming the alteration, deliver to the Registrar a certified copy of the order and, in the case of an order confirming the alteration, a copy of the memorandum as altered.

(8) The court may by order at any time extend the time for delivery of documents to the Registrar under *subsection (7)(b)* for such period as the court may think proper.

(9) If a CLG makes default in giving notice or delivering any document to the Registrar as required by *subsection (7)*, the CLG and any officer of it who is in default shall be guilty of a category 4 offence.

1186 Restriction of *section 32(1)* in relation to CLGs

(1) Other than in respect of making an amendment of the type specified in *subsection (2)*, *section 32(1)* shall not apply in relation to a CLG.

(2) The amendment referred to in *subsection (1)* is an amendment of the amount referred to in *section 1176(2)(e)* that is specified in the CLG's memorandum.

1187 Alteration of articles by special resolution

(1) Subject to the provisions of this Act and to the conditions contained in its memorandum, a CLG may, by special resolution, alter or add to its articles.

(2) Any alteration or addition so made in the articles shall, subject to the provisions of this Act, be as valid as if originally contained therein and be subject in like manner to alteration by special resolution.

1188 Power to alter provisions in memorandum which could have been contained in articles

(1) Subject to *subsection (2)*, *sections 32(4)* and *(5)* and *212*, any provision contained in a CLG's memorandum which could lawfully have been contained in articles instead of in the memorandum may, subject to the provisions of this section, be altered by the CLG by special resolution.

(2) If an application is made to the court for the alteration to be cancelled, it shall not have effect except in so far as it is confirmed by the court.

(3) This section shall not apply where the memorandum itself provides for or prohibits the alteration of all or any of the foregoing provisions, and shall not authorise any variation or abrogation of the special rights of any class of members.

(4) *Section 1184(3)* to *(6)* (other than *subsection (3)(b)*) and *section 1185* (other than *subsections (3)* to *(6)*) shall apply in relation to any alteration and to any application made under this section as they apply in relation to alterations and to applications made under those sections.

1189 Status of existing guarantee company

(1) In this section "existing guarantee company" means a company limited by guarantee, and not having a share capital, which—

(a) was incorporated under any former enactment relating to companies (within the meaning of *section 5*), and

(b) is in existence immediately before the commencement of this section.

(2) An existing guarantee company shall, on and from the commencement of this section, continue in existence and be deemed to be a CLG to which this Part applies.

(3) *Section 1190* contains provisions—

(a) for enabling such a company to continue to use, for a limited period, "limited" or "teoranta" in its name despite the foregoing status that it has assumed, and

(b) subject to certain exceptions, deeming the name of such a company, after a specified period and in default of its having changed its name in that fashion, to be altered by the replacement of—

(i) "company limited by guarantee" for "limited" at the end thereof, or

(ii) "cuideachta faoi theorainn ráthaíochta" for "teoranta" at the end thereof,

as the case may be.

(4) Reference, express or implied, in this Act to the date of registration of a company mentioned in a preceding subsection shall be read as a reference to the date on which the company was registered under the Joint Stock Companies Act 1862, the Companies (Consolidation) Act 1908 or the prior Companies Acts, as the case may be.

1190 Transitional provision — use of "limited" or "teoranta" by existing guarantee company

(1) In this section—

"existing guarantee company" has the same meaning as it has in *section 1189*;

"new provisions" means the provisions of this Part (and the relevant provisions of *Part 2* as applied by this Part) relating to the use of either of the required sets of words (or their abbreviations) set out in *subsection (2)*;

"transition period" means the period of 18 months beginning after the commencement of this section.

(2) For the purposes of this section, each of the following is a required set of words—

(a) company limited by guarantee,

(b) cuideachta faoi theorainn ráthaíochta.

(3) The reference—

(a) in the preceding definition of "new provisions", and

(b) in *subsection (4)*,

to provisions relating to the use of any words includes a reference to provisions conferring an exemption from the use of those words.

(4) During—

(a) the transition period, or

(b) if before the expiry of that period the company has changed its name to include either of the required sets of words, the period preceding the making of that change,

the provisions of the prior Companies Acts relating to the use of limited or teoranta (or their abbreviations) shall apply as respects the name of an existing guarantee company in place of the new provisions.

(5) On and from—

(a) the expiry of the transition period, or

(b) the company changing its name to include either of the required sets of words,

whichever happens first, the new provisions shall apply as respects the name of an existing guarantee company.

(6) Without prejudice to the generality of *subsection (5)* and subject, where appropriate, to *section 1180(9)* to *(12)*, on the expiry of the transition period (and the company has not changed its name before then to include either of the required sets of words), the name of an existing guarantee company, as set out in its memorandum, shall be deemed to be altered by the replacement of—

(a) "company limited by guarantee" for "limited" at the end thereof, or

(b) "cuideachta faoi theorainn ráthaíochta" for "teoranta" at the end thereof,

as the case may be.

(7) Where an existing guarantee company's name, as set out in its memorandum, is altered by virtue of *subsection (6)*, the Registrar shall issue to the company a fresh certificate of incorporation in respect of it, being a certificate of incorporation that is altered to meet the circumstances of the case.

Chapter 3
Share capital

1191 Limitation on offers by CLGs of securities to the public

Section 68 shall apply to a CLG as if the following subsection were substituted for *subsection (2)*:

"(2) A company shall—

(a) neither apply to have securities (or interests in them) admitted to trading or to be listed on, nor

(b) have securities (or interests in them) admitted to trading or listed on,

any market, whether a regulated market or not, in the State or elsewhere; however nothing in this subsection prohibits the admission to trading or listing (or an application being made therefor) on any market of debentures (or interests in them) for the purposes of any of *paragraphs (a)* to *(e)* of *subsection (3)*.".

1192 Application of *section 114* in relation to CLGs

In its application to this Part, *section 114* shall apply as if each reference in it to the acquisition and holding of shares in a company included, in a case where the holding company is a CLG, a reference to becoming, and being, a member of the company otherwise than by means of acquiring and holding shares.

1193 Uncertificated transfer of securities

Sections 1085 to *1087* shall apply to securities of a CLG as they apply to securities of a PLC.

Chapter 4
Corporate governance

1194 Directors

(1) A CLG shall have at least 2 directors.

(2) Nothing in *Parts 1* to *14* that makes provision in the case of a company having a sole director shall apply to a CLG.

1195 Limitation on number of directorships

For the purposes of this Part, *section 142* shall apply as if the following subsection were substituted for *subsection (1)*:

"(1) A person shall not, at a particular time, be a director of more than—

(a) 25 companies limited by guarantee, or

(b) 25 companies, one, or more than one, of which is a company limited by guarantee and one, or more than one, of which is any other type of company capable of being wound up under this Act.".

1196 Rotation of directors

(1) Each provision of this section applies save to the extent that the CLG's constitution provides otherwise.

(2) At the first annual general meeting of the CLG all the directors shall retire from office.

(3) At the annual general meeting in every subsequent year, one-third of the directors for the time being, or, if their number is not 3 or a multiple of 3, then the number nearest one-third shall retire from office.

(4) The directors to retire in every year shall be those who have been longest in office since their last election but as between persons who became directors on the same day, those to retire shall (unless they otherwise agree among themselves) be determined by lot.

(5) A retiring director shall be eligible for re-election.

(6) The CLG, at the meeting at which a director retires in any of the foregoing instances, may fill the vacated office by electing a person to it.

(7) In default of the CLG doing so, the retiring director shall, if offering himself or herself for re-election, be deemed to have been re-elected, unless—

(a) at such meeting it is expressly resolved not to fill such vacated office, or

(b) a resolution for the re-election of such director has been put to the meeting and lost.

1197 Remuneration of directors

(1) Each provision of this section applies save to the extent that the CLG's constitution provides otherwise.

(2) The remuneration of the directors of a CLG shall be such as is determined, from time to time, by the CLG in general meeting and such remuneration shall be deemed to accrue from day to day.

(3) The directors of a CLG may also be paid all travelling, hotel and other expenses properly incurred by them—

(a) in attending and returning from—

(i) meetings of the directors or any committee referred to in *section 160(9)*, or

(ii) general meetings of the CLG,

or

(b) otherwise in connection with the business of the CLG.

1198 Removal of directors

Section 146 shall apply to a CLG with the omission of *subsection (2)* (exclusion of section's application to a director holding office for life).

1199 Membership

(1) The subscribers to the memorandum of association of a CLG shall be deemed to have agreed to become members of the CLG, and, on its registration, shall be entered as members in its register of members.

(2) Such other persons—

(a) being persons—

(i) whom the directors admit to membership; or

(ii) who are admitted to membership, pursuant to provisions that the constitution may contain in that behalf, whether provisions that—

(I) provide a separate power to; or

(II) supplement or limit, or exclude,

any power of the directors in that regard;

and

(b) whose names are entered in its register of members,

shall be members of the CLG.

(3) The articles of a CLG shall state the number of members with which the company proposes to be registered.

(4) Where a CLG has increased the number of its members beyond the registered number, it shall, within 15 days after the date on which the increase was resolved on or took place, deliver particulars of the increase to the Registrar.

(5) If default is made by a CLG in complying with *subsection (4)*, the CLG and any officer of it who is in default shall be guilty of a category 4 offence.

(6) The articles of a CLG may state the maximum number of persons who may be members of the CLG, subject to the power of the directors to register an increase in the number of members.

(7) A member may resign his or her membership by serving notice to that effect upon the directors at the registered office of the CLG, such notice to expire no earlier than the date of service of the notice of resignation.

(8) Save where the constitution of a CLG provides otherwise, the directors may require a member to resign his or her membership by serving notice upon the member terminating his or her membership to expire no earlier than the date of service of the notice of termination.

(9) Save where the constitution of a CLG provides otherwise, every member shall have one vote.

(10) The death or bankruptcy of a member shall terminate his or her membership.

1200 Personation of member: offence

If any person falsely and deceitfully personates any member of a CLG and thereby—

(a) receives or endeavours to receive any money due to any such member, or

(b) votes at any meeting as if the person were the true and lawful member,

he or she shall be guilty of a category 2 offence.

1201 Register of members

Section 169 shall apply to a CLG with the following modifications:

(a) the following paragraph shall be substituted, in *subsection (1)*, for *paragraph (a)*:

"(a) the names and addresses of the members;";

and

(b) *subsection (5)* shall be omitted.

1202 CLG, with 2 or more members, may not dispense with holding of a.g.m.

Section 175(3) and *(4)* (which relate to dispensing with the holding of an annual general meeting) shall not apply to a CLG if it has more than one member.

1203 Convening of extraordinary general meeting on requisition

Section 178 shall apply to a CLG with the following modifications:

(a) *subsections (1)(a)* and *(2)* shall be omitted; and

(b) the following subsection shall be substituted for *subsection (3)*:

"(3) The directors of a company shall, on the requisition of one or more members holding, or together holding, at the date of the deposit of the requisition, not less than 10 per cent of the total voting rights of all the members having, at the date of the deposit, the right to vote at general meetings of the company, forthwith proceed duly to convene an extraordinary general meeting of the company.".

1204 Persons entitled to notice of general meetings

Section 180 shall apply to a CLG with the omission of *subsection (1)(b)* and *(c)* and *subsections (2)* to *(4)*.

1205 Proxies

Section 183 shall apply to a CLG with the following modifications:

(a) in *subsection (1)* there shall be inserted "and save to the extent that the constitution provides otherwise" after "Subject to *subsection (3)*";

(b) in [*subsection (9)*][a], the words "or the transfer of the share in respect of which the proxy is given" shall be omitted; and

[(c) in *subsection (10)*, there shall be substituted "such death or revocation" for "such death, insanity, revocation or transfer".][b]

Amendments

a Words substituted by C(A)A 2017, s 98(k)(i) (previously: "*subsection (8)*").

b Paragraph (c) substituted by C(A)A 2017, s 98(k)(ii).

1206 Votes of members

Section 188 shall apply to a CLG with the following modifications:

(a) the following subsection shall be substituted for *subsection (2)*:

"(2) Where a matter is being decided (whether on a show of hands or on a poll), every member present in person and every proxy shall have one vote, but so that no individual member shall have more than one vote.";

(b) *subsection (3)* shall be omitted; and

(c) the following subsection shall be substituted for *subsection (6)*:

"(6) No member shall be entitled to vote at any general meeting of a company unless all moneys immediately payable by him or her to the company have been paid.".

1207 Right to demand a poll

Section 189 shall apply to a CLG with the omission of *subsection (2)(d)*.

1208 Application of *section 193* in relation to a CLG

Section 193 shall apply to a CLG as if, in *subsection (1)*, after "Notwithstanding any provision to the contrary in this Act", there were inserted "and unless the constitution provides otherwise".

1209 Application of *section 198* in relation to a CLG

Section 198 shall apply to a CLG with the following modifications:

(a) the following paragraph shall be substituted for *paragraph (c)* of *subsection (4)*:

"(c) resolutions or agreements which have been agreed to by all the members of some class of membership but which if not so agreed to, would not have been effective for their purpose unless they had been passed by some particular majority or otherwise in some particular manner, and all resolutions or agreements which effectively bind all the members of any class of membership though not agreed to by all those members;";

and

(b) *paragraphs (d)* and *(e)* and *(g)* to *(k)* of *subsection (4)* shall be omitted.

1210 Application of *Chapter 5* of *Part 5* to a CLG

(1) Subject to *subsection (2)*, *Chapter 5* of *Part 5* shall apply to a CLG.

(2) For the purposes of that application, *Chapter 5* of *Part 5* shall operate, so far as it relates to shares in a company, or shares in a body corporate of the same group as that company belongs to, as if it excluded references to—

(a) that company where that company is a CLG, and

(b) such a body corporate where that body corporate is a CLG.

Chapter 5
Financial statements, annual return and audit

1211 Non-application of *Part 6* to CLGs that are credit institutions or insurance undertakings

Part 6 shall not apply to a CLG that is a credit institution or an insurance undertaking—

(a) to the extent provided by regulations made under section 3 of the European Communities Act 1972 to give effect to Community acts on accounts of credit institutions and insurance undertakings, respectively, or

(b) to the extent provided by any other enactment.

1212 Requirement for corporate governance statement and modification of certain provisions of *Parts 5* and *6* as they apply to CLGs

Chapter 3 of *Part 23* has effect in relation to, amongst other companies, a CLG that has debentures admitted to trading on a regulated market in an EEA state.

1213 Modification of definition of "IAS Regulation" in the case of CLGs

Section 1116 (modification of definition of "IAS Regulation") shall apply in the case of a CLG as it applies in the case of PLC.

1214 Application of *section 297* to a CLG

[...][a]

Amendments

a Section 1214 repealed by C(A)A 2017, s 3(1)(h).

1215 Disclosures by CLG that is credit institution

In addition to its having effect in relation to a public limited company, *section 1120* shall have effect in relation to a CLG.

1216 Disclosure of membership changes in CLG's financial statements

Section 318 (details of authorised share capital, allotted share capital and movements) shall not apply in relation to the financial statements of a CLG but where there are changes in the interests of members of a CLG in the financial year to which the financial statements of the CLG relate then particulars of those changes shall be given in the notes to those financial statements.

1217 Disapplication of *sections 325(1)(c)* and *329* to a CLG

Sections 325(1)(c) and *329* shall not apply to a CLG.

1218 Application of *sections 334*, *359* and *362* to a CLG

(1) *Section 334* shall apply to a CLG with the following modifications:

(a) the following subsection shall be substituted for *subsection (1)*:

"(1) Any member of a company may serve a notice in writing on the company stating that that member does not wish the audit exemption to be available to the company in a financial year specified in the notice.";

(b) *subsection (3)* shall be omitted; and

(c) the following subsection shall be substituted for *subsection (4)*:

"(4) For the avoidance of doubt, the reference in *subsection (1)* to the member's not wishing the audit exemption to be available to the company in a specified financial year is, if the company is a subsidiary undertaking, a reference to the member's not wishing the audit exemption to be available to the subsidiary undertaking irrespective of whether its holding company and any other undertakings in the group avail themselves of the audit exemption in that year.".

[...][a]

[...][b]

Amendments

a Subsection (2) repealed by C(A)A 2017, s 3(1)(i).
b Subsection (3) repealed by C(A)A 2017, s 3(1)(i).

1219 Qualification of *section 338* in the case of a CLG

Section 338 (circulation of statutory financial statements) shall apply to a CLG with the following modifications:

(a) in *subsection (1)(a)*, there shall be substituted "(but only if that person is entitled to receive notices of general meetings of the company)" for "(whether that person is or is not entitled to receive notices of general meetings of the company)"; and

(b) in *subsection (1)(b)*, there shall be substituted "(but only if that person is so entitled)" for "(whether that person is or is not so entitled)".

1220 Exemption from filing with Registrar financial statements, etc.

(1) Without prejudice to *subsections (4)* to *(6)* (which contain transitional provisions), *sections 347* and *348* shall not apply to a CLG if it satisfies the following conditions:

(a) it has been formed for charitable purposes; and

(b) it stands exempted from those sections by an order made by the relevant authority (which order the relevant authority is, by virtue of this section, empowered to make),

and the exemption provided by that order may, as the relevant authority considers appropriate, be either for an indefinite or a limited period.

(2) The following provisions have effect in relation to a CLG referred to in *subsection (1)*—

(a) unless the CLG is entitled to and has availed itself of the audit exemption conferred by *Chapter 15* or *16* of *Part 6*, the statutory auditors of the CLG shall prepare a separate report to the directors which—

(i) confirms that they audited the relevant statutory financial statements for the relevant financial year, and

(ii) includes within it the report made to the members of the CLG pursuant to *section 391*,

and

(b) a copy of the report prepared under *paragraph (a)* shall be annexed to the annual return delivered by the CLG to the Registrar.

(3) The reference in *subsection (2)* to a copy of the report prepared under *paragraph (a)* of it is a reference to a copy that satisfies the following conditions:

(a) it is a true copy of the original save for the difference that the signature or signatures on the original, and any date or dates thereon, shall appear in typeset form on the copy; and

(b) it is accompanied by a certificate of a director and the secretary of the company, that bears the signature of the director and the secretary in electronic or written form, stating that the copy is a true copy of the original (and the foregoing statement need not be qualified on account of the difference permitted by *paragraph (a)* as to the form of a signature or of a date).

(4) *Sections 347* and *348* shall not apply to an existing guarantee company that, immediately before the commencement of this section, stood exempted from the requirements of section 128 of the Act of 1963 by virtue of subsection (4)(c) or (5) of that section, but this is subject to *subsections (5)* and *(6)*.

(5) If, by reason of a change of circumstances set out in section 128(4) of the Act of 1963 relating to the company concerned (were that section 128(4) to remain in force after the commencement of *section 4* (repeals and revocations)), an existing guarantee company would no longer comply with that section 128(4), then, thereupon, *sections 347* and *348* shall apply to that company.

(6) If—

(a) circumstances arise affecting an existing guarantee company that stood exempted, immediately before the commencement of this section, from the requirements of section 128 of the Act of 1963 by virtue of subsection (5) of the latter, and

(b) those circumstances are such as would, but for the repeal of that section 128, warrant the relevant authority exercising the power of revocation that but, for that repeal, would have been available to them in relation to the particular order that had subsisted, under that subsection (5), in relation to that company,

then the relevant authority shall, by virtue of those circumstances, be empowered to declare in writing that *sections 347* and *348* shall, on and from a date specified in the declaration, apply to that company and, where the relevant authority so declares, *sections 347* and *348* shall apply to that company on and from the date so specified.

(7) In *subsection (8)*—

"electronic means" means those provided for under the Electronic Commerce Act 2000 and effected in compliance with any requirements of the Registrar of the kind referred to in sections 12(2)(b) and 13(2)(a) of that Act;

"required documents" means the copy of the report referred to in *paragraph (a)* of *subsection (3)*, accompanied by the certificate referred to in *paragraph (b)* of that subsection;

"required period" means the period referred to in *section 343(2)* or *(3)*, as the case may be, or, where that period stands extended in accordance with *section 343(5)* and *(6)*, that period as it stands so extended.

(8) Where a CLG makes its annual return by electronic means to the Registrar within the required period then, notwithstanding that the required documents have not been annexed to the annual return, the annual return shall be deemed to have been delivered to the Registrar within the required period with the foregoing documents annexed to it if those documents are delivered to the Registrar within 28 days after the date on which the annual return has been delivered to the Registrar by electronic means.

(9) In this section—

"existing guarantee company" has the same meaning as it has in *section 1189*;

"relevant authority" means—

(a) before the establishment day (within the meaning of the Charities Act 2009), the Commissioners of Charitable Donations and Bequests for Ireland; and

(b) on or after the foregoing day, the Charities Regulatory Authority.

1221 Application of *section 392* to a CLG

Section 392 (report to Registrar and Director: accounting records) shall apply to a CLG as if, in *subsection (6)*, there were substituted "its members" for "its shareholders".

1222 Application of *section 393* to a CLG

Section 393 (report to Registrar and Director: category 1 and 2 offences) shall apply to a CLG as if, in *subsection (4)*, there were substituted "its members" for "its shareholders".

Chapter 6
Liability of contributories in winding up

1223 Liability as contributories of past and present members and provision concerning winding up after certain re-registration

(1) Subject to *subsection (2)*, in the event of a CLG being wound up, every present and past member shall be liable to contribute to the assets of the CLG to an amount sufficient for payment of its debts and liabilities, and the costs, charges and expenses of the winding up, and for the adjustment of the rights of the contributories among themselves.

(2) The following qualifications apply in relation to *subsection (1)*:

(a) no contribution shall be required from any member exceeding the amount undertaken to be contributed by him or her to the assets of the CLG in the event of its being wound up;

(b) a past member shall not be liable to contribute if he or she has ceased to be a member for one year or more before the commencement of the winding up;

(c) a past member shall not be liable to contribute in respect of any debt or liability of the CLG contracted after he or she ceased to be a member;

(d) a past member shall not be liable to contribute unless it appears to the court that the existing members are unable to satisfy the contributions required to be made by them in pursuance of this Act;

(e) nothing in this Act shall invalidate any provision contained in any policy of insurance or other contract whereby the liability of individual members on the policy or contract is restricted, or whereby the funds of the CLG are alone made liable in respect of the policy or contract;

(f) a sum due to any member of the CLG, in his or her character of a member, by way of distributions, profits or otherwise, shall not be deemed to be a debt of the company, payable to that member in a case of competition between himself or herself and any other creditor not a member of the CLG, but any such sum may be taken into account for the purpose of the final adjustment of the rights of the contributories among themselves.

(3) Without prejudice to the application of that section to a CLG, and its adaptation generally, by *section 1173* of *section 665* (winding up of company that had been an unlimited company before re-registration), *paragraph (c)* of *section 665* shall apply as if the reference in it to *section 655(2)(a)* were, in the case of a CLG, a reference to *subsection (2)(a)* of this section.

Chapter 7
Examinerships

1224 Petitions for examinerships

Section 510 shall apply to a CLG as if the following subsections were substituted for *subsections (2)* and *(3)*:

"(2) Where the company referred to in *section 509* is an insurer or the holding company of an insurer, a petition may be presented only by the Central Bank, and *subsection (1)* shall not apply to the company.

(3) Where the company referred to in *section 509* is—

(a) a credit institution or the holding company of a credit institution,

(b) a company which one or more trustee savings banks have been reorganised into pursuant to an order under section 57 of the Trustee Savings Banks Act 1989, or

(c) a company which a building society has converted itself into under Part XI of the Building Societies Act 1989,

a petition may be presented only by the Central Bank, and *subsection (1)* shall not apply to the company.".

Chapter 8
Investigations

1225 Application of *section 747(2)* to CLGs

Section 747(2) shall apply to a CLG as if *paragraph (c)* were deleted therefrom.

Chapter 9
Public offers of securities, prevention of market abuse, etc.

1226 Application of *Chapters 1, 2* and *4* of *Part 23* to CLGs

Chapters 1, *2* and *4* of *Part 23*, so far as they are applicable to companies other than public limited companies, shall apply to a CLG.

PART 19
UNLIMITED COMPANIES

Chapter 1
Preliminary and definitions

1227 Interpretation (*Part 19*)

In this Part—

"constitution" shall be read in accordance with *section 1233* or *1234*, as the case may be;

"PUC" shall be read in accordance with *section 1228(1)(b)*;

"PULC" shall be read in accordance with *section 1228(1)(c)*;

"ULC" shall be read in accordance with *section 1228(1)(a)*.

1228 Three types of unlimited company and uniform words to be affixed to name

(1) This Part makes provision for, and there is permitted to be formed and registered under this Part, the following 3 types of unlimited company:

(a) a private unlimited company — referred to in this Part as a "ULC";

(b) a public unlimited company — referred to in this Part as a "PUC"; and

(c) a public unlimited company that has no share capital — referred to in this Part as a "PULC".

(2) Irrespective of the type of unlimited company that the particular company constitutes, the name of any such company shall, as provided under *section 1237* and subject to that section and *section 1247*, end with the words "unlimited company" or "cuideachta neamhtheoranta".

1229 References to unlimited company to mean ULC, PUC or PULC

A reference in this Part to an unlimited company shall, unless expressly provided otherwise, be read as a reference to any of the 3 types of unlimited company referred to in *section 1228*.

1230 Application of *Parts 1* to *14* to unlimited companies

(1) The provisions of *Parts 1* to *14* apply to an unlimited company except to the extent that they are disapplied or modified by—

(a) this section, or

(b) any other provision of this Part.

(2) For the purposes of that application, *section 10(1)* shall have effect as if it read:

> "(1) Unless expressly provided otherwise, a reference in *Parts 2* to *14* to a company is a reference to an unlimited company.".

(3) Any of *Parts 1* to *14* that makes provision by reference to—

(a) membership arising by virtue of a shareholding, or

(b) rights or incidents of membership, including the right to vote or receive a distribution, arising by virtue of a shareholding,

shall be read, in the case of a PULC, as making such provision in the analogous context in which membership, or rights or incidents of membership, may arise in the case of a PULC.

(4) *Subsection (3)* is without prejudice to the generality of the application and adaptation of *Parts 1* to *14* provided by *subsections (1)* and *(2)* or any specific adaptation provided by a subsequent section of this Part.

(5) The provisions of this Act specified in *Part 1* of the Table to this section shall not apply to an ULC.

(6) The provisions of this Act specified in *Part 2* of the Table to this section shall not apply to a PUC.

(7) The provisions of this Act specified in *Part 3* of the Table to this section shall not apply to a PULC.

(8) The specification in the foregoing Table of a provision (a "specified provision") of *Parts 1* to *14* also operates to disapply to the particular type of unlimited company concerned any other provision of those Parts (notwithstanding that it is not specified in that Table) that makes consequential, incidental or supplemental provision on, or in relation to, the specified provision.

Table

Part 1

Provisions disapplied to ULCs

Subject matter	Provision disapplied
Way of forming a private company limited by shares	*Section 17*
Company to carry on activity in the State and prohibition of certain activities	*Section 18*
Form of the constitution	*Section 19*
Effect of registration	*Section 25*
Provisions as to names of companies	*Section 26(1) to (4)*
Trading under a misleading name	*Section 27*
Amendment of constitution by special resolution	*Section 32(1)*
Capacity of private company limited by shares	*Section 38*
Security for costs	*Section 52*
Conversion of existing private company to private company limited by shares to which *Parts 1* to *15* apply	*Chapter 6* of *Part 2*
Returns of allotments	*Section 70(7)* and *(8)*
Variation in capital	*Chapter 4* of *Part 3* (other than *sections 83*, *89*, *90*, *92* and *93*)
Directors	*Section 128*
Certain particulars to be shown on all business letters	*Section 151(2)* to *(4)*
Majority written resolutions	*Section 194*

Subject matter	Provision disapplied
Supplemental provisions in relation to *section 194*	*Section 195*
Directors' compliance statement and related statement	*Section 225*
Liability as contributories of past and present members	*Section 655*
Payment of debts due by contributory to the company and extent to which set-off allowed	*Section 659*

Part 2
Provisions disapplied to PUCs

Subject matter	Provision disapplied
Way of forming a private company limited by shares	*Section 17*
Company to carry on activity in the State and prohibition of certain activities	*Section 18*
Form of the constitution	*Section 19*
Effect of registration	*Section 25*
Provisions as to names of companies	*Section 26(1) to (4)*
Trading under a misleading name	*Section 27*
Amendment of constitution by special resolution	*Section 32(1)*
Capacity of private company limited by shares	*Section 38*
Security for costs	*Section 52*
Allotment of shares	*Section 69*
Supplemental and additional provisions as regards allotments	*Section 70*
Variation in capital	*Chapter 4* of *Part 3* (other than *sections 83, 89, 90, 92* and *93*)
Directors	Section 128
Certain particulars to be shown on all business letters	*Section 151(2)* to *(4)*
Majority written resolutions	*Section 194*
Supplemental provisions in relation to *section 194*	*Section 195*
Directors' compliance statement and related statement	*Section 225*
[Qualification of company based on size of company	*Sections 280A* to *280G*][a]
Exemption from consolidation: size of group	[...][b]
Statutory financial statements must be audited (unless audit exemption availed of)	*Section 333*
Exclusions, exemptions and special arrangements with regard to public disclosure of financial information	*Chapter 14 of Part 6*
Audit exemption	*Chapter 15 of Part 6*
Special audit exemption for dormant companies	*Chapter 16 of Part 6*
Small and medium companies	*Section 377*
Liability as contributories of past and present members	*Section 655*
Payment of debts due by contributory to the company and extent to which set-off allowed	*Section 659*

Part 3
Provisions disapplied to PULCs

Subject matter	Provision disapplied
Way of forming a private company limited by shares	*Section 17*
Company to carry on activity in the State and prohibition of certain activities	*Section 18*
Form of the constitution	*Section 19*
Effect of registration	*Section 25*
Provisions as to names of companies	*Section 26(1)* to *(4)*
Trading under a misleading name	*Section 27*
Amendment of constitution by special resolution	*Section 32(1)*
Capacity of private company limited by shares	*Section 38*
Security for costs	*Section 52*
Conversion of existing private company to private company limited by shares to which *Parts 1* to *15* apply	*Chapter 6* of *Part 2*
Powers to convert shares into stock, etc.	*Section 65*
Shares	*Section 66*
Numbering of shares	*Section 67*
Allotment of shares and variation in capital	*Chapters 3* and *4* of *Part 3*
Transfer of shares	*Chapter 5* of *Part 3* (save *section 94* in so far as it relates to debentures)
Acquisition of own shares	*Chapter 6* of *Part 3* (save *sections 113* to *116*)
Procedures for declarations, payments, etc., of dividends and other things	*Section 124*
Supplemental provisions in relation to *section 124*	*Section 125*
Bonus issues	*Section 126*
Directors	*Section 128*
Share qualifications of directors	*Section 136*
Certain particulars to be shown on all business letters	*Section 151(2)* to *(4)*
Definition of member	*Section 168*
Majority written resolutions	*Section 194*
Supplemental provisions in relation to *section 194*	*Section 195*
Directors' compliance statement and related statement	*Section 225*
[Qualification of company based on size of company	*Sections 280A* to *280G*][c]
Holding of own shares	*Section 320(1)*
Directors' report as it relates to dividends	*Section 326(1)(d)*
Statutory financial statements must be audited (unless audit exemption availed of)	*Section 333*

Subject matter	Provision disapplied
Exclusions, exemptions and special arrangements with regard to public disclosure of financial information	*Chapter 14* of *Part 6*
Audit exemption	*Chapter 15* of *Part 6*
Special audit exemption for dormant companies	*Chapter 16* of *Part 6*
Small and medium companies	*Section 377*
Acquisition of shares	*Chapter 2* of *Part 9*
Liability as contributories of past and present members	*Section 655*
Payment of debts due by contributory to the company and extent to which set-off allowed	*Section 659*

Amendments

a Provision inserted by C(A)A 2017, s 76(a).

b Words repealed by C(A)A 2017, s 88(f)(ii).

c Provision inserted by C(A)A 2017, s 76(b).

Chapter 2
Incorporation and consequential matters

1231 Way of forming an unlimited company

(1) An unlimited company may be formed for any lawful purpose by any person or persons subscribing to a constitution and complying with the relevant provisions of—

(a) *Chapter 2* of *Part 2*, as applied by this Part, and

(b) this Part,

in relation to registration of an unlimited company.

(2) Without prejudice to the means by which an unlimited company may be formed under the relevant provisions referred to in *subsection (1)*, a company may be registered as an unlimited company by means of—

(a) the re-registration, or registration, as an unlimited company of a body corporate pursuant to *Part 20* or *22*,

(b) the merger of 2 or more companies pursuant to *Chapter 3* of *Part 9*, or

(c) the division of a company pursuant to *Chapter 4* of *Part 9*.

1232 Unlimited company to carry on activity in the State

An unlimited company shall not be formed and registered unless it appears to the Registrar that the company, when registered, will carry on an activity in the State, being an activity that is mentioned in its memorandum.

1233 The form of the constitution of an ULC or PUC

(1) Subject to *subsection (3)*, the constitution of an ULC or PUC shall be in the form of a memorandum of association and articles of association which together are referred to in this Part as a "constitution".

(2) The memorandum of association of an ULC or PUC shall state—

(a) its name,

(b) that it is, as the case may be, a private unlimited company or public unlimited company registered under this Part,

(c) its objects,

(d) the amount of share capital with which the company proposes to be registered and the division thereof into shares of a fixed amount, and

(e) the fact that its members have unlimited liability.

(3) The constitution of an ULC or PUC shall—

(a) in addition to the matters specified in *subsection (2)*, state the number of shares (which shall not be less than one) taken by each subscriber to the constitution,

(b) be in accordance with the form set out in—

(i) *Schedule 11* — in the case of an ULC, or

(ii) *Schedule 12* — in the case of a PUC,

or, in either case, as near thereto as circumstances permit,

(c) be printed in an entire format, that is to say the memorandum and articles shall be contained in the one document, being a document either in legible form or (as long as it is capable of being reproduced in legible form) in non-legible form, and

(d) either—

(i) be signed by each subscriber in the presence of at least one witness who shall attest the signature, or

(ii) be authenticated in the manner referred to in *section 888*.

(4) Where, subsequent to the registration of the constitution, an amendment of the memorandum of association is made affecting the matter of share capital, or another matter, referred to in *subsection (2)*, that subsection shall be read as requiring the memorandum to state the matter as it stands in consequence of that amendment.

1234 The form of the constitution of a PULC

(1) Subject to *subsection (3)*, the constitution of a PULC shall be in the form of a memorandum of association and articles of association which together are referred to in this Part as a "constitution".

(2) The memorandum of association of a PULC shall state—

(a) its name,

(b) that it is a public unlimited company, that has no share capital, registered under this Part,

(c) its objects, and

(d) the fact that its members have unlimited liability.

(3) The constitution of a PULC shall—

(a) be in accordance with the form set out in *Schedule 13* or as near thereto as circumstances permit,

(b) be printed in an entire format, that is to say the memorandum and articles shall be contained in the one document, being a document either in legible form or (as long as it is capable of being reproduced in legible form) in non-legible form, and

(c) either—

(i) be signed by each subscriber in the presence of at least one witness who shall attest the signature, or

(ii) be authenticated in the manner referred to in *section 888*.

(4) Where, subsequent to the registration of the constitution, an amendment of the memorandum of association is made affecting a matter referred to in *subsection (2)*, that subsection shall be read as requiring the memorandum to state the matter as it stands in consequence of that amendment.

1235 Supplemental provisions in relation to constitution referred to in *section 1233* or *1234* and continuance in force of existing memorandum and articles

(1) This section—

(a) contains provisions as to the articles of an unlimited company,

(b) provides that, in certain circumstances, a default position shall obtain in relation to the articles of an unlimited company, and

(c) continues in force the memorandum and articles of an unlimited company registered under the prior Companies Acts.

(2) In this section—

"mandatory provision" means a provision of any of *Parts 1* to *14* (as applied by this Part) or of this Part that is not an optional provision;

"optional provision" means a provision of any of *Parts 1* to *14* (as applied by this Part) or of this Part that—

(a) contains a statement to the effect, or is governed by provision elsewhere to the effect, that the provision applies save to the extent that the constitution provides otherwise or unless the constitution states otherwise, or

(b) is otherwise of such import.

(3) The articles of an unlimited company may contain regulations in relation to the company.

(4) So far as the articles of an unlimited company do not exclude or modify an optional provision, that optional provision shall apply in relation to the company.

(5) In the case of an ULC or PUC, articles, instead of containing any regulations in relation to the unlimited company, may consist solely of a statement to the effect that the provisions of the *Companies Act 2014* are adopted and, if the articles consist solely of such a statement, *subsection (4)* shall apply.

(6) In the case of a PULC, subject to the articles' compliance with *section 1259(3)* (articles must state the number of members with which the company proposes to be registered), articles of such an unlimited company may otherwise consist solely of a statement to the effect that the provisions of the *Companies Act 2014* are adopted and, if the articles contain such a statement, *subsection (4)* shall apply.

(7) The memorandum and articles of an unlimited company registered before the commencement of this section shall, save to the extent that they are inconsistent with a mandatory provision, continue in force but may be altered or added to under and in accordance with the conditions under which memorandums or articles, whenever registered, are permitted by this Act to be altered or added to.

(8) References in the provisions of a memorandum or articles so continued in force to any provision of the prior Companies Acts shall be read as references to the corresponding provision of this Act.

(9) To the extent that an unlimited company registered before the commencement of this section was, immediately before that commencement, governed by—

(a) the regulations of Part II or III of Table E in the First Schedule to the Act of 1963,

or

(b) the regulations of any Table referred to in section 3(9)(b), (c) or (d) of the Act of 1963,

it shall, after that commencement, continue to be governed by those regulations but—

(i) this is save to the extent that those regulations are inconsistent with a mandatory provision,

(ii) those regulations may be altered or added to under and in accordance with the conditions under which articles, whenever registered, are permitted by this Act to be altered or added to, and

(iii) references in the regulations to any provision of the prior Companies Acts shall be read as references to the corresponding provision of this Act.

1236 Effect of registration

(1) On the registration of the constitution of an unlimited company, the Registrar shall certify in writing that the company is incorporated and shall issue to the company a certificate of incorporation in respect of it.

(2) From the date of incorporation mentioned in the certificate of incorporation, the subscriber or subscribers to the constitution, together with such other persons as may from time to time become members of the unlimited company, shall be a body corporate with the name contained in the constitution, having perpetual succession and a common seal, but with such liability on the part of the members to contribute to

the assets of the company in the event of its being wound up as is mentioned in this Part.

(3) The certificate of incorporation issued under *subsection (1)* shall state that the company is—

(a) a private unlimited company,

(b) a public unlimited company, or

(c) a public unlimited company that has no share capital,

as the case may be.

(4) A certificate of incorporation issued under *subsection (1)* shall be conclusive evidence that the requirements of *section 21* and of this Chapter have been complied with, and that the unlimited company is duly registered under this Act.

(5) The persons who are specified in the statement required to be delivered to the Registrar by *section 21(1)(a)* as the directors, secretary or joint secretaries or assistant or deputy secretary or secretaries of the unlimited company to which the statement refers shall, on the incorporation of the company, be deemed to have been appointed as the first directors, secretary or joint secretaries or assistant or deputy secretary or secretaries, as the case may be, of the company.

(6) Any indication in the constitution, as delivered under *section 21* for registration, specifying a person as a director or secretary (including any assistant or deputy secretary) of a company shall be void unless such person is specified as a director or as secretary (or, as the case may be, assistant or deputy secretary) in the foregoing statement.

(7) *Subsection (5)* does not operate to deem a person appointed as a director or secretary (including any assistant or deputy secretary) of an unlimited company where—

(a) he or she is disqualified under this Act from being appointed a director, secretary, assistant or deputy secretary, as the case may be, of a company, or

(b) in the case of a director or secretary, a provision of this Act provides that the person's appointment as such in the circumstances is void.

1237 Provisions as to names of unlimited companies

(1) The name of an unlimited company shall end with one of the following:

— unlimited company;

— cuideachta neamhtheoranta.

(2) The words "unlimited company" may be abbreviated to "u.c." or "uc" (including either such abbreviation in capitalised form) in any usage after the company's registration by any person including the unlimited company.

(3) The words "cuideachta neamhtheoranta" may be abbreviated to "c.n." or "cn" (including either such abbreviation in capitalised form) in any usage after the company's registration by any person including the unlimited company.

(4) An unlimited company carrying on business under a name other than its corporate name shall register in the manner directed by law for the registration of

business names but the use of the abbreviations set out in *subsection (2)* or *(3)* shall not of itself render such registration necessary.

[...][a]

(6) This section is also subject to *section 1247* (which makes transitional provision for an existing unlimited company as regards its name).

Amendments

a Subsection (5) repealed by C(A)A 2017, s 3(1)(j).

1238 Trading under a misleading name

(1) Subject to *subsection (6)*, neither a body that is not an unlimited company nor an individual shall carry on any trade, profession or business under a name which includes, as its last part, the words "unlimited company", or "cuideachta neamhtheoranta" or abbreviations of those words.

(2) If a body or individual contravenes *subsection (1)*, the body or individual and, in the case of a body, any officer of it who is in default, shall be guilty of a category 3 offence.

(3) An unlimited company shall not, in the following circumstances, use a name which may reasonably be expected to give the impression that it is any type of a company other than an unlimited company or that it is any other form of body corporate.

(4) Those circumstances are circumstances in which the fact that it is an unlimited company is likely to be material to any person.

(5) If an unlimited company contravenes *subsection (3)*, the unlimited company and any officer of it who is in default shall be guilty of a category 3 offence.

(6) *Subsection (1)* shall not apply to any company—

(a) to which *Part 21* applies, and

(b) which has provisions in its constitution that would entitle it to rank as an unlimited company if it had been registered in the State.

1239 Capacity of an unlimited company

(1) An unlimited company shall have the capacity to do any act or thing stated in the objects set out in its memorandum.

(2) For the purposes of *subsection (1)*—

(a) the reference in it to an object includes a reference to anything stated in the memorandum to be a power to do any act or thing (whether the word "power" is used or not),

(b) if an object is stated in the unlimited company's memorandum without the following also being stated in relation to it, the capacity of the unlimited company extends to doing any act or thing that appears to it to be requisite, advantageous or incidental to, or to facilitate, the attainment of that object and that is not inconsistent with any enactment,

and a subsequent reference in this Part to an object of an unlimited company shall be read accordingly.

1240 Capacity not limited by the constitution of an unlimited company

(1) The validity of an act done by an unlimited company shall not be called into question on the ground of lack of capacity by reason of anything contained in the company's objects.

(2) A member of an unlimited company may bring proceedings to restrain the doing of an act which, but for *subsection (1)*, would be beyond the company's capacity but no such proceedings shall lie in respect of any act to be done in fulfilment of a legal obligation arising from a previous act of the company.

(3) Notwithstanding the enactment of *subsection (1)*, it remains the duty of the directors to observe any limitations on their powers flowing from the unlimited company's objects and action by the directors which, but for *subsection (1)*, would be beyond the unlimited company's capacity may only be ratified by the company by special resolution.

(4) A resolution ratifying such action shall not affect any liability incurred by the directors or any other person; if relief from any such liability is to be conferred by the unlimited company it must be agreed to separately by a special resolution of it.

(5) A party to a transaction with an unlimited company is not bound to enquire as to whether it is permitted by the company's objects.

1241 Alteration of objects clause by special resolution

(1) Subject to *subsection (2)*, an unlimited company may, by special resolution, alter the provisions of its memorandum of association by abandoning, restricting or amending any existing object or by adopting a new object and any alteration so made shall be as valid as if originally contained therein, and be subject to alteration in like manner.

(2) If an application is made to the court in accordance with this section for the alteration to be cancelled, it shall not have effect except in so far as it is confirmed by the court.

(3) Subject to *subsection (4)*, an application under this section may be made—

(a) in the case of—

(i) an ULC or a PUC by the holders of not less, in the aggregate, than 15 per cent in nominal value of the ULC's or PUC's issued share capital or any class thereof, or

(ii) in the case of any type of unlimited company, by not less than 15 per cent of the company's members,

or

(b) in any case, by the holders of not less than 15 per cent of the unlimited company's debentures, entitling the holders to object to alterations of its objects.

(4) An application shall not be made under this section by any person who has consented to or voted in favour of the alteration.

(5) An application under this section shall be made within 21 days after the date on which the resolution altering the unlimited company's objects was passed and may be made on behalf of the persons entitled to make the application by such one or more of their number as they may appoint in writing for the purpose.

(6) On an application under this section, the court may—

(a) make an order cancelling the alteration or confirming the alteration, either wholly or in part, and on such terms and conditions as it thinks fit, and

(b) if it thinks fit, adjourn the proceedings in order that an arrangement may be made to the satisfaction of the court for the purchase of the interests of dissenting members and may give such directions and make such orders as it may think expedient for facilitating or carrying into effect any such arrangement.

(7) An order under this section may, if the court thinks fit, provide for the purchase by the unlimited company of the shares of any members of the company and for the reduction accordingly of its company capital and may make such alterations in the constitution of the company as may be required in consequence of that provision; and such a purchase may be so ordered notwithstanding anything in *section 102*.

1242 Supplemental provisions in relation to section 1241

(1) Where an order under *section 1241* requires the unlimited company not to make any, or any specified, alteration in its constitution, then, notwithstanding anything in this Act, but subject to the provisions of the order, the unlimited company shall not have power, without the leave of the court, to make any such alteration in contravention of that requirement.

(2) Any alteration in the constitution of an unlimited company made by virtue of an order under *section 1241*, other than one made by resolution of the company, shall be of the same effect as if duly made by resolution of the company and the provisions of this Act shall apply to the constitution as so altered accordingly.

(3) Notice of the meeting at which the special resolution altering an unlimited company's objects is intended to be proposed shall be given to any holders of the company's debentures that entitle the holders to object to alterations of its objects; that notice shall be the same as that given to members of the company, so however that not less than 10 days' notice shall be given to the holders of any such debentures.

(4) If the written resolution procedure is used in the matter, notice, which shall not be less than 10 days, of the proposed use of that procedure shall, together with a copy of the proposed text of the resolution, be given to the debenture holders referred to in *subsection (3)*.

(5) In default of any provisions in the unlimited company's constitution regulating the giving to the foregoing debenture holders of notice referred to in *subsection (3)* or *(4)*, the provisions of *Part 4* or, as the case may be, of the unlimited company's constitution regulating the giving of notice to members shall apply.

(6) Where an unlimited company passes a resolution altering its objects—

(a) if no application is made under *section 1241* with respect to the alteration, it shall, within 15 days after the end of the period for making such an application, deliver to the Registrar a copy of its memorandum of association as altered, and

(b) if such an application is made, it shall—

(i) forthwith give notice of that fact to the Registrar, and

(ii) within 15 days after the date of any order cancelling or confirming the alteration, deliver to the Registrar a certified copy of the order and, in the case of an order confirming the alteration, a copy of the memorandum as altered.

(7) The court may, by order, at any time extend the time for delivery of documents to the Registrar under *subsection (6)(b)* for such period as the court may think proper.

(8) If an unlimited company makes default in giving notice or delivering any document to the Registrar as required by *subsection (6)*, the unlimited company and any officer of it who is in default shall be guilty of a category 4 offence.

1243 Application of *section 1017* to PUCs and PULCs

Section 1017 (official seal for sealing securities) shall apply to a PUC and a PULC as it applies to a PLC.

1244 Alteration of articles by special resolution

(1) Subject to the provisions of this Act and to the conditions contained in its memorandum, an unlimited company may, by special resolution, alter or add to its articles.

(2) Any alteration or addition so made in the articles shall, subject to the provisions of this Act, be as valid as if originally contained therein and be subject in like manner to alteration by special resolution.

1245 Power to alter provisions in memorandum which could have been contained in articles

(1) Subject to *subsection (2)*, *sections 32(4)* and *(5)* and *212*, any provision contained in an unlimited company's memorandum which could lawfully have been contained in articles instead of in the memorandum may, subject to the provisions of this section, be altered by the unlimited company by special resolution.

(2) If an application is made to the court for the alteration to be cancelled, it shall not have effect except in so far as it is confirmed by the court.

(3) This section shall not apply where the memorandum itself provides for or prohibits the alteration of all or any of the foregoing provisions, and shall not authorise any variation or abrogation of the special rights of any class of members.

(4) *Section 1241(3)* to *(7)* (other than *subsection (3)(b)*) and *section 1242* (other than *subsections (3)* to *(5)*) shall apply in relation to any alteration and to any application made under this section as they apply in relation to alterations and to applications made under those sections.

1246 Status of existing unlimited company

(1) In this section "existing unlimited company" means an unlimited company, whether it is a private or public such company having a share capital, or a public such one not having a share capital, which—

(a) was incorporated under any former enactment relating to companies (within the meaning of *section 5*), and

(b) is in existence immediately before the commencement of this section.

(2) An existing unlimited company shall, on and from the commencement of this section, continue in existence and be deemed to be—

(a) if it was a private unlimited company having a share capital before such commencement — an ULC to which this Part applies,

(b) if it was a public unlimited company having a share capital before such commencement — a PUC to which this Part applies, and

(c) if it was a public unlimited company not having a share capital before such commencement — a PULC to which this Part applies.

(3) *Section 1247* contains provisions—

(a) for enabling such a company to omit, for a limited period, "unlimited company" or "cuideachta neamhtheoranta" from its name despite the foregoing status that it has assumed, and

(b) deeming the name of such a company, after a specified period and in default of its having changed its name in that fashion, to be altered by (subject to *section 1237(5)*) the addition of—

(i) "unlimited company" at the end thereof, or

(ii) "cuideachta neamhtheoranta" at the end thereof,

as the case may be.

(4) Reference, express or implied, in this Act to the date of registration of a company mentioned in a preceding subsection shall be read as a reference to the date on which the company was registered under the Joint Stock Companies Act 1862, the Companies (Consolidation) Act 1908 or the prior Companies Acts, as the case may be.

1247 Transitional provision — omission of "unlimited company" or "cuideachta neamhtheoranta" by existing unlimited company

(1) In this section—

"existing unlimited company" has the same meaning as it has in *section 1246*;

"new provisions" means the provisions of this Part (and the relevant provisions of *Part 2* as applied by this Part) relating to the use of either of the required sets of words (or their abbreviations) set out in *subsection (2)*;

"transition period" means the period of 18 months beginning after the commencement of this section.

(2) For the purposes of this section, each of the following is a required set of words—

(a) unlimited company,

(b) cuideachta neamhtheoranta.

(3) During—

(a) the transition period, or

(b) if before the expiry of that period the company has changed its name to include either of the required sets of words, the period preceding the making of that change,

an existing unlimited company may omit the words "unlimited company" or "cuideachta neamhtheoranta" from its name.

(4) On and from—

(a) the expiry of the transition period, or

(b) the company changing its name to include either of the required sets of words,

whichever happens first, the new provisions shall apply as respects the name of an existing unlimited company.

(5) Without prejudice to the generality of *subsection (4)*, on the expiry of the transition period (and the company has not changed its name before then to include either of the required sets of words), the name of an existing unlimited company, as set out in its memorandum, shall, subject to *section 1237(5)*, be deemed to be altered by the addition of—

(a) "unlimited company" at the end thereof, or

(b) "cuideachta neamhtheoranta" at the end thereof,

as the case may be.

(6) Where an existing unlimited company's name, as set out in its memorandum, is altered by virtue of *subsection (5)*, the Registrar shall issue to the company a fresh certificate of incorporation in respect of it, being a certificate of incorporation that is altered to meet the circumstances of the case.

Chapter 3
Share capital

1248 Application of *section 68* to PUCs and PULCs

Section 68 shall apply to a PUC and a PULC as if the following subsection were substituted for *subsection (2)*:

"(2) A company shall—

(a) neither apply to have securities (or interests in them) admitted to trading or to be listed on; nor

(b) have securities (or interests in them) admitted to trading or listed on,

any market, whether a regulated market or not, in the State or elsewhere; however nothing in this subsection prohibits the admission to trading or listing (or an application being made therefor) on any market of debentures (or interests in them) for the purposes of any of *paragraphs (a)* to *(e)* of *subsection (3)*.".

1249 Authority to allot and pre-emption rights in the case of a PUC

Sections 1021 to *1023* shall apply to a PUC.

1250 Variation of rights attached to special classes of shares

Section 982 shall apply to a PUC and an ULC as if—

(a) each reference in it to a DAC were a reference to a PUC or an ULC, as the case may be, and

(b) in the case of a PUC, the reference in *subsection (3)(c)* to the giving, variation, revocation or renewal of an authority for the purposes of *section 69(1)* were a reference to the giving, variation, revocation or renewal of an authority for the purposes of *section 1021(1)*.

1251 Variation of company capital

Section 83 shall apply to an ULC and a PUC with the following modifications—

(a) "special resolution" shall be substituted for "ordinary resolution" in *subsection (1)*; and

(b) in *subsection (1)(b)*, the following shall be omitted:

> ", so however, that in the subdivision the proportion between the amount paid and the amount, if any, unpaid on each reduced share shall be the same as it was in the case of the share from which the reduced share is derived".

1252 Reduction of company capital

(1) Save to the extent that its constitution otherwise provides, an ULC or PUC may, by special resolution, reduce its company capital in any way it thinks expedient and, without prejudice to the generality of the foregoing, may thereby—

(a) extinguish or reduce the liability on any of its shares in respect of share capital not paid up,

(b) either with or without extinguishing or reducing liability on any of its shares, cancel any paid up company capital which is lost or unrepresented by available assets, or

(c) either with or without extinguishing or reducing liability on any of its shares, pay off any paid up company capital which is in excess of the wants of the company.

(2) A resolution shall not be valid for the purposes of *subsection (1)* if it would have the effect that the ULC or PUC no longer has any members.

(3) Without prejudice to any contrary provision of—

(a) the resolution for, or any other resolution relevant to, the reduction of company capital, or

(b) the ULC's or PUC's constitution,

a reserve arising from the reduction of an ULC's or PUC's company capital is to be treated for all purposes as a realised profit.

1253 Application of *section 94* to ULCs and PUCs

Section 94 shall apply to an ULC and a PUC as if the following subsection were substituted for *subsection (2)*:

"(2) The instrument of transfer of any share shall be executed by or on behalf of the transferor and the transferee.".

1254 Application of *section 114* in relation to PULCs

In its application to this Part, *section 114* shall apply as if each reference in it to the acquisition and holding of shares in a company included, in a case where the holding company is a PULC, a reference to becoming, and being, a member of the company otherwise than by means of acquiring and holding shares.

1255 Making of distributions unrestricted in the case of unlimited companies

Neither the provisions of *Chapter 7* of *Part 3* nor any rule of law on the making of distributions out of a company's assets shall apply in relation to an unlimited company.

1256 Uncertificated transfer of securities

Sections 1085 to *1087* shall apply to securities of a PUC or a PULC as they apply to securities of a PLC.

Chapter 4
Corporate governance

1257 Directors

(1) An unlimited company shall have at least 2 directors.

(2) Nothing in *Parts 1* to *14* that makes provision in the case of a company having a sole director shall apply to an unlimited company.

1258 Limitation on number of directorships

For the purposes of this Part *section 142* shall apply as if the following subsection were substituted for *subsection (1)*:

"(1) A person shall not, at a particular time, be a director of more than—

(a) 25 unlimited companies (of whatever type), or

(b) 25 companies, one, or more than one, of which is an unlimited company (of whatever type) and one, or more than one, of which is any other type of company capable of being wound up under this Act.".

1259 Membership of a PULC

(1) The subscribers to the memorandum of association of a PULC shall be deemed to have agreed to become members of the PULC, and, on its registration, shall be entered as members in its register of members.

(2) Such other persons—

(a) being persons—

(i) whom the directors admit to membership; or

(ii) who are admitted to membership, pursuant to provisions that the constitution may contain in that behalf, whether provisions that—

(I) provide a separate power to; or

(II) supplement or limit, or exclude,

any power of the directors in that regard;

and

(b) whose names are entered in its register of members,

shall be members of the PULC.

(3) The articles of a PULC shall state the number of members with which the company proposes to be registered.

(4) Where a PULC has increased the number of its members beyond the registered number, it shall, within 15 days after the date on which the increase was resolved on or took place, deliver particulars of the increase to the Registrar.

(5) If default is made in complying with *subsection (4)*, the PULC and any officer of it who is in default shall be guilty of a category 4 offence.

(6) The articles of a PULC may state the maximum number of persons who may be members of the PULC, subject to the power of the directors to register an increase in the number of members.

(7) A member may resign his or her membership by serving notice to that effect upon the directors at the registered office of the PULC, such notice to expire no earlier than the date of service of the notice of resignation.

(8) Save where the constitution of a PULC provides otherwise, the directors may require a member to resign his or her membership by serving notice upon the member terminating his or her membership to expire no earlier than the date of service of the notice of termination.

(9) Save where the constitution of a PULC provides otherwise, every member shall have one vote.

(10) The death of a member shall terminate his or her membership.

1260 Personation of member: offence

If any person falsely and deceitfully personates any member of a PULC and thereby—

(a) receives or endeavours to receive any money due to any such member, or

(b) votes at any meeting as if the person were the true and lawful member,

he or she shall be guilty of a category 2 offence.

1261 Register of members

Section 169 shall apply to a PULC with the following modifications:

(a) the following paragraph shall be substituted, in *subsection (1)*, for *paragraph (a)*:

"(a) the names and addresses of the members;";

and

(b) *subsection (5)* shall be omitted.

1262 Unlimited company, with 2 or more members, may not dispense with holding of a.g.m

Section 175(3) and *(4)* (which relate to dispensing with the holding of an annual general meeting) shall not apply to an unlimited company if it has more than one member.

1263 Application of *section 193* in relation to an unlimited company

Section 193 shall apply to an unlimited company as if, in *subsection (1)*, after "Notwithstanding any provision to the contrary in this Act", there were inserted "and unless the constitution provides otherwise".

Chapter 5
Financial statements, annual return and audit

1264 Definitions (*Chapter 5*)

In this Chapter—

"designated ULC" has the meaning assigned to it by *section 1274*;

"non-designated ULC" means a ULC that is not a designated ULC.

1265 Non-application of *Part 6* to unlimited companies that are credit institutions or insurance undertakings

Part 6 shall not apply to an unlimited company that is a credit institution or an insurance undertaking—

(a) to the extent provided by regulations made under section 3 of the European Communities Act 1972 to give effect to Community acts on accounts of credit institutions and insurance undertakings, respectively, or

(b) to the extent provided by any other enactment.

1266 Requirement for corporate governance statement and modification of certain provisions of *Parts 5* and *6* as they apply to PUCs and PULCs

Chapter 3 of *Part 23* has effect in relation to, amongst other companies, a PUC and a PULC that have debentures admitted to trading on a regulated market in an EEA state.

1267 Modification of definition of "IAS Regulation" in the case of PUCs and PULCs

Section 1116 (modification of definition of "IAS Regulation") shall apply in the case of a PUC and a PULC as it applies in the case of PLC.

[1267A Modification of definition of "ineligible entities" in case of PUCs and PULCs

A The definition of 'ineligible entities' in section 275(1) shall apply to a PUC or a PULC as if—

(a) in paragraph (c), 'undertakings,' were substituted for 'undertakings, or',

(b) in paragraph (d)(ii), 'shall be read accordingly, or' were substituted for 'shall be read accordingly;', and

(c) the following paragraph were inserted after paragraph (d):

'(e) are PUCs and PULCs;'.][a]

Amendments

a Section 1267A inserted by C(A)A 2017, s 77.

1268 Application of *section 297* to a PULC

[...][a]

Amendments

a Section 1268 repealed by C(A)A 2017, s 3(1)(k).

1269 Disclosures by unlimited company that is a credit institution

In addition to its having effect in relation to a public limited company, *section 1120* shall have effect in relation to an unlimited company.

1270 Disclosure of membership changes in PULC's financial statements

Section 318 (details of authorised share capital, allotted share capital and movements) shall not apply in relation to the financial statements of a PULC but where there are changes in the interests of members of a PULC in the financial year to which the financial statements of the PULC relate then particulars of those changes shall be given in the notes to those financial statements.

1271 Disapplication of *sections 325(1)(c)* and *329* to a PULC

Sections 325(1)(c) and *329* shall not apply to a PULC.

1272 Application of *section 362* to an ULC and obligation on other unlimited companies to have their financial statements audited

[...][a]

(2) The directors of a PUC shall arrange for the statutory financial statements of the PUC for a financial year to be audited by statutory auditors.

(3) The directors of a PULC shall arrange for the statutory financial statements of the PULC for a financial year to be audited by statutory auditors.

Amendments

a Subsection 1 repealed by C(A)A 2017, s 3(1)(l).

1273 Qualification of *section 338* in the case of a PULC

Section 338 (circulation of statutory financial statements) shall apply to a PULC with the following modifications:

(a) in *subsection (1)(a)*, there shall be substituted "(but only if that person is entitled to receive notices of general meetings of the company)" for "(whether that person is or is not entitled to receive notices of general meetings of the company)"; and

(b) in *subsection (1)(b)*, there shall be substituted "(but only if that person is so entitled)" for "(whether that person is or is not so entitled)".

[1274 No requirement to deliver financial statements, etc., with annual return in the case of certain ULCs

(1) Other than in the case of a designated ULC, *sections 347* and *348* (which require documents to be annexed to annual returns) shall not apply to an ULC.

(2) In this section "designated ULC" means—

(a) an ULC that at any time during the relevant financial year—

  (i) has been a subsidiary undertaking of an undertaking which was at that time limited,

  (ii) has had rights exercisable in respect of it by or on behalf of 2 or more undertakings which were at that time limited, being rights which if exercisable by one of the undertakings would have made the ULC a subsidiary undertaking of it, or

(iii) has been a holding company of an undertaking which was at that time limited,

(b) an ULC which is a credit institution or an insurance undertaking or the holding company of a credit institution or an insurance undertaking,

(c) an ULC, all of the members of which are—

(i) companies limited by shares or by guarantee,

(ii) unlimited companies, each of whose members is a limited company,

(iii) partnerships which are not limited partnerships, each of whose members is a limited company,

(iv) limited partnerships, each of whose general partners (within the meaning of the Limited Partnerships Act 1907) is a limited company, or

(v) any combination of the types of bodies referred to in the preceding subparagraphs of this paragraph and *paragraph (a)*, or

(d) an ULC, the direct or indirect members of which comprise any combination of ULCs and bodies referred to in paragraph (c) such that the ultimate beneficial owners enjoy the protection of limited liability.

(3) References in *subsection (2)* to a limited company, an unlimited company, a partnership or a limited partnership shall include references to a body which is not governed by the law of the State but which is comparable to such a limited company, an unlimited company, a partnership or a limited partnership, as may be appropriate.

(4) References in *subsection (2)(a)* to an undertaking being limited at a particular time are references to an undertaking (under whatever law established), the liability of whose members at that time is limited.

(5) In this section—

"general partner" has the same meaning as it has in the Limited Partnerships Act 1907;

"limited partnership" means a partnership to which the Limited Partnerships Act 1907 applies;

"partnership" has the same meaning as it has in the Partnership Act 1890.][a]

Amendments

a Section 1274 substituted by C(A)A 2017, s 78(1).

[1274A

Other than in the case of a designated ULC (within the meaning of *section 1274*), *Part 26* shall not apply to an ULC.][a]

Amendments

a Section 1274A inserted by C(A)A 2017, s 79.

1275 Application of *section 392* to a PULC

Section 392 (report to Registrar and Director: accounting records) shall apply to a PULC with the substitution, in *subsection (6)*, of "its members" for "its shareholders".

1276 Application of *section 393* to a PULC

Section 393 (report to Registrar and Director: category 1 and 2 offences) shall apply to a PULC with the substitution, in *subsection (4)*, of "its members" for "its shareholders".

1277 Documents to be annexed to annual return of non-designated ULC

(1) The statutory auditors of a non-designated ULC shall prepare, and furnish to the directors of the company, a separate report which—

(a) confirms that the statutory auditors audited the financial statements of the company for the relevant financial year, and

(b) includes within it the report made by them to the members of the company pursuant to *section 391* on those financial statements.

(2) Where a report is prepared in accordance with *subsection (1)* there shall be attached to the annual return of the non-designated ULC a copy of the report that satisfies the following conditions—

(a) it is a true copy of the original save for the difference that the signature or signatures on the original, and any date or dates thereon, shall appear in typeset form on the copy, and

(b) it is accompanied by a certificate of a director and the secretary of the non-designated ULC, that bears the signature of the director and the secretary in electronic or written form, stating that the copy is a true copy of the original (and the foregoing statement need not be qualified on account of the difference permitted by *paragraph (a)* as to the form of a signature or of a date).

(3) [...][a]

(4) [...][b]

(5) This section shall not apply if the non-designated ULC is entitled to, and has availed itself of, the audit exemption conferred by *Chapter 15* or *16* of *Part 6* in the financial year concerned.

Amendments

a Subsection (3) repealed by C(SA)A 2018, s 3(1)(j).

b Subsection (4) repealed by C(SA)A 2018, s 3(1)(j).

Chapter 6
Winding up

1278 Liability as contributories of past and present members

(1) Subject to *subsection (2)*, in the event of an unlimited company being wound up, every present and past member shall be liable to contribute to the assets of the unlimited company to an amount sufficient for payment of its debts and liabilities, and the costs, charges and expenses of the winding up, and for the adjustment of the rights of the contributories among themselves.

(2) The following qualifications apply in relation to *subsection (1)*:

(a) a past member shall not be liable to contribute if he or she has ceased to be a member for one year or more before the commencement of the winding up;

(b) a past member shall not be liable to contribute in respect of any debt or liability of the unlimited company contracted after he or she ceased to be a member;

(c) a past member shall not be liable to contribute unless it appears to the court that the existing members are unable to satisfy the contributions required to be made by them in pursuance of this Act;

(d) nothing in this Act shall invalidate any provision contained in any policy of insurance or other contract whereby the liability of individual members on the policy or contract is restricted, or whereby the funds of the unlimited company are alone made liable in respect of the policy or contract;

(e) a sum due to any member of the unlimited company, in his or her character of a member, by way of distributions, profits or otherwise, shall not be deemed to be a debt of the company, payable to that member in a case of competition between himself or herself and any other creditor not a member of the unlimited company, but any such sum may be taken into account for the purpose of the final adjustment of the rights of the contributories among themselves.

1279 Payment of debts due by contributory to the unlimited company and extent to which set-off allowed

(1) The court may make an order requiring any contributory for the time being on the list of contributories to pay, in a manner directed by the order, any money due from him or her or from the estate of the person whom he or she represents to the unlimited company, exclusive of any money payable by him or her or the estate by virtue of any call in pursuance of this Act.

(2) The court in making any such order may allow to the contributory by way of set-off any sum due to the contributory or to the estate which the contributory represents from the unlimited company on any independent dealing or contract with the

company, but not any money due to him or her as a member of the company in respect of any dividend or profit.

(3) When all the creditors are paid in full, any money due on any account whatever to a contributory from the unlimited company may be allowed to him or her by way of set-off against any subsequent call.

Chapter 7
Examinerships

1280 Petitions for examinerships

Section 510 shall apply to an unlimited company as if the following subsections were substituted for *subsections (2)* and *(3)*:

> "(2) Where the company referred to in *section 509* is an insurer or the holding company of an insurer, a petition may be presented only by the Central Bank, and *subsection (1)* shall not apply to the company.
>
> (3) Where the company referred to in *section 509* is—
>
> (a) a credit institution or the holding company of a credit institution,
>
> (b) a company which one or more trustee savings banks have been reorganised into pursuant to an order under section 57 of the Trustee Savings Banks Act 1989, or
>
> (c) a company which a building society has converted itself into under Part XI of the Building Societies Act 1989,
>
> a petition may be presented only by the Central Bank, and *subsection (1)* shall not apply to the company.".

Chapter 8
Investigations

1281 Application of *section 747(2)* to PUCs and PULCs

(1) *Section 747(2)* shall apply to a PUC as if the following paragraph were substituted for *paragraph (b)*:

> "(b) not less than 100 members of the company;".

(2) *Section 747(2)* shall apply to a PULC as if—

(a) the following paragraph were substituted for *paragraph (b)*: "(b) not less than 100 members of the company;";

and

(b) *paragraph (c)* were omitted therefrom.

Chapter 9
Public offers of securities, market abuse, etc.

1282 Application of *Chapters 1*, *2* and *4* of *Part 23* to PUCs and PULCs

Chapters 1, *2* and *4* of *Part 23*, so far as they are applicable to companies other than public limited companies, shall apply to a PUC and a PULC.

PART 20
RE-REGISTRATION

Chapter 1
Interpretation

1283 Interpretation (*Part 20*)

(1) In this Part—

"resultant company" means the company that a company re-registering becomes on the issue to the latter of a certificate of incorporation under *section 1285(6)*;

"resultant company type" means the type of company specified in the special resolution of a company under *section 1285(1)* as being the type of company which it wishes to be re-registered as;

"statement of compliance" shall be read in accordance with *section 1285(4)(c)*;

"type of company" means a company of a type that may be formed and registered under this Act.

(2) A word or expression used in this Part that is defined in a preceding Part of this Act shall, unless expressly provided otherwise, have the meaning given to it by that preceding Part.

Chapter 2
General provisions as to re-registration

1284 Company may re-register as another company type

(1) This Part permits a company, subject to compliance with certain requirements, to re-register as another type of company.

(2) This Part is in addition to—

(a) the provisions of *Chapter 6* of *Part 2* requiring or enabling an existing private company (within the meaning of *Part 2*) to re-register as a designated activity company limited by shares during the period specified in that Chapter,

(b) the provisions of *sections 1040* and *1041* concerning the re-registration of a PLC as another type of company where the effect of the PLC cancelling its own shares will be that the nominal value of the PLC's allotted share capital is brought below the authorised minimum.

1285 Procedure generally for re-registration

(1) Subject to *section 1286* and *Chapter 3*, a company may be re-registered as another type of company only if—

(a) a special resolution of the company, complying with *subsection (2)*, that it should be so re-registered is passed, and

(b) an application for the purpose, in the prescribed form and signed by a director or secretary of the company, is delivered to the Registrar together with the documents specified in *subsection (4)*.

(2) The special resolution shall—

(a) alter the company's constitution so that it states that the company is to be a company of the type that the company wishes to be re-registered as,

(b) make such other alterations in the company's constitution as are necessary to bring it in substance and in form into conformity with the requirements of this Act with respect to the constitution of the resultant company type, and

(c) make such other alterations in the company's constitution as are requisite in the circumstances.

(3) Without prejudice to the generality of *subsection (2)*, where the resultant company type is a private company limited by shares, the alteration required by that subsection shall include the replacement of the memorandum and articles of the re-registering company by a constitution in conformity with *section 19* and *Schedule 1* (but nothing in this section authorises the alteration of the rights and obligations of members of the re-registering company, or of other persons, as set out in its memorandum and articles and, accordingly, where necessary, the foregoing replacement constitution shall include such supplemental regulations as will secure those rights and obligations).

(4) The documents referred to in *subsection (1)* are—

(a) a copy of the special resolution that the company should re-register as another type of company,

(b) a copy of the constitution of the company as altered by the resolution,

(c) a statement in the prescribed form (in this Part referred to as a "statement of compliance") by a director or secretary of the company that the requirements of this Part as to re-registration as another type of company have been complied with by the company, including the passing of the special resolution for re-registration.

(5) The Registrar may accept the statement of compliance as sufficient evidence that the special resolution has been duly passed and the other conditions of this Part for re-registration have been satisfied and that the company is entitled to be re-registered as the type of company concerned.

(6) If, on an application for re-registration of a company as another type of company under *subsection (1)*, the Registrar is satisfied that a company is entitled to be so re-registered, the Registrar shall—

(a) retain the application and the other documents delivered to him or her under this Part, and

(b) issue to the company a certificate of incorporation in respect of it, being a certificate of incorporation that—

(i) is altered to meet the circumstances of the case, and

(ii) states that it is issued on re-registration of the company and the date on which it is issued.

(7) Upon the issue to a company of a certificate of incorporation on re-registration under *subsection (6)*—

(a) the company shall, by virtue of the issue of that certificate, become a company of the type described in the certificate, and

(b) any alterations in the constitution set out in the special resolution shall take effect accordingly.

(8) A certificate of incorporation issued on re-registration to a company under *subsection (6)* shall be conclusive evidence—

(a) that the requirements of this Part as to re-registration and of matters precedent and incidental thereto have been complied with, and

(b) that the company is the type of company which is set out in the certificate,

and, accordingly, the law applicable to the resultant company type shall, on and from the issue of the certificate, apply to the company.

(9) The re-registration of a company as another type of company pursuant to this Part shall not affect any rights or obligations of the company or render defective any legal proceedings by or against the company, and any legal proceedings which might have been continued or commenced against it in its former status may be continued or commenced against it in its new status.

(10) For the avoidance of doubt, references in *Part 6*, and in particular *section 349* (which exempts a company from having to annex financial statements to its first annual return), to the incorporation of a company are references to its original incorporation.

1286 Additional statements required of company that is to have a share capital on its re-registration

(1) In addition to the requirements of *section 1285*, in the case of a company, being a company which does not have a share capital, that proposes to re-register as a company which does have share capital, there shall, as part of the application under that section, be delivered to the Registrar—

(a) a statement under *subsection (2)* — in this section referred to as a "statement of initial shareholdings", and

(b) a statement under *subsection (3)* — in this section referred to as a "statement of share capital".

(2) The statement of initial shareholdings shall state with respect to each member of the company—

(a) the number and nominal value of the shares to be taken by him or her on re-registration, and

(b) the amount (if any) payable in respect of each share on re-registration, whether on account of the nominal value or by way of a premium.

(3) The statement of share capital—

(a) shall, if the resultant company will be other than a private company limited by shares, state with respect to the company's share capital to be allotted on re-registration—

(i) the total number of shares of the company,

(ii) the aggregate nominal value of those shares,

(iii) for each class of shares—

(I) the total number of shares of that class,

(II) the aggregate nominal value of shares of that class, and

(III) the amount paid up and the amount (if any) unpaid on each share (whether on account of the nominal value of the share or by way of premium);

or

(b) if the resultant company will be a private company limited by shares, state either (depending on whether it is to have an authorised share capital or not)—

(i) the particulars specified in *paragraph (a)(i)* to *(iii)*, or

(ii) that the share capital of the company shall, at the time of its re-registration, stand divided into shares of the fixed amount specified in the copy of the constitution delivered under *section 1285* and such of the other particulars specified in *paragraph (a)* as, having regard to that intended position, the circumstances permit to be stated.

1287 PLC's resolution to re-register as a private company limited by shares or DAC may be cancelled by court

(1) Subject to *subsection (2)*, where a special resolution by a PLC to be re-registered as a private company limited by shares or a designated activity company has been passed, an application to the court for the cancellation of the resolution may be made by—

(a) the holders of not less in the aggregate than 5 per cent in nominal value of the PLC's issued share capital or any class of the PLC's issued share capital (disregarding any shares held by the PLC as treasury shares), or

(b) not less than 50 of the PLC's members.

(2) An application shall not be made under this section by any person who has consented to or voted in favour of the resolution.

(3) An application under this section shall be made within 28 days after the date on which the resolution was passed and may be made on behalf of the persons entitled to make the application by such one or more of their number as they may appoint in writing for the purpose.

(4) If an application is made under this section—

(a) the PLC shall forthwith give notice of that fact to the Registrar, and

(b) within 15 days after the date of the court making its order on the application, or such longer period as the court may at any time direct, the PLC or the resultant company shall deliver to the Registrar a certified copy of the order.

(5) On the hearing of an application under this section, the court shall make an order either cancelling or confirming the resolution.

(6) The powers of the court on an application under this section extend to—

(a) providing that the re-registration, notwithstanding the confirmation, shall not take effect unless such terms and conditions as the court thinks fit and specifies are satisfied,

(b) if it thinks fit, adjourning the proceedings in order that an arrangement may be made to the satisfaction of the court for the purchase of the interests of dissentient members, and

(c) giving such directions and making such order as it thinks expedient for facilitating or carrying into effect any such arrangement.

(7) Without prejudice to the generality of *subsection (6)*, the order of the court may, if the court thinks fit—

(a) provide for the purchase by the PLC or the resultant company of the shares of any of its members and for the reduction accordingly of the PLC's or the resultant company's company capital, and

(b) make such alteration in the PLC's or the resultant company's constitution as may be required in consequence of that provision, and such a purchase may be so ordered notwithstanding anything in *section 102*.

(8) Where an order under this section requires the PLC or the resultant company not to make any, or any specified, alterations in its constitution, then, notwithstanding anything in this Act, but subject to the provisions of the order, the PLC or the resultant company shall not have power, without the leave of the court, to make any such alteration in contravention of that requirement.

(9) Any alteration in the constitution of a company (whether the PLC or the resultant company) made by virtue of an order under this section, other than one made by resolution of the company, shall be of the same effect as if duly made by resolution of the company, and the provisions of this Act shall apply to the constitution as so altered accordingly.

(10) If a company (whether the PLC or the resultant company) fails to comply with *subsection (4)*, the company and any officer of it who is in default shall be guilty of a category 3 offence.

1288 Re-registration upon reduction of company capital of a PLC

(1) If—

(a) the court makes an order confirming a reduction of the company capital of a PLC, and

(b) that reduction has the effect of bringing the nominal value of the company's allotted share capital below the authorised minimum,

the court may authorise the PLC to be re-registered as another type of company without its having passed a special resolution for that purpose.

(2) Where the court makes an order authorising a PLC to so re-register, the court shall specify in the order the alterations in the PLC's constitution to be made in connection with that re-registration.

(3) In its application to a PLC that applies to be re-registered as another type of company in pursuance of an authority given under *subsection (1)*, this Part shall have effect with the following modifications—

(a) references in *section 1285* to the special resolution of the company shall be read as references to the order of the court under *subsection (1)*,

(b) *section 1285(1)(a)* and *(2)* shall not apply and, in the event of an application to re-register the PLC as a private company limited by shares, *section 1290(a)* shall not apply, and, in the event of an application to re-register the PLC as a designated activity company, *section 1298(1)(a)* or *1299(1)(a)*, as the case may be, shall not apply, and

(c) *section 1285(6)* shall be read as if the following were substituted for all the words preceding *paragraphs (a)* and *(b)* of it:

> "(6) On receipt of an application for re-registration under this section made in pursuance of an order of the court under *section 1288(1)*, the Registrar shall —".

Chapter 3
Special requirements for re-registration

1289 What this Chapter does and references to relevant *Chapter 2* requirements

(1) This Chapter—

(a) makes provision in the following cases, namely—

(i) a case in which an application is not made under *section 1287*; and

(ii) a case in which an application is made under that section;

and, in the latter case, the provision made by this Chapter is by reference to the particular course that the application takes; and

(b) specifies requirements, additional to those in *Chapter 2*, that must be complied with in certain cases before a re-registration may be effected.

(2) In this Chapter a reference to the relevant *Chapter 2* requirements is a reference to—

(a) subject to *paragraph (b)*, the requirements of *section 1285*,

(b) in the case of a company that does not have a share capital and that proposes to re-register as a company that does have share capital, the requirements of *sections 1285* and *1286*.

1290 Particular requirements for re-registration as a private company limited by shares

A company may be re-registered as a private company limited by shares if, in addition to compliance by the company with the relevant *Chapter 2* requirements, the following requirements are complied with—

(a) where the company is a PLC—

(i) the period during which an application under *section 1287* for the cancellation of the special resolution has expired without any such application having been made, or

(ii) where such an application has been made, the application has been withdrawn, or

(iii) either—

(I) an order, not falling within clause (II), has been made under section 1287 confirming the resolution, or

(II) if an order has been made under that section confirming the resolution but providing that re-registration shall not take effect unless specified and terms and conditions are satisfied, those terms and conditions are satisfied,

and, in either case, a certified copy of that order has been delivered to the Registrar,

and

(b) where the company is an unlimited company, the special resolution required by *section 1285(1)(a)* includes a statement that the liability of the members of the resultant company is to be limited by shares and—

(i) if the resultant company is to have an authorised share capital, specifying what is to be that authorised share capital and the fixed amount of the shares into which that share capital is to be divided, or

(ii) if the resultant company is not to have an authorised share capital, specifying the fixed amount of the shares into which the company's share capital is to be divided.

1291 Particular requirements for re-registration of company as a PLC

(1) A company may be re-registered as a PLC if, in addition to compliance by the company with the relevant *Chapter 2* requirements and *section 1292*, the following requirements are complied with—

(a) the company delivers the following documents to the Registrar:

(i) a copy of a balance sheet of the company prepared as at a date not more than 7 months before the date on which the application for re-registration is received by the Registrar;

(ii) an unqualified report by the company's statutory auditors on that balance sheet;

(iii) a copy of a written statement by the statutory auditors of the company that, in their opinion, that, at the balance sheet date, the amount of the company's net assets was not less than the aggregate of its called-up share capital and undistributable reserves; and

(iv) a copy of any report prepared under [*section 1293*][a],

(b) the statement of compliance includes a statement by a director or secretary of the company confirming that, between the balance sheet date and the date of the making by the company of the application for re-registration, there has been no change in the financial position of the company that has resulted in the amount of the company's net assets becoming less than the aggregate of its called-up share capital and undistributable reserves, and

(c) where the company is an unlimited company, the special resolution required by *section 1285(1)(a)* includes a statement that the liability of the members of the resultant company is to be limited by shares and specifying what is to be the authorised share capital of the resultant company and the fixed amount of the shares into which that share capital is to be divided.

(2) The Registrar shall not, on foot of the application to re-register a company as a PLC, issue a certificate of incorporation under *section 1285(6)* if it appears to the Registrar that—

(a) by, either of the means specified in *section 84(2)*, a reduction of the company's company capital has taken place after the date of the passing of the special resolution that the company should be re-registered as a PLC, and

(b) the reduction has the effect of bringing the nominal value of the company's allotted share capital below the authorised minimum.

(3) A qualification shall be treated for the purposes of the definition of an "unqualified report" in *subsection (6)* as being not material in relation to any balance sheet if, but only if, the person making the report states in writing that the thing giving rise to the qualification is not material for the purposes of determining, by reference to that balance sheet, whether, at the balance sheet date, the amount of the company's net assets was not less than the aggregate of its called-up share capital and undistributable reserves.

(4) For the purposes of the making, in relation to the foregoing balance sheet, of a report falling within the definition of an "unqualified report" in *subsection (6)*, *section 290* and the other relevant provisions of *Part 6* (so far as applicable to balance sheets as distinct from the other elements of financial statements) shall be deemed to have effect in relation to that balance sheet with the following modifications.

(5) Those modifications are such modifications as are necessary by reason of the fact (if such is the case) that that balance sheet is prepared otherwise than in respect of a financial year.

(6) In this section—

"undistributable reserves" has the same meaning as in *section 1082*;

"unqualified report" means, in relation to the balance sheet of a company, a report stating without material qualification—

(a) that, in the opinion of the person making the report, the balance sheet complies with *section 290* and the other relevant provisions of *Part 6* (so far as applicable to balance sheets as distinct from the other elements of financial statements); and

(b) without prejudice to *paragraph (a)*, that in the opinion of that person, the balance sheet gives a true and fair view of the company's assets, liabilities and equity as at the balance sheet date.

Amendments

a Words substituted by C(SA)A 2018, s 47 (previously: "section 1292").

1292 Requirements as to share capital of a company applying to re-register as a PLC

(1) Subject to *subsection (2)*, a company shall not be re-registered under this Part as a PLC unless, at the time the special resolution that the company should be re-registered as a PLC is passed—

(a) the nominal value of the company's allotted share capital is not less than the authorised minimum,

(b) each of its allotted shares is paid up at least as to one-quarter of the nominal value of that share and the whole of any premium on it,

(c) where any share in the company or any premium payable on it has been fully or partly paid up by an undertaking given by any person that that person or another should do work or perform services for the company or another, the undertaking has been performed or otherwise discharged, and

(d) where shares have been allotted as fully or partly paid up to their nominal value or any premium payable on them otherwise than in cash and the consideration for the allotment consists of or includes an undertaking (other than one to which *paragraph (c)* applies) to the company either—

(i) that undertaking has been performed or otherwise discharged, or

(ii) there is a contract between the company and any person pursuant to which that undertaking must be performed within 5 years after that time.

(2) Subject to *subsection (3)*, any share allotted by the company—

(a) which was allotted prior to 13 October 1986, or

(b) which was allotted in pursuance of an employees' share scheme and by reason of which the company would, but for this subsection, be precluded under *subsection (1)(b)*, but not otherwise, from being re-registered as a PLC, may be disregarded for the purpose of determining whether *subsection (1)(b)* to *(d)* is complied with in relation to the company, and a share so disregarded shall be treated for the purposes of *subsection (1)(a)* as if it were not part of the allotted share capital of the company.

(3) A share shall not be disregarded by virtue of *subsection (2)(a)* if the aggregate in nominal value of that share and the other shares which it is proposed so to disregard is more than one-tenth of the nominal value of the company's allotted share capital (not including any share disregarded by virtue of *subsection (2)(b)*).

1293 Shares allotted by company applying to re-register as PLC between balance sheet date and passing of special resolution

(1) This section applies where—

(a) shares are allotted by a company applying to re-register as a PLC between the balance sheet date and the passing of the special resolution to re-register, and

(b) those shares have been allotted as fully or partly paid up as to their nominal value, or any premium on them, otherwise than in cash.

(2) Where this section applies the company shall not make an application for re-registration as a PLC under this Part unless, before the making of the application—

(a) the consideration for the allotment referred to in *subsection (1)* has been valued in accordance with the provisions of *Chapter 3* of *Part 17* that are applied by this section, and

(b) a report with respect to the consideration's value has been made to the company in accordance with those provisions during the 6 months immediately preceding the date of that allotment,

but this is subject to *subsection (4)*.

(3) Without prejudice to *subsection (4)*, the following provisions of *Chapter 3* of *Part 17*, namely—

(a) *section 1028(5) to (11)*,

(b) *section 1029(4)*, and

(c) *section 1030*,

shall apply for the purposes of this section as they apply for the purposes of *subsection (1)* of *section 1028* and as if the references in them to that *subsection (1)* were references to *subsection (2)* of this section and with any other necessary modifications.

(4) The provisions of *Chapter 3* of *Part 17* that operate to disapply the requirement under *section 1028(1)* for a valuation of the consideration referred to in that provision to be carried out (and the making of a report thereon) shall operate to disapply the requirement under *subsection (2)* for a valuation of the consideration referred to in that subsection to be carried out (and the making of a report thereon).

(5) For the purpose of those foregoing provisions (as they operate by virtue of the preceding subsection), those provisions shall apply as if the references in them to

subsection (1) of *section 1028* were references to *subsection (2)* of this section and with any other necessary modifications.

(6) In this section "balance sheet date" means the date as of which the balance sheet referred to in *section 1291(1)(a)* is prepared.

1294 Application of certain other provisions of *Part 17* on allotments to a company that passed resolution for re-registration

Sections 1025 to *1033* and *1036*, *1037* and *1038* shall apply to a company which has passed and not revoked a resolution that the company be re-registered a PLC as those sections apply to a PLC.

1295 Power of unlimited company to provide for reserve share capital on re-registration

An unlimited company having a share capital may, by its special resolution for re-registration as a limited company in pursuance of this Part, do either or both of the following things:

(a) increase the nominal amount of its share capital by increasing the nominal amount of each of its shares, but subject to the condition that no part of the increased capital shall be capable of being called up, except in the event and for the purposes of the company being wound up;

(b) provide that a specified portion of its uncalled share capital shall not be capable of being called up except in the event and for the purposes of the company being wound up.

1296 Particular requirements for re-registration of limited company as unlimited

(1) A limited company may be re-registered as an unlimited company if, in addition to compliance by the company with the relevant *Chapter 2* requirements, all the members of it have assented to its being so re-registered and the following requirements are complied with—

(a) the company delivers to the Registrar—

(i) the prescribed form of assent to the company's being re-registered as an unlimited company subscribed to by, or on behalf of, all members of the company, and

(ii) subject to *subsection (2)*, the financial statements specified in *subsection (3)* and the report specified in subsection (6),

and

(b) the statement of compliance includes confirmation by a director or secretary of the company that—

(i) the persons by whom, or on whose behalf, the form of assent referred to in *paragraph (a)* is subscribed constitute the whole membership of the company, and

(ii) if any of the members have not, themselves, subscribed that form, that the directors have taken all reasonable steps to satisfy themselves that each person who subscribed it on behalf of a member was lawfully empowered to do.

(2) *Subsection (1)(a)(ii)* does not apply if—

(a) within the period of 3 months prior to the date of the application to re-register, the company has delivered to the Registrar, in accordance with *Part 6*, an annual return with the financial statements required by that Part annexed to it, or

(b) the company was incorporated in that period of 3 months.

(3) The financial statements referred to in *subsection (1)(a)(ii)* are financial statements of the company covering a period that—

(a) ends on a date that is not more than 3 months prior to the date of the application to re-register, and

(b) subject to *subsection (4)*, is of at least 12 months duration.

(4) If, by reason of the company's recent incorporation, it is not possible for the duration of the foregoing period — that will be covered by the foregoing financial statements — to be one of 12 months, then the period covered by them shall be a period beginning on the date of the company's incorporation and ending on the first-mentioned date in *subsection (3)(a)*.

(5) The provisions of *Part 6* as the form and content of, and the notes to accompany, the financial statements required by that Part shall apply to the financial statements specified in *subsection (3)*.

(6) Unless the company would be entitled to avail itself of the audit exemption conferred by *Chapter 15* or *16* of that Part in respect of financial statements that are required to be prepared by that Part (being statements that would cover the period covered by the financial statements specified in *subsection (3)*), the provisions of *Part 6* as to the auditing of financial statements required to be prepared by that Part shall apply to the financial statements specified in *subsection (3)*; accordingly there shall accompany the latter statements that are delivered to the Registrar a report of the company's statutory auditors on them that complies with *Part 6*.

(7) For the purposes of this section—

(a) subscription to a form of assent by the personal representative of a deceased member of a company shall be deemed to be subscription by the member,

(b) an assignee in bankruptcy of a person who is a member of a company shall, to the exclusion of that person, be deemed to be a member of the company.

(8) Where a company is re-registered as an unlimited company, a person who at the time when the application for it to be re-registered was delivered to the Registrar, was a past member of the company and did not thereafter again become a member thereof shall not, in the event of the company's being wound up, be liable to contribute to the

assets of the company more than he or she would have been liable to contribute thereto had it not been so-registered.

(9) *Subsection (10)* applies if the provisions of *Part 6* on abridged financial statements (being statements that would cover the period covered by the financial statements specified in *subsection (3)*) could be availed of by the company with respect to the financial statements required by that Part to be prepared.

(10) Where this subsection applies, then the provisions of *Part 6* on abridged financial statements may be availed of by the company with respect to the financial statements specified in *subsection (3)* and those provisions shall have effect accordingly and the reference in *subsection (6)* to a report of the company's statutory auditors shall, if those provisions are availed of by the company, be read as a reference to a special report of those auditors referred to in *section 356*.

1297 Particular requirements for re-registration of company as a CLG

(1) A company may be re-registered as a company limited by guarantee if, in addition to compliance by the company with the relevant *Chapter 2* requirements, the following requirements are complied with—

- (a) where the company is a company with a share capital, all the members of it have assented to its being re-registered as a company limited by guarantee and the conditions specified in *subsection (2)* are satisfied, and
- (b) where the company is an unlimited company, in addition to the requirements of *paragraph (a)*, the special resolution required by *section 1285(1)(a)* includes a statement that the liability of the members of the resultant company is to be limited as provided for in the relevant alterations of its constitution made by that resolution.

(2) The conditions referred to in *subsection (1)(a)* are—

- (a) the company delivers to the Registrar the prescribed form of assent to the company's being re-registered as a company limited by guarantee subscribed to by, or on behalf of, all members of the company,
- (b) the statement of compliance includes confirmation by a director or secretary of the company that—
  - (i) the persons by whom, or on whose behalf, the form of assent referred to in *paragraph (a)* is subscribed constitute the whole membership of the company, and
  - (ii) if any of the members have not, themselves, subscribed that form, that the directors have taken all reasonable steps to satisfy themselves that each person who subscribed it on behalf of a member was lawfully empowered to do,

  and
- (c) unless the position concerning the allotted share capital of the company, at the date of the application for re-registration, is as referred to in *subsection (3)*, the court, on application to it by the company in that behalf, sanctions its re-registration as a company limited by guarantee and gives directions as to

how its company capital is to be treated in the framework of the resultant company.

(3) The position mentioned in *subsection (2)(c)*, concerning the company's allotted share capital, is that the following conditions are satisfied—

(a) no amount is paid up on it, and

(b) its nominal value does not exceed the aggregate maximum amount that the company's shareholders, who become members of the resultant company on the issue of the certificate of incorporation under *section 1285(6)*, would be liable to pay by virtue of the latter company's memorandum were the latter immediately then to be wound up.

(4) For the purposes of this section—

(a) subscription to a form of assent by the personal representative of a deceased member of a company shall be deemed to be subscription by the member,

(b) an assignee in bankruptcy of a person who is a member of a company shall, to the exclusion of that person, be deemed to be a member of the company.

1298 Particular requirements for re-registration of company as a DAC limited by shares

(1) A company may be re-registered as a DAC limited by shares if, in addition to compliance by the company with the relevant *Chapter 2* requirements, the following requirements are complied with:

(a) where the company is a PLC—

(i) the period during which an application under *section 1287* for the cancellation of the special resolution has expired without any such application having been made, or

(ii) where such an application has been made, the application has been withdrawn, or

(iii) either—

(I) an order, not falling within clause (II), has been made under *section 1287* confirming the resolution, or

(II) if an order has been made under that section confirming the resolution but providing that re-registration shall not take effect unless specified terms and conditions are satisfied, those terms and conditions are satisfied,

and, in either case, a certified copy of that order has been delivered to the Registrar;

and

(b) where the company is an unlimited company, the special resolution required by *section 1285(1)(a)* includes a statement that the liability of the members of the resultant company is to be limited by shares and specifying what is to be the authorised share capital of the resultant company and the fixed amount of the shares into which that share capital is to be divided.

1299 Particular requirements for re-registration of company as a DAC limited by guarantee

(1) A company may be re-registered as a DAC limited by guarantee if, in addition to compliance by the company with the relevant *Chapter 2* requirements, the following requirements are complied with—

(a) where the company is a PLC—

(i) the period during which an application under *section 1287* for the cancellation of the special resolution has expired without any such application having been made, or

(ii) where such an application has been made, the application has been withdrawn, or

(iii) either—

(I) an order, not falling within clause (II), has been made under *section 1287* confirming the resolution, or

(II) if an order has been made under that section confirming the resolution but providing that re-registration shall not take effect unless specified terms and conditions are satisfied, those terms and conditions are satisfied,

and, in either case, a certified copy of that order has been delivered to the Registrar,

(b) where the company is an unlimited company, the special resolution required by *section 1285(1)(a)* includes a statement that the liability of the members of the resultant company is to be limited as provided for in the relevant alterations of its constitution made by that resolution, and

(c) where the company is a company with a share capital, all the members of it have assented to its being re-registered as a DAC limited by guarantee and the conditions specified in *subsection (2)* are satisfied.

(2) The conditions referred to in *subsection (1)(c)* are—

(a) the company delivers to the Registrar the prescribed form of assent to the company's being re-registered as a DAC limited by guarantee subscribed to by, or on behalf of, all members of the company,

(b) the statement of compliance includes confirmation by a director or secretary of the company that—

(i) the persons by whom, or on whose behalf, the form of assent referred to in *paragraph (a)* is subscribed constitute the whole membership of the company, and

(ii) if any of the members have not, themselves, subscribed that form, that the directors have taken all reasonable steps to satisfy themselves that each person who subscribed it on behalf of a member was lawfully empowered to do,

and

(c) unless the position concerning the allotted share capital of the company, at the date of the application for re-registration, is as referred to in *subsection (3)*, the court, on application to it by the company in that behalf, sanctions its re-registration as a DAC limited by guarantee and gives directions as to how its company capital is to be treated in the framework of the resultant company.

(3) The position mentioned in *subsection (2)(c)*, concerning the company's allotted share capital, is that the following conditions are satisfied—

(a) no amount is paid up on it, and

(b) its nominal value does not exceed the aggregate maximum amount that the company's shareholders, who become members of the resultant company on the issue of the certificate of incorporation under *section 1285(6)*, would be liable to pay by virtue of the latter company's memorandum were the latter immediately then to be wound up.

(4) For the purposes of this section—

(a) subscription to a form of assent by the personal representative of a deceased member of a company shall be deemed to be subscription by the member,

(b) an assignee in bankruptcy of a person who is a member of a company shall, to the exclusion of that person, be deemed to be a member of the company.

Part 21
External Companies

Chapter 1
Preliminary

1300 Interpretation (*Part 21*)

(1) In this Part—

"1989 Directive" means Council Directive No. 89/666/EEC of 21 December 1989;

"2009 Directive" means Directive 2009/101/EC of 16 September 2009;

"accounting documents" means, in relation to a financial year of an external company, the following documents—

(a) the company's accounts for that period, including, if it has one or more subsidiaries, any consolidated accounts of the group;

(b) any annual report of the directors of the company for that period;

and *subsections (2)* and *(3)* supplement this definition;

"branch" has the same meaning as it has in the 1989 Directive;

"certified" means certified by—

(a) a director or secretary of the external company before any of the persons or other bodies specified in *paragraphs (b)* to *(d)*;

(b) any person authorised to take statutory declarations;

(c) any notary or notary public;

(d) a court;

in the prescribed manner to be a true copy or a correct translation;

"constitutive documents", in relation to an external company, means its memorandum of association and articles of association or its charter, statutes or other instrument constituting or defining its constitution;

"credit or financial institution" means a credit institution or financial institution to which Council Directive 89/117/EEC of 13 February 1989 applies;

["EEA company" means—

(a) a body corporate—

(i) which is incorporated in a state (other than the State) that is an EEA state, and

(ii) whose members' liability in respect of such body corporate is limited, or

(b) an undertaking—

(i) which is formed or incorporated in a state (other than the State) that is an EEA state,

(ii) whose members' liability in respect of such undertaking is unlimited, and

(iii) which is a subsidiary undertaking of a body corporate whose members' liability in respect of such body corporate is limited;][a]

"external company" means an EEA company or a non-EEA company;

"financial year" in relation to an external company, means the period for which the external company prepares its accounts in accordance with the law of the state in which it is incorporated;

["non-EEA company" means—

(a) a body corporate—

(i) which is incorporated in a state that is not an EEA state, and

(ii) whose members' liability in respect of such body corporate is limited, or

(b) an undertaking—

(i) which is formed or incorporated in a state that is not an EEA state,

(ii) whose members' liability in respect of such undertaking is unlimited, and

(iii) which is a subsidiary undertaking of a body corporate whose members' liability in respect of such body corporate is limited.][b]

(2) Subject to *subsection (3)*, "documents", in the definition of "accounting documents" in *subsection (1)*, means documents as audited in accordance with the laws of the state in which the external company is incorporated and, accordingly, "documents" in that definition includes the report of the auditors on—

(a) the accounts referred to in *paragraph (a)* of it, and

(b) any directors' annual report referred to in *paragraph (b)* of it.

(3) *Subsection (2)* does not apply if—

(a) in a case where the external company is an EEA company, the foregoing accounts have not (in circumstances permitted by the relevant Community act) been audited in accordance with the laws of the EEA state concerned, or

(b) in a case where the external company is a non-EEA company, the foregoing accounts have not (in circumstances permitted by the laws of the state concerned) been audited in accordance with those laws.

Amendments

a Definition substituted by C(A)A 2017, s 80(a).

b Definition substituted by C(A)A 2017, s 80(b).

1301 Application to external companies of certain provisions of *Parts 1* to *14*

(1) In this section "relevant external company" means an external company that satisfies the following conditions—

(a) either—

(i) after the commencement of this section, a branch in the State is established by the external company, or

(ii) immediately before that commencement, a branch in the State stands established by it,

and

(b) subject to *subsection (2)(b)*, the foregoing branch is not subsequently closed, or has not otherwise ceased to be established in the State, at the time this section falls to be applied.

(2) For the purposes of *subsection (1)*—

(a) in relation to the application of *Part 7* by this section, the relevant time that this section falls to be applied at shall be taken to be the time of the creation by the company of the charge, the acquisition by it of the property or the creation of the judgment mortgage referred to in *subsection (4)(a)*, *(b)* or *(c)*, as the case may be, and

(b) in relation to the application of *Part 13* by this section, it suffices, for a company to be a relevant external company, that it satisfies the condition specified in *paragraph (a)* of *subsection (1)*.

(3) *Section 132* shall apply to a relevant external company as it applies to a company referred to in *section 132*.

(4) Subject to *subsection (5)*, *Part 7* shall apply to—

(a) charges on property in the State which are created after the commencement of this section by a relevant external company,

(b) charges on property in the State which is acquired after that commencement by such a company, and

(c) judgment mortgages created after that commencement and affecting property in the State of such a company,

as that Part applies to charges created, or charges on property acquired, by a company referred to in that Part or, as the case may be, judgment mortgages affecting property of a company so referred to.

(5) Without prejudice to the application generally of the provisions of *Part 7* by *subsection (4)* and, in particular, the consequence of a charge being void under *section 409(1)*, the following provisions of that Part, namely, *sections 409(3)* and *(4)* and *410(2)*, may not, with respect to a charge created by a relevant external company, be availed of by the company or a person referred to in *section 410(2)* unless the company has complied with, as the case may be—

(a) *section 1302(1)* and *(2)*, or

(b) *section 1302(1)* and *(2)* as applied by *section 1304*.

(6) Subject to *subsection (7)*, *Parts 13* and *14* (other than *section 798*) shall apply to a relevant external company as *Part 13* or *14*, as the case may be, applies to a company referred to in that Part.

(7) The following provisions have effect as regards the foregoing application of *Parts 13* and *14*—

(a) in *section 747*—

(i) *paragraphs (a)* to *(d)* (which confer standing on certain persons to apply to have one or more competent inspectors appointed to investigate the affairs of a company) of *subsection (2)* shall not apply, and

(ii) the following shall be substituted for *paragraph (e)* of *subsection (2)*:

"(e) a person who is a creditor of the company, but only if the person is the company's creditor by reference to a liability which has arisen under and by virtue of business carried on in the State by the company.";

(b) *section 763* (investigation of share dealing by inspector appointed by Director) shall not apply;

(c) in *section 797* (court may order compliance by company or officer) "officer" shall include the one or more persons authorised by the relevant external company to ensure compliance with this Part;

(d) references to an insolvent company in *Chapters 3*, *5* and *6* of *Part 14* shall be read as including references to a relevant external company that is insolvent if, but only if, the latter is an unregistered company (within the meaning of *Chapter 3* of *Part 22*) that is being wound up pursuant to that Chapter;

(e) for the avoidance of doubt, the reference in *subsection (6)* to a company referred to in *Part 14* — so far as it is in *Chapter 3*, *4*, *5* or *6* of that Part that the reference occurs — includes, as well as a private company limited by shares, any other company referred to in *section 819(6)* where the following is the context—

(i) the context of the reference in *section 819(1)* to a person's being appointed or acting as a director or secretary of a company, or taking part in the formation or promotion of a company;

(ii) the context of *section 825*;

(iii) the context of *section 838*;

(iv) the context of a provision that otherwise imposes a restriction on a company by reference to the fact of its having a restricted person (within the meaning of *section 826*) or otherwise makes provision in consequence of that fact; and

(v) the context of a provision that otherwise makes provision in consequence of a person's being disqualified (within the meaning of *section 838*);

(f) in *section 879(1)*, for "*Parts 1* to *13* or *Part 15*" there shall be substituted "*Parts 1* to *13* or *Part 15* or *22*";

(g) in *section 880(1)*, for "*Parts 1* to *13* or *Part 15*" there shall be substituted "*Parts 1* to *13* or *Part 15* or *22*"; and

(h) the principal place of business in the State of the relevant external company shall be deemed to be its registered office.

(8) This section is in addition to *section 1311(2)* and *(3)* (which relate to the application of *sections 270* and *271* to external companies and certain persons having responsibilities in relation to them).

Chapter 2
Filing obligations of external companies

1302 Filing obligations of EEA company

(1) An EEA company that establishes a branch in the State shall, within 30 days after the date of its doing so, deliver to the Registrar a certified copy of its constitutive documents.

(2) An EEA company that establishes a branch in the State shall, within 30 days after the date of its doing so, notify the Registrar of, or as the case may be, deliver to the Registrar (in either case in the prescribed manner) the following particulars or matters—

(a) its name and legal form and the name of the branch if that is different from its name;

(b) a copy of its certificate of incorporation;

(c) the address of the branch;

(d) the activities at the branch;

(e) the place of registration of the company and the number under which it is registered;

(f) a list of its directors and secretary and any other persons who are authorised to represent the company in dealings with third parties and in legal proceedings together with the following particulars relating to each such person:

(i) present forename and surname and any former forename and surname;

(ii) date of birth;

(iii) usual residential address;

(iv) nationality;

(v) business occupation, if any;

(vi) particulars of any other directorships of bodies corporate, whether incorporated in the State or elsewhere, held by that person; and

(vii) the extent of that person's powers in relation to the activities of the branch;

(g) the name and addresses of some one or more persons resident in the State who is or are—

(i) authorised to accept service of documents required to be served on the EEA company, and

(ii) authorised to ensure compliance with the provisions of this Part together with a consent signed by each such person to act in that capacity;

(h) unless it is a credit or financial institution, copies of its latest accounting documents, that is to say the latest accounting documents—

(i) prepared in relation to a financial year of the company (in accordance with the laws of the EEA state in which it is incorporated), and

(ii) made public (in accordance with those laws) before the end of the period allowed for compliance with *subsection (1)* in respect of the branch, or if earlier, the date on which the company complies with *subsection (1)* in respect of the branch.

(3) An EEA company that establishes a branch in the State shall also deliver to the Registrar, in the prescribed manner, the following documents and notices within 30 days after the date of the occurrence of the event concerned, namely—

(a) any document making or evidencing an alteration in its constitutive documents,

(b) every amended text of its constitutive documents,

(c) notice of a change among the persons referred to in *subsection (2)(f)* or *(g)* or in any of the particulars relating to such persons, specifying the date of the change,

(d) notice of a change in the address referred to in *subsection (2)(c)* together with the new address of the branch,

(e) notice of the winding up of the company, the appointment of one or more liquidators, particulars concerning them and their powers and the termination of the winding up in accordance with disclosure by the company as provided for in Article 2(h), (j) and (k) of the 2009 Directive and particulars concerning insolvency proceedings, arrangements, compositions or any analogous proceedings to which the company is subject, and

(f) notice of the closure of the branch or its otherwise ceasing to be established in the State.

(4) *Section 149(12)* shall apply for the purposes of *subsection (2)(f)*.

(5) The reference in *subsection (2)(h)* to a copy of an accounting document is a reference to a copy that satisfies the following conditions—

(a) it is a true copy of the original save for the difference that the signature or signatures on the original, and any date or dates thereon, shall appear in typeset form on the copy; and

(b) it is accompanied by a certificate of a director and the secretary of the company, that bears the signature of the director and the secretary in electronic or written form, stating that the copy is a true copy of the original (and one such certificate relating to all of the accounting documents mentioned in *subsection (2)* suffices and the foregoing statement need not be qualified on account of the difference permitted by *paragraph (a)* as to the form of a signature or of a date).

(6) The documents and information referred to in *subsection (2)*, and in *subsection (3)*, other than *paragraphs (a)* and *(b)* of that subsection, shall be made available by the Registrar to the system of interconnection of registers.

(7) For the purposes of communications between registers (through the system of interconnection of registers) the Registrar shall assign a unique identifier to each branch which shall include elements to identify the branch as a branch in the State, to

identify the number assigned to the branch in the register and other appropriate elements to avoid identification errors.

(8) On receipt of information, through the system of interconnection of registers, that an EEA company, that has established a branch or branches in the State, has been wound up, dissolved or otherwise removed from the register in the state in which it is incorporated, the Registrar shall, as soon as practicable, enter in the register, in respect of each branch recorded in the register, the fact that the company has been so removed from the first-mentioned register save that this subsection shall not apply in any case in which the company has been so removed as a result of any change in the legal form of the company, a merger or division, or a cross border transfer of its registered office.

(9) If *subsection (1)*, *(2)* or *(3)* is not complied with by an EEA company, the company and any officer of it who is in default shall be guilty of a category 3 offence.

1303 Accounting documents to be filed by EEA company

(1) Subject to *subsection (7)*, for so long as a branch of it stands established in the State, an EEA company shall in each year deliver to the Registrar, in the prescribed manner, the following documents.

(2) Those documents are a copy of the accounting documents, for the financial year concerned, that the EEA company is required to cause to be prepared, and to be made public, in accordance with the laws of the EEA state in which it is incorporated.

(3) Those accounting documents shall be so delivered to the Registrar not later than 30 days after the last date upon which the EEA company was required to cause such accounting documents to be made public in accordance with the laws of the EEA state in which it is incorporated.

(4) The reference in *subsection (2)* to a copy of an accounting document is a reference to a copy that satisfies the following conditions—

(a) it is a true copy of the original save for the difference that the signature or signatures on the original, and any date or dates thereon, shall appear in typeset form on the copy, and

(b) it is accompanied by a certificate of a director and the secretary of the company, that bears the signature of the director and the secretary in electronic or written form, stating that the copy is a true copy of the original (and one such certificate relating to all of the accounting documents mentioned in *subsection (2)* suffices and the foregoing statement need not be qualified on account of the difference permitted by *paragraph (a)* as to the form of a signature or of a date).

(5) If this section is not complied with by an EEA company, the company and any officer of it who is in default shall be guilty of a category 3 offence.

(6) Without prejudice to the generality of *subsections (1)* and *(2)* of *section 865*, summary proceedings in relation to an offence under this section may be brought and prosecuted by the Registrar.

(7) This section shall not apply to a company that is a credit or financial institution.

1304 Filing obligations of non-EEA company

(1) If a non-EEA company establishes a branch in the State, the same requirements under *section 1302(1)* and *(2)* as apply to an EEA company's doing so shall apply to the non-EEA company and, accordingly, *section 1302(1)* and *(2)* shall apply to the non-EEA company, but with the following modifications.

(2) Those modifications are that—

(a) the following paragraph shall be substituted for *paragraph (e)* of *section 1302(2)*:

"(e) if the law of the state in which the company is incorporated requires entry in a register, the place of registration of the company and the number under which it is registered;";

and

(b) the following paragraphs shall be substituted for *paragraph (h)* of *section 1302(2)*:

"(h) unless it is a credit or financial institution, copies of its latest accounting documents, that is to say the latest accounting documents—

(i) prepared in relation to a financial year of the company (in accordance with the laws of the state in which it is incorporated), and

(ii) made public (in accordance with those laws), or, if not required by those laws to be made public, prepared as so mentioned, before the end of the period allowed for compliance with *subsection (1)* in respect of the branch, or if earlier, the date on which the company complies with *subsection (1)* in respect of the branch,

(i) each of the following so far as not ascertainable from its constitutive documents—

(i) the company's principal place of business,

(ii) the company's objects, and

(iii) the place where the company is incorporated.".

(3) A non-EEA company that establishes a branch in the State shall also deliver to the Registrar, in the prescribed manner, within 30 days after the date of the occurrence of the particular event referred to in *section 1302(3)(a)* to *(d)* or, as appropriate, *paragraph (b)* or *(c)* of this subsection—

(a) any document or notice referred to in *section 1302(3)(a) to (d)*,

(b) notice of the winding up of the company, the appointment of one or more liquidators, particulars concerning them and their powers and the termination of the winding up and particulars concerning insolvency proceedings, arrangements, compositions or any analogous proceedings to which the company is subject, and

(c) notice of the closure of the branch or its otherwise ceasing to be established in the State.

(4) *Section 1302(4)* (application of *section 149(12)*) applies for the purposes of *section 1302(2)(f)* as the latter has effect in relation to a non-EEA company by virtue of this section.

(5) *Section 1302(5)* applies for the purposes of *section 1302(2)(h)* as the latter has effect in relation to a non-EEA company by virtue of this section.

(6) If *section 1302(1)* or *(2)* (as applied by this section), or *subsection (3)*, is not complied with by a non-EEA company, the company and any officer of it who is in default shall be guilty of a category 3 offence.

1305 Accounting documents to be filed by non-EEA company

(1) Subject to *subsection (10)*, for so long as a branch of it stands established in the State, a non-EEA company shall in each year deliver to the Registrar, in the prescribed manner, the following documents.

(2) Those documents are a copy of the accounting documents, for the financial year concerned, that the non-EEA company is required to cause to be prepared, and, if such be the case, to be made public, in accordance with the laws of the state in which it is incorporated, but this is subject to *subsections (3)* and *(4)*.

(3) If there is no requirement, under the laws of the state in which it is incorporated, that accounting documents be caused to be prepared by it, the non-EEA company shall, subject to *subsection (10)*, for each year in which a branch of it stands established as mentioned in *subsection (1)*—

(a) cause to be prepared in accordance with—

(i) [the Accounting Directive (within the meaning of *Part* 6)][a], or

(ii) international financial reporting standards,

accounts and a directors' annual report on them, and

(b) unless the circumstances are such that auditing of those accounts is not required by the relevant Community act, cause those accounts and that annual report to be audited in accordance with [the Audit Directive (within the meaning of Part 27)][b].

(4) If a non-EEA company to which *subsection (2)* applies so opts, there may, instead of the accounting documents referred to in that subsection, be delivered by it, in the prescribed manner, to the Registrar—

(a) a copy of the accounts, and a directors' annual report on them, prepared as mentioned in *subsection (3)* (being accounts and such a report that have been audited as mentioned in *paragraph (b)* of that subsection unless the exception in that paragraph applies), and

(b) a copy of the auditor's report on those accounts and that annual report unless the foregoing exception applies.

(5) A copy of the accounting documents or accounts and other documents referred to in *subsection (2)* or *(4)*, as the case may be, shall be delivered to the Registrar not later than 30 days after—

(a) subject to *paragraph (b)*—

(i) in the case of those accounting documents, the last date on which, in accordance with the laws of the state in which it is incorporated, the non-EEA company was required to make public such accounting documents, or

(ii) in the case of the accounts and other documents referred to in *subsection (4)*, the last date on which, in accordance with those laws, the non-EEA company would have been required to make those accounts and other documents public were they accounting documents referred to in *subsection (2)*,

and

(b) if there is no requirement, under the laws of the state in which it is incorporated, that the non-EEA company cause to be published accounting documents that have been prepared by it, the date on which the preparation of those accounting documents or accounts and other documents is completed.

(6) In the case of a non-EEA company to which *subsection (3)* applies, a copy of the accounts and the directors' annual report referred to in that subsection and the auditor's report, if any, thereon, shall be delivered to the Registrar not later than 30 days after the date on which their preparation is completed.

(7) *Section 1303(4)* applies for the purposes of the construction of references in this section to a copy of accounting documents or accounts and other documents as it applies for the purpose of the construction of the reference to a copy of accounting documents in *section 1303(2)*.

(8) If this section is not complied with by a non-EEA company, the company and any officer of it who is in default shall be guilty of a category 3 offence.

(9) Without prejudice to the generality of *subsections (1)* and *(2)* of *section 865*, summary proceedings in relation to an offence under this section may be brought and prosecuted by the Registrar.

(10) This section shall not apply to a company that is a credit or financial institution.

Amendments

a Words substituted by C(A)A 2017, s 81 (previously: "Council Directive 78/660/EEC and, where appropriate, Council Directive 83/349/EEC").

b Words substituted by C(SA)A 2018, s 48 (previously: "the Audit Directive (within the meaning of the 2016 Audits Regulations").

1306 Return of capital by non-EEA company

(1) Subject to *subsection (2)*, a non-EEA company shall, at the same time as it delivers to the Registrar the accounting documents or accounts and other documents referred to in *section 1305*, deliver to the Registrar a statement, in the prescribed form, indicating the amount of the called up share capital of the company as of a date not earlier than 2 months before the date of the statement's delivery.

(2) *Subsection (1)* shall not apply where the information which would be contained in the foregoing statement is contained in the documentation referred to in *section 1302(1)* as applied by *section 1304(1)*.

Chapter 3
Disclosure in certain business documents and translation of documents

1307 Disclosure on letters and order forms

(1) For so long as a branch of an EEA company stands established in the State, every letter and order form that issues from or in respect of that branch shall bear the following particulars:

(a) the place of registration of the company and the number under which it is registered;

(b) the name of the company (if different from the name of its branch), its legal form and the address of its registered office;

(c) in the case of a company which is being wound up, the fact that that is so; and

(d) the fact that the branch is registered in the State and the number under which it is registered in the office of the Registrar.

(2) If on any foregoing letter or order form there is reference to the share capital of the EEA company, the company shall ensure that the reference is not stated otherwise than as a reference to the paid-up share capital of the company.

(3) For so long as a branch of a non-EEA company stands established in the State, every letter and order form that issues from or in respect of that branch shall bear the following particulars—

(a) the name of the company (if different from the name of its branch);

(b) if the law of the state in which the company is incorporated requires entry in a register, the place of registration of the company and the number under which it is registered; and

(c) the fact that the branch is registered in the State and the number under which it is registered in the office of the Registrar.

(4) If on any foregoing letter or order form there is reference to the share capital of the non-EEA company, the company shall ensure that the reference is not stated otherwise than as a reference to the paid-up share capital of the company.

(5) If *subsection (1)* or *(2)* is not complied with by an EEA company, the company and any officer of it who is in default shall be guilty of a category 3 offence.

(6) If *subsection (3)* or *(4)* is not complied with by a non-EEA company, the company and any officer of it who is in default shall be guilty of a category 3 offence.

1308 Notice of delivery to be published in CRO Gazette

The Registrar shall publish in the CRO Gazette, within 21 days after the date of such delivery, notice of the delivery to the Registrar under this Chapter of any document.

1309 Translation of documents

(1) Every document required to be delivered or notified by an external company to the Registrar under any of *sections 1302* to *1305* shall, if it is not in the Irish or English language, have annexed to it a certified translation of it in the Irish or English language.

(2) In any case of a discrepancy between the text, in its original language, of a document referred to in *subsection (1)* and the certified translation of it annexed as required by that subsection, the latter may not be relied upon by the external company against a third party. A third party may, nevertheless, rely on that translation against the external company, unless the company proves that the third party had knowledge of the text of the document in its original language.

(3) In *subsection (2)*, "third party" means a person other than the external company or a member, officer or employee of it.

Chapter 4
Service of documents

1310 Service of documents

(1) Subject to *subsection (2)*, any document required to be served on an external company referred to in *section 1302* or *1304* shall be sufficiently served if addressed to any person particulars of whom have been delivered to the Registrar under *section 1302(2)(g)* (or, as the case may be, that provision as applied by *section 1304*) and left at or sent by post to the address which has been so delivered.

(2) A document may be served on an external company referred to in *section 1302* or *1304* by leaving it at or sending it by post to any branch established by it in the State—

(a) where the external company makes default in delivering to the Registrar the particulars of a person resident in the State who is authorised to accept, on behalf of the company, service of the document, or

(b) if at any time all the persons whose particulars have been so delivered are dead or have ceased to so reside, or refuse to accept service on behalf of the external company, or for any reason it cannot be served.

(3) This section shall cease to apply to an external company on the expiration of 2 years after the date on which it has delivered the notice referred to in *section 1302(3)(f)* or, as the case may be, *section 1304(3)(c)*.

(4) If notice of a change among the persons referred to in *section 1302(2)(g)* or in any of the particulars relating to such persons has been delivered by the company

concerned to the Registrar in accordance with this Part, then the references in this section to any person, particulars in respect of whom have been delivered to the Registrar under the provision referred to in *subsection (1)*, shall be read having regard to the position that obtains in consequence of that change as so notified.

Chapter 5
Compliance

1311 Duty of securing compliance with this Part

(1) The duty of securing compliance by an external company with this Part shall, without prejudice to the duty of the external company concerned, also lie upon the one or more persons authorised by the external company to ensure compliance with this Part.

(2) *Sections 270* and *271* shall apply to an external company.

(3) If any person authorised, as mentioned in *subsection (1)*, by an external company would not otherwise be regarded as an officer of it for the purposes of *sections 270* and *271*, such a person shall be deemed to be an officer of the external company for the purposes of those sections.

PART 22
UNREGISTERED COMPANIES AND JOINT STOCK COMPANIES

Chapter 1
Application of Act to unregistered companies

1312 Application of certain provisions of Act to unregistered companies

(1) Subject to *subsections (2)* to *(7)*, the provisions specified in *Schedule 14* shall apply to all bodies corporate incorporated in and having a principal place of business in the State as if they were companies registered under this Act.

(2) The foregoing provisions shall not apply by virtue of this section to any of the following bodies—

(a) any body corporate incorporated by or registered under any public general statute,

(b) any body corporate not formed for the purpose of carrying on a business which has for its objects the acquisition of gain by the body or by the individual members thereof,

(c) any body corporate which is prohibited by statute or otherwise from making any distribution of its income or property among its members while it is a going concern or when it is being wound up, and

(d) any body corporate for the time being exempted by a direction given by the Minister for the purposes of this section,

each of which is referred to in this section as an "excluded body".

(3) The foregoing provisions shall apply also in like manner in relation to any unincorporated body of persons entitled by virtue of letters patent to any of the privileges conferred by the Chartered Companies Act 1837 and not registered under any other public general statute but subject to the like exceptions as are provided for in the case of bodies corporate by *paragraphs (b)*, *(c)* and *(d)* of *subsection (2)* (and any such incorporated body that is the subject of any of those exceptions is also referred to in this section as an "excluded body").

(4) *Subsections (5)* and *(6)* operate to—

(a) extend the effect of a certain provision (being a provision that excludes the application of provisions of this Act to public limited companies), or

(b) exclude the application of certain provisions of this Act,

to a body depending on whether it has, or, as the case may be, has not the status of a body that has securities admitted to trading on a regulated market in an EEA state (and a body that has securities admitted to such trading is referred to in those subsections as a "traded body").

(5) The provisions of [*section 1002*][a] that exclude the application of a provision of *Parts 1 to 14* to a public limited company shall (in so far as that provision would otherwise apply to a traded body by virtue of this section) operate to exclude the application of that provision to a traded body.

(6) In addition to the exceptions contained in *subsection (2)*, the following provisions specified in *Schedule 14*, namely—

(a) the several provisions of *Part 17*, and

(b) *Part 23*, shall not apply to a body unless it is a traded body.

(7) This section shall not repeal or revoke, in whole or in part, any enactment, charter or other instrument constituting or regulating any body in relation to which the foregoing provisions are applied by virtue of this section, but in relation to any such body, the operation of any such enactment, charter or instrument shall be suspended in so far as it is inconsistent with any of the foregoing provisions as they apply for the time being to that body.

(8) A body referred to in this section (other than an excluded body or one to which *subsection (9)* applies) and which has not already done so, shall forthwith deliver to the Registrar a certified copy of the charter, statutes, memorandum and articles or other instrument constituting or defining the constitution of the body.

(9) A body referred to in this section (other than an excluded body) and which comes into existence on or after the commencement of this section shall, within 3 months after the date of its coming into existence, deliver to the Registrar a certified copy of the charter, statutes, memorandum and articles or other instrument constituting or defining the constitution of the body.

(10) If default is made by a body in complying with *subsection (8)* or *(9)*, the body and any officer of it who is in default shall be guilty of a category 3 offence.

(11) In this section "public general statute" means an Act (as defined in section 2(1) of the Interpretation Act 2005) that either—

(a) was passed after 6 December 1922, not being—

(i) a private Act of the Oireachtas of Saorstát Éireann, or

(ii) a private Act of the Oireachtas;

or

(b) was passed on or before 6 December 1922, not being—

(i) a private Act, or

(ii) a local and personal Act,

of the parliament concerned.

Amendments

a Words substituted by C(A)A 2017, s 98(l) (previously: "*section 1004*").

1313 Minister's power to make regulations in relation to *Schedule 14*

(1) The Minister may, if he or she considers it necessary to do so in the interests of the orderly and proper regulation of the business of the bodies referred to in *section 1312*

(not being bodies referred to in that section as excluded bodies), make regulations adding to, or subtracting from, the list of the provisions of this Act specified in *Schedule 14*.

(2) Where it is proposed to make a regulation under this section a draft of the proposed regulation shall be laid before each House of the Oireachtas and the regulation shall not be made until a resolution approving of the draft has been passed by each such House.

Chapter 2
Registration of certain bodies (other than joint stock companies) as companies

1314 Definitions (*Chapter 2*)

In this Chapter—

"registration date" shall be read in accordance with *section 1323(2)*;

"registration resolution" shall be read in accordance with *section 1316(1)*.

1315 Registration as a company of body to which *section 1312(1)* applies

(1) A body corporate specified in *subsection (1)* of *section 1312*, not being—

(a) a body referred to in that section as an excluded body, or

(b) a joint stock company within the meaning of *Chapter 5*,

may apply to be registered under this Chapter as—

(i) a private company limited by shares,

(ii) a designated activity company,

(iii) a public limited company,

(iv) a company limited by guarantee, or

(v) an unlimited company,

but this is subject to the provisions of this Chapter and the appropriate requirements under the applicable Part of this Act being satisfied.

(2) Registration on foot of such an application shall not be invalid by reason that it has taken place with a view to the company's being wound up.

(3) Notwithstanding anything in this Part and, in particular, the definition of "joint stock company" in *Chapter 5*, *subsection (1)* applies to, amongst other bodies corporate, the Governor and Company of the Bank of Ireland and *Chapter 5* shall not apply to the latter body corporate.

(4) Notwithstanding anything in *paragraph (a)* of that subsection, *subsection (1)* applies to, amongst other bodies corporate, a society registered under the Industrial and Provident Societies Acts 1893 to 2014.

1316 Requirements for registration under this Chapter as company

(1) A body corporate shall not be registered under this Chapter as any particular type of company referred to in *section 1315* without the assent (in this Chapter referred to as a "registration resolution") to its registration as that type of company given by a

majority of such of its members as, being entitled so to do, vote in person or, where proxies are allowed, by proxy at a general meeting summoned for the purpose.

(2) In computing any majority under this section, when a poll is demanded, regard shall be had to the number of votes to which the member is entitled according to the regulations of the body corporate concerned.

(3) Before a registration resolution is moved, a statement in accordance with *subsection (4)* shall be sent, 21 days before the date of the moving of the resolution, by the body corporate concerned to every member of it entitled to notice of the meeting of it at which the registration resolution is to be moved.

(4) Every statement required by *subsection (3)* shall—

(a) state the type of company that the body corporate is proposed to be registered as,

(b) state the name of the proposed company,

(c) state the reasons for the proposal to register,

(d) summarise the principal implications of the registration for members, and

(e) indicate the place where there may be obtained or inspected, in either case free of charge, the memorandum of association and articles of association of the proposed company that comply, or, if the proposed company is a private company limited by shares, the constitution of it referred to in *section 19* that complies, with the requirements of this Act,

and copies of that memorandum and articles or that constitution shall, accordingly, be made available for such supply or inspection to or by every member entitled to the foregoing notice at the place so indicated.

(5) As long as a document referred to in *subsection (4)(e)* is also made available for such supply or inspection in hardcopy form, it shall be permissible to include in the foregoing statement, as well as the indication required by *subsection (4)(e)* concerning the hardcopy form, an indication that that document may be—

(a) inspected on, and

(b) downloaded and printed from,

a website of the body corporate free of charge.

(6) If an assent of the body corporate's members to such registration has (by means of a registration resolution in accordance with *subsection (1)*) been given, a body corporate may, in the prescribed form, apply to the Registrar to be registered under this Chapter as the type of company concerned.

(7) Such an application shall be made within 30 days after the date of the meeting at which that assent was given.

(8) Such an application shall be accompanied by the following documents:

(a) a copy of the statement required by *subsection (3)* and of the registration resolution, each certified by a director or other officer of the body corporate;

(b) a list showing the names and addresses of all persons who, on a date specified in the list (not being more than 28 days before the date on which the application is received by the Registrar) were members of the body corporate, specifying the shares or stock held by them respectively (distinguishing, in cases where the shares or stock are numbered, each share or unit of stock by its number);

(c) the nominal share capital of the body corporate and the number of shares into which it is divided, or the amount of stock of which it consists;

(d) the number of shares of the body corporate taken and the amount paid on each share; and

(e) the memorandum of association and articles of association of the proposed company.

1317 Particular requirements for registration of body corporate as a PLC

(1) A body corporate may be registered under this Chapter as a PLC if, in addition to the preceding section and *section 1318* being complied with, the following requirements are complied with—

(a) the body corporate delivers, with the application under *section 1316(6)*, the following documents to the Registrar—

(i) a copy of a balance sheet of the body prepared as at a date not more than 7 months before the date of receipt by the Registrar of the application,

(ii) an unqualified report by the body's statutory auditors on that balance sheet,

(iii) a copy of a written statement by those auditors that, at the balance sheet date, the amount of the body's net assets was not, in their opinion, less than the aggregate of its called-up share capital and undistributable reserves,

(iv) a copy of any report prepared under [*section 1319*][a], and

(v) a statement by a director or secretary of the body confirming—

(I) that the requirements of *section 1318* and *section 1319(2)* (where applicable) have been complied with, and

(II) that, between the balance sheet date and the date of the making by the body of application for registration, there has been no change in the financial position of the body that has resulted in the amount of the body's net assets becoming less than the aggregate of its called-up share capital and undistributable reserves,

and

(b) where the liability of the members of the body is unlimited, the registration resolution includes a statement that the liability of the members of the proposed company is to be limited by shares and specifying what is to be the authorised share capital of the proposed company and the fixed amount of the shares into which that share capital is to be divided.

(2) The Registrar may accept a statement under *paragraph (a)(v)* of *subsection (1)* as sufficient evidence that the requirements referred to in *clause (I)* of that provision have been complied with.

(3) The Registrar shall not, on foot of the application to register a body corporate under this Chapter as a PLC, issue a certificate of incorporation under *section 1323* if it appears to the Registrar that—

(a) by, either of the means specified in *section 84(2)(b)*, a reduction of the body's capital has taken place after the date of the passing of the registration resolution, and

(b) the reduction has the effect of bringing the nominal value of the body's allotted share capital below the authorised minimum.

(4) A qualification shall be treated for the purposes of the definition of an "unqualified report" in *subsection (7)* as being not material in relation to any balance sheet if, but only if, the person making the report states in writing that the thing giving rise to the qualification is not material for the purposes of determining, by reference to that balance sheet, whether, at the balance sheet date, the amount of the body corporate's net assets was not less than the aggregate of its called-up share capital and undistributable reserves.

(5) For the purposes of the making, in relation to the foregoing balance sheet, of a report falling within the definition of an "unqualified report" in *subsection (7)*, *section 290* and the other relevant provisions of *Part 6* (so far as applicable to balance sheets as distinct from the other elements of financial statements) shall be deemed to have effect in relation to that balance sheet with the following modifications.

(6) Those modifications are such modifications as are necessary by reason of the fact (if such is the case) that that balance sheet is prepared otherwise than in respect of a financial year.

(7) In this section—

"undistributable reserves" has the same meaning as in *section 1082*;

"unqualified report" means, in relation to the balance sheet of a body corporate, a report stating without material qualification—

(a) that, in the opinion of the person making the report, the balance sheet complies with *section 290* and the other relevant provisions of *Part 6* (so far as applicable to balance sheets as distinct from the other elements of financial statements); and

(b) without prejudice to *paragraph (a)*, that in the opinion of that person, the balance sheet gives a true and fair view of the body's assets, liabilities and equity as at the balance sheet date.

Amendments

a Words substituted by C(A)A 2017, s 98(m) (previously: "*section 1318*").

1318 Requirements as to share capital of body corporate applying to register as a PLC

A body corporate shall not be registered under this Chapter as a PLC unless, at the time the registration resolution is passed—

(a) the nominal value of the body's allotted share capital is not less than the authorised minimum,

(b) each of its allotted shares is paid up at least as to one-quarter of the nominal value of that share and the whole of any premium on it,

(c) where any share in the body or any premium payable on it has been fully or partly paid up by an undertaking given by any person that that person or another should do work or perform services for the body or another, the undertaking has been performed or otherwise discharged, and

(d) where shares have been allotted as fully or partly paid up to their nominal value or any premium payable on them otherwise than in cash and the consideration for the allotment consists of or includes an undertaking (other than one to which *paragraph (c)* applies) to the body either—

(i) that undertaking has been performed or otherwise discharged, or

(ii) there is a contract between the body and any person pursuant to which that undertaking must be performed within 5 years after that time.

1319 Shares allotted by body corporate applying to register as PLC between balance sheet date and passing of registration resolution

(1) This section applies where—

(a) shares are allotted by a body corporate applying to register under this Chapter as a PLC between the balance sheet date and the passing of the registration resolution, and

(b) those shares have been allotted as fully or partly paid up as to their nominal value, or any premium on them, otherwise than in cash.

(2) Where this section applies the body corporate shall not make an application under this Chapter to register as a PLC unless, before the making of the application—

(a) the consideration for the allotment referred to in *subsection (1)* has been valued in accordance with the provisions of *Chapter 3* of *Part 17* that are applied by this section, and

(b) a report with respect to the consideration's value has been made to the body in accordance with those provisions during the 6 months immediately preceding the date of that allotment, but this is subject to subsection (4).

(3) Without prejudice to *subsection (4)*, the following provisions of *Chapter 3* of *Part 17*, namely—

(a) *section 1028(5) to (11)*,

(b) *section 1029(4)*, and

(c) *section 1030*,

shall apply for the purposes of this section as they apply for the purposes of *subsection (1)* of *section 1028* and as if the references in them to that *subsection (1)* were references to *subsection (2)* of this section and with any other necessary modifications.

(4) The provisions of *Chapter 3* of *Part 17* that operate to disapply the requirement under *section 1028(1)* for a valuation of the consideration referred to in that provision to be carried out (and the making of a report thereon) shall operate to disapply the requirement under *subsection (2)* for a valuation of the consideration referred to in that subsection to be carried out (and the making of a report thereon).

(5) For the purpose of those foregoing provisions (as they operate by virtue of the preceding subsection), those provisions shall apply as if the references in them to *subsection (1)* of *section 1028* were references to *subsection (2)* of this section and with any other necessary modifications.

(6) In this section "balance sheet date" means the date as of which the balance sheet referred to in *section 1317(1)(a)* is prepared.

1320 Application of certain other provisions of *Part 17* on allotments to a body that passed resolution for registration as a PLC

Sections 1025 to *1033* and *1036*, *1037* and *1038* shall apply to a body corporate which has passed and not revoked a resolution that the body be registered under this Chapter as a PLC as those sections apply to a PLC.

1321 Regulations for special cases

(1) With respect to—

(a) an application that may be made by a body corporate, being a body corporate which does not have a share capital, to register under this Chapter as a company which does have a share capital, or

(b) an application that may be made by a body corporate to register under this Chapter as a company that is not a PLC,

the Minister may make regulations specifying requirements, additional to those contained in the preceding provisions of this Chapter, that must be complied with before the application may be acceded to by the Registrar.

(2) The requirements that may be so specified may, in the case of an application referred to in *subsection (1)(a)*, include requirements analogous to those in *section 1286*.

(3) Where it is proposed to make a regulation under this section a draft of the proposed regulation shall be laid before each House of the Oireachtas and the

regulation shall not be made until a resolution approving of the draft has been passed by each such House.

1322 Change of name for purposes of registration

(1) Subject to *subsection (2)*, where the name of a body seeking registration under this Chapter is one by which it may not be so registered by reason of the name being, in the opinion of the Registrar, undesirable, it may, with the approval of the Registrar signified in writing, change its name with effect from its registration under this Chapter.

(2) The like assent of the members of the body shall be required to the change of name as is by *section 1316(1)* required to the registration under this Chapter.

1323 Registration and its effects

(1) On compliance with the requirements of this Chapter with respect to registration, the Registrar shall certify in writing that the body applying for registration is incorporated, on a date specified by the Registrar, as the type of company specified in the application and shall issue to the company a certificate of incorporation in respect of it, and upon the foregoing date the company shall be so incorporated.

(2) In this Chapter, the foregoing date is referred to as the "registration date".

(3) A certificate issued under this section in respect of a company shall be conclusive evidence that the requirements of this Chapter in respect of registration and of matters precedent and incidental thereto have been complied with and that the company is duly registered under this Act.

(4) On and from the registration date the following provisions have effect:

(a) the provisions of this Act relating to the numbering of shares shall not apply to stock that had been issued, or shares, not numbered, that had been issued, by the company in its former status before that date;

(b) for the purposes of any provision of this Act which requires delivery of a document or return to the Registrar, the company shall not be obliged to so deliver any document or return, which relates to the period prior to the registration date, if it would not have been required to deliver such document or return had it not registered as a company;

(c) in the event of the company being wound up, every person shall be a contributory, in respect of the debts and liabilities of the company in its former status contracted before the registration date, who is liable to pay or contribute to the payment of—

(i) any debt or liability of the company in its former status contracted or incurred before that date,

(ii) any sum for the adjustment of the rights of the members among themselves in respect of any such debt or liability, or

(iii) the costs and expenses of winding up the company,

so far as relates to the foregoing debts or liabilities;

(d) in the event of the company being wound up, every contributory shall be liable to contribute to the assets of the company, in the course of the winding up, all sums due from him or her in respect of any such liability as is mentioned in *paragraph (c)*, and, in the event of the death or bankruptcy of any contributory, the provisions of this Act relating to the personal representatives of deceased contributories and to the assignees in bankruptcy of bankrupt contributories, respectively, shall apply.

(5) All property, real and personal (including things in action), belonging to or vested in a body corporate registering under this Chapter as a company, shall, on the registration date, pass to and vest in that company for all the estate and interest of the body corporate therein.

(6) Registration under this Chapter shall not affect—

(a) the rights or liabilities of the company in its former status in respect of any debt or obligation incurred, or any contract entered into by, to, with or on behalf of, it in its former status before the registration date, or

(b) the priority of any mortgage, charge, pledge or other security or encumbrance created by the company in its former status before the registration date.

(7) All actions and other legal proceedings which, at the registration date, are pending by or against the company in its former status, or any officer or member thereof, may be continued in the same manner as if the registration of it in its new status had not taken place.

1324 Supplemental provisions in relation to *section 1323*

Without prejudice to the generality of *section 1323(4)* to *(7)*, the following provisions shall have effect where a body corporate registers under this Chapter as a company, that is to say—

(a) a reference (express or implied) to the body corporate in any instrument made, given, passed, or executed before the registration date shall be read as a reference to the company,

(b) all contracts, agreements, conveyances, mortgages, deeds, leases, licences, other instruments, undertakings and notices (whether or not in writing) entered into by, made with, given to or by, or addressed to the body corporate (whether alone or with any other person) before the registration date and subsisting immediately before the registration date shall, to the extent that they were previously binding on and enforceable by, against, or in favour of the body corporate, be binding on and enforceable by, against, or in favour of the company as fully and effectually in every respect as if, instead of the body corporate, the company had been the person by whom they were entered into, with whom they were made, or to or by whom they were given or addressed as the case may be,

(c) an instruction, order, direction, mandate, or authority given to the body corporate and subsisting immediately before the registration date shall be deemed to have been given to the company,

(d) a security held by the body corporate as security for a debt or other liability to the body corporate incurred before the registration date shall be available to the company as security for the discharge of that debt or liability and, where the security extends to future or prospective debts or liabilities, shall be available as security for the discharge of debts or liabilities to the company incurred on or after the registration date, and, in relation to a security, the company, shall be entitled to all the rights and priorities (howsoever arising) and shall be subject to all liabilities to which the body corporate would have been entitled or subject if the body corporate had not become registered as a company,

(e) all the rights and liabilities of the body corporate as bailor or bailee of documents or chattels shall be vested in and assumed by the company,

(f) a negotiable instrument or order for payment of money which, before the registration date is drawn on or given to or accepted or endorsed by the body corporate or payable at a place of business of the body corporate shall, unless the context otherwise requires, have the same effect on and after the registration date as if it had been drawn on or given to or accepted or endorsed by the company instead of the body corporate or was payable at the place of business of the company,

(g) nothing effected or authorised by this Chapter—

(i) shall be regarded as placing the body corporate, or the company, or any other person, in breach of contract or confidence or as otherwise making any of them guilty of a civil wrong, or

(ii) shall be regarded as giving rise to a right to any person to terminate or cancel any contract or arrangement or to accelerate the performance of any obligation, or

(iii) shall be regarded as placing the body corporate or the company, or any other person in contravention or breach of any enactment or rule of law or contractual provision prohibiting, restricting or regulating the assignment or transfer of any property or the disclosure of any information, or

(iv) shall release any surety, wholly or in part, from any obligation, or

(v) shall invalidate or discharge any contract or security.

1325 Consequential repeals

(1) The statutes specified in *Part 1* of *Schedule 15* are repealed to the extent specified in the third column of that Part.

(2) The charters or instruments specified in *Part 2* of *Schedule 15* are revoked to the extent specified in the second column of that Part.

Chapter 3
Winding up of unregistered company

1326 *Chapter 3* — construction of expression "unregistered company"

For the purposes of this Chapter "unregistered company" includes any trustee savings bank licensed under the Trustee Savings Banks Act 1989, any partnership whether limited or not, any association and any company other than—

(a) a company as defined by *section 2(1)*,

(b) a partnership, association or company which consists of less than 8 members and is not formed outside the State.

1327 Restriction of this Chapter

This Chapter is subject to Chapters I (general provisions) and III (secondary insolvency proceedings) of the Insolvency Regulation.

1328 Winding up of unregistered companies

(1) Subject to the provisions of this Chapter, any unregistered company may be wound up under *Part 11* and all the provisions of *Part 11* relating to winding up shall apply to an unregistered company with the exceptions and additions mentioned in this section.

(2) The principal place of business in the State of an unregistered company shall, for all the purposes of the winding up, be deemed to be the registered office of the company.

(3) No unregistered company shall be wound up under this Act voluntarily.

(4) The circumstances in which an unregistered company may be wound up are as follows:

(a) if the company is dissolved or has ceased to carry on business or is carrying on business only for the purpose of winding up its affairs;

(b) if the company is unable to pay its debts;

(c) if the court is of the opinion that it is just and equitable that the company should be wound up.

(5) A petition for winding up a trustee savings bank licensed under the Trustee Savings Banks Act 1989 may be presented by the Minister for Finance as well as by any person authorised under the other provisions of this Act to present a petition for winding up a company.

(6) Where a company incorporated outside the State which has been carrying on business in the State ceases to carry on business in the State it may be wound up as an unregistered company under this Part notwithstanding that it has been dissolved or otherwise ceased to exist as a company under or by virtue of the laws of the country under which it was incorporated.

1329 Cases in which unregistered company shall be deemed to be unable to pay its debts

(1) In any of the following 4 cases, that is to say, those to which *subsections (2)* to *(5)* relate, an unregistered company shall be deemed to be unable to pay its debts for the purposes of this Chapter.

(2) This subsection relates to a case in which—

(a) a creditor, by assignment or otherwise, to whom the company is indebted in a sum exceeding €10,000 then due, has served on the company—

(i) by leaving at its principal place of business in the State,

(ii) by delivering to the secretary or some director or principal officer of the company, or

(iii) by serving otherwise in such manner as the court may approve or direct,

a demand in writing requiring the company to pay the sum so due, and

(b) the company has, for 21 days after the date of the service of the demand, neglected to pay the amount or to secure or compound for it to the satisfaction of the creditor.

(3) This subsection relates to a case in which—

(a) any action or other proceeding has been instituted against any person who is a member of the company for any debt or demand due, or claimed to be due, from the company or from the person in his or her character as member of it,

(b) notice in writing that that action or proceeding has been instituted has been served, by the means referred to in *subsection (2)(a)(i)*, *(ii)* or *(iii)*, on the company, and

(c) the company has not, within 10 days after the date of service of the notice, paid, secured or compounded for the debt or demand or procured the action or proceeding to be stayed or indemnified the defendant to his or her reasonable satisfaction against the action or proceeding and against all costs, damages and expenses to be incurred by the defendant by reason of the action or proceeding.

(4) This subsection relates to a case in which, in the State or in any state recognised by the Minister for the purposes of *section 1417* there has been returned unsatisfied execution or other process issued on a judgement, decree or order obtained in any court in favour of a creditor against—

(a) the company,

(b) any person, being a member of the company, in his or her character as such member, or

(c) any person authorised to be sued as nominal defendant on behalf of the company.

(5) This subsection relates to a case in which it is otherwise proved to the satisfaction of the court that the company is unable to pay its debts.

1330 Contributories in winding up of unregistered company

(1) In the event of an unregistered company being wound up, every person shall be deemed to be a contributory who is liable to pay or contribute to the payment of—

(a) any debt or liability of the company,

(b) any sum for the adjustment of the rights of the members among themselves, or

(c) the costs and expenses of winding up the company,

and every contributory shall be liable to contribute to the assets of the company, all sums due from him or her in respect of any such liability as is mentioned in the preceding paragraphs.

(2) In the event of the death or bankruptcy of any contributory, the provisions of this Act relating to the personal representatives of deceased contributories and to the assignees in bankruptcy of bankrupt contributories, respectively, shall apply.

1331 Power of court to stay or restrain proceedings

The provisions of this Act relating to staying and restraining actions and proceedings against a company at any time after the presentation of a petition for winding up and before the making of a winding-up order shall, in the case of an unregistered company where the application to stay or restrain is by a creditor, extend to actions and proceedings against any contributory of the company.

1332 Actions stayed on winding-up order

Where an order has been made for winding up an unregistered company, no action or proceeding shall be proceeded with or commenced against any contributory of the company in respect of any debt of the company, except by leave of the court and subject to such terms as the court may impose.

1333 Provisions of this Chapter to be cumulative

The provisions of this Chapter relating to unregistered companies shall be in addition to and not in restriction of any provisions contained in *Part 11* relating to winding up companies by the court and the court or liquidator may exercise any powers or do any act in the case of unregistered companies which might be exercised or done by it or him or her in winding up companies formed and registered under this Act.

Chapter 4
Provisions concerning companies registered, but not formed, under former Acts and certain other existing companies

1334 Application of Act to companies registered but not formed under former Companies Acts

(1) Subject to *subsection (2)*, this Act shall apply to every company registered (in a register kept in the State) but not formed under—

(a) the Joint Stock Companies Acts,

(b) the Companies Act 1862,

(c) the Companies (Consolidation) Act 1908, or

(d) the prior Companies Acts,

in the same manner as it is in *Chapter 5* declared to apply to companies registered but not formed under this Act.

(2) In this Act a reference, express or implied, to the date of registration shall, in the case of a company registered but not formed under a foregoing enactment, be read as a reference to the date at which the company was registered under—

(a) the Joint Stock Companies Acts,

(b) the Companies Act 1862,

(c) the Companies (Consolidation) Act 1908, or

(d) the prior Companies Acts,

as the case may be.

1335 Application of Act to unlimited companies re-registered as limited companies under certain former enactments

(1) Subject to *subsection (2)*, this Act shall apply to every unlimited company registered (in a register kept in the State) as a limited company in pursuance of—

(a) the Companies Act 1879, or

(b) section 57 of the Companies (Consolidation) Act 1908,

in the same manner as it applies to an unlimited company re-registered in pursuance of this Act as a limited company.

(2) In this Act a reference, express or implied, to the date of registration shall, in the case of an unlimited company registered as a limited company in pursuance of an enactment referred to in *paragraph (a)* or *(b)*, as the case may be, of *subsection (1)*, be read as a reference to the date on which it was registered as such in pursuance of the enactment referred to in that paragraph.

1336 Provisions as to companies registered under Joint Stock Companies Acts

(1) A company registered under the Joint Stock Companies Acts may cause its shares to be transferred in manner hitherto in use, or in such other manner as the company may direct.

(2) The power conferred by this Act on a company (not being a private company limited by shares) to alter its articles shall, in the case of an unlimited company formed and registered under the Joint Stock Companies Acts, extend to altering any regulations relating to the amount of capital or to its distribution into shares, notwithstanding that those regulations are contained in the memorandum.

Chapter 5
Registration of joint stock companies under this Act

1337 Interpretation (*Chapter 5*)

In this Chapter—

"joint stock company" means a company—

(a) having a permanent paid up or nominal share capital of fixed amount divided into shares, also of fixed amount, or held and transferable as stock, or divided and held partly in one way and partly in the other; and

(b) formed on the principle of having for its members the holders of those shares or that stock, and no other persons,

and such a company when registered with limited liability under this Chapter shall be deemed to be a company limited by shares;

"registration date" shall be read in accordance with *section 1343(2)*;

"registration resolution" shall be read in accordance with *section 1338(6)*.

1338 Companies capable of being registered

(1) With the exceptions and subject to the provisions contained in this section, any—

(a) company registered under the Joint Stock Companies Acts; or

(b) joint stock company,

may at any time register under this Chapter as—

(i) a private company limited by shares,

(ii) a designated activity company,

(iii) a company limited by guarantee, or

(iv) an unlimited company,

and the registration shall not be invalid by reason that it has taken place with a view to the company's being wound up.

(2) This section shall not apply to a company unless it has its registered office or principal place of business in the State.

(3) A company having the liability of its members limited by statute or letters patent, and not being a joint stock company, shall not register under this Chapter.

(4) A company, having the liability of its members limited by statute or letters patent, shall not register under this Chapter as an unlimited company or as a company limited by guarantee.

(5) A company that is not a joint stock company shall not register under this Chapter as a company limited by shares.

(6) A company shall not be registered under this Chapter as any particular type of company referred to in *subsection (1)* without the assent (in this Chapter referred to as a "registration resolution") to its registration as that type of company given, subject to

subsection (7), by a majority of such of its members as are present in person or by proxy at a general meeting summoned for the purpose.

(7) Where a company, not having the liability of its members limited by statute or letters patent, is about to register as a limited company, the majority required to assent as mentioned in *subsection (6)* shall consist of not less than three-fourths of the members present in person or by proxy at the meeting.

(8) Where a company is about to register as a company limited by guarantee, the assent to its being so registered shall be accompanied by a resolution declaring that each member undertakes to contribute to the assets of the company, in the event of its being wound up while he or she is a member, or within one year after the date on which he or she ceases to be a member—

(a) for payment of the debts and liabilities of the company contracted before he or she ceased to be a member,

(b) for payment of the costs and expenses of winding up, and

(c) for the adjustment of the rights of the contributories among themselves,

such amount as may be required, not exceeding an amount specified in the resolution.

(9) In computing any majority under this section when a poll is demanded, regard shall be had to the number of votes to which each member is entitled according to the regulations of the company.

(10) Section 1322 shall apply for the purposes of this section as it applies for the purposes of Chapter 2 with the substitution for the reference in subsection (2) of that section to section 1316(1) of a reference to subsection (6) or (7), as the case may be, of this section and any other necessary modifications.

1339 Requirements for registration of joint stock companies

Before the registration of a joint stock company under this Chapter as a company, there shall be delivered to the Registrar the following documents—

(a) a list showing the names, addresses and occupations of all persons who on a day named in the list, not being more than 6 days before the day of registration, were members of the company, specifying the shares or stock held by them respectively (distinguishing, in cases where the shares are numbered, each share by its number),

(b) a copy of any statute, charter, letters patent, deed of settlement, contract of co-partnery or other instrument constituting or regulating the company, and

(c) if the company is intended to be registered as a limited company, a statement specifying the following particulars in relation to that proposed limited company—

  (i) the nominal share capital of the company and the number of shares into which it is divided, or the amount of stock of which it consists,

  (ii) the number of shares taken and the amount paid on each share,

(iii) the name of the company with the addition of, as appropriate—

(I) "limited" or "teoranta",

(II) "designated activity company" or "cuideachta ghníomhaíochta ainmnithe",

(III) "company limited by guarantee" or "cuideachta faoi theorainn rathaiochta",

(IV) "unlimited company" or "cuideachta neamhtheoranta",

as the last word or words thereof, and

(iv) in the case of a company intended to be registered as a company limited by guarantee, the resolution declaring the amount of the guarantee.

1340 Verifications of lists of members and directors of company for purposes of registration

The lists of members and directors and any other particulars relating to the company required to be delivered under this Chapter to the Registrar shall be verified by a declaration of any 2 or more directors or other principal officers of the company.

1341 Registrar may require evidence as to nature of company

The Registrar may require such evidence as the Registrar thinks necessary for the purpose of satisfying himself or herself whether any company which proposes to be registered under this Chapter is or is not a joint stock company.

1342 Addition of "limited" or "teoranta", etc., to name

(1) Subject to *subsection (2)*, when a company registers under this Chapter with limited liability, the words—

(a) "limited" or "teoranta",

(b) "designated activity company" or "cuideachta ghníomhaíochta ainmnithe",

(c) "company limited by guarantee" or "cuideachta faoi theorainn rathaiochta",

as the case may be, shall form and be registered as part of its name.

(2) *Subsection (1)* shall not be taken as excluding the operation of *section 971* or *1180*.

(3) When a company registers under this Chapter with unlimited liability, the words "unlimited company" or "cuideachta neamhtheoranta" shall form and be registered as part of its name.

1343 Certificate of registration of existing company

(1) On compliance with the requirements of this Chapter with respect to registration, the Registrar shall certify in writing that the company applying for registration is incorporated, on a date specified by the Registrar, as the type of company specified in the application and shall issue to the company a certificate of incorporation in respect of it, and upon the foregoing date the company shall be so incorporated.

(2) In this Chapter, the foregoing date is referred to as the "registration date".

(3) A certificate issued under this section in respect of a company shall be conclusive evidence that the requirements of this Chapter in respect of registration and of matters precedent and incidental thereto have been complied with and that the company is duly registered under this Act.

1344 Effects of registration under this Chapter

(1) When a company is registered under this Chapter, the following provisions shall have effect.

(2) *Section 1323(5)* and *(6)* and, subject to *subsection (3)*, *section 1323(7)* shall apply to the company as they apply to a body corporate that has registered under *Chapter 2* as a company.

(3) Notwithstanding *section 1323(7)*, execution shall not issue against the effects of any individual member of the company on any judgment, decree or order obtained in any such action or proceeding as is mentioned in *section 1323(7)*, but in the event of the property and effects of the company being insufficient to satisfy the judgment, decree or order, an order may be obtained for winding up the company.

(4) *Subsection (5)* applies unless the company has registered under this Chapter as a private company limited by shares.

(5) All provisions contained in any statute or instrument constituting or regulating the company, including, in the case of a company registered as a company limited by guarantee, the resolution declaring the amount of the guarantee, shall be deemed to be conditions and regulations of the company, in the same manner and with the same incidents as if—

(a) so much of them as would, if the company had been formed under this Act, have been required to be inserted in the memorandum, were contained in a registered memorandum, and

(b) the residue of them were contained in registered articles.

(6) If the company has registered under this Chapter as a private company limited by shares, all provisions contained in any statute or instrument constituting or regulating the company shall be deemed to be conditions and regulations of the company, in the same manner and with the same incidents as if they were contained in a registered constitution.

(7) All the provisions of this Act shall apply to the company and the members, contributories and creditors thereof, in the same manner in all respects as if it had been formed under this Act, subject as follows—

(a) the provisions of this Act relating to the numbering of shares shall not apply to any stock that had been issued, or shares, not numbered, that had been issued, by the company in its former status before the registration date,

(b) subject to the provisions of this section, the company shall not have power to alter any provision contained in any statute relating to the company,

(c) subject to the provisions of this section, the company shall not have power, without the sanction of the Minister, to alter any provision contained in any letters patent relating to the company,

(d) the company shall not have power to alter any provision contained in a charter or letters patent relating to the objects of the company,

(e) in the event of the company being wound up, every person shall be a contributory, in respect of the debts and liabilities of the company in its former status contracted before registration, who is liable to pay or contribute to the payment of—

(i) any debt or liability of the company in its former status contracted or incurred before the registration date,

(ii) any sum for the adjustment of the rights of the members among themselves in respect of any such debt or liability,

(iii) the costs and expenses of winding up the company,

so far as relates to the foregoing debts or liabilities,

(f) in the event of the company being wound up, every contributory shall be liable to contribute to the assets of the company, in the course of the winding up, all sums due from him or her in respect of any such liability as is mentioned in *paragraph (e)*, and in the event of the death or bankruptcy of any contributory, the provisions of this Act relating to the personal representatives of deceased contributories and to the assignees in bankruptcy of bankrupt contributories, respectively, shall apply.

(8) The provisions of this Act relating to—

(a) the registration of an unlimited company as limited,

(b) the powers of an unlimited company on registration as a limited company to increase the nominal amount of its share capital and to provide that a portion of its share capital shall not be capable of being called up except in the event of winding up,

(c) the power of a limited company to determine that a portion of its share capital shall not be capable of being called up except in the event of winding up,

shall apply notwithstanding any provisions contained in any statute, charter or other instrument constituting or regulating the company.

(9) Nothing in this section shall authorise the company, not being a private company limited by shares, to alter any such provisions contained in any instrument constituting or regulating the company as would, if the company had originally been formed under this Act, have been required to be contained in the memorandum and are not authorised to be altered by this Act.

(10) None of the provisions of this Act (apart from *section 212(4)*) shall derogate from any power of altering its constitution or regulations which may, by virtue of any statute or other instrument constituting or regulating the company, be vested in the company.

(11) In this section "instrument" includes deed of settlement, contract of co-partnery and letters patent.

1345 Power to substitute memorandum and articles for deed of settlement

(1) Subject to *subsections (2)* to *(4)*, a company registered under this Chapter may, by special resolution, alter the form of its constitution by substituting a memorandum and articles for a deed of settlement.

(2) The provisions of *sections 974* and *975* relating to applications to the court for cancellation of alterations of the objects of a designated activity company and matters consequential on the passing of resolutions for such alterations shall, so far as applicable, apply to an alteration under this section with the following modifications:

(a) there shall be substituted for the copy of the altered memorandum, required to be delivered to the Registrar, a copy of the substituted memorandum and articles; and

(b) on the delivery to the Registrar of a copy of the substituted memorandum and articles or on the date when the alteration is no longer liable to be cancelled by order of the court, whichever last occurs, the substituted memorandum and articles shall apply to the company in the same manner as if it were a company registered under this Act, with that memorandum and those articles, and the company's deed of settlement shall cease to apply to the company.

(3) An alteration under this section may be made either with or without any alteration of the objects of the company under this Act.

(4) In this section "deed of settlement" includes any contract of co-partnery or other instrument constituting or regulating the company, not being a statute, charter or letters patent.

1346 Power of court to stay or restrain proceedings

The provisions of this Act relating to staying and restraining actions and proceedings against a company at any time after the presentation of a petition for winding up and before the making of a winding-up order shall, in the case of a company registered under this Chapter, where the application to stay or restrain is by a creditor, extend to actions and proceedings against any contributory of the company.

1347 Actions stayed on winding-up order

Where an order has been made for winding up a company registered under this Chapter, no action or proceeding shall be commenced or proceeded with against the company or any contributory of the company, in respect of any debt of the company except by leave of the court and subject to such terms as the court may impose.

PART 23
PUBLIC OFFERS OF SECURITIES, FINANCIAL REPORTING BY TRADED COMPANIES, PREVENTION OF MARKET ABUSE, ETC.

Chapter 1
Public offers of securities

1348 Interpretation (*Chapter 1*)

(1) In this Chapter—

"2003 Prospectus Directive" means Directive 2003/71/EC of the European Parliament and of the Council of 4 November 2003, including that Directive as it stands amended for the time being;

"body corporate" includes a company;

"EU prospectus law" means—

(a) the measures adopted for the time being by a Member State (including the State) or an EEA state, to implement the 2003 Prospectus Directive;

(b) any measures directly applicable in consequence of the 2003 Prospectus Directive and, without prejudice to the generality of this paragraph, includes the Prospectus Regulation; and

(c) any supplementary and consequential measures adopted for the time being by a Member State (including the State) or an EEA state in respect of the Prospectus Regulation;

"expert", save where a different construction in respect of that expression applies for the purposes of this Chapter by virtue of Irish prospectus law, includes engineer, valuer, accountant and any other individual or body (whether incorporated or unincorporated) the profession of whom, or the profession of members, officers or employees of which, gives authority to a statement made by the individual or body;

"Irish prospectus law" means—

(a) the measures adopted for the time being by the State to implement the 2003 Prospectus Directive (whether an Act of the Oireachtas, regulations under section 3 of the European Communities Act 1972, regulations under *section 1354* or any other enactment (other than, save where the context otherwise admits, this Chapter);

(b) any measures directly applicable in the State in consequence of the 2003 Prospectus Directive and, without prejudice to the generality of this paragraph, includes the Prospectus Regulation; and

(c) any supplementary and consequential measures adopted for the time being by the State in respect of the Prospectus Regulation;

"issuer" means a body corporate or other legal entity which issues or proposes to issue securities;

"local offer" means an offer of securities to the public in the State where—

(a) the offer expressly limits the amount of the total consideration for the offer to less than €5,000,000 (and the means by which that limit shall be calculated, in particular in the case of a series of such offers of securities, shall be the same as that provided for by regulations under *section 1354* in relation to analogous limits specified by those regulations for any purpose);

(b) the securities are other than those referred to in any of paragraphs (a) to (g) or paragraph (i) or (j) of Article 1(2) of the 2003 Prospectus Directive; and

(c) the offer is not of a kind described in Article 3(2) of the 2003 Prospectus Directive;

"Minister" means the Minister for Finance;

"offer of securities to the public" has the same meaning as it has in Irish prospectus law;

"offering document" means a document prepared for a local offer which document, if prepared in connection with an offer to which the 2003 Prospectus Directive applies, would be a prospectus;

"offeror" means a body corporate or other legal entity or an individual which or who offers securities to the public;

"promoter" means, subject to *subsection (5)*, a promoter who was a party to the preparation of a prospectus, or of the portion thereof containing an untrue statement;

"prospectus" means a document or documents in such form and containing such information as may be required by or under this Chapter or EU prospectus law, howsoever the document or documents are constituted, but does not include any advertisements in newspapers or journals derived from the foregoing;

"Prospectus Regulation" means Commission Regulation (EC) No. 809/2004 of 29 April 2004, implementing Directive 2003/71/EC of the European Parliament and of the Council as regards information contained in prospectuses as well as the format, incorporation by reference and publication of such prospectuses and dissemination of advertisements;

"securities" has the same meaning as it has in Irish prospectus law, and includes shares and debentures of a company.

(2) A word or expression that is used in this Chapter and is also used in the 2003 Prospectus Directive shall have in this Chapter the same meaning as it has in that Directive, unless—

(a) the contrary intention appears, or

(b) Irish prospectus law provides otherwise.

(3) For the purposes of this Chapter—

(a) a statement included in a prospectus shall be deemed to be untrue if it is misleading in the form and context in which it is included, and

(b) a statement shall be deemed to be included in a prospectus if it is contained therein or in any report or memorandum appearing on the face thereof or by reference incorporated therein.

(4) Without limiting the meaning of that expression in any other context in which it is used in this Chapter, "statement" in *section 1353(2)* (other than *paragraph (b)* thereof) and any other section of this Chapter that makes provision in respect of an expert, includes a report and a valuation.

(5) Nothing in this Chapter shall limit or diminish any liability which any person may incur under the general law.

(6) For the purposes of *sections 1349* and *1351*, the following persons shall be deemed not to be a promoter or a person who has authorised the issue of the prospectus—

(a) a professional adviser to any person referred to in *section 1349* acting as such,

(b) an underwriter or professional adviser to an underwriter acting as such.

(7) The person referred to as the "purchaser" in the following case shall be deemed to be an underwriter for the purposes of *subsection (6)(b)*.

(8) That case is one in which—

(a) a person (the "offeror") intends to make an offer of securities to the public; and

(b) another person (the "purchaser")—

(i) agrees to purchase those securities with the intention of their immediate resale, to give effect to that intention of the offeror, at a profit or subject to payment by the offeror to the purchaser of a commission; and

(ii) binds himself or herself to purchase, or procure the purchase of, any of the securities not so resold.

1349 Civil liability for misstatements in prospectus

(1) Subject to *sections 1350* and *1351*, the following persons shall be liable to pay compensation to all persons who acquire any securities on the faith of a prospectus for the loss or damage they may have sustained by reason of—

(a) any untrue statement included therein; or

(b) any omission of information required by EU prospectus law to be contained in the prospectus;

namely—

(i) the issuer who has issued the prospectus or on whose behalf the prospectus has been issued;

(ii) the offeror of securities to which the prospectus relates;

(iii) every person who has sought the admission of the securities to which the prospectus relates to trading on a regulated market;

(iv) the guarantor of the issue of securities to which the prospectus relates;

(v) every person who is a director of the issuer at the time of the issue of the prospectus;

(vi) every person who has authorised himself or herself to be named and is named in the prospectus as a director of the issuer or as having agreed to become such a director either immediately or after an interval of time;

(vii) every person being a promoter of the issuer;

(viii) every person who has authorised the issue of the prospectus (not being the competent authority designated under Irish prospectus law).

(2) In addition to the persons specified in *subsection (1)* as being liable in the circumstances there set out, an expert who has given the consent required by *section 1353* to the inclusion in a prospectus of a statement purporting to be made by him or her shall, subject to *sections 1350* and *1351*, be liable to pay compensation to all persons who acquire any securities on the faith of the prospectus for the loss or damage they may have sustained by reason of an untrue statement in the prospectus purporting to be made by him or her as an expert.

1350 Exceptions and exemptions

(1) A person shall not be liable under *section 1349* solely on the basis of a summary of a prospectus, including any translation thereof, unless it is misleading, inaccurate or inconsistent when read together with other parts of the prospectus.

(2) Subject to *subsection (4)*, a person shall not be liable under *section 1349* if he or she proves—

(a) that, having consented to become a director of the issuer, he or she withdrew, in writing, his or her consent before the issue of the prospectus, and that it was issued without his or her authority or consent; or

(b) that the prospectus was issued without his or her knowledge or consent and that, on becoming aware of its issue, he or she forthwith gave reasonable public notice that it was issued without his or her knowledge or consent; or

(c) that after the issue of the prospectus and before the acquisition of securities thereunder by the person referred to in *section 1349*, he or she, on becoming aware of any untrue statement therein or omission of material information required by EU prospectus law to be contained therein, withdrew, in writing, his or her consent thereto and gave reasonable public notice of the withdrawal and of the reason therefor; or

(d) that—

(i) as regards—

(I) every untrue statement not purporting to be made on the authority of an expert or of a public official document or statement;

(II) the omission from the prospectus of any information required by EU prospectus law to be contained therein;

he or she had reasonable grounds to believe, and did up to the time of the issue of the securities believe, that the statement was true or that the matter whose omission caused loss was properly omitted; and

(ii) as regards every untrue statement purporting to be a statement by an expert or contained in what purports to be a copy of or extract from a report or valuation of an expert, it fairly represented the statement, or was a correct and fair copy of or extract from the report or valuation, and he or she had reasonable grounds to believe and did up to the time of the issue of the prospectus believe that the person making the statement was competent to make it and, where required by *section 1353*, that that person had given his or her consent to the inclusion of the statement in the prospectus and had not withdrawn, in writing, that consent before the publication of the prospectus or, to the defendant's knowledge, before issue of securities thereunder; and

(iii) as regards every untrue statement purporting to be a statement made by an official person or contained in what purports to be a copy of or extract from a public official document, it was a correct and fair representation of the statement or copy of or extract from the document.

(3) In *subsections (4)* and *(5)* "by reason of the relevant consent", in relation to an expert, means by reason of his or her having given the consent required of him or her by *section 1353* to the inclusion in the prospectus of the statement concerned.

(4) *Subsection (2)* shall not apply in the case of an expert, by reason of the relevant consent, in respect of an untrue statement purporting to be made by him or her as an expert.

(5) An expert who, apart from this subsection, would be liable under *section 1349*, by reason of the relevant consent, in respect of an untrue statement purporting to be made by him or her as an expert shall not be so liable if he or she proves—

(a) that having given his or her consent to the inclusion in the prospectus of the statement, he or she withdrew it in writing before publication of the prospectus; or

(b) that, after publication of the prospectus and before the acquisition of securities thereunder by the person referred to in *section 1349*, on becoming aware of the untrue statement, withdrew his or her consent in writing and gave reasonable public notice of the withdrawal and of the reason therefor; or

(c) that he or she was competent to make the statement and that he or she had reasonable grounds to believe and did up to the time of such acquisition of the securities believe that the statement was true.

1351 Restriction of liability where non-equity securities solely involved

Where a prospectus is issued solely in respect of non-equity securities—

(a) only—

(i) the offeror or the person who has sought the admission of the securities to which the prospectus relates to trading on a regulated market; and

(ii) subject to, and to the extent provided in, *paragraph (c)*, the guarantor (if any);

and no other person referred to in *section 1349* shall be liable under that section in the circumstances in which that section applies unless—

(I) the prospectus expressly provides otherwise; or

(II) that other such person is convicted on indictment of an offence created by Irish prospectus law or an offence under *section 1357* in respect of the issue of that prospectus;

(b) neither *section 223(1)* nor *226(1)* shall apply to the directors or secretary of the issuer to the extent that such application would thereby impose a liability under *section 1349* on such directors or secretary; and

(c) no liability shall attach under *section 1349* to a guarantor of such securities save in respect of statements included in, or information omitted from, the prospectus that relate to the guarantor or the guarantee given by the guarantor.

1352 Indemnification of certain persons

(1) This section applies where—

(a) a prospectus contains the name of a person as a director of the issuer, or as having agreed to become a director thereof, and the person has not consented to become a director, or has withdrawn, in writing, his or her consent before the issue of the prospectus, and has not authorised or consented to the issue thereof; or

(b) the consent of an expert is required by *section 1353* to the inclusion in a prospectus of a statement purporting to be made by the expert and he or she either has not given that consent or has withdrawn, in writing, that consent before the issue of the prospectus.

(2) The directors of the issuer, except any without whose knowledge or consent the prospectus was issued, and any other person who authorised the issue thereof shall be liable to indemnify the person named as mentioned in *subsection (1)* or, as the case may be, whose consent was required as so mentioned against each of the following:

(a) all damages, costs and expenses to which the person may be made liable by reason of the person's name having been inserted in the prospectus or of the inclusion therein of a statement purporting to be made by the person as an expert, as the case may be;

(b) all costs and expenses in defending himself or herself against any action or legal proceeding brought against him or her in respect thereof.

1353 Expert's consent to issue of prospectus containing statement by him or her

(1) The prohibition in *subsection (2)* only applies in relation to a prospectus if EU prospectus law requires the inclusion in the prospectus of a statement of the kind referred to in *paragraph (b)* of that subsection.

(2) A prospectus including a statement that is attributed to an expert shall not be issued unless—

(a) the expert has given and has not, before publication of the prospectus, withdrawn, in writing, his or her consent to the inclusion in the prospectus of the statement in the form and context in which it is included, and

(b) a statement that the expert has given and has not withdrawn, in writing, that consent appears in the prospectus.

(3) If any prospectus is issued in contravention of this section, the issuer and every person who is knowingly a party to the issue thereof shall be guilty of a category 3 offence.

1354 Regulations (*Chapter 1*)

(1) The Minister may make regulations for the purposes of—

(a) giving effect to the 2003 Prospectus Directive; and

(b) supplementing and making consequential provision in respect of the Prospectus Regulation.

(2) Regulations under this section may contain such incidental, supplementary and consequential provisions as appear to the Minister to be necessary or expedient for the purposes of those regulations, including—

(a) provisions creating offences (but the regulations may only provide penalties in respect of a summary conviction for any such offence); and

(b) provisions revoking instruments made under other enactments.

(3) This section is without prejudice to section 3 of the European Communities Act 1972.

1355 Saver for existing Prospectus Regulations

(1) Regulations made under section 46 of the Investment Funds, Companies and Miscellaneous Provisions Act 2005 and in force immediately before the commencement of this section shall continue in force as if they were regulations made under *section 1354* and may be amended or revoked accordingly.

(2) Without prejudice to *Schedule 6* or to the generality of section 26(2)(f) of the Interpretation Act 2005, the reference in Regulation 107(4) of the Prospectus (Directive 2003/71/EC) Regulations 2005 (S.I. No. 324 of 2005) to section 47 of the Investment Funds, Companies and Miscellaneous Provisions Act 2005 shall, after the commencement of this section, be read as a reference to *section 1356*.

(3) The adaptation of reference effected by *subsection (2)* does not affect the operation of section 27 of the Interpretation Act 2005 as it concerns a prosecution initiated before or after the repeal by this Act of section 47 of the Investment Funds, Companies and Miscellaneous Provisions Act 2005 in respect of an offence referred to in that section 47 committed before that repeal.

1356 Penalties on conviction on indictment and defences in respect of certain offences

(1) A person who is guilty of an offence created by Irish prospectus law (being an offence expressed by that law to be an offence to which this section applies) shall, without prejudice to any penalties provided by that law in respect of a summary conviction for the offence, be liable, on conviction on indictment, to a fine not exceeding €1,000,000 or imprisonment for a term not exceeding 5 years or both.

(2) In any proceedings against a person in respect of an offence created by Irish prospectus law, it shall be a defence to prove—

(a) as regards any matter not disclosed in the prospectus concerned, that the person did not know it; or

(b) the contravention arose from an honest mistake of fact on the person's part; or

(c) the contravention was in respect of matters which, having regard to the circumstances of the case, was immaterial or as respects which, having regard to those circumstances, the person ought otherwise reasonably to be excused.

1357 Untrue statements and omissions in prospectus: criminal liability

(1) Where a prospectus is issued and—

(a) includes any untrue statement; or

(b) omits any information required by EU prospectus law to be contained in it;

any person who authorised the issue of the prospectus (not being the competent authority designated under Irish prospectus law) shall be guilty of a category 2 offence unless he or she proves—

(i) as regards an untrue statement, either that the statement was, having regard to the circumstances of the case, immaterial or that he or she honestly believed and did, up to the time of the issue of the prospectus, believe that the statement was true; or

(ii) as regards any information omitted, either that the omission was, having regard to the circumstances of the case, immaterial or that he or she did not know it; or

(iii) that the making of the statement or omission was otherwise such as, having regard to the circumstances of the case, ought reasonably to be excused.

(2) Without prejudice to the generality of *section 865(1)*, summary proceedings in relation to an offence under this section may be brought and prosecuted by the competent authority designated under Irish prospectus law.

(3) If at a trial for an offence under this section or an offence created by Irish prospectus law, the judge or jury has to consider whether the defendant honestly believed a particular thing or was honestly mistaken in relation to a particular thing, the presence or absence of reasonable grounds for such a belief or for his or her having been so mistaken is a matter to which the judge or jury is to have regard, in conjunction with any other relevant matters, in considering whether the defendant so believed or was so mistaken.

1358 Requirements about minimum subscriptions, matters to be stated in offer documentation in that regard, etc.

(1) No allotment shall be made of any share capital of a PLC offered for subscription unless—

(a) that capital is subscribed for in full, or

(b) the offer states that, even if the capital is not subscribed for in full, the amount of that capital subscribed for may be allotted in any event or in the event of the conditions specified in the offer being satisfied,

and, where conditions are so specified, no allotment of the capital shall be made by virtue of *paragraph (b)* unless those conditions are satisfied.

(2) Without prejudice to the generality of *subsection (1)*, where a prospectus states—

(a) the minimum amount which, in the opinion of the directors, must be raised from an issue of shares; and

(b) that no allotment shall be made of any of those shares unless that minimum amount has been subscribed and the sum payable on application for the amount so stated has been paid up;

then no such allotment shall be made unless that minimum amount has been subscribed and the foregoing sum so payable has been paid up.

(3) The amount stated in the prospectus as mentioned in *subsection (2)* shall be reckoned exclusively of any amount payable otherwise than in cash.

(4) Any condition requiring or binding any applicant for shares to waive compliance with any requirement of *subsections (1)* to *(3)* or *section 1359* as it applies to those subsections shall be void.

(5) *Subsections (2)* and *(3)* and, so far as it relates to those subsections, *subsection (4)* shall not apply to any allotment of shares subsequent to the first allotment of shares offered to the public for subscription.

1359 Supplemental provisions in relation to *section 1358*

(1) *Subsection (2)* applies where either—

(a) shares have been allotted in contravention of *section 1358(1)*; or

(b) the conditions referred to in *section 1358(2)* have not been satisfied on the expiration of 40 days after the date of first issue of the prospectus concerned.

(2) Where this subsection applies—

(a) all money received from applicants for shares shall be repaid forthwith after—

(i) in a case falling within *subsection (1)(a)*, the contravention referred to in that provision; or

(ii) in a case falling within *subsection (1)(b)*, the expiration of the period of 40 days referred to in that provision;

to the applicants without interest;

(b) if any such money is not so repaid after that contravention or, in a case falling within *subsection (1)(b)*, the expiration of 48 days after the date of first issue of the prospectus concerned, the directors of the PLC shall, subject to *subsection (3)*, be jointly and severally liable to repay that money with interest at the appropriate rate from that contravention or, as the case may be, the expiration of the 48th day.

(3) A director shall not be liable as mentioned in *subsection (2)(b)* if he or she proves that the default in the repayment of the money was not due to any misconduct or negligence on his or her part.

(4) *Section 1358(1)* shall apply in the case of shares offered as wholly or partly payable otherwise than in cash as it applies in the case of shares offered for subscription and—

(a) in *section 1358(1)* the word "subscribed" shall be read accordingly; and

(b) *section 1358(4)* and *subsections (1)* to *(3)* of this section shall accordingly apply in the first-mentioned case as they apply in the second-mentioned case, but with the following modifications.

(5) Those modifications are that references in *subsections (2)* and *(3)* to the repayment of money received from applicants for shares shall be read as including references to the return of any other consideration so received (including, if the case so requires, the release of the applicant from any undertaking) or, if it is not reasonably practicable to return the consideration, the payment of money equal to the value of the consideration at the time it was so received, and references to interest shall have effect accordingly.

1360 Further supplemental provisions in relation to *section 1358*: effect of irregular allotment

(1) An allotment made by a PLC to an applicant in contravention of *section 1358(1)* or *(2)* shall be voidable at the instance of the applicant within 30 days after the date of the allotment and not later, and shall be so voidable notwithstanding that the PLC is in the course of being wound up.

(2) Where an allotment is avoided under this section, the PLC shall, within 30 days after the date of avoidance, deliver to the Registrar a notice to that effect and *subsection (10)* of *section 1021* shall apply in relation to this subsection as it applies in relation to *subsection (9)* of that section.

(3) If any director of a PLC knowingly contravenes, or permits or authorises the contravention of, any of the provisions of *section 1358* with respect to allotment, he or she shall be liable to compensate the PLC and the allottee, respectively, for any loss, damage, costs or expenses which the PLC or allottee has sustained or incurred by reason of the contravention.

(4) No proceedings to recover any such loss, damage, costs or expenses shall be commenced after the expiration of 2 years after the date of the delivery to the Registrar of the return of allotments in question.

1361 Local offers

(1) An offering document prepared for a local offer shall contain the following statements in print in clearly legible type:

(a) on the front page or otherwise in a prominent position:

"This document,

— has not been prepared in accordance with Directive 2003/71/EC on prospectuses or any measures made under that Directive or the laws of Ireland or of any EU Member State or EEA treaty adherent state that implement that Directive or those measures,

— has not been reviewed, prior to its being issued, by any regulatory authority in Ireland or in any other EU Member State or EEA treaty adherent state,

and therefore may not contain all the information required where a document is prepared pursuant to that Directive or those laws.";

(b) elsewhere in the offering document:

(i) where the offering document contains information on past performance:

"*Past performance may not be a reliable guide to future performance.*";

(ii) where the offering document contains information on simulated performance:

"*Simulated performance may not be a reliable guide to future performance.*";

(iii) "*Investments may fall as well as rise in value.*";

(iv) where securities are described as being likely to yield income or as being suitable for an investor particularly seeking income from his or her investment, and where the income from the securities can fluctuate:

"*Income may fluctuate in accordance with market conditions and taxation arrangements.*";

(v) where the primary market for the securities or the currency of the underlying business is in a currency other than euro:

"*Changes in exchange rates may have an adverse effect on the value, price or income of the securities.*";

(vi) where the securities do not constitute a readily realisable investment:

"*It may be difficult for investors to sell or realise the securities and/or obtain reliable information about their value or the extent of the risks to which they are exposed.*".

(2) Any requirement of *subsection (1)* as to the inclusion of a particular statement in an offering document shall be regarded as satisfied if words substantially to the effect of that statement are instead included in that document.

(3) If an offeror fails to comply with *subsection (1)* the offeror shall be guilty of a category 3 offence.

(4) No offering document prepared for a local offer shall be issued by or on behalf of a PLC or in relation to an intended PLC unless, on or before the date of its publication, a copy of the offering document has been delivered to the Registrar.

1362 Exclusion of Investment Intermediaries Act 1995

(1) Any document issued in connection with an offer of securities by or on behalf of an issuer, offeror or person seeking admission of securities to trading on a regulated market shall not be regarded as constituting an investment advertisement within the meaning of section 23 of the Investment Intermediaries Act 1995.

(2) In *subsection (1)* "document" includes, in the case of a local offer, an offering document.

1363 Power to make certain rules and issue guidelines

(1) In this section "competent authority" means the competent authority designated under Irish prospectus law.

(2) The competent authority may make rules imposing or enabling the competent authority to impose requirements on persons on whom an obligation or obligations are imposed by Irish prospectus law, being requirements—

(a) to do or not to do specified things so as to secure that the provisions of Irish prospectus law are complied with and, in particular (without limiting the generality of this paragraph), to adopt specified procedures and use specified forms in the provision of information to the competent authority;

(b) to do or not to do specified things so as to secure the effective supervision by the competent authority of activities of the kind to which Irish prospectus law relates and, in particular (without limiting the generality of this paragraph), to make such reports or disclose such matters, at such times and in such manner, to the competent authority or other specified persons as are provided for by the rules or specified by the competent authority pursuant to the rules, being reports or a disclosure of matters that is or are required by virtue or in consequence of the operation of Irish prospectus law.

(3) Rules under this section may include rules providing for the manner in which or the matters by reference to which (or both) a determination is to be made of any issue as to whether a transaction or transactions is or are of a significant size for the purposes of the provisions of Irish prospectus law implementing Article 2(2)(a) of the 2003 Prospectus Directive.

(4) The reference in *subsection (2)* to an obligation imposed on a person by Irish prospectus law includes a reference to an obligation imposed on a person by virtue of the person's exercising a right or option provided under Irish prospectus law.

(5) Rules under this section may contain such consequential, incidental or supplemental provisions as the competent authority considers necessary or expedient.

(6) Rules under this section shall not contain any provision that is inconsistent with Irish prospectus law or require the provision of information to any person, the provision

of which is not reasonably related to the purposes for which the applicable provisions of the 2003 Prospectus Directive have been adopted.

(7) The provisions of Irish prospectus law that are expressed by that law to be made for the purpose of enabling the imposition of administrative sanctions shall apply in relation to a contravention of rules under this section as they apply in relation to a contravention of a provision of Irish prospectus law and, accordingly, a sanction that may be imposed pursuant to the first-mentioned provisions of Irish prospectus law in respect of a contravention of a provision of that law may, in accordance with that law, be imposed in respect of a contravention of rules under this section.

(8) The competent authority may issue guidelines in writing as to the steps that may be taken to comply with Irish prospectus law.

(9) Rules made under section 51 of the Investment Funds, Companies and Miscellaneous Provisions Act 2005 and in force immediately before the commencement of this section shall continue in force as if they were rules made under this section and may be amended or revoked accordingly.

1364 Certain agreements void

A condition—

(a) requiring or binding an applicant for securities to waive compliance with any requirement of—

(i) this Chapter; or

(ii) EU prospectus law;

or

(b) where EU prospectus law applies, purporting to affect him or her with notice of any contract, document or matter not specifically referred to in the prospectus concerned;

shall be void.

Chapter 2
Market abuse

[1365 Interpretation (*Chapter 2*)

(1) In this Chapter—

"Commission Implementing Directive" means Commission Implementing Directive (EU) 2015/2392 of 17 December 2015 on Regulation (EU) No. 596/2014 of the European Parliament and of the Council as regards reporting to competent authorities of actual or potential infringements of that Regulation;

"CSMA Directive" means Directive 2014/57/EU of the European Parliament and of the Council of 16 April 2014 on criminal sanctions for market abuse (market abuse directive);

"Irish market abuse law" means—

(a) regulations for the time being in force under section 3 of the European Communities Act 1972 made for the purpose of giving—

(i) full effect to provisions of the Market Abuse Regulation, or

(ii) effect to provisions of the Commission Implementing Directive or the CSMA Directive,

or both,

(b) any other enactment (other than, save where the context otherwise admits, this Chapter) enacted for the purpose of giving—

(i) full effect to provisions referred to in *paragraph (a)(i)* of this definition, or

(ii) effect to provisions referred to in *paragraph (a)(ii)* of this definition,

or both,

(c) any measures directly applicable in the State in consequence of the Market Abuse Regulation, and

(d) any supplementary and consequential measures adopted for the time being by the State in respect of the Market Abuse Regulation or either of the foregoing Directives;

"Market Abuse Regulation" means Regulation (EU) No. 596/2014 of the European Parliament and of the Council of 16 April 2014 on market abuse (market abuse regulation) and repealing Directive 2003/6/EC of the European Parliament and of the Council and Commission Directives 2003/124/EC, 2003/125/EC and 2004/72/EC;

"Minister" means the Minister for Finance.

(2) A word or expression that is used in this Chapter and is also used in the Market Abuse Regulation, the Commission Implementing Directive or the CSMA Directive shall have, in this Chapter, the same meaning as it has in that Regulation or either of those Directives, unless—

(a) the contrary intention appears, or

(b) Irish market abuse law provides otherwise.][a]

Amendments

a Section 1365 substituted by the Finance (Certain European Union and Intergovernmental Obligations) Act 2016, s 8(a), with effect from 26 October 2016.

1366 Regulations (*Chapter 2*)

[...][a]

Amendments

a Section 1366 repealed by the Finance (Certain European Union and Intergovernmental Obligations) Act 2016, s 8(b), with effect from 26 October 2016.

1367 Saver for existing Market Abuse Regulations

[...][a]

Amendments

a Section 1367 repealed by the Finance (Certain European Union and Intergovernmental Obligations) Act 2016, s 8(b), with effect from 26 October 2016.

1368 Conviction on indictment of offences under Irish market abuse law: penalties

[(1) In this section "offence created by Irish market abuse law" means an offence created by regulations falling within *paragraph (a)* of the definition of "Irish market abuse law" in *section 1365(1)*.

(2) A person who is guilty of an offence created by Irish market abuse law (being an offence expressed by that law to be an offence to which this section applies) shall—

(a) without prejudice to any penalties provided by that law in respect of a summary conviction for the offence, and

(b) notwithstanding section 3(3) of the European Communities Act 1972, be liable, on conviction on indictment, to a fine not exceeding €10,000,000 or imprisonment for a term not exceeding 10 years or both.][a]

Amendments

a Section 1368 substituted by the Finance (Certain European Union and Intergovernmental Obligations) Act 2016, s 8(c), with effect from 26 October 2016.

1369 Civil liability for certain breaches of Irish market abuse law

(1) If a person contravenes [Article 14 of the Market Abuse Regulation][a] the person shall be liable—

(a) to compensate any other party to the transaction concerned who was not in possession of the relevant information for any loss sustained by that party by reason of any difference between the price at which the financial instruments concerned were acquired or disposed of and the price at which they would have been likely to have been acquired or disposed of in such a transaction at the time when the first-mentioned transaction took place if that information had been generally available; and

(b) to account to the body corporate or other legal entity which issued the financial instruments concerned for any profit accruing to the first-mentioned person from acquiring or disposing of those instruments.

(2) If a person contravenes [Article 15 of the Market Abuse Regulation][b] the person shall be liable—

(a) to compensate any other party who acquired or disposed of financial instruments by reason of the contravention; and

(b) to account to the body corporate or other legal entity which issued the financial instruments concerned for any profit accruing to the first-mentioned person from acquiring or disposing of those instruments.

(3) *Subsections (1)* and *(2)* are without prejudice to any other cause of action which may lie against the person for contravening the provision concerned.

(4) An action under *subsection (1)* or *(2)* shall not be commenced more than 2 years after the date of the contravention concerned.

Amendments

a Words substituted by the Finance (Certain European Union and Intergovernmental Obligations) Act 2016, s 8(d)(i), with effect from 26 October 2016 (previously: "a provision of Irish market abuse law (being a provision the purpose of which is expressed by that law to be for the implementation of Article 2, 3 or 4 of the 2003 Market Abuse Directive)").

b Words substituted by the Finance (Certain European Union and Intergovernmental Obligations) Act 2016, s 8(d)(ii), with effect from 26 October 2016 (previously: "a provision of Irish market abuse law (being a provision the purpose of which is expressed by that law to be for the implementation of Article 5 of the 2003 Market Abuse Directive)").

1370 Supplementary rules, etc., by competent authority

(1) In this section "competent authority" means the competent authority designated under Irish market abuse law.

(2) The competent authority may make rules imposing or enabling the competent authority to impose requirements on persons on whom an obligation or obligations are imposed by Irish market abuse law, being requirements—

(a) to do or not to do specified things so as to secure that the provisions of Irish market abuse law are complied with and, in particular (without limiting the generality of this paragraph), to adopt specified procedures and use specified forms in the provision of information to the competent authority;

(b) to do or not to do specified things so as to secure the effective supervision by the competent authority of activities of the kind to which Irish market abuse law relates and, in particular (without limiting the generality of this paragraph), to make such reports or disclose such matters, at such times and in such manner, to the competent authority or other specified persons as are provided for by the rules or specified by the competent authority pursuant to the rules, being reports or a disclosure of matters that is or are required by virtue or in consequence of the operation of Irish market abuse law.

[...][a]

(4) Rules under this section may contain such consequential, incidental or supplemental provisions as the competent authority considers necessary or expedient.

(5) Rules under this section shall not contain any provision that is inconsistent with Irish market abuse law or require the provision of information to any person, the provision of which is not reasonably related to the purposes for which the applicable provisions of [the Market Abuse Regulation, the Commission Implementing Directive or the CSMA Directive][b] have been adopted.

(6) The provisions of Irish market abuse law that are expressed by that law to be made for the purpose of enabling the imposition of administrative sanctions shall apply in relation to a contravention of rules under this section as they apply in relation to a contravention of a provision of Irish market abuse law and accordingly, a sanction that may be imposed pursuant to the first-mentioned provisions of Irish market abuse law in respect of a contravention of a provision of that law may, in accordance with that law, be imposed in respect of a contravention of rules under this section.

(7) The competent authority may issue guidelines in writing as to the steps that may be taken to comply with Irish market abuse law.

[...][a]

Amendments

a Subsections (3) and (8) repealed by the Finance (Certain European Union and Intergovernmental Obligations) Act 2016, s 8(e)(ii), with effect from 26 October 2016.

b Words substituted by the Finance (Certain European Union and Intergovernmental Obligations) Act 2016, s 8(e)(i), with effect from 26 October 2016 (previously: "the Market Abuse Directive or the supplemental Directives").

1371 Application of Irish market abuse law to certain markets

(1) The Minister, after consultation with the competent authority designated under Irish market abuse law, may, by provisional order, provide that one or more provisions of Irish market abuse law that apply in relation to a market to which the [Market Abuse Regulation][a] applies shall, with such modifications if any, as are specified in the order, apply to a market specified in the order.

(2) The Minister may, by provisional order, amend or revoke a provisional order under this section (including a provisional order under this subsection).

(3) A provisional order under this section shall not have effect unless or until it is confirmed by an Act of the Oireachtas.

Amendments

a Words substituted by the Finance (Certain European Union and Intergovernmental Obligations) Act 2016, s 8(f), with effect from 26 October 2016 (previously: "2003 Market Abuse Directive").

Chapter 3
Requirement for corporate governance statement and application of certain provisions of Parts 5 and 6 where company is a traded company

1372 Definition (*Chapter 3*)

In this Chapter "traded company" means—

(a) a public limited company;

(b) a designated activity company;

(c) a company limited by guarantee; or

(d) a public unlimited company or a public unlimited company, that has no share capital;

that in the case of a public limited company has shares or debentures, or in the case of any of the other foregoing types of company has debentures, admitted to trading on a regulated market in an EEA state.

1373 Corporate governance statement in the case of a traded company

(1) Subject to *subsection (3)*, there shall be included in the directors' report referred to in *section 325* of a traded company a statement (which shall be known and is in this section referred to as a "corporate governance statement") in respect of the financial year concerned.

(2) The corporate governance statement shall be included as a specific section of the directors' report, and shall include, at least, all of the following information:

(a) a reference to—

(i) the corporate governance code—

(I) to which the company is subject and where the relevant text is publicly available; or

(II) which the company has voluntarily decided to apply and where the relevant text is publicly available;

and

(ii) all relevant information concerning corporate governance practices applied in respect of the company which are additional to any statutory requirement, and where the information on such corporate governance practices is available for inspection by the public;

(b) where the company departs, in accordance with any statutory provision, from a corporate governance code referred to in *clause (I)* or *(II)* of *paragraph (a)(i)*—

(i) an explanation by the company as to which parts of the corporate governance code it departs from in accordance with the statutory provision and the extent to which it departs from such code; and

(ii) the reasons for such departure;

and where the company has decided not to apply any provisions of a corporate governance code referred to in *clause (I)* or *(II)* of *paragraph (a)(i)*, the company shall explain its reasons for doing so;

(c) a description of the main features of the internal control and risk management systems of the company in relation to the financial reporting process;

(d) the information required under Regulation 21(2)(c), (d), (f), (h) and (i) of the European Communities (Takeover Bids (Directive 2004/25/EC)) Regulations 2006 (S.I. No. 255 of 2006), where the company is subject to those Regulations;

(e) a description of the operation of the shareholder meeting, the key powers of the shareholder meeting, shareholders' rights and the exercise of such rights;

(f) the composition and operation of the board of directors and the committees of the board of directors with administrative, management and supervisory functions.

(3) The information required under *subsection (2)* may be set out in a separate report published in conjunction with the directors' report in accordance with *subsection (4)* or *(5)*, or provided by a reference in the directors' report to where the separate report is publicly available on the website of the company, and where a separate report is provided, the corporate governance statement may contain a reference to the annual report where the information referred to in *subsection (2)(d)* is provided.

(4) Where a company prepares a corporate governance statement in the form of a separate report, such report shall be attached to every balance sheet, referred to in *section 341*, laid before the annual general meeting of the company and shall be signed on behalf of the directors by 2 of the directors of the company.

(5) Where a company prepares a corporate governance statement in the form of a separate report, a copy of such report shall—

(a) be published on the website of the company, and a statement that a copy of the report has been so published, together with the address of the website of the company, shall be included in the report of the directors of the company; or

(b) be annexed to the annual return of the company.

(6) The reference in *subsection (5)(b)* to a copy of the report is a reference to a copy that satisfies the following conditions:

(a) it is a true copy of the original save for the difference that the signature or signatures on the original, and any date or dates thereon, shall appear in typeset form on the copy; and

(b) it is accompanied by a certificate of a director and the secretary of the company, that bears the signature of the director and the secretary in electronic or written form, stating that the copy is a true copy of the original (and the foregoing statement need not be qualified on account of the difference permitted by *paragraph (a)* as to the form of a signature or of a date).

[(7) Where a company prepares a corporate governance statement, the statutory auditors of the company shall, in their report under *section 391* in respect of the company—

(a) provide an opinion, based on the work undertaken in the course of the audit, as to whether—

(i) the information given pursuant to *subsection (2)(c)* and *(d)* is consistent with the company's statutory financial statements in respect of the financial year concerned, and

(ii) such information has been prepared in accordance with this section,

(b) state whether, based on their knowledge and understanding of the company and its environment obtained in the course of the audit, they have identified material misstatements in the information given pursuant to *subsection (2)(c)* and *(d)* and, where they have so identified, give an indication of the nature of such misstatements, and

(c) state whether in their opinion, based on the work undertaken in the course of the audit, the information required pursuant to *subsection (2)(a)*, *(b)*, *(e)* and *(f)* is contained in the corporate governance statement.][a]

(8) *Subsection (2)(a)*, *(b)*, *(e)* and *(f)* shall not apply to a traded company which has only issued securities, other than shares, admitted to trading on a regulated market, unless such company has issued shares which are traded in a multilateral trading facility.

(9) In *subsection (8)* "multilateral trading facility" has the meaning assigned to it by Article 4(1), point (15) of Directive 2004/39/EC of the European Parliament and of the Council of 21 April 2004.

Amendments

a Subsection (7) substituted by European Union (Traded Companies – Corporate Governance Statements) Regulations 2015, reg 4, with effect from 2 October 2015, and again substituted by C(A)A 2017, s 82.

1374 Application of *section 225* to a traded company

Section 225 shall apply to a traded company as if, in *subsection (1)*:

(a) the following subparagraph were substituted for *subparagraph (ii)* of *paragraph (a)* of the definition of "relevant obligations":

"(ii) a serious Market Abuse offence, a serious Prospectus offence or a serious Transparency offence;";

and

(b) the following definition were inserted after the definition of "serious Prospectus offence":

" 'serious Transparency offence' means an offence referred to in *section 1382*;".

1375 Application of *sections 279* and *280* to a traded company excluded

(1) There is excluded from the definition of "relevant holding company" in *section 279(1)* a holding company that is a traded company.

(2) No category of holding company that is a traded company may be the subject of regulations under *section 280*.

1376 Application of *sections 290(7)(b)*, *293* and *362* to a traded company

(1) *Section 290(7)* shall apply to a traded company as if the following paragraph were substituted for *paragraph (b)*:

"(b) the company ceases to be a company with securities admitted to trading on a regulated market in an EEA state; or".

(2) In a case where a traded company has, at the end of its financial year, securities of it admitted to trading on a regulated market in an EEA state *section 293* shall apply to it as if—

(a) the following subsection were substituted for *subsection (3)*:

"(3) A company that is required to prepare group financial statements shall prepare the statements in accordance with international financial reporting standards and *section 295*.";

(b) the following subsection were substituted for *subsection (4)*:

"(4) Group financial statements prepared in accordance with international financial reporting standards and *section 295* shall be known, and are in this Act referred to, as 'IFRS group financial statements'.";

and

(c) *subsections (5)* to *(8)* were omitted.

(3) [*Section 362*][a] shall apply to a designated activity company and a company limited by guarantee as if the cases specified in that section in which the audit exemption, as referred to in *section 358* or *359*, as the case may be, is not available to a company, or a holding company and its subsidiary undertakings, included a case in which the company or holding company, as appropriate, is a traded company.

Amendments

a Words substituted by C(A)A 2017, s 84 (previously: "Without prejudice to its adaptation by *sections 994(2)* and *1218(3)*, *section 362*").

1377 Certain exemptions from consolidation of financial statements not available to traded company

(1) In a case where the lower holding company referred to in *section 299* is a traded company the following paragraph shall be added at the end of *subsection (4)* of that section:

"(f) the lower holding company does not have any shares, debentures or other debt securities admitted to trading on a regulated market in an EEA state.".

(2) In a case where the lower holding company referred to in *section 300* is a traded company the following paragraph shall be added at the end of *subsection (4)* of that section:

"(g) the lower holding company does not have any shares, debentures or other debt securities admitted to trading on a regulated market in an EEA state.".

1378 DAC or CLG that is a traded company may not file abridged financial statements

[*Sections 352* to *356*][a] shall not apply to a designated activity company or a company limited by guarantee that is a traded company.

Amendments

a Words substituted by C(A)A 2017, s 88(d) (previously: "*Sections 350* to *356*").

Chapter 4
Transparency requirements regarding issuers of securities admitted to trading on certain markets

1379 Interpretation (*Chapter 4*)

(1) In this Chapter—

"Minister" means the Minister for Finance;

"Transparency (Regulated Markets) Directive" means Directive 2004/109/EC of the European Parliament and of the Council of 15 December 2004 on the harmonisation of transparency requirements in relation to information about issuers whose securities are admitted to trading on a regulated market and amending Directive 2001/34/EC, including the first-mentioned Directive as it stands amended for the time being;

"transparency (regulated markets) law" means—

(a) the measures adopted for the time being by the State to implement the Transparency (Regulated Markets) Directive (whether an Act of the Oireachtas, regulations under section 3 of the European Communities Act 1972, regulations under *section 1380* or any other enactment (other than, save where the context otherwise admits, this Chapter));

(b) any measures directly applicable in the State in consequence of the Transparency (Regulated Markets) Directive and, without prejudice to the generality of this paragraph, includes any Regulation or Decision made by the Commission pursuant to the procedure referred to in Article 27(2) of that Directive; and

(c) any supplementary and consequential measures adopted for the time being by the State in respect of any Regulation or Decision made by the Commission in consequence of the Transparency (Regulated Markets) Directive pursuant to the foregoing procedure;

"supplemental Directive" means any Directive made by the Commission in consequence of the Transparency (Regulated Markets) Directive pursuant to the procedure referred to in Article 27(2) of that Directive.

(2) A word or expression that is used in this Chapter and is also used in the Transparency (Regulated Markets) Directive shall have in this Chapter the same meaning as it has in that Directive.

1380 Power to make certain regulations (*Chapter 4*)

(1) The Minister may make regulations for the purposes of—

(a) giving effect to the Transparency (Regulated Markets) Directive or any supplemental Directive; and

(b) supplementing and making consequential provision in respect of any Regulation or Decision made by the Commission in consequence of the first-mentioned Directive in *paragraph (a)* pursuant to the procedure referred to in Article 27(2) of that Directive.

(2) Regulations under this section may contain such incidental, supplementary and consequential provisions as appear to the Minister to be necessary or expedient for the purposes of those regulations, including—

(a) provisions creating offences (but the regulations may only provide penalties in respect of a summary conviction for any such offence); and

(b) provisions creating civil liability in respect of contraventions of the regulations so as to enable any person suffering loss thereby to recover compensation for that loss.

(3) Civil liability shall not be created by regulations under *subsection (2)* in respect of a contravention of regulations under this section save in respect of such a contravention that involves either—

(a) an untrue or misleading statement; or

(b) the omission from a statement of any matter required to be included in it;

being, in either case, a statement—

(i) that is contained in a publication made in purported compliance with a provision of transparency (regulated markets) law specified in the regulations; and

(ii) in respect of which a person suffers a loss by reason of the person's acquiring or contracting to acquire securities (or an interest in them) in reliance on that publication at a time when, and in circumstances in which, it was reasonable for the person to rely on that publication, and the following condition is fulfilled in respect of that publication.

(4) That condition is that a person discharging responsibilities within the issuer of the securities referred to in *subsection (3)* in relation to that publication (being responsibilities of a kind specified in regulations under this section)—

(a) knew the statement concerned to be untrue or misleading or was reckless as to whether it was untrue or misleading; or

(b) knew the omission concerned to be dishonest concealment of a material fact.

(5) Regulations under this section may also make, for the purposes of those regulations, provision analogous to that which is made by *Chapter 5* of *Part 5* and *Chapter 4* of *Part 17.*

(6) This section is without prejudice to section 3 of the European Communities Act 1972.

1381 Saver for existing Transparency Regulations

(1) Regulations made under section 20 of the Investment Funds, Companies and Miscellaneous Provisions Act 2006 and in force immediately before the commencement of this section shall continue in force as if they were regulations made under *section 1380* and may be amended or revoked accordingly.

(2) Without prejudice to *Schedule 6* or to the generality of section 26(2)(f) of the Interpretation Act 2005, the reference in Regulation 76(6) of the Transparency (Directive 2004/109/EC) Regulations 2007 (S.I. No. 277 of 2007) to section 21 of the Investment Funds, Companies and Miscellaneous Provisions Act 2006 shall, after the commencement of this section, be read as a reference to *section 1382*.

(3) The adaptation of reference effected by *subsection (2)* does not affect the operation of section 27 of the Interpretation Act 2005 as it concerns a prosecution initiated before or after the repeal by this Act of section 21 of the Investment Funds, Companies and Miscellaneous Provisions Act 2006 in respect of an offence referred to in that section 21 committed before that repeal.

1382 Conviction on indictment of offences under transparency (regulated markets) law

A person who is guilty of an offence created by transparency (regulated markets) law (being an offence expressed by that law to be an offence to which this section applies) shall, without prejudice to any penalties provided by that law in respect of a summary conviction for the offence, be liable, on conviction on indictment, to a fine not exceeding €1,000,000 or imprisonment for a term not exceeding 5 years or both.

1383 Supplementary rules, etc., by competent authority

(1) In this section "competent authority" means the competent authority designated under transparency (regulated markets) law for the purposes of the provisions of the Transparency (Regulated Markets) Directive (other than Article 24(4)(h) of that Directive).

(2) The competent authority may make rules imposing or enabling the competent authority to impose requirements on persons on whom an obligation or obligations are imposed by transparency (regulated markets) law, being requirements—

(a) to do or not to do specified things so as to secure that the provisions of transparency (regulated markets) law are complied with and, in particular (without limiting the generality of this paragraph), to adopt specified procedures and use specified forms in the provision of information to the competent authority;

(b) to do or not to do specified things so as to secure the effective supervision by the competent authority, of activities of the kind to which transparency (regulated markets) law relates and, in particular (without limiting the generality of this paragraph), to make such reports or disclose such matters, at such times and in such manner, to the competent authority or other specified persons, as are provided for by the rules or specified by the competent authority pursuant to the rules, being reports or a disclosure of matters that is or are required by virtue or in consequence of the operation of transparency (regulated markets) law.

(3) Rules under this section may, in particular, include rules necessary for the performance by the competent authority of the functions under Article 24 of the Transparency (Regulated Markets) Directive, other than paragraph (4)(h) of that Article.

(4) Rules under this section may contain such consequential, incidental or supplemental provisions as the competent authority considers necessary or expedient.

(5) Rules under this section shall not contain any provision that is inconsistent with transparency (regulated markets) law or require the provision of information to any person the provision of which is not reasonably related to the purposes for which the applicable provisions of the Transparency (Regulated Markets) Directive have been adopted.

(6) The provisions of transparency (regulated markets) law that are expressed by that law to be made for the purpose of enabling the imposition of administrative sanctions shall apply in relation to a contravention of—

(a) rules under this section; and

(b) rules adopted by the Supervisory Authority under *section 906(3)* concerning the matters that relate to its functions under *section 905(2)(m)*, as they apply in relation to a contravention of a provision of transparency (regulated markets) law and, accordingly, a sanction that may be imposed pursuant to the first-mentioned provisions of transparency (regulated markets) law in respect of a contravention of a provision of that law may, in accordance with that law, be imposed in respect of a contravention of rules referred to in either of the foregoing paragraphs.

(7) The competent authority may issue guidelines in writing as to the steps that may be taken to comply with transparency (regulated markets) law.

(8) Rules made under section 22 of the Investment Funds, Companies and Miscellaneous Provisions Act 2006 and in force immediately before the commencement of this section shall continue in force as if they were rules made under this section and may be amended or revoked accordingly.

1384 Application of transparency (regulated markets) law to certain markets

(1) The Minister, after consultation with the competent authority referred to in *section 1383(1)*, may, by provisional order, provide that one or more provisions of transparency (regulated markets) law that apply in relation to a market to which the Transparency (Regulated Markets) Directive applies shall, with such modifications, if any, as are specified in the order, apply to a market specified in the order.

(2) A provisional order under this section shall not have effect unless or until it is confirmed by an Act of the Oireachtas.

[*Chapter 5*

Application of section 393 to a company to which Part 23 applies

1384A Application of section 393 to a company to which Part 23 applies

(1) *Section 393* shall apply to a company to which this Part applies, as if—

(a) in *subsection (1)*, the following were substituted for "there are reasonable grounds for believing that a category 1 or 2 offence may have been committed by the company or an officer or agent of it,":

"there are reasonable grounds for believing that a category 1 or 2 offence, a serious Market Abuse offence, a Prospectus offence or a serious Transparency offence may have been committed by the company or an officer or agent of it,", and

(b) the following subsection were inserted after subsection (6):

"(7) In this section—

'serious Market Abuse offence' means an offence referred to in section 1368;

'serious Prospectus offence' means an offence referred to in section 1356;

'serious Transparency offence' means an offence referred to in section 1382."][a]

Amendments

a Chapter 5 inserted by C(A)A 2017, s 83.

PART 24
INVESTMENT COMPANIES

Chapter 1
Preliminary and interpretation

1385 Interpretation (*Part 24*)

(1) In this Part—

"investment company" has the meaning given to it by *section 1386*;

"Minister" means the Minister for Finance;

"management company" means a company designated by an investment company to undertake the management of the investment company;

"property" means real or personal property of whatever kind (including securities);

"sub-fund" means a portfolio of assets and liabilities maintained by an investment company in accordance with its articles and which has been approved by the Central Bank as a separate sub-fund of the investment company;

"UCITS Regulations" means the European Communities (Undertakings for Collective Investment in Transferable Securities) Regulations 2011 (S.I. No. 352 of 2011);

"umbrella fund" means an investment company which has one or more sub-funds and which is authorised by the Central Bank pursuant to *section 1395*.

(2) For the purposes of the application by this Part of certain provisions of the UCITS Regulations to investment companies, those provisions shall be read as one with this Part.

1386 Definition of "investment company" and construction of references to nominal value of shares, etc.

(1) In this Part "investment company" means a company (not being a company to which the UCITS Regulations apply) that is—

(a) a public limited company, the sole object of which is stated in its memorandum to be the collective investment of its funds in property with the aim of spreading investment risk and giving members of the company the benefit of the results of the management of its funds; and

(b) the articles or memorandum of which provide—

(i) that the actual value of the paid up share capital of the company shall at all times be equal to the value of the assets of any kind of the company after the deduction of its liabilities; and

(ii) subject to *subsection (2)*, that the shares of the company shall, at the request of any of the holders thereof, be purchased by the company directly or indirectly out of the company's assets.

(2) To the extent as may be approved and subject to such conditions as may be applied by the Central Bank, a company that otherwise falls within *subsection (1)* shall be regarded as an investment company within the meaning of this Part notwithstanding

that the articles or memorandum of it do not provide for the matters referred to in *subsection (1)(b)(ii)*.

(3) For the purposes of *subsection (1)(b)(ii)*, action taken by an investment company to ensure that the stock exchange value of its shares does not deviate from its net asset value by more than a percentage specified in its articles (which deviation shall not be so specified as greater than 5 per cent) shall be regarded as the equivalent of purchase of its shares by the investment company.

(4) The memorandum or articles of an investment company shall be regarded as providing for the matters referred to in *paragraphs (a)* and *(b)* of *subsection (1)* notwithstanding the inclusion in the memorandum or articles with respect thereto of incidental or supplementary provisions.

(5) A reference in any provision of this Act to the nominal value of an issued or allotted share in, or of the issued or allotted share capital of, a company shall, in the case of an investment company, be read as a reference to the value of the consideration for which the share or share capital (as the case may be) has been issued or allotted.

1387 Application of *Parts 1* to *14* to investment companies

(1) The provisions of *Parts 1* to *14* apply to an investment company save to the extent that they are—

(a) disapplied to public limited companies by *section 1002*; or

(b) disapplied by *subsection (3)* or modified by another provision of this Part.

(2) For the purposes of that application, *section 10(1)* shall have effect as if it read:

> "(1) Unless expressly provided otherwise, a reference in *Parts 2* to *14* to a company is a reference to an investment company.".

(3) In addition to those of them disapplied, as mentioned in *subsection (1)(a)*, the provisions of *Parts 1* to *14* specified in the Table to this section shall not apply to an investment company.

(4) The specification in the foregoing Table of a provision (a "specified provision") of *Parts 1* to *14* also operates to disapply to an investment company any other provision of those Parts (notwithstanding that it is not specified in that Table) that makes consequential, incidental or supplemental provision on, or in relation to, the specified provision.

Table

Subject matter	Provision disapplied
Nominal value of shares	*Section 66(1)* and *(2)(a)*
Allotment of shares	*Section 69(3)* and *(6)* to *(10)*
Allotment of shares	*Section 70(1), (2), (3), (7), (8), (10)* and *(11)*
Payment of shares	*Section 71(2), (3)* and *(5)*
Financial assistance	*Section 82*
Variation of company capital	*Section 83(3), (4)* and *(5)*

Subject matter	**Provision disapplied**
Reduction of company capital	*Section 84*
Notice to Registrar of certain alterations in share capital	*Sections 92* and *93*
Restriction on company acquiring its own shares	*Sections 102* and *103*
Acquisition of own shares	*Sections 105* to *107* and *109* to *112*
Holding by subsidiary of shares in its holding company	*Sections 114* to *116*
Restrictions on distribution of profits and assets	*Sections 117* to *123*
Procedure for declarations, payments, etc. of dividends and other things	*Sections 124* and *125*
Bonus issues	*Section 126*
Access to documents during business hours	*Section 127*
Audit committees	*Section 167*
Inspection of registers, provision of copies of information in them, etc.	*Sections 215* to *217*
Directors' compliance statement and related statement	*Section 225*
Holding of own shares or shares in holding company	*Section 320(1)*
Directors' report: acquisition or disposal of own shares	*Section 328*
Signature of statutory auditor's report to appear on certain copies	*Section 337(4)* and *(5)(b)*
Annual return and documents annexed to it	*Chapter 13* of *Part 6*
Exclusions, exemptions and special arrangements with regard to public disclosure of financial information	*Chapter 14* of *Part 6*
Audit exemption	*Chapter 15* of *Part 6*
Special audit exemption for dormant companies	*Chapter 16* of *Part 6*
Company may be required to contribute to debts of related companies	*Section 599*

1388 Application of *Part 17* to investment companies

(1) The provisions of *Part 17* apply to an investment company save to the extent that they are disapplied by *subsection (3)* or *(4)*.

(2) For the purposes of that application, references in *Part 17* to a public limited company (however expressed) shall be read as references to a public limited company that is an investment company.

(3) The definitions of "authorised minimum" and "authorised share capital" in *section 1000(1)* shall not apply to an investment company.

(4) The provisions of *Part 17* specified in the Table to this section shall not apply to an investment company.

Table

Subject matter	Provision disapplied
Ministerial power in relation to a defined expression	*Section 1000(2)*
Way of forming a PLC and form of its constitution	*Section 1004(1)* to *(4)* and *sections 1005* to *1007*
Restriction on commencement of business by a PLC	*Section 1010*
Power to allot certain securities and notification of allotments	*Section 1021(3)*, *(4)* and *(8)*
Pre-emption rights	*Sections 1022* and *1023*
Expert's report on non-cash consideration (requirements in respect thereof and dispensations therefrom)	*Sections 1028* to *1035*
Treatment of shares held by or on behalf of a PLC	*Sections 1040* and *1041*
Application of certain provisions of *section 82(6)* in relation to PLCs	*Section 1043*
Interests in shares: disclosure of individual and group acquisitions	*Chapter 4* of *Part 17*
Acquisition of own shares and certain acquisitions by subsidiaries	*Chapter 5* of *Part 17*
Distribution by a PLC	*Chapter 6* of *Part 17*
Application of *section 167* to PLC that is not a public-interest entity under S.I. No. 220 of 2010	*Section 1097*
Additional rights of shareholders in certain PLCs (provisions implementing Shareholders' Rights Directive 2007/36/EC)	*Sections 1099* to *1110*
Obligation to convene extraordinary general meeting in event of serious loss of capital	*Section 1111*
Reorganisations	*Chapter 13* of *Part 17*

1389 Adaptation of certain provisions of UCITS Regulations

Regulations 17(11), 40(2), 42(4)(d), 104(2), 125 to 127, 129 to 131, 134(1) to 134(9), 135(1) and 135(2) of the UCITS Regulations apply to an investment company as they apply to the bodies to which those Regulations relate subject to the following modifications—

(a) a reference in those Regulations to a term or expression specified in the second column of the Table to this section at any reference number shall be read, where the context admits, as a reference to the term or expression specified in the third column of that Table at that reference number; and

(b) references to cognate terms or expressions in those Regulations shall be read accordingly.

Table

Ref. No. (1)	**Term or expression referred to in UCITS Regulations (2)**	**Construction of term or expression for purposes of this section (3)**
1	"repurchase"	"purchase"
2	"these Regulations"	"*Part 24* of the *Companies Act 2014*"
3	"UCITS"	"investment company"
4	"unit"	"share"
5	"unit-holder"	"shareholder"

Chapter 2
Incorporation and registration

1390 Way of forming an investment company

(1) An investment company may be formed for any lawful purpose by any person or persons subscribing to a constitution and complying with the relevant provisions of—

(a) *Chapter 2* of *Part 2*, as applied by this Part; and

(b) this Part;

in relation to registration of an investment company.

(2) Without prejudice to the means by which an investment company may be formed under the relevant provisions referred to in *subsection (1)*, a company may be registered as an investment company by means of—

(a) the re-registration, or registration, as an investment company of a body corporate pursuant to *Part 20* or *22*;

(b) the merger of 2 or more bodies corporate pursuant to *Chapter 16* of *Part 17*;

(c) the division of a body corporate pursuant to *Chapter 17* of *Part 17*;

(d) the continuance, as an investment company, pursuant to *Chapter 9*, of a legal entity de-registering as a company in another jurisdiction; or

(e) the merger operation provided for by the European Communities (Cross-Border Mergers) Regulations 2008 (S.I. No. 157 of 2008).

(3) The liability of a member of an investment company at any time shall be limited to the amount, if any, unpaid on the shares registered in the member's name at that time.

(4) *Subsection (3)* is without prejudice to any other liability to which a member may be subject as provided by this Act.

1391 Investment company to carry on activity in the State

An investment company shall not be formed and registered unless it appears to the Registrar that the company, when registered, will carry on an activity in the State, being an activity that is mentioned in its memorandum.

1392 The form of an investment company's constitution

(1) Subject to *subsection (3)*, the constitution of an investment company shall be in the form of a memorandum of association and articles of association which together are referred to in this Part as a "constitution".

(2) The memorandum of association of an investment company shall state—

(a) its name;

(b) that it is a public limited company registered under this Part;

(c) its object as specified in *section 1386(1)(a)*;

(d) that the liability of its members is limited; and

(e) in respect of its share capital—

(i) that the share capital of the company shall be equal to the value for the time being of the issued share capital of the company;

(ii) the division of that share capital into a specified number of shares without assigning any nominal value thereto; and

(iii) that the issued share capital of the company for the time being shall not be less than a minimum amount nor more than a maximum amount specified in the memorandum.

(3) The constitution of an investment company shall—

(a) in addition to the matters specified in *subsection (2)*, state the number of shares (which shall not be less than one) taken by each subscriber to the constitution;

(b) be in accordance with the form set out in *Schedule 16* or as near thereto as circumstances permit;

(c) be printed in an entire format, that is to say the memorandum and articles shall be contained in the one document, being a document either in legible form or (as long as it is capable of being reproduced in legible form) in non-legible form; and

(d) either—

(i) be signed by each subscriber in the presence of at least one witness who shall attest the signature; or

(ii) be authenticated in the manner referred to in *section 888*.

(4) Where, subsequent to the registration of the constitution, an amendment of the memorandum of association is made affecting the matter of share capital, or another matter, referred to in *subsection (2)*, that subsection shall be read as requiring the memorandum to state the matter as it stands in consequence of that amendment.

1393 Supplemental provisions in relation to constitution and continuance in force of existing memorandum and articles

(1) This section—

(a) contains provisions as to the articles of an investment company;

(b) provides that, in certain circumstances, a default position shall obtain in relation to the articles of an investment company; and

(c) continues in force the memorandum and articles of an investment company to which Part XIII of the Act of 1990 applies.

(2) In this section—

"mandatory provision" means a provision of any of *Parts 1* to *14* or *Part 17* (as applied by this Part) or of this Part that is not an optional provision;

"optional provision" means a provision of any of *Parts 1* to *14* or *Part 17* (as applied by this Part) or of this Part that—

(a) contains a statement to the effect, or is governed by provision elsewhere to the effect, that the provision applies save to the extent that the constitution provides otherwise or unless the constitution states otherwise; or

(b) is otherwise of such import.

(3) The articles of an investment company—

(a) shall contain such regulations in relation to the investment company with respect to such aspects of the activity of collective investment referred to in *section 1386(1)(a)*, or matters related thereto, as are deemed appropriate; and

(b) may contain other regulations in relation to the investment company.

(4) So far as the articles of an investment company do not exclude or modify an optional provision, that optional provision shall apply in relation to the investment company.

(5) The memorandum and articles of an investment company to which Part XIII of the Act of 1990 applies and registered before the commencement of this section shall, save to the extent that they are inconsistent with a mandatory provision, continue in force but may be altered or added to under and in accordance with the conditions under which memorandums or articles, whenever registered, are permitted by this Act to be altered or added to.

(6) References in the provisions of a memorandum or articles so continued in force to any provision of the prior Companies Acts shall be read as references to the corresponding provision of this Act.

(7) To the extent that an investment company to which Part XIII of the Act of 1990 applies was, immediately before the commencement of this section, governed by the regulations of Part I of Table A in the First Schedule to the Act of 1963, it shall, after that commencement, continue to be governed by those regulations but—

(a) this is save to the extent that those regulations are inconsistent with a mandatory provision;

(b) those regulations may be altered or added to under and in accordance with the conditions under which articles, whenever registered, are permitted by this Act to be altered or added to; and

(c) references in the regulations to any provision of the prior Companies Acts shall be read as references to the corresponding provision of this Act.

1394 Status of existing investment company

(1) In this section "existing investment company" means an investment company to which Part XIII of the Act of 1990 applies and which—

(a) was incorporated under the prior Companies Acts; and

(b) is in existence immediately before the commencement of this section.

(2) An existing investment company shall, on and from the commencement of this section, continue in existence and be deemed to be an investment company to which this Part applies.

1395 Authorisation by Central Bank

(1) An investment company shall not carry on business in the State unless it has been authorised to do so by the Central Bank on the basis of criteria approved by the Minister.

(2) A person shall not carry on business on behalf of an investment company, in so far as relates to the purchase or sale of the shares of the investment company, unless the investment company has been authorised in the manner referred to in *subsection (1)*.

(3) The Central Bank shall not authorise an investment company to carry on business in the State unless the company has paid up share capital which, in the opinion of the Bank, will be sufficient to enable it to conduct its business effectively and meet its liabilities.

(4) An application by an investment company for the authorisation referred to in *subsection (1)* shall be made in writing to the Central Bank and contain such information as the Bank may specify for the purpose of determining the application (including such additional information as the Bank may specify in the course of determining the application).

(5) Where the Central Bank proposes to grant an authorisation to an investment company under this section and the Bank is satisfied that the company will raise capital by providing facilities for the direct or indirect participation by the public in the profits and income of the company, the Bank shall, in granting the authorisation, designate the company as a specially designated investment company which may raise capital in that manner, and "specially designated company" in this section and *section 1396* shall be read accordingly.

(6) An existing investment company (within the meaning of *section 1394*) that, immediately before the commencement of this section, is a designated company within the meaning of section 256(5) of the Act of 1990, shall be regarded as a specially designated company for the purposes of this section and *section 1396*; a reference in any other enactment to a designated company (within the meaning of that section 256(5)) shall, on and from the commencement of this section, be read as a reference to a specially designated company.

(7) In the event that a specially designated company does not provide facilities for the direct or indirect participation by the public in the profits and income of the company within a period, not greater than 6 months, which shall be specified in the authorisation under this section, the company shall, on the expiry of the period so specified, be deemed to have ceased to be a specially designated company; for the purposes of the application of this subsection to a company referred to in *subsection (6)* the foregoing reference to an authorisation under this subsection shall be read as a reference to an authorisation under section 256 of the Act of 1990 and, accordingly, a company referred to in *subsection (6)* is subject to the same cessation of its status, as is provided by this subsection for investment companies otherwise, where—

(a) the period specified in the authorisation under that section 256 expires after the commencement of this section; and

(b) the company has not provided facilities for the direct or indirect participation by the public in the profits and income of the company within that period.

(8) An investment company which is not a specially designated company shall not raise capital by providing facilities for the direct or indirect participation by the public in the profits and income of the company.

(9) If a company contravenes *subsection (1)* or *(8)*, the company and any officer of it who is in default shall be guilty of a category 2 offence.

(10) If a person contravenes *subsection (2)*, the person shall be guilty of a category 2 offence.

1396 Powers of Central Bank

(1) Notwithstanding any other powers which may be available to the Central Bank under any other enactment, the Central Bank may impose such conditions for the granting of an authorisation to a company under *section 1395* as it considers appropriate and prudent for the purposes of the orderly and proper regulation of the business of investment companies.

(2) Conditions imposed under *subsection (1)* may be imposed generally, or by reference to particular classes of company or business (including, but not limited to, whether or not an investment company is a specially designated company), or by reference to any other matter the Central Bank considers appropriate and prudent for the purposes of the orderly and proper regulation of the business of investment companies.

(3) The power to impose conditions referred to in *subsection (1)* includes a power to impose such further conditions from time to time as the Central Bank considers appropriate and prudent for the purposes of the orderly and proper regulation of the business of investment companies.

(4) As appropriate—

(a) conditions imposed by the Central Bank on an investment company may (without prejudice to the generality of *subsections (1)* to *(3)*) make provision for;

(b) as respects the person or other body referred to in *paragraph (iii)* or *(v)*, there is otherwise conferred on the Bank power to make provision for;

the following:

(i) the prudential requirements of the investment policies of the company;

(ii) without prejudice to *Chapter 1* of *Part 23* and regulations thereunder (so far as they are applicable to securities issued by companies of the closed-end type), prospectuses and other information disseminated by the company;

(iii) the vesting of the assets or specified assets of the company in a person nominated by the Central Bank with such of the powers or duties of a trustee with regard to the company as are specified by the Bank;

(iv) such other supervisory and reporting requirements and conditions relating to its business as the Central Bank considers appropriate and prudent to impose on the company from time to time for the purposes referred to in the foregoing subsections;

(v) supervisory and reporting requirements and conditions relating to the business of a management company as the Central Bank considers appropriate or prudent to impose on the management company from time to time.

(5) A company shall comply with any conditions relating to its authorisation or business imposed by the Central Bank.

(6) A person or other body referred to in *subsection (4)(iii)* or *(v)* in relation to whom requirements or conditions are imposed by the Central Bank in accordance with *subsection (4)* shall comply with such requirements or conditions.

(7) If a company fails to comply with a condition referred to in *subsection (5)*, the company and any officer of it who is in default shall be guilty of a category 2 offence.

(8) If a person or other body fails to comply with a requirement or condition referred to in *subsection (6)*, the person or body, and (in the case of a body) any officer of it who is in default, shall be guilty of a category 2 offence.

1397 Default of investment company or failure in performance of its investments

(1) An authorisation by the Central Bank under *section 1395* of an investment company shall not constitute a warranty by the Bank as to the creditworthiness or financial standing of that company.

(2) The Central Bank shall not be liable by virtue of that authorisation or by reason of its performance of the functions conferred on it by this Part in relation to investment companies for any default of the investment company unless the Bank acted in bad faith in performing such functions.

Chapter 3
Share capital

1398 Power of company to purchase own shares

(1) Subject to *subsection (2)*, the purchase by an investment company of its own shares shall be on such terms and in such manner as may be provided by its articles.

(2) An investment company shall not purchase its own shares, for the purposes referred to in *section 1386(1)(b)(ii)*, unless they are fully paid, but nothing in this subsection shall prevent a purchase being made in accordance with *section 1399(2)*.

(3) For the avoidance of doubt, nothing in this Act shall require an investment company to create any reserve account.

1399 Treatment of purchased shares

(1) Shares of an investment company which have been purchased by the company shall be cancelled and the amount of the company's issued share capital shall be reduced by the amount of the consideration paid by the company for the purchase of the shares.

(2) Notwithstanding *subsection (1)*, an umbrella fund may, for the account of any of its sub-funds, and in accordance with conditions imposed by the Central Bank pursuant to *section 1396*, acquire by subscription or transfer for consideration, shares of any class or classes, howsoever described, representing other sub-funds of the same umbrella fund provided that the acquisition is for a purpose otherwise than that provided for in *section 1386(1)(b)(ii)*.

Chapter 4
Financial statements

1400 Statutory financial statements

(1) To the extent that the use of any alternative body of accounting standards does not contravene any provision of *Part 6* (as that Part applies to investment companies)—

(a) a true and fair view of the assets and liabilities, financial position and profit or loss of an investment company may be given by the use by the investment company of those standards in the preparation of its Companies Act entity financial statements, and

(b) a true and fair view of the assets and liabilities, financial position and profit or loss of an investment company and its subsidiary undertakings as a whole may be given by the use by the investment company of those standards in the preparation of its Companies Act group financial statements.

(2) In this section—

"alternative body of accounting standards" means standards that accounts of companies or undertakings must comply with that are laid down by such body or bodies having authority to lay down standards of that kind in—

(a) United States of America;

(b) Canada;

(c) Japan; or

(d) any other prescribed state or territory;

as may be prescribed;

"relevant financial statements" means Companies Act entity financial statements or Companies Act group financial statements.

(3) Before making regulations for the purposes of *subsection (2)*, the Minister—

(a) shall consult with the Central Bank and the Supervisory Authority, and

(b) may consult with any other persons whom the Minister considers should be consulted.

(4) Regulations made under section 3(3) of the Act of 1990 prescribing, for the purposes of the definition of "alternative body of accounting standards" in section 260A(4) of the Act of 1990, bodies having authority to lay down standards of the kind referred to in that definition, and which regulations are in force immediately before the commencement of this section, shall continue in force as if they were regulations made under *section 12* for the purposes of *subsection (2)* and may be amended or revoked accordingly.

[1400A Modification of definition of "ineligible entities" in case of investment companies

The definition of 'ineligible entities' in *section 275(1)* shall apply to an investment company as if—

(a) in *paragraph (c)*, 'undertakings,' were substituted for 'undertakings, or',

(b) in *paragraph (d)(ii)*, 'shall be read accordingly, or' were substituted for 'shall be read accordingly;', and

(c) the following paragraph were inserted after paragraph (d):

'(e) are investment companies;'.][a]

Amendments

a Section 1400A inserted by C(A)A 2017, s 85.

1401 Requirement for corporate governance statement and modification of certain provisions of *Parts 5* and *6* as they apply to investment companies

Chapter 3 of *Part 23* has effect in relation to, amongst other companies, an investment company that has shares or debentures admitted to trading on a regulated market in an EEA state.

[1401A Filing of financial statements by investment company[a]

(1) An investment company shall, once in every year after the expiration of its first financial year, deliver to the Registrar, in the prescribed manner, copies of the documents referred to in *subsection (2)* not later than 11 months after the end of the company's financial year.

(2) The documents are as follows, namely:

(a) the statutory financial statements of the company for the financial year;

(b) the directors' report for the financial year;

(c) the statutory auditors' report on those financial statements and that directors' report.

(3) The reference in *subsection (1)* to a copy of a document is a reference to a copy that satisfies the following conditions:

(a) it is a true copy of the original save for the difference that the signature or signatures on the original, and any date or dates thereon, shall appear in typeset form on the copy;

(b) it is accompanied by a certificate of a director and the secretary of the company, that bears the signature of the director and the secretary in electronic or written form, stating that the copy is a true copy of the original (and one such certificate relating to all of the documents mentioned in *subsection (1)* suffices and the foregoing statement need not be qualified on account of the difference permitted by *paragraph (a)* as to the form of a signature or of a date).

(4) *Section 376* shall apply to an investment company as if the following subsection were substituted for *subsection (1)*:

> '(1) This section has effect where the directors of an investment company have prepared revised financial statements or a revised directors' report under [section 366][b] and a copy of the original statutory financial statements or directors' report, has been delivered to the Registrar under section 1401A.'.

(5) If an investment company fails to comply with the requirements of this section, the company and any officer of it who is in default shall be guilty of a category 3 offence.

(6) In *subsection (5)*, "officer" includes any shadow director and *de facto* director.]

Amendments

a Section 1401A inserted by C(A)A 2017, s 86.

b Words substituted by C(SA)A 2018, s 49 (previously: "section 367").

Chapter 5
Winding up

1402 Circumstances in which company may be wound up by the court

(1) *Section 569(1)(e)* shall not apply to an investment company but provision for the winding up of an investment company on the grounds that it is just and equitable to do so is made by this section.

(2) This section is in addition to the cases set out in *section 569* (so far as not disapplied by *subsection (1)*) in which an investment company may be wound up by the court.

(3) An investment company may be wound up by the court if the court is of opinion that it is just and equitable that the company should be wound up and the following conditions are satisfied—

(a) the petition for such winding up has been presented by the trustee of the company, that is to say, the person nominated by the Central Bank under *section 1396(4)(iii)* in respect of the company;

(b) that trustee has notified the company of its intention to resign as such trustee and 6 or more months have elapsed after the date of the giving of that notification without a trustee having been appointed to replace it;

(c) the court, in considering that petition, has regard to—

(i) any conditions imposed under *section 1396* in relation to the resignation from office of such a trustee and the replacement of it by another trustee; and

(ii) whether a winding up would best serve the interests of shareholders in the company;

and

(d) the petition for such winding up has been served on the company (if any) discharging, in relation to the first-mentioned company, functions of a management company.

Chapter 6
Restoration

1403 Restoration by the court

Section 741 shall apply to an investment company as if, in *subsection (1)(a)*, "2 years" were substituted for "20 years".

Chapter 7
Public offers of securities, prevention of market abuse, etc.

1404 Application of *Chapters 1, 2* and *4* of *Part 23* to investment companies

Chapters 1, *2* and *4* of *Part 23*—

(a) so far as they are applicable to companies other than public limited companies that fall within *Part 17*; and

(b) with the exception, in particular, of *sections 1358* to *1360*;

shall apply to an investment company.

Chapter 8
Umbrella funds and sub-funds

1405 Segregated liability of investment company sub-funds

(1) Notwithstanding any statutory provision or rule of law to the contrary, but subject to *Schedule 17*—

(a) any liability incurred on behalf of or attributable to any sub-fund of an umbrella fund shall be discharged solely out of the assets of that sub-fund; and

(b) no umbrella fund nor any director, receiver, examiner, liquidator, provisional liquidator or other person shall apply, nor be obliged to apply, the assets of any such sub-fund in satisfaction of any liability incurred on behalf of or attributable to any other sub-fund of the same umbrella fund;

whether such liability was incurred before, on or after 30 June 2005.

(2) *Schedule 17* provides that *subsection (1)* shall not apply to an umbrella fund which was authorised and commenced trading (as that latter expression is to be read in accordance with that Schedule) before 30 June 2005 unless the conditions specified in that Schedule are satisfied.

1406 Requirements to be complied with by, and other matters respecting, an umbrella fund to which *section 1405(1)* applies

(1) An umbrella fund to which *section 1405(1)* applies shall—

- (a) ensure that the words "An umbrella fund with segregated liability between sub-funds" are included in all its letterheads and in any agreement entered into by it in writing with a third party; and
- (b) disclose to a third party that it is a segregated liability umbrella fund before it enters into an oral contract with the third party.

(2) If an umbrella fund fails to comply with *subsection (1)(a)* or *(b)*, the umbrella fund and any officer of it who is in default shall be guilty of a category 3 offence.

(3) There shall be implied in every contract, agreement, arrangement or transaction entered into by an umbrella fund to which *section 1405(1)* applies the following terms, that:

- (a) the party or parties contracting with the umbrella fund shall not seek, whether in any proceedings or by any other means whatsoever or wheresoever, to have recourse to any assets of any sub-fund of the umbrella fund in the discharge of all or any part of a liability which was not incurred on behalf of that sub-fund;
- (b) if any party contracting with the umbrella fund shall succeed by any means whatsoever or wheresoever in having recourse to any assets of any sub-fund of the umbrella fund in the discharge of all or any part of a liability which was not incurred on behalf of that sub-fund, that party shall be liable to the umbrella fund to pay a sum equal to the value of the benefit thereby obtained by it; and
- (c) if any party contracting with the umbrella fund shall succeed in seizing or attaching by any means, or otherwise levying execution against, any assets of a sub-fund of an umbrella fund in respect of a liability which was not incurred on behalf of that sub-fund, that party shall hold those assets or the direct or indirect proceeds of the sale of such assets on trust for the umbrella fund and shall keep those assets or proceeds separate and identifiable as such trust property.

(4) All sums recovered by an umbrella fund as a result of any such trust as is described in *subsection (3)(c)* shall be credited against any concurrent liability pursuant to the implied term set out in *subsection (3)(b)*.

(5) Any asset or sum recovered by an umbrella fund pursuant to the implied term set out in *paragraph (b)* or *(c)* of *subsection (3)* or by any other means whatsoever or wheresoever in the events referred to in those paragraphs shall, after the deduction or payment of any costs of recovery, be applied so as to compensate the sub-fund affected.

(6) In the event that assets attributable to a sub-fund to which *section 1405(1)* applies are taken in execution of a liability not attributable to that sub-fund, and in so far as such assets or compensation in respect thereof cannot otherwise be restored to that sub-fund affected, the directors of the umbrella fund, with the consent of the custodian, shall certify or cause to be certified, the value of the assets lost to the sub-fund affected and transfer or pay from the assets of the sub-fund or sub-funds to which the liability was attributable, in priority to all other claims against such sub-fund or sub-funds, assets or sums sufficient to restore to the sub-fund affected, the value of the assets or sums lost to it.

1407 Further matters respecting an umbrella fund to which *section 1405(1)* applies

(1) Without prejudice to the other provisions of *sections 1405* and *1406*, *Schedule 17* and this section, a sub-fund of an umbrella fund is not a legal person separate from that umbrella fund, but an umbrella fund may sue and be sued in respect of a particular sub-fund and may exercise the same rights of set-off, if any, as between its sub-funds as apply at law in respect of companies and the property of a sub-fund is subject to orders of the court as it would have been if the sub-fund were a separate legal person.

(2) Nothing in *section 1405* or *1406*, *Schedule 17* or this section shall prevent the application of any enactment or rule of law which would require the application of the assets of any sub-fund in discharge of some or all of the liabilities of any other sub-fund on the grounds of fraud or misrepresentation and, in particular, by reason of the application of *section 443*, *557*, *604* or *608*.

(3) A sub-fund may be wound up in accordance with *section 569(1)(d)* or *586(2)* as if the sub-fund were a separate company but, in any such case, the appointment of the liquidator or any provisional liquidator and the powers, rights, duties and responsibilities of the liquidator or any provisional liquidator shall be confined to the sub-fund or sub-funds which is or are being wound up.

(4) For the purposes of *subsection (3)*, all references made in *section 569(1)(d)* or *586(2)*, and in all relevant provisions of this Act relating to the winding up of a company pursuant to *section 569(1)(d)* or *586(2)*, to one of the following words shall be read as follows:

(a) "company" shall be read as referring to the sub-fund or sub-funds which is or are being wound up;

(b) a "member" or "members" shall be read as referring to the holders of the shares in that sub-fund or sub-funds; and

(c) "creditors" shall be read as referring to the creditors of that sub-fund or sub-funds.

Chapter 9
Migration of funds

1408 Definitions (*Chapter 9*)

(1) In this Chapter—

"migrating company" means a body corporate which is established and registered under the laws of a relevant jurisdiction and which is a collective investment undertaking;

"registration documents" has the meaning given to it by *section 1409*;

"relevant jurisdiction", other than in *sections 1413* and *1414*, means the place, outside the State, prescribed under *subsection (2)* where the migrating company is established and registered at the time of its application under *section 1410.*

(2) The Minister may make regulations prescribing places, outside the State, for the purposes of the definition of "relevant jurisdiction" in *subsection (1)*, where he or she is satisfied that the law of the place concerned makes provision for migrating companies to continue under the laws of the State or for companies to continue under the laws of that place in a substantially similar manner to continuations under *section 1410.*

1409 "Registration documents"— meaning

(1) In this Chapter "registration documents", in relation to a migrating company, means the following documents:

(a) a copy, certified and authenticated in the prescribed manner, of the certificate of registration or equivalent certificate or document issued with respect to the migrating company under the laws of the relevant jurisdiction;

(b) a copy, certified and authenticated in the prescribed manner, of the memorandum and articles of the migrating company or equivalent constitutive document of the migrating company;

(c) a list setting out particulars in relation to the directors and secretary of the migrating company in accordance with the provisions of *section 149*;

(d) a statutory declaration, in the prescribed form, of a director of the migrating company made not more than 28 days before the date on which the application is made to the Registrar to the effect that—

  (i) the migrating company is, as of the date of the declaration, established and registered in the relevant jurisdiction, no petition or other similar proceeding to wind up or liquidate the migrating company has been notified to it and remains outstanding in any place, and no order has been notified to the migrating company or resolution adopted to wind up or liquidate the migrating company in any place;

(ii) the appointment of a receiver, liquidator, examiner or other similar person has not been notified to the migrating company and, at the date of the declaration, no such person is acting in that capacity in any place with respect to the migrating company or its property or any part thereof;

(iii) the migrating company is not, at the date of the declaration, operating or carrying on business under any scheme, order, compromise or other similar arrangement entered into or made by the migrating company with creditors in any place;

(iv) at the date of the declaration the migrating company has served notice of the proposed registration on the creditors of the migrating company;

(v) any consent or approval to the proposed registration in the State required by any contract entered into or undertaking given by the migrating company has been obtained or waived, as the case may be; and

(vi) the registration is permitted by and has been approved in accordance with the memorandum and articles of association or equivalent constitutive document of the migrating company;

(e) a declaration of solvency prepared in accordance with *section 1415*;

(f) a schedule of the charges or security interests created or granted by the migrating company that would, if such charges or security interests had been created or granted by a company incorporated under this Act, have been registrable under *Chapter 2* of *Part 7* and such particulars of those security interests and charges as are specified in relation to charges by *section 414*;

(g) notification of the proposed name of the migrating company if different from its existing name; and

(h) a copy of the memorandum and articles of the migrating company which the migrating company has resolved to adopt, which shall be in the Irish language or the English language, which shall take effect on registration under *section 1410* and which the migrating company undertakes not to amend before registration without the prior authorisation of the Registrar.

(2) If the original of any of the documents referred to in *subsection (1)* is not written in the Irish or the English language, then "registration documents" in this Chapter, in so far as that expression relates to such a document, means a translation of the document into the Irish or the English language certified as being a correct translation of it by a person who is competent to so certify.

1410 Continuation of foreign investment company

(1) A migrating company may apply to the Registrar to be registered as an investment company in the State by way of continuation.

(2) Where an application is made under *subsection (1)*, the Registrar shall not register the migrating company as an investment company in the State unless he or she is satisfied that all of the requirements of this Act in respect of the registration and of

matters precedent and incidental thereto have been complied with and, in particular, but without prejudice to the generality of the foregoing, he or she is satisfied that—

(a) the migrating company has delivered to the Registrar an application for the purpose, in the prescribed form and signed by a director of the migrating company, together with the registration documents;

(b) the name or, if relevant, the proposed new name of the migrating company has not been determined to be undesirable pursuant to *section 26*;

(c) the migrating company has delivered to the Registrar notice of the address of its proposed registered office in the State;

(d) the migrating company has applied to the Central Bank to be authorised to carry on business as an investment company under *section 1395* and the Central Bank has notified the migrating company and the Registrar that it proposes to authorise the migrating company to so carry on business.

(3) An application under this section shall be accompanied by a statutory declaration in the prescribed form made by a solicitor engaged for this purpose by the migrating company, or by a director of the migrating company, and stating that the requirements mentioned in *subsection (2)* have been complied with. The Registrar may accept such a declaration as sufficient evidence of compliance.

(4) The Registrar shall, as soon as is practicable after receipt of the application for registration, publish notice of it in the CRO Gazette.

(5) Where the Registrar receives a notification under *subsection (2)(d)*, the Registrar—

(a) may issue a certificate of registration of the migrating company by way of continuation of the migrating company as an investment company under the laws of the State; and

(b) if he or she issues such a certificate, shall enter in the register maintained for the purpose of *section 414*, in relation to charges and security interests of the migrating company specified in *paragraph (f)* of the definition of "registration documents" in *section 1409(1)*, the particulars specified by *section 414* which have been supplied by the migrating company.

(6) The migrating company shall, as soon as may be after being registered under *subsection (5)*, apply to be de-registered in the relevant jurisdiction.

(7) The Registrar shall enter in the register of companies the date of registration of the migrating company and shall forthwith publish notice in the CRO Gazette of the following matters:

(a) the date of the registration of the migrating company under this section;

(b) the relevant jurisdiction; and

(c) the previous name of the migrating company if different from the name under which it is being registered.

(8) From the date of registration, the migrating company shall be deemed to be an investment company formed and registered under this Part and shall continue for all

purposes under this Act, and the provisions of this Part shall apply to the migrating company, but this section does not operate—

(a) to create a new legal entity;

(b) to prejudice or affect the identity or continuity of the migrating company as previously established and registered under the laws of the relevant jurisdiction for the period that the migrating company was established and registered in the relevant jurisdiction;

(c) to affect any contract made, resolution passed or any other act or thing done in relation to the migrating company during the period that the migrating company was so established and registered;

(d) to affect the rights, authorities, functions and liabilities or obligations of the migrating company or any other person; or

(e) to render defective any legal proceedings by or against the migrating company.

(9) Without prejudice to the generality of *subsection (8)*—

(a) the failure of a migrating company to send to the Registrar the particulars of a charge or security interest created before the date of registration shall not prejudice any rights which any person in whose favour the charge was made or security interest created may have thereunder; and

(b) any legal proceedings that could have been continued or commenced by or against the migrating company before its registration under this section may, notwithstanding the registration, be continued or commenced by or against the migrating company after registration.

1411 Supplemental provisions in relation to *section 1410*

(1) The migrating company shall—

(a) notify the Registrar in the prescribed form; and

(b) notify the Central Bank;

within 3 days after the date of its de-registration in the relevant jurisdiction, of that de-registration.

(2) On registration of the migrating company under *section 1410(5)*, the Central Bank shall forthwith authorise the migrating company to carry on business under this Part.

(3) If there is any material change in any of the information contained in the statutory declaration mentioned in *paragraph (d)* of the definition of "registration documents" in *section 1409(1)* after the date of the declaration and before the date of the registration under *section 1410*, the director who made that statutory declaration, and any other director who becomes aware of that material change shall forthwith deliver a new statutory declaration to the Registrar relating to the change.

(4) If the migrating company fails to comply with any provision of *section 1410* or this section, the Registrar may send to the company by post a registered letter stating that, unless the migrating company rectifies the failure within 30 days after the date of the

letter and confirms that it has rectified the failure, a notice may be published in the CRO Gazette with a view to striking the migrating company off the register.

(5) If the failure mentioned in *subsection (4)* is not rectified within 30 days after the date of the sending of the letter referred to in that subsection, the Registrar may publish in the CRO Gazette a notice stating that, at the expiration of 1 month after the date of that notice, the migrating company mentioned therein will, unless the matter is resolved, be struck off the register, and the migrating company will be dissolved.

(6) At the expiration of the time mentioned in the notice, the Registrar may, unless cause to the contrary is previously shown by the migrating company, strike the company off the register, and shall publish notice thereof in the CRO Gazette, and on that publication, the migrating company shall be dissolved.

(7) For the purposes of this section, *section 736* shall apply as if the reference in it to *Chapter 1* of *Part 12* included a reference to this section and, accordingly, the other provisions of *Chapter 2* of that Part shall apply with any necessary modifications.

1412 Definitions for the purposes of de-registration provisions contained in *sections 1413* and *1414*

(1) In *sections 1413* and *1414*—

"applicant" means an investment company that applies under *section 1413* to be de-registered under *section 1414*;

"relevant jurisdiction" means the place, outside the State, prescribed under *subsection (2)* in which the investment company proposes to be registered;

"transfer documents", in relation to an applicant, means the following documents:

(a) a statutory declaration, in the prescribed form, of a director of the applicant made not more than 28 days before the date on which the application is made to the Registrar to the effect that—

(i) the applicant will, upon registration, continue as a body corporate under the laws of the relevant jurisdiction;

(ii) no petition or other similar proceeding to wind up or liquidate the applicant has been notified to the applicant and remains outstanding in any place, and no order has been notified to the applicant or resolution adopted to wind up or liquidate the applicant in any place;

(iii) the appointment of a receiver, liquidator, examiner or other similar person has not been notified to the applicant and, at the date of the declaration, no such person is acting in that capacity in any place with respect to the applicant or its property or any part thereof;

(iv) the applicant is not, at the date of the declaration, operating or carrying on business under any scheme, order, compromise or other similar arrangement entered into or made by the applicant with creditors in any place;

(v) the application for de-registration is not intended to defraud persons who are, at the date of the declaration, creditors of the applicant;

(vi) any consent or approval to the proposed de-registration required by any contract entered into or undertaking given by the applicant has been obtained or waived, as the case may be; and

(vii) the de-registration is permitted by the memorandum and articles of the applicant;

(b) a declaration of solvency prepared in accordance with the provisions of *section 1415*; and

(c) a copy of a special resolution of the applicant that approves the proposed de-registration and the transfer of the applicant to the relevant jurisdiction.

(2) The Minister may make regulations prescribing places, outside the State, for the purposes of the definition of "relevant jurisdiction" in *subsection (1)*, where he or she is satisfied that the law of the place concerned makes provision for bodies corporate that are substantially similar to applicants under *section 1413* to continue under the laws of the State in a substantially similar manner to continuations under *section 1410* or for companies to continue under the laws of that place.

1413 De-registration of companies when continued under the law of place outside the State

(1) An applicant which proposes to be registered in a relevant jurisdiction by way of continuation as a body corporate may apply to the Registrar to be de-registered in the State.

(2) Where an application is made under *subsection (1)*, the Registrar shall not de-register, under *section 1414*, the applicant as a company in the State unless he or she is satisfied that all of the requirements of this Act in respect of the de-registration and of matters precedent and incidental thereto have been complied with and, in particular, but without prejudice to the generality of the foregoing, he or she is satisfied that—

(a) the applicant has delivered to the Registrar an application for the purpose, in the prescribed form and signed by a director of the applicant, together with the transfer documents;

(b) the applicant has informed the Central Bank of its intention to be de-registered and the Central Bank has notified the Registrar that it has no objection to the de-registration, so long as the applicant complies with any conditions that the Central Bank may impose on the applicant; and

(c) the applicant has delivered to the Registrar notice of any proposed change in its name and of its proposed registered office or agent for service of process in the relevant jurisdiction.

(3) An application under this section shall be accompanied by a statutory declaration in the prescribed form made by a solicitor engaged for this purpose by the applicant, or by a director of the applicant, and stating that the requirements mentioned in *subsection (2)* have been complied with. The Registrar may accept such a declaration as sufficient evidence of compliance.

(4) The Registrar shall, as soon as is practicable after receipt of the application for de-registration, publish notice of it in the CRO Gazette.

(5) Where an application is made under *subsection (1)*, a person mentioned in *subsection (6)* may apply to the court, on notice to the applicant, the Central Bank, the Registrar and all creditors of the applicant, not later than 60 days after the date of the publication of the notice under *subsection (4)*, for an order preventing the proposal or passage of a resolution specified in *paragraph (c)* of the definition of "transfer documents" in *section 1412(1)* from taking effect in relation to the application, and the court may, subject to *subsection (9)*, make such an order accordingly.

(6) The following persons may apply for an order under *subsection (5)*:

(a) the holders of not less than 5 per cent of the issued share capital of the applicant and who have not voted in favour of the resolution; or

(b) any creditor of the applicant.

(7) Notice of an application for an order under *subsection (5)* may be given to the creditors concerned by publication in at least one national newspaper in the State.

(8) The Central Bank and the applicant concerned shall each be entitled to appear and be heard on an application made pursuant to *subsection (5)*.

(9) The court may make an order under *subsection (5)* only if it is satisfied that—

(a) the proposed de-registration of the applicant would contravene the terms of an agreement or arrangement between the applicant and any shareholder or creditor of the applicant; or

(b) the proposed de-registration would be materially prejudicial to any shareholder or creditor of the applicant and the interests of shareholders and creditors or both taken as a whole would be materially prejudiced.

(10) An order made under *subsection (5)* shall specify the period in respect of which it shall remain in force.

(11) An order of the court under *subsection (5)* is final and conclusive and not appealable.

1414 Supplemental provisions in relation to *section 1413*

(1) Unless the court orders otherwise, when one or more than one application is made under *section 1413(5)*, a resolution specified in *paragraph (c)* of the definition of "transfer documents" in *section 1412(1)* in relation to a company shall not take effect until—

(a) where the application or all the applications to the court are withdrawn—

(i) the day on which the resolution is passed;

(ii) the day next following the day on which the last outstanding application is withdrawn; or

(iii) the 31st day following the publication of the notice under *section 1413(7)*;

whichever is the latest; and

(b) where all applications to the court are not withdrawn—

(i) the day on which the resolution is passed;

(ii) the day specified in the order or, if no date is specified in the order, the day next following the day on which the period for which the order is specified to remain in force expires or otherwise ceases to be in force; or

(iii) the day next following the decision of the court;

whichever is the latest.

(2) When the applicant is registered as a company under the laws of the relevant jurisdiction, it shall give notice, in the prescribed form, to the Registrar of that fact within 3 days after the date of its becoming so registered, including its new name, if any, and, as soon as practicable after receiving that notice, the Registrar shall issue a certificate of de-registration of the applicant.

(3) The Registrar shall enter in the register of companies the date of the de-registration of the applicant and shall, within 7 days after the date of issue of the certificate under *subsection (2)*, publish in the CRO Gazette notice of the following matters:

(a) the date of the de-registration of the applicant under this section;

(b) the relevant jurisdiction; and

(c) the new name of the applicant if different from the name under which it was registered.

(4) From the date of registration of the applicant in the relevant jurisdiction, it shall cease to be a company for all purposes of this Act and shall continue for all purposes as a body corporate under the laws of the relevant jurisdiction, but this section does not operate—

(a) to create a new legal entity;

(b) to prejudice or affect the identity or continuity of the applicant as previously constituted under the laws of the State for the period that the applicant was so constituted;

(c) to affect any contract made, resolution passed or any other act or thing done in relation to the applicant during the period that the applicant was constituted under the laws of the State;

(d) to affect the rights, authorities, functions and liabilities or obligations of the applicant or any other person; or

(e) to render defective any legal proceedings by or against the applicant.

(5) Without prejudice to the generality of *subsection (4)*, any legal proceedings that could have been continued or commenced by or against the applicant before its de-registration under this section may, notwithstanding the de-registration, be continued or commenced by or against the applicant after registration.

1415 Statutory declaration as to solvency

(1) Where an application is made under *section 1410* or *1413*, a director of the migrating company or applicant, as the case may be, making the application shall

make a statutory declaration, in the prescribed form, stating that he or she has made a full inquiry into its affairs and has formed the opinion that it is able, at the time of the application, to pay its debts (being the debts identified for the purposes of *subsection (2)(b)*) as they fall due.

(2) A declaration under *subsection (1)* shall have no effect for the purposes of this section unless—

(a) it is made not more than 28 days before the date on which the application is made to the Registrar;

(b) it states the assets and liabilities of the migrating company or applicant as at the latest practicable date before the date of making of the declaration and in any event at a date not more than 3 months before the date of that making; and

(c) a report made by an independent person under *subsection (3)* is attached to the declaration, along with a statement by the independent person that he or she has given and has not withdrawn consent to the making of the declaration with the report attached to it.

(3) The report mentioned in *subsection (2)(c)* shall state whether, in the independent person's opinion, based on the information and explanations given to him or her, the opinion of the director mentioned in *subsection (1)* and the statement of the migrating company's or applicant's assets and liabilities referred to in *subsection (2)(b)* are reasonable.

(4) For the purposes of *subsection (3)*, the independent person shall be a person who, at the time the report is made, is—

(a) in the case of an application under *section 1410*, qualified to be the auditor of the migrating company under the laws of the relevant jurisdiction; and

(b) in the case of an application under *section 1413*, qualified to be the statutory auditor of the applicant.

(5) A director who makes a declaration under this section without having reasonable grounds for the opinion that the migrating company or applicant is able to pay its debts as they fall due shall be guilty of a category 2 offence.

(6) Where the migrating company or applicant is wound up within 1 year after the date on which the application is made to the Registrar and its debts are not paid or provided for in full within that year, it shall be presumed, unless the contrary is shown, that the director did not have reasonable grounds for his or her opinion.

PART 25
MISCELLANEOUS

Chapter 1
Provisions concerning foreign insolvency proceedings (including those covered by the Insolvency Regulation)

1416 Preliminary and interpretation (*Chapter 1*)

(1) In addition to their application to *Part 11*, *sections 1419* to *1428* shall apply to insolvency proceedings dealt with in *Part 10*.

(2) Save as provided in *section 1422* and except where the context otherwise requires, references in this Chapter to numbered Articles without qualification are references to Articles so numbered of the Insolvency Regulation.

1417 Recognition of winding up orders of non-European Union states and Denmark

(1) Any order made by a court of any state recognised for the purposes of this section and made for, or in the course of, winding up a company may be enforced by the High Court in the same manner in all respects as if the order has been made by the High Court.

(2) When an application has been made to the High Court under this section, an office copy of any order sought to be enforced shall be sufficient evidence of the order.

(3) In this section—

"company" means a body corporate incorporated outside the State;

"recognised" means recognised by order made by the Minister for the purposes of this section and no such order may be made in relation to a state that is a Member State (other than Denmark).

1418 Purpose of *sections 1419* to *1428*

The purpose of *sections 1419* to *1428* is to re-enact the European Communities (Corporate Insolvency) Regulations 2002 (S.I. No. 333 of 2002), apart from their provisions in so far as they relate to insolvency proceedings.

1419 Registration of judgments given in insolvency proceedings

(1) Without prejudice to Article 16(1) of the Insolvency Regulation, a liquidator appointed in insolvency proceedings who intends—

(a) to request under Article 21 of the Insolvency Regulation that notice of the judgment opening the proceedings and, where appropriate, the decision appointing him or her be published in the State; or

(b) to take any other action in the State under the Insolvency Regulation;

shall deliver to the Registrar a certified copy of the judgment and, where appropriate, of the decision appointing the liquidator.

(2) Registration under *subsection (1)* may also be effected by the Registrar on application by a liquidator who does not intend to take any action in the State under the Insolvency Regulation.

(3) The certified copy or copies mentioned in *subsection (1)* shall be accompanied by—

(a) if the judgment or decision is not expressed in the Irish or the English language, a translation, certified to be correct by a person competent to do so, into either of those languages;

(b) the prescribed form; and

(c) the prescribed fee.

(4) The Registrar shall issue a certificate of registration to the liquidator.

(5) In any proceedings a document purporting to be—

(a) a certified copy of a judgment opening insolvency proceedings or a decision appointing a liquidator in such proceedings, or

(b) a translation of such a document which is certified as correct by a person competent to do so,

shall, without further proof, be admissible as evidence of the judgment, the liquidator's appointment or the translation, unless the contrary is shown.

1420 Publication in relation to insolvency proceedings outside State

Section 711 shall apply to insolvency proceedings (as defined in *section 2(1)*) as it applies to insolvency proceedings (as defined in *section 710*).

1421 Registration of insolvency judgments

A request by a liquidator under Article 22 of the Insolvency Regulation that the judgment opening the insolvency proceedings be registered in a public register shall be made to the Registrar.

1422 Enforcement in State of insolvency judgments

(1) In this section—

"Brussels 1 Regulation" means Council Regulation (EC) No. 44/2001 of 22

December 2000 on jurisdiction and the recognition and enforcement of judgments in civil and commercial matters;

"insolvency judgment" means a judgment referred to in Article 25 of the Insolvency Regulation;

"Master" means the Master of the High Court.

(2) Except where the context otherwise requires, references in this section to numbered Articles without qualification are references to Articles so numbered of the Brussels 1 Regulation.

(3) Having regard to Article 68, references in Article 25 of the Insolvency Regulation to enforcement of insolvency judgments in accordance with certain Articles of the Brussels Convention are to be read as references to enforcement of those judgments in accordance with Articles 38 to 58.

(4) An application under the Brussels 1 Regulation for the enforcement in the State of an insolvency judgment shall be made to the Master.

(5) The Master shall determine the application by order in accordance with the Brussels 1 Regulation.

(6) The Master shall declare the insolvency judgment enforceable immediately on completion of the formalities provided for in Article 53 without any review under Articles 34 and 35 and shall make an enforcement order in relation to the judgment.

(7) An order under *subsection (5)* may provide for the enforcement of part only of the insolvency judgment concerned.

(8) An application to the Master under Article 39 for an enforcement order in respect of an insolvency judgment may include an application for any preservation measures the High Court has power to grant in proceedings that, apart from the provisions of this Chapter, are within its jurisdiction.

(9) Where an enforcement order is made, the Master shall grant any such preservation measures so applied for.

(10) For the purposes of this Chapter, references in Articles 42, 43, 45, 47, 48, 52, 53 and 57 to a declaration of enforceability are to be treated as references to an enforcement order under this section.

(11) Subject to the restrictions on enforcement contained in Article 47(3), if an enforcement order has been made respecting an insolvency judgment, the judgment—

- (a) shall, to the extent to which its enforcement is authorised by the enforcement order, be of the same force and effect as a judgment of the High Court; and
- (b) may be enforced by the High Court, and proceedings taken on it, as if it were a judgment of that Court.

1423 Interest on insolvency judgments and payment of costs

(1) Where, on application for an enforcement order respecting an insolvency judgment, it is shown—

- (a) that the judgment provides for the payment of a sum of money; and
- (b) that, in accordance with the law of the Member State in which the judgment was given, interest on the sum is recoverable under the judgment at a particular rate or rates and from a particular date or time;

the enforcement order, if made, shall provide that the person liable to pay the sum shall also be liable to pay the interest, apart from any interest on costs recoverable under *subsection (2)*, in accordance with the particulars noted in the order, and the interest shall be recoverable by the applicant as though it were part of the sum.

(2) An enforcement order may provide for the payment to the applicant by the respondent of the reasonable costs of or incidental to the application for the enforcement order.

(3) A person required by an enforcement order to pay costs shall be liable to pay interest on the costs as if they were the subject of an order for the payment of costs made by the High Court on the date on which the enforcement order was made.

(4) Interest shall be payable on a sum referred to in *subsection (1)(a)* only as provided for in this section.

1424 Currency of payments under enforceable insolvency judgments

(1) An amount payable in the State under an insolvency judgment by virtue of an enforcement order shall be payable in the currency of the State.

(2) If the amount is stated in the insolvency judgment in any currency except the currency of the State, payment shall be made on the basis of the exchange rate prevailing, on the date the enforcement order is made, between the currency of the State and any such currency.

(3) For the purposes of this section a certificate purporting to be signed by an officer of an authorised institution and to state the exchange rate prevailing on a specified date between a specified currency and the currency of the State shall be admissible as evidence of the facts stated in the certificate.

(4) In this section "authorised institution" means—

(a) a credit institution;

(b) a building society within the meaning of the Building Societies Act 1989;

(c) a trustee savings bank licensed under the Trustee Savings Banks Act 1989; or

(d) An Post.

1425 Preservation measures

(1) A request under Article 38 for measures to secure and preserve any of the debtor's assets in the State shall be made to the High Court.

(2) On such a request, the High Court—

(a) may grant any such measures that the court has power to grant in proceedings that, apart from the provisions of this Chapter, are within its jurisdiction; and

(b) may refuse to grant the measures sought if, in its opinion, the fact that, apart from this section, the court does not have jurisdiction in relation to the subject matter of the proceedings makes it inexpedient for it to grant the measures.

1426 Venue

The jurisdiction of the Circuit Court or District Court in proceedings that may be instituted in the State by a liquidator in exercise of his or her powers under Article 18 of the Insolvency Regulation may be exercised by the judge for the time being assigned—

(a) in the case of the Circuit Court, to the circuit, and

(b) in the case of the District Court, to the district court district, in which the defendant ordinarily resides or carries on any profession, business or occupation.

1427 Language of claims in relation to insolvency proceedings outside State

Section 714 shall apply to insolvency proceedings (as defined in *section 2(1)*) as it applies to insolvency proceedings (as defined in *section 710*).

1428 Non-recognition or non-enforcement of judgments

It shall be for the High Court to determine whether judgments referred to in Article 25(1), or insolvency proceedings or judgments referred to in Article 26, should not be recognised or enforced on grounds mentioned in those provisions.

Chapter 2
Other miscellaneous provisions

1429 Deemed consent to disclosure with respect to interest in shares or debentures acquired

The acquisition by any person of an interest in shares or debentures of a company registered in the State shall be deemed to be a consent by that person to the disclosure by the person, his or her agents or his or her intermediaries of any information required to be disclosed in relation to shares or debentures by or under this Act.

1430 Extension of *Chapter 1* of *Part 9* to any company liable to be wound up

Chapter 1 (other than *section 455*) of *Part 9* shall apply to any company liable to be wound up under this Act.

1431 Application of *sections 113* to *115* to bodies corporate generally

(1) In addition to its application where the company firstly referred to in *subsection (1)* of it is—

(a) a private company limited by shares; or

(b) by virtue of any of *Parts 16* to *24*, any other type of company,

section 113 shall apply to a body corporate that is not a company, and the foregoing reference in *subsection (1)* of it to a company, and the other relevant references in that section, shall be read accordingly.

(2) In addition to their application where the company firstly referred to in *subsection (1)* of either section is—

(a) a private company limited by shares; or

(b) by virtue of any of *Parts 16* to *22*, any other type of company,

sections 114 and *115* shall apply to a body corporate that is not a company, and the foregoing reference in *subsection (1)* of *section 114* or *115* to a company, and the other relevant references in either such section, shall be read accordingly.

1432 Saving for enactments providing for winding up under certain former Companies Acts

Nothing in *Part 11* or any other Part of this Act shall affect the operation of any enactment which provides for any association, partnership or company being wound up, or being wound up as a company or as an unregistered company under the Companies (Consolidation) Act 1908 or any enactment repealed by that Act.

1433 Application of *section 405* to every type of company and society

Section 405 shall apply to—

(a) any company within the meaning of *Chapter 4* of *Part 14*;

(b) any friendly society within the meaning of the Friendly Societies Acts 1896 to 2014; and

(c) any society registered under the Industrial and Provident Societies Acts 1893 to 2014;

as it applies to a private company limited by shares.

1434 Restriction of section 58 of the Solicitor's Act 1954

Notwithstanding section 58 of the Solicitor's Act 1954, a statutory auditor may draw or prepare any document for the purposes of this Act other than a deed or a constitution and, in the case of the latter (where the company is not a private company limited by shares), whether a memorandum of association or articles of association, or both.

1435 Prohibition of partnerships with more than 20 members

(1) No company, association or partnership consisting of more than 20 persons shall be formed for the purpose of carrying on any business (other than the business of banking), that has for its object the acquisition of gain by the company, association or partnership, or by the individual members thereof, unless—

(a) it is registered as a company under this Act;

(b) it is formed in pursuance of some other statute; or

(c) it is a partnership formed for the purpose of—

(i) carrying on practice as accountants in a case where each partner is a statutory auditor;

(ii) carrying on practice as solicitors in a case where each partner is a solicitor;

(iii) carrying on or promoting the business of thoroughbred horse breeding, being a partnership to which, subject to *subsection (5)*, the Limited Partnerships Act 1907 relates; or

(iv) the provision of investment and loan finance and ancillary facilities and services to persons engaged in industrial or commercial activities, being a partnership—

(I) that consists of not more than 50 persons; and

(II) to which, subject to *subsection (5)*, the Limited Partnerships Act 1907 relates.

(2) Subject to *subsection (3)*, the Minister may by order declare that the prohibition in *subsection (1)* shall not apply to a partnership that is of a description, and that has been or is formed for a purpose, specified in the order.

(3) The Minister shall not make an order under *subsection (2)* unless, after consultation with the Company Law Review Group, the Minister is satisfied that the public interest will not be adversely affected by the discontinuance, in consequence of the order, of the prohibition in *subsection (1)* in relation to the partnerships concerned.

(4) This section shall not apply to an investment limited partnership within the meaning of the Investment Limited Partnerships Act 1994.

(5) The provisions of section 4 (2) of the Limited Partnerships Act 1907 shall not apply to a partnership specified in *subsection (1)(c)* nor to a partnership specified in an order made under *subsection (2)*.

1436 Prohibition of banking partnership with more than 10 members

No company, association or partnership consisting of more than 10 persons shall be formed for the purpose of carrying on the business of banking, unless it is registered as a company under this Act, or is formed in pursuance of some other statute.

1437 Signing of statutory financial statements in case of credit institution registered after 15 August 1879

For the purposes of *section 324* as it applies to a credit institution that is—

(a) a company registered under this Act; or

(b) an existing company registered under a former enactment relating to companies (within the meaning of *section 5*) after 15 August 1879;

the statutory financial statements shall be signed by the secretary of the company and—

(i) where there are more than 3 directors of the company — by at least 3 directors of the company; and

(ii) where there are not more than 3 directors — by all the directors of the company.

1438 Audit by Comptroller and Auditor General of companies not trading for gain

(1) This section shall apply to a company which is not trading for the acquisition of gain by its members.

(2) The expression "statutory auditor" and the expression "audit of the statutory financial statements" shall, for the purposes of this Act, be deemed to include, respectively, the Comptroller and Auditor General and audit of the statutory financial statements by the Comptroller and Auditor General in any case in which he or she is appointed, under any enactment, auditor of a company to which this section applies.

(3) *Chapters 18*, *20* and *21* of *Part 6* [, *and Part 27*][a] shall not apply to the Comptroller and Auditor General in a case falling within *subsection (2)* nor to the audit of statutory financial statements by him or her in such a case.

Amendments

a Words inserted by C(SA)A 2018, s 50.

1439 Application of *sections 1402* and *1403* to companies that are UCITS

Each of the following—

(a) *section 1402* (circumstances in which company may be wound up by the court); and

(b) *section 1403* (restoration by the court);

shall, with the necessary modifications, apply to a company to which the European Communities (Undertakings for Collective Investment in Transferable Securities) Regulations 2011 (S.I. No. 352 of 2011) apply as those sections apply to an investment company.

1440 Relationship between *Chapters 1* and *2* of *Part 9* and Irish Takeover Panel Act 1997

(1) For the avoidance of doubt, nothing in *Chapter 1* or *2* of *Part 9* prejudices the jurisdiction of the Irish Takeover Panel under the Irish Takeover Panel Act 1997 with respect to a compromise or scheme of arrangement that is proposed between a relevant company (within the meaning of that Act) and its members or any class of them and which constitutes a takeover or other relevant transaction within the meaning of that Act and, accordingly, that Panel has, and shall be deemed always to have had, power to make rules under section 8 of that Act in relation to a takeover or other relevant transaction of the foregoing kind, to the same extent and subject to the like conditions, as it has power to make rules under that section in relation to any other kind of takeover or other relevant transaction.

(2) The Irish Takeover Panel, in exercising its powers under the Irish Takeover Panel Act 1997, and the court, in exercising its powers under *Chapter 1* or *2* of *Part 9*, shall each have due regard to the other's exercise of powers under that Act or either such Chapter, as the case may be.

1441 Eligibility to act as public auditor

[...][a]

Amendments

a Section 1441 repealed by C(SA)A 2018, s 3(1)(k).

1442 Certain captive insurers and re-insurers: exemption from requirement to have audit committee

Regulation 91(9) of the European Communities (Statutory Audits) (Directive 2006/43/EC) Regulations 2010 (S.I. No. 220 of 2010) is amended by inserting after subparagraph (d) the following:

"(da) a captive insurance undertaking or captive re-insurance undertaking (in each case within the meaning of Article 13 of Directive 2009/138/EC) which satisfies the following conditions—

(i) it is not owned by a credit institution within the meaning of Article 1(1) of Directive 2000/12/EC or by a group of such institutions, and

(ii) it has not issued transferable securities admitted to trading on a regulated market within the meaning of point 14 of Article 4(1) of Directive 2004/39/EC, or".

1443 Assurance company holding shares in its holding company

In the case of—

(a) a designated activity company,

(b) a public limited company, or

(c) an unlimited company,

that is an assurance company within the meaning of section 62 of the Insurance Act 1989, neither *section 113* nor *section 114*, other than *subsection (2)(b)(i)*, shall apply to shares subscribed for, purchased or held by it in its holding company pursuant to that *section 62*.

1444 Realised profits of assurance companies

(1) In the case of—

(a) a designated activity company,

(b) a public limited company, or

(c) a company limited by guarantee,

carrying on life assurance business, or industrial assurance business or both, any amount properly transferred to the profit and loss account of the company from a surplus in the fund or funds maintained by it in respect of that business and any deficit in that fund or those funds shall be respectively treated for the purposes of *Chapter 7* of *Part 3* as a realised profit and a realised loss, and, subject to the foregoing, any profit or loss arising on the fund or funds maintained by it in respect of that business shall be left out of account for those purposes.

(2) In *subsection (1)*—

(a) the reference to a surplus in any fund or funds of a company is a reference to an excess of the assets representing that fund or those funds over the liabilities of the company attributable to its life assurance or industrial assurance business, as shown by an actuarial investigation, and

(b) the reference to a deficit in any such fund or funds is a reference to the excess of those liabilities over those assets, as so shown.

(3) In this section—

"actuarial investigation" means an investigation to which section 5 of the Assurance Companies Act 1909 applies or provision in respect of which is made by regulations under section 3 of the European Communities Act 1972;

"life assurance business" and "industrial assurance business" have the same meaning they have as in section 3 of the Insurance Act 1936.

1445 Amendment of section 30 of Multi-Unit Developments Act 2011

Section 30 of the Multi-Unit Developments Act 2011 is amended, in subsection (1), by inserting "or, as the case may be, the Companies Registration Office Gazette" after "*Iris Oifigiúil*".

1446 Provision as to names of companies formed pursuant to statute

(1) This section applies to a company that—

(a) had been incorporated under a former enactment relating to companies (within the meaning of *section 5*) pursuant to, or in compliance with a requirement of, any statute; and

(b) by virtue of that statute was not required to include the word "limited" or "teoranta" in its name (or, as the case may be, the words "public limited company" or "cuideachta phoiblí theoranta" in its name).

(2) A company to which this section applies, notwithstanding its continuance in existence by a particular Part of this Act, shall not be subject to the requirement in that Part that its name end with a particular set of words.

(3) A company to which this section applies, notwithstanding its re-registration pursuant to *Chapter 6* of *Part 2* as a designated activity company, shall not be subject to the requirement in *Part 16* that its name end with a particular set of words.

1447 Disapplication of section 7 of Official Languages Act 2003

(1) Section 7 of the Official Languages Act 2003 shall not apply in relation to this Act.

(2) The text of this Act shall be made available electronically in each of the official languages as soon as practicable after its enactment.

1448 Provision in respect of certain discretion afforded by Commission Decision 2011/30/EU

[...][a]

Amendments

a Section 1448 repealed by C(SA)A 2018, s 3(1)(l).

[PART 26
PAYMENTS TO GOVERNMENTS

Chapter 1
Preliminary

1449 Interpretation

(1) In this Part—

"consolidated payment report" has the meaning assigned to it by section 1451;

"entity payment report" has the meaning assigned to it by section 1450;

"equivalent reporting requirements" means third country reporting requirements assessed as equivalent to the requirements of Chapter 10 of the Accounting Directive in accordance with Article 46 of that Directive;

"logging undertaking" means an undertaking which undertakes in primary forests the activity referred to in Section A, Division 02, Group 02.2 of Annex I to Regulation (EC) No. 1893/2006 of the European Parliament and of the Council of 20 December 2006[1] establishing the statistical classification of economic activities NACE Revision 2 as set out in *Table 1* of *Schedule 18*; and

"logging company" shall be read accordingly;

"mining or quarrying undertaking" means an undertaking which performs any activity involving the exploration, prospection, discovery, development, and extraction of minerals, oil, natural gas deposits or other materials, within the activities listed in Section B, Divisions 05 to 08 of Annex I to Regulation (EC) No. 1893/2006 of the European Parliament and of the Council of 20 December 2006[2] establishing the statistical classification of economic activities NACE Revision 2 as set out in Table 2 of Schedule 18; and

"mining or quarrying company" shall be read accordingly;

"payment" means an amount paid, whether in money or in kind, for relevant activities, where the payment includes any of the following:

(a) production entitlements;

(b) taxes levied on the income, production or profits of companies, excluding taxes levied on consumption such as value added taxes, personal income taxes or sales taxes;

(c) royalties;

(d) dividends, other than dividends paid by an undertaking to a government as an ordinary shareholder of that undertaking, where—

(i) the dividend is paid to the government on the same terms as to other ordinary shareholders, and

(ii) the dividend is not paid in lieu of production entitlements or royalties;

(e) signature, discovery and production bonuses;

(f) licence fees, rental fees, entry fees and other considerations for licences or concessions;

(g) payments for infrastructure improvements; "primary forest" has the same meaning as it has in Directive 2009/28/EC of the European Parliament and of the Council of 23 April 2009[3] on the promotion of the use of energy from renewable sources and amending and subsequently repealing Directives 2001/77/EC and 2003/30/EC;

"project" means operational activities that—

(a) are governed by—

(i) a single contract, licence, lease, concession or similar legal agreement, or

(ii) multiple contracts, licences, leases, concessions or similar legal agreements that are substantially interconnected, and

(b) form the basis for payment liabilities with a government;

"relevant undertaking" means an undertaking within the meaning of "ineligible entity"; and "relevant company" shall be read accordingly;

'relevant activities' means—

(a) the activity specified in *Table 1* of *Schedule 18* in primary forests, or

(b) any activity involving the exploration, prospection, discovery, development, and extraction of minerals, oil, natural gas deposits or other materials, within the economic activities specified in *Table 2* of *Schedule 18*;

'substantially interconnected' means forming a set of operationally and geographically integrated contracts, licences, leases or concessions or related agreements with substantially similar terms that are signed with a government, giving rise to payment liabilities.

(2) A word or expression that is used in this Part and is also used in Chapter 10 of the Accounting Directive has, unless the context otherwise requires, the same meaning in this Part as it has in Chapter 10 of the Accounting Directive.

References

1 OJ No. L 393, 30.12.2006, p.1.
2 OJ No. L 393, 30.12.2006, p.1.
3 OJ No. L 140, 5.6.2009, p.16.

Chapter 2

Obligation to prepare payment reports

1450 Obligation to prepare entity report on payments to governments

Subject to *sections 1454*, *1455* and *1456*, the directors of a company which is a large company or a relevant company shall, where such company is—

(a) a mining or quarrying company, or

(b) a logging company,

prepare and make available to the public each year a report on payments made to governments for each financial year (in this Part referred to as the "entity payment report").

1451 Obligation to prepare a consolidated payment report

(1) Subject to subsection (2) and sections 1454, 1456 and 1457, the directors of a holding company which is a large company or a relevant company shall—

(a) if the holding company is obliged to prepare group financial statements in accordance with section 293, and

(b) if the holding company or any of its subsidiary undertakings is—

(i) a mining or quarrying undertaking, or

(ii) a logging undertaking,

prepare and make available to the public each year a consolidated report on payments made to governments for each financial year of the holding company (in this Part referred to as a "consolidated payment report").

(2) This section shall not apply to the directors of—

(a) a holding company of a small group, except where any group undertaking is a relevant undertaking, or

(b) a holding company of a medium group, except where any group undertaking is a relevant undertaking.

Chapter 3
Content of payment reports

1452 Content of entity payment report

(1) A company shall in respect of its entity payment report, for each financial year, include the following in relation to its relevant activities:

(a) the government to which each payment has been made, including the country of that government;

(b) the total amount of payments made to each government;

(c) the total amount per type of payment made to each government;

(d) where those payments have been attributed to a specific project, the total amount per type of payment made for each such project and the total amount of payments for each such project.

(2) Where a company makes a payment that is not attributable to a specific project, it shall not be necessary in the entity payment report to allocate it to a specific project.

(3) A company shall not be required to include a payment in the entity payment report if—

(a) it is a single payment of an amount less than €100,000, or

(b) it forms part of a series of related payments within a financial year where the total amount of that series of payments is less than €100,000.

(4) Payments, activities and projects shall not be artificially split or aggregated to avoid the application of this Part.

(5) The disclosure of payments shall reflect the substance, rather than the form, of each payment, relevant activity or project concerned.

(6) Where payments in kind are made to a government, the entity payment report shall state the value of such payments in kind and, where applicable, the volume of those payments in kind, and the directors shall provide supporting notes to explain how the value of such payments in kind has been determined.

1453 Content of consolidated payment report

(1) A holding company shall in respect of its consolidated payment report, for each financial year, include the following information in relation to its relevant activities:

(a) the government to which each payment has been made, including the country of that government;

(b) the total amount of payments made to each government;

(c) the total amount per type of payment made to each government;

(d) where those payments have been attributed to a specific project, the total amount per type of payment made for each such project and the total amount of payments for each such project.

(2) A consolidated payment report shall include—

(a) any payments resulting from the relevant activities of a mining or quarrying undertaking, and

(b) any payments resulting from the relevant activities of a logging undertaking.

(3) Where an undertaking makes a payment that is not attributable to a specific project, it shall not be necessary in the consolidated payment report to allocate it to a specific project.

(4) A company shall not be required to include a payment in the consolidated payment report if—

(a) it is a single payment of an amount less than €100,000, or

(b) it forms part of a series of related payments within a financial year whose total amount is less than €100,000.

(5) Payments, activities and projects shall not be artificially split or aggregated to avoid the application of this Part.

(6) The disclosure of payments shall reflect the substance, rather than the form, of each payment, relevant activity or project concerned.

(7) Where payments in kind are made to a government, the consolidated payment report shall state the value of such payments in kind and, where applicable, the volume of those payments in kind, and the directors shall provide supporting notes to explain how the value of such payments in kind has been determined.

(8) In this section, "relevant activities", in relation to a holding company, means the activities of—

(a) the holding company, and

(b) any subsidiary undertaking included in the group financial statements of the holding company prepared in accordance with section 293.

Chapter 4
Payment reports: Exemptions and exclusions

1454 Exemption from preparation where certain payments included in consolidated payment report of holding company or higher holding undertaking

(1) The directors of a company that is a subsidiary or a holding company shall be exempt from preparing an entity payment report if any payments to governments made by the company are included in the consolidated payment report prepared by the holding company in accordance with *section 1451*.

(2) The directors of a company that is a subsidiary or a holding company shall be exempt from the requirement to prepare an entity payment report under *section 1450* or, in the case of a holding company, a consolidated payment report under *section 1451* if—

(a) any holding undertaking or higher holding undertaking of the company is subject to the provisions implementing Chapter 10 of the Accounting Directive in a Member State other than the State, and

(b) any payments to governments made by the company are included in the consolidated report drawn up by that holding undertaking.

1455 Exemption from preparation where company is subject to equivalent reporting requirements

The directors of a company shall be exempt from preparing an entity payment report if—

(a) the company is subject to equivalent reporting requirements, and

(b) the payments to governments made by the company are included in a report prepared in accordance with equivalent reporting requirements.

1456 Exemption from preparation where holding undertaking or higher holding undertaking is subject to equivalent reporting requirements

The directors of a company that is a subsidiary or a holding company are exempt from preparing an entity payment report under *section 1450* or, in the case of a holding company, a consolidated payment report under *section 1451* if—

(a) any holding undertaking or higher holding undertaking of the company is subject to the provisions implementing Chapter 10 of the Accounting Directive in a Member State other than the State,

(b) that holding undertaking or higher holding undertaking of the company that is governed by the laws of a Member State is subject to equivalent reporting requirements, and

(c) the payments to governments made by the company are included in a consolidated report drawn up to the same date, or an earlier date, in the same financial year, by that holding undertaking prepared in accordance with equivalent reporting requirements.

1457 Certain undertakings exempt from inclusion in a consolidated payment report

(1) Subject to *subsection (2)*, an undertaking, including a relevant undertaking, shall not be required to be included in a consolidated payment report where—

(a) severe long-term restrictions substantially hinder the holding company in the exercise of its rights over the assets or management of that undertaking,

(b) in extremely rare cases, the information necessary for the preparation of the consolidated payment report cannot be obtained without disproportionate expense or undue delay, or

(c) the interest of the holding company is held exclusively with a view to subsequent resale.

(2) The exemptions referred to in *subsection (1)* shall apply only if the holding company availed of the similar exemptions available under *section 303* in relation to that undertaking for the purposes of preparing its group financial statements in accordance with *section 293*.

Chapter 5
Approval and signing of payment reports

1458 Approval and signing of entity payment reports and consolidated payment reports

(1) An entity payment report prepared in accordance with *section 1450* and a consolidated payment report prepared in accordance with *section 1451* shall be approved by the board of directors and signed on their behalf by not less than 2 directors, where there are 2 or more directors.

(2) Without prejudice to the generality of section 11, where the company has a sole director, *subsection (1)* shall operate to require that director to approve and sign the entity payment report or consolidated payment report.

(3) Every copy of every entity payment report or consolidated payment report which is delivered to the Registrar or which is otherwise circulated, published or issued shall state the names of the persons who signed the payment report on behalf of the board of directors.

(4) If any copy of an entity payment report or a consolidated payment report is delivered to the Registrar or is otherwise circulated, published or issued without the payment report (the original of it as distinct from the copy) having been signed as required by this section or without the required statement of the signatories' names on the copy being

included, the company and any officer of it who is in default shall be guilty of a category 2 offence.

(5) In *subsection (4)*, 'officer' includes any shadow director and de facto director.

Chapter 6
Publication of payment reports

1459 Delivery of copy of entity payment reports and consolidated payment reports to Registrar

(1) A company, the directors of which are required to prepare—

(a) an entity payment report in accordance with *section 1450*, or

(b) a consolidated payment report in accordance with *section 1451*, shall deliver a copy of that entity payment report or consolidated payment report, as the case may be, to the Registrar within 11 months after the end of the financial year of the company.

(2) If a company to which *subsection (1)* applies fails to comply with the requirements of this section, the company and any officer of it who is in default shall be guilty of a category 3 offence.

(3) In *subsection (2)*, 'officer' includes any shadow director and de facto director.

1460 Delivery of copy of entity payment reports and consolidated payment reports prepared under equivalent reporting requirements to Registrar

(1) A company, the directors of which are exempt under *sections 1455* or *1456* from preparing an entity payment report or consolidated payment report, shall deliver to the Registrar a copy of any payment report or consolidated payment report prepared in accordance with equivalent reporting requirements within 28 days after such payment report is made available to the public under the equivalent reporting requirements.

(2) Where any document required to be delivered under this section is in a language other than the English language or the Irish language, there shall be annexed to the copy of that document delivered a translation of it into the English language or the Irish language, certified in the manner prescribed for the purposes of *section 348*.

(3) If a company to which *subsection (1)* applies fails to comply with the requirements of this section, the company and any officer of it who is in default shall be guilty of a category 3 offence.

(4) In *subsection (3)*, 'officer' includes any shadow director and *de facto* director.][a]

Amendments

a Part 26 inserted by C(A)A 2017, s 87.

[PART 27
STATUTORY AUDITS

Chapter 1
Preliminary and interpretation

1461 Interpretation (*Part 27 and Schedules 19 and 20*)

(1) In this Part and *Schedules 19* and *20*—

"2010 Audits Regulations" means the European Communities (Statutory Audits) (Directive 2006/43/EC) Regulations 2010 (S.I. No. 220 of 2010) revoked by Regulation 2(1) of the 2016 Audits Regulations;

"2016 Audits Regulations" means the European Union (Statutory Audits) (Directive 2006/43/EC, as amended by Directive 2014/56/EU, and Regulation (EU) No 537/2014) Regulations 2016 (S.I. No. 312 of 2016) revoked by section 3(6) of the Companies (Statutory Audits) Act 2018;

"AAPA report" shall be read in accordance with *section 930B(1)*;

"additional report to the audit committee" means the report submitted to the audit committee of a public-interest entity by the statutory auditor or audit firm carrying out statutory audits as referred to in Article 11 of Regulation (EU) No 537/2014;

"approved", in relation to a statutory auditor or audit firm, means approved under this Part;

"aptitude test" means an aptitude test referred to in *section 1476(1)*;

"audit committee", in relation to a public-interest entity, means the audit committee established for the entity under *section 1551*;

"Audit Directive" means Directive 2006/43/EC of the European Parliament and of the Council of 17 May 20065 on statutory audits of annual accounts and consolidated accounts, amending Council Directives 78/660/EEC and 83/349/EEC and repealing Council Directive 84/253/EEC, as amended by Directive 2014/56/EU of the European Parliament and of the Council of 16 April 20146 amending Directive 2006/43/EC on statutory audits of annual accounts and consolidated accounts;

"audit working papers", in relation to a statutory auditor or audit firm, means material (whether in the form of data stored on paper, film, electronic media or other media or otherwise) prepared by or for, or obtained by the statutory auditor or audit firm in connection with, the performance of the audit concerned, and includes—

(a) the record of audit procedures performed,

(b) relevant audit evidence obtained, and

(c) conclusions reached,

and a reference to audit working papers in relation to a Member State auditor or audit firm, or a third-country auditor or third-country audit entity, shall be read accordingly;

"auditing standards" means the standards adopted by the Supervisory Authority under *section 1526* in accordance with which statutory audits shall be carried out;

"client" has the meaning assigned to it by *section 934(1)*;

"Commission" means Commission of the European Union;

"counterpart authority" shall be construed in accordance with *section 1553*;

"disciplinary committee" has the meaning assigned to it by *section 900*;

"financial year"—

(a) in relation to the Supervisory Authority and an audited undertaking, shall be read in accordance with *section 288*, and

(b) in relation to a statutory auditor or audit firm, means any period in respect of which a profit and loss account or income statement is prepared by the auditor or audit firm for income tax or other business purposes, whether that period is of a year's duration or not;

"firm" includes a body corporate;

"Member State" means a Member State of the European Union or an EEA state;

"Member State audit firm" means an audit entity approved in accordance with the Audit Directive by the counterpart authority of another Member State to carry out audits of accounts or consolidated accounts as required by European Union law;

"Member State auditor" means an auditor approved in accordance with the Audit Directive by the counterpart authority of another Member State to carry out audits of accounts or consolidated accounts as required by European Union law;

"penalty" includes a sanction and a measure;

"public-interest entities" means undertakings that—

(a) have transferable securities admitted to trading on a regulated market of any Member State,

(b) are credit institutions,

(c) are insurance undertakings, or

(d) are undertakings that are otherwise designated, by or under any other enactment, to be entities referred to in point (d) of Article 2(13) of the Audit Directive;

"public register" shall be read in accordance with *section 1484*;

"recognised accountancy body" has the meaning assigned to it by *section 900*;

"Regulation (EU) No 537/2014" means Regulation (EU) No 537/2014 of the European Parliament and of the Council of 16 April 20147 on specific requirements regarding statutory audit of public-interest entities and repealing Commission Decision 2005/909/EC;

"relevant contravention" has the meaning assigned to it by *section 900*;

"relevant provisions" has the meaning assigned to it by *section 900*;

"relevant sanction" (except in *Chapter 9*) has the meaning assigned to it by *section 900*;

"standards" means those standards, as defined in *section 900*, of a prescribed accountancy body which is a recognised accountancy body;

"statutory audit" means an audit of entity financial statements or group financial statements in so far as—

(a) required by European Union law, or

(b) required by national law as regards small companies;

"statutory audit firm" means—

(a) an audit firm which is approved in accordance with this Part to carry out statutory audits, or

(b) an audit firm which is registered in accordance with section 1465 to carry out statutory audits;

"statutory auditor" means an individual who is approved in accordance with this Part to carry out statutory audits;

"third country" means a country or territory that is not a Member State or part of a Member State;

"third-country competent authority" means an authority in a third country with responsibilities, as respects auditors and audit entities in that country, equivalent to those of the Supervisory Authority.

(2) A reference in this Part or in *Schedule 19* or *20* to a registered third-country auditor or third-country audit entity is a reference to a third-country auditor or third-country audit entity registered under *Chapter 21*.

(3) A word or expression that is used in this Part or in *Schedule 19* or *20* and is also used in the Audit Directive shall have in this Part and that Schedule the same meaning as it has in the Audit Directive.

(4) A word or expression that is used in this Part or in *Schedule 19* or *20* and is also used in Regulation (EU) No 537/2014 shall have in this Part and that Schedule the same meaning as it has in that Regulation.

1462 Savings

(1) Subject to *Chapter 22*, the 2016 Audits Regulations, as in force immediately before the date of commencement of section 3(6) of the Companies (Statutory Audits) Act 2018—

(a) in so far as they related to the conduct of statutory audits and the duties and powers of statutory auditors and audit firms in relation thereto for financial years commencing before that date, shall continue to apply to the conduct of statutory auditors and audit firms in relation thereto for those financial years, and

(b) as regards each other matter provision for which was made by those Regulations before that date, shall continue to make such provision before that date.

(2) For the purposes only of enabling the 2016 Audits Regulations to operate, for the financial years referred to in *subsection (1)*, on and after the date referred to in that subsection, as those Regulations operated immediately before that date, a reference in

those Regulations to this Act or a provision of this Act shall be read as a reference to this Act or such provision, as the case may be, as in force immediately before that date.

1463 Application

Save where otherwise provided (including provided by Regulation (EU) No 537/2014), this Part applies—

(a) in so far as it relates to the conduct of statutory audits and the duties and powers of statutory auditors and audit firms in relation thereto, to the conduct of statutory audits for financial years commencing on or after the date referred to in *section 1462(1)*, and

(b) as regards each other matter provision for which is made by this Part, on and from that date.

Chapter 2
Approval of statutory auditors and audit firms

1464 Applications for approval, general principle as to good repute, etc.

(1) A recognised accountancy body may, on application made to it by an individual or a firm, approve, under this Part, the applicant as a statutory auditor or audit firm.

(2) A recognised accountancy body may, on foot of an application under *subsection (1)*, grant approval under this Part only to—

(a) individuals, or

(b) firms,

who are of good repute.

(3) A recognised accountancy body may, on application made to it by a third-country auditor and in accordance with *Chapter 20*, approve, under this Part, the applicant as a statutory auditor.

(4) *Subsection (5)* applies in the case of an application under *subsection (1)*—

(a) by a firm that is a Member State audit firm in the circumstances where it is not seeking registration in accordance with *section 1465*, or

(b) by a Member State auditor.

(5) For the purposes of this section, the fact that the applicant is a Member State audit firm or Member State auditor shall constitute conclusive evidence that the applicant is of good repute unless, arising out of the cooperation that the State is required to engage in by virtue of Part VIII of the Audit Directive, the counterpart authority in the Member State where the applicant is approved as a statutory audit firm or auditor has notified the Supervisory Authority or a recognised accountancy body that the counterpart authority has reasonable grounds for believing that the good repute of the audit firm or auditor has been seriously compromised.

(6) On approving a person as a statutory auditor or audit firm, a recognised accountancy body shall assign an individual identification number to the person.

(7) The recognised accountancy body shall maintain a record in writing of all numbers assigned by it under *subsection (6)*.

1465 Basis on which audit firms approved in other Member States may carry out audits in State

(1) An audit firm which is approved in another Member State shall be entitled to carry out statutory audits in the State if the key audit partner who carries out those audits on behalf of the audit firm, both at the time of registration (in accordance with subsection (2)) and at all times during the registration of the firm, complies with the requirements of *sections 1464* to *1472*.

(2) (a) An audit firm that wishes to carry out statutory audits in the State where the State is not its home Member State shall, before carrying out any such audit, register with the recognised accountancy body by which the key audit partner referred to in *subsection (1)* is approved.

(b) The recognised accountancy body shall ensure that an audit firm which complies with *subsection (1)* is registered in accordance with the requirements of *Chapter 5* and *Schedule 20*.

(3) (a) The recognised accountancy body shall register the audit firm if it is satisfied that the audit firm is registered with the counterpart authority in the audit firm's home Member State.

(b) Where the recognised accountancy body intends to rely on a certificate, issued by the counterpart authority in the home Member State, attesting to the registration of the audit firm in the home Member State, the recognised accountancy body may require that such certificate be issued on a date falling within the 3 months immediately preceding that date on which the recognised accountancy body is given that certificate.

(4) On registering the audit firm, the recognised accountancy body shall assign an individual identification number to the firm.

(5) The recognised accountancy body shall maintain a record in writing of all numbers assigned by it under *subsection (4)*.

(6) The recognised accountancy body shall inform the counterpart authority in the home Member State of the registration of the audit firm.

(7) Where a recognised accountancy body receives a notification from another Member State that an audit firm whose home Member State is the State has registered with the counterpart authority in the host Member State, the recognised accountancy body shall ensure that the registration is recorded in the public register.

1466 Restriction as to persons who may carry out statutory audits

Statutory audits shall be carried out only by—

(a) auditors or audit firms that are approved under this Part, or

(b) audit firms registered in accordance with *section 1465*.

1467 Restriction on acting as statutory auditor

A person shall not—

(a) act as a statutory auditor,

(b) describe himself or herself as a statutory auditor, or

(c) so hold himself or herself out as to indicate, or be reasonably understood to indicate, that he or she is a statutory auditor,

unless he or she has been approved in accordance with this Part.

1468 Restriction on acting as statutory audit firm

A firm shall not—

(a) act as a statutory audit firm,

(b) describe itself as a statutory audit firm, or

(c) so hold itself out as to indicate, or be reasonably understood to indicate, that it is a statutory audit firm,

unless it has been approved in accordance with this Part or registered in accordance with *section 1465*.

1469 Offence for contravening section 1466, 1467 or 1468

A person who contravenes *section 1466*, *1467* or *1468* shall be guilty of a category 2 offence.

1470 Conditions for approval as statutory auditor

A person shall not be eligible for approval as a statutory auditor unless he or she is—

(a) a member of a recognised accountancy body and holds an appropriate qualification as referred to in *section 1472,*

(b) a Member State auditor and complies with *section 1476*, or

(c) a third-country auditor and complies with *section 1476* and *Chapter 20*.

1471 Transitional provisions applicable to certain deemed approvals under Regulation 44 of 2016 Audits Regulations

(1) Subject to *sections 1479*, *1582* and *1583*, a deemed approval of a person as a statutory auditor continued in force under the 2016 Audits Regulations by virtue of Regulation 44(1) of those Regulations and in force immediately before the commencement of section 3(6) of the Companies (Statutory Audits) Act 2018 shall continue in force under this Part as if it were a deemed approval of that person as a statutory auditor under this Part.

(2) Subject to *sections 1480*, *1582* and *1583*, a deemed approval of a firm as a statutory audit firm continued in force under the 2016 Audits Regulations by virtue of Regulation 44(2) of those Regulations and in force immediately before the commencement of section 3(6) of the Companies (Statutory Audits) Act 2018 shall continue in force under this Part as if it were a deemed approval of that firm as a statutory audit firm under this Part.

1472 Appropriate qualification for purpose of section 1470(a)

(1) An individual holds an appropriate qualification, as required by *section 1470(a)*, if he or she holds a qualification granted by a recognised accountancy body whose standards relating to training and qualifications for the approval of a person as a statutory auditor are not less than those specified in *Schedule 19*.

(2) In *subsection (1)*, "qualification" means a qualification to undertake an audit of entity financial statements and group financial statements in so far as required by European Union law.

(3) A recognised accountancy body may exempt in writing a person who has passed a university or equivalent examination, or who holds a university degree or equivalent qualification, in one or more of the subjects referred to in the test of theoretical knowledge specified in *Schedule 19* if the body is satisfied that the passing of that examination, or the holding of that university degree or equivalent qualification, renders it unnecessary for the person to undergo that test in so far as those subjects are concerned.

(4) The Supervisory Authority shall, at such times as it thinks it appropriate to do so, issue guidelines to recognised accountancy bodies as to the specific matters that should be given regard to in reaching a decision under *subsection (3)* whether or not to grant an exemption under that subsection to a person.

1473 Conditions for approval as statutory audit firm

(1) In this section, references to a firm include references to a Member State audit firm if the firm is not seeking registration in accordance with *section 1465*.

(2) A firm shall not be eligible for approval as a statutory audit firm unless—

- (a) the individuals who carry out statutory audits in the State on behalf of the firm are approved as statutory auditors in accordance with this Part,
- (b) the majority of the voting rights in the firm are held by—
  - (i) individuals who are eligible for approval in the State or in any other Member State as statutory auditors,
  - (ii) audit firms approved as statutory audit firms in the State or in any other Member State, or
  - (iii) a combination of such individuals and audit firms,

  and
- (c) subject to *subsection (3)*, the majority of the members of the administrative or management body of the firm are—
  - (i) individuals who are eligible for approval in the State or in any other Member State as statutory auditors,
  - (ii) audit firms approved as statutory audit firms in the State or in any other Member State, or
  - (iii) a combination of such individuals and audit firms.

(3) Where the administrative or management body of a firm has no more than 2 members, then, for the purposes of *subsection (2)(c)*, one of those members shall satisfy at least the requirements of that subsection.

1474 Powers of Director

(1) The Director may demand of a person—

(a) acting as a statutory auditor or audit firm of an undertaking, or

(b) purporting to have obtained approval under this Part, or registration in accordance with *section 1465*, to so act,

the production of evidence of the person's approval under this Part or, if applicable, registration in accordance with *section 1465* in respect of any period during which the person so acted or purported to have obtained such approval.

(2) If the person concerned refuses or fails to produce the evidence referred to in *subsection (1)* within 30 days after the date of the demand referred to in that subsection, or such longer period as the Director may allow, the person shall be guilty of a category 3 offence.

(3) In a prosecution for an offence under this section, it shall be presumed, until the contrary is shown, that the defendant did not, within 30 days, or any longer period allowed, after the day on which the production was demanded, produce evidence in accordance with *subsection (1)*.

1475 Evidence in prosecutions under section 1474

(1) Subject to *subsection (2)*, in proceedings for an offence under *section 1474*, the production to the court of a certificate purporting to be signed by a person on behalf of a recognised accountancy body and stating that the defendant is not approved under this Part or, if applicable, is not registered in accordance with *section 1465*, by that recognised accountancy body shall be sufficient evidence, until the contrary is shown by the defendant, that the defendant is not so approved or registered, as the case may be.

(2) *Subsection (1)* shall not apply unless a copy of the certificate concerned is served by the prosecution on the defendant, by registered post, not later than 28 days before the day the certificate is produced in court in the proceedings concerned.

(3) If the defendant in those proceedings intends to contest the statement contained in such a certificate, he or she shall give notice in writing of that intention to the prosecution within 21 days, or such longer period as the court may allow, after the date of receipt by him or her of a copy of the certificate from the prosecution.

Chapter 3
Aptitude test

1476 Aptitude test to be passed

(1) Subject to *subsection (2)*, a Member State auditor or third-country auditor applying for approval as a statutory auditor in the State is required to sit and pass an aptitude test to demonstrate his or her knowledge of the enactments and practice that are relevant to statutory audits in the State.

(2) *Subsection (1)* shall not apply to a Member State auditor or third-country auditor if the recognised accountancy body is satisfied that he or she has otherwise demonstrated sufficient knowledge of the enactments and practice referred to in that subsection.

(3) The Supervisory Authority shall, at such time as it thinks it appropriate to do so, issue guidelines to each recognised accountancy body as to the specific matters that should be given regard to in reaching a decision under *subsection (2)* whether or not a person has demonstrated the knowledge referred to in *subsection (1)*.

(4) A recognised accountancy body may charge and impose on a Member State auditor or third-country auditor a fee (of an amount specified from time to time by the Minister sufficient to meet the body's administrative expenses in respect of the following) in respect of the administration of an aptitude test under this section in relation to him or her.

(5) A fee imposed under *subsection (4)* may, in default of payment, be recovered from the Member State auditor or third-country auditor concerned as a simple contract debt in any court of competent jurisdiction.

(6) The amount of a fee imposed under Regulation 49(4) of the 2016 Audits Regulations as those Regulations were in force immediately before the date of commencement of section 3(6) of the Companies (Statutory Audits) Act 2018 shall be the amount of the fee imposed under *subsection (4)* until such time as the Minister exercises his or her power under that subsection to specify a different amount of such fee.

1477 Scope of aptitude test

(1) The aptitude test shall—

- (a) be conducted in either the Irish language or the English language, and
- (b) relate only to the applicant's adequate knowledge of the enactments and practice that are relevant to statutory audits in the State.

(2) Subject to *subsection (3)*, the various matters that shall constitute the contents of the aptitude test shall be decided by the recognised accountancy body after it has received the approval of the Supervisory Authority to the contents of the test.

(3) A recognised accountancy body shall not alter the contents of an aptitude test approved under *subsection (2)* unless such alteration has been approved by the Supervisory Authority.

1478 Adequate standards to be applied in administration of aptitude test

(1) Subject to *subsection (2)*, a recognised accountancy body shall apply adequate standards in the administration of the aptitude test.

(2) No standards shall be used by a recognised accountancy body for the purposes of *subsection (1)* unless those standards have (with respect to that use) first been approved by the Supervisory Authority.

Chapter 4
Withdrawal of approval

1479 Grounds for mandatory withdrawal of approval in case of statutory auditor

(1) For the purposes of this section, the cases that can constitute circumstances of an auditor's good repute being seriously compromised include cases of professional misconduct or want of professional skill on the part of the auditor.

(2) Without prejudice to *section 1502* and subject to *subsections (4)* to *(6)*, a recognised accountancy body shall withdraw an approval of an auditor under this Part if, but only if—

(a) circumstances arise (involving acts or omissions on the part of the auditor) from which a recognised accountancy body can reasonably conclude that the auditor's good repute is seriously compromised,

(b) the auditor no longer falls within *section 1470(a)*, *(b)* or *(c)*, or

(c) in the case of a person who is a statutory auditor referred to in *section 1471(1)*—

(i) the auditor no longer falls within *section 1470(a)*,

(ii) the auditor is not registered as a statutory auditor in the public register, or

(iii) the auditor is not subject to the regulation of a recognised accountancy body.

(3) Unless there do not exist internal appeal procedures of a recognised accountancy body as referred to in *subsection (8)(a)*, references in *subsections (4)* to *(7)* to a recognised accountancy body shall be read as references to a recognised accountancy body acting through the disciplinary committee that deals with matters at first instance.

(4) Subject to *subsection (7)*, *subsection (5)* applies where, having—

(a) complied with the requirements of procedural fairness in that regard, and

(b) served any notices required for that purpose or as required by its investigation and disciplinary procedures,

a recognised accountancy body is satisfied that *subsection (2)(a)*, *(b)* or *(c)* applies in the case of an auditor.

(5) Subject to *subsection (7)*, the recognised accountancy body shall serve a notice in writing on the auditor stating that—

(a) it is satisfied that *subsection (2)(a)*, *(b)* or *(c)* applies in the case of the auditor,

(b) the auditor shall take specified steps to cause *subsection (2)(a)*, *(b)* or *(c)* to cease to apply to him or her within a specified period (which shall be not less than one month), and

(c) if those steps are not taken, it shall withdraw the approval of the auditor.

(6) Where the recognised accountancy body has served a notice under *subsection (5)* on a statutory auditor and the auditor has not, before the expiration of the specified period

referred to in *subsection (5)(b)*, taken the steps referred to in *subsection (5)(b)*, the recognised accountancy body shall withdraw the approval of the auditor under this Part.

(7) The procedure specified in *subsection (5)* need not be employed if the acts or omissions concerned referred to in *subsection (2)(a)* are such as, in the opinion of the recognised accountancy body, constitute professional misconduct or want of professional skill on the part of the auditor of a degree that employing that procedure would not be in the public interest but nothing in this subsection affects the application of the requirements of procedural fairness to the withdrawal of approval.

(8) If—

(a) there exist applicable internal appeal procedures of the recognised accountancy body, and

(b) the investigation and disciplinary procedures of the recognised accountancy body provide that a decision of its disciplinary committee, being a decision of a nature to which this section applies, shall stand suspended or shall not take effect until, as the case may be—

(i) the period for making an appeal under those procedures has expired without such an appeal having been made,

(ii) such an appeal has been made and the decision to withdraw the approval confirmed, or

(iii) such an appeal that has been made is withdrawn,

then, notwithstanding anything in the preceding provisions of this section, the operation of the withdrawal of approval by that disciplinary committee shall stand suspended until the occurrence of an event specified in *paragraph (b)(i), (ii)* or *(iii)*.

(9) *Subsection (10)* applies if—

(a) there exist applicable internal appeal procedures of the recognised accountancy body, and

(b) the investigation and disciplinary procedures of the recognised accountancy body do not provide, as referred to in *subsection (8)(b)*, for the decision of the disciplinary committee referred to in that provision to stand suspended or not to take effect.

(10) Notwithstanding the internal appeal procedures referred to in *subsection (9)(a)*, the auditor to whom the decision referred to in *subsection (8)(b)* relates may apply to the High Court for an order suspending the operation of the withdrawal pending the determination by the relevant appellate committee of an appeal that he or she is making under those procedures and, where such an application is made, *subsections (13)* to *(15)* apply to that application with—

(a) the substitution of references to an appeal under those internal appeal procedures for reference to an appeal under *section 1481*, and

(b) any other necessary modifications.

(11) If the relevant appellate committee referred to in *subsection (10)* is of the opinion, having regard to the particular issues that have arisen on that appeal, that, in the interests of justice, the disposal by it of an appeal referred to in that subsection ought to include its proceeding in the manner specified in *subsections (5)* and *(6)*, then, in disposing of that appeal, it shall proceed in the manner so specified.

(12) The recognised accountancy body shall take all reasonable steps to ensure that any appeal to the relevant appellate committee referred to in *subsection (10)* is prosecuted promptly and it shall be the duty of that appellate committee to ensure that any such appeal to it is disposed of as expeditiously as may be and, for that purpose, to take all such steps as are open to it to ensure that, in so far as is practicable, there are no avoidable delays at any stage in the determination of such an appeal.

(13) Where the recognised accountancy body has made a decision to withdraw the approval of an auditor under this Part (that is to say, a final decision of the recognised accountancy body on the matter after the internal appeal procedures (if any) of it have been employed and exhausted), the auditor may apply to the High Court for an order suspending the operation of the withdrawal pending the determination by the High Court of an appeal under *section 1481* that he or she is making against the withdrawal.

(14) On the hearing of an application under *subsection (13)*, the High Court may, as it considers appropriate and having heard the recognised accountancy body and, if it wishes to be so heard, the Supervisory Authority (which shall have standing to appear and be heard on the application)—

(a) grant an order suspending the operation of the withdrawal, or

(b) refuse to grant such an order,

and an order under *paragraph (a)* may provide that the order shall not have effect unless one or more conditions specified in the order are complied with (and such conditions may include conditions requiring the auditor not to carry out statutory audits save under the supervision of another statutory auditor or not to carry out such audits save in specified circumstances).

(15) The High Court may, on application to it by the auditor or the recognised accountancy body concerned, vary or discharge an order under *subsection (14)(a)* if it considers it just to do so.

(16) The procedures under this section are in addition to those procedures in the cases to which *section 930C(10)* to *(12)* apply, that are required by *section 930C(10)* to *(12)* to be employed.

1480 Grounds for mandatory withdrawal in case of statutory audit firm

(1) For the purposes of this section, the cases that can constitute circumstances of a statutory audit firm's good repute being seriously compromised include cases of professional misconduct or want of professional skill on the part of the audit firm or any of the one or more auditors through whom it acts.

(2) Without prejudice to *section 1502* and subject to *subsections (4)* to *(6)*, the recognised accountancy body shall withdraw an approval of an audit firm under this Part if, but only if—

(a) circumstances arise (involving acts or omissions on the part of the audit firm or auditor or auditors through whom it acts) from which the recognised accountancy body can reasonably conclude that the firm's good repute is seriously compromised,

(b) the audit firm (not being a firm referred to in paragraph (c)) no longer falls within *section 1473(2)(a)*, *(b)* and *(c)*, or

(c) in the case of a firm which is a statutory audit firm referred to in *section 1471(2)*, the firm no longer falls within *section 1473(2)(a)*.

(3) Unless there do not exist internal appeal procedures of the recognised accountancy body as referred to in *subsection (8)(a)*, references in *subsections (4)* to *(7)* to a recognised accountancy body shall be read as references to a recognised accountancy body acting through the disciplinary committee that deals with matters at first instance.

(4) Subject to *subsection (7)*, *subsection (5)* applies where, having—

(a) complied with the requirements of procedural fairness in that regard, and

(b) served any notices required for that purpose or as required by its investigation and disciplinary procedures,

the recognised accountancy body is satisfied that *subsection (2)(a)*, *(b)* or *(c)* applies in the case of an audit firm.

(5) Subject to *subsection (7)*, the recognised accountancy body shall serve a notice in writing on the audit firm stating that—

(a) it is satisfied that *subsection (2)(a)*, *(b)* or *(c)* applies in the case of the audit firm,

(b) the audit firm shall take specified steps to cause *subsection (2)(a)*, *(b)* or *(c)* to cease to apply to it within a specified period (which shall not be less than one month), and

(c) if those steps are not taken, it shall withdraw the approval of the firm.

(6) Where the recognised accountancy body has served a notice under *subsection (5)* on a statutory audit firm and the firm has not, before the expiration of the specified period referred to in *subsection (5)(b)*, taken the steps referred to in *subsection (5)(b)*, the recognised accountancy body shall withdraw the approval of the audit firm under this Part.

(7) The procedure specified in *subsection (5)* need not be employed if the acts or omissions concerned referred to in *subsection (2)(a)* are such as, in the opinion of the recognised accountancy body, constitute professional misconduct or want of professional skill on the part of the audit firm (or the auditor or auditors through whom it acts) of a degree that employing that procedure would not be in the public interest but nothing in this subsection affects the application of the requirements of procedural fairness to the withdrawal of approval.

(8) If—

(a) there exist applicable internal appeal procedures of the recognised accountancy body, and

(b) the investigation and disciplinary procedures of the recognised accountancy body provide that a decision of its disciplinary committee, being a decision of a nature to which this section applies, shall stand suspended or shall not take effect until, as the case may be—

(i) the period for making an appeal under those procedures has expired without such an appeal having been made,

(ii) such an appeal has been made and the decision to withdraw the approval confirmed, or

(iii) such an appeal that has been made is withdrawn,

then, notwithstanding anything in the preceding provisions of this section, the operation of the withdrawal of approval by that disciplinary committee shall stand suspended until the occurrence of an event specified in *paragraph (b)(i), (ii)* or *(iii)*.

(9) *Subsection (10)* applies if—

(a) there exist applicable internal appeal procedures of the recognised accountancy body, and

(b) the investigation and disciplinary procedures of the recognised accountancy body do not provide, as referred to in *subsection (8)(b)*, for the decision of the disciplinary committee referred to in that provision to stand suspended or not to take effect.

(10) Notwithstanding the internal appeal procedures referred to in *subsection (9)(a)*, the audit firm to which the decision referred to in *subsection (8)(b)* relates may apply to the High Court for an order suspending the operation of the withdrawal pending the determination by the relevant appellate committee of an appeal that it is making under those procedures and, where such an application is made, *subsections (13)* to *(15)* apply to that application with—

(a) the substitution of references to an appeal under those internal appeal procedures for reference to an appeal under *section 1481*, and

(b) any other necessary modifications.

(11) If the relevant appellate committee referred to in *subsection (10)* is of the opinion, having regard to the particular issues that have arisen on that appeal, that, in the interests of justice, the disposal by it of an appeal referred to in that subsection ought to include its proceeding in the manner specified in *subsections (5)* and *(6)*, then, in disposing of that appeal, it shall proceed in the manner so specified.

(12) The recognised accountancy body shall take all reasonable steps to ensure that any appeal to the relevant appellate committee referred to in *subsection (10)* is prosecuted promptly and it shall be the duty of that appellate committee to ensure that any such appeal to it is disposed of as expeditiously as may be and, for that purpose, to take all such steps as are open to it to ensure that, in so far as is practicable, there are no avoidable delays at any stage in the determination of such an appeal.

(13) Where the recognised accountancy body has made a decision to withdraw the approval of an audit firm under this section (that is to say, a final decision of the

recognised accountancy body on the matter after the internal appeal procedures (if any) of it have been employed and exhausted), the audit firm may apply to the High Court for an order suspending the operation of the withdrawal pending the determination by the High Court of an appeal under *section 1481* that it is making against the withdrawal.

(14) On the hearing of an application under *subsection (13)*, the High Court may, as it considers appropriate and having heard the recognised accountancy body and, if it wishes to be so heard, the Supervisory Authority (which shall have standing to appear and be heard on the application)—

(a) grant an order suspending the operation of the withdrawal, or

(b) refuse to grant such an order,

and an order under *paragraph (a)* may provide that the order shall not have effect unless one or more conditions specified in the order are complied with (and such conditions may include conditions requiring the audit firm not to carry out statutory audits save under the supervision of one or more statutory auditors or one or more statutory audit firms or not to carry out such audits save in specified circumstances).

(15) The High Court may, on application to it by the audit firm or the recognised accountancy body concerned, vary or discharge an order under *subsection (14)(a)* if it considers it just to do so.

(16) The procedures under this section are in addition to those procedures in the cases to which *section 930C(10)* to *(12)* apply, that are required by *section 930C(10)* to *(12)* to be employed.

1481 Appeals against withdrawal of approval

(1) Subject to *subsection (2)*, a person may appeal to the High Court against the withdrawal by the recognised accountancy body of approval under this Part of the person as a statutory auditor or audit firm.

(2) An appeal shall not lie under *subsection (1)* unless and until any applicable internal appeal procedures of the recognised accountancy body have been employed and exhausted by the person referred to in that subsection.

(3) An appeal under *subsection (1)* shall be made within one month—

(a) unless *paragraph (b)* applies, after the date of the withdrawal of approval, or

(b) after the confirmation of that withdrawal on foot of the internal appeal procedures of the recognised accountancy body having been employed.

(4) On the hearing of an appeal under *subsection (1)*, the High Court may—

(a) cancel the withdrawal of the approval, or

(b) confirm the withdrawal of the approval.

(5) The High Court may, on the hearing of an appeal under *subsection (1)*, consider evidence not adduced or hear an argument not made to the recognised accountancy body if the Court is satisfied that—

(a) there are cogent circumstances justifying the failure to adduce the evidence or make the argument to the recognised accountancy body, and

(b) it is just and equitable for the Court to consider the evidence or hear the argument, as the case may be.

(6) A notification of the outcome of an appeal under this section (or of any appeal from a decision of the High Court thereunder) shall be made by the recognised accountancy body to the same persons to whom a notification of a withdrawal of approval shall be made by *section 1482* and (where it applies) *section 1483*.

1482 Certain persons to be notified of withdrawal of approval

Without prejudice to *section 1483*, where the approval under this Part of a statutory auditor or audit firm is withdrawn for any reason by a recognised accountancy body, that fact and the reasons for the withdrawal shall be communicated by the recognised accountancy body to—

(a) the Supervisory Authority, and

(b) the Registrar,

as soon as possible, but not later than one month after the date of withdrawal of approval.

1483 Other persons to be notified of withdrawal of approval

(1) Where the approval under this Part of a statutory auditor is withdrawn for any reason by a recognised accountancy body, the recognised accountancy body shall, in addition to making the communication specified in *section 1482*, notify the relevant competent authorities of the host Member States, where the statutory auditor is also approved and entered in the public registers of those States pursuant to Articles 15 to 19 of the Audit Directive, of the fact of the withdrawal and the reasons for it.

(2) Where the approval under this Part of an audit firm is withdrawn for any reason by a recognised accountancy body, the recognised accountancy body shall, in addition to making the communication specified in *section 1482*, notify the relevant competent authorities of the host Member States, where the audit firm is also registered and entered in the public registers of those States pursuant to Articles 15 to 19 of the Audit Directive, of the fact of the withdrawal and the reasons for it.

(3) If the approval under this Part of a statutory auditor or audit firm is withdrawn by the Supervisory Authority, this section and *section 1482* (other than paragraph (a) of it) shall apply in relation to the withdrawal as if the references in them to the recognised accountancy body were references to the Supervisory Authority and with any other necessary modifications.

(4) The notifications under this section shall be made as soon as possible, but not later than one month after the date of withdrawal of approval.

Chapter 5
Public register

1484 Public register

(1) Subject to *subsection (2)* and *sections 887(2)*, *934C(2)(h)*, *1506(1)(h)*, *1573* and *1575*, the Registrar shall maintain a particular register (in this Part referred to as the "public register") which shall contain the information set out in Schedule 20 in relation to—

(a) statutory auditors and audit firms (other than audit firms which fall within *paragraph (b)* of the definition of "statutory audit firm"),

(b) third-country auditors and third-country audit entities, and

(c) audit firms approved in another Member State which have been registered in accordance with *section 1465*.

(2) Subject to *sections 1582* and *1583*, the public register referred to in Regulation 84 of the 2016 Audits Regulations, as that register was in being immediately before the date of commencement of section 3(6) of the Companies (Statutory Audits) Act 2018, shall, on and from that date, be deemed to be the public register referred to in *subsection (1)*, and the other provisions of this Part (including provisions relating to the removal or alteration of entries in the public register) shall apply to that register accordingly.

1485 Notification of information to Registrar

(1)(a) An auditor or audit firm (other than a statutory audit firm which falls within *paragraph (b)* of the definition of "statutory audit firm") shall, as soon as may be after he or she is approved under this Part as a statutory auditor or audit firm, notify the relevant information to the recognised accountancy body.

(b) A Member State audit firm shall, as soon as may be after it is registered in accordance with *section 1465*, notify the relevant information to the recognised accountancy body.

(c) A third-country auditor shall, as soon as may be after he or she is approved under this Part as a statutory auditor, notify the relevant information to the recognised accountancy body.

(2) On receipt of a notification under *subsection (1)* and its having carried out any verification of the information as seems to it to be necessary, the recognised accountancy body, as appropriate, shall notify to the Registrar—

(a) the relevant information contained in the notification, and

(b) (i) subject to *subparagraph (ii)*, the individual identification number assigned by it to the auditor, audit firm or third-country auditor under *section 1464(6)* or a Member State audit firm under *section 1465(4)*, and

(ii) where—

(I) under *section 1464(6)* or *1465(4)* such a number exists, and

(II) by reason of the circumstances referred to in *paragraph (b)* of the definition of "relevant information" in *subsection (4)*, the relevant information notified to the recognised accountancy body or Supervisory Authority does not include that number,

the number referred to in *paragraph 1(c)(ii)* or *2(g)* of *Schedule 20*.

(3) The notifications under *subsections (1)* and *(2)* shall each be made in such form and manner as the Registrar specifies.

(4) In this section, "relevant information" means the information set out in *paragraph 1* or *2*, as the case may be, of *Schedule 20*, other than that set out—

(a) in *subparagraph (b)* of that *paragraph 1* or *2*, or

(b) if, due to the simultaneous registration of a statutory audit firm and the statutory auditors that comprise that firm, the number there referred to is not available at that time, in *subparagraph (c)(ii)* of that *paragraph 1* or *subparagraph (g)* of that *paragraph 2*.

(5) For the avoidance of doubt, in the event that a recognised accountancy body is no longer recognised by the Supervisory Authority for the purposes of the relevant provisions or otherwise ceases to exist, the notifications under *subsections (1)* and *(2)* shall cease to have effect and the Registrar shall remove all information contained in such notifications from the public register.

1486 Prohibition on certain acts unless registered

(1) A person shall not—

(a) act as, or

(b) represent himself or herself, or hold himself or herself out, as being,

a person falling within a category of persons entered, or entitled to be entered, in the public register unless the person is entitled to be entered, and the name of the person is duly entered, in the public register.

(2) A person who contravenes *subsection (1)* shall be guilty of a category 2 offence.

1487 Obligation of statutory auditor or audit firm to notify certain information

(1) Each statutory auditor and audit firm and Member State audit firm shall, as soon as may be but not later than one month after the event, notify the recognised accountancy body of any change in the information contained in the public register relating to him or her.

(2) On receipt of a notification under *subsection (1)* and its having carried out any verification of the information stated to have changed as seems to it to be necessary, the recognised accountancy body shall notify the change in information to the Registrar without undue delay.

(3) The Registrar shall, as soon as may be but not later than one month after receipt of the notification referred to in *subsection (2)*, amend the public register to reflect the change of information so notified.

(4) A person who, without reasonable excuse, contravenes *subsection (1)* shall be guilty of a *category 4* offence.

1488 Information shall be signed

(1) Information notified under *section 1485(1)* or *1487(1)* by a statutory auditor or audit firm (including a Member State audit firm) shall be signed by the statutory auditor or, as the case may be, a person on behalf of the statutory audit firm.

(2) The signature referred to in *subsection (1)* may be an electronic signature (within the meaning of Article 3(10) of Regulation (EU) No 910/2014 of the European Parliament and of the Council of 23 July 20148 on electronic identification and trust services for electronic transactions in the internal market and repealing Directive 1999/93/EC) if the provision of a signature in that form complies with any requirements in that behalf of the Registrar of the kind referred to in section 13(2)(a) of the Electronic Commerce Act 2000.

(3) If information is notified under *section 1485(1)* or *1487(1)* without being signed as required by *subsection (1)*, the person concerned shall be guilty of a category 4 offence.

Chapter 6
Standards for statutory auditors

1489 Continuing education

(1) It shall, by virtue of this section alone, be a condition of a statutory auditor's approval (or, in the case of a statutory auditor referred to in *section 1471*, deemed approval) granted under this Part (or under any predecessor to this Part) that he or she shall take part in appropriate programmes of continuing education in order to maintain his or her theoretical knowledge, professional skills and values, including, in particular, in relation to auditing, at a sufficiently high level.

(2) The Supervisory Authority shall, at such times as it thinks it appropriate to do so, issue guidelines to the recognised accountancy bodies with regard to what constitutes compliance with the condition referred to in *subsection (1)*.

1490 Professional ethics

A recognised accountancy body shall subject statutory auditors and audit firms to principles of professional ethics, including at least their public interest function, their integrity and objectivity and their professional competence and due care.

1491 Independence, objectivity and professional scepticism

Statutory auditors and audit firms are subject to the independence, objectivity and professional scepticism requirements of *sections 1533* to *1544* and *1547*.

1492 Standards for purposes of sections 1489 to 1491

(1) A recognised accountancy body shall, in respect of statutory auditors and audit firms—

(a) have adequate standards requiring those auditors and audit firms to comply with the obligations specified in *sections 1489* to *1491*, and

(b) institute adequate arrangements for the effective monitoring and enforcement of compliance with such standards.

(2) No standards shall be used by a recognised accountancy body for that purpose unless those standards have (with respect to that use) first been approved by the Supervisory Authority in accordance with *section 905(2)(c)*.

1493 Arrangements for enforcement of standards

The arrangements for enforcement referred to in *section 1492(1)(b)* shall include, in accordance with *sections 1501* and *1502*, provision for—

(a) sanctions which include—

(i) at the discretion of the recognised accountancy body, in accordance with *section 1501*, the withdrawal of approval under this Part as a statutory auditor or audit firm,

(ii) appropriate penalties,

(iii) appropriate disciplinary measures,

(iv) appropriate regulatory sanctions,

and

(b) making available to the public information relating to the measures taken and the penalties imposed in respect of statutory auditors and audit firms.

Chapter 7
Quality assurance

1494 Quality assurance by Supervisory Authority of statutory audit of public-interest entities and third-country auditors, etc.

(1) The Supervisory Authority shall put in place a quality assurance system as set out in Article 26 of Regulation (EU) No 537/2014.

(2) The Supervisory Authority shall ensure that it has in place a quality assurance system of registered third-country auditors and third-country audit entities to whom this Part or Regulation (EU) No 537/2014 applies.

(3) *Sections 1496* and *1497* shall not apply to the statutory audit of entity and group financial statements of public-interest entities unless specified in Regulation (EU) No 537/2014.

(4) The Supervisory Authority may publish on its website the findings and conclusions of individual inspections undertaken as part of the quality assurance system referred to in *subsection (1)*.

1495 System of quality assurance to be put in place

(1) The Supervisory Authority, in accordance with this Part, shall oversee the quality assurance system implemented by the recognised accountancy bodies.

(2) A recognised accountancy body shall ensure that it has in place a system of quality assurance of—

(a) the body's members' activities as statutory auditors and audit firms of entities not referred to in *section 1494(1)* and *(2)*, and

(b) the activities, as statutory auditors and audit firms, of persons who, though not members of the recognised accountancy body, are persons in relation to whom the body may perform functions under the relevant provisions.

1496 Organisation of quality assurance system

(1) A recognised accountancy body shall organise its quality assurance system in such a manner that—

(a) the system is independent of the reviewed statutory auditors and audit firms,

(b) the funding for the system is secure and free from any possible undue influence by statutory auditors or audit firms,

(c) the system has adequate resources,

(d) the persons who carry out quality assurance reviews have appropriate professional education and relevant experience in statutory audit and financial reporting combined with specific training on quality assurance reviews,

(e) the selection of reviewers for specific quality assurance reviews is effected in accordance with an objective procedure designed to ensure that there are no conflicts of interest between reviewers and the statutory auditor or audit firm under review,

(f) the scope of quality assurance reviews of audits, supported by adequate testing of selected audit files, includes, except where otherwise agreed with the Supervisory Authority, an assessment of—

(i) compliance with applicable auditing standards and independence requirements,

(ii) the quantity and quality of resources spent,

(iii) the audit fees charged, and

(iv) the internal quality control system of the audit firm,

(g) each quality assurance review is the subject of a report in writing which includes the main conclusions of the review,

(h) a quality assurance review of each statutory auditor or audit firm takes place on the basis of an analysis of risk, at least, subject to *subsection (5)* and *section 1497*, every 6 years,

(i) statutory auditors and audit firms take all reasonable steps to ensure that recommendations arising from quality assurance reviews of them are implemented within a reasonable period,

(j) there is published annually by it the overall results of quality assurance reviews carried out by it in the year concerned, and

(k) quality assurance reviews are appropriate and proportionate in view of the scale and complexity of the activity of the reviewed statutory auditor or audit firm.

(2) For the purpose of *subsection (1)(e)*, at least the following criteria shall apply to the selection of reviewers:

(a) reviewers have appropriate professional education and relevant experience in statutory audit and financial reporting combined with specific training on quality assurance reviews;

(b) a person does not act as a reviewer in a quality assurance review of a statutory auditor or audit firm until at least 3 years have elapsed since that person ceased to be a partner or an employee of, or otherwise associated with, that statutory auditor or audit firm;

(c) reviewers shall declare (if such be the case) that there are no conflicts of interest between them and the statutory auditor and the audit firm to be reviewed.

(3) For the purpose of *subsection (1)(k)*, a recognised accountancy body, when undertaking quality assurance reviews of the statutory audits of entity or group financial statements of medium or small companies, shall take account of the fact that auditing standards adopted in accordance with Article 26 of the Audit Directive are designed to be applied in a manner that is proportionate to the scale and complexity of the business of the audited undertaking.

(4) If a statutory auditor or audit firm fails to take all reasonable steps to ensure that recommendations arising from a quality assurance review of him or her are implemented within a reasonable period, the recognised accountancy body shall take appropriate action, including, where applicable, subjecting the statutory auditor or audit firm, as the case may be, to the system of disciplinary actions or penalties referred to in the relevant provisions.

(5) The period of at least 6 years referred to in *subsection (1)(h)* shall be a continuation of the system that was in place under the 2010 Audits Regulations when the first quality assurance reviews were required to be completed and as that system was continued by the 2016 Audits Regulations.

1497 Quality assurance review deemed to include individual auditors in certain cases

For the purpose of *section 1496(1)(h)*, a quality assurance review conducted in relation to a statutory audit firm shall be regarded as a quality assurance review of all statutory auditors carrying out audits on behalf of the firm provided that the firm has a common quality assurance policy with which each such statutory auditor is required to comply.

1498 Right of recognised accountancy body as regards professional discipline

A recognised accountancy body shall have the right to take disciplinary actions or impose sanctions in respect of statutory auditors and audit firms who carry out audits and shall have procedures in place to facilitate the taking or imposition of such action or sanctions.

Chapter 8
Investigations and sanctions

1499 System of investigation and penalties

(1) Subject to *subsection (2)*, each recognised accountancy body shall, in respect of those auditors and audit firms in relation to whom, by virtue of *section 930C*, it may perform functions, institute arrangements to ensure that there are effective systems of investigations and penalties to detect, correct and prevent the inadequate execution of a statutory audit by those statutory auditors and audit firms.

(2) *Subsection (1)* shall not be construed to empower a recognised accountancy body referred to in that subsection to impose a penalty on a statutory auditor or audit firm of a public-interest entity in the case of a relevant contravention committed by that auditor or audit firm that relates (whether in whole or in part) to that entity.

1500 Privileges, etc.

(1) A witness before a recognised accountancy body is entitled to the same immunities and privileges as a witness before the High Court.

(2) Nothing in the arrangements referred to in *section 1499(1)* compels the disclosure by any person of any information that the person would be entitled to refuse to produce on the grounds of legal professional privilege or authorises the inspection or copying of any document containing such information that is in the person's possession or control.

(3) Any information produced or answer given by a person (howsoever described) in compliance with arrangements referred to in *section 1499(1)* may be used in evidence against the person in any proceedings whatsoever, save proceedings for an offence (other than perjury in respect of such an answer).

(4) A finding or decision of a recognised accountancy body under arrangements referred to in *section 1499(1)* is not a bar to any civil or criminal proceedings against the person (howsoever described) who is the subject of the finding or decision.

1501 Duty of each recognised accountancy body with regard to sanctions

(1) Each recognised accountancy body shall ensure that the contractual and other arrangements that exist between it and its members are such as enable the imposition by it of effective, proportionate and dissuasive penalties in respect of statutory auditors and audit firms in cases where statutory audits are not carried out by them in accordance with the relevant provisions.

(2) The contractual and other arrangements referred to in *subsection (1)* shall comply with the requirements of procedural fairness.

(3) By virtue of this section, the contractual and other arrangements referred to in *subsection (1)* that subsist for the time being between a recognised accountancy body and its members shall operate and have effect so as to enable the imposition by the recognised accountancy body—

(a) of penalties of a like character to those referred to in that subsection, and

(b) in the cases referred to in that subsection,

in respect of persons who, though not members of the recognised accountancy body, are persons in relation to whom it may, by virtue of *section 930C*, perform functions under the relevant provisions.

1502 Scope of penalties and publicity in relation to their imposition

(1) The penalties referred to in *section 1501*, provision for which shall be made by the means referred to in that section, shall, where appropriate, include withdrawal of approval under this Part or, if applicable, withdrawal of registration under *section 1465* and a temporary prohibition referred to in point (c) of Article 30a(1) of the Audit Directive and a temporary prohibition (in so far as it relates to a member of an audit firm) referred to in point (e) of that Article.

(2) *Subsection (1)* is without prejudice to *sections 1479* and *1480*.

(3) Unless there do not exist internal appeal procedures of a recognised accountancy body as referred to in *section 1479(8)(a)* or *1480(8)(a)*, the reference in *subsection (4)* to a recognised accountancy body shall be read as a reference to a recognised accountancy body acting through the disciplinary committee that deals with matters at first instance.

(4) Without prejudice to *section 930C(10)* to *(12)*, a recognised accountancy body may, save where, in its opinion, proceeding in this manner would not be in the public interest, adopt procedures analogous to those in *section 1479(4)* to *(6)* or *1480(4)* to *(6)* as regards affording the statutory auditor or audit firm an opportunity to rectify the matters that have occasioned the investigation concerned and the proposed exercise of the power of withdrawal of approval referred to in *subsection (1)*.

(5) If—

(a) there exist internal appeal procedures, as referred to in *section 1479(8)(a)* or *1480(8)(a)*, of a recognised accountancy body, and

(b) the investigation and disciplinary procedures of the recognised accountancy body provide that a decision of its disciplinary committee referred to in *subsection (3)*, being a decision of a nature to which this section applies, shall stand suspended or shall not take effect until, as the case may be—

(i) the period for making an appeal under those procedures has expired without such an appeal having been made,

(ii) such an appeal has been made and the decision to withdraw the approval confirmed, or

(iii) such an appeal that has been made is withdrawn,

then notwithstanding anything in the preceding provisions of this section, the operation of the withdrawal of approval by that disciplinary committee shall stand suspended until the occurrence of an event specified in paragraph (b)(i), (ii) or (iii).

(6) If—

(a) there exist internal appeal procedures, as referred to in *section 1479(8)(a)* or *1480(8)(a)*, of a recognised accountancy body, and

(b) the investigation and disciplinary procedures of the recognised accountancy body do not provide, as referred to in *subsection (5)(b)*, for the decision of the disciplinary committee referred to in that provision to stand suspended or not to take effect,

then, notwithstanding anything in those procedures, the auditor or audit firm to whom that decision relates may apply to the High Court for an order suspending the operation of the withdrawal pending the determination by the relevant appellate committee of an appeal that he or she is making under those internal appeal procedures.

(7) Where an application under *subsection (6)* is made to the High Court, *subsections (10)* to *(12)* apply to the application with—

(a) the substitution of references to an appeal under those internal appeal procedures for references to an appeal under *section 1481*, and

(b) any other necessary modifications.

(8) If the relevant appellate committee referred to in *subsection (6)* is of the opinion, having regard to the particular issues that have arisen on that appeal, that, in the interests of justice, the disposal by it of an appeal referred to in that subsection ought to include procedures analogous to those, as referred to in *subsection (4)*, provided by *section 1479(4)* to *(6)* or *1480(4)* to *(6)* being adopted by it, then, in disposing of that appeal, it shall adopt procedures analogous to those in *section 1479(4)* to *(6)* or *1480(4)* to *(6)*.

(9) A recognised accountancy body shall take all reasonable steps to ensure that any appeal to the relevant appellate committee referred to in *subsection (6)* is prosecuted promptly and it shall be the duty of that appellate committee to ensure that any such appeal to it is disposed of as expeditiously as may be and, for that purpose, to take all such steps as are open to it to ensure that, in so far as is practicable, there are no avoidable delays at any stage in the determination of such an appeal.

(10) Where a recognised accountancy body has made a decision to withdraw the approval of an auditor or audit firm under this section (that is to say, a final decision of the recognised accountancy body on the matter after the internal appeal procedures (if any) of it have been employed and exhausted), the auditor or audit firm may apply to the High Court for an order suspending the operation of the withdrawal pending the determination by the High Court of an appeal under *section 1481* that he or she is making against the withdrawal.

(11) On the hearing of an application under *subsection (10)*, the High Court may, as it considers appropriate and having heard the recognised accountancy body concerned and, if it wishes to be so heard, the Supervisory Authority (which shall have standing to appear and be heard on the application)—

(a) grant an order suspending the operation of the withdrawal, or

(b) refuse to grant such an order,

and an order under *paragraph (a)* may provide that the order shall not have effect unless one or more conditions specified in the order are complied with (and such conditions may include conditions requiring the auditor or audit firm not to carry out statutory audits save under the supervision of one or more other statutory auditors or audit firms or not to carry out such audits save in specified circumstances).

(12) The High Court may, on application to it by the auditor or audit firm or recognised accountancy body concerned, vary or discharge an order under *subsection (11)(a)* if it considers it just to do so.

(13) The fact of one or more—

(a) measures having been taken against, or

(b) one or more penalties having been imposed on,

a statutory auditor or audit firm by a recognised accountancy body shall be disclosed by the recognised accountancy body to the public and that disclosure shall, if the recognised accountancy body considers it appropriate, include such further particulars with respect to the matter as it thinks fit.

(14) Subject to *subsection (15)*, the manner of such disclosure, and the time at which it is made, shall be such as the recognised accountancy body determines to be appropriate.

(15) The recognised accountancy body shall establish, in writing, criteria the purpose of which is to govern the determination by it of the matters referred to in *subsection (14)*, and those criteria shall require the prior approval of the Supervisory Authority.

Chapter 9

Actions to be taken after decision by recognised accountancy body that statutory auditor or audit firm of public-interest entity has committed relevant contravention

1503 Definitions (Chapter 9)

In this Chapter—

"contravention concerned", in relation to a specified person, means the relevant contravention committed by the specified person in consequence of which the relevant decision was made;

"monetary sanction" means the monetary sanction referred to in *section 1506(1)(g)*;

"public notice of relevant sanction imposed", in relation to a specified person, means the publication in accordance with *section 1508(1)* of the specified person's particulars referred to in that section together with the other particulars referred to in that section;

"relevant decision", in relation to a specified person, means a decision under *section 1504(6)* by the Supervisory Authority to impose a relevant sanction on the specified person for the relevant contravention committed by the specified person;

"relevant sanction" means a sanction referred to in *section 1506(1)*;

"specified person" means the statutory auditor or audit firm the subject of a relevant decision.

1504 Initial actions to be taken after decision by recognised accountancy body that statutory auditor or audit firm of public-interest entity has committed relevant contravention

(1) Without prejudice to the generality of *sections 933*, *934* and *934E* and subject to *subsection (9)*, this section applies where—

(a) a recognised accountancy body has completed an investigation of a statutory auditor or audit firm of a public-interest entity and—

(i) has found that the auditor or audit firm has committed a relevant contravention that relates (whether in whole or in part) to that entity, and

(ii) would, but for *section 1499(2)*, be minded to impose a penalty on the auditor or audit firm for that contravention,

and

(b) the period within which an appeal (if any) referred to in *Chapter 8* may be made against the decision referred to in *paragraph (a)* has expired without any such appeal having been made or, if such an appeal has been made, that decision has been confirmed or the appeal has been withdrawn.

(2) The recognised accountancy body shall, as soon as is practicable after this section applies to a statutory auditor or audit firm of a public-interest entity and a relevant contravention committed by the auditor or audit firm, give the Supervisory Authority—

(a) particulars of the auditor or audit firm, the public-interest entity and the relevant contravention,

(b) copies of any reports arising out of the investigation, together with copies of any other documents relevant to the investigation, that explain how the recognised accountancy body conducted the investigation and reached the decision referred to in *subsection (1)(a)*, and

(c) particulars of the penalty referred to in *subsection (1)(a)(ii)*.

(3) Where the Supervisory Authority receives from the recognised accountancy body the particulars and copies referred to in *subsection (2)* but is not satisfied that it has sufficient information to perform its functions under *subsections (5)* to *(8)*, it may, by notice in writing given to the recognised accountancy body, require the body to provide it with such further information specified in the notice within the period (being a period of not less than 30 days from the body's receipt of the notice) specified in the notice.

(4) The recognised accountancy body shall comply with a notice under *subsection (3)* given to it.

(5) *Subsection (6)* applies where the Supervisory Authority receives from the recognised accountancy body the particulars and copies referred to in *subsection (2)* (and, if applicable, any further information required by a notice under *subsection (3)* given to that body) and, after considering those particulars and copies (and, if applicable, that further information), it is satisfied that the statutory auditor or audit firm has committed the relevant contravention and the Supervisory Authority is minded to impose a relevant sanction on the auditor or auditor firm for that contravention.

(6) Subject to *section 1511(3)* and *(4)*, the Supervisory Authority may impose a relevant sanction on the statutory auditor or audit firm of the public-interest entity for the relevant contravention and, for that purpose, it shall have regard to (but is not bound by) the penalty referred to in *subsection (1)(a)(ii)*.

(7) Where under *subsection (6)* the Supervisory Authority imposes a relevant sanction on the statutory auditor or audit firm of the public-interest entity for the relevant contravention, it shall, as soon as is practicable after so imposing such sanction, by notice in writing given to the recognised accountancy body, give particulars of the sanction imposed.

(8) Where the Supervisory Authority is not satisfied as referred to in *subsection (5)*, it shall, as soon as practicable after reaching that decision, by notice in writing given to the recognised accountancy body, advise the body that it is not so satisfied and the reasons therefor.

(9) (a) Subject to *paragraph (b)*, where a recognised accountancy body is minded to commence an investigation of a statutory auditor or audit firm in respect of a statutory audit of a public-interest entity, it shall, before commencing such investigation and in the interests of assisting the Supervisory Authority to make a decision as to whether or not, instead of the investigation, it would be more appropriate for the Supervisory Authority to take action under *section 934* or *934E*, give the Supervisory Authority particulars of the auditor or audit firm and the public-interest entity and the grounds on which it is so minded.

(b) The recognised accountancy body shall not commence an investigation referred to in *paragraph (a)* until it has the consent in writing of the Supervisory Authority to do so.

1505 Appeal against relevant decision

(1) Subject to *subsection (2)*, the specified person may appeal to the High Court against the relevant decision.

(2) An appeal under *subsection (1)* shall be brought within 3 months after the date on which the specified person was notified by the Supervisory Authority of the relevant decision.

1506 Sanctions which Supervisory Authority may impose on specified person

(1) Subject to *section 1507*, the Supervisory Authority may impose on the specified person one or more of the following sanctions in relation to the contravention concerned:

(a) a direction by the Supervisory Authority to the specified person that he or she cease the conduct giving rise (whether in whole or in part) to the contravention and to abstain from any repetition of that conduct;

(b) a direction by the Supervisory Authority to the specified person to remediate the conduct giving rise (whether in whole or in part) to the contravention;

(c) a reprimand or severe reprimand by the Supervisory Authority to the specified person in relation to the conduct giving rise (whether in whole or in part) to the contravention;

(d) a declaration by the Supervisory Authority that the statutory auditors' report concerned does not meet the requirements of *section 336* or *337* or, where applicable, Article 10 of Regulation (EU) No 537/2014;

(e) a direction by the Supervisory Authority to the specified person (being any one or more of a statutory auditor or key audit partner) prohibiting him or her, for the period specified in the direction (which may be up to and including an indefinite period), from carrying out statutory audits or signing statutory auditors' reports, or both;

(f) if the specified person is an audit firm, a direction by the Supervisory Authority to the firm, or to an officer, member or partner of the firm, or to both, prohibiting the firm or, as the case may be, the officer, member or partner, for the period specified in the direction (which may be up to and including an indefinite period) from performing functions—

(i) in the case of the firm, as an audit firm, or

(ii) in the case of the officer, member or partner, in audit firms or public-interest entities;

(g) subject to *section 1509*, a direction by the Supervisory Authority to the specified person to pay an amount, as specified in the direction but not exceeding—

(i) €100,000 in the case of a specified person who is an individual, or

(ii) in the case of a specified person which is an audit firm, €100,000 multiplied by the number of statutory auditors in the firm at the time that the relevant contravention occurred (and irrespective of whether any particular statutory auditor was or was not a party to the relevant contravention),

to the Supervisory Authority;

(h) an order excluding the specified person from having his or her particulars entered, or continuing to be entered, in the public register in respect of one or more recognised accountancy bodies.

(2) In default of payment of an amount referred to in *subsection (1)(g)*, the Supervisory Authority may recover that amount as a simple contract debt in any court of competent jurisdiction.

(3) A person the subject of a direction under *subsection (1)* shall comply with the direction.

(4) Where applicable, the Supervisory Authority shall direct the recognised accountancy body of which the specified person is a member to take any necessary action on foot of the imposition of a relevant sanction on the person and that body shall comply with the direction.

1507 Relevant circumstances to be considered in imposing relevant sanctions on specified person

In imposing a relevant sanction on a specified person, the Supervisory Authority shall consider the following circumstances:

(a) the gravity and duration of the contravention concerned;

(b) the degree of responsibility of the specified person;

(c) the financial strength of the specified person (including, in the case of a specified person who is not an individual, the total turnover of the specified person or, in the case of a specified person who is an individual, the annual income of the individual);

(d) the amount of profits gained or losses avoided by the specified person in consequence of the contravention concerned, in so far as they can be determined;

(e) the level of cooperation of the specified person with the Supervisory Authority and the recognised accountancy body of which the specified person is a member;

(f) previous relevant contraventions committed by the specified person.

1508 Publication of relevant sanction imposed on specified person, etc.

(1) Subject to *subsections (2)* and *(3)*, the Supervisory Authority shall, in so far as a relevant decision imposes a relevant sanction on a specified person, as soon as is practicable after—

(a) that decision has been confirmed by the High Court as referred to in *section 1511(3)*, or

(b) a decision of the High Court under *section 1511(2)(b)* has been made to impose a different relevant sanction on the specified person,

publish on its website particulars of the contravention concerned, particulars of the relevant sanction imposed and particulars of the specified person on whom the relevant sanction was imposed.

(2) Subject to *subsection (4)*, if there is an appeal from the High Court from a confirmation referred to in *subsection (1)(a)*, or a decision referred to in *subsection (1)(b)*, the Supervisory Authority shall as soon as may be, as it considers appropriate, publish particulars on its website of the status or outcome of the appeal.

(3) The Supervisory Authority shall publish the particulars, comprising a public notice of relevant sanction imposed, on an anonymous basis on its website in any one or more of the following circumstances:

(a) the Supervisory Authority, following an assessment of the proportionality of the publication of those particulars in accordance with *subsection (1)* in so far as personal data are concerned, is of the opinion that, in relation to the relevant sanction imposed on a specified person who is an individual, such publication would be disproportionate;

(b) the Supervisory Authority is of the opinion that the publication of those particulars in accordance with *subsection (1)* would jeopardise the stability of financial markets or an ongoing criminal investigation;

(c) the Supervisory Authority is of the opinion that the publication of those particulars in accordance with *subsection (1)* would cause disproportionate damage to the specified person.

(4) *Subsection (2)* shall not apply in any case where *subsection (3)* applies.

(5) The Supervisory Authority shall ensure that particulars published on its website in accordance with *subsection (1)* or *(2)* remain on its website for at least 5 years.

1509 Limitations on imposing monetary sanctions on specified person

(1) If the Supervisory Authority decides to impose a monetary sanction on a specified person, the Supervisory Authority shall not impose an amount—

(a) that would be likely to cause the specified person to cease business, or

(b) that would, if the specified person is an individual, be likely to cause the person to be adjudicated bankrupt.

(2) If the conduct engaged in by the specified person has given rise (whether in whole or in part) to 2 or more contraventions concerned, the Supervisory Authority shall not impose more than one monetary sanction on the person in respect of the same conduct.

1510 Specified person not to be liable to be penalised twice for same relevant contravention

(1) If the Supervisory Authority imposes a monetary sanction on a specified person and the conduct engaged in by the person that has given rise (whether in whole or in part) to the contravention concerned is an offence under the law of the State, the person shall not be liable to be prosecuted or punished for the offence under that law.

(2) The Supervisory Authority shall not impose a monetary sanction on a specified person if—

(a) the person has been charged with having committed an offence under a law of the State and has either been found guilty or not guilty of having committed the offence, and

(b) the offence involves the conduct engaged in by the person that has given rise (whether in whole or in part) to the contravention concerned.

1511 Appeals to and orders of High Court, including orders confirming relevant decisions of Supervisory Authority

(1) In an appeal under *section 1505*, the High Court may consider any evidence adduced or argument made, whether or not adduced or made to the Supervisory Authority or recognised accountancy body concerned.

(2) On the hearing of such an appeal, the High Court may make any order or give any direction as it thinks fit, including an order—

(a) confirming the decision under appeal, or

(b) modifying or annulling the decision.

(3) A relevant decision does not take effect until that decision is confirmed by the High Court either—

(a) on appeal under *section 1505*, or

(b) on application by the Supervisory Authority under *subsection (4)*.

(4) On application by motion on notice by the Supervisory Authority for an order confirming a relevant decision, the High Court may make an order confirming the decision or may refuse to make such an order.

Chapter 10
Appointment of statutory auditors or audit firms

1512 Prohibition of contractual clauses restricting choice of auditors

(1) *Section 380(6)* shall, with any necessary modifications, apply to an audited undertaking which is not a company and to which this Part applies as that section applies to an audited undertaking which is a company and to which this Part applies.

(2) An audited undertaking that is a public-interest entity shall directly and without delay report to the Supervisory Authority any contractual clause referred to in *section 380(6)* that purports to affect it and the circumstances which gave rise to that clause.

(3) The Supervisory Authority, on receipt of a report under *subsection (2)*, may share the report with—

(a) the Director,

(b) the Revenue Commissioners,

(c) the Workplace Relations Commission,

(d) the Central Bank, or

(e) any body responsible for the regulation of the public-interest entity.

1513 Selection procedures for statutory auditors or audit firms by public-interest entities

(1) Subject to *subsection (2)*, the following selection procedures apply, for financial years commencing on or after 17 June 2016, to the appointment of a statutory auditor or audit firm to a public-interest entity:

(a) the audit committee shall prepare a recommendation for the directors of the entity by carrying out the selection procedure specified in Article 16(3) of Regulation (EU) No 537/2014;

(b) the audit committee shall submit a recommendation to the directors of the entity for the appointment of statutory auditors or audit firms;

(c) the recommendation—

(i) shall be justified and contain at least 2 choices for the audit engagement and shall express a duly justified preference for one of them, and

(ii) shall state (if such be the case) that the recommendation is free from influence by a third party and that, on and from 17 June 2017, no clause of the kind referred to in *section 380(6)* has been imposed upon it;

(d) the proposal by the directors to the general meeting of shareholders or members of the entity for the appointment of statutory auditors or audit firms—

(i) shall include the recommendation referred to in *paragraph (b)* and the preference referred to in *paragraph (c)(i)*,

(ii) if it departs from the preference of the audit committee, shall justify the reasons for not following the recommendation of the audit committee, and

(iii) shall state if the statutory auditor or audit firm recommended by the directors participated in the selection procedure referred to in *subsection (2)(a)*.

(2) *Subsection (1)* shall not apply if—

(a) a selection procedure in accordance with Article 16(3) of Regulation (EU) No 537/2014 has been carried out in respect of the appointment of the statutory auditor or audit firm in relation to one or more of the preceding 9 financial years, and

(b) the statutory auditor or audit firm appointed by the public-interest entity was appointed for the previous financial year.

(3) Where the public-interest entity is exempt from the requirement for an audit committee under section 1551, this section applies to the directors of the public-interest entity.

(4) Where a public-interest entity relies on the provisions of *section 382*, *384* or *385*, the public-interest entity shall, as soon as is practicable, inform the Supervisory Authority of that fact.

(5) The appointment of an auditor or audit firm shall be invalid if the appointment contravenes a provision of this section.

(6) (a) Subject to *paragraph (b)*, a public-interest entity shall keep records demonstrating that the selection procedures referred to in *subsection (1)* have been carried out.

(b) The public-interest entity shall keep those records for at least 6 years from the date on which the selection procedures were completed.

(7) A person who contravenes *subsection (6)(a)* or *(b)* shall be guilty of a category 4 offence.

1514 Appointment of statutory auditors or audit firms by public-interest entities - informing the Supervisory Authority

(1) Subject to *subsection (2)*—

(a) where a statutory auditor or audit firm is first appointed by a public-interest entity on or after 17 June 2016, the statutory auditor or audit firm shall inform the Supervisory Authority within one month after the date of such appointment that the statutory auditor or audit firm has been appointed to hold office, and

(b) where a statutory auditor or audit firm which has complied with *paragraph (a)* is subsequently appointed by the same or a different public-interest entity, the statutory auditor or audit firm shall inform the Supervisory Authority within one month after the date of such appointment that the statutory auditor or audit firm has been appointed to hold office only if, immediately before the time of such appointment, the statutory auditor or audit firm held no such office with any public-interest entity.

(2) The information shall be submitted in such form and manner as the Supervisory Authority specifies and may be used by the Supervisory Authority in the performance of its functions.

(3) A person who contravenes *subsection (1)* shall be guilty of a category 3 offence.

1515 Removal of statutory auditors or audit firms by public-interest entities - supplementary provisions

(1) In the case of a statutory audit of a public-interest entity—

(a) shareholders representing 5 per cent or more of the voting rights or of the share capital, or

(b) the Supervisory Authority,

may bring a claim before the High Court for the removal of the statutory auditor or audit firm subject to there being good and substantial grounds for bringing such a claim before the Court.

(2) The grounds for bringing the claim before the High Court shall relate to—

(a) the conduct of the auditor or audit firm with regard to the performance of his or her duties as auditor of the public-interest entity or otherwise, or

(b) the petitioner's opinion that it is in the best interests of the public-interest entity to do so.

(3) For the purposes of *subsection (2)*—

(a) diverging opinions on accounting treatments or audit procedures cannot constitute the basis for the passing of any resolution for the purposes of that subsection, and

(b) "best interests of the public-interest entity" shall not include any illegal or improper motive with regard to avoiding disclosures or detection of any contravention by the entity of this Act.

1516 Directors' report to include date of last appointment of statutory auditor or audit firm

(1) The directors' report shall contain details of the date of appointment of the public-interest entity's statutory auditor or audit firm.

(2) Where a public-interest entity has sought an extension from the Supervisory Authority under *section 1548*, pursuant to Article 17(6) of Regulation (EU) No 537/ 2014, the directors' report shall also contain details of the extension granted.

(3) In this section, "directors' report" means the directors' report required by section 325.

Chapter 11
Confidentiality and professional secrecy

1517 Rules of confidentiality to apply

(1) The rules of confidentiality and secrecy of a recognised accountancy body (of which the statutory auditor or audit firm concerned is a member) shall apply with respect to information and documents to which a statutory auditor or audit firm has access when carrying out a statutory audit.

(2) The statutory auditor or audit firm, as the case may be, shall comply with those rules of confidentiality and secrecy.

(3) In the case of an audit firm registered in accordance with section 1465, the rules of confidentiality and secrecy of the recognised accountancy body of which the key audit partner who carries out the statutory audit on behalf of the audit firm is a member shall apply with respect to information and documents to which the audit firm (or a statutory auditor on behalf of the firm) has access when carrying out a statutory audit.

1518 Supplemental provisions in relation to section 1517

(1) *Section 1517* shall continue to apply with respect to the carrying out of a statutory audit notwithstanding—

- (a) that the statutory auditor or audit firm referred to in that section has ceased to be engaged in that audit, or
- (b) that the auditor or audit firm referred to in that section ceases to be—
  - (i) a statutory auditor or audit firm, or
  - (ii) an auditor or audit firm.

(2) Accordingly, in such a case—

- (a) the statutory auditor or, as the case may be, audit firm, or
- (b) the former such auditor or, as the case may be, audit firm,

shall continue to comply with the rules of confidentiality and secrecy concerned.

1519 Saving

(1) Nothing in *section 1517* or *1518* shall operate to prevent the recognised accountancy body from complying with its obligations under the relevant provisions.

(2) Nothing in *section 1517* or *1518* shall operate to impede the enforcement of the relevant provisions.

1520 Rules of confidentiality in relation to entities in third countries

(1) Where a statutory auditor or audit firm carries out a statutory audit of an undertaking which is part of a group whose holding undertaking is situated in a third country, the confidentiality and professional secrecy rules referred to in *section 1517(1)* shall not impede the transfer by the statutory auditor or the audit firm of relevant documentation concerning the audit work performed to the group auditor situated in a third country if such documentation is necessary for the performance of the audit of consolidated financial statements of the holding undertaking.

(2) A statutory auditor or an audit firm that carries out the statutory audit of an undertaking which has issued securities in a third country, or which forms part of a group issuing statutory consolidated financial statements in a third country, may only transfer the audit working papers or other documents relating to the audit of that undertaking that he or she holds to the competent authorities in the relevant third countries under the conditions set out in *Chapter 19*.

(3) The transfer of information to the group auditor situated in a third country shall comply with the Data Protection Acts 1988 to 2018 and Regulation (EU) 2016/679.

1521 Incoming statutory auditor or audit firm to be afforded access to information

Where a statutory auditor or audit firm is replaced by another statutory auditor or audit firm, the former statutory auditor or audit firm shall provide access to all relevant information concerning the audited undertaking and the most recent audit of that undertaking to the incoming statutory auditor or audit firm.

1522 Access by recognised accountancy body to audit documents

(1) Where it considers it reasonably necessary to do so for the purpose of performing a particular function under the relevant provisions, a recognised accountancy body may inspect and make copies of all relevant documents in the possession or control of a statutory auditor or audit firm; for that purpose, it may, by notice in writing served on a statutory auditor or audit firm, require the auditor or firm either (as shall be specified) to—

(a) furnish to it specified documents, or

(b) permit it to have access, under specified circumstances, to all relevant documents in the possession or control of the auditor or firm,

within a specified period.

(2) Without prejudice to the generality of *subsection (1)*, the powers under that subsection are exercisable in relation to a statutory auditor or audit firm where a complaint is made to a recognised accountancy body that the statutory auditor or audit firm has contravened a requirement of the relevant provisions.

(3) Where the powers under *subsection (1)* are exercisable, the following additional power may be exercised by a recognised accountancy body if it considers that the exercise of it is reasonably necessary to enable it to clarify any matter arising from its

inspection of the documents concerned, namely a power to require the statutory auditor or a member of the statutory audit firm to—

(a) attend before it, and

(b) explain any entry in the documents concerned and otherwise give assistance to it in clarifying the matter concerned.

(4) In this section, "specified" means specified in the notice concerned.

(5) Without prejudice to *subsection (6)*, if a person fails, without reasonable excuse, to comply with a requirement under *subsection (1)* or *(3)*, the person shall be guilty of a category 3 offence.

(6) Where a person fails to comply with a requirement under *subsection (1)* or *(3)*, the recognised accountancy body concerned may apply to the High Court for an order compelling compliance by the person with the requirement, and, on the hearing of such application, the Court may make such an order or such other order as it thinks just.

1523 Access by Supervisory Authority to information and documents held by recognised accountancy bodies or relevant persons

(1) Where it considers it reasonably necessary to do so for the purposes of performing a particular function under the relevant provisions, the Supervisory Authority may request information and inspect and make copies of all relevant documents in the possession or control of a recognised accountancy body or a relevant person; for that purpose, it may, by notice in writing served on the recognised accountancy body or relevant person, require the recognised accountancy body or relevant person either (as shall be specified) to—

(a) furnish to it specified documents or information, or

(b) permit it to have access, under specified circumstances, to all relevant documents in the possession or control of the recognised accountancy body or relevant person,

within a specified period.

(2) In this section, "relevant person" means—

(a) a member of a recognised accountancy body,

(b) a client or former client of the member,

(c) if the client or former client is a body corporate, a person who is or was an officer, employee or agent of the client or former client, or

(d) any person whom the Supervisory Authority reasonably believes has information or documents in relation to the particular function other than information or documents the disclosure of which is prohibited or restricted by law.

(3) Without prejudice to the generality of *subsection (1)*, the powers under that subsection are exercisable in relation to a recognised accountancy body or relevant person where a complaint is made to the Supervisory Authority that the recognised accountancy body or relevant person has contravened a requirement of the relevant provisions.

(4) Where the powers under *subsection (1)* are exercisable, the following additional power may be exercised by the Supervisory Authority if it considers that the exercise of it is reasonably necessary to enable it to clarify any matter arising from its inspection of the information or documents concerned, namely a power to require an officer of the recognised accountancy body or relevant person to—

(a) attend before it, and

(b) explain any entry in the information or documents concerned and otherwise give assistance to it in clarifying the matter concerned.

(5) In this section, "specified" means specified in the notice concerned.

(6) If a person fails, without reasonable excuse, to comply with a requirement under *subsection (1)* or *(4)*, the person shall be guilty of a category 3 offence.

(7) Nothing in this section derogates from the powers exercisable by the Supervisory Authority in the circumstances, and under the conditions, specified in *section 933* or *934*.

1524 Professional privilege

Nothing in this Chapter compels the disclosure by any person of any information that the person would be entitled to refuse to produce on the grounds of legal professional privilege.

1525 No liability for acts done in compliance with obligations imposed by relevant provisions

(1) No professional or legal duty to which a statutory auditor or audit firm is subject by virtue of his or her appointment as a statutory auditor or audit firm shall be regarded as contravened by reason of compliance with the obligations imposed by the relevant provisions.

(2) No liability to the undertaking audited or being audited, its shareholders, creditors, or other interested parties shall attach to the statutory auditor or audit firm by reason of such compliance.

(3) For the avoidance of doubt, nothing in this section affects the liability of a statutory auditor or audit firm for negligence or breach of duty in the conduct of a statutory audit by him or her.

Chapter 12
Auditing standards and audit reporting

1526 Auditing standards to be applied

(1) The Supervisory Authority shall adopt the auditing standards to be applied and statutory auditors and audit firms shall carry out statutory audits in accordance with those standards.

(2) On and from the adoption of international auditing standards, statutory auditors and audit firms shall carry out statutory audits in accordance with those standards.

(3) The reference in *subsection (2)* to the adoption of international auditing standards is a reference to the adoption by the Commission, in accordance with the procedure referred to in Article 26 of the Audit Directive, of international auditing standards.

(4) The Supervisory Authority may prescribe by regulations audit procedures or requirements, in addition to the international auditing standards adopted by the Commission under Article 26 of the Directive, only—

(a) if those audit procedures or requirements are necessary in order to give effect to legal requirements in the State relating to the scope of statutory audits, or

(b) to the extent necessary to add to the credibility and quality of financial statements.

(5) The Supervisory Authority shall communicate the audit procedures or requirements referred to in *subsection (4)* to the Commission at least 3 months before their entry into force or, in the case of requirements already existing at the time of adoption of an international auditing standard, at the latest within 3 months of the adoption of the relevant international auditing standard.

(6) In the case of the statutory audit of small companies, the Supervisory Authority may provide that the application of the auditing standards referred to in *subsection (1)* is to be proportionate to the scale and complexity of the activities of such companies and may take the measures necessary in order to ensure the proportionate application of the auditing standards to the statutory audits of small companies.

(7) In this section, "standards" include standards on professional ethics and internal quality control in addition to standards on auditing.

1527 Audit of group accounts – responsibility of group auditor

(1) Where a statutory audit of the group financial statements of a group is carried out—

(a) in relation to the group financial statements, the group auditor shall bear the full responsibility for the statutory auditors' report, and

(b) where the holding undertaking is a public-interest entity, the group auditor shall bear the full responsibility for ensuring that the requirements of Articles 10 and 11 of Regulation (EU) No 537/2014 are met in relation to the audit carried out on that public-interest entity.

(2) The group auditor shall—

(a) evaluate the audit work carried out by any auditors for the purpose of the group audit, and

(b) document the nature, timing and extent of the work carried out by those auditors, including the group auditor's review of the relevant parts of audit documentation.

(3) For the purposes of the group audit, auditors may be one or more of the following:

(a) statutory auditors;

(b) statutory audit firms;

(c) Member State auditors;

(d) Member State audit firms;

(e) third-country auditors;

(f) third-country audit entities.

(4) The group auditor shall carry out a review, and maintain documentation of such review, of the work of whoever referred to in *subsection (3)* performed audit work for the purposes of the group audit.

(5) The documentation referred to in *subsections (2)(b)* and *(4)* to be retained by the group auditor shall be such as enables the Supervisory Authority, or the recognised accountancy body where applicable, to conduct a quality assurance inspection or review, as the case may be, under *Chapter 7*.

(6) The group auditor shall request the agreement of the auditors concerned referred to in *subsection (3)(a)* to *(f)* to transfer relevant documentation during the carrying out of the audit of group financial statements as a condition of the reliance by the group auditor on the work of such auditors.

(7) (a) Where the group auditor is unable to secure an agreement referred to in *subsection (6)*, he or she shall take appropriate measures in order to form an audit opinion and inform the relevant Supervisory Authority or the recognised accountancy body where applicable.

(b) Such measures shall, as appropriate, include carrying out additional statutory audit work, either directly or by outsourcing the additional statutory audit work, in the relevant subsidiary.

(8) (a) The group auditor who is subject to a quality assurance inspection or review or an investigation concerning the statutory audit of the group financial statements of a group shall, when requested, make available to the Supervisory Authority or the recognised accountancy body where applicable the relevant documentation he or she retains concerning the audit work performed by the auditors concerned referred to in *subsection (3)(a)* to *(f)* for the purpose of the group audit, including any working papers relevant to the group audit.

(b) The Supervisory Authority may request additional documentation on the audit work performed by a statutory auditor or audit firm for the purpose of the group audit from the competent authorities in other Member States where applicable pursuant to *Chapter 17*.

1528 Further responsibility of group auditor

(1) Subject to *subsection (2)*, the Supervisory Authority may request additional documentation on the audit work performed by any third-country auditor or third-country audit entity on a holding undertaking or on a subsidiary undertaking of a group from the relevant competent authorities from third countries through the working arrangements referred to in *section 1568(1)(c)* or *1569(c)*.

(2) Where—

(a) a statutory audit of the group financial statements of a group is carried out, and

(b) a holding undertaking or subsidiary undertaking of the group is audited by one or more third-country auditors or third-country audit entities that have no working arrangements as referred to in *section 1568(1)(c)* or *1569(c)*,

the group auditor is responsible for ensuring proper delivery, when requested, to the Supervisory Authority of the additional documentation of the audit work performed by those auditors or audit entities, including the audit working papers relevant to the group audit.

(3) To ensure such delivery, the group auditor shall retain a copy of such audit documentation, or alternatively—

(a) agree, with one or more third-country auditors or third-country audit entities concerned, arrangements for the group auditor's proper and unrestricted access, upon request, to the documentation, or

(b) take any other appropriate action.

(4) Where audit working papers cannot, for legal or other reasons, be passed from a third country to the group auditor, the documentation retained by the group auditor shall include—

(a) evidence that he or she has undertaken the appropriate procedures in order to gain access to the audit documentation, and

(b) in the case of an impediment other than a legal one arising from legislation of the third country or countries concerned, evidence supporting the existence of such an impediment.

1529 Additional report to audit committee

(1) Where a public-interest entity is exempt from the requirement to have an audit committee, as provided for under this Part, the additional report to the audit committee shall be submitted to the directors of the public-interest entity.

(2) Subject to *subsection (1)*, the audit committee of a public-interest entity shall submit the additional report to the audit committee to the directors of the public-interest entity.

(3) The Supervisory Authority may set out additional requirements to those listed in points (a) to (p) of Article 11(2) of Regulation (EU) No 537/2014 in relation to the content of the additional report to the audit committee, or directors, as applicable, only where this provides further information to the audit committee on the audit work undertaken.

(4) The audit committee (or, if there is no audit committee, the directors of the public-interest entity) shall disclose the additional report to any of the following persons upon request where the information is required in order for the person to perform the person's functions:

(a) the Supervisory Authority;

(b) the Director;

(c) the Revenue Commissioners;

(d) the Workplace Relations Commission;

(e) the Central Bank;

(f) any body responsible for the regulation of the public-interest entity.

(5) A disclosure by the audit committee (or, if there is no audit committee, the directors of the public-interest entity) in accordance with *subsection (4)* shall not be treated, for any purpose, as a breach of any restriction of disclosure by that committee (or, as appropriate, such directors) imposed by or under any other enactment, rule of law or otherwise.

1530 Auditors' reporting obligations under Article 12 of Regulation (EU) No 537/2014

(1) Reports by statutory auditors or audit firms referred to in Article 12 of Regulation (EU) No 537/2014 shall be submitted to the Supervisory Authority unless they are already required to be submitted to the Central Bank under—

(a) Regulation 134(1) of, or Schedule 16 to, the European Communities (Undertakings for Collective Investment in Transferable Securities) Regulations 2011 (S.I. No. 352 of 2011),

(b) Regulation 52 of the European Union (Capital Requirements) Regulations 2014 (S.I. No. 158 of 2014), or

(c) Regulation 78 of the European Union (Insurance and Reinsurance) Regulations 2015 (S.I. No. 485 of 2015).

(2) The obligation imposed on a person by *subsection (1)* to disclose information that he or she has to the Supervisory Authority is in addition to, and not in substitution for, any other obligation that the person has to disclose information to the Supervisory Authority or any other person, but that subsection shall not require the first-mentioned person to disclose that information to the Supervisory Authority more than once.

(3) (a) The Central Bank may, by notice in writing given to a statutory auditor or audit firm, require the auditor or firm to give it, within the period specified in the notice, additional information if such information is necessary for effective financial market supervision as provided for in the law of the State.

(b) The statutory auditor or audit firm the subject of a notice under *paragraph (a)* shall comply with the notice.

Chapter 13
Record keeping

1531 Record keeping

(1) Statutory auditors and audit firms shall keep the documents and information referred to in Article 15 of Regulation (EU) No 537/2014 for a period of at least 6 years.

(2) Where a transaction, act or operation is the subject of an investigation, inquiry, claim, assessment, appeal or proceeding which has already commenced within that 6 year period, then the relevant documents and information shall be retained until such time as the investigation, inquiry, claim, assessment, appeal or proceeding has been concluded or for a period of at least 6 years, whichever is the longer.

Chapter 14
Objectivity

1532 Future viability

Without prejudice to the reporting requirements referred to in *sections 336*, *337* and *391* and, where applicable, Articles 10 and 11 of Regulation (EU) No 537/2014, the scope of the statutory audit shall not include assurance on the future viability of the audited undertaking or on the efficiency or effectiveness with which the directors of the undertaking have conducted or will conduct the affairs of the undertaking.

Chapter 15
Independence

1533 Requirement for independence - general

(1) During the period in which a statutory audit is being carried out—

(a) the statutory auditor or audit firm, as the case may be,

(b) in the latter case, any statutory auditor of the statutory audit firm, and

(c) any individual in a position to directly or indirectly influence the outcome of the statutory audit,

shall be independent of, and not involved in the decision-taking of, the audited undertaking.

(2) During the period in which a statutory audit is being carried out, a statutory auditor or audit firm, as the case may be, shall take all reasonable steps to ensure that his or her independence is not affected by—

(a) any existing or potential conflict of interest, or

(b) any business or other direct or indirect relationship,

involving the statutory auditor or audit firm carrying out the statutory audit.

(3) *Subsection (2)* also applies, with any necessary modifications, to—

(a) the network of the statutory auditor or audit firm,

(b) the managers, auditors, employees or any other individuals whose services are placed at the disposal or under the control of the statutory auditor or audit firm,

(c) any person directly or indirectly linked to the statutory auditor or audit firm by control, and

(d) managers, auditors, employees or any other individuals whose services are placed at the disposal or under the control of a person linked to the statutory auditor or audit firm by control.

(4) The obligations referred to in *subsections (1)* and *(2)* shall be required at least during both the period to which the financial statements to be audited relate and the period during which the statutory audit is carried out.

1534 Professional scepticism

(1) When carrying out a statutory audit, the statutory auditor or the audit firm shall—

(a) maintain professional scepticism throughout the audit,

(b) maintain professional scepticism when reviewing management estimates relating to fair values, the impairment of assets, provisions, and future cash flow relevant to the audited undertaking's ability to continue as a going concern, and

(c) recognise the possibility of a material misstatement due to facts or behaviour indicating irregularities, including fraud or error, notwithstanding the statutory auditor's or the audit firm's past experience of the honesty and integrity of the audited undertaking's management and of the persons charged with its governance.

(2) For the purposes of this section, 'professional scepticism' means an attitude that includes a questioning mind, being alert to conditions which may indicate possible misstatement due to error or fraud, and a critical assessment of audit evidence.

1535 Prohibited relationships – specific provisions to secure independence

(1) A statutory auditor or audit firm shall not carry out a statutory audit if there is any threat of self-review, self-interest, advocacy, familiarity, or intimidation, created by any direct or indirect financial, personal, business, employment or other relationship between—

(a) the statutory auditor or audit firm or network to which he or she belongs or any individual in a position to influence the outcome of the statutory audit, and

(b) the audited undertaking,

as a result of which an objective, reasonable and informed third party, taking into account the safeguards applied, would conclude that the statutory auditor's or audit firm's independence is compromised.

(2) Without prejudice to the generality of *subsection (1)*, a person shall not act as a statutory auditor of an undertaking if he or she is—

(a) an officer or servant of the undertaking,

(b) a person who has been an officer or servant of the undertaking within a period in respect of which accounts would fall to be audited by the person if he or she were appointed auditor of the undertaking,

(c) a parent, spouse, brother, sister or child of an officer of the undertaking,

(d) a person who is a partner of or in the employment of an officer of the undertaking,

(e) a person who is disqualified under this subsection for appointment as auditor of a body corporate that is a subsidiary or holding undertaking of the undertaking or a subsidiary of the undertaking's holding undertaking, or would be so disqualified if the body corporate were a company, or

(f) a person in whose name a share in the undertaking is registered, whether or not that person is the beneficial owner of the share.

(3) Without prejudice to the generality of *subsections (1)* and *(2)*, a statutory audit firm, regardless of its legal structure, shall not carry out a statutory audit of an undertaking if—

(a) any principal of the audit firm is an officer or servant of the undertaking,

(b) any principal of the audit firm has been an officer or servant of the undertaking within a period in respect of which accounts would fall to be audited by the firm if the firm was appointed auditor of the undertaking, or

(c) the firm is disqualified under this subsection for appointment as auditor of any other body corporate that is a subsidiary or holding undertaking of the undertaking or a subsidiary of the undertaking's holding undertaking, or would be so disqualified if the body corporate were a company.

(4) Without prejudice to the generality of *subsections (1)* to *(3)*, a person shall not carry out a statutory audit of an undertaking on behalf of a statutory audit firm if he or she is—

(a) a person in whose name a share in the undertaking is registered, whether or not that person is the beneficial owner of the share, or

(b) a parent, spouse, brother, sister or child of an officer of the undertaking.

1536 Prohibited relationships – financial or beneficial interest

(1) A statutory auditor, an audit firm, the key audit partner of an audit firm, the employees of the statutory auditor or audit firm, and any other individual whose services are placed at the disposal or under the control of the statutory auditor or audit firm and who is directly involved in statutory audit activities, and persons closely associated with them within the meaning of Article 1(2) of Commission Directive 2004/72/EC of 29 April 20049 implementing Directive 2003/6/EC of the European Parliament and of the Council as regards accepted market practices, the definition of inside information in relation to derivatives on commodities, the drawing up of lists of insiders, the notification of managers' transactions and the notification of suspicious transactions, shall not—

(a) hold or have a material and direct beneficial interest in, or

(b) engage in any transaction in any financial instrument issued, guaranteed, or otherwise supported by,

any audited undertaking within their area of statutory audit activities, other than interests owned indirectly through diversified collective investment schemes, including managed funds such as pension funds or life assurance.

(2) A statutory auditor, an audit firm, the key audit partner of the audit firm, the employees of the statutory auditor or audit firm, and any other individual referred to in *subsection (1)*, shall not participate in or otherwise influence the outcome of a statutory audit of any particular audited undertaking if he or she—

(a) owns financial instruments of the audited undertaking, other than interests owned indirectly through diversified collective investment schemes,

(b) owns financial instruments of any undertaking related to the audited undertaking, the ownership of which may cause, or may be generally perceived as causing, a conflict of interest, other than interests owned indirectly through diversified collective investment schemes, or

(c) has had an employment, business or other relationship with the audited undertaking within the period to which the financial statements to be audited relate and the period during which the statutory audit is carried out that may cause, or may be generally perceived as causing, a conflict of interest.

(3) A statutory auditor, an audit firm, the key audit partner of the audit firm, the employees of the statutory auditor or audit firm, and any other individual referred to in *subsection (1)*, shall not solicit or accept pecuniary or non-pecuniary gifts or favours from the audited undertaking or any undertaking related to an audited undertaking unless an objective, reasonable and informed third party would consider the value thereof as trivial or inconsequential.

1537 Prohibited relationships – mergers and acquisitions

(1) If, during the period to which the financial statements relate, an audited undertaking is acquired by, merges with, or acquires, another undertaking, the statutory auditor or audit firm shall identify and evaluate any current or recent interests or relationships, including any non-audit services provided to that undertaking, which, taking into account available safeguards, could compromise the statutory auditor's or audit firm's independence and ability to continue with the statutory audit after the effective date of the merger or acquisition.

(2) As soon as possible, and in any event within 3 months of the merger or acquisition referred to in subsection (1), the statutory auditor or audit firm shall take all such steps as may be necessary to terminate any current interests or relationships that would compromise his or her independence and shall, where possible, adopt safeguards to minimise any threat to his or her independence arising from prior and current interests and relationships.

1538 Threats to independence and other information to be recorded

A statutory auditor or audit firm shall document in the audit working papers all significant threats to his or her independence as well as the safeguards applied to mitigate those threats.

1539 Preparation for statutory audit and assessment of threats to independence

A statutory auditor or audit firm shall, before accepting or continuing an engagement for a statutory audit, assess and document the following:

(a) whether he or she complies with the requirements set out in *sections 1533* and *1535* to *1538*;

(b) whether there are threats to his or her independence and the safeguards applied to mitigate those threats;

(c) whether he or she has the competent employees, time and resources needed in order to carry out the statutory audit in an appropriate manner;

(d) whether, in the case of an audit firm, the key audit partner is approved as statutory auditor in the Member State requiring the statutory audit.

1540 Non-intervention by certain persons in execution of audit

Neither—

(a) the owners or shareholders of a statutory audit firm or the owners or shareholders of an affiliated firm, nor

(b) the members of the administrative, management or supervisory body of such a firm or of an affiliated firm,

shall intervene in the execution of a statutory audit in any way which jeopardises the independence and objectivity of the statutory auditor who carries out the statutory audit on behalf of the statutory audit firm.

1541 Internal organisation of statutory auditors and audit firms

(1) A statutory auditor or audit firm shall comply with the following organisational requirements:

(a) the audit firm shall establish appropriate policies and procedures to ensure that no person, including any partner, director, member or shareholder of the audit firm or of a firm in its network, intervenes in the carrying out of a statutory audit in any way which jeopardises the independence and objectivity of the statutory auditor who carries out the statutory audit on behalf of the audit firm;

(b) the statutory auditor or audit firm shall have sound administrative and accounting procedures, internal quality control mechanisms, effective procedures for risk assessment, and effective control and safeguard arrangements for information processing systems;

(c) the statutory auditor or audit firm shall establish appropriate policies and procedures to ensure that his or her employees and any other individuals whose services are placed at his or her disposal or under his or her control, and who are directly involved in the statutory audit activities, have appropriate knowledge and experience for the duties assigned;

(d) (i) the statutory auditor or audit firm shall establish appropriate policies and procedures to ensure that the undertaking by other persons of important audit functions is not done in such a way as to impair the quality of the statutory auditor's or audit firm's internal quality control and the ability of the competent authorities to supervise the statutory auditor's or audit firm's compliance with the obligations laid down in the relevant provisions;

(ii) the statutory auditor or audit firm shall ensure that any audit functions carried out by such other persons does not affect his or her responsibility towards the audited undertaking;

(e) the statutory auditor or audit firm shall establish appropriate and effective organisational and administrative arrangements to prevent, identify, eliminate or manage and disclose any threats to his or her independence as referred to in *sections 1533*, *1535* to *1539* and *1547*;

(f) the statutory auditor or audit firm shall establish appropriate policies and procedures for carrying out statutory audits, coaching, supervising and reviewing employees' activities and organising the structure of the audit file as referred to in *section 1543*;

(g) the statutory auditor or audit firm shall establish an internal quality control system to ensure the quality of the statutory audit so that—

(i) such system includes, at least, the policies and procedures referred to in *paragraph (f)*, and

(ii) responsibility for such system lies with a person who is qualified as a statutory auditor;

(h) the statutory auditor or audit firm shall use appropriate systems, resources and procedures to ensure continuity and regularity in the carrying out of his or her statutory audit activities;

(i) the statutory auditor or audit firm shall also establish appropriate and effective organisational and administrative arrangements for dealing with and recording incidents which have, or may have, serious consequences for the integrity of his or her statutory audit activities;

(j) the statutory auditor or audit firm shall have in place adequate remuneration policies, including profit-sharing policies, providing sufficient performance incentives to secure audit quality but the amount of revenue that the statutory auditor or audit firm derives from providing non-audit services to the audited undertaking shall not form part of the performance evaluation and remuneration of any person involved in, or able to influence the carrying out of, the audit;

(k) the statutory auditor or audit firm shall monitor and evaluate the adequacy and effectiveness of his or her systems, internal quality control mechanisms and arrangements established in accordance with the relevant provisions and take appropriate measures to address any deficiencies;

(l) the statutory auditor or audit firm shall—

(i) carry out an annual evaluation of the internal quality control system referred to in *paragraph (g)*, and

(ii) keep records of the findings of that evaluation and any proposed measure to modify the internal quality control system.

(2) A statutory auditor or audit firm shall communicate, in writing, his or her policies and procedures referred to in *subsection (1)* to the employees of the statutory auditor or audit firm.

(3) A statutory auditor or audit firm shall take into consideration the scale and complexity of his or her activities when complying with the requirements set out in *subsection (1)*.

(4) A statutory auditor or audit firm shall be able to demonstrate to the recognised accountancy body or Supervisory Authority that the policies and procedures designed to achieve compliance with this section are appropriate given the scale and complexity of activities of the statutory auditor or audit firm.

1542 Organisation of work of statutory auditors and audit firms

(1) An audit firm, when carrying out a statutory audit of an undertaking, shall designate at least one key audit partner who shall be actively involved in the carrying out of the statutory audit.

(2) An audit firm shall—

(a) provide the key audit partner with sufficient resources and with personnel that have the necessary competence and capabilities to discharge his or her duties appropriately, and

(b) ensure that the main criteria in selecting the key audit partner are securing audit quality, independence and competence.

(3) A statutory auditor, when carrying out a statutory audit of an undertaking, shall devote sufficient time to the engagement and shall assign sufficient resources to enable him or her to carry out his or her duties appropriately.

(4) A statutory auditor or audit firm shall keep records of any contraventions by him or her of the relevant provisions.

(5) A statutory auditor or audit firm shall keep records of any consequences of any contravention referred to in *subsection (4)*, including the measures taken to address such contravention and to modify his or her internal quality control system.

(6) A statutory auditor or audit firm shall prepare an annual report containing an overview of any measures taken pursuant to *subsection (5)* and, in the case of an audit firm, shall communicate that report internally to the partners or directors, as may be appropriate, of the audit firm.

(7) A statutory auditor or audit firm shall document each request made and advices received where he or she asks external experts for advice.

1543 Organisation of work of statutory auditors and audit firms - audit files

(1) A statutory auditor or audit firm shall maintain a client account record that includes the following data for each audit client:

(a) the name, address and place of business;

(b) in the case of an audit firm, the name of the key audit partner;

(c) the fees charged for the statutory audit and the fees charged for other services in any financial year.

(2) A statutory auditor or audit firm shall create an audit file for each statutory audit which shall be closed not later than 60 days after the date of signature of the statutory auditors' report concerned and, where applicable, the reports referred to in Articles 10 and 11 of Regulation (EU) No 537/2014.

(3) A statutory auditor or audit firm shall document and retain at least the data recorded pursuant to *section 1538*, and, where applicable, Articles 6 to 8 of Regulation (EU) No 537/2014 for a period of at least 6 years.

(4) A statutory auditor or audit firm shall retain any other data and documents that are of importance in support of the statutory auditors' report and, where applicable, the reports referred to in Articles 10 and 11 of Regulation (EU) No 537/2014 and for monitoring compliance with the relevant provisions and other applicable legal requirements.

(5) A statutory auditor or audit firm shall keep records of any complaints made in writing about the performance of the statutory audits carried out by him or her.

1544 Restrictions with regard to fees

A recognised accountancy body shall ensure that its standards include provisions that fees for statutory audits—

(a) are not to be influenced by, or determined by, the provision of additional services to the audited undertaking, and

(b) are not to be based on any form of contingency.

1545 Restrictions with regard to fees exemption on exceptional basis

(1) A statutory auditor or audit firm may, pursuant to Article 4(2) of Regulation (EU) No 537/2014, request the Supervisory Authority for an exemption from the limits in that Article on total fees for services provided by him or her to a public-interest entity for a period of up to 2 financial years on an exceptional basis.

(2) A request shall be made in such form and manner as the Supervisory Authority specifies.

(3) On receipt of a request in the form specified in *subsection (2)*, the Supervisory Authority shall—

(a) grant the exemption as requested,

(b) grant a shorter exemption than that requested, or

(c) refuse to grant the exemption.

(4) Where the Supervisory Authority, on receipt of a request for an exemption, considers that it requires additional information before making a decision under *subsection (3)*, it may give notice of that to the statutory auditor or audit firm that made the request.

(5) The notice referred to in *subsection (4)* shall set out the additional information required by the Supervisory Authority.

(6) On receipt of a response to the notice from the statutory auditor or audit firm containing the additional information referred to in *subsection (4)*, the Supervisory Authority shall—

(a) grant the exemption as requested,

(b) grant a shorter exemption than that requested, or

(c) refuse to grant the exemption.

(7) Where the Supervisory Authority grants an exemption under *subsection (3)* or *(4)*, it shall—

(a) do so on an exceptional and case by case basis only, and

(b) publish its decision on its website.

(8) Where the Supervisory Authority refuses to grant an exemption under *subsection (3)(c)* or *(6)(c)*, it shall provide reasons for its decision to the statutory auditor or audit firm.

1546 Rotation of key audit partner in cases of public-interest entities

The key audit partner responsible for carrying out a statutory audit of a public-interest entity shall cease his or her participation in the statutory audit of the entity not later than 5 years from the date of his or her first appointment to carry out such audit.

1547 Moratorium on taking up certain positions in audited undertakings or public-interest entities

(1) There shall not be taken up by—

(a) a statutory auditor who carries out a statutory audit of an undertaking, or

(b) the key audit partner who carries out, on behalf of an audit firm, a statutory audit of an undertaking,

any of the positions in that undertaking, specified in *subsection (2)*, before a period of at least one year has elapsed since the day following the end of his or her direct involvement as a statutory auditor or key audit partner from the audit engagement.

(2) The specified positions referred to in *subsection (1)* are—

(a) a key management position in the audited undertaking,

(b) a position on the audit committee, or where such committee does not exist, such body as performs the equivalent functions to the audit committee, of the audited undertaking, or

(c) a non-executive member position of the audited undertaking or a member's position of that undertaking.

(3) There shall not be taken up by—

(a) a statutory auditor who carries out a statutory audit of a public-interest entity, or

(b) the key audit partner who carries out, on behalf of an audit firm, a statutory audit of a public-interest entity,

any of the positions in that entity, specified in *subsection (4)*, before a period of at least 2 years has elapsed since the day following the end of his or her direct involvement as a statutory auditor or key audit partner from the audit engagement.

(4) The specified positions referred to in *subsection (3)* are—

(a) a key management position in the audited entity,

(b) a position on the audit committee, or where such committee does not exist, such body as performs the equivalent functions to the audit committee, of the audited entity, or

(c) a non-executive member position of the audited entity or a member's position of that entity.

(5) Where an employee or partner, other than the key audit partner, of a statutory auditor or audit firm, or any other individual whose services are placed at the disposal or under the control of the statutory auditor or audit firm, and when such employee, partner or other individual is personally approved as a statutory auditor, there shall not be taken up by such employee, partner or other individual any of the positions referred to in *subsections (2)* and *(4)*, before a period of at least one year has elapsed since the day following (should such occur) his or her involvement in the statutory audit engagement of that audited undertaking.

1548 Rotation of statutory auditor and audit firms in case of public-interest entities - extension

(1) A public-interest entity may, pursuant to Article 17(6) of Regulation (EU) No 537/2014, under exceptional circumstances request the Supervisory Authority for an extension to reappoint a statutory auditor or audit firm for a period of up to 2 years on an exceptional basis.

(2) The grounds for the exceptional basis may be events in the nature of mergers, acquisitions and special investigations but, in any case, it will be a matter for the Supervisory Authority to determine such grounds.

(3) A request shall be made in such form and manner as the Supervisory Authority specifies.

(4) On receipt of a request in the form specified in subsection (3), the Supervisory Authority shall—

(a) grant the extension as requested,

(b) grant a shorter extension than that requested, or

(c) refuse to grant the extension.

(5) Where the Supervisory Authority, on receipt of a request for an extension, considers that it requires additional information before making a decision under *subsection (4)*, it shall give notice of that to the public-interest entity that made the request.

(6) The notice referred to in *subsection (5)* shall set out the additional information required by the Supervisory Authority.

(7) On receipt of a response to the notice from the public-interest entity containing the additional information referred to in *subsection (5)*, the Supervisory Authority shall—

(a) grant the extension as requested,

(b) grant a shorter extension than that requested, or

(c) refuse to grant the extension.

(8) Where the Supervisory Authority grants an extension under *subsection (4)* or *(5)*, it shall—

(a) do so on an exceptional and case by case basis only, and

(b) publish its decision on its website.

(9) Where the Supervisory Authority refuses to grant an extension under *subsection (4)(c)* or *(7)(c)*, it shall provide reasons for its decision to the public-interest entity.

1549 Rotation – reports by statutory auditor and audit firm in case of public-interest entities

(1) If there is uncertainty as to the date on which a statutory auditor or audit firm began carrying out consecutive statutory audits for a public-interest entity (including due to firm mergers, acquisitions, or changes in ownership structure), the statutory auditor or audit firm shall immediately report (in accordance with Article 17(8) of Regulation (EU) No 537/2014 and in such form and manner as the Supervisory Authority specifies) such uncertainty to the Supervisory Authority.

(2) On receipt of a report in the form specified in subsection (1), the Supervisory Authority shall—

(a) determine the relevant date for the purposes of that subsection, or

(b) request additional information from the statutory auditor or audit firm before making a decision referred to in *paragraph (a)*.

(3) Where the Supervisory Authority, on receipt of a report, considers that it requires additional information from the statutory auditor or audit firm or public-interest entity before making a decision under *subsection (2)(a)*, it shall—

(a) give notice of that to the statutory auditor or audit firm or public-interest entity within 2 weeks after the receipt of the report, and

(b) set out, in the notice, the additional information required by the Supervisory Authority.

(4) On receipt of a response to the notice from the statutory auditor or audit firm or public-interest entity containing the additional information referred to in *subsection (3)*, the Supervisory Authority shall—

(a) determine the relevant date for the purposes of *subsection (1)*, and

(b) provide reasons for its decision to the statutory auditor or audit firm and public-interest entity.

1550 Provision of certain prohibited non-audit services by auditors of public-interest entities

(1) Subject to *subsection (2)*, a statutory auditor or audit firm carrying out the statutory audit of a public-interest entity, or any member of the network to which the statutory auditor or the audit firm belongs, may provide the following non-audit services to the audited entity, to its holding undertaking within the European Union or to its controlled undertakings (within the meaning of point (f) of Article 2(1) of the Transparency (Regulated Markets) Directive as defined in *section 1379*) within the European Union:

(a) tax services relating to—

(i) preparation of tax forms,

(ii) identification of public subsidies and tax incentives where support from the statutory auditor or audit firm in respect of such services is required by law,

(iii) support regarding tax inspections by tax authorities where support from the statutory auditor or audit firm in respect of such inspections is required by law,

(iv) calculation of direct and indirect tax and deferred tax, or

(v) provision of tax advice,

(b) valuation services, including valuations performed in connection with actuarial services or litigation support services.

(2) The non-audit services referred to in *subsection (1)* may only be provided as specified in that subsection if—

(a) they have no direct or have immaterial effect, separately or in the aggregate, on the audited financial statements,

(b) the estimation of the effect on the audited financial statements is comprehensively documented and explained in the additional report to the audit committee, and

(c) the principles of independence set out in this Part are complied with by the statutory auditor or audit firm.

(3) The audit committee or the directors of the public-interest entity, as applicable, shall, at such times as it or they, as the case may be, thinks or think it appropriate to do so, issue guidelines with regard to the non-audit services referred to in *subsection (1)*.

Chapter 16
Audit committees

1551 Audit committees for public-interest entities

(1) Subject to the other provisions of this section, the directors of each public-interest entity shall establish an audit committee for the entity.

(2) The majority of the members of the audit committee shall be non-executive directors of the public-interest entity, that is to say, directors—

(a) the terms of appointment of whom indicate or state that they are being appointed in a non-executive capacity, and

(b) who otherwise possess the requisite degree of independence (particularly with regard to each of them satisfying the condition in *subsection (3)*) so as to be able to contribute effectively to the committee's functions.

(3) The condition referred to in *subsection (2)(b)* is that the director does not have, and at no time during the period of 3 years preceding his or her appointment to the committee did have—

(a) a material business relationship with the public-interest entity, either directly, or as a partner, shareholder, director (other than as a non-executive director) or senior employee of a body that has such a relationship with the entity, or

(b) a position of employment in the public-interest entity.

(4) At least one of the directors referred to in *subsection (2)* shall be a person who has competence in accounting or auditing.

(5) For the purposes of *subsections (2)* and *(3)(a)*, a non-executive director is a director who is not engaged in the daily management of the public-interest entity or body concerned, as the case may be.

(6) The members of the audit committee as a whole shall have competence relevant to the sector in which the audited entity is operating.

(7) The chairman of the audit committee shall be appointed by its members and shall be independent of the audited entity.

(8) Any proposal of the directors of a public-interest entity with respect to the appointment of a statutory auditor or audit firm to the entity shall be based on a recommendation made to the directors by the audit committee.

(9) The statutory auditor or audit firm shall report to the audit committee of the public-interest entity on key matters arising from the statutory audit of the entity, and, in particular, on material weaknesses in internal control in relation to the financial reporting process.

(10)(a) Subject to *paragraph (b)*, *subsection (1)* shall not apply to public-interest entities which meet the criteria set out in points (f) and (t) of Article 2(1) of the 2003 Prospectus Directive provided that the functions assigned to an audit committee are performed by the board of directors as a whole.

(b) The chairman of the board of directors, being an executive member, shall not act as chairman while the board is performing the functions of the audit committee.

(11) Subsection (1) shall not apply to a public-interest entity if it is—

(a) a public-interest entity which is a subsidiary undertaking within the meaning of point 10 of Article 2 of the Accounting Directive if that entity fulfils the requirements set out in subsections (1) and (2) and Articles 11(1) and (2) and 16(5) of Regulation (EU) No 537/2014 at group level,

(b) any public-interest entity which is a UCITS (within the meaning of the UCITS Regulations as defined in section 1385), or an alternative investment fund (within the meaning of the European Union (Alternative Investment Fund Managers) Regulations 2013 (S.I. No. 257 of 2013)),

(c) subject to *subsection (12)*, any public-interest entity the sole business of which is to act as an issuer of asset backed securities as defined in point 5 of Article 2 of the Prospectus Regulation (within the meaning of *section 1348*), or

(d) any credit institution within the meaning of point 1 of Article 3(1) of Directive 2013/36/EU of 26 June 201310 on access to the activity of credit institutions and the prudential supervision of credit institutions and investment firms, amending Directive 2002/87/EC and repealing Directives 2006/48/EC and 2006/49/EC whose shares are not admitted to trading on a regulated market of any Member State and which has, in a continuous or repeated manner, issued only debt securities admitted to trading on a regulated market, provided that the total nominal amount of all such debt securities remains below €100,000,000 and that it has not published a prospectus under the 2003 Prospectus Directive.

(12) A public-interest entity that avails itself of the exemption under *subsection (11)(c)* shall, by means of a statement to that effect included in a published document, such as—

(a) in any annual report published by it, or

(b) in an annual return or other periodic statement delivered by it to the Registrar or Central Bank,

set forth the reasons for why it considers the establishment of an audit committee by it is not appropriate and, accordingly, why it has availed itself of that exemption.

(13)(a) Subject to paragraph (b), *subsection (1)* shall not apply to a captive insurance undertaking or captive reinsurance undertaking (in each case within the meaning of Regulation 3 of the European Union (Insurance and Reinsurance) Regulations 2015 (S.I. No. 485 of 2015)) provided that it has a body or bodies performing equivalent functions to an audit committee, established and functioning in accordance with provisions in place in the State in which the public-interest entity to be audited is registered (in such case the entity shall disclose on its website which body carries out those functions and how that body is composed).

(b) A captive insurance undertaking or captive reinsurance undertaking which falls within *paragraph (a)* shall satisfy the following conditions:

(i) it shall not be owned by a credit institution;

(ii) it shall not issue transferable securities admitted to trading on a regulated market.

(14) Without prejudice to the responsibility of the directors of the public-interest entity, the responsibilities of the audit committee shall include—

(a) informing directors of the entity of the outcome of the statutory audit and explaining how the statutory audit contributed to the integrity of financial reporting and what the role of the audit committee was in that process,

(b) monitoring the financial reporting process and submitting recommendations or proposals to the directors of the entity to ensure its integrity,

(c) monitoring the effectiveness of the entity's internal quality control and risk management systems and, where applicable, its internal audit, regarding the financial reporting of the entity, without breaching its independence,

(d) monitoring the statutory audit of the entity and group financial statements, in particular, its performance, taking into account any findings and conclusions by the Supervisory Authority pursuant to Article 26(6) of Regulation (EU) No 537/2014,

(e) reviewing and monitoring the independence of the statutory auditors or the audit firms in accordance with *sections 1535* to *1541* and Article 6 of Regulation (EU) No 537/2014, and, in particular, the appropriateness of the provision of non-audit services to the audited entity in accordance with Article 5 of that Regulation, and

(f) being responsible for the procedure for the selection of a statutory auditor or audit firm and recommending the statutory auditor or audit firm to be appointed in accordance with Article 16 of Regulation (EU) No 537/2014 except when Article 16(8) of that Regulation is applied.

(15) Subsection (8) applies to a proposal of the directors (with respect to the appointment of a statutory auditor or audit firm to a public-interest entity) made at any time after the establishment of the audit committee in respect of the entity.

(16) The other provisions of the relevant provisions with regard to the performance of a function by the audit committee apply with respect to financial statements of the public-interest entity for financial years beginning on or after the establishment of the audit committee in respect of the entity.

(17) A person who, without reasonable excuse, contravenes *subsection (12)* shall be guilty of a category 3 offence.

(18) *Section 167* shall not apply to a public-interest entity which is both a UCITS referred to in *subsection (11)(b)* and a company.

(19) In this section, '2003 Prospectus Directive' has the meaning assigned to it by *section 1348.*

Chapter 17
Cooperation with other Member States

1552 Cooperation with other Member States

(1) With regard to the cooperation that the State is required to engage in by virtue of Article 33 of the Audit Directive, the Supervisory Authority is assigned responsibility in that behalf.

(2) For the purpose of discharging that responsibility, the Supervisory Authority shall put in place appropriate mechanisms, including arrangements with competent authorities in other Member States.

1553 Specific requirements with regard to cooperation

(1) Subject to *section 1552*, the Supervisory Authority, the recognised accountancy bodies and the Registrar with functions relating to approval, registration, quality assurance, inspection and discipline under the relevant provisions shall cooperate with the counterpart authorities in other Member States and the relevant European Supervisory Authorities whenever necessary for the purpose of those authorities or bodies (or, as the case may be, the counterpart authorities) carrying out their respective

functions under the relevant provisions or, as the case may be, the laws of the other Member State concerned that implement the Audit Directive.

(2) Subject to *section 1552*, the Supervisory Authority, the recognised accountancy bodies and the Registrar with the foregoing functions under the relevant provisions shall render assistance to the counterpart authorities in other Member States and to the relevant European Supervisory Authorities and, in particular, shall exchange information and cooperate with them in investigations relating to the carrying out of statutory audits.

(3) In this section, 'counterpart authorities in other Member States' means competent authorities or bodies in other Member States with functions corresponding to those of the Supervisory Authority, the recognised accountancy bodies and the Registrar with regard to approval, registration, quality assurance, inspection and discipline under the relevant provisions.

1554 Confidentiality of information

(1) A person shall not disclose, except in accordance with law, information that—

(a) is obtained in performing functions under any provision of the relevant provisions, and

(b) has not otherwise come to the notice of members of the public.

(2) A person who contravenes *subsection (1)* shall be guilty of a category 3 offence.

1555 Supplemental provisions in relation to section 1554

Without prejudice to *section 1554*, the persons to whom that section applies shall include the following:

(a) a member or director or former member or director of any board or committee, howsoever called, of the Supervisory Authority, the recognised accountancy bodies or the Registrar;

(b) an employee or former employee of the Supervisory Authority, the recognised accountancy bodies or the Registrar;

(c) a professional or other advisor to the Supervisory Authority, the recognised accountancy bodies or the Registrar including a former advisor.

1556 Obligation to supply information required for certain purposes and saving concerning confidential information

(1) The Supervisory Authority or a recognised accountancy body shall, on request and without undue delay, supply any information required for the purpose referred to in *section 1553*.

(2) *Section 1554* shall not prevent the Supervisory Authority or a recognised accountancy body from complying with any such request or exchanging confidential information.

1557 Obligation of Supervisory Authority or recognised accountancy body to gather information

(1) Where necessary, the Supervisory Authority or a recognised accountancy body, on receiving a request referred to in *section 1556(1)*, shall, without undue delay, take the necessary measures to gather the required information.

(2) If the Supervisory Authority or a recognised accountancy body of whom a request under *subsection (1)* is made is not able to supply, without undue delay, the required information, it shall notify the counterpart authority in the other Member State that made the request of—

(a) the fact of the delay, and

(b) the reasons therefor.

1554 Application of section 1554 to certain information

Section 1554 shall apply to information received by the Supervisory Authority, a recognised accountancy body or the Registrar pursuant to the cooperation or exchange of information that is required of counterpart authorities of Member States by this Chapter.

1559 Requesting authority to be notified if its request not complied with

(1) If—

(a) the Supervisory Authority or a recognised accountancy body of whom a request referred to in *section 1556(1)* is made does not comply with the request, and

(b) the case is neither—

(i) one of a delay in complying with the request to which *section 1557(2)* relates, nor

(ii) one of a refusal to comply with the request on any of the grounds referred to in *section 1560*,

the Supervisory Authority or recognised accountancy body, as appropriate, shall notify the counterpart authority in the other Member State that made the request of the reasons for that failure to comply.

(2) If it is a recognised accountancy body as referred to in *subsection (1)(a)*, it shall also notify the Supervisory Authority of the reasons for the failure referred to in that subsection.

1560 Grounds for refusing request for information

(1) The Supervisory Authority or a recognised accountancy body may refuse to comply with a request referred to in *section 1556(1)* if—

(a) the ground referred to in point (a) of paragraph 4 of Article 36 of the Audit Directive applies,

(b) proceedings in any court in the State have already been initiated in respect of the same actions and against the same statutory auditor or audit firm, the subject of the request, or

(c) a final determination has already been made by the Supervisory Authority or recognised accountancy body in respect of the same actions and the same statutory auditor or audit firm, the subject of the request.

(2) A recognised accountancy body shall not exercise the power under *subsection (1)* to refuse to comply with a request save after consultation with the Supervisory Authority.

(3) The Supervisory Authority or a recognised accountancy body that refuses, under subsection (1), to comply with a request shall notify the counterpart authority in the other Member State that made the request of the reasons for the refusal.

(4) A recognised accountancy body, referred to in *subsection (3)*, shall also notify the Supervisory Authority of the reasons for the refusal referred to in that subsection.

1561 Use to which information may be put

(1) The Supervisory Authority or a recognised accountancy body may use relevant information only for the performance by it of its functions under the relevant provisions and then only in the context of steps it takes in—

(a) investigating and detecting failures to comply with the relevant provisions, and

(b) initiating and employing disciplinary procedures, or maintaining proceedings in any court, in respect of any such failures.

(2) Subject to *section 1552*, *subsection (1)* is without prejudice to any obligations, by virtue of any proceedings being maintained in any court, to which the Supervisory Authority or a recognised accountancy body or European Supervisory Authority is subject as regards the use to which it may put information referred to in that subsection and in the context of administrative or judicial proceedings specifically related to the performance of those functions.

(3) (a) The Supervisory Authority may transmit to the competent authorities in other Member States responsible for supervising public-interest entities, to central banks, to the European System of Central Banks and to the European Central Bank, in their capacity as monetary authorities, and to the European Systemic Risk Board, confidential information intended for the performance of their respective functions.

(b) Such authorities or bodies shall not be prevented from communicating, to the Supervisory Authority, information that the Supervisory Authority may need in order to perform its functions under Regulation (EU) No 537/2014.

(4) In this section, “relevant information” means information that the Supervisory Authority or a recognised accountancy body receives pursuant to the cooperation or exchange of information that is required of counterpart authorities of Member States in this Chapter.

1562 Counterpart authority to be notified of non-compliance with Audit Directive and Regulation (EU) No 537/2014

Where the Supervisory Authority or a recognised accountancy body forms, on reasonable grounds, the opinion that activities contrary to the provisions of the Audit Directive or of Regulation (EU) No 537/2014 are being, or have been, carried out on the territory of another Member State, it shall, as soon as possible—

(a) notify the counterpart authority in the other Member State of that opinion, and

(b) include in that notification specific details of the matter and the grounds for its opinion.

1563 Counterpart authority may be requested to carry out investigation

(1) In relation to activities that it suspects have been, or are being, carried on contrary to the provisions of the Audit Directive or Regulation (EU) No 537/2014, the Supervisory Authority or a recognised accountancy body may request the counterpart authority in another Member State to carry out an investigation in the territory of that Member State.

(2) A request under *subsection (1)* of the counterpart authority may be accompanied by a further request that one or more of the officers, or members of staff, of the Supervisory Authority or a recognised accountancy body be allowed to accompany officers, or members of staff, of the counterpart authority in the course of the investigation.

(3) A recognised accountancy body shall notify the Supervisory Authority of the making of a request by it under *subsection (1)* and, if such be the case, the making of the further request by it under *subsection (2)*.

1564 Duty of Supervisory Authority or recognised accountancy body to take certain action

(1) Where the Supervisory Authority or a recognised accountancy body receives a notification from—

(a) the entity specifically responsible, pursuant to the laws of another Member State that implement Article 36 of the Audit Directive, for ensuring the cooperation referred to in that Article, or

(b) the counterpart authority in another Member State,

that activities contrary to the provisions of the Audit Directive or Regulation (EU) No 537/2014 are being, or have been, carried on in the State, it shall take appropriate action under the relevant provisions.

(2) The Supervisory Authority or a recognised accountancy body shall inform the notifying entity or authority of the outcome of that action, and to the extent possible, of significant developments in the period pending that outcome.

(3) A recognised accountancy body shall—

(a) notify the Supervisory Authority of the taking by it of the action referred to in *subsection (1)*, and

(b) in addition to so informing, under *subsection (2)*, the notifying entity or authority of those matters, inform the Supervisory Authority of the outcome of that action, and to the extent possible, of significant developments in the period pending that outcome.

1565 Due consideration to be given to counterpart authority's request for investigation

(1) The Supervisory Authority or a recognised accountancy body shall give due consideration to a request made of it, pursuant to the laws of another Member State that implement Article 36 of the Audit Directive, to carry out an investigation in the State.

(2) If a request under *subsection (1)* is acceded to by the Supervisory Authority or a recognised accountancy body, the investigation shall be subject to the overall control of the Supervisory Authority or recognised accountancy body that receives the request.

(3) For the purpose of this section—

(a) the reference in *subsection (1)* to a request that is made pursuant to the laws of another Member State that implement Article 36 of the Audit Directive is a reference to such a request, whether or not it is accompanied by a further request (made pursuant to those laws) that one or more of the officers, or members of staff, of the requesting authority be allowed to accompany officers, or members of staff, of the Supervisory Authority or a recognised accountancy body in the course of the investigation, and

(b) the investigation is subject to the control as referred to in *subsection (2)* even if that further request is acceded to by the Supervisory Authority or a recognised accountancy body.

(4) A recognised accountancy body shall notify the Supervisory Authority—

(a) of the making of a request of it referred to in *subsection (1)*, and

(b) if the request is acceded to by it, of the fact of the request being so acceded to.

1566 Grounds for refusing request for investigation

(1) The Supervisory Authority or a recognised accountancy body may refuse to accede to a request referred to in *section 1565(1)* made of it or a further request of the kind referred to in *section 1565(3)(a)* made of it if—

(a) the ground referred to in point (a) of paragraph 6 of Article 36 of the Audit Directive applies,

(b) proceedings in any court in the State have already been initiated in respect of the same actions and against the same statutory auditor or audit firm, the subject of the request, or

(c) a final determination has already been made by the Supervisory Authority or a recognised accountancy body in respect of the same actions and the same statutory auditor or audit firm, the subject of the request.

(2) A recognised accountancy body referred to in *subsection (1)* shall not exercise the power thereunder to refuse to accede to a request save after consultation with the Supervisory Authority.

(3) The Supervisory Authority or a recognised accountancy body that refuses, under *subsection (1)*, to accede to a request shall notify the counterpart authority in the other Member State that made the request of the reasons for the refusal.

(4) A recognised accountancy body referred to in *subsection (3)* shall also notify the Supervisory Authority of the reasons for the refusal referred to in that subsection.

Chapter 18
Mutual recognition of regulatory arrangements between Member States

1567 Mutual recognition of regulatory arrangements between Member States

To the extent that the preceding provisions of this Part, or, where applicable, Regulation (EU) No 537/2014 do not operate to achieve the following effects in the law of the State, this Part or Regulation (EU) No 537/2014 and those preceding provisions (notwithstanding anything in them to the contrary) shall be read as operating, in a manner so that—

(a) (i) the principle of home-country regulation and oversight by the Member State in which the statutory auditor or audit firm is approved and the audited undertaking has its registered office is respected, and

(ii) without prejudice to *subparagraph (i)*, audit firms approved in one Member State that perform audit services in another Member State in accordance with *section 1465* shall be subject to quality assurance review in the home Member State and oversight in the host Member State of any audit carried out there,

(b) the imposition of additional requirements on a statutory auditor or audit firm in relation to the statutory audit concerning registration, quality assurance review, auditing standards, professional ethics and independence is prohibited in the case of—

(i) a statutory audit of consolidated financial statements, required by a Member State, of a subsidiary established in another Member State, and

(ii) an undertaking the securities of which are traded on a regulated market in another Member State to that in which it has its registered office, by that Member State, regarding the statutory audit of the accounts or consolidated accounts of that undertaking,

and

(c) a statutory auditor or audit firm, approved under *section 1464* or *Chapter 20*, which is registered in any Member State and provides audit reports concerning accounts or consolidated accounts in accordance with *section 1573*, the systems of oversight, quality assurance, investigation and sanctions of the Member State where registration took place will apply.

Chapter 19

Transfer of audit working papers, etc., to third-country competent authorities

1568 Transfer of audit documentation to third-country competent authority

(1) Subject to *section 1569*, audit working papers or other documents held by a statutory auditor or audit firm and inspection or investigation reports relating to the audits concerned may be transferred to a third-country competent authority only if the Supervisory Authority, on a request being made of it in that behalf by the first-mentioned authority, determines that the following conditions are complied with (and authorises such transfer accordingly), namely—

(a) those audit working papers or other documents relate to the audit of an undertaking which—

(i) has issued securities in the third country concerned, or

(ii) forms part of a group that issues group financial statements in the third country concerned,

(b) the third-country competent authority meets requirements which have been declared adequate in accordance with Article 47(3) of the Audit Directive,

(c) there are working arrangements on the basis of reciprocity agreed between the Supervisory Authority and the third-country competent authority, and

(d) the transfer of personal data to the third country concerned is in accordance with the Data Protection Acts 1988 to 2018 and Regulation (EU) 2016/679.

(2) The working arrangements referred to in *subsection (1)(c)* shall ensure that—

(a) justification as to the purpose of the request for audit working papers and other documents is provided by the third-country competent authority concerned,

(b) the audit working papers and other documents are only transferred if—

(i) an obligation similar to that provided by section 1554 is provided under the laws of the third country concerned in relation to persons whilst in, and in any period subsequent to their ceasing to be in, the employment of the third-country competent authority, and

(ii) the protection of the commercial interests of the audited undertaking, including its industrial and intellectual property, is not undermined,

(c) the third-country competent authority uses audit working papers and other documents only for the performance of its functions of public oversight, quality assurance and investigations that meet requirements equivalent to those of Articles 29, 30 and 32 of the Audit Directive, and

(d) the request from a third-country competent authority for audit working papers or other documents held by a statutory auditor or audit firm can be refused by the Supervisory Authority if—

(i) the first ground referred to in point (d) of paragraph 2 of Article 47 of the Audit Directive applies,

(ii) proceedings in any court in the State have already been initiated in respect of the same actions and against the same statutory auditor or audit firm, the subject of the request, or

(iii) a final determination has already been made by the Supervisory Authority in respect of the same actions and the same statutory auditor or audit firm, the subject of the request.

(3) The Supervisory Authority has, for the purposes of the performance of its functions under the preceding subsections (including the taking of any steps that necessitate the perusal by it of the papers and other documents concerned so as to determine whether the transfer should be refused on any of the grounds referred to in *subsection (2)(d)*), the power to require the statutory auditor or audit firm concerned to produce to it the audit working papers and other documents; the statutory auditor or audit firm shall comply with such a requirement made of him or her by the Supervisory Authority.

1569 Derogation from section 1568 in exceptional cases

By way of derogation from *section 1568*, the Supervisory Authority may, in exceptional cases, allow a statutory auditor or audit firm to transfer audit working papers and other documents directly to a third-country competent authority, provided that—

(a) an investigation has been initiated by that competent authority in the third country concerned,

(b) such transfer does not conflict with the obligations with which statutory auditors and audit firms are required to comply in relation to the transfer of audit working papers and other documents to the Supervisory Authority,

(c) there are working arrangements with the third-country competent authority of a reciprocal nature that allow the Supervisory Authority direct access to audit working papers and other documents of audit entities in the third country concerned,

(d) the third-country competent authority informs in advance the Supervisory Authority of each direct request for information, indicating the reasons therefor, and

(e) conditions similar to those specified in *section 1568(2)(a)* to *(d)* are satisfied.

1570 Particulars of working arrangements to be notified

(1) Where the Supervisory Authority enters into working arrangements with a third-country competent authority in accordance with *section 1568(1)(c)*, particulars of those working arrangements shall be published by the Supervisory Authority on its website without delay and those particulars shall include—

(a) the name of the third-country competent authority, and

(b) the jurisdiction in which it is established.

(2) Particulars of those working arrangements shall also be notified by the Supervisory Authority to the Commission.

1571 Joint inspections

The Supervisory Authority may perform the functions (whether in whole or in part) referred to in *section 905(2)(n)(iii)* in so far as such functions are part of a joint inspection under—

(a) Commission Implementing Decision (EU) 2016/1156 of 14 July 2016 on the adequacy of the competent authorities of the United States of America pursuant to Directive 2006/43/EC of the European Parliament and of the Council, or

(b) any other Commission Implementing Decision made pursuant to Article 47(3) of the Audit Directive on the adequacy of competent authorities for the purposes of joint inspections.

Chapter 20
International aspects

1572 Approval of third-country auditor

(1) Without prejudice to *Chapter 3* and subject to *subsection (2)*, a recognised accountancy body may approve a third-country auditor as a statutory auditor if that person has furnished proof that he or she complies with requirements equivalent to those specified in *sections 1464* and *1472*.

(2) A third-country auditor shall not be approved under *subsection (1)* unless reciprocal arrangements with the third country concerned are in place, that is to say arrangements that enable a statutory auditor to carry out audits in that third country—

(a) by virtue of the law of that third country, and

(b) on fulfilment by the statutory auditor concerned of requirements no more onerous than those specified by this section and *Chapter 3* for the third-country auditor's approval under *subsection (1)*.

Chapter 21
Registration and oversight of third-country auditors and third-country audit entities

1573 Registration of third-country auditors and third-country audit entities

(1)(a) Subject to *paragraph (b)*, *subsection (6)* and *section 1580*, the Supervisory Authority shall, in accordance with the relevant provisions of *Chapter 5* and Schedule 20, cause to be registered in each year in the public register every third-country auditor and third-country audit entity that indicates, in writing to it, his or her intention to provide an audit report concerning the accounts or consolidated accounts of an undertaking falling within *subsection (3)*.

(b) *Paragraph (a)* shall not apply to a third-country auditor or third-country audit entity that provides audit reports concerning the annual or group financial statements of undertakings incorporated in third countries in respect of which—

(i) the Commission has not yet made a decision that the public oversight, quality assurance and investigation and penalty systems for third-country auditors and third-country audit entities meet requirements which shall be considered equivalent to those of Articles 29, 30 and 32 of the Audit Directive, or

(ii) such a decision was made but for a specified period of time which has now expired.

(2) Registration in the public register pursuant to *subsection (1)* shall have effect for a period of 12 months from the date on which the registration is effected.

(3) The undertaking referred to in *subsection (1)* is one—

(a) incorporated outside the European Union, not being a collective investment undertaking, and

(b) whose transferable securities are admitted to trading on a regulated market in the State.

(4) There shall accompany the indication in writing by a third-country auditor or third-country audit entity referred to in *subsection (1)* a notification, in such form and manner as the Supervisory Authority specifies, of the following information (in relation to the auditor or audit entity) to it.

(5) That information is the information referred to in *paragraph 3* of *Schedule 20* but does not include the information referred to in *paragraph 1(b)* or *2(b)* (as applied by that *paragraph 3*) of that Schedule.

(6) *Subsection (1)* shall not apply if the undertaking referred to in that subsection is an issuer exclusively of outstanding debt securities for which one of the following applies:

(a) prior to 31 December 2010, the undertaking was admitted to trading on a regulated market, and the denomination per unit of which is at the date of issue at least €50,000 or, in case of debt securities denominated in another currency, equivalent, at the date of issue, to at least €50,000;

(b) from 31 December 2010, the undertaking was admitted to trading on a regulated market, and the denomination per unit of which is at the date of issue at least €100,000 or, in case of debt securities denominated in another currency, equivalent, at the date of issue, to at least €100,000.

(7) *Section 1487* shall apply to third-country auditors and third-country audit entities so registered with the substitution of references to the recognised accountancy body for references to the Supervisory Authority and any other necessary modifications.

(8) *Section 1488* shall apply, with any necessary modifications, to a notification of information by a third-country auditor or third-country audit entity under—

(a) *subsection (4)* to the Supervisory Authority, and

(b) *section 1487*, as applied by *subsection (7)*, to that Authority.

(9) In *subsection (3)*, "collective investment undertaking" does not include such an undertaking of the closed-ended type.

1574 Exemption from quality assurance

(1) The Supervisory Authority may exempt from *Chapter 7* a third-country auditor or third-country audit entity registered under *Chapter 5* pursuant to *section 1573* if a quality assurance review has, under another Member State's or third country's system of quality assurance, been carried out in relation to the auditor or audit entity during the 3 years preceding the making of the application.

(2) On the making of that application, if—

(a) the Supervisory Authority is satisfied that the quality assurance review referred to in *subsection (1)* has been carried out as referred to in that subsection, and

(b) the system of quality assurance referred to in that subsection has been assessed as equivalent in accordance with *section 1580*,

the Supervisory Authority shall grant the exemption and the third-country auditor or third-country audit entity shall be exempted from *Chapter 7* accordingly.

1575 Removal of third-country auditor or third-country audit entity registered in accordance with section 1573 from public register

(1) Subject to *subsections (2)* and *(3)*, the Supervisory Authority may require the Registrar, in the case of a third-country auditor or third-country audit entity registered pursuant to *section 1573*, to remove the third-country auditor or third-country audit entity from the public register if—

(a) the auditor or audit entity does not provide all the information or clarifications necessary for the renewal of his or her registration or does not pay the appropriate fee under *section 1579*, or

(b) the outcome of a quality assurance inspection or investigation and disciplinary process requires it.

(2) A third-country auditor or third-country audit entity the subject of a quality assurance inspection or investigation shall not be removed from the public register until the completion of that inspection or investigation.

(3) The Supervisory Authority shall not exercise its power under *subsection (1)* unless it has first given the third-country auditor or third-country audit entity concerned a reasonable opportunity, in the circumstances concerned, of making representations in writing on the grounds (which the Supervisory Authority shall make known to such auditor or entity) that the Supervisory Authority is minded to exercise such power.

(4) The Supervisory Authority shall, at such times as it thinks it appropriate to do so, issue guidelines with regard to what constitutes a reasonable opportunity referred to in *subsection (3)*.

(5) The Supervisory Authority may publish on its website the name of the third-country auditor or third-country audit entity that has been removed from the public register in accordance with this section along with the reasons for such removal.

1576 Audit by non-registered auditor or audit entity – consequence

Without prejudice to *section 1580* and unless *section 1573(6)* applies to it, an audit report provided by a third-country auditor or third-country audit entity concerning the accounts or consolidated accounts of an undertaking falling within *section 1573(3)* shall have no legal effect in the State if the third-country auditor or third-country audit entity that provides it is not registered under *Chapter 5*.

1577 Conditions for registration of third-country auditor or third-country audit entity

(1) The Supervisory Authority may cause to be registered a third-country auditor or third-country audit entity pursuant to *section 1573* only if—

(a) where the applicant for registration is an audit entity (referred to in this section as the "potential registrant"), the applicant satisfies so many of the conditions specified in *subsection (2)* as are applicable to an entity, and

(b) where the applicant for registration is an auditor (also referred to in this section as the "potential registrant"), the applicant satisfies so many of the conditions specified in *subsection (2)* as are applicable to an individual.

(2) The conditions are as follows:

(a) the majority of the members of the administrative or management body of the potential registrant meet requirements equivalent to those of *sections 1464* and *1472*;

(b) the third-country auditor carrying out the audit on behalf of the potential registrant meets requirements equivalent to those of *sections 1464* and *1472*;

(c) the audits of the accounts or consolidated accounts referred to in *section 1573(1)* are carried out in accordance with international auditing standards as referred to in *section 1526*, as well as the requirements referred to in *section 1491*, or with equivalent standards and requirements;

(d) the potential registrant publishes annually on a website, being a website maintained by or on behalf of the potential registrant, a report which includes the information referred to in Article 13 of Regulation (EU) No 537/2014 in relation to the year concerned or the potential registrant complies with equivalent disclosure requirements.

1578 Supervisory Authority may assess matter of equivalence for purposes of section 1577(2)(c)

(1) For so long as the Commission has not taken, in accordance with the procedure referred to in Article 48(2) of the Audit Directive, the decision under Article 45(6) of that Directive in relation to the matter of equivalence of standards and requirements referred to in *section 1577(2)(c)*, the Supervisory Authority may, for the purposes of that provision, make an assessment of that equivalence.

(2) When assessing the equivalence concerned, the Supervisory Authority shall use the general equivalence criteria established by the Commission in assessing whether the

audits of the financial statements referred to in *section 1573(1)* are carried out in accordance with the standards and requirements referred to in *section 1577(2)(c)*.

(3) The general equivalence criteria referred to in *subsection (2)* shall apply to all third countries.

1579 Certain fees chargeable by Supervisory Authority

(1)(a) For the purposes specified in *paragraph (b)*, the Supervisory Authority may charge and impose annual fees, where necessary on an interim basis, having obtained the Minister's consent and subject to *paragraph (c)*, on a third-country auditor or third-country audit entity referred to in *section 1573(1)*, in respect of registration, effected or provided in relation to the auditor or audit entity under and in accordance with this Part.

(b) Money received by the Supervisory Authority under this subsection may be used only for the purposes of meeting the Authority's reasonable administrative expenses in performing its functions and exercising its powers under *section 1573* and under any other provision of this Act that contains consequential or incidental provisions on, or in relation to, *section 1573*.

(c) The Supervisory Authority—

(i) shall submit the rationale for the level of fee to the Minister for approval before imposing a fee—

(I) initially when the fee is proposed, and

(II) at any time thereafter that the fee is proposed to be amended,

and

(ii) may charge fees on an annual basis to meet the reasonable administrative costs associated with the following tasks:

(I) the annual registration of such auditor or audit entity that is a statutory auditor or audit firm registered in a public register of a Member State pursuant to Articles 15 to 19 of the Audit Directive;

(II) the annual registration assessment and the annual registration of such auditor or audit entity that is not registered in a public register of a Member State pursuant to Articles 15 to 19 of the Audit Directive as a statutory auditor or audit firm.

(2)(a) For the purposes specified in *paragraph (b)*, the Supervisory Authority may charge and impose fees, where necessary on an interim basis, having obtained the Minister's consent and subject to *paragraph (c)*, on a third-country auditor or third-country audit entity referred to in *section 1573(1)* in respect of the oversight, quality assurance and the related matters of investigation, discipline and penalties, effected or provided in relation to the auditor or audit entity under and in accordance with the relevant provisions.

(b) Money received by the Supervisory Authority under this subsection may be used only for the purposes of meeting the Authority's reasonable administrative expenses in performing its functions and exercising its powers under *section*

930A, *Chapter 7* and this Chapter and under any other provision of this Act that contains consequential or incidental provisions on, or in relation to, *section 930A*, *Chapter 7* and this Chapter.

(c) The Supervisory Authority—

(i) shall establish criteria, as set out in *subsection (3)*, for charging and imposing fees on a third-country auditor or third-country audit entity referred to in *section 1573(1)*,

(ii) shall submit the criteria to the Minister for approval before imposing fees—

(I) initially when the criteria are established, and

(II) at any time thereafter that the criteria are amended,

(iii) may charge fees on an interim basis to meet the reasonable administrative costs associated with the functions of oversight, quality assurance and the related matters of investigation, discipline and penalties—

(I) before the function is performed,

(II) more than once, if necessary, during the performance of the function, and

(III) when the performance of the function is completed.

(3) Established criteria for charging and imposing fees on an interim basis on a third-country auditor or third-country audit entity referred to in *section 1573(1)* shall be based on costs incurred to meet the Supervisory Authority's reasonable administrative expenses in relation to—

(a) location (including any necessary and consequential travel costs),

(b) the testing of the internal quality control system undertaken (including the time taken to review audit firms),

(c) the number and nature of the Irish relevant audit clients,

(d) how many third-country auditors are within the firm,

(e) staffing resources, being how many staff are required, at what level and for what period,

(f) expertise required (including the use (if any) of consultants located outside the State to undertake on-site inspections),

(g) the nature and significance of the findings (including the time allocated to inspection, drafting the report and follow-up to the recommendations),

(h) associated miscellaneous costs (including the translation of working papers relevant to the audit), and

(i) legal and other costs.

(4) Notwithstanding that the particular audit of a public-interest entity has been carried out by a statutory auditor, no fee under this section shall be imposed on the statutory auditor if he or she was designated by a statutory audit firm to carry out the audit, and

the fees under this section shall, in those circumstances, be imposed on the statutory audit firm instead.

(5) A fee imposed under *subsection (1)* or *(2)* may, in default of payment, be recovered from the third-country auditor or third-country audit entity concerned as a simple contract debt in any court of competent jurisdiction.

1580 Exemptions in case of equivalence

(1) A third-country auditor or third-country audit entity may apply to the Supervisory Authority for an exemption from all or any of the provisions of *sections 1573* and *1574* on the basis that the third-country auditor or third-country audit entity is subject to systems of public oversight, quality assurance and investigations and penalties in the third country concerned that meet requirements equivalent to those of *section 930A*, *Chapter 7* and this Chapter.

(2) On the making of that application, if—

(a) the Commission has, in accordance with Article 46(2) of the Audit Directive, assessed the systems referred to in *subsection (1)* as meeting requirements equivalent to those in the corresponding provisions of the Audit Directive, and

(b) the Supervisory Authority is satisfied that the law of the third country concerned affords reciprocal rights to a statutory auditor or audit firm with regard to being granted corresponding exemptions under that law,

the Supervisory Authority may rely on the equivalence decided by the Commission, partially or entirely, and thus to disapply or modify the requirements in *sections 1573* and *1574* partially or entirely and the third-country auditor or third-country audit entity shall be partially or entirely exempted accordingly.

(3) The Supervisory Authority shall notify the Commission of the main elements of its cooperative arrangements with systems of public oversight, quality assurance and investigations and penalties of the third country concerned, arising out of arrangements it has entered into with that third country for the purposes of the reciprocity referred to in *subsection (2)(b)*.

1581 Investigations and sanctions

Sections 934 to *934I* shall, with any necessary modifications, apply to third-country auditors and third-country audit entities as those sections apply to statutory auditors and audit firms and audited entities.

Chapter 22
Savings for disciplinary proceedings in being

1582 Savings for disciplinary proceedings in being – 2010 Audits Regulations

(1) Nothing in the Companies (Statutory Audits) Act 2018 (and, in particular, provisions amending this Act) affect disciplinary proceedings in being before 17 June 2016 by a recognised accountancy body against any of its members and, accordingly, those proceedings may be continued on and after that date by that body against the member or members concerned.

(2) If, as a result of proceedings referred to in *subsection (1)* in relation to a person referred to in that subsection, the person's membership of the recognised accountancy body is terminated by the body or the body's approval (howsoever expressed) of the person to act as an auditor is withdrawn, then any deemed approval of the person as a statutory auditor or audit firm by virtue of *section 1471* ceases to have effect.

1583 Savings for disciplinary proceedings in being – 2016 Audits Regulations

(1) Nothing in the Companies (Statutory Audits) Act 2018 (and, in particular, provisions amending this Act) affect disciplinary proceedings (not being disciplinary proceedings referred to in *section 1582(1)*) in being before the date of commencement of section 3(6) of that Act by a recognised accountancy body against any of its members and, accordingly, those proceedings may be continued on and after that date by that body against the member or members concerned.

(2) If, as a result of proceedings referred to in *subsection (1)* in relation to a person referred to in that subsection, the person's membership of the recognised accountancy body is terminated by the body or the body's approval (howsoever expressed) of the person to act as an auditor is withdrawn, then any deemed approval of the person as a statutory auditor or audit firm by virtue of *section 1471* ceases to have effect.

1584 Savings for disciplinary proceedings in being – prescribed accountancy bodies

Nothing in the Companies (Statutory Audits) Act 2018 (and, in particular, provisions amending this Act) affect disciplinary proceedings (not being disciplinary proceedings referred to in *section 1582(1)* or *1583(1)*) in being before the date of commencement of section 3(6) of that Act by a prescribed accountancy body against any of its members and, accordingly, those proceedings may be continued on and after that date by that body against the member or members concerned.][a]

Amendments

a Part 27 inserted by C(SA)A 2018, s 51.

Schedules

SCHEDULE 1
FORM OF CONSTITUTION OF PRIVATE COMPANY LIMITED BY SHARES

Section 19.

CONSTITUTION
OF

[*name of company as below*]

1. The name of the company is: THE SOUTH EASTERN COUNTIES FLOORING AND TILING COMPANY LIMITED.
2. The company is a private company limited by shares, registered under *Part 2* of the *Companies Act 2014.*
3. The liability of the members is limited.
4. The share capital of the company is €50,000 divided into 50,000 shares of €1 each. / The share capital of the company is divided into shares of €1 each.
5. Supplemental Regulations (if any).

   We, the several persons whose names and addresses are subscribed, wish to be formed into a company in pursuance of this constitution, and we agree to take the number of shares in the capital of the company set opposite our respective names.

Names, Addresses and Descriptions of Subscribers	**Number of Shares taken by each Subscriber**
1. Mary Kelly Address: Description:	2,700
2. Alan Redmond Address: Description:	300
Total shares taken:	3,000

As appropriate:

signatures in writing of the above subscribers, attested by witness as provided for below; or

authentication in the manner referred to in *section 888*.

Dated the ______________ day of ______________ 20 ___

Witness to the above Signatures:

Name: ____

Address: ____

SCHEDULE 2
REPEALS AND REVOCATIONS

Section 4

PART 1
ACTS OF THE OIREACHTAS REPEALED

Number and Year	Short title	Extent of Repeal
No. 33 of 1963	Companies Act 1963	The whole Act
No. 31 of 1977	Companies (Amendment) Act 1977	The whole Act
No. 10 of 1982	Companies (Amendment) Act 1982	The whole Act
No. 13 of 1983	Companies (Amendment) Act 1983	The whole Act
No. 25 of 1986	Companies (Amendment) Act 1986	The whole Act
No. 27 of 1988	Bankruptcy Act 1988	Section 51(2)
No. 27 of 1990	Companies (Amendment) Act 1990	The whole Act
No. 33 of 1990	Companies Act 1990	The whole Act
No. 8 of 1999	Companies (Amendment) Act 1999	The whole Act
No. 30 of 1999	Companies (Amendment) (No. 2) Act 1999	The whole Act
No. 28 of 2001	Company Law Enforcement Act 2001	The whole Act
No. 44 of 2003	Companies (Auditing and Accounting) Act 2003	The whole Act
No. 12 of 2005	Investment Funds, Companies and Miscellaneous Provisions Act 2005	Parts 3, 4, 5 and 6
No. 41 of 2006	Investment Funds, Companies and Miscellaneous Provisions Act 2006	Parts 2 and 3
No. 20 of 2009	Companies (Amendment) Act 2009	The whole Act
No. 45 of 2009	Companies (Miscellaneous Provisions) Act 2009	Sections 1 to 4
No. 22 of 2012	Companies (Amendment) Act 2012	The whole Act
No. 46 of 2013	Companies (Miscellaneous Provisions) Act 2013	Sections 2 to 8

PART 2
STATUTORY INSTRUMENTS REVOKED

Number and Year	Citation	Extent of Revocation
S.I. No. 163 of 1973	European Communities (Companies) Regulations 1973	The whole Statutory Instrument
S.I. No. 137 of 1987	European Communities (Mergers and Divisions of Companies) Regulations 1987	The whole Statutory Instrument
S.I. No. 201 of 1992	European Communities (Companies: Group Accounts) Regulations 1992	The whole Statutory Instrument

Number and Year	Citation	Extent of Revocation
S.I. No. 395 of 1993	European Communities (Branch Disclosures) Regulations 1993	The whole Statutory Instrument
S.I. No. 275 of 1994	European Communities (Single Member Private Limited Companies) Regulations 1994	The whole Statutory Instrument
S.I. No. 437 of 2001	European Communities (Single-Member Private Limited Companies) Regulations 1994 (Amendment) Regulations 2001	The whole Statutory Instrument
S.I. No. 333 of 2002	European Communities (Corporate Insolvency) Regulations 2002	The whole Statutory Instrument
S.I. No. 765 of 2004	European Communities (Fair Value Accounting) Regulations 2004	The whole Statutory Instrument
S.I. No. 839 of 2004	European Communities (Companies) Regulations 2004	The whole Statutory Instrument
S.I. No. 49 of 2007	European Communities (Companies) (Amendment) Regulations 2007	The whole Statutory Instrument
S.I. No. 450 of 2009	European Communities (Directive 2006/46/EC) Regulations 2009	The whole Statutory Instrument
S.I. No. 83 of 2010	European Communities (Directive 2006/46/EC) (Amendment) Regulations 2010	The whole Statutory Instrument
S.I. No. 306 of 2011	European Communities (Mergers and Divisions of Companies) (Amendment) Regulations 2011	The whole Statutory Instrument
S.I. No. 304 of 2012	European Union (Accounts) Regulations 2012	The whole Statutory Instrument
S.I. No. 308 of 2012	Companies (Amendment) (No. 2) Act 1999 (Section 32) Order 2012	The whole Statutory Instrument

[SCHEDULE 3
ACCOUNTING PRINCIPLES, FORM AND CONTENT OF ENTITY FINANCIAL STATEMENTS

PART I
CONSTRUCTION OF REFERENCES TO PROVISIONS OF SCHEDULES

1. (1) Without prejudice to the generality of section 9 of the Interpretation Act 2005 and its application to the body of this Act and to *Schedules 1*, *2* and *5* to *18*—

   (a) a reference in this Schedule to a paragraph or Part is a reference to a paragraph or Part of this Schedule, unless it is indicated that a reference to some other enactment is intended,

   (b) a reference in this Schedule to a section is a reference to the section of the Part in which the reference occurs, unless it is indicated that a reference to some other enactment is intended, and

   (c) a reference in this Schedule to a subparagraph or clause is a reference to the subparagraph or clause of the provision in which the reference occurs, unless it is indicated that a reference to some other enactment is intended.

(2) Provisions providing for the interpretation of certain expressions appearing in this Schedule are contained in *Part VI*.

PART II
GENERAL RULES AND FORMATS

SECTION A
GENERAL RULES

2. (1) Subject to the provisions of this Schedule—

   (a) every balance sheet of a company shall show the items listed in either of the balance sheet formats set out in *Section B*, and

   (b) every profit and loss account of a company shall show the items listed in either of the profit and loss accounts formats so set out,

in either case in the order and under the headings and subheadings given in the format adopted.

(2) Notwithstanding *subparagraph (1)(a)*, in preparing the balance sheet of a company, the directors of the company may adapt one of the balance sheet formats in *Section B* so as to distinguish between current and non-current items in a different way, provided that—

   (a) the information given is at least equivalent to that which would have been required by the use of such format had it not been thus adapted, and

   (b) the presentation of those items is in accordance with generally accepted accounting principles or practice.

(3) Notwithstanding *subparagraph (1)(b)*, the directors of the company may prepare a statement of the performance of the company instead of a profit and loss account

and in doing so may adapt one of the profit and loss account formats in *Section B*, provided that—

(a) the information given is at least equivalent to that which would have been required by the use of such format had it not been thus adapted, and

(b) the presentation of those items is in accordance with generally accepted accounting principles or practice.

(4) *Subparagraph (1)* shall not be read as requiring the heading or sub-heading for any item in the balance sheet, or profit and loss account, of a company to be distinguished by any letter or number assigned to that item in the formats set out in *Section B*.

(5) So far as is practicable, the following provisions of this section shall apply to the balance sheet and profit and loss account of a company notwithstanding any adaptation pursuant to *subparagraphs (2) and (3)*.

3. (1) Where, in accordance with *paragraph 2(1)*, a company's balance sheet or profit and loss account for any financial year has been prepared by reference to one of the formats set out in *Section B* or where, in accordance with *paragraph 2(2) or 2(3)* one of the formats has been adapted, the directors of the company shall adopt the same format in preparing the financial statements for subsequent financial years unless, in their opinion, there are special reasons for a change.

(2) Where any change is made in the format adopted in preparing a balance sheet or profit and loss account of a company, the reasons for the change, together with full particulars of the change, shall be given in a note to the financial statements in which the new format is first adopted.

4. (1) Any item required in accordance with *paragraph 2* to be shown in the balance sheet or profit and loss account of a company may be shown in greater detail than that required by the format adopted.

(2) The balance sheet, or profit and loss account, of a company may include an item representing or covering the amount of any asset or liability or income or expenditure not otherwise covered by any of the items listed in the format adopted but the following shall not be treated as assets in the balance sheet of a company—

(a) preliminary expenses,

(b) expenses of and commission on any issue of shares or debentures, and

(c) costs of research.

(3) The balance sheet, or profit and loss account, of a company may include subtotals where their inclusion facilitates the assessment of the financial position or profit or loss of the company for the financial year concerned.

(4) Any items to which an Arabic number is assigned in any of the formats set out in *Section B* may be combined in the financial statements of a company—

(a) in any case where the individual amounts of such items are not material to assessing the financial position or profit or loss of the company for the financial year concerned, or

(b) in any case where the combination of such items facilitates that assessment.

(5) Where items are combined in a company's financial statements pursuant to *subparagraph (4)(b)*, the individual amounts of any items so combined shall be disclosed in a note to the financial statements.

(6) In preparing the balance sheet, or profit and loss account, of a company, the directors of the company shall adapt the arrangement and headings and sub-headings otherwise required by *paragraph 2* in respect of items to which an Arabic number is assigned in the format adopted, in any case where the special nature of the company's business requires such adaptation.

(7) Where an asset or liability relates to more than one of the items listed in either of the balance sheet formats set out in *Section B*, its relationship to other items shall be disclosed either under the item where it is shown or in the notes to the financial statements.

(8) The opening balance sheet for each financial year shall correspond to the closing balance sheet for the preceding financial year.

5. (1) Subject to *subparagraph (2)*, in respect of every item shown in the balance sheet, or profit and loss account, or notes thereto, of a company, the corresponding amount for the financial year immediately preceding that to which the balance sheet or profit and loss account relates shall also be shown and, if that corresponding amount is not comparable with the amount to be shown for the item in question in respect of the financial year to which the balance sheet or profit and loss account relates, the former amount may be adjusted, and particulars of the adjustment and the reasons therefor shall be given in a note to the financial statements.

(2) Corresponding amounts are not required for the movements in fixed assets during the year required by *paragraph 46(1)* and *(3)* or the movements in provisions required by *paragraph 54(1)* and *(2)*.

6. (1) Subject to *subparagraph (2)*, a heading or sub-heading corresponding to an item listed in the format adopted in preparing the balance sheet or profit and loss account of a company shall not be included in the balance sheet or profit and loss account, as the case may be, if there is no amount to be shown for that item in respect of the financial year to which the balance sheet or profit and loss account relates.

(2) *Subparagraph (1)* shall not apply in any case where an amount can be shown for the item in question in respect of the financial year immediately preceding that to which the balance sheet or profit and loss account relates, and that amount shall be shown under the heading or sub-heading required by the format adopted as aforesaid.

7. (1) Subject to *subparagraph (2)*, amounts in respect of items representing assets or income may not be set off in the financial statements of a company against amounts in respect of items representing liabilities or expenditure, as the case may be, or vice versa.

(2) *Subparagraph (1)* shall not apply in any case where such set off is in accordance with applicable accounting standards, provided that the gross amounts are disclosed in a note to the financial statements.

SECTION B
THE REQUIRED FORMATS FOR FINANCIAL STATEMENTS

Preliminary

8. References in this Part to the items listed in any of the formats set out in this Part are references to those items read together with any notes following the formats which apply to any of those items.
9. A number in brackets following any item in, or any heading to, any of the formats set out in this Part is a reference to the note of that number in the notes following the formats.
10. In the notes following the formats—
    (a) the heading of each note gives the required heading or subheading for the item to which it applies and a reference to any letters and numbers assigned to that item in the formats set out in this Part, and
    (b) references to a numbered format are references to the balance sheet format or (as the case may require) to the profit and loss account format of that number set out in this Part.

BALANCE SHEET FORMATS

Format 1

Assets

A. Fixed Assets

I. Intangible assets

1. Development costs
2. Concessions, patents, licences, trade marks and similar rights and assets (1)
3. Goodwill (2)
4. Payments on account

II. Tangible assets

1. Investment property
2. Land and buildings
3. Plant and machinery
4. Fixtures, fittings, tools and equipment
5. Payments on account and assets in course of construction

III. Financial assets

1. Shares in group undertakings
2. Loans to group undertakings
3. Participating interests

4. Loans to undertakings with which the company is linked by virtue of participating interests
5. Other investments other than loans
6. Other loans

B. Current Assets

I. Stocks

1. Raw materials and consumables
2. Work in progress
3. Finished goods and goods for resale
4. Payments on account

II. Debtors (3)

1. Trade debtors
2. Amounts owed by group undertakings
3. Amounts owed by undertakings with which the company is linked by virtue of participating interests
4. Other debtors
5. Called up share capital not paid
6. Prepayments
7. Accrued income

III. Investments

1. Shares in group undertakings
2. Other investments

IV. Cash at bank and in hand

C. Creditors: Amounts falling due within one year

1. Debenture loans (4)
2. Amounts owed to credit institutions
3. Called up share capital presented as a liability (8)
4. Payments received on account (5)
5. Trade creditors
6. Bills of exchange payable
7. Amounts owed to group undertakings
8. Amounts owed to undertakings with which the company is linked by virtue of participating interests
9. Other creditors including tax and social insurance (6)
10. Accruals
11. Deferred income (7)

D. Net current assets (liabilities)

E. Total assets less current liabilities

F. Creditors: Amounts falling due after more than one year

1. Debenture loans (4)
2. Amounts owed to credit institutions
3. Called up share capital presented as a liability (8)
4. Payments received on account (5)
5. Trade creditors
6. Bills of exchange payable
7. Amounts owed to group undertakings
8. Amounts owed to undertakings with which the company is linked by virtue of participating interests
9. Other creditors including tax and social insurance (6)
10. Accruals
11. Deferred income (7)

G. Provisions for liabilities

1. Retirement benefit and similar obligations
2. Taxation, including deferred taxation
3. Other provisions for liabilities

H. Capital and reserves

I. Called up share capital presented as equity(8)

II. Share premium account

III. Revaluation reserve

IV. Other reserves

1. Other undenominated capital
2. Reserve for own shares held
3. Reserves provided for by the constitution
4. Other reserves including the fair value reserve (specified as necessary)

V. Profit or loss brought forward (10)

VI. Profit or loss for the financial year (10).

Balance Sheet Formats

Format 2

ASSETS

A Fixed Assets

I. Intangible assets

1. Development costs

2. Concessions, patents, licences, trade marks and similar rights and assets (1)
3. Goodwill (2)
4. Payments on account

II. Tangible assets

1. Investment property
2. Land and buildings
3. Plant and machinery
4. Fixtures, fittings, tools and equipment
5. Payments on account and assets in course of construction

III. Financial assets

1. Shares in group undertakings
2. Loans to group undertakings
3. Participating interests
4. Loans to undertakings with which the company is linked by virtue of participating interests
5. Other investments other than loans
6. Other loans

B. Current Assets

I. Stocks

1. Raw materials and consumables
2. Work in progress
3. Finished goods and goods for resale
4. Payments on account

II. Debtors (3)

1. Trade debtors
2. Amounts owed by group undertakings
3. Amounts owed by undertakings with which the company is linked by virtue of participating interests
4. Other debtors
5. Called up share capital not paid
6. Prepayments
7. Accrued income

III. Investments

1. Shares in group undertakings
2. Other investments

IV. Cash at bank and in hand

Capital, Reserves and Liabilities

A. Capital and reserves

I. Called up share capital presented as equity (8)

II. Share premium account

III. Revaluation reserve

IV. Other reserves

1. Other undenominated capital
2. Reserve for own shares held
3. Reserves provided for by the constitution
4. Other reserves including the fair value reserve (specify as necessary)

V. Profit or loss brought forward (10)

VI. Profit or loss for the financial year (10)

B. Provisions for liabilities

1. Retirement benefit and similar obligations
2. Taxation, including deferred taxation
3. Other provisions for liabilities

C. Creditors (9)

1. Debenture loans (4)
2. Amounts owed to credit institutions
3. Called up share capital presented as a liability (8)
4. Payments received on account (5)
5. Trade creditors
6. Bills of exchange payable
7. Amounts owed to group undertakings
8. Amounts owed to undertakings with which the company is linked by virtue of participating interests
9. Other creditors including tax and social insurance (6)
10. Accruals
11. Deferred income (7)

Notes on the Balance Sheet Formats

(1) Concessions, patents, licences, trade marks and similar rights and assets

(Formats 1 and 2, items A. I. 2)

Amounts in respect of assets shall only be included in a company's balance sheet under this item if either—

(a) the assets were acquired for valuable consideration and are not required to be shown under goodwill, or

(b) the assets in question were created by the company itself.

(2) Goodwill

(Formats 1 and 2, items A. I. 3)

Amounts representing goodwill shall only be included to the extent that the goodwill was acquired for valuable consideration.

(3) Debtors

(Formats 1 and 2, items B. II. 1 to 7)

The amount falling due after more than one year shall be shown separately for each item included under debtors.

(4) Debenture loans

(Format 1, item C. 1 and F. 1 and Format 2, item C.1)

The amount of any convertible loans shall be shown separately and the terms and conditions under which those loans are convertible into share capital shall be disclosed in the notes to the financial statements.

(5) Payments received on account (Format 1, items C. 4 and F. 4 and Format 2, item C.4)

Payments received on account of orders shall be shown for each of these items in so far as they are not shown as deductions from stocks.

(6) Other creditors including tax and social insurance

(Format 1, items C. 9 and F. 9 and Format 2, item C.9)

The amount for creditors in respect of taxation and social insurance shall be shown separately from the amount for other creditors and in respect of taxation there shall be stated separately the amounts included in respect of income tax payable on emoluments to which Chapter 4 of Part 42 of the Taxes Consolidation Act 1997 applies, any other income tax, corporation tax, capital gains tax, value-added tax and any other tax.

(7) Deferred income

(Format 1, items C. 11 and F. 11 and Format 2, items C.11)

The amount in respect of Government grants, that is to say, grants made by or on behalf of the Government, included in this item shall be shown separately in a note to the financial statements unless it is shown separately in the balance sheet.

(8) Called up share capital

(Format 1, item C. 3, F. 3 and H. I, and Format 2, 'CAPITAL, RESERVES AND LIABILITIES' items A. I and C. 3)

In accordance with the accounting principle in paragraph 17, called up share capital shall be analysed between shares that are presented as liabilities and share capital.

(9) Creditors (Format 2, items C. 1 to 11)

Amounts falling due within one year and after one year shall be shown separately for each of these items and their aggregate shall be shown separately for all of these items.

(10) Profit and loss account

(Format 1, items H.V and VI, Format 2, 'CAPITAL, RESERVES AND LIABILITIES' items A.V and V.I)

These items may be combined where the appropriation of profit required by paragraph 53 is given at the foot of the profit and loss account or in a note to the financial statements.

PROFIT AND LOSS ACCOUNT FORMATS

Format 1 (15)

1. Turnover
2. Cost of sales (11)
3. Gross profit or loss
4. Distribution costs (11)
5. Administrative expenses (11)
6. Other operating income
7. Income from shares in group undertakings
8. Income from participating interests
9. Income from other financial assets (12)
10. Other interest receivable and similar income (12)
11. Value adjustments in respect of financial assets and investments held as current assets
12. Interest payable and similar expenses (13)
13. Tax on profit or loss
14. Profit or loss after taxation
15. Other taxes not shown under the above items
16. Profit or loss for the financial year (14)

Profit and Loss Account Formats

Format 2

1. Turnover
2. Variation in stocks of finished goods and in work in progress
3. Own work capitalised
4. Other operating income
5. (a) Raw materials and consumables
   (b) Other external expenses
6. Staff costs:
   (a) Wages and salaries
   (b) Social insurance costs
   (c) Other retirement benefit costs
   (d) Other compensation costs
7. (a) Depreciation and other value adjustments in respect of tangible and intangible fixed assets
   (b) Value adjustments in respect of current assets to the extent they exceed value adjustments that are normal in the undertaking concerned
8. Other operating expenses
9. Income from shares in group undertakings
10. Income from participating interests
11. Income from other financial assets (12)
12. Other interest receivable and similar income (12)
13. Value adjustments in respect of financial assets and investments held as current assets
14. Interest payable and similar expenses (13)
15. Tax on profit or loss
16. Profit or loss after taxation
17. Other taxes not shown under the above items
18. Profit or loss for the financial year (14)

Notes on the Profit and Loss Account Formats

(11) Cost of sales: Distribution costs: Administrative expenses

(Format 1, items 2, 4 and 5)

These items shall be stated after taking into account any necessary value adjustments for depreciation or diminution in value of assets.

(12) Income from other financial assets: other interest receivable and similar income

(Format 1, items 9 and 10; Format 2, items 11 and 12)

Income and interest derived from group undertakings shall be shown separately from income and interest derived from other sources.

(13) Interest payable and similar expenses

(Format 1, item 12; Format 2, item 14;)

The amount payable to group undertakings shall be shown separately.

(14) Profit or loss for the financial year

(Format 1, item 16; Format 2, item 18;)

The appropriation of profit required by *paragraph 53* may be given at the foot of the profit and loss account or in a note to the financial statements.

(15) Format 1

The amounts of any value adjustments for depreciation and diminution in value of tangible and intangible fixed assets falling to be shown under item 7(a) in Format 2 shall be disclosed in a note to the financial statements in any case where the profit and loss account is prepared by reference to Format 1.

PART III
ACCOUNTING PRINCIPLES AND VALUATION RULES

SECTION A
ACCOUNTING PRINCIPLES

Preliminary

11. Subject to *paragraph 18*, the amounts to be included in the financial statements of a company in respect of the items shown shall be determined in accordance with the principles set out in *paragraphs 12* to *17*.

Accounting principles

12. The company shall be presumed to be carrying on business as a going concern.

13. Accounting policies and measurement bases shall be applied consistently from one financial year to the next.

14. The amount of any item in the financial statements shall be determined on a prudent basis and in particular—

    (a) only profits realised at the financial year end date shall be included in the profit and loss account,

    (b) all liabilities which have arisen in the course of the financial year to which the financial statements relate or of a previous financial year shall be taken into account, even if such liabilities only become apparent between the financial year end date and the date on which the financial statements are signed under *section 324*, and

(c) all value adjustments for diminution in value shall be recognised, whether the result for the financial year to which the financial statements relate is a profit or loss.

15. All income and expenses relating to the financial year to which the financial statements relate shall be taken into account without regard to the date of receipt or payment.

16. In determining the aggregate amount of any item the amount of each individual asset or liability that falls to be taken into account shall be determined separately.

17. Items in the profit and loss account and balance sheet shall be accounted for and presented having regard to the substance of the reported transaction or arrangement in accordance with applicable accounting standards.

18. The provisions of this Schedule need not be complied with where the amounts involved are not material for the purpose of giving a true and fair view.

Departure from the accounting principles

19. If it appears to the directors of a company that there are special reasons for departing from any of the principles stated above in preparing the company's financial statements in any particular year, they may so depart, but particulars of the departure, the reasons for it and its effect on the balance sheet and profit and loss account of the company shall be stated in a note to the financial statements.

SECTION B
HISTORICAL COST ACCOUNTING RULES

Preliminary

20. Subject to *sections C* and *D*, the amounts to be included in respect of all items shown in a company's financial statements shall be determined in accordance with the rules set out in *paragraphs 21* to *30*.

FIXED ASSETS

General Rules

21. Subject to any value adjustment for depreciation or diminution in value made in accordance with *paragraph 22* or *23* the amount to be included in respect of any fixed asset shall be its purchase price or production cost.

Rules for depreciation and diminution in value

22. In the case of any fixed asset which has a limited useful economic life, the amount of—

(a) its purchase price or production cost, or

(b) where it is estimated that any such asset will have a residual value at the end of the period of its useful economic life, its purchase price or production cost less that estimated residual value, shall be reduced by value adjustments for depreciation calculated to write off that amount systematically over the period of the asset's useful economic life.

23. (1) Where a financial asset of a description falling to be included under item A. III of either of the balance sheet formats set out in *Part II* has diminished in value, value adjustments for diminution in value may be made in respect of it and the amount to be included in respect of it may be reduced accordingly; and any such value adjustments which are not shown separately in the profit and loss account shall be disclosed (either separately or in aggregate) in a note to the financial statements.

(2) Value adjustments for diminution in value shall be made in respect of any fixed asset which has diminished in value if the reduction in its value is expected to be permanent (whether its useful economic life is limited or not) and the amount to be included in respect of it shall be reduced accordingly; and any such value adjustments which are not shown separately in the profit and loss account shall be disclosed (either separately or in aggregate) in a note to the financial statements.

(3) Where the reasons for which any value adjustment was made in accordance with *subparagraphs (1)* or *(2)* have ceased to apply to any extent, that value adjustment shall be written back to the extent that it is no longer necessary; and any amounts written back in accordance with this subparagraph which are not shown in the profit and loss account shall be disclosed (either separately or in aggregate) in a note to the financial statements.

Rules for determining particular fixed asset items

24. (1) Notwithstanding that an item in respect of "development costs" is included under 'fixed assets' in the balance sheet formats set out in *Part II*, an amount may only be included in a company's balance sheet in respect of that item in special circumstances.

(2) If an amount is included in a company's balance sheet in respect of development costs, the following information shall be given in a note to the financial statements—

(a) the period over which the amount of those costs originally capitalised is being or is to be written off, and

(b) the reasons for capitalising the costs in question.

25. (1) The application of *paragraphs 21* to *24* in relation to goodwill and development costs (in any case where goodwill or development costs are treated as assets) and other intangible assets is subject to the following provisions of this paragraph.

(2) Subject to *subparagraph (3)*—

(a) the amount of the consideration for any goodwill acquired by a company,

(b) the amount of development costs capitalised, or

(c) the amount of other intangible assets recognised, shall be reduced by value adjustments for depreciation calculated to write off that amount systematically over the useful economic life of the goodwill, development costs or other intangible assets.

(3) Where, in exceptional circumstances, the useful life of goodwill acquired by a company or development costs or other intangible assets capitalised cannot be reliably estimated, the amounts referred to in *subparagraphs (2)(a)*, *(b)* and *(c)* shall be reduced by value adjustments for depreciation calculated to write off those amounts systematically over a period which shall be not more than 10 years.

(4) In any case where any goodwill acquired by a company is shown or included as an asset in the company's balance sheet, the period chosen for writing off the consideration for that goodwill and the reasons for choosing that period shall be disclosed in a note to the financial statements.

(5) Where, in accordance with *paragraph 23(2)*, a value adjustment for diminution in value has been recognised for goodwill, even if it is considered that the reason for the diminution in value has ceased to exist, the value adjustment shall not be reversed as required by *paragraph 23(3)*.

CURRENT ASSETS

26. Subject to *paragraph 27*, the amount to be included in respect of any current asset shall be its purchase price or production cost.

27. (1) If the net realisable value of any current asset is lower than its purchase price or production cost, the amount to be included in respect of that asset shall be the net realisable value.

(2) Where the reasons for which any value adjustment for diminution in value was made under *subparagraph (1)* have ceased to apply to any extent that value adjustment shall be written back to the extent that it is no longer necessary.

MISCELLANEOUS

Excess of money owed over value received as an asset item

28. (1) Where the amount repayable on any debt owed by a company is greater than the value of the consideration received in the transaction giving rise to the debt, the amount of the difference may be treated as an asset.

(2) Where any such amount exists—

(a) it shall be written off by reasonable amounts each year and shall be completely written off before repayment of the debt, and

(b) if the amount not written off is not shown as a separate item in the company's balance sheet, it shall be disclosed in a note to the financial statements.

DETERMINATION OF PURCHASE PRICE OR PRODUCTION COST

29. (1) The purchase price of an asset shall be determined by adding to the actual price paid any expenses incidental to its acquisition and by deducting from the actual price paid any income incidental to its acquisition.

(2) The production cost of an asset shall be determined by adding to the purchase price of the raw materials and consumables used the amount of the costs incurred by the company which are directly attributable to the production of that asset.

(3) In addition there may be included in the production cost of an asset—

(a) a reasonable proportion of the costs incurred by the company which are only indirectly attributable to the production of that asset, but only to the extent that they relate to the period of production, and

(b) interest on capital borrowed to finance the production of that asset, to the extent that it accrues in respect of the period of production,

provided, however, in a case within clause (b), that the inclusion of the interest in determining the cost of that asset and the amount of the interest so included is disclosed in a note to the financial statements.

(4) Distribution costs may not be included in production costs.

30. (1) Subject to the qualification mentioned in *subparagraph (2)*, the purchase price or production cost of—

(a) any assets which fall to be included under any item shown in a company's balance sheet under the general item "stocks", and

(b) any assets which are fungible assets (including investments), may be determined by the application of any of the methods mentioned in *subparagraph (3)* in relation to any such assets of the same class.

(2) The method chosen shall be one which appears to the directors to be appropriate in the circumstances of the company.

(3) The methods are—

(a) the method known as 'first in, first out' (FIFO),

(b) a weighted average price, and

(c) any other method reflecting generally accepted best practice.

(4) For the purpose of this paragraph, assets of any description shall be regarded as fungible if assets of that description are substantially indistinguishable from one another.

SECTION C
ALTERNATIVE ACCOUNTING RULES

Preliminary

31. (1) The rules set out in section B are referred to subsequently in this Schedule as the historical cost accounting rules.

(2) Those rules, with the omission of *paragraphs 20, 29* and *30*, are referred to subsequently in this Part as the depreciation rules; and references subsequently in this Schedule to the historical cost accounting rules do not include the depreciation rules as they apply by virtue of *paragraph 34*.

32. Subject to *paragraphs 34* to *37*, the amounts to be included in respect of assets of any description mentioned in *paragraph 33* may be determined on any basis so mentioned.

Alternative accounting rules

33. (1) Intangible fixed assets, other than goodwill, may be included at a market value determined as at the date of their last valuation.

(2) Tangible fixed assets may be included at a market value determined as at the date of their last valuation.

(3) Financial fixed assets may be included either—

(a) at a market value determined as at the date of their last valuation, or

(b) at a value determined on any basis which appears to the directors to be appropriate in the circumstances of the company,

but in the latter case particulars of the method of valuation adopted and of the reasons for adopting it shall be disclosed in a note to the financial statements.

(4) Participating interests in an associated undertaking may be included under the equity method of accounting.

Application of depreciation rules

34. (1) Where the value of any asset of a company is determined on any basis mentioned in *paragraph 33*, that value shall be, or (as the case may require) be the starting point for determining, the amount to be included in respect of that asset in the company's financial statements, instead of its purchase price or production cost or any value previously so determined for that asset; and the depreciation rules shall apply accordingly in relation to any such asset with the substitution for any reference to its purchase price or production cost of a reference to the value most recently determined for that asset on any basis mentioned in *paragraph 33*.

(2) The amount of any value adjustment for depreciation required in the case of any fixed asset by *paragraph 22* or *23* as it applies by virtue of *subparagraph (1)* is referred to subsequently in this paragraph as the adjusted amount; and the amount of any value adjustment which would be required by that paragraph in the case of that asset according to the historical cost accounting rules is referred to as the historical cost amount.

(3) Where *subparagraph (1)* applies in the case of any fixed asset, the amount of any value adjustment for depreciation in respect of that asset—

(a) included in any item shown in the profit and loss account in respect of amounts written off assets of the description in question, or

(b) taken into account in stating any item so shown which is required by note (11) of the notes on the profit and loss account formats set out in *Part II* to be stated after taking into account any necessary value adjustments for depreciation or diminution in value of assets included under it, may be the historical cost amount instead of the adjusted amount, provided that, if the amount of the value adjustment for depreciation is the historical cost amount, the amount of any difference between the two shall be shown separately in the profit and loss account or in a note to the financial statements.

Additional information in case of departure from historical cost accounting rules

35. (1) This paragraph applies where the amounts to be included in respect of fixed assets covered by any items shown in a company's financial statements have been determined on any basis mentioned in *paragraph 33*.

(2) The items affected and the basis of valuation adopted in determining the amounts of the assets in question in the case of each such item shall be disclosed in the notes to the financial statements on the accounting policies adopted by the company as required by *section 321*.

(3) In the case of each balance sheet item affected, the comparable amounts determined according to the historical cost accounting rules shall be shown separately in the balance sheet or in a note to the financial statements.

(4) In *subparagraph (3)*, references in relation to any item to the comparable amounts determined as there mentioned are references to—

(a) the aggregate amount which would be required to be shown in respect of that item if the amounts to be included in respect of all the assets covered by that item were determined according to the historical cost accounting rules, and

(b) the aggregate amount of the cumulative value adjustments for depreciation or diminution in value which would be permitted or required in determining those amounts according to those rules.

Revaluation Reserve

36. (1) With respect to any determination of the value of an asset of a company on any basis mentioned in *paragraph 33(1)* to *(3)*, the amount of any profit or loss arising from that determination (after allowing, where appropriate, for any value adjustments for depreciation or diminution in value made otherwise than by reference to the value so determined and any adjustments of any such value adjustments made in the light of that determination) shall be credited or, as the case may be, debited to a separate reserve (referred to in this paragraph as the "revaluation reserve").

(2) The amount of the revaluation reserve shall be shown in the company's balance sheet under a separate sub-heading in the position given for the item "revaluation reserve" under "Capital and Reserves" in Format 1 or 2 of the balance sheet formats set out in *Part II*.

(3) An amount may be transferred—

(a) from the revaluation reserve—

(i) to the profit and loss account, if the amount was previously charged to that account, or it represents realised profit, or

(ii) on capitalisation,

or

(b) to or from the revaluation reserve in respect of the taxation relating to any profit or loss credited or debited to the reserve,

and the revaluation reserve shall be reduced to the extent that the amounts transferred to it are no longer necessary for the purpose of the valuation methods used.

(4) In *subparagraph (3)(a)(ii)* "capitalisation", in relation to an amount standing to the credit of the revaluation reserve, means applying it in wholly or partly paying up unissued shares in the company to be allotted to members of the company as fully or partly paid shares.

(5) The revaluation reserve shall not be reduced except as mentioned in this paragraph.

(6) The treatment for taxation purposes of amounts credited or debited to the revaluation reserve shall be disclosed in a note to the financial statements.

Accounting for certain participating interests in entity financial statements

37. (1) Where in accordance with *paragraph 33(4)*, the interest of a company in an associated undertaking in which a participating interest is held, and the amount of profit or loss attributable to such an interest, are included in the financial statements by way of the equity method of accounting any goodwill arising shall be dealt with in accordance with *paragraphs 21* to *23* and *25*.

(2) Where the undertaking in which a participating interest is held is itself a holding undertaking, the net assets and profits or losses to be taken into account are those of the holding undertaking and its subsidiary undertakings (after making any consolidation adjustments).

(3) Where the cumulative profit attributable to the participating interest and recognised in the profit and loss account exceeds the cumulative amount of dividends received or receivable, the amount of the difference shall be placed in a separate reserve which may not be distributed to shareholders.

SECTION D
FAIR VALUE ACCOUNTING RULES

Inclusion of financial instruments at fair value

38. (1) Financial instruments that, under IFRS, may be accounted for in financial statements at fair value, may be so accounted for in financial statements to which the provisions of this Schedule apply, provided that the disclosures required by IFRS are made.

(2) In this paragraph, "fair value" means fair value determined in accordance with relevant IFRS.

Hedged items

39. A company may include any assets or liabilities, or identified portions of such assets or liabilities that qualify as hedged items under a fair value hedge accounting system at the amount required under that system.

Other assets that may be included at fair value

40. (1) This paragraph applies to—

(a) investment property, and

(b) living animals and plants, that, under relevant international financial reporting standards, may be included in financial statements at fair value.

(2) Such investment property and such living animals and plants may be included at fair value, provided that all such investment property or, as the case may be, all such living animals and plants are so included where their fair value can reliably be determined.

(3) In this paragraph, "fair value" means fair value determined in accordance with relevant IFRS.

Accounting for changes in fair value

41. (1) This paragraph applies where a financial instrument is valued at fair value in accordance with *paragraph 38* or *39* or where an asset is valued in accordance with *paragraph 40*.

(2) Notwithstanding *paragraph 14*, a change in the fair value of an investment property or living animal or plant shall be included in the profit and loss account.

(3) Notwithstanding *paragraph 14*, a change in the fair value of a financial instrument shall be accounted for in accordance with IFRS and to the extent the change in fair value is not included in the profit and loss account the amount of the change in value shall be credited or (as the case may be) debited to a separate reserve to be known as the "fair value reserve".

The fair value reserve

42. (1) The fair value reserve shall be adjusted when amounts therein are no longer necessary for the purposes of *paragraph 41(3)*.

(2) The treatment for taxation purposes of amounts credited or debited to the fair value reserve shall be disclosed in a note to the financial statements.

PART IV
INFORMATION REQUIRED BY WAY OF NOTES TO FINANCIAL STATEMENTS

Preliminary

43. (1) Any information required in the case of any company by the following provisions of this Part shall (if not given in the company's financial statements) be given by way of a note to those financial statements.

(2) These notes shall be presented in the order in which, where relevant, the items to which they relate are presented in the balance sheet and in the profit and loss account.

Information supplementing the balance sheet

44. *Paragraphs 45* to *58* require information which either supplements the information given with respect to any particular items shown in the balance sheet or is otherwise relevant to assessing the company's financial position in the light of the information so given.

Debentures

45. (1) If the company has issued any debentures during the financial year to which the financial statements relate, the following information shall be given:

(a) the reason for making the issue;

(b) the classes of debentures issued;

(c) in respect of each class of debentures, the amount issued and the consideration received by the company for the issue.

(2) Where any of the company's debentures are held by a nominee of or trustee for the company, the nominal amount of the debentures and the amount at which they are stated in the accounting records kept by the company in accordance with *section 281* shall be stated.

Fixed assets

46. (1) In respect of each item which is or would, but for *paragraphs 2(2)* and *4(4)(b)*, be shown under the general item "fixed assets" in the company's balance sheet, the following information shall be given:

(a) the appropriate amounts in respect of that item as at the date of the beginning of the financial year and as at the financial year end date respectively;

(b) the effect on any amount shown in the balance sheet in respect of that item of—

(i) any revision of the amount in respect of any assets included under that item made during that year on any basis mentioned in paragraph 33 or under the fair value accounting rules,

(ii) acquisitions during that year of any assets,

(iii) disposals during that year of any assets, and

(iv) any transfers of assets of the company to and from that item during that year.

(2) The reference in *subparagraph (1)(a)* to the appropriate amounts in respect of any item as at any date there mentioned is a reference to amounts representing the aggregate amounts determined, as at that date, in respect of assets falling to be included under that item—

(a) on the basis of purchase price or production cost (determined in accordance with *paragraphs 29* and *30*),

(b) on any basis mentioned in *paragraph 33*, or

(c) under the fair value accounting rules,

as the case may be (leaving out of account in each of clauses (a), (b) and (c) any value adjustments for depreciation or diminution in value).

(3) In respect of each item within *subparagraph (1)*—

(a) the cumulative amount of value adjustments for depreciation or diminution in value of assets included under that item as at each date mentioned in *subparagraph (1)(a)*,

(b) the amount of any such value adjustments made in respect of the financial year concerned,

(c) the amount of any changes made in respect of any such value adjustments during that year in consequence of the disposal of any assets, and

(d) the amount of any other changes made in respect of any such value adjustments during that year, shall also be stated.

47. Where any fixed assets of the company (other than listed investments) are included under any item shown in the company's balance sheet at an amount determined on any basis mentioned in *paragraph 33(1)* to *(3)*, the following information shall be given:

(a) the years (so far as they are known to the directors) in which the assets were severally valued and the several values;

(b) in the case of assets that have been valued during the financial year, the names of the persons who valued them or particulars of their qualifications for doing so and (in either case) the bases of valuation used by them.

Financial assets and investments held as current assets

48. (1) In respect of the amount of each item which is or would, but for *paragraphs 2(2)* or *4(4)(b)*, be shown in the company's balance sheet under the general items "financial assets" or 'investments held as current assets' there shall be stated how much of that amount is ascribable to listed investments.

(2) Where the amount of any listed investments is stated for any item in accordance with *subparagraph (1)*, there shall also be stated the fair value of those investments where it differs from the amount so stated.

Information about fair valuation of assets and liabilities

49. (1) This paragraph applies where financial instruments or assets other than financial instruments have been included at fair value by virtue of *paragraphs 38*, *39* or *40*.

(2) There shall be stated—

(a) the significant assumptions underlying the valuation models and techniques where fair values have been determined otherwise than by reference to market price in an active market,

(b) for each category of financial instruments or assets other than financial instruments, the fair value of the financial instruments or assets, other than financial instruments, in that category and the amounts—

(i) included in the profit and loss account, and

(ii) credited or debited to the fair value reserve, in respect of financial instruments or assets, other than financial instruments, in that category,

(c) for each class of derivative financial instrument, the extent and nature of the instruments including significant terms and conditions that may affect the amount, timing and certainty of future cash flows, and

(d) a table showing movements in the fair value reserve during the financial year.

50. Where the company has derivative financial instruments that it has not accounted for at fair value, there shall be stated for each class of such derivatives—

(a) the fair value of the derivatives in that class, if such a value can be determined in accordance with *paragraph 38*, and

(b) the extent and nature of the derivatives.

51. Where—

(a) a company has financial assets which could be included at fair value by virtue of *paragraph 38*,

(b) those assets are included in the company's financial statements at an amount in excess of their fair value, and

(c) the company has not made a value adjustment for the diminution in value of those assets in accordance with *paragraph 23(1)*, there shall be stated—

(i) the amount at which either the individual assets or appropriate groupings of those assets is stated in the company's financial statements,

(ii) the fair value of those assets or groupings, and

(iii) the reasons for not making a value adjustment for diminution in value of those assets, including the nature of the evidence that provides the basis for the belief that the amount at which they are stated in the financial statements will be recovered.

Information where investment property or living animals and plants included at fair value

52. (1) This paragraph applies where the amounts to be included in a company's financial statements in respect of investment property or living animals and plants have been determined in accordance with *paragraph 40*.

(2) The balance sheet items affected and the basis of valuation adopted in determining the amounts of the assets in question in the case of each such item shall be disclosed in the notes to the financial statements on the accounting policies adopted by the company as required by *section 321*.

Dividends, reserves and provisions for liabilities

53. (1) The profit and loss account, balance sheet or notes to the financial statements of a company for a financial year shall show—

(a) the aggregate amount of dividends paid in the financial year (other than dividends for which a liability existed at the immediately preceding financial year end date),

(b) the aggregate amount of dividends the company is liable to pay at the financial year end date (other than dividends for which a liability existed at the immediately preceding financial year end date),

(c) separately, any transfer between the profit and loss account reserve and other reserves,

(d) any other increase or reduction in the balance on the profit and loss account reserve since the immediately preceding financial year end date,

(e) the profit or loss brought forward at the beginning of the financial year, and

(f) the profit or loss carried forward at the end of the financial year.

(2) The aggregate amount of dividends proposed by the directors for approval of the members at the next general meeting shall be stated in a note to the financial statements.

54. (1) Where any amount is transferred—

(a) to or from any reserves,

(b) to any provision for liabilities, or

(c) from any provision for liabilities other than for the purpose for which the provision was established,

and the reserves or provisions for liabilities are or would, but for paragraph 4(4)(b), be shown as separate items in the company's balance sheet, the information mentioned in *subparagraph (2)* shall be given in respect of each such reserve or provisions for liabilities.

(2) The information, which is to be set out in tabular form, is—

(a) the amount of the reserves or provisions for liabilities as at the date of the beginning of the financial year and as at the financial year end date respectively,

(b) any amount transferred to or from the reserves or provisions for liabilities during that year, and

(c) the source and application respectively of any amounts so transferred.

(3) Particulars shall be given of each provision included in the item "other provisions for liabilities" in the company's balance sheet in any case where the amount of that provision is material.

Provision for taxation

55. The amount of any provision for deferred taxation shall be shown separately from the amount of any provision for other taxation.

Details of indebtedness

56. (1) In respect of each item shown under "creditors" in the company's balance sheet there shall be stated the aggregate amount of any debts included under that item which fall due for payment or repayment after the end of the period of 5 years beginning with the day next following the end of the financial year.

(2) Subject to *subparagraph (3)*, in relation to each debt falling to be taken into account under *subparagraph (1)*, the terms of payment or repayment and the rate of any interest payable on the debt shall be stated.

(3) If the number of debts is such that, in the opinion of the directors, compliance with *subparagraph (2)* would result in a statement of excessive length, it shall be sufficient to give a general indication of the terms of payment or repayment and the rates of any interest payable on the debts.

(4) In respect of each item shown under "creditors" in the company's balance sheet there shall be stated—

(a) the aggregate amount of any debts included under that item in respect of which any security has been given, and

(b) an indication of the nature of the securities so given.

(5) References in *subparagraph (1)* to an item shown under "creditors" in the company's balance sheet include references, where amounts falling due to creditors within one year and after more than one year are distinguished in the balance sheet—

(a) in a case within *subparagraph (1)*, to an item shown under the latter of those categories, and

(b) in a case within *subparagraph (4)*, to an item shown under either of those categories,

and references to items shown under 'creditors' include references to items which would, but for *paragraphs 2(2)* or *4(4)(b)*, be shown under that heading.

57. If any fixed cumulative dividends on the company's shares are in arrears, there shall be stated, distinguishing between those shares presented as a liability and other shares—

(a) the amount of the arrears, and

(b) the period for which the dividends or, if there is more than one class, each class of them are in arrears.

Guarantees and other financial commitments

58. (1) Particulars shall be given of any charge on the assets of the company to secure the liabilities of any other person, including, where practicable, the amount secured.

(2) Particulars and the total amount or estimated total amount shall be given with respect to any other financial commitment, guarantee or contingency not provided for in the balance sheet.

(3) An indication of the nature and form of any valuable security given by the company in connection with the commitments, guarantees or contingencies referred to in *subparagraph (2)* shall be given in the financial statements.

(4) The total amount of any commitments referred to in *subparagraph (2)* concerning retirement benefits shall be disclosed separately.

(5) Particulars, including details of significant assumptions underlying the valuation models, shall be given of retirement benefit commitments which are included in the balance sheet.

(6) Where any commitment referred to in *subparagraphs (4)* or *(5)* relates wholly or partly to retirement benefits payable to past directors of the company, separate particulars shall be given of that commitment.

(7) The aggregate amount of any commitments, guarantees or contingencies referred to in *subparagraph (2)* which are undertaken on behalf of or for the benefit of—

(a) any holding undertaking or fellow subsidiary undertaking of the company,

(b) any subsidiary undertaking of the company, or

(c) any undertaking in which the company has a participating interest,

shall be separately stated and those within each of clause (a), (b) and (c) shall also be stated separately from those within any other of those clauses.

Information supplementing the profit and loss account

59. *Paragraphs 60* to *63* require information which either supplements the information given with respect to any particular items shown in the profit and loss account or otherwise provides particulars of income or expenditure of the company or of circumstances affecting the items shown in the profit and loss account.

Separate statement of certain items of income and expenditure

60. Each of the following amounts shall be stated—

(a) the amount of interest on or any similar expenses in respect of—

(i) loans and overdrafts made to the company by credit institutions,

(ii) loans to the company from group undertakings,

(iii) loans of any other kind made to the company, and

(b) the amount of income from listed and unlisted investments.

Particulars of tax

61. (1) The basis on which the charge for corporation tax, income tax and other taxation on profits (whether payable in or outside the State) is computed shall be stated.

(2) Particulars shall be given of any special circumstances which affect the liability in respect of taxation on profits, income or capital gains for the financial year concerned or the liability in respect of taxation of profits, income or capital gains for succeeding financial years.

(3) The amount of the charge for corporation tax, income tax and other taxation on profits or capital gains, so far as charged to revenue, including taxation payable outside the State on profits (distinguishing where practicable between corporation tax and other taxation) shall be stated.

(4) The amounts referred to in *subparagraph (3)* shall be stated separately in respect of each of the amounts which is or would, but for *paragraph 4(4)(b)*, be shown under the following item in the profit and loss account, that is to say, "tax on profit or loss".

Particulars of turnover

62. (1) If, in the course of the financial year, the company has carried on business of 2 or more classes which, in the opinion of the directors, differ substantially from each other, there shall be stated in respect of each class (describing it) the amount of the turnover attributable to that class.

(2) If, in the course of the financial year, the company has supplied markets which, in the opinion of the directors, differ substantially from each other, the amount of the turnover attributable to each such market shall also be stated.

(3) In *subparagraph (2)*, "market" means a market delimited by geographical bounds.

(4) In analysing for the purposes of this paragraph the source (in terms of business or in terms of market) of turnover, the directors of the company shall have regard to the manner in which the company's activities are organised.

(5) For the purpose of this paragraph—

(a) classes of business which, in the opinion of the directors, do not differ substantially from each other shall be treated as one class, and

(b) markets which, in the opinion of the directors, do not differ substantially from each other shall be treated as one market,

and any amounts properly attributable to one class of business or (as the case may be) to one market which are not material may be included in the amount stated in respect of another.

(6) Where, in the opinion of the directors, the disclosure of any information required by this paragraph would be seriously prejudicial to the interests of the company, that information need not be disclosed, but the fact that any such information has not been disclosed shall be stated.

Exceptional items and miscellaneous matters

63. (1) Where any amount relating to any preceding financial year is included in any item in the profit and loss account, the effect shall be stated.

(2) The profit and loss account or the notes to the financial statements shall disclose information on the nature, amount and effect of individual items of income and expenditure that are exceptional by virtue of size or incidence.

(3) Any amount expended on research and development in the financial year, and any amount committed in respect of research and development in subsequent years, shall be stated.

(4) Where, in the opinion of the directors, the disclosure of any information required by *subparagraph (3)* would be prejudicial to the interests of the company, that information need not be disclosed, but the fact that any such information has not been disclosed shall be stated.

General information

64. *Paragraphs 65* to *67* require other information to be given in the notes to the financial statements.

Related party transactions

65. (1) Subject to *subparagraph (3)*, particulars shall be given in the notes to the financial statements of a company of transactions which have been entered into with related parties by the company if such transactions are material and have not been concluded under normal market conditions and the particulars shall include the amount of such transactions, the nature of the related party relationship and other information about the transactions which is necessary for an understanding of the financial position of the company.

(2) The provision of particulars and other information about individual transactions may be aggregated according to their nature, except where separate information is necessary for an understanding of the effects of related party transactions on the financial position of the company.

(3) *Subparagraph (1)* shall not apply to transactions which are entered into between 2 or more members of a group if any subsidiary undertaking which is party to the transaction is wholly owned by such a member.

(4) A word or expression that is used in this paragraph and is also used in IFRS has the meaning in this paragraph that it has in IFRS.

Foreign currencies

66. Where sums originally denominated in foreign currencies have been brought into account under any items shown in the balance sheet or profit and loss account, the basis on which those sums have been translated into euro or, if different, the functional currency of the company, shall be stated.

Events after the end of the financial year

67. The particulars and financial impact of material events that have occurred after the end of the financial year shall be given in the notes to the financial statements.

PART V
SPECIAL PROVISIONS WHERE A COMPANY IS A HOLDING COMPANY OR SUBSIDIARY UNDERTAKING

Dealings with or interests in group undertakings

68. (1) This Part applies where the company is a holding company, whether or not it is itself a subsidiary undertaking.

(2) Where a company is a holding company or a subsidiary undertaking and any item required by *Part II* to be shown in the company's balance sheet, in relation to group undertakings, includes—

(a) amounts attributable to dealings with or interests in any holding undertaking or fellow subsidiary undertaking, or

(b) amounts attributable to dealings with or interests in any subsidiary undertaking of the company,

the aggregate amounts within clauses (a) and (b), respectively, shall be shown as separate items, either by way of subdivision of the relevant item in the balance sheet or in a note to the company's financial statements.

Interests in debentures of holding company held by subsidiary undertakings

69. (1) Subject to *subparagraph (2)*, where the company is a holding company, the number, description and amount of the debentures of the company held by its subsidiary undertakings or their nominees shall be disclosed in a note to the company's financial statements.

(2) *Subparagraph (1)* does not apply in relation to any debentures—

(a) in the case of which the subsidiary undertaking is concerned as personal representative, or

(b) in the case of which it is concerned as trustee,

provided that in the latter case neither the company nor a subsidiary undertaking of the company is beneficially interested under the trust, otherwise than by way of security only for the purposes of a transaction entered into by it in the ordinary course of a business which includes the lending of money.

Holding undertakings preparing group financial statements

70. (1) Where a company is a subsidiary undertaking, the information specified in *subparagraphs (2)*, *(3)* and *(4)* shall be stated with respect to the holding undertaking of—

(a) the largest group of undertakings for which group financial statements are drawn up and of which the company is a member, and

(b) the smallest such group of undertakings.

(2) The name of the holding undertaking shall be stated.

(3) There shall be stated—

(a) if the holding undertaking is incorporated, the address of the holding undertaking's registered office or where the holding undertaking is incorporated outside the State, the registered office (howsoever described) of the holding undertaking in the country in which it is incorporated, or

(b) if it is unincorporated, the address of its principal place of business.

(4) If copies of the group financial statements referred to in subparagraph (1) are available to the public, there shall be stated the addresses from which copies of the financial statements may be obtained.

Provisions of general application

71. (1) This paragraph applies where a company is a holding company and either—

(a) does not prepare group financial statements, or

(b) prepares group financial statements which do not consolidate one or more of its subsidiary undertakings,

and references in this paragraph to subsidiary undertakings shall be read, in a case within clause (b), as references to such of the subsidiary undertakings of the company concerned as are not consolidated in the group financial statements.

(2) Subject to the following provisions of this paragraph, there shall be given in the notes to the company's entity financial statements—

(a) the reasons why subsidiary undertakings are not consolidated in group financial statements, and

(b) a statement—

(i) showing any qualifications contained in the reports of the statutory auditors of the subsidiary undertakings on their financial statements for their respective financial years ending with or during the financial year of the company, and

(ii) of any note or saving contained in those financial statements to call attention to a matter which, apart from the note or saving, would properly have been referred to in such a qualification,

in so far as the matter which is the subject of the qualification or note is not covered by the company's entity financial statements and is material from the point of view of its members.

(3) Subject to the following provisions of this paragraph, the aggregate amount of the total investment of the holding company in the shares of the subsidiary undertakings shall be stated in a note to the company's entity financial statements by way of the equity method of accounting.

(4) In so far as information required by any of the preceding provisions of this paragraph to be stated in a note to the company's entity financial statements is not obtainable, a statement to that effect shall be given instead in a note to those entity financial statements.

(5) Where, in any case within *subparagraph (1)(b)*, the company prepares group financial statements, references in the preceding subparagraphs to the company's entity financial statements shall be read as references to the group financial statements.

72. Where a company has subsidiary undertakings whose financial years did not end with that of the company, the following information shall be given in relation to each such subsidiary undertaking (whether or not consolidated in any group financial statements prepared by the company) by way of a note to the company's entity financial statements or (where group financial statements are prepared) to the group financial statements, that is to say—

(a) the reasons why the company's directors consider that the subsidiary undertakings' financial years should not end with that of the company, and

(b) the dates on which the subsidiary undertakings' financial years ending last before that of the company respectively ended or the earliest and latest of those dates.

PART VI
INTERPRETATION OF CERTAIN EXPRESSIONS IN SCHEDULE

Assets: Fixed or Current

73. For the purposes of this Schedule, assets of a company shall be taken to be fixed assets if they are intended for use on a continuing basis in the company's activities, and any assets not intended for such use shall be taken to be current assets.

Capitalisation

74. References in this Schedule to capitalising any work or costs are references to treating that work or those costs as a fixed asset.

Investment property

75. In this Schedule, 'investment property' means land or buildings (or both) held to earn rentals or for capital appreciation (or both).

Listed investments

76. In this Schedule, 'listed investments' means investments as respects which there has been granted a listing on—

(a) any regulated market or other stock exchange in the State,

(b) any regulated market or other stock exchange of repute in any other EEA state, or

(c) any stock exchange of repute in a state that is not an EEA state.

Loans

77. For the purposes of this Schedule, a loan shall be treated as falling due for payment, and an instalment of a loan shall be treated as falling due for payment, on the

earliest date on which the lender could require repayment or (as the case may be) payment, if the lender exercised all options and rights available to him or her.

Materiality

78. In this Schedule, 'material' means the status of information where its omission or misstatement could reasonably be expected to influence decisions that users make on the basis of the financial statements of the undertaking; and the materiality of individual items shall be assessed in the context of other similar items.

Value adjustments

79. (1) References in this Schedule to value adjustments for depreciation or diminution in value of assets are references to any amount written off by way of providing for depreciation or diminution in value of assets.

(2) Any reference in the profit and loss account formats set out in Part II to the depreciation of, or amounts written off, assets of any description is a reference to the movement in any value adjustment for depreciation or diminution in value of assets of that description.

Provisions

80. References in this Schedule to provisions for liabilities are references to any amount retained as reasonably necessary for the purpose of providing for any liability the nature of which is clearly defined and which exists at the financial year end date but, as respects the amount of which or the date on which it will be settled, there is uncertainty.

Purchase price

81. References in this Schedule (however expressed) to the purchase price of an asset of a company or of any raw materials or consumables used in the production of any such asset shall be read as including references to any consideration (whether in cash or otherwise) given by the company in respect of that asset or in respect of those materials or consumables (as the case may require).][a]

Amendments

a Schedule 3 substituted by C(A)A 2017, s 89(a) and Sch 1.

[SCHEDULE 3A
ACCOUNTING PRINCIPLES, FORM AND CONTENT OF ENTITY FINANCIAL STATEMENTS OF A COMPANY QUALIFYING FOR THE SMALL COMPANIES REGIME

PART I
CONSTRUCTION OF REFERENCES TO PROVISIONS OF SCHEDULE

1. (1) Without prejudice to the generality of section 9 of the Interpretation Act 2005 and its application to the body of this Act and to *Schedules 1*, *2* and *5* to *18*—

(a) a reference in this Schedule to a paragraph or Part is a reference to a paragraph or Part of this Schedule, unless it is indicated that a reference to some other enactment is intended,

(b) a reference in this Schedule to a section is a reference to the section of the Part in which the reference occurs, unless it is indicated that a reference to some other enactment is intended, and

(c) a reference in this Schedule to a subparagraph or clause is a reference to the subparagraph or clause of the provision in which the reference occurs, unless it is indicated that a reference to some other enactment is intended.

(2) Provisions providing for the interpretation of certain expressions appearing in this Schedule are contained in *Part VI*.

PART II
GENERAL RULES AND FORMATS

SECTION A
GENERAL RULES

2. (1) Subject to the provisions of this Schedule—

(a) every balance sheet of a company shall show the items listed in either of the balance sheet formats set out in *Section B*, and

(b) every profit and loss account of a company shall show the items listed in either of the profit and loss accounts formats so set out,

in either case in the order and under the headings and sub- headings given in the format adopted.

(2) Notwithstanding *subparagraph (1)(a)*, in preparing the balance sheet of a company, the directors of the company may adapt one of the balance sheet formats in *Section B* so as to distinguish between current and non-current items in a different way, provided that—

(a) the information given is at least equivalent to that which would have been required by the use of such format had it not been thus adapted, and

(b) the presentation of those items is in accordance with generally accepted accounting principles or practice.

(3) Notwithstanding *subparagraph (1)(b)*, the directors of the company may prepare a statement of the performance of the company instead of a profit and loss account and in doing so may adapt one of the profit and loss account formats in Section B, provided that—

(a) the information given is at least equivalent to that which would have been required by the use of such format had it not been thus adapted, and

(b) the presentation of those items is in accordance with generally accepted accounting principles or practice.

(4) *Subparagraph (1)* shall not be read as requiring the heading or sub-heading for any item in the balance sheet, or profit and loss

account, of a company to be distinguished by any letter or number assigned to that item in the formats set out in *Section B*.

(5) So far as is practicable, the following provisions of this Schedule shall apply to the balance sheet and profit and loss account of a company notwithstanding any adaptation pursuant to *subparagraphs (2)* and *(3)*.

3. (1) Where, in accordance with *paragraph 2(1)*, a company's balance sheet or profit and loss account for any financial year has been prepared by reference to one of the formats set out in *Section B* or where in accordance with *paragraph 2(2)* or *2(3)* one of the formats has been adapted, the directors of the company shall adopt the same format in preparing the financial statements for subsequent financial years unless, in their opinion, there are special reasons for a change.

(2) Where any change is made in the format adopted in preparing a balance sheet or profit and loss account of a company, the reasons for the change, together with full particulars of the change, shall be given in a note to the financial statements in which the new format is first adopted.

4. (1) Any item required in accordance with *paragraph 2* to be shown in the balance sheet or profit and loss account of a company may be shown in greater detail than that required by the format adopted.

(2) The balance sheet, or profit and loss account, of a company may include an item representing or covering the amount of any asset or liability or income or expenditure not otherwise covered by any of the items listed in the format adopted but the following shall not be treated as assets in the balance sheet of a company—

(a) preliminary expenses,

(b) expenses of and commission on any issue of shares or debentures, and

(c) costs of research.

(3) The balance sheet, or profit and loss account, of a company may include subtotals where their inclusion facilitates the assessment of the financial position or profit or loss of the company for the financial year concerned.

(4) Any items to which an Arabic number is assigned in any of the formats set out in *Section B* may be combined in the financial statements of a company—

(a) in any case where the individual amounts of such items are not material to assessing the financial position or profit or loss of the company for the financial year concerned, or

(b) in any case where the combination of such items facilitates that assessment.

(5) Where items are combined in a company's financial statements pursuant to *subparagraph (4)(b)*, the individual amounts of any items so combined shall be disclosed in a note to the financial statements.

(6) In preparing the balance sheet, or profit and loss account, of a company, the directors of the company shall adapt the arrangement and headings and sub-headings otherwise required by *paragraph 2* in respect of items to which an Arabic number is assigned in the format adopted, in any case where the special nature of the company's business requires such adaptation.

(7) Where an asset or liability relates to more than one of the items listed in either of the balance sheet formats set out in *Section B*, its relationship to other items shall be disclosed either under the item where it is shown or in the notes to the financial statements.

(8) The opening balance sheet for each financial year shall correspond to the closing balance sheet for the preceding financial year.

5. (1) Subject to *subparagraph (2)*, in respect of every item shown in the balance sheet, or profit and loss account, or notes thereto, of a company, the corresponding amount for the financial year immediately preceding that to which the balance sheet or profit and loss account relates shall also be shown and, if that corresponding amount is not comparable with the amount to be shown for the item in question in respect of the financial year to which the balance sheet or profit and loss account relates, the former amount may be adjusted, and particulars of the adjustment and the reasons therefor shall be given in a note to the financial statements.

(2) Corresponding amounts are not required for the movements in fixed assets during the year required by *paragraph 45(1)* and *(3)*.

6. (1) Subject to *subparagraph (2)*, a heading or sub-heading corresponding to an item listed in the format adopted in preparing the balance sheet or profit and loss account of a company shall not be included in the balance sheet or profit and loss account, as the case may be, if there is no amount to be shown for that item in respect of the financial year to which the balance sheet or profit and loss account relates.

(2) *Subparagraph (1)* shall not apply in any case where an amount can be shown for the item in question in respect of the financial year immediately preceding that to which the balance sheet or profit and loss account relates, and that amount shall be shown under the heading or sub-heading required by the format adopted as aforesaid.

7. (1) Subject to *subparagraph (2)*, amounts in respect of items representing assets or income may not be set off in the financial statements of a company against amounts in respect of items representing liabilities or expenditure, as the case may be, or *vice versa*.

(2) *Subparagraph (1)* shall not apply in any case where such set off is in accordance with applicable accounting standards, provided that the gross amounts are disclosed in a note to the financial statements.

SECTION B
THE REQUIRED FORMATS FOR FINANCIAL STATEMENTS

Preliminary

8. References in this Part to the items listed in any of the formats set out in this Part are references to those items read together with any notes following the formats which apply to any of those items.

9. A number in brackets following any item in, or any heading to, any of the formats set out in this Part is a reference to the note of that number in the notes following the formats.

10. In the notes following the formats—

    (a) the heading of each note gives the required heading or sub- heading for the item to which it applies and a reference to any letters and numbers assigned to that item in the formats set out in this Part, and

    (b) references to a numbered format are references to the balance sheet format or (as the case may require) to the profit and loss account format of that number set out in this Part.

Balance Sheet Formats

Format 1

A. Fixed Assets

   I. Intangible assets

      1. Development costs
      2. Concessions, patents, licences, trade marks and similar rights and assets (1)
      3. Goodwill (2)
      4. Payments on account

   II. Tangible assets

      1. Investment property
      2. Land and buildings
      3. Plant and machinery
      4. Fixtures, fittings, tools and equipment
      5. Payments on account and assets in course of construction

   III. Financial assets

      1. Shares in group undertakings
      2. Loans to group undertakings

3. Participating interests
4. Loans to undertakings with which the company is linked by virtue of participating interests
5. Other investments other than loans
6. Other loans

B. Current Assets

I. Stocks

1. Raw materials and consumables
2. Work in progress
3. Finished goods and goods for resale
4. Payments on account

II. Debtors (3)

1. Trade debtors
2. Amounts owed by group undertakings
3. Amounts owed by undertakings with which the company is linked by virtue of participating interests
4. Other debtors
5. Called-up share capital not paid
6. Prepayments
7. Accrued income

III. Investments

1. Shares in group undertakings
2. Other investments

IV. Cash at bank and in hand

C. Creditors: Amounts falling due within one year

1. Debenture loans (4)
2. Amounts owed to credit institutions
3. Called-up share capital presented as a liability (6)
4. Payments received on account (5)
5. Trade creditors
6. Bills of exchange payable
7. Amounts owed to group undertakings
8. Amounts owed to undertakings with which the company is linked by virtue of participating interests
9. Other creditors including tax and social insurance
10. Accruals
11. Deferred income

D. Net current assets (liabilities)

E. Total assets less current liabilities

F. Creditors: Amounts falling due after more than one year

1. Debenture loans (4)
2. Amounts owed to credit institutions
3. Called-up share capital presented as a liability (6)
4. Payments received on account (5)
5. Trade creditors
6. Bills of exchange payable
7. Amounts owed to group undertakings
8. Amounts owed to undertakings with which the company is linked by virtue of participating interests
9. Other creditors including tax and social insurance
10. Accruals
11. Deferred income

G. Provisions for liabilities

1. Retirement benefit and similar obligations
2. Taxation, including deferred taxation
3. Other provisions for liabilities

H. Capital and reserves

I. Called-up share capital presented as equity (6)

II. Share premium account

III. Revaluation reserve

IV. Other reserves

1. Other undenominated capital
2. Reserve for own shares held
3. Reserves provided for by the constitution
4. Other reserves including the fair value reserve (specified as necessary)

V. Profit or loss brought forward (8)

VI. Profit or loss for the financial year (8)

Balance Sheet Formats

Format 2

ASSETS

A. Fixed Assets

I. Intangible assets

1. Development costs
2. Concessions, patents, licences, trade marks and similar rights and assets (1)
3. Goodwill (2)
4. Payments on account

II. Tangible assets

1. Investment property
2. Land and buildings
3. Plant and machinery
4. Fixtures, fittings, tools and equipment
5. Payments on account and assets in course of construction

III. Financial assets

1. Shares in group undertakings
2. Loans to group undertakings
3. Participating interests
4. Loans to undertakings with which the company is linked by virtue of participating interests
5. Other investments other than loans
6. Other loans

B. Current Assets

I. Stocks

1. Raw materials and consumables
2. Work in progress
3. Finished goods and goods for resale
4. Payments on account

II. Debtors (3)

1. Trade debtors
2. Amounts owed by group undertakings
3. Amounts owed by undertakings with which the company is linked by virtue of participating interests
4. Other debtors
5. Called-up share capital not paid
6. Prepayments
7. Accrued income

III. Investments

1. Shares in group undertakings
2. Other investments

IV. Cash at bank and in hand

CAPITAL, RESERVES AND LIABILITIES

A. Capital and reserves

I. Called-up share capital presented as equity (6)

II. Share premium account

III. Revaluation reserve

IV. Other reserves

1. Other undenominated capital
2. Reserve for own shares held
3. Reserves provided for by the constitution
4. Other reserves including the fair value reserve (specify as necessary)

V. Profit or loss brought forward (8)

VI. Profit or loss for the financial year (8)

B. Provisions for liabilities

1. Retirement benefit and similar obligations
2. Taxation, including deferred taxation
3. Other provisions for liabilities

C. Creditors (7)

1. Debenture loans (4)
2. Amounts owed to credit institutions
3. Called-up share capital presented as a liability (6)
4. Payments received on account (5)
5. Trade creditors
6. Bills of exchange payable
7. Amounts owed to group undertakings
8. Amounts owed to undertakings with which the company is linked by virtue of participating interests
9. Other creditors including tax and social insurance
10. Accruals
11. Deferred income

NOTES ON THE BALANCE SHEET FORMATS

(1) Concessions, patents, licences, trade marks and similar rights and assets

(Formats 1 and 2, items A. I. 2)

Amounts in respect of assets shall only be included in a company's balance sheet under this item if either—

(a) the assets were acquired for valuable consideration and are not required to be shown under goodwill, or

(b) the assets in question were created by the company itself.

(2) Goodwill

(Formats 1 and 2, items A. I. 3)

Amounts representing goodwill shall only be included to the extent that the goodwill was acquired for valuable consideration.

(3) Debtors

(Formats 1 and 2, items B. II. 1 to 7)

The amount falling due after more than one year shall be shown separately for each item included under debtors.

(4) Debenture loans

(Format 1, item C. 1 and F. 1 and Format 2, item C.1)

The amount of any convertible loans shall be shown separately.

(5) Payments received on account

(Format 1, items C. 4 and F. 4 and Format 2, item C.4)

Payments received on account of orders shall be shown for each of these items in so far as they are not shown as deductions from stocks.

(6) Called-up share capital

(Format 1, item C. 3, F. 3 and H. I, and Format 2, 'CAPITAL, RESERVES AND LIABILITIES' items A. I and C. 3)

In accordance with the accounting principle in paragraph 17, called-up share capital shall be analysed between shares that are presented as liabilities and share capital.

(7) Creditors

(Format 2, items C. 1 to 11)

Amounts falling due within one year and after one year shall be shown separately for each of these items and their aggregate shall be shown separately for all of these items.

(8) Profit and loss account

(Format 1, items H.V and VI, Format 2, 'CAPITAL, RESERVES AND LIABILITIES' items A.V and VI)

These items may be combined where the appropriation of profit required by *paragraph 48* is given at the foot of the profit and loss account or in a note to the financial statements.

Profit and Loss Account Formats

Format 1 (13)

1. Turnover
2. Cost of sales (9)
3. Gross profit or loss
4. Distribution costs (9)
5. Administrative expenses (9)
6. Other operating income
7. Income from shares in group undertakings
8. Income from participating interests
9. Income from other financial assets (10)
10. Other interest receivable and similar income (10)
11. Value adjustments in respect of financial assets and investments held as current assets
12. Interest payable and similar expenses (11)
13. Tax on profit or loss
14. Profit or loss after taxation
15. Other taxes not shown under the above items
16. Profit or loss for the financial year (12)

Profit and Loss Account Formats

Format 2

1. Turnover
2. Variation in stocks of finished goods and in work in progress
3. Own work capitalised
4. Other operating income
5. (a) Raw materials and consumables

   (b) Other external expenses
6. Staff costs:

   (a) Wages and salaries

   (b) Social insurance costs

   (c) Other retirement benefit costs

   (d) Other compensation costs
7. (a) Depreciation and other value adjustments in respect of tangible and intangible fixed assets

(b) Value adjustments in respect of current assets to the extent they exceed value adjustments that are normal in the undertaking concerned

8. Other operating expenses
9. Income from shares in group undertakings
10. Income from participating interests
11. Income from other financial assets (10)
12. Other interest receivable and similar income (10)
13. Value adjustments in respect of financial assets and investments held as current assets
14. Interest payable and similar expenses (11)
15. Tax on profit or loss
16. Profit or loss after taxation
17. Other taxes not shown under the above items
18. Profit or loss for the financial year (12)

NOTES ON THE PROFIT AND LOSS ACCOUNT

FORMATS

(9) Cost of sales: Distribution costs: Administrative expenses

(Format 1, items 2, 4 and 5)

These items shall be stated after taking into account any necessary value adjustments for depreciation or diminution in value of assets.

(10) Income from other financial assets: other interest receivable and similar income

(Format 1, items 9 and 10; Format 2, items 11 and 12)

Income and interest derived from group undertakings shall be shown separately from income and interest derived from other sources.

(11) Interest payable and similar expenses

(Format 1, item 12; Format 2, item 14)

The amount payable to group undertakings shall be shown separately.

(12) Profit or loss for the financial year

(Format 1, item 16; Format 2, item 18)

The appropriation of profit required by paragraph 48 may be given at the foot of the profit and loss account or in a note to the financial statements.

(13) Format 1

The amounts of any value adjustments for depreciation and diminution in value of tangible and intangible fixed assets falling to be shown under item 7(a) in Format 2 shall be shown separately in any case where the profit and loss account is prepared by reference to Format 1.

PART III
ACCOUNTING PRINCIPLES AND VALUATION RULES

SECTION A
ACCOUNTING PRINCIPLES

Preliminary

11. Subject to *paragraph 18*, the amounts to be included in the financial statements of a company in respect of the items shown shall be determined in accordance with the principles set out in *paragraphs 12* to *17*.

Accounting principles

12. The company shall be presumed to be carrying on business as a going concern.
13. Accounting policies and measurement bases shall be applied consistently from one financial year to the next.
14. The amount of any item in the financial statements shall be determined on a prudent basis and in particular—
    (a) only profits realised at the financial year end date shall be included in the profit and loss account,
    (b) all liabilities which have arisen in the course of the financial year to which the financial statements relate or of a previous financial year shall be taken into account, even if such liabilities only become apparent between the financial year end date and the date on which the financial statements are signed under *section 324*, and
    (c) all value adjustments for diminution in value shall be recognised, whether the result for the financial year to which the financial statements relate is a profit or loss.
15. All income and expenses relating to the financial year to which the financial statements relate shall be taken into account without regard to the date of receipt or payment.
16. In determining the aggregate amount of any item the amount of each individual asset or liability that falls to be taken into account shall be determined separately.
17. Items in the profit and loss account and balance sheet shall be accounted for and presented having regard to the substance of the reported transaction or arrangement in accordance with applicable accounting standards.
18. The provisions of this Schedule need not be complied with where the amounts involved are not material for the purpose of giving a true and fair view.

Departure from the accounting principles

19. If it appears to the directors of a company that there are special reasons for departing from any of the principles stated above in preparing the company's financial statements in any particular year, they may so depart, but particulars of the departure, the reasons for it and its effect on the balance sheet and profit and loss account of the company shall be stated in a note to the financial statements.

SECTION B
HISTORICAL COST ACCOUNTING RULES

Preliminary

20. Subject to *sections* C and *D*, the amounts to be included in respect of all items shown in a company's financial statements shall be determined in accordance with the rules set out in *paragraphs 21* to *30*.

FIXED ASSETS

General rules

21. Subject to any value adjustment for depreciation or diminution in value made in accordance with *paragraph 22* or *23*, the amount to be included in respect of any fixed asset shall be its purchase price or production cost.

Rules for depreciation and diminution in value

22. In the case of any fixed asset which has a limited useful economic life, the amount of—

(a) its purchase price or production cost, or

(b) where it is estimated that any such asset will have a residual value at the end of the period of its useful economic life, its purchase price or production cost less that estimated residual value,

shall be reduced by value adjustments for depreciation calculated to write off that amount systematically over the period of the asset's useful economic life.

23. (1) Where a financial asset of a description falling to be included under item A. III of either of the balance sheet formats set out in Part II has diminished in value, value adjustments for diminution in value may be made in respect of it and the amount to be included in respect of it may be reduced accordingly; and any such value adjustments which are not shown separately in the profit and loss account shall be disclosed (either separately or in aggregate) in a note to the financial statements.

(2) Value adjustments for diminution in value shall be made in respect of any fixed asset which has diminished in value if the reduction in its value is expected to be permanent (whether its useful economic life is limited or not) and the amount to be included in respect of it shall be reduced accordingly; and any such value adjustments which are not shown separately in the profit and loss account shall be disclosed (either separately or in aggregate) in a note to the financial statements.

(3) Where the reasons for which any value adjustment was made in accordance with *subparagraph (1)* or *(2)* have ceased to apply to any extent, that value adjustment shall be written back to the extent that it is no longer necessary; and any amounts written back in accordance with this subparagraph which are not shown in the profit and loss account shall be disclosed (either separately or in aggregate) in a note to the financial statements.

Rules for determining particular fixed asset items

24. (1) Notwithstanding that an item in respect of 'development costs' is included under 'fixed assets' in the balance sheet formats set out in *Part II*, an amount may only be included in a company's balance sheet in respect of that item in special circumstances.

(2) If an amount is included in a company's balance sheet in respect of development costs, the following information shall be given in a note to the financial statements—

(a) the period over which the amount of those costs originally capitalised is being or is to be written off, and

(b) the reasons for capitalising the costs in question.

25. (1) The application of *paragraphs 21* to *24* in relation to goodwill and development costs (in any case where goodwill or development costs are treated as assets) and other intangible assets is subject to the following provisions of this paragraph.

(2) Subject to *subparagraph (3)*—

(a) the amount of the consideration for any goodwill acquired by a company,

(b) the amount of development costs capitalised, or

(c) the amount of other intangible assets recognised,

shall be reduced by value adjustments for depreciation calculated to write off that amount systematically over the useful economic life of the goodwill, development costs or other intangible assets.

(3) Where, in exceptional circumstances, the useful life of goodwill acquired by a company or development costs or other intangible assets capitalised cannot be reliably estimated, the amounts referred to in *subparagraph (2)(a)*, *(b)* and *(c)* shall be reduced by value adjustments for depreciation calculated to write off those amounts systematically over a period which shall be not more than 10 years.

(4) In any case where any goodwill acquired by a company is shown or included as an asset in the company's balance sheet, the period chosen for writing off the consideration for that goodwill and the reasons for choosing that period shall be disclosed in a note to the financial statements.

(5) Where, in accordance with *paragraph 23(2)*, a value adjustment for diminution in value has been recognised for goodwill, even if it is considered that the reason for the diminution in value has ceased to exist, the value adjustment shall not be reversed as required by *paragraph 23(3)*.

CURRENT ASSETS

26. Subject to *paragraph 27*, the amount to be included in respect of any current asset shall be its purchase price or production cost.

27. (1) If the net realisable value of any current asset is lower than its purchase price or production cost, the amount to be included in respect of that asset shall be the net realisable value.

(2) Where the reasons for which any value adjustment for diminution in value was made under *subparagraph (1)* have ceased to apply to any extent that value adjustment shall be written back to the extent that it is no longer necessary.

MISCELLANEOUS

Excess of money owed over value received as an asset item

28. (1) Where the amount repayable on any debt owed by a company is greater than the value of the consideration received in the transaction giving rise to the debt, the amount of the difference may be treated as an asset.

(2) Where any such amount exists—

(a) it shall be written off by reasonable amounts each year and shall be completely written off before repayment of the debt, and

(b) if the amount not written off is not shown as a separate item in the company's balance sheet, it shall be disclosed in a note to the financial statements.

DETERMINATION OF PURCHASE PRICE OR PRODUCTION COST

29. (1) The purchase price of an asset shall be determined by adding to the actual price paid any expenses incidental to its acquisition and by deducting from the actual price paid any income incidental to its acquisition.

(2) The production cost of an asset shall be determined by adding to the purchase price of the raw materials and consumables used the amount of the costs incurred by the company which are directly attributable to the production of that asset.

(3) In addition there may be included in the production cost of an asset—

(a) a reasonable proportion of the costs incurred by the company which are only indirectly attributable to the production of that asset, but only to the extent that they relate to the period of production, and

(b) interest on capital borrowed to finance the production of that asset, to the extent that it accrues in respect of the period of production,

provided, however, that in a case within clause (b), the inclusion of the interest in determining the cost of that asset and the amount of the interest so included is disclosed in a note to the financial statements.

(4) Distribution costs may not be included in production costs.

30. (1) Subject to the qualification mentioned in *subparagraph (2)*, the purchase price or production cost of—

(a) any assets which fall to be included under any item shown in a company's balance sheet under the general item "stocks", and

(b) any assets which are fungible assets (including investments),

may be determined by the application of any of the methods mentioned in *subparagraph (3)* in relation to any such assets of the same class.

(2) The method chosen shall be one which appears to the directors to be appropriate in the circumstances of the company.

(3) The methods are—

(a) the method known as 'first in, first out' (FIFO),

(b) a weighted average price, and

(c) any other method reflecting generally accepted best practice.

(4) For the purpose of this paragraph, assets of any description shall be regarded as fungible if assets of that description are substantially indistinguishable from one another.

SECTION C
ALTERNATIVE ACCOUNTING RULES

Preliminary

31. (1) The rules set out in *Section B* are referred to subsequently in this Schedule as the historical cost accounting rules.

(2) Those rules, with the omission of *paragraphs 20, 29* and *30* are referred to subsequently in this Part as the depreciation rules; and references subsequently in this Schedule to the historical cost accounting rules do not include the depreciation rules as they apply by virtue of paragraph 34.

32. Subject to *paragraphs 34* to *37*, the amounts to be included in respect of assets of any description mentioned in *paragraph 33* may be determined on any basis so mentioned.

Alternative accounting rules

33. (1) Intangible fixed assets, other than goodwill, may be included at a market value determined as at the date of their last valuation.

(2) Tangible fixed assets may be included at a market value determined as at the date of their last valuation.

(3) Financial fixed assets may be included either—

(a) at a market value determined as at the date of their last valuation, or

(b) at a value determined on any basis which appears to the directors to be appropriate in the circumstances of the company,

but in the latter case particulars of the method of valuation adopted and of the reasons for adopting it shall be disclosed in a note to the financial statements.

(4) Participating interests in an associated undertaking may be included under the equity method of accounting.

Application of depreciation rules

34. (1) Where the value of any asset of a company is determined on any basis mentioned in *paragraph 33*, that value shall be, or (as the case may require) be the starting point for determining, the amount to be included in respect of that asset in the company's financial statements, instead of its purchase price or production cost or any value previously so determined for that asset; and the depreciation rules shall apply accordingly in relation to any such asset with the substitution for any reference to its purchase price or production cost of a reference to the value most recently determined for that asset on any basis mentioned in *paragraph 33*.

(2) The amount of any value adjustment for depreciation required in the case of any fixed asset by *paragraph 22* or *23* as it applies by virtue of *subparagraph (1)* is referred to subsequently in this paragraph as the adjusted amount; and the amount of any value adjustment which would be required by that paragraph in the case of that asset according to the historical cost accounting rules is referred to as the historical cost amount.

(3) Where *subparagraph (1)* applies in the case of any fixed asset, the amount of any value adjustment for depreciation in respect of that asset—

(a) included in any item shown in the profit and loss account in respect of amounts written off assets of the description in question, or

(b) taken into account in stating any item so shown which is required by note (9) of the notes on the profit and loss account formats set out in *Part II* to be stated after taking into account any necessary value adjustments for depreciation or diminution in value of assets included under it,

may be the historical cost amount instead of the adjusted amount, provided that, if the amount of the value adjustment for depreciation is the historical cost amount, the amount of any difference between the two shall be shown separately in the profit and loss account or in a note to the financial statements.

Additional information in case of departure from historical cost accounting rules

35. (1) This paragraph applies where the amounts to be included in respect of fixed assets covered by any items shown in a company's financial statements have been determined on any basis mentioned in *paragraph 33*.

(2) The items affected and the basis of valuation adopted in determining the amounts of the assets in question in the case of each such item shall be disclosed in the notes to the financial statements on the accounting policies adopted by the company as required by *section 321*.

(3) In the case of each balance sheet item affected the comparable amounts determined according to the historical cost accounting rules shall be shown separately in the balance sheet or in a note to the financial statements.

(4) In *subparagraph (3)*, references in relation to any item to the comparable amounts determined as there mentioned are references to—

(a) the aggregate amount which would be required to be shown in respect of that item if the amounts to be included in respect of all the assets covered by that item were determined according to the historical cost accounting rules, and

(b) the aggregate amount of the cumulative value adjustments for depreciation or diminution in value which would be permitted or required in determining those amounts according to those rules.

Revaluation Reserve

36. (1) With respect to any determination of the value of an asset of a company on any basis mentioned in *paragraph 33(1)* to *(3)*, the amount of any profit or loss arising from that determination (after allowing, where appropriate, for any value adjustments for depreciation or diminution in value made otherwise than by reference to the value so determined and any adjustments of any such value adjustments made in the light of that determination) shall be credited or, as the case may be, debited to a separate reserve (referred to in this paragraph as the 'revaluation reserve').

(2) The amount of the revaluation reserve shall be shown in the company's balance sheet under a separate sub-heading in the position given for the item "revaluation reserve" under "Capital and Reserves" in Format 1 or 2 of the balance sheet formats set out in *Part II*.

(3) An amount may be transferred—

(a) from the revaluation reserve—

(i) to the profit and loss account, if the amount was previously charged to that account, or it represents realised profit, or

(ii) on capitalisation, or

(b) to or from the revaluation reserve in respect of the taxation relating to any profit or loss credited or debited to the reserve and the revaluation reserve shall be reduced to the extent that the amounts transferred to it are no longer necessary for the purpose of the valuation methods used.

(4) In *subparagraph (3)(a)(ii)* "capitalisation", in relation to an amount standing to the credit of the revaluation reserve, means applying it in wholly or partly paying up unissued shares in the company to be allotted to members of the company as fully or partly paid shares.

(5) The revaluation reserve shall not be reduced except as mentioned in this paragraph.

(6) The treatment for taxation purposes of amounts credited or debited to the revaluation reserve shall be disclosed in a note to the financial statements.

Accounting for certain participating interests in entity financial statements

37. (1) Where in accordance with *paragraph 33(4)*, the interest of a company in an associated undertaking in which a participating interest is held, and the amount of profit or loss attributable to such an interest, are included in the financial statements by way of the equity method of accounting, any goodwill arising shall be dealt with in accordance with *paragraphs 21* to *23* and *25*.

(2) Where the undertaking in which a participating interest is held is itself a holding undertaking, the net assets and profits or losses to be taken into account are those of the holding undertaking and its subsidiary undertakings (after making any consolidation adjustments).

(3) Where the cumulative profit attributable to the participating interest and recognised in the profit and loss account exceeds the cumulative amount of dividends received or receivable, the amount of the difference shall be placed in a separate reserve which may not be distributed to shareholders.

SECTION D
FAIR VALUE ACCOUNTING RULES

Inclusion of financial instruments at fair value

38. (1) Financial instruments that, under IFRS, may be accounted for in financial statements at fair value, may be so accounted for in financial statements to which the provisions of this Schedule apply, provided that the disclosures required by IFRS are made.

(2) In this paragraph, "fair value" means fair value determined in accordance with relevant IFRS.

Hedged items

39. A company may include any assets or liabilities, or identified portions of such assets or liabilities that qualify as hedged items under a fair value hedge accounting system at the amount required under that system.

Other assets that may be included at fair value

40. (1) This paragraph applies to—

(a) investment property, and

(b) living animals and plants,

that, under relevant international financial reporting standards, may be included in financial statements at fair value.

(2) Such investment property and such living animals and plants may be included at fair value, provided that all such investment property or, as the case may be, all such living animals and plants are so included where their fair value can reliably be determined.

(3) In this paragraph, "fair value" means fair value determined in accordance with relevant IFRS.

Accounting for changes in fair value

41. (1) This paragraph applies where a financial instrument is valued at fair value in accordance with *paragraph 38* or *39* or where an asset is valued in accordance with paragraph 40.

(2) Notwithstanding *paragraph 14*, a change in the fair value of an investment property or living animal or plant shall be included in the profit and loss account.

(3) Notwithstanding *paragraph 14*, a change in the fair value of a financial instrument shall be accounted for in accordance with IFRS and to the extent the change in fair value is not referred to in the profit and loss account, the amount of the change in value shall be credited or (as the case may be) debited to a separate reserve to be known, for the purpose of this Schedule as the "fair value reserve".

The fair value reserve

42. The fair value reserve shall be adjusted when amounts therein are no longer necessary for the purposes of *paragraph 41(3)*.

PART IV
INFORMATION REQUIRED BY WAY OF NOTES TO FINANCIAL STATEMENTS

Preliminary

43. (1) Any information required in the case of any company by the following provisions of this Part shall (if not given in the company's financial statements) be given by way of a note to those financial statements.

(2) These notes shall be presented in the order in which, where relevant, the items to which they relate are presented in the balance sheet and in the profit and loss account.

Information supplementing the balance sheet

44. *Paragraphs 45* to *51* require information which either supplements the information given with respect to any particular items shown in the balance sheet or is otherwise relevant to assessing the company's financial position in the light of the information so given.

Fixed assets

45. (1) In respect of each item which is or would, but for *paragraphs 2(2)* and *4(4)(b)*, be shown under the general item 'fixed assets' in the company's balance sheet, the following information shall be given:

(a) the appropriate amounts in respect of that item as at the date of the beginning of the financial year and as at the financial year end date respectively;

(b) the effect on any amount shown in the balance sheet in respect of that item of—

(i) any revision of the amount in respect of any assets included under that item made during that year on any basis mentioned in paragraph 33 or under the fair value accounting rules,

(ii) acquisitions during that year of any assets,

(iii) disposals during that year of any assets, and

(iv) any transfers of assets of the company to and from that item during that year.

(2) The reference in *subparagraph (1)(a)* to the appropriate amounts in respect of any item as at any date there mentioned is a reference to amounts representing the aggregate amounts determined, as at that date, in respect of assets falling to be included under that item—

(a) on the basis of purchase price or production cost (determined in accordance with *paragraphs 29* and *30*),

(b) on any basis mentioned in *paragraph 33*, or

(c) under the fair value accounting rules,

as the case may be, (leaving out of account in each of clauses (a), (b) and (c) any value adjustments for depreciation or diminution in value).

(3) In respect of each item within *subparagraph (1)*—

(a) the cumulative amount of value adjustments for depreciation or diminution in value of assets included under that item as at each date mentioned in *subparagraph (1)(a)*,

(b) the amount of any such value adjustments made in respect of the financial year concerned,

(c) the amount of any changes made in respect of any such value adjustments during that year in consequence of the disposal of any assets, and

(d) the amount of any other changes made in respect of any such value adjustments during that year,

shall also be stated.

Information about fair valuation of assets and liabilities

46. (1) This paragraph applies where financial instruments or assets other than financial instruments have been included at fair value by virtue of *paragraph 38*, *39* or *40*.

(2) There shall be stated—

(a) the significant assumptions underlying the valuation models and techniques where fair values have been determined otherwise than by reference to market price in an active market,

(b) for each category of financial instruments or assets other than financial instruments, the fair value of the financial instruments or assets other than financial instruments in that category and the amounts—

(i) included in the profit and loss account, and

(ii) credited or debited to the fair value reserve,

in respect of financial instruments or assets other than financial instruments in that category,

(c) for each class of derivative financial instrument, the extent and nature of the instruments including significant terms and conditions that may affect the amount, timing and certainty of future cash flows, and

(d) a table showing movements in the fair value reserve during the financial year.

Information where investment property or living animals and plants included at fair value

47.(1) This paragraph applies where the amounts to be included in a company's financial statements in respect of investment property or living animals and plants have been determined in accordance with *paragraph 40*.

(2) The balance sheet items affected and the basis of valuation adopted in determining the amounts of the assets in question in the case of each such item shall be disclosed in the notes to the financial statements on the accounting policies adopted by the company as required by *section 321*.

Appropriation of profit and loss account

48. The profit and loss account, balance sheet or notes to the financial statements of a company for a financial year shall show—

(a) the aggregate amount of dividends paid in the financial year (other than dividends for which a liability existed at the immediately preceding financial year end date),

(b) the aggregate amount of dividends the company is liable to pay at the financial year end date (other than dividends for which a liability existed at the immediately preceding financial year end date),

(c) separately, any transfer between the profit and loss account reserve and other reserves,

(d) any other increase or reduction in the balance on the profit and loss account reserve since the immediately preceding financial year end date,

(e) the profit or loss brought forward at the beginning of the financial year, and

(f) the profit or loss carried forward at the end of the financial year.

49. (1) Where any amount is transferred to or from any revaluation reserves and the revaluation reserves are or would, but for *paragraph 2(2)* or *4(4)(b)*, be shown as separate items in the company's balance sheet, the information mentioned in *subparagraph (2)* shall be given in respect of each such reserve.

(2) The information, which is to be set out in tabular form, is—

(a) the amount of the reserves as at the date of the beginning of the financial year and as at the financial year end date respectively,

(b) any amount transferred to or from the reserves during that year, and

(c) the source and application respectively of any amounts so transferred.

Details of indebtedness

50. (1) In respect of each item shown under 'creditors' in the company's balance sheet there shall be stated the aggregate amount of any debts included under that item which fall due for payment or repayment after the end of the period of 5 years beginning with the day next following the end of the financial year.

(2) In respect of each item shown under 'creditors' in the company's balance sheet there shall be stated—

(a) the aggregate amount of any debts included under that item in respect of which any security has been given, and

(b) an indication of the nature of the securities so given.

(3) References in *subparagraph (1)* to an item shown under 'creditors' in the company's balance sheet include references, where amounts falling due to creditors within one year and after more than one year are distinguished in the balance sheet—

(a) in a case within *subparagraph (1)*, to an item shown under the latter of those categories, and

(b) in a case within *subparagraph (2)*, to an item shown under either of those categories,

and references to items shown under 'creditors' include references to items which would, but for *paragraph 2(2)* or *4(4)(b)*, be shown under that heading.

Guarantees and other financial commitments

51. (1) Particulars shall be given of any charge on the assets of the company to secure the liabilities of any other person, including, where practicable, the amount secured.

(2) Particulars and the total amount or estimated total amount shall be given with respect to any other financial commitment, guarantee or contingency not provided for in the balance sheet.

(3) An indication of the nature and form of any valuable security given by the company in connection with the commitments, guarantees or contingencies referred to in *subparagraph (2)* shall be given in the financial statements.

(4) The total amount of any commitments referred to in *subparagraph (2)* concerning retirement benefits shall be disclosed separately.

(5) Particulars, including details of significant assumptions underlying the valuation models shall be given of retirement benefit commitments which are included in the balance sheet.

(6) Where any commitment referred to in *subparagraph (4)* or *(5)* relates wholly or partly to retirement benefits payable to past directors of the company, separate particulars shall be given of that commitment.

(7) The aggregate amount of any commitments, guarantees or contingencies referred to in *subparagraph (2)* which are undertaken on behalf of or for the benefit of—

(a) any holding undertaking or fellow subsidiary undertaking of the company,

(b) any subsidiary undertaking of the company, or

(c) any undertaking in which the company has a participating interest,

shall be separately stated and those within each of clause (a), (b) and (c) of this subparagraph shall also be stated separately from those within any other of those clauses.

Information supplementing the profit and loss account

52. *Paragraph 53* requires information which either supplements the information given with respect to any particular items shown in the profit and loss account or otherwise provides particulars of income or expenditure of the company or of circumstances affecting the items shown in the profit and loss account.

Exceptional items

53. The profit and loss account or the notes to the financial statements shall disclose information on the nature, amount and effect of individual items of income and expenditure that are exceptional by virtue of size or incidence.

General information

54. *Paragraphs 55* and *56* require other information to be given in the notes to the financial statements.

Related party transactions

55. (1) Subject to *subparagraphs (3)* and *(4)*, particulars shall be given in the notes to the financial statements of a company of transactions which have been entered into with related parties by the company if such transactions are material and have not been concluded under normal market conditions and the particulars shall include the amount of such transactions, the nature of the related party relationship and other information about the transactions which is necessary for an understanding of the financial position of the company.

(2) The provision of particulars and other information about individual transactions may be aggregated according to their nature, except where separate information is necessary for an understanding of the effects of related party transactions on the financial position of the company.

(3) *Subparagraph (1)* shall not apply to transactions which are entered into between 2 or more members of a group if any subsidiary undertaking which is party to the transaction is wholly owned by such a member.

(4) *Subparagraph (1)* applies only to related parties that are—

(a) the holders of participating interests in the company,

(b) undertakings in which the company holds a participating interest, and

(c) directors of the company or of a holding company of the company.

(5) A word or expression that is used in this paragraph and is also used in IFRS has the meaning in this paragraph that it has in IFRS.

Events after the end of the financial year

56. The particulars and financial impact of material events that have occurred after the end of the financial year shall be given in the notes to the financial statements.

PART V
SPECIAL PROVISIONS WHERE A COMPANY IS A HOLDING COMPANY OR SUBSIDIARY UNDERTAKING

Dealings with or interests in group undertakings

57. This Part applies where the company is a holding company, whether or not it is itself a subsidiary undertaking.

Holding undertaking of smallest group preparing group financial statements

58. (1) Where a company is a subsidiary undertaking, the information specified in *subparagraphs (2)* and *(3)* shall be stated with respect to the holding undertaking of the smallest group of undertakings for which group financial statements are drawn up and of which the company is a member.

(2) The name of the holding undertaking shall be stated.

(3) There shall be stated—

(a) if the holding undertaking is incorporated, the address of the holding undertaking's registered office or where the holding undertaking is incorporated outside the State, the registered office (howsoever described) of the holding undertaking in the country in which it is incorporated, or

(b) if it is unincorporated, the address of its principal place of business.

PART VI
INTERPRETATION OF CERTAIN EXPRESSIONS IN SCHEDULE

Assets: Fixed or Current

59. For the purposes of this Schedule, assets of a company shall be taken to be fixed assets if they are intended for use on a continuing basis in the company's activities, and any assets not intended for such use shall be taken to be current assets.

Capitalisation

60. References in this Schedule to capitalising any work or costs are references to treating that work or those costs as a fixed asset.

Investment property

61. In this Schedule, "investment property" means land or buildings (or both) held to earn rentals or for capital appreciation (or both).

Loans

62. For the purposes of this Schedule, a loan shall be treated as falling due for payment, and an instalment of a loan shall be treated as falling due for payment, on the earliest date on which the lender could require repayment or (as the case may be) payment, if the lender exercised all options and rights available to him or her.

Materiality

63. In this Schedule, 'material' means the status of information where its omission or misstatement could reasonably be expected to influence decisions that users make on the basis of the financial statements of the undertaking; and the materiality of individual items shall be assessed in the context of other similar items.

Value adjustments

64. (1) References in this Schedule to value adjustments for depreciation or diminution in value of assets are references to any amount written off by way of providing for depreciation or diminution in value of assets.

(2) Any reference in the profit and loss account formats set out in Part II to the depreciation of, or amounts written off, assets of any description is a reference to the movement in any value adjustment for depreciation or diminution in value of assets of that description.

Provisions

65. References in this Schedule to provisions for liabilities are references to any amount retained as reasonably necessary for the purpose of providing for any liability the nature of which is clearly defined and which exists at the financial year end date but, as respects the amount of which or the date on which it will be settled, there is uncertainty.

Purchase price

66. References in this Schedule (however expressed) to the purchase price of an asset of a company or of any raw materials or consumables used in the production of any such asset shall be read as including references to any consideration (whether in cash or otherwise) given by the company in respect of that asset or in respect of those materials or consumables (as the case may require).][a]

Amendments

a Schedule 3A substituted by C(A)A 2017, s 89(b) and Sch 2.

[SCHEDULE 3B

ACCOUNTING PRINCIPLES, FORM AND CONTENT OF FINANCIAL STATEMENTS OF A COMPANY QUALIFYING FOR THE MICRO COMPANIES REGIME

PART I

CONSTRUCTION OF REFERENCES TO PROVISIONS OF SCHEDULE

1. (1) Without prejudice to the generality of section 9 of the Interpretation Act 2005 and its application to the body of this Act and to *Schedules 1, 2* and *5* to *18*—

(a) a reference in this Schedule to a paragraph or Part is a reference to a paragraph or Part of this Schedule, unless it is indicated that a reference to some other enactment is intended,

(b) a reference in this Schedule to a section is a reference to the section of the Part in which the reference occurs, unless it is indicated that a reference to some other enactment is intended, and

(c) a reference in this Schedule to a subparagraph or clause is a reference to the subparagraph or clause of the provision in which the reference occurs, unless it is indicated that a reference to some other enactment is intended.

(2) Provisions providing for the interpretation of certain expressions appearing in this Schedule are contained in *Part V*.

PART II

GENERAL RULES AND FORMATS

SECTION A

GENERAL RULES

2. (1) Subject to the provisions of this Schedule—

(a) every balance sheet of a company shall show the items listed in either of the balance sheet formats set out in *Section B*, and

(b) every profit and loss account of a company shall show the items listed in the profit and loss accounts format so set out,

in either case in the order and under the headings given in the format adopted.

(2) *Subparagraph (1)* shall not be read as requiring the heading for any item in the balance sheet, or profit and loss account, of a company to be distinguished by any letter or number assigned to that item in the formats set out in *Section B*.

3. (1) Where, in accordance with *paragraph 2(1)(a)*, a company's balance sheet for any financial year has been prepared by reference to one of the formats set out in *Section B*, the directors of the company shall adopt the same format in preparing the financial statements for subsequent financial years unless, in their opinion, there are special reasons for a change.

(2) Where any change is made in the format adopted in preparing a balance sheet of a company, the reasons for the change, together with full particulars of the change,

shall be given in a note to the financial statements in which the new format is first adopted.

4. (1) Any item required in accordance with *paragraph 2* to be shown in the balance sheet or profit and loss account of a company may be shown in greater detail than that required by the format adopted.

(2) The balance sheet or profit and loss account of a company may include an item representing or covering the amount of any asset or liability or income or expenditure not otherwise covered by any of the items listed in the format adopted but the following shall not be treated as assets in the balance sheet of a company—

(a) preliminary expenses,

(b) expenses of and commission on any issue of shares or debentures, and

(c) costs of research.

(3) The balance sheet or profit and loss account of a company may include subtotals where their inclusion facilitates the assessment of the financial position or profit or loss of the company for the financial year concerned.

(4) Where an asset or liability relates to more than one of the items listed in either of the balance sheet formats set out in *Section B*, its relationship to other items shall be disclosed either under the item where it is shown or in the notes to the financial statements.

(5) The opening balance sheet for each financial year shall correspond to the closing balance sheet for the preceding financial year.

5. In respect of every item shown in the balance sheet, or profit and loss account, or notes thereto, of a company, the corresponding amount for the financial year immediately preceding that to which the balance sheet or profit and loss account relates shall also be shown and, if that corresponding amount is not comparable with the amount to be shown for the item in question in respect of the financial year to which the balance sheet or profit and loss account relates, the former amount may be adjusted, and particulars of the adjustment and the reasons therefor shall be given in a note to the financial statements.

6. (1) Subject to *subparagraph (2)*, a heading corresponding to an item listed in the format adopted in preparing the balance sheet or profit and loss account of a company shall not be included in the balance sheet or profit and loss account, as the case may be, if there is no amount to be shown for that item in respect of the financial year to which the balance sheet or profit and loss account relates.

(2) *Subparagraph (1)* shall not apply in any case where an amount can be shown for the item in question in respect of the financial year immediately preceding that to which the balance sheet or profit and loss account relates, and that amount shall be shown under the heading required by the format adopted as aforesaid.

7. (1) Subject to *subparagraph (2)*, amounts in respect of items representing assets or income may not be set off in the financial statements of a company against amounts in respect of items representing liabilities or expenditure, as the case may be, or *vice versa*.

(2) *Subparagraph (1)* shall not apply in any case where such set off is in accordance with applicable accounting standards, provided that the gross amounts are disclosed in a note to the financial statements.

SECTION B
THE REQUIRED FORMATS FOR FINANCIAL STATEMENTS
Preliminary

8. References in this Part to the items listed in any of the formats set out in this Part are references to those items read together with any notes following the formats which apply to any of those items.

9. A number in brackets following any item in, or any heading to, any of the formats set out in this Part is a reference to the note of that number in the notes following the formats.

10. In the notes following the formats—
   (a) the heading of each note gives the required heading for the item to which it applies and a reference to any letters and numbers assigned to that item in the formats set out in this Part, and
   (b) references to a numbered format are references to the balance sheet format of that number set out in this Part.

BALANCE SHEET FORMATS

Format 1

A. Called up share capital not paid
B. Fixed assets
C. Current assets
D. Prepayments and accrued income
E. Creditors: amounts falling due within one year
F. Net current assets (liabilities)
G. Total assets less current liabilities
H. Creditors: amounts falling due after more than one year
I. Provisions for liabilities
J. Accruals and deferred income
K. Capital and reserves

Format 2

ASSETS

A. Called up share capital not paid
B. Fixed assets
C. Current assets
D. Prepayments and accrued income

CAPITAL, RESERVES AND LIABILITIES

A. Capital and reserves

B. Provisions for liabilities

C. Creditors (1)

D. Accruals and deferred income

NOTE ON THE BALANCE SHEET FORMATS

(1) Creditors

(Format 2, "CAPITAL, RESERVES AND LIABILITIES", item C)

Amounts falling due within one year and after one year shall be shown separately.

PROFIT AND LOSS ACCOUNT FORMAT

1. Turnover
2. Other income
3. Cost of raw materials and consumables
4. Staff costs
5. Value adjustments and other amounts written off assets
6. Other expenses
7. Tax
8. Profit or loss

PART III
ACCOUNTING PRINCIPLES AND VALUATION RULES

SECTION A
ACCOUNTING PRINCIPLES

Preliminary

11. Subject to *paragraph 18*, the amounts to be included in the financial statements of a company in respect of the items shown shall be determined in accordance with the principles set out in *paragraphs 12* to *17*.

Accounting principles

12. The company shall be presumed to be carrying on business as a going concern.
13. Accounting policies and measurement bases shall be applied consistently from one financial year to the next.
14. The amount of any item in the financial statements shall be determined on a prudent basis and in particular—

    (a) only profits realised at the financial year end date shall be included in the profit and loss account,

(b) all liabilities which have arisen in the course of the financial year to which the financial statements relate or of a previous financial year shall be taken into account, even if such liabilities only become apparent between the financial year end date and the date on which the financial statements are signed under *section 324*, and

(c) all value adjustments for diminution in value shall be recognised, whether the result for the financial year to which the financial statements relate is a profit or loss.

15. All income and expenses relating to the financial year to which the financial statements relate shall be taken into account without regard to the date of receipt or payment.

16. In determining the aggregate amount of any item the amount of each individual asset or liability that falls to be taken into account shall be determined separately.

17. Items in the profit and loss account and balance sheet shall be accounted for and presented having regard to the substance of the reported transaction or arrangement in accordance with applicable accounting standards.

18. The provisions of this Schedule need not be complied with where the amounts involved are not material for the purpose of giving a true and fair view.

Departure from the accounting principles

19. If it appears to the directors of a company that there are special reasons for departing from any of the principles stated above in preparing the company's financial statements in any particular year, they may so depart, but particulars of the departure, the reasons for it and its effect on the balance sheet and profit and loss account of the company shall be stated in a note to the financial statements.

SECTION B
HISTORICAL COST ACCOUNTING RULES

Preliminary

20. The amounts to be included in respect of all items shown in a company's financial statements shall be determined in accordance with the rules set out in *paragraphs 21* to *30*.

FIXED ASSETS

General rules

21. Subject to any value adjustment for depreciation or diminution in value made in accordance with *paragraph 22* or *23*, the amount to be included in respect of any fixed asset shall be its purchase price or production cost.

Rules for depreciation and diminution in value

22. In the case of any fixed asset which has a limited useful economic life, the amount of—

(a) its purchase price or production cost, or

(b) where it is estimated that any such asset will have a residual value at the end of the period of its useful economic life, its purchase price or production cost less that estimated residual value,

shall be reduced by value adjustments for depreciation calculated to write off that amount systematically over the period of the asset's useful economic life.

23. (1) Where a financial asset of a description falling to be included under item A. III of either of the balance sheet formats set out in *Part II* has diminished in value, value adjustments for diminution in value may be made in respect of it and the amount to be included in respect of it may be reduced accordingly; and any such value adjustments which are not shown separately in the profit and loss account shall be disclosed (either separately or in aggregate) in a note to the financial statements.

(2) Value adjustments for diminution in value shall be made in respect of any fixed asset which has diminished in value if the reduction in its value is expected to be permanent (whether its useful economic life is limited or not) and the amount to be included in respect of it shall be reduced accordingly; and any such value adjustments which are not shown separately in the profit and loss account shall be disclosed (either separately or in aggregate) in a note to the financial statements.

(3) Where the reasons for which any value adjustment was made in accordance with *subparagraph (1)* or *(2)* have ceased to apply to any extent, that value adjustment shall be written back to the extent that it is no longer necessary; and any amounts written back in accordance with this subparagraph which are not shown in the profit and loss account shall be disclosed (either separately or in aggregate) in a note to the financial statements.

Rules for determining particular fixed asset items

24. (1) Notwithstanding that an item in respect of "development costs" is included under "fixed assets" in the balance sheet formats set out in *Part II*, an amount may only be included in a company's balance sheet in respect of that item in special circumstances.

(2) If an amount is included in a company's balance sheet in respect of development costs, the following information shall be given in a note to the financial statements—

(a) the period over which the amount of those costs originally capitalised is being or is to be written off, and

(b) the reasons for capitalising the costs in question.

25. (1) The application of *paragraphs 21* to *23* in relation to goodwill and development costs (in any case where goodwill or development costs are treated as assets) and other intangible assets is subject to the following provisions of this paragraph.

(2) Subject to *subparagraph (3)*—

(a) the amount of the consideration for any goodwill acquired by a company,

(b) the amount of development costs capitalised, or

(c) the amount of other intangible assets recognised,

shall be reduced by value adjustments for depreciation calculated to write off that amount systematically over the useful economic life of the goodwill, development costs or other intangible assets.

(3) Where, in exceptional circumstances, the useful life of goodwill acquired by a company or development costs or other intangible assets capitalised cannot be reliably estimated, the amounts referred to in *subparagraph (2)(a), (b)* and *(c)* shall be reduced by value adjustments for depreciation calculated to write off those amounts systematically over a period which shall be not more than 10 years.

(4) In any case where any goodwill acquired by a company is shown or included as an asset in the company's balance sheet, the period chosen for writing off the consideration for that goodwill and the reasons for choosing that period shall be disclosed in a note to the financial statements.

(5) Where, in accordance with *paragraph 23(2)*, a value adjustment for diminution in value has been recognised for goodwill, even if it is considered that the reason for the diminution in value has ceased to exist, the value adjustment shall not be reversed as required by *paragraph 23(3)*.

CURRENT ASSETS

26. Subject to *paragraph 27*, the amount to be included in respect of any current asset shall be its purchase price or production cost.

27. (1) If the net realisable value of any current asset is lower than its purchase price or production cost, the amount to be included in respect of that asset shall be the net realisable value.

(2) Where the reasons for which any value adjustment for diminution in value was made under *subparagraph (1)* have ceased to apply to any extent that value adjustment shall be written back to the extent that it is no longer necessary.

MISCELLANEOUS

Excess of money owed over value received as an asset item

28. (1) Where the amount repayable on any debt owed by a company is greater than the value of the consideration received in the transaction giving rise to the debt, the amount of the difference may be treated as an asset.

(2) Where any such amount exists—

(a) it shall be written off by reasonable amounts each year and shall be completely written off before repayment of the debt, and

(b) if the amount not written off is not shown as a separate item in the company's balance sheet, it shall be disclosed in a note to the financial statements.

DETERMINATION OF PURCHASE PRICE OR PRODUCTION COST

29. (1) The purchase price of an asset shall be determined by adding to the actual price paid any expenses incidental to its acquisition and by deducting from the actual price paid any income incidental to its acquisition.

(2) The production cost of an asset shall be determined by adding to the purchase price of the raw materials and consumables used the amount of the costs incurred by the company which are directly attributable to the production of that asset.

(3) In addition there may be included in the production cost of an asset—

(a) a reasonable proportion of the costs incurred by the company which are only indirectly attributable to the production of that asset, but only to the extent that they relate to the period of production, and

(b) interest on capital borrowed to finance the production of that asset, to the extent that it accrues in respect of the period of production,

provided, however, that in a case within clause (b), the inclusion of the interest in determining the cost of that asset and the amount of the interest so included is disclosed in a note to the financial statements.

(4) Distribution costs may not be included in production costs.

30. (1) Subject to the qualification mentioned in *subparagraph (2)*, the purchase price or production cost of—

(a) any assets which fall to be included in the general item 'stocks' shown in a company's balance sheet, and

(b) any assets which are fungible assets (including investments),

may be determined by the application of any of the methods mentioned in *subparagraph (3)* in relation to any such assets of the same class.

(2) The method chosen must be one which appears to the directors to be appropriate in the circumstances of the company.

(3) The methods are—

(a) the method known as 'first in, first out' (FIFO),

(b) a weighted average price, and

(c) any other method reflecting generally accepted best practice.

(4) For the purpose of this paragraph, assets of any description shall be regarded as fungible if assets of that description are substantially indistinguishable from one another.

PART IV
INFORMATION REQUIRED BY WAY OF NOTES TO FINANCIAL STATEMENTS

Preliminary

31. (1) Any information required in the case of any company by the following provisions of this Part shall (if not given in the company's financial statements) be given by way of a note to those financial statements.

(2) These notes shall be presented in the order in which, where relevant, the items to which they relate are presented in the balance sheet and in the profit and loss account.

Information supplementing the balance sheet

32. *Paragraphs 33* to *35* require information which either supplements the information given with respect to any particular items shown in the balance sheet or is otherwise relevant to assessing the company's financial position in the light of the information so given.

Appropriation of profit and loss account

33. The profit and loss account, balance sheet or notes to the financial statements of a company for a financial year shall show—

(a) the aggregate amount of dividends paid in the financial year (other than dividends for which a liability existed at the immediately preceding financial year end date),

(b) the aggregate amount of dividends the company is liable to pay at the financial year end date (other than dividends for which a liability existed at the immediately preceding financial year end date),

(c) separately, any transfer between the profit and loss account and other reserves,

(d) any other increase or reduction in the balance on the profit and loss account since the immediately preceding financial year end date,

(e) the profit or loss brought forward at the beginning of the financial year, and

(f) the profit or loss carried forward at the end of the financial year.

Details of indebtedness

34. In respect of 'creditors' shown in the company's balance sheet there shall be stated—

(a) the aggregate amount of any debts included under that item in respect of which any security has been given, and

(b) an indication of the nature of the securities so given.

Guarantees and other financial commitments

35. (1) Particulars shall be given of any charge on the assets of the company to secure the liabilities of any other person, including, where practicable, the amount secured.

(2) Particulars and the total amount or estimated total amount shall be given with respect to any other financial commitments, guarantees or contingencies not provided for in the balance sheet.

(3) An indication of the nature and form of any valuable security given by the company in connection with the commitments, guarantees or contingencies referred to in *subparagraph (2)* shall be given in the financial statements.

(4) The total amount of any commitments within *subparagraph (2)* concerning retirement benefits shall be disclosed separately.

(5) Particulars shall be given of retirement benefit commitments which are included in the balance sheet.

(6) The aggregate amount of any commitments, guarantees or contingencies referred to in *subparagraph (2)* which are undertaken on behalf of or for the benefit of—

(a) any holding undertaking or fellow subsidiary undertaking of the company,

(b) any subsidiary undertaking of the company, or

(c) any undertaking in which the company has a participating interest,

shall be separately stated and those within each of clauses (a), (b) and (c) shall also be stated separately from those within any other of those clauses.

PART V
INTERPRETATION OF CERTAIN EXPRESSIONS IN SCHEDULE

Assets: fixed or current

36. For the purposes of this Schedule, assets of a company shall be taken to be fixed assets if they are intended for use on a continuing basis in the company's activities, and any assets not intended for such use shall be taken to be current assets.

Materiality

37. In this Schedule, "material" means the status of information where its omission or misstatement could reasonably be expected to influence decisions that users make on the basis of the financial statements of the undertaking. The materiality of individual items shall be assessed in the context of other similar items.

Value adjustments

38. (1) References in this Schedule to value adjustments for depreciation or diminution in value of assets are references to any amount written off by way of providing for depreciation or diminution in value of assets.

(2) Any reference in the profit and loss account format set out in Part II to amounts written off assets is a reference to the movement in any value adjustment for depreciation or diminution in value of assets of that description.

Provisions

39. References in this Schedule to provisions are references to any amount retained as reasonably necessary for the purpose of providing for any liability the nature of which is clearly defined and which exists at the financial year end date but, as respects the amount of which or the date on which it will be settled, there is uncertainty.

Purchase price

40. References in this Schedule (however expressed) to the purchase price of an asset of a company or of any raw materials or consumables used in the production of any such asset shall be read as including references to any consideration (whether in cash or otherwise) given by the company in respect of that asset or in respect of those materials or consumables (as the case may require).][a]

Amendments

a Schedule 3B substituted by C(A)A 2017, s 89(c) and Sch 3.

[SCHEDULE 4
ACCOUNTING PRINCIPLES, FORM AND CONTENT OF GROUP FINANCIAL STATEMENTS

PART I
CONSTRUCTION OF REFERENCES TO PROVISIONS OF SCHEDULE

1. Without prejudice to the generality of section 9 of the Interpretation Act 2005 and its application to the body of this Act and to *Schedules 1*, *2* and *5* to *18*—

(a) a reference in this Schedule to a paragraph or Part is a reference to a paragraph or Part of this Schedule, unless it is indicated that a reference to some other enactment is intended, and

(b) a reference in this Schedule to a subparagraph or clause is a reference to the subparagraph or clause of the provision in which the reference occurs, unless it is indicated that a reference to some other enactment is intended.

PART II
GENERAL RULES AND FORMATS

GENERAL RULES

2. (1) Group financial statements shall comply, except for any necessary modifications to take account of differences between group financial statements and entity financial statements, with the provisions of *Schedule 3* as if the undertakings included in the consolidation (the "group") were a single company.

(2) In particular, for the purposes of *paragraph 68* of *Schedule 3* as it applies to group financial statements—

(a) any subsidiary undertakings of the holding company not dealt with in the group financial statements shall be treated as a subsidiary undertaking of the group, and

(b) if the holding company is itself a subsidiary undertaking, the group shall be treated as a subsidiary undertaking of any holding undertaking of the holding company, and the reference to fellow subsidiary undertakings shall be read accordingly.

3. (1) The group balance sheet and group profit and loss account shall consolidate in full the information contained in the separate balance sheets and profit and loss accounts of the holding company and of the subsidiary undertakings included in the consolidation, subject to the adjustments required or permitted by the following provisions of this Schedule and to such other adjustments (if any) as may be appropriate in accordance with generally accepted accounting practice.

(2)If the financial year of a subsidiary undertaking dealt with in the group financial statements differs from that of the holding company, the group financial statements shall be drawn up—

(a) from the entity financial statements of the subsidiary undertaking for its financial year last ending before the end of the holding company's financial year provided that the financial year ended no more than 3 months before that of the holding undertaking and *subparagraph (3)* is complied with, or

(b) from interim financial statements drawn up by the subsidiary undertaking as at the end of the holding company's financial year.

(3) Where the group financial statements are drawn up from entity financial statements of a subsidiary undertaking referred to in *subparagraph (2)(a)*, account shall be taken and, where appropriate, disclosure shall be made of important events concerning the assets and liabilities, the financial position and the profit or loss of the subsidiary undertaking between the subsidiary undertaking's financial year end date and that of the holding company.

AMENDMENTS TO FORMATS IN SCHEDULE 3

Non-controlling interests

4. (1) In applying Balance Sheet Formats 1 and 2 set out in *Part II of Schedule 3* to group financial statements a separate item under the heading "Non-controlling Interests" shall be shown—

(a) in Format 1 after item H, and

(b) in Format 2 under the general heading "CAPITAL, RESERVES AND LIABILITIES", between items A and B.

(2) The amount to be shown under the heading "Non-controlling Interests" referred to in *subparagraph (1)* shall be the amount of share capital and reserves attributable to shares in subsidiary undertakings consolidated in the group financial statements held by or on behalf of persons other than the holding company and its subsidiary undertakings.

5. (1) In applying Profit and Loss Account Formats 1 and 2 set out in Part II of Schedule 3 to group financial statements, the profit or loss for the year shown as—

(a) in Format 1, item 16, and

(b) in Format 2, item 18,

shall be attributed between amounts due to "Non-controlling Interests" and equity holders of the holding company.

(2) The amount to be shown under the heading "Non-controlling Interests" in accordance with *subparagraph (1)* shall be the amount of any profit or loss for the year attributable to shares in subsidiary undertakings consolidated in the group financial statements held by or on behalf of persons other than the holding company and its subsidiary undertakings.

Other changes

6. (1) The formats set out in *Part II of Schedule 3* shall have effect in relation to group financial statements with the following modifications.

(2) In the Balance Sheet Formats, the items headed "Participating interests", that is—

(a) in Format 1, item A.III.3, and

(b) in Format 2, item A.III.3 under the heading "ASSETS",

shall be replaced by 2 items, "Interests in associated undertakings" and "Other participating interests".

(3) In the Profit and Loss Account Formats, the items headed "Income from participating interests", that is—

(a) in Format 1, item 8, and

(b) in Format 2, item 10,

shall be replaced by 2 items, "Income from interests in associated undertakings" and "Income from other participating interests".

PART III

ACCOUNTING PRINCIPLES AND VALUATION RULES

ACCOUNTING PRINCIPLES

General

7. In determining the amounts to be included in the group financial statements, the accounting principles and valuation rules contained in *Part III of Schedule 3* shall apply and shall be applied consistently within those group financial statements.

8. (1) Subject to *subparagraph (2)*, a holding company shall apply the same methods of valuation in drawing up its group financial statements as it applies in drawing up its entity financial statements unless the group and entity financial statements are drawn up under different accounting standards; and if so the applicable accounting standards shall be disclosed in the notes to the group and entity financial statements and the reasons given.

(2) *Subparagraph (1)* shall not apply where, in the opinion of the directors, a departure from that paragraph is necessary for the purpose of giving a true and fair view.

(3) Where there is any application of *subparagraph (2)*, the particulars of the departure and the reasons therefor shall be disclosed in the notes to the group financial statements.

9. (1) Where the assets and liabilities to be included in the group financial statements have been valued or otherwise determined by undertakings included in the consolidation according to accounting rules differing from those used in the group financial statements, the values or amounts shall be adjusted so as to accord with the rules used for the group financial statements.

(2) The adjustments referred to in this paragraph need not be made if they are not material for the purpose of giving a true and fair view.

(3) If, in the opinion of the directors of the holding company, there are special reasons for departing from *subparagraph (1)* they may do so but particulars of any such departure, the reasons therefor and its effect shall be stated in the notes to the group financial statements.

Preparing the consolidation

10. (1) Group financial statements shall show the assets, liabilities and financial position as at the end of the financial year and the profit or loss for the financial year of the holding company and the undertakings included in the consolidation as if they were a single undertaking.

(2) In particular—

(a) debts and claims between the undertakings included in the consolidation shall be eliminated in preparing the group financial statements,

(b) income and expenditure relating to transactions between the undertakings included in the consolidation shall be eliminated in preparing the group financial statements, and

(c) where profits and losses resulting from transactions between the undertakings included in the consolidation are included in the book values of assets, they shall be eliminated in preparing the group financial statements,

however clauses (a) to (c) need not be complied with where the amounts involved are not material for the purpose of giving a true and fair view.

11. (1) The methods of consolidation shall be applied consistently from one financial year to the next.

(2) If, in the opinion of the directors of the holding company, there are special reasons for departing from *subparagraph (1)* they may do so but particulars of any such departure, the reasons therefor and its effect shall be stated in the notes to the group financial statements.

Accounting for an acquisition

12. (1) *Paragraphs 13* to *16* apply where an undertaking becomes a subsidiary undertaking of the holding company.

(2) That event is referred to in those provisions as an "acquisition" and references to the undertaking acquired or acquired undertaking shall be read accordingly.

13. An acquisition shall be accounted for by the acquisition method of accounting unless the conditions for accounting for it as a merger as set out in *paragraph 15* are satisfied and the merger method of accounting is adopted.

14. (1) The acquisition method of accounting is as described in *subparagraphs (2)* to *(6)*.

(2) The identifiable assets and liabilities of the undertaking acquired shall be included in the consolidated balance sheet at their fair values as at the date of acquisition.

(3) The income and expenditure of the undertaking acquired shall be brought into the group financial statements only as from the date of acquisition.

(4) There shall be calculated the difference between the acquisition cost of the interest in the shares of the acquired undertaking incurred by the undertakings included in the group financial statements, and the interest of the undertakings

included in the group financial statements in the adjusted capital and reserves of the undertaking acquired.

(5) For the foregoing purpose—

"acquisition cost" means the amount of any cash consideration and the fair value of any other consideration, together with such amounts (if any) in respect of fees and other expenses of the acquisition as the holding company may determine to have been incurred in relation to the acquisition;

"adjusted capital and reserves of the undertaking acquired" means its capital and reserves at the date of the acquisition after adjusting the identifiable assets and liabilities of the undertaking to fair values as at that date.

(6) The resulting amount—

(a) if positive, shall be treated as goodwill and the provisions of *Schedule 3* in relation to goodwill shall apply, and

(b) if negative, shall be treated as negative goodwill and may be transferred to the profit and loss account in accordance with the accounting principles in *Part III* of *Schedule 3*.

15. The conditions for accounting for an acquisition as a merger are—

(a) that all of the entities involved in the business combination are ultimately controlled by the same party both before and after the business combination,

(b) that such control is not transitory, and

(c) that adoption of the merger method accords with generally accepted accounting principles or practice.

16. (1) The merger method of accounting is as set out in *subparagraphs (2)* to *(6)*.

(2) The assets and liabilities of the undertaking acquired shall be brought into the group financial statements at the amount at which they stand in the acquired undertaking's financial statements, subject to any adjustment authorised or required by this Part.

(3) The income and expenditure of the acquired undertaking shall be included in the group financial statements for the entire financial year, including the period before the acquisition.

(4) The group financial statements shall show corresponding amounts relating to the previous financial year as if the undertaking had been included in the consolidation throughout that year.

(5) There shall be set off against the aggregate of—

(a) the appropriate amount in respect of any shares issued by the acquiring company in consideration for the acquisition of shares in the acquired undertaking, and

(b) the fair value of any other consideration for the acquisition of shares in the acquired undertaking, determined as at the date when those shares were acquired, the nominal value of the issued share capital of the acquired undertaking held by the undertakings consolidated in the group financial statements.

(6) The resulting amount shall be shown as an adjustment to the consolidated reserves.

(7) In *subparagraph (5)(a)*, the "appropriate amount" in respect of the shares issued shall be determined in accordance with the requirements of *sections 71* to *75*.

17. Where an acquisition has taken place in the financial year and the merger method of accounting has been adopted, the notes to the financial statements shall disclose—

(a) the address of the acquired undertaking's registered office or where the acquired undertaking is incorporated outside the State, the registered office (howsoever described) of the acquired undertaking in the country in which it is incorporated,

(b) the name of the ultimate controlling party referred to in *paragraph 15(a)*,

(c) the address of that controlling party's registered office or where the controlling party is incorporated outside the State, the registered office (howsoever described) of the controlling party in the country in which it is incorporated, and

(d) the information referred to in *paragraph 16(6)*.

18. (1) Where a group is acquired, *paragraphs 12* to *17* apply with the following adaptations.

(2) References to shares of the acquired undertaking shall be read as references to shares of the holding undertaking of the group acquired.

(3) Other references to the acquired undertaking shall be read as references to the group acquired; and references to the assets and liabilities, income and expenditure and capital and reserves of the acquired undertaking shall be read as references to the assets and liabilities, income and expenditure and capital and reserves of the group after making the set offs and other adjustments required by this Part in the case of group financial statements.

Changes in the composition of the group

19. If the composition of the undertakings consolidated in the group financial statements has changed significantly in the course of a financial year, the group financial statements shall include information which makes the comparison of successive sets of group financial statements meaningful.

ACCOUNTING FOR JOINT VENTURES AND ASSOCIATES IN GROUP FINANCIAL STATEMENTS

Joint ventures

20. (1) Where a holding company or one of its subsidiary undertakings consolidated in the group financial statements manages another undertaking jointly with one or more undertakings not consolidated in the group financial statements, that other undertaking (the "joint venture") may, if it is not a subsidiary undertaking of the

holding company, be proportionally consolidated in the group financial statements in proportion to the rights in its capital held by the holding company or the subsidiary undertakings consolidated in the group financial statements, as the case may be.

(2) The provisions of this Schedule relating to the preparation of consolidated financial statements shall apply, with any necessary modifications, to the inclusion of joint ventures in the consolidated financial statements by proportional consolidation in accordance with *subparagraph (1)*.

Associated undertakings

21. (1) In *paragraph 22*, "associated undertaking" means an undertaking in which an undertaking consolidated in the group financial statements has a participating interest and over whose operating and financial policy it exercises a significant influence and which is not—

   (a) a subsidiary undertaking of the holding company, or

   (b) a joint venture proportionally consolidated in accordance with *paragraph 20*.

(2) Where an undertaking holds 20 per cent or more of the voting rights in another undertaking, it shall be presumed to exercise such an influence over it unless the contrary is shown.

(3) The voting rights in an undertaking means the rights conferred on shareholders in respect of their shares or, in the case of an undertaking not having a share capital, on members, to vote at general meetings of the undertaking on all or substantially all matters.

(4) The provisions of *section 7(5)* and *(6)* with respect to determining whether shares are held in a body corporate and with respect to reckoning the amount of voting rights held apply, with any necessary modifications, in determining for the purpose of this paragraph whether an undertaking holds 20 per cent or more of the voting rights in another undertaking.

22. (1) The interest of an undertaking consolidated in the group financial statements in an associated undertaking, and the amount of profit or loss attributable to such an interest, shall be shown in the group financial statements by way of the equity method of accounting including dealing with any goodwill arising in accordance with *paragraphs 21* to *23* and *25* of *Schedule 3*.

(2) Where the associated undertaking is itself a holding undertaking, the net assets and profits or losses to be taken into account are those of the holding undertaking and its subsidiary undertakings (after making any consolidation adjustments).

(3) The equity method of accounting need not be applied if the amounts in question are not material for the purpose of giving a true and fair view.

Participating interest

23. (1) Subject to *subparagraph (5)*, in *paragraph 21* and this paragraph, "participating interest" means an interest held by one undertaking in the equity shares of another undertaking which it holds on a long term basis for the purpose of securing a

contribution to that undertaking's own activities by the exercise of control or influence arising from or related to that interest.

(2) The reference in *subparagraph (1)* to an interest in equity shares includes—

(a) an interest which is convertible into an interest in equity shares, and

(b) an option to acquire equity shares or any such interest, and an interest or option falls within clause (a) or (b)

notwithstanding that the equity shares to which it relates are, until the conversion or the exercise of the option, unissued.

(3) Where an undertaking holds an interest in equity shares and such an interest represents 20 per cent or more of all such interests in the other undertaking it shall be presumed to hold that interest on the basis and for the purpose mentioned in *subparagraph (1)* unless the contrary is shown.

(4) For the purpose of this paragraph an interest held on behalf of an undertaking shall be treated as held by it.

(5) In the balance sheet and profit and loss formats set out in *Part II* of *Schedule 3*, "participating interest" does not include an interest in a group undertaking.

PART IV
INFORMATION REQUIRED BY WAY OF NOTES TO GROUP FINANCIAL STATEMENTS

24. Without prejudice to *paragraph 2*, the notes to the group financial statements shall, in addition to providing the information required by *Schedule 3*, also state the information required by *paragraphs 25* to *31*.

25. Where sums originally denominated in currencies, other than the currency in which the group financial statements are presented, have been brought into account under any items shown in the balance sheet or profit and loss account, the basis on which those sums have been translated into the currency in which the group financial statements are presented shall be stated.

26. In respect of the aggregate of the amounts shown in the group balance sheet under the heading 'creditors' there shall be stated the information required by *paragraph 56* of *Schedule 3* as if references in that paragraph to a company were to the company and its subsidiary undertakings taken as a whole.

27. In relation to each joint venture proportionally consolidated, there shall be stated the nature of the joint management arrangement.

28. In disclosing the information in relation to particulars of staff required by *section 317*, there shall be shown separately the average number of persons employed by undertakings that are proportionally consolidated.

29. In relation to acquisitions taking place in the financial year, there shall be stated in the notes to the group financial statements—

(a) the name and registered office of the acquired undertaking or where the acquired undertaking is incorporated outside the State, the registered office (howsoever described) of the acquired undertaking in the country in which it is incorporated, or

(b) where a group was acquired, the name and registered office of the holding undertaking of that group or where the holding undertaking is incorporated outside the State, the registered office (howsoever described) of the holding undertaking in the country in which it is incorporated, and

(c) whether the acquisition has been accounted for by the acquisition method or the merger method of accounting.

30. (1) Where a holding company prepares group financial statements, the following information shall be given with respect to each undertaking which is a subsidiary undertaking of the holding company at the end of the financial year:

(a) whether the subsidiary undertaking is included in the consolidation and, if it is not, the reasons for excluding it from the consolidation;

(b) a statement identifying which of the conditions specified in *section 7(2)* is the undertaking a subsidiary undertaking of its immediate holding undertaking.

(2) *Paragraph (1)(b)* need not be applied if the subsidiary undertaking is an undertaking within the description of *section 7(2)(a)(iii)* or *(iv)* and the immediate holding undertaking holds the same proportion of shares in the undertaking as it holds voting rights.

31. *Paragraph 65* of *Schedule 3* shall, in the case of group financial statements, apply to all transactions entered into by the holding company, or any subsidiary undertaking included in the consolidation, with related parties, being transactions of the kind referred to in that paragraph but not being intra-group transactions.

PART V
MISCELLANEOUS MATTERS

Deferred tax

32. Deferred tax balances shall be recognised on consolidation where it is probable that a charge to tax or a reduction in tax payable will arise within the foreseeable future for one of the undertakings included in the consolidation.][a]

Amendments

a Schedule 4 substituted by C(A)A 2017, s 89(d) and Sch 4.

[SCHEDULE 4A

ACCOUNTING PRINCIPLES, FORM AND CONTENT OF GROUP FINANCIAL STATEMENTS FOR COMPANIES SUBJECT TO THE SMALL COMPANIES REGIME

PART I

CONSTRUCTION OF REFERENCES TO PROVISIONS OF SCHEDULE

1. Without prejudice to the generality of section 9 of the Interpretation Act 2005 and its application to the body of this Act and to Schedules 1, 2 and 5 to 18—

   (a) a reference in this Schedule to a paragraph or Part is a reference to a paragraph or Part of this Schedule, unless it is indicated that a reference to some other enactment is intended, and

   (b) a reference in this Schedule to a subparagraph or clause is a reference to the subparagraph or clause of the provision in which the reference occurs, unless it is indicated that a reference to some other enactment is intended.

PART II

GENERAL RULES AND FORMATS

GENERAL RULES

2. (1) Group financial statements shall comply, except for any necessary modifications to take account of differences between group financial statements and entity financial statements, with the provisions of Schedule 3A as if the undertakings included in the consolidation (the 'group') were a single company.

   (2) In particular, for the purposes of paragraph 57 of Schedule 3A as it applies to group financial statements—

   (a) any subsidiary undertakings of the holding company not dealt with in the group financial statements shall be treated as a subsidiary undertaking of the group, and

   (b) if the holding company is itself a subsidiary undertaking, the group shall be treated as a subsidiary undertaking of any holding undertaking of the holding company, and the reference to fellow subsidiary undertakings shall be read accordingly.

3. (1) The group balance sheet and group profit and loss account shall consolidate in full the information contained in the separate balance sheets and profit and loss accounts of the holding company and of the subsidiary undertakings included in the consolidation, subject to the adjustments required or permitted by the following provisions of this Schedule and to such other adjustments (if any) as may be appropriate in accordance with generally accepted accounting practice.

   (2)If the financial year of a subsidiary undertaking dealt with in the group financial statements differs from that of the holding company, the group financial statements shall be drawn up—

   (a) from the entity financial statements of the subsidiary undertaking for its financial year last ending before the end of the holding company's financial year provided that the financial year ended no more than 3 months before that of the holding undertaking and subparagraph (3) is complied with, or

(b) from interim financial statements drawn up by the subsidiary undertaking as at the end of the holding company's financial year.

(3) Where the group financial statements are drawn up from entity financial statements of a subsidiary undertaking referred to in subparagraph (2)(a), account shall be taken and, where appropriate, disclosure shall be made of important events concerning the assets and liabilities, the financial position and the profit or loss of the subsidiary undertaking between the subsidiary undertaking's financial year end date and that of the holding company.

AMENDMENTS TO FORMATS IN SCHEDULE 3A

Non-controlling interests

4. (1) In applying Balance Sheet Formats 1 and 2 set out in *Part II* of *Schedule 3A* to group financial statements a separate item under the heading 'Non-controlling Interests' shall be shown—

(a) in Format 1 after item H, and

(b) in Format 2 under the general heading "CAPITAL, RESERVES AND LIABILITIES", between items A and B.

(2) The amount to be shown under the heading 'Non-controlling Interests' referred to in subparagraph (1) shall be the amount of share capital and reserves attributable to shares in subsidiary undertakings consolidated in the group financial statements held by or on behalf of persons other than the holding company and its subsidiary undertakings.

5. (1) In applying Profit and Loss Account Formats 1 and 2 set out in *Part II* of *Schedule 3A* to group financial statements the profit or loss for the year shown—

(a) in Format 1, item 16, and

(b) in Format 2, item 18,

shall be attributed between amounts due to "Non-controlling Interests" and equity holders of the holding company.

(2) The amount to be shown under the heading "Non-controlling Interests" in accordance with subparagraph (1) shall be the amount of any profit or loss for the year attributable to shares in subsidiary undertakings consolidated in the group financial statements held by or on behalf of persons other than the holding company and its subsidiary undertakings.

Other changes

6. (1) The formats set out in *Part II* of *Schedule 3A* shall have effect in relation to group financial statements with the following modifications.

(2) In the Balance Sheet Formats, the items headed "Participating interests", that is—

(a) in Format 1, item A.III.3, and

(b) in Format 2, item A.III.3 under the heading "ASSETS",

shall be replaced by 2 items, "Interests in associated undertakings" and "Other participating interests".

(3) In the Profit and Loss Account Formats, the items headed "Income from participating interests", that is—

(a) in Format 1, item 8, and

(b) in Format 2, item 10,

shall be replaced by 2 items, "Income from interests in associated undertakings" and "Income from other participating interests".

PART III
ACCOUNTING PRINCIPLES AND VALUATION RULES

ACCOUNTING PRINCIPLES

General

7. In determining the amounts to be included in the group financial statements, the accounting principles and valuation rules contained in *Part III* of *Schedule 3A* shall apply and shall be applied consistently within those group financial statements.

8. (1) Subject to *subparagraph (2)*, a holding company shall apply the same methods of valuation in drawing up its group financial statements as it applies in drawing up its entity financial statements unless the group and entity financial statements are drawn up under different accounting standards; and if so the applicable accounting standards shall be disclosed in the notes to the group and entity financial statements and the reasons given.

(2) *Subparagraph (1)* shall not apply where, in the opinion of the directors, a departure from that paragraph is necessary for the purpose of giving a true and fair view.

(3) Where there is any application of *subparagraph (2)*, the particulars of the departure and the reasons therefor shall be disclosed in the notes to the group financial statements.

9. (1) Where the assets and liabilities to be included in the group financial statements have been valued or otherwise determined by undertakings included in the consolidation according to accounting rules differing from those used in the group financial statements, the values or amounts shall be adjusted so as to accord with the rules used for the group financial statements.

(2) The adjustments referred to in this paragraph need not be made if they are not material for the purpose of giving a true and fair view.

(3) If, in the opinion of the directors of the holding company, there are special reasons for departing from *subparagraph (1)* they may do so but particulars of any such departure, the reasons therefor and its effect shall be stated in the notes to the group financial statements.

Preparing the consolidation

10. (1) Group financial statements shall show the assets, liabilities and financial position as at the end of the financial year and the profit or loss for the financial year of the holding company and the undertakings included in the consolidation as if they were a single undertaking.

(2) In particular—

(a) debts and claims between the undertakings included in the consolidation shall be eliminated in preparing the group financial statements,

(b) income and expenditure relating to transactions between the undertakings included in the consolidation shall be eliminated in preparing the group financial statements, and

(c) where profits and losses resulting from transactions between the undertakings included in the consolidation are included in the book values of assets, they shall be eliminated in preparing the group financial statements,

however clauses (a) to (c) need not be complied with where the amounts involved are not material for the purpose of giving a true and fair view.

11. (1) The methods of consolidation shall be applied consistently from one financial year to the next.

(2) If, in the opinion of the directors of the holding company, there are special reasons for departing from *subparagraph (1)*, they may do so but particulars of any such departure, the reasons therefor and its effect shall be stated in the notes to the group financial statements.

Accounting for an acquisition

12. (1) *Paragraphs 13* to *16* apply where an undertaking becomes a subsidiary undertaking of the holding company.

(2) That event is referred to in those provisions as an 'acquisition' and references to the undertaking acquired or acquired undertaking shall be read accordingly.

13. An acquisition shall be accounted for by the acquisition method of accounting unless the conditions for accounting for it as a merger as set out in *paragraph 15* are satisfied and the merger method of accounting is adopted.

14. (1) The acquisition method of accounting is as described in *subparagraphs (2)* to *(6)*.

(2) The identifiable assets and liabilities of the undertaking acquired shall be included in the consolidated balance sheet at their fair values as at the date of acquisition.

(3) The income and expenditure of the undertaking acquired shall be brought into the group financial statements only as from the date of acquisition.

(4) There shall be calculated the difference between the acquisition cost of the interest in the shares of the acquired undertaking incurred by the undertakings included in the group financial statements, and the interest of the undertakings

included in the group financial statements in the adjusted capital and reserves of the undertaking acquired.

(5) For the foregoing purpose—

"acquisition cost" means the amount of any cash consideration and the fair value of any other consideration, together with such amounts (if any) in respect of fees and other expenses of the acquisition as the holding company may determine to have been incurred in relation to the acquisition;

"adjusted capital and reserves of the undertaking acquired" means its capital and reserves at the date of the acquisition after adjusting the identifiable assets and liabilities of the undertaking to fair values as at that date.

(6) The resulting amount—

(a) if positive, shall be treated as goodwill and the provisions of *Schedule 3A* in relation to goodwill shall apply, and

(b) if negative, shall be treated as negative goodwill and may be transferred to the profit and loss account in accordance with the accounting principles in *Part III* of *Schedule 3A*.

15. The conditions for accounting for an acquisition as a merger are—

(a) that all of the entities involved in the business combination are ultimately controlled by the same party both before and after the business combination,

(b) that such control is not transitory, and

(c) that adoption of the merger method accords with generally accepted accounting principles or practice.

16. (1) The merger method of accounting is as set out in *subparagraphs (2)* to *(6)*.

(2) The assets and liabilities of the undertaking acquired shall be brought into the group financial statements at the amount at which they stand in the acquired undertaking's financial statements, subject to any adjustment authorised or required by this Part.

(3) The income and expenditure of the acquired undertaking shall be included in the group financial statements for the entire financial year, including the period before the acquisition.

(4) The group financial statements shall show corresponding amounts relating to the previous financial year as if the undertaking had been included in the consolidation throughout that year.

(5) There shall be set off against the aggregate of—

(a) the appropriate amount in respect of any shares issued by the acquiring company in consideration for the acquisition of shares in the acquired undertaking, and

(b) the fair value of any other consideration for the acquisition of shares in the acquired undertaking, determined as at the date when those shares were acquired, the nominal value of the issued share capital of the acquired undertaking held by the undertakings consolidated in the group financial statements.

(6) The resulting amount shall be shown as an adjustment to the consolidated reserves.

(7) In *subparagraph (5)(a)*, the "appropriate amount" in respect of the shares issued shall be determined in accordance with the requirements of *sections 71* to *75*.

17. Where an acquisition has taken place in the financial year and the merger method of accounting has been adopted, the notes to the financial statements shall disclose—

   (a) the address of the acquired undertaking's registered office or where the acquired undertaking is incorporated outside the State, the registered office (howsoever described) of the acquired undertaking in the country in which it is incorporated,

   (b) the name of the ultimate controlling party referred to in *paragraph 15(a)*,

   (c) the address of that controlling party's registered office or where the controlling party is incorporated outside the State, the registered office (howsoever described) of the controlling party in the country in which it is incorporated, and

   (d) the information referred to in *paragraph 16(6)*.

18. (1) Where a group is acquired, *paragraphs 12* to *17* apply with the following adaptations.

(2) References to shares of the acquired undertaking shall be read as references to shares of the holding undertaking of the group acquired.

(3) Other references to the acquired undertaking shall be read as references to the group acquired; and references to the assets and liabilities, income and expenditure and capital and reserves of the acquired undertaking shall be read as references to the assets and liabilities, income and expenditure and capital and reserves of the group after making the set offs and other adjustments required by this Part in the case of group financial statements.

Changes in the composition of the group

19. If the composition of the undertakings consolidated in the group financial statements has changed significantly in the course of a financial year, the group financial statements shall include information which makes the comparison of successive sets of group financial statements meaningful.

ACCOUNTING FOR JOINT VENTURES AND ASSOCIATES IN GROUP FINANCIAL STATEMENTS

Joint ventures

20. (1) Where a holding company or one of its subsidiary undertakings consolidated in the group financial statements manages another undertaking jointly with one or more undertakings not consolidated in the group financial statements, that other undertaking (the "joint venture") may, if it is not a subsidiary undertaking of the

holding company, be proportionally consolidated in the group financial statements in proportion to the rights in its capital held by the holding company or the subsidiary undertakings consolidated in the group financial statements, as the case may be.

(2) The provisions of this Schedule relating to the preparation of consolidated financial statements shall apply, with any necessary modifications, to the inclusion of joint ventures in the consolidated financial statements by proportional consolidation in accordance with *subparagraph (1)*.

Associated undertakings

21. (1) In *paragraph 22*, "associated undertaking" means an undertaking in which an undertaking consolidated in the group financial statements has a participating interest and over whose operating and financial policy it exercises a significant influence and which is not—

(a) a subsidiary undertaking of the holding company, or

(b) a joint venture proportionally consolidated in accordance with *paragraph 20.*

(2) Where an undertaking holds 20 per cent or more of the voting rights in another undertaking, it shall be presumed to exercise such an influence over it unless the contrary is shown.

(3) The voting rights in an undertaking means the rights conferred on shareholders in respect of their shares or, in the case of an undertaking not having a share capital, on members, to vote at general meetings of the undertaking on all or substantially all matters.

(4) The provisions of *section 7(5)* and *(6)* with respect to determining whether shares are held in a body corporate and with respect to reckoning the amount of voting rights held apply, with any necessary modifications, in determining for the purpose of this paragraph whether an undertaking holds 20 per cent or more of the voting rights in another undertaking.

22. (1) The interest of an undertaking consolidated in the group financial statements in an associated undertaking, and the amount of profit or loss attributable to such an interest, shall be shown in the group financial statements by way of the equity method of accounting including dealing with any goodwill arising in accordance with *paragraphs 21* to *23*, and *25* of *Schedule 3A*.

(2) Where the associated undertaking is itself a holding undertaking, the net assets and profits or losses to be taken into account are those of the holding undertaking and its subsidiary undertakings (after making any consolidation adjustments).

(3) The equity method of accounting need not be applied if the amounts in question are not material for the purpose of giving a true and fair view.

Participating interest

23. (1) Subject to *subparagraph (5)*, in *paragraph 21* and this paragraph "participating interest" means an interest held by one undertaking in the equity shares of another undertaking which it holds on a long term basis for the purpose of securing a

contribution to that undertaking's own activities by the exercise of control or influence arising from or related to that interest.

(2) The reference in *subparagraph (1)* to an interest in equity shares includes—

(a) an interest which is convertible into an interest in equity shares, and

(b) an option to acquire equity shares or any such interest, and an interest or option falls within clause (a) or (b)

notwithstanding that the equity shares to which it relates are, until the conversion or the exercise of the option, unissued.

(3) Where an undertaking holds an interest in equity shares and such an interest represents 20 per cent or more of all such interests in the other undertaking it shall be presumed to hold that interest on the basis and for the purpose mentioned in *subparagraph (1)* unless the contrary is shown.

(4) For the purpose of this paragraph an interest held on behalf of an undertaking shall be treated as held by it.

(5) In the balance sheet and profit and loss formats set out in Part II of Schedule 3A, 'participating interest' does not include an interest in a group undertaking.

PART IV
INFORMATION REQUIRED BY WAY OF NOTES TO GROUP FINANCIAL STATEMENTS

24. Without prejudice to *paragraph 2*, the notes to the group financial statements shall, in addition to providing the information required by *Schedule 3A*, also state the information required by *paragraphs 25* to *31*.

25. Where sums originally denominated in currencies, other than the currency in which the group financial statements are presented, have been brought into account under any items shown in the balance sheet or profit and loss account, the basis on which those sums have been translated into the currency in which the group financial statements are presented shall be stated.

26. In respect of the aggregate of the amounts shown in the group balance sheet under the heading 'creditors', there shall be stated the information required by *paragraph 50* of *Schedule 3A* as if references in that paragraph to a company were to the company and its subsidiary undertakings taken as a whole.

27. In relation to each joint venture proportionally consolidated, there shall be stated the nature of the joint management arrangement.

28. In disclosing the information in relation to staff numbers required by *section 317*, there shall be shown separately the average number of persons employed by undertakings that are proportionally consolidated.

29. In relation to acquisitions taking place in the financial year, there shall be stated in the notes to the group financial statements—

(a) the name and registered office of the acquired undertaking or where the acquired undertaking is incorporated outside the State, the registered office (howsoever described) of the acquired undertaking in the country in which it is incorporated, or

(b) where a group was acquired, the name and registered office of the holding undertaking of that group or where the holding undertaking is incorporated outside the State, the registered office (howsoever described) of the holding undertaking in the country in which it is incorporated, and

(c) whether the acquisition has been accounted for by the acquisition method or the merger method of accounting.

30. *Paragraph 55* of *Schedule 3A* shall, in the case of group financial statements, apply to all transactions entered into by the holding company, or any subsidiary undertaking included in the consolidation, with related parties that are—

(a) the holders of participating interests in the holding company or any subsidiary undertaking,

(b) undertakings in which the holding company or any subsidiary undertaking holds a participating interest, or

(c) directors of the holding company or of a higher holding undertaking.

31. (1) Where a holding company prepares group financial statements, the following information shall be given with respect to each undertaking which is a subsidiary undertaking of the holding company at the end of the financial year:

(a) whether the subsidiary undertaking is included in the consolidation and, if it is not, the reasons for excluding it from consolidation;

(b) a statement identifying which of the conditions specified in *section 7(2)* is the undertaking a subsidiary undertaking of its immediate holding undertaking.

(2) *Paragraph (1)(b)* need not be applied if the company is a company within the description of *section 7(2)(a)(iii)* or *(iv)* and the immediate holding undertaking holds the same proportion of shares in the undertaking as it holds voting rights.

PART V
MISCELLANEOUS MATTERS
Deferred tax

32. Deferred tax balances shall be recognised on consolidation where it is probable that a charge to tax or a reduction in tax payable will arise within the foreseeable future for one of the undertakings included in the consolidation.][a]

Amendments

a Schedule 4A substituted by C(A)A 2017, s 89(e) and Sch 5.

SCHEDULE 5
LIST OF COMPANIES FOR CERTAIN PURPOSES OF ACT (INCLUDING, IN PARTICULAR, *SECTIONS 142, 350, 362* AND *510*)

Section 142

1. A company that is an authorised investment firm within the meaning of the European Communities (Markets in Financial Instruments) Regulations 2007 (S.I. No. 60 of 2007).
2. A company that is an authorised market operator.
3. A company that is an associated undertaking or a related undertaking, of an authorised investment firm or an authorised market operator, within the meaning of the European Communities (Markets in Financial Instruments) Regulations 2007 (S.I. No. 60 of 2007).
4. A company to which Chapter VII, VIII or IX of Part II of the Central Bank Act 1989 applies.

[5. A company or undertaking engaged in the business of accepting deposits or other repayable funds from the public and granting credit for its own account.][a]

6. A company that is an associated body of a building society within the meaning of the Building Societies Act 1989.
7. A company that is an associated enterprise of a credit institution within the meaning of the European Communities (Credit Institutions) (Consolidated Supervision) Regulations 2009 (S.I. No. 475 of 2009).
8. An investment company within the meaning of *Part 24*.
9. A company that is a management company, trustee or custodian within the meaning of *Part 24* or of Part 2 of the Investment Funds, Companies and Miscellaneous Provisions Act 2005.
10. A company that is an undertaking for collective investment in transferable securities within the meaning of the European Communities (Undertakings for Collective Investment in Transferable Securities) Regulations 2011 (S.I. No. 352 of 2011).
11. A company that is a management company or trustee of an undertaking for collective investment in transferable securities within the meaning of the European Communities (Undertakings for Collective Investment in Transferable Securities) Regulations 2011 (S.I. No. 352 of 2011).
12. A company that is a management company or trustee of a unit trust scheme within the meaning of the Unit Trusts Act 1990.
13. A company that is a general partner or custodian of an investment limited partnership within the meaning of the Investment Limited Partnerships Act 1994.
14. A company that has close links (within the meaning of the European Union (Capital Requirements) Regulations 2014 (S.I. No. 158 of 2014)) with an

authorised investment firm referred to in *paragraph 1* or a company referred to in *paragraph 5*.

15. Any other company the carrying on of business by which is required, by virtue of any enactment or instrument thereunder, to be authorised by the Central Bank.

16. A company that is the holder of an authorisation within the meaning of—

    (a) Regulation 2 of the European Communities (Non-Life Insurance) Regulations 1976 (S.I. No. 115 of 1976);

    (b) Regulation 2 of the European Communities (Non-Life Insurance) Framework Regulations 1994 (S.I. No. 359 of 1994);

    (c) Regulation 2 of the European Communities (Life Assurance) Regulations 1984 (S.I. No. 57 of 1984); or

    (d) Regulation 2 of the European Communities (Life Assurance) Framework Regulations 1994 (S.I. No. 360 of 1994).

17. A company that is an insurance intermediary within the meaning of the Insurance Act 1989.

18. A company that is an excepted body within the meaning of the Trade Union Acts 1871 to 1990.

Amendments

a Paragraph 5 substituted by C(SA)A 2018, s 52.

SCHEDULE 6
FURTHER SAVINGS AND TRANSITIONAL PROVISIONS

Section 5.

Continuity of company law not affected

1. The continuity of the operation of the law relating to companies shall not be affected by the substitution of this Act for the prior Companies Acts.

Status (generally) of instruments made under prior Companies Acts

2. Notwithstanding anything in section 26(2)(d) of the Interpretation Act 2005, no instrument made under any of the prior Companies Acts shall continue in force save as provided for in this Schedule.

Certain regulations saved

3. Any regulations made under section 28 or 48 of the Companies (Auditing and Accounting) Act 2003 and in force before the commencement of *Chapter 2* of *Part 15* shall continue in force as if made under the corresponding provision of that Chapter and may be amended or revoked accordingly.

Certain superannuation schemes saved

4. Every scheme made under section 9 of the Company Law Enforcement Act 2001 or section 20 of the Companies (Auditing and Accounting) Act 2003 and in force before the commencement of *Chapter 2* or *3*, as the case may be, of *Part 15* shall continue in force as if made under the corresponding provision of that Chapter and may be amended or revoked accordingly.

Certain other instruments saved

5. (1) As provided for in *section 1355*, *1367* or *1381*, as appropriate—

   (a) the Prospectus (Directive 2003/71/EC) Regulations 2005 (S.I. No. 324 of 2005) and any regulations amending those regulations;

   (b) the Market Abuse (Directive 2003/6/EC) Regulations 2005 (S.I. No. 342 of 2005) and any regulations amending those regulations;

   (c) the Transparency (Directive 2004/109/EC) Regulations 2007 (S.I. No. 277 of 2007) and any regulations amending those regulations,

   shall continue in force and may be amended or revoked under *section 1354*, *1366* or *1380*, as appropriate, accordingly.

   (2) The Companies Act 1990 (Uncertificated Securities) Regulations 1996 (S.I. No. 68 of 1996) shall continue in force and may be amended or revoked under *section 1086* accordingly.

   (3) As provided for in *section 1400(4)*, the Companies Act 1990 (Prescribed Alternative Accounting Standards Bodies) Regulations 2005 (S.I. No. 382 of 2005) and any regulations amending those regulations shall continue in force and may be amended or revoked under *section 12* accordingly.

Applicability of offence investigation and other powers in case of offences under prior Companies Acts

6. (1) For the purposes of the exercise of any power conferred by this Act, a reference in the provision concerned of this Act to an offence under a provision or provisions of this Act shall be read as including a reference to an offence under the corresponding provision or provisions of the prior Companies Acts.

(2) Without prejudice to the generality of *subparagraph (1)*, that subparagraph applies to the exercise of any power of investigation or search, entry or seizure conferred by this Act and, in particular, as respects the operation of any condition precedent, provided in the provision concerned of this Act, with respect to the power's exercise.

(3) *Section 789* applies to a search warrant issued under section 20 of the Act of 1990 as it applies to a search warrant issued under *section 787*.

Continuity of law relating to disqualifications and restrictions, etc.

7. (1) Without prejudice to the generality of *paragraph 1*, the continuity of the law relating to disqualifications and restrictions is not affected by the substitution of *Chapters 3*, *4* and *6* of *Part 14* for Part VII of the Act of 1990.

(2) Without prejudice to the generality of *paragraph 1*, any disqualification or declaration of restriction (within the meaning of Part VII of the Act of 1990) provided, made or granted under that Part and in force before the commencement of the corresponding provision of *Part 14* shall continue in force and operate as a disqualification or declaration of restriction provided, made or granted under that corresponding provision.

(3) Without prejudice to the generality of *paragraph 6*, *section 839* (automatic disqualification on conviction of certain indictable offences) operates with respect to the circumstances of a person's being convicted of an indictable offence under the prior Companies Acts as it operates with respect to the circumstances of a person's being convicted of an indictable offence under this Act.

(4) Without prejudice to the generality of *paragraph 6*, the powers of the court under *section 842* (court may make disqualification order) are exercisable by reference to matters or things done or omitted to be done under the prior Companies Acts as they are exercisable by reference to matters or things done or omitted to be done under this Act.

(5) *Chapter 5* (Disqualification and Restriction Undertakings) of *Part 14* shall be read as being operative and as applicable in a case where the Director has reasonable grounds for the belief referred to in *section 850(2)* or *852(2)* by reference to matters or things done or omitted to be done, or circumstances, under the prior Companies Acts as they are operative and applicable in a case where the Director has reasonable grounds for such belief by reference to matters or things done or omitted to be done, or circumstances, under this Act.

Continuation of acts not completed

8. (1) Any thing commenced under a provision of the prior Companies Acts, before the repeal, by this Act, of that provision, and not completed before that repeal, may be continued and completed under the corresponding provision of this Act.

(2) Without prejudice to the generality of the preceding subparagraph or *paragraph 1*, any petition presented for the winding up of a company or the appointment of an examiner to a company before the repeal of the provision concerned of the prior Companies Acts but not disposed of before the commencement of the corresponding provision of this Act may be proceeded with and heard under that corresponding provision and, likewise any subsequent act, application or proceeding in any such matter commenced but not completed before the corresponding provision of this Act is commenced may be so done, proceeded with or heard.

(3) However, in any such case, the court concerned shall, subject to *subparagraph (4)*, have jurisdiction to make whatever order it thinks appropriate for ensuring the smooth transition from the law and procedure under the prior Companies Acts to the law and procedure under this Act (that is to say, this Act and the rules of court as they have been brought into conformity with this Act as mentioned in *section 564(4)*) and that jurisdiction of the court shall extend, in a case where a liquidator has proceeded to take substantive steps in a winding up ordered by the court before the commencement of the relevant provision of *Part 11*, to making a direction that the functions of the court officer known as "the Examiner" that were performable under the rules of the court, before they were so brought into conformity, shall be performable in that winding up.

(4) In exercising the jurisdiction referred to in *subparagraph (3)*, the court shall bear in mind the extent to which a power of a liquidator that is exercisable under the relevant provisions of *Part 11* and also was exercisable under the relevant provisions of the prior Companies Acts may be exercised without the sanction of the court under the first-mentioned provisions.

(5) Notwithstanding anything in this paragraph or elsewhere, *sections 646* to *648* (liquidator's remuneration) shall not apply to a winding up commenced before the commencement of the relevant provisions of *Part 11* and the matters dealt with by those sections shall be governed by the relevant provisions of the prior Companies Acts and the rules of court in force before the commencement of the first-mentioned provisions, and the second-mentioned provisions and rules of court shall, despite *section 4*, continue in force for that purpose accordingly.

(6) Without prejudice to the generality of *subparagraph (1)* or *paragraph 1*, any investigation by inspectors appointed under the Act of 1990 before the commencement of the relevant provisions of *Part 13* but not completed before that commencement may be continued and completed under those relevant provisions.

Reckoning of periods of time in cases of acts continued under this Act

9. (1) Where any thing commenced under the prior Companies Acts but not completed before the commencement of the corresponding provision of this Act is continued to be carried on under that corresponding provision but the time specified in that provision for completing the thing is less than the time specified in that behalf in the repealed provision then, notwithstanding that corresponding provision, the period of time within which the thing may be completed under it shall be that specified in the repealed provision.

(2) In the converse case (that is to say, a case in which a greater period of time is specified in the corresponding provision of this Act than that specified in the repealed provision), the thing concerned may be completed within that greater period of time.

New Nomenclature for Certain Matters

10. (1) Without prejudice to the generality of *paragraph 1*, neither the use of the expression "financial statements" in this Act, as distinct from the expression "accounts" used in the prior Companies Acts, nor the use, with respect to associated matters concerning accounts and financial reporting, in this Act of expressions different from those used in those other Acts affects the validity of the preparation, auditing, circulation or laying of documents or the delivery of them to the Registrar, being documents that—

(a) are prepared in respect of a financial year beginning before the commencement of this Schedule and ending thereafter; and

(b) bear a description by reference to the nomenclature used in the prior Companies Acts.

(2) Without prejudice to the generality of *paragraphs 1* and *8*, the use of the expression "independent expert" in this Act, as distinct from the expression "independent accountant" used in the Companies (Amendment) Act 1990, does not affect the continued performance, after the commencement of this Schedule, by a person engaged before that commencement (by reference to that former nomenclature) of his or her functions in relation to an actual or prospective examinership.

References in enactments to provisions of prior Companies Acts

11. (1) A reference in any enactment to a provision of the prior Companies Acts, being a provision that is repealed by this Act and which corresponds to a provision of this Act, shall, unless the context otherwise requires, be read as a reference to that provision of this Act.

(2) Without prejudice to the generality of *subparagraph (1)*—

(a) the reference in Regulation 22(2) of the European Communities (Takeover Bids (Directive 2004/25/EC)) Regulations 2006 (S.I. No. 255 of 2006) to section 204 of the Act of 1963 shall be read as a reference to *Chapter 2* of *Part 9*;

(b) the reference in Regulation 81 of the Transparency (Directive 2004/109/EC) Regulations 2007 (S.I. No. 277 of 2007) to Chapter 2 of Part IV of the Act of 1990 shall be read as a reference to *Chapter 4* of *Part 17*; and

(c) the references in section 30 of the Multi-Unit Developments Act 2011 to section 311 or 311A of the Act of 1963 or section 12 or 12B of the Companies (Amendment) Act 1982, or to a particular provision of any such section, shall be read as references to *Chapter 1* or, as appropriate, *Chapter 2* of *Part 12* or, as the case may be, the corresponding provision of either such Chapter.

(3) Nothing in this paragraph affects *section 6* (construction of references in other Acts to companies registered under the Companies (Consolidation) Act 1908 and Act of 1963).

Provisions as to status of companies restored to register, having been struck off under former enactments

12. (1) Without prejudice to any specific provision in this Act in that behalf and the subsequent provisions of this paragraph, the provisions of this Act that shall apply to a company—

(a) struck off the register under any former enactment relating to companies (within the meaning of *section 5*); and

(b) subsequently restored to the register, whether under—

(i) the former enactment referred to in *section 744(3)*;

(ii) *Chapter 2* of *Part 12*; or

(iii) section 30 of the Multi-Unit Developments Act 2011,

shall be those applicable to the type of company that corresponds to the type of company to which the company belonged before it was so struck off.

(2) Without prejudice to *subparagraphs (3)* and *(4)*, where any of this Act's provisions, as applicable to a particular type of company, operates differently by reference (however the matter is expressed) to the length of time that has elapsed after the provision's commencement, then the reference in *subparagraph (1)* to the provisions of this Act that are applicable to a type of company shall, in the case of that particular provision, be read as a reference to that provision as it is applicable to a company of the type concerned at the time of the particular company's restoration to the register (and then at a future date, as the case may be, as it is so applicable at that future date).

(3) If the company's type, before being so struck off, was that of a private company limited by shares and the date on which the company is restored to the register under *Chapter 2* of *Part 12* or section 30 of the Multi-Unit Developments Act 2011 is subsequent to the expiry of the transition period (within the meaning of *Chapter 6* of *Part 2*), then, subject, in the case of a restoration under *section 738* or *741*, to any direction or order of the court under *section 742*, *section 61(1)(a)* and *(b)* shall apply in relation to the company notwithstanding that the company was not an existing private company within the meaning of that *Chapter 6* and,

accordingly, the company shall, on the date of its restoration to the register, be deemed to be a private company limited by shares to which *Parts 1* to *15* apply and the other provisions of *section 61* shall apply to it with any necessary modifications.

(4) *Subparagraph (3)* shall similarly apply (where the company's type, before being so struck off, was that of a private company limited by shares) if, by virtue of *subsection (3)* of *section 744*, the former enactment referred to in that subsection applies to the application for the company's restoration but with the modification that the reference in that subparagraph to a particular provision under which the application for restoration is made, or to a particular provision under which a direction or order of the court is made, shall be read as a reference to the corresponding provision of the former enactment concerned.

(5) If in any respect any difficulty arises during the period of 20 years after the commencement of *Chapter 2* of *Part 12* in bringing into operation that Chapter as it relates to a case falling within any of *subparagraphs (1)* to *(4)*, the Minister may by regulations do anything which appears to the Minister to be necessary or expedient for bringing that Chapter into operation as it relates to such a case.

(6) The Minister's power to make regulations under *subparagraph (5)* extends to removing difficulties in cases in which a private company limited by shares was—

(a) struck off the register under any former enactment relating to companies (within the meaning of *section 5*); and

(b) restored to the register under—

(i) the former enactment referred to in *section 744(3)*;

(ii) *Chapter 2* of *Part 12*; or

(iii) section 30 of the Multi-Unit Developments Act 2011,

and, before the date it is so restored, there has elapsed a length of time that, in the Minister's opinion, represents a substantial portion (or greater) of the transition period (within the meaning of *Chapter 6* of *Part 2*).

Application of paragraph 12 to companies whose dissolution is declared void

13. *Paragraph 12* shall, with any necessary modifications, apply to a company the dissolution of which is declared under *section 708* to have been void as it applies to a company restored to the register under an enactment referred to in that paragraph (but subject to any order the court may make under *section 708* in making such a declaration).

Authorisations, designations and approvals under Part XIII of the Act of 1990

14. Every authorisation, designation and approval under Part XIII of the Act of 1990 (including any condition imposed thereunder) that is in force immediately before the commencement of *Part 24* shall continue in force as if granted, made or imposed under *Part 24* and may be the subject of the like exercise of powers

thereafter as authorisations, designations, approvals and conditions generally under *Part 24*.

Generality of Interpretation Act 2005 not affected

15. Save for any express limitation by this Schedule of that Act's terms, this Schedule is without prejudice to the generality of the Interpretation Act 2005.

Specific transitional provisions not affected

16. This Schedule is in addition to the special provision made in certain provisions of this Act for transitional matters as they relate to those provisions and, in the event of conflict between this Schedule and such special provisions, those special provisions prevail as they relate to those matters.

SCHEDULE 7
FORM OF CONSTITUTION OF DESIGNATED ACTIVITY COMPANY LIMITED BY SHARES

Section 967.

CONSTITUTION
OF
[*name of company as below*]

MEMORANDUM OF ASSOCIATION

1. The name of the company is: THE SAFE SKIES SOFTWARE DESIGNATED ACTIVITY COMPANY.
2. The company is a designated activity company limited by shares, that is to say a private company limited by shares registered under *Part 16* of the *Companies Act 2014*.
3. The objects for which the company is established are the development, production and sale of computer software designed to enhance the safety of aviation and the doing of all such other things as are incidental or conducive to the attainment of the above object.
4. The liability of the members is limited.
5. The share capital of the company is €200,000, divided into 200,000 shares of €1 each.

ARTICLES OF ASSOCIATION

The following Regulations shall apply to the company:

[or, instead of the immediately foregoing words, the following sentence:-]*

The provisions of the *Companies Act 2014* are adopted.

**See section 968(5)*

We, the several persons whose names and addresses are subscribed, wish to be formed into a company in pursuance of this constitution, and we agree to take the number of shares in the capital of the company set opposite our respective names.

Names, Addresses and Descriptions of Subscribers	Number of Shares taken by each Subscriber
1. Patrick McKenna Address: Description:	300
2. Bridget McCloy Address: Description:	2,700
Total shares taken:	3,000

As appropriate:

signatures in writing of the above subscribers, attested by witness as provided for below; or

authentication in the manner referred to in *section 888*.

Dated the______________ day of ______________ 20 ___

Witness to the above Signatures:

Name: ____

Address: ____

SCHEDULE 8
FORM OF CONSTITUTION OF DESIGNATED ACTIVITY COMPANY LIMITED BY GUARANTEE

Section 967.

CONSTITUTION
OF
[*name of company as below*]

MEMORANDUM OF ASSOCIATION

1. The name of the company is: THE WESTERN COUNTIES TOURISM DEVELOPMENT DESIGNATED ACTIVITY COMPANY.
2. The company is a designated activity company limited by guarantee, that is to say a private company limited by guarantee and having a share capital registered under *Part 16* of the *Companies Act 2014*.
3. The objects for which the company is established are the promotion of tourism in the western counties of Ireland by providing facilities for tourists and the doing of all such other things as are incidental or conducive to the attainment of the above object.
4. The liability of the members is limited.
5. Every member of the company undertakes to contribute to the assets of the company, if the company is wound up while he or she is a member or is wound up within one year after the date on which he or she ceases to be a member, for—
   (a) the payment of the debts and liabilities of the company contracted before he or she ceases to be a member, and the costs, charges and expenses of winding up; and
   (b) the adjustment of the rights of contributories among themselves,

such amount as may be required, not exceeding €50.

6. The share capital of the company is €10,000, divided into 10,000 shares of €1 each.

ARTICLES OF ASSOCIATION

The following Regulations shall apply to the company:

[or, instead of the immediately foregoing words, the following sentence:-]*

The provisions of the *Companies Act 2014* are adopted.

**See section 968(5)*

We, the several persons whose names and addresses are subscribed, wish to be formed into a company in pursuance of this constitution, and we agree to take the number of shares in the capital of the company set opposite our respective names.

Names, Addresses and Descriptions of Subscribers	**Number of Shares taken by each Subscriber**
1. Ann Larkin Address: Description:	1,000
Total shares taken:	1,000

As appropriate:

signature in writing of the above subscriber, attested by witness as provided for below; or

authentication in the manner referred to in *section 888*.

Dated the ______________ day of ______________ 20__

Witness to the above Signatures:

Name: ____

Address: ____

SCHEDULE 9

FORM OF CONSTITUTION OF PUBLIC LIMITED COMPANY

Section 1006.

CONSTITUTION

OF

[*name of company as below*]

MEMORANDUM OF ASSOCIATION

1. The name of the company is: THE NORTHERN MINING PUBLIC LIMITED COMPANY.
2. The company is a public limited company, registered under *Part 17* of the *Companies Act 2014*.
3. The objects for which the company is established are the mining of minerals of all kinds and the doing of all such other things as are incidental or conducive to the attainment of the above object.
4. The liability of the members is limited.
5. The share capital of the company is €30,000, divided into 30,000 shares of €1 each.

ARTICLES OF ASSOCIATION

The following Regulations shall apply to the company:

[or, instead of the immediately foregoing words, the following sentence:-]*

The provisions of the *Companies Act 2014* are adopted.

**See section 1007(5)*

We, the several persons whose names and addresses are subscribed, wish to be formed into a company in pursuance of this constitution, and we agree to take the number of shares in the capital of the company set opposite our respective names.

Names, Addresses and Descriptions of Subscribers	**Number of Shares taken by each Subscriber**
1. Jerry O'Donovan Address: Description:	5
2. Agnieska Mooney Address: Description:	375
3. Cormac Vayner Address: Description:	225

Names, Addresses and Descriptions of Subscribers	**Number of Shares taken by each Subscriber**
4. Colleen Parsons Address: Description	55
Total shares taken:	660

As appropriate:

signature in writing of the above subscribers, attested by witness as provided for below; or

authentication in the manner referred to in *section 888*.

Dated the ______________ day of ______________20___

Witness to the above Signatures:

Name: ____

Address: ____

SCHEDULE 10
FORM OF CONSTITUTION OF COMPANY LIMITED BY GUARANTEE

Section 1176.

CONSTITUTION

OF

[*name of company as below*]

MEMORANDUM OF ASSOCIATION

1. The name of the company is: THE UNIVERSITY FOUNDATION COMPANY LIMITED BY GUARANTEE.
2. The company is a company limited by guarantee, registered under *Part 18* of the *Companies Act 2014*.
3. The objects for which the company is established are the raising of funds for the furtherance of education and research carried out by Irish universities and the doing of all such other things as are incidental or conducive to the attainment of the above object.
4. The liability of the members is limited.
5. Every member of the company undertakes to contribute to the assets of the company, if the company is wound up while he or she is a member or is wound up within one year after the date on which he or she ceases to be a member, for—

   (a) the payment of the debts and liabilities of the company contracted before he or she ceases to be a member, and the costs, charges and expenses of winding up; and

   (b) the adjustment of the rights of contributories among themselves,

   such amount as may be required, not exceeding €1.

ARTICLES OF ASSOCIATION

The following Regulations shall apply to the company:

1. The number of members with which the company proposes to be registered is 4.

[In addition to the immediately foregoing words, the following sentence may be included:-]*

The provisions of the *Companies Act 2014* are adopted.

**See section 1177(5).*

We, the several persons whose names and addresses are subscribed, wish to be formed into a company in pursuance of this constitution.

Names, Addresses and Descriptions of Subscribers
1. Francis McMaster Address: Description:
2. Colleen D. Cahill Address: Description:
3. Guy Tabarie Address: Description:
4. Akosa Martins Address: Description:

As appropriate:

signature in writing of the above subscribers, attested by witness as provided for below; or

authentication in the manner referred to in *section 888*.

Dated the ________________ day of ________________20___

Witness to the above Signatures:

Name: ____

Address: ____

SCHEDULE 11
FORM OF CONSTITUTION OF PRIVATE UNLIMITED COMPANY HAVING A SHARE CAPITAL

Section 1233.

CONSTITUTION

OF

[*name of company as below*]

MEMORANDUM OF ASSOCIATION

1. The name of the company is: BIG WAREHOUSE UNLIMITED COMPANY.
2. The company is a private unlimited company having a share capital, registered under *Part 19* of the *Companies Act 2014*.
3. The objects for which the company is established are the design and manufacture of clothing, and the doing of all such other things as are incidental or conducive to the attainment of the above object.
4. The share capital of the company is €200,000, divided into 200,000 shares of €1 each.
5. The liability of the members is unlimited.

ARTICLES OF ASSOCIATION

The following Regulations shall apply to the company:

[or, instead of the immediately foregoing words, the following sentence:-]*

The provisions of the *Companies Act 2014* are adopted.

**See section 1235(5)*

We, the several persons whose names and addresses are subscribed, wish to be formed into a company in pursuance of this constitution, and we agree to take the number of shares in the capital of the company set opposite our respective names.

Names, Addresses and Descriptions of Subscribers	**Number of Shares taken by each Subscriber**
1. Henry Klein Address: Description:	300
2. Brendan Pettit Address: Description:	2,700

Names, Addresses and Descriptions of Subscribers	Number of Shares taken by each Subscriber
3. Frances Little Address: Description:	500
Total shares taken:	3,500

As appropriate:

signature in writing of the above subscribers, attested by witness as provided for below; or

authentication in the manner referred to in *section 888*.

Dated the _______________ day of _______________20___

Witness to the above Signatures:

Name: ____

Address: ____

SCHEDULE 12
FORM OF CONSTITUTION OF PUBLIC UNLIMITED COMPANY HAVING A SHARE CAPITAL

Section 1233.

CONSTITUTION

OF

[name of company as below]

MEMORANDUM OF ASSOCIATION

1. The name of the company is: ALL BREEDS DOG CARE UNLIMITED COMPANY.
2. The company is a public unlimited company having a share capital, registered under *Part 19* of the *Companies Act 2014*.
3. The objects for which the company is established are the provision of general care, kennelling and grooming services in respect of all breeds of dog and the doing of all such other things as are incidental or conducive to the attainment of the above object.
4. The share capital of the company is €400,000, divided into 200,000 shares of €2 each.
5. The liability of the members is unlimited.

ARTICLES OF ASSOCIATION

The following Regulations shall apply to the company:

[or, instead of the immediately foregoing words, the following sentence:-]*

The provisions of the *Companies Act 2014* are adopted.

**See section 1235(5)*

We, the several persons whose names and addresses are subscribed, wish to be formed into a company in pursuance of this constitution, and we agree to take the number of shares in the capital of the company set opposite our respective names.

Names, Addresses and Descriptions of Subscribers	Number of Shares taken by each Subscriber
1. Duncan Moloney Address: Description:	600
2. John Berry Address: Description:	850

Names, Addresses and Descriptions of Subscribers	Number of Shares taken by each Subscriber
3. Melissa Smith Address: Description:	500
4. Dermot O'Kelly Address: Description:	100
Total shares taken:	2,050

As appropriate:

signature in writing of the above subscribers, attested by witness as provided for below; or

authentication in the manner referred to in *section 888*.

Dated the ______________ day of ______________20___

Witness to the above Signatures:

Name: ____

Address: ____

SCHEDULE 13
FORM OF CONSTITUTION OF PUBLIC UNLIMITED COMPANY NOT HAVING A SHARE CAPITAL

Section 1234.

CONSTITUTION

OF

[name of company as below]

MEMORANDUM OF ASSOCIATION

1. The name of the company is: THE OLD HEAD LEISURE UNLIMITED COMPANY.
2. The company is a public unlimited company not having a share capital, registered under *Part 19* of the *Companies Act 2014*.
3. The objects for which the company is established are the provision of guided tours (including treks on foot or by means of bicycle) in and around the coastal areas of the counties of Kerry, Cork, Waterford and Wexford and the doing of all such things as are incidental or conducive to the attainment of the above object.
4. The liability of the members is unlimited.

ARTICLES OF ASSOCIATION

The following Regulations shall apply to the company:

1. The number of members with which the company proposes to be registered is 5.

[In addition to the immediately foregoing words, the following sentence may be included:-]*

The provisions of the *Companies Act 2014* are adopted.

**See section 1235(6).*

We, the several persons whose names and addresses are subscribed, wish to be formed into a company in pursuance of this constitution.

Names, Addresses and Descriptions of Subscribers
1. Máire de Barra Address: Description:
2. Carla Stewart Address: Description:
3. Liam Wallis Address: Description:

Names, Addresses and Descriptions of Subscribers
4. Emmett O'Toole Address: Description:
5. Jane Grey Address: Description:

As appropriate:

signature in writing of the above subscribers, attested by witness as provided for below; or

authentication in the manner referred to in *section 888*.

Dated the ________________ day of ________________20___

Witness to the above Signatures:

Name: ____

Address: ____

SCHEDULE 14
PROVISIONS APPLIED TO UNREGISTERED COMPANIES

Section 1312.

Subject matter	Provision applied
Interpretation generally	*Section 2*
Periods of time	*Section 3*
Definition of "subsidiary"	*Section 7*
Definitions of "holding company", "wholly owned subsidiary" and "group of companies"	*Section 8*
Construction of references to directors, board of directors and interpretation of certain other plural forms	*Section 11*
Amendment of constitution by special resolution and publication of certain notices	*Section 32(3)* and *section 33(1)(b)* to *(h)* and *(2)*
Registered person	*Section 39*
Persons authorised to bind company	*Section 40*
Pre-incorporation contracts	*Section 45*
Registered office of company	*Section 50*
Service of documents	*Section 51*
Share premium	*Section 71(5)*
Restriction of *section 71(5)* in the case of mergers	*Section 72*
Restriction of *section 71(5)* in the case of group reconstructions	*Section 73*
Supplementary provisions in relation to *sections 72* and *73*	*Section 74*
Financial assistance for acquisition of shares	*Section 82*
Reduction in company capital and associated provisions and court procedures	*Sections 84* to *87*
Rectification of dealings in shares	*Section 100*
Acquisition of own shares	*Chapter 6* of *Part 3*
Distributions	*Chapter 7* of *Part 3*
Access to documents during business hours	*Section 127*
Validity of acts of director or secretary	*Section 135*
Register of directors and secretaries	*Section 149*
Supplemental provisions (including offences) in relation to *section 149*	*Section 150*
Particulars to be shown on all business letters of company	*Section 151*
Summary Approval Procedure	*Chapter 7* of *Part 4* (in so far as it relates to *sections 82*, *84* and *239*)
Remedy in case of oppression	*Section 212*

Subject matter	Provision applied
Form of registers, minutes, etc.	*Section 213*
Use of computers, etc. for certain company records	*Section 214*
Inspection of registers, provision of copies of information in them and service of notices	*Chapter 10* of *Part 4* (in so far as it relates to provisions applied by *section 1312*)
Power of court to grant relief to officers of company	*Section 233*
Anticipated claim: similar power of relief as under *section 229*	*Section 234*
Any provision exempting officers of company from liability void (subject to exceptions)	*Section 235*
Evidential provisions with respect to loans, other transactions, etc., between company and directors	*Chapter 3* of *Part 5*
Substantive prohibitions or restrictions on loans to directors and other particular transactions involving conflict of interest	*Chapter 4* of *Part 5*
Disclosure of interests in shares and debentures	*Chapter 5* of *Part 5*
Meaning of "in default" in context of sanctions specified in respect of officers (whether directors or secretaries or not)	*Section 270*
Presumption that default permitted and certain defence	*Section 271*
Financial statements, annual return and audit	*Part 6*
Definition (*Part 7*)	*Section 408*
Registration of charges and priority	*Chapter 2* of *Part 7*
Examinerships	*Part 10*
Investigations	*Part 13*
Court may order compliance by company or officer	*Section 797*
Disclosure orders	*Chapter 2* of *Part 14*
Restrictions on, and disqualification of, directors	*Chapters 3* to *6* of *Part 14*
Provisions relating to offences generally	*Chapter 7* of *Part 14*
Additional general offences	*Chapter 8* of *Part 14*
Evidential matters	*Chapter 9* of *Part 14*
Fees	*Section 889*
Inspection and production of documents kept by Registrar	*Section 891*
Admissibility of certified copy or extract	*Section 892*
Certificate by Registrar admissible as evidence of facts stated	*Section 893*
Capacity of a PLC	*Section 1011*
Official seal for sealing securities	*Section 1017*
Share capital	*Chapter 3* of *Part 17*
Interests in shares: disclosure of individual and group acquisitions	*Chapter 4* of *Part 17*

Subject matter	Provision applied
[Application of *sections 310 to 313*	*Section 1120*][a]
Mergers and divisions	*Chapters 16* and *17* of *Part 17*
Public Offers of Securities, Financial Reporting by Traded Companies, Prevention of Market Abuse, etc.	*Part 23* (other than *section 1374*)

Amendments

a Words "Application of sections 310 to 313" and "Section 1120" inserted by Companies Act 2014 (section 1313) Regulations 2016, reg 3.

SCHEDULE 15
REPEALS AND REVOCATION IN RELATION TO UNREGISTERED COMPANIES

Section 1325.

PART 1
STATUTES REPEALED

Session and Chapter or Number and Year	Short title	Extent of repeal
21 & 22 Geo III, c 16	Bank of Ireland Act 1781	The whole Act so far as unrepealed
31 Geo III, c 22	Bank of Ireland Act 1791	The whole Act so far as unrepealed
37 Geo III, c 50	Bank of Ireland Act 1797	The whole Act so far as unrepealed
48 Geo III, c 103	Bank of Ireland Act 1808	The whole Act so far as unrepealed
1 & 2 Geo IV, c 72	Bank of Ireland Act 1821	The whole Act so far as unrepealed
8 & 9 Vic, c 37	Bankers' (Ireland) Act 1845	So much of the Act as is unrepealed other than sections 25, 26 and 27
23 & 24 Vic, c 31	Bank of Ireland Act 1860	The whole Act
27 & 28 Vic, c 78	Bank Notes (Ireland) Act 1864	The whole Act
35 & 36 Vic, c 5	Bank of Ireland Charter Amendment Act 1872	The whole Act so far as unrepealed
55 & 56 Vic, c 48	Bank Act 1892	Sections 1, 3, 6 and 7
No. 4 (Private) of 1929	Bank of Ireland Act 1929	The whole Act so far as unrepealed
No. 1 (Private) of 1935	Bank of Ireland Act 1935	The whole Act so far as unrepealed
No. 23 of 1961	Finance Act 1961	Section 37
No. 24 of 1971	Central Bank Act 1971	Section 51

PART 2
INSTRUMENTS OR CHARTERS REVOKED

Instrument or Charter	Extent of revocation
Commission (27 July 1782)	The whole instrument
Charter of the Governor and Company of the Bank of Ireland (10 May 1783)	The whole Charter

SCHEDULE 16
FORM OF CONSTITUTION OF INVESTMENT COMPANY

Section 1392.

CONSTITUTION

OF

[name of company as below]

MEMORANDUM OF ASSOCIATION

1. The name of the company is: THE HIGH SCORE INVESTMENT PUBLIC LIMITED COMPANY.
2. The company is a public limited company, registered under *Part 24* of the *Companies Act 2014*.
3. The object for which the company is established is the collective investment of its funds in property with the aim of spreading investment risk and giving members of the company the benefit of the results of the management of its funds.
4. The liability of the members is limited.
5. The share capital of the company shall be equal to the value for the time being of the issued share capital of the company.
6. *[Unless this is provided for in the articles of association]* The actual value of the paid up share capital of the company shall at all times be equal to the value of the assets of any kind of the company after the deduction of its liabilities.
7. The share capital of the company is divided into 1,000,000 shares.
8. The issued share capital of the company for the time being shall not be less than €5,000,000 nor more than €20,000,000.
9. *[Unless this is provided for in the articles of association or the company has the approval of the Central Bank not to so provide]* The shares of the company shall, at the request of any of the holders thereof, be purchased by the company directly or indirectly out of the company's assets.

ARTICLES OF ASSOCIATION

1. Regulations in relation to the company with respect to such aspects of the activity of collective investment referred to in *section 1386(1)(a)*, or matters related thereto, as are deemed appropriate.
2. Unless the memorandum of association provides for this, the matter referred to in *paragraph 6* above.

3. Unless the memorandum of association provides for this or the company has the approval of the Central Bank not to so provide, the matter referred to in *paragraph 9* above.
4. Other regulations (if any).

We, the several persons whose names and addresses are subscribed, wish to be formed into a company in pursuance of this constitution, and we agree to take the number of shares in the capital of the company set opposite our respective names.

Names, Addresses and Descriptions of Subscribers	**Number of Shares taken by each Subscriber**
1. Thomas Friel Address: Description:	5
2. George Mooney Address: Description:	375
3. Cormac O'Hara Address: Description:	225
4. Sarah Weizmann Address: Description:	55
Total shares taken:	660

As appropriate:

signature in writing of the above subscribers, attested by witness as provided for below; or

authentication in the manner referred to in *section 888*.

Dated the ______________ day of ______________20___

Witness to the above Signatures:

Name: ____

Address: ____

SCHEDULE 17
CONDITIONS TO BE SATISFIED FOR APPLICATION OF SEGREGATED LIABILITY TO SUB-FUNDS OF INVESTMENT COMPANY TRADING BEFORE 30 JUNE 2005

Section 1405

Conditions for segregated liability to apply to sub-funds

1. (1) *Section 1405(1)* shall not apply to an umbrella fund which was authorised and commenced trading (as that latter expression is to be read in accordance with this Schedule) before 30 June 2005 unless—

(a) the members of the umbrella fund shall have resolved by special resolution that the provisions of *section 1405(1)* should apply to that umbrella fund; and

(b) the special resolution has taken effect in accordance with *paragraph 2*.

(2) For the purposes of this Schedule, an umbrella fund shall be deemed to have commenced to trade before 30 June 2005 if—

(a) shares, other than the subscriber shares issued for the purposes of incorporation of the umbrella fund, were issued in any sub-fund of that umbrella fund before 30 June 2005 and one or more of those shares remained in issue on that date; or

(b) the umbrella fund, or any person acting on its behalf, entered into an agreement with a third party before 30 June 2005, which remained in force on that date and pursuant to which the assets of any sub-fund may be applied in satisfaction of any liability incurred on behalf of or attributable to any other sub-fund of the same umbrella fund.

Taking effect of special resolution referred to in paragraph 1

2. (1) If no application to the court is made pursuant to *paragraph 5*, a special resolution passed pursuant to *paragraph 1(1)* shall take effect on the date on which such resolution is passed or the 31st day after the date of service of notice on creditors issued pursuant to *paragraph 3(1)(b)*, whichever is the later.

(2) If an application is, or applications are, made to the court pursuant to *paragraph 5*, a special resolution pursuant to *paragraph 1(1)* shall not take effect until—

(a) in the event that all applications made are withdrawn, the day on which such resolution is passed or the day next following the withdrawal of the last outstanding application, whichever is the later, subject to this day being no earlier than the 31st day after the date of service of notice on creditors issued pursuant to *paragraph 3(1)(b)*; and

(b) in the event that all applications made are not withdrawn, whichever of the following is the later, that is to say, the later of the day on which such resolution is passed, and:

(i) where an order is granted by the court pursuant to *paragraph 5* or on appeal pursuant to *paragraph 6*, the date specified in that order or, if no such date is specified, the day next following the date on which the period for which the order is specified to remain in force expires or, as appropriate, following the day on which it otherwise ceases to be in force; or

(ii) where no appeal against any decision of the court is lodged pursuant to *paragraph 6*, the day next following the date on which the period for such an appeal in relation to the last such determination of the court shall have elapsed; or

(iii) where an appeal is lodged against any decision of the court pursuant to *paragraph 6*, the day next following the date on which the last outstanding such appeal is disposed of or withdrawn,

unless a court has otherwise ordered under *paragraph 5* or *6*.

Certain requirements concerning notice of meeting to consider special resolution

3. (1) Any notice of a meeting at which a special resolution of the type referred to in *paragraph 1(1)* is intended to be proposed—

(a) shall be accompanied by audited financial statements for the umbrella fund which—

(i) include a statement of the assets and liabilities of each sub-fund of the umbrella fund; and

(ii) are prepared as at a date which is not more than 4 months before the date on which the notice convening the meeting is served,

and such a statement is referred to subsequently in this paragraph and *paragraph 4* as a "statement of assets and liabilities";

(b) shall be given to all creditors of the umbrella fund, accompanied by a copy of the statement of assets and liabilities, in accordance with the provisions of *paragraph 4*; and

(c) shall be delivered to the Registrar, accompanied by the statement of assets and liabilities, no later than the third day after the date on which the notice is first sent to members of the umbrella fund.

(2) If the means provided under *section 193* (unanimous written resolutions) are proposed to be used to pass the special resolution, the following provisions have effect—

(a) notice in writing of the proposed use of those means for that purpose shall be served on all members of the umbrella fund (and such notice shall not be valid if less than 30 days elapse between the date of service of it and the date of the signing of the resolution by the last member to sign);

(b) each of the requirements under *subparagraph (1)* with respect to the notice of a meeting shall apply to the notice in writing under *clause (a)*; and

(c) references in *subparagraph (1)* to the notice of a meeting shall be read as references to the notice in writing under *clause (a)*,

and references elsewhere in this Schedule to the notice of a meeting shall be read accordingly.

Notice to creditors of meeting to consider special resolution under paragraph 1(1)

4. (1) The requirement in *subparagraph (1)(a)* of *paragraph 3* to give all creditors of the umbrella fund notice of the meeting referred to in that paragraph shall be regarded as having been complied with if—

(a) a notice in writing, accompanied by the statement of assets and liabilities, is sent to each relevant creditor of a sub-fund; and

(b) a notice is published in at least one national newspaper, stating that the umbrella fund intends to avail itself of *section 1405(1)* and that an application may be made in accordance with *paragraph 5* for an order pursuant to that paragraph.

(2) For the purpose of this paragraph, a relevant creditor of a sub-fund is any creditor for whom provision was made, in accordance with the articles of association, in the net asset value of the sub-fund calculated—

(a) in the case of a sub-fund in respect of which the net asset value is not calculated on a daily basis, as at the last valuation point for that sub-fund before the date of service of the notice pursuant to *paragraph 3(1)(b)*; and

(b) in the case of a sub-fund in respect of which the net asset value is calculated on a daily basis, as at the second last valuation point for that sub-fund.

Application to court opposing special resolution under paragraph 1(1)

5. (1) An application may be made to the court in accordance with this paragraph for an order preventing any resolution passed, or proposed to be passed, pursuant to *subparagraph (1)* of *paragraph 1* from taking effect in relation to any umbrella fund referred to in that paragraph.

(2) An order under this paragraph may be granted only if the court considers that it would be just and equitable to do so.

(3) Each order granted pursuant to this paragraph shall specify the period in respect of which the order shall remain in force and, without prejudice to the powers of the court to specify such period, may specify that the order shall cease to be in force on the date on which the applicant ceases to be a creditor of the umbrella fund or the date on which the applicant consents to the application of *section 1405(1)* to that umbrella fund, whichever is the later.

(4) An application under this paragraph may only be made by a relevant creditor or relevant creditors constituting not less than 1 per cent in number of the creditors of any sub-fund, or the debts owed to whom account for not less than 1 per cent in value of the debts owed by any sub-fund, in each case as provided for in the net asset value of that sub-fund referred to in *paragraph 4*.

(5) Any application pursuant to this paragraph shall be made by a relevant creditor within 28 days after the date of service of the notice referred to in *paragraph 3(1) (b)*, and may be made on behalf of the creditors entitled to make the application by one or more of their number as they may appoint in writing for such purpose.

(6) Notice of an application to the court for the purposes of this paragraph shall be sent by the relevant creditor or relevant creditors to the umbrella fund and to the Central Bank within 2 days after the date on which the application is made, and the umbrella fund and the Central Bank shall each be entitled to appear and be heard on an application made pursuant to this paragraph.

(7) In considering whether it is just and equitable to make an order pursuant to this paragraph, the court shall have regard to the following matters:

(a) the terms of any agreement or arrangement between the creditor or creditors and the umbrella fund or its delegates;

(b) the course of dealings between the creditor or creditors and the umbrella fund or its delegates;

(c) the conduct of the umbrella fund or its delegates towards the creditor or creditors;

(d) the extent to which the umbrella fund or its delegates represented to the creditor or creditors that the umbrella fund would have recourse to the assets of any other sub-fund to discharge the liabilities owed to the creditor or creditors;

(e) the extent to which it was reasonable for the relevant creditor or relevant creditors to expect to have recourse to the assets of any other sub-fund;

(f) any other matters which the court shall deem relevant.

Appeal from decision of court under paragraph 5

6. (1) Any creditor who has made an application pursuant to *paragraph 5*, or the umbrella fund in respect of which the application is made, may appeal to the Supreme Court against any decision of the court in respect of that application.

(2) Notice of any such appeal shall be lodged within 5 days after the date on which the order is perfected by the court.

(3) Notice of any appeal lodged by the umbrella fund shall be sent to the Central Bank and to the relevant creditor or relevant creditors who made the application pursuant to *paragraph 5* within 2 days after the date on which the appeal is made.

(4) Notice of any appeal by the party which made the application pursuant to paragraph 5 shall be sent to the Central Bank and to the umbrella fund within 2 days after the date on which the appeal is made.

[SCHEDULE 18
TABLE OF ACTIVITIES RELEVANT TO THE DEFINITIONS OF "LOGGING UNDERTAKING" AND "MINING OR QUARRYING UNDERTAKING" IN SECTION 1449

ANNEX I TO REGULATION (EC) NO. 1893/2006

TABLE 1

Section A – Agriculture, Forestry and Fishing

Division	Group	Class	Description	International Standard Industrial Classification Revision 4
02	02.2	02.20	Logging	0220

TABLE 2

Section B – Mining and Quarrying

Division	Group	Class	Description	International Standard Industrial Classification Revision 4
05			Mining of coal and lignite	
	05.1		Mining of hard coal	0510
	05.2	05.20	Mining of lignite	0520
06			Extraction of crude petroleum and natural gas	
	06.1	06.10	Extraction of crude petroleum	0610
	06.2	06.20	Extraction of natural gas	0620
07			Mining of metal ores	
	07.1	07.10	Mining of iron ores	0710
	07.2		Mining of non-ferrous metal ores	
		07.21	Mining of uranium and thorium ores	0721
		07.29	Mining of other non-ferrous metal ores	0729
08			08	08
	08.1		Quarrying of clay stone, sand and	
		08.11	Quarrying of ornamental and building stone, limestone, gypsum, chalk and slate	0810 (part of)
		08.12	Operation of gravel and sand	0810 (part of)
	08.9		Mining and quarrying not elsewhere classified	

Division	Group	Class	Description	International Standard Industrial Classification Revision 4
		08.91	Mining of chemical and fertiliser minerals	0891
		08.92	Extraction of peat	0892
		08.93	Extraction of salt	0893
		08.99	Other mining and quarrying not elsewhere classified	0899][a]

Amendments

a Schedule 18 substituted by C(A)A 2017, s 89(f) and Sch 6.

[SCHEDULE 19
STANDARDS RELATING TO TRAINING AND QUALIFICATIONS FOR APPROVAL OF INDIVIDUAL AS STATUTORY AUDITOR

Section 1472

1. An individual shall have attained university entrance or equivalent level and then—
   (a) completed a course of theoretical instruction,
   (b) undergone practical training, and
   (c) passed an examination of professional competence which is of at least the standard required in the State for university final or equivalent examination level.

2. (1) The examination of professional competence referred to in *paragraph 1* shall be such as guarantees the necessary level of theoretical knowledge of subjects relevant to statutory audit and the ability to apply such knowledge in practice. Part at least of that examination shall be in writing.

   (2) The test of theoretical knowledge included in the examination shall include the following subjects in particular:
   (a) general accounting theory and principles;
   (b) legal requirements and standards relating to the preparation of entity and group financial statements;
   (c) international accounting standards;
   (d) financial analysis;
   (e) cost and management accounting;
   (f) risk management and internal control;
   (g) auditing and professional skills;
   (h) legal requirements and professional standards relating to statutory audit and statutory auditors;
   (i) international auditing standards as referred to in *section 1526*;
   (j) professional ethics and independence.

3. The examination shall also include at least the following subjects in so far as they are relevant to auditing:
   (a) company law and corporate governance;
   (b) the law of insolvency and similar procedures;
   (c) tax law;
   (d) civil and commercial law;
   (e) social security law and employment law;
   (f) information technology and computer systems;
   (g) business, general and financial economics;
   (h) mathematics and statistics;

(i) basic principles of the financial management of undertakings.

4. (1) In order to ensure the ability to apply theoretical knowledge in practice, a test of which is included in the examination, a trainee shall complete a minimum of 3 years practical training in, amongst others, the auditing of entity financial statements, group financial statements or similar financial statements. A substantial part of such practical training shall be in statutory audit work and at least two thirds of such practical training shall be completed with a statutory auditor or an audit firm approved in any Member State.

(2) All such training shall be carried out with persons who a recognised accountancy body is satisfied possess, to an adequate standard, the ability to provide practical training.][a]

Amendments

a Schedule 19 inserted by C(SA)A 2018, s 53(a) and Sch 1.

[SCHEDULE 20
INFORMATION REQUIRED, BY CHAPTER 5 OF PART 27, TO BE SUPPLIED AND ENTERED IN PUBLIC REGISTER

Section 1484

Statutory auditors

1. In relation to a statutory auditor, the public register shall contain at least the following information:

   (a) the name and address of the auditor;

   (b) the number under which the auditor is entered in that register;

   (c) if applicable—

      (i) the name and address and the website address (if any) of the statutory audit firm by which the auditor is employed, or with whom he or she is associated as a partner or otherwise, and

      (ii) the number under which that statutory audit firm is entered in that register;

   (d) the name and address of the recognised accountancy body responsible for the regulation of the auditor;

   (e) if he or she is so registered with one or more recognised accountancy bodies, counterpart authorities or third-country competent authorities—

      (i) particulars of his or her registration—

         (I) as a statutory auditor, with each recognised accountancy body or counterpart authority and the name of each such body or authority, and

         (II) as an auditor, with each third-country competent authority and the name of such authority,

      and

      (ii) the number under which he or she is registered with each such body or authority;

   (f) without prejudice to subparagraph (e), with regard to the auditor's status (if such be the case) as a Member State statutory auditor, the name and address of each counterpart authority responsible, in relation to him or her, for—

      (i) approval as referred to in Article 3 of the Audit Directive,

      (ii) quality assurance as referred to in Article 29 of the Audit Directive and Article 26 of Regulation (EU) No 537/2014,

      (iii) investigations and sanctions as referred to in Chapter VII of the Audit Directive and Articles 23 and 24 of Regulation (EU) No 537/2014,

      (iv) public oversight as referred to in Article 32 of the Audit Directive, and

(v) performing the functions provided for in Regulation (EU) No 537/2014 and for ensuring the provisions of that Regulation are applied as referred to in Article 20 of that Regulation.

Statutory audit firms and audit firms approved in another Member State

2. In relation to a statutory audit firm, the public register shall contain at least the following information:

(a) the name and address of the audit firm;

(b) the number under which the audit firm is entered in that register;

(c) the legal form of the audit firm;

(d) the primary contact person in the audit firm and contact details;

(e) the address of each office in the State of the audit firm and the website address (if any) of the audit firm;

(f) the name of every individual employed by or associated as partner or otherwise with the audit firm who is approved as a statutory auditor under *Part 27*;

(g) the number under which that individual is entered in the register;

(h) the name and address of the recognised accountancy body responsible for the regulation of the audit firm in the State;

(i) the names and addresses of the owners of, or as appropriate, shareholders in, the audit firm;

(j) the names and addresses of the directors, or other members of, as appropriate—

(i) the board of directors,

(ii) the board of management, or

(iii) other administrative or management body,

of the audit firm (but where the audit firm comprises a partnership with no management structure, the provision of the address of each individual named, under *subparagraph (f)*, as partner suffices);

(k) if applicable, the fact of the audit firm's membership of a network and either—

(i) a list of the names and addresses of member firms and affiliates of the network, or

(ii) an indication of where such information is publicly available;

(l) if the audit firm is so registered with one or more counterpart authorities or third-country competent authorities—

(i) particulars of the firm's registration—

(I) as a statutory audit firm, with each counterpart authority and the name of the authority,

(II) as an audit firm, with such third-country competent authority and the name of such authority, and

(III) as an audit firm approved in another Member State, who has registered in accordance with Article 3a of the Audit Directive,

and

(ii) the number under which the firm is registered with each such authority;

(m) without prejudice to *subparagraph (l)*, with regard to the audit firm's status (if such be the case) as a Member State statutory audit firm, the name and address of each counterpart authority responsible, in relation to it, for—

(i) approval as referred to in Article 3 of the Audit Directive,

(ii) where the audit firm is registered in the public register of another Member State pursuant to Article 3a of the Audit Directive and the State is its home Member State—

(I) the fact that the firm is so registered, and

(II) the name of the host Member State and the counterpart authority in the host Member State,

(iii) quality assurance as referred to in Article 29 of the Audit Directive and Article 26 of Regulation (EU) No 537/2014,

(iv) investigations and sanctions as referred to in Chapter VII of the Audit Directive and Articles 23 and 24 of Regulation (EU) No 537/2014,

(v) public oversight as referred to in Article 32 of the Audit Directive, and

(vi) performing the functions provided for in Regulation (EU) No 537/2014 and for ensuring the provisions of that Regulation are applied as referred to in Article 20 of that Regulation;

(n) where the audit firm is registered in the public register pursuant to Article 3a(3) of the Audit Directive with the State as its host Member State—

(i) the fact that the firm is so registered, and

(ii) the name of the home Member State and the counterpart authority in the home Member State.

Third-country auditors and third-country audit entities

3. (1) In relation to the case provided by *section 1573* of the registration of a third-country auditor or third-country audit entity, the public register shall contain at least the information specified in the provisions of paragraph 1 or, as the case may be, 2 (as, in either case, those provisions are applied by *subparagraph (2)*).

(2) The provisions of *paragraph 1* or *2*, as the case may be, apply for the purposes of this paragraph save so much of them as are inapplicable in the case of a third-country auditor or third-country audit entity, as appropriate.

(3) Third-country auditors or third-country audit entities so registered shall be clearly indicated in the register as such and not as statutory auditors or audit firms.